May 21–23, 2014
Houston, Texas, USA

I0036647

Association for Computing Machinery

Advancing Computing as a Science & Profession

GLSVLSI'14
Proceedings of the 2014
Great Lakes Symposium on VLSI

Sponsored by:
ACM SIGDA

Technical Supporters:
CEDA, CAS, and IEEE

**Association for
Computing Machinery**

Advancing Computing as a Science & Profession

The Association for Computing Machinery
2 Penn Plaza, Suite 701
New York, New York 10121-0701

ISBN: 978-1-4503-2816-6 (Digital)

ISBN: 978-1-4503-3079-4 (Print)

Additional copies may be ordered prepaid from:

ACM Order Department
PO Box 30777
New York, NY 10087-0777, USA

Phone: 1-800-342-6626 (USA and Canada)
+1-212-626-0500 (Global)
Fax: +1-212-944-1318
E-mail: acmhelp@acm.org
Hours of Operation: 8:30 am – 4:30 pm ET

Printed in the USA

GLSVLSI'14 Chairs' Welcome

Welcome to the 24th edition of the Great Lakes Symposium on VLSI (GLSVLSI) 2014 held in Houston, Texas. GLSVLSI is a premier venue for the dissemination of manuscripts of the highest quality in all areas related to VLSI, devices and system level design. The venue of this year's GLSVLSI is Houston, which not only has a "Lake Houston" nearby but also is located right next to "Great Gulf of Mexico". You will enjoy the beautiful scenery surrounding Houston as well as the program over the two and a half days of this year's GLSVLSI activity.

As for the technical meeting, GLSVLSI 2014 was a resounding success: 179 papers were submitted, including authors from 30 different countries, of which 49 papers were accepted for oral presentation at the symposium (a 27.4% acceptance rate). With poster papers, a total of 76 papers will be presented at the symposium and published in the conference proceedings. The final technical program consists of 29 full presentations and 20 short presentations in 15 oral sessions and 27 posters in two poster sessions. Of these papers in the program, 55.8% are from North America, 18.2 % from Asia, 20.8% from Europe, and 5.2% from South America/Australia.

GLSVLSI 2014 starts on Wednesday, May 21st, in the morning with an invited keynote talk "VLSI Systems for Neurocomputing and Health Informatics" by Keshab Parhi, University of Minnesota, followed by technical sessions on Reliability, CAD, Energy Efficient Systems, and System Design Methodologies, and an inspiring and entertaining dinner keynote talk "Create, then Innovate" by Gene Frantz. Then, the technical program continues on Thursday, May 22nd with the second invited keynote talk "Smart Nodes of Internet of Things (IoT): A Hardware Perspective View & Implementation" by Edgar Sanchez-Sinencio, Texas A&M University, followed by technical sessions which present the latest industrial and academic research covering topics such as Fault-tolerance, Application-specific Circuits and Systems, Reconfigurable Elements, and System-level Optimization. The conference will end by the noon of Friday, May 23rd after the third keynote talk "EDA for Extreme Scale Systems" by Alex Jones, University of Pittsburgh, and sessions on topics of Reconfigurable Systems, Analog Design, Low Power Design, and Emerging Technologies during the morning. Overall, there are 15 regular sessions in the technical program including a session where the "best paper award" candidates will have the opportunity to present their outstanding work.

Putting together GLSVLSI'14 was a team effort. We first thank the authors for providing the content of the program. We are grateful to the program committee, who worked very hard in reviewing papers and providing feedback for authors. Finally, we thank the hosting university, our sponsor, and ACM SIGs. We hope that you will find this program interesting and thought-provoking and that the symposium will provide you with a valuable opportunity to share ideas with other researchers and practitioners from institutions around the world.

Joseph R. Cavallaro
GLSVLSI'14 General co-Chair
Rice University, USA

Tong Zhang
GLSVLSI'14 General co-Chair
Rensselaer Polytechnic Inst. USA

Alex K. Jones
GLSVLSI'14 Program co-Chair
University of Pittsburgh, USA

Hai (Helen) Li
GLSVLSI'14 Program co-Chair
University of Pittsburgh, USA

Table of Contents

Poster Session 1

Session: Energy Efficient Systems
Session Chair: Alberto Macii *(Politecnico di Torino, Italy)*

Session: Design Methodology
Session Chair: Ke Chen *(Oracle Corporation, USA)*

Gala Dinner Keynote
Session Chair: Joseph Cavallaro *(Rice University, USA)*

Keynote II
Session Chair: Joseph Cavallaro *(Rice University, USA)*

Session: Reliability, Resiliency, Robustness II
Session Chair: Dimin Niu *(Samsung Research, USA)*

Session: Application Specific Designs

Session Chair: Houman Homayoun *(George Mason University, USA)*

Session: Memory Designs

Session Chair: Nikolaos Papandreou *(IBM Research-Zurich)*

Session: Fault Tolerance

Session Chair: Ann Gordon-Ross *(University of Florida, USA)*

Poster Session 2

Session Chair: Prasun Ghosal *(Indian Institute of Engineering Science and Technology, Shibpur, India)*

Session: Reconfigurable Systems

Session Chair: Xi Chen *(Qualcomm Technology Inc., USA)*

Session: Analog Design

Session Chair: Saraju Mohanty *(University of North Texas, USA)*

Session: Low Power Design

Session Chair: Akash Kumar *(National University of Singapore, Singapore)*

Session: Emerging Technologies

Session Chair: Zhenyu Sun *(Broadcomm Inc., USA)*

GLSVLSI 2014 Conference Organization

General Chairs: Joseph R. Cavallaro *(Rice University, USA)*
Tong Zhang *(Rensselaer Polytechnic Inst., USA)*

Program Chair: Alex K. Jones *(University of Pittsburgh, USA)*
Hai (Helen) Li *(University of Pittsburgh, USA)*

Web Chair: Theocharis Theocharides *(University of Cyprus, CYPRUS)*

Proceedings Chair: Laleh Behjat *(University of Calgary, Canada)*

Publicity Chair: Miroslav Velev *(Aries Design Automation, USA)*

Steering Committee: David Atienza *(EPFL, Switzerland)*
José Ayala *(Univ. Complutense Madrid, Spain)*
Iris Bahar *(Brown University, USA)*
Sanjukta Bhanja *(University of South Florida, USA)*
Erik Brunvand *(University of Utah, USA)*
Yehea Ismail *(American University in Cairo, Egypt)*
Fabrizio Lombardi *(Northeastern University, USA)*
Enrico Macii *(Politecnico di Torino, Italy)*
Gang Qu *(University of Maryland, USA)*
Ken Stevens *(University of Utah, USA)*
Yuan Xie *(Pennsylvania State University, USA)*
Zhiyuan Yan *(Lehigh University, USA)*
John Lach *(University of Virginia, USA)*
Hai Zhou *(Northwestern University, USA)*

Program Committee: ***VLSI Design Track***
Track Chair: Saraju Mohanty *(University of North Texas, USA)*
Track Chair: Sudeep Pasricha *(Colorado State University, USA)*
Youcef Bouchebaba *(ST Microelectronics, Canada)*
Andreas Burg *(EPFL, Switzerland)*
Yangdong Deng *(Tsinghua University, China)*
Prasun Ghosal *(Bengal Engineering and Science University, Shibpur)*
Manish Goel *(Texas Instruments, USA)*
Houman Homayoun *(George Mason University, USA)*
Antonio Jimenez *(Instituto de Microelectrónica de Sevilla, Spain)*
Selcuk Kose *(University of South Florida, USA)*
Sébastien Le Beux *(École Centrale de Lyon, France)*
Karthikeyan Lingasubramanian *(University of Alabama at Birmingham, USA)*

Program Committee (continued):

Marisa López-Vallejo *(Universidad Politécnica de Madrid (UPM), Spain)*
Chao Lu *(Purdue University, Indiana, USA)*
Rabi Mahapatra *(Texas A&M University, USA)*
Martin Margala *(University of Massachussets, Lowell, USA)*
Brett Meyer *(McGill University, Canada)*
Alberto Nannarelli *(Danmarks Tekniske Universitet - DTU, Denmark)*
Ashoka Sathanur *(Philips, Netherlands)*
Zhijie Shi *(University of Connecticut, USA)*
James Stine *(Oklahoma State University, USA)*
Aida Todri-Sanial *(Laboratoire d'Informatique, de Robotique et de Microélectronique de Montpellier, France)*
Miroslav Velev *(Aries Design Automation, USA)*

VLSI Circuit Track

Track Chair: Emre Salman *(State University of New York, Stony Brook, USA)*
Track Chair: Lei Wang *(University of Connecticut, USA)*
Xi Chen *(Qualcomm Inc., USA)*
Selcuk Kose *(University of South Florida, USA)*
Chrysostomos Nicopoulos *(University of Cyprus, Cyprus)*
Marvin Onabajo *(Northeastern University)*
Theo Theocharides *(University of Cyprus, Cyprus)*
Diego Vázquez-García De La Vega *(Consejo Superior de Investigaciones Científicas, Spain)*

CAD Track

Track Chair: Laleh Behjat *(University of Calgary, Canada)*
Track Chair: Gabriela Nicolescu *(École Polytechnique de Montréal, Canada)*
Nadine Azemard *(Laboratoire d'Informatique, de Robotique et de Microélectronique de Montpellier, France)*
Giovanni Beltrame *(École Polytechnique de Montréal, Canada)*
Youcef Bouchebaba *(ST Microelectronics, Canada)*
Francesco Bruschi *(Politecnico di Milano, Italy)*
Maciej Ciesielski *(University of Massachusetts, USA)*
Philippe Coussy *(Universite de Bretagne-Sud, France)*
Rolf Drechsler *(University of Bremen, Germany)*
Fabrizio Ferrandi *(Politecnico di Milano, Italy)*
Niraj Jha *(Princeton University, USA)*
Yan Luo *(Oracle Inc. USA)*
Brett Meyer *(McGill University, Canada)*
Vivek S Nandakumar *(University of California, Santa Barbara, USA)*
Massimo Poncino *(Politecnico di Torino, Italy)*
Matteo Sonza Reorda *(Politecnico di Torino, Italy)*
Jelena Trajkovic *(Concordia University, Canada)*
Wei Zhang *(Nanyang Technological University, Singapore)*

Program Committee (continued):

Low-Power Track

Track Chair: Baris Taskin *(Drexel University, USA)*
Track Chair: Yong-Bin Kim *(Northeastern University, USA)*
Antonio Acosta *(Consejo Superior de Investigaciones Científicas, Spain)*
Alberto Bocca *(Politecnico di Torino, Italy)*
Andrea Calimera *(Politecnico di Torino, Italy)*
Koushik Chakraborty *(Utah State University, USA)*
Minsu Choi *(Missouri University of Science and Technology, USA)*
Ayse Coskun *(Boston University, USA)*
Domenik Helms *(Institut für Informatik Oldenburg, Germany)*
Kyung Ki Kim *(Daegu University, South Korea)*
Vonkyung Kim *(Oracle Inc., USA)*
Marisa Lopez-Vallejo *(Universidad Politécnica de Madrid, Spain)*
Alberto Macii *(Politecnico di Torino, Italy)*
Alberto Nannarelli *(Danmarks Tekniske Universitet - DTU, Denmark)*

Testing Track

Track Chair: Erik Larsson *(Lund Technical University, Sweden)*
Track Chair: Jennifer Dworak *(Southern Methodist University, USA)*
Chih-Tsun Huang *(National Technical University of Taiwan, Taiwan)*
Nicola Nicolici *(McMaster University, Canada)*
Ozgur Sinanoglu *(New York University Abu Dhabi)*
Haralampos Stratigopoulos *(Tima Laboratory, France)*
Spyros Tragoudas *(Southern Illinois University, USA)*
Xiaoqing Wen *(Kyushu Institute of Technology, Japan)*

Post-CMOS VLSI and Emerging Technologies Track

Track Chair: Kartik Mohanram *(University of Pittsburgh, USA)*
Track Chair: Guangyu Sun *(Pennsylvania State University, USA)*
Shamik Das *(MITRE, USA)*
Dhireesha Kudithipudi *(Rochester Institute of Technology, USA)*
Sébastien Le Beux *(Lyon Institute of Nanotechnology, France)*
Dimin Niu *(Samsung Research, USA)*
Zhenyu Sun *(Broadcom Inc., USA)*
Mehdi Tahoori *(Kalrsuhe Institute of Technology, Germany)*
Himanshu Thapliyal *(Qualcomm Inc., USA)*
Jishen Zhao *(Pennsylvania State University, USA)*

Additional reviewers:

Nabila Abdessaied	Paul Leons
Tariq Ahmad	Haroon Mahmood
Wisam Aljubouri	Kevin Martin
Phaninder Alladi	Vineeth Mohan
Mohamed Aly	Ahish Nagabharan
Nagamani An	Nasibeh Nasiri
Hassan Anwar	Katayoun Neshatpour
Paolo Burgio	Yuchi Ni
Sairahul Chalamalasetti	Oghenekarho Okobiah
Chun-Hsiang Chang	Piotr Olejarz
Hari Chauhan	Jin Ouyang
Cyrille Chavet	Ashok K. Palaniswamy
Junlin Chen	Jacopo Panerati
Ke Chen	Shafigh Parsazad
Xianmin Chen	Luke Pierce
Kazem Cheshmi	Nils Przigoda
Kevin Cushon	Mohammad Rad
Chandra Dara	Logan Rakai
Nima K. Darav	Axel Reimer
Amin Farshidi	William Reohr
Junpeng Feng	Ehsan Saboori
Ping Gao	Onur Sahin
Dhruva Ghai	Arun Sathanur
Mahadevan Gomathisankaran	Oren Segal
Na Gong	Jawar Singh
Peter Grossmann	Mathias Soeken
Mohammad Hajkazemi	Flemming Stassen
Guoxian Huang	Aysa F. Tabrizi
Wenjie Huang	Valerio Tenace
Jayashree Hv	Ozan Tuncer
Pablo Ituero	Ridvan Umaz
Reyhaned Jabbarvand	Gianvito Urgese
Fulya Kaplan	Orhun A. Uzun
Oliver Keszöcze	Wim Vanderbauwhede
Lars Kosmann	Jinhui Wang
Elias Kougianos	Ke Wang
Ulrich Kuehne	Adam Watkins
Marco Lattuada	Ali Zahrai
Hoang M. Le	Tiansheng Zhang
Joseph Lenox	Qiaosha Zou

GLSVLSI 2014 Sponsor & Supporters

Sponsor:

siG
special interest group on
acm
da
design automation

Technical Supporters:

CEDA
IEEE Council on Electronic Design Automation

CAS
IEEE CIRCUITS AND SYSTEMS SOCIETY

◆IEEE

VLSI Systems for Neurocomputing and Health Informatics

GLSVLSI'2014 Invited - Keynote Talk Abstract

Keshab K. Parhi
Department of Electrical and Computer Engineering
University of Minnesota
Minneapolis, MN 55455
parhi@umn.edu

ABSTRACT

Ubiquitous access to computers, cell phones, internet, personal digital devices, cameras and TV can be attributed to advances in the very large scale integration (VLSI) technology and the advances in circuit design to operate circuits at Gigahertz rates. One of the mysteries that we have not been able to unravel is the understanding of how the brain works from different perspectives. Reverse engineering the brain has been identified as one of the grand challenge problems by the National Academies. Advances in sensor technologies and imaging modalities such as electroencephalogram (EEG), intra-cranial electroencephalogram (iEEG), magnetoencephalogram (MEG), and magnetic resonance imaging (MRI) allow us to collect data from hundreds of electrodes from the brain at sample rates ranging from 256 Hz to 15kHz. These data can be key to not only understanding brain functioning and brain connectivity at macro and micro levels in healthy subjects but also in identifying patients with neurological and mental disorder. Extracting the appropriate biomarkers using spectral-temporal-spatial signal processing approaches and classifying states using machine learning approaches can assist clinicians in predicting and detecting seizures in epileptic patients, and in identifying patients with mental disorder such as schizophrenia, depression and personality disorder. The biomarkers can be tracked to design personalized therapy and effectiveness of therapy by closed loop drug delivery or closed loop neuromodulation, i.e., brain stimulation either by invasive or non-invasive means using electrical or magnetic stimulation. High-performance VLSI system design is critical to not-only increasing battery life of VLSI chips for neuromodulation but also for reducing computation time by orders of magnitude in analyzing MRI signals. Another grand challenge problem identified by the National Academies is Advanced Health Informatics. Analysis of health data is key to monitoring biomarkers and delivering drugs as needed. VLSI system design of biomarkers and disease state classification is again critical in improving the health and quality of life of human beings.

In this talk, I will highlight the emerging opportunities in high-performance low-power VLSI system design for neurocomputing and health informatics at various scales. At macroscale, the goal is to design small low-power implantable or wearable devices that can be used to monitor biomarkers and trigger an alarm signal to alert an abnormal state of the brain such as an impending seizure. At microscale, extracting thousands of connections from structural and functional MRI can require many hours or even a day for one subject and one set of parameters using parallel computers. The challenge here is to design parallel multicore computer architectures and compiler tools that can reduce the time for microscale analysis of MRI to an hour or less. I will describe research in my group in use of signal processing and machine learning approaches to identify and track various neurological and mental disorders. I will present some results on VLSI design of feature extractors such as power spectral density (PSD) and classifiers such as support vector machines (SVMs). I will present diabetic retinopathy screening using fundus image analysis and machine learning as an example to illustrate opportunities in design of embedded systems for health informatics. Significant research needs to be pursued in this area. My presentation will hopefully inspire further research in this emerging and important field of embedded VLSI system design for neuro, bio and health informatics.

Categories and Subject Descriptors

B.7.1 [**Integrated Circuits**]: Types and Design Style; I.2.1 [**Artificial Intelligence**]: Applications and Expert Systems; J.3 [**Computer Applications**]: Life and Medical Sciences

Keywords

Embedded system design, machine learning, pattern recognition, classification, biomarker, signal processing, neuromodulation, health informatics, data analysis, epilepsy, mental disorder, retinopathy, support vector machine, power spectral density.

Biography

Keshab K. Parhi received the B.Tech. degree from the Indian Institute of Technology (IIT), Kharagpur, in 1982, the M.S.E.E. degree from the University of Pennsylvania, Philadelphia, in 1984, and the Ph.D. degree from the University

GLSVLSI'14, May 21–23, 2014, Houston, Texas, USA.
ACM 978-1-4503-2816-6/14/05.
http://dx.doi.org/10.1145/2591513.2597168.

of California, Berkeley, in 1988. He has been with the University of Minnesota, Minneapolis, since 1988, where he is currently Distinguished McKnight University Professor and Edgar F. Johnson Professor in the Department of Electrical and Computer Engineering. He has published over 500 papers, has authored the textbook VLSI Digital Signal Processing Systems (Wiley, 1999) and coedited the reference book Digital Signal Processing for Multimedia Systems (Marcel Dekker, 1999). Dr. Parhi is widely recognized for his work on high-level transformations of iterative data-flow computations and for developing a formal theory of computing for design of digital signal processing systems. His current research addresses VLSI architecture design and implementation of signal processing, communications and biomedical systems, error control coders and cryptography architectures, high-speed transceivers, stochastic computing, secure computing, and molecular computing. He is also currently working on intelligent classification of biomedical signals and images, for applications such as seizure prediction and detection, schizophrenia classification, biomarkers for mental disorder, brain connectivity, and diabetic retinopathy screening.

Dr. Parhi is the recipient of numerous awards including the 2013 Distinguished Alumnus Award from IIT, Kharagpur, India, 2013 Graduate/Professional Teaching Award from the University of Minnesota, 2012 Charles A. Desoer Technical Achievement award from the IEEE Circuits and Systems Society, the 2004 F. E. Terman award from the American Society of Engineering Education, the 2003 IEEE Kiyo Tomiyasu Technical Field Award, the 2001 IEEE W. R. G. Baker prize paper award, and a Golden Jubilee medal from the IEEE Circuits and Systems Society in 2000. He was elected a Fellow of IEEE in 1996. He has served on the editorial boards of the IEEE TRANSACTIONS ON CIRCUITS AND SYSTEMS - PART I and PART II, VLSI Systems, Signal Processing, Signal Processing Letters, and Signal Processing Magazine, and served as the Editor-in-Chief of the IEEE TRANSACTIONS ON CIRCUITS AND SYSTEMS -PART I (2004-2005 term), and currently serves on the Editorial Board of the Springer Journal of Signal Processing Systems. He has served as technical program cochair of the 1995 IEEE VLSI Signal Processing workshop and the 1996 ASAP conference, and as the general chair of the 2002 IEEE Workshop on Signal Processing Systems. He was a distinguished lecturer for the IEEE Circuits and Systems society during 1996-1998. He served as an elected member of the Board of Governors of the IEEE Circuits and Systems society from 2005 to 2007.

Hardening QDI Circuits against Transient Faults Using Delay-Insensitive Maxterm Synthesis

Matheus T. Moreira, Ricardo A. Guazzelli, Guilherme Heck and Ney L. V. Calazans

GAPH – FACIN – Pontifícia Universidade Católica do Rio Grande do Sul

Av. Ipiranga, 6681 Partenon Porto Alegre/RS – Brazil

{matheus.moreira, ricardo.guazzelli, guilherme.heck}@acad.pucrs.br, ney.calazans@pucrs.br

ABSTRACT

The correct functionality of quasi-delay-insensitive asynchronous circuits can be jeopardized by the presence and propagation of transient faults. If these faults are latched, they will corrupt data validity and can make the whole circuit to stall, given the strict event ordering constraints imposed by handshaking protocols. This is particularly concerning for the delay-insensitive minterm synthesis logic style, widely adopted by asynchronous designers to implement combinatory quasi-delay-insensitive logic, because it makes extensive use of C-elements and these components are rather vulnerable to transient effects. This paper demonstrates that this logic style submits C-elements to their most vulnerable states during operation. It accordingly proposes the alternative use of the delay-insensitive maxterm synthesis for hardening QDI circuits against transient faults. The latter is a logic style based on the return-to-one 4-phase protocol. Although this style also relies on extensive usage of C-elements, the states where these components are most vulnerable are avoided. Results display improvements of over 300% in C-elements tolerance to transient faults, in the best case.

Categories and Subject Descriptors

B.8.1 [**Hardware**]: Reliability, Testing, and Fault-Tolerance

General Terms

Design, Reliability.

Keywords

delay-insensitive maxterm synthesis; quasi-delay-insensitive; return-to-one; robustness; transient faults.

1. INTRODUCTION & RELATED WORK

The ever increasing demand for more complex systems and the possibility of integrating billions of transistors in a single chip brought designers to the boundaries of the synchronous paradigm capability. The efficient distribution of a global clock signal in modern, complex designs poses a very complex task. Albeit techniques and tools to help this exist, they can lead to overheads in power and area [1]. Also, as power budgets get tighter, motivated by battery-based appliances demand, and performance gets over-

constrained by aggressive technologies' process variations, traditional design techniques become unsustainable [2] [3]. In fact, the International Technology Roadmap for Semiconductors predicts that a shift on integrated circuits design paradigm is required to provide further improvements [4].

In this scenario, asynchronous techniques emerge as a promising solution to cope with technological problems faced by synchronous designers. Such techniques may employ several alternative templates [5]. However, according to Martin and Nyström in [1], the majority of current asynchronous circuits rely on the quasi-delay-insensitive (QDI) delay model, using 4-phase handshaking coupled to 1-of-n delay-insensitive (DI) codes. This is mainly because this template enables simple timing closure and analysis while maintaining insensitivity to wire and gates delay, given that the isochronic fork [6] constraint is respected [7]. For such circuits, different design styles support building combinational logic. Among them, a very popular style is the Delay-Insensitive Minterm Synthesis (DIMS) [5]. One reason behind the wide adoption of DIMS is the fact that it allows the use of semi-custom design approaches, as it requires only C-elements [5] and conventional gates and supports different DI codes that accept the use of Return-to-Zero (RTZ) 4-phase handshake protocols [5].

Although DIMS logic allows achieving delay insensitivity, as any logic circuit it is not insensitive to Single Event Transients (SETs) affecting its signals. These faults are unavoidable in CMOS technologies and can be caused by effects such as glitches produced by crosstalk noise, radiation or charge sharing [8]. In fact, the correct functionality of a DIMS circuit can be easily jeopardized if a glitch propagates to inputs that directly feed C-elements, because these components are quite vulnerable to transient faults [9] [10]. The same problem arises if a glitch is generated in an internal node or in the output of the C-element. Depending on the C-element internal state, glitches large enough can be latched, which produces a Single Event Upset (SEU). This is particularly problematic because DIMS logic relies on the extensive usage of C-elements and SEUs can corrupt their stored data.

This work presents a comprehensive analysis of the analog behavior of C-elements of an in-house library called ASCEnD [11] for all their states, under the presence of glitches in their inputs. We identify situations where this component is more vulnerable and identify the associated critical points. Results show that in DIMS logic blocks, C-elements are often subjected to their most vulnerable states, requiring smaller glitches to produce SEUs. To harden QDI circuits against such faults, we propose the usage of Delay-Insensitive Maxterm Synthesis (DIMxS), which is similar to DIMS but is based in the Return-to-One (RTO) 4-phase handshake protocol [12]. In DIMxS, the states where C-elements are most vulnerable are avoided. Simulation results indicate an increase in tolerance of glitches in the inputs of such components of over 300% in the best case.

2. RETURN-TO-ONE HANDSHAKING

QDI templates require the choice of a DI code and a handshake protocol. Classically, the RTZ 4-phase protocol is used in 1-of-n DI codes, where n 0s represent a spacer and valid code words are those that contain a single 1. Fig. 1(a) shows the RTZ 1-of-2 code, which uses two wires, called D.1 and D.0, to carry a single bit of information. A '0' bit is denoted by D.0 at 1, and a '1' bit by D.1 at 1. In 1-of-n RTZ conventions, any code word with more than a wire at 1 is invalid data. Fig. 2(a) shows data transmission in a system using the RTZ protocol. Communication starts with all wires at 0 (all-0s). Next, the sender puts data in the channel (D.0, D.1) which is acknowledged by the receiver with the ack signal. After the sender receives ack, it produces a spacer to end communication. The receiver then lowers the ack signal, after which another communication can take place.

Wire Name	Spacer	Bit '0'	Bit '1'	Wire Name	Spacer	Bit '0'	Bit '1'
D.1	0	0	1	D.1	1	1	0
D.0	0	1	0	D.0	1	0	1

Fig. 1. 4-phase 1-of-2 data encoding for (a) RTZ and (b) RTO protocols.

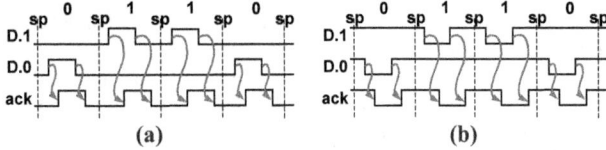

Fig. 2. Example of 4-phase (a) RTZ and (b) RTO 1-of-2 data transmission, where sp stands for spacers.

The RTO 4-phase protocol [12] is similar to RTZ. One difference is that valid data values are reversed compared to RTZ. Fig. 1(b) shows conventions for a 1-of-2 code based on RTO. Spacers are represented by n wires at 1 (all-1s). A '1' bit is denoted by D.1 at 0 and a '0' bit by D.0 at 0. As Fig. 2(b) shows, differently from RTZ, RTO data transmission starts after the all-1s value is in the data channel. As soon as the sender puts valid data in channel (D.0, D.1) the receiver may acknowledge it, by lowering the ack signal. Next, all data wires must return to 1 to produce a spacer. When the spacer is detected by the receiver, it raises the ack signal and new data can follow. Thus, RTO-RTZ domain interfaces for 1-of-n codes require only n inverters. As a generalization, an RTO D.x wire logical value can be translated from RTZ by Eq. (1).

$$\forall x, 0 \leq x \leq n-1 : RTO(D.x) = \neg RTZ(D.x) \tag{1}$$

Here, expressions RTO(D.x) and RTZ(D.x) correspond to wire logic values in the RTO and RTZ domains, respectively. In this way, according to Martin [6], the conversion of data from one domain to another is DI. Throughout this work 1-of-2 codes will be employed, but all presented techniques can be adjusted to any 1-of-n code in a straightforward way.

3. C-ELEMENTS, SETS AND SEUS
3.1 Background

A C-element is a basic gate in QDI design, which is used for the synchronization of events. Fig. 3(a) shows its symbol. Basically, the output Q of a 2-input C-element will only switch to 1 when both inputs are at 1 and to 0 when both inputs are at 0. In any other case, the output will remain with its previous value. Alternative CMOS transistor topologies for C-elements are the Sutherland, Martin and van Berkel, showed in Fig. 3 (b), (c) and (d) respectively [13]. The logic stack (1) is the part of the circuit that

is responsible for making the output to switch when both inputs have the same logic value, by charging/discharging the internal node nd0, which feeds the output inverter (2). When inputs are different, the output logic value is kept through the feedback mechanism (3).

Pontes et al. [14] and Bastos et al. [15] demonstrated that C-elements can be rather vulnerable to transient faults. When operating as a buffer (A=B), the worst consequence is the generation of a SET in the output, which will propagate as a glitch. However when operating as a memory (A≠B) this SET can be latched and generate an SEU. For instance, Fig. 4 shows the state transition graph of a 2-input C-element considering SEU and SET generation, as reported in [14]. The graph on Fig. 4 shows that when both inputs are at the same logic value, the output assumes this logic value and enters in a stable state where Q=A=B. During this state, any effect that causes the output to switch will not generate an SEU because the inputs ensure the output value. In fact, the result is the generation of an SET, where the output will incorrectly switch for a moment and then switch back, given that A=B, generating a glitch. But when A≠B, the C-element relies only on its internal memory scheme to keep the output. If the output switches incorrectly, this transition will be latched and generate an SEU. This fault will not be forced back to the correct value, because A≠B. Throughout this paper we refer to C-element memorizing states as vulnerable states.

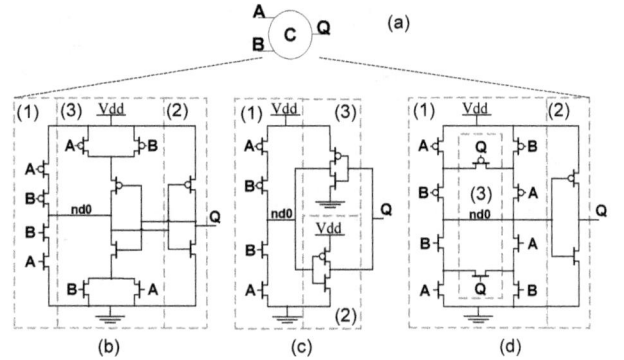

Fig. 3. C-element symbol (a) and Sutherland (b), Martin (c) and van Berkel (d) topologies [13]. For each topology (1) is the logic stack, (2) is the output inverter and (3) is the feedback mechanism.

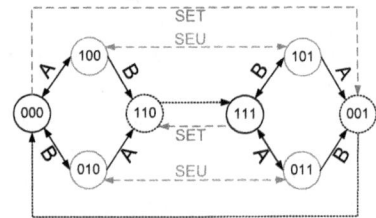

Fig. 4. State transition graph (ABQ) of a C-element considering SET and SEU effects [14]. Full-line nodes are static states. Dotted-line nodes are transition (unstable) states. Dashed lines are transitions that generate SETs or SEUs in the output. Dotted lines are transitions from unstable to stable states.

Some previous works explored the susceptibility of C-elements to transient faults. Mohammadi et al. [16] explore the effects of charge sharing on C-elements internal nodes. They demonstrate that glitches caused by such effects are a significant source of potential failure and propose modifications in C-element topology to alleviate the problem. A similar work [17] proposes rearranging transistors to alleviate the generated glitches and avoid SEU generation. Vaidyanathan et al. [18] evaluate the sensitivity of C-elements to radiation effects and propose a new transistor topology to increase robustness. None of these works presents a solution to cope with glitches that are propagated to the output, which will end up in the input of another cell, potentially a C-element in DIMS. Bastos et al. [15] identify all the vulnerable logic states of C-elements, including possible propagation of transient faults in the inputs and demonstrate that the correct choice of transistor topology can mitigate, but not eliminate the problem. These authors propose a technique for further improvements, which consists in increasing internal nodes capacitance for filtering transient faults, but this incurs in additional delay/power/area penalties.

The revised works propose modifications in the C-element at the circuit level for hardening QDI circuits against transient faults, which degrade performance and increase area. Also, most do not explore techniques for coping with possible transient faults that can propagate to the inputs of C-elements. Using the components of the ASCEnD library [11], we note that fault generation is facilitated when the output of a C-element is at logic 0. In fact, considering radiation effects in the output of a C-element [14], state 111 (refer to Fig. 4) requires a charge 39% bigger than state 000 to generate a SET and states 011 and 101 require 36% and 3% bigger charges than states 010 and 100, respectively, for generating SEUs. This work presents simulation results for all scenarios where 2-input C-elements are at vulnerable states, injecting 0 to 1 and 1 to 0 glitches of varying sizes to the inputs in order to quantify how vulnerable the components are in each state, defining states to avoid. In this way, problems generated by transient faults can be mitigated without incurring delay/power/area penalties.

3.2 Experiments

In a first experiment, we simulate the three C-element topologies described in Fig. 3 for vulnerable states (100, 010, 101 and 011 from Fig. 4). For each state, we simulate the injection of a trapezoidal glitch in the input that can cause the output to switch. In other words, for states 100 and 010, 0 to 1 glitches were injected in B and A, respectively. For states 101 and 011, 1 to 0 glitches were injected

in A and B, respectively. Such glitches had a varying height from 5 mV to 1 V in steps of 5 mV and a varying width, from 1 ps to 200 ps, in steps of 1 ps. Note that for 1 to 0 glitches the height was given as a negative variation. According to the work presented in [19], such setup provides a realistic analysis. Performing such investigation required a total of 200*200*4=160,000 simulation scenarios for each C-element, totalizing 480,000 simulations. Experiments use the Spectre simulator, from Cadence, employing post-layout extraction C-elements from ASCEnD [11], designed using a 65nm bulk CMOS technology from STMicroelectronics. Extractions occur for typical fabrication process and typical operating conditions (1 V and 25 C). Also, for all scenarios, C-elements have an output load equivalent to four inverters of the same driving strength input capacitances (FO4). Gates were also extracted for worst and best fabrication process and simulated using worst (125C and 0.9V) and best (-40C and 1.1V) operating conditions, for a total of 4,320,000 simulation scenarios. However, given that results vary only quantitatively and not qualitatively, and given the big volume of data, we only present results for the typical fabrication process under typical operating conditions. During simulation, we measure the variation in the voltage of the output for each scenario. The obtained results are summarized by Fig. 5. Results for Martin are showed in Fig. 5(a) and (b), for Sutherland in Fig. 5(c) and (d) and for van Berkel in Fig. 5(e) and (f). The first line of charts presents the results collected for 1 to 0 glitches (Glitch Down). Accordingly, in these charts, the worst case between 011 and 101 was collected. Similarly, the second line of charts present worst case for 0 to 1 glitches (Glitch Up), collected as the worst case between 010 and 100 states. Note that the points where the charts of the first line reach the bottom indicate scenarios (combination of a height and width for a glitch) that generate a SEU, because the output switched its logic value. The same applies to the points in the charts of the second line that reach the top. We refer to points in the frontier of those cases that generate SEUs as critical points, since they represent the minimum width for each glitch height (or vice-versa) that produces SEUs.

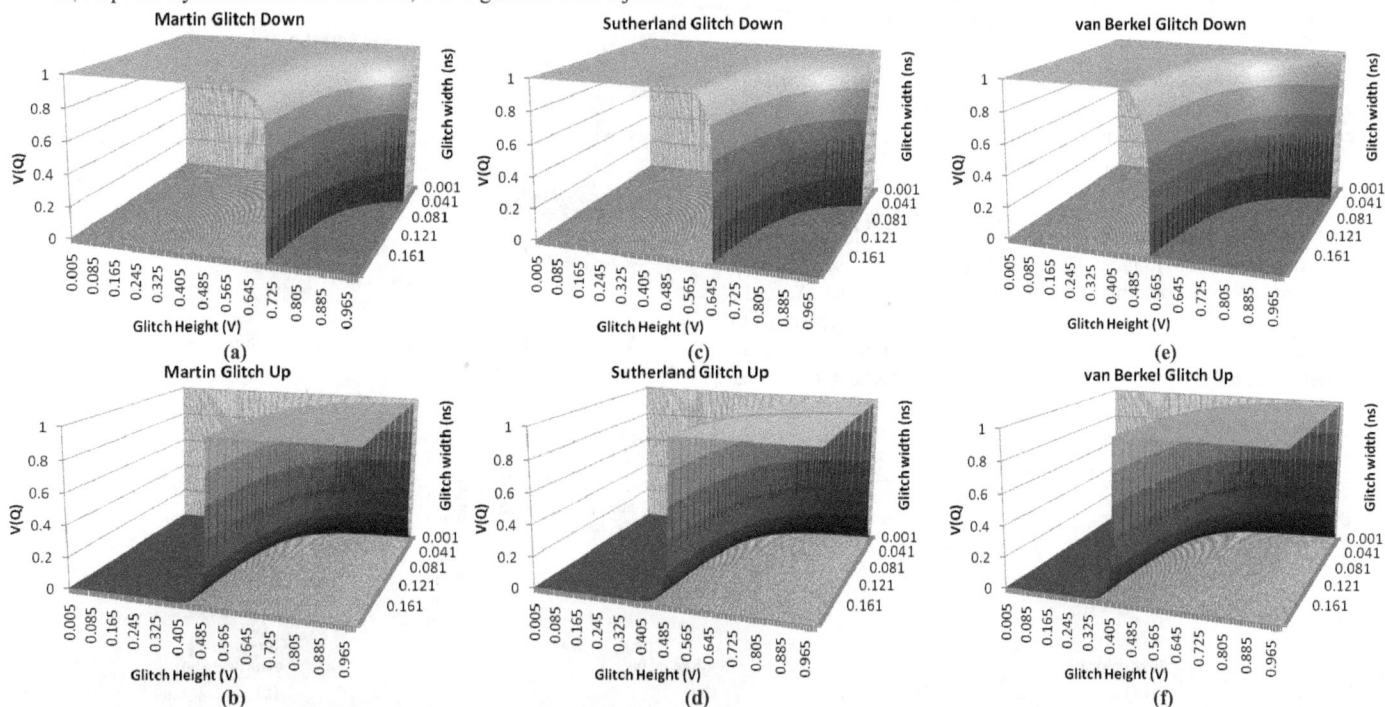

Fig. 5. Output voltage variation in the Martin (a) and (b), Sutherland (c) and (d) and van Berkel (e) and (f) topologies. Glitch Up stands for 010 and 100 scenarios and Glitch Down stands for 011 and 101 scenarios, where the worst case result was collected.

Note that critical points for the Martin topology are much bigger than those of Sutherland and van Berkel, displaying the increased robustness of this topology and confirming results pointed in [15]. However, one interesting characteristic of C-elements that no work available in the literature reports (as far as the authors could verify), is the big discrepancy between critical points for 0 to 1 and 1 to 0 glitches. Analyzing the critical points of the charts of second line of Fig. 5, it is clear that they are much smaller than those of the charts of the first line. What is more alarming is that for the Martin C-element, for instance, 0 to 1 glitches with heights of roughly 0.5 V can already generate SEUs, while for 1 to 0 glitches the minimum height is of over 0.7 V. Also, for the same topology, the minimum width for 0 to 1 glitches to produce an SEU is 22 ps, while for 1 to 0 glitches it is 42 ps. A similar analysis applies to the other two topologies. In this way, it is clear that vulnerable states where the output of the C-element is fixed at 0 are much more sensitive to glitches in the inputs than those where the output is at 1.

Another perspective of the results allows us to quantify this sensitivity more easily. Fig. 6 presents the isolated critical points for the Martin (a), Sutherland (b) and van Berkel (c) topologies, obtained from those of Fig. 5. Accordingly, the minimum heights for generating SEUs in the outputs of these C-elements for 0 to 1 glitches are roughly 0.5 V, 0.5 V and 0.4 V, respectively. For 1 to 0 glitches these values change to 0.7 V, 0.65 V and 0.55 V, respectively. Also, for the same heights, 1 to 0 glitches require much bigger widths than 0 to 1 glitches to produce SEUs. The right Y axis of the charts of Fig. 6 quantifies how bigger these widths need to be. For a worst case, these values are of 91%, 127% and 135% for Martin, Sutherland and van Berkel, respectively. However, the worst case is the one where glitches have bigger heights. If we evaluate the effects of glitches with small heights, the obtained improvements are much more significant, reaching up to 311%, 237% and 215% for Martin, Sutherland and van Berkel, respectively. This means that for the Martin topology, which is preferable for robust applications, 1 to 0 glitches in the inputs require almost two times the width of 0 to 1 glitches to generate SEUs in worst case and over four times in the best case.

Optimizations in DIMS logic may also employ inverted C-elements, as reported by Sokolov in [20]. However, as far as we could verify, no work available in current literature evaluates the effects of transient faults on these components.

In a second experiment, we generated the same 4,320,000 simulation scenarios, however this time using inverted C-elements from the ASCEnD-ST65 library. The critical points were isolated and compared to those obtained for non-inverted C-elements. Accordingly, in most cases we observed improvements in the tolerance of 0 to 1 glitches on the inputs. However for 1 to 0 glitches in general results are worse. Fig. 7 depicts the obtained results for Martin,

Sutherland and van Berkel C-element topologies. Note that Glitch Up still stands for 0 to 1 glitches in the inputs while Glitch Down stands for 1 to 0 glitches, albeit the output is inverted. As the chart shows, inverted C-elements tolerate 36%, 45% and 120% wider 0 to 1 glitches for Martin, Sutherland and van Berkel, in the worst case. These values reach 135%, 51% and 166%, respectively in the best case. These results indicate that using inverted C-elements can mitigate transient faults effects for 0 to 1 glitches. However, for 1 to 0 glitches this is not the case. As Fig. 7 shows, for Martin and Sutherland topologies improvements are typically negative, indicating that the components are more sensitive for 1 to 0 glitches. For the van Berkel, results oscillate around 0, which indicate that neither inverted nor non-inverted implementations can be said to tolerate wider 1 to 0 glitches.

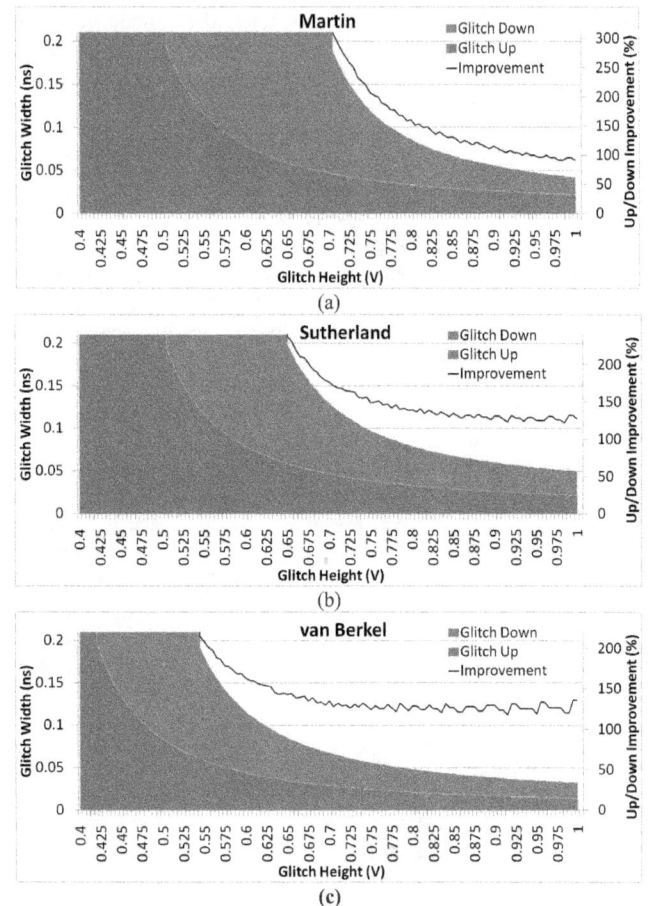

Fig. 6. Isolated critical points for Martin (a), Sutherland (b) and van Berkel (c) topologies.

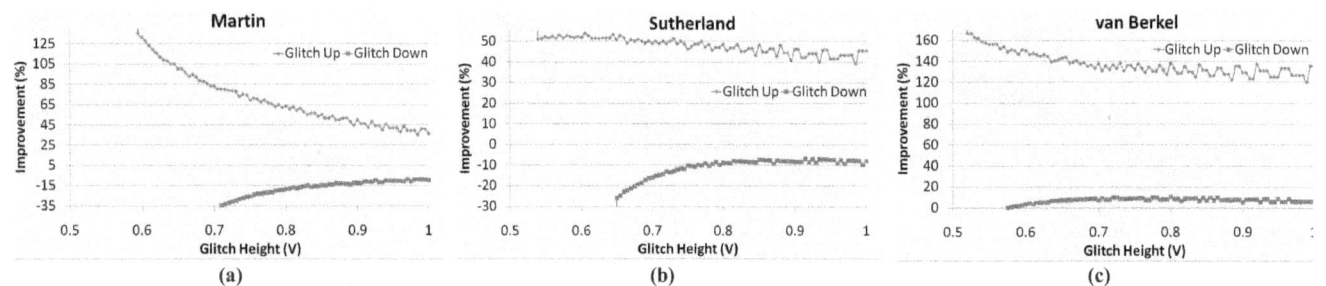

Fig. 7. Optimization provided by inverted C-elements compared to non-inverted ones for the Martin (a), Sutherland (b) and van Berkel (c) topologies.

The obtained results point that for non-inverted C-elements vulnerable states where the output was 1 tolerate bigger and wider glitches. One of the reasons behind this is the fact that in such states, glitches on the inputs of PMOS transistors are those that can generate faults, while in vulnerable states where the output is at 0, fault generation depends of glitches on the inputs of NMOS transistors. The latter are known to work much faster than the former.

4. HARDENING QDI CIRCUITS AGAINST TRANSIENT FAULTS

We demonstrated that submitting C-elements to vulnerable states with 1 in the output rather than those with 0 in the output allows mitigating problems caused by glitches in the inputs during such states, which enables hardening QDI circuits against transient faults. An analysis of the behavior of DIMS logic blocks reveals that the C-elements in this logic are often submitted to vulnerable states with 0s in the output. Meanwhile, in DIMxS blocks subject to vulnerable states, C-elements components have 1s in the outputs. Hence, we propose the usage of DIMxS for mitigating problems caused by transient faults in QDI circuits.

The DIMS logic style is a popular way of implementing combinational logic in QDI circuits. DIMS relies on the generation of the minterms for a given set of variables using C-elements, which are then combined through ORs to perform a given function, similar to two-level logic implementations used e.g. in PLAs. This style is useful to implement circuits with any 1-of-n DI code and employing 4-phase handshaking. Fig. 8(a) presents an example of a 2-input DIMS AND logic block, assuming an 1-of-2, RTZ, 4-phase handshaking template. Given that in this template a spacer precedes each valid data transmission, the reset (start) state for this circuit is all inputs at 0, which sets all internal nodes M00, M01, M10 and M11 to 0 as well. As soon as there are valid data in inputs A and B (represented by their 1-of-2 wires A.0, A.1, B.0 and B.1), one of the internal nodes will be set to 1, switching the output signal directly or triggering the OR gate, which will switch the output. For instance, if both inputs are 1 (A.1=1 and B.1=1), M11 will be set to 1, writing logic 1 in Q.1. The remaining internal nodes will still be at logic 0, keeping Q.0 in 0. This produces a logic 1 in the output. On the other hand, if at least one input is 0, as soon as both inputs have their values available in the C-elements inputs, either M00, M01 or M10 will be set to 1, writing 1 in Q.0, through the OR gate. Q.1 will still hold a 0, due to the previous spacer.

The construction of DIMxS circuits is similar to DIMS. Fig. 8(b) for instance, shows the schematic of a 2-input DIMxS AND logic block, assuming an 1-of-2, RTO, 4-phase handshaking. However, in this case, every data transmission is preceded by an all-1s spacer and C-elements generate the maxterms for the set of inputs, which are combined through an AND that implements the function output. In this way, the value of each signal of a DIMxS block is exactly the inverse of those of a DIMS block during operation, respecting Equation (1). Also, previous works demonstrate that DIMxS is more power efficient than DIMS, as reported in [21] and [22].

Fig. 9(a) shows the transition diagram for the 2-input DIMS and DIMxS AND blocks. Communications always start with two spacers. Next, valid data is inserted in both inputs, producing an output. Then, inputs must return to spacers so that new values can follow. The state of each C-element for the DIMS AND, for each state of Fig. 9(a) appears in Fig. 9(b). The only state where no C-element is at a vulnerable state is with two input spacers. For all other 8 states there are always two C-elements vulnerable. This shows that the problem cannot be ignored, as most of the time components are vulnerable. Given that in RTZ spacers are represented by the all-0s codeword, as Fig. 9(b) shows, vulnerable states of C-elements in DIMS blocks are always with a 0 in the output. Fig. 9(c) presents the same analysis for a similar DIMxS logic block. In this case, there is also a single state where C-elements are not vulnerable. However, in all remaining vulnerable states, components have 1s in the output, because spacers in RTO are represented by the all-1s codeword. From Fig. 8(a) it is clear that any fault generated by C-elements C0, C1, C2 or C3 corrupt the values of M00, M01, M10 or M11, causing the circuit to operate incorrectly. The same is valid for the equivalent DIMxS circuit in Fig. 8(b). Therefore, we believe that employing DIMxS rather than DIMS logic blocks mitigates problems caused by transient effects, as these effects are more expressive when the output of C-elements is at logic 0. To do so, RTO must be adopted in the design rather than RTZ. This can be done globally or locally in the circuit.

This approach does not require modifications in the C-elements and does not increase area or power [21]. The only modification is in the protocol assumption, which requires the usage of DIMxS rather than DIMS. In other words, OR gates are replaced by AND gates. Also, according to Equation (1), the translation of RTZ signals to RTO requires only inverters. However, because C-elements are usually employed for constructing QDI sequential and combinational components, inverted C-elements could be used for components in the borders between RTZ and RTO. In fact, results also indicate that using inverted C-elements is beneficial for mitigating problems caused by transient effects. These components could also be employed for DIMS logic optimizations such as those proposed in [20]. The equivalent state of each C-element of such optimized blocks is the same as the one in Fig. 9(c), given the inverted output. However, albeit the obtained results show that improvements could be obtained, these are much more modest than the ones obtained by using DIMxS. Therefore, we strongly advise the usage of DIMxS for hardening QDI circuits against transient faults.

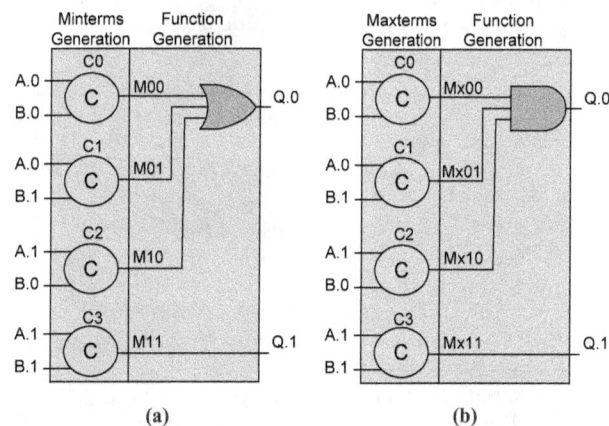

Fig. 8. Schematics for 2-input, 1-of-2 AND in (a) DIMS and (b)DIMxS

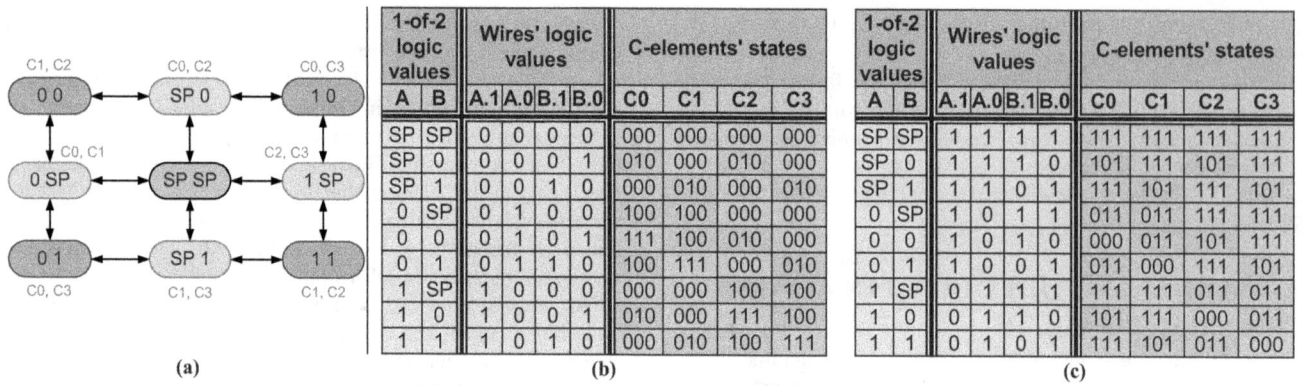

Table (a) — Transition diagram labels

	C1, C2		C0, C2		C0, C3
	0 0	↔	SP 0	↔	1 0
	C0, C1				C2, C3
	0 SP	↔	SP SP	↔	1 SP
	0 1	↔	SP 1	↔	1 1
	C0, C3		C1, C3		C1, C2

(b)

1-of-2 logic values		Wires' logic values				C-elements' states			
A	B	A.1	A.0	B.1	B.0	C0	C1	C2	C3
SP	SP	0	0	0	0	000	000	000	000
SP	0	0	0	0	1	010	000	010	000
SP	1	0	0	1	0	000	010	000	010
0	SP	0	1	0	0	100	100	000	000
0	0	0	1	0	1	111	100	010	000
0	1	0	1	1	0	100	111	000	010
1	SP	1	0	0	0	000	000	100	100
1	0	1	0	0	1	010	000	111	100
1	1	1	0	1	0	000	010	100	111

(c)

1-of-2 logic values		Wires' logic values				C-elements' states			
A	B	A.1	A.0	B.1	B.0	C0	C1	C2	C3
SP	SP	1	1	1	1	111	111	111	111
SP	0	1	1	1	0	101	111	101	111
SP	1	1	1	0	1	111	101	111	101
0	SP	1	0	1	1	011	011	111	111
0	0	1	0	1	0	000	011	101	111
0	1	1	0	0	1	011	000	111	101
1	SP	0	1	1	1	111	111	011	011
1	0	0	1	1	0	101	111	000	011
1	1	0	1	0	1	111	101	011	000

(a)   (b)   (c)

Fig. 9. Comparing DIMS and DIMxS. (a) Transition diagram for 2-input DIMS and DIMxS AND blocks; (b) States of the C-elements for a 2-input DIMS AND; (c) States of the C-elements for a 2-input DIMxS AND. Inputs are assumed to be encoded using the 1-of-2 code. SP stands for spacer.

5. CONCLUSIONS

In this work authors demonstrated that C-elements of DIMS circuits are often subjected to states that are more prone to generate SEUs. In fact, from the 9 possible states of a 2 input DIMS logic block, 8 states submit 50% of the C-elements in the block to such states. We propose DIMxS for implementing combinational logic for QDI circuits, which alleviates the problem by keeping C-elements more time in robust states. Results indicate that in these states, components tolerate glitches 311% wider than in equivalent DIMS states, in the best case, and 91% in the worst case. Also, no modifications are required in the C-elements' internal topology. The only modification is in the asynchronous template assumption. As future work, we will perform an evaluation of the behavior of DIMS and DIMxS blocks for near- and sub-threshold voltages.

6. ACKNOWLEDGMENTS

This work was partially supported by the CAPES-PROSUP (under grant 11/0455-5) and FAPERGS (under grant 11/1445-0). Authors acknowledge the support of CNPq under grants 310864/2011-9 (N.Calazans) and 142079/2013-8 (M.Moreira).

7. REFERENCES

[1] A. Martin and M. Nyström, "Asynchronous techniques for system-on-chip design," Proceedings of the IEEE, 94(6), 2006, pp.1089-1120.

[2] N. Ekekwe, "Power dissipation and interconnect noise challenges in nanometer CMOS technologies," IEEE Potentials, 29(3), May 2010, pp. 26–31.

[3] K. Chang and J. Chang, "Synchronous-Logic and Asynchronous-Logic 8051 Microcontroller Cores for Realizing the Internet of Things: A Comparative Study on Dynamic Voltage Scaling and Variation Effects," IEEE Journal on Emerging and Selected Topics in Circuits and Systems, 3(1), March 2013, pp. 23–34.

[4] International Technology Roadmap for Semiconductors, 2011 Edition - Design Chapter, available at http://www.itrs.net, 2013, 52p.

[5] P. Beerel, R. Ozdag, and M. Ferretti, "A Designer's Guide to Asynchronous VLSI," Cambridge University Press, Cambridge, 2010, 337 p.

[6] A. J. Martin, "The Limitations to Delay-Insensitivity in Asynchronous Circuits," in MIT Conference on Advanced Research in VLSI, 1990, pp. 263-278.

[7] W. J. Bainbridge, W. B. Toms, D. A. Edwards, and S. B. Furber, "Delay-insensitive, point-to-point interconnect using m-of-n codes," in ASYNC, 2003, pp. 132-140.

[8] J. M. Rabaey, A Chandrakasan, and B. Nikolic, "Digital Integrated Circuits a Design Perspective," Pearson Education, 2003, 761p.

[9] K. van Berkel, "Beware the isochronic fork," Integration, the VLSI Journal, 13(2), June 1992, pp. 103–128.

[10] F. Ouchet, K. Morin-Allory, and L. Fesquet, "Delay Insensitivity Does Not Mean Slope Insensitivity!," in ASYNC, 2010, pp. 176–184.

[11] M. T. Moreira, B. Oliveira, J. J. H. Pontes and N. L. V. Calazans. "A 65nm Standard Cell Set and Flow Dedicated to Automated Asynchronous Circuits Design," in SoCC, 2011, pp. 99-104.

[12] M. T. Moreira, R. A. Guazzelli, and N. L. V. Calazans. "Return-to-One Protocol for Reducing Static Power in C-elements of QDI Circuits Employing m-of-n Codes," in SBCCI, 2012, 6p.

[13] M. T. Moreira, B. Oliveira, F. G. Moraes, and N. L. V. Calazans, "Impact of C-elements in Asynchronous Circuits," in ISQED, 2012, pp. 438-444.

[14] J. J. H. Pontes, N. L. V. Calazans, and P. Vivet, "Adding Temporal Redundancy to Delay Insensitive Codes to Mitigate Single Event Effects," in ASYNC, 2012, pp. 142–149.

[15] R. Bastos, G. Sicard, F. Kastensmidt, M. Renaudin, and R. Reis, "Evaluating transient-fault effects on traditional C-element's implementations," in IOLTS, 2010, pp. 35–40.

[16] S. Mohammadi, S. Furber, and J. Garside, "Designing robust asynchronous circuit components," IEE Proceedings - Circuits, Devices and Systems, 150(3), 2003, pp. 161–166.

[17] M. T. Moreira, B. Oliveira, F. G. Moraes, and N. L. V. Calazans, "Charge Sharing Aware NCL Gates Design," in DFT, 6p. 2013.

[18] B. Vaidyanathan, and Y. Xie, "Soft error analysis and optimizations of C-elements in asynchronous circuits," in SELSE, 2006, pp. 2–5.

[19] M. Omaña, D. Rossi and C. Metra, "Model for Transient Fault Susceptibility for Combinational Circuits," Journal of Electronic Testing, 2004, 20(5), pp. 501-509.

[20] D. Sokolov, "Automated synthesis of asynchronous circuits using direct mapping for control and data paths," PhD Thesis, University of Newcastle, 2006. 203p.

[21] M. T. Moreira, R. A. Guazzelli, and N. L. V. Calazans, "Return-to-One DIMS Logic on 4-phase m-of-n Asynchronous Circuits," in ICECS, pp. 669-672, 2012.

[22] M. T. Moreira, J. Pontes, and N. L. V. Calazans, "Tradeoffs Between RTO and RTZ in WCHB QDI Asynchronous Design," in ISQED, 2014, pp 692-699.

System-level Reliability Exploration Framework for Heterogeneous MPSoC

Zheng Wang, Chao Chen
Anupam Chattopadhyay
MPSoC Architectures, RWTH Aachen University
52074 Aachen, Germany
{wang, anupam}@umic.rwth-aachen.de
ccbrucer@gmail.com

Piyush Sharma
Department of Electrical Engineering
IIT Patna, India
piyush.ee10@iitp.ac.in

ABSTRACT

Power density of digital circuits increased at alarming rate for deep sub-micron CMOS technology, turning reliability into a serious design concern. On the other hand, growing task complexity with strict performance budget forced designers to adopt complex, heterogeneous MPSoCs as the implementation choice. Several commercial system-level design platforms exist currently for design, exploration and implementation of MPSoC. In this paper, we propose a system-level reliability exploration framework by extending a commercial system-level design flow. Using this framework, a heterogeneous MPSoC is designed which can accept a custom mapping algorithm based on the MPSoC topology before the actual task deployment. The dynamic reliability-aware task management is able to consider the desired reliability constraints of tasks as well as reliability levels of the system components. We report our experimental findings using state-of-the-art benchmark applications.

Categories and Subject Descriptors

B.8.1 [**Performance and Reliability**]: Reliability, Testing, and Fault-Tolerance

Keywords

System-level Design; Reliability Exploration; Task Mapping

1. INTRODUCTION

With reduced transistor size in deep sub-micron CMOS technology, the performance and power density of processor have increased dramatically. High power density on the semiconductor chips increases failure rate and consequently reduces device lifetime as well as causes soft errors [10]. Furthermore, processor soft errors are caused by external radiations, such as cosmic rays [34], even at ground level [25]. These trends forced digital design community to consider reliability as a serious design concern.

Architectural fault tolerance techniques have been intensively studied in the past, in relation to manufacturing defects. With runtime, soft errors becoming more prominent than ever, these fault tolerance techniques have received a

renewed attention. On the other hand, as the design complexity grows, Multi-Processor System-on-Chip (MPSoC) becomes the state-of-the-art architecture for high performance and low power applications. The design trend of complex, multi-core systems puts stronger focus on systematic high-level design flow against traditional Register Transfer Level (RTL)-based design flow. To this end, SystemC, which is a library of C++ functions supporting concurrent process simulation, has become the standard design approach for complex SoC modeling. On top of SystemC kernels, several platform simulation tools are proposed by Electronic System Level (ESL) tool vendors.

It is necessary to integrate reliability exploration in system-level design, where efficient support in tools, platforms and algorithms is required. For instance, while there exist dedicated processor-specific fault-injection studies [9][26], generic system-level fault injection is relatively less explored [22]. This is compounded by the fact that, heterogeneous MPSoC platform with customized interconnect topology consists of processing elements with varying robustness. Furthermore, reliability-aware system-level task mapping technique should consider the reliability requirement of individual tasks. All these aspects need to be addressed together for a system-level reliability exploration platform.

In this work, we first present an efficient fault injection technique for SoC components, such as processor IPs, bus and memory. The fault injection tools developed are conveniently used for system-level reliability exploration. For processors IPs such as ARM9 [2], fault injection is realized by the integrated high-level programming interface of SystemC components, which is inherited directly from the platform support package of abstract processor models. With regard to bus and memories, new fault injection interfaces are inserted to facilitate runtime fault injection.

Taking advantage of the fault injection technique, a heterogeneous multiprocessor platform consisting of processor IPs and customized modules for executing Kahn Process Network (KPN)-like [18] streaming applications is developed. The processing elements and communication channels are equipped with fault injection properties. Executing on the centralized task manager, a novel firmware initializes user-defined KPN task graph and dynamically updating system interconnect topology. The task-mapping algorithm can be easily integrated through interface in the firmware, thereby scheduling KPN applications accordingly. We further investigate the mapping technique in the presence of various reliability requirements among KPN tasks and different levels of reliability among heterogeneous processing elements. A combined task/core-reliability-aware task mapping heuristic is then presented. Our key contributions are:

- System-level fault injection for individual components.

- Firmware for user defined task and system topology.

- Mapping technique considering task/core reliability level.

The rest of the paper is organized as follows. Section II discusses the related work. Section III introduces the system-level fault injection techniques. The reliability exploration platform is presented in Section IV. The usability of the proposed approaches is shown in Section V. Finally, Section VI closes the paper with conclusion and future work.

2. RELATED WORK

2.1 Processor Fault Injection

Processor reliability can be investigated through simulation-based fault injection which has been studied across design abstraction layers. This is done through altering of simulation states such as register values at particular time instance. At circuit-level faults can be accurately simulated [21], but it is also the most time consuming. Alternatively, gate-level [7] and RTL [12][17][3] fault simulation explores the trade-off between simulation speed and accuracy. In [9], it is shown that a significant accuracy improvement is achieved via circuit-level reliability analysis compared to software-level analysis [8] at the cost of more than 1 order of magnitude speedup. However, the accuracy gap is reportedly much less for cycle-accurate processor descriptions when compared to RTL or gate-level reliability analysis[31][32]. This is due to the fact that information exposure in cycle-accurate processor simulation model is quite close to the RTL.

2.2 System-level Fault Injection

System-level fault injection using SystemC models are primarily done using Code Modification (CM) method, which requires time-consuming model recompilation. Fin *et al*[15] presents an environment for stuck-at fault injection into SystemC models by adoption of *mutants* techniques. In [5], a similar approach is shown for the fault injection on finite state machines. In [22] the authors present configurable fault injection through mutated TLM communication functions. *Saboteur*-based approaches are presented in [27] and [24], where specific fault injection modules are used for managing the injected faults. Few works have been carried out for Simulation Commands (SC) based methods, which avoid model recompilation. In [23] the authors take advantage of the *reflective property* provided by specific programming languages such as Java to implement the SC technique. However, the work is done on Java software models. The work in [4] further extends the reflective property of Python language to build a software interface interacting with user commands. Such methods can inject faults on all the public members. The experiments in the work are carried out only for simple modules such as FIR and FSM.

2.3 Reliability-aware Task Mapping

Task mapping approaches on MPSoC have been intensively investigated in recent past. A detailed survey on those can be found in [29]. With regard to the techniques improving device lifetime, [13] discusses approaches for addressing the lifetime optimization in terms of Mean Time To Failure (MTTF). Coskun *et al* [11] presented a temperature-aware mapping that leads to increased lifetime. A wear-based heuristic is proposed in [16] to improve the system lifetime.

On the other hand, several papers target reliable mapping in presence of transient faults. In [19] the authors propose a remapping technique aimed towards determining task migrations with the minimum cost while minimizing the throughput degradation. In [28] a scenario-based design flow for mapping streaming applications onto heterogeneous on-chip many-core systems is presented. [14] evaluates several remapping algorithms for single fault scenarios by using

Integer Linear Programming (ILP) under faulty core constraints. Several proposed heuristics also perform optimization to minimize communication traffic and total execution time.

Though reliability is treated by several research works for efficient task management, the proposed mapping techniques have not yet considered the intrinsic differences of reliability levels among different processing units. This is presumably due to the lack of system-level reliability exploration frameworks. The ERSA architecture [20] addresses this issue by adopting one Super Reliable Core (SRC) and multiple Relaxed Reliable Cores (RRCs) and manages the tasks according to the vulnerability of the cores. In this work, we propose a reliability exploration framework to aid the development of such platforms and furthermore, explore core/task-level reliability-aware remapping techniques.

3. SYSTEM-LEVEL FAULT INJECTION

In this section, we explain the strategies for fault injection on system level modules such as processors, bus and memory.

3.1 Processor fault injection

For processor-level fault injection, we adopt a commercial processor design flow [30], which is based on the language LISA. Fault injection for LISA-based processors has been proposed in [31], where the LISA Application Programming Interface (API) is used for modifying the processor states during execution. To integrate LISA processor model into the platform, a SystemC wrapper is constructed which inherits all the methods including the API functions of the processor model. Taking advantage of LISA API interfaces, high-level processor models are subjected to fault injection with fairly accurate reliability estimation [31]. The system-level techniques apply the same methodology so that similar accuracy is achieved. The fault injection flow is briefly explained in the following.

3.1.1 The setup phase

By using LISA compiler, SystemC simulation models for the LISA processor are generated, where all the declared resources are exposed for fault injection. A user-friendly GUI is provided to generate fault configurations such as timing, location and amounts of faults in an XML file. The SystemC processor model reads the fault configuration file, which is used later for scheduling and injection of faults.

3.1.2 The simulation phase

LISA APIs are interactively used for simulating the processor models. Several methods such as model initialization, cycle based execution, get and set resources values are used to inject the faults based on user configurations. Resource value tracing method is used for dumping simulation results as Value Change Dump (VCD) file. The simulation phase consists of several steps: First, the fault configurations is parsed by the XML parser to create queue-based data structures. Second, the tracing resources specified in the configuration file are added to the simulation tracing list. When the simulation starts, a scheduler is triggered to inject the faults based on the faults injection time. The executed program finally runs until the end of simulation.

3.1.3 The evaluation phase

For estimating reliability, *Error Manifestation Rate* (EMR) is used as the metric. EMR is defined as the percentage of experiments, for which an error is detected on the processor-memory interface. Various EMR values among heterogeneous processors indicates the different fault tolerant abilities against soft error. One example can be refered in [33] where processor with protected ALU shows less EMR value than unprotected one under the same fault condition.

3.2 Bus fault injection

Compared to the processor model, fault injection in the system bus is considerably simplified due to its few communication states while the transmitted data is provided as an argument of the data transport function. Even without the API support, such transmitted data can be subjected to fault injection by changing its value at specific time instances directly. Similar to the processor models, faults are specified in the configuration file. During model initialization, the fault configuration is parsed and sorted into the fault queue according to their injection time. When data transport function is called, the scheduler detects whether a fault needs to be injected to the data before the actual data transmission according to the fault injection time.

3.3 Memory fault injection

Contrary to processor and bus models, memory models in SystemC specification are not required to be clock-sensitive for a pure behavioral simulation. However, decisions of fault injection need to be made according to the current simulation time. For this purpose, an extra clock-sensitive SystemC method which maintains a clock counter is created for time-based fault injection, where the clock counter is continuously checked against the fault injection time. The proposed method can also be applied to other clock-insensitive modules. In the fault configuration phase, user needs to provide detailed memory array indices for fault injection target or select a statistical distribution for the same.

4. RELIABILITY EXPLORATION

In this section, the reliability exploration platform and task management methodologies are introduced. Figure 1 illustrates an exemplary heterogeneous MPSoC platform with a mapping example of KPN application. It is noted that KPN nodes have different reliability levels due to the application properties, which can be defined by software developer. For instance, higher reliability levels can be assigned to node P3 and P6 in Figure 1 due to higher degree of edges. From the architecture side, the ability to integrate customized processor helps improving core-level reliability. In Figure 1 the PD_RISC processors are protected with architecture-level fault tolerance features such as Error Correction Code (ECC) and Triple Modular Redundancy (TMR). During task mapping, task with high reliability level are preferred to be mapped on more reliable cores. To realize initial task mapping and run-time remapping, the run-time manager core, which is protected by both ECC and TMR, executes a firmware for task scheduling and monitoring under fault injection. The firmware is novel in the sense that it supports arbitrary platform topology and user defined task graphs through its API. Timer on individual processor informs the manager core whether the monitored processor is in unresponsive state and requires to be reset. The shared memory implements channels containing data tokens for communication between processors with synchronization features. Several novel features of the platform are presented in the following.

4.1 Customized processor integration

Taking advantage of Synopsys Processor Designer, customized processor in both RTL and SystemC package can be automatically generated from high-level descriptions. The PD_RISC core used as run-time manager and reliable processing elements (PEs) is a mixed 16 and 32 bits instruction set processor with 6 pipeline stages. Reliability extensions are implemented via additional LISA operations and resources. The processor-bus interface can be chosen among TLM 2.0 and AHB types depending on the applied bus system. Fault injection technique in Section 3 is applied for individual processor.

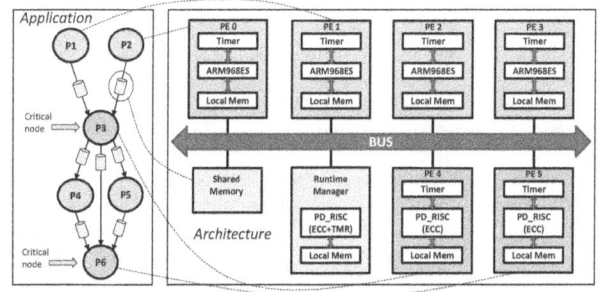

Figure 1: KPN tasks mapping to MPSoC considering node reliability level

4.2 Run-time manager firmware

The extensibility of MPSoC platform requires support from the run-time manager for a dynamic platform topology specification, which considers not only system interconnects but also core reliability indexes due to intrinsic differences of fault tolerant abilities among heterogeneous cores. Both KPN application and platform topology are defined by the APIs shown in Figure 2.

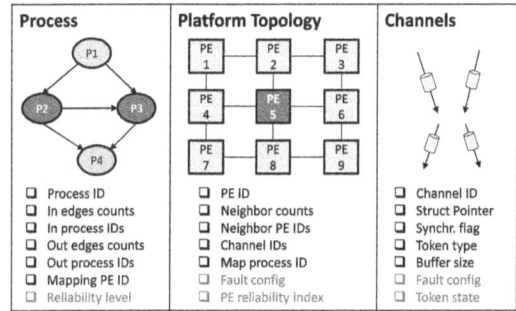

Figure 2: Data structures for platform initialization

4.2.1 Application graph

Basic fields are used to describe the KPN task graph such as process ID and connecting processes. The firmware also maintains a look-up-table in the local memory of each PE for the function definition corresponding to the process ID. For reliability-directed mapping, user can provide reliability level for each process manually. A successful task mapping assigns PE ID to all the processes.

4.2.2 Platform topology

Specific fields are required to represent the platform topology for each PE such as neighboring PE nodes and connecting channels. For instance, bus based platform in Figure 1 is configured as a fully connected processor network. Architecture level reliability index for each core is defined according to the EMR metric in Section 3.1.3. Detailed EMR evaluation for heterogeneous processors is referred in [33]. Besides, fault configuration is provided on each core for the purpose of fault injection.

4.2.3 Channels

Channels implement not only inter-PE communication but also data synchronizations. Token type and buffer sizes are defined based on user inputs. Regarding the implementation, channels can be realized in different ways depending on the emulation platform. A NoC platform relates channels directly to its physical links. For a bus-based platform, channels are implemented as data structures in shared memory according to the topology to emulate generic styles of interconnects, which gets automatically analyzed from topology graph. Fault injection in channels are implemented as bit manipulation in the data elements of channel structure, where a fault configuration file is provided for each channel. A specific *token state* field is used to pass the current task execution state to the following channels. It can be realized as an integer, whose value is incremented each time the start node (P1 in Figure 2) processes one token. When the same token is finished processing by the end node (P4), its value is updated in the shared memory. Such mechanism helps retrieving the processing state when run-time task remapping happens. After remapping, the start node can directly process the next token.

4.2.4 State transition

Upon system initialization, the manager initializes KPN processes, topology and channels according to user-provided information while PEs wait for task assignment. After a successful initial mapping the PEs begin to perform individual tasks and token state begins to pass down the channels. The manager keeps checking the status of all PEs. We consider the worst case that unresponsive PE is not able to be restarted. Under such case whenever one PE is unresponsive, the platform topology is updated by removing the faulty PE and its edges from the topology graph. A task remapping phase then follows up. In case of mapping failure, the run-time manager terminates the system. A successful mapping will interrupt all PEs for task switching while current token state is retrieved to continue processing the erroneous token. The mapping algorithm can be realized as either complete run-time mapping or based on design-time analysis [29].

4.3 Core reliability directed task mapping

While focusing on core reliability-aware task mapping, the performance/power differences among heterogeneous processors are currently disregarded. Besides, it is limited that only one task can be mapped to one PE, which implies a static global communication cost for a fixed KPN system. The focus of the remapping algorithm is to accept the core/task reliability constraint and generate a mapping with low overhead. A heuristic recursive mapping algorithm is developed in Algorithm 1. It maps tasks sequentially. Once a task is mapped successfully, the mapping of next dependent task in the task graph starts. Otherwise, the task will be mapped to other remaining processors. If such a task cannot be mapped to any remaining processor, the recursive algorithm returns and changes the previous task mapping. The algorithm stops when a successful mapping for all tasks are achieved.

Algorithm 1 Mapping task to platform recursively

INPUTS: PE: Topology graph **TA:** Task graph
OUTPUT: PE $\Leftrightarrow$ **TA**
1: **function** RUNMAP(PE, TA)
2:     $sort\_PE\_node$
3:     $sort\_TA\_node$
4:     $status = recursiveMap(0)$ ▷ init recursive mapping
5:     **return** $status$
6: **end function**
7:
8: **function** RECURSIVEMAP($task\_id$)
9:     **if** $task\_id == task\_Count$ **then**
10:         **return** $Success$ ▷ last task has been mapped
11:     **end if**
12:     **for** $pe\_id = 1$ to PE_Count **do**
13:         **if** $mapT2P(task\_id, pe\_id)$ **then**   ▷ mapping plug-in
14:             $binding(PE[pe\_id], TA[task\_id])$
15:             **if** $recursiveMap(task\_id + 1) == Success$ **then**
16:                 **return** $Success$ ▷ recursive mapping success
17:             **else**
18:                 $PE(pe\_id) \rightarrow t\_id = null$
19:             **end if**   ▷ recursion fail, clear parent decision
20:         **end if**
21:     **end for**
22:     **return** $Fail$
23: **end function**

Algorithm 2 shows the procedure which decides Task-PE mapping according to the constraints. Two constraints are presented while further ones considering other performance can be easily integrated.

Algorithm 2 Decision with edges and reliability constraints

1: **function** MAPT2P($task\_id, pe\_id$)
2:     **if** $PE(pe\_id) \rightarrow Degree < TA(task\_id) \rightarrow Degree$ **then**
3:         **return** $Fail$ ▷ meet task edges constraint
4:     **end if**
5:     **if** $PE(pe\_id) \rightarrow relia\_ind < TA(task\_id) \rightarrow relia\_lev$ **then**
6:         **return** $Fail$ ▷ meet reliability requirement
7:     **end if**
8:     $neighbors\_ids = get\_task\_neighbors(task\_id)$
9:     **for all** $neighbors\_ids$ **do**
10:         $pe\_neb\_id = TA(neighbors\_ids) \rightarrow p\_id$
11:         **if** $pe\_neb\_id! = null$ **then**
12:             **if** $is\_pe\_neighbors(pe\_neb\_id, pe\_id)$ **then**
13:             **else**
14:                 **return** $Fail$
15:             **end if**
16:         **end if**   ▷ ensure task neighbors are topological neighbors
17:     **end for**
18:     **return** $Success$
19: **end function**

4.3.1 Task degree constraint

The 1-to-1 mapping constraint implies a possible mapping only when the count of node edges in task graph is not larger than the count of PE links in topology graph. Besides, connecting tasks in KPN graph should also be topological neighbors. The search procedure in Algorithm 1 starts by sorting both processes and PEs in descending order of their degrees, which reduces the time for finding a possible mapping. During mapping, if the number of PE links is smaller than required, the mapping fails. Otherwise, the task will check whether its dependent tasks, which have already been mapped, can reach it as topological neighbors.

4.3.2 Core reliability constraint

A successful mapping ensures that the reliability indexes of all PEs are not less than the tasks' reliability level, which is considered every time before the mapping decision.

5. EXPERIMENTAL RESULTS

In this section, we present several experimental studies with our proposed techniques. First, system-level fault injection experiments on a heterogeneous MPSoC are performed. Second, real-world KPN tasks are implemented on the customized MPSoC platform described in section 4. Consequently, the effectiveness of run-time manager and core/task reliability-aware mapping is illustrated.

5.1 System level fault injection

The Operating System Application Specific Instruction-set Processor (OSIP) [6] is a hardware accelerator of OS kernel providing support for mapping, scheduling and synchronization in heterogeneous MPSoCs. OSIP-based MP-SoC system is used to verify the effects of system level fault injection. Modeled using Synopsys Platform Architect [1], the platform consists of 7 ARM926EJ-S processors as PEs and 1 OSIP. Two applications have been investigated.

5.1.1 H.264 decoder

The application decodes H.264 data into video stream. ARM PEs dynamically get their task assignments from the OSIP. Fault configurations are parsed into the SystemC models of PEs. Note that currently no faults are injected into the OSIP. Figure 3 shows the impacts of faulty simulation compared with fault free simulation, where several effects are shown such as pixel error, unresponsive PE and fail to process.

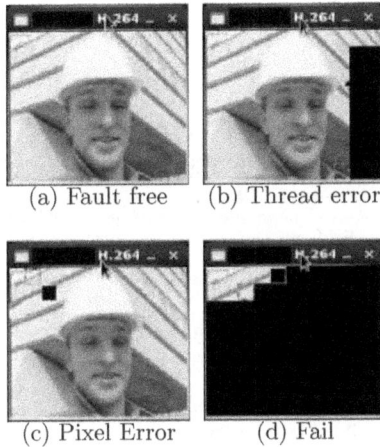

(a) Fault free (b) Thread error

(c) Pixel Error (d) Fail

Figure 3: H.264 decoder with fault injection

5.1.2 Median filter

Median filter implementation on OSIP reduces image noise by using PEs. Figure 4(a) and 4(b) show the original image with noise and the image after filtering respectively. A fault-tolerant implementation of median filter is executed on OSIP, which schedules additional tasks to other PEs whenever one PE is unresponsive. Downcount timers are implemented to restart the unresponsive PEs so that they get new tasks from the OSIP to continue processing. Currently the downcount time is set as 3× of the regular processing time for one data token. Within such time if no pixel has been processed the PE is considered to be in *hanging state*. Several experiments are conducted which are shown in Figure 4(c). The first experiment runs without fault injection, whereas for the rest experiments 100 bit-flip faults are injected on one PE. It can be observed from the Figure 4(c) that without monitoring timers, the processing overhead increases significantly as the number of hanging PEs grows. However, only a slight overhead occurs when timers are equipped, which is caused during task re-allocation.

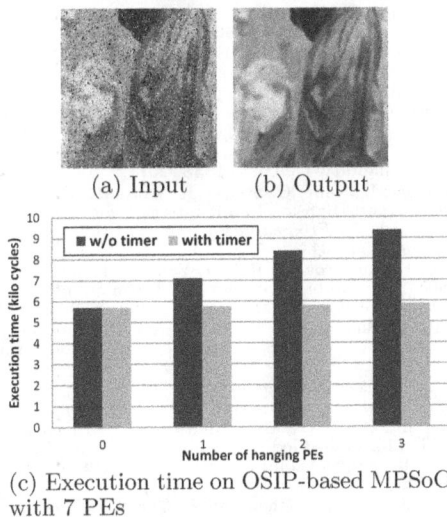

(a) Input (b) Output

(c) Execution time on OSIP-based MPSoC with 7 PEs

Figure 4: Median filter reliability exploration

5.2 Core-reliability-aware task mapping

The efficacy of the mapping technique is explored with an audio processing application, shown as a KPN graph in Figure 5. The application is mapped onto a heterogeneous MPSoC platform with 16 PEs. The filter block task is assigned

with a high reliability constraint according to its degree. To demonstrate the usage of proposed mapping algorithm, the platform consists PD_RISC processors with ECC protection on its program counter register (PC), which is labeled as 'H' while the rest ARM processors are labeled as 'L'.

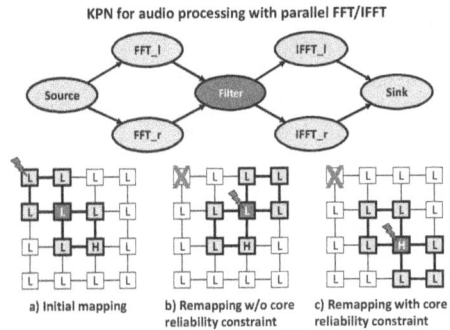

Figure 5: KPN tasks mapping onto 16 PE platform

5.2.1 Algorithm constraints

Initially a fixed mapping as in 5a) is forced for all the tasks. Upon single bit fault injection into the PC register, the ARM processor without ECC protection is likely to fall into unresponsive state which activates the run-time manager for task remapping. When only edge count constraint is applied, the tasks are mapped as in Figure 5b), where the filter task is still prone to the faults on an unreliable PE. However, a core-reliability-aware mapping schedules tasks as in Figure 5c), where further single bit-flip fault injection on the filter application does not hang the system due to the ECC protected program counter. Table 1 shows the required cycles of fault simulation to process 10 data tokens using different mapping algorithms. When the core reliability constraint is considered, an overhead of 1.2% is caused by task migration, while the system hangs when only edge count constraint is applied.

Mapping constraints	Cycles count w/o faults	Cycle count with faults	Cycle increased
edge count only	18,173k	Hang	Hang
edge count+core reliability	18,173k	18,387k	1.2%

Table 1: Mapping exploration with different algorithm constraints

5.2.2 Topology and PE types

Further mapping explorations with different topology and PE types are performed as in Figure 6. A platform with mesh topology suffers from 3 unresponsive PEs as in 6e). One extra high reliable core does not facilitate further remapping as shown in 6f). In the contrary, a topology with more links such as nearest neighbor (NN) realize further mappings, where up to 5 unresponsive PEs are tolerant as in 6i). When further highly reliable core is deployed, remapping is still achieved with 6 hanging PEs as shown in 6k). No further mapping is possible with 7 hanging PEs.

Experiments are conducted where single bit-flip faults are injected to the PC registers of PEs as shown in Figure 6. Table 2 shows the required cycles to process 10 data tokens with regard to various topologies and PE types where up to 7 PEs become unresponsive during execution. It is shown that NN topology with 2 highly reliable PEs can tolerate up to 6 hanging PEs whereas Mesh suffers from 3 hanging PEs. The remapping task itself takes 143 kcycles on the supervisor core for 16-PE Mesh topology and 138 kcycles for the same using NN topology. In NN it is easier and faster to find a possible mapping according to the task degree constraint

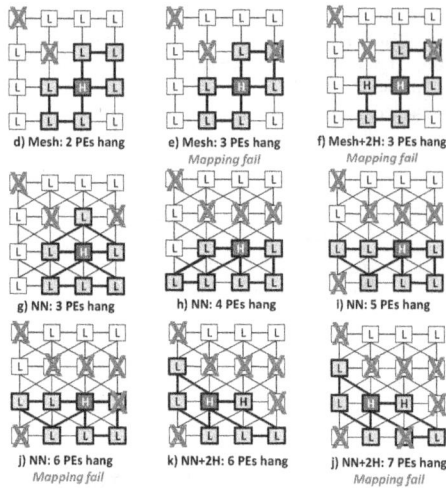

Figure 6: Mapping exploration for 7 KPN nodes

since all processor nodes have more edges than those in Mesh for executing the same KPN task. However, the increased amount of channels implies the trade-off between topology complexity and possibility of successful mapping. The overhead differences caused by varying number of reliable cores for the same topology and number of hanging PEs are minor since only difference of a few cycles is incurred during PE initialization.

Hanging PE count	Cycle count (kcycles)					
	Mesh			NN		
	1H PE	2H PEs	+(%)	1H PE	2H PEs	+(%)
0	18,173	18,173	0	18,168	18,168	0
1	18,387	18,387	1.2	18,375	18,375	1.1
2	18,621	18,621	2.5	18,602	18,602	2.4
3	Hang	Hang	-	18,831	18,831	3.6
4	Hang	Hang	-	19,063	19,063	4.9
5	Hang	Hang	-	19,297	19,297	6.2
6	Hang	Hang	-	Hang	19,542	7.6
7	Hang	Hang	-	Hang	Hang	-

Table 2: Exploration with topology and PE types

6. CONCLUSION

In this paper a system-level reliability exploration framework is presented based on a commercial design flow. A mapping algorithm for process networks considering reliability level of individual tasks is illustrated. A heterogeneous MPSoC platform with user-defined architecture topology and its ability of integrating customized processors with reliability extension show the usability of the proposed mapping technique. Future work includes the systematic exploration with core reliability constraint against other performance metrics as well as study of further cross-layer reliability approaches. Low-overhead dynamic task remapping will also be explored.

7. REFERENCES

[1] Synopsys platform architect introduction. Accessed: 2013-07-21.
[2] ARM. http://www.arm.com/products/processors/classic/arm9/index.php.
[3] J. C. Baraza, J. Gracia, D. Gil, and P. J. Gil. A prototype of a vhdl-based fault injection tool: description and application. Journal of Systems Architecture, 47(10):847–867, 2002.
[4] C. Bolchini, A. Miele, and D. Sciuto. Fault models and injection strategies in systemc specifications. In 11th EUROMICRO Conf. on Digital System Design - Architectures, Methods and Tools, DSD '08.
[5] F. Bruschi, F. Ferrandi, and D. Sciuto. A framework for the functional verification of systemc models. Int. J. Parallel Program., 33(6):667–695, Dec. 2005.
[6] J. Castrillon, D. Zhang, T. Kempf, B. Vanthournout, R. Leupers, and G. Ascheid. Task management in mpsocs: an asip approach. ICCAD'09.
[7] H. Cha, E. Rudnick, J. Patel, R. Iyer, and G. Choi. A gate-level simulation environment for alpha-particle-induced transient faults. IEEE Trans. Comput., 45(11):1248–1256, Nov. 1996.
[8] D. Chen, G. Jacques-Silva, Z. Kalbarczyk, R. Iyer, and B. Mealey. Error behavior comparison of multiple computing systems: A case study using linux on pentium, solaris on sparc, and aix on power. In 14th IEEE Pacific Rim International Symposium on Dependable Computing, PRDC '08.
[9] H. Cho, S. Mirkhani, C. Cher, J. A. Abraham, and S. Mitra. Quantitative evaluation of soft error injection techniques for robust system design. In Proceedings of the 50th Annual Design Automation Conference, DAC '13.
[10] C. Constantinescu. Trends and challenges in vlsi circuit reliability. IEEE Micro, 23(4):14–19, 2003.
[11] A. K. Coskun, T. S. Rosing, and K. C. Gross. Temperature management in multiprocessor socs using online learning. DAC '08.
[12] D. Kammler, J. Guan, G. Ascheid, R. Leupers and H. Meyr. A fast and flexible Platform for Fault Injection and Evaluation in Verilog-based Simulations. SSIRI '09.
[13] A. Das, A. Kumar, and B. Veeravalli. Reliability-driven task mapping for lifetime extension of networks-on-chip based multiprocessor systems. In Conference on Design, Automation and Test in Europe, DATE '13.
[14] O. Derin, D. Kabakci, and L. Fiorin. Online task remapping strategies for fault-tolerant network-on-chip multiprocessors. In Fifth ACM/IEEE International Symposium on Networks-on-Chip, NOCS '11.
[15] A. Fin, F. Fummi, and G. Pravadelli. Amleto: A multi-language environment for functional test generation. In Proceedings IEEE International Test Conference, ITC '01.
[16] A. S. Hartman and D. E. Thomas. Lifetime improvement through runtime wear-based task mapping. CODES+ISSS '12.
[17] E. Jenn, J. Arlat, M. Rimén, J. Ohlsson, and J. Karlsson. Fault injection into vhdl models: The mefisto tool. In Twenty-Fourth International Symposium on Fault-Tolerant Computing (FTCS), pages 66–75, 1994.
[18] G. Kahn. The semantics of simple language for parallel programming. In IFIP Congress '74.
[19] C. Lee, H. Kim, H. Park, S. Kim, H. Oh, and S. Ha. A task remapping technique for reliable multi-core embedded systems. CODES/ISSS '10.
[20] L. Leem, H. Cho, J. Bau, Q. Jacobson, and S. Mitra. Ersa: error resilient system architecture for probabilistic applications. In Design, Automation and Test in Europe, DATE '10.
[21] R. Leveugle and A. Ammari. Early seu fault injection in digital, analog and mixed signal circuits: A global flow. DATE '04.
[22] M. Michael and D. Große and R. Drechsler. Analyzing dependability measures at the Electronic System Level. In Forum on Specification & Design Languages, FDL '11.
[23] E. Martins and A. C. A. Rosa. A fault injection approach based on reflective programming. DSN '00.
[24] S. Misera, H. T. Vierhaus, L. Breitenfeld, and A. Sieber. A mixed language fault simulation of vhdl and systemc. DSD '06.
[25] E. Normand. Single event upset at ground level. IEEE Transactions on Nuclear Science, 43(6):2742–2750, 1996.
[26] S. Rehman, M. Shafique, F. Kriebel, and J. Henkel. Reliable software for unreliable hardware: embedded code generation aiming at reliability. CODES+ISSS, 2011.
[27] K. Rothbart, U. Neffe, C. Steger, R. Weiss, E. Rieger, and A. Muehlberger. High level fault injection for attack simulation in smart cards. In Proceedings of the 13th Asian Test Symposium, ATS '04.
[28] L. Schor, I. Bacivarov, D. Rai, H. Yang, S. Kang, and L. Thiele. Scenario-based design flow for mapping streaming applications onto on-chip many-core systems. CASES '12.
[29] A. Singh, M. Shafique, A. Kumar, and J. Henkel. Mapping on multi/many-core systems: survey of current and emerging trends. DAC '13.
[30] Synopsys. Processor Designer http://www.synopsys.com/Systems/BlockDesign/processorDev.
[31] Z. Wang and C. Chen and A. Chattopadhyay. Fast reliability exploration for embedded processors via high-level fault injection. In International Symposium on Quality Electronic Design, ISQED, 2013.
[32] Z. Wang, K. Singh, C. Chen and A. Chattopadhyay. Accurate and efficient reliability estimation techniques during adl-driven embedded processor design. In Design Automation and Test in Europe, DATE, pages 547–552, 2013.
[33] Z. Wang, R. Li and A. Chattopadhyay. Opportunistic redundancy for improving reliability of embedded processors. In 8th IEEE International Design and Test Symposium (IDT), 2013.
[34] J. Ziegler and W. Lanford. The effect of sea level cosmic rays on electronic devices. In IEEE International Solid-State Circuits Conference. Digest of Technical Papers, volume XXIII, pages 70–71, 1980.

A TSV-cross-link-based Approach to 3D-clock Network Synthesis for Improved Robustness

Rickard Ewetz[†], Anirudh Udupa[‡], Ganesh Subbarayan[‡], Cheng-Kok Koh[†]

[†]School of Electrical and Computer Engineering, [‡]School of Mechanical Engineering

Purdue University

West Lafayette, IN 47907-2035, USA

{rewetz, audupa, ganeshs, chengkok}@purdue.edu

ABSTRACT

To obtain high yield for 3D ICs, random open defects, process variations, and thermal induced stress are key issues that must be addressed when synthesizing 3D clock networks. Current research on 3D clock synthesis often focuses on the construction and optimization of a 3D clock tree topology. Moreover, extra circuitry has been proposed to enable pre-bond testing and substitution of through silicon vias (TSVs) with random open defects. However, tree structures inherently have limited robustness to variations and may suffer failures arising from defects and/or process variations. To counter such problems, we propose to use TSVs to add redundancy in a 3D clock network. The proposed 3D network would have a complete 2D clock network on each die, facilitating pre-bond testing. Also, cross links would be inserted within each die using wires and across dies using TSVs to improve timing robustness within each die and across dies, respectively. Moreover, clock buffers are placed outside of zones that have high TSV-induced stress that could influence carrier mobility. Experimental results show that the proposed 3D clock networks have no failures due to random open defects, and on the average have 53% lower skew compared to 3D tree structures.

Categories and Subject Descriptors

B.7.2 [**Hardware, Integrated Circuits**]: Design Aids

General Terms

Algorithms, Design, Performance, Reliability.

Keywords

VLSI CAD; Physical Design; 3D-Clock Network; TSVs.

1. INTRODUCTION

In today's high performance designs, strict timing constraints must be met to guarantee correct functionality of

GLSVLSI'14, May 21–23, 2014, Houston, Texas, USA.

Copyright 2014 ACM 978-1-4503-2816-6/14/05 ...$15.00.

http://dx.doi.org/10.1145/2591513.2591584.

an IC. However meeting timing constraints when considering process, voltage, and temperature (PVT) variations is very challenging. It has been observed that the quality of a 2D clock network can deteriorate significantly under such variations. In 2009 and 2010 ISPD [15], two clock synthesis contests were held to emphasize the importance of clock network synthesis. Several studies, [6, 10, 14] for example, have addressed the robustness issue of 2D clock networks.

The robustness issue of 3D clock networks is even more challenging. First, TSVs may fail because of random open defects [7]. Such TSV failures can result in a bad chip. Second, the PVT variations across different dies on a 3D IC may be drastically different. Third, TSVs cause thermal-mechanical stress that can change the carrier mobility of nearby buffers, thereby affecting the timing. Another complication is pre-bond testing. To reduce manufacturing cost, each die in a 3D IC must be tested individually before bonding. Therefore, extra circuitry must be added to complete a functional 2D clock network on each die. Such circuitry is disabled in the normal operation of the 3D IC [5].

Some of these issues have been addressed recently. TSV reliability and overhead minimization are addressed in [3, 8]. In [9], a 3D clock tree synthesis algorithm reduces skew induced by thermal variations. In [17], a statistical approach for minimizing inter-die variations and TSV-induced stress is presented. Reduction of the pre-bond circuitry has been explored in [5].

In this paper, we consider random open defects, timing robustness, and testability at the same time. The key is to introduce redundancy in the 3D clock network in order to handle random open defects and PVT variations. A solution is to use cross links to provide redundant paths from the clock source to the clock sinks. Essentially, we construct a 3D clock tree with TSV cross links inserted between the dies and wire cross links within the dies. Moreover, a complete clock network exists on each die, thereby simplifying the pre-bond testing circuitry.

The proposed synthesis algorithm has the following general flow: As subtrees are being constructed on each die, cross links are inserted to improve the robustness. For cross links connecting clock wires on the same die, wires are used, and for cross links connecting clock wires on different dies, TSVs are used. Also, buffer locations are determined with the goal of avoiding regions that experience undue TSV-induced stress that may affect carrier mobility. Experimental results show that the proposed 3D clock networks have no failures caused by random open defects in TSVs. On the average, the proposed 3D clock networks have 53% lower skew compared to 3D tree structures.

2. PROBLEM DEFINITION

We extend the clock synthesis problem defined in the ISPD 2010 [15] contest to consider 3D ICs. We also modify the problem definition so that we can account for spatially correlated process variations, random open defects, and thermal-mechanical stress.

Sequential elements in a clock network are called clock sinks and they are distributed across all dies. These sinks are to be connected to a clock source, which reside on a particular die, using wires, inverters, and TSVs. The same wire library and inverter library, both based on a 45 nm technology, provided in the ISPD contest are used. They specify the wires and inverters available. However, we modify the library to also include the same inverters but with a modified mobility $u0$ for the NMOS and PMOS transistors. The TSV available is the same as in [17]. Some placement restrictions exist; inverters, TSVs, and blockages may not overlap.

The difference in the arrival times of a clock signal at a pair of sinks is called skew and is the measure of the timing quality of a clock network. Each pair of sinks will generate a skew in each simulation. The worst skew of among all the sink pairs is called worst global clock skew (wGCS). The worst skew of a pair of sinks separated by less than a specified local skew distance (LSD) is called the worst local clock skew (wLCS). When measuring LSD, we project all sinks onto a single die and measure the 2D distance between sinks. Each simulation will result in a wLCS and a wGCS.

As in ISPD contests, each synthesized clock network is evaluated by 500 Monte Carlo simulations using NGSPICE [11], with the network being subject to PVT variations, random open defects, and TSV-induced stress as follows: Inverters are subject to power supply variations, and wires and TSVs are subject to width variations. The variations are modeled as $\pm\triangle$ around the nominal values. Moreover, the voltage variations are generated using spatial correlation as described in [1]. Because of random open defects, each TSV has a failure probability of f. When a TSV fails, it is split into two parts. Each such part loads the network without realizing the original connection. Moreover, buffers experience changes in the carrier mobility depending on its relative location and orientation to nearby TSVs because of thermal-mechanical stress.

Each simulation represents the testing of a chip. The tested chip is classified as bad if the wLCS violates a specified skew constraint or if the slew at any point in the clock network violates a specified slew constraint. The yield is defined as the percentage of good chips among all tested chips. For consistency with the ISPD contest, we also denote the 95th percentile of the wLCS's as 95% LCS. Similarly, the 95th percentile of wGCS is denoted as 95% GCS.

2.1 Random open defects and critical connections

In a 3D clock network inter-die connections (each realized by one or more TSVs) may fail since TSVs can have random open defects [7]. The failure of a inter-die connection may lead to a chip failure in two different ways. First of all, the failure of an inter-die connection may result in two disjoint clock networks. Moreover, even if a complete 3D-network

remains after an inter-die connection has failed, the timing may have degraded enough to create a a chip failure.

In a 3D tree each inter-die connection is *critical*. A 3D tree can be constructed with One *Critical* Connection (OCC) or with Multiple *Critical* Connections (MCC) between two adjacent dies. We refer to them as an OCC-Tree (Figure 1(a)) or an MCC-Tree (Figure 1(b)), respectively.

An example of a *non-critical* connection is illustrated in Figure 1(c). Figure 1(c) is obtained by adding a TSV cross link to an OCC-Tree. A TSV cross link is a link connecting two points of a 3D tree residing in adjacent dies. A cross link has traditionally been defined to be a wire between two points in a clock network on the same die [12, 10]. We refer to such a cross link as a *wire cross link*. In this work, we generalize the definition of cross link to connect two points on two adjacent dies in a 3D clock network. Correspondingly a *TSV cross link* would be a wire-TSV-wire connection between two points on adjacent dies in a 3D tree (see Figure 1(c)).

Both wire and TSV cross links are *non-critical* because each cross link is typically inserted between two points in the clock tree that have the same delay (or even better, same voltage waveform). In other words, cross links are designed to deliver minimal (or no) current in an ideal situation. Therefore, if a cross link fails, the remaining network will still be functional.

A cross link simply adds an alternative path from the source to some sink(s). Even if *non-critical* TSV cross link has been inserted as in Figure 1(c), the initial *critical* connection remains *critical*. This is because if the *critical* connection fails the timing may change significantly.

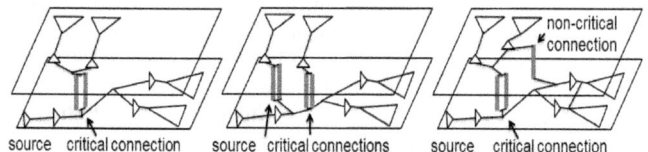

(a) OCC-Tree. (b) MCC-Tree. (c) TSV- and wire cross link.

Figure 1: Critical and non-critical inter-die connections.

To limit chip failures, the number of *critical* connections should be reduced or extra circuitry should be inserted. Two methods that use extra circuitry to avoid failures are the double TSV method and the TSV Fault-tolerant Unit (TFU) method [8]. In [8], circuits that used TFUs had higher skew than circuits that used double TSVs. As our focus is on meeting tight skew constraints, all *critical* connections in this work will be realized with two or more TSVs.

2.2 Timing robustness

2.2.1 PVT variations

For a 3D clock network, the PVT variations across different dies may be drastically different. Moreover, the stacking of dies may also cause further degradation in supply voltage and alter the thermal profile.

To evaluate whether a 3D tree structure can meet the skew requirement, we perform the following experiment. For a given 3D circuit, we construct a clock tree with the assumption that all TSVs are ideal i.e., the capacitance and resistance of each TSVs is 0. This is equivalent to having all the sinks projected onto one die. We refer to this construction as the Projected Tree method or the P-Tree method. The constructed clock tree is then evaluated with Monte Carlo simulations as described earlier. Details of the 3D circuits used and the simulation parameters are found in Section 5. The skews are provided in Table 2. It is clear that a 3D tree structure will not meet the skew requirements as even P-Trees cannot meet those requirements.

It is commonly known that non-tree structures are more robust to process variations. Several non-tree clock topologies, including meshes [14], multilevel fusion trees [6], and trees with cross links [10] have been used to construct more robust clock networks. Such non-tree networks involve constructing alternate paths to provide redundancy.

2.2.2 Thermal induced stress

Thermal-mechanical stress can also cause timing issues [17]. The stress is caused by a mismatch of the coefficient of thermal expansion (CTE) between the copper fill in a TSV ($16.7ppm/°C$) and the adjacent silicon ($2.3ppm/°C$). This thermal-mechanical stress can affect the carrier mobility of the transistors in a buffer. The change in carrier mobility is dependent on the carrier type and the orientation θ between the transistor channel and the TSV [4]. Therefore, buffers placed close to TSVs must account for TSV-induced stress. In Figure 2.2.2, the changes in carrier mobility for NMOS and PMOS transistors with $\theta = 0$ are illustrated. Transistors placed in the red and blue zones experience an increase and an decrease in carrier mobility, respectively. As we can see from the figure there is a mismatch between the PMOS and NMOS mobility.

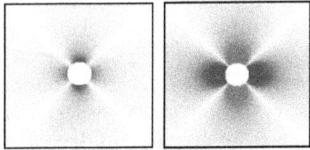

Figure 2: Changes in carrier mobility for PMOS (left) and NMOS (right).

Since a buffer has both NMOS and PMOS transistors, it would be best to avoid the colored zones completely to avoid further timing complications. In [17], it was shown that these changes in carrier mobility can introduce a significant skew in a 3D-clock tree.

3. PROPOSED 3D CLOCK NETWORK

From Section 2.2 it is clear that a 3D tree will not meet the timing constraints. A non-tree structure with redundancy between and within each die is needed to meet the constraints. At the same time, a *critical* inter-die connection needs to be realized with two or more TSVs, resulting in higher capacitance. Therefore, in this work we propose to use *non-critical* TSV cross links between the dies to provide the necessary redundancy needed. As TSV cross links are *non-critical* single TSVs can be used. To provide inter-die redundancy we chose to use wire cross links. We acknowledge that the intra-die redundancy could be provided with other methods as in [6, 10, 14]. We chose to explore constructing a 3D tree with TSV/wire cross links because earlier studies suggested that cross links were a cheap option. In the following we discuss some design considerations, how the 3D tree is selected, and some aspects regarding TSV/wire cross links.

3.1 3D tree topology

The 3D tree in our proposed structure can be constructed either as an OCC-Tree or as an MCC-Tree. Naturally, a

trade-off between wire length and the number of *critical* connections exists. The trade-off has been studied in depth in previous works [5, 9, 17].

Another design consideration is testability of circuits. A functional 2D network is needed on each die for pre-bond testing. If fewer inter-die connections are used, less pre-bond circuitry is needed to complete a functional 2D network on each die. Note that the OCC-Tree has a complete 2D network on each die (see Figure 1(a)). We choose to construct an OCC-Tree (with cross links inserted) to minimize the number of inter-die connections and enable easy testability, as there is one complete clock subtree in each die.

3.2 TSV and wire cross links

Cross links were developed to provide redundancy in a clock network while allowing the network to still be treated almost as a tree structure. By definition all cross links, wire or TSV, are *non-critical* connections. In [12], a wire cross link is modeled as two capacitors at the ends of a resistor, i.e., a π-type circuit. Moreover, if a resistor is inserted to connect two nodes with zero skew, these two nodes will still have zero skew after the insertion. Based on this several wire cross link insertion techniques have been developed [12].

The cross link insertion methods in [12, 10] first identifies the locations for cross link insertion. The cross link capacitance are added to these nodes, and a zero-skew clock tree is constructed with these additional cross link capacitances taken into account. The resistors of these cross links are then added after the tree construction. The redundant path introduced can reduce the effect of PVT variations as follows: Adding a cross link between nodes u and w will reduce the skew sensitivity of a sink pair i and j if they are located in the subtrees T_u and T_w, respectively, where T_u and T_w are two subtree rooted at node u and w.

This method can be easily generalized to handle TSV cross links by converting the wire-TSV-wire connection into a π-type RC circuit.

The argument that a resistor of a cross link can be added without affecting the skew/timing provides an explanation why a TSV cross link is a *non-critical* connection. As a resistor can be added (inserting a TSV cross link) without affecting the skew, it can be removed (when there is an open defect) without affecting the skew.

In our proposed methodology, a cross link is inserted between two subtrees only when the two subtrees are *local*, i.e., the there exist sinks that are separated by less than LSD and they belong to the two different subtrees. We insert links between such local subtrees as the local clock skews (LCS) are what we are interested in optimizing (Section 2).

3.3 Summary

To meet the timing constraints under PVT variations we propose to construct an OCC-Tree with *non-critical* TSV cross links and wire cross links. The TSV cross links provide the redundancy needed between the dies. Any type of redundancy could have been used within each die. We chose to use wire cross links for consistency in the approach. Also, the structure facilitates pre-bond testing as a complete 2D network exists on each die.

4. METHODOLOGY

Our clock network synthesis (CNS) flow builds the clock network bottom up. The basic idea is that we construct a clock network on each die with cross links spanning within the dies and between the dies. This is implemented by merging subtrees as described in Section 4.1 until all subtrees are sufficiently large. Next, wire cross links are inserted between subtrees on the same die as described in Section 4.2. This is followed by a selection of a driving buffer for each subtree with details in Section 4.3. That completes the construction of the first stage subtrees, i.e., subtrees that are each driven by a buffer. Above the layer of driving buffers of the first stage subtrees, TSV cross links are inserted as described in Section 4.4. The buffers of the first stage subtrees are treated as the sinks of subsequent clock tree construction. Merging (Section 4.1) and buffer selection (Section 4.3) are performed interchangeably on each die to build subtrees of stage 2 and above until a single root exists on all dies, where each stage contains subtrees that are each driven by a buffer. The roots of the individual dies are then routed and merged to the die where the clock source is located. The roots of the dies are merged to a final root and routed to the source. After the network construction is complete the entire network is tuned and embedded top down. As we have very few *critical* connections in the proposed 3D clock network, we use four parallel TSVs (instead of two TSVs) for each *critical* connection between adjacent dies. The flow can be seen in Figure 3. An illustration of the topology is found in Figure 4.

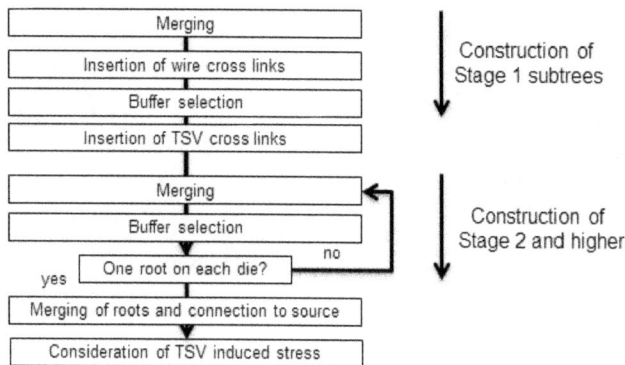

Figure 3: Proposed clock synthesis flow.

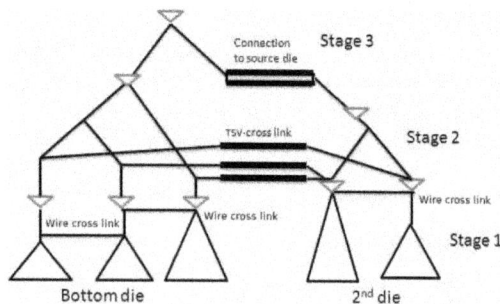

Figure 4: A sample of the proposed 3D clock network.

4.1 Merging

Subtrees in each stage are generated with iterative merges. Merges are performed using the DME approach outlined in [2]. To select subtrees to be merged, we alternate between two metrics iteratively. The first metric selects the pair of subtrees that needs the least wiring capacitance [2]. The second metric finds the subtree with the least delay and then

merges it with the subtree requiring the least wiring capacitance. This process is facilitated with a Nearest Neighbor Graph (NNG). After merging, the newly merged subtree is checked to ensure that it satisfies the slew constraint S_{slew}. If it does not, it is un-merged and the nodes are locked from further merging. After all subtrees are locked, buffer selection is performed for all subtrees in stage 2 and above. For the first stage subtrees, wire cross links are first inserted before the buffer selection step.

4.2 Insertion of wire cross links

Wire cross links are inserted within each die after the generation of first stage subtrees. For each pair of subtrees that are *local* and on the same die, we include the pair in a set P. We process the pairs of subtrees in P in the following order: Pick the pair that has the subtree s with the least delay. This subtree may appear in several pairs within P. We pick the pair with the least total delay. We insert a wire cross link between this pair as described below.

For the subtree with a smaller delay in the pair, we attach a wire to the top of it to match the delays of the two subtrees. The length of the wire is analytically determined using the Elmore delay model. After the delays have been equalized, a wire cross link is inserted between the two root nodes. The pair is then removed from P. The delays of all the subtrees is updated and a new pair is selected until P is empty. Note that a subtree may participate in this process many times.

4.3 Buffer selection

In [1], buffers have been shown to be effective in handling spatially correlated variations. In this work, we use the same 45nm technology library, which contains two inverters, as in the ISPD 2010 contest. An inverter library is formed by connecting multiple inverters in parallel. Next, a buffer library is formed by connecting two inverters in series. For each subtree, we select the smallest buffer that can drive the subtree without violating the slew constraint S_{slew}.

4.4 Insertion of TSV cross links

We insert inter-die TSV cross links above the first layer of buffers between local subtrees (or more precisely, networks, since they have wire cross links) that resides in different dies.

The insertion of the TSV cross links is similar to the insertion of wire cross links. However, the generation of the set of subtree pairs P for TSV cross links insertion is slightly different. For each pair, we use the distance as the cost to insert TSV cross link between them. For each subtree, we only insert the pair with the least cost into P.

Next, we insert TSV cross links in the same fashion as we insert wire cross links, with the following exception: If both of the subtrees in the pair already have a TSV cross link attached, we do not add a TSV cross link for that pair.

4.5 Handling placement restrictions

In 3D clock networks, buffers, blockages and TSVs may not overlap. Although no previous works have directly addressed placement restrictions for TSVs, buffers, and blockages at the same time, a legal placement solution can "easily" be obtained by considering the restrictions in the bottom up construction of the clock tree. The methods applied are simple extension and combinations of the work in [14, 18]. However these techniques cannot be applied to ensure that buffers are placed outside zones with mobility changes. This is because TSV and buffer locations are not known until after the top down embedding [2]. To address this issue, we present a buffer re-placement technique.

Similar to [13, 17], we determine the changes changes in carrier mobility due to thermal-mechanical stress induced by a single TSV with an analytical model [16]. Next, the stress is converted to changes in carrier mobility through a piezo-resistive model [4]. When multiple TSVs are placed closely, the total change in mobility is obtained through super-position, as in [13, 17].

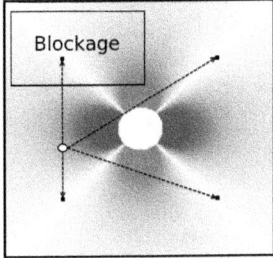

After the top down embedding, buffers with significant changes in carrier mobility are identified. Adjustments of the (x, y) location of these buffers is considered to neutralize the changes. For each buffer, a set of (dx, dy) moves are evaluated. As the most important factor for a clock network is robustness, we select a target location that reduces the changes in mobility to below $< |0.5\%|$, while requiring the smallest displacement in (dx, dy). As a heuristic approach, we consider four locations that are on the $y = x$

Figure 5: Arrows show relocation options for a buffer along the four directions to neutralize changes in carrier mobility.

and $y = -x$ lines, originating from the closest TSV, as shown in Figure 4.5. A line is drawn from the original buffer location to each of these locations, and points along these lines are considered to be target locations of the buffer. Of course, some of these target locations are non-ideal as they fall in the red or blue zones of a TSV or may be blocked by a blockage. With this method, we avoid performing perturbation of the buffer locations manually as in [13].

5. EXPERIMENTAL RESULTS

Our algorithm is implemented in C++ and the experiments are run on a quad core 3.1 GHz Linux machine with 7.7 GB Memory. Eight 3D circuits BM01-08 are constructed by stacking combination of benchmark circuits, named ispd01–08, from the 2010 ISPD contest. Table 1 lists the constructed 3D circuits. All stacked benchmark circuits ispd01–08 are scaled to the size of the bottom most benchmark circuit. The local clock skew constraint, slew constraint and local skew distance are defined based on those of the circuits residing in the bottom-most die. The skew constraint and LSD for each circuit is found in Table 1. The slew constraint is 100 ps for all circuits.

Table 1: 3D circuits constructed by stacking and scaling 2010 ISPD benchmark circuits.

Ckt	bottom	2nd	3ed	4th	Skew (ps)	LSD (um)
BM01	ispd01	ispd02	-	-	7.50	600
BM02	ispd03	ispd04	-	-	4.99	370
BM03	ispd05	ispd06	-	-	7.50	600
BM04	ispd07	ispd08	-	-	7.50	600
BM05	ispd01	ispd02	ispd04	-	7.50	600
BM06	ispd06	ispd07	ispd08	-	7.50	600
BM07	ispd06	ispd05	ispd07	ispd03	7.50	600
BM08	ispd05	ispd03	ispd06	-	7.50	600

Voltage variations, denoted as $\triangle V$, are generated with a uniform distribution ranging between $\pm 7.5\% V_{DD}$ [15]. Wire width [15] and TSV diameter variations, which are $\pm 5\%$ of

Table 2: Comparison of clock networks synthesized by the OCC-Tree, P-Tree and Cross methods. An '*' indicates that the solution does not meet the skew requirement.

Ckt	Method	Tsv num	Yield (%)	95% LCS (ps)	95% GCS (ps)	Cap (fF)	Run time (s)
01	OCC-Tree	4	2	*15.04	16.99	284881	1979
	P-Tree	-	26	*11.86	14.79	235348	1571
	Cross	130	97	7.33	13.59	481132	2877
02	OCC-Tree	4	12	*10.06	10.55	61080	490
	P-Tree	-	36	*8.36	9.64	56598	455
	Cross	33	100	3.91	5.71	78617	690
03	OCC-Tree	4	78	*9.30	9.78	52062	307
	P-Tree	-	86	*8.37	9.81	47922	291
	Cross	28	100	5.06	6.42	76772	387
04	OCC-Tree	4	63	*9.60	10.07	70073	520
	P-Tree	-	79	*8.83	9.72	64510	489
	Cross	37	100	4.28	5.33	113623	702
05	OCC-Tree	8	0	*17.50	19.12	386565	3681
	P-Tree	-	12	*11.65	15.34	283283	2432
	Cross	186	76	*8.98	13.07	647560	4776
06	OCC-Tree	12	44	*10.51	10.64	87254	943
	P-Tree	-	75	*8.89	9.17	76769	872
	Cross	51	100	3.96	4.33	136172	1070
07	OCC-Tree	24	26	*11.80	12.11	108427	1400
	P-Tree	-	57	*9.03	9.51	92271	1258
	Cross	74	99	3.70	6.43	162818	1630
08	OCC-Tree	8	47	*10.22	10.94	89818	632
	P-Tree	-	80	*8.78	9.73	78786	543
	Cross	55	100	5.22	6.15	133967	855
	OCC-Tree			1.00		1.00	
	P-Tree			0.88		0.87	
	Cross			0.47		1.54	

nominal width and diameter, respectively, are also generated with a uniform distribution. The TSVs used have a diameter of $4um$, a capacitance of $28fF$, and a resistance of 0.053Ω [17]. The probability of a random open defect is set to be 0.01 [8]. If the TSV suffers an open defect it is split into two parts with the sizes of the two parts determined with a random uniform probability. The 45nm PTM library is modified to PMOS and NMOS models with mobility changes of -50% to $+50\%$ in 1% increments.

In this section we compare our work, referred to as "Cross", against "P-Trees" and "OCC-Trees" constructed on the same benchmarks. Note that a P-Tree is in fact an MCC-Tree with ideal TSVs (zero resistance and capacitance). It is not surprising that the P-Trees have the lowest cost, and that the proposed "Cross" solutions are more expensive compared to both P-Trees and OCC-Trees. We did not compare with existing approaches in 3D clock synthesis because the *nominal* skews (without variations) reported in these studies—as high as 20 ps in [18] and 13 ps in [17] (where the skew is determined without SPICE[17])—are already higher than the local skew constraints that are considered here, and the cost is at best similar to that of P-Trees. Recall, this work targets 7.5 ps skew constraints while affected by variations as in the 2010 ISPD [15] clock contest. For skew constraints of 15 ps or more no redundancy is needed and a 3D-tree topology may indeed be a better option. For such constraints a detailed comparisons should be made with [17] and [18].

The yield loss for the P-Trees is mainly caused by the vulnerability of tree structures to variations. There are three main reasons for the yield loss of the OCC-Trees. First, an OCC-Tree is also a tree structure. Second, it is a 3D tree structure, which has different levels of variations across dies.

Third, as a 3D structure, it may also suffer yield loss because of the random open defects in TSVs.

The LCS (within-die and inter-die) and GCS are better for the P-Tree method than the OCC-Tree method in most cases. However, both P-Tree method and OCC-Tree method are not able to meet the stringent skew constraints. In contrast, our proposed structure with wire and TSV cross links can improve the yield significantly. Moreover, the synthesized structures have on the average 42%, and 53% lower local clock skews compared those generated by P-Tree and OCC-Tree methods, respectively.

All 3D circuits, except BM05, have a yield of 97% or higher. BM05 is a 3-die circuit with the largest and most difficult circuits from the 2010 ISPD contest. The problem is made even more challenging because we model the variations with spatial correlation. Even with these additional challenges, we can obtain a yield of 76%, more than $6X$ that of P-Trees. The improved robustness comes with a 54% increase in capacitance compared to the OCC-Trees. While this increase may look substantial, it is still in line or better than what have been reported in the literature for 2D clock synthesis. For example, meshes and multilevel fusion trees can have $2.3\times–5\times$ [14] and $1.6\times$ [6] higher capacitance, respectively, compared to a tree structure. As can be seen in Table 2, we have over designed a few circuits. This suggests that further capacitance reduction could be obtained by reducing the number of cross links.

We also show the effectiveness of our method in reducing changes in carrier mobility in Table 3. The table shows the maximum change in carrier mobility (among all the BMs) before the buffers are moved. As can be seen, all buffers can successfully be moved out of the colored zones of TSVs, resulting in at most 0.5% change in carrier mobility.

Table 3: Avoidance of changes in carrier mobility.

Ckt.	Optimizing buffer placment.	
	Before opt.	After opt.
	|Max mobility %|	|Max mobility %|
BM01-08	4.38	< 0.5

Table 4: Comparison of pre- and post- bonding.

Ckt	Pre			Post		
	Mean (ps)	95% (ps)	max (ps)	Mean (ps)	95% (ps)	max (ps)
01	6.39	8.46	10.54	5.05	6.87	9.57
02	2.26	3.24	4.07	2.74	3.17	5.19
03	4.47	6.44	8.34	3.66	4.23	6.35
04	3.25	4.93	6.81	3.23	3.74	5.62
05	6.45	8.46	9.89	5.01	6.62	8.99
06	2.21	3.31	4.61	2.06	2.90	3.91
07	2.41	3.50	4.88	2.14	3.03	3.98
08	2.93	4.30	5.53	2.76	4.01	5.08
Norm.	1.11	**1.22**	1.13	1.00	1.00	1.00

As our proposed network has a complete clock network on each die, the only pre-bond circuitry required is a buffer to drive the root node on each die. We show in Table 4 that the skews of the bottom-most die in the eight 3D circuits when they are evaluated separately. To perform this evaluation, we assume that each TSV present will load the 2D network on each die with half of its capacitance and half of its resistance. In Table 4, we present the result of pre-bond testing of the bottom-most die. We also present the skews within the bottom-most die after bonding. We can note a 1–1.5

ps higher skew in pre-bond testing. This is likely caused by timing imbalance introduced by the TSV loading.

We believe that the problem can be resolved if we consider pre-bond testing explicitly in the synthesis process. We will explore that in the future.

6. CONCLUSIONS AND FUTURE WORK

In this paper, we proposed a 3D clock network structure that uses TSVs to introduce redundancy for improving timing and criticality. Experimental results showed that our proposed structures does not suffer failures caused by random open defects and the timing performance is significantly improved, even under PVT variations and changes in carrier mobility caused by thermal-mechanical stress induced by TSVs.

7. ACKNOWLEDGMENTS

This work was supported in part by the NSF under award CCF-1065318 and SRC under task 1292-074.

8. REFERENCES

[1] S. Bujimalla and C.-K. Koh. Synthesis of low power clock trees for handling power-supply variations. ISPD '11, 2011.

[2] M. Edahiro. A clustering-based optimization algorithm in zero-skew routings. DAC, pages 612 – 616, 1993.

[3] A.-C. Hsieh, T. Hwang, M.-T. Chang, M.-H. Tsai, C.-M. Tseng, and H.-C. Li. TSV redundancy: architecture and design issues in 3D IC. DATE, pages 711 – 722, 2010.

[4] H. Irie, K. Kita, K. Kyuno, and A. Toriumi. In-plane mobility anisotropy and universality under uni-axial strains in nand p-MOS inversion layers on (100), (110), and (111) Si. In *Electron Devices Meeting*, pages 225–228, 2004.

[5] T.-Y. Kim and T. Kim. Clock tree synthesis with pre-bond testability for 3D stacked IC designs. DAC '10, pages 723–728, 2010.

[6] D.-J. Lee and I. L. Markov. Multilevel tree fusion for robust clock networks. ICCAD, pages 632–639, 2011.

[7] I. Loi, S. Mitra, T. H. Lee, S. Fujita, and L. Benini. A low-overhead fault tolerance scheme for TSV-based 3D network on chip links. ICCAD '08, pages 598 – 602, 2008.

[8] C.-L. Lung, Y.-S. Su, S.-H. Huang, Y. Shi, and S.-C. Chang. Fault-tolerant 3D clock network. DAC '11, pages 645 – 651, 2011.

[9] J. Minz, X. Zhao, and S. K. Lim. Buffered clock tree synthesis for 3D ICs under thermal variations. ASP-DAC, pages 504 – 509, 2008.

[10] T. Mittal and C.-K. Koh. Cross link insertion for improving tolerance to variations in clock network synthesis. ISPD '11, pages 29–36, 2011.

[11] NGSPICE. http://ngspice.sourceforge.net/.

[12] A. Rajaram, J. Hu, and R. Mahapatra. Reducing clock skew variability via cross links. DAC, pages 18–23, 2004.

[13] J. seok Yang, K. Athikulwongse, Y.-J. Lee, S.-K. Lim, and D. Pan. TSV stress aware timing analysis with applications to 3D-IC layout optimization. DAC, pages 803–806, 2010.

[14] X.-W. Shih, C.-C. Cheng, Y.-K. Ho, and Y.-W. Chang. Blockage-avoiding buffered clock-tree synthesis for clock latency-range and skew minimization. ASP-DAC, pages 395–400, 2010.

[15] C. Sze. ISPD 2010 high performance clock network synthesis contest: Benchmark suit and results. 2010.

[16] A. Udupa, G. Subbarayan, and C.-K. Koh. Analytical estimates of stress around a doubly periodic arrangement of through-silicon vias. *Microelectronics Reliability*, pages 63–69, 2013.

[17] J.-S. Yang, J. Pak, X. Zhao, S. K. Lim, and D. Pan. Robust clock tree synthesis with timing yield optimization for 3D-ICs. ASP-DAC, pages 621 – 626, 2011.

[18] X. Zhao and S.-K. Lim. Through-silicon-via-induced obstacle-aware clock tree synthesis for 3D ICs. ASP-DAC, pages 347–352, 2012.

A Feasibility Study on Robust Programmable Delay Element Design based on Neuron-MOS Mechanism

Renyuan Zhang
Japan Advanced Institute of
Science and Technology
1-1 Asahidai, Nomi, Ishikawa,
923-1292 Japan
rzhang@jaist.ac.jp

Mineo Kaneko
Japan Advanced Institute of
Science and Technology
1-1 Asahidai, Nomi, Ishikawa,
923-1292 Japan
mkaneko@jaist.ac.jp

ABSTRACT

The feasibility of programmable delay elements (PDEs) design based on Neuron-MOS mechanism is investigated in this work. By applying the capacitor coupling technology, the charging/discharging current of a clock buffer can be digitally programmed to generate various switching delay without static power consumption. No any additional transistor is introduced into the charging/discharging path, that reduces the performance fluctuation due to process variations for MOS transistors. From the circuit simulation results, the delay change of proposed PDE is less than one third compared to that of the conventional PDE circuits. In order to reduce the temperature sensitivity, another Neuron-MOS-based PDE circuit is also suggested by employing a temperature insensitive reference-current-generator. This type of PDE circuit achieves a delay change within 0.1% when the temperature fluctuates from $25°C$ to $75°C$. In general, both types of suggested PDE circuits achieve better or fair performances over the robustness, power consumption and delay range.

Categories and Subject Descriptors

B.7.1 [**Integrated Circuits**]: VLSI (very large scale integration)

1. INTRODUCTION

Nowadays the complexity and operating clock frequency of vary large scale integrated (VLSI) circuits increase greatly. The timing problems in most of VLSI sequential circuits become noticeably serious. In addition, VLSI circuits and their clock distributions suffer from process and temperature variations. In order to prevent timing errors even improve speed performances, the tuning of clock skew is necessary after the chip fabrication in many applications. From some reported works, the Post-Silicon clock Skew Tuning (PSST) technology is very helpful to improve the reliability and performance-yield of VLSI circuits [1, 2, 3, 4]. The

GLSVLSI'14, May 21–23, 2014, Houston, Texas, USA.
Copyright 2014 ACM 978-1-4503-2816-6/14/05 ...$15.00.
http://dx.doi.org/10.1145/2591513.2591591.

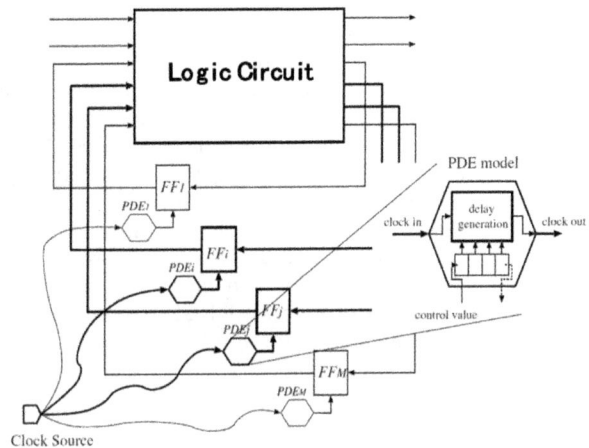

Figure 1: Sequential circuits including PDEs, which are programmed by digital input patterns.

programmable delay element (PDE) circuits were developed to realize various switching delays, which are controlled by input patterns as shown in Fig. 1. Usually, the clock skew is expected to be programmed digitally.

Many prototypes of PDEs have been developed [5, 6, 7, 8, 9] during past decades. Since a PDE circuit can be considered as a clock buffer between the common clock source and some specific sequential circuits, the essence of a PDE is to control the charging/discharging time inner the buffer stage. In this sense, there are two strategies for designing PDE circuits. One is to increase the load inner buffer stages; another lies on controlling the value of charging/discharging current. Several works employing the former strategy realized the delay tuning by inverter-chains [5], but not programmed digitally. A similar prototype was reported to build PDEs using so-called "shunt capacitors" [4], which is digitally programmable. However, the charging/discharging of additional load-capacitor (usually incomplete) results in the uncontrollability on either edge of rising or falling. Their chip area and power consumption are also considered as demerits. To solve these problems, the prototype employing so-called "current starve" strategy was proposed [6, 7, 8, 9]. A small charging/discharging current is generated by the current mirror and a set of long channel transistors controlled by power-supply-voltage V_{dd} or 0 on gates. The delay programmability is improved by using this technology.

The modern VLSI sequential circuits always operate with high clock frequencies. Obviously, the PDE tuning resolution could even be much finer than the clock frequency. Furthermore, PDEs also suffer from the variations due to the temperature and fabrication process. Thus, the stability and reliability of PDEs are seriously concerned.

The purpose of this work is to develop reliable PDE circuits with well performances over programmability, power consumption and delay range. It is noticed the Neuron-MOS mechanism is very efficient to realize multi-bit computations [10]. Emulating this mechanism, the capacitor-coupling on the gate of a standard MOS transistor could realize similar behaviors [11], even with a very high frequency [12]. Two types of PDE circuits were proposed in this paper on the basis of capacitor-coupling. One of these PDEs implements Neuron-MOS mechanism directly on the transistors of a standard inverter, which introduces no any addition transistor into the charging/discharging path. Without static power consumption, the delay change due to process variations (3% on the transistor's size for instance) is less than one third compared to that of conventional PDE circuits. Another type of PDE circuit is proposed employing a reference-current-generator [13, 14, 15], in which the reference current is digitally programmed by a Neuron-MOS-like transistor. With the consideration of temperature fluctuation from $25^\circ C$ to $75^\circ C$, the delay change is less than 0.1%. In general, both types of suggested PDE circuits achieve better or fair performances over the robustness, power consumption and delay range.

2. PROPOSED PDE CIRCUITS

Two types of PDE circuits were proposed in this paper on the basis of Neuron-MOS mechanism. All the devices including MOS transistors, capacitors and resistors are available in a standard CMOS process technology. The target is to design digitally programmable delay elements with a high reliability.

2.1 Neuron-MOS mechanism and capacitor-coupling behaviors

The structure of Neuron-MOS is an n-channel transistor with a gate electrode which is electrically floating [10]. As illustrated in Fig. 2, n input gates are capacitively coupled to the floating gate. The terminal voltages and various capacitive coupling coefficients are defined as $V_1, V_2, \cdots, V_n$ and $C_1, C_2, \cdots, C_n$ respectively, where ϕ_F is the floating-gate potential. The gate capacitance between the floating-gate and substrate is defined as C_0. $Q_0, Q_1, Q_2, \cdots, Q_n$ denote the electronic charges stored on the coupling capacitors. The charge Q_F stored on the floating-gate is calculated as:

$$Q_F = Q_0 + \sum_{i=1}^{n} -Q_i = \sum_{i=0}^{n} C_i(\phi_F - V_i)$$
$$= \phi_F \sum_{i=0}^{n} C_i - \sum_{i=0}^{n} C_i V_i. \qquad (1)$$

It is assumed the no charge injection occurs during device operation (namely, $Q_F = 0$), and the substrate is grounded. Then, the potential on the gate of the MOS transistor can be obtained as:

$$\phi_F = \frac{C_1 V_1 + C_2 V_2 + \cdots + C_n V_n}{C_{TOT}}, \qquad (2)$$

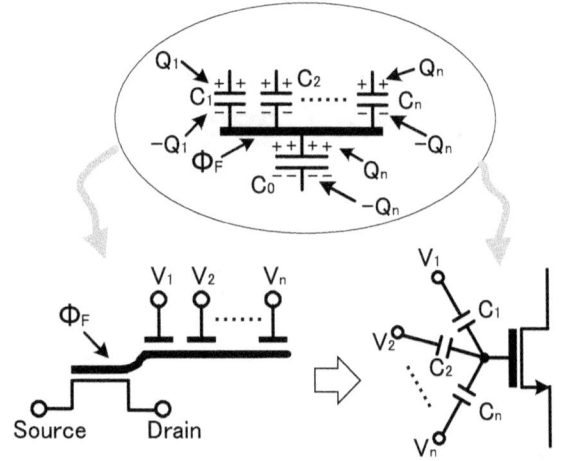

Figure 2: Structure of Neuron-MOS transistor and its equivalent model by using standard devices (regular MOS transistor and capacitors).

where

$$C_{TOT} = \sum_{i=0}^{n} C_i. \qquad (3)$$

In this paper, we assume the gate capacitance of Neuron-MOS is sufficiently small compared to the terminal capacitors.

It is possible to emulate the Neuron-MOS mechanism by using standard devices (MOS transistor and a set of capacitors) as shown in Fig. 2 [11]. A set of terminal capacitors were coupled on the gate of a standard MOS transistor. The potential on the gate can be dynamically tuned by terminal input voltages according to Eq. 2. In this manner, an additional function can be realized on the gate of transistor before the consideration of the circuit in which it is implemented. The capacitance values are designed according to the demanded function. Namely, even an input pattern in the form of digitals generate an analog control signals on the gate of transistor.

An obvious benefit of the coupling-capacitance mechanism is that all the capacitors are not actually charged or discharged during the operations. This phenomenon implies a potential of computations in a low power and high speed fashion. Only the ratio among coupling capacitances is concerned rather than the capacitance values. Thus, it is allowed to use smaller capacitors to reduce the chip area.

2.2 Proposed PDE circuit with simplest charging/discharging path (Type-1)

A low power PDE circuit is designed with simplest charging/discharging path as shown in Fig. 3. Here, only the delay on the rising edge is concerned, which is realized by the control of discharging inner the buffer stage. In the case of falling edge, similar circuit can be easily implemented on the charging path (effecting the p-channel transistor). The delay is programmed by a four bits input digital signals represented by V_1, V_2, V_3, V_4 (or b_1, b_2, b_3, b_4 in the form of digital bits). The input of this PDE is a clock signal from the common clock source; the output is a delayed clock signal distributed to relevant sequential circuits.

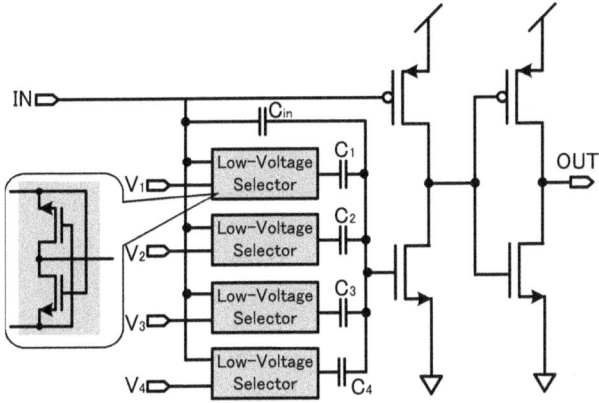

Figure 3: Proposed PDE circuit with simplest charging/discharging path (Type-1), which consists of a Neuron-MOS-based inverter and a regular inverter. Four-bit digital signals are used as coding input to program delay.

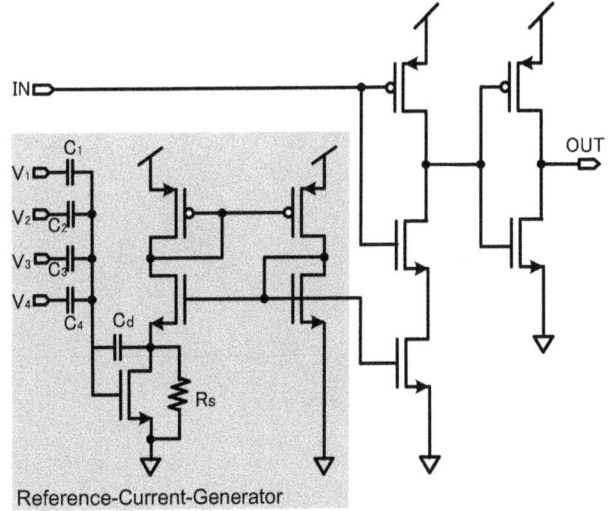

Figure 4: Proposed PDE circuit employing a current-reference-generator. Neuron-MOS mechanism is adapted to generate a digitally programmable reference-current.

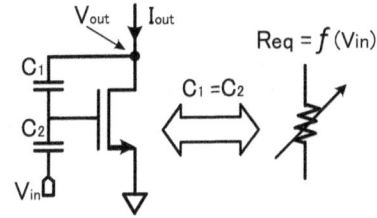

Figure 5: The resistor is emulated by a MOS transistor and a set of coupling capacitors employing Neuron-MOS mechanism. Its resistance value is tunable by applying a input voltage V_{in}.

In essence, the proposed PDD circuit consists of two inverters in chain as a buffer stage. The first inverter is designed to generate a "starve current" on the discharging path according to the input coding. It is followed by a regular inverter connected to the output terminal. A set of capacitors are introduced to the gate of transistors in the first inverter (only n-channel MOS is discussed here), which couples the clock input and control coding terminals. The ratio of coupling capacitors is set as $C_1 : C_2 : C_3 : C_4 = 1 : 2 : 4 : 8$ to reflect the weight of each coding bit. An additional capacitor C_{in} is applied between floating gate and clock input, which contributes to generate a small discharging current when all the programming inputs are set as zero.

A set of "low-voltage selectors" are designed between the inputs and floating gate. Since the MOS transistor with floating gate is the only switching device on the discharging path, the turn-off state during the static phase is seriously concerned. The low-voltage selector is a two-input and one-output module, which consists of two n-channel MOS transistors cross-connected by gates and sources. It always outputs a voltage as same as the lower one out of two inputs. During the static phase, all terminals of coupling capacitors are grounded by input clock regardless of program coding inputs. Thus, the unexpected discharging is prevented in the static state. During the switching phase (discharging in this case), the terminals of coupling capacitors are set as zero or V_{CLK}, where V_{CLK} is the voltage of input clock. Considering the ratio of coupling capacitances, the potential of floating gate is given by:

$$\phi_F \approx \frac{b_1 \cdot V_{CLK} + 2b_2 \cdot V_{CLK} + 4b_3 \cdot V_{CLK} + 8b_4 \cdot V_{CLK}}{15},$$
(4)

where $b_i = 0$ or 1. The starve current is generated by this gate voltage; and the delay inner the buffer stage is programmed digitally.

Since the digital programmability is achieved by capacitance coupling, there is no any static power consumption theoretically; and the dynamic power is aways less than that of a regular inverter. Compared to a regular inverter, the

proposed buffer stage does not introduce any additional devices into the discharging path. Thus, variations of semiconductor devices have less effect than that of conventional current-starve-based PDEs. Regarding the chip area, coupling capacitors are not actually charged, which means small values of capacitances are sufficient.

However, a basic MOS transistor switch is still sensitive to the temperature. In this sense, a temperature compensation technology is considered as described in the following part.

2.3 Proposed PDE circuit employing reference-current-generator (Type-2)

It is very common to use a process, voltage and temperature (PVT) insensitive circuitry for generating stable reference current [13, 14, 15]. In this work, we introduce a basic reference-current-generator with temperature compensation into the PDE design. The challenge is to realize a digital programmability on the generated current.

Our proposed PDE circuit employing a current-reference-generator is illustrated in Fig. 4. The structure of a basic reference-current-generator consists of four MOS transistors and a resistor. Two branches have equal currents flowing

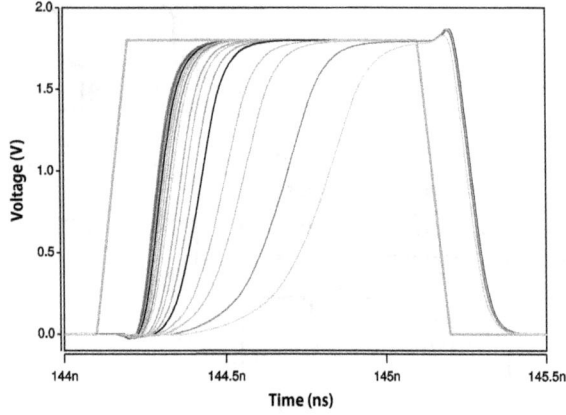

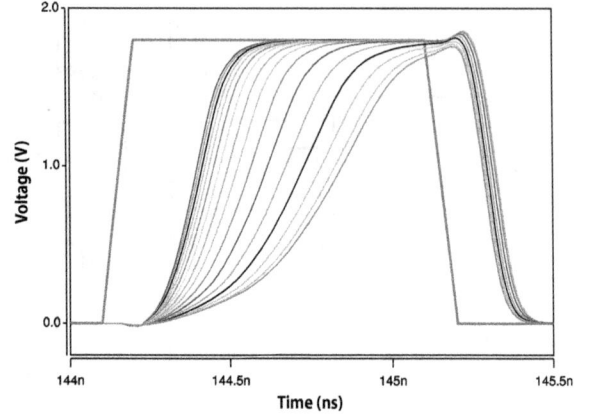

Figure 6: Input clock and delayed signals are captured by circuit simulation results for proposed PDE of Type-1. Sixteen cases are verified by the combination of 4-bit program coding.

Figure 7: Input clock and delayed signals are captured by circuit simulation results for proposed PDE of Type-2.

in them. As it was well analyzed in some works [13], the current in each branch is given by:

$$I = U_T \cdot R \cdot ln(\frac{S_2 S_4}{S_1 S_3}), \qquad (5)$$

where U_T is the thermal voltage, S_i is the transistor aspect ratio, and R is the resistance in this circuit, respectively.

In order to produce a programmable current, a tunable resistance is designed employing Neuron-MOS mechanism as shown in Fig. 5. The current flowing in this transistor is

$$I_{out} = K \cdot [(V_{gs} - V_{th})V_{ds} - \frac{V_{ds}^2}{2}], \qquad (6)$$

where K is the conduction factor; V_{gs}, V_{ds}, and V_{th} are the gate-to-source, drain-to-source, and threshold voltage, respectively. Under the condition of $C_1 = C_2$, the gate-to-source voltage is given by:

$$V_{gs} = \phi_F \approx \frac{V_{in} + V_{out}}{2}. \qquad (7)$$

Substituting it into Eq. 6, the output current is obtained as:

$$I_{out} = K \cdot V_{out}(\frac{V_{in}}{2} - V_{th}). \qquad (8)$$

In this sense, this circuit can be approximately treated as a linear resistance with a equivalent resistance value of $R_{eq} = 1/[K \cdot (\frac{V_{in}}{2} - V_{th})]$. Then, the reference-current is generated by:

$$I = U_T \cdot (R_{eq}//R_s) \cdot ln(\frac{S_2 S_4}{S_1 S_3}). \qquad (9)$$

This reference-current is applied in the discharging path of clock buffer.

To program the reference-current digitally, a set of coupling capacitors are applied on the gate of Neuron-MOS. The ratio of capacitance values are defined by $C_1 : C_2 : C_3 : C_4 = 1 : 2 : 4 : 8$ under the condition of $C_1 + C_2 + C_3 + C_4 = C_d$. In this manner, the delay of clock buffer is programmed by a 4-bit input pattern. The robustness against temperature of the employed reference-current-generator is sufficient for our application. In addition, the process variations have less effect than that of conventional starve-current-based PDEs.

3. CIRCUIT SIMULATION RESULTS

In order to verify the operations and performance of the proposed PDEs (both types), the designed circuits are simulated in a $0.18\mu m$ CMOS technology. A clock signal with the frequency of $450MHz$ is used in the simulations.

3.1 Programmability of delay generation

A configuration of 4-bit program coding is set in all simulations. The circuit simulation results for sixteen cases of delay demand are illustrated in Fig. 6 according to the program coding from $b_1 b_2 b_3 b_4 = 1111$ to $b_1 b_2 b_3 b_4 = 0000$. As it is shown in this result, the proposed PDE of Type-1 achieved wide delay range. The minimum delay almost equals to the inherent delay of regular inverters. Since there is no any additional device on the discharging path, it is possible to generate a sufficiently small delay if necessary. Figure 7 shows the circuit simulation results of the proposed PDE of Type-2. It also achieves all sixteen delayed signals as expected. By using a stable reference-current for discharging the load inner the buffer stage, the linearity of programmability is expected to be improved. Theoretically, the maximum delays of both types could cover the entire half-clock-cycle if necessary.

For a fair comparison, a conventional PDE circuit [8] with exactly same output load is designed in the same $0.18\mu m$ CMOS technology. The delay programmability of PDE circuits is simulated as shown in Fig. 8. Thanks to the simplest discharging path, the proposed PDE of Type-1 performs a wide range of delay programmability. Its minimum delay is about $140ps$ when the input coding is set as $b_1 b_2 b_3 b_4 = 1111$, which is same as the inherent delay of regular inverter buffer. The proposed PDE of Type-2 achieves better linearity compared to conventional PDE circuit with the similar delay range.

3.2 Robustness against variation and temperature

To verify the robustness of proposed PDE circuits against process variations, circuit simulation results are shown in Fig. 9. A general investigation is made in this simulation when a global mismatch of 3% on transistors' sizes is con-

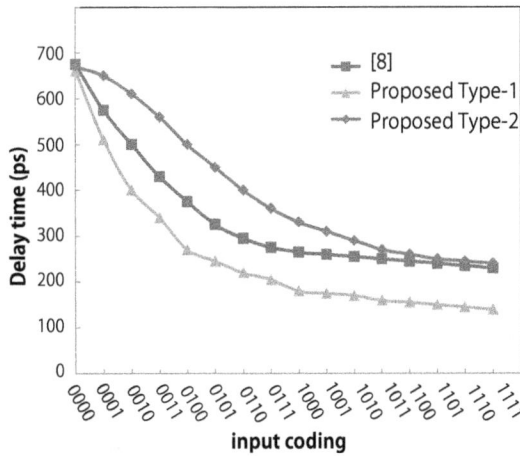

Figure 8: Delay programmability of a conventional [8] and proposed PDE circuits (both types) is simulated with exactly same output load.

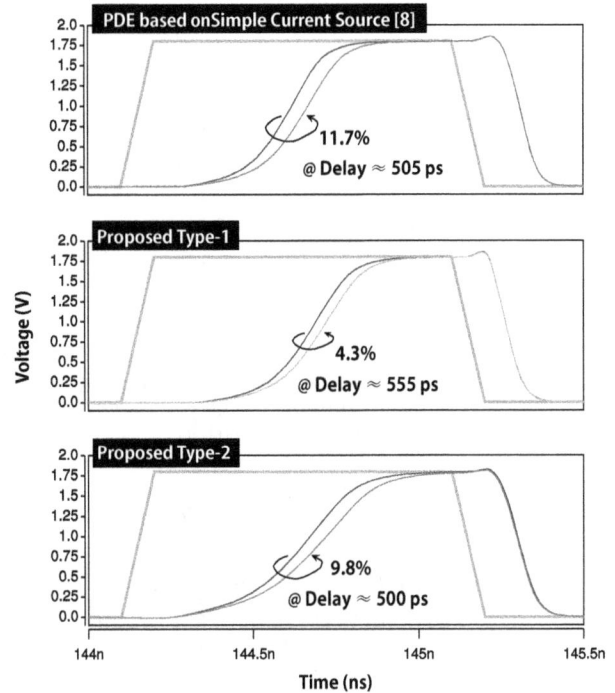

Figure 9: When a global mismatch of 3% on transistors' sizes is considered, the generated delays of PDE circuits are noticeably different from expected values.

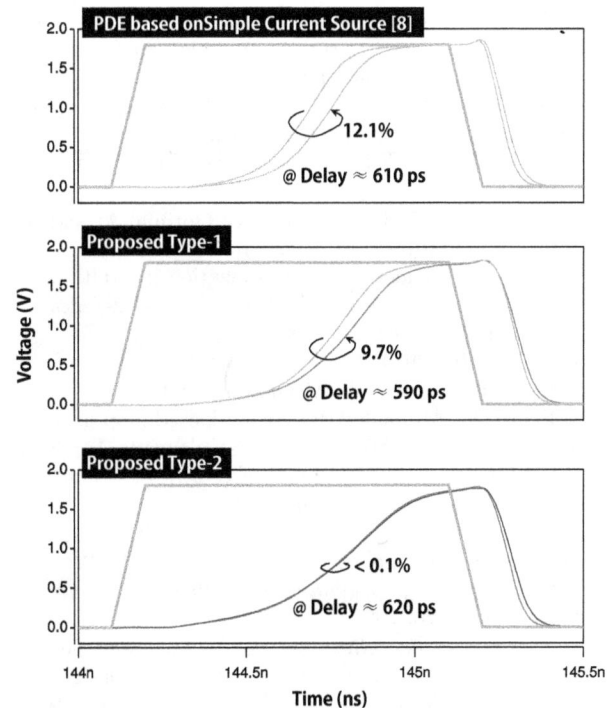

Figure 10: Delay is changed when temperature fluctuates from $25°C$ to $75°C$. Proposed PDE of Type-2 achieves best robustness among these three PDE circuits.

sidered. From the simulation results, the proposed Type-1 achieves best robustness out of these three PDEs. The robustness of proposed Type-2 is also improved due to the use of PVT-insensitive reference-current-generator. The temperature insensitivity is verified as shown in Fig. 10. Since a basic but satisfying temperature-compensation technology is applied in the proposed PDE of Type-2, the delay change of this circuit is less than 0.1% when temperature fluctuates from $25°C$ to $75°C$. The situation with a delay around $600ps$ (a large delay in fact) is considered for instance in this simulation. It is noticed the delay changes due to the variations and temperature become more serious when the expected delay increases.

3.3 Comparisons

The comparisons between conventional and proposed PDE circuits are made in Tab. 1. Compared to the conventional PDEs, the proposed circuits (both types) achieve similar or better performances over power, range and robustness. However, two types of PDEs suggested in this work appear different merits. The one with simplest discharging path (Type-1) performs low power, wide range and robust to process variations; Type-2 is insensitive to the temperature fluctuation. Regarding the chip area, Neuron-MOS mechanism is helpful to reduce the area occupied by capacitors since all of them are not actually charged. Namely, very small capacitance value is sufficient for coupling. Furthermore, the proposed PDEs avoid to employ long channel transistors (large sizes), which is necessary in conventional current-starve-based PDEs. In this sense, it is possible to fabricate the suggested PDEs within smaller chip area than conventional prototypes.

4. CONCLUSIONS

The feasibility to design PDE circuits based on Neuron-MOS mechanism is studied in this work. By applying capacitor coupling technology, the digital programmability for generating various delays is realized in stead of long channel transistors. Two types of PDE circuits were suggested with different merits. In general, both types achieve similar

Table 1: Performance comparisons.

	[8]	Proposed Type-1	Proposed Type-2
Delay range (ps)	235 ~	140 ~	240 ~
Static power (Max.)	32 μW	0	36μW
Delay change (3%var. on size)	11.7% (delay $\approx$ 505ps)	4.3% (delay $\approx$ 555ps)	9.8% (delay $\approx$ 500ps)
Delay change (25$^{\circ}C$ ~ 75$^{\circ}C$)	12.1% (delay $\approx$ 610ps)	9.7% (delay $\approx$ 590ps)	< 0.1% (delay $\approx$ 620ps)

or better performances than conventional PDEs over power consumption, delay range, robustness against process variations and temperatures. From the circuit simulation results, the type with simplest discharging path (type-1) performs a wide range of and robust delay without any static power consumption; Type-2 achieves a small delay change of 0.1% when the temperature fluctuates from 25$^{\circ}C$ to 75$^{\circ}C$.

5. ACKNOWLEDGMENTS

The authors would like to thank the VLSI Design and Education Center (VDEC) of the University of Tokyo in collaboration with Rohm Corporation, Toppan Printing Corporation, Synopsys, Inc., Cadence Design Systems, Inc., and Mentor Graphics, Inc.

6. REFERENCES

[1] J. P. Fishburn. Clock Skew Optimization. *IEEE Trans. Computers*, 39(7):945–951, 1990.

[2] M. Kaneko. Timing-test scheduling for constraint-graph based post-silicon skew tuning. In *Proc. IEEE Int. Conf. Computer Design*, pages 460–465, 2012.

[3] M. Y. C. Kao, K. -T. Tsai, and S. -C. Chang. A robust architecture for post-silicon skew tuning. In *Proc. IEEE/ACM Int. Conf. Computer-Aided Design*, pages 474–778, 2011.

[4] K.-H. Lim and D. Joo, T. Kim. An Optimal Allocation Algorithm of Adjustable Delay Buffers and Practical Extensions for Clock Skew Optimization in Multiple Power Mode Designs. *IEEE Trans. Computer-Aided Design of Integrated Circuits and Systems*, 32(3):392–405, 2013.

[5] J. Jasielski, S. Kuta, W. Machowski, and W. Kolodziejski. An analog dual delay locked loop using coarse and fine programmable delay elements. In *Proc. IEEE Int. Conf. Mixed Design of Integrated Circuits and Systems*, pages 185–190, 2013.

[6] N. R. Mahupatra, A. Tureent, and S. V. Gurimellu. Comparison and analysis of delay elements. In *Proc. IEEE Midwest Symposium on Circuits and Systems*, pages II-473–476, 2002.

[7] J. -L. Yang, C. -W. Chao, and S. -M. Lin. Tunable Delay Element for Low Power VLSI Circuit Design. In *Proc. IEEE Region Conf. TENCON*, pages 1–4, 2006.

[8] M. Maymandi-Nejad and M. Sachdev. A digitally programmable delay element: design and analysis. *IEEE Trans. Very Large Scale Integration (VLSI) Systems*, 11(5):871–878, 2003.

[9] J. B. Kobenge and H. Yang. A power efficient digitally programmable delay element for low power VLSI applications. In *Proc. IEEE Asia Symposium on Quality Electronic Design*, pages 83–87, 2009.

[10] T. Shibata and T. Ohmi. A functional MOS transistor featuring gate-level weighted sum and threshold operations. *IEEE Trans. Electron Devices*, 39(6):1444–1455, 1992.

[11] P. Hasler and T. S. Lande. Overview of floating gate devices, circuits and systems. *IEEE J. Solid State Circuits*, 48(1):1–3, 2001.

[12] T. Shibata, R. Zhang, Steven P. Levitan, Dmitri Nikonov, and George Bourianoff. CMOS Supporting Circuitries for Nano-Oscillator-Based Associative Memories. In *Proc. IEEE Int. Workshop on Cellular Nanoscale Networks and their Applications*, pages 1–4, 2012.

[13] K. Uy, P. Reyes-Abu, and W. Chung. A high precision temperature insensitive current and voltage reference generator. *World Academy of Science, Engineering and Technology*, 50:966–969, 2009.

[14] Y. -S. Park, H. -R. Kim, J. -H. Oh, Y. -K. Choi, and B. -S. Kong. Compact 0.7-V CMOS voltage/current reference with 54/29-ppm/$^{\circ}C$ temperature coefficient. In *Proc. IEEE Int. SoC Design Conf.*, pages 496–499, 2009.

[15] V. S. Babu, P. S. Haseena, and M. R. Baiju. A Floating Gate MOSFET Based Current Reference with Subtraction Technique. In *Proc. IEEE Computer Society Annual Symposium on VLSI*, pages 206–209, 2010.

Horizontal Benchmark Extension for Improved Assessment of Physical CAD Research

Andrew B. Kahng[†‡], Hyein Lee[†] and Jiajia Li[†]
[†]ECE and [‡]CSE Departments, University of California at San Diego
La Jolla, CA, 92093
abk@ucsd.edu, hyeinlee@ucsd.edu, jil150@ucsd.edu

ABSTRACT

The rapid growth in complexity and diversity of IC designs, design flows and methodologies has resulted in a benchmark-centric culture for evaluation of performance and scalability in physical-design algorithm research. Landmark papers in the literature present *vertical benchmarks* that can be used across multiple design flow stages; *artificial benchmarks* with characteristics that mimic those of real designs; artificial benchmarks with *known optimal solutions*; as well as benchmark suites created by major companies from internal designs and/or open-source RTL. However, to our knowledge, there has been no work on *horizontal benchmark* creation, i.e., the creation of benchmarks that enable maximal, comprehensive assessments across commercial and academic tools at one or more specific design stages. Typically, the creation of horizontal benchmarks is limited by mismatches in data models, netlist formats, technology files, library granularity, etc. across different tools, technologies, and benchmark suites. In this paper, we describe methodology and robust infrastructure for "horizontal benchmark extension" that permits maximal leverage of benchmark suites and technologies in "apples-to-apples" assessment of both industry and academic optimizers. We demonstrate horizontal benchmark extensions, and the assessments that are thus enabled, in two well-studied domains: place-and-route (four combinations of academic placers/routers, and two commercial P&R tools) and gate sizing (two academic sizers, and three commercial tools). We also point out several issues and precepts for horizontal benchmark enablement.

1. INTRODUCTION

Scaling of integrated system complexities, along with rapid changes in both SOC architectures and underlying process technologies, continue to demand improvements of VLSI CAD algorithms and tool capabilities. Particularly in the academic research context, *benchmarks* have been widely adopted as the basis for evaluation and comparison of VLSI CAD algorithms and optimizations [1] [21]. Evaluations mainly focus on solution quality and runtime; optimization domains include synthesis, partitioning, placement, clock tree synthesis, global routing, gate sizing, and other aspects of IC implementation. Since the mid-1980s, various benchmark suites and methods for artificial benchmark generation have been published, as reviewed in Section 2 below [4] [3] [2] [7] [9] [15].

At a high level, benchmarks in VLSI CAD (and, specifically, physical design) may be classified as **real** (derived from actual designs), **artificial** (intended to mimic aspects of real designs, and often the product of parameterizable generators), and **artificial with known optimal solutions** (realistic, but with optimal solutions embedded in the benchmark construction). On the other hand, **vertical** benchmarks [14] explicitly seek to enable evaluation of CAD tool performance across a span of several flow stages, via representations at multiple levels of abstraction.

For nearly three decades, VLSI CAD benchmarks, and their use, have faced the same quandary. Essentially, "leading-edge", "real" designs embody high-value intellectual property of their creators, and cannot be easily released; "old" or "artificial" benchmarks potentially drive CAD research in stale or wrong directions. Thus, when "real" benchmarks are released to the academic research community, their influence can be enormous, as was seen with the ISPD98 partitioning benchmark suite from IBM [2]. Further, the difficulty of obtaining real, leading-edge designs as open drivers for research raises an obvious challenge: **How can we *maximally* leverage available benchmarks as enablers of (physical) CAD research?**

To our knowledge, no previous work pursues the *maximal* assessment of academic research and its prevailing industry context (i.e., across various process/library technologies, benchmark circuits, and tools), at one or more particular flow stages, while such maximal assessment would reveal tools' suboptimality, and thus guide the improvements of tools' quality. Such "horizontal" evaluations are usually blocked by gaps between data models and formats of academic benchmark suites, versus those used in industry CAD tool flows.[1] Many benchmarks are constructed for particular technologies with specific library [36] granularity and naming conventions, which limits assessment. Underlying problem formulations may be mismatched to industry use cases, further hampering assessment.

In this work, we pursue the goals of *horizontal benchmarks* and *benchmark extension*, which together seek to maximize "apples-to-apples" assessment at one or more particular design stages, across different benchmarks, technologies, and tools. We use sizing and P&R (placement and routing), which are the topics of recent ISPD contests, to illustrate the challenges of, and our resulting methodologies for, horizontal benchmark enablement. For **benchmarks**, we report transformed sizing-oriented benchmarks (i.e., ISPD12/13 [18] [19]), placement-oriented benchmarks (i.e., ISPD11 [25]) and real designs (from OpenCores [37]). For **technologies**, we show mappings across ISPD12/13 contest and 28/45/65/90nm foundry technologies. Given the resulting horizontal benchmark suite, for **tools** we demonstrate the feasibility of apples-to-apples assessment among two academic sizers and three commercial tools in the sizing domain, and among four academic P&R tools and three commercial tools in the P&R domain. Comparison to commercial tools allows a better assessment of academic tools' capability. The scope of our efforts is depicted in Figure 1. The website [28] gives all conversion scripts, tool runscripts, and horizontal benchmark datasets that we describe in this paper.

We make several high-level observations. First, our work does not simply convert data formats to be used across different tools. Rather, we address at a number of levels the key challenge of horizontal benchmark enablement, namely, how missing information can be reasonably filled in, and/or which

---

[1] We recognize and applaud initiatives such as OpenAccess [39] and the now-inactive OAGear [40]. These data model and infrastructure projects offer the promise of universal data model and 'star topology, rather than clique topology' of interfaces and converters. However, given the long-standing incompleteness of open data models (e.g., with respect to timing flows) as well as the small number of key targets (ISPD benchmark formats, LEF/DEF and Verilog standards) we take a less elegant, and more pragmatic and brute-force, approach to achieving the desired enablement.

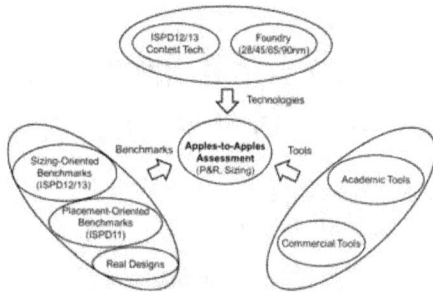

Figure 1: Scope of this work. We enable extensive assessment across different technologies, benchmarks and tools.

information should be simplified or hidden from tools, such that useful studies become possible. Second, the deeper contribution of our work is in enabling new questions to be explored: Can we better assess academic solver quality and scalability, in order to better assess potential gaps between the leading edge of academic research and industry contexts? Third, we emphasize that throughout our paper we use the term "benchmark" as a noun, and not as a verb. Our work is in the same spirit as OAGear [40], the GSRC Bookshelf [46] and works such as [5] – i.e., we hope that horizontal benchmarks will help industry and academia identify the most fruitful targets for academic research, as well as the potential impact of new academic research results.[2]

Our contributions may be summarized as follows.

- We propose and demonstrate *horizontal benchmarks* that allow maximum leverage of industry-provided benchmark data, and maximal "apples-to-apples" assessment of academic research tools in industry contexts (hence, technology evaluation and transfer) across benchmarks, technologies and tools, which will provide indications to designers on how to improve their tools' robustness/performance.

- We enumerate a number of challenges in horizontal benchmark creation, along with our solution approaches.

- We demonstrate the feasibility of apples-to-apples assessments in the P&R and sizing domains, using a rich mix of academic benchmark and real design data, four distinct process technologies, and a number of academic and commercial optimizers.

- Our infrastructure for horizontal benchmark extension and enablement (conversion scripts, tool runscripts, mapped benchmarks) is available on the web [28] for use by industry and academia.

The rest of this paper is organized as follows. Section 2 briefly reviews related work on academic benchmark suites and generators. In Section 3, we describe issues and challenges of horizontal benchmark enablement – both general issues, and issues specific to P&R or sizing – along with our solution approaches. Section 4 describes our experimental setup and results that demonstrate the feasibility of horizontal assessment in the P&R and sizing domains. Section 5 gives our conclusions and some perspectives on broader issues pertaining to horizontal benchmark enablement.

2. RELATED WORKS

Previous literature on benchmark generation (a recent review is given in [21]) addresses two main categories of benchmarks. **Real benchmarks** are derived from actual (but not too recent, for IP protection reasons) industrial designs. Figure 2 shows gate count over time in largest MPU products (per the 2011 ITRS [33]) and in largest circuits of notable benchmark suites. Superficially, gate counts in real designs have increased by 22× since 1998, while over the same 15-year period the gate count of the largest benchmark netlists has increased by 12×; there is currently still a "1000×" gap (indicated by the scale difference

---

[2]We do not advocate "benchmarking" (the verb) or any other activity that is in violation of commercial tool licenses.

between two y-axes). More realistically, the gap between academic benchmark and real design complexities can be estimated (based on gate count) at 5× ∼ 20×, when we calibrate to individual hard macros and top-level netlists in modern SOCs, or flat ASIC designs.[3] **Artificial benchmarks** are algorithmically generated, typically for a specific field or problem domain such as row-based placement or power grid analysis. The primary concern in artificial benchmark generation has been to capture salient attributes of real designs, such that academic CAD research is appropriately driven to intercept future industry needs. Thus, artificial benchmarks have attempted to match such parameters of real designs as Rent exponent, fanin/fanout distribution, path depth, etc. Important directions have included randomization techniques, and methods to generate artificial benchmarks with known optimal solutions. We briefly review examples of each benchmark type.

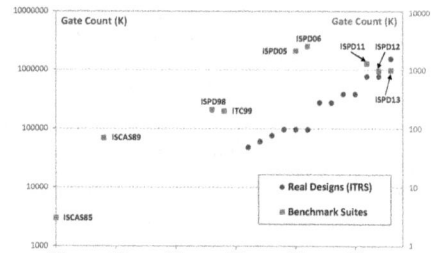

Figure 2: Gate count trajectories of largest MPU products [33] and largest designs in benchmark suites. Data in blue use the left y-axis, and data in red use the right y-axis.

Benchmark Suites Based on Real Designs. The highly influential **MCNC** benchmark suites [3] [4], published in the 1980s, have been used in various CAD applications such as automatic test pattern generation (ATPG), logic synthesis, netlist partitioning, and placement. The largest instance in the ISCAS-89 benchmark suite has ∼70K gates and ∼3K flip-flops. The **ISPD98** benchmark suite [2], developed for netlist partitioning applications, includes 18 circuits with module counts up to ∼210K. Since the benchmark circuits are generated from IBM internal designs, functionality, timing and technology information is removed. The **ITC99** benchmark suite [10] from the same time frame contains both RTL and gate-level benchmarks, the largest of which has ∼200K gates and ∼7K flip-flops, targeted at ATPG algorithm evaluation.

Over recent ISPD contests, the **ISPD05** and **ISPD06** benchmarks [31] respectively afford up to 2.1M and 2.5M placeable modules in the mixed-size placement context. The **ISPD11** suite [25] is derived from industrial ASIC designs and aims at routability-driven placement; it goes beyond earlier placement benchmarks by introducing non-rectangular fixed macros and associated pins that reside on metal layers, with up to 1200K modules (standard cells, macros and IO pins). For gate sizing and Vt-swapping, the **ISPD12** benchmark suite [18] adds library timing models (.lib, or Liberty table model format [36]) for a cell library with 11 combinational cells (each with 3 Vt variants and 10 sizes) and one sequential cell, along with a simplified SPEF with a single lumped capacitance for each net. The **ISPD13** suite [19] adds more detailed RC modeling and incorporates an industry timer in the evaluation. Instance complexity reaches 982K instances.

Artificial Benchmark Suites. Previous artificial benchmark generation approaches include *circ/gen* [13], *gnl* [22] and the work of [11]. A valuable class of methods produces instances with *known optimal solutions*. The **PEKO** placement benchmark generator [7] achieves a net-degree distribution similar to (ISPD98) IBM netlists as well as a constructive placement solution with known minimum wirelength. To improve realism (PEKO benchmarks have a single cell size, and all nets are local), **PEKU** [9] generates instances with known upper bounds on optimal wirelength. Nets in PEKU instances are long; a hybrid of PEKO and PEKU allows users to specify the percentage of short nets in the benchmarks. Generation

---

[3]There may be a chicken-egg dynamic here: growth of hard macro gate counts in SOC designs is limited by scaling of capacity (i.e., QoR/runtime sweetspot) of EDA tools, which has slowed in recent years.

of artificial instances with known optimal solutions has also been achieved for gate sizing optimizations [12]; an extension in [15] produces instances that resemble real designs in terms of gate count, path depth, fanin/fanout distribution and Rent parameter.

3. CHALLENGES

We now discuss challenges of horizontal benchmark extension, focusing on recent ISPD suites and actual designs.[4] The most obvious challenge in benchmark extension, arising from IP protection and limited scope of target problem formulations, is that benchmarks typically omit information. Partitioning instances (ISPD98) omit cell sizes and signal directions; placement instances (ISPD06/11) omit/obfuscate cell functions and combinational-sequential distinctions; global routing instances (ISPD07/08) omit cell functions and pin locations; etc. Thus, we must make a number of judgment calls as to how to best fill in missing information to achieve "benchmark extension". To (i) enable academic and industry optimizers to be run on the same testcases, and (ii) extend placement benchmarks to sizing benchmarks, we are faced with many options. These include, for example, criteria for mapping a placeable cell in a placement benchmark to a timable cell in a sizing benchmark; setting of timing, max fanout and other constraints; creation of interconnect parasitics; etc. The exemplary issues shown in Table 1 are addressed in the next three subsections.

Table 1: Sample issues in horizontal benchmark enablement.

Issue	Summary
A1	Missing logic function information in ISPD11 benchmarks
A2	Need timable benchmarks with parasitic information for sizing
B1	Commercial tools handle richer constraints and design rules
B2	ISPD12/13 technology does not provide LEF file
C1	Commercial sizers require timing-feasible benchmarks
C2	Granularity of libraries varies across different technologies

3.1 Formats, Data Models, and Libraries

We illustrate horizontal benchmark extension using selected instances from the ISPD11, ISPD12 and ISPD13 benchmark suites, along with two designs from the OpenCores website [37]. The first challenge is different formats (see Table 2): ISPD11 benchmarks are in Bookshelf format [46], ISPD12/13 benchmarks are .v netlists (i.e., structural Verilog), and real designs are described as RTL. Further, cell function information is removed from ISPD11 benchmarks. To enable horizontal assessment, our solution maps all benchmarks to .v netlists, which enables us to synthesize real implementations in arbitrary technology libraries; for ISPD11 benchmark circuits, we map nodes to cells in a given target technology. Apples-to-apples assessment in the P&R domain then requires us to also generate DEF [35] by performing floorplanning, power planning, and placement of primary inputs and outputs.

Table 2: Data formats/models for ISPD benchmark types

Design stage	Tool	Required file format
Placement	Commercial	.v, .lib, (DEF), LEF
	Academic	.nodes, .nets, .wts, .pl, .scl, .shapes
Global routing	Commercial	.v, .lib, DEF, LEF
	Academic	.gr or .nodes, .nets, .pl, .scl, .shapes, .route
Sizing	Commercial	.v, .lib, DEF, LEF, SPEF, .sdc
	Academic	.v, .lib, SPEF, .sdc

A second basic challenge in horizontal extension is that many academic tools are "hard-wired" to particular technology definitions. When assessing "legacy" tools that are no longer under active development, extra stpdf of enablement are required to migrate benchmarks across multiple technologies. For example, different cell libraries might vary in granularity (number of cell sizes, number of Vt flavors), available logic functions, or naming conventions, and this makes technology migrations not so straightforward. Figure 3 depicts our flow to extend benchmarks horizontally across multiple technologies. Explanations of sample issues (shown in Table 1), and our corresponding approaches, are as follows.[5]

---

[4] In our experience, horizontal extension of artificial, as opposed to real, netlists does not bring any fundamentally different challenges. Thus, while our discussion below focuses on real instances, it is largely orthogonal to the real vs. artificial dichotomy.

[5] Due to space constraints, more complete documentation is given at [28].

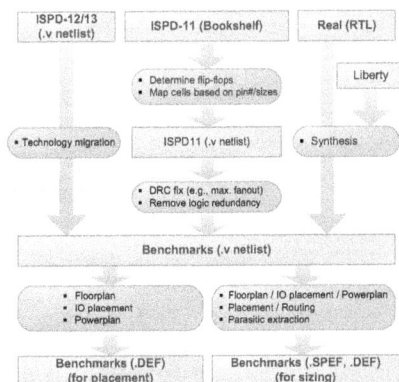

Figure 3: Flow to extend benchmark circuits across technologies.

Issue A1: In ISPD11 benchmarks, logic function information is removed and only node (i.e., cell, macro, pin) sizes and connectivity information are provided. To address this issue, **our approach** maps nodes of a placement benchmark to cells in a given Liberty/LEF pair, based on cell pin count and cell width. We first determine sequential cells.[6] We then map other nodes to combinational cells in the given LEF based on cell width and pin count. We normalize widths of nodes with the same pin count in the benchmarks to a particular range (e.g., [0, 1]). Then, we normalize cells with the corresponding pin count to the same range. Based on the normalized width values, we randomly assign cells from Liberty to nodes of the ISPD11 benchmark. Since we do not consider design functionality during cell mapping, logic redundancy can result, and we therefore use *Synopsys DC Compiler* [42] to simplify the netlist with Boolean transforms. When we migrate a resulting benchmark to another technology, we preserve functionality but scale footprint accordingly.

Issue A2: Timing paths are not considered in placement benchmarks. For instance, there are many floating nets (i.e., driving cell information is missing), notably in ISPD11 benchmarks, which lead to unconstrained timing paths. In addition, parasitic information is missing in placement benchmarks. **Our approach** adds additional primary inputs, to which we connect the floating nets. We determine the number of additional primary inputs based on Rent's rule (we use a Rent exponent value of 0.55 in the implementations reported below), and distribute floating nets evenly to the additional primary inputs. Further, we perform low-effort placement and routing and extract parasitic information from the routed designs.

3.2 Enablement of P&R Assessments

Figure 4 shows our enablement of P&R assessments. The inputs of the standard industry flow are LEF, DEF (or .v) and Liberty files. Conversion between LEF/DEF and Bookshelf formats enables assessment across commercial and academic tools. We implement placement with both commercial and academic placers; we then perform global routing on the resultant placement solutions using both commercial and academic tools. Detailed routing is feasible only with commercial tools. To enable apples-to-apples assessments across academic and commercial tools, we modify technology files and apply conversions between different formats. Explanations of sample issues (shown in Table 1), and our corresponding approaches, are as follows.

Issue B1: Commercial tools have multiple objectives and need to satisfy many design rules (e.g., antenna and maximum current density rules) and constraints (e.g., multi-mode/multi-corner timing, maximum fanout, etc.) while academic tools have only a specific objective. Our goal is to compare performance in terms of the specific objective, not to compare overall tool quality. In light of this goal, **our approach** intentionally drives the commercial tools to optimize for a specific objective that we want

---

[6] Given that area of a flip-flop is typically $\sim5\times$ the area of a NAND gate of similar driving strength, we bucket nodes having width of 25-32 units as flip-flops in ISPD11 benchmarks. Our identification of sequential cells has been confirmed by checking against a golden list of sequential cells provided by contest organizers [25].

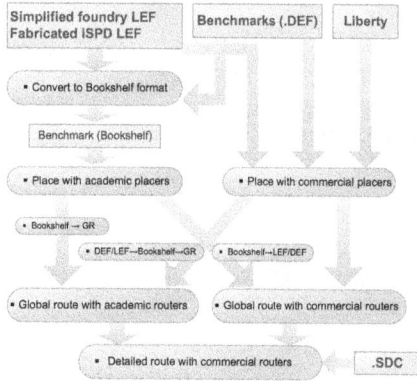

Figure 4: Enablement flows for horizontal P&R assessment.

to evaluate, by removing various extraneous rules that are defined in the LEF file. We use the simplified LEF file in placement and routing with both academic and commercial tools.

Issue B2: No technology (LEF) file is provided with ISPD12/13 benchmarks. To enable P&R of ISPD12/13 benchmarks using commercial tools, **our approach** constructs a new LEF file that incorporates technology information (e.g., metal pitch, width) from the foundry LEF. To generate cell LEF, we extract the pin area of X1 cells in the foundry LEF; based on this, we generate rectangular pins with the same area and height. Currently, we only distribute pins evenly inside each cell – then, based on the generated X1 cells, we scale width, pin area and on-grid pin locations linearly with drive strength to derive the LEF for larger cells.[7]

3.3 Enablement of Gate Sizing Assessments

We also enable horizontal evaluation across academic and industry tools for gate sizing (i.e., post-routing leakage reduction), as depicted in Figure 5. The cell sizing/Vt-swapping optimization reduces leakage *while preserving a timing signoff*. While commercial tools can consider, e.g., an area increase constraint, to achieve a fair assessment we only study tools in a pure leakage minimization use context. Inputs to sizing tools are netlist (.v), interconnect parasitics (SPEF), timing constraints (.sdc) and timing/power Liberty (.lib).

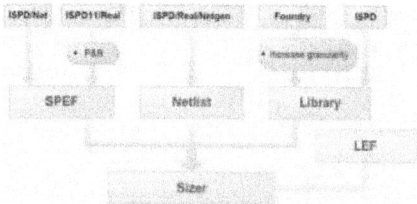

Figure 5: Enablement flows for horizontal sizer assessment.

Issue C1: Academic tools developed for the ISPD12/13 gate sizing contests must perform timing legalization as well as leakage minimization with a fixed set of SPEF parasitics, since no timing-feasible solution is provided. On the other hand, the use model for commercial "post-route leakage recovery" tools is to preserve a timing signoff (with fixed SPEF from a complete detailed route) while minimizing leakage. In other words, the industry tools assume a starting timing-feasible solution. For a fair assessment, we obtain timing-feasible solutions for all testcases. **Our approach** uses the academic tool [17] to perform timing recovery and changes .sdc files to generate timing-feasible solutions.

Issue C2: For assessment across different technologies, we would like to ensure that input netlists and sizing/Vt solution spaces are preserved across technologies. Varying library granularity poses a challenge, e.g., there are 10 sizes of inverters in ISPD12/13

[7]Particularly for mapping to advanced (≤ 28nm) foundry technologies, we recognize the need to improve awareness of porosity, pin accessibility, and related considerations.

Liberty, but a different number of sizes in a foundry Liberty. This would lead to less consistent results across technologies due to the changed solution space; thus, it is difficult to assess tools' quality across technologies. To match the number of cell variants, **our approach** increases library granularity so that all different technologies have the same sizing solution space. We generate new cells by interpolating/extrapolating based on timing information (cell delay, output transition time) of existing cells, exploiting logical effort analysis for cells of each given type. Last, we approximate leakage power and pin capacitance values by fitting second-order models to the values of existing cells.

4. EXPERIMENTAL RESULTS

We experimentally validate our horizontal benchmark enablements in two ways: (i) P&R studies; and (ii) sizing studies. In each way, we first assess tools' performance on different benchmarks, then, in different technologies. Last, we select the largest benchmark in each domain and perform maximal comparison, where we compare among different technologies and tools. Our studies use benchmark circuits with multiple sources and original purposes, as listed in Table 3. We use five distinct: ISPD12/13, and foundry 28nm FDSOI, 45GS, 65GP, and 90LP.

Table 3: Benchmark circuits.

Benchmark	Name	Gate Count (P&R)	Gate Count (Sizing)
ISPD13-1	des_perf	113112	113112
ISPD13-2	netcard	982258	982258
ISPD13-3	cordic	42903	42903
ISPD13-4	matrix_mult	156440	156440
ISPD12-1	b19	219268	219268
ISPD11-1	superblue1	817297	651533
ISPD11-2	superblue12	1286948	895309
ISPD11-3	superblue18	467261	385882
Real-1	jpeg_encoder	83241	83241
Real-2	leon3mp	473986	473986

4.1 P&R

We perform horizontal assessments using both academic and commercial P&R tools, across five technologies. Table 4 lists our experiments, where cPlacer1, cPlacer2 and cRouter1 are P&R functions (mapping not given here) in *Cadence SoC Encounter vEDI13.1* [30] and *Synopsys IC Compiler vH-2013.03-SP3* [41].

Table 4: Apples-to-apples assessments in P&R domain.

	Benchmark	Tech	Tool
Expt 1	ISPD13-{1-4}, ISPD12-1, ISPD11-{1-3}, Real-{1-2}	28nm	cPlacer1, mPL6
Expt 2	ISPD13-2, ISPD11-2	ISPD, 28/45/65/90nm	cPlacer1, mPL6
Expt 3	ISPD11-2	ISPD, 28/65nm	cPlacer1, cPlacer2, cPlacer3, NTUPlace3, mPL6, FastPlace3.1
Expt 4	ISPD13-2	28nm	cPlacer1, mPL6, cRouter1, BFG-R,

Expt 1 assesses solution quality (HPWL) and runtime of one commercial placer and one academic placer, using circuits from ISPD11/12/13 benchmark suites and real designs, with foundry 28nm technology. Results in Table 5 show that the academic tool achieves better HPWL, but consumes more runtime especially on large benchmarks. For a "fair comparison", awareness of timing and electrical design constraints is disabled in the commercial tool, where these issues (timing, DRVs) are not yet well-considered by any academic placers.

Expt 2 assesses placement solutions of one commercial placer and one academic placer across five different technologies. Results in Table 6 again show the academic tool in most cases achieving less HPWL with larger runtime, consistently across technologies.

Expt 3 illustrates horizontal assessment across two commercial and three academic placers, and across three distinct technologies, using the ISPD11-2 benchmark. Results in Table 7 show that solution quality is fairly consistent in the commercial tools, but varies more widely across the academic tools. More critically, the tool rankings that might be inferred using the ISPD technology are quite different from those that might be inferred in 28nm and 65nm technologies, which raises the possibility of greater suboptimality for academic tools in industry technologies.

Table 7: Expt 3. Comparison across placers. Benchmark: ISPD11-2. "-" indicates that no feasible solution is obtained within 48 CPU-hours.

Tech	cPlacer1		cPlacer2		NTUPlace3		mPL6		FastPlace3.1	
	HPWL (mm)	Runtime (min)	HPWL (mm)	Runtime (min)	HPWL (mm)	Runtime (min)	HPWL (mm)	Runtime (min)	HPWL (mm)	Runtime (min)
ISPD	50300	263	46100	103	47300	1330	73300	32	40400	88
28nm	36400	328	41500	29	-	-	32000	1212	48200	130
65nm	58800	335	65000	30	-	-	51100	657	73200	141

Table 5: Expt 1. Placer assessment across benchmark circuit types.

Benchmark	cPlacer1		mPL6	
	HPWL (mm)	Runtime (min)	HPWL (mm)	Runtime (min)
ISPD13-1	1040	12	868	7
ISPD13-2	31800	185	35800	313
ISPD13-3	224	3	178	3
ISPD13-4	1478	18	1338	11
ISPD12-1	1535	34	1360	853
ISPD11-1	19660	159	18260	547
ISPD11-2	36400	328	32000	1212
ISPD11-3	13960	94	12140	282
Real-1	954	10	800	6
Real-2	29400	273	17600	268

Table 6: Expt 2. Placer assessment across technologies.

Benchmark	Tech	cPlacer1		mPL6	
		HPWL (mm)	Runtime (min)	HPWL (mm)	Runtime (min)
ISPD13-2	ISPD	47200	149	39900	177
	28nm	31800	185	35800	313
	45nm	33600	221	31200	185
	65nm	50200	273	43400	172
	90nm	67500	327	55400	148
ISPD11-2	ISPD	50300	263	40400	88
	28nm	36400	328	32000	1212
	45nm	42600	307	37100	781
	65nm	58800	335	51100	657
	90nm	78600	449	73800	719

Table 8: Expt 4. Integration of routers in assessment (at 28nm).

Benchmark	Placer	GlobRouter	WL (mm)	%Overflow
ISPD13-2	mPL6	BFG-R	50.7	68.8
		cRouter1	48.0	71.8
	cPlacer1	BFG-R	47.9	47.1
		cRouter1	44.7	59.3
ISPD13-3	mPL6	BFG-R	0.68	0.0
		cRouter1	0.23	1.0
	cPlacer1	BFG-R	0.75	0.0
		cRouter1	0.27	1.1

Table 9: Apples-to-apples assessments in sizing domain.

	Benchmark	Tech	Tool
Expt 5	ISPD13-{1-4}, ISPD12-1, ISPD11-{2-3}, Real-1	28nm	cSizer1, UFRGS
Expt 6	ISPD13-2, ISPD11-2	ISPD, 28/45/65nm	cSizer1, UFRGS
Expt 7	ISPD13-2	ISPD, 28/65nm	cSizer1, cSizer2, cSizer3, Trident, UFRGS

academic sizers, in general, tend to spend more time and resources (e.g., memory), compared with the commercial sizers.

Table 10: Expt 5. Assessment of sizers on various benchmarks.

Benchmark	cSizer1			UFRGS		
	Leak (mW)	WNS (ns)	Runtime (min)	Leak (mW)	WNS (ns)	Runtime (min)
ISPD13-1	2.5	0.0	6.0	2.5	0.0	9.3
ISPD13-2	27.8	0.5	64.0	27.7	-3.7	73.5
ISPD13-3	0.4	0.0	6.8	0.4	0.0	3.0
ISPD13-4	1.1	0.0	13.5	1.0	-0.1	18.4
ISPD12-1	2.1	0.4	21.9	2.1	-0.2	28.0
ISPD11-2	30.4	2.7	155.0	30.4	-14.8	241.1
ISPD11-3	25.9	118.3	48.5	25.9	136.8	106.0
Real-1	1.4	0.0	4.2	1.3	-0.3	7.2

Last, to further exercise the horizontal benchmark enablement of Figure 4, and to incorporate global routers into our assessments, we run global routing (with identical *ggrid* definitions) using both commercial and academic tools. Inputs are placement solutions for the ISPD13-2 and ISPD13-3 testcases obtained using commercial and academic placers. Results in Table 8 show that global routing solutions have wirelength roughly consistent with HPWL of placement solutions. At the same time, we notice in the academic tool BFG-R some possible effects of a contest-induced focus on reduction of overflows: a de-emphasis of the wirelength metric might be the cause of longer wirelength (e.g., on the ISPD13-3 testcase) compared to the commercial router. Perhaps a more interesting aspect of this study is that it starts to show the wide-ranging possibilities from "maximal horizontal benchmark enablement": a gate sizing testcase is mapped to a production 28nm FDSOI library, placed with both commercial and academic placers, and global-routed with identical *ggrid* topology by both commercial and academic global routers (!). Potential additional studies abound – e.g., in a future study we will vary the number of routing layers for both placement and global routing comparison.

4.2 Sizing

Table 9 shows our setup of sizing assessments. As with P&R, we enable apples-to-apples assessment of commercial and academic sizers across multiple benchmarks and technologies. cSizer1, cSizer2 and cSizer3 are the leakage optimization tool *BlazeMO v2013* [29], and leakage optimization functions in *Synopsys IC Compiler vH-2013.03-SP3* [41] and *Cadence SoC Encounter vEDI13.1* [30] (mapping not given here).

Expt 5 compares final leakage and runtime of one commercial and one academic sizer on a range of benchmark types (sizing-oriented benchmarks, placement-oriented benchmarks, and real designs) with 28nm foundry technology. Interconnect RC parasitics (SPEF) are generated after P&R, and the clock period constraint is $1.2 \times$ the longest combinational path delay in the extracted and timed netlist.[8] We have observed in results that

Expt 6 assesses a commercial (cSizer1) and an academic (UFRGS) sizer with four foundry technologies. Results in Table 11 show that cSizer1 is worse than UFRGS in both solution quality and runtime, when evaluated using the ISPD contest technology. On the other hand, with 28nm, 45nm and 65m foundry technologies, cSizer1 achieves better solution quality with smaller runtime. The change in tool superiority across technologies, despite our enablement of identical sizing and multi-Vt solution space across technologies (recall issue **C1** in Section 3.3), raises the possibility that the academic sizer is somehow specialized to the ISPD technology.[9]

Expt 7 illustrates the horizontal assessment across three commercial and two academic sizers, and across three distinct technologies. Results in Table 12 show differences in ranking between the ISPD technology and industry technologies, which may indicate the potential for improvement of academic tools' robustness.[10]

5. CONCLUSIONS

In this work, we have proposed and implemented "horizontal benchmark extensions" to maximally leverage available benchmark testcases across multiple optimization domains. We enable new assessments of academic research at one or more design stages, within industrial tool/flow contexts, across multiple technologies, and across multiple types of benchmarks.

---

[8]The Real-1 benchmark, and the ISPD11-2 and ISPD11-3 instances derived from placement-oriented benchmarks, have "somewhat odd" WNS values after leakage optimization, as a result of this methodology.

[9]Anecdotally, participants in the 2013 Gate Sizing Contest observed that the ISPD technology was unusual in many respects, notably the non-monotonicity of delay and leakage benefits across sizes such as X3 gates.

[10]We make two comments. (i) The version of UFRGS that we study, obtained from the tool's authors, has a known inability to handle interconnect delay correctly; this can result in negative WNS values. The relative tool performance is similar across technologies, which suggests that testcases generated by our methodology are not biased to any particular technology; on the other hand, our SPEF generation may be especially challenging to the UFRGS binary. (ii) The results for cSizer3 are certainly unusually poor, but we have double-confirmed the reported numbers.

Table 12: Expt 7. Comparison across sizers. Benchmark: ISPD13-2.

Tech	cSizer1 Leak (mW)	WNS (ns)	Runtime (min)	cSizer2 Leak (mW)	WNS (ns)	Runtime (min)	cSizer3 Leak (mW)	WNS (ns)	Runtime (min)	Trident Leak (mW)	WNS (ns)	Runtime (min)	UFRGS Leak (mW)	WNS (ns)	Runtime (min)
ISPD	5231.6	-0.01	55.0	5591.5	0.0	31.6	3899.1	-125.4	80.5	5233.1	0.0	179.8	5184.1	-0.2	46.0
28nm	27.8	0.5	64.0	27.8	0.7	35.0	27.5	-851.2	98.0	29.4	1.4	43.7	27.7	-3.7	73.5
65nm	45.8	0.4	49.5	45.9	0.5	34.0	45.0	-283.9	104.5	46.0	1.2	46.8	45.4	-2.6	77.3

Table 11: Expt 6. Assessment of sizers across technologies.

Benchmark	Tech	cSizer1 Leak (mW)	WNS (ns)	Runtime (min)	UFRGS Leak (mW)	WNS (ns)	Runtime (min)
ISPD13-2	ISPD	5231.6	-0.01	55.0	5184.1	-0.2	46.0
	28nm	27.8	0.5	64.0	27.7	-3.7	73.5
	45nm	35.9	1.2	77.5	35.5	-5.8	95.6
	65nm	45.8	0.4	49.5	45.4	-2.6	77.3
ISPD11-2	ISPD	7143.8	14.8	77.0	6341.8	16.6	192.0
	28nm	30.4	2.7	155.0	30.4	-14.8	241.1
	45nm	39.8	96.5	127.2	39.4	302.6	367.0
	65nm	50.2	25.8	67.5	50.1	-56.8	262.9

In the domains of P&R and gate sizing, we describe several challenges to horizontal benchmark enablement as well as our proposed solution approaches and methodologies. We demonstrate benchmark constructions that are mapped to five technologies and consumed by academic and commercial tools for placement, routing (both global and detailed) and sizing. Experimental results suggest that academic tools can outperform industry tools on very specific objectives, but that over-focusing on a single objective can incur penalties in the multi-objective, highly constrained optimizations that arise in practical VLSI physical design contexts. Our results also point out that (i) academic tools can scale more poorly than commercial tools, and that (ii) the rank-ordering of tools by benchmark outcomes can be highly sensitive to choice of testcases and technology.

Our ongoing work pursues further horizontal benchmark constructions, e.g., to encompass clock network synthesis (ISPD09/10) and routability-driven placement (ICCAD13) benchmark suites while preserving their relevant characteristics. Connecting legacy methods for artificial testcase generation to current tool flows and formats is also of interest. Moreover, we seek benchmark constructions that can create more challenging, realistic benchmarks (e.g., benchmarks that explicitly test the ability to handle multiple objective and constraint types). Last, we believe that horizontal benchmark enablement can enable better exploration of the gaps between academic optimizers and real-world design contexts: certainly, improved understanding of "where things break" (cell counts, obstacles, aspect ratios, utilizations, library density, design rules, RC and signoff corners, etc.) can only help guide academic research.

6. ACKNOWLEDGMENTS

We are grateful to the authors of the academic tools studied [6] [8] [16] [17] [20] [26] for providing binaries of their optimizers for use in our study.

7. REFERENCES

[1] S. N. Adya, M. C. Yildiz, I. L. Markov, P. G. Villarrubia, P. N. Parakh and P. H. Madden, "Benchmarking for Large-Scale Placement and Beyond", *IEEE TCAD* 23(4) (2004), pp. 472-487.

[2] C. J. Alpert, "The ISPD98 Circuit Benchmark Suite", *Proc. ISPD*, 1998, pp. 80-85.

[3] F. Brglez, D. Bryan and K. Koźmiński, "Combinational Profile of Sequential Benchmark Circuits", *Proc. ISCAS*, 1989, pp. 1929-1933.

[4] F. Brglez and H. Fujiwara, "Recent Algorithms for Gate-Level ATPG with Fault Simulation and Their Performance Assessment", *Proc. ISCAS*, 1985, pp. 663-698.

[5] A. E. Caldwell, A. B. Kahng, A. A. Kennings and I. L. Markov, "Hypergraph Partitioning for VLSI CAD: Methodology for Heuristic Development, Experimentation and Reporting", *Proc. DAC*, 1999, pp. 349-354.

[6] T. F. Chan, J. Cong, J. R. Shinnerl and K. Sze, "mPL6: Enhanced Multilevel Mixed-Size Placement", *Proc. ISPD*, 2006, pp. 212-214.

[7] C. C. Chang, J. Cong and M. Xie, "Optimality and Scalability Study of Existing Placement Algorithms", *Proc. ASP-DAC*, 2003, pp. 621-627.

[8] T.-C. Chen, T.-C. Hsu, Z.-W. Jiang and Y.-W. Chang, "NTUplace: A Ratio Partitioning Based Placement Algorithm for Large-Scale Mixed-Size Designs", *Proc. ISPD*, 2005, pp. 236-238.

[9] J. Cong, M. Romesis and M. Xie, "Optimality, Scalability and Stability Study of Partitioning and Placement Algorithms", *Proc. ISPD*, 2003, pp. 88-94.

[10] F. Corno, M. S. Reorda and G. Squillero, "RT-Level ITC'99 Benchmarks and First ATPG Results", *IEEE Design & Test of Computers* 17(3) (2000), pp. 44-53.

[11] J. Darnauer and W. W.-M. Dai, "A Method for Generating Random Circuits and Its Application to Routability Measurement", *Proc. FPGA*, 1996, pp. 66-72.

[12] P. Gupta, A. B. Kahng, A. Kasibhatla and P. Sharma, "Eyecharts: Constructive Benchmarking of Gate Sizing Heuristics", *Proc. DAC*, 2010, pp. 592-602.

[13] M. D. Hutton, J. Rose, J. P. Grossman and D. Corneil, "Characterization and Parameterized Generation of Synthetic Combinational Circuits", *IEEE TCAD* 17(10) (1998), pp. 985-996.

[14] C. Inacio, H. Schmit, D. Nagle, A. Ryan, D. E. Thomas, Y. Tong and B. Klass, "Vertical Benchmarks for CAD", *Proc. DAC*, 1999, pp. 408-413.

[15] A. B. Kahng and S. Kang, "Construction of Realistic Gate Sizing Benchmarks With Known Optimal Solutions", *Proc. ISPD*, 2012, pp. 153-160.

[16] A. B. Kahng, S. Kang, H. Lee, I. L. Markov and P. Thapar, "High-Performance Gate Sizing with a Signoff Timer", *Proc. ICCAD*, 2013, pp. 450-457.

[17] V. S. Livertamento, C. Guth, J. L. Güntzel and M. O. Johann, "Fast and Efficient Lagrangian Relaxation-Based Discrete Gate Sizing", *Proc. DATE*, 2013, pp. 1855-1860.

[18] M. M. Ozdal, C. Amin, A. Ayupov, S. M. Burns, G. R. Wilke and C. Zhuo, "ISPD-2012 Discrete Cell Sizing Contest and Benchmark Suite", *Proc. ISPD*, 2012, pp. 161–164. http://archive.sigda.org/ispd/contests/12/ispd2012_contest.html.

[19] M. M. Ozdal, C. Amin, A. Ayupov, S. M. Burns, G. R. Wilke and C. Zhuo, "An Improved Benchmark Suite for the ISPD-2013 Discrete Cell Sizing Contest", *Proc. ISPD*, 2013, pp. 168–170. http://www.ispd.cc/contests/13/ispd2013_contest.html.

[20] J. A. Roy and I. L. Markov, "High-performance routing at the nanometer scale", *Proc. ICCAD*, 2007, pp. 496–502.

[21] L. Srivani and V. Kamakoti, "Synthetic Benchmark Digital Circuits: A Survey", *IETE Technical Review* 29(6) (2012), pp. 442-448.

[22] D. Stroobandt, P. Verplaetse and J. V. Campenhout, "Generating Synthetic Benchmark Circuits for Evaluating CAD Tools", *IEEE TCAD* 19(9) (2000), pp. 1011-1022.

[23] D. Sylvester and K. Keutzer, "Getting to the Bottom of Deep Submicron", *Proc. ICCAD*, 1998, pp. 203-211.

[24] N. Viswanathan, IBM Corporation, *personal communication*, November 2011.

[25] N. Viswanathan, C. J. Alpert, C. Sze, Z. Li, G.-J. Nam and J. A. Roy, "The ISPD-2011 Routability-Driven Placement Contest and Benchmark Suite", *Proc. ISPD*, 2011, pp. 141-146. http://www.ispd.cc/contests/11/ispd2011_contest.html.

[26] N. Viswanathan, M. Pan and C. Chu, "FastPlace 3.0: A Fast Multilevel Quadratic Placement Algorithm with Placement Congestion Control", *Proc. ASP-DAC*, 2007, pp. 135-140.

[27] X. Yang, M. Wang, K. Eguro and M. Sarrafzadeh, "A Snap-On Placement Tool", *Proc. ISPD*, 2000, pp. 153-158.

[28] Horizontal Benchmarks Project Website. http://vlsicad.ucsd.edu/A2A

[29] Blaze MO. http://www.tela-inc.com

[30] Cadence Design Systems. http://www.cadence.com

[31] ISPD05/06 benchmarks. http://archive.sigda.org/ispd2005/contest.htm, http://archive.sigda.org/ispd2006/contest.html

[32] ISPD website. http://www.ispd.cc

[33] ITRS 2011 edition reports. http://public.itrs.net/reports.html

[34] IWLS contest. http://www.iwls.org/challenge/index.html

[35] LEF DEF reference. http://www.si2.org/openeda.si2.org/projects/lefdef

[36] Liberty Technical Advisory Board. http://www.opensourceliberty.org

[37] OpenCores. http://opencores.org

[38] Research Data Alliance. http://rd-alliance.org

[39] Si2 OpenAccess. http://www.si2.org/?page=69

[40] Si2 OpenAccess Gear. http://www.si2.org/openeda.si2.org/help/group_ld.php?group=73

[41] Synopsys. http://www.synopsys.com

[42] Synopsys Design Compiler User Guide. http://www.synopsys.com/Tools/Implementation/RTLSynthesis/DCUltra/Pages

[43] Synopsys PrimeTime User's Manual. http://www.synopsys.com

[44] TAU contest. http://www.tauworkshop.com

[45] UCLA/UCSD Sizing Optimizers. http://vlsicad.ucsd.edu/SIZING/optimizer.html

[46] VLSI CAD Bookshelf, A. E. Caldwell, A. B. Kahng and I. L. Markov. http://vlsicad.eecs.umich.edu/BK

OCV-Aware Top-Level Clock Tree Optimization

Tuck-Boon Chan‡, Kwangsoo Han‡, Andrew B. Kahng†‡,
Jae-Gon Lee§ and Siddhartha Nath†
†CSE and ‡ECE Departments, UC San Diego, §Samsung Electronics Co., Ltd.
tbchan@ucsd.edu, kwhan@eng.ucsd.edu, abk@cs.ucsd.edu,
altair.lee@samsung.com, sinath@cs.ucsd.edu

ABSTRACT

The clock trees of high-performance synchronous circuits have many clock logic cells (e.g., clock gating cells, multiplexers and dividers) in order to achieve aggressive clock gating and required performance across a wide range of operating modes and conditions. As a result, clock tree structures have become very complex and difficult to optimize with automatic clock tree synthesis (CTS) tools. In advanced process nodes, CTS becomes even more challenging due to on-chip variation (OCV) effects. In this paper, we present a new CTS methodology that optimizes clock logic cell placements and buffer insertions in the top level of a clock tree. We formulate the top-level clock tree optimization problem as a linear program that minimizes a weighted sum of timing slacks, clock uncertainty and wirelength. Experimental results in a commercial 28nm FDSOI technology show that our method can improve post-CTS worst negative slack across all modes/corners by up to 320ps compared to a leading commercial provider's CTS flow.

1. INTRODUCTION

In a modern SOC, *clock logic cells* (CLCs), such as clock gating cells (*CGCs*), multiplexers (*MUXes*) and dividers (*DIVs*), are required in the clock tree to achieve different performance and power saving requirements. To enable multi-mode operation and dynamic voltage frequency scaling (DVFS), large numbers of clocks are generated to drive flip-flops (FFs) in an SOC.[1] Balancing the clock trees of multiple clocks is challenging because timing constraints depend on clock periods, and on the process, voltage and temperature (PVT) corners. Furthermore, as on-chip variation (OCV) increases, *clock uncertainties* (derates) on the launch and capture paths can increase. Clock tree synthesis (CTS) must find optimal branching points in the clock tree to minimize clock uncertainties due to OCV on *non-common paths* [9][16][17]. Figure 1 (left) illustrates the clock balancing problem due to CLCs in a clock tree and the impact due to OCV. Due to the CLCs, the clock arrival times at FF groups are skewed. Moreover, the clock tree splits near the clock source; this leads to long non-common paths between the FF groups. As shown in Figure 1 (right), we can insert buffers to balance the clock, and optimize placement of the CLCs to reduce the non-common paths.

1.1 Motivation for Clock Tree Optimization

Given a clock tree, we represent the *top-level clock tree* as a hypergraph, $G_{top}(V_{top}, E_{top})$, in which V_{top} is a set of CLCs and the transitive fanin cells of the CLCs. E_{top} is a set of nets that connect the cells in V_{top}. Figure 2 shows a top-level clock tree

---

[1] Both synchronous and asynchronous clocks can exist in an SOC. Our work focuses on balancing synchronous clocks in an SOC.

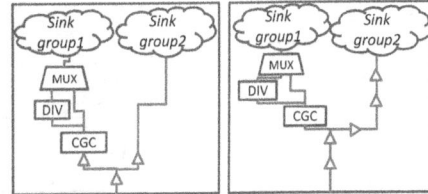

Figure 1: Clock tree synthesis problems.

with a CLC and three bottom-level buffered clock trees. In most cases, sophisticated EDA tools and CTS algorithms are able to achieve good solutions for the bottom-level clock trees. However, *achieving a good solution for the top-level clock tree can be problematic* when there are critical paths across the FF groups between different bottom-level clock trees. The requirements to balance the top-level clock are not obvious due to the complex structure of the tree (see Figure 6). Fixing the critical paths across the FF groups can be difficult at the bottom-level clock trees due to tight timing constraints among FFs within the same group. To optimize timing across FF groups, we propose to **balance the top-level clock tree while preserving the bottom-level clock trees**. For example, in Figure 2, if we increase the delay $d(1,2)$ on the net between *pins 1* and *2* from 2ns to 4ns, we can change the skew between *FF groups 1* and *2* from 2ns to 0ns, thereby meeting the timing target of *critical path A* which has a clock period of 3ns. Note that varying the delay on the top-level clock tree does not affect *critical path B* (but, the OCV derating on a longer top-level path will be larger), which has both its launch and capture FFs in the same group. Therefore, we only need to consider the requirements to balance clock across FF groups, thereby simplifying the top-level clock tree optimization problem. Since problems arise in the top-level tree due to CLCs, our work focuses on optimizing the placement of CLCs and insertion of buffers in the *top-level clock tree*.

1.2 Previous Work

Rajaram and Pan [16] propose CTS algorithms to optimize the chip-level clock tree across different PVT corners. They use quadratic programming to reallocate clock pins of IP blocks to reduce non-common paths in the chip-level clock tree. After clock pins are reallocated, buffers are inserted up to each pin, and subtrees are merged recursively in the same manner as the *deferred-merge embedding* (DME) algorithm [6]. The algorithm only inserts buffers that minimize the difference in clock latency among subtrees across PVT corners. Although the chip-level CTS work in [16] accounts for delay variation across PVT corners and timing penalty on non-common paths, it does not consider CLCs, timing between FF groups, or wirelength, all of which make CTS a challenging task. As illustrated in Figure 1, the placement of CLCs should also be considered during CTS as it can significantly affect the non-common paths in the tree. Other works [20][18] seek to minimize the effect of OCV during CTS, but do not address the issues of CTS with CLCs across multi-corner or multi-mode (MCMM) scenarios. Lung et al. [12] propose a linear programming (LP) based clock skew optimization [8] which accounts for delay variation across PVT corners. They also present a method to map the required delays obtained from the LP to actual circuits. While mapping delays, they use updated timing information to dynamically adjust buffer delays. Although this work addresses the MCMM clock skew minimization problem, it does not consider the effects of non-common paths and CLC placement. There are many previous works on buffer insertion for CTS (e.g., [1][4]), but they do not consider clock trees with CLCs which have different timing requirements depending on the operating modes and FF groups. Papa et al. [15] minimize worst negative slack (WNS) at a single PVT corner by optimizing the placement and buffering of datapaths. They do not consider multiple PVT corners and they do not balance the top-level clock trees.

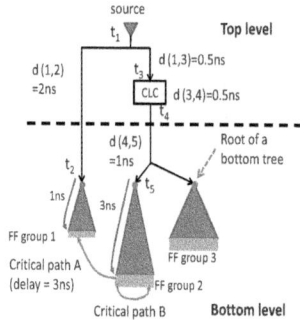

Figure 2: Example of balancing a clock tree by varying $d(i,j)$.

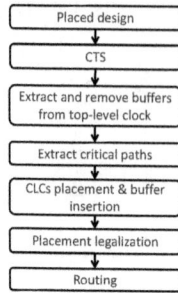

Figure 3: Overview of our CTS flow.

1.3 Our Work

To address the top-level CTS problem mentioned above, we propose a *new* CTS flow that accounts for the effects of CLCs as well as delay variations due to MCMM and OCV. The basic idea of our approach is to *automatically* identify the requirements to balance clocks based on the timing critical paths and use them to drive the CTS. The flow shown in Figure 3 starts with a placed design and performs *conventional CTS* to obtain a clock tree. We then extract the top-level clock tree (see Algorithm 1) and remove buffers in the top-level clock tree. Within the remaining (bottom-level) clock trees, we extract timing-critical FF-to-FF paths to identify the timing requirements for clock balancing. Based on these requirements, we construct a linear program (LP) to optimize the placement of CLCs and the delay on nets (achieved by inserting buffers) in the top-level clock tree. Unlike the routing algorithm proposed by Oh et al. [13] which minimizes the total wirelength of a routing tree, we include CLCs and Steiner point locations as variables in the LP, so that the LP-based optimization can account for the cost of non-common paths. With the physical locations of CLCs and Steiner points of the routes, we insert buffers in the top-level clock tree, legalize the placement and route the clock tree. The advantages of our methodology are as follows.

- Preserving the bottom-level clock trees affords more accurate timing information for the top-level clock tree optimization.[2]

- Since the top-level clock tree has many fewer instances, we can perform runtime-intensive optimizations which cannot be practically applied to the bottom-level clock tree.

- Introducing our new top-level clock tree placement optimization enables fixing of suboptimal CLC placements which have already been determined during the preceding placement stage.

- Buffer insertion and CLC placement optimization can achieve reductions of non-common path timing penalties, which are not achievable using local/incremental optimizations.

The key contributions of our work are summarized as follows.

- We propose a new automated clock tree synthesis methodology that optimizes the CLC placements and buffer insertion in the top-level clock tree.

- We propose an LP-based clock tree optimization method which accounts for routing resources (i.e., wirelength), circuit timing and the impact of non-common paths.

[2] In this work, we optimize only the top-level clock tree. Joint optimization of the top- and bottom-level trees is a direction of ongoing work.

- Our method improves WNS by up to 320ps, and reduce the top-level clock wirelength by up to 50% compared to a default CTS flow.

- As part of our validation process, we develop generators for testcases that represent clock tree structures typically found in high-speed IPs (e.g., graphics accelerators) and real-world SOCs.

In the remainder of this paper, Section II describes our top-level clock tree optimization methodology. Section III describes experimental setup and our experimental results. In Section IV, we summarize our work and outline directions for future research.

2. CLOCK TREE OPTIMIZATION

We now explain the top-level clock tree optimization problem and our approach. In the following, we use *condition*, k, to denote that a timing value is specific to a PVT corner, clock group and timing analysis type (setup or hold). For example, with two PVT corners, two operating modes, two clock groups and two timing analysis types, k will range from $1, 2, ..., 16$.

2.1 Problem Statement

Formally, the top-level CTS problem is defined as follows.
Objective: Minimize the weighted sum of (i) worst negative slack, (ii) total negative slack (TNS), (iii) clock uncertainty and (iv) wirelength of a clock tree [16].
Input: Placed design; list of CLCs; timing constraints (.sdc).
Output: An optimized placement of CLCs and clock buffers, clock routing of the top-level clock tree.

We model the cost of clock uncertainty $Z_k(a,b)$ on a critical path between FFs a and b as the sum of delays of the non-common launch and capture clock paths in the critical path. The non-common path delays are normalized to the clock period (CP) of the path using factor α_k.

$$Z_k(a,b) = \alpha_k \{ \sum_{i \in h_a, j \in h_b} d_k(i,j) - \sum_{i,j \in (h_a \cap h_b)} 2d_k(i,j) \} \quad (1)$$
$$\alpha_k = 1/\text{CP at condition } k$$

where h_a denotes a launch/capture path from a clock source to FF a, and $d_k(i,j)$ is the delay between pin i and j.

2.2 Our Approach

We formulate the top-level clock tree balancing problem as a linear program by assuming that we can vary (i) the delay $d_{ref}(i,j)$ from an output pin i to its fanout input pin j at a *reference condition*;[3] (ii) locations of CLCs; and (iii) Steiner points in the clock net (for a given topology). Although wire delay is normally nonlinear with respect to wirelength, we approximate $d_{ref}(i,j)$ as a linear function of distance between pin i and j assuming buffer insertion (as noted in, e.g., [15], the delay of a net with uniformly spaced buffers is linearly proportional to the number of stages).[4]

The main objective of the LP is to minimize the weighted sum of worst negative slack S_{wns}, the total negative slack S_{tns}, non-common paths, $Z_k(a,b)$, and total wirelength $U(i,j)$.[5] Note that we weight the $Z_k(a,b)$ proportional to its original *negative* slack (i.e., $1 - s_k^0(a,b)$) such that the LP focuses on reducing the non-common path delay on timing paths. The critical paths and their original slacks $s_k^0(a,b)$ are extracted after the buffer removal step in Figure 3 by performing static timing analysis (STA).

To represent negative slack $s_k'(a,b)$ in the LP, we use Constraints (3) and (4) such that $s_k'(a,b) = 0$ when $s_k(a,b) > 0$. S_{wns} and S_{tns} are defined in Constraints (5) and (6), respectively. Since circuit designers may treat hold and setup slacks differently, we use a

[3] The reference condition is {SS process corner, $0.85V, 125°C$}.

[4] A buffered net has relatively linear delay vs. distance even in advanced technology nodes. For example, the stage delay in a uniformly buffered-chain is almost the same except for the first few stages. Adding an additional stage will increase the delay by a fixed amount. To account for the non-linearity within a single stage delay, our buffer insertion algorithm detour wires to match the required delay obtained from our LP.

[5] Our objective function is different from [16]. They do not consider wirelength and the timing between FF groups.

weight $\gamma_k \geq 0$ to set the ratio of importance (i.e., normalization ratio) of setup and hold slacks. The value of γ_k can be different for hold or setup analysis, as indicated by the condition k. We represent the timing slacks $s_k(a,b)$ for each timing-critical path between FFs a and b as a function of the original slack, original clock skew $\lambda_k(a,b)$, and the clock arrival times ($t_{ref}(a)$) in Constraint (7). Because delay and slack vary according to PVT corners and timing analysis type, we normalize the slacks across different conditions to a reference corner by using scaling factors η_k, following the approach in [12]. $\zeta = 1$ if the path is a setup-critical path and $\zeta = -1$ if the path is a hold-critical path. $t_{ref}(a)$ is the sum of delays along the path h_a (Constraint (8)).

Objective:

$$\text{Min } -w_{wns} \cdot S_{wns} - w_{tns} \cdot S_{tns} + w_{wl} \cdot \sum_{e(i,j) \in E_{top}} U(i,j)$$

$$+ w_{ncp} \cdot \sum_{k,a,b} (1 - s_k^0(a,b)) \cdot Z_k(a,b) + w_{dis} \cdot \sum_i M(i,i_0) \quad (2)$$

Subject to:

$$s_k'(a,b) \leq \alpha_k \cdot s_k(a,b), \ \forall a,b,k \quad (3)$$

$$s_k'(a,b) \leq 0, \qquad \forall a,b,k \quad (4)$$

$$S_{wns} \leq \gamma_k \cdot s_k'(a,b), \forall a,b,k \quad (5)$$

$$S_{tns} = \sum_{a,b,k} \gamma_k \cdot s_k'(a,b) \quad (6)$$

$$\eta_k \cdot s_k(a,b) = \eta_k \cdot (s_k^o(a,b) - \lambda_k(a,b)) + \zeta(t_{ref}(a) - t_{ref}(b)) \quad (7)$$

$$t_{ref}(a) = \sum_{i,j \in h_a} d_{ref}(i,j) \quad (8)$$

$$d_{ref}(i,j) \geq \beta_{ref} \cdot U(i,j) \quad (9)$$

$$Z_k(a,b) = \alpha_k \{ \sum_{i \in h_a, j \in h_b} d_k(i,j) - \sum_{i,j \in (h_a \cap h_b)} 2d_k(i,j) \} \quad (10)$$

$$M(i,j) = m_x(i,j) + m_y(i,j) \quad (11)$$

$$m_x(i,j) \geq (p_x(j) - p_x(i)), m_x(i,j) \geq 0 \quad (12)$$

$$m_y(i,j) \geq (p_y(j) - p_y(i)), m_y(i,j) \geq 0 \quad (13)$$

$$M(i,i_0) = m_x(i,i_0) + m_y(i,i_0) \quad (14)$$

$$m_x(i,i_0) \geq (p_x(i) - p_x(i_0)), m_x(i,i_0) \geq 0 \quad (15)$$

$$m_y(i,i_0) \geq (p_y(i) - p_y(i_0)), m_y(i,i_0) \geq 0 \quad (16)$$

$$0 \leq p_{\{x,y\}}(i) \leq F_{\{x,y\}} \quad (17)$$

The values of $\lambda_k(a,b)$ and the cell delays in $d_{ref}(i,j)$ are constants in the LP, and are extracted from STA reports after the buffer removal step in our flow. In Constraint (9), we model the delay $d_{ref}(i,j)$ between pins i and j as a linear function of the Manhattan distance $U(i,j)$ between the pins. β_{ref} is a conversion factor to convert the Manhattan distance to delay at the reference condition. We obtain the value of β_{ref} using the optimal repeater length method in [2]. The value of β_{ref} is 30ps per 100μm for a 8X buffer in the 28nm foundry FDSOI standard cell library that we use in our experiments. We calculate $Z_k(a,b)$ in Constraint (10). The Manhattan distances are calculated using Constraints (11)–(13). The location of a pin i is specified by variables $p_x(i)$ and $p_y(i)$, which represent the x and y coordinates of the pin. The bounds for $p_x(i)$ and $p_y(i)$ are specified in Constraint (17). F_x and F_y are the upper bounds for the pin coordinates along the x and y axes, i.e., the dimensions of the design's floorplan.

To avoid unnecessary cell displacements, we add a *displacement cost* $M(i,i_0)$ in the objective function [15]. The displacement cost is defined as the sum of Manhattan distances between the original cell locations ($[p_x(i_0), p_y(i_0)]$) and their corresponding cell locations ($[p_x(i), p_y(i)]$) after optimization. $M(i,i_0)$ is calculated using Constraints (14)–(16). Since the displacement cost will force the LP to "pull" the cells to their original locations, we use a very small weighting factor ($w_{dis} = 0.001$) as the cell displacement cost.

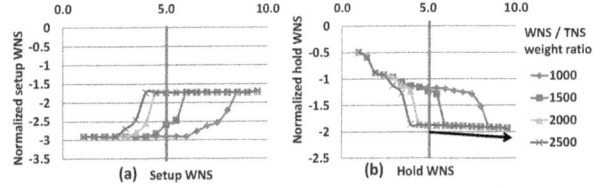

Figure 4: Normalized (a) setup WNS and (b) hold WNS obtained by solving the LP for different γ_k and w_{wns}/w_{tns}.

We apply uniform weights for TNS and non-common path delays, i.e., $w_{tns} = 1$, $w_{ncp} = 1$. Since the typical values of total wirelength in a top-level clock tree is much larger than the timing slacks we set $w_{wl} = 0.001$ such that the cost in the LP is not dominated by the wirelength.

Figures 4(a) and 4(b) respectively show the setup and hold WNS (both normalized to their corresponding clock periods) obtained by solving the LP for different values of γ_k. As we sweep γ_k from 1 to 10, the setup WNS obtained from the LP improves but the hold WNS worsens. When we sweep the w_{wns}/w_{tns} ratio, the setup and hold WNS are not affected when $\gamma_k \leq 3$. However, when $\gamma_k > 3$, the cost in the LP is dominated by the setup WNS and increasing the w_{wns}/w_{tns} ratio will improve the setup WNS. Since the hold time violations are relatively easy to fix by inserting buffers, we prioritize setup slacks when we select the γ_k and w_{wns}/w_{tns} weight ratios. In our experiments, we use $\gamma_k = 5$ and $w_{wns}/w_{tns} = 2000$ because we experimentally observe that by increasing γ_k further does not improve the setup WNS but makes hold WNS worse (black arrow in Figure 4(b)). We use the same values of the weighting factors across all testcases. It is also possible to apply different combinations of values of weighting factors, run the flows in parallel, and choose the best CTS solution.

2.3 Implementation Heuristics

Given a design with an initial clock tree, $G(V,E)$, and a subset of vertices $V_{CLC} \subseteq V$ corresponding to CLCs, we extract the top-level clock net using Algorithm 1.[6] First, we create a list V_{top} of all transitive fanin cells of the CLCs. In Lines 2–4, we remove all the clock routes connected to the fanin cells. In Lines 5–12, we check each cell in V_{top}, remove all the buffers and reconnect the nets accordingly.

Algorithm 1 Extract top-level clock tree

> **Procedure** *Extract_top*()
> **Input :** $G(V,E)$, V_{CLC}
> **Output:** $G(V_{top}, E_{top})$
> 1: $V_{top} \leftarrow$ transitive fanins of all $v \in V_{CLC}$;
> 2: **for all** $e(u,v) \in E$; $u,v \in V_{top}$ **do**
> 3:   Remove clock routing for $e(u,v)$;
> 4: **end for**
> 5: $E_{top} \leftarrow \emptyset$
> 6: **for** $v \in V_{top}$ **do**
> 7:   **if** v is a buffer **then**
> 8: $(v.parent).children \leftarrow v.children$;
> 9: $V_{top} \leftarrow V_{top} \setminus \{v\}$;
> 10: $E_{top} \leftarrow E_{top} \cup \{e(v.parent, v.children)\}$;
> 11:   **end if**
> 12: **end for**
> 13: Return $G(V_{top}, E_{top})$;

In the top-level clock balancing problem, the LP optimizes the delays from an output pin to input pins in every net. For nets with more than one fanout, we modify the net into a binary tree by inserting Steiner points. The purpose of this step is to include the locations of the Steiner points as variables in the LP so as to optimize the non-common paths. Given a net, $G_{net}(V,E)$, and its driving pin, v_r, we apply Algorithm 2 to obtain a binary tree. In Lines 8–16, we find the pin pair that minimize the metric $\Delta L'$ which is defined as the sum of the difference in *sink latency*[7] and the delay

---

[6]We obtain V_{CLC} by assuming all CLCs are in the top-level clock tree.

[7]The sink latency $L(u)$ of a pin u is the maximum latency from u to any FF in the transitive fanout of u.

due to the Manhattan distance between these pins.[8] In Lines 17–25, we merge the pin pair that has minimum $\Delta L'$ by creating a new Steiner point. We define the x and y coordinates of the new Steiner point as the average of the x and y coordinates of the merged pins (Lines 21–22). The sink latency of the Steiner point is defined as the maximum sink latency of the merged pins (Line 20). The procedure *split_net()* is invoked repeatedly until all driving pins have a single connection (to a Steiner point). Figure 5 illustrates our Steiner point insertion algorithm. In the first iteration, we merge pins j_2 and j_3 because they have the smallest ΔL and Manhattan distance. Pins j_2 and j_3 are then connected to Steiner point $j_{2'}$ (red square). The location of $j_{2'}$ is defined by the average of the x and y coordinates of pins j_2 and j_3. In the second iteration, we merge pins j_1 with $j_{2'}$ because they have a smaller $\Delta L'$ even though the Manhattan distance between pins j_1 and $j_{2'}$ is larger than the Manhattan distance between pins j_4 and $j_{2'}$. In the last iteration, we merge j_4 and $j_{1'}$. Note that our algorithm selects the pins to merge based on the sum of Manhattan distance and the difference in sink latency. This is different from the algorithm in [7] which selects the pins based on Manhattan distance only. For example, the algorithm in [7] will merge j_2 and j_3, followed by j_4 and j_1. As shown in Figure 5 (the upper-right clock tree), the algorithm in [7] will lead to a clock tree that will require more buffers to be inserted (red arrows) to balance the clock latencies (green arrows) compared to the tree produced by our algorithm (the lower-right clock tree).

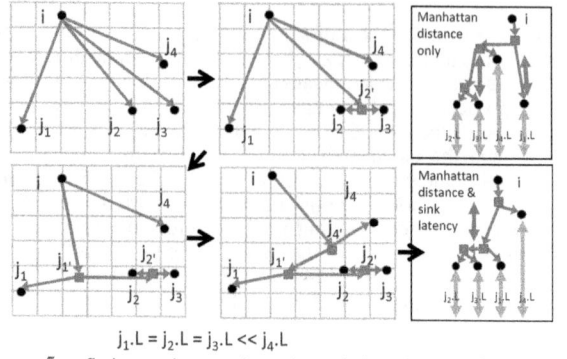

$$j_1.L = j_2.L = j_3.L \ll j_4.L$$

Figure 5: Steiner point creation. In each iteration, we find a pair of pins (black circles) or Steiner points with the minimum $\Delta L'$ (sum of scaled Manhattan distance and difference in sink latency) and connect them to a new Steiner point (red square).

of net and buffer delays (d_{est}) exceeds the required delay between the pins i and j (d_{req}). In Lines 15–21, we calculate the minimum wirelength required to insert n buffers. If this wirelength is less than or equal to the Manhattan distance between pins i and j, $M(i, j)$, we place the buffers in an L-shaped (y-axis first, followed by x-axis) manner. Otherwise, we place the buffers in a U-shaped manner because total wirelength is $> M(i, j)$. U-shaped placement is the general case, and L-shaped is a special case of U-shape when total wirelength is $\leq M(i, j)$.

Algorithm 2   Create Steiner points

Procedure *split_net()*
Input : $G_{net}(V, E), v_r \in V$
Output: $G'_{net}(V', E')$

1: $V' \leftarrow V$;
2: **if** ($|v_r.child| < 2$) **then**
3:    $E' \leftarrow E$;
4: **else**
5:    $E' \leftarrow \emptyset$;
6:    **while** ($|v_r.child| \geq 2$) **do**
7:       $min\_\Delta L' \leftarrow \infty$;
8:       **for** ($u_1, u_2 \in v_r.child$) **do**
9:          $\Delta L(u_1, u_2) \leftarrow |u_1.L - u_2.L|$;
10:          $\Delta L'(u_1, u_2) \leftarrow \beta_k \cdot M(u_1, u_2) + \Delta L(u_1, u_2)$;
11:          **if** ($\Delta L'(u_1, u_2) \leq min\_\Delta L'$) **then**
12:             $u_{min1} \leftarrow u_1$;
13:             $u_{min2} \leftarrow u_2$;
14:             $min\_\Delta L' \leftarrow \Delta L'(u_1, u_2)$;
15:          **end if**
16:       **end for**
17:       Create a new Steiner point $u' \notin V$;
18:       $v_r.child \leftarrow v_r.child \setminus \{u_{min1}, u_{min2}\}$;
19:       $u'.child \leftarrow \{u_{min1}, u_{min2}\}$;
20:       $u'.L \leftarrow max(u_{min1}.L, u_{min2}.L)$;
21:       $p_x(u') \leftarrow (p_x(u_{min1}) + p_x(u_{min2}))/2$;
22:       $p_y(u') \leftarrow (p_y(u_{min1}) + p_y(u_{min2}))/2$;
23:       $v_r.child \leftarrow v_r.child \cup \{u'\}$;
24:       $V' \leftarrow V' \cup \{u'\}$;
25:       $E' \leftarrow E' \cup \{e(u', u_{min1}), e(u', u_{min2})\}$;
26:    **end while**
27:    $E' \leftarrow E' \cup \{e(v_r, u')\}$;
28: **end if**
29: Return $G'_{net}(V', E')$;

By solving the LP, we obtain cell locations, clock routes (Steiner point locations) and net delays in the top-level clock tree. Next, we insert buffers in the top-level clock tree to guide clock routing and control clock skews. For each two-pin net in the optimized top-level clock tree, we insert buffers according to the steps described in Algorithm 3. In Line 1, we initialize the variable n, which indicates the number of inserted buffers, to 1. In Lines 2–14, we calculate the number of buffers required to meet the delay target as a function of net delays and buffer delays. M_{buf} is the minimum required spacing between two buffers.[9] The **while** loop exits when the sum

---

Algorithm 3   Insert buffers

Procedure *insert_buffers()*
Input : pins i and j, $d_{req}(i, j)$
Output: inserted buffers

1: $n \leftarrow 1$;
   // calculate number of buffers to meet required delay
2: **while** (1) **do**
3:    $l \leftarrow M(i, j)/(n+1)$;
4:    **if** ($l < M_{buf}$) **then**
5:       $l \leftarrow M_{buf}$;
6:    **end if**
7:    $d_{est} \leftarrow (n+1) \times d_w(l) + (n-1) \times d_g(c_{in\_buf} + c_w(l)) + d_g(c_{in}(j) + c_w(l))$;
8:    **if** ($d_{est} > d_{req}(i, j)$) **then**
9:       $n \leftarrow n - 1$;
10:       break;
11:    **else**
12:       $n \leftarrow n + 1$;
13:    **end if**
14: **end while**
15: **if** ($n > 0$) **then**
16:    **if** ($M_{buf} \times n > M(i, j)$) **then**
17:       Detour wire and place n buffers in U-shape;
18:    **else**
19:       Place n buffers in L-shape;
20:    **end if**
21: **end if**

---

3. EXPERIMENTS

To test the effectiveness of our methodology, we require testcases with complex top-level clock trees. Since existing benchmarks [10][23] typically lack complex top-level clock trees, we generate testcases based on common clock tree structures typically found in high-speed SOCs and IPs [21][22]. The clock structures of our testcases are shown in Figures 6(a)–(f). We use dual-Vt 28nm foundry FDSOI libraries and implement each testcase at two operating modes – {1.25GHz at 0.95V} and {1.667GHz at 1.20V}. We perform placement and routing (P&R) using a commercial tool and use *Synopsys PrimeTime vH-2013.06-SP2* [25] for timing analysis. Table 1 shows the timing analysis parameters in our experiments.

3.1 Testcase Description and Generation

Testcases from Tsay [19], Kahng and Tsao [10] and ISPD-2009/2010 [23] CNS contest benchmarks lack CLCs and are insufficient to create complex top-level clock hierarchies. Kahng et al. [11] improve CTS testcases by adding CLCs (Figures 3(a) and 3(b) in [11]) but two key elements ignored: (1) combinational

---

[8] We convert the Manhattan distance to delay by a conversion factor β_k at the reference condition.

[9] We use $M_{buf} = 5\mu m$ in our experiments.

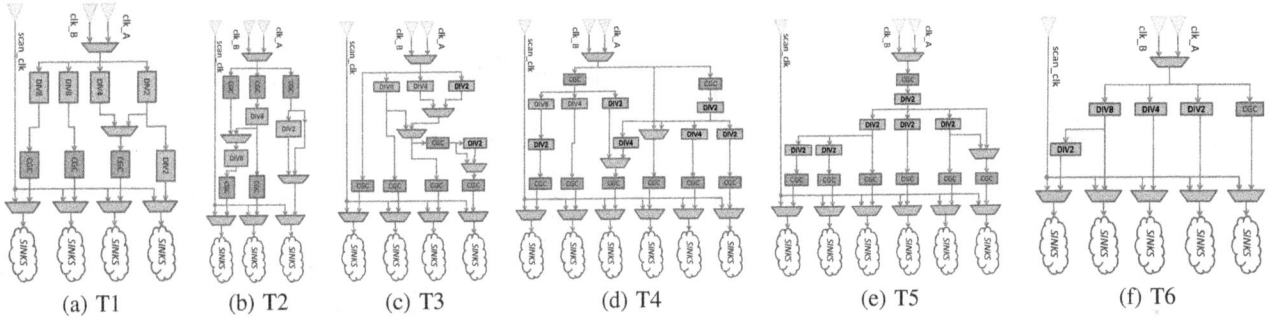

| (a) T1 | (b) T2 | (c) T3 | (d) T4 | (e) T5 | (f) T6 |

Figure 6: Clock structures of our testcases.

Table 1: Timing analysis setup.

Parameter	Value
PVT corner for setup analysis at the 1.250GHz mode	SS, 0.85V, 125C
PVT corner for hold analysis at the 1.250GHz mode	FF, 1.05V, 125C
PVT corner for setup analysis at the 1.667GHz mode	SS, 1.10V, 125C
PVT corner for hold analysis at the 1.667GHz mode	FF, 1.30V, 125C
Clock uncertainty	$0.15 \times$ clock period
Maximum transition for clock paths	0.055ns
Maximum transition for data paths	$0.125 \times$ clock period
Timing derate on net delay (early/late)	0.90 / 1.19
Timing derate on cell delay (early/late)	0.90 / 1.05
Timing derate on cell check (early/late)	1.10 / 1.10

logic between FF groups and hence critical paths between FF groups; and (2) multiple clock sources. The CTS problem becomes difficult when synchronous and asynchronous clocks need to be balanced across multiple FF groups. We improve over [11] by (1) adding combinational logic with varying number of stages between FF groups, (2) adding multiple synchronous and asynchronous clocks, (3) using CLCs at different hierarchies to make the clock balancing problem very complex, (4) creating multiple top-level clock hierarchies, and (5) performing CTS with MCMM and OCV constraints.

Figures 6(a)–(f) show the six testcases T1–T6 used in our experiments. These testcases use three clock sources typically seen in SOC designs [21] and can have large fanouts (e.g., >1000 FFs). The clock source *m_clk* is from the crystal oscillator, *clk* is the output of a PLL and *scan_clk* is the test clock. Clock sources *m_clk* and *clk* are used to implement low-power modes of operation, such as DVFS. The testcases use three kinds of dividers (*DIV2, DIV4, DIV8* in figures), a glitch-free clock MUX, and integrated clock gating cells (CGCs) as CLCs. Outputs of all dividers are sources of generated clocks; the generated clocks typically drive FFs for debug/tracing, IO and other peripheral logic.

To implement variable stages of combinational logic, we use *NetGen* [26] and vary #stages from 15 to 30. To model different critical paths, we connect FFs across groups as well as within the same group using these logic stages. To obtain floorplan dimensions that resemble SOCs, we use multiple instantiations of an interface logic module (ILM) of the *jpeg_encoder* design from OpenCores [24]. We create a netlist with the top module *x5_jpeg*, in which we instantiate the *jpeg_encoder* design five times, perform SP&R and generate an ILM. Note that in this paper, we do not optimize the bottom-level clock tree. Therefore, instantiation of the same *x5_jpeg* multiple times (instead of using different modules) does not change the outcome of our experiments. We connect multiple instances of the ILM using combinational logic stages. For all CLCs, we implement custom netlists in the 28nm foundry FDSOI technology, and group FFs within the CLCs into their own skew groups so that these FFs do not affect global skew and latencies. The path latencies of FF groups are controlled by changing timing constraints and the number of stages of combinational logic between the groups. To allow a blockage-free placement region for the CLCs, we place ILM blocks (hard macros for the CTS tools) in an L-shaped manner along the periphery of the core as shown in Figure 7(a).

All testcases contain bidirectional paths, i.e., both launch and capture FFs appear in FF groups that are driven by the fastest clock and other slower clocks. In addition, the fastest clock drives around 90% of the FFs that do not belong to the ILMs. Table 2 shows #CLCs, #cells, the FFs not in ILM, FFs in the ILM, FFs at

the ILM boundary, and the area of each testcase (design in table). Testcases T2, T3 and T6 contain critical paths between FFs from two different clocks, one with large latency and the other with small latency. The CTS problem is complicated by the need to balance skew between these FF groups. Testcases T1–T4 contain multiple generated clocks and reconvergent paths between these clocks. These testcases make the CTS problem complex because skew needs to be balanced between fast and slow clocks. In testcases T3–T5, the control signals of CGCs are generated by *clk*, which makes the latency of the signal to the enable pin of the CGCs very critical. Besides balancing skews, CTS also needs to balance the critical path delays of the enable signal to the CGCs along with the clock latency. To report timing paths across clocks accurately, we set the path multiplier in the Synopsys Design Constraint (SDC) [3] file for paths between all clocks.

Table 2: Benchmark designs.

Design	#CLCs	#Cells	#Flip-flops			Area
			$\notin$ ILM	$\in$ ILM	Boundary	(mm^2)
T1	17	1.93M	10K	202.7K	1.7K	3.75×3.00
T2	12	1.93M	10K	202.7K	1.7K	3.75×3.00
T3	18	1.93M	12K	202.7K	1.7K	3.75×3.00
T4	24	1.93M	12K	202.7K	1.7K	3.75×3.00
T5	18	1.93M	8K	202.7K	1.7K	3.75×3.00
T6	13	1.92M	7K	202.7K	1.7K	3.75×3.00

3.2 Experimental Results

Table 3 summarizes the key metrics of the clock tree before (**I** = Initial, produced by a commercial tool) and after (**O** = Optimized) applying our top-level clock tree optimization. Rows 1–14 in Table 3 show the results at the post-CTS stage, while Rows 15–28 show the results at the end of the implementation flow (after datapath routing).[10]

Post-CTS stage: Our optimization flow reduces the total wirelength of the top-level clock tree by 53% to 68% across all six testcases. Figure 7 shows that wirelength reduces because our flow clusters the CLCs such that the clock tree does not split near the clock entry points. The large wirelength reduction suggests that the initial CLC placements by EDA tools may not be aware of the CTS requirements. The smaller wirelength enables the optimized clock tree to also reduce the number of buffers. In testcases T4 and T5, the number of buffers is larger, as our optimization flow inserts more buffers in the clock tree to improve timing slack. To estimate switching power, we extract gate and wire capacitances of the top-level clock tree. Rows 5–6 in Table 3 show that our flow can reduce the switching power in the top-level clock tree by 12% to 40% for all testcases, including testcases T4 and T5, where the number of buffers increases.

Our flow also improves the setup WNS and TNS by up to 550ps and 255ns, respectively (Rows 7–10). Hold WNS and TNS are also improved except for testcase T6, in which the hold WNS and TNS worsen by 110ps and 780ps, respectively (Rows 11–14). Our optimization flow can worsen hold WNS and TNS because we focus on improving the setup slacks ($\gamma_k = 5$). The tradeoff between setup and hold slacks is based on the following assumptions: (1) hold time violations are easier to fix in post-CTS implementation

---

[10]We apply the default clock tree optimization, routing and design optimization commands in the EDA tool after CTS. We do not compare our work with previous work as their algorithms cannot be applied to our testcases.

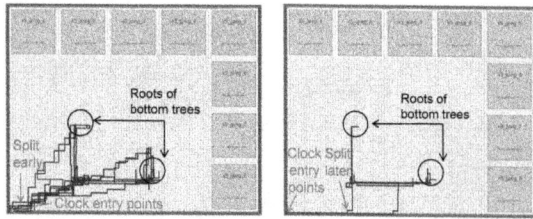

(a) Initial clock tree. (b) Optimized clock tree.

Figure 7: Initial (a) and optimized (b) clock trees for testcase T6. Wiring of the top-level clock trees is shown in black. Our flow splits common paths farther from the clock root compared to the initial clock tree. As a result, the total wirelength in the top-level clock tree is reduced from 45mm to 22mm.

Table 3: Post-CTS results. I: Initial, O: Optimized.

	Testcase:		T1	T2	T3	T4	T5	T6
				Post-CTS				
1	Top-level	I (um)	18086	19261	41476	38830	34009	36052
2	wirelength	O (um)	8442	8614	13193	14389	14186	15104
3	Total-level	I	163	210	361	298	322	253
4	buffers	O	152	167	242	301	421	226
5	Switching	I (uW)	875	1018	1639	1515	1557	1315
6	power	O (uW)	590	692	969	1210	1360	987
7	Worst	I (ns)	-0.05	-0.10	-0.37	-0.65	-0.55	-0.32
8	setup WNS	O (ns)	-0.04	0.00	-0.36	-0.55	0.00	-0.20
9	Total	I (ns)	-0.41	-0.25	-48.47	-1034.38	-8.39	-40.56
10	setup TNS	O (ns)	-0.17	0.00	-45.47	-779.46	0.00	-12.78
11	Worst	I (ns)	0.00	0.00	-0.40	-0.04	0.00	-0.04
12	hold WNS	O (ns)	0.00	0.00	-0.40	-0.01	0.00	-0.15
13	Total	I (ns)	0.00	0.00	-130.12	-0.21	0.00	-0.09
14	hold TNS	O (ns)	0.00	0.00	-128.23	-0.05	0.00	-0.87
				Post-datapath routing				
15	Top-level	I (um)	26261	30779	58223	50432	48761	44794
16	wirelength	O (um)	15750	19097	33982	27342	28570	22051
17	Total-level	I	163	215	357	300	322	252
18	buffers	O	152	170	248	306	427	226
19	Switching	I (uW)	885	1100	1748	1592	1616	1337
20	power	O (uW)	638	729	1042	1220	1374	968
21	Worst	I (ns)	-0.03	0.00	-0.05	-0.58	-0.32	-0.19
22	setup WNS	O (ns)	0.00	0.00	0.00	-0.46	0.00	-0.18
23	Total	I (ns)	-0.05	0.00	-0.06	-883.50	-3.03	-10.81
24	setup TNS	O (ns)	0.00	0.00	0.00	-609.02	0.00	-1.10
25	Worst	I (ns)	0.00	0.00	-0.37	-0.04	0.00	0.00
26	hold WNS	O (ns)	0.00	0.00	-0.10	-0.11	-0.04	-0.05
27	Total	I (ns)	0.00	0.00	-19.82	-0.14	0.00	0.00
28	hold TNS	O (ns)	0.00	0.00	-5.46	-0.78	-0.08	-0.33
29	Total timing paths in LP		16K	20K	72K	40K	28K	11K
				Runtime (minutes)				
30	Extract timing		45	37	176	71	71	25
31	Formulate LP		36	26	165	51	36	9
32	Place & legalization		8	4	6	5	6	5
33	Clock routing		7	4	5	4	5	5
34	Total		96	71	352	131	118	44

stages, and (2) some of the hold time violations are fixed by the increased wire delays in the routing stage.

In Rows 30–34 of Table 3, we report runtimes of the main procedures in our optimization flow. We spend most of the time to extract timing information and to formulate the LP.[11] CLC placement, buffer insertion, legalization and routing only take 10 minutes in total because there are not many cells in the top-level clock tree. The total runtime is 135 minutes on average. Testcase T3 has a higher runtime because it has more timing-critical paths than other testcases (Row 29).

Post-datapath routing stage: To study the benefits of our optimization flow, we also compare the post-routing results between the initial and the optimized clock trees. The results in Table 3 show that all designs with the optimized clock tree have the same or improved setup WNS compared to the designs with the initial clock tree (Rows 21–24). The improvement in setup WNS at the post-routing stage is up to 320ps. Although some testcases with the optimized clock tree have worse hold slacks (i.e., testcases T4, T5 and T6), the differences are less than 100ps. The results in Rows 15–16 shows that our optimization flow reduces the total wirelength by 38% to 51% across all six testcases. The improvements are smaller as compared to the post-CTS stage because the total wirelength of the initial and optimized clock trees

---

[11]Solving the LP takes less than 30 seconds.

both increase at the post-routing stage due to wiring of the signal nets. Total number of buffers and switching power at the post-routing stage are similar to values seen at the post-CTS stage.

4. CONCLUSIONS

Designing a balanced top-level clock tree with multiple clock sources is very complex as we need to consider MCMM, OCV and timing constraints across FF groups. We develop a CTS methodology that optimizes CLC placement and buffer insertion, and that minimizes non-common paths between FF groups. We formulate the top-level CTS problem as the minimization of a weighted sum of WNS, TNS, clock uncertainty due to OCV and wirelength. We solve this problem using LP and develop heuristic flows to insert Steiner points and buffers, which are required elements of a top-level CTS solution. We also develop generators for testcases that resemble clock tree structures typically found in high-speed SOCs. We validate our optimization flow on testcases from our generators and achieve up to 51% reduction in wirelength for the top-level clock tree, and 320ps improvement in WNS, compared to a leading commercial CTS tool. Our future work includes (i) handling obstacles, (ii) accounting for *optimal* buffering solutions, (iii) creating testcases to capture other important SOC elements such as memory controller and multimedia blocks, and (iv) joint optimization of the top- and bottom-level clock trees.

5. REFERENCES

[1] C. J. Alpert, M. Hrkic, J. Hu, A. B. Kahng, J. Lillis, B. Liu, S. T. Quay, S. S. Sapatnekar, A. J. Sullivan and P. Villarrubia, "Buffered Steiner Trees for Difficult Instances", *Proc. ISPD*, 2001, pp. 4-9.

[2] H. B. Bakoglu, *Circuits, Interconnects, and Packaging for VLSI*. Reading, MA: Addison-Wesley, 1990.

[3] J. Bhasker and R. Chadha, *Static Timing Analysis for Nanometer Designs: A Practical Approach*, Springer, 2009.

[4] Y.-Y. Chen, C. Dong and D. Chen, "Clock Tree Synthesis Under Aggressive Buffer Insertion", *Proc. DAC*, 2010, pp. 86-89.

[5] C. Chen, C. Kang and M. Sarrafzadeh, "Activity-Sensitive Clock Tree Construction for Low Power", *Proc. ISLPED*, 2002, pp. 279-282.

[6] T.-H. Chao, Y.-C. Hsu, J.-M. Ho, K. D. Boese and A. B. Kahng, "Zero Skew Clock Routing with Minimum Wirelength", *IEEE Trans. on Circuits and Systems* 39(11) (1992), pp. 799-814.

[7] M. Edahiro, "A Clustering-Based Optimization Algorithm in Zero-Skew Routings", *Proc. DAC*, 1993, pp. 612-616.

[8] J. P. Fishburn, "Clock Skew Optimization", *IEEE Trans. on Computers* 39(7) (1990), pp. 945-951.

[9] E. G. Friedman, "Clock Distribution Networks in Synchronous Digital Integrated Circuits", *IEEE Proceedings*, 89(5) (2001), pp. 665-692.

[10] A. B. Kahng and C.-W. A. Tsao, "VLSI CAD Software Bookshelf: Bounded-Skew Clock Tree Routing", Version 1.0, 2000. *http://vlsicad.ucsd.edu/GSRC/bookshelf/Slots/BST/*

[11] A. B. Kahng, B. Lin and S. Nath, "High-Dimensional Metamodeling for Prediction of Clock Tree Synthesis Outcomes", *Proc. SLIP*, 2013.

[12] C.-L. Lung, H.-C. Hsiao, Z.-Y. Zeng and S.-C. Chang, "LP-Based Multi-Mode Multi-Corner Clock Skew Optimization", *Proc. VLSI-DAT*, 2010, pp. 335-338.

[13] J. Oh, I. Pyo and M. Pedram, "Constructing Lower and Upper Bounded Delay Routing Trees Using Linear Programming", *Proc. DAC*, 1996, pp. 401-404.

[14] U. Padmanabhan, J. M. Wang and J. Hu, "Robust Clock Tree Routing in the Presence of Process Variations", *IEEE Trans. on CAD* 27(8) (2008), pp. 1385-1397.

[15] D. A. Papa, T. Luo, M. D. Moffitt, C. N. Sze, Z. Li, G.-J. Nam, C. J. Alpert and I. L. Markov, "RUMBLE: An Incremental Timing-Driven Physical-Synthesis Optimization Algorithm", *IEEE Trans. on CAD* 27(12) (2008), pp. 2156-2168.

[16] A. Rajaram and D. Z. Pan, "Robust Chip-Level Clock Tree Synthesis", *IEEE Trans. on CAD* 30(6) (2011), pp. 877-890.

[17] V. Ramachandran, "Construction of Minimal Functional Skew Clock Trees", *Proc. ISPD*, 2012, pp. 119-120.

[18] J.-L. Tsai, "Clock Tree Synthesis for Timing Convergence and Timing Yield Improvement in Nanometer Technologies", *Ph.D. Thesis*, Electrical and Computer Engineering, University of Wisconsin-Madison, 2005.

[19] R.-S. Tsay, "Exact Zero-Skew", *Proc. ICCAD*, 1991, pp. 336-339.

[20] D. Velenis, M. C. Papaefthymiou and E. G. Friedman, "Reduced Delay Uncertainty in High Performance Clock Distribution Networks", *Proc. DATE*, 2003, pp. 68-73.

[21] Broadcom Corporation (networking infrastructure physical design principal engineer), *personal communication*, November 2013.

[22] Samsung Electronics Corporation (System LSI application processor principal engineer), *personal communication*, November 2013.

[23] *ISPD CNS Contest*. http://ispd.cc/contests/09/ispd09cts.html

[24] *OpenCores*. http://opencores.org

[25] *Synopsys PrimeTime User's Manual*. http://www.synopsys.com/Tools/Implementation/Signoff/PrimeTime/Pages/

[26] *UC Benchmark Suite for Gate Sizing*. http://vlsicad.ucsd.edu/SIZING/bench/artificial.html

Modeling of the Charging Behavior of Li-Ion Batteries based on Manufacturer's Data

Alessandro Sassone   Donghwa Shin   Alberto Bocca

Alberto Macii   Enrico Macii   Massimo Poncino

Department of Control and Computer Engineering
Politecnico di Torino, 10129 Torino, Italy

ABSTRACT

The market of portable devices, wireless sensors, electric vehicles and storage systems has grown enormously in recent years. As a consequence, batteries and related technologies have become one of the major topics for researchers.

Due to the large variety of applications in which batteries are involved, battery modeling is becoming an extremely important research topic. This relevance is witnessed by the number of papers addressing battery modeling.

This paper proposes a methodology to build a battery model for the charge phase of secondary Lithium-Ion batteries resorting on data available in battery datasheets.

The distinguishing feature of the proposed modeling methodology is that, even if the amount of information regarding the battery charge provided by manufacturers is, in most of the cases, very limited, it is able to extract anyway a model of the charging phase with a good amount of accuracy.

Simulation results show, in fact, that the proposed model is able to accurately track the charge behavior with an average error of 1.35%.

Categories and Subject Descriptors

J.6 [**Computer-Aided Engineering**]: Computer-aided design (CAD); I.6.4 [**Simulation and Modeling**]: Model Validation and Analysis; I.6.5 [**Simulation and Modeling**]: Model Development.

General Terms

Design, Verification

Keywords

Battery charging, Battery Modeling, Simulation, Datasheet, Validation.

GLSVLSI'14, May 21–23 2014, Houston, TX, USA.
Copyright 2014 ACM 978-1-4503-2816-6/14/05$15.00.
http://dx.doi.org/10.1145/2591513.2591592.

1. INTRODUCTION

Battery modeling is a very popular research topic due to its impact in many application domains, including portable electronics, power systems, automotive, and aerospace. Such popularity is reflected by huge amount of papers describing a variety of models with different semantics, complexities and levels of detail (see [1] for an exhaustive survey on the various types of models proposed). Among the many alternatives, in recent years, there has been a general alignment in all the application domains towards the use of battery models based on *electrical equivalent circuits*, whose main advantage is that they can be co-simulated with standard circuit simulators [2, 3, 4]. The many variants of electrical models proposed differ in the specific effects that are modeled and therefore their degree of accuracy (and relative complexity of the circuit equivalent).

Two are the main characteristics that are typical of these models. The first is that they *represent a template of models*, i.e., a circuit that includes resistances, capacitances and voltage/current generators whose actual values must be appropriately calculated for a specific instance of a battery. This calculation can be done either by using measurement (as done in most cases), or using data available in datasheets [5, 6, 7, 8]. In the latter case, the accuracy of the model is subject to the actually available data.

The second characteristic is that most of these models *focus on the discharge process*; this is mostly due to the fact that battery discharge is driven by the demand of current by the load, which can exhibit the most disparate load profiles. Conversely, the behavior of the battery during *charge* is considered to be less interesting because the charge current profile normally follows some pre-defined standard "protocols".

Although many of the proposed models claim to be suitable for both charge and discharge by simply inverting the sign of the load current, a thorough validation of their validity for the charge process is seldom carried out.

However, charge is an important part of the battery operational life; it also affects the discharge behavior, in particular when multiple charge-discharge cycles are analyzed. As an example of this effect, the amount of current injected into the battery during the charge affects the usable capacity at the end of the charge. In practice, a larger current implies speeding up the charge process (i.e., chemical reaction), which has negative effects on the physical characteristics of the battery materials [9]. Therefore, the amount of charge current affects the capacity loss across charge cycles and higher current ages the battery faster.

Another relevant issue related to charge is the development of advanced *charge protocols* that differ the standard one based on the *Constant Current-Constant Voltage (CC-CV)* scheme [10, 11, 12]. It would be very helpful to be able to simulate, with reasonable accuracy, those charge protocols without the need of measuring them, avoiding therefore both the cost and time of measurements.

This paper presents a methodology for building a battery model of the charge phase in Lithium-ion batteries that is based solely on data that are available in a datasheet. The latter feature has an important consequence on the analytical power of the model. All battery datasheets report only data for the recommended CC-CV charge protocol, and almost invariably only for the recommended current level. This implies that the amount of information to build the model is quite limited. We thus need to extrapolate the missing information required to populate the model by using some data relative to the discharge process. However, unlike existing approaches that use only data relative to the discharge process to characterize the model parameters even for estimating the charge process, we use discharge data only to integrate the scarce data available about the charge.

Simulation results show that our model, in spite of its underlying simplicity, is able to accurately replicate (with an average error of 1.35%) the charge behavior under conditions that are different from those used for its characterization, paving the way to its usage for validating more complex charge protocols.

The paper is organized as follows. Section 2 introduces related studies including battery models as well as charging protocols. Section 3 describes the proposed battery model for the charge phase based on manufacturer's data. Section 4 presents the results of model validation, while Section 5 concludes this paper.

2. BACKGROUND

2.1 Modeling of batteries

Battery models can be mostly categorized into analytical and electrical circuit-equivalent ones. The former are based on the analysis of chemical processes that characterize the physical behavior of the batteries (e.g., [13, 14, 15]). The latter ones are based on the idea of emulating the curves describing the various battery effects by mean of a linear RC circuit that includes current and voltage generators. These circuit-equivalent models are preferable both for their efficiency as well as for the possibility of co-simulating them with the circuit description.

Out of the many circuit equivalent proposed, the one presented in [16] is now regarded as a de-facto basic standard model. This model is characterized based on typical discharge curves (e.g., voltage vs. state of charge, usable capacity vs. current load, etc.) that can be either obtained by measurements or derived from available information in datasheets. Figure 1 shows the circuit equivalent of the model. The left part models the capacity information while the right one represents the transient behavior. The resistance and the RC elements denote the internal impedance of a cell. The dependence of the voltage on the state of charge (SOC) is modeled by bridging the two circuit parts via a voltage controlled generator $V_{OC}(V_{SOC})$.

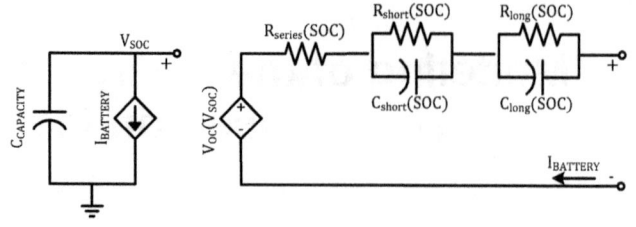

Figure 1: Battery model of [16].

Although the model can track both the charge and discharge processes, since they differ just in the sign of the current that is used as input of the model, in [16] the validation is carried out only for the discharge phase.

As a matter of fact, the charge phase should be considered separately from the discharging model. This is also motivated by the well-known fact that a battery exhibits different internal resistances during charging and discharging [17]. Therefore, modeling of the charging phase requires different electrical components in the equivalent circuits with respect to the ones used to model the discharging behavior, as also reported in [18], in which the electrical circuit takes into account characteristics of both phases. This is effectively achieved by using two sub-models for the impedance in parallel (right section of the circuit) with different values of the RC components, which are activated in a mutually exclusive way via diodes..

2.2 Battery Charge Protocols

The standard way to charge Li-ion batteries consists of two main phases. The battery is initially charged at a constant current (typically in the range 0.7–0.8C) until its voltage reaches the pre-determined limit (4.1 or 4.2 V) followed by a constant voltage charging until the current declines to a pre-determined low value. This method is called constant current-constant voltage (CC-CV) charging. This protocol is required, in particular the second phase, to avoid overcharging that can be very critical and hazardous in Li-ion batteries. Another reason for CC-CV as a standard charge protocol lies in its simplicity for implementation into chargers. As an example, Figure 2 shows the typical CC-CV curves reported in most datasheets. The one in the figure refers to a Sony UP383562 [19].

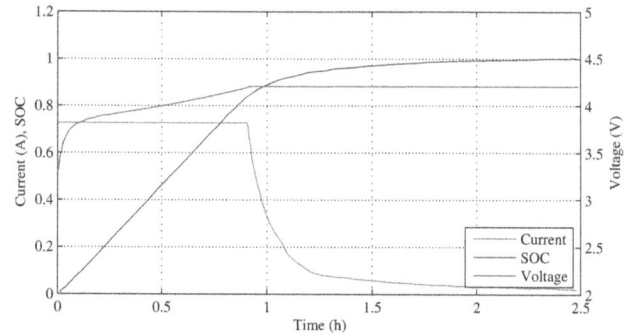

Figure 2: Typical CC-CV charging protocol.

We notice that the SOC initially grows linearly (integral of current), while the voltage also grows. At the end of the

CC phase, the voltage has reached a value very close to the final one, but the charge process continues to achieve maximal filling (in the figure there is still approximately a 20% SOC to be filled after the CC phase). The definition of the end-of-charge period depends on the specific battery, and can occur when reaching (i) a minimum current, (ii) a maximum voltage level, or (iii) a total charge time.

With the main objective of speeding up the charge process without affecting too much the wearout of the battery, various alternative charging protocols for Li-ion batteries have been analyzed, such as pulsed charge, constant power, or multi-stage constant current ([9, 12]).

Testing of such charge protocols is typically done by measurements. As a matter of fact, battery models such as the one of [16] could in principle be used to simulate battery charge protocols; however, they must necessarily resort to measurements to characterize the models, because datasheets almost always include only data relative to a CC-CV protocol. This is quite different from the discharge process, which is normally described with various levels of details in datasheets.

The approach of [5] tries to overcome this problem by introducing an equivalent-circuit model for the charge phase, which however relies on a set of charge data that are claimed to be derived from datasheets, but are not typically available in commercial batteries. Therefore, this approach does not offer a practical solution to the problem.

In this paper we try to bridge this gap by proposing a methodology for modeling the charging phase of a battery (with a distinct model from that of discharge) that uses solely the information provided by typical datasheets for charge, i.e., the CC-CV profile. In order to complement the limited information provided by datasheet about charge, we extrapolate other information from discharge data to build up a reliable model.

3. MODELING THE CHARGE PHASE

As discussed in the previous section, the charge process of a Li-ion battery is typically simulated using battery models that are characterized using data obtained from the discharge process. This is true in particular for methods that do not rely on measurements and use only datasheet information. As a matter of fact, datasheets normally report discharge curves of many types (e.g., for various C-rates, in some cases even curves for pulsed currents) whereas the only information about charge consists in the specification of the CC-CV protocol. This is reasonable because a datasheet is supposed to provide information about battery usage rather than data from which to extract a simulation model.

From the modeling perspective, the limited information about charge prevents the use of rich and accurate models such as that of [16] for modeling of the charge process, unless discharge data are used. One problem in using battery discharge data for representing the battery charge is that it is well-known that a battery exhibits different values of the internal resistance during the charge and discharge phases. Therefore, even if a richer model is used, the characterization is based on inaccurate information.

In order to overcome the latter problem we use a simplified version of the equivalent circuit proposed in [16], in which only the resistive (ohmic) part of the internal impedance of Figure 1 is kept, consistently with the fact that the CC-CV

protocol requires constant charging current. The simplified circuit-based model is shown in Figure 3.

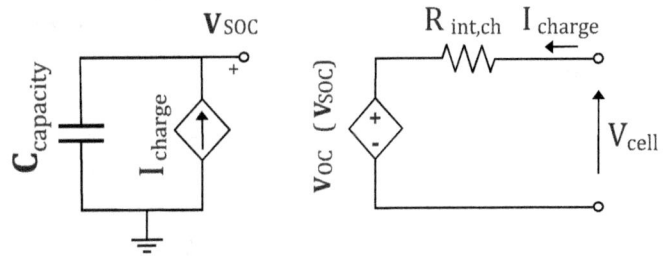

Figure 3: Simplified circuit model for charging.

Even such simplified model, however, cannot be characterized using solely the information provided by CC-CV curves. As a matter of fact, for deriving the internal resistance ($R_{int,ch}$) we would need at least **two** charge curves corresponding to different charging currents.

To solve this problem, we derive the missing information by using available data relative to the discharge process. This differs from previous modeling approaches based on datasheets information only, which **only** use information about discharge to generate a model that is claimed to be accurate for charge as well.

3.1 Estimation of Charging Resistance

By simple analysis of the right section of the equivalent circuit of Figure 3, the internal resistance during the charge can be expressed as:

$$R_{int,ch} = \frac{V_{cell}(SOC) - OCV}{I_{charge}} \qquad (1)$$

where V_{cell} is the actual battery cell voltage and OCV is the Open-Circuit Voltage (i.e., the voltage generator $V_{OC}(V_{SOC})$ in Figure 3). In Equation 1, $R_{int,ch}$ and OCV are unknowns and must be calculated.

The first step consists of the extraction of the OCV from the discharge curves. In this operation there is a slight approximation; while apparently the OCV is unique, in practice, there is a slight difference due to a small hysteresis in the charge vs. discharge process [20].

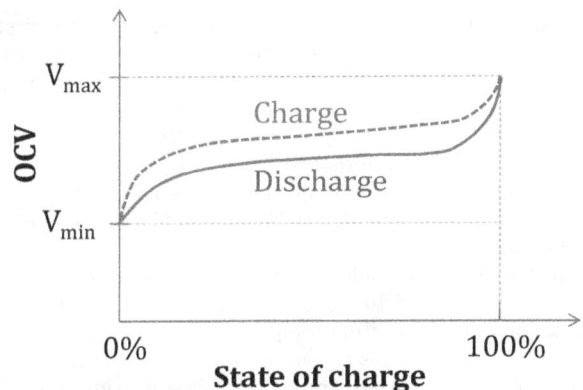

Figure 4: Example of OCV hysteresis.

As Figure 4 shows, for a given SOC value the OCV depends on whether the state is reached during charge or discharge.

41

Nevertheless, the error is relatively small and approximately constant across various SOC levels.

Therefore, OCV can be calculated from discharge curves that are typically provided in datasheets. Figure 5 shows the V_{cell} vs. SOC curves for the Sony battery of [19]. Notice that curves for different discharge rates are provided.

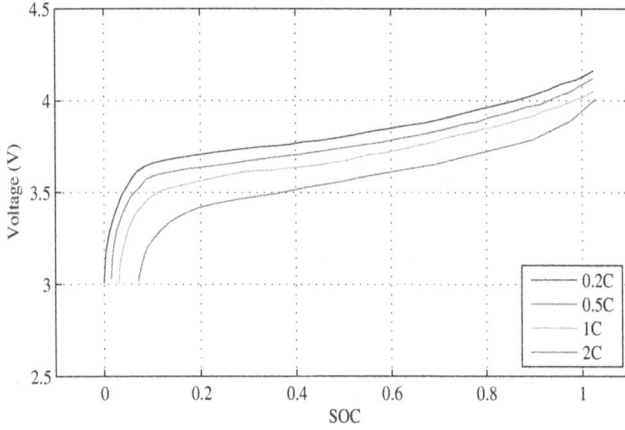

Figure 5: Voltage vs. SOC for constant current discharge rates (C-rates) for the battery of [19].

OCV is thus extracted as a function of SOC from these curves. The curves are tabulated and define the values of $V_{OC}(V_{SOC})$ in the model.

At this point the only unknown is $R_{int,ch}$, which can be easily derived from Equation 1 using the value of I_{charge} specified in the CC phase of the charge protocol.

4. EXPERIMENTS

The aim of this section is to validate the proposed model and assess its accuracy against typical manufacturer's data. The battery model (circuit of Figure 3) is written and simulated in the Matlab environment. Values of the model parameters are derived directly from the datasheets and do not require any measurement.

4.1 Model Characterization and Self-Validation

The Sony UP383562 datasheet [19] was selected for the first validation of the model; this battery represents the typical scenario in terms of available information. Using the data from voltage vs. SOC curves at different C-rates (Figure 5) and the CC-CV charging profile (Figure 2), OCV was first derived and then the internal charging resistance with Equation 1. The applied current and the end-of-charge period are the recommended ones, i.e., $0.72A$ in the CC phase, and a total charge time of 2.5h.

After the model was built, we re-applied the same current profile to the model to assess the "noise" incurred by the extraction of the data from the plots. The charge profile estimated by the model is shown in Figure 6. The curves are related to voltage, current and resistance as function of SOC. As shown in Figure 6, the proposed methodology is able to reproduce the charging profile almost perfectly: the simulated battery voltage coincides with the one extracted from the datasheet (the two curves are completely overlapped). The OCV is always below the battery voltage due to the

opposing charging resistance, as expected from the circuit at the base of the model.

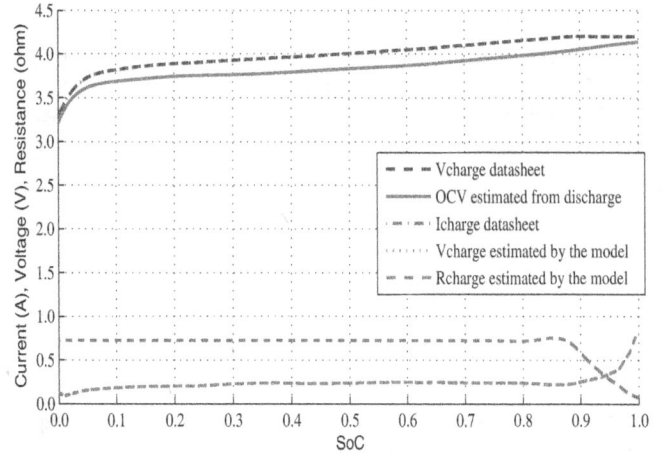

Figure 6: Charge Profile as Function of SOC: Model validation vs. battery datasheet information (Sony UP383562 - 760mAh Lithium-ion cell).

4.2 Model Validation

The second experiment targets the cross-validation of the model, i.e., checking whether the model is able to replicate a behavior under input conditions that are different from those used for the characterization.

To this purpose, we chose the battery datasheet of the Saft Lithium-ion MP 174565 Integration^{TM} cell [21]. This represents one of the few cases where multiple information about charge are provided; in particular, three different charge profiles are reported (1C, 0.5C, and 0.2C currents for the CC phase)

We used then only one of the three curves for model characterization, and applied the same approach as for the self-validation, i.e., used discharge curves for the deriving the OCV plus the charge curve to derive the internal resistance. The cross-validation consisted then in applying the other two current values (in the CC phase) and checking the resulting error.

We selected the 1C rate as the charge profile used for characterization. This choice is motivated by the fact that this value is the closest to the typical rate used for the charge for Lithium-ion batteries (0.8C–1C).

Figure 7 shows the charge profile estimated by the model with the application of the 0.2C rate. For the end-of-charge period a total time of 6.2h was used (the recommended charge time goes from 6 to 7 h). The obtained voltage curve replicates the curve from the datasheet with an average error of $65mV$ (about 1.7% of the battery nominal voltage).

The charge profile estimated by the model with the application of the 0.5C rate is shown in Figure 8. In this case a total time of 3.5h was used to simulate the charge process (the recommended charge time goes from 3 to 4 h). The obtained average error of the model is of $38mV$ (about 1.0% of the battery nominal voltage).

These curves demonstrate an important property of our model: *even using a single CC-CV profile (with a given C-rate in the CC phase), and integrating it with some discharge curve to*

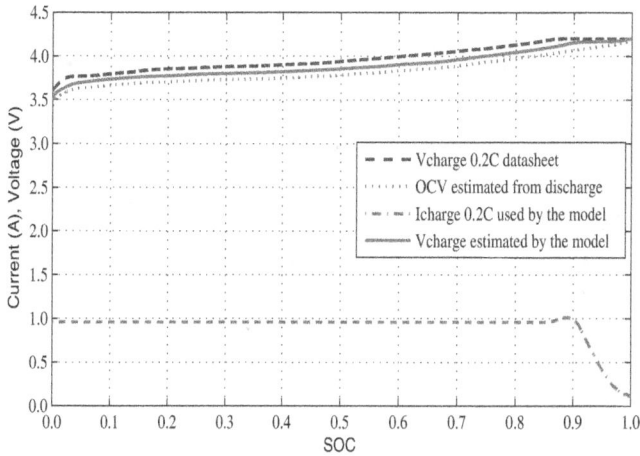

Figure 7: Charge profile at 0.2C as function of SOC: Model validation using 1C charge profile vs. battery datasheet information (Saft MP 174565 - 4.8Ah Lithium-ion cell).

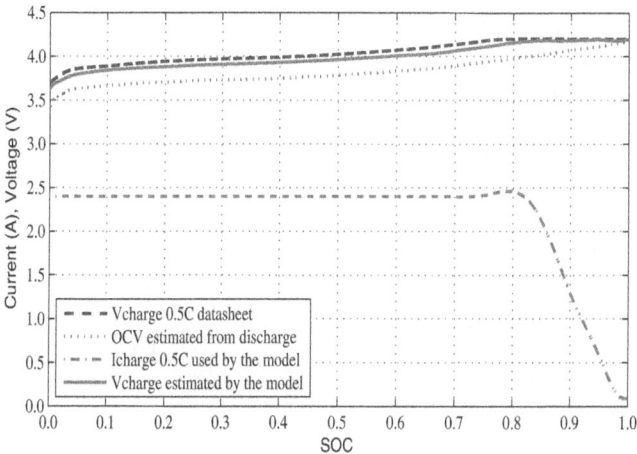

Figure 8: Charge profile at 0.5C as function of SOC: Model validation using 1C charge profile vs. battery datasheet information (Saft MP 174565 - 4.8Ah Lithium-ion cell).

derive the OCV, it is possible to estimate the charge behavior of another CC-CV profile (with a C-rate different from the one used in characterization).

This allows us to use this model to simulate with a good level of accuracy non standard charge protocols (i.e., different from CC-CV): by using a piecewise linear approximation of a charge current load, the charge conditions would not be so different from the ones used in a scenario like the one of Figure 8.

4.3 Avoiding the Use of Discharge Information

As mentioned in Section 3, we could avoid resorting to discharge data to extract the OCV, if at least two charge profiles are available; in this case, it is possible to estimate

both model parameters, OCV and internal resistance, directly from charge data.

We therefore tested this solution on the Saft MP 174565 cell, in particular, we used the charge curves relative to the 1C and 0.2C current rates to characterize the model, which was then simulated using the charge profile of to the 0.5C rate. The estimation results are shown in Figure 9.

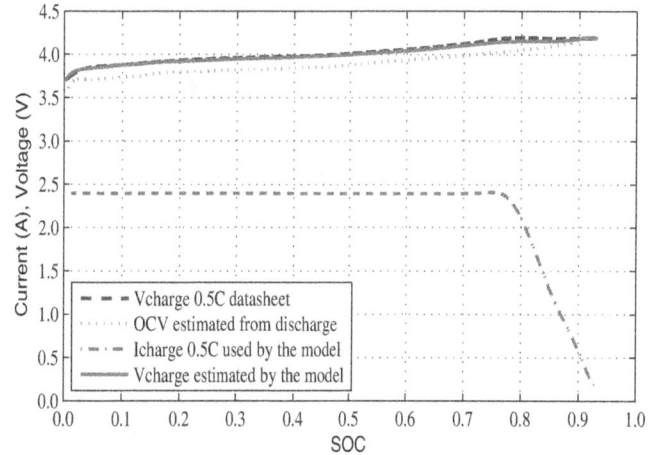

Figure 9: Charge profile at 0.5C as function of SOC: Model validation using only 1C and 0.2C charge profiles vs. battery datasheet information (Saft MP 174565 - 4.8Ah Lithium-ion cell).

The simulation has been stopped at around $SOC = 93\%$ since the model shows an intrinsic limitation on the $R_{int,ch}$ extraction in the CV phase. The average error for the voltage curve estimation is of $16mV$ (about 0.4% of the battery nominal voltage). This is an even better accuracy than the previous experiments, but is somehow expected: since we are using two curves both referring to the charge process, the calculation of the OCV and resistance is more accurate. This result shows another important feature of the proposed model, i.e., that the availability of just two different CC-CV charge profiles provides enough information to build an accurate model for any CC-CV profile.

5. CONCLUSION

We presented a methodology for modeling the CC-CV protocol charging phase of Li-ion batteries, in which only information from datasheet is considered for extracting the parameters values of the model. In the cases (as for most batteries) where only a single CC-CV curve is available, our methodology uses discharge information to characterize the model.

Simulation results show that the proposed model, in the case the battery datasheet provides only one charge profile, is able to replicate the battery charge behavior with an average error of 1.35%. The error decreases at 0.4% if the datasheet provides more charging profiles.

Despite its simplicity the model fills a gap in battery modeling because it can be used to simulate non standard charge protocols, which will be the subject of our future research on this topic.

6. REFERENCES

[1] M.R. Jongerden and B.R. Haverkort. Battery Modeling. *Technical Report TR-CTIT-08-01*, University of Twente, The Netherlands, 2008.

[2] L. Benini, A. Macii, E. Macii, M. Poncino, "Discharge current steering for battery lifetime optimization," *ISLPED'02: International Symposium on Low Power Electronics and Design*, pp.118-123, 2002.

[3] L. Benini, G. Castelli, A. Macii, E. Macii, M. Poncino, and R. Scarsi. Discrete-Time Battery Models for System-Level Low-Power Design. *IEEE Transactions On Very Large Scale Integration (VLSI) Systems*, Vol. 9 n. 5, pp. 630-640, 2001.

[4] L. Benini, G. Castelli, A. Macii, E. Macii, R. Scarsi, "Battery-driven dynamic power management of portable systems," *ISSS'00: 13th International Symposium on System Synthesis*, pp. 25-30, 2000.

[5] J.V. Barreras, E. Schaltz, S.J. Andreasen, T. Minko. Datasheet-based modeling of Li-Ion batteries. *2012 IEEE Vehicle Power and Propulsion Conference (VPPC 2012)*, pages 830-835. IEEE, October 2012.

[6] M. Dubarry, B.Y. Liaw. Development of a universal modeling tool for rechargeable lithium batteries. *Journal of Power Sources*, 174(2):856-860, 2007.

[7] N.K. Medora, A. Kusko. Dynamic battery modeling of lead-acid batteries using manufacturers' data. *IEEE Twenty-Seventh International Telecommunications Energy Conference (INTELEC 2005)*, pages 228-232. IEEE, 18-22 September 2005.

[8] M. Petricca, D. Shin, A. Bocca, A. Macii, E. Macii, M. Poncino. An Automated Framework for Generating Variable-Accuracy Battery Models from Datasheet Information. *IEEE International Symposium on Low Power Design (ISLPED 2013)*, pages 365-370. IEEE, 4-6 September 2013.

[9] S.S. Zhang. The effect of the charging protocol on the cycle life of a Li-ion battery. *Journal of Power Sources*, 161(2):1385-1391, October 2006.

[10] J. Li, E. Murphy, J. Winnick, P. A. Kohl. The effects of pulse charging on cycling characteristics of commercial lithium-ion batteries. *Journal of Power Sources*, 102(1):302-309, 2001.

[11] P.H.L. Notten, J.H.G. Op het Veld, J.R.G. van Beeka. Boostcharging Li-ion batteries: A challenging new charging concept. *Journal of Power Sources*, 145(1):89-94, 2005.

[12] R. Klein et al. Optimal Charging Strategies in Lithium-Ion Battery. *2011 American Control Conference (ACC)*, pages 382-387. IEEE, June 29 - July 01, 2011.

[13] M. Doyle, T.F. Fuller, and J. Newman. Modeling of Galvanostatic Charge and Discharge of the Lithium/Polymer/Insertion Cell. *Journal of The Electrochemical Society*, 140(6):1526-1533, 1993.

[14] D. Rakhmatov. Battery voltage modeling for portable systems. *ACM Transactions on Design Automation of Electronic Systems (TODAES)* 14(2): Article 29, March 2009.

[15] Y. Ye, Y. Shi, N. Cai, J. Lee, X. He. Electro-thermal modeling and experimental validation for lithium ion battery. *Journal of Power Sources*, 199(1):227-238, 2012.

[16] M. Chen and G.A. Rincón-Mora. Accurate Electrical Battery Model Capable of Predicting Runtime and I-V Performance. *IEEE Transactions On Energy Conversion*, 21(2):504-511, June 2006.

[17] S.J. Moura, J.C. Forman, S. Bashash, J.L. Stein, and H.K. Fathy. Optimal Control of Film Growth in Lithium-Ion Battery Packs via Relay Switches. *IEEE Transactions On Industrial Electronics*, 58(8):3555-3566, August 2011.

[18] H.L. Chan, D. Sutanto. A new battery model for use with battery energy storage systems and electric vehicles power systems. *IEEE Power Engineering Society Winter Meeting*, pages 470-475. IEEE, 23-27 January 2000.

[19] Sony Corporation. *Lithium Ion Rechargeable Batteries Technical Handbook*.

[20] M.A. Roscher, O. Bohlen, and J. Vetter. OCV Hysteresis in Li-Ion Batteries including Two-Phase Transition Materials. *International Journal of Electrochemistry*, 2011:Article ID 984320, 2011.

[21] SAFT. Rechargeable lithium-ion battery MP 174565 Integration™. www.saftbatteries.com/force_download/MP_174565_INT.pdf (at December 2013).

High Level Energy Modeling of Controller Logic in Data Caches

Preeti Ranjan Panda[1], Sourav Roy[2], Srikanth Chandrasekaran[3], Namita Sharma[1],
Jasleen Kaur[1], Sarath Kumar Kandalam[1], and Nagaraj N.[1]
[1]Indian Institute of Technology Delhi, New Delhi, India
[2]Freescale Semiconductor India Pvt. Ltd., Noida, India
[3]IEEE (Standards),Bangalore, India

ABSTRACT

In modern embedded processor caches, a significant amount of energy dissipation occurs in the controller logic part of the cache. Previous power/energy modeling tools have focused on the core memory part of the cache. We propose energy models for two of these modules – Write Buffer and Replacement logic. Since this hardware is generally synthesized by designers, our power models are also based on empirical data. We found a linear dependence of the per-access write buffer energy on the write buffer depth and write width. We validated our models on several different benchmark examples, using different technology nodes. Our models generate energy estimates that are within 4.2% of those measured by detailed power simulations, making the models valuable mechanisms for rapid energy estimates during architecture exploration.

Categories and Subject Descriptors

B.3.2 [**Memory Structures**]: Design Styles—*Cache Memories*

Keywords

Data Caches; Energy Modeling; Synthesis; Write Buffer

1. INTRODUCTION

Accurate performance and energy models of memory and cache sub-systems are necessary in order to aid the architecture exploration of modern processors and systems-on-chip. The regularity in the cache design allows for relatively fast energy/power modeling at a very high level of abstraction. Cache modeling for area, timing, and power has received considerable attention in recent times. Figure 1(a) shows a high level view of the major components in a data cache. Other than the core memory array and decoders, the cache controller blocks including replacement logic (RPL), write buffer, and cache coherence logic also contribute to the cache energy dissipation. In this work, we attempt to improve the cache energy model by incorporating the energy contribution of other components in cache design, such as the write buffer and RPL. Analytical models such as CACTI could still be used for the memory component. Unlike the memory array, the controller logic portion of the cache is

seldom custom-designed, and usually synthesized from high-level HDL descriptions in practice; thus the power modeling is not very amenable to analytical treatment at the layout level, and we take an empirical approach for energy estimation.

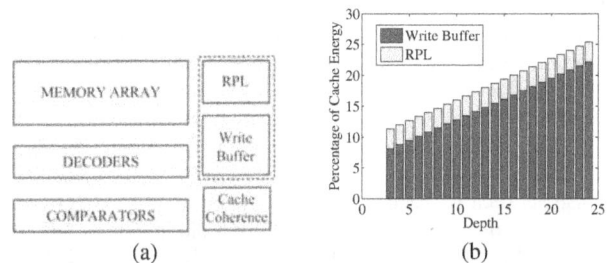

Figure 1: (a) Data cache controller components modelled for energy (b) Controller energy as a percentage of cache energy

Early dynamic and leakage energy models for caches reported in [1, 2] are incorporated into CACTI [3]. The power numbers estimated by CACTI could be improved by incorporating more details of the cache design such as the controller. Similar approaches at analytical power modeling are attempted by tools such as ORION [4], which performs an analytical quantification of dynamic and leakage power within router elements of an interconnect network. NVSim [14] generates energy estimates for non-volatile memory structures based on different technologies such as NAND flash, PCRAM, and STT-RAM, using principles similar to CACTI. In this paper we take the route of empirical models derived from power simulations, which is useful for synthesized logic.

To illustrate the importance of estimating cache controller energy, let us study the total energy of the controller blocks as a fraction of the energy due to the rest of the cache, including memory array, decoders, and comparators. This would give us an idea of the energy component that is typically ignored by standard cache power models such as CACTI.

Figure 1(b) shows the variation of the fraction of cache energy contributed by controller blocks, as *write buffer depth* controller parameter is varied for a 16 KB, 16-way data cache, for an *FIR* filter application. Since controller logic modules, such as write buffers, are not modeled in CACTI-style tools, their energy estimates could be off by 12-25%, as shown in Figure 1(b). Large write buffers are common in several modern embedded processor designs (e.g., the Cavium Octeon [9] has a 2KB write buffer in each core) and ignoring their energy implications could lead to serious energy underestimates, causing misleading performance/power trade-offs during design space exploration. The RPL energy is relatively small, and stays unchanged as it is independent of the write buffer depth.

We attempt to estimate the per-access energy for the cache controller in terms of high-level parameters such as write buffer depth, write width, and cache associativity. This model can then be combined with CACTI energy models to determine the total energy per access.

2. DESIGN DETAILS

In this section, we discuss the design of two important cache controller components: write buffer and replacement logic. We identify the typical functionality assigned to these modules and generic principles used in their implementation. Naturally, the actual details are likely to differ across different implementations. Nevertheless, the basic principles remain unchanged, and the nature of the equations derived for the energy models will be substantially similar, though a new one-time energy characterization will be needed to generate the correct set of co-efficients used for each variation of implementation and library/technology. The energy modeling strategy for the components is discussed in Section 4.

2.1 Write Buffer

The write buffer is used in data caches to reduce write stalls, which occur when the processor is suspended while accessing the next memory level. The write buffer stores the data to be written and sends it to next level memory whenever the data bus is free. It allows overlapping of processor execution and memory update. A write buffer may be present between L1-cache and the L2-cache and also between L2-cache and the main memory. The path from the processor directly to the write buffer is valid in case of write-through caches only. In this paper, we consider the write buffer between the L1-cache and L2-cache, as shown in Figure 2.

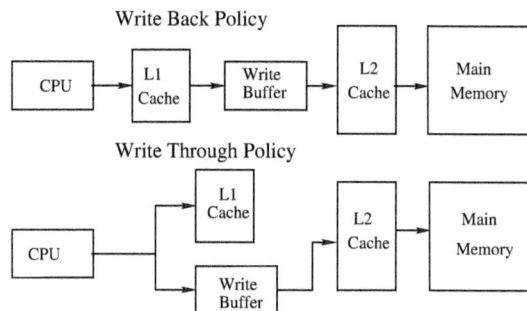

Figure 2: Write buffer interface for a cache write

A generic write buffer architecture is shown in Figure 3. In a write-back cache, the write buffer stores a complete cache line at once and sends the line word by word to the next level memory. The write buffer architecture is mainly divided into Address array, Comparator array, Data array, and Control Logic. The data array stores the data lines to be written, and the address array stores their addresses. The comparator array compares the incoming address with the stored ones and returns the matching line. Some LSB bits are omitted from the address, depending on the line size (e.g., 8 words per line means that 3 LSB address bits can be omitted). The maximum number of cache lines stored in a write buffer is termed its *Depth*. The write buffer can be configured in various different ways. The architecture parameters are described below [10].

2.1.1 Cache Write Policy

The write buffer architecture is dependent on the cache write policy. In write-back caches, an entire cache line is written to the write buffer at once, while in write-through caches, only a single word is

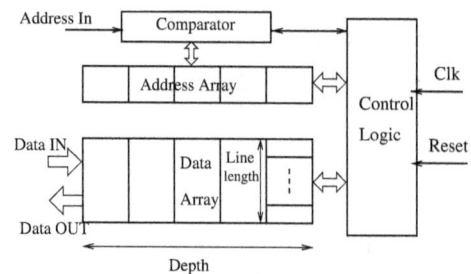

Figure 3: Write Buffer Architecture

written at a time. The write buffer in write-through caches requires additional control logic because validity information is associated with every word.

2.1.2 Word Coalescence

For write-through caches, a word is written on every write, and by spatial locality of writes, the probability of subsequent writes being to recently accessed lines, is high. This is captured by coalescing multiple writes into the same line, and writing to the next level memory only once. This also reduces energy by avoiding the redundancy of storing the same address multiple times. To maintain this status, an update bit is added for each word in the line, which helps in identifying the valid words to send to the next level memory. Write-back caches do not require coalescing as the data is moved line by line.

2.1.3 Retirement order and Retirement Policy

The order of writing data from the write buffer to L2-cache depends on the *retirement order* of the write buffer, which is typically FIFO (First-In First-Out). The data is moved to L2-cache only after a minimum number of entries are filled, which is determined by the write buffer *Retirement Policy*. The Alpha21164 [11] processor uses *retire-at-2* policy, which means that the data will not be moved to L2-cache until 2 or more valid entries are present in the write buffer. In case of write-through cache, a higher retire-at value increases the probability of word coalescing. The probability of load hazard stall (described below) increases with a higher retire-at value. From the energy perspective, the search operation for every read miss dissipates more energy with a higher retire-at value.

2.1.4 Load Hazard Policy

Access to the write buffer may stall the CPU for various reasons. The buffer may be full, or may be involved in a transfer to L2 when there is a cache read miss. One condition that is determined by the write buffer parameter is the *load hazard* – this occurs if the requested data of a cache read miss is present in the write buffer. On a load hazard stall, the data is *flushed* from the write buffer and fetched back to L1-cache. The different types of load hazard policies are:

- *Flush full* – the entire write buffer is emptied and the data is moved to L2-cache.

- *Flush partial* – the write buffer is emptied until the required entry is moved to L2-cache.

- *Flush-item only* – only a specific entry is moved from the write buffer to the L2-cache. In the above three policies, data is fetched from the L2-cache back to L1-cache as in the case of a load miss.

- *Read from write buffer* – the data is directly read from the write buffer to the L1-cache.

2.2 Cache Line Replacement Logic

Replacement policy in a set-associative cache refers to the identification of the cache block/line to be replaced within a set on a read or write miss, and is key to the performance of the cache [12]. Different possible replacement policies are: Least Recently Used (True LRU – replace the line that was accessed earliest), Pseudo Least Recently Used (Pseudo LRU or PLRU – a simpler practical implementation of LRU), First In First Out (replace the line that entered first) and Random replacement policy (replace a line at random). Variants of LRU are commonly used in practical systems because they yield relatively good performance. In this section, we outline the typical implementation of True LRU and Pseudo LRU policies.

True LRU

True LRU is based on the observation that the block that has been used least recently is the one which is less likely to be used again in the near future. A queue is maintained of the way numbers for each set, representing the order of accesses of each way (Figure 4(a)). On a *miss*, the line at the tail is replaced, and the new line is inserted at the head of the queue (Line '11' in Figure 4(b)). A *hit* to a line causes the corresponding way number to become the new head of the queue (Line '01' in Figure 4(c)).

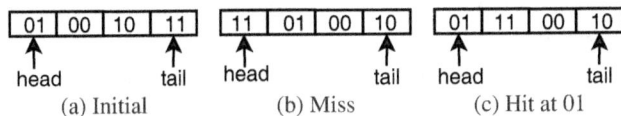

Figure 4: Working of the True LRU queue

Pseudo LRU

Pseudo LRU (PLRU) [5, 6] is an attempt to reduce the hardware complexity of implementing LRU, while still retaining its essence. It has been used in several commercial processor implementations such as those from Intel's x86 series [7], IBM's Power Architecture family, and Freescale's PowerPC G4 [8].

A binary search tree with $(N-1)$ nodes is used, where N is the associativity, where each node has a flag bit to record the latest traversal information. In Figure 5(a), the leaf nodes represent the different ways of the 4-way associative cache, and the 3 internal nodes (which are stored as 3 bits) represent the direction (0/1 for left/right) traversed in the previous access. Assume that the initial state for nodes 2,1,0 is "100". On a *miss*, the LRU block is replaced followed by the complementation of bits in the traversed path. To find the LRU block, we follow the stored path from the root node. In Figure 5(b), the line to be replaced is stored in way 2 ("10"). The new state is "001". On a *hit*, the values at the nodes along the path are complemented. In Figure 5(c), a hit to way 1 ("01") causes an update in the LRU bits to "111". This strategy is an approximation of the LRU algorithm, but leads to simpler hardware.

3. MODELING METHODOLOGY

The logic blocks we have chosen for modeling are generally synthesized by designers, so we have taken a synthesis-based route for power modeling. A layout-based approach (such as the one used by CACTI) may not be very appropriate because: (1) the controller style logic used here is not very amenable to the geometric treatment at layout level used in such tools; and (2) even though some relatively regular sub-blocks are present, the final design of such peripheral blocks is typically synthesized in the industry, not

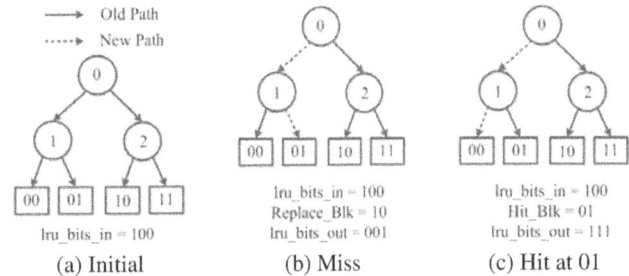

Figure 5: Working of the Pseudo LRU replacement policy

custom-designed. Hence, the proposed approach is actually likely to result in a closer match.

We started with a hardware description model written for the sub-systems. A synthesis-based approach was taken to generate the detailed implementations. The parameters affecting the per-access energy were identified, and energy equations were built based on these observations using some of the configurations. Test cases were generated to determine the coefficients of the equations identified by fitting data obtained by detailed power simulations of the models.

The co-efficients used in the equations would change when a new library/technology is used. The suggested methodology is that, when a new library is used, the initial one-time characterization process is re-done and the curve fitting is performed to generate a new set of co-efficients, giving us the new energy models.

4. BUILDING THE POWER MODEL

In this section, we attempt to identify the high-level parameters that affect the energy consumption of the cache controller modules, and propose simple equations to model the energy.

4.1 Write Buffer

We study the energy implications of various write buffer configuration parameters in this section.

4.1.1 Buffer Depth and Write Width

The write buffer depth represents the maximum number of entries that can be buffered before retirement to the higher level memory is initiated. Depth is one of primary determinants of write buffer energy, since a register array is used for storing the lines to be written, and accesses to this structure cause energy dissipation proportional to its size. Possible operations in each cycle are: Read operation, Write operation, Read+Write operation, or no operation. For each operation, the control logic block generates the corresponding signals. Similarly, the number of bits written together (the write width) in one write operation also determines the energy. In our write buffer energy model, the energy is proportional to the product of the depth and write width. Note that this width is different depending on whether the L1 cache is a write-through or write-back. In write-through caches, the width is one word, whereas in write-back caches, the width equals the line size.

4.1.2 Hamming Distance

Since data is frequently written to the write buffer, the hamming distance between the current data and the previous data could be a candidate determining dynamic energy. However, our experiments with benchmark programs (Section 5.3) indicated a negligible difference in modeling error of the energy estimates, by the incorporation of hamming distance information. This led us to ignore this parameter, and we do not discuss the implications further.

4.1.3 Retirement Policy

The variation in retire-at policy typically does not affect the energy of write-back caches significantly. Figure 6 shows a slice though this design space – the total energy due to retire-at-2 is compared with that due to retire-at-4, for write-back caches, on some typical benchmarks.

However, higher retire-at policy helps write-through caches in avoiding the storage of redundant addresses, and increases word coalescing possibilities. The difference, in case of write-through caches, shows up in reduced/increased number of write buffer accesses. Further, there is a difference in the control logic hardware of the write buffer. Bits are maintained for each line, with the number being proportional to the buffer depth. It is expected that part of the energy model exhibiting a linear dependence on the depth, also captures this dependence for the write-through cache.

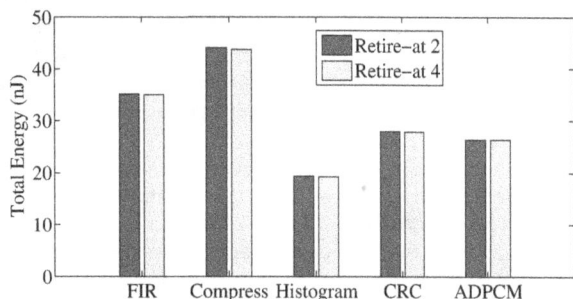

Figure 6: Energy variation with different retire-at values at depth=9

4.1.4 Load Hazard Policy

The various load hazard policies were discussed in Section 2.1. From the power or energy perspective, for the first three cases (Flush full, Flush partial, Flush item-only) the data and addresses blocks are identical, but for the last case (Read from Write Buffer), extra ports are added from the data array to read from the write buffer.

The above parameters are used for power modeling of the data array and address array in the write buffer. For control logic, the parameters used are the active cycles and transitions between active and inactive cycles. The plots in Figure 7 illustrate the variation of energy per operation with the write buffer depth for operations in data array. Each of these energy values can be expressed as a linear function of depth and write width of the write buffer:

$$\text{Energy\_est} = a \times \text{Depth} \times \text{Write Width} + b \times \text{Depth} + c \quad (1)$$

The individual energy components are then multiplied by the number of cycles with only reads, only writes, and simultaneous reads and writes. These parameters can be obtained from a processor/cache simulator.

The load hazard policy used also leads to changes in the controller energy, caused by the bits stored in the controller for every buffer entry. This leads to the $(b \times \text{Depth})$ expression in the Equation 1. The variation in *retire-at policy* affects only the number of operations in the control logic block.

The leakage power is independent of the operation being performed and varies linearly with the depth and width (write-width and address width) (Figure 7). The set of co-efficients obtained by the modeling are omitted due to lack of space.

The energy for each write buffer component can be evaluated by summing up the energies for each type of operation relevant to the

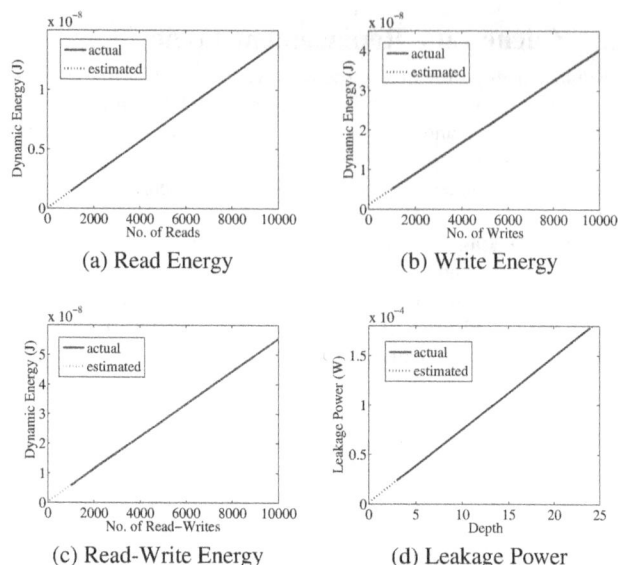

(a) Read Energy   (b) Write Energy

(c) Read-Write Energy   (d) Leakage Power

Figure 7: Energy for different operations for Data array

component. For the data and address arrays, the operation types are: Read, Write, and simultaneous Read-Write. For the control logic, the operation types are the number of active cycles and the number of transitions. The total energy for write buffer can be estimated as:

$$Energy_{WB} = Energy_{DA} + Energy_{AA} + Energy_{CL}$$
$$+ Leakage\ Power \times Simulation\ time \quad (2)$$

where $Energy_{DA}$, $Energy_{AA}$, and $Energy_{CL}$ are the energy due to data array, address array, and control logic respectively, and Leakage Power refers to the total leakage power estimated for all the three components.

4.2 Replacement Policy Logic

4.2.1 True LRU

For the True LRU policy, a queue of N entries is maintained, where N is the cache associativity. Each entry identifies the way, requiring $\log_2 N$ bit (Figure 4). Thus, $(N \times \log_2 N)$ bits are needed to maintain the queue. These bits are stored along with other control bits in the Tag array of the cache, and the corresponding energy for accessing the bits need not be separately modeled (tools such as CACTI already account for this energy). However, we still need to add the energy in the combinational logic that generates the next state from the present queue bits. We observe that the combinational logic takes the $N \times \log_2 N$ bit values from the queue, and N bit values from the comparators (to determine matches), and propose an energy function where the dynamic and leakage energy are linear functions of these two numbers. The energy equations are of the form:

$$E_{hit} = A_2 N \log_2 N + A_1 N + A_0 \quad (3)$$

where E_{hit} is the energy of a single hit. The equation is similar for misses.

We further observe that the power consumed by a hit operation is, in general, different from the power consumed by a miss operation, because of different line re-organizations within the cache set. Hence, different sets of co-efficients are derived for hits and misses. We generated traces consisting of random sequences of hits to different ways (similarly for misses), and plotted the data obtained from power simulations. Co-efficients for Equation 3 were

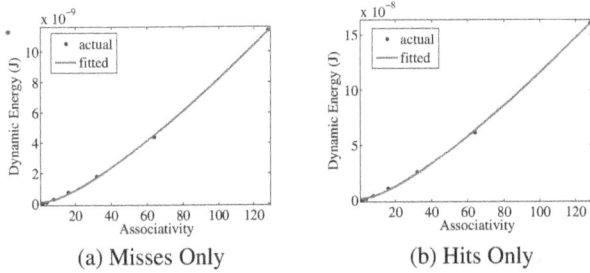

(a) Misses Only (b) Hits Only

Figure 8: Modeling dynamic energy for True LRU

obtained by fitting the empirical data to the curve. The total energy due to replacement logic would be estimated by first observing the hit- and miss-counts in a performance simulation, and using an equation of the form:

$$\text{Dynamic Energy} = hit\_count \times E_{hit} + miss\_count \times E_{miss} \quad (4)$$

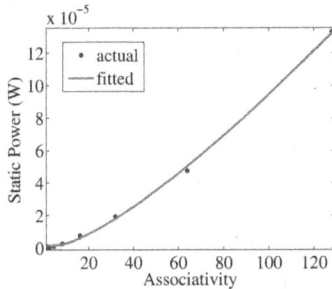

Figure 9: Modeling leakage power for True LRU

The power simulation data generated for dynamic energy and leakage power for the True LRU implementation, is plotted in Figures 8 and 9. The set of co-efficients derived from the above modeling, for a 90nm library, is given in Table 1.

Table 1: Model co-efficients for True LRU for 90nm library

Co-efficients	$(A_2 N log_2 N + A_1 N + A_0)$		
	Leakage Power (W)	Dynamic Energy (J)	
		E_{hit}	E_{miss}
A_2	2.717E-07	6.687E-10	2.346E-10
A_1	-8.887E-07	-1.356E-9	9.022E-10
A_0	2.768E-06	6.400E-9	-1.647E-9

4.2.2 PLRU

PLRU is an approximation of the LRU policy, using fewer $(N - 1)$ bits, where N is the cache associativity. The power consumed by a hit operation is not much different from the power consumed by a miss operation. Hence, we propose a model for dynamic energy that is a linear function of N. The leakage power model is also linear in N, where the area (which is the primary determinant of leakage) is estimated to be proportional to N because a flip-flop is required for each bit. The equation is:

$$B_1 N + B_0 \quad (5)$$

The power simulation data for PLRU is plotted in Figure 10. The co-efficients derived from the above modeling, for a 90nm library, are shown in Table 2.

The RPL block was experimentally found to account for less than 4% of the cache energy. The PLRU implementation dissipates lesser energy than True LRU, accounting for less than 1%. Considering the percentage contributions of the replacement policies, we

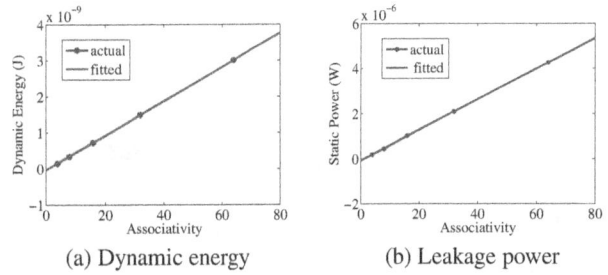

(a) Dynamic energy (b) Leakage power

Figure 10: Modeling dynamic energy and leakage power for PLRU

Table 2: Model co-efficients for PLRU at 90nm

$(B_1 N + B_0)$	Co-efficients	
	B_1	B_0
Leakage Power (W)	6.800E-08	-8.700E-08
Dynamic Energy (J)	4.800E-11	-3.900E-11

may conclude that the simplifications used in the energy modeling are justified.

5. EXPERIMENTAL VALIDATION

5.1 Setup

To validate our cache controller energy modeling approach, we first developed and synthesized – using a Cadence toolflow starting from RTL Compiler and a 90nm ASIC library – a few different configurations of the controller, and performed power simulations using the access traces mentioned earlier, to generate the co-efficients of the energy equations. We first determined the minimum number of data points (depths) to be considered to obtain a reasonably accurate model. Our experiments showed that the co-efficients derived from just four data points (write buffer depth) generated models with similar errors to those generated with large number of up to 10 points. Details are omitted due to lack of space.

We used Simplescalar [13], augmented by a detailed implementation of the write buffer and RPL, to generate the access traces for several application programs. For each application, we noted all the high-level parameters needed for the energy estimates, such as the number of cache hits, write buffer reads/writes, etc. The synthesized controller designs were then taken through detailed power simulation on Synopsys Primepower. The measured and estimated energy values were compared to assess the accuracy of the energy models. Because of limited space, we present comparisons of estimated and measured energy values for variations of selected configuration parameters.

5.2 Validation with Applications

The applications selected for validation are from the Mediabench Benchmark suite. Figure 11(a) summarizes the percentage error when the energy estimate for the cache controller is compared with the measured energy, for different depth values of the write buffer. Other parameters were held constant for this experiment: associativiy was 4-way with a PLRU policy, word width was 32 bits, address width was 32 bits, line size was 8 words. The maximum error for the write buffer was 3.5%, and the maximum error for RPL was 0.5%.

Figure 12 shows the estimation errors for the RPL blocks for the PLRU and True LRU logic blocks, for the ADPCM benchmark. We notice that the PLRU estimates exhibit much smaller errors than those for True LRU. The overall error is dominated by the write

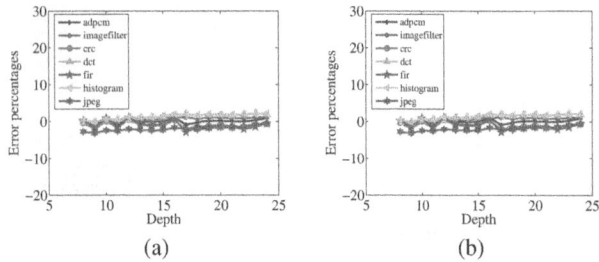

Figure 11: Cache controller energy estimation errors for (a) different applications using 90nm technology (b) model including Hamming Distance

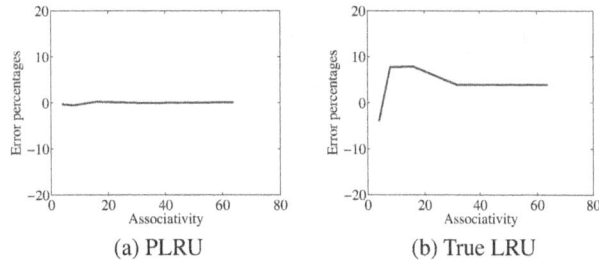

Figure 13: (a) Estimation errors for 65nm library (b) Controller energy variation with line size in write-back and write-through caches

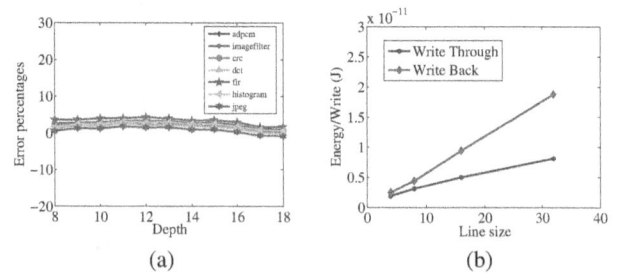

(a) PLRU   (b) True LRU

Figure 12: Estimation errors for RPL for ADPCM

buffer numbers because of the relatively large energy values of the write buffer.

5.3 Hamming Distance parameter

In Figure 11(b) we plot the estimation errors for the cache controller energy by using an energy model that takes into account the Hamming Distance between successive data values. As a comparison with Figure 11(a) shows, the error difference due to this improved model is negligible. The parameter is hence suitable for exclusion from the model, as it would avoid the additional bookkeeping associated with computing the distances on every access.

5.4 Validation on a Different Library

We used a 65nm ASIC library to separately validate our modeling methodology. New equation co-efficients were generated as described earlier, and power simulations were carried out. The errors in energy estimates for the controller plotted in Figure 13(a), by varying the write buffer depth, indicates a similar overall observation – the maximum error is 4.2%.

5.5 Validation on Write-back vs. Write-through Caches

We compared the cache controller energy variations on write-back and write-through caches, when the line size is varied. According to our models, the write-back cache controller exhibits a larger variation with line size because the write-width is the entire line width. For write-through, the width is fixed, but there is a small variation in the control logic block because of additional bits maintained. This effect is clearly observed in Figure 13(b), where the respective curves have different slopes.

6. CONCLUSION AND FUTURE WORK

We presented energy models for estimating the energy consumed by the write buffer and replacement logic of data caches. Our energy model for the write buffer uses a simple equation that captures the write buffer depth and the write width. The energy equation for replacement policy logic block depends on the cache associativity. Experimental validation of the model with different benchmarks and technology nodes indicate an estimation error within 4.2% of the energy values generated by detailed power simulation. The energy model can be extended in the future to incorporate the contribution of cache coherence protocols, which becomes an important component of cache controllers in on-chip multiprocessors.

7. ACKNOWLEDGMENTS

This research was partially supported by an SRC research grant from Freescale. We are grateful for their support. We also thank Puneet Ginoria and Himanshu Gupta for their partial support with the experiments.

8. REFERENCES

[1] M. B. Kamble and K. Ghose, "Analytical energy dissipation models for low-power caches," ISLPED, 1997

[2] M. Mamidipaka and N. Dutt, "An enhanced power estimation model for on-chip caches," UC Irvine, Tech. Rep., September 2004.

[3] N. Muralimanohar, R. Balasubramanian, and N. P. Jouppi, "Architecting efficient interconnects for large caches with CACTI 6.0," IEEE Micro, 28(1), 2008

[4] A. Kahng, B. Li, L.-S. Peh, and K. Samadi, "Orion 2.0: A power-area simulator for interconnection networks," TVLSI, 20(1), 2012.

[5] J. Handy, *The cache memory book*. San Diego, CA, USA: Academic Press Professional, Inc., 1993.

[6] H. Ghasemzadeh, S. Sepideh Mazrouee, and M. R. Kakoee, "Modified Pseudo LRU Replacement Algorithm," ECBS 2006

[7] "Ultra Low-Power Intel486ÂŹ Embedded Processor." http://www.intel.com/design/intarch/prodbref/272713.htm

[8] "Powerpc g4 architecture white paper." http://cache.freescale.com/files/product/doc/G4WP.pdf

[9] http:www.caviumnetworks.com

[10] K. Skadron and D. W. Clark, "Design Issues and Tradeoffs for Write Buffers," HPCA 1997

[11] DEC, "Alpha 21164 microprocessor, hardware reference manual," Tech. Rep. EC-QAEQD-TE, 1996.

[12] J. L. Hennessy and D. A. Patterson, *Computer Architecture - A Quantitative Approach*. Elsevier, 1990.

[13] "The SimpleScalar Architectural Research Tool, version 3.0." http://www.simplescalar.com/

[14] X. Dong et al., "NVSim: A Circuit-Level Performance, Energy, and Area Model for Emerging Nonvolatile Memory." TCAD, 31(7), 2012.

3D-SWIFT: a High-performance 3D-stacked Wide IO DRAM[*]

Tao Zhang, Cong Xu,
Yuan Xie
Penn State University
{zhangtao, czx102,
yuanxie}@cse.psu.edu

Ke Chen
Oracle Corporation
ke.c.chen@oracle.com

Guangyu Sun
Peking University
gsun@pku.edu.cn

ABSTRACT

Wide IO has been standardized as a low-power, high-bandwidth DRAM for embedded system. The performance of Wide IO, however, is limited by the power constraint and unexploited fine-grained memory parallelism. In this work, we propose a novel architecture, 3D-SWIFT, that achieves high access parallelism by partitioning a memory bank into sub-banks with a fine access granularity, which takes advantage of 3D die-stacking. The power constraint is naturally eliminated by the fine-grained structure due to the reduced activation power. Moreover, we propose sub-bank autonomy and introduce corresponding management policies to enable an intelligent interface protocol. Thanks to sub-rank autonomy, the overhead of tracking huge concurrent accesses in the memory controller is significantly reduced, making our 3D-SWIFT architecture scalable for future memory systems. We evaluate our 3D-SWIFT and the results show that 3D-SWIFT can achieve 87.6% performance improvement compared to the state-of-the-art Wide IO.

1. INTRODUCTION

As an early adoption of 3D integration, 3D-stacked DRAM is a promising technology for overcoming the barriers in DRAM scaling, thereby offering an opportunity to break the "memory wall" with improved DRAM cell density (capacity) and wire routing resources (connectivity), as well as reduced wire length (latency and power) [1, 2, 3, 4, 5, 6]. In particular, Wide IO DRAM [1] has been standardized by JEDEC as a high bandwidth and low-power 3D DRAM for embedded SoC system. A Wide IO DRAM has four channels that are independent of each other. Each channel is 128-bit wide with single data rate. The Wide IO follows the low-power design methodology of LPDDR so that it removes the delay lock loop (DLL) and on-die termination (ODT) logic and applies lower supply voltage to achieve low static power.

Unfortunately, Wide IO does not take full advantage of the die-stacking since it has to comply with conventional DRAM structure where the bank size is large and the number of banks is small. In addition, the increasing number of channels in turn mandates more memory controllers (MCs) and interconnects between them, bringing in issues that may hinder its popularity. As 3D die-stacking eliminates (or at least alleviates) most of the physical limitations,

it provides the opportunity to further enhance memory parallelism with novel memory architecture. In this work, we propose *3D-SWIFT* to enable a fine-grained memory architecture so as to improve performance in Wide IO. The contributions of our work can be summarized as follows.

- **Fine-grained 3D DRAM structure.** We find that the power constraint can suppress the performance of Wide IO DRAM. To eliminate the power constraint, a bank in 3D-SWIFT is further divided into multiple sub-banks and each sub-bank has the ability to independently serve a memory request and provide an entire cacheline. Once there is a memory access, only the target sub-bank is activated. In this way, the fine-grained access reduces the activation/precharge current and thus enables higher memory parallelism. To our best knowledge, this is the first work that takes into account power constraint in designing high-performance Wide IO.

- **Sub-bank "autonomy".** Leveraging the close-page row-buffer management policy, sub-bank autonomy is developed to combine the commands RAS, CAS and PRE as REQ to activate a sub-bank, carry on the data burst, and close the sub-bank *automatically*. We devise a packet-based interface protocol accordingly to simplify the memory transaction. Moreover, by making use of the rich routing resource on the logic die, a wide data bus is employed to deliver a full cacheline in one cycle.

- **Simplified memory controller design.** 3D-SWIFT takes into account the design complexity of MCs. By leveraging the sub-bank autonomy and packet-based protocol, a MC of 3D-SWIFT can be integrated into the processor die so that it is visible to the processor for the system-level optimization.

2. BACKGROUND AND MOTIVATION

In conventional DDR*x* family, the pin count constraint is a major factor that limits the memory bandwidth due to the packaging limitation. The long off-chip memory bus implemented with the transmission line mandates the trade-off between a high operating frequency and the channel capacity because of the load and signal integrity. In addition, since all DRAM devices (chips) in a rank work in lockstep, DDR*x* exposes an extremely large logic row while only a small fraction of data is delivered for each memory access (see Figure 1a). Even though the data overfetching is beneficial for applications with high spatial locality, the fixed device association limits bank-level parallelism since few banks are visible to the MC.

Once we relocate the DRAM from off-chip to on-chip, multiple DRAM dies can be stacked together to increase the cell density. The Wide IO (Figure 1b) is applicable for memory bandwidth improvement for two reasons. First of all, the pin-out constraint is eliminated and the on-chip I/O bus replaces the long off-chip transmission lines. Moreover, the compact DRAM layout reduces

---

[*]This work is supported in part by SRC Grants, NSF (1017277, 1213052, and 1218867), NSF China (61202072), 863 Program of China (2013AA013201), and AMD Gift Grant.

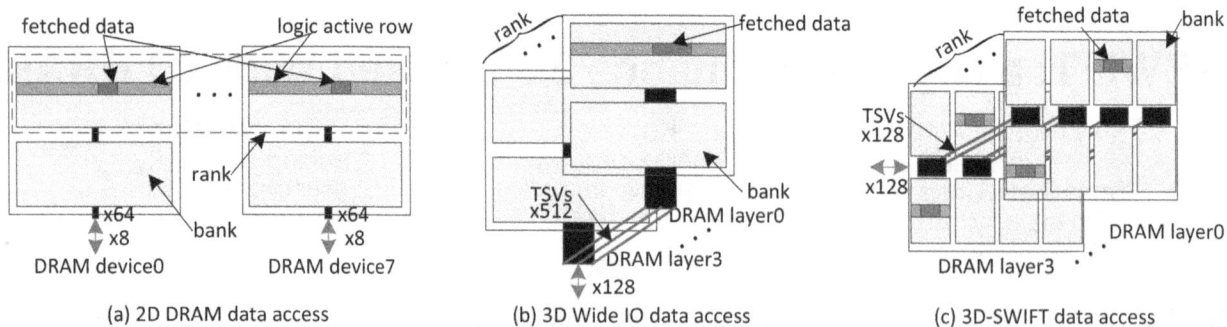

Figure 1: Data access mechanisms in different memories. (a) DDR3: the data is distributed over all devices in a rank. Only a small fraction of row is fetched in each memory access; (b) Wide IO: the data is placed in a large row and no individual device exists. Still only a portion of data is fetched; (c) 3D-SWIFT: the width of fetched data matches cacheline width. The rest of a row is idle.

memory access latency as well as power consumption. Despite the benefits a Wide IO provides, some new problems emerges and need to be solved carefully:

• **More restricted power and current density constraints.** A new problem in Wide IO is the requirement of low-power design, which is critical for the success of 3D DRAM due to the increasing power density [7]. Since no DLL or ODT is employed, the background power is dramatically reduced and the burst and activation/precharge power now starts to dominate in the Wide I/O DRAM. As illustrated in Figure 1b, the entire row is activated but only a portion of data is fetched, which still indicates large power redundancy. In addition, considering the power supply challenges in 3D ICs [8, 9], the power constraint becomes more restricted in 3D context. Therefore, Wide IO has conservatively switched the restriction on memory accesses from four-bank activation window (tFAW) to two-bank activation window (tTAW) and extended the window width from 30ns to 50ns (the lower the better for performance) [1].

As shown in Figure 2, with a large tTAW constraint (tTAW=50ns), no further improvement is observed even if the bank-level parallelism is augmented as the bank number increases from 8 to 64. In other words, the power constraint can significantly suppress the bank-level-parallelism in a rank (channel), which has also been verified in [10] when close-page row buffer management policy is applied. Once the power constraint is eliminated (tTAW=0ns), the performance gain can be up to 44% when increasing the bank number from 8 to 64. Moreover, by getting rid of tTAW constraint, the bank-level parallelism can further provide 14% performance improvement. As a result, neglecting the power constraint and simply increasing the bank number or bank size in 3D DRAM is not a wise choice in terms of either performance or power. Instead, 3D DRAM design should carefully cope with the power constraint to make sure it does not incur performance degradation.

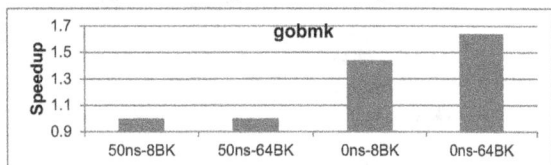

Figure 2: The impact of power constraint on 3D DRAM. The simulation is done with 8/64 banks(BK) and tTAW=50ns/0ns (see Section 5 for the details of simulation setups).

• **Increased design complexity of memory controller.** The second problem is that the increasing number of channels one Wide IO provides can result in higher design complexity of memory controllers. For example, eight independent channels have been implemented by Tezzaron [3]. While more channels can effectively improve the bandwidth, the need of multiple MCs induces noticeable

area overhead when MCs are deployed in the processor die. These MCs are required to have either peer-coordination [11] or smart application assignment [12] to achieve better memory performance, which aggravates the design complexity. Alternatively, HMC [2] puts the memory controller on the logic layer, which leaves little room for a system designer to conduct further system optimization on the MC for the better communication with 3D DRAM [13].

3. 3D-SWIFT–A NOVEL WIDE IO DRAM

As shown in Figure 3, 3D-SWIFT re-maps a 2D DRAM that has nine devices (eight for data and one for ECC) and eight banks per device into the 3D-stacked DRAM. With respect to the process optimization, 3D-SWIFT separates control and interface logics from DRAM cells and put them in the logic layer as other state-of-the-art 3D DRAM does. Note that 3D-SWIFT is extensible when more ranks are employed. Those ranks can be either stacked vertically or placed horizontally as neighbors. Like HMC, multiple 3D-SWIFTs can be populated on the interposer to increase the memory capacity.

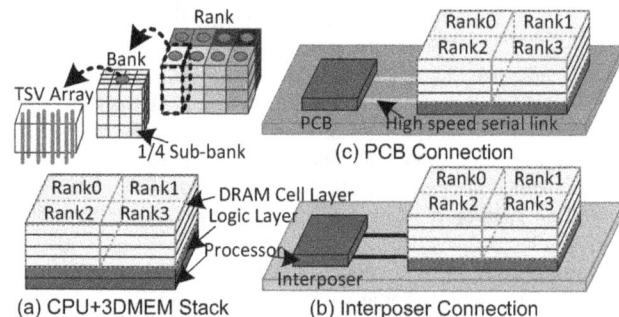

Figure 3: 3D-SWIFT memory subsystem and possible applications. (a) 3D-SWIFT directly stacks on the top of CPU; (b) 3D-SWIFT is connected to CPU by interposer; (c) 3D-SWIFT is placed on PCB with high speed links. Multiple 3D-SWIFTs can be populated to provide large memory capacity (not shown).

3.1 Fine-grained Memory Architecture

Without loss of generality, we use an example DRAM design with specific configurations to demonstrate the 3D-SWIFT design. To enable the fine-grained memory access, a 128M-bit ($16K \times 8K$) bank is further split into 16 identical sub-banks so that each sub-bank is sized by 16384×512 to provide a full cache line. As a consequence, a device with eight banks has 128 sub-banks and totally 2,048 sub-banks are available in 4 channels within the four layers. As multiple DRAM layers are provided, each sub-bank can be further folded [14]. For example, when there are four layers, only four sub-banks belonging to the same bank are on one layer. Since a sub-bank can serve a memory request independently, 3D-SWIFT can significantly improve the memory parallelism. In particular, *TAW constraint can be eliminated* since ideally 3D-SWIFT allows as many as $2\times16=32$ sub-banks to be activated in pipeline due to the reduction of active row size[1], which always holds with 1/cycle request rate and tRC row cycle (in this work, tRC=36ns=15cycles). Furthermore, the 16 identical sub-banks guarantee that 3D-SWIFT can provide sustained bandwidth even in the the worst case, where all requests access the same bank but no sub-bank conflict occurs.

3.2 Sub-bank Autonomy

In traditional DDR*x* protocol, MC and DRAM work in a **master-slave** manner. As a master, MC must send various commands, including RAS (row activation), CAS (column read/write) and PRE (precharge), to order the target DRAM bank to complete a data transaction. These commands can only be issued under various timing constraints (tRAS, tRCD, tRP, etc.). As MC is a queuing system, commands can be rescheduled to maximize row buffer hit rate and/or bank-level parallelism. The growing design complexity of the scheduler, however, incurs large hardware overhead and makes MC error-prone.

To offload MC's complexity, 3D-SWIFT employs the sub-bank autonomy, in which each sub-bank can automatically go through the state transition loop without intervention from MC. To enable the sub-bank autonomy, one sub-bank should be aware of the timing stamp to complete the state transition. Thanks to the deterministic access latency listed above, a transition generator can be deployed to easily signal the sub-bank when to move. As a result, a new **client-server** relation is established between MC and 3D-SWIFT: Whenever there is a new memory request, MC (client) only needs to send the request to 3D-SWIFT and then wait for the sub-bank's response. Once a sub-bank (server) detects a request, the sub-bank carries on the transition and completes the data transfer automatically. As a result, 3D-SWIFT eliminates the complicated and area-consuming scheduler in MC.

3.3 Packet-based Interface Protocol

With respect to the sub-bank autonomy, a simple packet-based interface protocol is developed to simplify MC's interface design. As shown in Figure 4, MC sends a REQ with a full memory address and read/write signal to 3D-SWIFT. After tRCD+CL cycles, MC should receive the data on the data bus if it is a read, or put the write data on the data bus in the case of a write. Multiple memory requests can be issued in pipeline as long as these requests do not cause sub-bank conflict, which happens once a request reference to a busy sub-bank. As a result, even though overfetching is disabled, a series of back-to-back requests can be issued to mimic the open-page overfetching. In addition, the request pipeline can also be used to support a DMA transfer that usually has a larger data size than a cacheline, in which case MC generates multiple memory requests in burst to 3D-SWIFT.

To enable the sub-bank autonomy, the automatic state transition shown in Figure 4 must be designed so that the sub-bank knows how to move forward to complete data transaction. A dedicated transition generator is deployed as a timer to signal the sub-rank to complete transition (see Figure 5). According to the cycle number of tRC, (15cycles), a 4-bit counter is sufficient to count the cycle number in the transition generator. Whenever one of the control signals "Data phase", "Pre phase" or "Idle" is asserted, the sub-

---

[1]In fact, the number of concurrent active sub-banks in 3D-SWIFT is less than 16 because of the 2-cycle data burst and the read/write turn-around overhead.

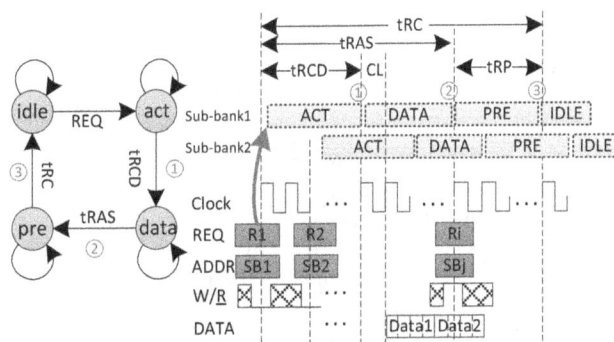

Figure 4: Packet-based interface protocol. Memory controller only issues REQ to initiate a memory access. The sub-bank can complete the data transfer and precharge to close the row automatically.

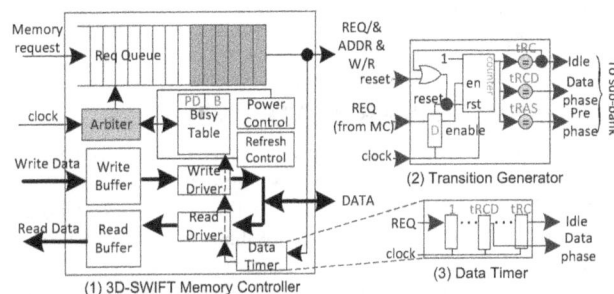

Figure 5: Memory controller design in 3D-SWIFT. (1) Memory controller; (2) Transition generator; (3) Data timer. The length of the counter and shifter are determined by the cycle number of tRC.

bank automatically moves to the next state till the time it returns to idle.

3.4 The Design of Memory Controller

As mentioned, the proposed packet-based interface protocol can significantly reduce the design complexity and area overhead of MC. Unlike a conventional MC that needs to maintain a bank status table for guarding the timing constraints, a 3D-SWIFT MC (Figure 5) only needs to affirm the freedom from sub-bank conflict with simple logic. In addition, command queues are removed to improve area efficiency. Considering the negligible footprint of the data timer, 3D-SWIFT is able to reduce MC's area and make it simpler for verification.

Different from HMC, of which the MC is transparent to the user, the smaller MC in 3D-SWIFT can be integrated into the processor die with few pin-outs. As a consequence, processor designers can apply system-level optimization on the "visible" MC. We believe this is meaningful for the wide adoption of 3D-SWIFT.

Busy Table. As MC is responsible to avoid sub-bank conflict, a busy table is deployed to track sub-banks' status. As shown in Figure 5, one table entry has two bits: 1) the "busy" bit tells whether the sub-bank is idle ('0') or busy ('1'); and 2) the "PowerDown" bit indicates if the sub-bank is in PowerDown mode. Since the size of busy table is relatively small (4,096bits), a 512B multi-port (4R4W) register file is simply employed. The area and power of the busy table is estimated based on [15].

Data Timer As mentioned in Section 3.2, MC and 3D-SWIFT have the agreement that they know exactly when to put the data on the data bus. Different from a sub-bank that gets the information from the transition generator, MC completes the data transfer with the assistance of a data timer. The data timer is in fact a bit shifter

Table 1: Hardware Implementation Summary

Name	Type	Area	Power
Rank decoder & Device decoder	5-32dec	58.92μm^2	9.40μW
Bank decoder	3-8dec	13.41μm^2	2.05μW
Subbank decoder	4-16dec	27.87μm^2	4.68μW
Transition generator	counter	55.75μm^2	18.71μW
Data timer	shifter	93.25μm^2	35.85μW
Row address register	register	101.61μm^2	35.92μW
Busy table [15]	regfile	0.02mm^2	25mW

that has tRC bits. Figure 5 illustrates the function of the data timer. A valid request sets the left-most bits to indicate a data transfer is scheduled. Once the "Data phase" is asserted, MC knows there should be a data transfer in the following cycle. The "Idle" phase notifies MC to clear the busy bit in busy table. Two data timers are used to distinguish the data read and write. They also help MC meet the bus turn-around constraint.

4. DESIGN OVERHEAD ANALYSIS

Since DRAM is very cost-sensitive and area is the major contributor to the memory cost, we strive to minimize the area overhead of our sub-bank design in 3D-SWIFT. In this section, we elaborate the floorplan of the 3D-SWIFT with sub-bank design in addition to the description in Section 3.

Sub-bank DRAM Floorplan. In general, our goal is to increase the data width per mat to output all bits in the sense amplifier (i.e., row buffer) without introducing extra metal layer or area overhead on wire interconnect. Figure 6 shows the 3D-SWIFT floorplan inside a bank which consists of 16 sub-banks. As shown, each sub-bank has 8 mats on one layer, with a total size of 8Mb over four layers. Note that we keep a consistent mat size with the same 512 wordlines and 512 bitlines as in the conventional DRAM design. To minimize the overhead on intra-bank wiring incurred by the sub-bank partitioning, we leverage similar design as in the prior fine-grained 3D DRAM design [14].

In the conventional 2D DRAM, since each mat outputs 4 data bits, there are 512/4=128 column select lines per mat. Note that the numbers of column select lines (M3) and global data lines (M3) in a mat are complementary, meaning that the product of the two numbers is in fact the total number of bitlines of a mat. Alternatively, in 3D-SWIFT we can switch the usage of the wires and have 128 data lines and 4 column select lines. This is easily accomplished by flipping the direction of the three-state driver that connects the column select line and data line (the driver input is the sense amplifier output). In this way, the output of a mat is increased by 128/4=32 times without incurring any area overhead or wire routing overhead. In order to provide the full 512 bits from each mat's sense amplifier to feed an entire cache line, we use an internal burst length of 4.

Simply switching the column select line and global data line is at the risk of increasing the data line access latency, because the original column select lines are usually densely routed above the mats and are relatively narrow and slow. Specifically, the new global data line has a pitch of only 8F (while F is feature size=45nm). Fortunately, because we can partition the bank and sub-bank into different die layers (connected with TSVs), the length of the global dataline (equal to the height of the bank) is effectively shortened by four folds. In addition, we can layout the TSVs in the middle ground between the mats and share the TSVs between the half sub-banks on two sides as shown in Figure 6, which further reduces the data line length by half. In this way, the wire latency and power consumption is effectively reduced to 1/8 of the original.

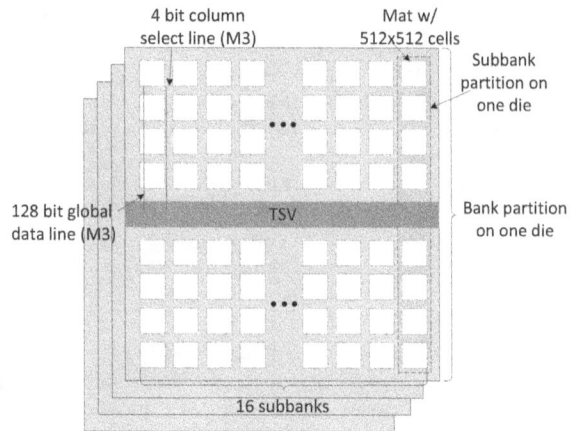

Figure 6: The Floorplan of 3D-SWIFT. A sub-bank consists of 32 mats and each mat is 256Kb (512×512).

Area Overhead. Based on the above-mentioned design, we basically eliminate the data wire routing overhead. The area overhead now comes from two parts: 1) the address/command buses and the row drivers routed to the individual sub-banks because they need to be accessed independently. 2) The TSV layout overhead. Here we assume that all sub-banks in a bank share a common 128-bit wide TSV data bus. We modified CACTI-3DD [16] to model the sub-banked 3D DRAM with the aforementioned configurations, and compare the results against a Wide IO design with the same memory capacity and mat size. The results show that our design has only a negligible 1.6% area overhead with each DRAM die size as 29.3mm^2.

Specifically for the TSV overhead part, according to ITRS' projection [17], the size of TSV will quickly shrink to 2-4μm. Based on the published 3D DRAM prototype [5, 6], the TSV used in this work is set as 2μm wide, 6μm high, and has 4μm pitch. The TSV count is calculated as follows. In one bank, there are 128 TSVs for data delivery. In addition, one redundant TSV is inserted to address the TSV reliability issue [18]. Given 14-bit row address and 5-bit control signals, one bank needs 147 TSVs with a total number of 4,704 TSVs employed in each layer, which consumes about 0.075mm^2 as one TSV takes 16μm^2.

In addition, the wire model in CACTI-3DD is used to calculate the bus delay, where 1mm wire introduces 0.087ns delay and TSV has 0.03ns delay at 45nm technology. Since the RC delay is proportional to the wire length, the longest path, which crosses four layers and goes from the corner to the center, is around 5.35mm and thus introduces 0.58ns delay. Compared to the 2.5ns clock period, the signal propagation delay does not incur extra bus latency (in cycle).

Control Logic Overhead. Except the busy table, all control logics in the 3D-SWIFT and MC have been implemented and verified by ModelSim. All designs are further synthesized by Design Compiler with TSMC 45nm technology for the area and power analysis. Table 1 shows the synthesis results.

As the MC of 3D-SWIFT can be integrated into the processor die, it does not consume any area in 3D-SWIFT. The main area overhead caused by the control logic is from the dedicated row address register. Given 2,048 sub-banks in 3D-SWIFT, the row address register consumes 0.21mm^2 area in total (four layers). Similarly, the area overhead of transition generator is 0.12mm^2, if each sub-bank also has a dedicated generator. In fact, the number of transition generators can be reduced to the value of tRC (in cycle) by sharing the generators among all sub-banks, as at least one

Table 2: Simulation Platform Configuration

System	
Cores	4, ALPHA, out-of-order
CPU Clock Freq.	3 GHz
LDQ/STQ/ROB Size	32 / 32 / 128 entries
Issue/Commit Width	8 / 8
L1-D/L1-I Cache	32kB / 32kB 2-way 2-cycle latency
D-TLB/I-TLB Size	64 / 48 entries
L2 Cache	Shared, Snooping, 4MB, LRU 8-way, 15-cycle latency
Memory	
2D	JEDEC-DDR3, 2GB, 2 ranks 8 banks($\times$8), 64-bit bus, 800MHz (1.6GHz DDR) tRAS-tRCD-tRP-tTAW: 28-10-10-24
3D-WIDE	128-bit/channel, 4-channel, 400MHz tRAS-tRCD-tRP-tTAW: 20-8-8-20
3D-SWIFT	128-bit/channel, 4-channel, 400MHz tRAS-tRCD-tRP-tTAW: 20-8-8-**0**

Table 3: Benchmark Classification

	#Benchmarks(MPKI)
H	[1]bzip2(45.89), [2]bwaves(36.62), [3]zeusmp(19.37), [4]gobmk(37.69), [5]sjeng(33.51), [6]lbm(26.44), [7]STREAM(34.43)
M	[8]milc(5.13), [9]cactusADM(7.85), [10]leslie3d(8.33), [11]libquantum(6,94), [12]wrf(7.33), [13]astar(1.01)
L	[14]soplex(0.16), [15]gamess(0.12), [16]gromacs(0.14), [17]sphinx3(0.08), [18]gcc(0.12), [19]hmmer(0.08), [20]GemsFDTD(0.001), [21]namd(0.04)
Mix$H$	mix1: bzip2, bwaves, zeusmp, lbm mix2: lbm sjeng, gobmk, stream mix3: bzip2, sjeng, zeusmp, stream mix4: zeusmp , bwaves, gobmk, lbm
Mix$M$	mix1: milc, cactusADM, leslie3d, wrf mix2: astar, libquantum, wrf, milc mix3: cactusADM, leslie3d, astar, libquantum mix4: wrf, libquantum, leslie3d, astar
Mix$L$	mix1: gcc, gamess, gromacs, namd mix2: GemsFDTD, soplex, hmmer, sphinx3 mix3: gcc, soplex, gromacs, sphinx3 mix4: GemsFDTD, gamess, hmmer, namd

transition generator is free after a row cycle. However, the shared transition generators induce the internal multiplexing logic and distribution network. Therefore, we insist on the dedicated transition generator. Accounting for the address decoder, the area overhead caused by control logic circuit is 0.35mm^2, which is only 1.2% of one layer.

5. EXPERIMENT

5.1 Evaluation Methodology

In this work, we adopt gem5 [19] as our simulation platform. We modified the DRAMSim2 [20] and successfully integrated it to gem5 as the DRAM model. The SPEC2006 [21] and STREAM [22] benchmarks are employed as multi-programmed benchmarks. Normalized Instructions-Per-Cycle (IPC) is used as the speedup criteria. Table 2 shows the gem5 setup during the simulation. In this work, two memory systems are developed as our reference models. **2D** is the base model that simulates a commodity JEDEC DDR3-1600 SDRAM. **3D-WIDE** is a Wide IO DRAM model that leverages the wider memory bus to deliver the burst data. For the fairness of comparison, even though 3D-WIDE has four independent channels, all channels are used as ranks and connected to a single MC. In addition, the data bus in 3D-WIDE runs at 400MHz with double data rate, which is envisioned as the next generation Wide IO. FR-FCFS scheduling scheme [23] is used in 2D and 3D-WIDE, to maximize the row buffer hit rate, whilst FCFS is deployed in 3D-SWIFT due to the close-page policy. The key timing parameters are shown at the bottom of the table. Note that the tTAW of 3D-SWIFT is 0 to indicate that it eliminates the power constraint.

5.2 Performance Analysis

Single-core Simulation. Firstly, we characterize the benchmark in the single-core simulation. We run each SPEC2006 CPU benchmark with reference input size for 100 million instructions to warm up the cache and another 100 million instructions for the statistics. According to the miss per kilo instructions (MPKI) of last level cache (LLC), we classify the benchmarks into three categories. The symbols H, M, and L stand for the applications that have high (>10), medium ([1, 10]), and low memory intensity (<1), respectively. Only eight benchmarks are selected as the representatives of L class because the rest have almost the same results. Table 3 lists the classification and the corresponding MPKIs. All selected benchmarks are numbered as shown in the table.

The performance result of signle-core simulation is shown in Figure 7a. 3D-WIDE experience 13.5% performance drop on average. The performance degradation of 3D-WIDE mainly stems from its larger access latency, which adversely affects the memory parallelism. The results from H and M benchmarks indicate that 3D-WIDE has poor performance with memory-intensive applications. In contrast, 3D-SWIFT only has small performance loss in some H and M benchmarks. On average 3D-SWIFT achieves 17.8% and 38.4% performance improvement over 2D and 3D-WIDE, respectively.

In particular, cactusADM has 2.18X improvement with 3D-SWIFT. Note that cactusADM has absolutely random accesses as the row buffer hit rate is 0. Therefore, 3D-SWIFT can fully take advantage of sub-bank activation to maximize the memory concurrency. This observation indicates that 3D-SWIFT is more promising in a multi-core system in which the intensive memory requests are more likely to be random due to the interference among applications.

Four-Core Simulation. We randomly select benchmarks from each category for four-core simulation. The mixed benchmarks are listed at the bottom of Table 3 and Figure 7b presents the results. Similar to the single-core simulation, 3D-SWIFT performs better in H and M benchmarks. In general, 3D-SWIFT achieves 64.7% (58.2%) and 87.6% (67.3%) improvement over 2D, and 3D-WIDE, respectively for H-Mix (M-Mix) benchmarks. The application interference that destroys the data locality and makes the memory request more random is the main reason for the performance improvement, as observed in [24].

Impact of Power Constraint (tTAW). As mentioned, the tTAW becomes larger (50ns) in [1]. We intentionally apply a 20ns tTAW to 3D-WIDE to see the impact of tTAW. As shown in Figure 8a, tTAW has significant impact on the memory-intensive applications. Particularly, STREAM has 21.5% performance drop compared with larger tTAW. On average, 8.5% performance degradation is observed, which results from the more restricted power constraint on Wide IO. As a result, 3D DRAM design should carefully cope with the power constraint and 3D-SWIFT is one of potential solutions.

Address Mapping. As shown in Figure 8b, we evaluate the impact of three address mapping schemes: "bank(b):subbank(sb):row(r)", "b:r:sb", and "r:sb:b" and compare it to the baseline "r:b:sb" which maximizes the sub-bank-level parallelism. First of all, there is no difference to prioritize the sub-bank-level (r:b:sb) or bank-level parallelism (r:sb:b) since both levels can be accessed in parallel. In contrast, both b:r:sb and b:sb:r introduces significant performance drop. The reason is these two schemes suppress the sub-bank-level

(a) Single-core

(b) Four-core

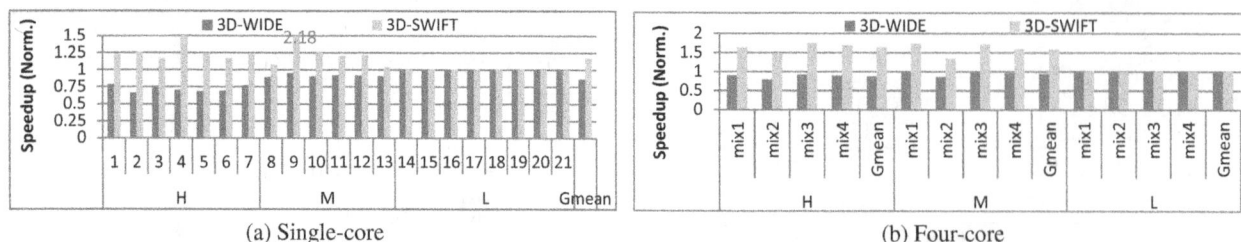

Figure 7: Performance results of single-core and 4-core simulation. All results are normalized to 2D DRAM design.

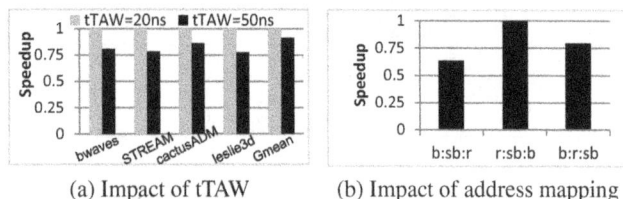

(a) Impact of tTAW   (b) Impact of address mapping

Figure 8: Sensitivity Study. (a) Impact of tTAW; (b) Performance with different address mapping schemes. "r"–row, "b"–bank, "sb"–sub-bank.

parallelism. In particular, b:sb:r is the worst case since it maps a large continuous memory space to a single sub-bank, where lots of sub-bank conflicts are fired so that following memory requests must stall and access the sub-bank sequentially. As a result, the overall performance drops by 33.5% and some applications even experiences 75% degradation. Therefore, 3D-SWIFT adopts r:b:sb as the solution.

6. CONCLUSION

In this work, we propose a fine-grained 3D-stacked Wide IO DRAM architecture–3D-SWIFT, to exploit high memory parallelism for improving performance and power efficiency. Sub-bank autonomy and packet-based interface protocol are devised to simplify the MC design. The experiment results show that 3D-SWIFT can achieve 64.7% and 87.6% performance improvement than conventional 2D DRAM and 3D Wide IO, respectively. The results indicates the promising future of 3D-SWIFT.

7. REFERENCES

[1] JEDEC Solid State Technology Association, "JEDEC Standard: Wide I/O Single Data Rate Specification," http://www.jedec.org/standards-documents/results/jesd229, Dec. 2011.

[2] J. T. Pawlowski, "Hybrid Memory Cube," *HotChip'11*, Aug. 2011.

[3] Tezzaron, "Octopus 8-Port DRAM for Die-Stack Applications," http://www.tezzaron.com/memory/Octopus.html, 2010.

[4] U. Kang, H. Chung, S. Heo, S.-H. Ahn, H. Lee *et al.*, "8Gb 3D DDR3 DRAM Using Through-Silicon-Via Technology," in *ISSCC'09*, Feb. 2009, pp. 130–131.

[5] T. Zhang, Y. Xie *et al.*, "A Customized Design of DRAM Controller for on-chip 3D DRAM Stacking," in *CICC'10*, Sep. 2010, pp. 1–4.

[6] D. H. Kim, K. Athikulwongse, M. Healy, M. Hossain, M. Jung *et al.*, "3D-MAPS: 3D Massively Parallel Processor with Stacked Memory," in *ISSCC'12*, Feb. 2012, pp. 188–190.

[7] M. Ghosh and H.-H. S. Lee, "Smart Refresh: An Enhanced Memory Controller Design for Reducing Energy in Conventional and 3D Die-Stacked DRAMs," in *MICRO'40*, Dec. 2007, pp. 134–145.

[8] P. Jain, D. Jiao, X. Wang, and C. H. Kim, "Measurement, Analysis and Improvement of Supply Noise in 3D ICs," in *VLSI Circuits Digest*, Jun. 2011, pp. 46–47.

[9] M. B. Healy and S. K. Lim, "Power-Supply-Network Design in 3D Integrated Systems," in *ISQED'11*, Mar. 2011, pp. 223–228.

[10] B. Jacob, S. W. NG, and D. T. Wang, *Memory Systems: Cache, DRAM, Disk.* Morgan Kaufmann, 2007.

[11] Y. Kim, D. Han, O. Mutlu, and M. Harchol-Balter, "ATLAS: A Scalable and High-performance Scheduling Algorithm for Multiple Memory Controllers," in *HPCA'16*, Jan. 2010, pp. 43–54.

[12] S. P. Muralidhara, L. Subramanian, O. Mutlu, M. Kandemir, and T. Moscibroda, "Reducing Memory Interference in Multicore Systems via Application-Aware Memory Channel Partitioning," in *MICRO'44*, Dec. 2011, pp. 374–385.

[13] HPCWire, "NVIDIA Bill Dally Talks 3D Chips and More at GTC."

[14] D. H. Woo, N. H. Seong, and H.-H. S. Lee, "Pragmatic Integration of an SRAM Row Cache in Heterogeneous 3-D DRAM Architecture Using TSV," *TVLSI*, pp. 1–13, Dec. 2011.

[15] T. Shah, "Fabmem: A Multiported RAM and CAM Compiler for Superscalar Design Space Exploration," *Thesis*, 2010.

[16] K. Chen, S. Li, N. Muralimanohar, J. H. Ahn, J. Brockman, and N. Jouppi, "CACTI-3DD: Architecture-level Modeling for 3D Die-stacked DRAM Main Memory," in *DATE'12*, Mar. 2012, pp. 33–38.

[17] International Technology Roadmap for Semiconductors, http://www.itrs.net/, 2009.

[18] A.-C. Hsieh, T. Hwang, M.-T. Chang, M.-H. Tsai, C.-M. Tseng, and H.-C. Li, "TSV Redundancy: Architecture and Design Issues in 3D IC," in *DATE'10*, Mar. 2010, pp. 166–171.

[19] N. Binkert, B. Beckmann, G. Black, S. K. Reinhardt, A. Saidi *et al.*, "The gem5 Simulator," *Computer Architecture News*, vol. 39, no. 2, pp. 1–7, Aug. 2011.

[20] P. Rosenfeld, E. Cooper-Balis, and B. Jacob, "DRAMSim2: A Cycle Accurate Memory System Simulator," *Computer Architecture Letters*, vol. 10, no. 1, pp. 16–19, Jan.–Jun. 2011.

[21] Standard Performance Evaluation Corporation, "SPEC2006 CPU," http://www.spec.org/cpu2006.

[22] J. D. McCalpin, "STREAM Benchmark," http://www.cs.virginia.edu/stream.

[23] S. Rixner, W. J. Dally, U. J. Kapasi, P. Mattson, and J. D. Owens, "Memory Access Scheduling," in *ISCA'27*, Jun. 2000, pp. 128–138.

[24] A. N. Udipi, N. Muralimanohar, N. Chatterjee, R. Balasubramonian, A. Davis, and N. P. Jouppi, "Rethinking DRAM Design and Organization for Energy-constrained Multi-cores," in *ISCA'37*, Jun. 2010, pp. 175–186.

Minimum Implant Area-Aware Gate Sizing and Placement

Andrew B. Kahng[†‡] and Hyein Lee[†]

[†]ECE and [‡]CSE Departments, University of California at San Diego

abk@ucsd.edu, hyeinlee@ucsd.edu

ABSTRACT

With reduction of minimum feature size, the *minimum implant area* (MinIA) constraint is emerging as a new challenge for the physical implementation flow in sub-22nm technology. In particular, the MinIA constraint induces a new problem formulation wherein gate sizing and V_t-swapping must now be linked closely with detailed placement changes. To solve this new problem, we propose heuristic methods that fix MinIA violations and reduce power with gate sizing while minimizing placement perturbation to avoid creating extra timing violations. Compared to recent versions of commercial P&R tools, our methodologies achieve significant reductions (up to 100%) in the number of MinIA violations under timing/power constraints.

1. INTRODUCTION

As minimum feature sizes decrease, physical design rules have become tighter. Geometric constraints for layout that arise from limits of patterning technology are described as design rules in technology files such as LEF [17]. Each layer has width, spacing, minimum-area, etc. rules which can affect the legality of standard-cell placement. Implant (active) layers, which indicate regions for ion implantation, determine the threshold voltage (V_t) of transistors. Figure 1 shows the implant region in standard cells and an example *minimum implant area* (MinIA) layer rule in the LEF file. As shown in the figure, the polygons of implant layers have drawn dimensions typically matched to the width of standard cells.

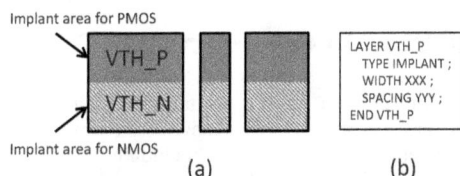

Figure 1: (a) Illustration of implant layer regions in standard cells. (b) An example of an implant layer rule in a LEF5.7 file.

MinIA layer rules affect multi-V_t standard cell-based designs; the multi-V_t regime is essential to achieve low-leakage, high-performance design implementations [4]. Traditional timing- and routability-driven placement of cells with multiple V_t values can result in a small island of a given V_t that cannot meet the MinIA layer rule. A small cell that cannot meet the MinIA rule must be abutted with cells having the same V_t, so as to form a wider implant layer polygon. That is, a narrow cell cannot be sandwiched between different-V_t cells. Figure 2 shows an example of a MinIA violation. The dotted line indicates the minimum width of the V_{t_2} implant layer. A narrow cell c_2 with V_{t_2} is surrounded by V_{t_1} cells, and this violates the MinIA (equivalently, width) constraint. We note that the impact of the MinIA rule can be huge when

the proportion of small-width cells in the netlist is large; this is a common scenario especially in cost-driven, low-power mobile IC products. We have studied how "thin" a netlist can be. For example, in a *jpeg* netlist synthesized from OpenCores [19] using a 28nm FDSOI foundry library, the smallest and second-smallest cell widths comprise ~18% and ~23% of the total number of instances, respectively.

The (minimum width and spacing) design rules for implant layers have not been critical before, as cell sizes have been large enough to cover these minimum rules. Hence, up until recent technology generations, placement and gate sizing/V_t-swapping methods have not had to consider these rules, since any legal cell placement would be correct with respect to the MinIA criterion. However, as cell sizes have continued to shrink in advanced process nodes, even as the wavelength used in 193i optical lithography remains constant, the MinIA rule has become larger than the minimum width of standard cells (e.g., INV×1 cell). MinIA rules constrain cell placement starting with the foundry "20nm" (64nm minimum metal pitch) node, due to the minimum pattern size limits and cell library (diffusion layer layout) strategies.

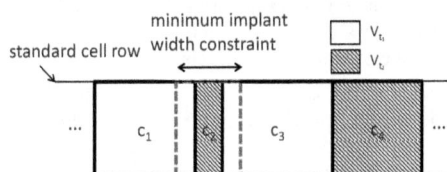

Figure 2: An example of the minimum implant area violation. The dotted line indicates the minimum width constraint of the implant layer. The cell instance c_2 (V_{t_2}) violates the constraint as it is narrow and sandwiched by two cells (c_1 and c_3) that have a different V_t (V_{t_1}).

The minimum width constraint of implant layers changes the traditional placement and post-layout gate sizing problems. That is, beyond existing constraints such as timing, power and area, additional *geometric* information of cells must be considered. A major change to the traditional sizing problem formulation is that even downsizing and V_t-swapping operations must comprehend spatially adjacent cell instances and whitespace in order to avoid creation of sandwiched narrow cells. Further, placement algorithms must comprehend V_t assignment of spatially adjacent cell instances, as well as whitespace, for the same reason. Therefore, the two problems cannot be solved independently. A unified method that considers both cell size/V_t and placement together is needed.

Case study of P&R tools. Recently, commercial P&R tools have claimed that minimum implant area rules are considered during the implementation, given that filler cells with active layers can be used to improve active density and manage STI stress effects [15]. Commercial P&R tools apparently fix the minimum implant area violations by inserting filler cells at the final design stage. For example, Mentor Graphics *Olympus* [18] has a utility to define an implant layer group for filler cells, so that each narrow cell can be padded filler cells having the same implant type. Cadence *Encounter Digital Implementation System (EDI)* [16] checks and fixes implant area violations according to the rules specified in LEF, during placement and filler cell insertion. Synopsys *IC Compiler (ICC)* [21] offers a *Voltage-threshold-aware filler cell insertion* flow according to which users can define the V_t filler cells to be inserted between different V_t regions. For example, users can insert NVT filler cells between NVT and HVT cells, and LVT filler cells between LVT and NVT cells. In our case studies of P&R tools, we assign HVT filler cells to HVT-NVT and HVT-LVT pairs, and NVT filler cells to NVT-LVT pairs. We have tested commercial P&R tools using two small netlists (*dma* and *aes*) synthesized from OpenCores [19] RTL, and a 45nm foundry library along with intentionally tightened MinIA constraints. The minimum implant layer rules are defined in LEF. The portion of each V_t type in the testcases is evenly distributed so as to heighten the number of MinIA rule violations. The utilizations in the *dma* and *aes* implementations are 77% and 82%, respectively. Figure 3(c) shows example commands used with current P&R tools. After routing, the tools' built-in filler cell insertion flows are applied. The results shown in Figure 3 (a) and (b) show that commercial P&R tools cannot fix all of the MinIA violations by simply inserting filler cells.

This work. We have discussed how MinIA rules change the gate sizing and placement problems, and we have observed that commercial P&R tools can handle this new issue only to a limited extent. To our knowledge, no work in the research literature has tried to solve MinIA violations systematically, for both gate sizing and placement. The main contributions of our work are summarized as follows.

- We redefine traditional placement and gate sizing problems in view of the minimum implant layer constraint.
- We propose methods to minimize MinIA violations and optimize power under the MinIA constraint with placement perturbation and gate sizing/V_t-swapping.
- Our proposed methods are implemented with C++ programs and incorporated into a standard P&R flow. Our methods are validated with a commercial tool and 45nm foundry library with a range of MinIA constraints.

The remainder of this paper is organized as follows. In Section 2, we review relevant prior work. Section 3 describes various problem formulations that consider both gate sizing and placement under minimum implant layer constraints. To address these problems, we introduce a heuristic approach for sequential sizing and placement considering minimum implant layer rules. The overall flow of our optimization is described in Section 4. Section 5 provides experimental results and analysis. We give conclusions and ongoing research directions in Section 6.

2. PREVIOUS WORK

Gate sizing, and co-optimization with placement. Traditional gate sizing, which optimizes power and delay of circuits using size (gate width), V_t, and gate length of cells, has been extensively reviewed in [12]. Co-optimization of placement and gate sizing has had limited previous consideration. Lee and Gupta [11] suggest LP-based gate sizing considering an ECO cost, which is computed with respect to power and area and modeled as a linear function of several parameters. The objective is to minimize "power + ECO cost". Luo et al. [14] minimize power by combining placement, sizing and V_t-swapping optimizations using a slack management technique. The placement, sizing and V_t-swapping phases are performed sequentially.

Linear (1-D) placement. Since MinIA violations do not occur between standard cell rows, the associated problem of obtaining a MinIA-legal placement can be treated as a type of linear (1-D) placement. In the related literature, Kahng et al. [10] and Brenner et al. [1] consider the problem of placing a set of cells in a single row with a fixed horizontal ordering, with the objective of minimizing the (weighted) sum of net bounding box perimeters. The paper [8] evaluates several techniques to legalize cell overlaps in row-based placements, so as to improve metrics of routability and routed wirelength. In [3], Gupta et al. describe a dynamic programming (DP) based technique for Assist-Feature Correctness (AFCorr) in

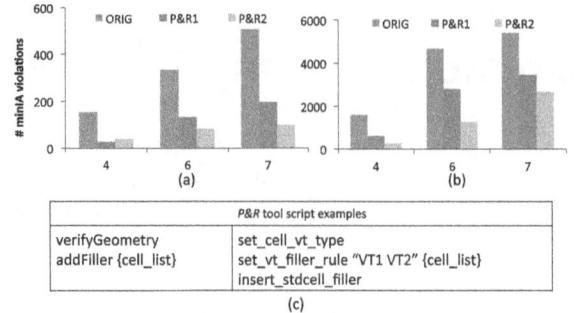

Figure 3: Minimum implant area violation fix results from two commercial tools (P&R1 and P&R2) through filler cell insertion, for two testcases: (a) *dma* and (b) *aes*. The x-axis shows the minimum implant width constraints in the number of grids. (c) The commands used for filler cell insertion flow.

detailed placement of standard-cell designs. Their implementation achieves improved depth of focus and CD control, and subsequent works from the same group use similar DP methods to address leakage and other objectives.

Layout effect-aware placement. STI stress-aware placement has tangential similarity to our MinIA placement, in the sense that solutions can seek to increase implant area; however, the main objective is different. Joshi et al. [5] propose stress as a means to achieve an optimal power-performance tradeoff. They study how stress-induced performance enhancements are affected by layout properties, and they improve standard-cell layouts to achieve maximum performance gain with dual-V_t assignment. Kahng et al. [9] combine detailed placement and active-layer fill insertion to exploit STI stress for performance improvement. Chakraborty et al. [2] propose an active area sizing aware cell-level delay model which forms the basis of linear programming to achieve either maximum performance, or target performance under a resource budget. Li et al. [13] present a methodology to determine optimal STI well width; using geometric programming, they also solve a STI stress aware placement optimization formulation.

3. PROBLEM FORMULATION

Given a placed standard-cell design[1] with potential MinIA rule violations, our ultimate goal is to find location and sizing/V_t assignment for each cell, so as to achieve minimum power without any violation of design constraints – including timing, placement legality, and MinIA rule constraints. Implicitly, our problem formulation assumes the following. (1) We do not consider violations that occur inside of a cell; individual cells are assumed correct by construction. (2) We assume that the minimum width of an implant region inside a cell is always the same as the cell width. (3) We do not consider the height of implant regions within a cell; again, correctness by construction is assumed. To optimize power considering both timing and geometry information, we combine gate sizing and ECO placement to address MinIA-aware gate sizing and placement problem:

Problem: *MinIA-aware sizing and placement*

Minimize: $\sum_{\forall c} P(c)$

Subject to:

$$S(c) > 0 \qquad \text{(T1)}$$
$$T_r(c) < T_{r_{max}} \qquad \text{(T2)}$$
$$W_e(c) < I_{min}(V_t(c)), \ \forall c \qquad \text{(P1)}$$
$$\text{No overlap in placement} \qquad \text{(P2)}$$

Here, (T1) and (T2) are the timing-related constraints: (T1) is the setup (max path delay) slack constraint, and (T2) is the maximum transition time constraint. (P1) and (P2) are the placement-related

---

[1] Possibly, the design is routed as well, depending on preferences regarding parasitic estimation accuracy versus turnaround time.

constraints: (P1) is the minimum implant area constraint, and (P2) is the placement legality (non-overlapping) constraint. Additional constraints such as max capacitance, hold time checks, and various other physical design rules can be transparently considered within the approaches that we propose. We omit discussion of these for simplicity of exposition.

Table 1: Notations used in this work. Note that $W_e(c)$ is the maximum width of any contiguous region of an implant layer in c. Also note that $B(c)$ includes minimum implant area violations.

Notation	Meaning
$P(c)$	leakage power of cell c
$V_t(c)$	threshold voltage of cell c
$S(c)$	timing slack of cell c
$T_r(c)$	transition time of cell c
$T_{r_{max}}$	max transition time constraint
$W_e(c)$	effective implant layer width of cell c
$B(c)$	violations caused by cell c in placement
$\{N(c)\}$	neighbor cells of cell c
$I_{min}(V_t)$	minimum implant area constraint for V_t
m_k	a potential sizing solution

When we optimize both sizing and ECO placement via any sequential/iterative procedure, it is clear that gate sizing will minimize power at the cost of potential violations (in particular, with respect to MinIA placement rules), and that these violations must be fixed by an ECO placement step. Further, the sizing and placement problems naturally have different objectives and constraints. How we combine the two problems in a single framework will induce any of several basic heuristic approaches:

Heur1. Size cells freely (enforcing only the (T1)(T2) constraints, as is traditional in gate-sizing formulations), and fix placement at a later stage (enforcing all of (T1)(T2)(P1)(P2)).

Heur2. Constrain sizing to enforce all placement and design rules (i.e., with enforcement of (T1)(T2)(P1)(P2)).

Heur3. Size cells with partial constraints of placement (enforcing (T1)(T2) constraints, and relaxed (P1)(P2) constraints), such that only a small number of violations require fixing at the ECO placement stage.

We observe that **Heur1** may achieve the best power reduction with its sizing optimization, but may also result in a large number of MinIA violations in placement. At the other extreme, **Heur2** may achieve only limited power reduction since all potential sizing moves for each cell are restricted by placement. **Heur3** may be viewed as a compromise between the two methods. We note that **Heur3** gives the best results in our experiments reported in Section 5 below.

A truly simultaneous optimization of sizing and placement for MinIA fixing is not obvious to us at this point: it appears difficult to explore the entire solution space since there are so many combinations of sizes, locations, V_t assignments, and filler cell assignments. For now, we have pursued sequential optimization of sizing and placement, with (i) a sizing heuristic that considers placement, and (ii) placement perturbation heuristics to fix post-sizing MinIA violations. For the placement optimization stage, we define a *MinIA-aware placement* problem, derived from the *MinIA-aware sizing and placement* problem, in which the objective is to minimize the number of violations:

Problem: *MinIA-aware placement*

Minimize: $\sum_{\forall c} B(c)$

Subject to: $S_c > 0$ (T1)

$T_r(c) < T_{r_{max}}$ (T2)

The **Experiment 1** discussion in Section 5 below assesses our placement algorithms in the context of this *MinIA-aware placement* problem.

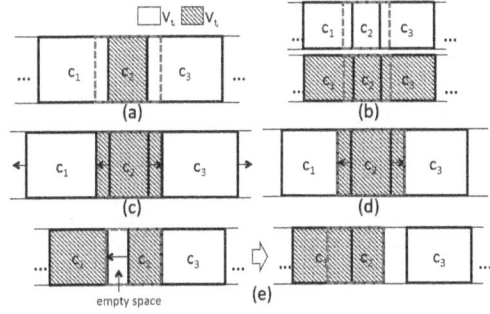

Figure 4: Available fixing approaches for MinIA rule violations. A given violation, depicted in (a), can be fixed by using (b) V_t-swapping, or (c) moving a neighbor cell, or (d) downsizing a neighbor, or (e) moving the narrow cell.

4. OUR APPROACHES

We now discuss our gate sizing and placement approaches considering MinIA constraints.

4.1 Minimum implant area-aware placement

Levers to solve MinIA rule violation. If violators of MinIA constraints have enough spacing around them, then the violations can be easily fixed by inserting same-V_t filler cells, thereby increasing the width of the implant area. However, when the spacing is insufficient, we must change cell size/V_t or perturb the placement, such that the implant layer region of the narrow cell can match up with an adjacent (abutting) implant layer region. Figure 4 illustrates four ways to fix a given violation. Suppose that cell c_2 with V_{t_2} violates the MinIA constraint, and that c_1 and c_3 are neighbor cells with V_{t_1}, as shown in Figure 4(a). First, we can fix the violation either by swapping V_t of c_2 to V_{t_1} or by swapping V_t of c_1 and c_3 to V_{t_2}; this is shown in Figure 4(b). Second, we can push out (i.e., shift) c_1 and c_3 to create spacing for filler cell insertion, as shown in Figure 4(c). Third, c_1 and c_3 can be downsized to create spacing around c_2, as shown in Figure 4(d). Fourth, the violator can be relocated so that it becomes abutted to a same-V_t cell, c_1 in Figure 4(e).

Algorithm 1 *MinIA*-aware Placement Heuristic

Procedure $fixMinImpVio(c, \{I_{min}\}, D)$
Input : a cell c, a set of min implant constraints $\{I_{min}\}$, a netlist D, a placement of D
Output : a sizing/location solution for $c \in D$

1: **for all** cell $c \in D$ **do**
2:    $s \leftarrow 0$;
3:    **for all** cell $n \in \{N(c)\}$ **do**
4:      $s \leftarrow s +$ spacing of c to n;
5:    **end for**
6:    $MinImpSlack \leftarrow c.width - I_{min}(V_t(c))$;
7:    **if** $s + MinImpSlack \geq 0$ **then** insert filler cells;
8: **end for**
9: **if** #violations is zero **then** return success;
10: **for all** cell $c \in D$ **do**
11:    **if** cell c violates **then** $ChangeVtCell(c)$;
12: **end for**
13: **if** #violations is zero **then** return success;
14: **for all** cell $c \in D$ **do**
15:    **if** cell c violates **then** $MoveNCell(c)$;
16: **end for**
17: **if** #violations is zero **then** return success;
18: **for all** cell $c \in D$ **do**
19:    **if** cell c violates **then** $DownSizeNCell(c)$;
20: **end for**
21: **if** #violations is zero **then** return success;

Heuristic approach for fixing minimum implant area violations. Algorithm 1 shows the overall flow of our heuristic approach, which is based on the four MinIA violation-fixing approaches noted above. First, whitespace around violating cells is calculated (Line 3). If there is enough spacing, sufficient width of same-V_t filler cells is inserted to fix the violation (Line 8). In the next step, V_t-swapping is performed for the violating cell or its neighbor cells with *ChangeV$_t$Cell* (Line 13). For any violations remaining after this step, there is no space for insertion of filler cells and V_t-swapping is unavailable due to timing constraints. Thus, we try to create spacing by changing the placement. We first try to move neighbor cells (Line 17).[2] Then, downsizing of neighbor cells (Line 21) can be tried if those cells are not timing-critical. Note that these steps can be performed in a different order – e.g., downsizing of neighbor cells can be performed before moving cells. The particular sequence of optimizations of steps used in our flow has been experimentally determined. Filler insertion is performed first, since it does not require any cost. Our studies of the permutations of V_t-*swapping*, *moving* and *downsizing cells* indicate that downsizing of cells occurs very rarely, since many cells are small and timing violations can result. With respect to V_t-swapping and moving cells, the results are better when V_t-swapping is performed first (e.g. #MinIA violations of V_t-*swapping-first* and *moving-first* are 155 and 44, respectively, for the *jpeg* testcase). We also note that our heuristic flow executes steps occur in an order that minimizes perturbation of placement or sizing.

Subroutine 1 Functions for *MinIA*-aware Placement Heuristic

1: **Procedure** *ChangeV$_t$Cell(c)*
2: Input : a cell c
3: Output : V_t solutions for c and its neighbor cells
4: // Change V_t of the violator
5: $V_{t_{orig}} \leftarrow V_t(c)$;
6: **for all** cell $n \in \{N(c)\}$ **do**
7: $\quad V_t(c) \leftarrow V_t(n)$;
8: $\quad w \leftarrow$ total width of c and $\{N(c)\}$;
9: $\quad$ **if** $w \geq I_{min}(V_t(c))$ && c does not violate timing **then** return success;
10: $\quad$ **else** $V_t(c) \leftarrow V_{t_{orig}}$;
11: **end for**
12: // V_t-swapping for neighbors
13: **for all** cell $n \in \{N(c)\}$ **do**
14: $\quad V_{t_{orig}} \leftarrow V_t(n)$; $V_t(n) \leftarrow V_t(c)$;
15: $\quad$ **if** n violates timing **then**
16: $\quad\quad V_t(n) \leftarrow V_{t_{orig}}$; continue;
17: $\quad$ **end if**
18: $\quad w \leftarrow$ total width of c and its neighbor cells;
19: $\quad$ **if** $w \geq I_{min}(V_t(c))$ **then** return success;
20: **end for**

1: **Procedure** *MoveNCell(c)*
2: Input : a cell c
3: Output : location solutions for c's neighbor cells
4: $n_{cl} \leftarrow$ the left neighbor cell; $n_{cr} \leftarrow$ the right neighbor cell;
5: $s \leftarrow$ spacing of c to n_{cl} and n_{cr};
6: $MinImpSlack \leftarrow c.width - I_{min}(V_t(c))$;
7: **if** n_{cl} has leftside space Δ **then**
8: $\quad d \leftarrow max(-(MinImpSlack + s), \Delta)$; Move n_{cl} by d; $s \leftarrow s + d$;
9: **end if**
10: **if** $s + MinImpSlack < 0$ **then**
11: $\quad$ **if** n_{cr} has rightside space Δ **then**
12: $\quad\quad d \leftarrow max(-(MinImpSlack + s), \Delta)$; Move n_{cr} by d; $s \leftarrow s + d$;
13: $\quad$ **end if**
14: **end if**
15: **if** $s + MinImpSlack \geq 0$ **then**
16: $\quad$ insert filler cells; return success;
17: **else**
18: $\quad$ return fail;
19: **end if**

Details of two levers are described in Subroutine 1. *ChangeV$_t$Cell* tries V_t-swapping for c, using any V_t in $\{N(c)\}$, and checks timing and MinIA violations. If there is any violation, the V_t-swapping of c is reverted (Line 10). In a similar way, V_t-swapping of neighbor cells is tried. *MoveNCell(c)* moves neighbor

cells to create additional space. It first checks whitespace around the left and right neighbor cells and moves these cells if possible, similar to [9]. We limit the movement of cells to avoid large perturbation of placement, in light of the timing impact of cell placement.[3]

Our minimum implant area-aware placement can be used standalone, in an ECO methodology, to fix MinIA violations. We evaluate our approach with various minimum implant area constraints in Section 5, **Experiment 1**.

4.2 Minimum implant area-aware gate sizing

Our gate sizing method is based on sensitivity-guided gate sizing [6] [7]. In addition to timing constraints, we consider the placement constraints (P1)(P2) described in Section 3. Our objective is to minimize power without creating any additional (P1)(P2) violations.

Algorithm 2 *MinIA*-aware Gate Sizing Heuristic

Procedure *GSMinImp($\{I_{min}\}, D$)*
Input : minimum implant constraints $\{I_{min}\}$, a netlist D, a placement of D, a set of timing constraints
Output : a sizing solution
1: $M \leftarrow \emptyset$
2: **for all** cell c in the netlist D **do**
3: $\quad$ **if** c is downsizable **then**
4: $\quad\quad m_k.c \leftarrow c$; $m_k.m \leftarrow downsize$; $m_k.cost \leftarrow \Delta TNS$;
5: $\quad\quad m_k.sensitivity \leftarrow \Delta Leakage/m_k.cost$;
6: $\quad\quad M \leftarrow M \cup m_k$;
7: $\quad$ **end if**
8: $\quad$ **if** c_i is not a highest V_t cell **then**
9: $\quad\quad m_k.c \leftarrow c$; $m_k.m \leftarrow V_t$ upscaling; $m_k.cost \leftarrow \Delta TNS$;
10: $\quad\quad V_{t_{orig}} \leftarrow V_t(c_i)$;
11: $\quad\quad V_t(c) \leftarrow$ higher V_t; // placement cost calculation
12: $\quad\quad \{N(c)\} \leftarrow \{N(c)\} \cup c$;
13: $\quad\quad$ **for all** $n \in \{N(c)\}$ **do**
14: $\quad\quad\quad$ **if** n violates $I_{min}(V_t(n))$ **then**
15: $\quad\quad\quad\quad$ **if** fixable by V_t-swapping/sizing/move of neighbors n **then**
16: $\quad\quad\quad\quad\quad m_k.cost \leftarrow m_k.cost + CalCost(n)$;
17: $\quad\quad\quad\quad$ **else**
18: $\quad\quad\quad\quad\quad$ break; continue to the next c_i;
19: $\quad\quad\quad\quad$ **end if**
20: $\quad\quad\quad$ **end if**
21: $\quad\quad$ **end for**
22: $\quad\quad V_t(c) \leftarrow V_{t_{orig}}$; $m_k.sensitivity \leftarrow \Delta Leakage/m_k.cost$; $M \leftarrow M \cup m_k$;
23: $\quad$ **end if**
24: **end for**
25: **while** $M \neq \emptyset$ **do**
26: $\quad$ Pick a m_k with maximum *sensitivity* in M; Commit m_k; $M \leftarrow M \setminus m_k$;
27: $\quad$ *STA()*;
28: $\quad$ Fix the extra MinIA violations;
29: $\quad$ **if** $!feasible()$ **then** restore m_k;
30: **end while**

For each gate, we check whether the potential sizing produces violations that require placement perturbations or sizing of neighbor cells to be resolved. If the neighbor cells need to be changed or relocated, we estimate the timing impact on neighbor cells and add this to the sensitivity function. During gate sizing to recover power, a gate can be downsized or its V_t can be swapped to a higher threshold voltage. Downsizing a gate can produce violations, but if neighbor cells do not consume the whitespace created by downsizing, the violations can be easily cured by inserting filler cells. However, when a gate is V_t-swapped and creates violations by itself or in relation to its neighbor cells, possible fixing methods should be carefully explored. Algorithm 2 describes our sizing flow. $\Delta Leakage/cost$ is used as our sensitivity function. The default cost is the change in total negative slack

---

[2]We do not need to try moving the target cell (Figure 4(e)) as this case could have been fixed at the filler cell insertion stage.

[3]We observe that up to 10 placement grids of movement will change timing by less than 2 ps with the 45nm foundry library. We allow perturbation of cell location by up to 10 grids.

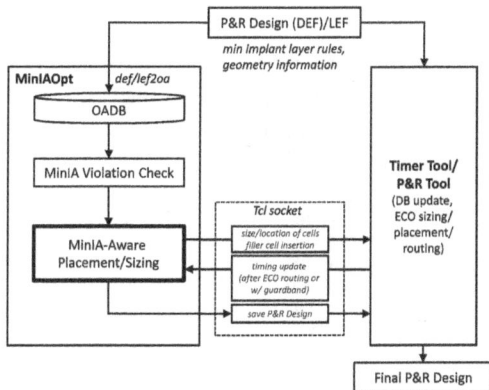

Figure 5: Overall flow of our optimizer, *MinIAOpt*.

(*TNS*). When MinIA violations occur, we additionally calculate potential decrease (worsening) of *TNS* from changing neighbor cells to fix the violations (*CalCost()*, Line 16). This calculated cost is then added to *cost* so that the *sensitivity* decreases.

4.3 Overall flow

Figure 5 shows the overall flow of our optimizer, *MinIAOpt*. A DEF file of a routed netlist, and LEF files for geometry information of standard cells and technology information including the minimum implant layer rules, are converted into *OpenAccess* [20] DB using *def/lef2oa* parsers. The minimum implant area-aware gate sizing is performed to reduce leakage power with considerations of geometry information. Further minimum implant area-aware placement optimization can be performed to fix MinIA violations without creating new timing violations. For both stages, a *Tcl* socket interface is used to enable the communication between the P&R tool and/or timer tool and our optimizer. Via this interface, *MinIAOpt* can send commands to insert filler cells, size/V_t-swap cells and change the locations of cells, as well as obtain updated timing information after ECO routing. We also can use a quick timing estimation from timer tools without ECO routing to achieve faster runtime while sacrificing some accuracy.[4]

5. EXPERIMENTAL RESULTS

5.1 Experimental setup

Our program is written in C++, and the interface to support DEF/LEF [17] is implemented using the *OpenAccess 2.6* [20] API. We use a *Tcl*-socket interface (*Tcl/Tk 8.4* [23]) to communicate with P&R and timer tools similar to Trident2.0 [7] and SensOpt [24]. We have applied our proposed method to a set of open-source designs [19], which we synthesize from RTL using *Synopsys Design Compiler H-2013.03-SP3* [22]. For P&R, we use *Cadence Encounter Digital Implementation System XL 13.1* [16]. Implementations in all experiments are with a 45nm foundry technology and library.

Table 2 shows the testcases used in our experiments. We compare to the result of a simple filler cell insertion performed by a commercial P&R tool with high-utilization testcases that are synthesized with a standard implementation flow. We test various MinIA constraints to understand the scaling of algorithm performance with instance difficulty (e.g., reflecting MinIA constraints in future technology nodes). The utilization, the distribution of cell V_t values[5], and the percentage of smaller

cells (% Mincells) with width less than the minimum implant area constraints all affect the difficulty of a given testcase. We use various minimum implant width constraints *Const*1, *Const*2 and *Const*3, corresponding to four, six and seven, respectively. In the 45nm library, 3%, 12% and 28% of standard cells are narrower than these constraints. Also, to study the sensitivity of the results to the difficulty of problem instances, we intentionally tweak the V_t cell distribution of *aes* and generate *aes_var** so that the same placement will have various numbers of MinIA violations. All experiments are performed on a 2.5GHz Intel Xeon Linux workstation.

Table 2: Testcases used in the experiments. *WS, Period, Leak* are worst slack, clock period and leakage power, respectively, after routing, before filler cell insertion stage.

Bench	#Inst	Util (%)	Mincells (%)	V_t(H/N/L) (%)	WS (ps)	Period (ns)	Leak (mW)
dma	1168	78	59	78/4/16	137	1.0	0.050
mpeg	7121	82	64	83/6/9	39	1.25	0.363
aes	9611	75	84	95/1/2	21	1.5	0.238
jpeg	44911	81	68	82/8/8	36	1.6	2.413
aes_var1	9611	75	84	40/30/30	39	2.1	0.129
aes_var2	9611	75	84	60/20/20	82	2.4	0.106
aes_var3	9611	75	84	80/10/10	137	2.5	0.080

5.2 Experimental results

Experiment 1: Evaluation of MinIA-fix algorithms. Our first experiment evaluates the MinIA-fix algorithm under power and timing constraints. In Table 3, *Commercial P&R* indicates the result of simple filler cell insertion performed by a commercial P&R tool. *Δ#Vio.(%)* shows the absolute (relative) change in number of MinIA violations compared to the original number of violations (negative numbers indicate that the number of violations is reduced). *Commercial P&R* does not change the design, and the runtime is almost zero. However, it fixes only 36% of MinIA violations in the worst case (i.e., 64% of violations remain), and 74% on average across all testcases. By contrast, our heuristic substantially reduces the number of MinIA violations (97% in the worst case, and by 99% on average). Note that the WS of all testcases is positive even though *ΔWS* is negative for the case of *mpeg* with *Const*3, *aes_var2* and *aes_var3*. *Fill (%)* indicates the portion of the total area occupied by filler cells. We see that the numbers are very small, which means that whitespace is not all consumed by filler cells. The *CPU total/tool* shows the total runtime, and the time consumed by the socket interface between external tools (i.e., P&R and timer tool) and our optimizer. Nearly all of the total runtime is consumed by external tools, since the operations used during the optimization such as adding filler cells, moving and/or sizing a cell take *O(few seconds per operation)*.

Experiment 2: MinIA-aware sizing. Our second experiment evaluates three approaches – free sizing (**Heur 1**), restricted sizing (**Heur 2**) and MinIA-aware sizing (**Heur 3**) with our heuristic approach (Algorithm 2) in terms of leakage power, timing and the number of MinIA violations. *Const*3 is used for the minimum implant width constraint. Table 4 shows **Heur 1**, **Heur 2** and **Heur 3** results after sizing. Although the leakage power values are smallest with **Heur 1**, the increase in number of MinIA violations is up to 151% of the original number of MinIA violations. With **Heur 2**, the leakage power values are high since the sizing is prevented from creating any violation for the target cell. The increase in number of violations comes from the impact of sizing on neighbor cells. **Heur 3** shows near-zero or small increase in MinIA violations with less leakage power than **Heur 2**. In the **Heur 3** results, we see that solution quality in terms of leakage and

---

[4]For any change of cells, ECO routing should be performed and timing should be updated accordingly. But, performing ECO routing for each cell change takes too much time to be practically feasible. To compensate for the inaccuracy, a timing guardband can be used.

[5]The percentage of each V_t type relative to the total number of cells. H/N/L indicates HVT, NVT and LVT %, respectively.

Table 3: Results for a simple filler insertion and our heuristic method.

Bench	MinIA Const	Orig. #Vio.	Commercial P&R Δ #Vio. (%)	Heuristic Δ WS (ps)	Δ Leak (mW)	Fill (%)	Δ #Vio. (%)	CPU total / tool (min)
dma	Const1	71	-53 (-75)	0	0.000	0.4	-71 (-100)	1.9 / 1.0
	Const2	128	-93 (-73)	0	0.000	1.7	-128 (-100)	2.1 / 1.1
	Const3	193	-151 (-78)	0	0.000	2.5	-193 (-100)	2.0 / 1.1
mpeg	Const1	183	-155 (-85)	0	0.000	0.1	-183 (-100)	4.6 / 3.7
	Const2	453	-322 (-71)	-1	0.000	0.7	-451 (-100)	5.9 / 5.0
	Const3	693	-515 (-74)	-18	0.000	1.0	-689 (-99)	6.7 / 5.8
aes	Const1	338	-327 (-97)	0	0.000	0.5	-338 (-100)	5.1 / 4.1
	Const2	978	-868 (-89)	0	0.000	2.6	-978 (-100)	8.2 / 7.2
	Const3	1146	-1005 (-88)	0	0.000	3.4	-1146 (-100)	8.7 / 7.8
jpeg	Const1	1341	-1186 (-88)	0	0.001	0.3	-1341 (-100)	25.3 / 24.3
	Const2	3865	-3079 (-80)	0	0.004	1.5	-3850 (-100)	73.8 / 72.9
	Const3	7864	-6077 (-77)	0	-0.002	2.5	-7820 (-99)	168.7 / 167.7
aes_var1		2955	-1069 (-36)	28	0.001	10.8	-2863 (-97)	32.3 / 31.4
aes_var2	Const3	2558	-1106 (-43)	-51	-0.002	8.5	-2492 (-97)	25.0 / 24.1
aes_var3		1816	-1014 (-56)	-84	-0.002	4.1	-1792 (-99)	15.6 / 14.7

Table 4: Results for our heuristic sizing algorithm. *Const3* is used for the minimum implant width constraint in this experiment.

Benchmarks	WS (ps) Heur1	Heur2	Heur3	Leak (mW) Heur1	Heur2	Heur3	Δ #Vio. (%) Heur1	Heur2	Heur3	CPU total / tool (min) Heur1	Heur2	Heur3
dma	3	131	**4**	0.046	0.048	**0.047**	64 (33)	50 (26)	**0 (0)**	7 / 5	5 / 3	**7 / 5**
mpeg2	3	19	**19**	0.298	0.315	**0.309**	376 (54)	164 (24)	**9 (1)**	43 / 41	27 / 26	**34 / 33**
aes	6	18	**18**	0.184	0.213	**0.203**	1734 (151)	814 (71)	**412 (36)**	98 / 96	51 / 50	**69 / 68**
jpeg	-5	9	**10**	1.898	2.109	**1.954**	4861 (62)	2921 (37)	**659 (8)**	1209 / 1207	663 / 662	**1093 / 1091**

timing is nearly maintained, while the number of MinIA violations is greatly reduced.

Additionally, we have applied our placement heuristic to the results of sizing. For *aes*, we observe that 22% of MinIA violations still remain in the result of **Heur 1**, while 3-4% of those are left for **Heur 2** and **Heur 3**. Note that the MinIA violations may increase the total area and power even though the initial leakage power might be less with **Heur 1**.

6. CONCLUSIONS

In this work, we have addressed a new gate sizing/V_t-swapping and placement problem with the *minimum implant area* (MinIA) constraint. The MinIA constraint presents a new challenge to the physical implementation flow in sub-22nm technology, and requires true co-optimization of placement and gate sizing/V_t-swapping. We have proposed sizing and placement heuristics that optimize power and fixes MinIA violations while minimizing placement perturbation. Compared to commercial P&R tools, our methods achieve significant reductions in the number of MinIA violations under timing/power constraints.

Our current heuristics cannot guarantee to minimize the perturbation of placement and/or the number of violations, though they are straightforward and easy to apply. Hence, similar to [3], we intend to study the use of dynamic programming to solve single-row placement with MinIA fixing. Procedure *fixRowMinImpVio()* sketches such an approach. Our ongoing work includes implementation of, and analysis of results from, dynamic programming based optimizations.

Procedure *fixRowMinImpVio*($\{I_{min}\}, R, \{T\}$)
Input : minimum implant constraints $\{I_{min}\}$, a placement of a standard-cell row R, a set of timing constraints $\{T\}$
Output : a sizing/placement solution for R
$\{c_i.sol\} \leftarrow \emptyset$;
// $\{c_i.sol\}$ = sizing/placement solutions from the left-most cell to the ith cell
for $i = 1$ to k **do**
   for all $\{l, v, s\}$, where $l = -W$ to W, $v =$ LVT, NVT, HVT, $s = -S$ to S **do**
     // $l = \Delta$ cell location, $v = V_t$, $s = \Delta$ cell size
     $Cost(c_{i,l,v,s}) \leftarrow \min_{j \in \{c_{i-1}.sol\}} Cost(\{c_{i,l,v,s}, j\})$
     // $Cost(*)$ = cost of power and minIA violations
     $\{c_i.sol\} \leftarrow \{c_i.sol\} \cup c_{i,l,v,s}.sol$;
   end for
end for
$sol \leftarrow$ the minimum cost solution in $\{c_k.sol\}$;
return sol;

---

7. REFERENCES

[1] U. Brenner and J. Vygen, "Faster Optimal Single-Row Placement with Fixed Ordering", *Proc. DATE*, 2000, pp. 117-121.

[2] A. Chakraborty, S. X. Shi and D. Z. Pan, "Stress Aware Layout Optimization Leveraging Active Area Dependent Mobility Enhancement", *IEEE Trans. on CAD* 29(10) (2010), pp. 1533-1545.

[3] P. Gupta, A. B. Kahng and C.-H. Park, "Detailed Placement for Improved Depth of Focus and CD Control", *Proc. ASPDAC*, 2005, pp. 343-348.

[4] ITRS Low-Power Design Technology Roadmap, Design Chapter Table DESN14, 2011. http://public.itrs.net/reports.html

[5] V. Joshi, B. Cline, D. Sylvester, D. Blaauw and K. Agarwal, "Leakage Power Reduction Using Stress-Enhanced Layouts", *Proc. DAC*, 2008, pp. 912-917.

[6] J. Hu, A. B. Kahng, S. Kang, M.-C. Kim and I. L. Markov, "Sensitivity-Guided Metaheuristics for Accurate Discrete Gate Sizing", *Proc. ICCAD*, 2012, pp. 233-239.

[7] A. B. Kahng, S. Kang, H. Lee, I. L. Markov and P. Thapar, "High-Performance Gate Sizing with a Signoff Timer", *Proc. ICCAD*, 2013, pp. 450-457.

[8] A. B. Kahng, I. L. Markov and S. Reda, "On Legalization of Row-Based Placements", *Proc. GLSVLSI*, 2004, pp. 214-219.

[9] A. B. Kahng, P. Sharma and R. O. Topaloglu, "Exploiting STI Stress for Performance", *Proc. ICCAD*, 2007, pp. 83-90.

[10] A. B. Kahng, P. Tucker and A. Zelikovsky, "Optimization of Linear Placements for Wirelength Minimization with Free Sites", *Proc. ASPDAC*, 1999, pp. 241-244.

[11] J. Lee and P. Gupta, "Incremental Gate Sizing for Late Process Changes", *Proc. ICCD*, 2010, pp. 215-221.

[12] J. Lee and P. Gupta, "Discrete Circuit Optimization", *Foundations and Trends in Electronic Design Automation* 6(1) (2012), pp. 1-120.

[13] J. Li, B. Yang, X. Hu, Q. Dong and S. Nakatake, "STI Stress Aware Placement Optimization Based On Geometric Programming", *Proc. GLSVLSI*, 2009, pp. 209-214.

[14] T. Luo, D. Newmark and D. Z. Pan, "Total Power Optimization Combining Placement, Sizing and Multi-Vt Through Slack Distribution Management", *Proc. ASPDAC*, 2008, pp. 352-357.

[15] L. Remy, P. Coll, F. Picot, P. Mico and J.-M. Portal, "Definition of an Innovative Filling Structure for Digital Blocks: the DFM Filler Cell", *Proc. ICECS*, 2009, pp. 73-76.

[16] Cadence SOC Encounter User Guide. http://www.cadence.com/products/di/first_encounter/pages/default.aspx

[17] LEF DEF reference. http://www.si2.org/openeda.si2.org/projects/lefdef

[18] Mentor Graphics Olympus-SoC. http://www.mentor.com/products/ic_nanometer_design/place-route/olympus-soc

[19] OpenCores: Open Source IP-Cores, http://www.opencores.org

[20] Si2 OpenAccess. http://www.si2.org/?page=69

[21] Synopsys IC Compiler User Guide. http://www.synopsys.com/Tools/Implementation/PhysicalImplementation/Pages/ICCompiler.aspx

[22] Synopsys Design Compiler User Guide. http://www.synopsys.com/Tools/Implementation/RTLSynthesis/DCUltra/Pages

[23] Tcl/Tk Built-in Commands Manual. http://www.tcl.tk/man/tcl8.4/TclCmd

[24] UCSD SensOpt Leakage Optimizer (A. B. Kahng and S. Kang, 2010-2011), http://vlsicad.ucsd.edu/SIZING/optimizer.html

A Multi-stage Leakage Aware Resource Management Technique for Reconfigurable Architectures

Nam Khanh Pham
Department of Electrical and
Computer Engineering
National University of
Singapore
a0095804@nus.edu.sg

Amit Kumar Singh
Department of Electrical and
Computer Engineering
National University of
Singapore
amit.singh@nus.edu.sg

Akash Kumar
Department of Electrical and
Computer Engineering
National University of
Singapore
akash@nus.edu.sg

ABSTRACT

Shrinking size of transistors has enabled us to integrate more and more logic elements into FPGA chips leading to higher computing power. However, it also brings serious concern to the leakage power dissipation of the FPGA devices. One of the major reasons for leakage power dissipation in FPGA is the utilization of prefetching technique to minimize the reconfiguration overhead (delay) in Partially Reconfigurable (PR) FPGAs. This technique creates delays between the reconfiguration and execution parts of a task, which may lead up to 44% leakage power of FPGA since the SRAM-cells containing reconfiguration information cannot be powered down. In this work, a resource management approach containing *scheduling*, *placement* and *post-placement* stages has been proposed to address the aforementioned issue. In scheduling stage, a leakage-aware cost function is derived to cope with the leakage power. The placement stage uses a cost function that allows designers to decide a trade-off between performance and leakage-saving. The post-placement stage employs a heuristic approach and shows further improvements. Experiments show that our approach can achieve large leakage savings for both synthetic and real life applications with acceptable extended deadline. Furthermore, different variants of the proposed approach can reduce leakage power by 40-65% when compared to a performance-driven approach and by 15-43% when compared to state-of-the-art works.

Categories and Subject Descriptors

B.7 [**Integrated Circuits**]: Design Aids; B.7.1 [**Integrated Circuits**]: Types and Design Styles—*Gate arrays*

General Terms

Design

Keywords

Resource management; FPGA; leakage aware

1. INTRODUCTION

Field-programmable gate arrays (FPGAs) are promising candidates for digital circuit implementation because of their growing density and speed, short design cycle, and steadily decreasing cost. Furthermore, most of the FPGA devices nowadays can be partially

reconfigured at run time, i.e., a configuration can be loaded into part of the device while the rest of the system continues operating. This feature obviously provides greater flexibility and more powerful computing ability. However, these advantages come with additional problems related to reconfiguration time and power dissipation.

A drawback of FPGA due to its hardware redundancy is its inefficiency in term of power consumption when compared to ASIC components [12] [16]. In practice, an FPGA circuit implementation may use only a fraction of the hardware resource but the power is dissipated in both the used and the unused components. The total power consumption includes static (leakage) and dynamic power [17], and their contribution into the total power consumption heavily depends on the circuit technology. Beyond 65 nm technology, leakage power becomes an increasingly dominant component of total power dissipation [24]. This has motivated us to focus our work on reducing the leakage power dissipation.

Configuration prefetching [9] is a widely adopted technique for reducing the reconfiguration delay in Partially Reconfigurable (PR) FPGA. In prefetching, a task is loaded into the FPGA as soon as possible and this may result in overlap between the configuration part of the waiting task (to be executed) with the execution part of operating tasks, facilitating for reduced reconfiguration overhead (time). However, even after the task is loaded (prefetched), it may not execute and wait until few other tasks complete due to involved dependencies. Such waiting introduces delays between the configuration and execution part of the same task. During the delay interval, the SRAM-cells of the FPGA (containing bits of the waiting task to be executed) cannot be powered down to avoid the loss of configuration data from the cells. Therefore, the cells dissipate a significant amount of power.

Motivational Example: Fig. 1 presents an example to demonstrate aforementioned issues. In this example, the task graph on the left-hand side is scheduled on an FPGA platform with prefetching technique. During the interval between R3 and E3, the logic blocks of columns 1 and 2 can be powered down to remove leakage wastes. However, since the SRAM-cells of these columns cannot be powered down as the configuration data will be lost, they consume a considerable amount of power. As SRAM cells leakage contributes $\approx 38\%$ to FPGA leakage [22] (up to 44% for Spartan-3 family [21]), reducing FPGA SRAM leakage is of paramount importance.

In order to reduce leakage, a scheduling approach needs to be developed aiming at allocating reconfiguration and execution parts as close as possible while keeping task dependencies, timing and architecture constraints into account. Several works have been proposed to solve this problem [25], [10]. However, these works attempt to address the leakage problem in a single phase of the resource management process (details in later sections). As a result, the leakage power cannot be significantly reduced. It has also been

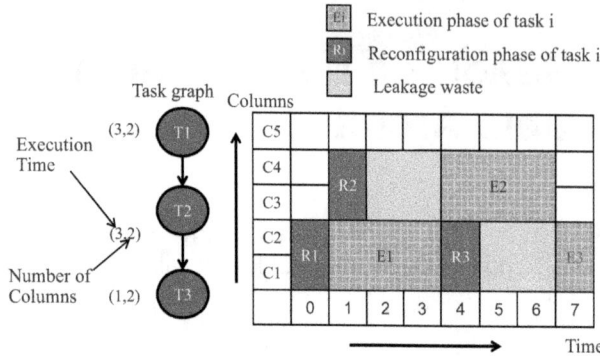

Figure 1: Example of Leakage Waste caused by Prefetching Technique

observed that there exists a trade-off between leakage savings and performance [25]. However, the trade-off analysis by employing the existing approaches is not efficient. A high degradation in performance is noticed in order to achieve small amount of leakage savings. To tackle the problem in a comprehensive perspective towards achieving high leakage reductions, we propose a multi-stage resource management approach consisting of three stages. Our main contributions to each stage are as follows:

- **Scheduling:** A list-scheduling algorithm has been developed with a specific priority function that is customized for addressing the leakage power reduction.

- **Placement:** A cost function has been derived for the placement stage to further reduce the leakage power. This function provides designers a flexibility to manage the trade-off between performance and leakage savings.

- **Post-placement:** A post-placement heuristic has been proposed to improve the scheduling results (leakage savings) from previous stages.

In our multi-stage approach, the application to be executed is processed iteratively in the scheduling and placement stage, where in each iteration the scheduling stage defines next application task to be placed in the placement stage by using a dynamic priority scheme (details in a later section). The placement stage identifies the FPGA column to map the task. Once all the application tasks are mapped, the post-placement stage tries to reduce gaps between configuration and execution parts for all the application tasks in order to improve results obtained from earlier stages. *To the best of our knowledge, this is the first work that considers leakage optimization in multiple stages while considering application deadline.*

Paper Organization: Section 2 presents state-of-the-art related to leakage power reduction. Section 3 provides the targeted FPGA architecture, application model and problem definition. The main contributions are presented in Section 4. In Section 5, experimental results are reported and Section 6 provides the conclusion.

2. RELATED WORK

There are various techniques reported in literature to reduce the leakage power of FPGAs. At *architecture level*, Calhoun et al. [4] introduce a fine-grained leakage control scheme using sleep transistors [15]. Fei Li *et al.* [13] proposed the programmable supply voltage (V_{dd}) in FPGAs. Elements on critical path are provided high supply voltage to ensure high performance, while components on noncritical path are supplied with low voltage and unused part of the device is switched-off. The leakage power of FPGAs significantly depends upon the threshold voltage (V_T) and an approach using high V_T transistors is proposed in [6]. A profound survey of leakage reduction techniques for SRAMs has been provided in [5].

At *system level*, works focusing on leakage power problems are fewer than those of the architecture level [14]. Bharadwaj *et al.* [3]

propose a design methodology that groups temporal locality design into cluster. The authors also develop a power state controller for effectively switching the states of the cluster. Addressing the leakage problem from system level as well, Zapater *et al.* has proposed an empirical model for leakage components and used it to design a energy-efficient control mechanism for servers in data centers [26].

Task graph scheduling for FPGA is an extensively studied topic [1, 2, 18, 20]. In [18], an efficient technique to schedule real-life applications on FPGA is proposed, but partial reconfiguration and resource constraint has not been considered. Most of the scheduling methods for FPGA focus on specific problems related to reconfiguration overhead and defragmentation. Ahmadinia *et al.* [1] combined scheduling and placement method for 2D FPGA architecture using cluster-based method to improve the performance by 20% and task rejection by 16.2%. Christoph *at el.* [20] integrated an online placement into a scheduling algorithm using small tasks first and earliest deadline first techniques. However, they do not take into account prefetching technique and resource constraint due to single reconfiguration controller pertaining to PR FPGA. The first work that considered both prefetching technique and resource constraint was introduced by Banerjee *at el.* [2]. The scheduling and placement models are included with the partitioning stage to form a complete HW-SW co-design approach for PR systems. The linear placement model in this work is later adopted by Yuh *et al.* [25] and Hsieh *et al.* [10] to address the leakage power issues.

Yuh *et al.* [25] first introduced the idea of using scheduling approach to mitigate the leakage issue. The authors utilized the scheduling and placement results from [2] and on top of that they developed a post-placement heuristic to reduce the delays between execution and reconfiguration parts. They also proposed an exact ILP solution to perform the post-placement in order to verify the effectiveness of the heuristic. Since their work tackles the leakage optimization after the tasks are already allocated onto the FPGA, the existing placement results may not allow their approach to significantly eliminate the leakage power. To achieve maximal leakage saving, our work addresses the leakage problem in all phases of the resource management process: *scheduling stage*, *placement stage* and *post-placement stage*.

With the same model and target, Hsieh *et al.* [10] introduced another approach to reduce the leakage waste. Their method consists of 3 phases: *binding*, *priority dispatching* and *split-aware placing*. First, the reconfiguration and execution parts of all tasks are combined together in the binding phase so that the leakage power is minimal. Then, each task is assigned a priority value based on the position of the task in the task graph. Finally, while placing the tasks into FPGA architecture, the split-aware placer checks for the deadline. If the deadline is violated, the placer splits the reconfiguration and the execution phase of the task. While the work in [10] tried to solve the leakage problem in the placement phase only, we propose a more complete solution having multiple stages. Furthermore, the scheduling algorithms in [10] used static priority, which is computed before the actual scheduling process takes place. The static priority is computed based on the characteristic of the task graph and remains unchanged during the scheduling process. In contrast, our algorithm dynamically recalculates the priorities of all available tasks every time a task is allocated onto the FPGA. Therefore, our algorithm updates the current available resource of the FPGA, leading to a better scheduling decision.

Table 1 summarizes the distinction of our work in comparison to the closely related works reported in the literature. As can be seen, existing works perform leakage aware optimization in scheduling, placement, or post-placement stages, whereas our approach performs optimization in all the stages. Further, unlike most of the approaches that consider static priorities of tasks, our approach considers dynamic priorities.

Table 1: Comparison of various approaches

Features	Ref. [2]	Ref. [25]	Ref. [10]	Our work
Scheduling	Performance driven	No	Performance driven	Leakage aware
Placement	Performance driven	No	Leakage aware	Leakage aware
Post placement	No	Leakage aware	No	Leakage aware
Priority of tasks	Dynamic	No	Static	Dynamic

3. SYSTEM MODEL AND PROBLEM DEFINITION

The **targeted architecture** used in this work is 1 dimensional (1D) FPGA, where the configurable logic blocks (CLBs) are arranged in fixed vertical columns, and a task occupies an integral number of columns. Moreover, the device supports dynamic partial reconfiguration: a part of the platform can be configured while other parts operate without interruption. The basic configuration unit is a column. A task can be deployed on an adjacent set of columns, and the reconfiguration time of the task is proportional to the number of columns. Such an architecture is similar to Xilinx FPGA Virtex family [23]. The device can be configured by a bitstream through configuration ports like JTAG or ICAP. However, both configuration ports are managed by only one configuration controller. Therefore, two different tasks cannot be reconfigured at the same time. Such architectural constraint plays a critical role in the process of scheduling and placement. Another key element realizing the benefits of scheduling algorithm on FPGA are sleep transistors. It is assumed that unused CLBs can be totally powered off by the sleep transistors integrated in the device. Based on this assumption, each column can be independently controlled by a sleep transistor [25].

Task model: We consider only hardware tasks, i.e., a task can be synthesized and implemented on the FPGA platform. In comparison to software tasks, hardware tasks have some additional parameters related to the required hardware area and configuration time. Directed acyclic graph (DAG) is used to represent the task set of an application. An example of the task graph model is presented in Fig. 1. In the DAG, each node u represents a task, while an edge $e(u; v)$ indicates the dependency between tasks u and v.

A task has two components: reconfiguration and execution. Reconfiguration part is scheduled under the architectural constraint (only one reconfiguration controller) while scheduling of execution part depends on the data dependencies, where a linear task placement model as that of [2] has been adopted. In the scheduling process, the communication overhead between tasks is ignored due to two reasons: *1)* tasks communicate with each other through a shared memory with the same latency and cost; and *2)* this latency is negligible in comparison to runtime reconfiguration overhead (time) and execution time.

Scheduling Problem

The problem targeted in this paper considers following set of input, constraints and objective.

- **Input:** The application task graph and FPGA architecture (number of columns, 1 reconfiguration controller and 1D architecture).

- **Constraints:** Task graph dependency for execution parts, reconfiguration controller constraint for reconfiguration part and sequential relation between the reconfiguration and execution parts of the same task.

- **Objective:** Minimize leakage power dissipation because of the delays between the reconfiguration and execution parts, minimize schedule length.

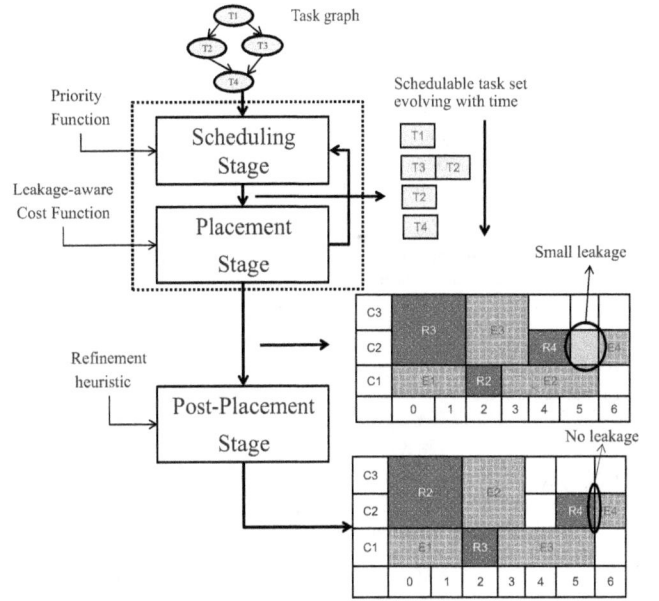

Figure 2: Multi-stage Scheduling Scheme

4. PROPOSED MULTI-STAGE RESOURCE MANAGEMENT APPROACH

An overview of the proposed resource management approach is provided in Fig.2. The approach has 3 stages: *Scheduling, Placement* and *Post-placement*. At first, the application task graph is processed iteratively in the first two stages (Scheduling and Placement). In each iteration, the Scheduler will define the next task coming to the Placer by a dynamic priority scheme, which means that the priorities of all the schedulable tasks are changed after each iteration. The Placer then decides the column where the task should be mapped and update the current status of the platform for the Scheduler. After all the tasks in task graph are allocated into the platform, the refinement heuristic in Post-Placement Stage will further improve the result from previous stages.

4.1 Scheduling Stage

Algorithm 1 presents our algorithm for the scheduling phase. At each step, all schedulable tasks whose parents have been scheduled are stored in a set of ready task $- S$. Then, the scheduler calculates the dynamic priorities of all tasks in set S according to a priority function defined by Equation 1. Thereafter, it chooses the task with highest priority to pass to the placer. As mentioned in Section 2, we use a dynamic priority function so that the scheduling process can adapt with the current status of the FPGA. Since the priority function has a strong impact on the schedule quality, it is carefully designed to address both leakage saving and performance requirement. The function includes different components that reflect the affection of constraints (FPGA architecture and task graph dependency) as well as optimization targets (leakage saving and schedule length) on scheduling decision. Our priority function is described as follows:

$$F = \alpha BT + \sigma C - \beta EET - \gamma ERT - \mu LK \qquad (1)$$

$$LK = C * (EET - (RT + ERT)) \qquad (2)$$

where,

BT : bottom level of the task that represents the length of the longest path in task graph starting from this task;

EET: earliest execution time of the task;

ERT: earliest reconfiguration time of the task;

C : number of columns required by the task;

RT : the reconfiguration time of the task;

Algorithm 1 Leakage Aware Task Scheduling Algorithm

Input: Task graph G=(U,V)
Output: Schedule with minimal LK
1: Put source tasks $\{t_i \in U : \mathbf{pred}(t_i) = \emptyset\}$ into set **S**
    // **S** − Set of schedulable tasks
2: **while S** $\neq \emptyset$ **do**
3:    Calculate priorities of unscheduled tasks in **S** (by Equation 1)
4:    Choose the task t with maximum priority
5:    Choose the best column C for task t (by Algorithm 2)
6:    Schedule task t starting from column C
7:    **if** child tasks of t are not already added to **S then**
8:       Add new available tasks to **S**
9:    **end if**
10:   Remove task t from **S**
11: **end while**

LK : leakage waste caused by scheduling the task. The leakage waste is the product of the used columns and the delay between reconfiguration and execution parts.

EET, ERT and LK are dynamic factors and are computed in scheduling process based on the current status of the partial schedule. Since these variables are fundamentals for scheduling problem, the details of their calculation can be found in basic textbook about task scheduling, such as [19]. $\alpha, \beta, \gamma, \sigma, \mu$ are coefficients related to each factor and used to determine the intensity of their impact on the cost function. The signs of elements in the function are given based on their impact on the schedule: tasks requiring larger columns should be placed earlier to increase the space for other tasks; tasks with higher bottom level (close to leaf tasks) should be scheduled first because they strongly affect the schedule length. Additionally, tasks with minimal EET, ERT and LK should be chosen for the desired optimization objective. As shown in Fig.2 the output of the scheduling stage is a set of schedulable tasks with the task of the highest priority in the front of the set. This highest priority task is then transferred to Placement Stage to be allocated onto the FPGA. Since we are using a dynamic priority scheme, both the schedulable task set and the priorities of tasks in the set are changed every time a task is placed in FPGA.

4.2 Placement stage

After getting the task with highest priority, the placer applies the steps in **Algorithm 2** to allocate the task into physical column(s) of FPGA. When a task comes to this stage, the algorithm scans all the columns to find available positions for the task and for each available position, the cost function is computed. Then, the task is placed into the position with minimal cost value. Here, also the cost function is also designed to optimize for both performance and leakage waste, which is presented as follows:

$$G = \frac{a}{10} * LK + (1 - \frac{a}{10}) * EST \qquad (3)$$

where, LK and EST represent leakage power and earliest start time for a placement; a is the leakage-schedule length trade-off coefficients, which can be used to provide a balance between the two optimization goals. Therefore, the cost function not only facilitates to reduce the leakage dissipation but also provides designer the ability to manage the trade-off between performance (schedule length) and leakage saving. The trade-off values can be achieved by adjusting the value of a in Equation 3. By increasing the value of a, designer can save more leakage power with a longer schedule length.

Fig. 2 demonstrates the placement results from the first 2 stages of our approach. It is expected to have small leakage power as a result of above optimization techniques as shown in the figures.

Algorithm 2 Leakage Aware Placement Algorithm

Input: Task t, set of columns **P**
Output: column C- with minimal LK
1: **for** each column $c_i \in$ **P do**
2:    Schedule task t starting from column c_i
3:    Calculate cost of placing t on c_i (by Equation 3)
4: **end for**
5: Choose the column C with minimal cost function

Algorithm 3 Leakage Aware Post-placement Algorithm

Input: Task graph G=(U,V), Tasks' placement after placement stage
Output: Optimized placement of tasks
1: **for** each leaf task $t_i \in$ **U do**
2:    Schedule configuration and execution of task t_i by considering architectural constraint
3:    **while** *parents of* $t_i \neq \emptyset$ **do**
4:       Find reconfiguration costs for parent tasks of t_i by Equation 4
5:       Sort reconfigurations in descending order based on cost
6:       Schedule reconfigurations considering architectural constraints
7:       Select parents one by one from maximum to minimum cost as t_i
8:    **end while**
9:    Move executions close to reconfigurations if dependencies do not violate
10: **end for**

4.3 Post-placement Heuristic

Our post-placement heuristic is presented in Algorithm 3. The heuristic takes task graph & tasks' placement as input and provides optimized placement of tasks so that leakage power due to delays between reconfigurations and executions is further minimized. The heuristic first schedules leaf tasks to maintain the same finish time towards meeting the timing deadline. For each leaf task, it's parent tasks are evaluated for their reconfiguration costs and scheduled by taking architectural constraints into account. The cost is computed as follows

$$C = lw * NC - sw * SP \qquad (4)$$

where, NC and SP are the number of occupied columns and range of reconfiguration space, respectively. The lw and sw are the weights to be given to NC and SP respectively, which determine the leakage power dissipation.

After all the tasks are scheduled, the executions are tried to place close to the respective reconfigurations if dependencies are not violated. This helps us to achieve placement that contains reconfigurations and executions close to each other as shown in Fig. 2, leading to reduced leakage power.

5. EXPERIMENTAL RESULTS

A series of experiments are conducted to demonstrate the performance of our resource management approach. Three versions of our scheduling and placement approach with different value of constant a in Equation 3 (a=1, a=2, a=10) are compared with following existing approaches: performance-driven algorithm (PDA) proposed in [2], Enhanced Leakage Aware Algorithm (ELAA) employed in [10], the ILP and Iterative Refinement (ITE) heuristic approach proposed in [25]. The PDA does not consider the leakage waste in the scheduling process, and has been used as the baseline approach for comparisons. ELAA demonstrates high performance when dealing with the leakage problem [10]. One important target in this work is to examine the trade-off between leakage saving and the schedule length, so no deadline (in terms of schedule length) is set for the trade-off analysis. The results from our post-placement approach are compared to that of [25].

Our algorithm is implemented in Java language and experiments are performed on an Intel Core i7 2.26GHz CPU with 4 GB RAM.

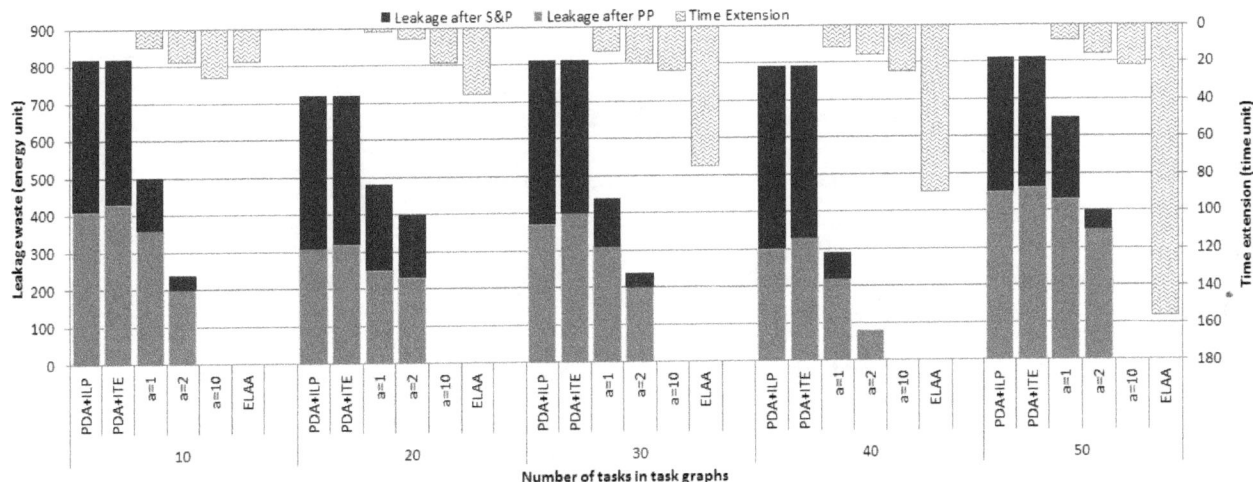

Figure 3: Leakage and Schedule Length when employing Different Approaches

The experiments are performed with real-life task graphs and synthetic task sets generated by the TGFF tool [8]. For the synthetic case, five task sets are considered. Each task set contains 10 task graphs with different level of parallelism; and each task in the task graph requires 10 to 50 columns and has the execution time from 1 to 9 time units. The FPGA platform is considered to have a fixed number of columns as 100. For real-life task graphs, JPEG encoder [2], MP3 decoder [11] and MPEG4 decoder [7] are considered with their specifications provided in respective references in order to demonstrate the applicability of our approach for real-life scenarios.

The criteria of the comparison are schedule length, leakage waste, and the runtime of the algorithms. The schedule length is measured in time unit, while the leakage waste is measured in energy unit, which is the power dissipation of one column during 1 time unit. The leakage waste of a particular task is computed by Eqn. 2. The leakage waste of the task graph after scheduling is the sum of leakage waste of all its tasks. For leakage waste of a task set, leakage values of all the contained task graphs are added. Further, as sleep transistors are used to stitch-off the unused SRAM cells for each column, the leakage waste for a task before its configuration and after the execution is considered as zero.

5.1 Leakage Waste and Schedule Length

Fig. 3 presents the leakage waste and schedule length (in terms of time extension over baseline approach PDA) of all the approaches over the five task sets. The whole bars present the leakage waste obtained after Scheduling and Placement (S&P) stage, while the lower parts of the bars describe the leakage waste after applying Post-Placement (PP) methods. Therefore, for existing approaches, the whole bars describe the leakage waste of PDA methods, and the lower part of each bar is the leakage after post-placement refinement (PDA+ITE or PDA+ILP). The time extension is the extended deadline required for leakage reduction. It is computed by subtracting the schedule length of each approach to the schedule length of the baseline (PDA) and these values are presented by columns with reversed direction (up to down). The horizontal axis declares notations for different approaches. For example, the first two notations PDA+ILP and PDA+ITE denote two approaches used in [25], where PDA is used in Scheduling and Placement (S&P) phase and either ILP or ITE is used in Post Placement phase.

It can be seen from Fig. 3 that all versions of our approach achieve better leakage saving when compared with the two approaches in [25]. Furthermore, when the number of tasks is large (greater than 10), our approach with $a = 10$ can reach the optimal leakage saving (leakage waste = 0) with smaller extension in time

when compared to ELAA. On an average, our approach adopted with the parameter $a = 1$ and $a = 2$ shows leakage power savings of 40% and 65% respectively when compared to PDA. Furthermore, when compared with existing approach PDA+ITE, our approach achieves 15% and 43% more leakage savings with parameter $a = 1$ and $a = 2$, respectively. The reason behind superior results by our approach over other approaches is that we consider leakage optimization first in scheduling and placement stages and then in post-placement stage as well. The optimization in scheduling and placement stages results in minimize delays between configurations and executions, and the post-placement stage try to further minimize the left delays in order to reduce the leakage dissipation. However, other approaches tackle the leakage optimization in only one stage (e.g., in placement stage in ELAA [10] and in post-placement stage in [25]).

5.2 Post-placement Leakage Waste and Algorithm Runtime

In this experiment, we examine the leakage saving and runtime of 3 post-placement methods ILP, ITE in [25], and our proposed heuristic. The methods are executed with the same inputs, which are the placement results from PDA. The deadline of all the task graphs are set to the schedule length of our approach when achieving optimal value of leakage saving (i.e., $a = 10$).

Table 2 shows leakage waste and algorithm runtime for various post-placement methods. As can be seen from Table 2, in many cases, all the post-placement methods are unable to totally eliminate the leakage dissipation over the PDA placement. However, for the same deadline, our multi-stage approach can achieve the optimal solution (leakage waste = 0) as described earlier. This signifies the advantages of our comprehensive strategy that addresses the leakage problem throughout the resource management process. Although our scheduling and placement stages achieve high leakage savings, they still can leave spaces between reconfiguration and execution parts of many tasks. Our post-placement stage tries to reallocate reconfigurations and executions so that the spaces between them are minimized in order to achieve further leakage savings. Table 2 shows that our post-placement heuristic can produce better leakage results than ITE. Additionally, our heuristic obtains the results in a smaller runtime.

5.3 Case-study: Real-life Applications

We applied different scheduling approaches on real-life applications: JPEG encoder [2], MP3 decoder [11] and MPEG4 decoder [7] as mentioned earlier. Table 3 shows leakage waste and schedule length for real-life applications. The notations used in

Table 2: Leakage waste and algorithm runtime of post-placement methods

Algorithms	Number of tasks in task graphs									
	10		20		30		40		50	
	Leakage	Runtime (s)	Leakage	Runtime (s)	Leakage	Runtime (s)	Leakage	Runtime (s)	Leakage	Runtime (s)
PDA+ILP	0	2.278	40	12.451	60	25.812	0	50.24	60	199.24
PDA+ITE	20	2.46E-04	80	4.32E-04	180	8.17E-04	80	1.14E-03	80	3.69E-03
PDA + Our heuristic	20	2.15E-04	80	4.36E-04	100	3.66E-04	80	4.32E-04	80	5.02E-04

this experiment are the same as those in previous experiments. The ELAA and our approach with $a = 10$ always achieve the optimal value of leakage waste (zero) with some extension in schedule length. Therefore, leakage in these cases does not need any improvement by Post-placement methods and not applicable (NA) has been mentioned for the same. As can be seen from the table, for MPEG and JPEG, our approach with $a = 1$ can obtain the same results as that of approach *PDA+ITE*. However, when it comes to MP3 decoder, the advantage of our comprehensive strategy becomes obvious. Due to low quality solution in the first two phases, the ITE approach cannot remove all the leakage from initial placement of previous phases. In contrast, all stages of our approach still work well to get maximum leakage saving.

Table 3: Leakage waste and schedule length for real-life applications

		PDA+ITE	a=1	a=10	ELAA
MPEG	Schedule length	44	44	53	57
	Leakage S&P	140	80	0	0
	Leakage PP	0	0	NA	NA
JPEG	Schedule length	22	23	24	29
	Leakage S&P	60	20	0	0
	Leakage PP	20	20	NA	NA
MP3 decoder	Schedule length	50	57	61	63
	Leakage S&P	270	30	0	0
	Leakage PP	270	30	NA	NA

6. CONCLUSION

We present a multi-stage resource management approach to tackle the leakage power problem in Partially Reconfigurable FPGAs. Our multi-stage approach employs leakage-aware priority function in scheduling stage, leakage-performance trade-off function in placement stage and a heuristic in post-placement stage. A series of experiments are performed to highlight the advantages of the proposed approach over existing works. The results demonstrate that the proposed approach dominates the existing approaches when the application task graph contains higher number of tasks. Additionally, experiments show that our approach can always achieve the optimal value as a comprehensive strategy is adopted, whereas other single-stage methods may not achieve the optimal value. Furthermore, our approach also provides the flexibility to the designers to achieve trade-off values between leakage saving and performance. In the future, we plan to examine the dependencies between task graph parameters and coefficient a to enhance the schedule quality. Extending the problem for two-dimensional FPGAs is also a promising direction.

7. ACKNOWLEDGMENT

This work is supported by Singapore Ministry of Education Academic Research Fund Tier 1, grant number R-263-000-B02-112.

8. REFERENCES

[1] A. Ahmadinia, C. Bobda, and J. Teich. A dynamic scheduling and placement algorithm for reconfigurable hardware. *Organic and Pervasive Computing–ARCS 2004*, pages 443–465, 2004.

[2] S. Banerjee, E. Bozorgzadeh, and N. Dutt. Physically-aware hw-sw partitioning for reconfigurable architectures with partial dynamic reconfiguration. In *DAC*, pages 335–340, 2005.

[3] R. Bharadwaj et al. Exploiting temporal idleness to reduce leakage power in programmable architectures. In *ASP-DAC*, pages 651–656, 2005.

[4] B. Calhoun, F. Honore, and A. Chandrakasan. Design methodology for fine-grained leakage control in mtcmos. In *ISLPED*, pages 104–109, 2003.

[5] A. Calimera et al. Design techniques and architectures for low-leakage srams. *Circuits and Systems I: Regular Papers, IEEE Transactions on*, pages 1992–2007, 2012.

[6] L. Ciccarelli, A. Lodi, and R. Canegallo. Low leakage circuit design for fpgas. In *CICC*, pages 715–718, 2004.

[7] J. Cong and K. Gururaj. Energy efficient multiprocessor task scheduling under input-dependent variation. In *DATE*, pages 411–416, 2009.

[8] R. Dick, D. Rhodes, and W. Wolf. Tgff: task graphs for free. In *CODES*, pages 97–101, 1998.

[9] S. Hauck. Configuration prefetch for single context reconfigurable coprocessors. In *FPGA*, pages 65–74, 1998.

[10] J. Hsieh et al. An enhanced leakage-aware scheduler for dynamically reconfigurable fpgas. In *ASP-DAC*, pages 661–667, 2011.

[11] P. Kumar and L. Thiele. Thermally optimal stop-go scheduling of task graphs with real-time constraints. In *ASP-DAC*, pages 123–128. IEEE Press, 2011.

[12] I. Kuon and J. Rose. Measuring the gap between fpgas and asics. *TCAD*, 26:203–215, 2007.

[13] F. Li, Y. Lin, and L. He. Field programmability of supply voltages for fpga power reduction. *TCAD*, 26:752–764, 2007.

[14] A. Raghunathan, N. K. Jha, and S. Dey. *High-Level Power Analysis and Optimization*. 1998.

[15] A. Sathanur et al. Row-based power-gating: a novel sleep transistor insertion methodology for leakage power optimization in nanometer cmos circuits. *VLSI*, 19:469–482, 2011.

[16] M. Shafique, L. Bauer, and J. Henkel. Remis: Run-time energy minimization scheme in a reconfigurable processor with dynamic power-gated instruction set. In *ICCAD*, pages 55–62, 2009.

[17] A. K. Singh et al. Energy optimization by exploiting execution slacks in streaming applications on multiprocessor systems. In *DAC*, pages 115:1–115:7, 2013.

[18] A. K. Singh et al. Mapping real-life applications on run-time reconfigurable noc-based mpsoc on fpga. In *FPT*, pages 365–368, 2010.

[19] O. Sinnen. *Task scheduling for parallel systems*, volume 60. 2007.

[20] C. Steiger, H. Walder, and M. Platzner. Heuristics for online scheduling real-time tasks to partially reconfigurable devices. *FPGA*, pages 575–584, 2003.

[21] T. Tuan, S. Kao, A. Rahman, S. Das, and S. Trimberger. A 90nm low-power fpga for battery-powered applications. In *FPGA*, pages 3–11, 2006.

[22] T. Tuan and B. Lai. Leakage power analysis of a 90nm fpga. In *CICC*, pages 57–60, 2003.

[23] Xilinx. Partial reconfiguration user guide. Technical report.

[24] S. Yang et al. Accurate stacking effect macro-modeling of leakage power in sub-100 nm circuits. In *VLSI Design, 2005. 18th International Conference on*, pages 165–170, 2005.

[25] P. Yuh et al. Leakage-aware task scheduling for partially dynamically reconfigurable fpgas. *TODAES*, 14:52, 2009.

[26] M. Zapater et al. Leakage and temperature aware server control for improving energy efficiency in data centers. In *DATE*, pages 266–269, 2013.

A Performance Enhancing Hybrid Locally Mesh Globally Star NoC Topology

Tuhin Subhra Das [†], Prasun Ghosal [†‡], Saraju P. Mohanty [‡], Elias Kougianos [‡]
[†] Bengal Engineering and Science University, Shibpur, Howrah 711103, WB, India
[‡] University of North Texas, Denton, TX 76203, USA
tuhinbcrec@gmail.com, prasun@ieee.org, Saraju.Mohanty@unt.edu, eliask@unt.edu

ABSTRACT

With the rapid increase in the chip density, Network-on-Chip (NoC) is becoming the prevalent architecture for today's complex chip multi processor (CMP) based systems. One of the major challenges of the NoC is to design an enhanced parallel communication centric scalable architecture for the on chip communication. In this paper, a hybrid Mesh based Star topology has been proposed to provide low latency, high throughput and more evenly distributed traffic throughout the network. Simulation results show that a maximum of 62% latency benefit (for size 8×8), 55% (for size 8×8), and 42% (for size 12×12) throughput benefits can be achieved for proposed topology over mesh with a small area overhead.

Categories and Subject Descriptors

B.7.1 [**Hardware Integrated Circuits**]: Types and Design Styles—*Advance technologies*

Keywords

NoC topology; Throughput; Latency; Load balancing; Performance.

1. INTRODUCTION

To cater modern day's complex high performance processing needs network on chips (NoC) are getting much more attention by the researchers day by day. To provide the massively parallel distributed communication environment during on-chip communication among hundreds of processing cores on an NoC, design of an efficient network topology with proper routing, flow control, deadlock prevention, and scalability plays an important role.

Novel contributions of this paper: The major contributions of this paper include the development of a new hybrid Locally Mesh Globally Star (LMGS) NoC topology with an objective to design a balanced network with low network latency benefit. Besides this, system performance improvement in terms of high throughput as well as low packet loss rate have been studied and optimized. A novel routing scheme also has been proposed to distribute packet more evenly throughout the network and thus to make system much more reliable by reducing channel contention problem.

GLSVLSI'14, May 21–23, 2014, Houston, Texas, USA.
ACM 978-1-4503-2816-6/14/05.
http://dx.doi.org/10.1145/2591513.2591544.

2. BACKGROUND AND MOTIVATION

In some recently proposed topologies viz. star-type 2D mesh [2], L2STAR [3], low latency based topology [7] researchers have followed some hybrid techniques to improve the performance. Objective is to design a low latency based parallel scalable architecture. Most of these approaches suffer from either higher node degree or from channel contention problem with increase in network size. In this paper, we overcome these limitations due to latency, throughput, and scalability through our proposed hybrid topology.

3. PROPOSED HYBRID NOC TOPOLOGY

Proposed hybrid topology (see Fig. 1) offers the advantages of both mesh and hierarchical star [5]. It facilitates both long distance and short distance traffic by using two different types of connections at different levels. Usually a mesh facilitates short distance local traffic, whereas star is used to facilitate long distance traffic.

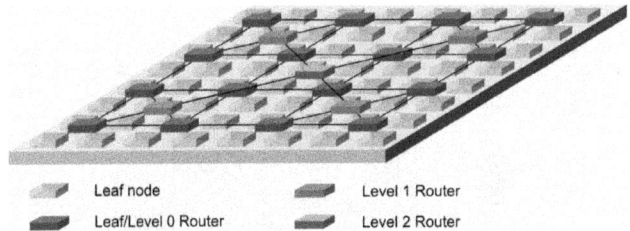

Figure 1: Proposed Hybrid topology for N=4

Some important parameters of an $M \times M$ sized proposed architecture are shown in Table 1, where, $M = 2^m$ for $m = 2, 3, \ldots, n$.

4. EXPERIMENTAL RESULTS

4.1 Experiments for Performance Evaluation

NS-2 simulator [1] is used for simulation that provides NAM (Network Animator) that helps to visualize network operation in real time by tracking data flow. Tcl scripts are used to create four different types of topologies of sizes 4×4, 8×8, and 12×12. Each router at leaf level (i.e. at level-0) is connected to its neighbour router as well as next higher level router by a maximum channel bandwidth of 1Mb. Routers at next higher level (i.e. at level-1) are connected to same level and next higher level router by double i.e. 2 Mb. Thus for a 4×4 sized proposed topology total eight 2Mb channels are required. A single IP core is assumed to be connected to each leaf level router. UDP is selected for communication protocol. Each source (i.e. UDP agent) is attached to an *exponential* traffic generator. Traffic ON and OFF periods are set to 2 ms and

Table 1: Important parameters of proposed architecture.

Bisection width	$M + 4$
Maximum node degree of non-leaf router	7
Maximum node degree of leaf router ($N = 4$)	9
Maximum node degree of leaf router ($N = 1$)	6
Maximum number of IP cores connected to a network where N is number of IP cores connected to each leaf level router.	$M \times M \times N$

0.1 ms respectively. Each node uses a *DropTail* queue with maximum size of 8. Link delay for short and long channels are set to 0.1 and 0.12 milliseconds respectively. A communication scenario has been defined by selecting 15-27% of nodes to generate traffic and by running simulation for 15 seconds.

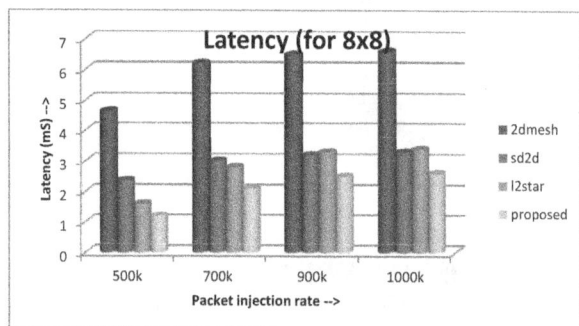

Figure 2: Packet latency vs network load for 8×8 sized topology.

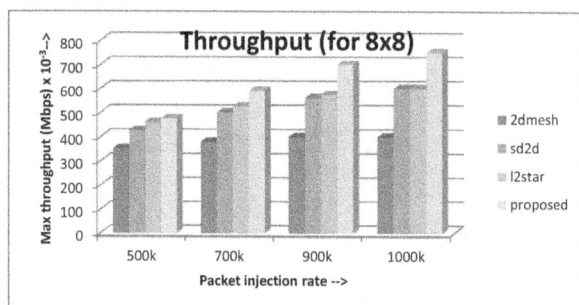

Figure 3: Max throughput vs network load for 8×8 sized topology.

4.2 Simulation Results and Discussion

Network performance parameters e.g. network latency, throughput, and packet loss rate are calculated based on the information retrieved by Perl scripts from output trace files for different topologies with varying network loads. Latency benefits of 30%, 30%, and 64% (for 8×8 size) compared to SD2D [4], L2STAR [3], and simple mesh have been observed for proposed topology (see Fig. 2). Packet delay for proposed topology reaches threshold at higher loads compared to others. Improvements of 20%, 20%, and 55% in maximum throughput compared to SD2D, L2STAR, and simple 2D mesh respectively are observed for proposed topology of size 8×8 (see Fig. 3), and 14%, 27%, and 42% respectively for 12×12 (see Fig. 4). Packet loss rate is negligible compared to others signifying lower channel contention problem. A comparison on required additional area has been calculated followed by a method proposed by Suboh *et al.* in [6]. A 31% to 13% area overhead has been ob-

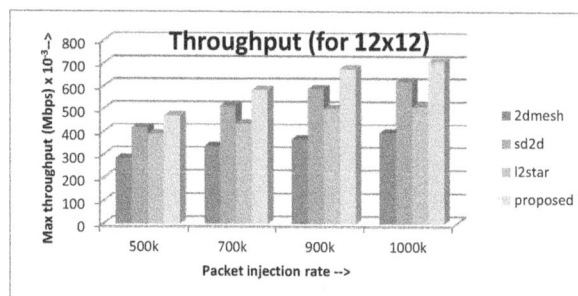

Figure 4: Max throughput vs network load for 12×12 sized topology.

served by varying N from 1 to 4 for proposed topology over 2D mesh of size 8×8.

5. CONCLUSION

A considerable amount of improvement in latency as well as throughput and packet drop rate has been achieved through the proposed hybrid topology with a small area overhead. Future works may be extended to minimize the area overhead as well as channel contention problems further.

6. REFERENCES

[1] The Network Simulator-NS-2. Online. Available: http://www.isi.edu/nsnam/ns/.

[2] K.-J. Chen, C.-H. Peng, and F. Lai. Star-type architecture with low transmission latency for a 2D mesh NOC. In *IEEE Asia Pacific Conference on Circuits and Systems (APCCAS)*, pages 919–922, 2010.

[3] P. Ghosal and T. S. Das. L2STAR: A Star Type level-2 2D Mesh architecture for NoC. In *Asia Pacific Conference on Postgraduate Research in Microelectronics and Electronics (PrimeAsia)*, pages 155–159, 2012.

[4] P. Ghosal and T. S. Das. Network-on-chip routing using Structural Diametrical 2D mesh architecture. In *Third International Conference on Emerging Applications of Information Technology (EAIT)*, pages 471–474, 2012.

[5] Z. Song, G. Ma, and D. Song. Hierarchical Star: An Optimal NoC Topology for High-Performance SoC Design. In *International Multisymposiums on Computer and Computational Sciences (IMSCCS '08)*, pages 158–163, 2008.

[6] S. Suboh, M. Bakhouya, J. Gaber, and T. El-Ghazawi. Analytical modeling and evaluation of network-on-chip architectures. In *International Conference on High Performance Computing and Simulation (HPCS)*, pages 615–622, 2010.

[7] X. Wang and L. Bandi. A low-area and low-latency network on chip. In *23rd Canadian Conference on Electrical and Computer Engineering (CCECE)*, pages 1–5, 2010.

VLSI Implementation of Linear MIMO Detection With Boosted Communications Performance

[Extended Abstract]

Dominik Auras, Dominik Rieth, Rainer Leupers, Gerd Ascheid
Institute for Communication Technologies and Embedded Systems
RWTH Aachen University, 52056 Aachen, Germany
auras@ice.rwth-aachen.de

ABSTRACT

A novel class of linear soft-input soft-output detectors featuring boosted communications performance is introduced. Compared to state-of-the-art linear detectors, the detector has an SNR gain of up to 2.4 dB. We shortly summarize the algorithm, and sketch a suitable architecture. The corresponding ASIC implementation shows the feasibility and efficiency of the concept. It achieves the IEEE 802.11n standard's peak data rate of 600 Mbit/s.

Categories and Subject Descriptors

C.3 [**Special-Purpose and Application-Based Systems**]: Signal processing systems

Keywords

Multiple-input multiple-output (MIMO) wireless transmission; soft-input soft-output (SISO) detection; VLSI architecture

1. INTRODUCTION

In this extended abstract, we present the ***Expectation Propagation based MIMO Detector ASIC***, shortly EPIC. It belongs to a novel class of linear MIMO detectors for BICM-ID systems that combines suitable VLSI implementation properties, like a purely feed-forward and deeply pipelineable structure, with an improved communications performance. The underlying idea is derived from a recent publication [3] on detection algorithms using the Expectation Propagation framework.

2. EPIC DETECTOR

The EPIC detector resembles a regular SISO MMSE MIMO detector, *boosted* with an initial SO-only MMSE MIMO detection in the first receiver iteration, when the message from the channel decoder is not available.

GLSVLSI'14, May 21–23, 2014, Houston, Texas, USA.
ACM 978-1-4503-2816-6/14/05.
http://dx.doi.org/10.1145/2591513.2591551.

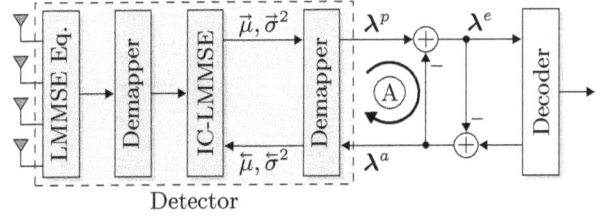

Figure 2: MIMO BICM-ID Receiver Model

Fig. 2 depicts the proposed detector. The first two blocks internal to the detector are a default LMMSE detector. It provides prior knowledge in terms of LLRs and its filter's output to the IC-LMMSE detector, that comprises the other two blocks. This second internal detector is slightly modified in order to process the extended prior knowledge. During the iterations between EPIC detector and decoder, we use only the IC-LMMSE detector with all modifications disabled.

The information exchange between the four internal blocks uses Gaussian distributions. The message parameters for the equalizers are $\vec{\mu}_t$ and $\vec{\sigma}_t^2$, and for demappers we use $\breve{\mu}_t$ and $\breve{\sigma}_t^2$. Both combined according to $\mu_t/\sigma_t^2 = \breve{\mu}_t/\breve{\sigma}_t^2 + \vec{\mu}_t/\vec{\sigma}_t^2$ and $1/\sigma_t^2 = 1/\breve{\sigma}_t^2 + 1/\vec{\sigma}_t^2$ represent the current belief on the transmit symbols with parameters μ_t and σ_t^2. The proposed EPIC detector's algorithm is listed as Alg. 1.

Algorithm 1: EPIC Detector

---

if *1st Receiver Iteration ($\lambda^a = 0$)* **then**
  $\vec{\mu}_t, \vec{\sigma}_t^2 = $ LMMSE-Det$(\boldsymbol{y}, \boldsymbol{H}, N_0)$
    $\lambda^{\text{int}} = $ demap$(\vec{\mu}_t, \vec{\sigma}_t^2)$
  $\mu_t, \sigma_t^2 = $ map(λ^{int})
  $\breve{\mu}_t, \breve{\sigma}_t^2 = $ gaussdiv$(\mu_t, \sigma_t^2, \vec{\mu}_t, \vec{\sigma}_t^2)$
else
  $\breve{\mu}_t, \breve{\sigma}_t^2 = $ map(λ^a)
$\vec{\mu}_t, \vec{\sigma}_t^2 = $ IC-LMMSE-Det$(\boldsymbol{y}, \boldsymbol{H}, N_0, \breve{\mu}_t, \breve{\sigma}_t^2)$
  $\lambda^e = $ demap$(\vec{\mu}_t, \vec{\sigma}_t^2)$

The function *gaussdiv* bridges the two internal detectors. It "divides" two Gaussian distributions. To this end, we compute $\breve{\sigma}_t^2 = (1/\sigma_t^2 - 1/\vec{\sigma}_t^2)^{-1}$ and $\breve{\mu}_t = \breve{\sigma}_t^2 (\mu_t/\sigma_t^2 - \vec{\mu}_t/\vec{\sigma}_t^2)$ from the inputs of the filter and the mapper. We also assume to use the decoder's posterior LLRs, and we neglect the prior knowledge in the final demapping. This means that both subtraction points in Fig. 2 are omitted.

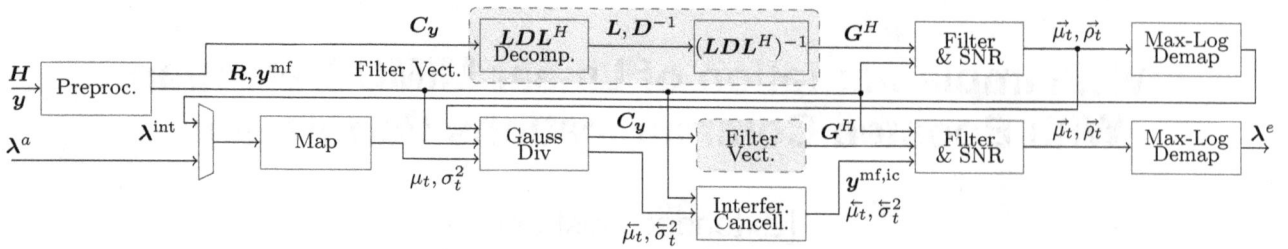

Figure 1: EPIC Architecture Design.

3. ARCHITECTURE

The architecture for our algorithm is designed to support the IEEE 802.11n standard's peak data rate of $\Theta_b = 600$ Mbit/s.

3.1 Overview

The architecture, depicted in Fig. 1, is organized into a coarse-grained pipeline of multi-cycle processing units (PUs), taking 18 clock cycles per pipeline cycle. Pipeline and PU design resemble that in [1,2,4]. For a clock frequency of $f_{clk} = 540$ MHz, the design sustains a data rate of $\Theta_b = \frac{rN_tK}{18}f_{clk} = 600$ Mbit/s or equivalently a code bit throughput of $\Theta_c = 720$ MBit/s.

There are two possible configurations. When no decoder feedback is available, the processing starts with the *Preprocessing* PU, proceeds with the upper internal detector (four PUs), and continues with the lower internal detector comprising seven PUs. Otherwise, the upper chain is disabled. The input λ^a is fed to the mapper PU. We use the *GaussDiv* unit only partially. Depending on the configuration, the processing latency is either $L = 11 \cdot 18$ clock cycles, or $L = 7 \cdot 18$ clock cycles. The throughput is constant for both.

4. IMPLEMENTATION RESULTS

Our proof-of-concept ASIC meets the IEEE 802.11 standard's peak data rate. The purpose is to show the efficiency and feasibility of the EPIC detector.

4.1 Algorithmic Performance

We simulated the system to obtain the frame error rate (FER) over SNR for the $\Theta_b = 600$ Mbit/s mode of the IEEE 802.11n standard, assuming $N_t = 4$, 64-QAM ($K = 6$) and the code rate $r = 5/6$. The simulation includes the bit-accurate model of our EPIC, and a model of the MMSE-PIC [4] excluding finite word-length effects.

The communications performance of the EPIC over the MMSE-PIC is measured at 10% FER. Our simulations show that the EPIC achieves the 10% FER at up to 2.4 dB less than the MMSE-PIC. As we expected, the biggest advantage is in the first receiver iteration. Subsequently, since the EPIC is then a default IC-LMMSE detector, the gains are most likely resulting from the improved first iteration. With more receiver iterations, the gap to the MMSE-PIC becomes smaller. For example, while the MMSE-PIC gains 4.2 dB from the first to the second receiver iterations, it is only 3.1 dB for the EPIC. Furthermore, the EPIC seems to perform best at lower code rates.

4.2 ASIC Implementation

We synthesized the proposed architecture with Synopsys Design Compiler G-2012.06 in topographical mode using a 90nm standard-performance CMOS library. The ASIC achieves a maximum clock frequency of 627 MHz, yielding a maximum throughput of $\Theta_c = 822$ Mbit/s. This variant occupies 334 kGE. The most area-throughput efficient design runs at 588 MHz and occupies a total area of 302.8 kGE.

Table 1: Comparison to other reported detectors

	This work	[4]
Number of antennas	4×4	4×4
Modulation order	≤ 64	≤ 64
Algorithm	EPIC	MMSE-PIC
Technology	90 nm	90 nm
Throughput Θ_c [Mbit/s]	784	757
Detection area [kGE]	302.8	384.2[a]
A-TP Eff. [Mbit/s/kGE]	2.59	1.97

[a] Area for chip IO interface excluded

In Tbl. 1, data for the EPIC and the MMSE-PIC [4] is shown. The comparison bases on the area-throughput efficiency. We can see that this implementation of the EPIC is smaller and slightly faster than the MMSE-PIC. However, while we currently have only post-synthesis results, the MMSE-PIC has been fabricated. As outlook, we plan to layout the architecture to allow a more reasonable comparison.

Acknowledgment

This work has been supported by the UMIC Research Centre, RWTH Aachen University.

5. REFERENCES

[1] D. Auras, R. Leupers, and G. Ascheid. Efficient VLSI architectures for matrix inversion in soft-input soft-output MMSE MIMO detectors. In *Proc. IEEE ISCAS*, 2014. accepted for publication.

[2] D. Auras, R. Leupers, and G. Ascheid. A novel reduced-complexity soft-input soft-output MMSE MIMO detector: Algorithm and efficient VLSI architecture. In *Proc. IEEE ICC*, 2014. accepted for publication.

[3] M. Senst and G. Ascheid. How the framework of expectation propagation yields an iterative IC-LMMSE MIMO receiver. In *Proc. IEEE GLOBECOM*, pages 1 – 6, 2011.

[4] C. Studer, S. Fateh, and D. Seethaler. ASIC implementation of soft-input soft-output MIMO detection using MMSE parallel interference cancellation. *IEEE J. Solid-State Circuits*, 46(7):1754 –1765, 2011.

Energy Optimal Sizing of FinFET Standard Cells Operating in Multiple Voltage Regimes Using Adaptive Independent Gate Control

Yue Fu[1], Yanzhi Wang[2], Xue Lin[2], Shahin Nazarian[2], and Massoud Pedram[2]

[1]Oracle Corporation, [2]University of Southern California

{yuefu, yanzhiwa, xuelin, snazaria, pedram}@usc.edu

ABSTRACT

FinFET has been proposed as an alternative for bulk CMOS in the ultra-low power designs due to its more effective channel control, reduced random dopant fluctuation, higher ON/OFF current ratio, lower energy consumption, etc. The characteristics of FinFETs operating in the sub/near-threshold region are very different from those in the strong-inversion region. This paper introduces an analytical transregional FinFET model with high accuracy in both subthrehold and near-threshold regions. The unique feature of independent gate controls for FinFET devices is exploited for achieving a tradeoff between energy consumption and delay, and balancing the rise and fall times of FinFET gates. This paper proposes an effective design framework of FinFET standard cells based on the adaptive independent gate control method such that they can operate properly at all of subthreshold, near-threshold and super-threshold regions. The optimal voltage for independent gate control is derived so as to achieve equal rise and fall times or minimal energy-delay product at any supply voltage level.

Categories and Subject Descriptors

B.8.2 [**Performance and Reliability**]: Performance Analysis and Design Aids

Keywords

FinFET; near-threshold; independent gate control

1. INTRODUCTION

FinFET device, a special quasi-planar double gate (DG) device, has been proposed as an alternative for the bulk CMOS when technology scales beyond 32nm technology [1][2]. In double-gate FinFET circuits, each fin contains two gates, a *front gate* and a *back gate*. The thickness T_{si} of a single fin equals to the silicon channel thickness. The current flows from the source to drain along the wafer plan. In this structure, each fin is essentially the parallel connection of the *front-gate-controlled FET* and the *back-gate-controlled FET*, both with width H equal to the height of each fin. It is proved in [2][3] that FinFET devices can enhance the energy efficiency, ON/OFF current ratio, and soft-error immunity compared with bulk CMOS devices. FinFET devices also show better voltage scalability because of less leakage power consumption [3]. We observe that the minimum energy point (MEP) (~200 mV) of FinFET lies in the subthreshold or near-threshold region, which is typically lower than the bulk CMOS

circuits (> 300 mV). Therefore, the FinFET devices outperform bulk CMOS devices in ultra-low power designs by allowing for higher voltage scalability.

One of the unique features for FinFET devices is the independent gate control method, i.e., the front gate and the back gate of a FinFET device can be controlled by different voltages, which enables more power margin and flexible circuit designs [5]. Furthermore, due to the capacitor coupling of the front gate and the back gate, the threshold of the front-gate-controlled FET varies in response to the back-gate biasing, and vice versa. Cakici et al. [4] used independent-gate FinFETs in the pull-down network of an SRAM cell to keep the ~20 pA/um standby power budget. The authors of [5] studied gate sizing and negative biasing on the back gate and showed significant power reduction.

Many burst-mode applications require high performance for brief time periods between extended sections of low performance operation [6]. Digital circuits supporting such burst-mode applications should work on both near-threshold regions and super-threshold regions for brief time periods. The characteristics of FinFETs operating in the sub/near-threshold region are very different from those in the strong-inversion region. In this paper, we target at designing a robust FinFET standard cell library that achieves *equal rise and fall times* or *minimum energy-delay product* at any supply voltage level, including all of the subthreshold, near-threshold, and super-threshold regions.

First, we notice that the conventional FinFET models are expressed in a piecewise fashion with a breakpoint at or near the threshold voltage V_{th}, separating the super-threshold region where the strong-inversion model is applied [7] and the sub-threshold region where the exponential dependency model is applied. We apply the simple empirical model [8] for the FinFETs operating in both the subthreshold and the near-threshold regimes. This model results in a maximum of 7.76% inaccuracy compared with the HSpice simulation results.

Based on the accurate transregional model, we develop the robust FinFET standard cell library operating at multiple supply voltage levels. We exploit the adaptive independent gate control method, i.e., applying different voltage levels for independent gate control at different supply voltage levels. We start from the FinFET gates designed for equal rise and fall times in the super-threshold region. We define two optimization problems of (i) achieving equal rise and fall times and (ii) minimizing energy-delay product of the FinFET circuit at any supply voltage level. The optimal solution of the first problem achieves the minimum circuit delay, but not necessarily achieves the minimum energy-delay product. In the optimal solution of the second problem, the rise and fall times of the FinFET gates are not necessarily balanced. We derive and find the optimal voltage for independent gate control at any supply voltage level, such that objective (i) or (ii) is achieved. Experimental results using ISCAS benchmarks on 32nm Predictive Technology Model (PTM) for FinFETs [9] show that

GLSVLSI'14, May 21–23, 2014, Houston, Texas, USA.

ACM 978-1-4503-2816-6/14/05

http://dx.doi.org/10.1145/2591513.2591555

the proposed design optimization framework achieves up to 64% reduction in energy-delay product.

2. EXPERIMENTAL RESULTS

We test the proposed optimization framework based on adaptive independent gate control on a set of benchmark circuits, including inverter chains and synthesized ISCAS benchmark circuits. We perform simulations on the 32nm PTM for FinFETs.

Figure 1 illustrates the circuit delay optimization results on a 20-stage inverter chain by adjusting V_{BN} under different V_{DD} levels. One can observe that the independent gate control method achieves more significant reduction in circuit delay when V_{DD} is lower (i.e., in the subthreshold or near-threshold regions.) We observe that the circuit delay can be reduced by up to 48.5% when comparing with the same circuit without independent gate control in the subthrehold or near-threshold regions. This circuit delay reduction is achieved through speeding up the N-type FETs that are relatively weaker in the sub/near-threshold regions.

Figure 2 and Figure 3 illustrate the optimization results on the energy-delay product using adaptive independent gate control (applying different V_{BN} voltage values under different V_{DD} levels), on a 20-stage inverter chain and the ISCAS C432 benchmark, respectively. Table 1 show more results on the reduction of energy-delay product using optimal adaptive independent gate control method. We conclude that (i) the energy-delay product of a circuit can be reduced by up to 64% when comparing with the same circuit without independent gate control; (ii) we achieve more significant reduction in energy-delay product when V_{DD} is lower (i.e., in the subthreshold or near-threshold regions) or when the activity factor α is larger.

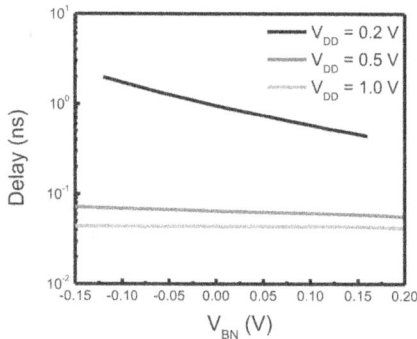

Figure 1. Delay optimization of a 20-stage inverter chain by adjusting V_{BN} under different V_{DD} levels.

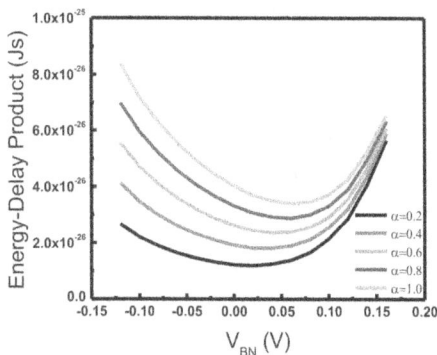

Figure 2. Energy-delay product optimization results on a 20-stage inverter chain by adjusting V_{BN} with different activity factors (V_{DD} = 0.2 V).

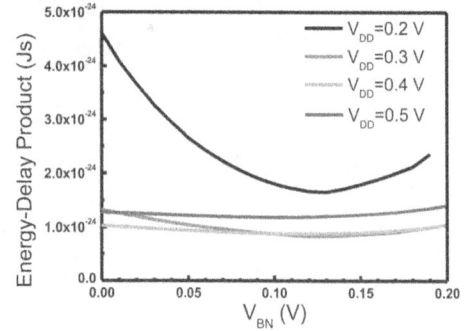

Figure 3. Energy-delay product optimization results of ISCAS85' Benchmark C432 by applying different V_{BN} at different V_{DD} levels.

Table 1. Comparison results on energy-delay product when the adaptive independent gate control method is applied for minimize energy-delay product.

	Baseline (Js)	Optimized (Js)
20-stage inverter chain (V_{DD} = 0.2 V)	4.017×10^{-26}	3.392×10^{-26}
20-stage inverter chain (V_{DD} = 0.3 V)	1.688×10^{-26}	1.518×10^{-26}
C432 (V_{DD} = 0.2 V)	4.615×10^{-24}	1.652×10^{-24}
C432 (V_{DD} = 0.3 V)	1.321×10^{-24}	8.276×10^{-25}
C499 (V_{DD} = 0.12 V)	9.709×10^{-26}	8.660×10^{-26}
C499 (V_{DD} = 0.2 V)	8.124×10^{-27}	7.099×10^{-27}

3. ACKNOWLEDGMENTS

This research is sponsored in part by grants from the PERFECT program of the Defense Advanced Research Projects Agency.

4. REFERENCES

[1] E. J. Nowak, I. Aller, T. Ludwig, K. Kim, R. V. Joshi, C.-T. Chuang, K. Bernstein, and R. Puri, "Turning silicon on its edge," *IEEE Circuits and Devices Magazine*, 2004, 20 – 31.

[2] T. Sairam, W. Zhao, and Y. Cao, "Optimizing FinFET technology for high-speed and low-power design", in *Proc. of Great Lakes Symp. VLSI*, 2007.

[3] F. Crupi, M. Alioto, J. Franco, P. Magnone, M. Togo, N. Horiguchi, and G. Groeseneken, "Understanding the basic advantages of bulk FinFETs for sub- and near-threshold logic circuits from device measurements," *IEEE Trans. on Circuits and Systems II*, vol. 59, no. 7, July 2012.

[4] T. Cakici, K. Kim, and K. Roy, "FinFET based SRAM design for low standby power applications," *ISQED*, 2007.

[5] A. Muttreja, N. Agarwal, and N. K. Jha, "CMOS logic design with independent gate FinFETs," in *Proc. Intl. Symp. Computer Design*, vol. 20, pp. 560 – 567, 2007.

[6] B. H. Calhoun, A. Wang, N. Verma, and A. Chandrakasan, "Sub-threshold design: the challenges of minimizing circuit energy," *ISLPED*, 2006.

[7] N. Waste and D. Harris, *CMOS VLSI Design: A Circuits and Systems Perspective*, Pearson publisher, 2008.

[8] D. M. Harris, B. Keller, J. Karl, and S. Keller, "A transregional model for near-threshold circuits with application to minimum-energy operation," in *ICM*, 2010.

[9] W. Zhao and Y. Cao, "New generation of Predictive Technology Model for sub-45nm early design exploration," *IEEE Transactions on Electronic Devices*, vol. 53, no. 11, pp. 2816 – 2823, Nov. 2006.

A High Resolution Area Efficient Digital Pulse Width Modulator with Process and Temperature Calibration Designed for Digital Controlled DC/DC Converters

Jing Lu
Department of Electrical and Computer Engineering
Northeastern University
Boston, MA, USA
jinglu@ece.neu.edu

Yong-Bin Kim
Department of Electrical and Computer Engineering
Northeastern University
Boston, MA, USA
ybk@ece.neu.edu

ABSTRACT

In this paper, a 12-bit high resolution, power and area economy Digital Pulse Width Modulator (DPWM) with process and temperature calibration is proposed for digital controlled DC-DC converter. It adopts the differential delay cell so as the size is minimized compared to the single ended one. Voltage controlled inverter is built to be a deferential delay cell. Both the delay cell is optimized and the additional control node makes the calibration possible. The process and temperature monitors provides the desired feature aimed to calibrate the frequency variation caused by the process corner and temperature factors, which allows this delay line can be served as a clock. The lookup table combines different situation and output proper control voltage to the delay cell. Each module is verified by simulation and whole block is working properly under different corner using 0.18um technology.

Categories and Subject Descriptors

B.7.0 [**Integrated Circuits**]: General

General Terms

Management, Performance, Design

Keywords

Dealy-line DPWM, Process Monitor, Temperature Monitor, Flash-ADC, look-up table

1. INTRODUCTION

The basic concept of digital controlled DC-DC converter is illustrated in Figure 1, taking Buck for example [1]. First, the voltage difference between Buck's sensed output voltage V_{fb} and a reference voltage V_{ref} is quantized by an ADC and a digital error signal $e[n]$ is generated. Then the error signal $e[n]$ is processed by a digital computing unit, which may include digital compensator, protection function and other control algorism. Combining all the control information, a duty ratio $d[n]$ is output to the DPWM. DPWM is a digital to time converter. It will generate a pulse width modulated signal by the $d[n]$ at fixed frequency. And finally, the pulsed can control the on/off state of the power switches and so as to regulate the output to a targeted value.

GLSVLSI'14, May 21–23, 2014, Houston, Texas, USA.
ACM 978-1-4503-2816-6/14/05.

With the detailed structure analysis of digital controlled DC/DC converter, one can tell that the major disadvantage is the limited resolution of ADC and DPWM, compared to the theoretically infinite resolution of an analog controlled converter. Meanwhile, the resolution of DPWM should always be higher than the ADC to prevent an unstable state called limit-cycle [2]. Therefore a high resolution DPWM is always demanded in such a system. Reference [3] runs simulation on the output precision versus the resolution of ADC and the resolution of DPWM. The result shows that the optimum precision is reached when the DPWM is 12-bit and the ADC is approximately 11-bit. Beyond this resolution, the output ripple becomes the limiting factor of the output accuracy.

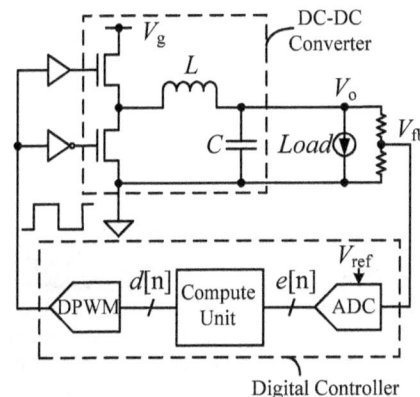

Figure 1. Conventional digital DC-DC converter architecture

The purpose of this paper is to design a 12-bit hybrid DPWM which incorporates a low 6-bit delay line based digital to time converter (DTC) with process and temperature calibration and high 6-bit counter based DTC. Usually the delay line DTC excels in its low power but occupies more silicon area. On the other hand, the counter based DTC utilizes 2^n times faster clock to realize n-bit DTC, which impose design stress on the high speed clock and excessive power consumption. The hybrid structure combines the advantageous of two methods and significantly counteracts their drawbacks, which makes it a majority choice. Furthermore voltage controlled differential inverter delay cell is proposed in this paper. The differential structure can save as much as 37.5% area [3]. The voltage controlled inverter is economic in size and convenience in fine tuning the delay time for its additional voltage control node. Furthermore, process and temperature calibration circuit are proposed to address the delay time dependency on process and temperature. The calibration voltage is connected the voltage control node of that differential voltage controlled inverter. The overall design is completed on 0.18um technology.

2. Hybrid differential DPWM

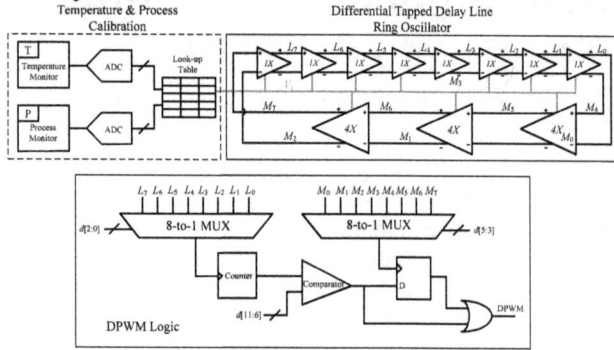

Figure 2. Proposed 12-bit hybrid DPWM with process and temperature calibration

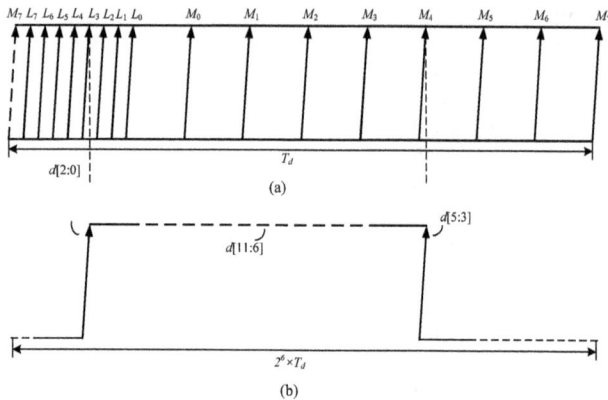

Figure 3. Time chart of the proposed DPWM

The conventional hybrid DPWM is analyzed in [4]. A tapped delay line and a digital counter together with comparator are used to build the structure. This structure adopts the advantageous of small size counter based DPWM and small power consumption of delay-line based DPWM. Reference further improved this structure by employing differential delay line cells. What's more, [3] utilizes the delay-line ring oscillator frequency as the clock of the counter comparator part, so that a high frequency clock generation circuit is saved. However, the structure proposed in [3] suffers two major problems. One is its delay cell is an analog differential amplifier, which needs common feedback loop and causing the delay cell is much larger than conventional digital delay cells. The other one is delay line highly dependent on the process and temperature factors, in case that a stable supply voltage can be guaranteed. This results that the switching frequency will vary as the process and temperature. To overcome the problem mentioned above, a novel 12-bit DPWM with process and temperature calibration is proposed in Figure 2. Eight 1X cells and three 4X cells are connected into a ring oscillator frame. The low 3-bit [L0-L7] and middle 3-bit [M0-M7] are tapped out as denoted in Figure 2. The one period time chart is shown in Figure 3 (a). The starting one is L7 to L0 and M0 to M7. The Low 3-bit determines the starting edge of the pulse, and the high six bits [H6-H11] determines how many period is added, and the middle three bits determine the falling edge of the pulse. The total period is $2^6 \times T_d$. The delay cell is composed of a differential voltage controlled inverter [6]. The calibration is worked as this: first, the process and temperature monitor keep monitoring the process and temperature information and output an analog output [7]. The output is converted to digital code by two 2-bits flash ADC. Combining different situation of process and temperature, an idea voltage is output to the delay line through a loop-up table. The detailed circuits are given in the following section.

3. CONCLUSION

This paper developed the architecture of a 6-bit differential delay line with process and temperature calibration. The utilization of this delay line was given in a high resolution DPWM. The basic delay cell was investigated and voltage controlled delay line is chosen to be the one, for it has the targeted delay time and controllable delay time, and small in size. Furthermore, it can be easily configured into differential mode. With the additional phase provided by differential mode, the 6-bit delay-line cell can be largely reduced, which in turn save area and power. Facing the common problem of process and temperature suffered by most delay cells, a process and temperature monitor circuits are proposed and analyzed in the paper, and the simulation results is listed after each circuits with process monitor is insensitive to temperature and temperature monitor is insensitive to process variation. The output of each monitor is encoded and different situation can be combined to right control voltage to the voltage controlled inverter delay cell. At the point, the delay time of each cell, or the frequency of this ring-oscillator delay line can be under controlled. All the circuits are implemented on 0.18um process. Simulation results have verified all the assumptions right. The whole structure works very well.

4. ACKNOWLEDGMENTS

Our thanks to Dongbu to support the 0.18um technology.

5. REFERENCES

[1] Patella, B. J.; Prodic, A.; Zirger, A. and Maksimovic D. 2003. High frequency digital PWM controller IC for DC/DC converters. In *IEEE Transactions on Power Electronic*. Vol. 18. Issue 1. Part 2. Pp: 438-446. 2003.

[2] Peterchev, A. V.; Sanders, S. R. 2003. Quantization resolution and limit cycling in digitally controlled PWM converters. In *IEEE Transactions on Power Electronic*. Vol. 18. Issue 1. Part: 2. Pp: 208-215. 2007.

[3] Foong, H. C.; Zheng, Y.; Tan, Y. K.; and Tan, M. T. 2012. Fast-transient integrated digital DC-DC converter with predictive and feedforward control. In IEEE Transactions on Circuits and Systems 1: Regular Papers. Vol. 59, Issue 7, pp: 1567-1576. 2012.

[4] Syed, A.; Ahmed, E.; Maksimovic, D.; Alarcon, E. 2004 Digital pulse width modulator architectures. In 2004 IEEE 35th Annual Power Electronics Specialists Conference, PESC 04. Vol. 6, pp: 4689-4695.

[5] Peterchev, A. V.; Xiao, J.; Sanders, S. R. 2003. Architecture and IC implementation of a digital VRM controller. In IEEE Transactions on Power Electronics. Vol. 18. Issue: 1. Part: 2. Pp: 356-364.

[6] Mahapatra, N. R.; Garimella, S. V.; Taree, A. 2000. An empirical and analytical comparison of delay elements and a new delay element design. In Procceddings IEEE Computer Society Workshop on VLSI, 2000. Pp: 81-86.

[7] Kim, K. K.; and Kim, Y. B. 2009. A novel adaptive design methodology for minimum leakage power considering PVT variations on nanoscale VLSI systems. In IEEE Transactions on Very Large Scale Integration (VLSI) systems. Vol. 17. Issue 4. Pp: 517-528.

WeDBless : Weighted Deflection Bufferless Router for Mesh NoCs

Simi Zerine Sleeba
Model Engineering College
Kochi, India
simi@mec.ac.in

John Jose
Rajagiri School of Engineering
& Technology, Kochi, India
johnj@rajagiritech.ac.in

Mini M.G.
Model Engineering College
Kochi, India
mininair@mec.ac.in

ABSTRACT

Bufferless NoC routers employing deflection routing are gaining popularity due to their power and area efficiency. We propose WeDBless, a bufferless deflection router that reduces deflection rate of flits by employing port allocation based on weighted deflection of flits. The proposed method directs the frequently misrouted flits towards their destination by increasing their probability of getting a productive output port. Our evaluations on synthetic traffic patterns show that WeDBless achieves significant reduction in deflection rate, average flit latency and improvement in network saturation point compared to the state-of-the-art bufferless router and reduced complexity in route computing logic.

Categories and Subject Descriptors

C.2.1 [**Network Architecture and Design**]: Network Communication

Keywords

Deflection rate; output port selection; latency reduction

1. INTRODUCTION & BACKGROUND

Efficient microarchitecture and cost effective routing algorithms are highly essential characteristics for NoC routers. Traditional virtual channel routers (VCR) employ buffers in the input ports. Buffers contribute significantly to dynamic and static power [1, 3]. With an aim of reducing chip area and power, bufferless deflection routers are introduced [3]. In a bufferless deflection router, all flits arriving at the input ports have to pass through one of the output ports at the end of the pipeline cycle. This can lead to misrouting of flits and hence can increase the latency of flits. Effective output port selection in deflection routers is a critical design issue.

The baseline bufferless router, BLESS [3] uses an age based flit ranking scheme for output port selection. Because of the sequential port allocation scheme, the router pipeline

GLSVLSI'14, May 21–23, 2014, Houston, Texas, USA.
ACM 978-1-4503-2816-6/14/05.
http://dx.doi.org/10.1145/2591513.2591559.

latency in BLESS is high, leading to lower operating frequency of the network. This performance issue in BLESS is addressed in CHIPPER [2] by parallel port allocation. CHIPPER makes sure that the highest priority flit(golden flit) is assigned the productive port in every router. But it leads to increase in deflection rate compared to BLESS since all non-golden flits are assigned random ports. In this paper, we briefly describe the working of Weighted Deflection Bufferless (WeDBless) router and analyse the experimental results.

2. WEDBLESS ROUTER

We introduce a novel routing algorithm for bufferless deflection routers which prioritises flits based on Weighted Deflection Count(WDC) and assigns output ports based on Directional Weights (DW). WDC and DWs are computed in each router and are incorporated in the flit itself. A small side buffer which buffers one ejection ready flit is also provided to reduce deflections. Reduction in the deflection rate leads to reduction of dynamic power occuring due to unproductive flit movement in the network. We also propose a simple logic that precomputes the productive routes of a flit in the succeeding router by adjusting the DWs of the flit.

Concept of Weighted Deflection Count :
In WeDBless, WDC of a flit will be 0 at the time of its injection into the network. This WDC is updated at the end of the router pipeline by incrementing or decrementing its value. Frequently deflected flits will have higher WDC value than less deflected ones. Priority is assigned to flits such that flits with high WDC will have higher priority in output port selection.

The four DWs of a flit represent its preference for the four output ports. The DWs can take any one of the three values, -1,+1 or +2 which are coded using 2 bits each. For a flit, the DW of a fully productive output port will be -1 (least weight) whereas DW of partially non-productive ports will be +1 (medium weight). DWs of output ports that deflect flits to the opposite side of destination will be +2 (maximum weight). As an example, if the flit's destination lies in the same column and towards south of the current router, then DWs in the north, south, east and west directions are +2, -1, +1 and +1 respectively. In order to incorporate the WDC and DWs, we use additional 14 bits in the flit header; 6 bits for WDC and 8 bits for DWs.

Router Pipeline:
WeDBless uses a two stage pipeline with one cycle latency each. In the WeDBless architecture as shown in Figure 1,

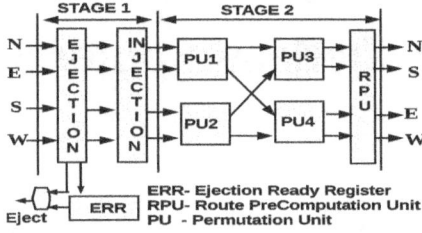

Figure 1: WeDBless router pipeline.

incoming flits enter the router pipeline through input ports (shown on left) and move towards output port (shown on right) through various units. Ejection and Injection constitute the first cycle of the router pipeline which is similar to the pipeline architecture of CHIPPER [2]. In the Ejection unit, we provide an Ejection Ready Register(ERR) which buffers one among the multiple flits destined to the local core. This buffering serves to reduce deflections due to such flits roaming around the network.

In the next pipeline stage, flits pass through the permutation network at the end of which output ports are alloted to them. WeDBless router uses the permutation network proposed in CHIPPER for output port selection. In the port allocation stage, a flit competes to occupy the output port with lowest DW. After port allocation, the DW value of allotted output port is added to the WDC of the flit. The incrementing and decrementing of WDC using DWs helps to maintain its value between 0 and 63.

The Route Precomputation Unit (RPU) is placed at the end of the router pipeline and after this unit, flits proceed to the next router through the flit channel. The RPU recalculates the four DWs of the flit for the next router. It consists of simple hardware which can increment, decrement or retain the previous value of DWs of the flit depending on which output port is allocated to it.

3. EXPERIMENTAL METHODOLOGY

We model BLESS and CHIPPER router designs with two cycle latency by modifying the traditional cycle accurate NoC simulator, Booksim [1]. We also model the WeDBless router design by making modifications to the CHIPPER simulation model as mentioned in Section 2. We conduct all evaluations using single flit packets. Using synthetic traffic patterns, we conduct experiments for 8x8 mesh network. After providing sufficient warm up, we collect the deflection rate and average flit latencies for various flit injection rates from zero load to saturation.

Results:

Deflection of flits through the network causes unnecessary dissipation of dynamic power. The aim of WeDBless is to minimise these deflections and achieve energy efficiency for the NoC. Average deflection rate is computed as the average number of deflections encountered per flit. From evaluations using synthetic traffic, we observe that WeDBless reduces the deflection rate by a maximum of 56% compared to CHIPPER as shown in Figure 2. The unique routing mechanism in WeDBless reduces deflections in three ways : (1) by computing more than one productive paths for a flit (2) by increasing WDC value for deflected flits so that they win desired output ports in the succeeding router's ar-

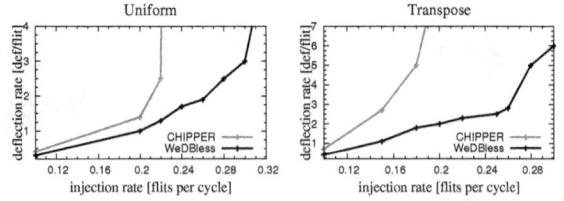

Figure 2: Avg. deflection rate for 8×8 mesh

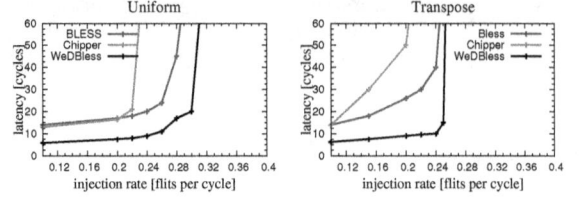

Figure 3: Avg. flit latency for 8×8 mesh

bitration (3) by providing an ERR that buffers one among multiple flits destined to the local core.

Reduction in deflection rate leads to lower average latency as well. For uniform traffic, WeDBless improves the network saturation point by 8% compared to BLESS. The introduction of ERR and the concept of port allocation using WDC are responsible for the reduction in latency for WeDBless compared to BLESS. Compared to CHIPPER, WeDBless exhibits improvement in network saturation point by 55% for transpose traffic and 26% for uniform traffic as shown in Figure 3.

4. CONCLUSION

We proposed a novel bufferless deflection router for mesh NoCs that reduces the deflection rate and average latency of flits in the network. We used Weighted Deflection Count to rank flits and Directional Weights to prioritise output ports for a flit. We also presented a simple and effective method to precompute the routes of a flit by recomputing the directional weights . Future work on WeDBless router consists of evaluating the network using benchmark applications and analysing the application level speed up. Further, power and area modelling of WeDBless router shall be conducted to prove the energy savings obtained due to the reduced deflection rate.

5. ACKNOWLEDGMENT

This work is supported in part by grant from UGC under MOMA-MANF scheme.

6. REFERENCES

[1] W. Dally and B. Towles. *Principles and Practices of Interconnection Networks*. Morgan Kaufmann, USA, 2004.

[2] C. Fallin, C. Craik, and O. Mutlu. Chipper: A low-complexity bufferless deflection router. In *17th International Symposium on High Performance Computer Architecture*, pages 144–155. IEEE Computer Society, 2011.

[3] T. Moscibroda and O. Mutlu. A case for bufferless routing in on chip networks. In *36th Annual International Symposium on Computer Architecture*, pages 196–207. ACM, 2009.

Trade-off between Energy and Quality of Service Through Dynamic Operand Truncation and Fusion

Wenchao Qian, Robert Karam and Swarup Bhunia
Case Western Reserve University, Cleveland, Ohio, USA
{wxq18,rak65,skb21}@case.edu

ABSTRACT

Energy efficiency has emerged as a major design concern for embedded and portable electronics. Conventional approaches typically impact performance and often require significant design-time modifications. In this paper, we propose a novel approach for improving energy efficiency through judicious fusion of operations. The proposed approach has two major distinctions: (1) the fusion is enabled by operand truncation, which allows representing multiple operations into a reasonably sized lookup table (LUT); and (2) it works for large varieties of functions. Most applications in the domain of digital signal processing (DSP) and graphics can tolerate some computation error without large degradation in output quality. Our approach improves energy efficiency with graceful degradation in quality. The proposed fusion approach can be applied to trade-off energy efficiency with quality at run time and requires virtually no circuit or architecture level modifications in a processor. Using our software tool for automatic fusion and truncation, the effectiveness of the approach is studied for four common applications. Simulation results show promising improvements (19-90%) in energy delay product with minimal impact on quality.

Categories and Subject Descriptors

B.8.1 [**Hardware**]: Performance and Reliability—*Reliability, Testing, and Fault-Tolerance*; C.5.4 [**Computer Systems Organization**]: Computer System Implementation—*VLSI Systems*; H.3.3 [**Information Systems**]: Information Search and Retrieval—*Information Search and Retrieval*

Keywords

Operation Fusion; Energy Efficiency; DSP; Quality of Service

1. INTRODUCTION

Energy efficiency has emerged as an important design constraint for embedded and portable electronics [1]. Design

GLSVLSI'14, May 21–23, 2014, Houston, Texas, USA.
ACM 978-1-4503-2816-6/14/05.
http://http://dx.doi.org/10.1145/2591513.2591561.

of energy-efficient systems can be accomplished by using design-time or run-time approaches. However, in general, they incur considerable performance overhead and often require circuit and architecture-level modifications. Truncation of input operand has been explored earlier in energy reduction [2]. However, they are applied at design time and are typically applicable to custom hardware. Memory based computing is another approach that provides an opportunity to reduce the computation energy through the use of LUTs [4].

In this paper, we propose a novel approach for improving energy efficiency in DSP and graphics applications through operation fusion and judicious truncation of operands. some applications are tolerant to output errors within an acceptable range based on the application requirements [2]. The proposed approach maps a complex fused operation into a lookup operation. Hence, it requires virtually zero design modifications and can be effective to reduce the number of operations. By ignoring a certain number of least significant bits, the LUT can be limited to an acceptable size, reducing the memory space and energy requirements while sacrificing the Quality of Service (QoS) or accuracy. We have presented the overall approach and proposed an efficient fusion process. We have developed a software tool to implement the fusion and truncation steps from the control and data flow graph, to create the LUT entries and to evaluate the trade-off between energy and accuracy. Using our tool, we have analyzed the effectiveness of the proposed approach for four representative applications. Our analysis shows 19 - 90% improvement in energy efficiency with only a modest loss of quality.

2. OVERALL APPROACH

The overall approach is described as follows. At design-time, input applications are first examined for opportunities for fusion. Once suitable operations are fused, the corresponding LUT content are generated. During run time, on-demand truncation schemes are applied to the complex fused functions to improve the energy efficiency and memory space. After a specific scheme is applied, the required LUTs are loaded into memory, and LUT operations is executed accessing memory to the correct address to retrieve the result. When finished, the QoS requirements are re-evaluated, and the truncation scheme is adjusted as needed.

Fusion incorporates three routines: (i) fusion of random LUT-based operations, (ii) fusion of bit-sliceable operations, and (iii) fusion of custom datapath operations. We have developed a heuristic for partitioning a target application into multi-input multi-output operations. The vertices inside each partition are fused to form a single vertex to be mapped as a LUT operation [3]. LUT implementation is enabled by truncating some insignificant bits from input operands, if they have large bitwidth (than a threshold), otherwise the LUT size will grow exponentially.

The memory-based computing paradigm calls for storing not only the data itself, but also the LUT content, in the same memory space. By involving the OS in the LUT storage process, the system is run-time configurable using the address containing the LUT content. In address generation, the base address represents the operation type, while the operands are combined in a shuffled pattern to form the offset address. This allows a lookup of a specific function output given by the two input operands. The operands form two different offset address, but use the same base address, as they are both inputs to the same function type. The LUT content needs to be computed and loaded only one time, further improving the energy required for repeated execution of the same kernel.

Loading the correct values, however, is not trivial, since any change into the number of truncated bits results in different offset addresses for given inputs. We store values in the reverse order, with the truncations being done from the MSBs. Hence, truncating each bit will disable part of the LUT content. In other words, useful entries will be stored in consecutive blocks, making the memory management trivial.

For applications that can tolerate a small amount of output error, input and/or output truncation becomes an attractive option for reducing the lookup table size and access energy, since the LUT size varies exponentially with the input bitwidth. Truncating few LSB bits often allow the output value to remain more or less the same, thus inducing graceful degradation in QoS.

The proposed approach is amenable for automation, and we have developed a software tool that can automatically identify the operations to fuse, perform appropriate operand truncation, create LUT content, and replace a cluster of fused operations into one lookup operation.

3. SIMULATION RESULTS

We have implemented and simulated several representative applications from the DSP and graphics domains, including a two-dimensional discrete cosine transform, color interpolation, finite impulse response filtering, and the discrete wavelet transform. These applications are compute-intensive, and may potentially benefit from LUT implementations; but more importantly, they can tolerate small amount of output error. The baseline implementation used a 16-bit adder for addition, a 16-bit lookup table for multiplication, and an operating frequency of 500MHz. Energy values were obtained using Synopsys Design Compiler for 32nm process models, while the memory access parameters were generated with CACTI. Finally, we assumed that all lookup table and datapath operations are completed in a single cycle. For a certain output bit width, LUT energy values are the same for different input sizes. This is because we assume that the total cache size does not change and run-time reconfiguration is being used to write the proper size of LUT content into cache according to input and output bit width. We evaluate the output quality using Peak Signal-to-Noise Ratio (PSNR) for color interpolation and DCT, and Mean Squared Error (MSE) for DWT and FIR (uniform and preferential trunca-

tions). Simulation results in Fig. 1 show promising improvements (19-90%) in energy delay product with a minimal impact on quality.

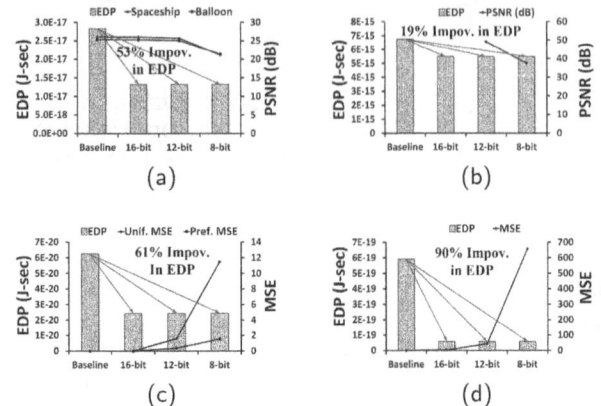

Figure 1: Comparison of EDP-quality for: (a) 2D-DCT, (b) color interpolation, (c) FIR, (d) DWT.

4. CONCLUSION

We have presented fusion approach enabled by judicious operand truncation that allows trade-off between energy efficiency and quality for signal processing and graphics applications. It utilizes the embedded memory of a processor to realize lookup-based evaluation of a fused operation. Thus, the proposed approach requires virtually no design modifications and can be used to trade-off energy versus accuracy at run-time. To minimize the quality impact associated with truncation, we have presented a preferential truncation strategy that optimally chooses the bits to truncate for an application. The approach is amenable to automation, and we have developed a software tool to evaluate it for four common applications. The proposed approach can be easily combined with existing run-time energy management schemes such as voltage scaling or adaptive body biasing.

5. ACKNOWLEDGEMENTS

The research has been funded in part by National Science Foundation (NSF) Grants #1002090 and #0964514.

6. REFERENCES

[1] N. Banerjee, G. Karakonstantis and K. Roy, "Process Variation Tolerant Low Power DCT Architecture," *DATE*, 2007.

[2] K. Kunaparaju, S. Narasimhan and S. Bhunia, "VaROT: Methodology for Variation-Tolerant DSP Hardware Design Using Post-Silicon Truncation of Operand Width," *VLSI Design*, 2011.

[3] J. Cong and S. Xu, "Technology mapping for fpgas with embedded memory blocks," *FPGA*, 1998.

[4] S. Paul and S. Bhunia, "Dynamic Transfer of Computation to Processor Cache for Yield and Reliability Improvement," *IEEE Trans. on VLSI systems*, 2011.

A Novel Low-Power and In-Place Split-Radix FFT Processor

Zhuo Qian
University of Massachusetts Lowell
Lowell, MA,USA
Zhuo_Qian@student.uml.edu

Martin Margala
University of Massachusetts Lowell
Lowell, MA,USA
Martin_Margala@uml.edu

ABSTRACT

Split-radix Fast Fourier Transform (SRFFT) approximates the minimum number of multiplications by theory among all the FFT algorithms. Since multiplications significantly contribute to the overall system power consumption, SRFFT is a good candidate for implementation of a low power FFT processor. In this paper we present a novel low power SRFFT processor using a modified radix-2 butterfly structure. With the proposed butterfly unit, the address generation scheme for conventional radix-2 FFT could be applied to SRFFT and therefore it can avoid the complexity of address generation and interim data registers. Simulation results show that compared with a conventional radix-2 implementation, power consumption of the new processor is reduced by an amount of 11.7% and 18.3% for 16-point and 32-point FFT respectively.

Categories and Subject Descriptors

B.7.1 [**Integrated Circuits**]: Algorithms Implemented in Hardware

Keywords

Radix-2; Split-Radix FFT; Low Power

1. INTRODUCTION

Discrete Fourier Transform (DFT) is one of the fundamental operations used for various signal processing and communication applications. Fast Fourier transform is a fast version of DFT algorithm which was developed by Cooley and Tukey in 1965 [1]. In 1984, Duhamel and Hollman [2] developed a new FFT algorithm called Split-Radix FFT (SRFFT). Their algorithm requires least multiplications and additions among all the known algorithms with input length N equals to 2^m (m is any natural number)

In general, all hardware implementations of FFT processors can be categorized into two main groups: pipelined architecture or shared-memory architecture. Pipelined architecture offers speed advantages but it requires more hardware resources at the same time. On the other hand, although shared-memory based architecture is slow, it requires least amount of hardware resources and it is often implemented with the "in-place" strategy, meaning that the two outputs of the butterfly unit can be written back to the same memory locations of the two inputs and replace the old data within one clock cycle. Previous research has focused on implementing SRFFT with pipelined architecture because the irregularity of split radix butterfly structure will lead to either complex control logic or extra registers to buffer interim data if using shared-memory technique.

GLSVLSI'14, May 21–23, 2014, Houston, Texas, USA.
ACM 978-1-4503-2816-6/14/05.
http://dx.doi.org/10.1145/2591513.2591563

In this paper, we implement a shared-memory, in-place and low power SRFFT processor using the proposed radix-2 butterfly structure. One advantage of using radix-2 butterfly is that the in-place memory addressing scheme could be adopted. Furthermore, the size of proposed butterfly structure remains constant as the FFT size increases. Compared with the reference design in [3], our proposed design offers a significant dynamic power reduction especially when it comes to large points of FFT.

2. DESIGN OF EACH MODULE
2.1 Modified Butterfly Structure

The new butterfly unit is shown in figure 1. First, the main difference between the proposed butterfly and conventional radix-2 butterfly is the extra multiplier that is placed at the upper leg of the butterfly unit. Second, in SRFFT algorithm, radix-2 stages are used for even half components and radix-4 are used for odd half components, which results in an "L" shaped butterfly. Our proposed unit can be seen as a combination of the "L" shaped butterfly and standard radix-2 butterfly. Note that in figure 1 both the adders and multipliers are complex arithmetic units. When we need to multiply twiddle factors, data go through the multiplier path. Otherwise, data just go to output. To prevent unnecessary switching activity, we put tristate buffer in the multiplier path. In [5], Loeffler mentioned a technique which calculates complex multiplications using only 3 real multiplications and 3 additions instead of 4 real multiplications and 2 additions. Using this technique, there are totally 6 real multipliers in our design.

2.2 Address Generation for RAMs and ROMs

In shared-memory architecture, FFT data that need to be processed are stored in RAMs. Pease [4] showed that in conventional radix-2 FFT, for every butterfly addresses of the two input data differ in their parity, therefore N-point FFT can be organized in two memory banks (RAM) according to the parity of their addresses. We observe that the flow graphs of conventional FFT and SRFFT are the same except for the location and value of twiddle factors, hence in-place and conflict-free memory addressing scheme for radix-2 FFT can also be applied to SRFFT. In 2007, Xiao [3] proposed a new in-place memory addressing scheme for radix-2 FFT. Based on our butterfly architecture Xiao's algorithm could be applied to address generation of SRFFT data.

However, when it comes to address generation of twiddle factors which are stored in ROMs, we cannot simply adopt Xiao's method, since conventional radix-2 FFT only has twiddle factors at the lower leg of butterfly unit while SRFFT has twiddle factors located at both the upper leg and lower leg. In our implementation, we use a decoder which takes the combination of pass counter P and butterfly counters B as inputs, and generates the address of twiddle factors as well as control signals for the tristate buffer. This fact suggests two ROMs are required, one for the upper leg twiddle factors and the other for the lower leg ones. The complete block diagram of SRFFT processor is shown in figure 2.

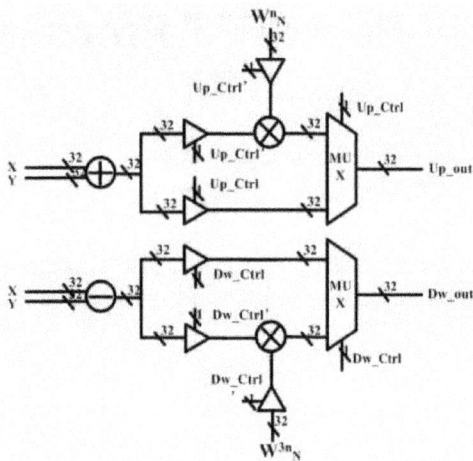

Figure 1. Proposed butterfly structure

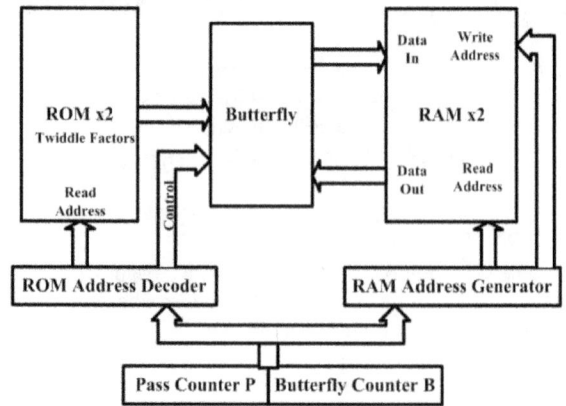

Figure 2. FFT block diagram

Table I
Synthesis Results and Power Comparison under Different FFT Size

FFT Size	Xiao's design [3]				Proposed design				
	Cell Count /Area (mm^2)	Delay (ns)	Static Power (mW)	Dynamic Power (mW)	Cell Count /Area(mm^2)	Delay (ns)	Static Power (mW)	Dynamic Power (mW)	Total Power Saving Ratio
8-point	4374/0.159	4.25	0.081	0.655	6017/0.219	4.91	0.132	0.710	—
16-point	5744/0.208	4.27	0.109	1.407	7305/0.261	4.94	0.161	1.178	11.7%
32-point	8118/0.298	4.39	0.159	1.830	9787/0.357	5.07	0.209	1.416	18.3%

3. IMPLEMENTATION RESULTS

In order to compare power consumption, we implemented the reference design in [3] and the proposed design with an input size of 8-point, 16-point and 32-point FFT respectively. Both FFT algorithms are written in VHDL 93 and synthesis is done using OSU gscl45nm library. Waveform simulation and power analysis are performed in NCsim and Cadence RTL Compiler. Power estimation is based on the switching activity file of 10 complete FFT operations generated by NCsim at 50MHz and 1.1 V.

Table I shows the simulation results of the overall implementation. First, for an 8-point FFT the proposed design consumes more power than the reference design because in this input size, both SRFFT algorithm and conventional radix-2 algorithm have the same number of complex multiplications. But when it comes to 16-point and 32-point FFT, compared with Xiao's design, the proposed architecture saves 11.7% and 18.3% of total power consumption respectively. Second, in terms of static power the proposed design is always larger than the reference design. However, in the technology we are using static power is only about 10% of total power consumption, therefore reducing dynamic power is the key part to minimize overall system power consumption. Because the number of multiplications required by SRFFT algorithm significantly decreases as the FFT size increases, it is reasonable to assume the proposed architecture will save more power and have higher power saving ratio when it comes to larger points of FFT.

4. CONCLUSION

In this paper we present a novel low power SRFFT processor using shared-memory-based architecture which is extensible to any 2^n-point FFT. Discussion is made on module design and implementation of SRFFT. Based on our proposed butterfly structure, the address generation algorithm for conventional radix-2 FFT could be applied to SRFFT. In contrast to pipelined architecture, shared-memory architecture is not designed for high speed or real time signal processing. Although the proposed design has a longer critical path delay, which is introduced by the multiplexer and tristate buffer, compared with conventional radix-2 FFT processor our implementation has the advantage of low power consumption, therefore it is very attractive for portable and wireless application where power is a critical design parameter.

5. REFERENCES

[1] J.W.Cooley and J.W.Tukey, "An algorithm for the machine calculation of complex Fourier series," *Math. Comput.*, 19:297–301, 1965

[2] P. Duharnel and H. Hollmann, "Split radix FFT algorithm," *Electronic Lett*ers, 20(1):14-16, 1984

[3] X. Xiao, E. Oruklu and J. Saniie, "An Efficient FFT Engine with Reduced Addressing Logic," *IEEE Transactions on Circuits and Systems II: Express Briefs*, 55(11):1149 - 1153, 2008.

[4] M. C. Pease, "Organization of large scale Fourier processors," *JACM*, 16(3):474-482, 1969

[5] C.Loeffler and A. Lightenberg, "Practical fast 1-DCT algorithms with 11 Multiplications," in *Proceedings of the International Conference on Acoustics, Speech and Signal Processing*, pp. 988-991, 1989.

H.264 8x8 Inverse Transform Architecture Optimization

Fabio Pereira   André Borin   Altamiro Susin

Programa de Pós-graduação em Microeletrônica (PgMicro)
Universidade Federal do Rio Grande do Sul – Brasil
Av. Osvaldo Aranha, 103
fabio.irigon@gmail.com, borin@inf.ufrgs.br, altamiro.susin@ufrgs.br

ABSTRACT

This paper presents a resource optimized hardware solution to perform the H.264 8x8 inverse transform. Row/column decomposition is used, arithmetic units are re-used and the transpose memory is replaced by a shift register. The architecture is able to perform 8x8 integer transform calculation in 144 cycles with as few as 431 LUTs on a Xilinx virtex 6 FPGA for 16-bit resolution. To enable the module to process all inverse transforms in H.264, the number of LUTs is increased to 681. When used to calculate all transforms for H.264 videos, the design supports resolutions up to 1280x720@30fps when running at 84 MHz.

Categories and Subject Descriptors

B.5.1 **[Register Transfer Level Implementation]**: Design - *Styles*

General Terms

Algorithms, Design.

Keywords

H.264; inverse transform; Hardware Implementation

1. INTRODUCTION

The H.264 [1] is a widely used standard for video applications introducing, several algorithms to increase video compression efficiency. One of such algorithms is the 8x8 integer transform.

The difference between the predicted images and the original image is called "residual" and is the input to the transformation module on the video encoder. The outputs of the module are called transform coefficients. On the decoder, the transformed coefficients, are used by the inverse transform module to generate the residuals. The residuals can then be added to the predicted image to generate the reconstructed image.

For the H.264 integer transforms, the row/column decomposition was proposed in several works [2], [3], using either one or two 1-dimension transform modules (1DT). In those designs the 2D transform is divided in two 1D steps. In this paper, focusing on area reduction, a modified version of the 1DT block will be presented. Then a minimalistic architecture using the proposed module will be introduced.

GLSVLSI'14, May 21–23, 2014, Houston, Texas, USA.
ACM 978-1-4503-2816-6/14/05.
http://dx.doi.org/10.1145/2591513.2591564

2. H.264 INVERSE TRANSFORM ALGORITHM:

The inverse transform algorithm receives a matrix of transform coefficients and generates matrix of residuals. In all transforms supported by H.264 the 2D-transforms can be split into two 1D-transforms, by first applying a set of operations in each row of the input matrix of transformed coefficients, storing the outputs as a matrix of intermediary values, and finally applying the same procedure in each column of the intermediary values, generating the final transformed values. Fig. 1 shows the operations performed in one row/column ($d_0 - d_7$) in the 8x8 inverse transform.

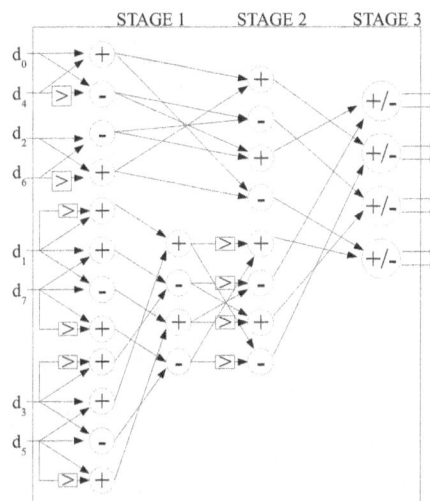

Figure 1: original 1DT

The 4x4 transform is a sub-set of the 8x8 transform algorithm, and the 4x4 Hadamard inverse transform is implemented by the same sub-set just replacing two operands by the right-shift result of those operands. The 2D-2x2 Hadamard transform can be calculated with the same operations as the 1D-4x4 Hadamard.

3. THE PROPOSED SOLUTION:

Looking at the stage 1 and stage 2 of the 1D 8x8 inverse transform, we can see that the even and odd arguments are calculated independently in stages 1 and 2 and those outputs are processed together only in stage 3.

The idea is to create a single 4 input and 4 output sub-module to calculate the odd elements of stages 1 and 2 of the 8x8 transform. Then those outputs are stored, and the same module is reused to calculate the even coefficients. This sub-module will be called M1DT_core. The outputs of the M1DT_core for the odd and even coefficients can then be all processed together to generate the final outputs. The left of Fig. 2 shows the M1DT architecture.

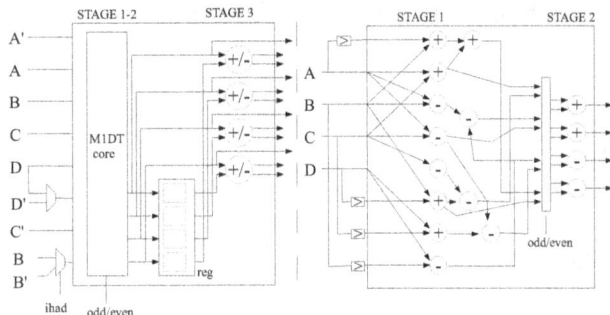

Figure 2: M1DT architecture and the M1DT core

We define 4 inputs {A, B, C, D} for our module, and the right shifted version of those inputs are represented by {A', B', C', D'}. When the odd part of the 8x8 matrix is selected, the inputs (A, B, C, D) will be set to {d1, d3, d5, d7}, otherwise to {d0, d2, d4, d6}. The 4 adders/subtractors in the even part of step 1 are a subset of the twelve adder/subtractors used in the odd part of step 1. Step 2 is composed of 8 operations, 4 additions and 4 subtractions. By placing a 2x1 multiplexer on each input of these units we can perform odd and even operations of the steps 1 and 2 of the 8x8 inverse transform, with 7 adders and 9 subtractors instead of the 14 adders and 10 subtractors required for parallel calculation, of course with some extra multiplexing and lower throughput. The right of Fig 2 shows the internal connections for the M1DT_core, with all connections being 16 bit wide.

An architecture using the M1DT module was implemented aimed for applications where high throughput is not mandatory. A shift-register is used in place of the usual transpose memory. Three multiplexers control the unit: MA selects external input or intermediate results from the shift-register, MC chooses odd, even or the four inputs when 4x4 algorithm should be used, and MB is used to select which column of intermediate results will be stored. Fig 3 shows the layout.

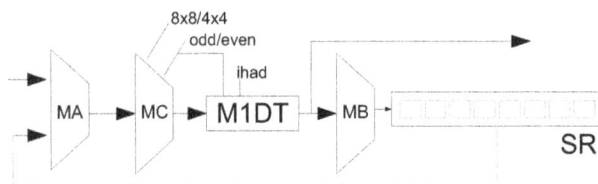

Figure 3: The proposed architecture

4. RESULTS AND COMPARISONS:

In order to evaluate our proposed design, we implemented the architecture used by [2] and [3] targeting only the 8x8 transform. The pipelining registers, quantization module and output multiplexer used in the original works were removed, the bit width of all the operators was set to 16-bit, and all the multiplexers and operators for the smaller transforms were not included. We named them "Implemented A" and "Implemented B" respectively. All designs were only able to fully execute the 8x8 transform, synthesized with the same tool, to the same target platform (Xilinx Virtex 6) and the results and the original implementations are shown in table 1.

Table 1: Comparison with other architectures

Design:	LUTs/FFs	Add/Sub	Support	Thput(8x8):
Proposed	430/253	24	8x8	8/18 samp/cyc
Implemented A	898/1051	32/40	8x8	4 samp/cyc
Implemented B	966/135	64	8x8	1 samp/cyc
Original [1]	———	32/40	all	4 samp/cyc
Original [2]	2887/251	64	8x8+Q	1 samp/cyc

When the control and multiplexers for all the transforms are added to the proposed solution, the number of LUTs is increased to 681, which is still very low. Even with the lower throughput, the module would have to run at 85 MHz to support 1280x720@30fps to when used for all transforms.

5. CONCLUSION

This paper showed an optimized implementation of the H.264 8x8 transform. Row/Column decomposition and arithmetic re-use have been employed to reduce the number of used logic elements. The proposed solution is suitable to HD videosystems as part of a full decoder or as an accelerator IP.

6. ADDITIONAL AUTHORS

Alexsandro Bonatto – *Instituto Federal de Educação, Ciência e Tecnologia* - alexsandro.bonatto@ufrgs.br

Marcelo Negreiros – *Universidade Federal do Rio Grande do Sul* - negreiro@eletro.ufrgs.br

7. REFERENCES

[1] ITU –T. 2005. Recommendation H.264 & ISO/TEC 14496-10 AVC, Advanced Video Coding for Generic Audiovisual Services, 2005 version 3

[2] - Y. C. Chao, H. H. Tsai, Y. H. Lin, J. F. Yang, and B. D. Liu. 2007. A novel design for computation of all transforms in H.264/AVC decoders. *in IEEE Int. Conf. Multimedia Expo*, pp. 1914–1917 (Jul 2007)

[3] J. S. Park, T. Ogunfunmi. 2009. A New Hardware Implementation of the H.264 8x8 Transform and Quantization. 2009 *in Acoustics, Speech and Signal Processing, IEEE International Conference on.* (2009)

Energy-efficient Wireless Network-on-Chip Architecture with Log-Periodic On-Chip Antennas

Md Shahriar Shamim,
Naseef Mansoor,
Amlan Ganguly
Rochester Institute of Technology
(ms5614,nxm4026,amlan.gang
uly)@rit.edu

Aman Samaiyar
Delhi Technological University
aman.samaiyar@dce.edu

Sujay Deb,
Shobha Sunndar Ram
Indraprastha Institute of Technology
(sdeb,shobha)@iiitd.ac.in

ABSTRACT

On-chip wireless interconnects have emerged as a promising alternative to conventional wireline interconnects in Network-on-Chip (NoC) fabrics for multicore systems. However, it is not practical in the immediate future to arbitrarily scale up the number of wireless links without innovations in the physical layer. Here, we explore the design of a directional on-chip antenna based on a log-periodic structure. In this paper we propose the design of a wireless NoC (WiNoC) architecture with concurrent wireless links using these directional on-chip antennas. Through cycle accurate simulations we demonstrate that this novel WiNoC architecture attains better performance and energy efficiency compared to the state-of-the-art token based WiNoC of similar topology.

Categories and Subject Descriptors

C.2.1 **[Computer-Communication Networks]**: Network Architecture and Design

General Terms

Performance, Design.

Keywords

Network-on-Chip; wireless interconnect; directional antenna.

1. INTRODUCTION

In the era of multicore chips the number of cores per chip is predicted to increase up to several hundreds in the near future. Networks-on-Chips (NoCs) have emerged as a communication backbone for such systems. Conventional NoCs with metal/dielectric based interconnects are not scalable in terms of performance and energy consumption due to long multi-hop wireline paths. On-chip wireless interconnects are shown to alleviate this problem by introducing direct long-range links [1]. Many on-chip wireless architectures are explored with different physical layer design technologies. However, the CMOS process-compatible zig-zag antennas [1] widely studied in on-chip environments so far do not have good directional characteristics. Moreover, creating multiple millimeter-wave transceivers tuned to non-overlapping channels to enable concurrent links is an extremely challenging problem. Therefore some wireless NoC (WiNoC) architectures adopt a token passing based wireless medium access mechanism to transmit data over the shared

GLSVLSI'14, May 21–23, 2014, Houston, Texas, USA.
ACM 978-1-4503-2816-6/14/05
http://dx.doi.org/10.1145/2591513.2591566

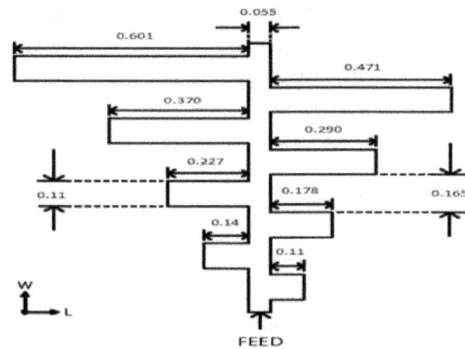

Figure 1. On-chip planar log periodic antenna with dimensions in mm

wireless channel. Although this is a simple distributed mechanism without the need for any centralized synchronization, only a single transmitter can access the wireless channel at any given instant of time. This limits the performance benefits of the wireless interconnection although multiple transceivers are deployed over the entire NoC. In this paper, we propose to use log periodic on-chip directional antennas to enable multiple concurrent links, which will eventually improve performance and energy efficiency of the WiNoC.

2. WIRELESS NOC ARCHITECTURE

The architecture and consequently the performance of the WiNoC with directional antennas (DWiNoC) strongly depend on the physical layer design strategy, which are discussed in this section.

2.1 Physical Layer

In this section we discuss the directional log-periodic antenna we propose to use in the DWiNoC. Planar log periodic antennas (PLPA) are very popular and widely studied for their ease of manufacturing and for their wide-band properties [2]. In this paper, we propose the design for an on-chip planar log-periodic antenna with wide bandwidth and high end-fire directivity in the millimeter wave frequency range. The generalized design parameters allow the flexibility towards designing the antennas for specified frequencies. The design of the log-periodic antenna adopted in this paper with eight teeth is shown in Figure. 1. The sizes of the teeth increase in a logarithmic manner. The dimensions mentioned in the figure are specifically for 60 GHz and can be scaled appropriately for any desired frequency of operation within micro and millimeter wave range. The longest dimension of the antenna is 1.1825 mm that is comparable to the wavelength of the signal in the dielectric medium.

A wireless interconnect can be implemented by establishing a communication link between antennas on the same substrate with one antenna in the end-fire region of another. We adopt the transceiver design from [1] where a simple non-coherent On-Off Keying (OOK) based transceiver is demonstrated for power-efficiency.

2.2 Topology and routing of the DWiNoC

The topology of the proposed DWiNoC is a small-world network where the wireline links between switches are established following an inverse power-law distribution discussed in [3]. This strategy of developing a small-world network has been shown to be most efficient in terms of wiring costs.

The location of the WIs is optimized for minimum average distance or hop-count between source-destination pairs while ensuring that no WI is in the path of communication between other pairs of WIs. This optimization is performed following a Simulated Annealing based heuristics while observing the following constraints:

1) Linearity constraints: There will be no such node in any pairs that will be in the end-fire region of other antennas.

2) Angularity constrains: There will be no such element in any pairs that will be in the same line passing through the side lobes of any other antenna as seen in Figure 2.

Following these constraints in the SA optimization we are able to establish concurrent links, which do not interfere with each other and design the DWiNoC with the minimum average hop-count. In the DWiNoC data is transferred via wormhole routing using virtual channel (VC) based NoC switches. Deadlock is avoided by using a forwarding-table based routing over precomputed shortest paths determined by Dijkstra's algorithm.

3. EXPERIMENTAL RESULTS

In this section, we demonstrate the characteristics of the PLPA antennas and evaluate the performance and energy efficiency of the proposed DWiNoC architecture. In this work, the NoC architecture is characterized using a cycle accurate simulator accounting for those flits that reach the destination as well as those that are dropped. The width of all wired links is considered to be same as the flit size, which is considered to be 32 bits. We consider a moderate packet size of 64 flits for all our experiments. Similar to the wired links, we have adopted wormhole routing in the wireless links too.

3.1 Antenna characteristics and link budget analysis

The 60 GHz on-chip PLPA is simulated using FEM based HFSS software. Here, a 10-20 Ω-cm silicon substrate is considered. The radiation patterns of the antenna in the azimuth and elevation plane are shown in Figure 2. It demonstrates the end-fire beamwidth of the on-chip PLPA is 33°. Similarly, the half-power beamwidth along the elevation, is 30°.

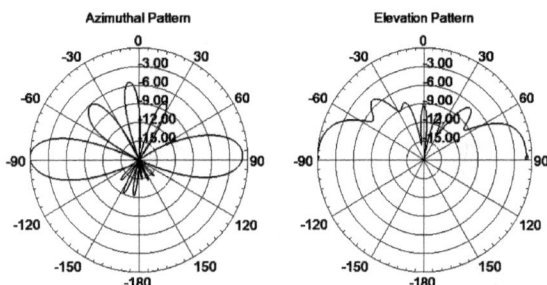

Figure 2. Radiation pattern along the azimuthal and elevation plane

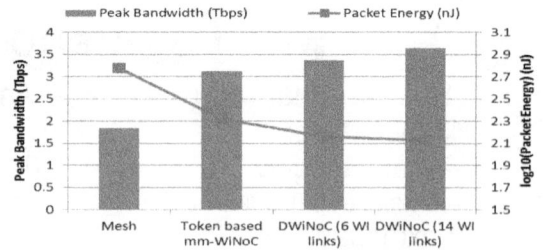

Figure 3. Peak bandwidth and packet energy dissipation of various NoC architectures for 64-core system

3.2 Performance Evaluation of the DWiNoC

In this section, we evaluate the peak bandwidth and energy efficiency of the proposed directional antenna based DWiNoC architecture for a 64-core system with uniform random traffic distribution and the results are shown in Figure 3. We also compare it with a conventional wireline mesh and the token-based WiNoC with similar topology. We found that our proposed architecture achieves higher bandwidth and lower packet energy compared to both mesh and token based WiNoC. The token based WiNoC has higher bandwidth and about three times less packet energy compared to mesh of the same system size due to the efficient small-world network topology and energy-efficient wireless links. However, in the token-based WiNoC only a single wireless link is active at any given point of time. We have evaluated the directional antenna based DWiNoC with similar number of WIs (6 links or 12 WIs for the 64 core system) as the token based WiNoC optimized for best performance. Even for the same overheads in wireless transceivers we see that the proposed architecture achieves higher bandwidth and lower packet energy compared to the token-based system due to multiple concurrent wireless links. On increasing the number of concurrent links to 14 with 28 WIs, we observe that the packet energy and bandwidth are further improved compared to the DWiNoC with 6 links.

4. CONCLUSIONS

In this paper we present the design of a wireless NoC architecture with directional log-periodic antennas. Through system level simulations we demonstrate that such a WiNoC is capable of improving the performance and reduce packet energy dissipation compared to the state-of-the-art token passing based WiNoC as well as a conventional electronic mesh based NoC.

5. ACKNOWLEDGEMENTS

This work is supported in part by the US National Science Foundation, under grant CCF1162123.

6. REFERENCES

[1] S. Deb, A. Ganguly, P. P. Pande, B. Belzer, and D. Heo, "Wireless NoC as Interconnection Backbone for Multicore Chips: Promises and Challenges," *IEEE J. on Emerging and Selected Topics in Circuits and Systems*, vol. 2, no. 2, pp. 228–239, 2012.

[2] Z. N. Chen, M. J. Ammann, X. Qing, X. H. We, T. S. P. See and A. Cai, "Planar antennas", *IEEE Microw. Mag.*, vol. 7, no. 6, pp. 63-73, Dec. 2006.

[3] A. Ganguly, P. Wettin, K. Chang, and P. Pande, "Complex network inspired fault-tolerant NoC architectures with wireless links," in *IEEE/ACM International Symposium on Networks on Chip (NoCS)*, pp. 169–176, 2011.

Customizing an Open Source Processor to Fit in an Ultra-Low Power Cluster with a Shared L1 Memory

Michael Gautschi[1], Davide Rossi[2], Luca Benini[1,2]

[1] Integrated Systems Laboratory
ETH Zurich, Switzerland
{gautschi,benini}@iis.ee.ethz.ch

[2] Electrical, Electronic, and Information Engineering
University of Bologna, Italy
{davide.rossi, luca.benini}@unibo.it

ABSTRACT

The OpenRISC processor core, featuring a flat pipeline and a low area footprint has been integrated in a multi-core ultra-low power (ULP) cluster with a shared multi-banked memory to exploit parallelism in the near-threshold regime. The micro-architecture has been optimized to support a shared L1 memory and to achieve a high value of instructions per cycle (IPC) per core. The proposed architecture achieves IPC results in the range of 0.88 and 1 in a set of benchmark applications which is an improvement of up to 83% with respect to the original OpenRISC implementation.

Implemented in 28 nm FDSOI technology, the proposed design achieves 177 MOPS when supplied at 0.6 V near-threshold voltage. The energy efficiency at this workload is 90.07 MOPS/mW which is an improvement of 50% with respect to what can be achieved with an OpenRISC cluster based on the original micro-architecture.

Categories and Subject Descriptors

B.7.1 [**Integrated Circuits**]: Types and Design Styles—*Microprocessors and Microcomputers*
; C.1.1 [**Processor Architectures**]: Single Data Stream Architectures—*RISC/CISC, VLIW Architectures*

General Terms

Design, Performance

Keywords

VLSI; Ultra-Low Power; Processor; RISC; OpenRISC; Many-core Cluster; Parallel Computing; IPC; 28 nm FDSOI

1. OPENRISC CLUSTER INTEGRATION

Today's deeply embedded sensing systems [9][4] require ever-increasing processing performance while operating in ULP and maintaining extreme energy efficiency up to 1 GOPS/mW. Because of the quadradic dependency of

GLSVLSI'14, May 21–23, 2014, Houston, Texas, USA.
ACM 978-1-4503-2816-6/14/05.
http://dx.doi.org/10.1145/2591513.2591569.

power and supply voltage, it is more energy efficient to process workloads at a reduced speed and lower voltage [6]. Processor clusters in advanced process technologies such as 28 nm FDSOI achieve a high energy efficiency if operated in the near-threshold voltage regime. It was shown [1] that a multi-core architecture consumes 62% less power with respect to its single core equivalent. Our cluster in Fig. 1 features 4 processing elements (PE) and a shared scratchpad memory, realized with 8 tightly coupled data memory (TCDM) banks. TCDM is accessed through a low-latency interconnect (LIC) [2] to maximize the computational efficiency of each core. The key feature when targeting high energy efficiency is an optimized core micro-architecture to achieve near-unitary IPC while keeping the complexity low. In the context of a shared-L1 cluster, it is not the pipeline of the PE itself which limits the maximum frequency but the return path of the shared memory. A flat pipeline as in the ARM Cortex M series [7] which is currently dominating the low-power, low-cost market for 32b architecutres is suitable for the cluster. However, ARM is a proprietary instruction set architecture (ISA) and RTL implementations are not publicly available. The Open Cores community [5] offers a functionally comparable 32b ISA, featuring a flat pipeline and a low area footprint which makes it suitable to be integrated in the ULP-cluster, as it allows for high IPC even in presence of control flow and data dependencies.

The 32b *or1200* implementation [3] has been used as PE with a private 2 KB I$ in a cluster which consists of 8 4 KB TCDM banks. Implemented in 28 nm FDSOI, a critical path of 5.3 ns from TCDM (3.8 ns memory access time) back to the register file of the core was measured in a slow-slow corner at 0.6 V and −40 °C. Using a single core and a hot I$, IPC has been analyzed and multiplications, branching and the load/store interface have been identified as main sources for IPC-losses. An improved micro-architecture with additional write ports at the register file to get rid of the blocking behaviour of the multiplier and the load/store interface is presented in Fig. 2. The multiplier is pipelined once, and the core is only stalled if data hazards have been detected. In addition, zero overhead branching has been employed by moving the branch computation to the second stage of the pipeline and forwarding the flag for conditional branches to the *genPC* unit.

The optimized micro-architecture of the OpenRISC allows to achieve up to 83% higher IPC values as illustrated in Fig. 3 in a collection of branch, storage, and computational

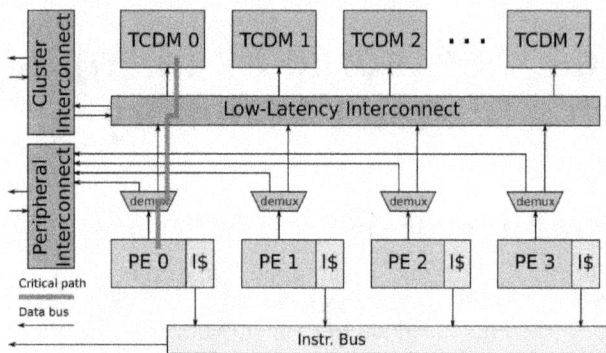

Figure 1: ULP-cluster with 4 PEs and 8 TCDM banks connected by a low-latency interconnect.

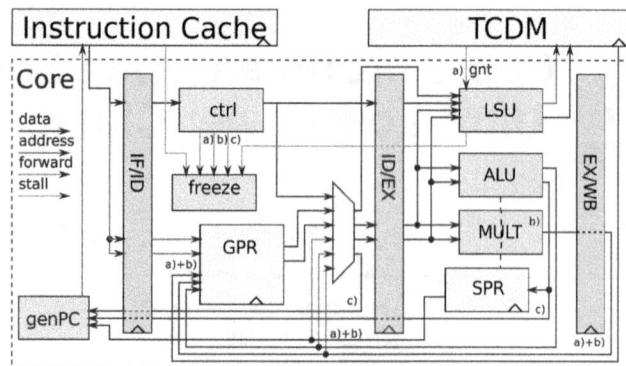

Figure 2: Architectural modifications to minimize stalls related to a) load/store operations, b) multiplications and c) branches.

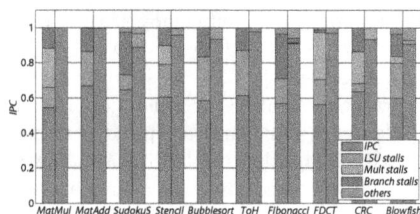

Figure 3: IPC and profiling comparison between the original and the improved micro-architecture.

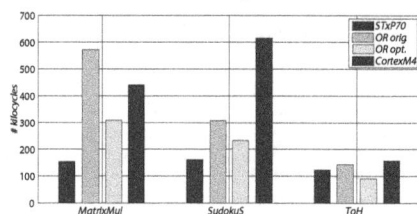

Figure 4: Run time comparison assuming a fixed frequency.

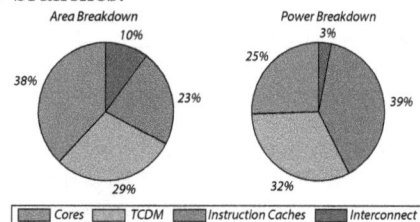

Figure 5: Area and power distribution of the cluster.

intensive benchmark programs. Implemented in 28 nm FD-SOI the cluster achieves a maximum frequency of 188 MHz in a slow-slow corner at 0.6 V. In this conditions an average power consumption of $10.98\,\mu W/MHz$ was measured when executing a matrix multiplication. With automatic clock gating, 90% of the registers are gated which reduces the power consumption during stalls to $2.13\,\mu W/MHz$. The higher IPC allows each core to achieve 177 MOPS, when supplied with 0.6 V which equals an energy efficiency of 90.07 MOPS/mW while the original micro-architecture requires a supply voltage of 0.68 V to process this workload. Thanks to the higher computational efficiency, the improved micro-architecture is 50% more energy efficient, while the area of the optimized core did only increase by 5%.

Fig. 4 shows that the optimized OpenRISC is competitive with the ARM Cortex M4, but worse than the STxP70 [8]. Although the IPC performance of the optimized OpenRISC version is nearly optimal, the instruction set and the compiler are different to the other cores. The STxP70 is a dual issue processor with a complex and bigger architecture than our OpenRISC architecture and is therefore able to execute programs faster.

Finally, Fig. 5 shows an area and power breakdown of the complete cluster which takes up $0.255\,mm^2$. Due to a low leakage technology, total leakage is only $0.8\,\mu W$ at $-40\,°C$ and $781\,\mu W$ or 5.98% of total dynamic power at $125\,°C$. The cores require 38% of the area while at the same time, they only consume 25% of the power. Hence, it is important to optimize the computational efficiency of the cores in order to also minimize the amount of power consumed by the I\$ and TCDM. Future work will focus on improving the power consumption in memories as it is dominant.

2. ACKNOWLEDGMENTS

We would like to thank the OpenRISC community for their effort in the design of an open source processor. This work was supported by the FP7 project PHIDIAS (318013).

3. REFERENCES

[1] A. Dogan et al. 'Low-Power Processor Architecture Exploration for Online Biomedical Signal Analysis'. *IET'12*, 6(5):279–286.

[2] A. Rahimi et al. 'A Fully-Synthesizable Single-Cycle Interconnection Network for Shared-L1 Processor Clusters'. In *DATE'11*, pages 1–6.

[3] D. Lampret. 'OpenRISC 1200 IP Core Specification'. 2010.

[4] M. Hanson et al. 'Body Area Sensor Networks: Challenges and Opportunities'. *Computer*, 42(1):58–65, 2009.

[5] Open Cores. 'http://www.opencores.org'.

[6] R. Dreslinski et al. 'Near-Threshold Computing: Reclaiming Moore's Law through Energy Efficient Integrated Circuits'. *Proceedings of the IEEE*, 98(2):253–266, 2010.

[7] D. Seal. *'ARM Architecture Reference Manual'*. Pearson Education, 2000.

[8] Y. Janin et al. 'Designing Tightly-Coupled Extension Units for the STxP70 Processor'. In *DATE'13*, pages 1052–1053.

[9] G.-Z. Yang and M. Yacoub. 'Body Sensor Networks'. 2006.

Performance Modeling of Virtualized Custom Logic Computations

Michael J. Hall   Roger D. Chamberlain
Department of Computer Science and Engineering
Washington University in St. Louis
{mhall24, roger}@wustl.edu

ABSTRACT

Virtualization of custom logic computations (i.e., by sharing a fixed function across distinct data streams), provides a means of reusing limited hardware resources. This is common practice in traditional processors where more than one user can share processor resources. In this paper, we virtualize a custom logic block using C-slow techniques to support fine-grain context-switching. We then develop and present an analytic model for several performance measures (throughput, latency, input queue occupancy) for both fine- and coarse-grained context switching. Next, we calibrate the analytic performance model with empirical measurements. We then validate the model via discrete-event simulation and use the model to predict the performance and develop optimal schedules for virtualized logic computations.

Categories and Subject Descriptors

B.5.2 [**Register-Transfer-Level Implementation**]: Optimization; B.8.2 [**Performance and Reliability**]: Performance Analysis and Design Aids

1. INTRODUCTION

Virtualization of computational resources provides a way by which hardware resources can be reused or shared. Sharing is a common technique for utilizing available hardware resources for computing such as DSP blocks, memory controllers, memory bandwidth, and IP cores.

We have developed a model of the performance of a virtualized fixed logic computation. Our interest is in supporting a set of distinct data streams that all wish to perform the same computation. Virtualizing the logic computation involves sharing hardware resources and context-switching each distinct data stream into the hardware. This context switch can be either fine-grained (in which context is changed each clock cycle) or coarse-grained (in which the state of the computation is swapped out to a secondary memory). With the model, we can then tune a schedule for optimal performance.

To virtualize a function, consider a hardware block (HW) with an Nx1 input multiplexer and 1xN output demultiplexer. This block is a function implemented in custom logic. N distinct data streams (each with a dedicated input and output port) share the single instance of the HW block. These data streams are then multiplexed into the custom logic block, processed, and then demultiplexed back into independent streams. When the logic function is purely combinational (i.e., feed-forward), inputs from any data stream can be presented to the HW block at each clock cycle, even if it is deeply pipelined. In this case, there are no constraints on scheduling. When the logic function is sequential (i.e., has feedback) and has been deeply pipelined, this imposes scheduling constraints. Once a data element from a particular stream has been delivered to the HW block, the stream has to wait a number of clock ticks equal to the pipeline depth before it can provide a subsequent data element from that same stream.

Pipelined logic circuits having feedback can be context switched to compute multiple data streams concurrently. The pipelined logic adds latency and decreases single stream throughput since it takes multiple clock cycles (corresponding to the number of pipeline stages) to compute a single result and feed it back to the input. If the number of pipeline stages is C, then this circuit is said to be C-slowed since a single computation takes C times more clock cycles (often mitigated by a higher clock *rate*). C-slow is a technique described by Leiserson and Saxe [2] by which each register is replaced by C registers and then retimed to balance the registers throughout the combinational logic.

When the number of contexts to be supported, N, is greater than the pipeline depth, C, coarse-grained context switching can be used, swapping out whatever state is stored in the circuit to a secondary memory. In general, this will incur some cost, S, representing the overhead of a context switch.

2. MODELING AND CALIBRATION

The queueing model computes the effective service rate for each context to be

$$\mu_s = \frac{R_S}{(R_S N + SN/C) \cdot t_{CLK}} \text{ elements/s} \quad (1)$$

where R_S is the number of rounds of C fine-grain contexts that execute in a round-robin schedule before a context switch to a secondary memory (schedule period).

It follows that the total achievable throughput, T_{TOT}, is then $N \cdot \mu_s$. The wait time at the head of the queue is,

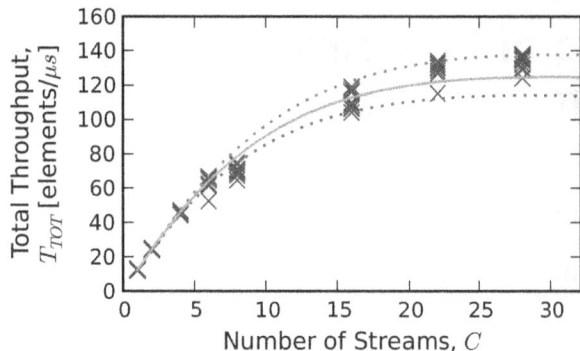

Figure 1: Total achievable throughput plot. The number of streams is the logic pipeline depth, C, and $N = C$). For each value of C, 10 data points were taken.

likewise, determined to be

$$W_h = \frac{(R_S (N - C) + SN/C)^2 \cdot t_{CLK}}{2 (R_S N + SN/C)}$$

which can be used with classic queueing model results to compute latency.

We use an AES encryption cipher in CBC block mode (that has a feedback path) as the experimental vehicle to calibrate the clock period, t_{CLK}, in the model. In our implementation, the individual block cipher is fully unrolled forming a long combinational function up to 14 rounds (the AES 256-bit standard) [3]. We target a Xilinx Virtex-4 XC4VLX100 FPGA and use the Xilinx ISE 13.4 tools for synthesis, place, & route of the hardware designs.

We compute the total throughput, T_{TOT}, as $1/t_{CLK}$, and plot the observed data values from the synthesis, place, & route runs and a model prediction fitted to the data in Figure 1. The solid line represents the model prediction. The dotted lines represent confidence intervals on the model [1] (computed as a 95% confidence for 10 future observations).

The model does a reasonably good job of characterizing the shape of the curve. Most, although clearly not all, of the measured data points are within the confidence intervals. Second, throughput initially increases linearly (at low stream counts) but eventually levels off and adding additional streams does not provide any significant throughput gains. Finally, the maximum throughput achievable is present at 16 streams and higher.

3. RESULTS

We use our model with the calibrated t_{CLK} to predict latency and total throughput performance (shown in Figure 2) as a function of offered load and schedule period (R_S). The latency plot is initially high at low R_S due to queueing delay, but drops steeply as R_S increases due to the total achievable throughput also increasing. Latency then hits a minimum at the knee and next gradually increases due to wait time caused by the larger R_S in the round-robin schedule. The total achievable throughput plot increases as R_S increases because the cost of a context switch, S, is amortized by the higher schedule period. To optimize for both latency and throughput, we computed a figure of merit (FoM) defined

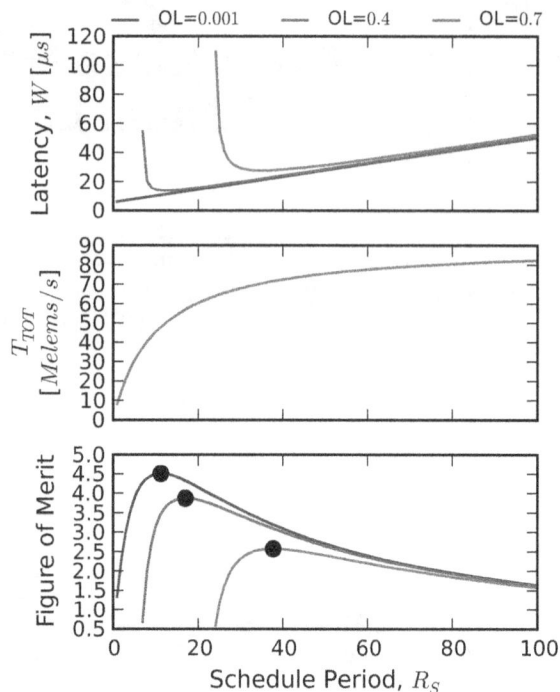

Figure 2: Latency (top), total achievable throughput (middle), and figure of merit (bottom) at three different offered loads (OL) versus the schedule period, R_S. C is 10, N is 100, S is 100, and t_{CLK} is calibrated using model in Figure 1.

as T_{TOT}/W (total throughput divided by latency). A plot of the figure of merit shows that it is initially low (due to low throughput and high latency), increases to a peak (the optimal value), and then decreases gradually (since latency is increasing faster than throughput).

Solving for the maximum FoM optimizes the schedule period, R_S, concurrently for high throughput and low latency.

4. CONCLUSIONS

Analytic models are developed for achievable throughput, latency (including traditional queueing, increased queueing due to hierarchical scheduling, and compute time), and occupancy of the input buffers. Using the models, we demonstrate the ability to choose an optimal schedule period as a function of one (or more) input parameters.

5. ACKNOWLEDGMENT

This research was supported by NSF grant CNS-0931693.

6. REFERENCES

[1] R. Jain. *The Art of Computer System Performance Analysis: Techniques for Experimental Design, Measurement, Simulation and Modeling.* John Wiley & Sons, Inc., New York, 1991.

[2] C. Leiserson and J. Saxe. Retiming synchronous circuitry. *Algorithmica*, 6:5–35, June 1991.

[3] NIST. FIPS-197: Advanced Encryption Standard. *Federal Information Processing Standards (FIPS) Publications*, Nov. 2001.

Scheduling of PDE Setting and Timing Tests for Post-Silicon Skew Tuning with Timing Margin

[Extended Abstract]

Mineo Kaneko
Japan Advanced Institute of Science and Technology
1-1 Asahidai, Nomi-shi, Ishikawa, Japan
mkaneko@jaist.ac.jp

ABSTRACT

Post-Silicon clock-Skew Tuning (PSST) is a promising technology for improving performance-yield of VLSIs under process variations. On the other hand, the resultant circuit after PSST should be also robust for run-time timing variations due to the change of temperature, power supply noise, etc. So, post-silicon skew tuning problem considering timing margin arises. In this work, the timing margin in the context of PSST is defined in terms of control values for programmable delay elements (PDEs), and a novel PDE tuning algorithm considering timing margin is proposed. The key component of our PDE tuning procedure is a timing test considering timing margin, in which we need to use a set of different PDE settings (μ-margin PDE test-settings) from a designed (target) PDE setting. Discussions done in this work are devoted to reducing test cost in terms of the number of timing test as well as PDE setting cost in terms of the number of μ-margin PDE test-settings.

Categories and Subject Descriptors

B.8 [**Performance and Reliability**]: Reliability, Testing, and Fault-Tolerance; B.7 [**Integrated Circuits**]: Miscellaneous

Keywords

Delay variation, clock skew, delay test, setup timing constraint, hold timing constraint

1. PDE SETTING WITH TIMING MARGIN

This work is based on the same concept of "timing margin in control values" proposed in our previous work "Timing-Test Scheduling for Constraint-Graph based Post-Silicon Skew Tuning" (Proc. ICCD, pp.460-465, 2012), but proposes a quite different strategy to guarantee the timing margin, which is called "μ-margin timing test". In order to guarantee the

GLSVLSI'14, May 21–23, 2014, Houston, Texas, USA.
ACM 978-1-4503-2816-6/14/05.
http://dx.doi.org/10.1145/2591513.2591571.

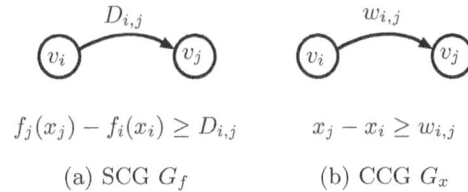

$$f_j(x_j) - f_i(x_i) \geq D_{i,j} \qquad x_j - x_i \geq w_{i,j}$$

(a) SCG G_f \qquad (b) CCG G_x

Figure 1: An edge of skew constraint graph (a), and an edge of control-value constraint graph (b).

robustness against run-time variations, only the monotonicity of PDE delay with respect to its control value is assumed in our μ-margin timing test, while a kind of linearity is assumed in the previous work.

If we consider a standard sequential circuit together with PDEs on a clock distribution tree, the correct operation of the circuit is guaranteed by the *setup timing constraint* and the *hold timing constraint*, both of which can be represented in the form

$$f_j(x_j) - f_i(x_i) > D_{i,j}$$

where $f_j(x_j)$ is a PDE delay for FF_j generated with its integral control value x_j, and $D_{i,j}$ is a constant determined by the signal propagation delay from FF_i to FF_j (or vice versa), setup time (or hold time) of a flip-flop, etc.

In order to capture the situation of timing requirement of a circuit under consideration, we will introduce a skew constraint graph (SCG) G_f. Each vertex v_i of G_s corresponds to a PDE PDE_i ($f_i(x_i)$), and an edge $(v_i, v_j) \in E(G_f)$ with its edge weight $D_{i,j}$ represents a timing constraint in the form given above. If all necessary edge weights is given, and PDE delay can take any real value, feasible PDE delays can be computed as the longest path lengths from an auxiliary introduced source vertex to all other PDE vertices on G_f.

Transforming the concept of skew constraint graph into the control value domain, the constraints on control values will be maintained by another graph called control-value constraint graph (CCG) G_x. In G_x, an control value x_i for PDE_i is associated with an vertex $v_i \in V(G_x)$. G_x has the same topology with G_f, and an edge (v_i, v_j) with its edge weight $w_{i,j}$ implies

$$x_j - x_i \geq \text{`` a constant } w_{i,j} \text{''},$$

for $1 \leq i \leq M$ and $1 \leq j \leq M$.

2. μ-MARGIN PDE SETTING

We will define a timing margin in control-value domain as follows.

DEFINITION 1 (μ-MARGIN PDE DESIGN-SETTING).
For given PDE design-setting x_i for PDE_i and x_j for PDE_j and a nonnegative integer μ, the timing test (the setup timing test for signal paths from FF_i to FF_j and the hold timing test for signal paths from FF_j to FF_i) with PDE setting (PDE test-setting) x_i^* for PDE_i and x_j^* for PDE_j such that

$$x_i \leq x_i^* \qquad (1)$$
$$x_j^* \leq x_j \qquad (2)$$
$$x_j^* - x_i^* \leq x_j - x_i - \mu \qquad (3)$$

is called "μ-margin timing test".

If μ-margin timing test passes successfully, the given PDE design-setting is called "μ-margin PDE design-setting".

Despite a specified (designed) clock arrival timing by PDE setting x_i and x_j, we will use a severe clock arrival timing for the setup timing requirement for paths from FF_i to FF_j and the hold timing requirement for paths from FF_j to FF_i, which is realized by PDE test-setting x_i^* and x_j^*. If both the setup and the hold timing test pass successfully, the designed PDE setting x_i and x_j is considered as μ-margin PDE design-setting. Our objective of PSST is to find μ-margin PDE design-setting for each fabricated sequential circuit.

3. PDE TEST-SETTING PROBLEM

Supposing that a sequential circuit as well as its CCG G_x, a PDE design-setting $(x_1, \cdots, x_M)$, and a timing margin in control value $\mu \in N$ are given, we will check whether the PDE design-setting is a μ-margin PDE design-setting or not by applying the μ-margin timing test. The problem to find PDE test-setting(s) arises here since PDE test-setting for the μ-margin timing test is not unique, and in many cases a single test-setting is not enough.

In the following, if the control-value assignment x_i^* to FF_i and x_j^* to FF_j is a μ-margin PDE test-setting, we will say that the PDE test-setting x_i^* and x_j^* covers the edge (v_i, v_j) in G_x.

Fig.2-(a) shows an instance of CCG together with a PDE design-setting, and (b) is one possible PDE test-setting pattern for timing margin $\mu = 2$. This setting pattern covers bold edges only in the same figure. It means that the timing requirements associated with those bold edges are tested by this PDE test-setting. For the other edges represented with thin broken lines, we need to prepare other PDE test-setting pattern(s). (c) and (d) in Fig.2 are two other PDE test-settings needed for completing μ-margin timing test for this circuit.

In a practical situation, we will employ the scan chain technique for applying timing test. A similar chaining technique will be also needed for setting control values to PDEs. In order to reduce the total cost for PDE tuning, we need to save the cost of PDE setting as well as the cost of timing test.

4. THE OTHER CONTRIBUTIONS

The rest of this work includes

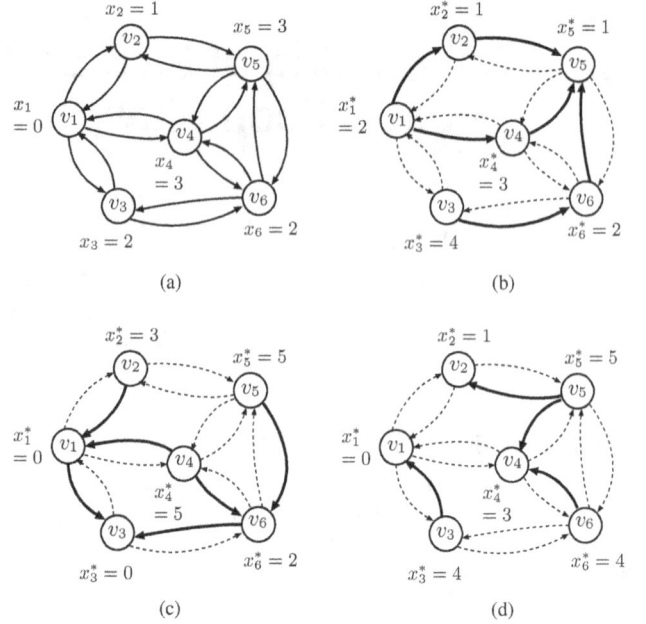

Figure 2: CCG and PDE design-setting are shown in (a), while (b), (c) and (d) are three PDE test-setting patterns for timing test considering timing margin $\mu = 2$. Using these three patterns, all edges in the given CCG are covered by μ-margin timing test.

(1) Bounds on the number of PDE test-settings:

The minimum number of PDE test-settings for a given CCG depends on the structure of the CCG and PDE designed-setting. We have two theorems about the lower bound on the number of PDE test-settings.

Theorem 1: For any CCG G_x, at most $2\lceil lg(|V(G_x)|)\rceil$ PDE test-setting patterns are enough to cover all edges in Gx.

Theorem 2: There exists a CCG which needs at least $\lceil lg(|V(G_x)|)\rceil$ PDE test-setting patterns to cover all edges in G_x.

(2) μ-margin PDE Tuning Based on Timing Test:

Our PDE tuning starts with an initial PDE design-setting (e.g., $x_i = 0$ for each PDE_i). We apply μ-margin timing test to a given PDE design-setting, and update PDE design-setting when the μ-margin timing test reports "timing failure". This procedure is repeated until we have a PDE design-setting (μ-margin PDE setting) for which no μ-margin timing failure is reported.

(3) Experimental results:

Through computer simulation of PDE tuning procedure to randomly generated delay-varying circuits, the effectiveness of our PDE tuning algorithm as well as the robustness of the circuits tuned by our method against run-time delay variations have been shown.

An Area Efficient Low Power High Speed
S-Box Implementation Using Power-Gated PLA

Ho Joon Lee and Yong-Bin Kim [*]
Northeastern University
360 Huntington Ave.
Boston, United States

ABSTRACT

Advanced Encryption Standard (AES) is one of the most common symmetric encryption algorithms. The hardware complexity in AES is dominated by AES substitution box (S-Box), which is considered as one of the most complicated and costly part of the system because it is the only non-linear structure. This paper presents a low power design of Rijndael S-Box for the SubByte transformation using power-gating and PLA design techniques to reduce area and leakage power during stand-by mode. The proposed design is implemented using 110nm standard CMOS process with 1.2V power supply. The proposed design reduces the total leakage power and the total transistor count to 10% and 50% of the conventional design, respectively while improving the speed performance by ten times.

Categories and Subject Descriptors

B.6.1 [**Logic Design**]: Design Styles—*Logic array*; B.7.1 [**Integrated Circuits**]: Types and Design Styles—*Algorithms implemented in hardware, Gate arrays, VLSI*

General Terms

Cryptography, Power Gate, Low Power

Keywords

AES, PLA, Power Gate, S-Box

1. INTRODUCTION

The AES algorithm that has been used most widely is based on Rijndael algorithm, which was developed by Joan Daemen and Vincent Rijnmen. It was announced by National Institute of Standards and Technology (NIST) in 1997

*The authors are with the Department of Electrical and Computer Engineering, Northeastern University, Massachusetts, USA (e-mail: hjlee@ece.neu.edu; ybk@ece.neu.edu).

as AES algorithm[2] according to the primary criteria of security, performance, efficiency in software and hardware, flexibility, and implementability.

The AES cipher involves repetitive round operations. Each round operation, SubBytes has been shown to be the performance limiting step, being several times slower than the other three steps (ShiftRows, MixColums, and round key) required in AES algorithm. In general, SubBytes operation occupies half of the total delay time and 20% of the circuit area[5]. This paper focuses on the way to implement the SubBytes (S Box) operational unit efficiently to improve the overall encryption algorithm performance.

This paper proposes the S-box circuit implementation using PLA architecture and power gating scheme for the leakage reduction at nanoscale technology node to reduce leakage power when the SubBytes transformation is not active based on the mode introduce by [1]. The circuit design of the proposed architecture has been performed with 110 nm standard CMOS technology with post layout performance verification.

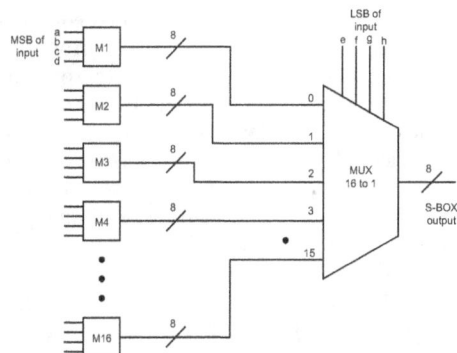

Figure 1: S-Box architecture using combinational logic.

2. PROPOSED POWER-GATED PLAS BASED DESIGN

[1] implemented the S-Box using the combinational random logic and a 16:1 bit mux as shown in Figure 1. In this paper, S-Box design based on the model introduced in [1] is presented using Programmble Logic Array (PLA) and power-gating techniques for power and area efficient solution. The previously proposed S-Box design in [1] is implemented with combinational logic as an effort to solve the

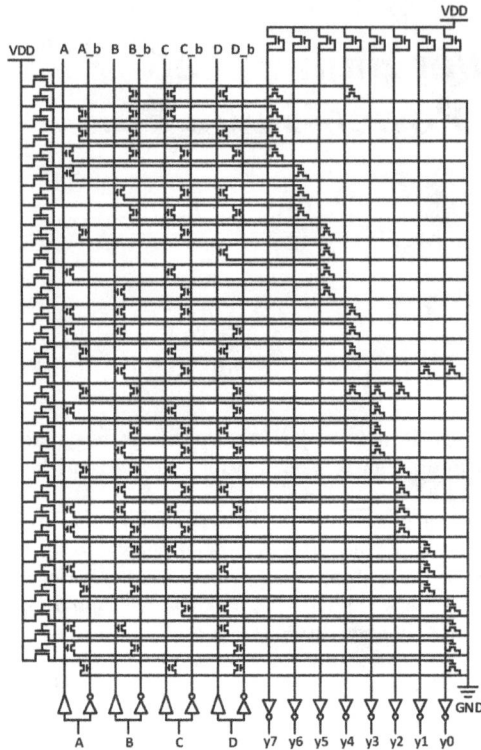

Figure 2: Proposed M1 implementation with PLA.

Table 1: Performance and transistor count comparison

Architecture	Dealy(ns)	Total no. of transistors
Proposed	0.963	2977
Prev 1[4]	10.802	7270
Prev 2[3]	14.653	-
Prev 3[1]	7.745	-

Table 2: Standby and leakage current comparison

Architecture	Standby power	Leakage current
Proposed(Non PG)	7.548mW	6.28mA
Proposed(PG)	0.658nW	0.541nA

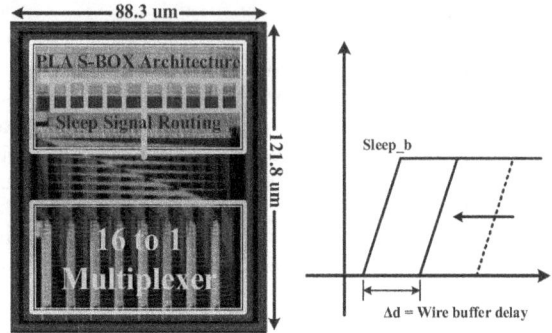

Figure 3: Custom Layout of the proposed S-Box architecture.

unbreakable delay incurred by look-up table(LUT) based architecture and to reduce the critical path delay by using composite filed arithmetic.

The proposed circuit is highly optimized for performance, area, and power by taking advantages of full custom design approach. Programmable Logic Array (PLA) is kind of programmable logic device used to implemented combinational logic circuits that has many min terms. The proposed Module 1 (M1) implementation with PLA structure is shown in the Figure 2. The transistor size of the PLA has been optimized considering the wire load of every signal line and the pre-charge device. The SubByte transformation is considered as a very complex design and it causes high area and power dissipation in AES. Power-gating technique is applied to the proposed architecture to reduce leakage current during standby mode.

3. EXPERIMENTAL RESULTS

Table 1 compares the previous S-Box design and our proposed PLAs architecture in terms of delay and transistor count. It is observed that our proposed PLA based S-Box design has efficient area compared to other three approaches. It also shows that the delay of our proposed S-Box is at least seven times faster than previous architecture.

In the Table 2, shows the power gating simulation results. As shown in the Table 2, the proposed power-gated PLA based S-Box architecture saves a huge power during standby mode.

Figure 3 shows the layout of the proposed PLA based S-Box design with 110nm CMOS technology library. The power overhead in the proposed approach is about 5% and the speed overhead due to the RC parasitic is 9%.

4. DISCUSSION & CONCLUSION

In this paper, a new design approach for S-Box design is presented using PLA and power-gated techniques, and its performance was analyzed and compared with the conventional S-Box designs. The proposed S-Box architecture demonstrates advantages in terms of area, speed, and power consumption.

5. REFERENCES

[1] N. Ahmad, R. Hasan, and W. Jubadi. Design of aes s-box using combinational logic optimization. In *Industrial Electronics Applications (ISIEA), 2010 IEEE Symposium on*, pages 696–699, 2010.

[2] J. Damen and V. Rijnmen. *The Design of Rijndael*. Springer Verlag, New York, 2002.

[3] C. Nalini, P. Anandmohan, D. Poomaiah, and V. Kulkarni. Compact designs of subbytes and mixcolumn for aes. In *Advance Computing Conference, 2009. IACC 2009. IEEE International*, pages 1241–1247, 2009.

[4] R. Rachh and P. Ananda Mohan. Implementation of aes s-boxes using combinational logic. In *Circuits and Systems, 2008. ISCAS 2008. IEEE International Symposium on*, pages 3294–3297, 2008.

[5] S. M. K. T. Satoh, A. and S. Munetoh. A compact rijndael hardware architecture with s-box optimization. *Proceedings of the 7th International Conference on the Theory and Application of Cryptology and Information Security*, 2248:239–254, November 2001.

FPGA Based Implementation of a Genetic Algorithm for ARMA Model Parameters Identification

Hocine Merabti and Daniel Massicotte
Laboratoire des Signaux et Systèmes Intégrés
Department of Electrical and Computer Engineering
Université du Québec à Trois-Rivières
{Hocine.Merabti, Daniel.Massicotte}@uqtr.ca

ABSTRACT

In this paper, we propose an FPGA implementation of a genetic algorithm (GA) for linear and nonlinear auto regressive moving average (ARMA) model parameters identification. The GA features specifically designed genetic operators for adaptive filtering applications. The design was implemented using very low bit-wordlength fixed-point representation, where only 6-bit wordlength arithmetic was used. The implementation experiments show high parameters identification capabilities and low footprint.

Categories and Subject Descriptors

C.3 [**Special-purpose and application-based systems**]: Signal Processing Systems

Keywords

Genetic algorithms, ARMA, System Identification, Adaptive filtering, Non-linear systems, Low wordlength arithmetic, FPGA

1. INTRODUCTION

System identification is a major issue in signal processing and various other fields [1].ARMA models have been involved in many time series analysis studies. Using adaptive filtering techniques to identify the parameters of an ARMA model is a common practice. However, addressing nonlinear models require the use of nonlinear adaptive filtering algorithms, which are generally much more complex than linear techniques.

Recently, several research works brought up the use of GAs to address adaptive filtering problems [2-3]. This interest is driven by the ability of these algorithms to search and find the global solution for the optimization problem whether the system is linear or nonlinear. Another benefit of using GAs is the robustness to the quantization effect, thanks to their natural weights updating mechanism which does not require arithmetic operations [4]. However, all the proposed works in the literature for adaptive filtering using GA, consider sequential processor based software implementations only.

In this work, we propose a field programmable gate array (FPGA) implementation of a GA for linear and nonlinear ARMA model parameters identification. The GA with specifically designed

GLSVLSI'14, May 21–23, 2014, Houston, Texas, USA.
ACM 978-1-4503-2816-6/14/05.
http://dx.doi.org/10.1145/2591513.2591579

genetic operators for adaptive filtering applications, and the ARMA identification problem were studied in [5]. This algorithm was designed with a special focus on computation load reduction and robustness increase to the quantization effect in low wordlength fixed-point processing environment, which makes it very attractive for hardware implementations. The target GA based identification system is modeled in very high speed integrated circuits hardware description language (VHDL) and implemented in FPGA using 6-bits wordlength arithmetic.

2. GA OPERATION

The flowchart of the implemented GA is shown in Figure 1. The operation begins by generating a random initial population $P(0)$. Individuals forming the population are called chromosomes, each represents the concatenated binary coded parameters (genes), which in our case are the potential ARMA model coefficients. The fitness function is then applied to every chromosome of the population. Next, the fitness scores calculated by the previous operation are used by the selection mechanism to select the two chromosomes that will participate in the crossover operation. After that, the offspring generated by the crossover is passed through the mutation device. The resulting chromosome is used to form the new population $P(g+1)$. Once the newly formed population is complete, the process (fitness function, selection, crossover and mutation) is repeated till the user defined generation G is reached.

3. IMPLEMENTATION RESULTS

The GA based ARMA identification system [5] was implemented on the XILNIX Spartan-6 xc6slx4-3tqg144 FPGA. A population of 16 chromosomes and a smoothing window size of B=16 were used. To test the robustness to the quantization effect, low fixed-

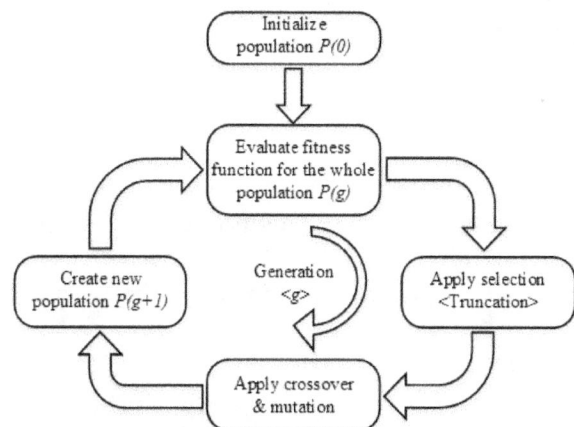

Figure 1. GA flow chart.

point wordlength arithmetic environment was considered, where all arithmetic operations were implemented using the Q5 format (1 sign bit and 5 fractional bits).

The post place and route implementation results and the timing performance achieved are presented in Table 1 and Table 2, respectively. No DSP slice or block memory have been used in the design, LUTs were used instead for faster performance. The design used 83% of the total device logic, and was able to provide a processing rate of 320 Kilo Generation/second.

Table 1. Post place-and-route implementation summary

Resource utilization	Available	Used
Slice registers	4800	889 (18%)
Slice LUTs	2400	1415 (58%)
Total Slices	600	498 (83%)

Table 2. Timing performance

Parameters	Rate
Maximum clock frequency	105 MHz
Maximum group rate	320 KGen/sec

The signal processing performance analysis is done on the Signal to Quantization Noise Ratio (SQNR)

$$SQNR(n) = 10\log\left(\sum_{i=1}^{M} w_i^2 \bigg/ \sum_{i=1}^{M}\left(w_i - \hat{w}_i(n)\right)^2\right)(dB) \qquad (1)$$

where w_i is the exact coefficient, and $\hat{w}_i$ is the estimated coefficient. M is the number of coefficients, it has a value of $M = 7$ in this study.

To investigate the ability of the GA to successfully identify the ARMA coefficients, 10 independent realizations were performed.

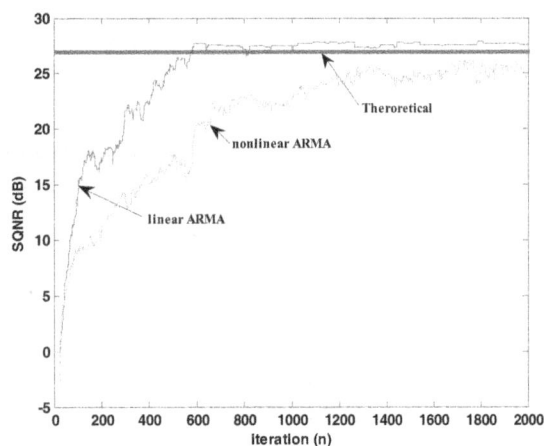

Figure 2. System identification performance results.

In each realization, system signals are produced for randomly generated coefficients. This corresponds to the second scenario studied in [5].

Figure 2 shows the average SQNR of all realizations for the linear and the nonlinear identification problems. A theoretical SQNR is given as a reference metric, it is calculated by using the Q5 truncation quantization of the perfect floating-point coefficients, and it has a mean value of 26.9 dB.

The implemented GA converges to a steady state with an SQNR of 27.6 dB at generation 600 for the linear identification, it is 0.7 dB more than the theoretical SQNR. This gain of performance is justified by the ability of the GA to perform rounding by altering the coefficients LSBs through the optimization process.

For nonlinear identification, the GA still capable of estimating the system parameters with a maximum SQNR of 24.7 dB, which is 2.2 dB below the theoretical SQNR and 2.9 dB lower than the performance achieved in linear identification. This is very interesting given the strong nonlinearity considered in the study. 1200 generations were required for the GA to converge to steady state.

4. CONCLUSION

An FPGA implementation of a GA for linear and nonlinear auto regressive moving average (ARMA) model parameters identification has been presented. The design considered low wordlength fixed-point arithmetic processing environement. The implementation shows high signal processing performances and low resources cost, where only 6-bits worlength fixed-point arithmetic was used in all operations.

5. ACKNOWLEDGMENTS

The authors wish to thank the National Sciences and Engineering Research Council of Canada (NSERC) for financial support.

6. REFERENCES

[1] T. Cassar, K. P. Camilleri, and S. G. Fabri, "Order Estimation of Multivariate ARMA Models," *IEEE Journal of Selected Topics in Signal Processing,* vol. 4, pp. 494-503, 2010.

[2] V. Duong and A. R. Stubberud, "System identification by genetic algorithm," *IEEE Aerospace Conference Proceedings,* 2002, pp. 5-2331-5-2337 vol.5.

[3] Cheng-Yuan, C. and C. Deng-Rui, "Active Noise Cancellation Without Secondary Path Identification by Using an Adaptive Genetic Algorithm," *IEEE Transactions on Instrumentation and Measurement,* 59(9), 2010, pp. 2315-2327.

[4] D. Massicotte and D. Eke, "High robustness to quantification effect of an adaptive filter based on genetic algorithm," *IEEE Northeast Workshop on Circuits and Systems (NEWCAS),* 2007, pp. 373-376.

[5] H. Merabti and D. Massicotte, "Towards Hardware Implementation of Genetic Algorithms for Adaptive Filtering Applications," *IEEE Canadian Conference on Electrical and Computer Engineering (CCECE),* 2014, to appear.

Highly Adaptive and Congestion-aware Routing for 3D NoCs

Manoj Kumar
Malaviya National Institute of
Technology, Jaipur, India
bohra.manoj1980@gmail.com

Vijay Laxmi
Malaviya National Institute of
Technology, Jaipur, India
vlgaur@gmail.com

Manoj Gaur
Malaviya National Institute of
Technology, Jaipur, India
gaurms@gmail.com

Masoud Daneshtalab
University of Turku, Turku,
Finland
masdan@utu.fi

Seok-Bum Ko
University of Saskatchewan,
Saskatoon, Canada
seokbum.ko@usask.ca

Mark Zwolinski
University of Southampton,
Southampton, United Kingdom
mz@ecs.soton.ac.uk

ABSTRACT

In this paper, we propose a novel highly adaptive and congestion aware routing algorithm 3D meshes which is equally applicable to 2D meshes as well. The proposed algorithm allows cyclic dependencies in channel dependency graph (CDG) providing higher degree of adaptiveness. The algorithm uses congestion-aware channel selection strategy that results balanced distribution of traffic flows across the network. A packet follows non-minimal paths only when minimal paths are congested at the neighboring channels. The deadlock avoidance methodology adopted by our algorithm remains cost-efficient as it uses one extra virtual channel along each of Y and Z dimensions to achieve deadlock freedom.

Categories and Subject Descriptors

C.2.1 [**Network Architecture and Design**]: Network communications

Keywords

On-chip Networks; congestion; deadlock-freedom; routing algorithms; non-minimal routes

1. INTRODUCTION

On-chip interconnection networks are discussed and researched in past few years as a promising communication paradigm for MCSoCs and CMPs architectures. Efficiency and performance of NoCs is highly dependent on the routing algorithm we select. Higher the degree of adaptiveness of routing algorithm, lower is the probability for a packet to enter faulty or congested area. Thus, the focus of this research is to enhance the performance of routing algorithm by increasing degree of adaptiveness (allowing more number of minimal paths), use of less number of virtual channels for deadlock and providing congestion awareness.

GLSVLSI'14, May 21–23, 2014, Houston, Texas, USA.
ACM 978-1-4503-2816-6/14/05.
http://dx.doi.org/10.1145/2591513.2591581.

2. PROPOSED WORK

The proposed method uses turn model, which is *major* improvement and 3D-extension of the 2D turn model used by Mad-y algorithm [4]. The proposed method provides additional minimal and non-minimal paths between source and destination than Mad-y. It allows some 0-degree, 180-degree and 90-degree turns, which were prohibited in Mad-y. However, these allowed turns create cycles in CDG, but we have shown that proposed routing method is deadlock free using Duato's theorem [3]. Duato has proved that cycles can be allowed in CDG if extended channel dependency graph (ECDG) is acyclic. Goal of proposed method is to enhance the capability of existing virtual channels in Mad-y to route packets minimally or non minimally around network "hot spots". Figure 1a shows turn model representation of Mad-y routing algorithm. It prohibits following routing turns.

1. 90-degree turns: $N2$-W, $S2$-W, E-$N1$ and E-$S1$ (Figures 1a(i) and 1a(ii)).
2. 0-degree turns: $S2$-$S1$ and $N2$-$N1$ (Figure 1a(iii)).
3. 180-degree turns: all prohibited.

An acyclic CDG requirement to avoid deadlocks places unnecessary, thus avoidable restrictions on the routing turns in a routing algorithm. Mad-y routing method is proved deadlock-free using acyclic CDG [2]. Thus, its routing function cannot use all qualified turns to forward packets through less congested areas. The proposed method imposes substantially fewer restrictions on routing turns, thus it provides more minimal and non-minimal paths between source and destination. It deploys double-yz network that uses one virtual channel along X dimension ($+X$:*east*, $-X$:*west*), two virtual channels along Y dimension ($+Y$:*north*, $-Y$:*south*) and Z dimension ($+Z$:*up*, $-Z$:*down*) to achieve high degree of adaptiveness. Figure 1 shows turn model representation for different planes (YZ, XY and XZ). A packet is permitted to use first virtual channel at any time as shown in Figures 1b(i), 1b(ii) and 1c(i). It can use second virtual channel only if it has already routed to negative directions (west and south) of all lower dimensions. It is allowed to take 180-degree turn from west to east, south to north and down to up only if it has completed routing in west, south and down directions, respectively.

For XY-*plane*, proposed method imposes following constraints on routing turns:

1. It prohibits two 90-degree turns $S2$-W and $N2$-W (Figure 1c(ii)).

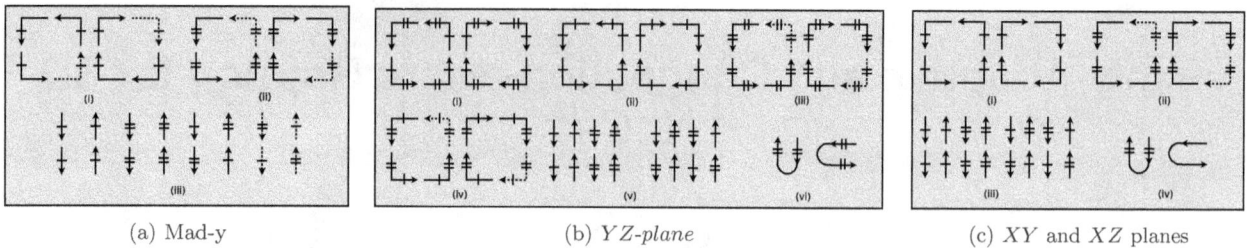

| (a) Mad-y | (b) YZ-plane | (c) XY and XZ planes |

Figure 1: Turn models for proposed method (solid lines for permitted turns and dash lines for prohibited turns)

2. It allows 0-degree turns $S1$-$S1$, $N1$-$N1$, $S2$-$S2$ and $N2$-$N2$ (Figure 1c(iii)). It allows 0-degree turns $S1$-$S2$, $N1$-$N2$, $S2$-$S1$ and $N2$-$N1$ (Figure 1c(iii)), with some restrictions. It allows these restricted turns only when packet does not need to be forwarded further west.

3. It permits some 180-degree turns (Figure 1c(iv)).

For YZ-plane, proposed method imposes following constraints on routing turns:

1. It prohibits four 90-degree turns $U2$-$S1$, $U2$-$S2$, $D2$-$S1$ and $D2$-$S2$ (Figures 1b(iii) and 1b(iv)).

2. It allows 0-degree turns $U1$-$U1$, $D1$-$D1$, $U2$-$U2$ and $D2$-$D2$ (Figure 1b(v)). It allows 0-degree turns $U1$-$U2$, $U2$-$U1$, $D1$-$D2$ and $D2$-$D1$ (Figure 1b(v)), with some restrictions. It allows these restricted turns only when packet does not need to be forwarded further west or south. Similarly, we can find allowed and restricted 0-degree turns for north and south as well.

3. It permits some 180-degree turns (Figure 1b(vi)).

For XZ-plane, constraints on routing turns can be deduced in similar fashion as in XY-plane.

Functionality of proposed method is divided into two phases: route computation and output channel selection. On the basis input channel (on which packet has arrived) and relative position of destination node with respect to current node, routing function computes a set of output channels using turn model explanation discussed above. By comparing turn models as shown in Figures 1a and 1c, we can conclude that our method results in a larger set of output channels due to high degree of adaptiveness than Mad-y. Selection function selects one output channel from the set of output channels provided by the route computation function. Our selection function first checks all qualified output channels corresponding to shortest routes and forwards the packet to the output channel in which the corresponding next hop node has its congestion status flag set to zero (and possibly, corresponding to *non-escape channels*). If the congestion status flags of all next hop nodes on shortest routes are set to one, the congestion status flag of each eligible non-minimal route is inspected. If there exist such non-minimal routes, which are not congested, our method selects one of the output channel to forward the packet (and possibly, corresponding to *non-escape channels*). Our method prefers adaptive output channels over escape channels (output channels which are used to escape from deadlocks), because it results in increased probability of escape output channels being available when they are required to avoid deadlocks.

3. RESULTS DISCUSSION

We modified and extended NIRGAM [1] to evaluate proposed method. For all experiments, we consider $4 \times 4 \times 4$ mesh. Packet size and virtual channel size are set to 6 and 8 flits, respectively. The simulator is warmed up for $5,000$ cycles. Congestion threshold is set to 66% of total buffer size.

As communication performance parameter, we consider latency (delay). To evaluate proposed work in a more realistic scenario, we consider E3S benchmark suite. We select four application suites automotive/industrial, networking, consumer and office-automation. Figure 2 shows average packet latency normalized to XYZ routing. Proposed method provides lower latency than other methods across all four application suites. It shows the greatest performance gain on consumer application traces. Average performance gain of our method is up to 28% across all selected benchmarks vs XYZ and 11% vs other adaptive algorithms.

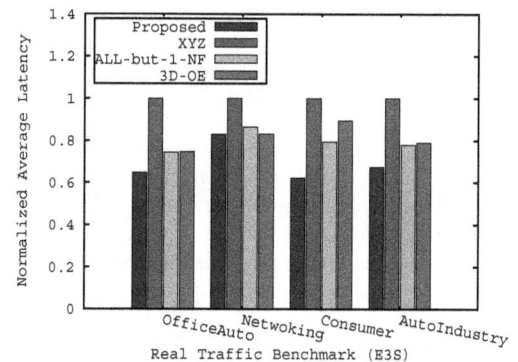

Figure 2: Performance for application traces

4. CONCLUSION AND FUTURE WORK

Network congestion may result into increased communication latency and power consumption, thus can severely degrade performance of on chip networks. Acyclic channel dependency graph for deadlock freedom results into lower degree of adaptiveness. In this paper, we presented a novel and improved turn model for 3D meshes. We also proposed a low cost, highly adaptive routing algorithm to mitigate congestion based on proposed turn model. Future work is focused on incorporating global congestion and extending proposed method for n-dimensional meshes.

Acknowledgment

This research is partially supported by UK India Education and Research Initiative grant for the collaborative project on HiPER NIRGAM (2011-2014).

5. REFERENCES

[1] Nirgam:. http://wiki.mnit.ac.in/mediawiki/index.php/Nirgam/.

[2] W. J. Dally and C. L. Seitz. Deadlock-free Message Routing in Multiprocessor Interconnection Networks. *Computers, IEEE Transactions on*, 100(5):547–553, 1987.

[3] J. Duato. A Necessary and Sufficient Condition for Deadlock-free Adaptive Routing in Wormhole Networks. *Parallel and Distributed Systems, IEEE Transactions on*, 6(10):1055–1067, 1995.

[4] C. J. Glass and L. M. Ni. Maximally Fully Adaptive Routing in 2D Meshes. In *International Conference on Parallel Processing, volume I*, pages 101–104, 1992.

Adaptive Compressive Sensing for Low Power Wireless Sensors

Adam Watkins*, Venkata Naresh Mudhireddy*, Haibo Wang and Spyros Tragoudas

Department of Electrical and Computer Engineering
Southern Illinois University, Carbondale 62901
watkins@engr.siu.edu, mudhireddy@siu.edu, zhwang@siu.edu, spyros@engr.siu.edu

ABSTRACT

Compressive sensing has been demonstrated as an appealing technique in the implementation of low-power sensors. This work studies the feasibility and potential power savings by adaptively adjusting the sampling rates in compressive sensing operations, which is referred to as adaptive compressive sensing in this paper. The results reveal that the sparsity of many biomedical sensor signals varies over time and hence it is possible to perform such adaptive operations. The study also shows that the adaptive operation can lead to significant reduction on sensor node power consumption.

Categories and Subject Descriptors

B.8.2 [**Performance and Reliability**]: Performance Analysis and Design Aids

General Terms

Measurement, Performance, Design, Verification

Keywords

Sensor, Low Power, Power Estimation, Compressive Sensing

1. INTRODUCTION

Compressive sensing (CS) is a relatively new technique that allows the reconstruction of a signal from limited measurements [1, 2], if the signal is sparse with regard to a mathematical basis. Due to this desirable feature, it has been used in a wide range of applications, including image capturing [3], radar [4], ultra-wide band (UWB) communications [5], in order to reduce hardware complexity, minimize system operation, or relax circuit performance requirements at the sensing end. Recently, CS techniques had been used in the implementation of low-power sensors [6, 7]. One of its most astonishing features in low-power sensor applications is that it potentially allows the sensor signal to be sampled at rates lower than the Nyquist Rate, which is the theoretical minimum sampling rate in conventional data acquisition systems. Reduced sampling rates allow sensing devices to be less frequently stimulated [6], and also cut the amount of data being wirelessly transmitted [7], both of which help minimize sensor node power consumption. Most of such reported low-power sensors focus on biomedical applications since many biomedical signals are sparse with respect to wavelet or Gabor functions [6, 7] and there are increasing demands for low-power implantable or wearable biomedical devices.

* Both authors contribute to this work equally.

At present, the sampling rates, also referred to as measurement size, in the CS operations of these low-power sensors are fixed according to prior knowledge of signal sparsity, and hence do not change during sensing operations. As to be discussed in Section 2, the required CS measurement size is affected by signal sparsity, which may vary over the time. Hence, it is naturally expected that the CS measurement size, or sampling rate, should follow the variations of signal sparsity. We refer to the CS operations, in which the sampling rates are adaptively adjusted according to the signal sparsity variations, as *adaptive compressive sensing (ACS)*. The work in [8] also exploits signal sparsity variations to dynamically adjust sampling rate. It targets image applications and does not investigate the potential power saving by ACS. The approach in [9] adaptively adjusts the coefficients in the mathematic basis that are used in the reconstruction of the signal. It does not change the sampling rate at the sensing end.

The need for ACS operation depends on whether signal sparsity significantly varies over the time, which is strongly application dependent. This work examines a larger number of real biomedical sensor signals collected from the *Multiparameter Intelligent Monitoring in Intensive Care* (MIMIC II) database [10] to study the sparsity variations of these signals as well as the required CS measurement sizes at different time periods. It shows that the sparsity characteristics and the required measurement sizes of many biomedical sensor signals do vary over the time and hence it is possible to perform ACS for such signals.

With the obtained signal characteristics, this work further investigates the potential power savings by applying ACS in wireless sensors. The study assumes that the power consumption of the wireless transmitter dominates the overall power consumption of the sensor node, which is true for most wireless sensors [11, 12]. A generic power model is used to estimate the power consumption of the transmitter along with the signal sparsity characteristics. The results demonstrate significant power savings using ACS techniques, compared to conventional CS techniques.

The rest of the paper is organized as follows. A brief review of CS theory is provided in Section 2. It explains the rationale of ACS operation. Section 3 describes the procedure for studying signal sparsity variation and the required measurement sizes for the selected signals. The wireless transmitter power model is presented in Section 4 and the overall simulation flow for studying potential power savings by ACS is described in Section 5. Experimental results are presented in Section 6 and the paper is concluded in Section 7.

2. Overview of CS Operation

Assume that vector x contains N outputs of a sensor in the time domain. With a basis matrix ψ, x can be projected into another domain as a vector denoted by c. The relation among x, ψ and c is given in Equation 1. If the number of nonzero (or significant) terms in c is significantly smaller than N, signal x is called sparse with respect to basis ψ.

$$x = \psi \cdot c \qquad (1)$$

In CS operation, signal x is not directly transmitted, digitized or sensed, depending at which stage the CS operation is performed. For the simplicity of discussion, we assume that the CS operation is performed after sensor signal digitization [7]. Thus, the data to be transmitted, denoted by vector y, is a set of random combinations of the original sensor signal x. The expression of y is:

$$y = \Phi \cdot x \qquad (2)$$

where Φ is called the measurement matrix. It has the dimension of M×N and M<N. The size of vector y is M, which is often called the measurement size. Note that vector y, the data to be transmitted, has less data points than the original signal x.

The receiver has prior knowledge of ψ and Φ. Based on received vector y, it solves for coefficient vector c from Equation 3. Once c is obtained, the original signal x can be reconstructed using Equation 1.

$$y = \Phi \cdot \psi \cdot c \qquad (3)$$

Since M<N, there exists multiple solutions for Equation 3. Typically, an l_1-minimization problem is formulated as shown by Relation 4 to find the solution of c that contains the minimum number of significant terms. This solution is often the correct projection of signal x at the domain defined by matrix ψ.

$$minimize\ \|c\|_{l1}\ subject\ to\ y = \Phi \cdot \psi \cdot c \qquad (4)$$

It is shown that a signal can be recovered by the above approach with high probability if the measurement size M meets the following lower bound requirement [2]:

$$M \geq K \log \frac{N}{K} \qquad (5)$$

where K is the number of non-zero or significant terms in vector c. The value of K is directly related to the signal sparsity. If the sparsity of a signal changes over the time, the above relation indicates that the required minimum measurement size in CS operation will also change. This observation motivates our study.

3. Investigating the Feasibility of ACS

This section describes the procedure used to study the feasibility of performing ACS operations. The signals used in the study are biomedical signals collected from MIMIC database. The described procedure can be also applied to other signals as well. In this study, the obtained sensor signal vectors are partitioned into different blocks or windows and each block contains 1024 data points. The data contained in each window correspond to vector x that is referred to in Section 2. The selection of 1024 as the N value is arbitrary which does not significantly affect the validity of the study. The Gabor matrix, whose values are described by Equation 6, is used in the study as the basis matrix ψ since many biomedical signals are sparse with respect to it [6].

$$[\Psi]_{i,j} = \cos(\frac{2\pi(i-1)(j-1)}{2N})e^{\frac{-(i-1)^2(j-\frac{N}{2})^2}{\omega N^2}} \qquad (6)$$

In the above equation, i and j represent the row and column index of the matrix element; ω is related to the width of the Gaussian kernel in the Gabor domain. A random binary measurement matrix [6] is used to generate signal y according to Equation 2. To recover the coefficients, the CVX l_1-minimization solver [27, 28] is used to solve the l_1-minimization problem described by Relation 4.

For each data window, a binary search based algorithm is used to find the minimum measurement size M such that the reconstructed signal from CS operation meets the accuracy requirements. The key steps of the search algorithm are shown in Figure 1. In the search process, for each M value being examined, the aforementioned CS operations are performed and the error between the reconstructed signal and the original signal is compared with a threshold. If the error is larger than the threshold, the measurement size is increased; otherwise, it is reduced. This process continues until the upper bound (max) and lower bound (min) converge.

```
Generate Gabor Basis Matrix ψ
M=N/2
max=N
min=0
for j=1:log2(N)
    {
        Generate NxM Measurement Matrix Φ
        y=Φ*f
        minimize ||c|| subject to y=Φψc
        x_rec=ψ⁻¹c
        x_avg=(∑ᵢᴺ xᵢ)/N
        error=|x-x_rec|/|x-x_avg|
        if error < threshold
            min=M
        else
            max=M
        M=(max+min)/2
    }
```

Figure 1: Algorithm of searching minimum measurement size.

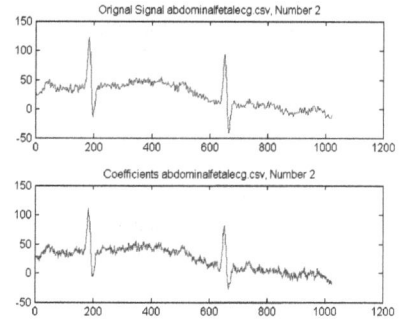

Figure 2: Comparison between the original (top) and recovered (bottom) signals.

In the study, it was observed that if a signal had a significant DC bias the calculated error could be influenced by the bias. To avoid this problem, the error equation defined below is used to measure the accuracy of the reconstructed signals.

$$error = \frac{\|x - x\_rec\|}{\|x - x\_avg\|} \qquad (7)$$

where x is the original signal; x_rec is the recovered signal; and x_avg is the DC offset level of the signal which is calculated as follows:

$$x\_avg = \frac{\sum_i^N x_i}{N} \qquad (8)$$

The error threshold is set to be 0.2 in this work. Our simulations for various types of signals indicate that with the 0.2 error threshold the recovered and original signals are close. As an example, Figure 2 compares the original signal and the signal that is recovered with the measurement size selected based on the 0.2 error threshold.

4. Power Model of Wireless Sensor Node

This section develops power estimation models for a generic wireless sensor node. It will be used to compare sensor node power consumptions with ACS or conventional CS operations. The block diagram of a generic wireless sensor node is shown in Figure 3. We assume that the sensor node power consumption is dominated by its RF transmitter circuit [7]. Hence, only the power consumption of the major circuit blocks inside the transmitter are estimated. To achieve this goal, we derived a power model for the charge scaling DAC circuit. For the rest of the blocks, we adopted the power models in [12]. However, many of the technology or circuit dependent coefficients used in these models are not reported in literature. Hence, we estimate these parameters based on recently reported circuits.

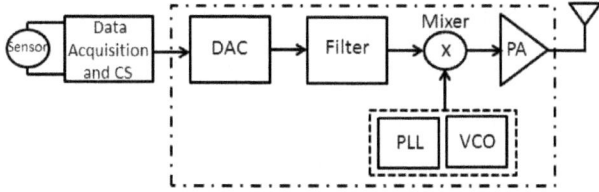

Figure 3: wireless sensor block diagram

DAC Power model: charge scaling (CS) DAC is typically used in applications that have a tight power budget and relatively slow data rate. The block diagram of an n-bit CS DAC is shown in Figure 4, where C is the unit capacitance of the circuit.

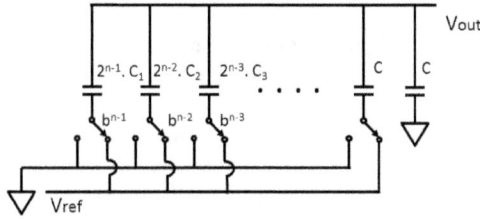

Figure 4: Capacitive DAC

Assume that the DAC input code is D. During the conversion, D*C capacitance is connected to V_{ref} and the rest of the capacitance $(2^n-D)*C$ is tied to ground. Thus, the equivalent capacitance to be charged is:

$$C_{eq}^D = \frac{(2^n * C - D * C) * (D * C)}{(2^n * C - D * C) + (M * C)}$$

$$= (D * C) - \frac{1}{2^n} D^2 * C \quad (9)$$

Assume all the codes have equal possibility to appear at the DAC input port, the average capacitance to be charged to V_{ref} can be estimated as:

$$C_{avg} = \frac{\sum_{D=0}^{2^n-1} C_{eq}^D}{2^n}$$

$$= \frac{C}{2^n} \left(\sum_{D=0}^{2^n-1} D - \frac{1}{2^N} \sum_{D=0}^{2^n-1} D \right)$$

$$= \frac{C}{3} 2^{n-1} - \frac{C}{6.2^n}$$

$$\approx \frac{C}{3} 2^{n-1} \quad (10)$$

Thus, the power consumption for charging the capacitor array is:

$$P_{cap} = C_{avg} . V_{ref}^2 . f_{conv} \quad (11)$$

The above equation does not include the power consumption of switches that control the capacitor array. To include that, a proportional constant k_{cap} can be introduced and the power estimation equation can be written as:

$$P_{cap} = (1 + k_{cap}) C_{avg} . V_{ref}^2 . f_{conv} \quad (12)$$

Filter Power Model: a system-level power model for a general reconstruction filter is [12]:

$$P_{filter} = \eta . KT . f_c . Q . \left(\frac{S}{N} \right)^2 \quad (13)$$

where K is Boltzmann constant; T is the absolute temperature; f_c is the filter corner frequency; $\left(\frac{S}{N} \right)$ is signal to noise ratio, Q is the filter quality factor, and η is a proportionality constant that depends on filter topology. Since there is no reported η value in literature, Table 1 lists three η values that are computed based on three recently reported filter circuits [13, 14, 15]. It shows that the η values for circuits in [13, 14] are reasonably close; but the η value for the filter in [15] is much larger compared with the other two values. This is because the above power model is derived with the assumption that KT/C noise dominates the circuit noise performance, which is likely true for the circuits in [13, 14]. Since the pass-band frequency in [15] is very low, device 1/f noise likely dominates the circuit noise performance and this may result in a large η value. Nevertheless, the values listed in the table provide useful guidelines for selecting η values in later power estimation experiments.

Table 1: Values of η for different filters

Ref.	f_c	Power	η
[13]	13.6MHz	0.47mW	365.92
[14]	8.58MHz	1.16mW	180
[15]	240Hz	453nW	9.12×10^5

Mixer power model: a simplified mixer power model is given in [12]:

$$P_{mixer} = k_{mixer} . \frac{G}{NF} \quad (14)$$

where G is the conversion gain; NF is the noise figure and k_{mixer} is a coefficient that is associated with circuit design and fabrication technologies. Based on the circuits in [16, 23], the values of k_{mixer} are calculated and listed in Table 2. It indicates that k_{mixer} is likely in the range from several to tens milli-watts.

Table 2: k_{mixer} values for two recently reported mixer circuits

Ref.	G	NF	Power	k_{mixer}
[16]	16.2dB	18.5dB	9mW	15.28×10^{-3}
[23]	3.8dB	8.4dB	1.95mW	5.6×10^{-3}

PLL power model: it is proposed to use the following equation to estimate PLL power consumption [12]:

$$P_{PLL} = b_1 . C_1 . F_{LO} . V_{dd}^2 + b_2 . C_2 . F_{ref} . V_{dd}^2 \quad (15)$$

where b1 and b2 are coefficients; C_1 and C_2 are parasitic loading capacitances; f_{LO} and f_{ref} are local oscillator and reference frequencies. Since C_1 and C_2 are rarely reported in literature and they are proportional to CMOS technology feature size λ, we propose to modify the above model as:

$$P_{PLL} = A_1 . \lambda . F_{LO} . V_{dd}^2 + A_2 . \lambda . F_{ref} . V_{dd}^2 \quad (16)$$

where A_1 and A_2 are the new circuit dependent coefficients. Since there are two variables in the above model, we use a data regression method to extract A1 and A2 values based on three recently reported PLL circuits [17, 18, 19]. This leads to A1=1.4×10^{-6} and A2=1.6×10^{-4}. Although the sample size (number of circuits) used in the regression is small from statistic perspective, the resultant coefficients as well as the power model still can be used in the study since the focus of this study is to explore the power saving trends and potentials

VCO power model: LC-tank oscillators are often used in wireless transmitters and their power consumption can be estimated by [12]:

$$P_{VCO} = \left(\beta \frac{V_{dd}^2}{L^2 . \omega^2} \right) \qquad (17)$$

where ω is the oscillation frequency in angular form; L is the inductance value; and β is a circuit and technology dependent coefficient. For three recently reported VCO circuits [18, 19, 20], the calculated β values are listed in Table 3.

Table 3: β values of different VCO circuits

Ref.	f_o	L	Vdd	Power	β
[18]	2.4GHz	6nH	1.2V	0.4mW	2.27
[19]	1.8GHz	10nH	1V	0.38mW	4.86
[20]	1.83GHz	10nH	1.2V	0.58mW	5.33

Power amplifier (PA) power model: The PA power consumption is affected by its efficiency η_{PA} and output power P_{out} as:

$$P_{PA} = \frac{P_{out}}{\eta_{PA}} \qquad (18)$$

Several recently reported PA circuits [18, 21, 22] used in short distance wireless transmitters are either class AB or C amplifiers. Their efficiencies range from 25% to 32.4%. The desired output power is determined by receiver sensitivity P_r, target transmission distance D, RF signal wavelength λ_{RF}, antenna gains G_t, G_r and transmission loss l due to multipath and obstacles. This is described as:

$$P_{out} = \frac{P_r . l}{G_t . G_r} \left(\frac{4\pi . D}{\lambda_{RF}} \right)^2 \qquad (19)$$

In this study, P_{out} is computed using the following values: P_r=-80dBm, l=21dB [25], G_t=1dBi [24] and G_r=3dBi [26], D=10m and the RF signal frequency of 2.4GHz.

Based on the above discussion, we select the parameters summarized in Table 4 in estimating the power consumption of a wireless transmitter, whose performance metrics fit in typical low-power short range sensor applications. Note that the same set of parameters is used to estimate the power consumption of sensor nodes with ACS or conventional CS operations.

Table 4: Power model parameter values used in this study

Circuit Block	Circuit Parameters	Values
DAC	N	8
	C	50fF
	K	0.05
	f_conv	100KHz
Filter	fc	40KHz
	Q	5
	SNR	50dB
	η	1×10^5
Mixer	k_{mixer}	10×10^{-3}
	G	0dBm
	NF	10dBm
PLL	A_1	1.4×10^{-6}
	A_2	1.6×10^{-4}
	f_{LO}	2.4GHz
	f_{ref}	22MHz
VCO	A	2.3
	f_{osc}	2.4GHz
	L	6nH
PA	η_{PA}	28%
	P_{out}	-3dBm

5. Study of Potential Power Saving by ACS

The experimental flow for studying the potential power savings by ACS is shown in Figure 5. As discussed in Section 3, the sensor signals are first partitioned into different time windows (sub blocks) with the window size of N (N=1024 in this study). The procedure shown in Figure 1 is used to find the minimum (optimal) measurement size M for each sub block of data. Subsequently, the power consumption for transmitting the measurement vector y for each sub block is estimated according to the optimal M value. The total power consumption, which is the sum of the power of the sub blocks, is the power consumption using ACS. As a comparison, the power consumption of the same sensor node using a conventional compressive sensing technique is also estimated similarly. The significant difference between the two is the following. In ACS approach, the M value fed to the power estimator for each sub block changes according to signal sparsity. On the contrary, in the conventional compressive sensing approach, the same M value is used in power estimation and hence the largest M value among all the sub blocks is used.

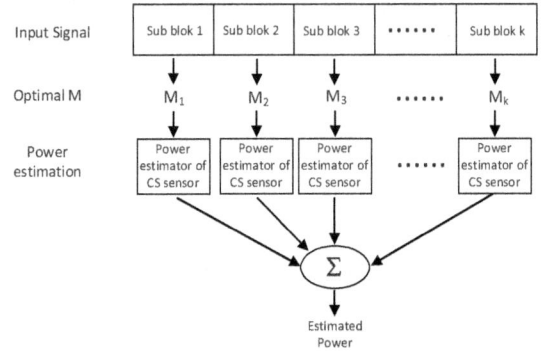

Figure 5. Power estimation flow

The power estimation procedure for a given M value is described as follows. First, the original signal from the database reveals the time duration $t_{sensing}$ that the N data points are collected. With compressive sensing or ACS, only M data points are transmitted during this period. The time taken by the transmitter to send out the M data points is referred to as transmitter active time; and it can be estimated as follows:

$$t_{active} = \frac{M}{R} \qquad (20)$$

where R is the transmission rate of the transmitter, which is related to the DAC conversion rate.

If t_{active} is smaller than $t_{sensing}$, we assume that the transmitter can switch to sleep mode to save power. Since the processes of switching the transmitter into sleep mode and later waking it up take time and consume power, switching the transmitter into sleep mode is only performed when the sensor has adequate time to complete the sleep-wake-up sequences and when it does result in power saving. These two criteria are described by the relations below:

$$t_{sleep} = \frac{N-M}{R} - t_{A2S} - t_{wakeup} > 0 \qquad (21)$$

$$(P_{active} - P_{sleep}) \cdot t_{sleep} > E_{A2S} + E_{wakeup} \qquad (22)$$

where t_{A2S}, E_{A2S}, t_{wakeup} and E_{wakeup} are the time and energy for switching the device into sleep mode and to wake the device up, respectively; t_{sleep} is the time that the device is in the sleep mode; P_{active} and P_{sleep} are the power consumption during active and sleep modes.

Note that the above estimation neglects the potential power overhead caused by conducting ACS operation. Since the ACS operation does not require significant modification for the measurement circuits that have been used in conventional compressive sensing approaches. We expect the power overhead of the measurement circuit, due to performing ACS, will not be significant compared to the power savings at the wireless transmitter.

6. SIMULATION RESULTS

6.1 Variations of Signal Sparsity and Minimum Measurement Size

This section presents the findings about signal sparsity variations as well as the changes of minimum measurement sizes for biomedical sensor signals obtained from MIMIC database. The procedure discussed in Section 3 is implemented in Matlab. When conducting the experiments, we examined four packages, CVX, l_1-magic, ISAL1 and GPSR [27, 31], to solve the formulated l_1-minimization problem. We found that the CVX package results in more accurate signal recovery for most sensor signals used in our study.

A large number of sensor signals are examined in this study. It is found that many sensor signals manifest sparsity variations. As a result, their minimum measurement size can change dramatically over the time. Figure 6 summarizes the maximum changes on the desirable measurement sizes for various sensor signals over the time durations being examined in the study. In addition, Table 5 lists more detailed information about the changes in measurement sizes for four types of sensor signals. It lists the optimal measurement sizes for different time durations.

Table 5: Variations of signal sparsity and measurement sizes.

Signal	Block	1	2	3	4	5	6
Fetal ECG	*M*	351	609	407	417	307	399
Cap	*M*	443	961	977	857	969	385
Stress	*M*	191	209	201	187	575	193
PPG	*M*	231	118	169	141	255	237

6.2 Potential power saving by ACS

Following the experiment flow highlighted in Section 5, the potential power saving by ACS operations are investigated. It is assumed that the wireless transmitter can have both active and sleep modes. The active power is estimated using the power model developed in Section 4. The sleep mode current consumption and active-to-sleep mode transition time are obtained from [21] and given as 0.8 nA and 100 µs respectively. Table 6 shows the potential power savings for sensor signals whose characteristics are listed in Table 5. Both the power consumptions of the conventional CS sensor nodes and the ACS sensor nodes are estimated and listed in the table. It shows that for the signals being examined the potential power savings by ACS range from 17.2% to 47.3%.

Table 6. Results of the power estimation simulation

Signal	Conv. CS	ACS	Power Savings
Fetal ECG	3.08 mW	2.31 mW	25%
Cap	4.57 mW	3.75 mW	17.2%
Stress	2.98 mW	1.57 mW	47.3%
PPG	1.55 mW	1.27 mW	18.1%

7. CONCLUSION

In this work, we investigate signal sparsity variations as well as the changes of the required minimum measurement sizes in compressive sensing operations for a wide range of biomedical sensor signals. The findings indicate that many sensor signals exhibit fluctuations on signal sparsity, which are large enough to justify adaptively changing measurement sizes during sensing operations. Such adaptive compressive sensing helps further reduce power consumption of sensor nodes. Using a system-level power model of a generic wireless transmitter, the sensor node power consumption with conventional CS and ACS are compared. It shows that significant power can be saved by using ACS.

8. ACKNOWLEDGEMENT

This research has been supported by the NSF I/UCRC for Embedded Systems at SIUC, and funded in part by the National Science Foundation under Grant No. 0856039. Any opinions, findings, and conclusions or recommendations expressed in this material are those of the author(s) and do not necessarily reflect the views of the National Science Foundation.

9. REFERENCES

[1] Donoho, D.L. Compressed sensing. IEEE Transactions on Information Theory 52, 4 (2006), 1289–1306.

[2] Candès, E.J., Romberg, J.K., and Tao, T. Stable signal recovery from incomplete and inaccurate measurements. *Communications on Pure and Applied Mathematics 59*, 8 (2006), 1207–1223.

[3] Han, B., Wu, F., and Wu, D. Image representation by compressed sensing. *15th IEEE International Conference on Image Processing, 2008. ICIP 2008*, (2008), 1344–1347.

[4] Kyriakides, I. Adaptive Compressive Sensing and Processing of Delay-Doppler Radar Waveforms. *IEEE Transactions on Signal Processing 60*, 2 (2012), 730–739.

[5] Zhang, P., Hu, Z., Qiu, R.C., and Sadler, B.M. A Compressed Sensing Based Ultra-Wideband Communication System. *IEEE International Conference on Communications, 2009. ICC '09*, (2009), 1–5.

[6] Baheti, P.K. and Garudadri, H. An Ultra Low Power Pulse Oximeter Sensor Based on Compressed Sensing. *Sixth International Workshop on Wearable and Implantable Body Sensor Networks, 2009. BSN 2009*, (2009), 144–148.

[7] Chen, F., Chandrakasan, A.P., and Stojanovic, V. A signal-agnostic compressed sensing acquisition system for wireless and implantable sensors. *2010 IEEE Custom Integrated Circuits Conference (CICC)*, (2010), 1–4.

[8] Warnell, G., Reddy, D., and Chellappa, R. Adaptive rate compressive sensing for background subtraction. *2012 IEEE International Conference on Acoustics, Speech and Signal Processing (ICASSP)*, (2012), 1477–1480.

[9] Soni, A. and Haupt, J. Efficient adaptive compressive sensing using sparse hierarchical learned dictionaries. *2011 Conference Record of the Forty Fifth Asilomar Conference on Signals, Systems and Computers (ASILOMAR)*, (2011), 1250–1254.

[10] Saeed, M., Villarroel, M., Reisner, A.T., et al. Multiparameter Intelligent Monitoring in Intensive Care II (MIMIC-II): A public-

access intensive care unit database. *Critical care medicine 39*, 5 (2011), 952–960.

[11] Zhang, Y., Zhang, F., Shakhsheer, Y., et al. A Batteryless 19 W MICS/ISM-Band Energy Harvesting Body Sensor Node SoC for ExG Applications. *IEEE Journal of Solid-State Circuits 48*, 1 (2013), 199–213.

[12] Li, Y., Bakkaloglu, B., and Chakrabarti, C. A System Level Energy Model and Energy-Quality Evaluation for Integrated Transceiver Front-Ends. *IEEE Transactions on Very Large Scale Integration (VLSI) Systems 15*, 1 (2007), 90–103.

[13] Ye, L., Shi, C., Liao, H., and Huang, R. A 0.47mW 6th-order 20MHz active filter using highly power-efficient Opamp. *2011 IEEE International Symposium on Circuits and Systems (ISCAS)*, (2011), 1640–1643.

[14] Ismail, S.H., Soliman, E.A., and Mahmoud, S.A. Cascaded third-order tunable low-pass filter using low voltage low power OTA. *2011 13th International Symposium on Integrated Circuits (ISIC)*, (2011), 488–491.

[15] Lee, S.-Y. and Cheng, C.-J. Systematic Design and Modeling of a OTA-C Filter for Portable ECG Detection. *IEEE Transactions on Biomedical Circuits and Systems 3*, 1 (2009), 53–64.

[16] Chenjian, W. and Zhiqun, L. A 0.18 μm CMOS up-conversion mixer for wireless sensor networks application. *2011 International Conference on Wireless Communications and Signal Processing (WCSP)*, (2011), 1–4.

[17] Vidojkovic, M., Liu, Y.-H., Huang, X., Imamura, K., Dolmans, G., and de Groot, H. A fully integrated 1.7 -2.5GHz 1mW fractional-N PLL for WBAN and WSN applications. *2012 IEEE Radio Frequency Integrated Circuits Symposium (RFIC)*, (2012), 185–188.

[18] Liu, Y.-H., Huang, X., Vidojkovic, M., et al. A 2.7nJ/b multi-standard 2.3/2.4GHz polar transmitter for wireless sensor networks. *Solid-State Circuits Conference Digest of Technical Papers (ISSCC), 2012 IEEE International*, (2012), 448–450.

[19] Tanguay, L.-F. and Sawan, M. A Fully-Integrated 580 μW ISM-Band Frequency Synthesizer for Implantable Medical Devices. *International Symposium on Signals, Circuits and Systems, 2007. ISSCS 2007*, (2007), 1–4.

[20] Moradi, A., Zgaren, M., and Sawan, M. A 0.084 nJ/b FSK transmitter and 4.8 μW OOK receiver for ISM-band medical sensor networks. *New Circuits and Systems Conference (NEWCAS), 2013 IEEE 11th International*, (2013), 1–4.

[21] Van Langevelde, R., Van Elzakker, M., van Goor, D., Termeer, H., Moss, J., and Davie, A.J. An ultra-low-power 868/915 MHz RF transceiver for wireless sensor network applications. *IEEE Radio Frequency Integrated Circuits Symposium, 2009. RFIC 2009*, (2009), 113–116.

[22] Kopta, V., Pengg, F., Le Roux, E., and Enz, C. A 2.4-GHz low power polar transmitter for wireless body area network applications. *New Circuits and Systems Conference (NEWCAS), 2013 IEEE 11th International*, (2013), 1–4.

[23] Sapone, G. and Palmisano, G. A 0.25- μm CMOS Low-Power Up-Conversion Mixer for 3.1-5 GHz Ultra-Wideband Applications. *Research in Microelectronics and Electronics 2006, Ph. D.*, (2006), 457–460.

[24] Alomainy, A., Hao, Y., and Pasveer, F. Numerical and Experimental Evaluation of a Compact Sensor Antenna for Healthcare Devices. *IEEE Transactions on Biomedical Circuits and Systems 1*, 4 (2007), 242–249.

[25] Receiver Sensitivity. http://www.digi.com/technology/rf-articles/receiver-sensitivity.

[26] Dual-radio, Three-stream 802.11n Wireless Access Point. http://www.merunetworks.com/collateral/data-sheets/ds-wireless-access-points-for-high-density-environments-ap332.pdf.

[27] Michael Grant and Stephen Boyd. CVX: Matlab software for disciplined convex programming, version 2.0 beta. http://cvxr.com/cvx, September 2013.

[28] Michael Grant and Stephen Boyd. Graph implementations for nonsmooth convex programs, Recent Advances in Learning and Control (a tribute to M. Vidyasagar), V. Blondel, S. Boyd, and H. Kimura, editors, pages 95-110, Lecture Notes in Control and Information Sciences, Springer, 2008. http://stanford.edu/~boyd/graph_dcp.html.

[29] Candes, E.J. and Romberg, J. l1-MAGIC: Recovery of Sparse Signals via Convex Programming. 2005. http://users.ece.gatech.edu/~justin/l1magic/downloads/l1magic.pdf.

[30] 1.Lorenz, D., Pfetsch, M., and Tillmann, A. Solving Basis Pursuit: Heuristic Optimality Check and Solver Comparison. 2011.

[31] Figueiredo, M.A.T., Nowak, R.D., and Wright, S.J. Gradient Projection for Sparse Reconstruction: Application to Compressed Sensing and Other Inverse Problems. *IEEE Journal of Selected Topics in Signal Processing 1*, 4 (2007), 586–597.

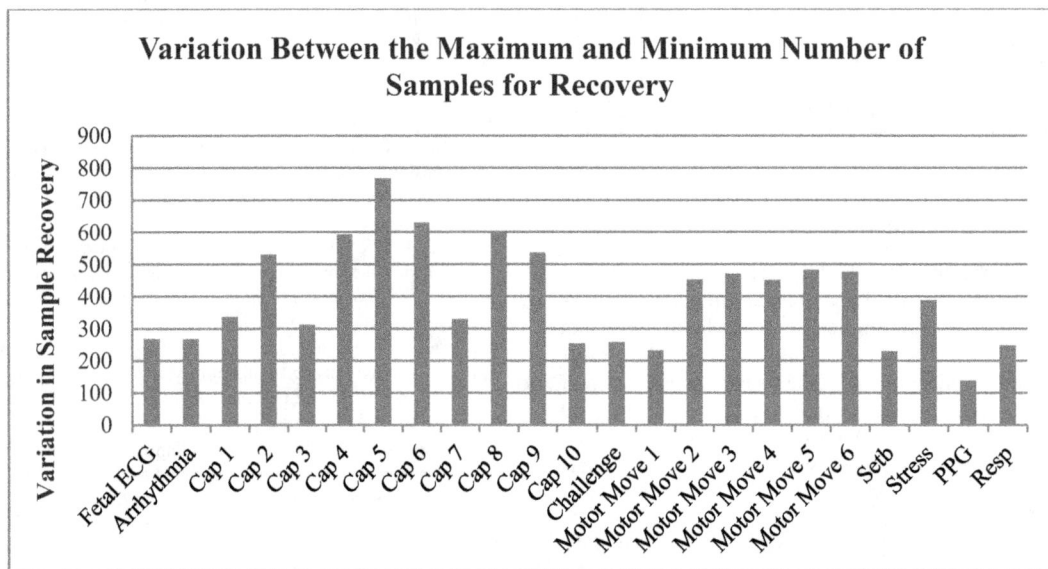

Figure 6: The variation between the maximum and minimum number of samples over 6 windows.

Regulator-Gating: Adaptive Management of On-Chip Voltage Regulators

Selçuk Köse
Department of Electrical Engineering
University of South Florida
Tampa, Florida
kose@usf.edu

ABSTRACT

Design-for-power has become one of the primary objectives with the continuous demand to improve the battery life of mobile devices or minimize the cooling costs of servers. To save power and mitigate thermal emergencies, circuits typically enter reduced power states when the workload is light. Voltage regulators, however, operate indifferently under varying workload conditions due to the lack of different operating modes. When a voltage regulator is optimized for a particular load current, significant power is dissipated during voltage conversion while delivering a different load current. Adaptive activity management of on-chip voltage regulators based upon the workload information is exploited in this paper to force each on-chip regulator to operate in its most power-efficient load current. In the proposed regulator-gating (ReGa) technique, regulators are adaptively turned on (off) when the current demand is high (low) to improve the voltage conversion efficiency. With the proposed ReGa technique, the overall voltage conversion efficiency from the battery or off-chip power supply to the output of on-chip voltage regulators is improved ~3×.

Categories and Subject Descriptors

B.7.1 [**Hardware**]: INTEGRATED CIRCUITS

Keywords

On-chip voltage regulation; parallel voltage regulation; power management

1. INTRODUCTION

With continuous advancements in the semiconductor industry, transistors with smaller than 20 nm feature size have enabled the integration of multi-billion transistors on a single die [13, 28, 34]. With the failure of Dennard's scaling [1], however, only a fraction of the transistors on a die can operate at full voltage/frequency to not exceed the thermal design power (TDP) [8]. A large proportion of the circuit blocks is either inactive (dark silicon) or in a reduced-power state (dim silicon) at any given time to satisfy the power and

thermal constraints [4, 5]. Despite the significant amount of research and growing necessity for a holistic power optimization technique, existing efforts to minimize power dissipation are typically not coherent. The existing research efforts are disjointed into two pieces: i) the dynamic and static power loss at the load circuits is minimized or ii) the power loss during power-conversion is minimized.

There is a growing trend for integrating the voltage regulators fully on-chip [10, 18, 19, 27] to improve the quality of voltage delivered to the load circuits. Voltage regulators are typically designed to provide the highest power-conversion efficiency when delivering a particular output current regime (*i.e.*, typically the maximum current for LDO and SC regulators). Since dynamically changing the design parameters of a voltage regulator under different workloads is difficult, existing power management techniques suffer from increased voltage conversion losses during idle states when the current demand is low [16, 30] and regulator efficiency is reduced. A new parallel voltage regulation architecture and regulator management technique are proposed in this paper to improve the voltage conversion efficiency at different utilization levels.

The related background and motivation for the proposed voltage regulator management technique are presented in the next section. The proposed regulator-gating technique is explained in Section 3 with a sample system of parallel voltage regulators. The overall power efficiency improvement and the proposed management of regulator-gating are also offered in this section. The paper is concluded in Section 4.

2. BACKGROUND AND MOTIVATION

More than 32% of the overall battery power is dissipated during high-to-low voltage conversion before even reaching the load circuits in modern mobile platforms [22]. The primary reason for this huge power loss is that power delivery networks are designed to satisfy the stringent noise requirements under *worst-case* loading conditions, which is typically the full utilization of the overall chip computing and memory resources when the current demand is the highest.

Parallel voltage regulation has been widely used for buck and SC regulators to reduce the output voltage ripple by interleaving multiple regulators with phase shifted switching frequencies [31, 32]. Advantages of interleaved regulation include reduced filter size for buck converters, improved load response, and higher efficiency [26]. The interleaved architectures, however, have not been exploited until recently to regulate voltage close to the load circuits to minimize

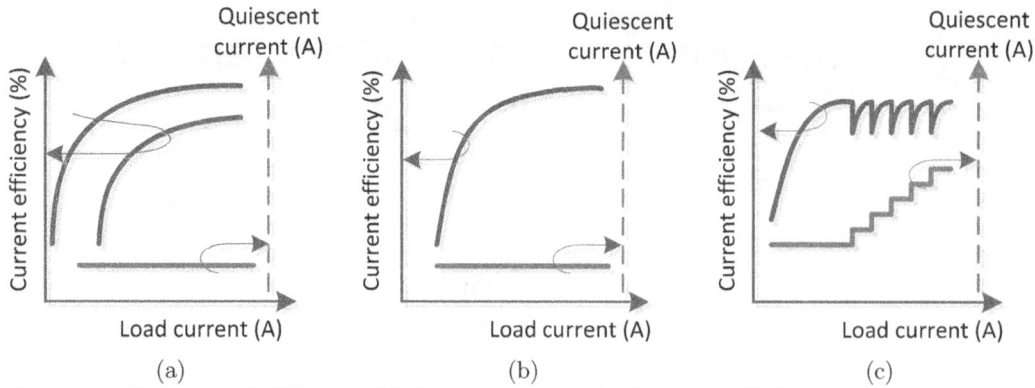

Figure 1: Current efficiency of different LDO regulators. a) Current efficiency of an LDO regulator is significantly degraded when the quiescent current increases at light load currents [20]. b) Current efficiency of an LDO regulator increases monotonically with the load current when the quiescent current is constant [12]. c) Adaptively controlling the quiescent current based upon the load current can improve the current efficiency [23].

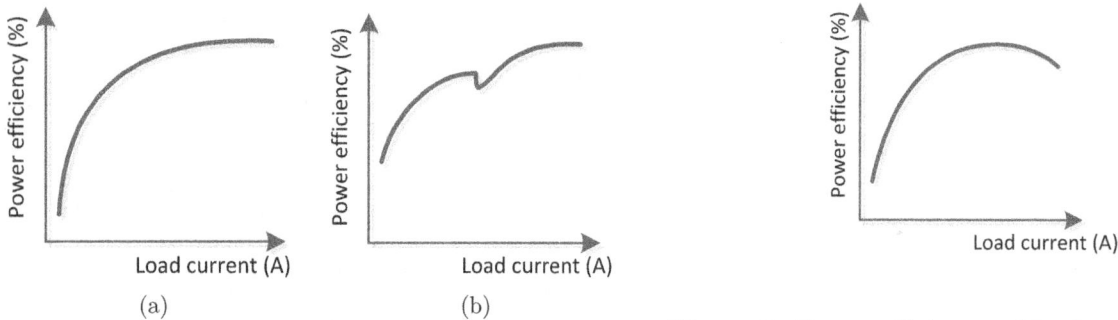

Figure 2: Power efficiency of different SC regulators. a) The power efficiency of a SC regulator is not necessarily monotonic but the maximum efficiency is typically obtained while delivering maximum output current [33]. b) Different techniques can be used to improve the efficiency at light load currents [27].

Figure 3: Power efficiency of buck converters. The efficiency graph exhibits a non-monotonic behavior and the maximum power efficiency is not obtained at the full output current [11, 25].

noise [7, 35]. Distributed on-chip voltage regulation is an emerging research area where multiple voltage regulators are connected in parallel, delivering current to the same power network close to the load circuits [2,3,6,7,17,21,35]. Although challenges such as device mismatch, offset voltages among parallel regulators, overall system stability, and balanced current sharing need to be considered, distributed voltage regulation can provide sub-nanosecond load regulation to attain high performance under increased temporal and spatial workload variations in modern ICs. Bulzacchelli *et al.* achieved 500 ps transient response time with a system of eight distributed LDO regulators [6]. Ten LDO regulators and a buck converter are connected in parallel to provide 1.4 amps maximum current in a commercial cellular handset chip [2]. Recently, Lai *et al.* provided detailed guidelines to ensure stability of a distributed voltage regulation system composed of LDO regulators [21] based on a hybrid stability theory. Publications from ST-Ericsson [2] and IBM [6] clearly demonstrate that there is a growing interest not only from academia but also from industry to realize distributed on-chip voltage regulation.

One very important observation that is exploited in this paper is that regulators are optimized at a particular output current, assuming that the regulator typically operates at that particular current regime [29]. The voltage conversion efficiency during the idle periods is therefore significantly degraded since the regulators are almost always designed to provide the highest power efficiency at higher load current [30]. Aggressive power saving mechanisms are currently implemented as a result of the modern ICs exhibiting frequent idle periods [24]. It is projected that more than half of the circuit needs to be idle at 8 nm technology node [5] to satisfy the TDP requirement in server processors or to improve the battery life in mobile processors. Sinkar *et al.* analyzed the potential power savings from workload-aware voltage regulator optimization for a single buck converter and proposed an optimization based on frequency and phase count of the regulator, achieving 34% lower overall power consumption [30].

The power efficiency of low-dropout (LDO) regulators, switched capacitor (SC) regulators, and buck converters are illustrated in Figs. 1, 2, and 3, respectively. The current efficiency of an LDO regulator depends on the quiescent current consumption within the regulator. Although the efficiency of an LDO regulator can be improved by adaptively changing the the quiescent current, current efficiency is significantly

(a) LDO

(b) DLDO

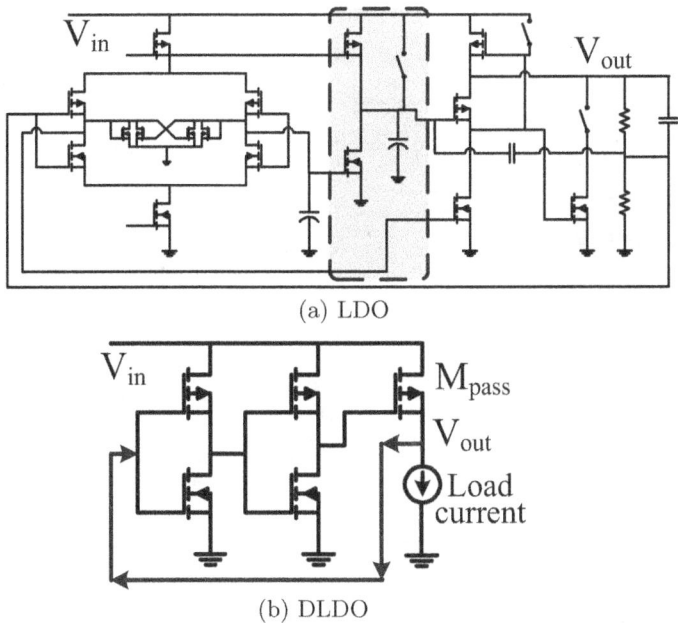

Figure 4: Voltage regulators used in the analysis. a) LDO proposed by Lai *et al.* [20] and b) modified DLDO regulator used in this paper to achieve fast load regulation.

Figure 5: Illustration of a distributed power network with 7 LDO and 3 DLDO voltage regulators connected in parallel.

degraded at light load currents, as shown in Fig. 1 [12,20,23]. The power efficiency of an SC regulator typically increases with the output current as shown in Fig. 2a [33]. Although advanced techniques can be used to improve the efficiency at light load currents, as illustrated in Fig. 2b, the efficiency is typically significantly degraded while providing light output current [27]. The power efficiency of a buck converter exhibits a non-monotonic behavior and efficiency is degraded when the load current exceed a certain value. Similar to the other regulator types, the power efficiency of a buck converter is minimized while delivering light load current, as shown in Fig. 3 [11,25].

As compared to the conventional schemes where the power network is designed targeting the full utilization of the overall chip area, the proposed technique will provide an adaptive power delivery infrastructure that is tailored to provide high voltage conversion efficiency during both fully-utilized and under-utilized modes of operation. One of the primary challenges is to realize a voltage regulator with fast (*a couple of nanoseconds*) turn on and off capability. Voltage regulators with fast turn on and off capability tailored to achieve an adaptive *regulator-gating* methodology are investigated in this paper.

3. REGULATOR-GATING

3.1 Proof of Concept

A distributed power delivery network is constructed with parallel LDO and digital-LDO (DLDO) regulators to provide a *proof of concept* for the proposed ReGa methodology. Although similar results have been obtained with parallel SC and DLDO regulators, in the interest of limited space,

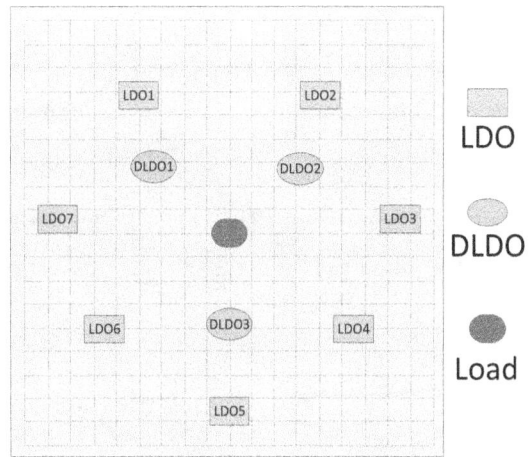

preliminary results from the system designed with LDO and DLDO regulators are reported in this paper since parallel LDO regulators tend to have more stability problems and are considered to be more difficult to realize.

A DLDO regulator with two skewed inverters to sense the changes at the output voltage and to generate a transient signal to control the gate voltage of a pass transistor M_{pass}, permitting an instant response to transient changes is shown in Fig. 4b. A drop at the output voltage V_{out} causes the pass transistor to provide higher current due to the increased gate voltage. This DLDO regulator is similar to the circuit proposed in [9] with certain differences. The voltage sense portion of the circuit is simpler and a single pass transistor is used without a pull-down NMOS transistor. Due to the smaller area of the sense transistors, multiple copies of this modified DLDO regulator can be distributed across the die in parallel with LDO regulators and can provide a fast response time of ∼400 ps (see Fig. 6). Multiple copies of these DLDO regulators are connected in parallel with the LDO regulator proposed by Lai *et al.* in [20]. The inverting amplifier stage of the LDO regulator, shown in dotted box in Fig. 4a, has been modified to enhance the dynamic response while minimizing the quiescent current consumption at this stage.

Seven LDO and three DLDO regulators are connected to a small power network with 400 nodes, as depicted in Fig. 5. The current contribution from individual regulators to the power grid is shown in Fig. 6 when the load current demand increases from 11 mA to 80 mA. While only one LDO regulator (LDO 7) is sufficient to provide a robust 11 mA current to the load, the rest of the LDO regulators turn on and start providing current to the power grid when the load current demand increases to 80 mA. DLDO regulators turn on immediately after sensing a voltage drop at the power grid and provide instant current to the grid while the LDO regulators are turning on, as shown in Fig. 6. The DLDO regulators remain active only for a couple of nanoseconds (∼4 ns) until the LDO regulators turn on. The DLDO regulators are self-activated, whereas the LDO regulators are controlled by the system-level (global) controller, as explained in the next subsections.

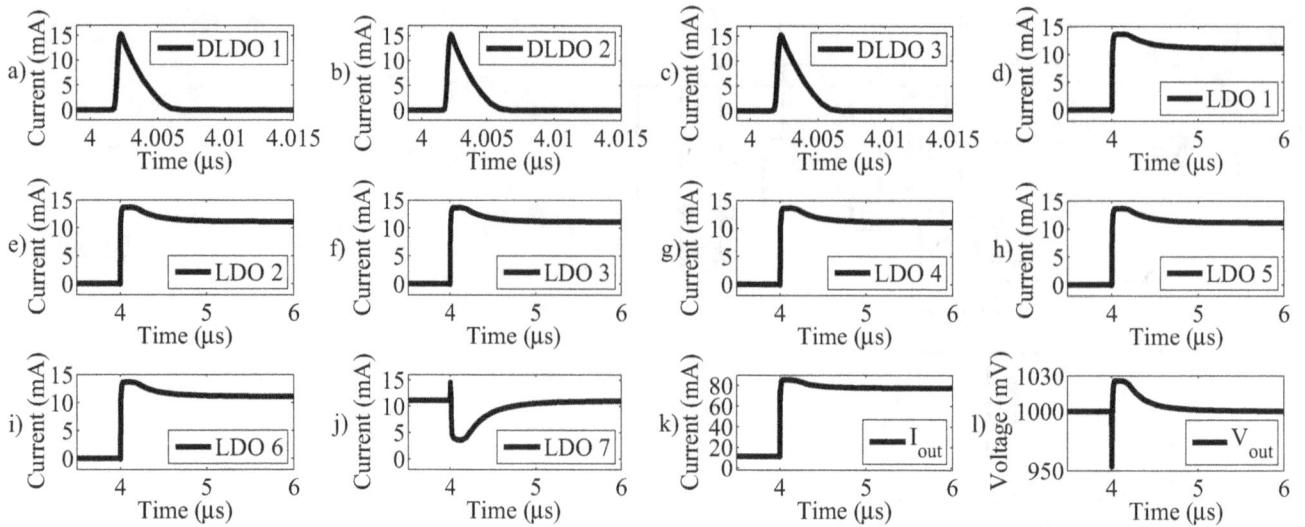

Figure 6: Response time of multiple LDO and DLDO regulators connected in parallel to the same power grid when the load current is increased from 11 mA to 80 mA.

3.2 Regulator Gating to Improve Overall Power Efficiency

The current efficiency of the LDO regulators is around 98% (~300 μA quiescent current while providing 11 mA current). The quiescent current increases while providing a lower output current, as discussed in [20], and doubles to ~600 μA when the output current is lower than 2 mA. In this case, the current efficiency of the LDO regulator becomes 2/2.6=~77%. The increase in the quiescent current is typically observed when an LDO regulator has an AB amplifier type output stage. In the case study where the load current is 11 mA, a single LDO regulator provides the required current with 98% current efficiency. If all of the seven LDO regulators were active while providing 11 mA load current, each LDO regulator would contribute less than 2 mA current to the load with a current efficiency of less than 77%. Without regulator-gating, the total power dissipated during voltage conversion while providing 11 mA load current is $V_{in} * I_{in} - V_{out} * I_{out} = 1.2$ V * (11 mA + 7 * 0.6 mA) - 1 V * 11 mA = 7.24 mW. Alternatively, with regulator-gating, the total power dissipated during voltage conversion is $V_{in} * I_{in} - V_{out} * I_{out} = 1.2$ V * 11.3 mA - 1 V * 11 mA = 2.56 mW. This preliminary study demonstrates that power delivery system is ~3× more power-efficient with ReGa when certain regulators are gated during the idle periods of time. If the idle period lasts 1 ms, the energy savings will be greater than 8 μj for this sample circuit.

On-chip voltage regulation introduces certain overheads, such as area and reduced power efficiencies. In spite of these overheads, on-chip voltage regulation can enable per-core-DVFS, lower the on-chip noise, and reduce the number of dedicated I/O pins [15]. The primary overheads of ReGa assuming that the system already has on-chip voltage regulation are summarized below.

Speed of ReGa: With the utilization of DLDO regulators, the turn on time is decreased to sub-nanosecond range (400 ps in our example). For most of the applications, this turn on time does not degrade system performance.

Area overhead of ReGa Assuming that the power delivery network already has control circuitry for power/clock gating, on-chip voltage or current sensors, and performance counters, the area overhead of ReGa will be the additional area requirement for the DLDO regulators. Please note that DLDO regulators already exist in certain designs without ReGa [9]. When a firmware is used, there is no additional area overhead for ReGa power management.

Power overhead of ReGa The additional power overhead of the proposed ReGa methodology occurs during turning on and off voltage regulators. The power dissipation to turn on an LDO is less than ~0.1 mW, and the power dissipated by the DLDO is negligible (i.e. ~0.02 mW) when providing 15 mA output current.

3.3 Proposed Regulator-Gating Management

The proposed ReGa control methodology is based on two control loops: i) local control and ii) global control, as illustrated in Fig. 7. A local control provides a sub-nanosecond response to the transient changes in the supply voltage. DLDO regulators are immediately activated based on a simple voltage feedback and provide instant current to the power grid in ~400 ps. When the voltage emergency is over (i.e., the transient spike is mitigated), these burst mode DLDO regulators are self-deactivated and wait for another interrupt to be activated. Alternatively, a global control loop continuously monitors the overall power consumption of the distributed regulators and compares this information with the available power budget dictated by the system-level controller. If the power consumption exceeds the available power budget limit, certain regulators are turned off. Global and local control loops are fundamentally separate during normal operation, however, the global control loop can override the local control at any time during the operation and can permanently turn off the regulators which are actually controlled locally. When the global controller turns a voltage regulator off, the local control loop cannot turn the regulator on unless the global controller asserts the turn on signal. The proposed power management system is partially imple-

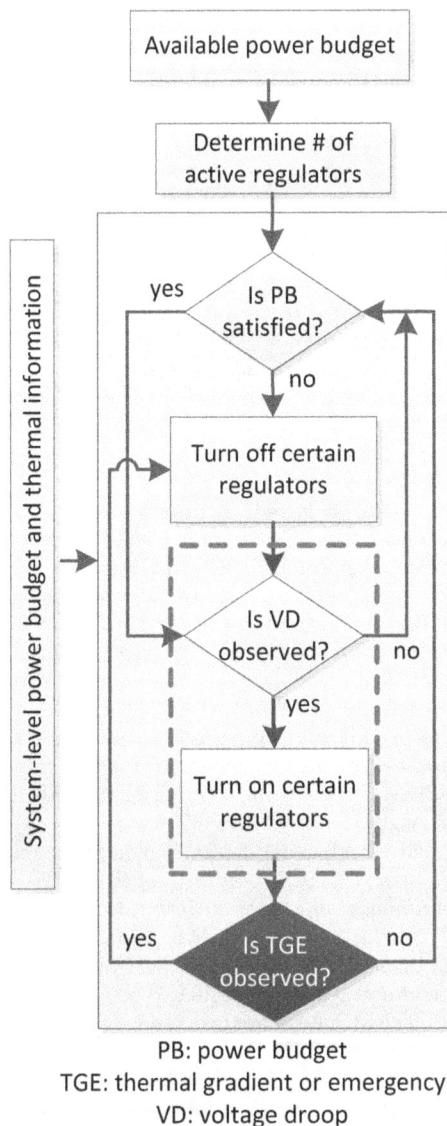

PB: power budget
TGE: thermal gradient or emergency
VD: voltage droop

Figure 7: Proposed regulator gating (ReGa) technique. The local control, which is shown with the dotted box, has been implemented in this paper.

mented at the circuit level as demonstrated in the previous section that includes the local control and a portion of the global control which is illustrated in the dotted box in Fig. 7.

4. FUTURE WORK

Since the ReGa technique is orthogonal to other power management techniques, ReGa can be implemented within an existing power management flow with negligible area and power overhead. The system-level workload information to control the DVFS, power-gating, and clock-gating will be leveraged in the proposed ReGa methodology and there will be no additional overhead for workload prediction. A requirement for the proposed methodology is the design of a flexible system-level controller to balance the competing objectives of power, noise, and temperature based upon the data obtained from distributed sensors at runtime. The system-level controller will employ power allocation decisions based on multiple objective optimal control [14]. Distributed sensors within the power management system will report the power, temperature, and noise requirements to the system-level controller, which also considers workload estimations while allocating available power to local regulators through the local controllers. This hierarchical power management organization will be implemented to control the activity of the individual voltage regulators. The stability and feasibility of the overall power management system will also be evaluated.

5. CONCLUSIONS

More than 32% of the overall power is dissipated during voltage conversion in modern integrated circuits. A new power management technique, regulator-gating, is proposed in this paper to improve the voltage conversion efficiency by adaptively controlling the activity of individual voltage regulators within a system of parallel on-chip voltage regulators. The proposed regulator-gating technique achieves $\sim 3\times$ lower power consumption during voltage conversion in a sample circuit with seven LDO and three DLDO regulators which are connected in parallel. A modified DLDO regulator is utilized to achieve fast turn on capability A power management technique to control the regulator-gating is proposed and partially implemented. The related overheads of the proposed technique are addressed.

6. REFERENCES

[1] R. H. e. Dennard. Design of ion-implanted mosfet's with very small physical dimensions. *IEEE Journal of Solid-State Circuits*, 9(5):256–268, October 1974.

[2] A. J. D. *et al.* A fully integrated power-management solution for a 65nm cmos cellular handset chip. In *Proceedings of the IEEE International Solid-State Circuits Conference*, pages 382–384, February 2011.

[3] F. L. *et al.* Embedded cmos distributed voltage regulator for large core loads. In *Proceedings of the IEEE European Solid-State Circuits Conference*, pages 521–524, September 2003.

[4] G. V. *et al.* Conservation Cores: Reducing the Energy of Mature Computations. In *Proceedings of the International Conference on Architectural Support for Programming Languages and Operating Systems*, pages 205–218, March 2010.

[5] H. E. *et al.* Dark silicon and the end of multicore scaling. In *Proceedings of the International Symposium on Computer Architecture*, pages 365–376, June 2011.

[6] J. F. B. *et al.* Dual-loop system of distributed microregulators with high dc accuracy, load response time below 500 ps, and 85-mv dropout voltage. *IEEE Journal of Solid-State Circuits*, 47(4):863–874, April 2012.

[7] P. Z. *et al.* Optimization of on-chip switched-capacitor dc-dc converters for high-performance applications. In *Proceedings of the IEEE/ACM International Conference on Computer-Aided Design*, pages 263–270, November 2012.

[8] W. H. *et al.* Many-core design from a thermal perspective. In *Proceedings of the IEEE/ACM Design Automation Conference*, pages 746–749, June 2008.

[9] Y. O. *et al.* 0.5-v input digital low-dropout regulator (ldo) with 98.7% current efficiency in 65 nm cmos.

IEICE Transactions on Electronics, 94(6):938–944, June 2011.

[10] J. Guo and K. N. Leung. A 6-μW Chip-Area-Efficient Output-Capacitorless LDO in 90-nm CMOS Technology. *IEEE Journal of Solid-State Circuits*, 45(9):1896–1905, September 2010.

[11] P. e. Hazucha. A 233-MHz 80%-87% Efficient Four-Phase DC-DC Converter Utilizing Air-Core Inductors on Package. *IEEE Journal of Solid-State Circuits*, 40(4):838–845, April 2005.

[12] P. e. Hazucha. Area-Efficient Linear Regulator with Ultra-Fast Load Regulation. *IEEE Journal of Solid-State Circuits*, 40(4):933–940, April 2005.

[13] R. Jakushokas, M. Popovich, A. V. Mezhiba, S. Kose, and E. G. Friedman. *Power Distribution Networks with On-Chip Decoupling Capacitors, Second Edition*. Springer, 2011.

[14] P. P. Khargonekar and M. A. Rotea. Multiple objective optimal control of linear systems: the quadratic norm case. *IEEE Transactions on Automatic Control*, 36(1):14–24, January 1991.

[15] W. Kim, M. S. Gupta, G.-Y. Wei, and D. Brooks. System level analysis of fast, per-core dvfs using on-chip switching regulators. In *Proceedings of the IEEE International Symposium on High Performance Computer Architecture*, pages 123–134, February 2008.

[16] S. Kose. Thermal Implications of On Chip Voltage Regulation Upcoming Challenges and Possible Solutions. In *Proceedings of the IEEE/ACM Design Automation Conference*, June 2014.

[17] S. Kose and E. G. Friedman. Distributed on-chip power delivery. *IEEE Journal on Emerging and Selected Topics in Circuits and Systems*, 2(4):704–713, December 2012.

[18] S. Kose, S. Tam, S. Pinzon, B. McDermott, and E. G. Friedman. An Area Efficient On-Chip Hybrid Voltage Regulator. In *Proceedings of the IEEE International Symposium on Quality Electronic Design*, pages 398–403, March 2012.

[19] S. Kose, S. Tam, S. Pinzon, B. McDermott, and E. G. Friedman. Active Filter Based Hybrid On-Chip DC-DC Converters for Point-of-Load Voltage Regulation. *IEEE Transactions on Very Large Scale Integration (VLSI) Systems*, 21(4):680–691, April 2013.

[20] S. Lai and P. Li. A fully on-chip area-efficient cmos low-dropout regulator with fast load regulation. *Analog Integrated Circuits and Signal Processing*, 72(2):925–1030, February 2012.

[21] S. Lai, B. Yan, and P. Li. Stability assurance and design optimization of large power delivery networks with multiple on-chip voltage regulators. In *Proceedings of the IEEE/ACM International Conference on Computer-Aided Design*, pages 247–254, November 2012.

[22] W. e. Lee. Power conversion efficiency characterization and optimization for smartphones. In *Proceedings of the IEEE/ACM International Symposium on Low Power Electronics and Design*, pages 103–108, July-August 2012.

[23] M. e. Luders. A fully-integrated system power aware ldo for energy harvesting applications. In *Proceedings*

of the IEEE Symposium on VLSI Circuits, pages 244–245, June 2011.

[24] D. Meisner, B. T. Gold, and T. F. Wenisch. PowerNap: Eliminating Server Idle Power. In *Proceedings of the International Conference on Architectural Support for Programming Languages and Operating Systems*, pages 205–216, March 2009.

[25] M. D. Mulligan, B. Broach, and T. H. Lee. A constant-frequency method for improving light-load efficiency in synchronous buck converters. *IEEE Power Electronics Letters*, 3(1):24–29, March 2005.

[26] X. Peng, Y.-C. Ren, Y. Mao, and F. C. Lee. A family of novel interleaved dc/dc converters for low-voltage high-current voltage regulator module applications. In *Proceedings of the Annual IEEE International Power Electronics Specialists Conference*, pages 1507–1511, June 2001.

[27] Y. Ramadass, A. Fayed, B. Haroun, and A. Chandrakasan. A 0.16 mm^2 Completely On-Chip Switched-Capacitor DC-DC Converter Using Digital Capacitance Modulation for LDO Replacement in 45 nm CMOS. In *Proceedings of the IEEE International Solid-State Circuits Conference*, pages 208–209, February 2010.

[28] R. J. e. Riedlinger. A 32 nm 3.1 billion transistor 12-wide-issue itanium processor for mission-critical servers. In *Proceedings of the IEEE International Solid-State Circuits Conference*, pages 84–86, February 2011.

[29] G. e. Schrom. Optimal design of monolithic integrated dc-dc converters. In *Proceedings of the IEEE International Conference on Integrated Circuit Design and Technology*, pages 1–3, May 2006.

[30] A. A. Sinkar, H. Wang, and N. S. Kim. Workload-aware voltage regulator optimization for power efficient multi-core processors. In *Proceedings of the Conference on Design, Automation and Test in Europe*, pages 1134–1137, March 2012.

[31] N. e. Sturcken. A switched-inductor integrated voltage regulator with nonlinear feedback and network-on-chip load in 45 nm soi. *IEEE Journal of Solid-State Circuits*, 47(8):1935–1945, August 2012.

[32] F. Su, W.-H. Ki, and C.-Y. Tsui. Regulated switched-capacitor doubler with interleaving control for continuous output regulation. *IEEE Journal of Solid-State Circuits*, 44(4):1112–1120, April 2009.

[33] T. e. Umeno. New switched-capacitor dc-dc converter with low input current ripple and its hybridization. In *Proceedings of the IEEE International Midwest Symposium on Symposium on Circuits and Systems*, pages 1091–1094, August 1990.

[34] J. e. Warnock. 5.5 ghz system z microprocessor and multi-chip module. In *Proceedings of the IEEE International Solid-State Circuits Conference*, pages 46–47, February 2013.

[35] P. Zhou, D. Jiao, C. H. Kim, and S. S. Sapatnekar. Exploration of on-chip switched-capacitor dc-dc converter for multicore processors using a distributed power delivery network. In *Proceedings of the IEEE Custom Integrated Circuits Conference*, pages 1–4, September 2011.

Logic Block and Design Methodology for Via-Configurable Structured ASIC Using Dual Supply Voltages

Ta-Kai Lin
Computer Science and Engineering
Yuan Ze University
Chung-Li, 320 Taiwan
camino0605@hotmail.com

Kuen-Wey Lin
Computer Science
National Chiao Tung University
Hsin-Chu, 300 Taiwan
s966047@mail.yzu.edu.tw

Chang-Hao Chiu, Rung-Bin Lin
Computer Science and Engineering
Yuan Ze University
Chung-Li, 320 Taiwan
csrlin@cs.yzu.edu.tw

ABSTRACT

This paper presents a via-configurable logic block and a design methodology for realizing fine-grained dual-supply-voltage structured ASIC. Experiments with a 90nm process technology show that, given various timing budgets, our approach can achieve up to 44% energy reduction with 1.6% area overhead on level converters. Compared with *GECVS*, our approach converts up to 39% more high-supply voltage gates into low-supply voltage gates.

Categories and Subject Descriptors

B.7.2 [**Integrated Circuits**]: Design Aids – *Layout*.

General Terms

Algorithms, Performance, Design, Experimentation.

Keywords

Structured ASIC, Via configurable, Dual supply voltage, Low power, Standard cell, Level converter.

1. INTRODUCTION

Structured ASIC [1,2] has a pre-fabricated yet configurable logic fabric formed by metal- or via-configurable logic blocks (VCLB). Via-configurable logic fabric uses fewer customizable mask layers and hence has a lower NRE cost, but gives a lower degree of freedom to designing a circuit. To leverage standard-cell design tools, a VCLB's layout must be instrumental to creation of standard cells that employ only one type of VCLB [3,4]. Due to this requirement, we have difficulty finding a VCLB that can take advantage of process advancements such as multi-threshold voltage designs or take advantage of design methodology advancements such as dual-supply voltage assignment. The work in [5] proposed a VCLB that facilitates power-gating for leakage power reduction. Although dual-supply voltage deployment [6,7] can lead to a large power reduction, to the best of our knowledge, we are the first to propose a VCLB and a methodology to enable

structured ASIC designs using dual-supply voltages. We employ a fine-grained approach that freely mixes high-voltage gates (HG) with low-voltage gates (LG) in a layout design, in stark contrast to a row-based [8-10] or voltage-island approach [11, 12].

In this article we first present a VCLB that can realize combinational logic gates, D flip-flops, and level-converters (LC). The VCLB enables a standard cell like design. We build an HG and an LG cell library of 150 cells respectively based on this VCLB. We then implement a slack budgeting tool to distribute available slacks to the gates on non-critical paths. We develop a post-placement methodology to replace HG's with LG's based on available slacks. Experiments run for test circuits designed with a 90nm process technology show that, given various timing budgets, our dual-supply-voltage structured ASIC achieves up to 44% energy reduction per switching with 1.6% area overhead on LC's. Compared with *GECVS*, our approach converts up to 39% more high-supply voltage gates into low-supply voltage gates. Nevertheless, the effectiveness of our methodology highly depends on timing requirement tightness.

The reset of this paper is organized as follows. Section 2 reviews some dual supply-voltage methodologies. Section 3 presents a VCLB for our dual supply-voltage structured ASIC. Section 4 proposes our dual supply-voltage design methodology. Section 5 gives some experimental results. Last section draws conclusions.

2. RELATED WORK

A dual supply-voltage design employs two different logic gates, LG and HG. Basically, LG's are on non-critical paths for saving power whereas HG's are on critical paths for maintaining chip performance. An LC (level-converter) should be deployed between an LG and an HG when the LG drives the HG. Two major approaches are widely used for determining whether a logic gate should be an LG or an HG. Extended Clustered Voltage Scaling (ECVS) approach [9] starts from a design having only HG's and then converts HG's level-by-level into LG's by making a traversal from flip-flops backward toward the primary inputs. Greedy ECVS (GECVS) approach [13] uses a sensitivity cost that considers slack changes and power saving on each gate to determine whether a logic gate should be an HG or an LG. It replaces an HG with maximum sensitivity by an LG. ECVS and GECVS are done before placement.

Power distribution is an important issue for applying dual supply-voltage methodology. High-voltage supply (VDDH) and low-voltage supply (VDDL) must co-exist in the same chip. Hence, placement of logic cells determines how VDDL and VDDH are distributed. There are three placement methods in general. One method is to cluster logic cells of the same supply voltage into

GLSVLSI'14, May 21–23, 2014, Houston, Texas, USA.
Copyright is held by the owner/author(s). Publication rights licensed to ACM.
ACM 978-1-4503-2816-6/14/05...$15.00.
http://dx.doi.org/10.1145/2591513.2591601

cell rows [8,9]. The HG cell rows may interleave LG cell rows. Some variants [10] of this method are to use left part of the rows for LG's and right part of the rows for HG's. This approach eases the distribution of supply voltages and reduces routing resource usage. Another method is to construct clusters of HG's and clusters of LG's to form voltage islands [11, 12]. The standard cells used by each of the above methods need only one power rail, either a VDDH rail or a VDDL rail. Nevertheless, all the above methods reduce the degree of freedom on cell placement. The third method is to place logic cells, regardless of HG's or LG's, just like ordinary standard cells. This method need not customize typical standard cell design tools for placement optimization and power distribution. However, a logic cell must be designed with two power supply rails. This may increase logic cell areas but will simplify power network deployment and reduce higher metal layer resource usage. This approach is also called fine-grained dual-supply methodology. Our work adopts this approach.

There are some LC's [14-16] designed for dual supply-voltage methodology. Some LC's are integrated into a flip-flop so that a high-voltage flip-flop can be directly driven by an LG. In our work we use a standalone LC from [16] as shown in Figure 1. Our study with a 90nm technology shows that the LC in [16] has better timing performance than the one in [15] given the same amount of power dissipation. Note that the P-transistor's source of the inverter at the LC output is connected to VDDH.

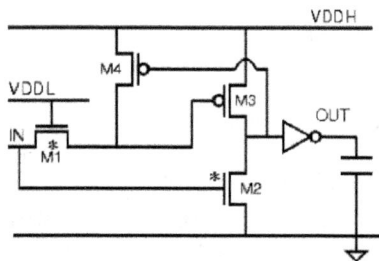

Figure 1. Level converter used in this work employing low threshold voltage transistors (marked by *).

3. VCLB SUPPORTING DUAL SUPPLY-VOLTAGE DESIGNS

Both the circuit implementation and relevant tool development for our structured ASIC are akin to VCLB layout design. There are a number of VCLB's in the literature, especially those from [3]. Each of those VCLB's enables a standard cell-like design so that standard cell design tools can be best leveraged for structured ASIC, so will our VCLB be designed in this way. Basically, a VCLB should be composable so that we can use multiple VCLB instances to implement complex logic gates. In this article, we will use *VCLB* to denote also a VCLB instance if its meaning in the context is clear. Furthermore, we will use *logic gate* and *cell* interchangeably. As mentioned before, we would employ a VDDL and a VDDH rail in our VCLB for achieving maximum placement flexibility. Figure 2 shows the stick diagram of our VCLB. Figure 3 gives the corresponding layout based on a commercial 90nm process technology. This VCLB has five pairs of P/N transistors and some predefined ME1 and ME2 wires. We can use some vias (denoted by *VI1*) between ME1 and ME2 to configure this VCLB into a combinational gate, a sequential gate, or an LC. Some jumpers on the left and right boundaries enable

composability. Pins are on ME2. Wires and diffusions do not have bends for better manufacturability.

Although our VCLB has a similar structure as the ones from [3], it has some distinct features that enable a fine-grained dual supply-voltage design. We place an ME2 VDDH rail at the top boundary so that row abutment can lead to a wider VDDH rail. Besides, we place an ME2 VDDL rail just right below the VDDH rail and two ME1 wires within two dotted regions A and B on the upper right and left corners as shown in Figure 2. Each of the two wires is connected to the VDDL rail by two *VI1*'s. When two cell rows abut in the way shown in Figure 4, the four ME1 wires at the center of the figure, respectively from the four VCLB's, abut seamlessly to form a large metal piece that connects the VDDL rails of the two adjacent rows. In addition, three ME1 jumpers respectively on the left and right boundaries of a VCLB can also abut on the corresponding jumpers of a neighboring VCLB. In this way we can simply employ the wires provided by the VCLB instances to implement more complex logic gates. This enables composability. Note that the N-well in this VCLB must not be too close to the left, right, and top boundaries so that N-wells of any two abutted VCLB's powered by different supply voltages will be at least separated by a minimum distance. An N-well tap within dotted region C shown in Figure 2 can be configured to connect the N-well to VDDL or VDDH. A configurable substrate tap is located at the center of the bottom boundary. We always drop a *VI1* from GND rail to this substrate tap. In addition, we have some vertical ME1 wires extended upward from the active area to the top boundary. We can connect these wires to either the VDDH or VDDL rail to configure this VCLB into an HG or LG.

Figure 5 shows an implementation of the LC in Figure 1 using our VCLB. We use some *VI1*'s to realize this circuit. On the left of the figure, one *VI1* is employed to connect the sources of two P-transistors to VDDH. At the center, one *VI1* is used to connect the polysilicone gate of an N-transistor to VDDL. On the right, one *VI1* is used to connect the source of a P-transistor to VDDH. A *VI1* is dropped from VDDH to the well tap to connect the N-well to VDDH. Note that the sources of all the P-transistors in this LC are driven by VDDH and hence the N-well should also be connected to VDDH. Based on a 90nm process technology, we have used this VCLB to implement an HG cell library and an LG cell library, each of which has more than 150 cells. We set VDDH=1.2V and VDDL=1.0V.

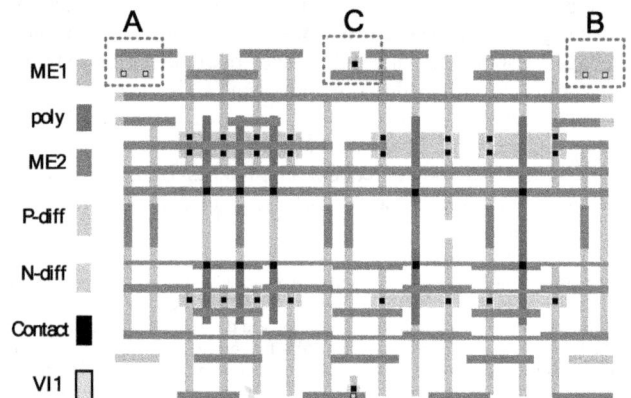

Figure 2. Stick diagram of our VCLB.

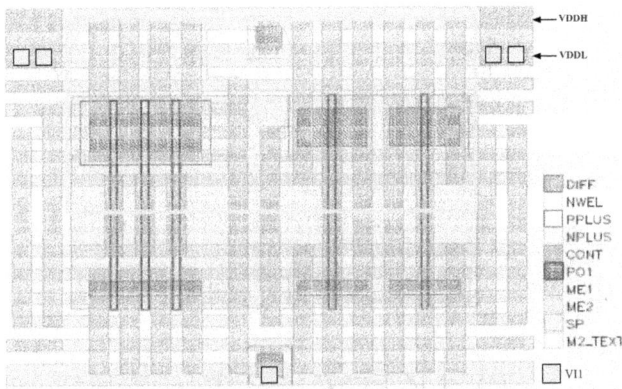

Figure 3. A VCLB for our dual supply-voltage structured ASIC.

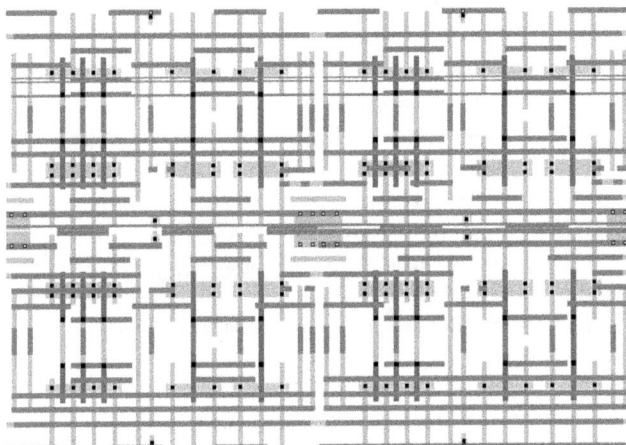

Figure 4. Abutment of cell rows, formed by abutment of VCLB instances. Also showing abutment of VDDH rails and joining of VDDL rails on adjacent rows.

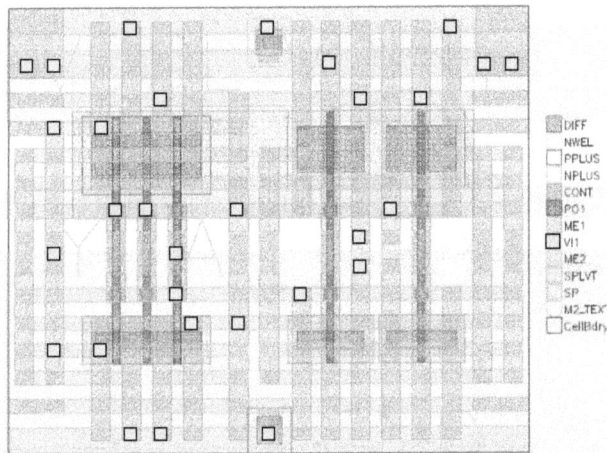

Figure 5. An implementation of the LC circuit in Figure 1 using our VCLB.

4. DUAL-SUPPLY STRUCTURED ASIC DESIGN METHODOLOGY

Our dual-supply structured ASIC design flow starts with a placement design which consists of only HG's. A placement design provides more accurate delay information such that timing

performance can be better maintained during replacing HG's with LG's. The basic principle of the replacement is to make use of the slack on non-critical paths. Hence, in this work we implement an incremental timing analyzer that can efficiently update slacks of a logic gate after replacing some HG's by LG's. We also implement a slack budgeting method to allocate as large slacks as possible to the candidate HG's for being replaced by some LG's. Finally, we develop a replacement method that converts HG's on non-critical paths into LG's. This involves developing a method to determine the locations of inserted LC's.

4.1 Incremental Timing Analyzer

We implement an incremental timing analyzer [17] in order to update timing information efficiently after we replace some HG's with LG's. Similar to other incremental timing analysis, ours will identify the part of a design where timing is affected by replacement and update signal arrival times, required signal arrival times, and hence the slacks for the affected logic gates promptly.

Given an HG that has been replaced by an LG, we need update the signal arrival times and slews of downstream logic gates starting from the logic gates that drive the LG. For example, as shown in Figure 6, if g4 is replaced by an LG, the delay of g4 will increase. Because the input capacitance of g4 will change, the output slew and cell delay of g4's predecessors i.e., g3 and g7, will be affected. Hence, we should start to perform incremental timing analysis from g3 and g7. All the gates falling in the fanout cone originated from g3 and g7 should be updated with new timing information. For this we perform a breath-first traversal through the fanout cone. At the same time, we propagate signal slews along the paths backward. If new slew at an input of a logic gate is the same as the old one (or very close to the old one), we stop slew propagation along the underlying path. Proper slew propagation is essential to achieving more accurate timing analysis. On the course of slew propagation, we must also recalculate the signal arrival times of the logic gates in the fanout cone. Once this is done, we compute the required signal arrival times of the logic gates backward reachable from the logic gates whose delays have been updated. Accordingly, we update the slacks of logic gates affected by replacement of an HG with an LG.

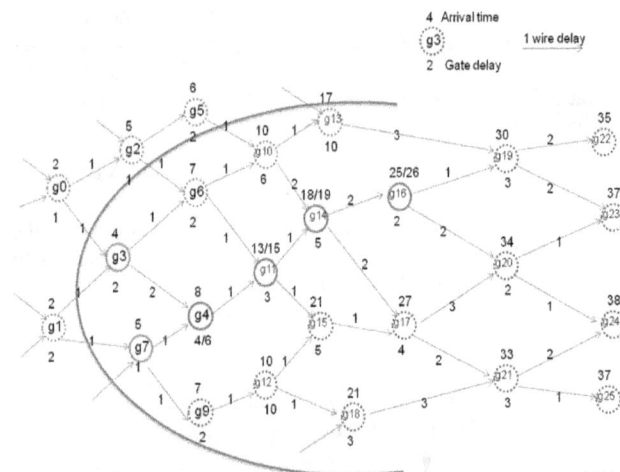

Figure 6. Slew and delay propagation for incremental timing analysis.

4.2 Slack Budgeting

We adopt the slack budgeting method developed in [6] for our work. First, we model a circuit as a transitive closure graph G_m. Slack budgeting is performed iteratively. In each iteration we find out a maximum independent set, denoted by *MINS*, of cells which has a maximum slack value, denoted by S_{max}. We also find out the second largest slack value, denoted by S_{max-1}. Then, the cells in the *MINS* are assigned a slack value $\varepsilon = S_{max} - S_{max-1}$ This process is repeated until all slacks are distributed to the cells. This method attempts to maximize the total amount of slacks assigned to logic cells in a circuit. Basically, if a cell in a *MINS* is assigned a slack value equal to or smaller than ε, then such an assignment will not influence the amount of slack value being assigned to another cells in the *MINS*. A cell may be included into a *MINS* many times. Hence, the assigned slack values should be accumulated. The assigned slacks will be employed to determine whether an HG can be replaced by an LG. The following subsection presents a replacement methodology based on the incremental timing analyzer and slack budgeting method.

4.3 Post-Placement Dual-Supply-Voltage Methodology

Our methodology takes a placement xx.def file, a timing library xx.lib file, a layout library xx.lef file, and a constraint file as inputs. The methodology takes an iterative approach to replacing HG's with LG's as shown in Figure 7. A design initially consists of only HG's. Let *delay_gap*() be the delay difference as a result of replacing an HG by an LG. Cell delay is calculated based on input slew and capacitance load. Elmore delay of a net is calculated based on the routing topology obtained by FLUTE [18]. First, the methodology calculates the slacks of cells by performing a static timing analysis [17]. It then performs slack budgeting [6] to distribute slacks to the gates on non-critical paths (lines (4)~(11)). When the accumulated slack assigned to an HG is larger than the corresponding *delay_gap*(), the HG cell can be replaced by an LG counterpart (lines (12)~(15)). The methodology must then determine where to insert LC's and which LC's should be removed (line 16). If an LC should be inserted, a location must be determined. The reason why an LC should be removed is due to combining of several LC's on the same net into one LC. Once LC insertion and/or LC removal is done, an incremental timing analysis is performed to check whether there is any timing violation (line (17)). If any timing violation exists, the replacement of HG's by LG's should be undone (lines (18)~(21)). In this situation, the methodology tries to convert one HG at a time into an LG (lines (22)~(29)). The above process is repeated until no slacks can be distributed.

The reason why an LC should be inserted is because an HG being replaced by an LG drives at least one HG. Hence, we must insert an LC onto a net driven by the LG, i.e., the one that replaces the underlying HG. Using Figure 8 as an example, we explain how to determine the location of an LC on a net driven by an LG (denoted by D here). Below are the major steps.

Step 1. Cluster all the HG's and D into a group.

Step 2. Use FLUTE [18] to construct a new Steiner tree for the cells in the group as shown Figure 8(a).

Step 3. Find a wire segment which is connected to D and place an LC at the middle of the wire segment. This is shown in Figure 8(b).

Step 4. Use FLUTE to construct a Steiner tree again to connect D and all the LG cells as shown in Figure 8(c).

Dual-Supply-Voltages-Assignment-Methodology ( ) {
(1)　　**Perform** timing analysis to calculate arrival times, required arrival times, and slacks of all the cells;
(2)　　**Initialize** a set Q; // Q holds the HG's being distributed with non-zero slack values
(3)　　**Do**{
(4)　　　　**Find** a MINS of HG's from G_m ;
(5)　　　　**Calculate** $\varepsilon = S_{max} - S_{max-1}$;
(6)　　　　**Increase** cell delay of all the cells in the MINS by ε ;
(7)　　　　**For** (each cell c in the MINS){
(8)　　　　　　**If** (c is not in Q)
(9)　　　　　　**then Put** it into Q with a distributed slack ε ;
(10)　　　　　**else Increase** the slack distributed to c by ε ;
(11)　　　　} // end *For*
(12)　　　　**For** (each cell q in Q) {
(13)　　　　　**If** (slack distributed to q is larger than *delay_gap()*)
(14)　　　　　**then Replace** q by the corresponding LG;
(15)　　　　} // end *For*
(16)　　　　**Insert** or **remove** level converter();
(17)　　　　**Do** incremental timing analysis();
(18)　　　　**If** (no timing violation)
(19)　　　　**then Remove** all q's converted into LG's from Q;
(20)　　　　**else** {
(21)　　　　　**Do** recovery();　//Undo replacement
　　　　　　　// Now replacing one q in Q at a time
(22)　　　　　**For** (each q whose assigned slack $\geq$ *delay_gap()*) {
(23)　　　　　**Replace** q by an LG;
(24)　　　　　**Insert** or **remove** level converter() ;
(25)　　　　　**Do** incremental timing analysis();
(26)　　　　　**If** (timing violation)
(27)　　　　　**then Do** recovery();
(28)　　　　　**Remove** q from Q;
(29)　　　　　} // end *For*
(30)　　　　} // end *else*
(31)　　} **until** ($\varepsilon = 0$)
(32)　　}

Figure 7. Post-placement dual-supply voltage methodology.

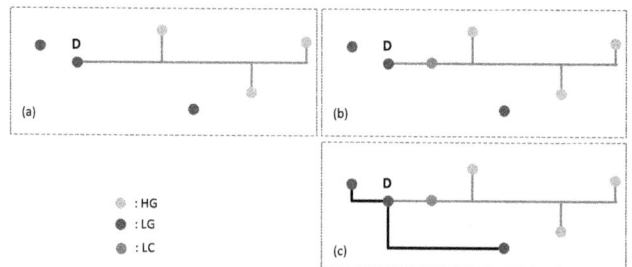

Figure 8. Determining a placement location for an LC.

In Step 3 we could also place D at a point where would minimize the sum of the delay from D to the LC and the delay from the LC to the longest driven cell. Note that in Step 4 we can also first remove the wire from D to the LC and then construct a Steiner tree for the LC, D, and all the LG's.

After LC insertion, we generate a DEF file with LC's. Since LC's may overlap other logic gates, we perform layout legalization using Cadence SOC Encounter. Note that we have to adjust the core utilization of a design to a proper number, said 90%, because LC insertion causes an increase in total cell area. Alternatively, we can start with a lower core utilization. Without doing so, we will not be even able to obtain a legalized placed design, not to mentioning a routable design. Once a design is routed, we perform post-layout timing analysis using SOC Encounter.

5. EXPERIMENTAL RESULTS

We employ some ITC99 benchmark circuits to test our methodology. Results are summarized in Table 1. A commercial 90nm process technology is used for implementing our VCLB. Two cell libraries, one having 150 LG's and the other having 150 HG's, are respectively created using our VCLB. We set VDDH=1.2V and VDDL=1.0V. The logic gates are characterized using a commercial characterization tool for timing delay and power dissipation. For each test circuit, we first give a very tight timing constraint for logic synthesis using the HG cell library. A so-obtained circuit denoted by *HGdes* consists of only HG's. After placing and routing *HGdes*, we use SOC Encounter to obtain the longest path delay of *HGdes*. The delay is denoted by *base_delay*. We then perform our dual supply-voltage synthesis using (100+*alpha*)/100* *base_delay* as timing constraint for each circuit, where *alpha*=0 denotes no timing relaxation and *alpha* > 0 denotes *alpha*% relaxation (denoted by *alpha*% *R* in Table 1) in timing constraint. Table 1 gives the percentage of LG's in a circuit and energy saving per switching with varying percentages of timing constraint relaxation. LC% in the table denotes the percentage of LC's used in a circuit. LG% denotes the percentage of HG's being converted into LG's. As one can see, our approach can achieve up to 44% energy reduction per switching of our dual-supply-voltage structured ASIC with 1.6% area overhead on LC's. The two large circuits b19 and b17 have better energy savings. As to the longest path delay, the one for *HGdes* is actually equal to the *base_delay* for the corresponding circuit. For example, the longest path delay of *HGdes* for b15 is 3.73ns which is also the *base_delay* of b15 used for setting timing constraints. As one can see, to a certain extent the timing performances of b15, b17, b20 are well maintained. However, there is a large discrepancy between the resulted longest path delay and the targeted path delay of b19, especially for the cases of no relaxation and 10% relaxation. One reason for this might be that the driving capability of LC is not large enough to drive large loads due to elongated wire length caused by cell legalization. The reason for poor cell legalization might be just having too many LC's that need to be legalized. Note that energy saving highly depends on the difference between the two supply voltages and how tight a circuit's timing requirement is. A tight-timing requirement will result in a smaller energy saving. Basically, a poor replacement rate corresponds to a poor energy reduction. This phenomenon is clearly observed for b20.

We also implement GECVS method for making a comparison with ours. Table 2 shows the results obtained by GECVS with 10%, 30%, and 50% relaxation in timing constraint. Compared with the results obtained by our method, GECVS inserts much more LC's but converts much fewer HG's into LG's. With respect to the case of no relaxation, 10% relaxation, and 30% relaxation,

our approach converts on average 34%, 25%, and 39% more HG's into LG's than GECVS does. The reason for this is that GECVS has less degree of freedom for replacing HG's by LG's and cannot make best use of available slacks.

Table 1. Percentages of LG's used and energy savings per switching (energy unit: nJ)

ckts	timing constraint	longest path delay(ns)	# of gates	LC%	LG %	run time (min)	energy per switching (pJ)	energy saving %
b15	HGdes	3.73	5253	0.0	0	NA	55.61	0
	No relax	3.99	6411	18.1	54.3	8	61.86	-11
	10% R	4.13	6312	16.8	62.2	4	57.82	-4
	20% R	4.54	6059	13.3	70.4	4	53.47	4
	30% R	4.65	5946	11.7	75.3	4	50.33	10
b17	HGdes	3.82	16067	0.0	0	NA	178.36	0
	No relax	4.18	19605	18.1	50.4	32	178.61	0
	10% R	4.29	18948	15.2	63.3	26	160.19	10
	20% R	5.18	18527	13.3	70.8	20	175.40	2
	30% R	4.52	17971	10.6	77.6	22	138.01	23
b19	HGdes	9.08	78310	0.0	0	NA	1159	0
	No relax	19.37	82688	5.3	86.9	102	1151	1
	10% R	15.77	82186	4.7	89.6	91	833	28
	20% R	13.9	80711	3.0	93.9	83	665	43
	30% R	14.1	79578	1.6	97	68	645	44
b20	HG des	5.69	10262	0.0	0	NA	118.35	0
	No relax	6.83	12607	18.6	53.3	19	169.96	-44
	10% R	6.97	12133	15.4	63.2	17	151.75	-28
	20% R	7.54	11994	14.4	66.2	31	146.93	-24
	30% R	7.58	11362	9.7	79.6	16	125.44	-6

Table 2. Comparison of our results with that obtained by GECVS

circuits	timing constraint	# of gates	LC%	LG%	runtime (min)
b15	HGdes	5253	0	0	NA
	No relax	5370	3.52	28.54	14
	10% R	5370	28.25	42.02	11
	30% R	7045	26.46	31.95	15
	50% R	7153	27.57	35.45	13
b17	HGdes.	16067	0	0	0
	No relax	20729	22.49	24.39	47
	10% R	21359	24.78	33.78	33
	30% R	21516	25.33	31.22	32
	50% R	21610	25.65	36.09	27
b19	HGdes	78310	0	0	NA
	No relax	107115	26.89	43.65	579
	10% R	87573	10.58	74.09	337
	30% R	87041	10.03	77.2	604
	50% R	86749	9.73	81.03	617
b20	HGdes	10262	0	0	NA
	No relax	11739	12.58	10.58	67
	10% R	12548	18.22	29.65	59
	30% R	12315	16.67	32.8	54
	50% R	12315	24.92	36.84	59

6. CONCLUSIONS

This work presented a via-configurable logic block (VCLB) that enables dual supply-voltage designs for structured ASIC. It also presented a post-placement dual supply-voltage design methodology based on the VCLB. This work demonstrated for the first time the feasibility of doing dual supply-voltage designs for via-configurable structured ASIC. The results showed that dual-supply-voltage structured ASIC can achieve considerably smaller energy consumption, depending on voltage difference between two supply rails, available timing budgets, etc.

7. REFERENCES

[1] Ran, Y. and Marek-Sadowska, M. 2006. Designing via-configurable logic blocks for regular fabric. *IEEE Trans. on VLSI Systems*. Vol. 14, No. 1 (Jan. 2006), 1-14.

[2] Teifel, J., Flores, R. S., Pearson, S., Begay, C., Ma, K. K., and Palmer, J. 2012. ViArray Standard Platforms: Rad-Hard Structured ASICs for Digital and Mixed-Signal Applications. *IEEE Aerospace Conference* (2012), 1-9.

[3] Tung, H. H., Lin, R. B., Li, M. C., and Heish, T. H. 2012. Standard cell like via-configurable logic blocks for structured ASIC in an industrial design flow. *IEEE Trans. on VLSI Systems*, Vol. 20, No. 12, (Dec. 2012), 2184-2197.

[4] Liu, H. H., Lin, R. B., and Tseng, I. L. 2013. Relocatable and resizable SRAM synthesis for via configurable structured ASIC. In *Proc. IEEE ISQED* (2013), 494-501.

[5] Chen, S. Y., Lin, R. B., Tung, H. H., and Lin, K. W. 2010. Power gating design for standard-cell-like structured ASICs. In *Proc. DATE* (Mar. 2010), 514-519.

[6] Chen, C., Srivastava, A., and Sarrafzadeh, M. 2001. On gate level power optimization using dual-supply voltages," *IEEE Trans. On VLSI Systems*, Vol.9, No.5, (Oct. 2001), 616-629.

[7] Chi, J. C., Lee, H. H., Tsai, S. H., and Chen Chi, M., 2007. Gate level multiple supply voltage assignment algorithm for power optimization under timing constraint. *IEEE Trans. on VLSI Systems*, Vol.15, no.6, (June 2007), 637-648.

[8] Usami, K., Igarashi, M., Ishikawa, T., Kanazawa, M., Takahashi, M., Hamada, M., Arakida, H., Terazawa, T., and Kuroda, T. 1998.

[9] Usami, K., Igarashi, M., Minami, F., Ishikawa, T., Kanzawa, M., Ichida, M., and Nogami, K.. 1998. "Automated low-power technique exploiting multiple supply voltages applied to a media processor. *IEEE Journal of Solid-State Circuits*, Vol.33, No.3, (Mar. 1998), 463-472 .

Design methodology of ultra low-power MPEG4 codec core exploiting voltage scaling techniques. *Design Automation Conference*, (June 1998), 483-488.

[10] Yeh, C., Kang, Y., Shieh, S., and Wang, J. 1999. Layout techniques supporting the use of dual supply voltages for cell-based designs. *Design Automation Conference*, (June 1999), 62-67.

[11] Hu, J., Shin, Y., Dhanwada, N., and Marculescu, R., 2004. Architecting voltage islands in core-based system-on-a-chip designs. *ISLPED*, (Aug. 2004), 180-185.

[12] Wu, H., Liu, I. M., Wong, M. D. F., and Wang, Y., 2005. Post-Placement Voltage Island Generation Under Performance Requirement. *Proc. ICCAD*, (Nov. 2005), 309-316.

[13] Kulkarni, S. H, Srivastava, A. N., and Sylvester, D., 2004. A new algorithm for improved VDD assignment in low power dual VDD systems. *ISLPED*, (Aug. 2004), 200-205.

[14] Diril, A. U., Dhillon, Y. S., Chatterjee, A., and Singh, A. D., 2005. Level-shifter free design of low power dual supply voltage CMOS circuits using dual threshold voltages. *IEEE Trans. on VLSI Systems,* Vol.13, No.9, (Sept. 2005), 1103-1107.

[15] Ishihara, F., Sheikh, F., and Nikolic, B., 2004. Level conversion for dual-supply systems. *IEEE Trans. on VLSI Systems*, Vol.12, No.2, (Feb. 2004), 185-195.

[16] Kulkarni, S. H. and Sylvester, D., 2004. High performance level conversion for dual VDD design. *IEEE Trans. on VLSI Systems*, Vol.12, No.9, (Sept. 2004), 926-936.

[17] Lee, J. F. and Tang, D. T., 1995. An algorithm for incremental timing analysis. In *Proc. DAC*, (June1995), 696-701.

[18] Chu, C., 2004. FLUTE: fast Lookup table based wirelength estimation technique. In *Proc. ICCAD*, (Nov. 2004), 696-701.

Squash: A Scalable Quantum Mapper Considering Ancilla Sharing

Mohammad Javad Dousti, Alireza Shafaei, and Massoud Pedram
Department of Electrical Engineering, University of Southern California, Los Angeles, CA, U.S.A.
{dousti, shafaeib, and pedram}@usc.edu

ABSTRACT

Quantum algorithms for solving problems of interesting size often result in circuits with a very large number of qubits and quantum gates. Fortunately, these algorithms also tend to contain a small number of repetitively-used quantum kernels. Identifying the quantum logic blocks that implement such quantum kernels is critical to the complexity management for realizing the corresponding quantum circuit. Moreover, quantum computation requires some type of quantum error correction coding to combat decoherence, which in turn results in a large number of ancilla qubits in the circuit. Sharing the ancilla qubits among quantum operations (even though this sharing can increase the overall circuit latency) is important in order to curb the resource demand of the quantum algorithm. This paper presents a multi-core *reconfigurable quantum processor* architecture, called *Requp*, which supports a layered approach to mapping a quantum algorithm and ancilla sharing. More precisely, a scalable quantum mapper, called *Squash*, is introduced, which divides a given quantum circuit into a number of quantum kernels—each kernel comprises k parts such that each part will run on exactly one of k available cores. Experimental results demonstrate that Squash can handle large-scale quantum algorithms while providing an effective mechanism for sharing ancilla qubits.

Categories and Subject Descriptors

B.7.2 [**Integrated Circuits**]: Design Aids – *Placement and routing.*

Keywords

Quantum computing; mapping; physical design; scalable algorithms; ancilla sharing.

1. INTRODUCTION

Mapping quantum circuits directly to a quantum fabric is a challenging task due to the gigantic size of quantum circuits. These circuits comprise of two parts: a netlist of *quantum logical operations* followed by the *quantum error correction* (QEC) circuit. The QEC increases the circuit size by one or two orders of magnitude depending on the decoherence degree and the desired fidelity of results. To handle this growth in the size, circuits are mapped in two levels. The lower-level mapping, which is done by the *physical-level mapper*, maps a universal set of quantum operations in a fault-tolerant fashion followed by an appropriate QEC circuit to a given *physical machine description* (PMD). In the higher-level mapping, which is performed by the *logical-level mapper*, the *logical* circuit is mapped to an abstraction of the PMD assuming that the universal set of fault-tolerant quantum operations is provided by the lower level. This approach addresses the

GLSVLSI '14, May 21 - 23 2014, Houston, TX, USA
Copyright is held by the owner/author(s). Publication rights licensed to ACM.
ACM 978-1-4503-2816-6/14/05$15.00.
http://dx.doi.org/10.1145/2591513.2591523

increase in size by the QEC in the first level very well, but it does not help for the second level. Real-size quantum circuits (even without QEC) are so large that traditional mappers introduced by previous researchers cannot efficiently handle them [1].

Reference [2] shows that Shor's factorization algorithm for a 1024-bit integer has 1.35×10^{15} physical instructions. Assuming that the one-level $[\![7,1,3]\!]$ Steane code is used in this implementation, each logical operation results in about 10^5 physical instructions. Hence, this algorithm has almost 1.35×10^{10} logical operations. As can be seen, the physical-level mapper can handle the low-level QEC in a reasonable time as the number of physical instructions is not so high (~10^5 physical instructions). On the other hand, mapping 1.35×10^{10} logical operations is very time consuming.

Fortunately, quantum circuits can be partitioned into multiple quantum computational stages. These stages tend to contain a small number of repetitively-used quantum kernels. This means that mapping one instance of these kernels is sufficient. For instance, Figure 1 shows the phase estimation algorithm which is the core of many well-known and useful quantum algorithms such as Shor's factorization algorithm [3] and quantum random walk [4]. As can be seen, in this circuit the controlled unitary is a kernel which is repeated n times throughout the circuit with different exponents (throughout stages 2 to $n + 1$). The exponent denotes the number of repetitions for the corresponding circuit. Clearly, identifying the quantum kernels and avoiding the remapping can exponentially improve the mapping speed for this circuit.

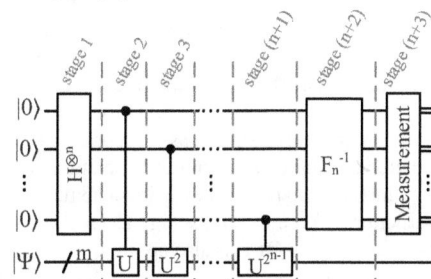

Figure 1. Quantum circuit representation of the phase estimation algorithm [3]. The computational stages are identified in this circuit.

Another major stumbling block for realizing a scalable quantum computer is the limited amount of physical qubits. Each logical operation is implemented in a fault-tolerant manner based on the adopted QEC code, and using a certain amount of *physical data qubits* and *physical ancilla qubits*. Physical data qubits are uniquely belong to their corresponding logical qubits, and hence cannot be shared. However, physical ancilla qubits, which are used to store intermediate information, may participate in the QEC circuit of various logical operations at different time instances. This reuse of ancilla qubits is referred to as *ancilla sharing*. Escalating the ancilla sharing increases the latency of the entire circuit while saving the precious quantum resources and vice versa. This trade-off is similar to the well-known area-delay trade-off in the VLSI circuits.

This paper introduces a novel quantum architecture, called *reconfigurable quantum processor architecture* (Requp), in order to address the problem of ancilla sharing. Requp has k quantum cores each of which contains a *quantum reconfigurable compute region*

(QRCR), a dedicated quantum cache, and a quantum memory. Quantum cores are arranged on a 2-D mesh topology. Each QRCR has a constrained amount of ancilla qubits while trying to share this limited resource among several quantum operations so as to minimize the latency. The major contribution of this architecture lies in its reconfigurability where it supports quantum operations with different number of ancilla qubits. This difference is quite substantial and neglecting it leads to over provisioning of quantum physical qubits.

Using the kernel extraction method and the proposed architecture (Requp) mentioned above, a scalable quantum mapper, called _scalable quantum mapper considering ancilla sharing_ (Squash), is introduced. Squash initially divides the given circuit into a number of quantum kernels. For each kernel, it builds a _quantum operation dependency graph_ (QODG) based on the data dependency among the operations. QODG is then partitioned into k sub-graphs and bound to the quantum cores. These sub-graphs are subsequently scheduled and mapped to the Requp with k quantum cores. Finally, results of mapping for each quantum kernel are combined in order to generate the entire mapping of the given circuit.

The rest of this paper is organized as follows: Section 2 explains the basics of quantum computing as well as the related work. Section 3 presents the new architecture (Requp), whereas Section 4 explains the proposed mapper (Squash). Experimental results are presented in Section 5, and finally Section 6 concludes the paper.

2. PRELIMINARIES AND PRIOR WORK

2.1 Quantum Computing Basics

A quantum bit, _qubit_, is a physical object (e.g., an ion or a photon) that carries data in quantum circuits. Qubits interact with each other through _quantum gates_. Depending on the underlying quantum computing technology, a universal set of quantum gates is available at the physical level. More precisely, each quantum fabric is natively capable of performing a universal set of one and two-qubit instructions (also called _physical instructions_). However, the importance of fault-tolerant quantum computation dictates the quantum circuits to be generated from _fault-tolerant_ (FT) quantum operations. A universal (but redundant) set of FT operations includes H, S, T, T†, X, Y, Z, and CNOT operations [3], which may differ from physical instructions supported at the physical level. Fortunately, each FT quantum operation (or quantum operation for short) can be realized by using a composition of these physical instructions. Accordingly, a logical level circuit contains quantum operations where QEC is also applied.

A quantum circuit fabric is arranged as a 2-D array of identical _cells_. Each cell contains sites for creating qubits, reading them out, performing instructions on one or two physical qubits, and resources for routing qubits (or equivalently swapping their information to the neighboring qubit). In practice, however, an abstract _quantum architecture_ (QA) is built which hides the physical information and the QEC details. Operation sites in this QA are capable of performing any quantum operation. The QA is also equipped with syndrome extraction circuitries following the quantum operation in order to prevent error propagation that may have been introduced by the quantum operation.

A _quantum compilation/synthesis_ tool generates a reversible quantum circuit composed of quantum operations. Every qubit in the output circuit is called a _logical_ qubit, which is subsequently encoded into several _physical_ qubits in order to detect and correct potential errors on qubits. Physical qubits are comprised of two types: 1) _physical data qubits_ and 2) _physical ancilla qubits_. Physical data qubits carry the encoded data of the logical qubits. Based on the type and the concatenation level of the QEC, a logical qubit is encoded to seven or more physical data qubits. On the other hand, physical ancilla qubits are used as scratchpads and can

be _shared_ among different logical qubits for the error correction procedure.

A _high-level mapping_ tool schedules, places, and routes the logical circuit on the QA. To achieve this, the quantum algorithm is initially modeled as a _quantum operation dependency graph_ (QODG), in which nodes represent quantum operations and edges capture data dependencies [1]. More precisely, operation O_j depends on operation O_i if O_i and O_j share at least one qubit and O_j is the first operation after O_i in the circuit that uses this (these) shared qubit(s). This dependency is shown as $O_i \rightarrow O_j$. For instance, Figure 2 depicts an FT implementation of a 3-input Toffoli operation [5] along with its QODG.

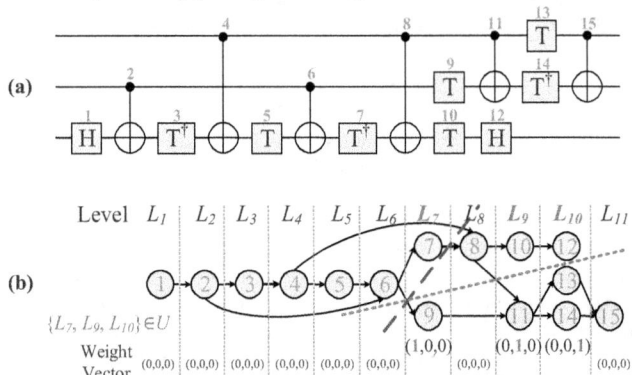

Figure 2. (a) FT implementation of a three-input Toffoli circuit [5], (b) the corresponding QODG where each node represents a circuit operation. Detailed steps of the 2-way partitioning algorithm are also illustrated.

Next, the QODG is mapped to the desired QA. The latency of the quantum algorithm mapped to the QA can be calculated as the length of the longest path (critical path) in the mapped QODG, where the length of a path in the QODG is in turn the summation of latencies of operations located on that path plus routing latencies of their qubit operands [1]. Critical path of the mapped QODG may not be the same as the original QODG, since the latter does not contain routing latencies. This can change the scheduling slacks, and hence may increase the critical path of the entire graph.

2.2 Prior Work

• **Quantum Architectures.** Metodi _et al._ propose the first QA called _quantum logic array_ (QLA) which is a 2-D array of super-cells called _tiles_ [6]. Each tile comprises of an $n \times n$ array of cells so as a logical operation can fit in. Thaker _et al._ observe that the parallelism in the quantum circuits is very limited [7]. Hence, they suggest the _compressed QLA_ (CQLA) which separates the array into two regions: _memory_ and _compute_. In the memory region, the qubits which do not participate in any operation at the current time are stored. These qubits absorb less noise and hence require a lighter error correction scheme. In other words, the error correction needs fewer physical ancilla qubits for every physical data qubit (a ratio of 1 to 2). On the other hand, the qubits in the compute region actively participate in the quantum operations. Hence they require a much larger number of ancilla qubits. Since the compute region occupies much smaller area than the memory region, this new architecture helps saving a lot of unnecessary physical ancilla qubits which are used in QLA. Memory region is also further broken down into the cache and the global memory to address the qubit locality issue required by the compute region.

• **Quantum Mapping Techniques.** The quantum mapping problem, similar to the corresponding problem in the traditional VLSI area, is known as a hard problem. Whitney _et al._ suggest a CAD flow for mapping a quantum circuit fault-tolerantly to an ion-trap fabric [2]. To address the scalability issue, they adopt the two-level (physical and logical) mapping. Other levels of hierarchy are handled manually without any automation. Jones *et al.* propose a five-layer stack for implementing a quantum computer [8]. This work does not show how to overcome the complexity of the "*logical layer*" and tries to address other complexities in the design by adding more layers. In [1], we have suggested to use a quick estimation method called *LEQA* to calculate the circuit latency instead of a full-fledged mapping. Even though this approach is quite fast, it does not provide the detailed mapping. Moreover, it requires a flattened high-level netlist as the input which requires a huge amount of disk space to store the netlist and a large memory in order to store its data structures. Additionally, LEQA does not consider the ancilla sharing problem. Although several heuristics have been proposed in the literature for solving the quantum mapping problem, none of them is able to deal with large circuits [2][6][7][9][10].

3. PROPOSED ARCHITECTURE

The CQLA architecture reviewed in the previous section assumes that the number of required ancilla qubits for all of the logical operations followed by the QEC is the same. Hence, CQLA accounts for a certain amount of physical ancilla qubits for every logical operation in the compute region. However, this assumption is not true. An important subset of logical operations, called *non-transversal* operations, requires more ancilla than *transversal* operations. It has been proven that every universal logical operation set contains at least one non-transversal gate which varies based on the employed QEC [11]. Table 1 summarizes the ancilla requirements for two typical QEC codes and various logical operations. As can be seen, a non-transversal operation requires half an order of magnitude (in the *Steane code*) up to more than one order of magnitude (in the *Bacon-Shor code*) more ancilla qubits compared to that of transversal operations. Moreover, a two-qubit transversal operation (like CNOT) requires twice ancilla qubits compared to that of a one-qubit transversal operation.

Table 1. Ancilla requirements for various QEC codes and operations

QEC	Operation Type	Operation	# of Ancilla Qubits
Steane [[7,1,3]]	Transversal	X, Y, Z, H, S	28
		CNOT	56
	Non-Transversal	T	100
Bacon-Shor [[9,1,3]]	Transversal	X, Y, Z, H	18
		CNOT	36
	Non-Transversal	S	58
		T	309

With this observation, the compute region cannot be a pre-allocated area with a fixed number of ancilla qubits for all of operations; otherwise, it leads to an overestimation of the required ancilla. Hence, we propose the *quantum reconfigurable compute region* (QRCR) which distributes the ancilla qubits in the compute region based on the dispatched operations. In other words, the ancilla qubits are *shared* among the operations which are being executed based on their ancilla qubit requirements. To further speed up the computation and eliminate the overhead of qubit routing, a hierarchical memory design is adopted. The first level of the hierarchy is the *quantum cache* which stores qubits that are immediately needed after the execution of the current operations in the QRCR. The second level is the *quantum memory* which keeps the rest of the qubits. Using this hierarchy, the overhead of the routing delay can be mostly hidden. More precisely, the routing delay is substantially smaller than the delay of logical operations, because the routing involves qubit movement (or information swap) which can be done directly by using fast primitive operation(s), whereas logical operations require time consuming QECs. The only considerable routing delay is the time required to load the qubits from the quantum cache to the QRCR.

Figure 3 (a) depicts a *quantum core* which is comprised of a QRCR, a quantum cache, and a quantum memory. As can be seen,

QRCR is located at the center and surrounded by the quantum cache followed by the quantum memory. The highly shaded areas inside the QRCR have higher number of ancilla, whereas lightly shaded areas contain lesser ancilla. The arrangement of ancilla changes during the runtime of a quantum algorithm based on the operations being executed.

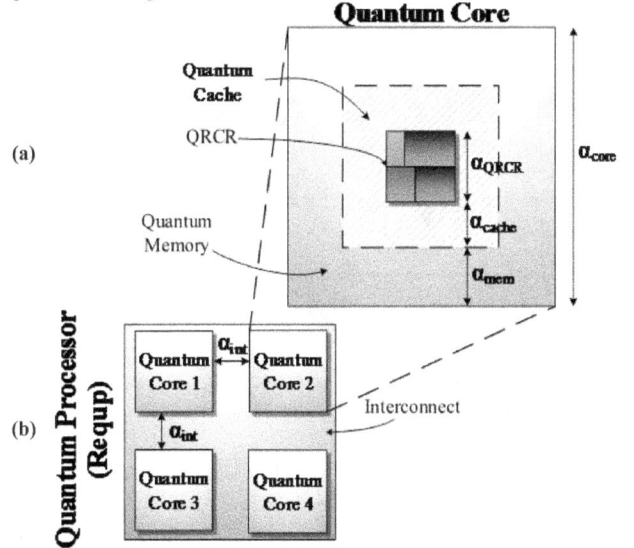

Figure 3. (a) Structure of a quantum core (b) Structure of a quad-core Requp

In large-scale algorithms, the size of the cache and the memory may grow. This increases the qubit routing delay which was already hidden by the long delay of logical operations. To avoid this effect, we further extend the quantum core architecture to the *reconfigurable quantum processor architecture* (Requp). A Requp contains multiple reconfigurable quantum cores which are connected to each other by *quantum interconnects*. Quantum interconnects are physically implemented similar to the rest of the quantum physical fabric. Here, this distinction is made for clarity. A quad-core Requp is shown in Figure 3 (b).

4. SQUASH

This section introduces a *scalable quantum mapper considering ancilla sharing* (Squash). Squash adopts Requp as its underlying fabric abstraction. It takes a netlist of quantum operations in the *quantum assembly* (QASM) format [12], a QEC code description similar to Table 1, the number of quantum cores (k), the delay of a qubit travelling the extent of one grid cell (called *qubit unit-distance delay* and denoted by β_{PMD}), interconnect width (α_{int}), a coefficient which models the effect of memory size on the routing speed (γ_{mem}), and the total ancilla budget (A). The quantum operation set is limited to the fault-tolerant operation set. The output of Squash is a circuit mapped to the designated fabric. Algorithm 1 presents the steps involved in Squash.

As it is explained previously, early work found that quantum algorithms offer limited parallelism [7]. By investigating various quantum algorithms, including the phase estimation algorithm which is at the basis of many well-known and useful quantum algorithms (such as Shor's factorization algorithm [3] and quantum random walk [4]), we realized that quantum algorithms can be divided into major *computational stages* which cannot be run in parallel, i.e., they should be executed serially. The main reason is due to the *no-cloning theorem*, which does not allow a qubit to be replicated. This limitation forbids any fan-out in a quantum circuit. As a result, scheduling of computational stages becomes a trivial task— they should be run serially. Moreover, these stages tend to contain a small number of repetitively-used quantum kernels. Mapping only one instance of these kernels significantly reduces

Algorithm 1: Squash

Input: A QASM, a QEC code, Requp parameters (i.e., number of quantum cores (k), qubit unit-distance delay (β_{PMD}), interconnect width (α_{int}), and memory size effect on the routing coefficient (γ_{mem})), and total ancilla budget (A)

Output: Mapped circuit of the given quantum algorithm

1. Identify a set of quantum kernels $S = \{S_1, \ldots, S_m\}$
2. **For** each S_i in S
3.   Generate a QODG for the operations in S_i (QODG$_i$)
4.   K-way partition the QODG$_i$ to get $\mathcal{P}_i = \{\mathcal{P}_{i,1}, \ldots, \mathcal{P}_{i,k}\}$
5.   Calculate the routing delay matrix d
6.   Bind each $\mathcal{P}_{i,j}$ to one of the quantum cores
7.   Map each $\mathcal{P}_{i,j}$ to the designated quantum core
8. **End For**
9. **Return** mapping of $\{\mathcal{P}_{i,j} | 1 \leq i \leq m, 1 \leq j \leq k\}$.

the runtime overhead. Accordingly, the first line of Algorithm 1 identifies a list of candidates for the quantum kernels. Moreover, in the for-loop block (lines 3 to 7), the algorithm maps each of the kernels separately. Then, the entire mapping solution can be constructed by properly ordering the mapping results for each of the kernels (line 9).

In the rest of this section, the details of mapping a quantum kernel to the given Requp is explained (i.e., the for-loop body). Line 3 generates a QODG as explained in Section 2. Next, it is broken into k parts such that k quantum cores can execute these parts simultaneously while having the minimum amount of inter-core communication (line 4). Next, the routing delay matrix is calculated, which comprises of the qubit routing delay between every pair of quantum cores (line 5). Each part is then bound (line 6), and finally mapped (line 7) to a quantum core.

4.1 QODG K-Way Partitioning

A standard k-way partitioning algorithm takes a graph, and divides its node set into k disjoint parts such that the parts are balanced in terms of their size and a minimum number of edges are cut. Using this method, the same workload is assigned to each quantum core, while inter-core communication is minimized. However, there is no guarantee that parts can be executed in parallel which is in fact a desired metric in order to reduce the runtime. As an example, consider the QODG shown in Figure 2 (b), and assume a 2-way partitioning is needed. A standard graph partitioning algorithm may suggest the dashed cut which partitions the graph into two parts with almost equal number of nodes. Unfortunately, this solution does not allow any parallelism. On the other hand, the dotted cut, even though one part has twice as many nodes as the other one, is a better solution as parts can be executed simultaneously.

In order to guide the partitioning algorithm to produce parts that can be run in parallel, we employ the technique proposed in [13] which adopts the *multi-constraint graph partitioning* (MCGP) method [14]. The MCGP method assigns an n_{con}-dimensional weight vector to each node, and then balances the total sum of the weight values among the parts in each dimension while minimizing the edge cut. The weight vector for each QODG node is calculated as follows. Initially, the QODG is levelized. Let n_i be the number of nodes at level i (L_i), $U = \{L_i | n_i \geq k\}$, and $n_{con} = |U|$ (i.e., the number of levels that contain more than $k - 1$ nodes.) Then, weight vectors of size n_{con} are assigned to each node. For nodes that are at level $L_i \notin U$, the weight vector is set to zero vector. For other nodes, we first assign a label to each level $L_i \in U$ using the one-hot coding scheme. This label will be used as the weight vector for all of the nodes within the same level. Hence, by using one-hot coding, a unique dimension of the weight vector is assigned to all nodes at level $L_i \in U$. Therefore, the MCGP method is forced to partition these nodes into distinct parts so that the total

weight in the corresponding dimension for each part is balanced. An example for the 2-way MCGP is shown in Figure 2 (b).

4.2 Routing Delay Matrix Calculation

In this phase, based on the information obtained from the partitioning step, the quantum core is characterized in order to find the accurate qubit routing delays between each pair of cores. Note that it is not necessary to use the same quantum core configuration for all of the quantum kernels, because it is just an abstraction to simplify the mapping and hide the technology details. For this purpose, four parameters, namely α_{QRCR}, α_{core}, α_{cache}, and α_{mem} (which are shown in Figure 3) are initially calculated. The approach is to derive the number of physical qubits each area should accommodate and then the desired distances are calculated accordingly. α_{QRCR} can be obtained by

$$\alpha_{QRCR} = \left\lceil \sqrt{\frac{A/k}{A_{min}} \cdot L_{code} + (A/k - \frac{D_{max}}{2})} \right\rceil, \quad (1)$$

where A_{min} is the minimum ancilla qubit requirement among quantum operations, L_{code} is the QEC code length, and D_{max} is the maximum number of data qubits a core may accommodate. For instance, for the Steane code listed in Table 1, $A_{min} = 28$ and $L_{code} = 7$. D_{max} can be calculated by referring to the partitioned set of operations for each core. The first summation term in Equation (1) accounts for the maximum number of physical data qubits the QRCR may host, whereas the second term accounts for the physical ancilla qubits. Note that A/k is the ancilla budget per core. Furthermore, $\frac{D_{max}}{2}$ ancilla qubits are reserved for the error correction of data qubits in the cache and the memory. As mentioned earlier, for the QEC of every two data qubits in the cache or the memory, one ancilla qubit is enough. α_{core} is determined by

$$\alpha_{core} = \left\lceil \sqrt{D_{max} \cdot L_{code} + A/k} \right\rceil. \quad (2)$$

As suggested in [7], α_{cache} can be set such that the cache area becomes twice as large as the QRCR area. Hence, α_{cache} can be calculated as

$$\alpha_{cache} = min\left\{ \left\lceil \frac{\sqrt{3}-1}{2} \alpha_{QRCR} \right\rceil, \frac{\alpha_{core} - \alpha_{QRCR}}{2} \right\}. \quad (3)$$

A minimum value is calculated in order to avoid over provisioning of resources for the cache, i.e., the cache plus QRCR area should not be larger than the area of the core. Finally, α_{mem} can be derived based on the values of α_{QRCR}, α_{cache}, and α_{core}:

$$\alpha_{mem} = \left\lceil \frac{\alpha_{core}}{2} - \frac{\alpha_{QRCR}}{2} - \alpha_{cache} \right\rceil. \quad (4)$$

Using these four parameters, the communication delay for routing a qubit from the QRCR of core x to the QRCR of core y can be calculated as

$$d_{x,y} = \begin{cases} n_{x,y}(\alpha_{core} + \alpha_{int})\beta_{PMD}, & x \neq y \\ \frac{(\alpha_{QRCR} + \alpha_{cache} + \gamma_{mem}\alpha_{mem})}{2}\beta_{PMD}, & x = y \end{cases} \quad (5)$$

where $n_{x,y}$ is the Manhattan distance between core x and core y. The first case ($x \neq y$) is considered as the inter-core routing delay, whereas the second case ($x = y$) accounts for the delay of transferring a qubit from the cache (or possibly the memory) into the QRCR. Coefficient γ_{mem} ensures the proper contribution of the memory size to the routing delay of a qubit. In other words, if the memory size becomes large enough, then the routing delay cannot be overshadowed by the long operation delay, and hence should be considered in the routing delay calculation. We capture this effect with the γ_{mem} coefficient.

4.3 Resource Binding

After partitioning the QODG, the resultant parts should be bound to the quantum cores such that the total routing delay of qubits between cores is minimized. Since the scheduling of the QODG is not known at this step, we cannot focus on minimizing the total routing delay of the operations on the critical path. Furthermore, the scheduling requires this binding information in order to properly schedule two dependent operations assigned to two different quantum cores.

The binding problem can be formulated as follows:

$$\min \sum_{m=1}^{k} \sum_{n=1}^{k} \sum_{x=1}^{k} \sum_{y=1}^{k} a_{m,n} a_{x,y} d_{n,y} w_{m,x} \qquad (6)$$

subject to

$$\sum_{n=1}^{k} a_{m,n} = 1, \text{ for } 1 \leq m \leq k, \qquad (7)$$

$$\sum_{m=1}^{k} a_{m,n} = 1, \text{ for } 1 \leq n \leq k, \qquad (8)$$

where $a_{m,n}$ is a binary variable, which is 1 if $\mathcal{P}_{i,m}$ is bound to quantum core n and 0 otherwise, and $w_{m,x}$ denotes the number of qubits that traverse from part $\mathcal{P}_{i,m}$ to $\mathcal{P}_{i,x}$. The objective function (6) is the sum of inter-core communication delays while constraints (7) and (8) ensure a one-to-one assignment between parts and quantum cores. Since k is fairly small, the computation time to solve the resulting *0-1 quadratic program* (0-1 QP) is of little concern.

4.4 Mapping

The objective of scheduling the QODG on k quantum cores is to minimize the overall latency while ensuring that the number of ancilla qubits used in each quantum core is no more than the given budget. The aforesaid scheduling problem is similar to the well-known *minimum-latency resource-constraint multi-cycle* (MLRC-MC) scheduling problem [15] in high-level synthesis with the following difference. The MLRC-MC problem does not deal with the cost of moving data among resources whereas in our formulation the resources (i.e., quantum cores) lie on a given grid, and therefore, their average communication costs can be pre-calculated (see Equation (5)). More precisely, our problem formulation is as follows.

$$\min \mathcal{L} \qquad (9)$$

subject to

$$\sum_{O_x \in \mathcal{P}_{i,j}} \sum_{y=0}^{T_x-1} b_{x,z-y} A_{O_x} \leq A/k, \ 1 \leq z \leq \mathcal{L}_{init}, 1 \leq j \leq k \ (10)$$

$$\sum_{j=1}^{\mathcal{L}_{init}} b_{x,y} = 1, \forall O_x, \qquad (11)$$

$$S_x + T_x + d_{m,n} \leq S_y, \ O_x \rightarrow O_y, O_x \in C_m \text{ and } O_y \in C_n, \quad (12)$$

$$S_x + T_x - 1 \leq \mathcal{L}, \forall O_x \text{ without any successors}, \qquad (13)$$

where $\mathcal{L}$ is the total number of scheduling levels, T_x is the delay of operation O_x, $b_{x,y}$ is a binary variable which is 1 if O_x is scheduled to start at scheduling level y and 0 otherwise, A_{O_x} denotes the ancilla requirement of operation O_x, $\mathcal{L}_{init}$ is an upper bound for the total number of scheduling levels ($\mathcal{L}$), S_x is equal to the scheduling level where O_x is scheduled, i.e., $b_{x,S_x} = 1$, and $O_x \in C_m$ means that operation O_x is bound to quantum core m. Equation (10) sets a constraint on the total number of ancilla that each core can use at each scheduling level. Equation (11) ensures that all of the operations are scheduled. Equation (12) makes sure that dependent operations are properly scheduled, i.e., an operation starts after its predecessor in the QODG is finished. Equation (13) assures that the operations in the last scheduling level are scheduled to finish their execution before or at the scheduling level $\mathcal{L}$. We modified the list scheduling method presented in [16] as described above to solve the scheduling problem.

Using the Requp architecture, the ancilla sharing problem is solved during the scheduling. Moreover, the placement problem has already been solved in the prior step (i.e., resource binding step). Additionally, as it is explained earlier, the routing delay is hidden by the operation delay. Hence, a simple routing algorithm like the xy-routing fits well for the purpose of transferring qubits (or equivalently swapping their information) through the interconnection network of Requp.

5. EXPERIMENTAL RESULTS

Squash is developed in Java. It uses METIS 5 [14] as the partitioning engine and Gurobi 5.6 [17] for solving the 0-1 QP. A computer with an Intel Core i7-3770 CPU running at 3.40 GHz and 8GB of memory is employed for the experiments.

The $[\![7,1,3]\!]$ Steane code with the information presented in Table 1 is adopted as the QEC code. Moreover, the input variables of Squash are set as follows: $\beta_{PMD}=10 \ \mu s$, $\alpha_{int} = 3$, and $\gamma_{mem} = 0.2$. Squash is not limited to a particular quantum technology; however, the ion-trap technology is selected since it is the most promising method for realizing quantum circuits to date [18]. The delay of quantum operations in this technology is taken from [19].

In the rest of this section, first the latency-ancilla count trade-off in quantum circuits is studied using Squash. Then the optimum number of quantum cores for a representative benchmark is found. After that, the resource requirement of Requp, CQLA, and QLA are analytically compared. Finally, Squash is compared with the state-of-the-art mapper.

• **Investigating the latency-ancilla count trade-off:** As it is explained earlier, ancilla qubits are precious resources in quantum computers. Increasing the total ancilla budget lowers the circuit latency and vice versa. In order to study this effect using Squash, the *binary welded tree* (BWT) algorithm [20] is selected as the benchmark and compiled with Scaffold Compiler (which is introduced in [21]) to produce a QASM file. The number of quantum cores (k) is set to 4. The trade-off between latency and the ancilla budget (A) is shown as a Pareto curve in Figure 4. As can be seen, the delay value saturates at $A = 800$. This means that the circuit does not require more than 800 ancilla qubits.

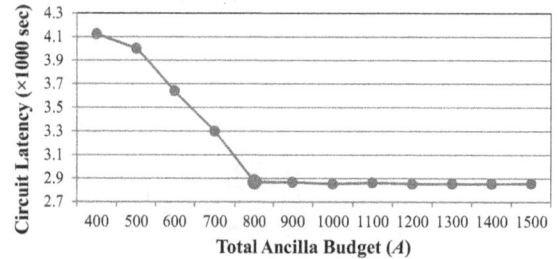

Figure 4. Latency-ancilla count trade-off for the BWT algorithm using a quad-core Requp architecture

• **Finding the optimum number of quantum cores:** One of the Squash input parameters is the quantum core count (k). The optimum value for this parameter varies based on the parallelism inside a given circuit. The quantum core count is just an abstraction and has no relation with the usage of quantum physical resources. However, Squash has a higher runtime for smaller values of k, because the size of the weight vector for partitioning is larger. Figure 5 shows the latency of the BWT algorithm as a function of quantum core count when $A = 800$. It can be seen that the optimal latency is achieved when k is set to 2. However, $k = 4$ is preferred since the runtime of Squash for this case is 15 times faster than that of the former case.

• **Resource usage comparison among Requp, CQLA, and QLA architectures:** In the QLA architecture, every qubit requires to be placed in a quantum tile. Each tile needs to support all types of quantum operations and their respective QEC codes. Hence, in the case of one-level $[\![7,1,3]\!]$ Steane code, the required ancilla in this architecture is equal to 100×(total qubit count). CQLA limits this value to the maximum number of parallel operations the architecture should be able to execute. For instance, if z parallel operations are supported (which is significantly smaller than the total qubit count), 100×z ancilla qubits are required. Requp improves this resource limitation by considering the fact that all of the parallel operations may not require the maximum number of ancilla qubits (i.e., 100). Therefore, Requp allows to run at most $(100/28) \times z$ operations at the same time while still having the same worst case parallelism as CQLA. This discussion reveals that Requp performs more efficiently in the average case compared to CQLA and behaves as bad as CQLA in the worst case.

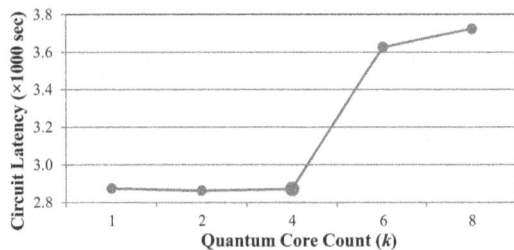

Figure 5. Finding the optimum number of quantum cores for the BWT algorithm

• **Comparison between Squash and QSPR:** In this section, the performance and the quality of results produced by Squash is compared with that of *QSPR* which is introduced in [10]. QSPR is a full-fledged quantum mapper which is recently improved to support the QLA architecture [1]. Unfortunately, no quantum mapper for the CQLA architecture is available for the comparison.

Various sizes of the BWT algorithm is compiled based on a parameter called s. This parameter is varied from 3 to 19, where $s = 19$ is the problem size of interest. (For the previous experiments, s was set to 5.) Figure 6 compares the circuit latency mapped by Squash and QSPR. As can be seen, Squash could achieve better results in all of problem sizes. This is due to the improved qubit routing mechanism in Squash. As it was explained earlier, Squash hides most of the routing delay by parallelizing it with the execution of logical operations.

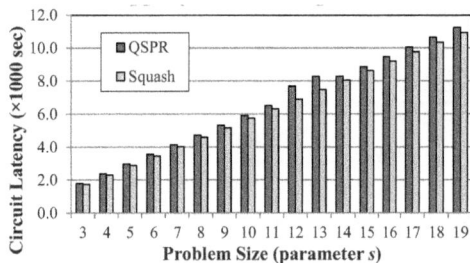

Figure 6. Comparison of the circuit latency mapped by QSPR and Squash

Figure 7 compares the runtime of QSPR and Squash. As can be seen, for very small problem sizes ($s < 8$), QSPR is slightly faster than Squash. However, as the problem size grows, the runtime of QSPR radically increases, whereas the runtime of Squash does not change. This phenomenon is due to the fact that QSPR handles a large netlist of quantum operations, whereas Squash maps only the quantum kernels which grow very slowly compared to the main circuit size. Also note that when $s > 15$, QSPR runtime rapidly grows due to the inefficient handling of large netlists.

6. CONCLUSION

Quantum circuits for solving real-size problems are gigantic. As a result, quantum mappers have difficulty in mapping them to quantum fabrics. Moreover, current quantum mappers cannot properly handle the ancilla sharing problem which allows reducing the resource demand (even though it is achieved at the cost of increased latency). To address these two key problems, a scalable quantum mapper, called Squash, was introduced. Squash uses a novel multi-core reconfigurable quantum processor architecture, called Requp, which supports a layered approach to mapping a quantum algorithm and enables ancilla sharing. Experimental results demonstrated that Squash can handle large-scale quantum

algorithms while providing an effective mechanism for sharing ancilla qubits.

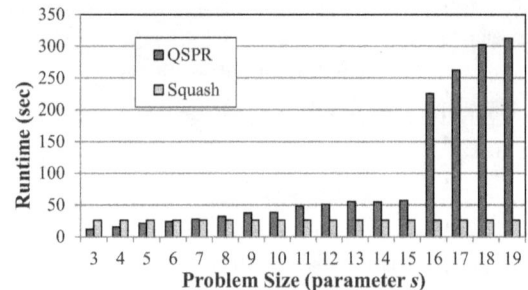

Figure 7. Comparison of mapping results between QSPR and Squash

7. ACKNOWLEDGMENTS

The authors would like to thank Professor Todd Brun for his valuable comments about the calculation of ancilla requirements for various QEC codes and operations.

This research was supported in part by the Intelligence Advanced Research Projects Activity (IARPA) via Department of Interior National Business Center contract number D11PC20165.

8. REFERENCES

[1] M. J. Dousti and M. Pedram, "LEQA: Latency Estimation for a Quantum Algorithm Mapped to a Quantum Circuit Fabric," in *DAC*, 2013.

[2] M. G. Whitney et al., "A Fault Tolerant, Area Efficient Architecture for Shor's Factoring Algorithm," in *ISCA*, 2009.

[3] M. A. Nielsen and I. L. Chuang, *Quantum Computation and Quantum Information*. Cambridge University Press, 2010.

[4] S. E. Venegas-Andraca, *Quantum walks for computer scientists*. Morgan & Claypool Publishers, 2008.

[5] V. V. Shende and I. L. Markov, "On the CNOT-cost of TOFFOLI gates," *QIC*, vol. 9, no. 5, pp. 461–486, 2009.

[6] T. S. Metodi et al., "A Quantum Logic Array Microarchitecture: Scalable Quantum Data Movement and Computation," in *MICRO*, 2005.

[7] D. D. Thaker et al., "Quantum Memory Hierarchies: Efficient Designs to Match Available Parallelism in Quantum Computing," in *ISCA*, 2006.

[8] N. C. Jones et al., "Layered Architecture for Quantum Computing," *Phys. Rev. X*, vol. 2, no. 3, p. 031007, 2012.

[9] L. Kreger-Stickles and M. Oskin, "Microcoded Architectures for Ion-Tap Quantum Computers," in *ISCA*, 2008.

[10] M. J. Dousti and M. Pedram, "Minimizing the Latency of Quantum Circuits During Mapping to the Ion-Trap Circuit Fabric," in *DATE*, 2012.

[11] B. Zeng et al., "Transversality Versus Universality for Additive Quantum Codes," *IEEE Trans. Inf. Theory*, vol. 57, no. 9, pp. 6272–6284, 2011.

[12] "Quantum Architectures: qasm2circ." [Online]. Available: http://www.media.mit.edu/quanta/qasm2circ.

[13] M. Tanaka and O. Tatebe, "Workflow Scheduling to Minimize Data Movement Using Multi-constraint Graph Partitioning," in *CCGRID*, 2012.

[14] G. Karypis and V. Kumar, "Multilevel Algorithms for Multi-constraint Graph Partitioning," in *Supercomputing*, 1998.

[15] C.-T. Hwang et al., "A Formal Approach to the Scheduling Problem in High Level Synthesis," *IEEE TCAD*, vol. 10, no. 4, pp. 464–475, 1991.

[16] G. D. Micheli, *Synthesis and Optimization of Digital Circuits*. McGraw-Hill, 1994.

[17] "Gurobi Optimizer." [Online]. Available: http://www.gurobi.com.

[18] T. D. Ladd et al., "Quantum computers," *Nature*, vol. 464, no. 7285, pp. 45–53, 2010.

[19] H. Goudarzi et al., "Design of a Universal Logic Block for Fault-Tolerant Realization of any Logic Operation in Trapped-Ion Quantum Circuits," *Quantum Inf. Process.*, pp. 1–33, Jan. 2014.

[20] A. M. Childs et al., "Exponential Algorithmic Speedup by a Quantum Walk," in *Proceedings of the Theory of Computing*, 2003.

[21] A. JavadiAbhari et al., "ScaffCC: A Framework for Compilation and Analysis of Quantum Computing Programs," in *CF*, 2014.

Design and Analysis of Robust and Wide Operating Low-Power Level-Shifter for Embedded Dynamic Random Access Memory

Kenneth Ramclam
Computer Science and Engineering
University of South Florida
Tampa, Florida-33647
Kramclam@mail.usf.edu

Swaroop Ghosh
Computer Science and Engineering
University of South Florida
Tampa, Florida-33647
Sghosh@cse.usf.edu

Abstract— Level shifters (LS) are crucial components in low power design where the die is segregated in multiple voltage domains. LS are used at the voltage domain interfaces to mitigate sneak path current. Another important application of LS is in high voltage drivers for designs where voltage boosting is needed for performance and functionality. We explore one such application in embedded Dynamic Random Access Memories (eDRAM) where LS is employed in the wordline path. Our investigation reveals that leakage power of LS can pose a serious threat by lowering the wordline voltage and subsequently affecting the speed and retention time of eDRAM. Furthermore the delay of LS under worse case process corners can cause functional discrepancies. We propose low-power pulsed-LS with supply gating to circumvent these issues. Our analysis indicate that pulsed-LS can improve the worst case speed from 2.7%-43%. We also propose power-gating for LSs to improve the retention time and bandwidth with minimal power and area overhead.

Categories and Subject Descriptors

B.6[LOGIC DESIGN] Design Styles – *Combinational Logic*
B.7[INTEGRATED CIRCUITS] Types and Design Styles – *Advance Technologies*

Keywords

Wide-operating Level shifters; eDRAM; Low-Power

I. INTRODUCTION

Supply voltage scaling is an effective knob to reduce the power consumption and has been exploited extensively on various parts of micro-processors to control both dynamic and leakage power consumption [1]. Since the optimal voltage for each part could be different, the die is segregated into several voltage domains. For example, cache voltage is typically higher than core voltage. Level shifters (LS) are needed whenever the voltage domain is crossed. Although this application of LS is important, the number of level shifters in the die is limited to few thousands. Therefore power and performance of LS does not pose a significant threat. We investigate the application of LS in embedded memory where the number of these components could be in the order of 4-5 sigma.

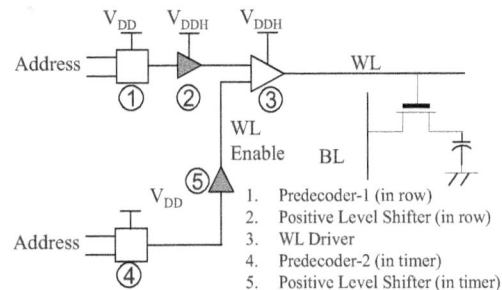

Fig. 1 Level shifters in the wordline driver path

1. Predecoder-1 (in row)
2. Positive Level Shifter (in row)
3. WL Driver
4. Predecoder-2 (in timer)
5. Positive Level Shifter (in timer)

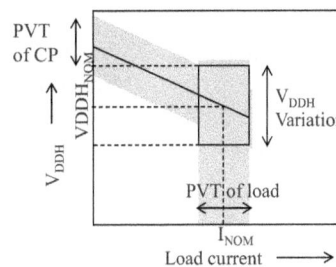

Fig. 2 V_{DDH} variation due to PVT variation in charge pump and load current.

Embedded Dynamic Random Access Memory (eDRAM)[2] employs high voltage (HV) on the gate (i.e., the wordline) of access transistor to write a full logical '1' on the storage element. Therefore the wordline (WL) driver is operated on the high voltage supply (V_{DDH}) with dedicated charge pumps to support the high voltage circuitries. The WL predecoder employs LS to convert nominal voltage (V_{DD}) to high voltage. The HV is typically generated by using a dedicated charge pump (CP) [3]. The emerging memories such as Spin-Transfer Torque Random Access Memory (STTRAM) also employ HV on the access transistor to reduce the write failure while maintaining small bitcell footprint for improved memory density. Fig. 1 shows the simplified diagram of WL path for memory arrays where LSs are employed in both WL predecoder (typically located in the row driver) and WL enable (typically located in the timer). The detailed structure of the WL path is explained in Section II.

The prime complexity involved in designing the LS for embedded memory is due to the fact that V_{DDH} can vary depending on PVT and load current [3]. This can be understood from the cartoon in Fig. 2 that shows CP output vs. load current behavior and the impact of PVT variations. Both CP output and load current can vary due PVT fluctuation and has a cumulative impact on V_{DDH} variation. This is on top of access dependent load current variation

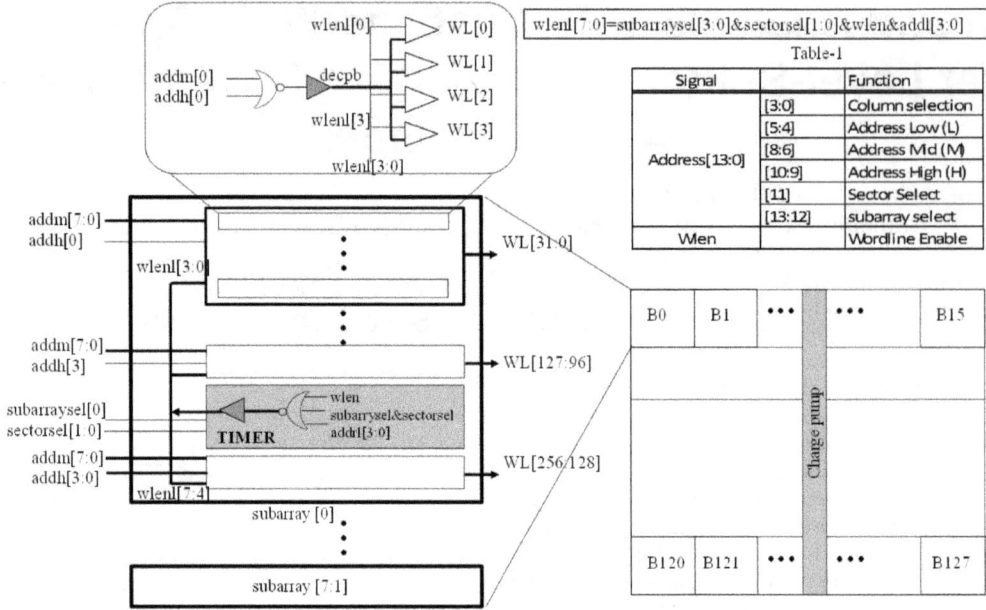

Fig. 3 Wordline driver design for eDRAM subarray

In the figure:

wlenl[7:0]=subarraysel[3:0]&sectorsel[1:0]&wlen&addl[3:0]

Table-1

Signal		Function
Address[13:0]	[3:0]	Column selection
	[5:4]	Address Low (L)
	[8:6]	Address Mid (M)
	[10:9]	Address High (H)
	[11]	Sector Select
	[13:12]	subarray select
Wlen		Wordline Enable

(explained in Section II). Therefore, the functionality of LS has to be guaranteed for a wide range of V$_{DDH}$. Other challenge with LS design involves (a) tight area budget as the LS should fit within the array with minimum area overhead, (b) the LS transistors should be protected to avoid reliability degradation due to NBTI, PBTI and HCI [4] and (c) reducing the leakage of the LS to alleviate the burden from charge pump and save standby power.

Level shifters are well studied circuits and numerous design approaches have been proposed in literature to improve its robustness, area and power consumption. A contention mitigated LS (CMLS) is proposed in [5] that uses stacked PMOS transistors to mitigate the contention from PMOS in conventional DCVS (differential cascade voltage switch) LS [6]. A pass transistor based LS (LSpg) and several flavors to mitigate the contention to improve delay and reduce power has been described [7]. Another work [8] proposed a 2-step LS to reduce the load from charge pump during LS toggling. A new approach to embed the LS in flip-flops (FF) is introduced in [9]. By using LS FF, the area overhead can be minimized and interfacing between two different voltage levels can be made seamless. In order to address the issue of interfacing between high voltage IO and logic operating at subthreshold voltages, new LS topology is presented in [10]. Although the above techniques are low-overhead, low-power and robust they are not designed to operate at wide range of supply voltages. An error correcting LS is described in [11] to convert very low voltage to very high voltage. A novel technique to mitigate the contention in conventional DCVS LS and enable wide range of operation is introduced in [12]. Although effective the large area overhead associated with this technique would prevent its application in eDRAM wordline selection.

This paper provides an in-depth analysis of the design issues related to LS shifters for embedded memory arrays. In summary, we make following contributions in this paper,

- We provide comprehensive analysis of LS operating conditions (in terms of leakage and performance) for eDRAM.
- Our study shows that delay and power of LS can affect the functionality and retention time of eDRAM.

- We propose and evaluate a novel wide-operating pulsed LS for mitigating contention in LS. We also propose a power gating technique for robustness and low-power.
- We provide a system level analysis of eDRAM outlining the need for low power peripheral to maintain high performance and retention.

The rest of the paper is organized as follows. In Section II, we describe the memory architecture and operating conditions of LS. The impact of V$_{DDH}$ on leakage and functionality of LS is discussed in Section III. The low-power and wide-operating pulsed LS design is also presented. The system level analysis is described in Section IV. Finally, conclusions are drawn in Section V.

II. MEMORY ARCHITECTURE

In this section, first we present the memory architecture (including bank and subarray level design) to describe the wordline driver design. This is followed by CP modeling and analysis.

A. Wordline Driver Design

Fig. 3 shows the 32MB eDRAM array that contains 128 banks each with 256KB capacity. Each bank consists of 8 subarrays. Each subarray contains 256 rows and 1024 columns. The detailed subarray and 128KB eDRAM bank architecture [13] for NOR style WL driver is also illustrated. The raw address is predecoded into high, mid and low outside array and shipped to the subarrays for further decoding. The addressing structure for the bank is shown Table-1. The wordline selection is done based on predecoded address, wordline enable and subarray select. The wordline decoding is done in following manner

$$for(i = 0; i < length(addrh); i + +)\{$$
$$\quad for(j = 0; j < length(addrm); j + +)\{$$
$$\quad\quad for(k = 0; k < length(addrl); k + +)\{$$
$$\quad\quad WL[2^7 * sectorsel + 2^5.i + 2^3.j + k] =$$
$$\quad\quad Subarraysel\&Wlen\&Addh[i]\&Addm[j]\&Addl[k]$$
$$\quad\quad \}$$
$$\quad \}$$
$$\}$$

The LS are present iWL driver after predecoding stage as well as in timer. The total number of LS per bank is 544 (i.e., ((256/4)+4)x8). For the 32MB array, the total number of LS is 69632 (i.e., 544x128). The HV circuitries including WL driver and LS are supported by a dedicated charge pump. The charge pump load contains the leakage power of idle banks and active power of selected banks. For this study, we consider 4 types of access patterns: (a) 1 bank access (1B or 1X), (b) 2 bank access (2B or 2X), (c) 4 bank access (4B or 4X) and (d) 8 bank access (8B or 8X). Note that the access modes are bandwidth dependent. 1B is suitable for low bandwidth while 8B is suitable for high bandwidth. Furthermore, the bank accesses can be interleaved to avoid supply droop. The V_{DDH} load current is given by the summation of dynamic current drawn by the HV circuitries of active banks and leakage power of inactive banks. For 1B mode, leakage power dominates the total load whereas in 8B mode, dynamic power also becomes significant.

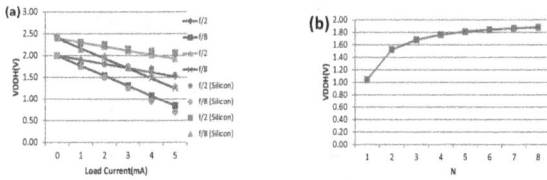

Fig. 4 (a) CP modeling and comparison with Silicon data and, (b) mitigating V_{DDH} droop by increasing the number of CPs.

B. Charge Pump Modeling

For accurate estimation of VDDH and low power design of LS it is important to model and integrate CP in the analysis. In this work, we perform curve fitting of silicon data for the voltage doubler design [3] to model CP. If the number of CPs per 32MB memory array is N and supply voltage is V_{DD} then the output voltage is given by

$$V_{DDH} = 2V_{DD} - \left(\frac{I_{load}}{N}\right)\left(\frac{\Delta}{5.2 x 10^{-3}}\right) \qquad (1)$$

Where Δ=0.5 (1.2) for f/2 (f/8). Fig. 4(a) shows that above model closely matches silicon data. It can be observed that V_{DDH} droops significantly due to increase in load current. In our analysis we employ multiple CPs to compensate for larger load (Fig. 4(b)). Note that the downside of employing multiple CP (increasing N) is two-fold: (a) area overhead and (b) possibility of very high voltage (closer to $2V_{DD}$) at the HV circuits which may experience reliability degradation.

C. Impact of V_{DDH} Variation on Retention Time

Read operation in eDRAM is destructive due to charge sharing between bitcell and bitline and writeback is essential to maintain the functional integrity. The writeback voltage depends on WL voltage (since NMOS access transistor cannot pass a full high signal) which in turn depends on V_{DDH}. Degradation in writeback voltage is manifested as poor retention time (i.e., the maximum amount of time before which the bitcell can be read correctly). This issue is further illustrated in Fig. 5(g).

III. ANALYSIS OF LEVEL SHIFTER

In this section, we describe the LS designs and analyze them in terms of power and delay. We also propose a pulsed LS and power-gating to improve the delay, robustness and power dissipation.

A. LS Design Challenges

The primary challenge of designing LS is to ensure its robustness across all V_{DDH}, process skews and random variations. For example, the design requirements for $V_{DDH}= V_{DDH}(min)$ may conflict with the design for $V_{DDH}=V_{DDH}(max)$. Similarly, the designs for FS and SF corners could conflict with each other. These challenges are further elaborated in Section IIID.

B. Simulation Setup

The simulations are carried out with predictive 22nm HP models [14]. Fast (slow) corner is modeled by reducing (adding) 150mV in the transistor threshold voltage (V_{TH}). We have simulated at five process corners namely TT (typical nmos and pmos), FS (fast nmos, slow pmos), SF (fast pmos, slow nmos), SS (slow nmos, slow pmos) and FF (fast nmos, fast pmos). The random variations are modeled by adding V_{TH} with $(\mu, \sigma) = (0, 50mV)$. Since there are 69K LS present in the memory system, 4.5 sigma analysis is performed in these corners to ensure the functionality of the LS. For analysis of LS stability V_{DDH} is varied between $V_{DDH}(min)$ and $V_{DDH}(max)$. The $V_{DDH}(min)=V_{DDL}=1V$ and $V_{DDH}(max)=1.8V$. Nominal room temperature (25C) is used for delay simulations whereas hot temperature (90C) is used for leakage estimations. A total of 20 charge pumplets have been assumed for leakage simulations.

C. Analysis of Baseline Level Shifter

Fig. 5(a) and 5(c) depicts two common LS designs [6] [7]- LSnom and LSpg. The pros of LSnom lie in its simplicity and symmetrical nature whereas the con is its area overhead. Due to symmetricity, LSnom experiences contention in both directions. Since V_{DDH} can vary from low to high voltages the PMOS is kept small. The NMOS is sized such that it is strong enough to win the contention with PMOS under all VDDH and process skews. In our simulation the NMOS is sized 5X than PMOS to ensure robustness under 4.5sigma at all process skews. The LS is sized to drive FO4 load. Fig. 5(b) plots the $(\mu+4.5\sigma)$ rise and fall delay points obtained using Monte Carlo for all process skews. It can be observed that the rise delay is worse when V_{DDH} is low and the PMOS transistor is slow (SS and FS corners). At higher voltages (and SF corner), the fall delay gets worse due to stronger PMOS transistor. Furthermore, the plot also reveals the challenge in designing LS that can operate at wide range of voltages without impacting the propagation delay.

LSpg is low overhead and preferable for area constrained applications. The sizing of LSpg is done to mitigate the stability and robustness under all process and voltage conditions. Compared to LSnom, this structure experiences contention in only one direction. Fig. 5(c) shows the contention between {P2, P3} and {N1, N2} at SF corner when V_{DDH} is $V_{DDH}(max)$. The sizing should be done so that {N1, N2} wins the fight with {P2, P3} and node 'fb' is pulled down to turn {P0, P1} ON (for fast rise delay). The same sizing conflicts when $V_{DDH}=V_{DDH}(min)$ and {P2, P3} is too weak to pull node 'fb' to turn {P0, P1} OFF. This results in contention between {P0, P1} and N0 as both are ON simultaneously (slow fall delay). We consider these conflicting requirements for sizing the LS. Fig. 5(d) shows the path delay simulated at room temperature. It can be observed that rise delay is worse at low V_{DDH} whereas fall delay is worse at high V_{DDH} (@SS corner). This is an outcome of weak NMOS and relatively strong PMOS due to very good V_{GS} at high V_{DDH}(@SS corner). The leakage vs. V_{DDH} applied is depicted in Fig. 5(e). The V_{DDH} applied and V_{DDH} obtained is also shown. The corresponding droop in V_{DDH} (due to LS leakage) is also plotted in Fig. 5(f). It can be observed that the LS leakage can significantly affect the CP output voltage. Therefore the LS and WL drivers receives less than required V_{DDH} degrading the writeback voltage of bitcell and degrading the retention time.

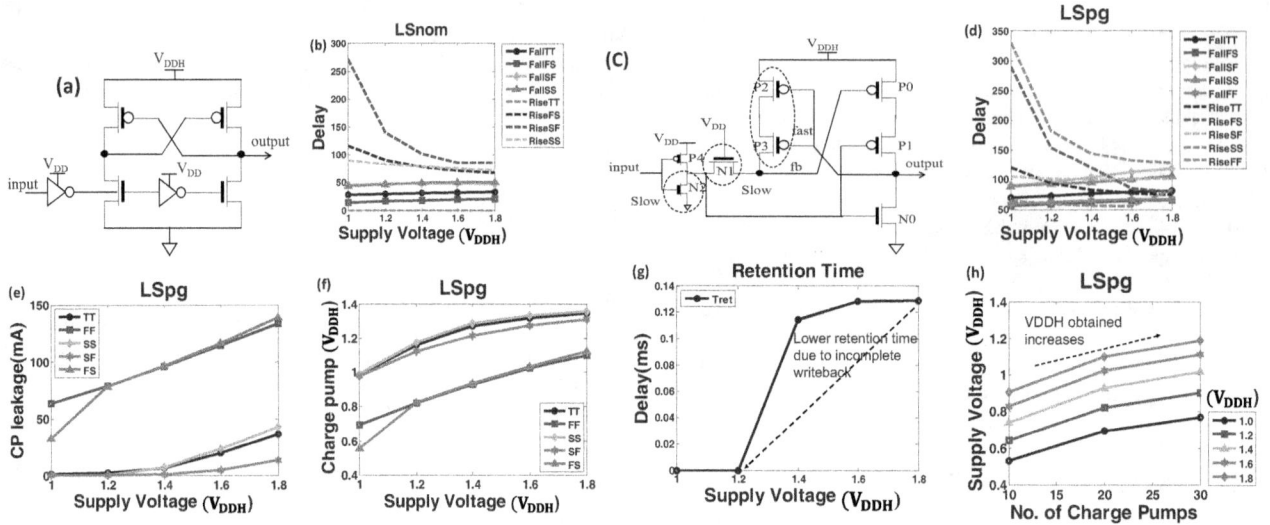

Fig. 5 Analysis of conventional LS: (a) &(b) DCVS LS and corresponding plot showing (μ+4.5σ) delay under process variations, (c) & (d) pass-gate LS (LSpg) and corresponding plot showing (μ+4.5σ) delay, (e) & (f) CP leakage vs. supply voltage and corresponding values of actual voltage received from CP is also plotted for different corners. It can be observed that charge pump output droops for fast corners due to higher leakages and actual V_{DDH} is lower than the desired values, (g) impact of lower V_{DDH} on retention time. It is evident that the retention time reduces to 0us if the V_{DDH} is less than 1.4V and (h) plot showing that V_{DDH} can be boosted by increasing the number of CPs (FF corner is used for this simulation).

We have simulated a single eDRAM bitcell and the results are depicted in Fig. 5(g). For this simulation we have used the bitcell capacitance to be 20fF and bitline capacitance to be 50fF. The circuit simulations are carried out at FF corner and 90C. It can be noted that the retention time reduces with lower V_{DDH} values. This can be attributed to incomplete writeback during read/write access since the NMOS access transistor cannot pass a full logic '1' and the bit is restored to a value much lower than 1V. For the simulations we define the retention time to be the time by which the bitcell losses so much charge that it is unable to develop 100mV differential. From the plot it is evident that retention time can be reduced to 0us due to droop in V_{DDH}. These results outline the need for designing low-power LS.

One possible alternative to avoid the V_{DDH} droop is to increase the number of CPs that can supply the leakage and maintain high V_{DDH}. Fig. 5(h) shows that the number of CP can be increased to 30 in order to regain the voltage lost due to leakage. However, increasing the CP is associated with extra power consumption.

D. Robust and Fast Pulsed Level Shifter Design

It can be noted from previous Section that the delay associated with LSpg can be attributed to the contention between P1 and {N1,N2} at high voltages. We propose a pulsed-LSpg (pLSpg) to mitigate this contention. The pLSpg design splits the supply of feedback and pull-up PMOS transistors and droops the supply of feedback transistor {P2, P3} during up-conversion (0$\rightarrow$1 transition). The weakening of feedback PMOS reduces the contention on the node 'fb' and assist easy flipping. We have implemented the pLSpg design with the described voltage drooping mechanism as shown in Fig. 6(e). The delay is very sensitive to the amount of droop but the pulsewidth shows a strong impact as well. Both the amount and duration of V_{DDH} droop determines the propagation delay of LS as shown in Fig. 6(a). A narrow pulse doesn't improve delay significantly because the droop time is insufficient to fully mitigate the contention. Fig. 6(a) also illustrates the rise delay vs. pulse duration for different amount of droop. It can be noticed that the benefit of droop saturates after 40%. This is due to the fact that the contention is already mitigated and extra drooping doesn't help.

Similar argument holds true for pulsewidth more than 50-100ps. The regions dominated by contention and PMOS pull-up are also indicated. The waveforms of feedback node (fb) obtained through circuit simulation is illustrated in Fig. 6(b) for 40% and 60% droop. The waveform without droop is also shown for reference. The reduction in contention at 'fb' is evident from this result.

In order to estimate benefit of pLSpg under process variation, we simulated 5000 Monte Carlo points with 60% droop and Δ=100ps for all process corners and V_{DDH} values. The choice of Δ is based on all corner simulation. The worst case rise delays for SF and SS (which are worst case corners in terms of rise delay) are shown in Fig. 6(c) and 6(d). For the sake of comparison, the worst case of LSpg is also plotted. It can be observed that as much as 30% reduction in worst case rise delay is possible at V_{DDH}=1.8V@SS with the proposed pLSpg. This is very beneficial because the best retention time can be seen when V_{DDH}=1.8V. The benefit of feedback weakening is least at V_{DDH}=1V due to absence of contention.

The salient feature of the droop circuit is that it fully operates on V_{DDL} rail eliminating the need of level conversion for control signals. There are two components of the circuit, (a) programmable pulse generator that can modulate the width of pulse duration adaptively and, (b) droop circuit to disconnect the supply from LS and pull it down. The pulse generator senses the rise transition on input and generates a pulse which is in sync with the input. The pulse is fed to PMOS transistor Pd0 to disconnect LS from V_{DDH}. Note that Pd0 will be weakly ON since the pulse input is on V_{DDL} rail. Nevertheless, it will reduce DC current between V_{DDH} and ground when NMOS transistors ND0, ND1 and ND2 start to the pull-down node V_{droop}. It is possible to fully disconnect V_{DDH} in order to enable fast droop and eliminate DC current however that would require pulse np to be level shifted to V_{DDH} rail (which will create timing complexities). In order to avoid the area and delay overhead we keep the droop circuitry on V_{DDL} rail. Pull-down NMOS transistors Nd1 and Nd2 are diode connected to clamp the droop to $2V_{TN}$ above ground. This is done to ensure fast pull-back and lower static power.

126

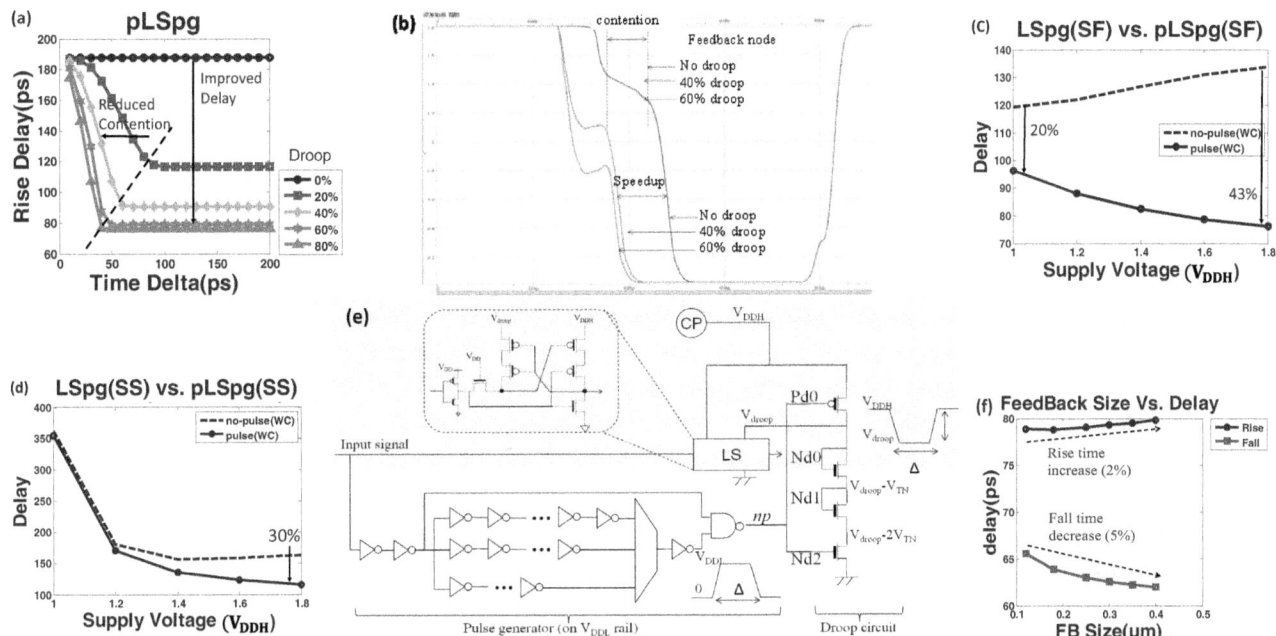

Fig. 6 Design and analysis of pulsed LS: (a) worst case delay vs. pulsewidth for different amounts of droop in pLSpg, (b) waveform of feedback node (fb) showing the contention mitigation with droop. The pulsewidth is kept 100ps for this simulation, (c) & (d) worst case delay points for a voltage range of 1V to 1.8V simulated at SF and SS corners with pLSpg. (e) Schematic of pLSpg design. The split path for feedback transistor that is controlled by droop circuit is shown in inset, (f) plot showing the trade-off between rise and fall delay by feedback transistor upsizing. As much as 5% improvement in fall delay is possible with less than 2% impact in rise delay.

Note that the proposed circuit provides ~60% droop however multiple droop legs could be added or sizing of Nd2 could be dynamically changed to control the magnitude of droop. The pulse generator and the droop circuit are shared among 64 LS (i.e., per subarray) to minimize the area overhead. The area overhead of the droop circuit is <1% since it is shared by 64 LS present in the subarray. The power overhead is 56uW which is <1%.

Note that pLSpg requires pulsing the supply only during rising transition. This is due to the fact the worst case delay is dominated by rise delay. Furthermore, pulsing does not help fall transition due to absence of contention in the falling edge. However, the proposed technique provides opportunity to make trade-off between rise and fall delay. This can be achieved by upsizing the feedback PMOS transistors P2 and P3 which turn-off P0 quickly so that N0 can pull-down easily. The corresponding effect on rise time is minimal since the contention is fully eliminated through pulsing. Fig. 6(f) illustrates the rise and fall delay with upsizing of feedback transistors. It can be observed that the fall delay improvement is minimal since P1 already makes weakens pull-up strength.

E. Design for Low Power

From section IIIC it is evident that leakage power of LS poses a threat to functionality and retention time of eDRAM design. We propose a power gated LS to sleep the inactive decoders in order to mitigate the leakage. Fig. 7(a) shows the comparison of leakage with supply and ground gating for different applied V_{DDH}. It can be observed that supply gating provides better leakage saving (8X) at high V_{DDH} compared to ground gating (which shows slightly better results for low V_{DDH}). Therefore we select supply gating as the enabling leakage saving mechanism for pLSpg.

Note that sleep transistor sizing is non-trivial because the leakage saving and the wakeup time have conflicting sizing requirement. In order to determine the reasonable size we sweep the transistor width and compare the leakage and wake-up delay (Fig. 7(b) and 7(c)).

Based on the result obtained we choose 9um to be the sleep transistor size where the wake-up delay is minimized. The sleep signal is controlled by early subarrayselect. When the subarray is activated the LS is woken up. If the LS wakes up late, the wordline driver will be weak and the access latency will go down. For hiding the wakeup latency we require subarryselect to arrive 1 cycle early (assuming 2GHz operating frequency). Fig. 7(d) shows the V_{DDH} obtained and V_{DDH} applied at WC leakage corner (FF). It can be noted that gated pLS can improve the CP output voltage by 34% due to lower leakage. This increases the retention time to 120us (from 0us). The latency is impacted by 1 clock cycle that can be hided.

IV. SYSTEM LEVEL ANALYSIS

In previous section we presented analysis of passgate LS and design of a novel low-power and robust pulsed-LS. In this section, we present system level analysis of the eDRAM memory for various access modes as introduced in Section IIA.

A. System Modeling

Fig. 8(a) shows the system model that is used for simulation. The LSs are divided into three sections- awake, active and sleep. The number of sleep, awake and active LS is determined by the access mode. For example, 1X mode will wake up 64 LS (since they share a common sleep transistor) with 1 LS being active. The remaining LS will remain in sleep mode (total number of LS=69K). Similarly, 2X will wake up 128LS with 2 LS being active and so forth. The equations describing number of active, awake and sleeping LS as well as PMOS power-gating sizes for each of the sections can be seen in Fig. 8(a). Note that the leakage of the waked up LSs is higher than that of sleep mode LSs and therefore they will present extra load to the CP. Apart from that the LS which is fired will draw dynamic current. For the sake of accurate estimation of V_{DDH} due to leakage the CP model is also included in the simulation.

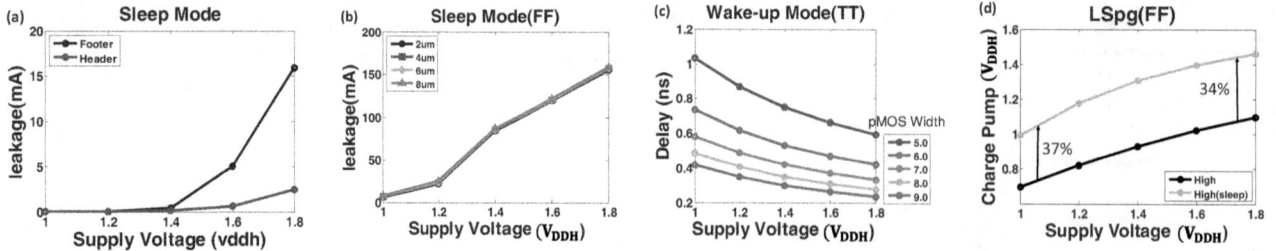

Fig. 7 Low-power LS design by using power-gating: (a) leakage vs. V_{DDH} for header and footer transistor (TT corner), (b) & (c) impact of transistor size on leakage and wake-up time. Leakage is simulated at FF while delay is simulated at TT corner. The sleep transistor is chosen to ensure wake-up time of 1 cycle (250ps) and (d) simulation showing 34%-37% improvement in V_{DDH} by using the sleep transistor.

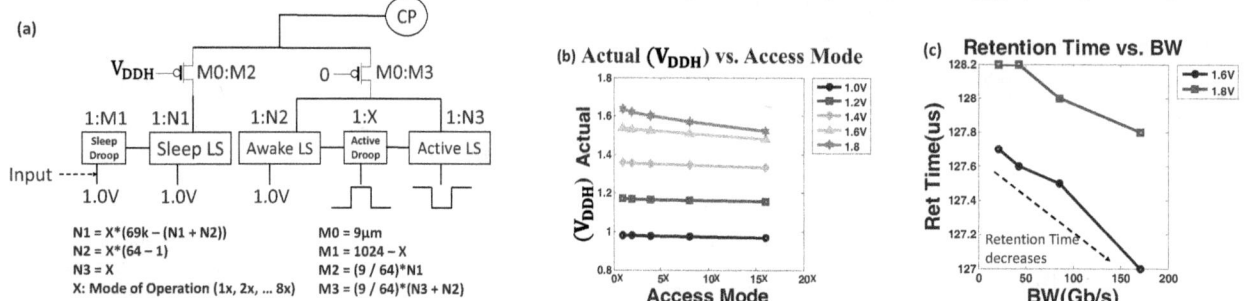

Fig. 8 System level analysis: (a) simulation model showing sleeping, awake and active LS and corresponding droop circuitries. The size of PMOS sleep transistor and total number of instantiations of sleep, active and awake LSs (i.e., N1, N2, N3, M1, M2 and M3) are also depicted, (b) plot indicating the V_{DDH} obtained vs. access modes for different V_{DDH} applied and (c) bandwidth vs. retention. A higher bandwidth corresponds to lower retention due to V_{DDH} droop and incomplete writeback.

B. Simulation Results

The plot of V_{DDH} obtained for different operating modes are drawn for different V_{DDH} applied in Fig. 8(b). The simulation is performed at 90C and FF corner for worst case leakage. A total of 10 CPs are assumed in this simulation. It can be observed that V_{DDH} obtained from CP decreases as the access mode increases (i.e., for 8X and 16X). The access time is assumed to be 3ns meaning that the active bank cannot be accessed for atleast 3ns (which is equivalent to 12 cycles@4GHz). This access period is determined by the sense, writeback and precharge time. In our simulation, sense time is 1 cycle, precharge time is 1 cycle and remaining 10 cycles are allocated for writeback.

The bandwidth vs. retention time is plotted in Fig. 8(c). It can be observed from Fig. 8(b) that 8X mode results in maximum droop in V_{DDH}. This corresponds to poor retention time however the bandwidth obtained is maximum in this case. 1X mode improves the retention time due to less droop in V_{DDH} but the corresponding bandwidth is also low. This indicate that higher bandwidth from the memory can be sustained by lowering the retention time which translates to higher refresh power. This trend is shown in Fig. 8(c). Note that the present model of the system does not account for loading due to wordline driver which is a crucial component of leakage and active power. Nevertheless the conclusions drawn remain same. Future model will be improved to comprehend wordline driver leakage for better accuracy and estimation.

V. CONCLUSIONS

We studied level-shifters for application in eDRAM. Our investigation revealed that leakage power of the LS circuitries could play an important role in determining the retention time and functionality. Our study also indicated that conventionally designed LS may fail to meet the timing requirement due to wide CP voltage variation. We proposed a novel low overhead power gated pulsed LS to break the dependency of LS speed on CP output variation and enable fast level conversion and higher retention time. Our system level simulation indicated the presence of an interesting trade-off between bandwidth, leakage power of LS and standby power of system that is governed by retention time.

VI. ACKNOWLEDGEMENT

This paper is based on work supported by Semiconductor Research Corporation (#2442.001)

REFERENCES

[1] S. Rusu, et al. "A 65-nm dual-core multithreaded Xeon® processor with 16-MB L3 cache." JSSC, 2007.

[2] PW Diodato, "Embedded DRAM: more than just a memory", IEEE Communications Magazine, 2000.

[3] D. Somasekhar et al. "Multi-phase 1 Ghz voltage doubler charge pump in 32 nm logic process." JSSC, 2010.

[4] R. Vattikonda, et al. "Modeling and minimization of PMOS NBTI effect for robust nanometer design." DAC, 2006.

[5] C. Q. Tran, et al. "Low-power high-speed level shifter design for block-level dynamic voltage scaling environment." ICICDT, 2005.

[6] J. M. Rabaey, et al. Digital integrated circuits. Prentice hall, 2002. (rab)

[7] S. H. Kulkarni, et al. "High performance level conversion for dual V_{DD} design." TVLSI, 2004.

[8] A. Raychowdhury, et al. "PVT-and-aging adaptive wordline boosting for 8T SRAM power reduction." ISSCC, 2010.

[9] F. Ishihara, et al."Level conversion for dual-supply systems." TVLSI, 2004.

[10] I. J. Chang, et al. "Robust level converter for sub-threshold/super-threshold operation: 100 mV to 2.5 v." TVLSI, 2011.

[11] Y. Osaki, et al. "A low-power level shifter with logic error correction for extremely low-voltage digital CMOS LSIs." JSSC, 2012.

[12] Y. Kim, et al. "LC2: Limited contention level converter for robust wide-range voltage conversion." VLSIC, 2011.

[13] S. Ghosh, et al. "NOR Logic Word Line Selection", WO Patent 2,012,087,473, 2012.

[14] Predictive technology model, ASU, http://www.asu.edu/~ptm.

A Study on the use of Parallel Wiring Techniques for Sub-20nm Designs

Rickard Ewetz[†], Wen-Hao Liu[‡], Kai-Yuan Chao[‡‡], Ting-Chi Wang[††], Cheng-Kok Koh[†]

[†]School of Electrical and Computer Engineering, Purdue University, West Lafayette, USA
[‡]Block Implementation, ICD, Cadence Design Systems, Taiwan
[‡‡]Intel Corporation, Hillsboro, USA
[†††]Department of Computer Science, National Tsing Hua University, Hsinchu, Taiwan
rewetz@purdue.edu, whliu@cadence.com, kaiyuan.chao@intel.com,
tcwang@cs.nthu.edu.tw, chengkok@purdue.edu

ABSTRACT

Wire sizing can be used to reduce the delays of critical nets. However, because of the forbidden pitch issue in sub-20nm designs, wide wires may no longer be an attractive solution because of the restrictive wire spacing requirement from advanced lithography. In this work, we investigate the suitability of the parallel wiring technique, in which multiple parallel wires are used to route the same net, as an alternative to routing a net using a single wide wire. In particular, we study the trade offs between parasitics, timing, power, and routing resources. Our study reveals that wire sizing using both parallel wires and wide wires can be advantageous. Moreover, if high layout densities are required, parallel wiring can be a viable approach in solving timing problems for sub-20nm designs.

Categories and Subject Descriptors

B.7.2 [**Hardware, Integrated Circuits**]: Design Aids

General Terms

Algorithms, Design, Performance.

Keywords

VLSI; Physical Design; Interconnects; Routing; Parallel Wires.

1. INTRODUCTION

Wire sizing can be used to improve the performance of interconnects. It has also been used to reduce high current densities to avoid failures from electromigration. However, recent challenges in lithography have generated design rules regulating spacing requirements and layout densities, which make wire sizing using wide wires a less desirable solution.

To enable sub 20-nm technologies, several manufacturing techniques, such as double patterning lithography (DPL),

optical proximity correction (OPC), process window aware OPC (PW-OPC) and retargeting, are required. In DPL, two lithography exposures are used to print target shapes with smaller pitch [2, 12]. In OPC and PW-OPC, optimization is performed to obtain an optimal mask for a given target shape [8, 6, 3, 11]. However, if the target shapes are not lithography friendly, even such techniques may not be able to make the shapes printable. To overcome poor target shapes, retargeting [23, 1, 24] can modify ill-formed target shapes until the constraints in a process window are met.

One key issue is that wider wires require more spacing to generate lithography friendly layout [25]. At the same time higher layout density is required to maintain yield and scaling cost economy. To extend the efficacy of existing wire sizing techniques in sub-20 nm design, it may be necessary to realize a wide wire using multiple narrow parallel wires. This paper presents a study to gain insight of the performance of wire sizing using parallel wires as compared to wire sizing using wider wires. In addition, we present a hybrid method that uses both wide wires and parallel wires, should the layout density requirement permit. Specifically we evaluate the effectiveness of wire sizing using only wide wires, only parallel wires, and a combination of both, in terms of delay, power, and routing resources.

We observed that the performance of wire sizing using parallel and/or wide wires is dependent on the available routing resources and density requirements. In general, wide wires have lower parasitic capacitances. However, parallel wiring is more flexible with respect to routing resources and density constraints and is the only feasible method to size a net when high layout densities are required.

The rest of the paper is organized as follows: In Section 2, a set of wiring patterns is introduced. In Section 3, our experimental setup is described. In Section 4, the wiring patterns are analyzed with respect to parasitics. In Section 5, we analyze the performance of different wiring patterns when the wires of a net is sized using different techniques. In Section 6, we outline future challenges and potentials for optimization using parallel wires. Finally, we conclude the paper in Section 7.

2. WIRING PATTERNS

A metal layer is divided into a set of tracks. Wires of minimum width W (or $1W$) are assigned and routed in such tracks. Wires of twice the width (denoted $2W$) can be routed using two tracks. Moreover, there must be spacing or empty track(s) between two wires. Let S be the minimum spacing and it is typical for advanced technology to set $S = W$. In sub-20 nm technology, the spacing must be equal or wider than that of the width of the wire. Obtaining a high layout density within a region become a problem when wide wires require a wide spacing. In particular, if a wire of width nW needs a spacing of nS, the layout density of a design within a region would be negatively affected. For this study, we consider the routing area occupied by a net to include the wire (or wires in the case of parallel wiring) and the two adjacent empty tracks. Moreover, we assume that the adjacent empty tracks are of the minimal required spacing, i.e., if nS is the required spacing, we would not use $(n+1)S$.

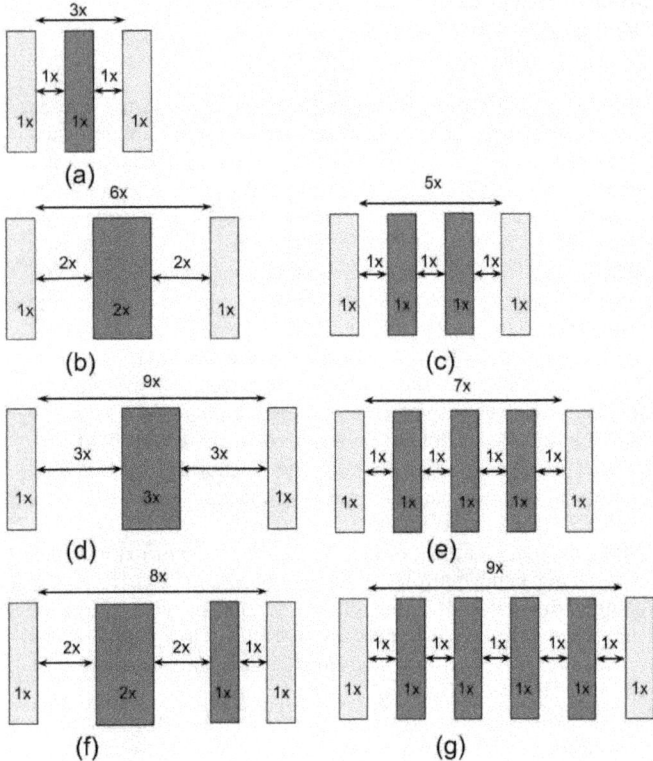

Figure 1: Wiring patterns using at most 9 tracks.

In Figure 1, we show in (a), (b), and (d) a middle red wire with $1W$, $2W$, and $3W$ widths, respectively. The adjacent empty space beside the red wire are of dimension $1S$, $2S$, and $3S$, respectively. We denote the wiring patterns in Figures 1(a), (b), and (d) as (1S-1W-1S), (2S-2W-2S), and (3S-3W-3S), respectively. The sum of the numeric terms in each wiring pattern indicates the total number of tracks required, under the assumption that 1S and 1W each occupies a track.

In order to achieve high layout density in each local region, parallel wiring is a compelling solution. Two parallel narrow wires, each of width $1W$, has effectively similar resistance as a single wire of width $2W$. Wiring patterns in (c) and (e) of Figure 1, denoted as (1S-1W-1S-1W-1S) and (1S-1W-1S-1W-1S-1W-1S), realize wires of widths $2W$ and $3W$, respectively.

In fact, there are multiple wiring patterns to realize a wire of width $3W$. Other than the wiring pattern in (e) of Figure 1, the pattern in (f), denoted as (2S-2W-2S-1W-1S), or its mirror image (1S-1W-2S-2W-2S), which is not shown

in the figure, also realizes a wire of width $3W$. First, the wiring patterns in (d), (e), and (f) of Figure 1 require different numbers of tracks: 9, 7, and 8, respectively. Second, the coupling capacitance is different for each of the wiring patterns. In Section 3.2, it is shown that wiring pattern (d) has the lowest coupling capacitance and (e) has the highest coupling capacitance among the patterns (d)–(f). As the coupling capacitance directly affects the timing performance and the power consumption of a net, the different wiring patterns represent a trade-off among timing, power, and routing resources.

If fact, for the 9 tracks required of the (3S-3W-3S) wiring pattern, one could also use the 9 tracks for 4 $1W$ wires, which could be used as 4 parallel wires of a single net to further reduce the wiring resistance. Alternatively, it could be used for routing two nets, both of effective width $2W$, or one of effective width $3W$ and one of $1W$. In other words, using only tracks of $1W$ (and spacing of $1S$), routing perhaps can be more flexible, and different wiring patterns may be advantageous in different scenarios.

3. EXPERIMENTAL SETUP

To analyze the trade-offs among routing resources, timing, and power, we perform an experiment to compare traditional wire sizing and parallel wiring techniques. We shall do that with a set of nets obtained from a ICCAD 2012 placement contest benchmark circuit, namely, superblue3 [22]. The placement solution of superblue3 is obtained by SimPLR (ICCAD 2012 placement contest winner) [10]. A global routing solution of the placement is then generated using a publicly available academic routing tool NCTUgr [15]. Next, a subset of the routed nets of various lengths and fan-outs are selected for this study.

In this study, we perform wire sizing on the set of selected nets. The wire sizing is performed using either wire segments of different widths or segments of multiple parallel wires. The wire sizing solutions are then evaluated in terms of timing, power, and routing resources. For routing resources, we consider the total routing area required for both the wiring tracks and spacing tracks.

To obtain the timing and power of each net, we perform an extraction of the resistive and capacitive parasitics for each selected net. In the evaluation each selected net is driven by an inverter using the inverter library from the ISPD 2010 clock synthesis contest [20] (smallest library we have available). The input to the inverter is a ramp with 100 ps slew. The delay of each net is determined using NGSPICE [17].

We shall describe the wire sizing algorithm and the process for extracting parasitics in the remainder of this section.

3.1 Wire sizing or selection of wiring patterns

Wire sizing has been used to satisfy the timing constraints of critical nets. Several works [4, 5, 19] used wire sizing to optimize a weighted-sum of sink delays. In [21], an optimal buffer insertion algorithm to minimize the maximum sink delay in an RC-tree under the Elmore delay model was presented. The algorithm could also be adapted to perform optimal buffer insertion to meet required arrival time constraints at all sinks. In [13, 14], the work of [21] was extended to handle simultaneous buffer and wire sizing.

The optimal wire sizing solutions for the selected nets of superblue3 are obtained based on the wire sizing algorithm of [13, 14]. The only difference here is that instead of choosing a width for a wire segment, the problem is that of selecting a suitable wiring pattern for the segment. Here, wires of different widths are also wiring patterns available for selection.

We shall provide a simple review of the wire sizing algorithm in [13, 14] using an example illustrated in Figure 2. Consider the problem of selecting a wire pattern to realize each edge in the interconnect tree in Figure 2 such that the maximum delay from the root to the sink (or leaf) nodes is minimized. Let wn denote the number of wiring patterns available.

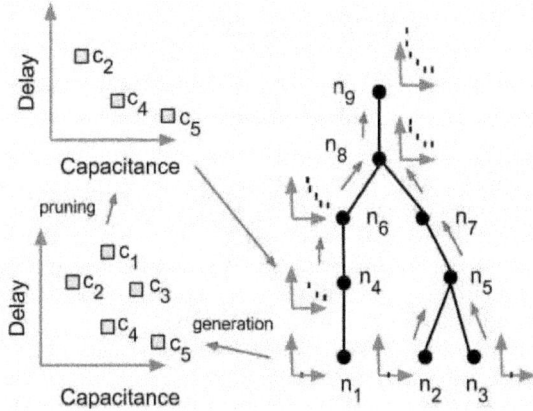

Figure 2: Illustration of how candidate solutions are propagated towards the root of an interconnect tree in the wire sizing algorithm.

A candidate solution is created at each leaf node (n_1, n_2, and n_3). Each candidate c_i stores the maximal downstream delay to any leaf and the total downstream capacitance, denoted as ($cap_i, delay_i$). For a leaf node n_i, the candidate solution has zero delay and the capacitance of the leaf node itself. Next, each candidate solution is propagated toward the root node (driver). When a candidate is propagated over an edge, all possible wiring patterns are enumerated to realize the edge traversed, i.e., every candidate solution at a node results in wn candidates at its parent node. The downstream capacitance and maximal delay of each new candidate depends on the candidate from which it was created and the wiring pattern realizing the traversed edge.

In Figure 2, the single candidate at node n_1 is propagated to node n_4, generating wn new candidates at node n_4 (in this example, $nw = 5$). If the candidates at node n_4 are examined, they all most likely have different downstream capacitances and delays. For each candidate of n_4, labeled c_1, c_2, c_3, c_4, and c_5, its corresponding downstream capacitance and delay are shown in the plot next to the node. In the plot, the horizontal axis is the downstream capacitance and the vertical axis is the maximum delay to the leaf node.

Consider candidate solutions c_1 and c_2. As the capacitance and delay of c_1 are both higher than those of c_2, we say that c_1 is dominated by c_2. A dominated candidate can never be a part of the optimal solution and may therefore be pruned. Similarly candidate c_3 is dominated by candidate c_4.

When the propagation of candidate solutions results in two branches meeting together at a node, a candidate ($cap_l, delay_l$) from the left branch should be combined with

a candidate ($cap_r, delay_r$) from the right branch to create a new candidate solution as follows:

$$(cap_l + cap_r, \max(delay_l, delay_r)).$$

If there are m candidates on the left and n candidates on the right, the total number of non-dominated candidates can be shown to be at most $m + n - 1$. Consequently, for a RC tree that is a strictly binary tree, the complexity of this algorithm is polynomial [14].

To apply the above algorithm, we extend the existing wire sizing algorithm to be a wire pattern selection algorithm. A library of wiring patterns is created. In the library, each wiring pattern has an associated per-unit-length resistance and per-unit-length capacitance. In the next section, we present the extraction of parasitics for each wiring pattern included in the library. Moreover, we will also show that the wire sizing algorithm can be made more efficient as we do not have to consider generating wn candidate solutions for each candidate solution that is propagated upstream.

3.2 Extraction of parasitics

The capacitive coupling of 3D structures can be computed using fastCap [16] or FFTCAP [18]. Such programs consider finding the capacitive coupling of n ideal conductors in a lossless dielectric medium. The capacitive coupling matrix C is defined to be $q = Cp$ where $q \in R^n$ is the charge on the n ideal conductors and $p \in R^N$ is the potential of the n ideal conductors. In the following, we use wires and conductors interchangeably.

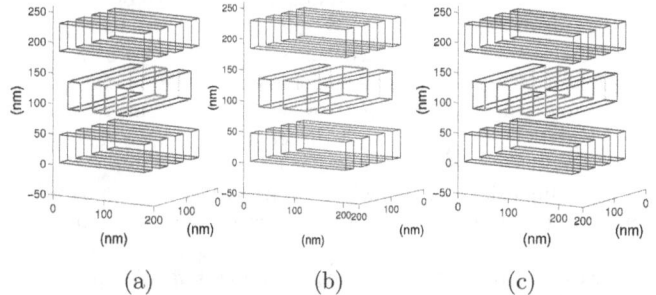

(a)   (b)   (c)

Figure 3: The respective figures shows the modeling of wiring patterns (1S-1W-1S), (2S-2W-2S), and (1S-1W-1S-1W-1S) for capacitance extraction. The capacitance extraction of other wiring patterns is carried out with similar models.

As capacitive coupling is known to be local [7], we consider the following layout structure for capacitance extraction: The wiring pattern of interest is sandwiched between two $1W$ wires, as shown in Figure 1. This set of wires reside in the middle layer of a 3-layer structure. The top and bottom layers of wires are of minimum width ($1W$) and minimum spacing ($1S$). Moreover, the wires on the bottom and top layers, shown in blue in Figure 3, are of orthogonal direction to the wiring pattern of interest and are sufficiently long to cover the lateral span of the wires in the middle layer. In Figure 3, we show in red three wiring patterns of interest, namely, (1S-1W-1S), (2S-2W-2S), and (1S-1W-1S-1W-1S). Adjacent wires to the red wiring patterns in the same layer are shown in yellow, as in Figure 1.

FastCap computes a wire coupling matrix C given a system of wires. Each element C_{ij} in C corresponds to the capacitive coupling between wires i and j. For some wiring patterns two or more wires may belong to the same net. Such wires should be treated as one net and not multiple separate wires. The $n \times n$ wire coupling matrix C for a system of n wires should be transformed into an equivalent $m \times m$ net coupling matrix $\bar{C}$, where m is the number of nets, realized with n wires. In such a net coupling matrix, each net_i $(1 \leq i \leq m)$ is realized with k_i parallel wires and $\sum_{i=1}^{m} k_i = n$.

Each element $\bar{C}_{ij}$ can be computed by summing up the charge on the wires realizing net_i when the potential on all wires realizing net_j is set to 1 and the potential of all other wires is set to 0. The charge on each wire given the potential on each wire can be computed from $Cv = q$ (where C is obtained using FastCap).

Assume a system of n wires. Let $\bar{r}_i = [r^1, \dots, r^n]^T$ be a vector where $r^t = 1$ if wire t belongs to net i, otherwise $r^t = 0$. Then $\bar{C}_{ij} = \bar{r}_i^T C \bar{r}_j$. The complete equivalent capacitance matrix $\bar{C}$ can be obtained as follows:

$$R = [\bar{r}_1, \dots, \bar{r}_m], \qquad (1)$$
$$\bar{C} = R^T C R.$$

The coupling of the wiring pattern of interest is obtained (in the worst case) as the sum of the capacitive coupling to all the other nets in the equivalent coupling matrix. For each wiring pattern, a per-unit-length capacitance is computed and stored in the wiring pattern library.

The effective resistance of the minimum width wires is given in the ITRS roadmap predictions for 2014 [9]. The effective resistivity in the roadmap is adjusted to obtain the resistance of wires that are $2W$ and $3W$ under the assumption that all wires of $1W$, $2W$ and $3W$ have the same lining thickness. Consequently, a wider wire has relatively thinner lining compared to a narrow wire. It also means that the resistance of a $2W$ wire is lower when compared to the effective resistance of two parallel $1W$ wires.

The dimensions of the wires, relative dielectric constant, effective resistance in the wiring patterns are taken from the ITRS roadmap predictions for 2014 [9]. The wires in $M1$ are 24 nm wide and have a height of 45.6 nm. The pitch is 48 nm and the vertical spacing between two layers is 45.6 nm. The effective relative dielectric constant is 4.2 and the effective resistance is $6.0 u\Omega$-cm.

4. IMPLICATIONS OF EXTRACTED PARASITICS

The extracted resistive and capacitive parasitics for each of the different wiring patterns shown in Figure 1 are plotted in Figure 4, where the horizontal axis is for the wire resistance and the vertical axis is for the wire capacitance. For each data point in the plot, we label the wiring pattern that produces that point, as well as the total number of tracks required by that wiring pattern.

From Figure 4, we can see that there are wiring patterns whose resistive and capacitive parasitics are both higher than those of some other wiring patterns. Let R_i and C_i be the resistive and capacitive parasitics of wiring pattern i. If there are two wiring patterns i and j, it should be clear that if $R_i > R_j$ and $C_i > C_j$, when a candidate solution $(cap, delay)$ is being propagated upstream through an tree edge and the wire sizing algorithm has to generate wn candidate solutions from $(cap, delay)$, the new candidate

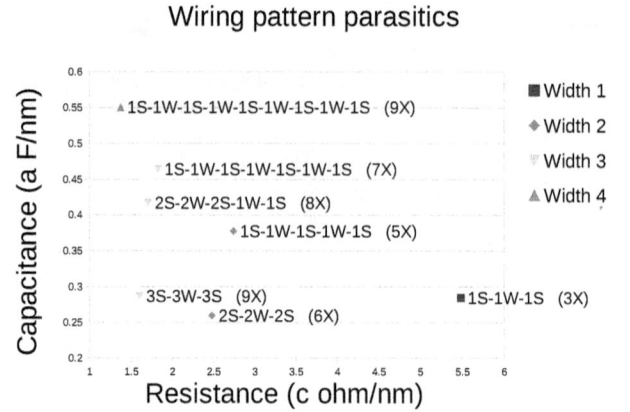

Figure 4: Illustration of the capacitance-resistance tradeoff between different wiring patterns.

solution generated using pattern i would have a higher capacitance and maximum delay than the solution generated using pattern j. In other words, wiring pattern i should not be considered in the first place. We say that wiring pattern i is dominated by wiring pattern j. In other words, the wiring pattern library should maintain only a set of non-dominated wiring patterns for an efficient implementation of the wire sizing algorithm.

However, we would like to point out that domination of wiring patterns is context-dependent. In Figure 4, we find that (3S-3W-3S) dominates both (2S-2W-2S-1W-1S) and (1S-1W-1S-1W-1S-1W). Moreover, (2S-2W-2S-1W-1S) also dominates (1S-1W-1S-1W-1S-1W). However, in some situation, there may only be 8 routing tracks available and a strict density constraint stating that the maximum spacing allowed is a spacing of $1S$. In such a situation, the only feasible wiring pattern of the three that would allow an effective wire width of $3W$ is (1S-1W-1S-1W-1S-1W). Therefore we say that the wiring patterns exhibit conditional dominance.

In the following, we give a few other scenarios. First, we introduce a density requirement parameter D, which denotes the maximum allowed spacing, i.e., spacing of width wider than D tracks is not permitted.

1. If there are 9 tracks available and $D = 1$, the patterns that should be considered would be (1S-1W-1S-1W-1S-1W-1S-1W-1S), (1S-1W-1S-1W-1S-1W-1S), (1S-1W-1S-1W-1S), and (1S-1W-1S).

2. If there are 9 tracks available and $D = 2$, the patterns that should be considered would be (1S-1W-1S-1W-1S-1W-1S-1W-1S), (2S-2W-2S-1W-1S) (and its mirror image), and (2S-2W-2S).

3. If there are 9 tracks available and $D = 3$, the patterns that should be considered would be (1S-1W-1S-1W-1S-1W-1S-1W-1S), (3S-3W-3S), and (2S-2W-2S).

In general, we draw the following conclusions: (1) Wiring patterns with wide spacing reduces the capacitance. (2) Wiring patterns using wide wires are advantageous if the routing resources are available and density constraint requirements allow larger spacing. (3) Wiring patterns using parallel wires are more flexible to different resource and density constraints.

However, it is important to note that the plot in Figure 4 is obtained with manufacturing parameters obtained from the ITRS roadmap. Different non-dominated wiring patterns will be obtained if these manufacturing parameters change. For example, with a small change in the manufacturing parameters, (1S-1W-1S) may not be dominated by (2S-2W-2S).

5. ANALYSIS OF WIRE SIZING SOLUTIONS

In this section we evaluate the wire sizing techniques using variable width wires or parallel wires. To this end, we create three different wiring pattern libraries. In the first library, denoted by *WL1*, wide wires are allowed. In the second library, denoted as *WL2*, only parallel wires are allowed. In the third library, denoted as *WL3*, is a hybrid library that allow wiring patterns using both wide and parallel wires. The wiring patterns for each library is shown in Table 1.

Table 1: Wiring pattern libraries *WL1*, *WL2*, and *WL3*.

WL1	WL2	WL3
1S-1W-1S	1S-1W-1S	1S-1W-1S
2S-2W-2S	1S-1W-1S-1W-1S	1S-1W-1S-1W-1S
3S-3W-3S	1S-1W-1S-1W-1S-1W-1S	2S-2W-2S
	1S-1W-1S-1W-1S-1W-1S-1W-1S	1S-1W-1S-1W-1S-1W-1S
		2S-2W-2S-1W-1S
		1S-1W-1S-1W-1S-1W-1S-1W-1S
		3S-3W-3S

Then, we perform wire sizing to minimize the maximum delay with two scenarios. In the first scenario, we set the available routing tracks for each wire segment in a net to be 9 tracks. In the second scenario, the number of available routing tracks is 7. In both cases, the density constraint parameter D is set to be 2, and the wiring pattern libraries are then pruned accordingly based on the discussions in Section 4.

The results on timing, power, and routing resource utilization are shown in Figure 5. Not surprisingly, we find that the hybrid library *WL3*, which has access to all wiring patterns, can achieve the best timing results on all of the nets. When we compare between *WL1* (wide wires) and *WL2* (parallel wires), the results are dependent on the routing resources available and the properties of the different nets. With 9 wiring tracks available, the parallel wiring technique can achieve better timing result compared to that of the wide wiring technique for 4 out of 6 nets. However, when the number of wire tracks is 7, the parallel routing technique cannot use the pattern (1S-1W-1S-1W-1S-1W-1S-1W-1S) and the performance of the parallel wiring technique is worse. In fact, the library *WL1* can achieve lower maximum delays on all 6 nets compared to the parallel wire library *WL2*.

The parallel wire library *WL2* consumes the most power as the available wiring patterns have minimal spacing to neighboring nets, and therefore higher coupling capacitances. Another reason for the parallel wiring technique to consume more power is that the goal of minimizing maximum delay will inherently use wider wires (more parallel wires), leading to higher overall capacitance and higher power consumption.

The number of routing tracks used by the wide wire library *WL1* are for most nets less than those used by the parallel wire library *WL2* or the hybrid library *WL3*. However, the power and routing resources could be reduced substantially if they were considered in the optimization. Optimization of other metrics given a maximum delay constraint has been addressed in [14] and the technique in [13] could be adopted to use a library of wiring patterns.

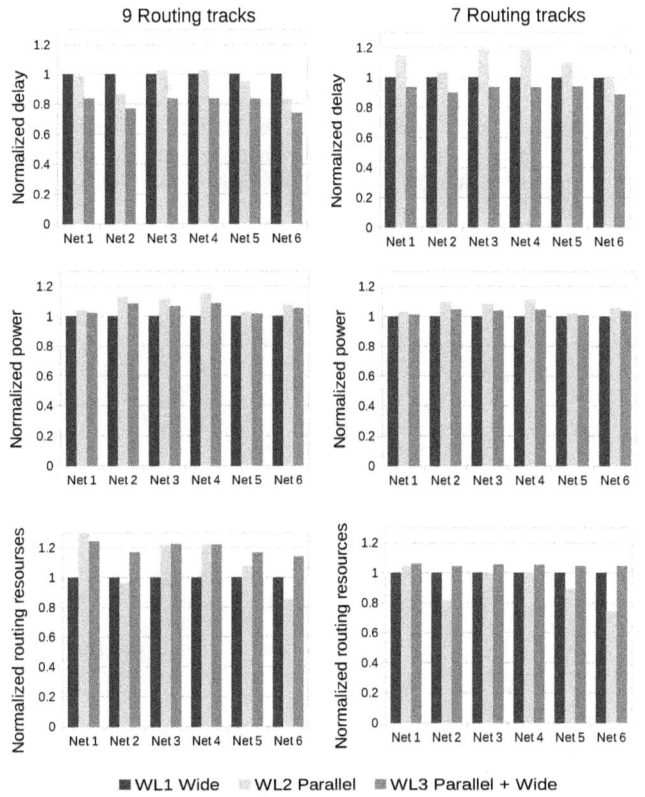

Figure 5: Wire sizing of six nets with 9 tracks available (left) and 7 tracks available (right) under a density constraint allowing a maximum spacing width of $2S$.

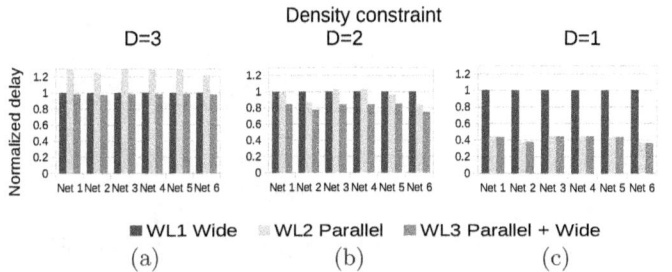

Figure 6: Wire sizing of six nets with 9 tracks available and a maximum spacing of $3S$ in (a) $2S$ in (b) and $1S$ in (c).

Next, the six nets are sized again under three different scenarios. In each scenario 9 routing tacks are available and the density constraint is set to $D = 3$, $D = 2$, and $D = 1$ respectively. The wire pattern libraries are again pruned as described in Section 4. The normalized delays in each scenario are shown in Figure 6. From the figure is can be observed that when high density layouts are required, wire sizing using parallel wires becomes increasingly advantageous compared to wire sizing using wide wires. In fact, when the density constraints is set to $D = 1$ wire sizing can only be performed using parallel wires (the pruned wire pattern library *WL2* contains the same wire patterns as the hybrid wire pattern library *WL3*). From Figure 6(c) it is clear that the parallel wires can improve the timing even under such strict density constraints.

6. IMPLICATIONS ON ROUTING

It should be evident by now that wire sizing using parallel wires is not really a technically challenging problem, because an existing algorithm can be adapted to perform the task in a fairly straightforward manner. However, the use of parallel wires does present new opportunities and challenges to routing.

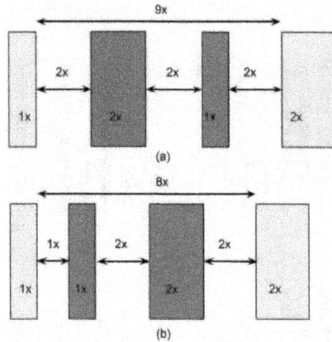

Figure 7: Illustration of the impact of ordering non symmetric routing patterns depending on context.

In Figure 7(a), we show the routing of three nets, with the left net being assigned a width of $1W$, the middle net a width of $3W$, and the right net a width of $2W$. If instead, we use the mirror image of the parallel wiring pattern in (a), we can route the middle net with 8 tracks nets, as shown in Figure 7(b). This implies that routing have to be performed with wire sizing taken into account.

This example illustrates that the net ordering and track assignment can have impact on the required number of tracks required for global routing. However, the net ordering or track assignment step is typically performed after global routing. The inter-dependency of global routing and net ordering have to be considered in the development of future routing tools. Moreover, the example demonstrates that the problem of simultaneous wire sizing of multiple nets sharing routing resources can be challenging.

7. CONCLUSIONS AND FUTURE WORK

As wider wires require wider spacing, sizing nets with wide wires may lead to density problems in sub-20nm designs. Therefore, realizing a net with multiple parallel wires is an alternative approach. In this paper we have investigated the parasitics and performance of routing a net with parallel wires compared to with wider wires. The performance is shown to be very dependent on the routing resources available and density constraints. In the future we plan to apply simultaneous wire sizing of multiple nets using parallel wires. We also plan to study issues related to crosstalk noise.

8. ACKNOWLEDGMENTS

This work was supported in part by the National Science Foundation under award CCF-1065318 and the Semiconductor Research Corporation under task 1292-074.

9. REFERENCES

[1] K. B. Agarwal and S. Banerjee. Integrated model-based retargeting and optical proximity correction. *SPIE*, pages 79740F–79740F–10, 2011.

[2] T. Ando, M. Takeshita, R. Takasu, Y. Yoshii, J. Iwashita, S. Matsumaru, S. Abe, and T. Iwai. Pattern freezing process free litho-litho-etch double patterning. *SPIE*, pages 71402H–71402H–8, 2008.

[3] N. B. Cobb and A. Zakhor. Large-area phase-shift mask design. *SPIE*, pages 348–360, 1994.

[4] J. Cong and C.-K. Koh. Simultaneous driver and wire sizing for performance and power optimization. *Very Large Scale Integration Systems*, pages 408–425, 1994.

[5] J. Cong, K. Leung, and D. Zhou. Performance-driven interconnect design based on distributed RC delay model. *DAC*, pages 606–611, 1993.

[6] C.-C. Fu, Y. Tungsheng, and D. R. Stone. Enhancement of lithographic patterns by using serif features. *Electron Devices*, pages 2599–2603, 1991.

[7] T. Gao and C. Liu. Minimum crosstalk channel routing. *ICCAD*, pages 692–696, 1993.

[8] K. Harazaki, Y. Hasegawa, Y. Shichijo, H. Tabuchi, and K. Fujii. High accurate optical proximity correction under the influences of lens aberration in 0.15 μm logic process. *Microprocesses and Nanotechnology Conference*, pages 14–15, 2000.

[9] ITRS: Roadmap 2011. http://www.itrs.net/links/2011itrs/home2011.html.

[10] M.-C. Kim, J. Hu, D. Lee, and I. L. Markov. A simplr method for routability-driven placement. *ICCAD*, pages 80–84, 2011.

[11] A. Krasnoperova, J. A. Culp, I. Graur, S. Mansfield, M. Al-Imam, and H. Maaty. Process window OPC for reduced process variability and enhanced yield. *SPIE*, pages 1200–1211, 2006.

[12] D. Laidler, P. Leray, K. Dhave, and S. Cheng. Sources of overlay error in double patterning integration schemes. *SPIE*, pages 69221E–69221E–11, 2008.

[13] J. Lillis, C.-K. Cheng, and T.-T. Y. Lin. Optimal wire sizing and buffer insertion for low power and a generalized delay model. *ICCAD*, pages 138–143, 1995.

[14] J. Lillis, C.-K. Cheng, and T.-T. Y. Lin. Simultaneous routing and buffer insertion for high performance interconnect. *GLSVLSI*, pages 148–155, 1996.

[15] W.-H. Liu, W.-C. Kao, Y.-L. Li, and K.-Y. Chao. Nctu-gr 2.0: Multithreaded collision-aware global routing with bounded-length maze routing. *on CAD of Integrated Circuits and Systems*, pages 709–722, 2013.

[16] K. Nabors and J. White. FastCap: A multipole accelerated 3-D capacitance extraction program. *Computer-Aided Design of Integrated Circuits and Systems*, pages 1447–1459, 1991.

[17] NGSPICE. http://ngspice.sourceforge.net/.

[18] J. Phillips and J. White. A precorrected-FFT method for electrostatic analysis of complicated 3-D structures. *Computer-Aided Design of Integrated Circuits and Systems*, pages 1059–1072, 1997.

[19] S. Sapatnekar. RC interconnect optimization under the elmore delay model. *DAC*, pages 387–391, 1994.

[20] C. Sze. ISPD 2010 high performance clock network synthesis contest: Benchmark suit and results. *ISPD*, pages 143–143, 2010.

[21] L. van Ginneken. Buffer placement in distributed RC-tree networks for minimal elmore delay. *Circuits and Systems*, pages 865–868, 1990.

[22] N. Viswanathan, C. Alpert, C. Sze, Z. Li, and Y. Wei. ICCAD-2012 CAD contest in design hierarchy aware routability-driven placement and benchmark suite. *ICCAD*, pages 345–348, 2012.

[23] E. Yang, C. H. Li, X. H. Kang, and E. Guo. Model-based retarget for 45nm node and beyond. *SPIE*, pages 727428–727428–8, 2009.

[24] A. Yehia Hamouda, J. Word, M. Anis, and K. S. Karim. Aerial image retargeting (AIR): achieving litho-friendly designs. *SPIE*, pages 797411–797411–8, 2011.

[25] H. Zhang, Y. Deng, J. Kye, and M. D. F. Wong. Impact of lithography retargeting process on low level interconnect in 20nm technology. *SLIP*, pages 3–10, 2012.

Create, then Innovate

Gene A Frantz
Rice University
Houston, Texas 77005
genf@rice.ecu

ABSTRACT

Innovation seems to be a measure of success for most technologists. We are proud of our innovations which have significantly contributed to society. But we seem not to speak much about creativity and how it relates to innovation. Is creativity part of the innovation process? Or is the innovation process the result of creativity? This talk will suggest an interesting set of definitions that put these two concepts into perspective. Examples will be shown that will support this proposed definitions.

Categories and Subject Descriptors

A.2 [Reference]: dictionaries, encyclopedias

General Terms

Creativity, Innovation, Business

Keywords

Impossible, answer, visionary, vision, Innovate, Create

Bio

Gene A Frantz is a Professor in the Practice at Rice University. He took this position after 39 years at Texas Instruments where he retired as TI's Principal Fellow. For the last 30 years he applied his passion for finding new opportunities and for creating new businesses utilizing TI's digital signal processing technology taking, a leadership role in starting businesses within the corporate structure. As a result, he is a recognized leader in DSP technology both within TI and throughout the industry. He received is BSE from the University of Central Florida, his MSEE from Southern Methodist University and his MBA from Texas Tech University.

Frantz is a Fellow of the IEEE, holds 48 patents in the area of memories, speech, consumer products and DSP, has written more than 100 Papers and articles and continually presents at Universities and conferences worldwide. Frantz has been recognized as an industry expert and has been widely quoted in the media due to his tremendous knowledge and vision in DSP.

GLSVLSI'14, May 21–23, 2014, Houston, Texas, USA.
ACM 978-1-4503-2816-6/14/05.

Smart Nodes of Internet of Things (IoT): A Hardware Perspective View & Implementation

Edgar Sánchez-Sinencio
Texas A&M University
Analog and Mixed-Signal Center
College Station, TX 78758 USA
s-sanchez@tamu.edu

ABSTRACT

A lot of efforts have been done on software layer to propose the idea of Internet of Things (IoT). However, the functionality of IoT highly depends on the implementation of its end nodes. And there is little attention about realization of such IoT Smart Nodes. As mixed signal IC researchers, we analyze the urgent needs of IoT Smart Nodes and their implementation challenges. We focus this talk on the two of the most important practical issues: energy harvesting & regulating, and wireless transceiver.

A high efficient self-sustained energy harvester inside the Smart Nodes can power numerous possibilities to IoT network. For the various inputs, it should accommodate nonlinear energy sources and achieve Maximum Power Point Tracking (MPPT).

As it is considered the most power hungry part, the wireless transceiver in the IoT Smart Nodes needs special focus to minimize its power consumption. The transceiver should adapt its power consumption based on the available amount of the energy and the amount of the transferred data in time.

Categories and Subject Descriptors

C.2.1 [**Network Architecture and Design**]: Network communications, Wireless communication; C.3 [**Special-Purpose and Application-Based Systems**]: Real-time and embedded systems; B.7.1 [**Integrated Circuits**]: VLSI (very large scale integration)

General Terms

Algorithms, Measurement, Performance, Design, Reliability, Experimentation.

Keywords

Internet of Things; Mixed Signal IC; Smart Nodes; Energy Harvesting and Regulating; Wireless Transceiver.

BIOGRAPHY

Edgar Sánchez-Sinencio was born in Mexico City, Mexico. He received the degree in communications and electronic engineering (Professional degree) from the National Polytechnic Institute of Mexico, Mexico City, the M.S.E.E. degree from Stanford University, Stanford, CA, USA, and the Ph.D. degree from the University of Illinois at Urbana-Champaign, IL, USA, in 1966, 1970, and 1973, respectively. He is currently the TI J. Kilby Chair Professor and Director of the Analog and Mixed-Signal Center at Texas A&M University, College Station, TX, USA. His current interests are in the area of harvesting techniques, power management, ultra-low power analog circuits, data converters and medical electronics circuit design. He has graduated 57 M.Sc. and 40 Ph.D. students. He is a co-author of six books on different topics, including RF circuits, low-voltage low-power analog circuits, and neural networks.

Dr. Sánchez-Sinencio is a former Editor-in-Chief of IEEE TRANSACTIONS ON CIRCUITS AND SYSTEMS II and a former IEEE CAS Vice President-Publications. In November 1995 he was awarded an Honoris Causa Doctorate by the National Institute for Astrophysics, Optics and Electronics, Mexico. This degree was the first honorary degree awarded for microelectronic circuit-design contributions. He is a co-recipient of the 1995 Guillemin-Cauer Award for his work on cellular networks. He received the Texas Senate Proclamation # 373 for Outstanding Accomplishments in 1996. He was also the co-recipient of the 1997 Darlington Award for his work on high-frequency filters. He received the IEEE Circuits and Systems Society Golden Jubilee Medal in 1999. He is the recipient of the prestigious IEEE Circuits and Systems Society 2008 Technical Achievement Award. He was the IEEE Circuits and Systems Society's Representative to the IEEE Solid-State Circuits Society during 2000–2002. He was a member of the IEEE Solid-State Circuits Society Fellow Award Committee from 2002 to 2004. He is currently a Distinguished Lecturer of the IEEE Circuits and Systems Society (2012–2013). His website is http://amesp02.tamu.edu/~sanchez/.

GLSVLSI'14, May 21–23, 2014, Houston, Texas, USA.
ACM 978-1-4503-2816-6/14/05.
http://dx.doi.org/10.1145/2591513.2597169

WriteSmoothing: Improving Lifetime of Non-volatile Caches Using Intra-set Wear-leveling

Sparsh Mittal, Jeffrey S. Vetter and Dong Li
Future Technologies Group, Oak Ridge National Laboratory
Oak Rige, Tennessee, USA 37830
{mittals,vetter,lid1}@ornl.gov

ABSTRACT

Driven by the trends of increasing core-count and bandwidth-wall problem, the size of last level caches (LLCs) has greatly increased. Since SRAM consumes high leakage power, researchers have explored use of non-volatile memories (NVMs) for designing caches as they provide high density and consume low leakage power. However, since NVMs have low write-endurance and the existing cache management policies are write variation-unaware, effective wear-leveling techniques are required for achieving reasonable cache lifetimes using NVMs. We present WriteSmoothing, a technique for mitigating intra-set write variation in NVM caches. WriteSmoothing logically divides the cache-sets into multiple modules. For each module, WriteSmoothing collectively records number of writes in each way for any of the sets. It then periodically makes most frequently written ways in a module unavailable to shift the write-pressure to other ways in the sets of the module. Extensive simulation results have shown that on average, for single and dual-core system configurations, WriteSmoothing improves cache lifetime by 2.17× and 2.75×, respectively. Also, its implementation overhead is small and it works well for a wide range of algorithm and system parameters.

Categories and Subject Descriptors

B.3.2 [**Hardware**]: MEMORY STRUCTURES—*Cache memories*; B.8.m [**Hardware**]: PERFORMANCE AND RELIABILITY—*Miscellaneous*

Keywords

Non-volatile memory; device lifetime; cache memory; intra-set write variation; wear-leveling; write endurance

1. INTRODUCTION

To meet the demands of increasing number of on-chip cores and circumvent the problem of memory bandwidth-wall, modern processors are using very large last level caches. For example, Intel's Itanium 9560 processor uses 32MB last level cache (LLCs) [1]. Conventionally, processor caches have been designed using SRAM since it provides low access latency and has high write

GLSVLSI'14, May 21–23, 2014, Houston, Texas, USA.
Copyright 2014 ACM 978-1-4503-2816-6/14/05 ...$15.00.
http://dx.doi.org/10.1145/2591513.2591525.

endurance. However, SRAM has large leakage power consumption and hence, large LLCs designed with SRAM consume huge amount of power and chip area [13]. For example, the leakage power of the LLCs contributes to 63% and 56% of the total leakage power in Xeon Tulsa and Core 2 Penryn processors respectively, which corresponds to 30% and 20% of the total power in these processors [11].

To address this issue, researchers have explored use of non-volatile memories, such as resistive RAM (ReRAM), spin transfer torque RAM (STT-RAM) and phase change memory (PCM) for designing on-chip caches [6,9,18]. NVMs provide high density and scalability, consume very low leakage power and intrinsically avoid the need of refresh operations for maintaining data-integrity (unlike embedded DRAM devices) [12]. A crucial limitation of NVMs, however, is that their write endurance is orders of magnitude smaller than that of SRAM and DRAM. This low endurance value may lead to very small device lifetimes. For example, while the write endurance of SRAM and DRAM is in excess of 10^{15}, the write endurance of ReRAM, STT-RAM and PCM are only 10^{11}, 4×10^{12} and 10^8, respectively [8,10,16,18].

Further, the conventional cache management policies have been designed for optimizing performance and energy-efficiency, and they do not take the write endurance into account. In an attempt to leverage temporal locality, they may significantly increase the number of writes on a few cache blocks. This may cause those blocks to fail much earlier than the anticipated lifetime assuming uniform write distribution. As an example, conventional selective-way based cache reconfiguration approaches (e.g. [14]) only control the *number* of turned-off ways and do not control *which* ways will be selected for being turned-off. Thus, they are likely to keep the same ways turned-on (or turned-off) during the entire execution of the program which may exacerbate the problem of limited write-endurance. Similarly, with LRU (least-recently used) replacement policy, the most recently used data are expected to be repeatedly accessed and hence, the number of writes to the physical blocks which store these data is expected to increase much more than those in the remaining ways. To illustrate this, we take the example of povray benchmark from SPEC06 suite and execute it with a ReRAM L2 cache (the simulation parameters are shown in Section 5). We observe that due to write-variation, the cache lifetime is observed to be only **2.3 days**, although assuming an ideal uniform write-distribution to all L2 cache blocks, the lifetime would be **38.7 years**. This clearly shows the need of a wear-leveling technique.

In this paper, we present WriteSmoothing, a technique for improving cache lifetime by mitigating intra-set write variation. WriteSmoothing logically divides the cache-sets into multiple modules, for example, in a cache with 4096 sets and 32 modules, each module contains 128 sets. WriteSmoothing works on the following key idea: if the intra-set write variation in a module is larger than a threshold, then the most heavily written cache ways can be temporarily made "unavailable" which will shift the write-pressure on the remaining ways. Different cache ways are made unavailable in rotation and this leads to wear-leveling which improves the cache lifetime (Section 3). WriteSmoothing does not require static profiling or modification of program binary and its overhead is very small (Section 4).

We perform exhaustive simulations using an x86-64 simulator and benchmarks from SPEC CPU2006 suite and HPC (high performance computing) field (Section 5). Results have shown that WriteSmoothing is effective in reducing the intra-set write variation which leads to increase in cache lifetime (Section 6). For single and dual-core systems, the average improvement in cache lifetime are $2.17\times$ and $2.75\times$, respectively. Also, WriteSmoothing has very small effect on performance and energy efficiency. Additional experiments show that WriteSmoothing works well for different system and algorithm parameters.

2. BACKGROUND AND RELATED WORK

Improvement in lifetime of NVM caches can be obtained by reducing the number of writes and uniformly distributing them over different blocks (wear-leveling). The reduction in number of writes is achieved by using additional levels of caches [2] or write coalescing buffers [17] and avoiding redundant writes [9, 20]. These approaches are orthogonal and complementary to our technique, and hence, can be synergistically integrated with it.

Since caches show both inter-set and intra-set write variation [13], wear-leveling can be performed at the level of inter-set [5, 18] or intra-set [18]. In this paper, we propose an intra-set wear-leveling technique. Intra-set write variation increases with increasing associativity and it can be larger than inter-set write variation for some workloads hence, addressing it is extremely important ([18], also see Section 6). Further, WriteSmoothing can be integrated with the techniques for mitigating inter-set write variation and error correction/detection to improve the cache lifetime even further.

Wang et al. [18] propose an intra-set wear-leveling technique, which works by periodically flushing the block seeing a write-hit to change the cache block location of the hot data-item. A limitation of this technique is that it does not detect the write-variation present in the application and thus, it may blindly flush the cache. This is especially harmful for applications which have small write-variation but high write intensity. Moreover, while attempting to uniformly spread the writes to the cache, it may increase the writes on the main memory leading to contention, energy loss and endurance issues in main memory.

3. SYSTEM ARCHITECTURE

Background and Notations: We logically divide the cache-sets into multiple (e.g. 32) "modules", where each module contains several sets. We collect the number of cache writes for each way at the granularity of a single module. For example, if the cache has 32 modules, 4096 sets and 8 ways, then a group of 128 sets form one module and a total of 32×8 counters are used. The 8 counters for module 0 record the number of writes in each way for any of the sets numbering 0 to 127 and so on. We term the way of each module as a "sub-way".

Let S, A, B and T denote the number of cache sets, associativity, block-size and tag-size, respectively. In this paper, we assume, B = 64B and T = 40bits. Also, let $w_{i,j}$ denote the number of writes on any block at set i and way-index j. Further, let W_{avg} denote the

average number of writes on all the blocks. Then, the coefficient of intra-set write variation (IntraV) for the entire cache is defined as follows [18],

$$IntraV = \frac{100}{S \cdot W_{avg}} \sum_{i=1}^{S} \sqrt{\frac{\sum_{j=1}^{A} \left(w_{i,j} - \sum_{r=1}^{A} w_{i,r}/A \right)^2}{A - 1}} \quad (1)$$

Note that compared to [18], we express IntraV as percentage and hence, multiply the value by 100. Similarly, we can define the IntraV for each module (called ModuleIntraV). Let M denote the number of cache-modules and $e_{m,j}$ denote the writes on sub-way j of a module m. Let $E_{m,avg}$ denote the average writes on all the sub-ways of module m. Then, we have

$$ModuleIntraV[m] = \frac{100}{E_{m,avg}} \sqrt{\frac{\sum_{j=1}^{A} \left(e_{m,j} - \sum_{r=1}^{A} e_{m,r}/A \right)^2}{A - 1}} \quad (2)$$

3.1 Key Idea

WriteSmoothing works on the idea that if the ModuleIntraV[m] for a module m is greater than a threshold λ, then the data in the most-frequently written (MFW) way can be transferred to that in the least-frequently written way and the MFW way can be temporarily made unavailable, which helps in shifting the future write-pressure to the remaining blocks. The MFW way is expected to store hot data, and thus, future writes are expected to be redirected especially to the least-frequently written way. If desired, the unavailable way can be turned-off to save leakage energy, however, we do not implement this in our experiments since NVMs consume negligible amount of leakage power. Although WriteSmoothing works to directly reduce *intra-set* write-variation, by virtue of working at the granularity of cache module, it accounts for *inter-set* write-variation also.

In a module, WriteSmoothing makes the same physical cache-way unavailable for all the sets, although in different sets of a module, the actual position of the most frequently written way may be different. To address this issue, we can minimize the number of cache sets in a module (i.e., $M = S$), such that each cache set has a set of counters to track each way. However, this incurs a large profiling overhead. Hence, the choice of M provides a balance between profiling overhead and accuracy. We study the sensitivity of wear-leveling to the choice of M in Section 6.2. The general conclusion based on our study is that for a reasonably large value of M (e.g. 32 or 64), its effect on wear-leveling is small.

3.2 Algorithm Description

Algorithm 1 shows the pseudo-code for WriteSmoothing, which runs after K cycles (e.g. K = 5 million) and can be a kernel module. The algorithm works as follows. For each module, ModuleIntraV is computed. Wear-leveling for any module is only performed if the ModuleIntraV is greater than λ. This helps in minimizing the algorithm overhead for workloads with small write-variation. The algorithm searches for the sub-way with the highest and the lowest $nWrite$ values and transfers the data from W_{max} sub-way to W_{min} sub-way. The TransferDataBetweenSubWays function copies valid data from the W_{max} sub-way to the W_{min} sub-way. If this data-item is clean, it is only copied if the destination data-item is invalid, otherwise it is flushed. If this data-item is dirty, it is copied regardless of the state of destination data-item. The reason for this is that the data-item at W_{max} location is expected to be hot and hence, keeping it in cache is likely to be beneficial. The Make-

Algorithm 1: Algorithm for WriteSmoothing

1. Let $IsAvailable[0:M-1][0:A-1]$ show whether a particular sub-way is available
2. Let $nWrite[0:M-1][0:A-1]$ denote the writes on each sub-way
3. Let $ModuleIntraV[0:M-1]$ denote the IntraV for each module (calculated from $nWrite$ values)
4. **for** *each module m* **do**
5.   Let $NumUnavailable[m]$ show the total number of unavailable ways in module m
6.   **if** $ModuleIntraV[0:M-1] > \lambda$ **then**
7.   Let W_{max} be the sub-way with the highest number of writes where $IsAvailable[m][W_{max}]$ is TRUE
8.   Let W_{min} be the sub-way with the least number of writes
9.   TransferDataBetweenSubWays(m,W_{max},W_{min})
10.   MakeUnavailable(m, W_{max})
11.   `/* If the number of unavailable ways in m has become larger than Z, make the least written way available */`
12.   **if** $NumUnavailable[m] > Z$ **then**
13.   Let W_{low} be the sub-way with the least number of writes among all sub-ways w, such that $W_{low} \neq W_{min}$ and $IsAvailable[m][W_{max}]$ is FALSE
14.   MakeAvailable(m, W_{low})
15.   **end**
16.   **else**
17.   **if** $NumUnavailable[m] > 0$ **then**
18.   Let W_{low} be the sub-way with the least number of writes among all sub-ways w, such that $IsAvailable[m][W_{max}]$ is FALSE
19.   MakeAvailable(m, W_{low})
20.   **end**
21.   **end**
22. **end**

Unavailable function write-backs the dirty data and flushes clean valid data of a sub-way and marks it as unavailable for the next interval. The MakeAvailable function simply marks a sub-way as available for the next interval.

If the number of unavailable ways in a module increases greater than Z, a single least-frequently written way is made available to keep the performance loss small. Note that at any point of time, the number of unavailable ways in different modules can be different. This is an important feature of our technique which helps in accounting for inter-set write variation and also keeping the performance loss small.

In processors with higher number of cores, not all the cores may run applications at the same time. Also, with private LLC or partitioned shared LLC, the cache space of each application is optimized for performance by exploiting temporal locality. In these scenarios, the write-variation is expected to be high and hence, we expect that with increasing number of cores, the benefits of WriteSmoothing will increase further.

4. IMPLEMENTATION AND OVERHEAD ASSESSMENT

Storage Overhead: We assume 40-bit counters for recording $nWrite$ values. Also, the data transfer between sub-ways is performed using a temporary buffer, as used in previous works [19] which has 128 registers, each 64B wide. These registers can also be used as intermediate storage for computing ModuleIntraV, since this happens in series (and not in parallel) with data-transfer. Thus, the percentage overhead of WriteSmoothing implementation compared to the L2 cache can be computed as

$$Overhead = \frac{(M \times A \times 40) + (128 \times 64 \times 8)}{S \times A \times (B + T)} \times 100 \quad (3)$$

As an example, for a 4MB, 16-way cache with 32 modules, this $Overhead$ is only 0.24% of the L2 cache. Assuming some additional logic for computation and data-transfer, we conservatively take 0.5% as the upper bound of the overhead of WriteSmoothing, which is very small.

Latency and Energy Overhead: We assume that for each module, computing ModuleIntraV takes 40 cycles. For each module which undergoes wear-leveling, 60 cycles are consumed for selecting W_{max}. In Section 6.2 we also conduct experiments assuming $4\times$ higher overhead of computation and data-transfer and observe that the performance and energy loss of WriteSmoothing still remains small. Transfer of data takes $L_W + 4$ cycles, where L_W is the write latency of L2 NVM cache (shown in Table 1) and 2 cycle each is consumed in writing 64B data to and from the buffer over a 32B-wide bus. The extra writes due to algorithm execution are accounted in the number of L2 writes, used for computing energy, lifetime etc. Note that since the algorithm runs after a few million cycles, its overhead is easily amortized over the interval-length. Moreover, a small increase in latency of LLC is easily hidden by the instruction-level parallelism (ILP). Thus, WriteSmoothing has minimal effect on performance, as confirmed by our experiments (see Section 6.1).

5. EXPERIMENTAL METHODOLOGY

Simulation Infrastructure: We use interval-core model in Sniper x86-64 multicore simulator [3]. The frequency of processor is 2GHz. L1 I/D caches are 32KB 4-way LRU caches and are private to each core. L2 cache is shared among cores and its parameters are shown in Table 1, which are obtained using NVsim tool [7]. In this paper, we assume a ReRAM L2 cache, and based on it, WriteSmoothing can be easily applied to caches designed with other NVMs. Due to their properties, NVMs are more suitable to be used as last level caches and not first level caches. For this reason, in this paper, we assume that NVM is used for designing the L2 cache and apply WriteSmoothing algorithm in the L2 cache. The latency of main memory is 220 cycles. The peak memory bandwidth for single and dual-core systems are 10 and 15GB/s, respectively and contention is also modeled.

Table 1: Parameters for ReRAM L2 Cache

	2MB	4MB	8MB	16MB
Hit latency (ns)	4.33	4.13	4.74	6.21
Miss latency (ns)	1.47	1.44	1.55	1.81
Write latency (ns)	21.72	21.55	21.87	23.09
Hit Energy (nJ)	0.524	0.547	0.646	0.679
Miss Energy (nJ)	0.204	0.188	0.194	0.200
Write Energy (nJ)	0.834	0.851	0.925	0.967
Leakage Power (W)	0.204	0.325	0.785	1.118

Workloads: All 29 SPEC CPU2006 benchmarks with *ref* inputs and 5 benchmarks from HPC field (shown as italics in Table 2) are taken as single-core workloads. Using these, 17 dual-core multiprogrammed workloads are randomly created such that each benchmark is used exactly once. These workloads are shown in Table 2.

Evaluation Metrics: We show the results on 1.) Relative lifetime 2.) IntraV 3.) Weighted speedup (called relative performance) [14] 4.) Percentage energy loss and 5.) Absolute increase in MPKI (miss per kilo-instructions). The lifetime is defined as the inverse of the maximum number of writes on any block. We model

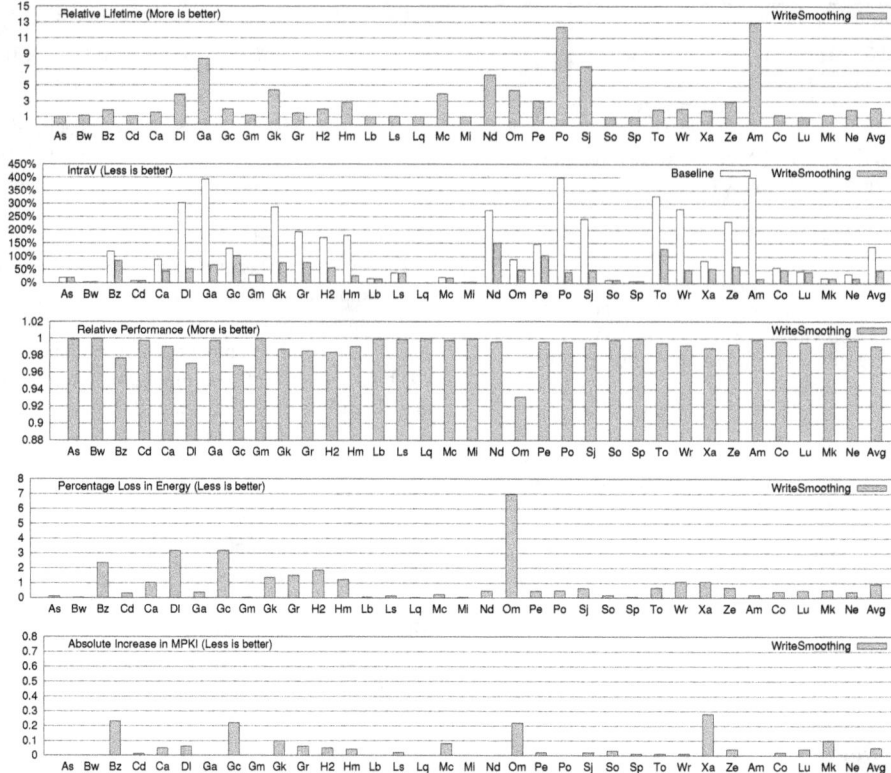

Figure 1: WriteSmoothing Results for Single-core System

Table 2: Workloads Used in the Paper

Single-core workloads and their acronyms
As(astar), Bw(bwaves), Bz(bzip2), Cd(cactusADM), Ca(calculix)
Dl(dealII), Ga(gamess), Gc(gcc), Gm(gemsFDTD), Gk(gobmk)
Gr(gromacs), H2(h264ref), Hm(hmmer), Lb(lbm), Ls(leslie3d)
Lq(libquantum), Mc(mcf), Mi(milc), Nd(namd), Om(omnetpp)
Pe(perlbench), Po(povray), Sj(sjeng), So(soplex), Sp(sphinx)
To(tonto), Wr(wrf), Xa(xalancbmk), Ze(zeusmp), *Am(amg2013)*
Co(CoMD), Lu(LULESH), Mk(MCCK), Ne(Nekbone)
Dual-core workloads (Using acronyms shown above)
AsDl, GcGa, BzXa, LsLb, GkNe, OmGr, NdCd, CaTo
SpSo, LqPo, SjWr, GmMk, PeZe, HmH2, BwMi, McLu, CoAm

the energy of L2 cache, which is computed using parameters from Table 1 and includes the contribution of extra writes due to algorithm execution (see Section 4). The energy consumed by the counters is orders of magnitude smaller than that consumed by the L2 cache and hence, is ignored. For dual-core system, we have also computed the fair speedup [15] and have found the fair speedup to be almost the same as weighted speedup. Thus, WriteSmoothing does not cause unfairness. For brevity, we omit these results. Speedup values are averaged using geometric mean and the remaining metrics are averaged using arithmetic mean [15]. Simulations are performed till each core runs 500M instructions. In dual-core system, the program which finishes earlier is allowed to run, but its IPC is only recorded for the first 500M instructions. Remaining metrics are computed for the entire simulation (following well-established simulation methodology [4, 14, 15]).

6. EXPERIMENTAL RESULTS

6.1 Main Results

Figure 1 and 2 show the results for single and dual-core, respectively, which are obtained using the following parameter values: Z

= 3, K = 5M cycles, λ =15%, 16-way set-associativity, 4MB L2 with M = 32 for single-core system and 8MB L2 with M = 64 for dual-core system. Our baseline is a cache which uses LRU replacement policy but does not use any wear-leveling technique.

We now analyze the results. Firstly, for some workloads, baseline IntraV can be as high as 400%, for example Ga (gamess), Po (povray), Am(amg2013). Also, we observe that on average, for single and dual-core system, 87.8% and 89.3% of the write accesses happen to just the MRU way of the 16-way cache (figure omitted for brevity). This highlights the need of using an intra-set wear-leveling technique for achieving reasonable cache lifetime. On average, for the single and the dual-core systems, improvement in lifetime are 2.17× and 2.75×, respectively. For some workloads, the improvement in lifetime is more than 10×, for example, Po, Am and LqPo (libquantum-povray). For a few other workloads, such as Ga, Sj (sjeng), GcGa (gcc-gamess), CoAm (CoMD-amg2013), the improvement in lifetime is more than 7×. This shows the effectiveness of WriteSmoothing.

WriteSmoothing reduces the IntraV from 136.6% to 45.7% for single-core system, and from 136.4% to 49.2% for dual-core system. As seen from the figure on relative lifetime and IntraV, the improvement in lifetime achieved depends on the intra-set variation present in the original application. By virtue of computing ModuleIntraV, WriteSmoothing performs shifting and incurs its overhead only when the intra-set write variation in original application is high. Thus, for applications such as Lb (lbm), Lq, Sp (sphinx), Mi (milc), LsLb (leslie3d-lbm) etc., WriteSmoothing does not incur performance or energy overhead. This feature is especially beneficial for workloads such as Lb, which have very high write intensity but low intra-set write variation. For the single and the dual-core systems, relative performance values are 0.99× and 0.99×, respectively. The reason WriteSmoothing maintains the performance

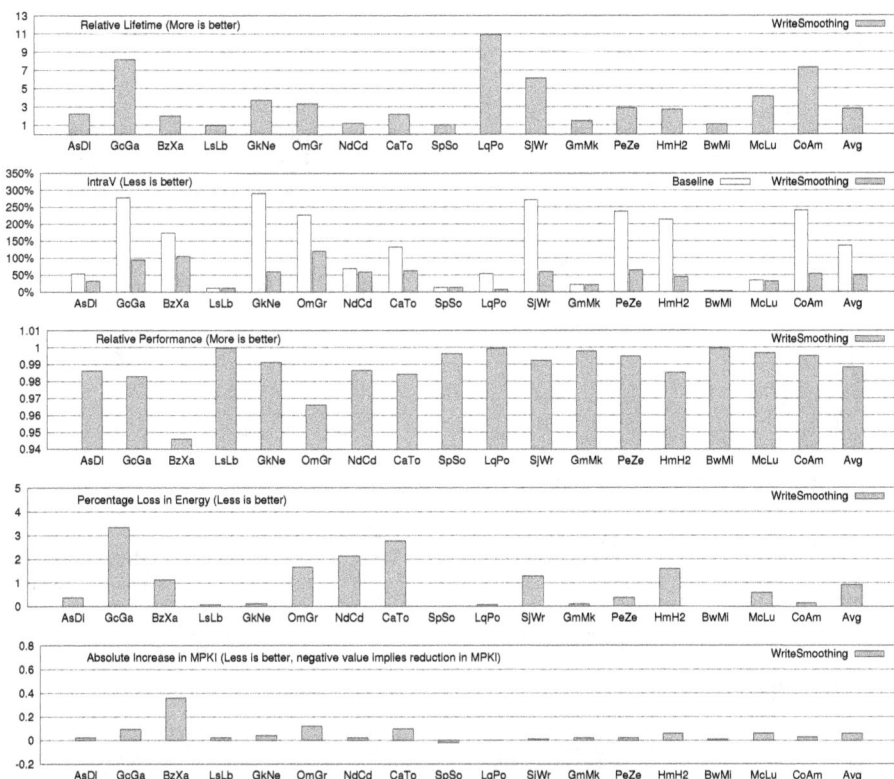

Figure 2: WriteSmoothing Results for Dual-core System

close to $1\times$ is that it makes cache ways unavailable only when the intra-set write-variation is high, which happens when the application does not fully utilize the cache and a few ways remain unused. In such a case, making some ways unavailable does not significantly harm the performance. Only Om (omnetpp) and BzXa (bzip2-xalan) show relative performance less than $0.95\times$, since these workloads are very sensitive to L2 cache performance.

For the single and the dual-core systems, on average, increase in MPKI are 0.05 and 0.06, respectively and loss in energy are 0.93% and 0.92%, respectively. These values are very small and thus, WriteSmoothing does not increase the DRAM traffic appreciably, which is a significant improvement over previous data-invalidation based techniques (e.g. [5,18]), which lead to increased DRAM traffic. Our wear-leveling approach also provides the benefit of write density minimization [13] which can help in lowering the chip-temperature and cooling cost. Moreover, NVMs offer high density and low leakage power compared to SRAM and WriteSmoothing addresses the crucial limitation of NVMs, namely their limited write endurance. For these reasons, a small increase in miss-rate and energy may be acceptable. Further, as we show in Section 6.2, by changing the algorithm parameters (viz. M, λ, K and Z), a designer can strike a balance between acceptable algorithm implementation overhead and desired improvement in lifetime.

6.2 Parameter Sensitivity Results

We now evaluate the sensitivity of WriteSmoothing for different parameters. The results are summarized in Table 3. Except the parameter mentioned, the values of all parameters are same as used in the default case. For comparison purposes, the value with default case is also shown.

Change in Number of Modules (M): On increasing M, the granularity of wear-leveling is also increased leading to higher improvement in lifetime. However, this also leads to a small increase in the algorithm implementation overhead. Opposite is seen on reducing the number of modules.

Change in Threshold λ: Reducing λ increases the aggressiveness of wear-leveling, which increases the improvement in the lifetime at the cost of a small increase in energy loss, and vice-versa.

Change in Interval Size (K): Smaller value of interval size leads to more frequent wear-leveling which improves the cache lifetime, although it leads to a small increase in energy loss due to more frequent data-transfer. At 10M cycle interval size, the opportunity of wear-leveling is missed, although due to reduced data-transfer, the energy loss is also reduced.

Change in Maximum Unavailable Ways (Z): Change in Z does not monotonically affect the improvement in lifetime, since different applications have different associativity requirements and cache usage intensity. Change in Z has very small effect on the energy loss and increasing Z increases the energy loss since the effective cache associativity is reduced. Considering these factors, for a 16-way cache, a value of $Z = 3$ or $Z = 4$ is suitable.

Higher algorithm overhead: We evaluate WriteSmoothing assuming a latency overhead which is $4\times$ that of shown in Section 4 (i.e. 160 cycles for computing ModuleIntraV and 240 cycles for selecting W_{max}). As shown in Table 3, the relative performance still remains $0.99\times$ and energy loss is small (close to 1%). This confirms that, due to the reasons mentioned in Section 4, overhead of WriteSmoothing is quite small.

Change in Associativity (A): For a fixed capacity, a cache with lower associativity has higher miss-rate and smaller number of replacement candidates, which reduces the non-uniform distribution of writes, leading to smaller value of IntraV. This is evident from the values of IntraV for baseline cache and can also be understood by considering the extreme cases, viz. a direct-mapped cache and

Table 3: Parameter Sensitivity Results (Rel. = Relative, LT. = Lifetime, WrSm = WriteSmoothing, Perf. = Performance, Energy loss values are in percentage.). Default values are shown in Section 6.1.

	Rel. LT.	IntraV Base	IntraV WrSm	Rel. Perf.	Energy Loss	Δ MPKI
Single-core System						
Default	2.17	136.6	45.7	0.99	0.93	0.05
M =8	1.80	136.6	50.2	0.99	0.83	0.04
M =16	1.94	136.6	47.7	0.99	0.85	0.04
M =64	2.49	136.6	43.6	0.99	1.03	0.06
M =128	2.61	136.6	41.3	0.99	1.15	0.06
λ =10%	2.26	136.6	42.8	0.99	1.26	0.08
λ =20%	2.00	136.6	48.7	0.99	0.72	0.04
K =3M	2.18	136.6	44.3	0.99	1.06	0.05
K =10M	2.03	136.6	51.0	0.99	0.74	0.05
Z =2	2.07	136.6	48.2	0.99	0.83	0.04
Z =4	2.21	136.6	44.6	0.99	1.00	0.05
⇑ Overhead	2.13	136.6	45.3	0.99	1.07	0.05
8-way	1.72	107.1	34.4	0.99	1.14	0.07
32-way	2.37	167.7	60.7	0.99	0.73	0.05
2MB L2	1.82	103.7	37.6	1.00	0.46	0.02
8MB L2	2.58	175.4	53.8	0.98	2.00	0.10
Two-core System						
Default	2.75	136.4	49.2	0.99	0.92	0.06
M =16	2.20	136.4	53.1	0.99	0.82	0.05
M =32	2.25	136.4	51.1	0.99	0.87	0.05
M =128	3.25	136.4	47.3	0.99	1.02	0.06
M =256	3.85	136.4	45.1	0.98	1.19	0.07
λ =10%	3.25	136.4	45.3	0.98	1.22	0.08
λ =20%	2.37	136.4	52.6	0.99	0.76	0.04
K =3M	2.75	136.4	49.2	0.99	1.00	0.06
K =10M	2.63	136.4	51.9	0.99	0.79	0.05
Z =2	2.61	136.4	51.0	0.99	0.85	0.05
Z =4	2.68	136.4	49.0	0.99	0.98	0.06
⇑ Overhead	2.75	136.4	49.1	0.99	1.09	0.06
8-way	2.11	106.6	38.9	0.98	2.14	0.08
32-way	3.80	170.0	61.6	0.99	0.98	0.05
4MB L2	2.22	100.9	42.2	0.99	1.16	0.05
16MB L2	2.99	171.0	58.1	0.98	1.80	0.08

a fully-associative cache. WriteSmoothing works well for all associativity values and improves lifetime in proportion to the write-variation present in the baseline. For dual-core system with 32-way cache, the lifetime improvement is 3.8×.

Change in Cache Capacity: Since applications have fixed working set size, an increase in cache size improves the hit-rate and thus, only a few blocks are repeatedly accessed and cache evictions are reduced. This leads to higher write-variation, as evident from IntraV values. Depending on IntraV, WriteSmoothing provides large improvement in lifetime, with only small loss in performance and energy.

For all the above parameters, relative performance is greater than 0.97× and increase in MPKI is less than 0.11, which confirm that WriteSmoothing works well for a wide range of system and algorithm parameters.

7. CONCLUSION

Addressing the limitations posed by low write-endurance of NVMs is essential for making them a universal memory solution. In this paper, we presented WriteSmoothing, a technique for improving lifetime of non-volatile caches by minimizing intra-set write variation. Exhaustive evaluation over different benchmarks, algorithm and system parameters have shown that WriteSmoothing is effective in improving cache lifetime and incurs very small loss in performance and energy. Our future work will focus on integrating WriteSmoothing with write-minimization techniques to improve the cache lifetime even further.

8. REFERENCES

[1] http://download.intel.com/newsroom/archive/Intel-Itanium-processor-9500_ProductBrief.pdf.

[2] J. Ahn and K. Choi. Lower-bits cache for low power STT-RAM caches. In *ISCAS*, pages 480–483, 2012.

[3] T. E. Carlson et al. Sniper: Exploring the level of abstraction for scalable and accurate parallel multi-core simulations. In *SC*, 2011.

[4] M. Chaudhuri. Pseudo-LIFO: the foundation of a new family of replacement policies for last-level caches. In *MICRO*, 2009.

[5] Y. Chen et al. On-chip caches built on multilevel spin-transfer torque RAM cells and its optimizations. *J. Emerg. Technol. Comput. Syst.*, 9(2):16:1–16:22, 2013.

[6] X. Dong et al. Circuit and microarchitecture evaluation of 3D stacking magnetic RAM (MRAM) as a universal memory replacement. In *DAC*, pages 554–559, 2008.

[7] X. Dong et al. NVsim: A circuit-level performance, energy, and area model for emerging nonvolatile memory. *IEEE TCAD*, 31(7):994–1007, 2012.

[8] Y. Huai. Spin-transfer torque MRAM (STT-MRAM): Challenges and prospects. *AAPPS Bulletin*, 2008.

[9] Y. Joo et al. Energy-and endurance-aware design of phase change memory caches. In *DATE*, pages 136–141, 2010.

[10] Y.-B. Kim et al. Bi-layered RRAM with unlimited endurance and extremely uniform switching. In *VLSIT*, pages 52–53. IEEE, 2011.

[11] S. Li et al. CACTI-P: Architecture-level modeling for SRAM-based structures with advanced leakage reduction techniques. In *ICCAD*, pages 694–701, 2011.

[12] S. Mittal. A Cache Reconfiguration Approach for Saving Leakage and Refresh Energy in Embedded DRAM Caches. Technical report, Iowa State University, USA, 2013.

[13] S. Mittal. A survey of architectural techniques for improving cache power efficiency. *Sustainable Computing: Informatics and Systems*, 2013.

[14] S. Mittal et al. FlexiWay: A Cache Energy Saving Technique Using Fine-grained Cache Reconfiguration. In *IEEE ICCD*, pages 100–107, 2013.

[15] S. Mittal et al. MASTER: A Multicore Cache Energy Saving Technique using Dynamic Cache Reconfiguration. *IEEE TVLSI*, 2013.

[16] M. K. Qureshi et al. *Phase change memory: From devices to systems*, volume 6. Morgan & Claypool Publishers, 2011.

[17] G. Sun et al. A novel architecture of the 3D stacked MRAM L2 cache for CMPs. In *HPCA*, pages 239–249, 2009.

[18] J. Wang et al. i²WAP: Improving non-volatile cache lifetime by reducing inter- and intra-set write variations. In *HPCA*, pages 234–245, 2013.

[19] X. Wu et al. Hybrid cache architecture with disparate memory technologies. In *ISCA*, pages 34–45, 2009.

[20] P. Zhou et al. Energy reduction for STT-RAM using early write termination. In *ICCAD*, pages 264–268, 2009.

Reliability-Aware Cross-Point Resistive Memory Design

Cong Xu†, Dimin Niu†, Yang Zheng†, Shimeng Yu‡, Yuan Xie†
†Pennsylvania State University, {czx102,dun118,yxz184,yuanxie}@cse.psu.edu
‡Arizona State University, shimeng.yu@asu.edu

ABSTRACT

The transition metal oxide (TMO) resistive random access memory (ReRAM) has been identified as one of the most promising candidates for the next generation non-volatile memory (NVM) technology. Numerous TMO ReRAMs with different materials have been developed and demonstrate attractive characteristics, such as fast read/write speed, low power consumption, high integrated density, and good scalability. Among them, the most attractive characteristic of ReRAM is its cross-point structure which features a $4F^2$ cell size. However, the existence of sneak current and voltage drop along the wire resistance in a cross-point array brings in extra design challenges. In addition, a robust ReRAM design needs to deal with both soft and hard errors. In this paper, we summarize mechanisms of both soft and hard errors of ReRAM cells and propose a unified model to characterize different failure behaviors. We quantitatively analyze the impact of cell failure modes on the reliability of cross-point array. We also propose an error resilient architecture which avoids unnecessary writes in the hard error detection unit. Experimental results show that our design can extend the lifetime of ReRAM up to 75% over the design without hard error detections and up to 12% over the design with "write-verify" detection mechanism.

1. INTRODUCTION

As the scaling of traditional DRAM and Flash are facing many severe challenges, some emerging non-volatile memory technologies (NVM), such as Phase Change Memory (PCM), Spin-transfer-torque RAM (STT-RAM), and Resistive RAM (ReRAM) evolve as promising candidates for next generation memory systems. Among them, the TMO based ReRAM has shown excellent features, including low power, fast access speed, small cell size, good scalability, as well as back-end-of-the-line (BEOL) CMOS process compatibility.

Soft and hard errors are vital concerns when designing a memory system. A soft error is a random, recoverable upset-ting of the information stored in a memory cell, while a hard error is a permanent corruption of a memory cell resulting from physical defects. Although most emerging non-volatile memory technologies are not charge-based storage, they still suffer from soft and hard errors. The presence of hard errors normally results from the limited endurance compared to DRAM and SRAM technologies. The cause of soft error is distinctive for each NVM. For example, soft errors of PCM refer to the resistance drift behaviors, or the thermal disturbance from adjacent cells. As for STT-RAM, the stochastic properties imply that both write and read operations can bring in soft errors. For ReRAM, soft errors are caused by the retention failures of the cell, and hard errors are due to the limited endurance of the cell. In the presence of both soft and hard errors, the reliability of ReRAM array, especially for its unique cross-point structure, becomes a serious design challenge. Specifically, there is no isolation between cells in a cross-point array, and thus a single cell failure can affect the read/write noise margin when reading/writing a cell in the same row or column with one or more bad cells.

Most prior work on NVM reliability tackles either soft errors [1, 2] or hard errors [3, 4] assuming only a single type of error exists in the target NVM technology, which makes them less effective under some practical cases. Therefore, it is necessary to consider the co-existence of both soft errors and hard errors when designing an error resilient architecture. Conventionally, once an error is detected, a "rewrite-read-verify" (also called "write-verify") is often involved to determine whether it is a hard error or soft error. However, this approach may bring in additional writes which further wear out the memory cells. Hence, it is critical to avoid such unnecessary writes.

The major contributions of this paper are:

- We systematically studied the mechanisms of both soft and hard errors of ReRAM and proposed a unified model to characterize their behaviors.

- We analyzed the impact of different types of failure on the reliability of a cross-point ReRAM array, and identified that some types of failure affect read noise margin most while others may affect worst-case write noise margin and write energy.

- We proposed an error resilient architecture to deal with both soft and hard errors for ReRAM design. A key innovation in our design is the hard error detection unit. We avoid the unnecessary writes by determining the error type based on the unique characteristics of retention failure (soft error) and each type of endurance failure (hard error).

This work is supported in part by SRC grants, NSF 1218867, 1213052. This material is based upon work supported by the Department of Energy under Award Number DE - SC0005026.

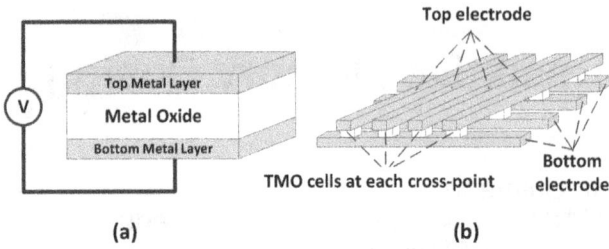

Figure 1: An overview of (a) TMO MIM structure and (b) a cross-point ReRAM array.

2. PRELIMINARIES

In this section, the background of TMO ReRAM is presented. Then the cross-point architecture of ReRAM array is introduced.

2.1 Background of ReRAM Technology

A schematic view of the Metal-Insulator-Metal (MIM) structure of a TMO ReRAM cell is shown in Figure 1a. The ReRAM cell has a very simple structure: a TMO based storage layer sandwiched by two metal layers of electrodes, named top electrode (TE) and bottom electrode (BE). To store information in the cell, low resistance state (LRS or ON-state) and high resistance state (HRS or OFF-state) are used to represent the logic "1" and "0", respectively. As shown in Figure 1a, in order to switch an ReRAM cell between the LRS and the HRS, an external voltage with specified polarity, magnitude, and duration is required. According to the switching behaviors, the ReRAM can be classified into two categories: the bipolar and the unipolar ReRAM. For a unipolar ReRAM cell, the resistance switching only depends on the magnitude of the external voltage applied across the cell. In contrast, for a bipolar ReRAM cell, the LRS-to-HRS switching (aka RESET operation) and the HRS-to-LRS switching (aka SET operation) occur at different voltage polarities. In this work, we focus on bipolar ReRAM technology as they are more commonly used in cross-point memory.

2.2 ReRAM Array Structure

As shown in Figure 1b, in the cross-point structure, each ReRAM cell is sandwiched by a TE and a BE at each cross-point of the array without access device. In this structure, each cell only occupies an area of $4F^2$ (F is the feature size of the fabrication technology), which is the theoretical smallest cell area for a single-layer memory structure. Such a simple structure make ReRAM a low cost-per-bit memory technology.

As mentioned, the write operations (SET and RESET) of an ReRAM cell require external voltage across the cell with specified magnitude and duration. To write a cell in the cross-point array, the wordline and bitline(s) connected to the cells should be selected (or activated). In addition, the other unselected wordlines and bitlines are set to a certain voltage or left floating to avoid disturbance of other cells in the array. However, even with proper write schemes [5], the sneak current of the half-selected cells along with the current of selected cells result in significant IR drop on the wire resistance, reducing the amount of voltage drop on the selected cells. As for a read operation, the selected wordline is biased at V_{read} while all the other wordlines and bitlines are grounded. Then the state of the selected cells are read out by the sense amplifiers connected to the selected bitlines.

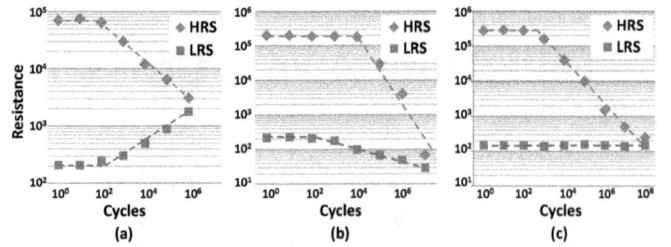

Figure 2: Types of endurance failure (hard errors) in TMO ReRAM cell: (a) Type I, (b) Type II, and (c) Type III.

3. FAILURE IN A CROSS-POINT ARRAY

In the cross-point structure, the reliability issues come from two different sources: structural error and cell error. The structural error is determined by the special organization of the cross-point array. The impact of voltage drop, sneak current, write/read schemes, as well as data pattern on the array reliability are well studied in literatures [5–7]. They show that the structural errors can be mitigated with exhaustive worst-case design. However, it is difficult to eliminate cell errors. To implement a reliable ReRAM array, specialized detection circuitry are required. In this section, we first discuss the resistance switching behaviors of ReRAM cell. Based on the discussion, mechanisms and modeling of soft errors and hard errors of ReRAM cell are presented. Then, the impact of the cell errors at the array design is evaluated.

3.1 ReRAM switching mechanism

Several studies have been conducted to reveal the physical mechanisms of the resistance switching behaviors. The filamentary model is widely accepted to explain the resistance switching phenomenon in the TMO ReRAM [8]: switchings between LRS and HRS are caused by the formation and rupture of the nanoscale conductive filaments (CFs) at the anode interface of the cell. For forming operation can be considered as a "preset" operation of the ReRAM cell.

3.2 ReRAM soft and hard errors modeling

Soft errors of the ReRAM cell come from the retention failure. The retention failure is a recoverable upset of the resistance of the cell. The retention failure can either be a sudden resistance drop of the HRS cell (HRS failure) or an abrupt resistance increasing of the LRS cell (LRS failure). The retention failure behaviors result from the random generation of the Vo (HRS failure), and the recombination of Vo with oxygen ions (LRS failure). Both of them imply that the retention failure is a stochastic process. Theoretically, either the HRS failure or the LRS failure can happen, but in many practical cases the LRS failure dominates under low current operation [9]. Given the operating range of write current in our design, the soft errors are dominated by the LRS failure ("1"-to-"0" flip).

In order to quantify the retention failure behavior, the cumulative failure probability is employed. A simplified model of the cumulative failure probability can be expressed as [10],

$$F(t) = 1 - (1-p)^{\alpha t} \qquad (1)$$

where α is a constant value, t is the retention time, and p is the generation probability of the Vo which is calculated as,

$$p = e^{(qVl/2d-\varepsilon_V)/kT} \qquad (2)$$

Table 1: Parameters of a Cross-Point Array

Metric	Description	Value(s)
$A_{\mathbf{cell}}$	Cell Size	$4F^2$
R_w	Wire Resistance	0.65Ω
$V_{\mathbf{write}}$	Write voltage of selected wordline	$\pm 2V$
$V_{\mathbf{write}}/2$	Write voltage of half selected lines	$\pm 1V$
$V_{\mathbf{SB}}$	Voltage of selected bitline	0
$V_{\mathbf{read}}$	Read voltage	$0.5V$
K_r	Nonlinearity of ReRAM Cell	40
N	Number of wordlines or bitlines	$128,256,512$

where q is the electric quantity of the Vo, V is the applied voltage on the TMO layer, l is the lattice constant, d is the length of the filament's ruptured region, and ε_V is the formation energy of the Vo.

Different from soft errors, the hard errors result from the limited endurance of the ReRAM cell compared to traditional DRAM/SRAM technologies. The endurance failure is caused by a gradual resistance change over the write cycles. According to different behaviors and physical mechanisms, the endurance failures are classified into three categories [11],

1. Type I Failure: This failure is caused by the generation of extra oxide layer at the anode during the SET operations. This layer prevents the movement of the oxygen ions and results in R_{LRS} increment or R_{HRS} decrement.

2. Type II Failure: The programming voltage generated extra Vo, which directly increases the diameter of the CFs. In this failure, both of the R_{LRS} and the R_{HRS} decrease gradually.

3. Type III Failure: This failure results from the undesired consumption of the oxygen ions at stored in the anode. In this case, the combination probability of Vo and oxygen ions will reduce. Thus the R_{HRS} decreases while the R_{LRS} keeps constant.

We proposed a unified model of different types of endurance failure, in which the resistance change can be expressed as,

$$R = R_0(1 + \frac{sgn(c-c_0)+1}{2}\beta(c-c_0)^\gamma) \qquad (3)$$

where R_0 is the initial resistance of LRS or HRS, c_0 is the start cycle that the endurance degradation is observed, and β and γ represent the direction and rate of the resistance change. The results in Figure 2 show that our model with different parameters fits well with experimental data of each failure type [11].

3.3 Impact of different types of failure

A soft error is a recoverable error and is essentially a resistance state transition without applying external voltages. We conclude that soft errors can only affect the information stored in the cells where the endurance failures arise, and will not affect the other cells in the cross-point array. To overcome the soft error, normally some form of the ECC is introduced. We will discuss the corresponding design overheads in Section 4.

Compared to the soft errors, the hard errors are more sereve, especially for the cross-point structure. In general, the reliability concerns about the hard errors are in three aspects: (1) the decreased ratio of $R_{\mathrm{HRS}}/R_{\mathrm{LRS}}$ may degrade the read noise margin and eventually result in a read failure. This problem appears in all the three types of failure; (2)

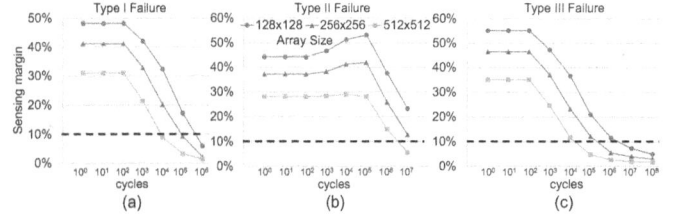

Figure 3: Read noise margin degradation in various array sizes for (a) type I failure, (b) type II failure, (c) type III failure.

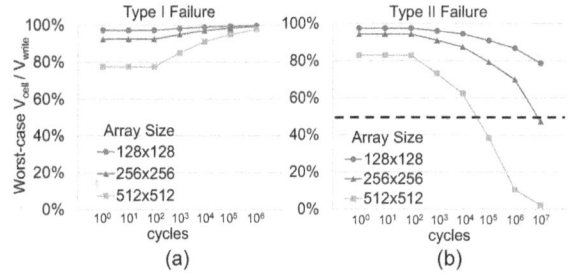

Figure 4: Worst-case voltage drop over cycles in various array size for (a) type I , (b) type II failure

the reduction of R_{LRS} increases the amount of sneak current and thus reduces the worst-case voltage drop on the furthest cell in a cross-point array. This can cause a write failure of the selected cell [5]; (3) the reduction of R_{LRS} also increases the total energy consumption of a cross-point array during the write operation. There are chances that all the activated arrays are under worst-case or near worst-case scenarios, and the total power consumption for a given chip may violate the peak power budget. Breaking power limits will result in unexpected IR drops or excessive current, and even make electro-migration worse etc. (2) and (3) only exist in type II failure in which the R_{LRS} decreases over write cycles.

Figure 3 shows the read noise margin over cycles with various array sizes for different types of failure. The baseline parameters of a cross-point array in summarized in Table 1. We also assume that there is no variation in the initial resistance or resistance degradation rate of the cells in a cross-point array. In other words, we fix the constants in Equation 3. As seen in Figure 3, for type I and III failure, the resistance noise margins degrade gradually because either the R_{HRS} decreases or/and the R_{LRS} increases. However, the trend is different for type II failure. As its R_{LRS} starts to increase earlier than its R_{HRS} starts to decrease, the resistance ratio is boosted and the sensing margin is improved. Even after its R_{HRS} starts to decrease, its read noise margin may continue to go up a little (i.e. by 5%) over a few cycles until a high reduction ratio of R_{HRS} is reached. In fact, the reduction of R_{LRS} helps the cross-point array maintain a reasonable read noise margin in type II failure, compared with type I and III failure. The larger the array size is, the earlier its sensing margin goes below the sensing boundary.

To ensure successful write operations in a cross-point ReRAM design, the cross-point array is always designed for the worst case: (1) V_{write} is large enough so that the furthest cell has enough voltage drop to switch its state given the worst-case data pattern stored in other cells in the cross-point array; (2) V_{write} can not exceed twice the threshold switching voltage to ensure that the half-selected cell which has a voltage drop of $V_{\mathrm{write}}/2$ is not disturbed; (3) the overall write energy

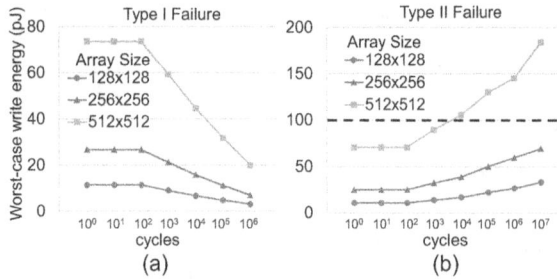

Figure 5: Worst-case write energy per array in various array size for (a) type I (b) type II failure

does not break the power limits. It has been identified that R_{LRS} is the key parameter for designing a cross-point array in terms of worst-case voltage drop and write energy. Since the R_{LRS} is not affected in type III failure, the worst-case write noise margin and write energy are well maintained over cycles for such type of failure. Figure 4 illustrates the worst-case voltage on the furthest cell in a cross-point array over cycles with various array sizes for type I and II failure. Not surprisingly, the voltage drop becomes better over time for type I failure as its R_{LRS} continues to increase. However, the reduction of R_{LRS} poses a significant reliability issue on type II failure. For example, the voltage drop of a 512×512 array can go below half of V_{write} after 10^5 write cycles, and will inevitably cause a write failure [5]. The problem is alleviated in smaller array sizes, but a 256×256 array cannot work reliably after 10^7 write cycles even its read noise margin is still acceptable according to Figure 3b.

The write energy of a cross-point array are much higher than its 1T1R counterpart because all the cells and wire resistance in a cross-point array is consuming energy during the write operation. Given the peak power budget and the number of activated arrays simultaneously, the write energy of a cross-point array should not exceed an upper bound. It is straightforward that the worst-case write energy occurs when all the cells in a cross-point are in LRS. Figure 4 illustrates such worst-case write energy of a cross-point array over cycles with various array sizes. For type I failure, the worst-case energy goes down as its R_{LRS} increases over time. For type II failure, the worst-case energy can increase by several times with the reduction of R_{LRS}. For example, the write energy of a 512×512 array doubles after 10^5 write cycles.

In summary, ReRAM with type I and type III failure suffers from small read noise margin problems and encounters occasional read failures as the resistance ratio of cells shrinks, but they are almost write failure free once the worst-case design is determined during manufacturing. For type II failure, the write failure is a more severe problem due to the reduction of its R_{LRS}. Even writing a good cell with no bad cells may fail if some half-selected cells have reduced R_{LRS}. For all types of failure, there is a clear trade-off between the lifetime and the array size of a cross-point array. The smaller the array size is, the longer the lifetime is. There is an important choice to make for balancing reliability and density at the design stage.

4. ERROR RESILIENCE DESIGN

Most prior work on NVM reliability tackles either soft errors [1, 2] or hard errors [3, 4]. However, a reliable cross-point ReRAM design should be resilient to both soft and hard errors. In our design, we proposed an error resilient architecture to improve the reliability of the system. We classify each failure event into soft error or hard error based on the characteristics of each error type. The basic flow of our detection-handle mechanism is listed step by step,

- If the ECC, which can be as simple as a single-error correcting and double-error detecting (SEC-DED) code, detects a correctable error during a read operation, the data are sent to the read request after correction. At the same time, the hard error detection is triggered.

- The hard error detection unit will determine whether the failed cell is a retention failure (soft error) or an endurance degradation (hard error). It will take extra steps if necessary. The design of the hard error detection unit heavily depends on the failure type, and will be discussed later in this section.

- If the failure event is identified as a hard error, the hard-error tolerating technique must be involved, such as ECP [4] or DPM [3]. In our design we adopt a light version of ECP. However, additional work is required for type II failure. This is because if we simply leave the bad cell as it is, this cell can serve as a half-selected cell when writing a different block address next time. After accumulating a lot of bad cells, there are chances that some of the half-selected cells in a write operation are bad cells and they have lower R_{LRS} than other normal LRS cells, resulting in an unintentional write failure even if the selected cell works perfectly. Therefore, we will apply a RESET pulse on any bad cell in type II failure once it is detected. This ensures the resistance of the bad cell is not smaller than the initial low resistance of a normal cell.

4.1 Hard error detection unit

Most hard error detection works in a "rewrite-read-verify" (or "write-verify" for short) way. The approach is briefly explained as follows. After the error is specified, the correct data are written back, and immediately followed by a read operation. If the read succeed and ECC reports no error, then the previous error was identified as a soft error. If the ECC reports an error in the same location again, this cell will be marked as a bad cell.

The key drawback of this approach is that there is one additional write operation every time when the ECC is triggered. If the soft error rates are high and they trigger the ECC more frequently than the hard errors do, the cells will wear out even earlier.

Our solution to this problem is to identify the error type by leveraging the rational behind each error type in ReRAM. One key observation as discussed in Section 3.2 is that the soft errors of ReRAM cells with low write current are dominated by LRS failure ("1"-to-"0" flip). If there is no write failure and the ECC detects that a cell is identified as "1" while it is supposed to be "0", it cannot be a soft error. In other words, an erroneous "1" in type I and III failure is determined as a hard error. However, the characteristics of each failure type in ReRAM endurance degradation make the design of the hard error detection unit different from each other.

4.1.1 Type I failure

Figure 6 demonstrates the hard error detection mechanism for type I failure. As mentioned, an erroneous "1" is determined as a hard error. While for an erroneous "0", there are two possibilities: an increased R_{LRS} due to cycling

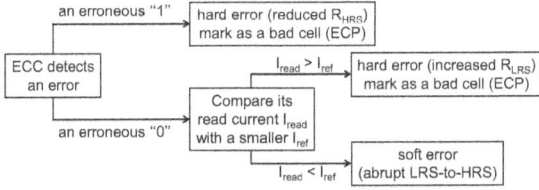

Figure 6: Hard error detection for type I failure.

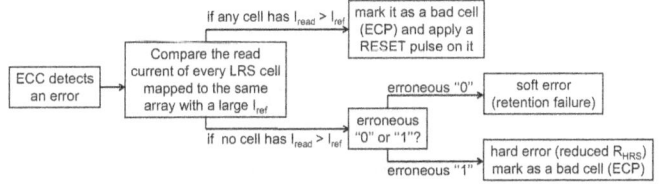

Figure 7: Percentage of available capacity versus the number of writes to ReRAM for type I failure, with various array sizes of (a) 128x128, (b)256x256, (c)512x512

or an abrupt LRS-to-HRS jump due to retention failure. Given that the resistance changes gradually and the erroneous cell was not marked as a bad cell, the increased ΔR_{LRS} is expected to be much smaller than an abrupt LRS-to-HRS jump. Therefore, the erroneous cell is read again and its read current is compared with another reference current I_{ref} which is smaller than the one used for normal read operation (I_{ref0}). If its read current I_{read} is greater than I_{ref}, it indicates that the cell has a modest resistance value, indicating a hard error. Thus ECP will mark it as a bad cell. Otherwise the cell has a high resistance value, indicating a soft error.

The design is essentially based on a three-level output sense amplifier. Normally the reference current I_{ref0} for read operation is generating by averaging the current from two complementary cells: one cell in LRS while the other in HRS, that is,

$$I_{ref0} = \frac{I_{LRS} + I_{HRS}}{2} \qquad (4)$$

In our design, the reference current I_{ref} is generated from a partially-RESET reference cell.

$$I_{ref} = m \times I_{HRS} \quad (m > 1) \qquad (5)$$

where m is the factor of multiplication. The area overhead of such sense amplifier design is estimated to be less than 5% of the total NVM chip area [12].

In order to evaluate the effectiveness of our hard error detection unit, we choose an ECP_6 scheme with 6 correction pointers that can mark up to 6 bad cells in a 512-bit memory block. We assign 10% variations for both β and γ in Equation 3. The soft error rates are calculated using Equation 1. We do not assume wear-leveling techniques in our simulations. Figure 7 shows the fraction of memory blocks that survive given the number of block writes to ReRAM built in different array sizes. The baseline ECP without any hard error detection assumes every error reported by ECC is marked as a bad cell and occupies one correction pointer in ECP. Therefore, it has the worst lifetime though there is no associated hardware, performance, and energy overhead for detecting hard errors. Compared to the baseline, the "write-verify" detection scheme improves the lifetime signif-

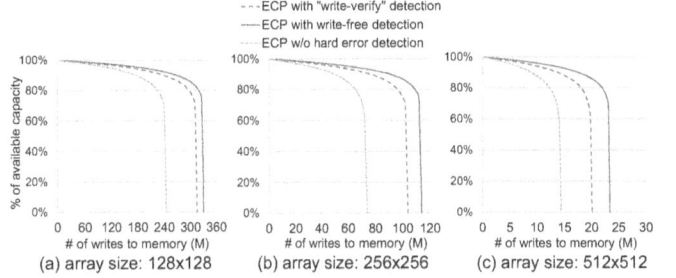

Figure 8: Hard error detection for type II failure.

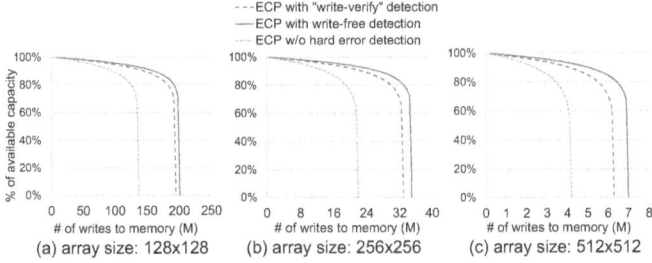

Figure 9: Percentage of available capacity versus the number of writes to ReRAM for type II failure, with various array sizes of (a) 128x128, (b)256x256, (c)512x512

icantly because the soft errors are identified, avoiding unintentional usage of correction pointers in ECP. The detection mechanism we propose further enhances the endurance curve because it does not involve unnecessary writes during the detection procedure. Our approach are more effective for ReRAM with larger cross-point array as they are more vulnerable to errors. Another advantage of our scheme over the conventional "write-verify" scheme is that the latency and energy overheads associated with the unnecessary writes are saved given that reads are much faster and more energy-efficient than writes in NVM.

4.1.2 Type II failure

The unique characteristic of type II failure is its R_{LRS} can decrease over cycles, resulting in a write failure. In practical, more than one LRS cell in a memory block can be mapped to the same cross-point array, and they are fully selected during the write operation. The current of these fully biased LRS cells contributes the most to the total current of the selected wordline and thus causes a significant IR drop on the wire. If the furthest selected cell fails to have enough voltage drop, the primary reason is that some of the fully selected LRS cells have degraded R_{LRS} values. The secondary reason is that there have accumulated a large number of degraded LRS cells among the half-selected cells. Our design tries to avoid the latter case.

Figure 8 illustrates the hard error detection mechanism for type II failure. As the ΔR_{LRS}-induced write failure is the primary concern in the reliability issue, each time the ECC detects an error, it will read all the "1"s in the memory block that mapped to the same cross-point array with the erroneous cell again. The read current of these cells (including the erroneous cell) is compared with a large reference current level I_{ref} to determine whether if there is notable R_{LRS} reduction in the cell. If the read current of any LRS cell is greater than the I_{ref}, the cell is marked as a bad cell by ECP. Then we apply a RESET pulse on the bad cell. As long as the cell is RESET to a higher level than the initial R_{LRS}, the cell will not be responsible for any write failure no matter whether it is fully selected or half-selected during a future write operation. If no LRS cell in the array show sig-

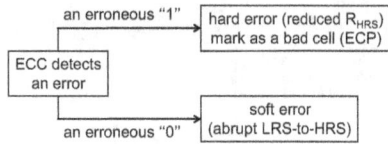

Figure 10: Hard error detection for type III failure.

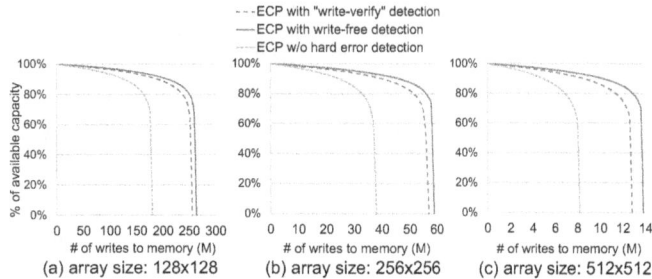

Figure 11: Percentage of available capacity versus the number of writes to ReRAM for type III failure, with various array sizes of (a) 128x128, (b)256x256, (c)512x512

nificant R_{LRS} degradation, then we determine an erroneous "1" is caused by decreased R_{HRS} (hard error) and the cell is simply marked as a bad cell by ECP. No RESET operation is required for such cell since it is already in its HRS.

Figure 9 shows the percentage of surviving memory blocks for type II failure. The improvement of our design over the "write-verify" detection scheme is more significant than it is for type I failure. This is because checking more than one cells after the ECC is triggered provides a wider error coverage range. For ReRAM with 512x512 arrays, our design extends the lifetime by more than 12% compared to conventional "write-verify" detection scheme.

4.1.3 Type III failure

Detecting a hard error in type III failure is relatively easy since its R_{LRS} almost keeps constant. In this case, an erroneous "1" indicated by the ECC is identified to be a hard error as a result of R_{HRS}. In contrast, an erroneous "0" is identified to be a soft error as a result of retention failure. Figure 11 shows the percentage of surviving memory blocks for type III failure. Given that our detection approach for this type of failure is almost free, the improvement over the conventional hard error detection schemes is significant.

5. CONCLUSION

ReRAM is a promising candidate for next-generation non-volatile memory technology. The high density cross-point structure is the most attractive memory organization for low-cost ReRAM. However, due to the lack of isolation between cells in a cross-point array, the resistance degradation over write cycles observed in ReRAM cells will have a significant impact on the reliability of such structure. Our analysis shows that type I and III failure suffer from read noise noise margin degradations while type II failure has to deal with additional write issues including reduced voltage drop and increased write energy. Instead of a write-intensive hard error detection mechanism, we design effective hard error detection units for each failure type without involving write operations. Our design enables a soft error and hard error resilient architecture which extends the lifetime of ReRAM by up to 75% over the design without hard error detections

and up to 12% over the design with "write-verify" detection mechanism.

6. REFERENCES

[1] G. Sun, E. Kursun, J. Rivers, and Y. Xie, "Exploring the vulnerability of cmps to soft errors with 3d stacked non-volatile memory," in *IEEE 29th International Conference on Computer Design (ICCD)*, 2011, pp. 366–372.

[2] N. H. Seong, S. Yeo, and H.-H. S. Lee, "Tri-level-cell phase change memory: toward an efficient and reliable memory system," in *Proceedings of the International Symposium on Computer Architecture (ISCA)*, 2013, pp. 440–451.

[3] E. Ipek, J. Condit, E. B. Nightingale, D. Burger, and T. Moscibroda, "Dynamically replicated memory: Building reliable systems from nanoscale resistive memories," in *Proceedings of the Fifteenth Edition of ASPLOS on Architectural Support for Programming Languages and Operating Systems*, 2010, pp. 3–14.

[4] S. Schechter, G. H. Loh, K. Straus, and D. Burger, "Use ecp, not ecc, for hard failures in resistive memories," in *Proceedings of the international symposium on Computer architecture (ISCA)*, 2010, pp. 141–152.

[5] D. Niu, C. Xu, N. Muralimanohar, N. P. Jouppi, and Y. Xie, "Design Trade-offs for High Density Cross-point Resistive Memory," in *Proceedings of the ACM/IEEE International Symposium on Low Power Electronics and Design (ISLPED)*, 2012, pp. 209–214.

[6] J. Liang and H.-S. Wong, "Cross-point memory array without cell selectors -device characteristics and data storage pattern dependencies," *IEEE Transactions on Electron Devices*, vol. 57, no. 10, pp. 2531 –2538, Oct 2010.

[7] Y. Deng, P. Huang, B. Chen, X. Yang, B. Gao, J. Wang, L. Zeng, G. Du, J. Kang, and X. Liu, "RRAM cross-point Array With Cell Selection Device: A Device and Circuit Interaction Study," *IEEE Transactions on Electron Devices*, vol. 60, no. 2, pp. 719–726, 2013.

[8] H.-S. Wong, H.-Y. Lee, S. Yu, Y.-S. Chen, Y. Wu, P.-S. Chen, B. Lee, F. Chen, and M.-J. Tsai, "Metal Oxide RRAM," *Proceedings of the IEEE*, vol. 100, no. 6, pp. 1951–1970, 2012.

[9] Y. Chen *et al.*, "Improvement of data retention in HfO2/Hf 1T1R RRAM cell under low operating current," in *IEEE InternationalElectron Devices Meeting (IEDM)*, 2013, pp. 10.1.1–10.1.4.

[10] B. Gao, H. Zhang *et al.*, "Modeling of Retention Failure Behavior in Bipolar Oxide-Based Resistive Switching Memory," *Electron Device Letters, IEEE*, vol. 32, no. 3, pp. 276–278, 2011.

[11] B. Chen, Y. Lu, B. Gao, Y. H. Fu, F. Zhang, P. Huang, Y. Chen, L. Liu, X. Liu, J. Kang, Y. Y. Wang, Z. Fang, H. Y. Yu, X. Li, X. Wang, N. Singh, G. Q. Lo, and D.-L. Kwong, "Physical mechanisms of endurance degradation in TMO-RRAM," in *IEEE InternationalElectron Devices Meeting (IEDM)*, 2011, pp. 12.3.1–12.3.4.

[12] X. Dong and Y. Xie, "AdaMS: Adaptive MLC/SLC phase-change memory design for file storage," in *Design Automation Conference (ASP-DAC), 2011 16th Asia and South Pacific*, 2011, pp. 31–36.

Using Adaptive Read Voltage Thresholds to Enhance the Reliability of MLC NAND Flash Memory Systems

Nikolaos Papandreou, Thomas Parnell, Haralampos Pozidis,
Thomas Mittelholzer, Evangelos Eleftheriou
IBM Research - Zurich
{npo, tpa, hap, tmi, ele}@zurich.ibm.com

Charles Camp, Thomas Griffin, Gary Tressler, Andrew Walls
IBM Systems and Technology Group
{camp, tgriff, gtressle, awalls}@us.ibm.com

ABSTRACT

NAND Flash memory is not only the ubiquitous storage medium in consumer applications, but has also started to appear in enterprise storage systems as well. MLC and TLC Flash technology made it possible to store multiple bits in the same silicon area as SLC, thus reducing the cost per amount of data stored. However, at current sub-20nm technology nodes, MLC Flash devices fail to provide the levels of raw reliability, mainly cycling endurance, that are required by typical enterprise applications. Advanced signal-processing and coding schemes are needed to improve the Flash bit error rate and thus elevate the device reliability to the desired level. In this paper, we report on the use of adaptive voltage thresholds in the read operation of NAND Flash devices. We discuss how the optimal read voltage thresholds can be determined, and assess the benefit of adapting the read voltage thresholds in terms of cycling endurance, data retention and resilience to read disturb.

Categories and Subject Descriptors

B.7.1 [**Integrated Circuits**]: [Memory technologies]

General Terms

Design, Reliability

Keywords

NAND Flash, characterization, signal processing

1. INTRODUCTION

Flash memory, in particular of the NAND type, has become the ubiquitous storage medium in consumer applications in recent years, and in many cases even enabled new such applications. MLC and later TLC Flash cells made it possible to store two and three bits in the same silicon area as SLC cells at minimal additional manufacturing complexity, thus significantly reducing the cost per amount of data stored. The deterioration in device reliability brought about by MLC technology is tolerable for consumer applications, which benefited tremendously from the effective drop in cost.

More recently, and partially sparked by the inability of the HDD industry to deliver sizeable latency improvements, Flash memory devices have also started finding a place in enterprise applications. In this case, large performance benefits, in particular in random I/O throughput, were the decisive factor. Although the first enterprise storage systems were based on SLC Flash, a shift to MLC (and even TLC) Flash is recently being observed, mainly because of the significant cost reduction that is achievable. However, the use of MLC or TLC Flash brings with it an inevitable deterioration in device reliability and performance. Specifically, because the margin between adjacent signal levels in MLC Flash is narrower than in SLC, smaller voltage threshold shifts, which are caused by successive program/erase cycles, read disturbs and data retention effects, may cause level overlap and thus a deterioration of the raw bit error rate. As a result, Flash manufacturers qualify MLC Flash for much lower endurance than SLC.

It has quickly become apparent that the raw endurance of MLC Flash does not suffice for enterprise applications. This has forced memory manufacturers to launch an alternative version of MLC Flash devices, called enterprise-class MLC (or eMLC), which offer higher endurance than MLC at the cost of a moderate increase in write latency and higher price. However, at the current sub-20nm technology nodes, even eMLC Flash fails to provide the levels of raw reliability, mainly cycling endurance, that are required by typical enterprise applications. Advanced signal-processing and coding schemes are needed to improve the Flash bit error rate and thus elevate the device reliability to the desired levels [1].

In this paper, we report on the use of adaptive voltage thresholds in the read operation of NAND Flash devices. We describe a method to extract the optimal read voltage thresholds at different points in the device lifetime based on several reads of a Flash page. We demonstrate that a simple adaptive algorithm can track the optimal read voltage thresholds in the course of both program/erase cycling as well as data retention. Furthermore, we show that by using

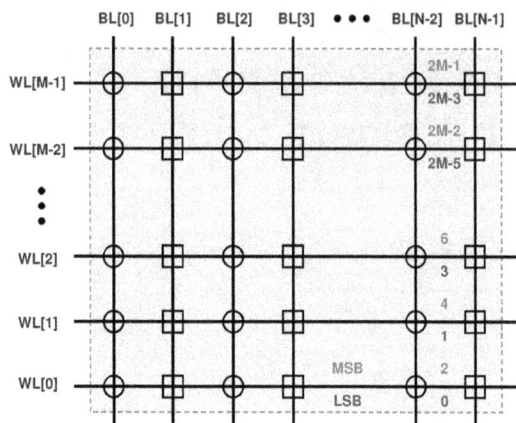

Figure 1: Illustration of NAND memory array and page programming order. Each cell stores 2 bits of information. LSB and MSB define the lower and upper page, respectively. The page programming order is selected so as to minimize CCI.

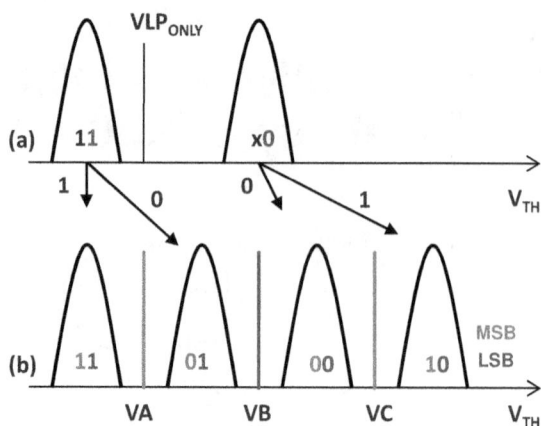

Figure 2: Programming of 2 bits per cell takes place in steps where (a) first the LSB (lower page) and then (b) the MSB (upper page) is programmed. Thresholds VA, VB, VC are used for detecting the 2 bits of information in each cell.

adaptive read thresholds rather than fixed ones it is possible to achieve large cycling endurance gains, as well as an increased resiliency to read disturb effects.

2. WRITING AND READING OPERATIONS IN MLC NAND FLASH

In NAND Flash, information is written to or read from the memory array in the form of a page, the size of which depends on the array design and can vary among chip vendors and technology nodes. A group of pages form a block and before a page in a block can be re-programmed the entire block has to be erased. After erasing, all pages in the block are reset to the erased state. Figure 1 illustrates the organization of an MLC NAND memory block. The block array consists of M word lines (WLs) and N bit-lines (BLs). Each page is defined by the cells of a WL and contains either the LSB (least significant bit) or the MSB (most significant bit) of the 2-bit information stored on the cells of the corresponding WL. In the former case the page is usually referred as lower page and in the latter case as upper page [2].

Information storage in the NAND cells is achieved by a programming mechanism that modifies the threshold voltage (V_{TH}) of each cell to multiple discrete levels. By applying a read bias voltage, one can detect each of the levels and thus the information stored in the cells. To store 2 bits per cell, first the lower page (LSB) has to be programmed, followed by the upper page (MSB). Figure 2 illustrates a typical process for programming the 2 bits in a NAND Flash cell. After the block has been erased, the cells of each WL are in the erased state (11). In the first step, the LSB is stored by programming the lower page. This process will either leave the cells in the erased state or will program the cells to an intermediate state (x0), depending on the LSB. In the second step, the MSB is stored by programming the upper page. The final state of each cell will depend on both LSB and MSB as Figure 2 shows. For data recovery, three read voltage thresholds denoted VA, VB and VC are used when both 2 bits of information have been programmed in the memory cells. When only the lower page has been programmed, a single voltage threshold is used to detect

the LSB. The principle illustrated in Figure 2 is extended to lower, middle and upper page programming for 3 bit per cell devices (TLC) [3].

Achievement of tight threshold voltage distributions after programming is critical for the reliability of the device. As the technology moves to lower scaling dimensions, the available threshold voltage (V_{TH}) window for level programming is reduced. Various algorithms and technology advancements have been proposed by memory manufacturers to achieve a high degree of control for both the erased and the programmed level distributions [4]. One of the factors that can disturb the programmed state of a cell is the so-called cell-to-cell interference (CCI) due to parasitic capacitive coupling between neighboring cells [5]. CCI will disturb the threshold voltage of a victim cell when the so-called aggressor cells are being programmed. The aggressor cells are the neighboring cells that belong to the same or the adjacent WL. Figure 1 shows the page programming order which is selected so that the CCI effects are minimized during page programming [6].

3. CHARACTERIZATION RESULTS FROM MLC NAND DEVICES

Figure 3 illustrates a typical testing procedure to characterize and evaluate the reliability and performance of a NAND Flash device. In the first part, the device under test is subjected to repeated program and erase (P/E) cycles, where t_C and T_C denote the total cycling test duration and the ambient temperature, respectively. Cycling stress has been shown to increase the density of defects in the tunnel oxide of the NAND cell, which results in charge trapping [7]. The second part of the testing procedure involves baking the device at an ambient temperature T_B for a total time of t_B. In the post-cycling data-retention part, de-trapping of previously trapped charges takes place [8], which affects the stability of the threshold voltage distribution and thus the reliability of the device.

The procedure described above is usually accelerated by using high ambient temperatures for both the cycling and the data-retention parts. The time and temperature param-

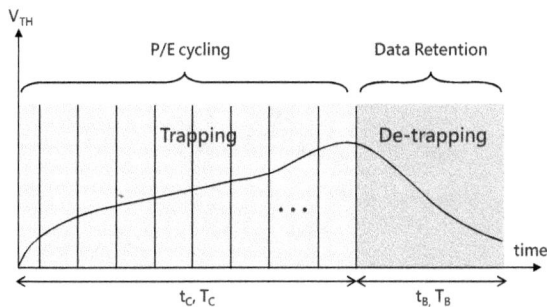

Figure 3: Schematic illustration of a typical NAND Flash reliability testing procedure that involves a first part of P/E cycling followed by a data retention part where the device is baked at high temperature.

eters of the testing procedure are carefully selected so that the accelerated test conditions are equivalent to the device operating conditions in the field. For the determination of the time-temperature parameters an Arrhenius law is generally adopted by using a constant activation energy of the order of $E_a = 1.1$ eV [9], [10].

Figure 4 presents characterization results from a 1x MLC NAND device. The threshold voltage distribution was extracted during both the cycling as well as the data-retention phases of the characterization test. Figure 4(a) shows three snapshots of the extracted threshold voltage distribution of a representative page in a block at a number of P/E cycles that correspond to 0.3X, 1X and 3X of the nominal device cycling endurance specification. The histogram of the readback signal is an estimate of the pdf of the programmed MLC states, i.e., states 01, 00, 10 in Figure 2. The repeated cycling stress results in a positive (right) shift and broadening of the multilevel distributions due to charge trapping. Figure 4(b) shows the effect of post-cycling data retention. The device under test was baked at high temperature for a total time period that is equivalent to 2 months at 40C. Due to charge de-trapping the MLC distributions exhibit a negative (left) shift and further broadening.

The results in Figure 4 demonstrate the effects of P/E cycling and data retention on the threshold voltage distributions. Apart from the broadening of the level distributions, a positive or negative shift is observed depending on the underlying physical mechanism, which implies that detecting the stored data by using fixed voltage thresholds is not optimal in terms of bit error rate. On the contrary, varying the voltage thresholds (VA, VB and VC in Figure 2) by an adaptive mechanism should enable better tracking of the changing device conditions and thus result in bit error rate improvement and associated device lifetime extension. In the following section we demonstrate the performance of such a mechanism based on characterization results from 1x MLC NAND devices.

4. ADAPTIVE READ VOLTAGE THRESH-OLDS

In a Flash system it is highly desirable to read using the voltage thresholds that minimize the raw bit error rate (RBER) at all times. If significant reductions in RBER can be obtained by changing the read voltage thresholds then it is possible to improve the performance of a Flash system in

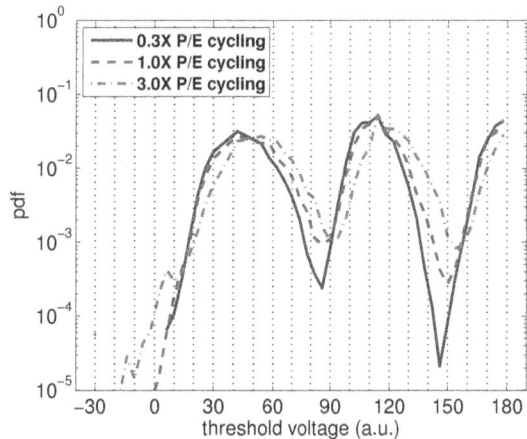

(a) Change of readback signal distributions during P/E cycling

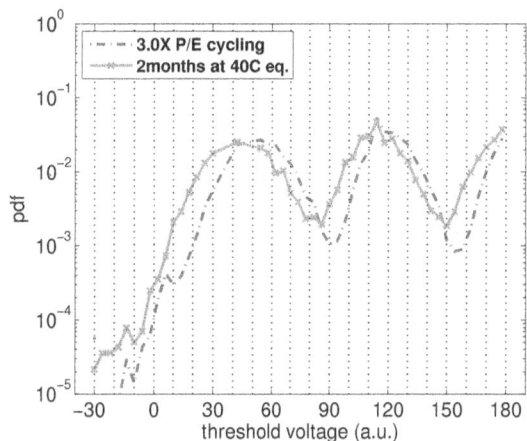

(b) Change of readback signal distributions during high temperature data retention bake

Figure 4: Characterization of MLC distributions in 1x MLC NAND Flash during accelerated reliability testing.

a number of ways. One way to benefit from reduced RBER might be an endurance enhancement: cells may be subjected to a greater number of program/erase cycles (or reads) before the number of raw bit errors exceeds the correction capability of the ECC engine and user information can no longer be retrieved. Conversely, rather than extending endurance one may prefer to take advantage of the improved RBER by reducing the correction capability of the ECC engine and thus increasing the coding efficiency of the system. In this section we begin by discussing various ways to estimate the optimal read voltage thresholds throughout the lifetime of a flash device. We then proceed to demonstrate the performance enhancement that arises from adapting the read voltage thresholds using experimental results from a 1x MLC NAND device.

4.1 Determining the optimal threshold voltages

In a typical Flash chip is possible to change the read voltage thresholds by issuing a command to the chip that applies a set of fixed voltage offsets $(\Delta A, \Delta B, \Delta C)$ to the three nominal read voltage thresholds (VA,VB,VC) independently. Let $\vec{R}_m^{(L)}(\Delta B)$ denote the binary vector of length N obtained upon reading the lower page of the m-th word line with the threshold voltage $(VB + \Delta B)$. Similarly, let $\vec{R}_m^{(U)}(\Delta A, \Delta C)$ denote the binary vector of the same length obtained upon reading the upper page of the m-th word line with the pair of threshold voltages: $(VA + \Delta A, VC + \Delta C)$. The number of raw bit errors observed when reading with a given set of read offsets can be expressed as:

$$E_m^{(L)}(\Delta B) \;=\; \sum_{n=0}^{N-1} X_{m,n}^{(L)} \oplus R_{m,n}^{(L)}(\Delta B) \qquad (1)$$

$$E_m^{(U)}(\Delta A, \Delta C) \;=\; \sum_{n=0}^{N-1} X_{m,n}^{(U)} \oplus R_{m,n}^{(U)}(\Delta A, \Delta C) \quad (2)$$

where $\vec{X}_m^{(U/L)}$ is the user information stored and the operator $\oplus$ denotes binary addition (XOR). It should be noted that in order to obtain the user information one must rely on the ECC engine to correct the raw bit errors that contaminate the read-back data. If the number of raw bit errors exceeds the correction capability of the code then the ECC engine will return an uncorrectable status. It is possible that at a given point in the device lifetime, some set of read offsets lead to uncorrectable read-back events, while others do not and hence we are able to extend endurance by finding the optimal read offsets.

We define the optimal voltage shifts for the m-th word line to be the set of shifts $(\Delta \hat{A}_m, \Delta \hat{B}_m, \Delta \hat{C}_m)$ that minimize the number of raw bit errors:

$$\Delta \hat{B}_m \;=\; \arg\min_{\Delta B} \left(E_m^{(L)}(\Delta B) \right) \qquad (3)$$

$$(\Delta \hat{A}_m, \Delta \hat{C}_m) \;=\; \arg\min_{\Delta A, \Delta C} \left(E_m^{(U)}(\Delta A, \Delta C) \right) \qquad (4)$$

If L is the number of read offset values provided by the Flash manufacturer then the minimization of (3) requires L reads and the minimization of (4) requires L^2 reads since all pairs of shifts $(\Delta A, \Delta C)$ must be evaluated. Even if performed very infrequently, this exhaustive search approach will be costly in terms of latency since $L(L + 1)$ reads are required for every word line of the flash device.

A number of approaches for adapting the read voltage thresholds have been proposed in the literature. One approach [11] involves dynamically adapting the voltage thresholds using read-back data from progressive reads and the assumption that the underlying statistics are Gaussian. While this approach correctly identifies the crucial issue of read latency in adapting the read voltage thresholds, characterization data (see for example [12]) suggests that the underlying cell threshold voltage distributions are actually highly asymmetric with exponential tails. A different approach is that of [13] where balanced coding (or the storage of extra metadata) is proposed to efficiently determine the read voltage threshold dynamically.

In this work we chose instead to use a simple algorithm that periodically re-adapts the read voltages for a given word line using only 6 reads (3 reads per page). No additional coding overhead is required and no assumptions are made about the statistics other than the assumption that the optimal voltage thresholds are slowly varying with respect to

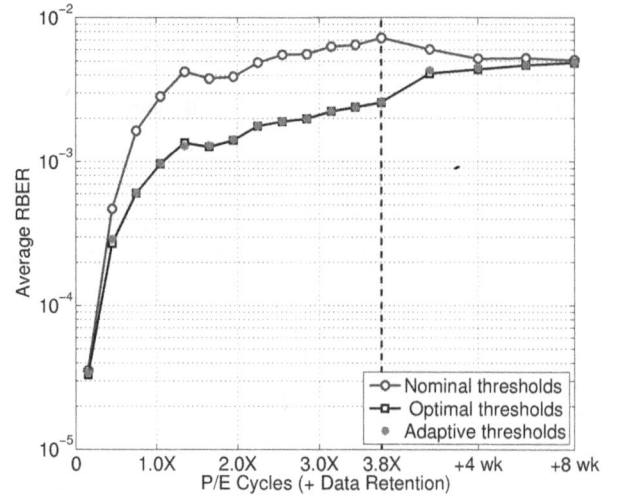

(a) RBER performance

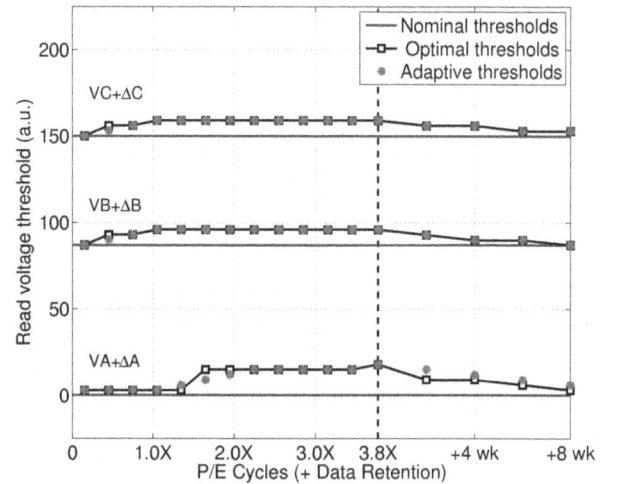

(b) Tracking of optimal read voltages

Figure 5: Adaptation of voltage thresholds during cycling and data-retention

the number of program/erase cycles (or indeed reads) that a word line has been subjected to. We will show in the next section that such an algorithm is capable of tracking the optimal thresholds very closely while incurring a very small latency overhead.

4.2 Performance Analysis

A characterization experiment was designed to evaluate the benefit of adapting the read voltage thresholds as follows: a block from a sample of 1x MLC NAND Flash was subjected to 3.8X the nominal number of program/erase cycles (1X) based on the device specification. The cycling was performed at 55C with a 260s dwell time between consecutive program/erase cycles. A read sweep is performed periodically on 6 pages (belonging to 3 word lines) of the device using the read offset command. The data obtained from these read sweeps allows computing the average RBER us-

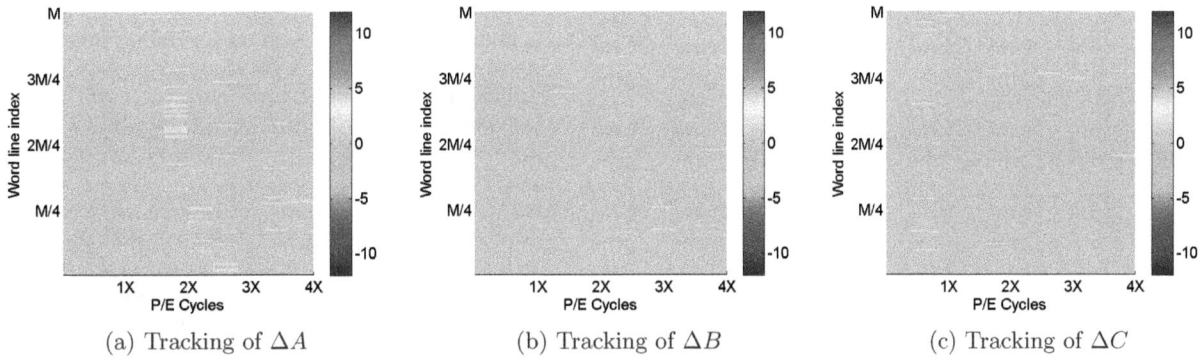

(a) Tracking of ΔA (b) Tracking of ΔB (c) Tracking of ΔC

Figure 6: Tracking of optimal read voltage thresholds

ing the nominal voltage thresholds, the optimal thresholds (found by exhaustive search) and the thresholds as determined by the adaptive algorithm. These pages have been chosen in such a way to ensure that the average RBER across these 6 pages is representative of the average RBER across the entire block. After the cycling phase of the experiment the Flash chip was subjected to a 48 hour data retention bake at 67.9C (equivalent to 8 weeks at 40C) with intermittent read sweeps every 12 hours (equivalent to 2 weeks at 40C).

The average RBER at each read sweep is shown in Figure 5(a). We observe that the read thresholds found by the adaptive algorithm provide an average RBER that is very close to that obtained when using the optimal read thresholds during both cycling and data retention. Furthermore, the endurance improvement from adapting the thresholds during the cycling phase is found to be a factor of 3.8: for instance if the ECC is designed to tolerate a RBER of 2.6×10^{-3} then by adapting the read voltage thresholds it is possible to extend endurance from around 1X program/erase cycles to around 3.8X. An interesting observation is that while the RBER reduction from using the optimal thresholds is large during the cycling phase of the experiment, during the retention phase the nominal thresholds seem to improve and the gain from using the optimal thresholds diminishes. To understand this characteristic behavior it helps to study the evolution of the optimal (and adaptive) read voltage thresholds during the experiment in relation to the nominal thresholds.

In Figure 5(b) the optimal thresholds are plotted for one of the word lines under test and compared with the nominal thresholds (horizontal solid lines). The adaptive thresholds are also plotted as star markers. It can be observed that during cycling the optimal thresholds shift upwards and above the nominal thresholds and thus using these increased read voltages can reduce the RBER significantly. Conversely, during the data retention phase the optimal thresholds shift back down, approaching the nominal thresholds again, and therefore we should expect the nominal thresholds to perform close to the optimal ones.

A second experiment was designed to verify that the adaptive algorithm is capable of tracking the optimal thresholds for every word line in the Flash block (as opposed to just 6 pages in the previous experiment). In this experiment one block of 1x MLC NAND Flash memory was subjected to 4X the nominal number of program/erase cycles given by the

device specification but this time the cycling was performed very quickly using a 1s dwell time at room temperature. The read offset sweep is performed on all pages within the block every 0.4X cycles. Each time the read sweep occurs we run the adaptive algorithm to re-optimize the voltage thresholds and run the exhaustive search for comparison. In Figure 6 the difference between the optimal voltage thresholds and the adaptive voltage thresholds is plotted as a color map. A very close tracking is observed throughout the cycling for all word lines (the units represented by different colors can be compared with the units of Figure 5(b)).

Finally an experiment was designed to demonstrate that adapting the read voltage thresholds can improve resilience of a Flash system to read disturb effects. A block of 1x MLC NAND Flash memory (from a different device to the one used in the previous experiments) was cycled to 3X the nominal number of P/E cycles given in the device specification. Immediately after the cycling phase the same Flash block was subjected to 10Y consecutive reads of every page in the block. The nominal number of reads Y is defined in the device specification as the number of reads that can be performed at the end of life before data must be relocated. A read sweep is performed every 0.3X cycles during the cycling phase and every Y reads during the read phase. Using the data that was obtained we were able to determine the RBER performance using the nominal thresholds, the optimal thresholds (determined by exhaustive search) and the adaptive thresholds. In Figure 7(a) it can be seen that by adapting the read voltage thresholds it is possible to obtain a factor of 10 improvement in the number of reads that can be achieved without exceeding RBER $= 2 \times 10^{-3}$. In Figure 7(b) we show the behavior of the optimal (and adaptive) read voltage thresholds during the reading phase of the experiment for one of the word lines of the block under test. We notice that while a significant BER improvement has been obtained, the optimal thresholds themselves do not change significantly during the reading phase of the experiment. A small upward shift of ΔA is observed at 5Y reads, suggesting that the primary effect of extreme read disturbs is an upwards shift of the erase distribution.

5. CONCLUSIONS

MLC NAND Flash memory plays a continuously increasing role in current enterprise storage systems. To comply with the high reliability requirements of such systems, how-

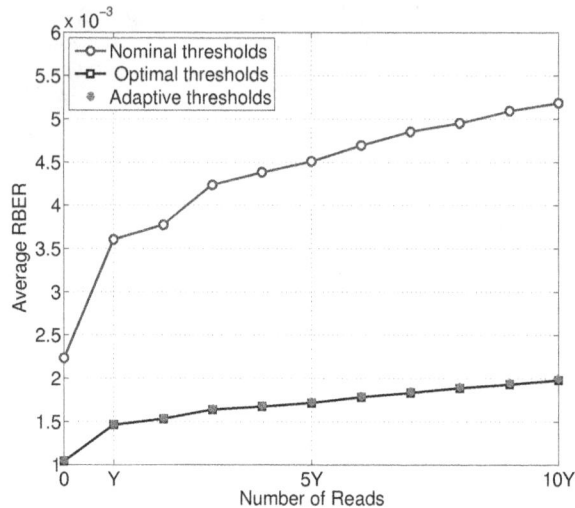

(a) RBER performance

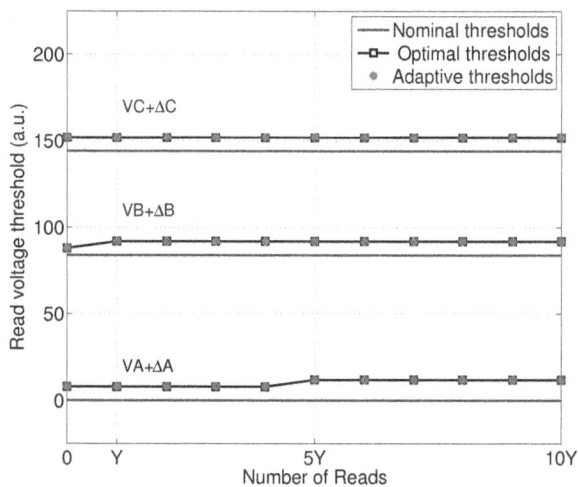

(b) Tracking of voltage thresholds

Figure 7: Adaptation of voltage thresholds during read disturb

ever, the raw endurance of MLC Flash and its resiliency to read disturb effects need to be significantly extended. We have shown that the use of variable voltage thresholds leads to large raw BER reductions and thus large endurance gains and increased resiliency to read disturb, as compared to fixed thresholds. Moreover, we have demonstrated that a practical algorithm is able to estimate and track the optimal read voltage thresholds both during device program/erase cycling and during data retention.

6. ACKNOWLEDGMENTS

We gratefully acknowledge Urs Egger from IBM Research – Zurich for designing the characterization platform used in this work, and the Flash characterization teams at IBM Systems and Technology Group for their support with Flash devices and parts.

7. REFERENCES

[1] H. Shim, S.-S. Lee, B. Kim, et al. Highly reliable 26nm 64Gb MLC E2NAND (Embedded-ECC & Enhanced-efficiency) flash memory with MSP (Memory Signal Processing) controller. In *VLSI Technology (VLSIT), 2011 Symposium on*, pages 216–217, 2011.

[2] R.-A. Cernea, L. Pham, F. Moogat, et al. A 34 MB/s MLC write throughput 16 Gb NAND with all bit line architecture on 56 nm technology. *IEEE Journal of Solid-State Circuits*, 44(1):186–194, January 2009.

[3] B. Park, S. Cho, M. Park, et al. Challenges and limitations of NAND flash memory devices based on floating gates. In *2012 IEEE International Symposium on Circuits and Systems (ISCAS)*, pages 420–423, May 2012.

[4] S. Aritome. NAND Flash innovations. *IEEE Solid-State Circuits Magazine*, 5(4):21–29, 2013.

[5] J.-D. Lee, S.-H. Hur, and J.-D. Choi. Effects of floating-gate interference on NAND flash memory cell operation. *IEEE Electron Device Letters*, 23(5):264–266, May 2002.

[6] K.-T. Park, M. Kang, D. Kim, et al. A zeroing cell-to-cell interference page architecture with temporary LSB storing and parallel MSB program scheme for MLC NAND flash memories. *IEEE Journal of Solid-State Circuits*, 43(4):919–928, April 2008.

[7] N. Mielke, H. Belgal, I. Kalastirsky, et al. Flash EEPROM threshold instabilities due to charge trapping during program/erase cycling. *IEEE Transactions on Device and Materials Reliability*, 4(3):335–344, May 2004.

[8] J.-D. Lee, J.-H. Choi, D. Park, and K. Kim. Effects of interface trap generation and annihilation on the data retention characteristics of flash memory cells. *IEEE Transactions on Device and Materials Reliability*, 4(1):110–117, March 2004.

[9] N. Mielke, H. Belgal, A. Fazio, Q. Meng, and N. Righos. Recovery effects in the distributed cycling of flash memories. In *Proc. 44th Annual IEEE International Reliability Physics Symposium*, pages 29–35. IEEE, March 2006.

[10] M. Calabrese, C. Miccoli, C. Compagnoni, et al. Accelerated reliability testing of flash memory: Accuracy and issues on a 45nm NOR technology. In *2013 International Conference on IC Design Technology (ICICDT)*, pages 37–40. IEEE, May 2013.

[11] B. Peleato, R. Agarwal, J. Cioffi, M. Qin, and P. Siegel. Towards minimizing read time for NAND flash. In *Global Communications Conference (GLOBECOM), 2012 IEEE*, pages 3219–3224, 2012.

[12] Y. Cai, E. Haratsch, O. Mutlu, and K. Mai. Threshold voltage distribution in MLC NAND flash memory: Characterization, analysis, and modeling. In *Design, Automation Test in Europe Conference Exhibition (DATE), 2013*, pages 1285–1290, 2013.

[13] F. Sala, R. Gabrys, and L. Dolecek. Dynamic threshold schemes for multi-level non-volatile memories. *IEEE Transactions on Communications*, 61(7):2624–2634, July 2013.

A New Methodology for Reduced Cost of Resilience

Andrew B. Kahng†‡, Seokhyeong Kang† and Jiajia Li†
†ECE and ‡CSE Departments, University of California at San Diego
La Jolla, CA, 92093
abk@ucsd.edu, shkang@vlsicad.ucsd.edu, jil150@ucsd.edu

ABSTRACT

Resilient design techniques are used to (i) ensure correct operation under dynamic variations; and (ii) improve design performance (e.g., through *timing speculation*). However, significant overheads (e.g., 17% and 15% energy penalties due to throughput degradation and additional circuits) are incurred by existing resilient design techniques. For instance, resilient designs require additional circuits to detect and correct timing errors. Further, when there is an error, the additional cycles needed to restore a previous correct state degrade throughput, which diminishes the performance benefit of using resilient designs. In this work, we propose a methodology for resilient design implementation to minimize the costs of resilience in terms of power, area and throughput degradation. Our methodology uses two levers: selective-endpoint optimization (i.e., sensitivity-based margin insertion) and clock skew optimization. We integrate the two optimization techniques in an iterative optimization flow which comprehends toggle rate information and the tradeoff between cost of resilience and margin on combinational paths. Our proposed flow achieves energy reductions of up to 19% and 21% compared to a conventional design (with only margin used to attain robustness) and a brute-force implementation, respectively. These benefits increase in the context of an adaptive voltage scaling strategy.

Categories and Subject Descriptors: B.7.2 [Design Aids]: Placement and routing

Keywords: Low power, resilient design, design optimization, cost reduction

1. INTRODUCTION

IC products in advanced technology nodes are susceptible to dynamic variations that manifest via supply voltage droop, temperature fluctuation, cross-coupling, aging, and other mechanisms. To ensure correct functionality and robustness, traditional IC implementation methodologies build guardband into clock frequencies and design signoffs – notably, timing signoff at worst-case corners and for hold-time correctness. However, it is well-recognized that designing for worst-case conditions incurs considerable power and performance overheads. *Better Than Worst-Case design* [3], where an error checker and corresponding recovery mechanism enable typical-case optimization, can significantly reduce overdesign compared to traditional methodologies. A similar idea for guardband reduction has been proposed by Bowman et al. in [5], where several techniques for dynamic variation tolerance (i.e., resilient designs) are presented.

Resilient designs trade off design robustness against design quality (performance, power and area), and are used to ensure correctness against variation and improve performance [7] [9] [10] [12] [13] [18]. *Razor* [10] is a well-known technique to detect

GLSVLSI'14, May 21–23, 2014, Houston, Texas, USA.
Copyright 2014 ACM 978-1-4503-2816-6/14/05 ...$15.00.
http://dx.doi.org/10.1145/2591513.2591600.

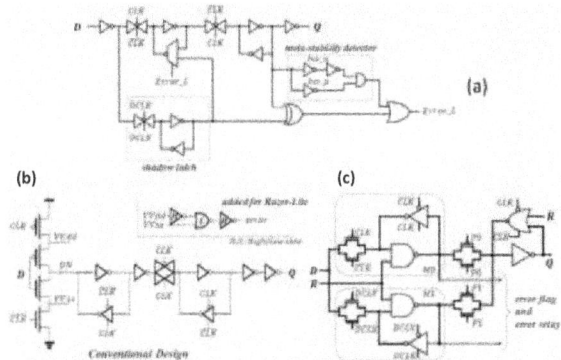

Figure 1: Structure of (a) Razor, (b) Razor-Lite and (c) TIMBER flip-flops.

and correct timing errors due to frequency, temperature and voltage variations. Razor detects timing violations by supplementing error-tolerant flip-flops with *shadow latches*. A shadow latch strobes the output of a logic stage at a fixed delay after the main flip-flop; if a timing violation occurs, the main flip-flop and shadow latch will have different values, signaling the need for correction. Correction involves recovery using the correct value(s) stored in the shadow latch(es). In the following discussion, we define the maximum timing violation (worst negative slack) that a resilient design can tolerate as the *safety margin* of the corresponding design.

By allowing timing errors, resilient designs are also used to improve performance. An example is *timing speculation* [19], which increases the clock frequency and exploits error detection and recovery mechanisms to correct the resulting errors. Timing improvement from resilient designs can further lead to power and area benefits over conventional designs. In other words, we can reduce the power and area of logic cells in a fanin cone by using the error-tolerant register at the endpoint.

However, resilient designs require additional circuits or cycles to detect and correct timing errors. Figure 1 shows the structure of Razor, Razor-Lite [17] and TIMBER [7] flip-flops. All have additional circuits, and hence power and area overheads, compared to a conventional flip-flop. For instance, Razor has its shadow latch and other error-tolerant circuits (comparator, multiplexer and OR-gate). When compared to a conventional flip-flop, the total power overhead of Razor flip-flop is 30% [9]. Although the power overhead has been significantly reduced in a recent work [17], the additional cycles needed to recover from errors can still lead to performance degradation. Moreover, error-tolerant circuits are vulnerable to hold violations. Designers must ensure that benefits (in terms of performance, and/or area and power reduction from the error resilience) outweigh the additional costs of error-tolerant circuits.

In this work, we perform in-depth studies of the tradeoff between the overhead of error-tolerant circuits and the cost of the traditional timing optimizations, with the goal of assessing 'true' benefits of resilient design techniques. We propose two effective design optimization techniques – *selective-endpoint optimization*, and *clock skew (useful skew) optimization* [1] [11] – to minimize the costs of resilience, i.e., (i) power and area overhead of resilient circuits, and (ii) throughput degradation due to additional cycles for error recovery. Since our work currently focuses on optimization at the post-placement stage, we do not yet consider the cost of hold

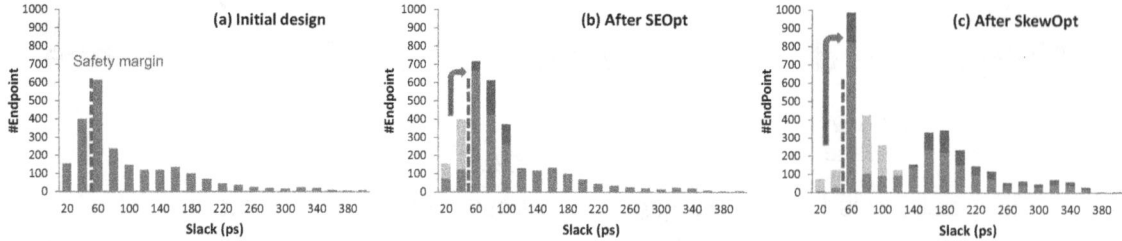

Figure 2: Slack distribution of endpoints in (a) original design; (b) design with only selective-endpoint optimization; and (c) design with combined selective-endpoint and useful skew optimization. Red dotted lines indicate required safety margin. Design: FPU (OpenSPARC T1). Technology: 28nm FDSOI.

violations due to resilient design implementation. However, our optimization flow can easily be combined with existing short-path padding optimizations (e.g., [20]). Our contributions include the following.

- We propose an optimization methodology for resilient designs to reduce the cost of resilience. Our method exploits both error-tolerant registers and clock skew scheduling.

- We study the benefits and cost of resilient design implementations, where we trade off among (i) power and area overheads of error-tolerant registers, (ii) optimization of logic cells in the fanin cone, and (iii) throughput degradation due to timing errors.

- We assess the opportunities of resilient designs across different error-tolerant registers designs as well as in the adaptive voltage scaling (AVS) context.

The rest of this paper is organized as follows. Section 2 presents related work. Section 3 formulates the problem to reduce the cost of resilience and describes our methodology for implementing low-cost resilience. Section 4 presents our experimental results and analysis, and Section 5 summarizes and concludes the paper.

2. RELATED WORK

A number of resilient design techniques have been proposed that allow timing errors with different error detection and correction mechanisms. These previous works can be roughly classified into two categories. In the first category, designs use replica circuits for error masking. These designs typically incur large power and area overheads due to its additional circuits. In the second category, designs use error-tolerant registers to detect timing errors. Although circuit power and area overheads can be smaller, rollback or instruction reply is required to recover from timing errors. The additional cycles for error recovery lead to throughput degradation.

Replica Circuits for Error Masking. A well-known technique compares output values in each cycle using redundant hardware circuits. *Paceline* [13] employs a *leader-checker* which checks timing errors due to overclocking. *CPipe* [18] enables reliable overclocking through core-replication. The outputs of the main combinational logic are compared with those of the duplicated logic in each cycle. Choudhury et al. [8] synthesize error-masking circuits and use 2-to-1 multiplexers to mask errors at the output of critical paths. Similarly, Yuan et al. [22] mask errors by adding redundant approximation logic which has higher speed than the original circuit. *TIMBER* flip-flops and latches [7] enable online timing error masking via time-borrowing from the successive pipeline stage, and hence do not require additional cycles to recover from an error. This kind of approach provides error resilience with high reliability, but also incurs significant power and area overheads due to the redundant logic circuits.

Error-Tolerant Registers with Error Recovery. Razor and related works [4] [9] [10] [17] replace registers with specialized flip-flops which detect and correct timing errors on each endpoint by capturing the correct value at shadow latches with a delayed clock. Razor [10] can correct timing errors within a specific safety margin of the error-tolerant register. *Razor II* [9] provides analysis of the Razor flip-flop – with respect to timing constraints, safety margin and clocking scheme – and reduces complexity and area of

the Razor flip-flop. A more recent work – *Razor-Lite* [17] – further reduces the area and power penalties of error-tolerant registers. *STEM* [4] improves the capability of error-detection with a second shadow latch.

Resilient Design Optimization. With the above error-tolerant registers, various design-level optimization techniques [8] [14] [15] [16] [19] [22] have been proposed which identify and optimize critical paths that are frequently exercised during operation. However, these works typically fail to holistically consider the costs of the error-tolerant circuits during the optimization. For example, Choudhury et al. [8] reduce the area and power penalties of resilient designs. However, their method simply applies resilient techniques to timing-critical paths, and ignores the tradeoff between the benefits of resilience and the costs of margin insertion for data paths.

3. IMPLEMENTATION METHODOLOGY

In this section, we define a resilience cost reduction problem and describe our optimization flow for low-cost resilient design implementation. Our flow uses two optimization techniques – *selective-endpoint optimization* (SEOpt) and *clock skew optimization* (SkewOpt) – to minimize resilience overheads of energy, area and throughput degradation. Figure 2 illustrates the basic idea of our optimization approach. In the initial resilient design (a), a large number of endpoints have timing violations at the target frequency (with respect to the safety margin), and error-tolerant registers or error-masking circuits are used for those endpoints. In our selective-endpoint optimization (b), we tightly optimize a set of selected endpoints to reduce the resilience overheads. During clock skew optimization (c), we increase timing slacks of endpoints having timing violations by optimizing the clock-arrival time at individual endpoints, further reducing the resilience overheads. In our optimization flow, we iteratively perform SEOpt and SkewOpt to minimize the cost of resilient design.

3.1 Resilience Cost Reduction Problem

We solve the following **resilience cost reduction problem**. Given an RTL design along with (i) throughput requirements, (ii) power and area overheads as well as safety margin for each type of error-tolerant register, and (iii) number of cycles needed to recover from an error: implement the design to attain minimum energy, comprehending the energy penalties of additional circuits and the throughput degradation due to rollback or instruction replay.

We calculate design energy based on total power and throughput information, i.e.,

$$Energy = \frac{Power}{TP} \quad (1)$$

where TP is the throughput of the design. TP is estimated based on error rate information [19] as

$$TP = \frac{1 - ER}{T} + \frac{ER}{r \cdot T} \quad (2)$$

where ER is the total error rate of the design, T is the clock period, and r is the number of cycles needed to recover from an error. Thus, for an accurate design, the throughput is $1/T$.

We further estimate the error rate based on toggle information of flip-flops (including toggles of both negative-slack and positive-slack fanin paths) [16] as

$$ER = \alpha \cdot \frac{\sum(TG_{ff} \cdot \frac{\sum TG_{p\_neg}}{\sum TG_{p\_all}})}{\sum TG_{ff}} \qquad (3)$$

where TG_{ff} is the toggle rate of a flip-flop, TG_{p_neg} and TG_{p_all} are respectively the toggle rates of negative-slack fanin paths and all fanin paths to the flip-flop, and α is a parameter to compensate pessimism due to (i) the fact that errors can occur in one cycle and (ii) the existence of false paths. We empirically use $\alpha = 0.35$ in our experiments.

3.2 Selective-Endpoint Optimization

We propose *selective-endpoint optimization* (SEOpt) to minimize the resilient design cost (primarily area, power and throughput degradation). Our SEOpt trades off between the costs of resilience and of data path optimization. In other words, we selectively increase margins at the endpoints with timing violations; this allows us to replace the error-tolerant registers with conventional ones and/or to remove replica circuits. However, these margins incur area and power cost in combinational logic cones. Therefore, key questions are (i) '*which endpoints should be optimized?*', and (ii) '*how many endpoints should be optimized?*'.

For Question (i), area and power of combinational cells in the fanin cone of an endpoint will increase when we add slack margin for the endpoint. Further, each endpoint will exhibit a different cost function due to the margin insertion. For instance, the optimization cost increases significantly for an endpoint which has a large number of timing-critical fanin cells (i.e., negative-slack cells in the fanin cone of the endpoint). Therefore, to reduce the optimization cost, we should preferentially optimize endpoints which are less sensitive to slack margin insertion. In SEOpt, we propose sensitivity functions for endpoints to estimate the potential optimization cost, based on which we select endpoints for optimization. Note that the sensitivity function of an endpoint indicates the performance vs. power and/or area tradeoff of the corresponding fanin cone. We study five sensitivity functions for a given timing endpoint p:

$$SF1(p) = |slack(p)| \qquad (4)$$

$$SF2(p) = |slack(p)| \times num_{cri}(p) \qquad (5)$$

$$SF3(p) = |slack(p)| \times \frac{num_{cri}(p)}{num_{total}(p)} \qquad (6)$$

$$SF4(p) = |slack(p)| \times \sum_{c \in fanin(p)} Pwr(c) \qquad (7)$$

$$SF5(p) = \sum_{c \in fanin(p)} (|slack(c)| \times Pwr(c)) \qquad (8)$$

$slack(p)$ indicates the worst negative slack of endpoint p; $num_{cri}(p)$ and $num_{total}(p)$ respectively indicate the number of critical cells (i.e., cells with negative timing slacks) and total cell count in the fanin cone of the endpoint p; c indicates the combinational cells in the fanin cone; and $slack(c)$ and $Pwr(c)$ are respectively the worst negative slack of any path through cell c and the power of cell c.

To study the performance of each sensitivity function, we sort the endpoints in increasing order of a given sensitivity function. Then, we optimize the top $k\%$ endpoints in the sorted list, where we increase k from 0 to 100 with a step size of 5. Figure 3 shows power and area resulting from selective-endpoint optimizations based on five sensitivity functions. In this example, the safety margin is 10% of the clock period.[1] We observe that SEOpt based on SF2 and SF5 incurs smaller penalties with respect to power and area. We use SF5 in the experiments reported in Section 4.

---

[1] In [7], safety margins of 10%, 20% and 30% of clock period are studied.

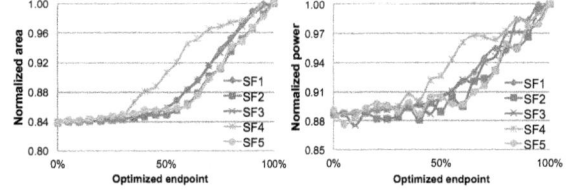

Figure 3: Cell area and total power resulting from selective-endpoint optimization with different sensitivity functions.

For Question (ii), optimizing more endpoints reduces the number of error-tolerant registers required. However, the cost of this optimization (i.e., area and power penalty on data paths) also increases. We iteratively increase the number of endpoints to be optimized and select the solution with minimum cost (e.g., a function of area and/or power).

3.3 Clock Skew Optimization

To further reduce the number of error-tolerant registers and minimize the timing errors, we use *clock skew optimization* (SkewOpt) which maximizes the timing slacks on endpoints with timing violations. In SkewOpt, we formulate the clock skew optimization problem as a maximum mean weight cycle problem [2]. This is due to the fact that the maximum achievable timing slack of a path is determined by the maximum average slack of a cycle (i.e., a loop formed by timing paths) which contains the corresponding path. We use the *parametric shortest path* algorithm [21] to determine the maximum mean weight cycle. The algorithm as we have implemented it is described in Algorithm 1. We first construct a graph G where each endpoint corresponds to a vertex and each timing path corresponds to two edges (i.e., one for the setup constraint and one for the hold constraint) (Line 1). The weights of edges indicate setup/hold slacks of timing paths in the corresponding flop-to-flop logic cones.

In SkewOpt, we optimize setup timing slacks of endpoints with error-tolerant registers (with respect to hold constraints and setup constraints on other paths). Based on the above, we classify edges in the graph into two categories – (i) *parameterized edges* and (ii) *non-parameterized edges* – where timing corresponding to parameterized edges will be optimized, while non-parameterized edges will serve as constraints during the optimization. We define parameterized edges based on setup constraints on timing paths having timing violations with respect to the safety margin, and we define non-parameterized edges based on hold/setup constraints on other paths. We formulate the constraints in SkewOpt as

$$x_q + \underbrace{(T - d_q - d_{p,q}^{max} - t_q^{setup} - t_{p,q}^{margin})}_{s_{p,q}} - \lambda \geq x_p \ (q \in R) \qquad (9)$$

$$x_q + \underbrace{(T - d_q - d_{p,q}^{max} - t_q^{setup} - t_{p,q}^{margin})}_{s_{p,q}} \geq x_p \ (q \notin R) \qquad (10)$$

$$x_p + \underbrace{(d_p - d_{p,q}^{min} - t_q^{hold} - d_q)}_{s_{p,q}} \geq x_q \ (\forall q) \qquad (11)$$

where T is the clock period; x_p is the clock arrival time of endpoint p; d_p is the clock-to-Q delay of p; $d_{p,q}^{max}$ and $d_{p,q}^{min}$ are, respectively, the maximum and minimum path delay from p to q; t_q^{setup} and t_q^{hold} are the setup and hold times of q; and $t_{p,q}^{margin}$ is the required safety margin between p and q. R is the set of endpoints which use error-tolerant registers, and λ is the *parameter* which will indicate the slack change. Constraint (9) corresponds to a parameterized edge in the constructed graph with an edge weight of $(s_{p,q} - \lambda)$. Constraints (10) and (11) are respectively induced by setup and hold constraints on a given non-parameterized edge in the constructed graph with an edge weight of $s_{p,q}$.

159

Algorithm 1 Clock Skew Optimization (SkewOpt)

Procedure $SkewOpt(N)$

1. $G(V, E) \leftarrow$ construct graph corresponding to N
2. Initialize solution graph $G'(V, \emptyset)$
3. $V \leftarrow \{r\} \cup V$; $E \leftarrow \{e(r,p)\} \cup E$, $\forall p \neq r$; $w(r,p) \leftarrow 0$, $\forall p \neq r$
4. $E_T \leftarrow \{e(r,p)\}$, $\forall p \neq r$
5. Update $p\_w(p)$, $\forall p \in V$
   // $p\_w(p) = \sum w(p_i, p_j)$, $\forall e(p_i, p_j) \in$ shortest path from r to p
6. **while** $|E| > 1$ **do**
7. $\lambda_{min} \leftarrow +\infty$
8.   **for all** $p \in E$ but $\notin E_T$ **do**
9. $\lambda_{p,q} \leftarrow$ Solve $p\_w(p) + w(r,q) = p\_w(q)$
10.   **if** $\lambda_{p,q} < \lambda_{min}$ **then**
11. $\lambda_{min} \leftarrow \lambda_{p,q}$
12. $e_{min} \leftarrow e(p,q)$
13.   **end if**
14.   **end for**
15. $E_T \leftarrow E_T \cup \{e(p,q)\}$
16. $\lambda \leftarrow \lambda_{min}$
17.   Remove edges from E_T with the same head as e_{min}
18.   **if** there is a cycle in E_T **then**
19. $slack(p,q) \leftarrow \lambda_{min}$, $\forall e(p,q) \in cycle$
20.   Add all edges on cycle to G'
21. $E \leftarrow E \setminus \{e(p,q) \mid e(p,q) \in cycle\}$
22.   Contract all vertices on cycle into p_{new}
23.   Update E and E_T
24.   **end if**
25. **end while**
26. Traverse G' to calculate x_q based on $slack(p,q)$ and x_p
27. $N_{sol} \leftarrow$ apply x_p, $\forall p$ to N
28. **return** N_{sol}

Algorithm 2 Combined Optimization (CombOpt)

Procedure $CombOpt(N)$

1. Run STA to initialize slack values for the netlist N
2. $P \leftarrow \emptyset$
3. **for all** timing endpoints p in the netlist N **do**
4.   **if** $slack(p) < 0$ **then**
5. $p.sensitivity \leftarrow |slack(p)| \times fanin(p)$
6. $P \leftarrow P \cup \{p\}$
7.   **end if**
8. **end for**
9. $m \leftarrow |P|/k$
10. $C_{min} \leftarrow \infty$
11. **for** $i = 0$; $i < m$; $i \leftarrow i+1$ **do**
12.   Pick the top k endpoints P_i with minimum $sensitivity$ in P;
13. $N_i \leftarrow TimingOpt(N_{i-1}, P_i)$
14. $N_i \leftarrow SkewOpt(N_{i-1})$
15.   Run incremental $STA(N_i, P_i)$
16.   **for all** endpoint p in P **do**
17.   **if** $slack(p) \geq 0$ **then**
18.   Replace error-tolerant register by conventional register at p
19.   **end if**
20.   **end for**
21. $C_i \leftarrow COST(N_i)$
22.   **if** $C_i < C_{min}$ **then**
23. $C_{min} \leftarrow C_i$
24. $N_{min} \leftarrow N_i$
25.   **end if**
26. $P \leftarrow P - P_i$
27.   Update $sensitivity$ of all endpoints in P
28. **end for**
29. **return** N_{min}

In the graph G, we always maintain a tree to store edges corresponding to timing-critical paths. We initialize the tree by inserting a dummy vertex (i.e., root r) and dummy edges connecting r and other vertices (Lines 3-4). Then, we continuously add edges corresponding to the most timing-critical paths to the tree (Lines 7-15) and remove dummy edges that share the same head with the added edge (Line 17). When adding an edge to the tree results in a cycle[2], we coalesce the cycle (including vertices and edges on the cycle) into one vertex (Lines 18-24). The edges on the cycle are added to the solution graph and the optimized slacks are stored. We assign to the parameterized edges weights equal to the summation of weights (i.e., slacks) on the cycle divided by the number of parameterized edges on the cycle, and assign zero slack to the non-parameterized edges on the cycle. That is, timing paths with conventional registers as endpoints will have zero slack with respect to the safety margin if they are in a maximum mean weight cycle with critical paths with error-tolerant registers as endpoints. Note that assigning new weights indicates the change of clock arrival times. Therefore, we update the weights of edges incident to vertices on the cycle. Then, we optimize slacks on the updated graph. We iteratively determine and optimize the most critical maximum mean weight cycle until there is only one edge in the graph (i.e., no more cycles can be determined). Last, we traverse the solution graph and calculate the clock arrival times based on the optimized path slacks (Line 26).

Although the above algorithm improves timing slacks on paths with timing-violated endpoints, it is not aware of error rates. To enable error-rate awareness and reduce the cost of throughput degradation, we extract the toggle rate information of each timing path and replace Constraint (9) by

$$x_q + \frac{s_{p,q}}{1 + \beta \cdot TG(p,q)} - \lambda \geq x_p \ (q \in R) \tag{12}$$

where $TG(p,q)$ indicates the toggle rate of the maximum-delay path between endpoints p and q, and β is a weighting factor (we set $\beta = 2$ in our experiments).

3.4 Proposed Optimization Flow

As mentioned in Section III-B, SEOpt reduces cost of resilience via optimization on data paths. However, such an optimization incurs power and area overheads on combinational cells, and its performance is limited on timing-critical paths (i.e., upsizing and buffer insertion cannot remove timing violations on timing-critical paths that have already been optimized with these levers). On the other hand, SkewOpt does not lead to power and area penalty on data paths, but its performance is limited by the total available timing slacks in the design (i.e., it only migrates timing slacks from timing non-critical paths to timing-critical paths, but cannot generate additional slacks) and the topology of the sequential graph (i.e., the benefits of SkewOpt are limited when there are many cycles consisting of timing-critical paths).

To minimize the cost of resilience, we combine the SEOpt and SkewOpt methods and execute them iteratively. The basic idea is that we use SEOpt to create timing slacks on data paths with low power penalty; then, we use SkewOpt to migrate the timing slacks on non-critical paths and the created timing slacks from SEOpt to critical-timing paths which have high-sensitivity endpoints. In this way, we reduce the number of error-tolerant registers without incurring large power penalty on data paths.

Algorithm 2 describes our combined optimization, which we call *CombOpt*, to reduce the error-resilience overhead. The procedure takes as input a netlist N which has error-tolerant registers on endpoints with timing violations. The procedure runs static timing analysis (STA) and computes a sensitivity value for each endpoint p (Lines 1-8). We use the sensitivity function SF5 as described above. The procedure finds all fanin cells by tracing backward from the endpoint register using depth-first search. During the fanin-

---

[2]Since we always add the edge corresponding to the most timing-critical path to the tree, the resulting cycle is the most critical maximum mean weight (i.e., slack) cycle.

cone tracing, we count only the timing-critical fanin cells since non-critical fanin cells have little effect on the cost of endpoint optimization. The procedure optimizes the top k endpoints according to the sensitivity in each iteration (i.e., SEOpt) (Lines 12-13). $TimingOpt(N,P)$ (Line 13) represents a timing optimization on the set of endpoints P in netlist N. We perform SkewOpt after optimization on the fanin cones of the top k endpoints (Line 14). $ISTA(N,P)$ (Line 15) is an incremental static timing analysis (STA) after the optimization. If the timing slack of endpoint p becomes positive, the procedure replaces the register of p with a conventional register. Then, the cost of the netlist ($COST(N)$) is updated. After the iterations of endpoint optimization, the procedure finds a netlist (N_{min}) which has a heuristically minimized cost in terms of area and/or power consumption.

4. EXPERIMENTAL RESULTS

4.1 Experimental Setup

We conduct experiments with four sub-modules (Table 1) from the *OpenSPARC T1* processor [26]. The modules are implemented with commercial 28nm FDSOI libraries; synthesis is performed with *Synopsys Design Compiler H-2013.03-SP3* [27], and placement and routing are performed with *Cadence EDI System 13.1* [24]. Runtime is reduced by adopting a restricted library of 90 commonly used cells (40 combinational and five sequential, with dual-V_T flavors). We use three error-tolerant flip-flops in our experiments, with overheads of power, area (estimated based on extra transistor count), and throughput as given in Table 2.

In our experiments, (i) we model power penalty by multiplying the total power of the error-tolerant flip-flops by the corresponding power overhead; (ii) we model area overhead by scaling the size of flip-flops in LEF; and (iii) we model safety margin using the SDC file (using original clock period + safety margin as the clock period for implementation, but specifying the original clock period as the maximum delay on paths with conventional flip-flops as endpoints). To obtain switching activity and accurate error rate (i.e., to determine α in Equation (3)), we perform gate-level simulation using *Cadence NC-Verilog v8.2* [23]. Figure 4 compares the actual error rates and estimated error rates at different supply voltages. Our estimated error rates roughly match the actual values. To find timing slack and power values at specific voltages, we prepare Synopsys Liberty (.lib) files for each voltage from 1.20V to 0.50V in 20mV increments, using *Synopsys SiliconSmart v2013.06-SP1* [29].

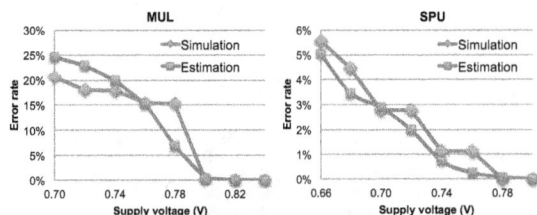

Figure 4: Actual error rates vs. estimated error rates at different voltages.

Table 1: Testcases from OpenSPARC T1.

module	description	# of cells	area (um^2)
FPU	floating point adder	12986	34633
EXU	integer execution	17614	58721
MUL	integer multiplier	13162	40693
SPU	stream processing	8066	28150

Table 2: Penalties of error-tolerant flip-flops.

design	Razor	Razor-Lite	TIMBER
power penalty	30% [9]	~0% [17]	100% [7]
area penalty	182% [17]	33% [17]	255% [6]
# of recovery cycles	5 [19]	11 [17]	0 [7]

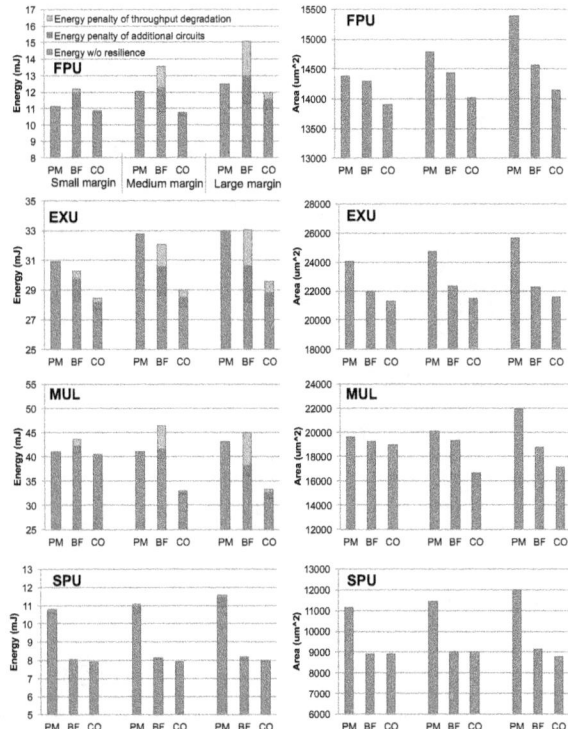

Figure 5: Energy and area results from different implementation methodologies – pure-margin (PM), brute-force (BF) and CombOpt (CO).

4.2 Methodology Comparison

In our first experiment, we compare area and energy results of CombOpt with (i) pure-margin designs[3] and (ii) a brute-force methodology where we first implement designs without considering the safety margin, then replace with error-tolerant registers any points having timing violations with respect to the required margin. We use Razor flip-flops for error resilience in this experiment. We compare our methodology at three different safety margins, where large margin, medium margin and small margins are respectively 15%, 10% and 5% of the clock period (0.8ns).

Figure 5 shows that the benefits of CombOpt increase with the required safety margin. We observe that CombOpt achieves up to 19% (6% on average) energy and 14% (4% on average) area reduction compared to the brute-force method, and up to 21% (16% on average) energy and 17% (14% on average) area reduction compared to the conventional pure-margin method.

4.3 Different Error-Tolerant Flip-Flops

In our second experiment, we study the cost of different error-tolerant flip-flops. We compare designs implemented with Razor, Razor-Lite and TIMBER types of error-tolerant flip-flops. We implement the designs with the brute-force methodology mentioned above, and CombOpt.

Table 3 shows results for the MUL testcase, where we assume a safety margin of 10% of the clock period. Using the brute-force method, we observe 17% and 15% energy penalties due to throughput degradation and additional circuit overheads in designs using Razor-Lite and TIMBER flip-flops, respectively. We also observe that CombOpt significantly reduces the number of error-tolerant flip-flops (by 60%, 56% and 62% for Razor-Lite, Razor and TIMBER, respectively). Such reductions can be enabling to the energy- and area-feasibility of resilient designs.

---

[3]We define a *pure-margin design* as one wherein only timing margins are inserted to ensure correct operation under dynamic variation.

Table 3: Comparison among different error-tolerant flip-flops.

design	Razor-Lite	Razor	TIMBER
method	brute-force		
total energy (mJ)	43.58	44.95	44.18
energy w/o resilience (mJ)	36.21	36.06	37.49
energy w/ additional circuits (mJ)	0.00	2.08	6.69
energy w/ throughput penalty (mJ)	7.36	6.82	0.00
# of error-tolerant flip-flops	893	927	895
total cell area (μm^2)	19063	18751	19361
method	CombOpt		
total energy (mJ)	31.68	33.25	35.35
energy w/o resilience (mJ)	31.10	31.40	32.26
energy w/ additional circuits (mJ)	0.00	1.15	3.09
energy w/ throughput penalty (mJ)	0.58	0.69	0.00
# of error-tolerant flip-flops	361	409	342
total cell area (μm^2)	17070	17138	17239

4.4 Energy Reduction from AVS

In our last experiment, we study the energy reduction of resilient design in an adaptive voltage scaling context. We compare energy of designs implemented with the brute-force method and our CombOpt at different supply voltages. In addition, we implement pure-margin designs at each voltage as references. Figure 6 shows results for our four testcases. The designs implemented with CombOpt achieve significant energy reduction with voltage scaling. This is because our optimization comprehends the toggle information and tradeoff between power consumption on combinational cells and error-tolerant registers; this results in less energy penalty from throughput degradation and additional circuits. Note that although throughput degradation increases at lower supply voltages, the total power also reduces. This leads to the observed decrease in energy cost of throughput degradation at lower supply voltages for most cases. However, further downscaling of the supply voltage is limited by the safety margin. We also observe that the benefits of resilience can be design-dependent: a design with larger error rate (e.g., FPU) derives less benefit from resilience because of large recovery overheads. From our proposed optimization (CombOpt), we achieve 11% and 18% energy reduction on average compared to the brute-force and conventional (pure-margin) methods, respectively.

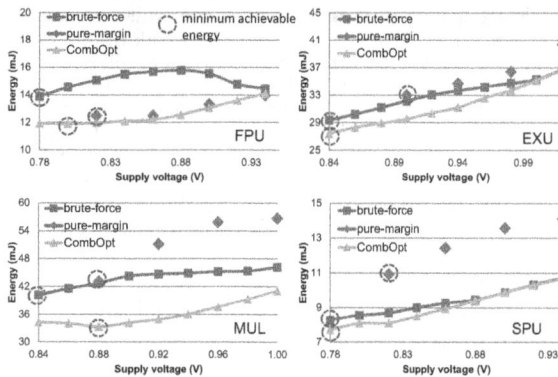

Figure 6: Energy consumption with voltage scaling, and minimum achievable energy for each method.

5. CONCLUSION

By allowing timing errors, resilient design techniques can reduce design effort and obtain power and area benefits over conventional designs which always operate correctly. However, throughput and circuit power and/or area overheads can diminish the benefits of resilient design.

In this work, we provide a new design flow for mixing of resilient and non-resilient circuits within a given implementation, so as to minimize the overhead of error resilience. We propose a *selective-endpoint optimization*, which reduces timing-critical endpoints with small cost of timing optimization. We also propose a *clock skew optimization*, specifically targeted to a resilient design

methodology, which improves robustness to process, voltage and temperature variations. Our proposed optimization techniques achieve significant energy reductions – up to 19% and 21% – compared to conventional (pure-margin) design and a brute-force resilience implementation, respectively. In an adaptive voltage scaling context, our method shows further benefits of error resilience.

A number of research directions remain open. In particular, our ongoing work seeks to (1) implement an entire physical design flow for error-resilient systems including error-detection network and hold margin consideration, (2) build a unified framework for simultaneous data- and clock-path optimization, and (3) study the impact of process variation on resilient design methodologies.

6. REFERENCES

[1] C. Albrecht, B. Korte, J. Schietke and J. Vygen, "Cycle Time and Slack Optimization for VLSI-Chips", *Proc. ICCAD*, 1999, pp. 232–237.

[2] C. Albrecht, B. Korte, J. Schietke and J. Vygen, "Maximum Mean Weight Cycle in a Digraph and Minimizing Cycle Time of a Logic Chip", *Discrete Applied Mathematics* 123(1-3) (2002), pp. 103–127.

[3] T. Austin, V. Bertacco, D. Blaauw and T. Mudge, "Opportunities and Challenges for Better Than Worst-Case Design", *Proc. ASP-DAC*, 2005, pp. 2–7.

[4] N. D. P. Avirneni, V. Subramanian and A. K. Somani, "Low Overhead Soft Error Mitigation Techniques for High-Performance and Aggressive Systems", *Proc. DSN*, 2009, pp. 185–194.

[5] K. Bowman, J. Tschanz, C. Wilkerson, S.-L. Lu, T. Karnik, V. De and S. Borkar, "Circuit Techniques for Dynamic Variation Tolerance", *Proc. DAC*, 2009, pp. 4–7.

[6] C.-H. Chen, Y. Tao and Z. Zhang, "Efficient In Situ Error Detection Enabling Diverse Path Coverage", *Proc. ISCAS*, 2013, pp. 773–776.

[7] M. Choudhury, V. Chandra, K. Mohanram and R. Aitken, "TIMBER: Time Borrowing and Error Relaying for Online Timing Error Resilience", *Proc. DATE*, 2010, pp. 1554–1559.

[8] M. R. Choudhury and K. Mohanram, "Masking Timing Errors on Speed-Paths in Logic Circuits", *Proc. DATE*, 2009, pp. 87–92.

[9] S. Das, C. Tokunaga, S. Pant, W.-H. Ma, S. Kalaiselvan, K. Lai, D. M. Bull and D. T. Blaauw, "Razor II: In Situ Error Detection and Correction for PVT and SER Tolerance", *Proc. ISSCC*, 2008, pp. 400–622.

[10] D. Ernst, N. S. Kim, S. Das, S. Pant, R. Rao, T. Pham, C. Ziesler, D. Blaauw, T. Austin, K. Flautner and T. Mudge, "Razor: A Low-Power Pipeline Based on Circuit-Level Timing Speculation", *Proc. MICRO*, 2003, pp. 7–18.

[11] J. P. Fishburn, "Clock Skew Optimization", *IEEE Trans. on Computers* 39(7) (1990), pp. 945–951.

[12] S. Ghosh and K. Roy, "CRISTA: A New Paradigm for Low-Power and Robust Circuit Synthesis Under Parameter Variations Using Critical Path Isolation", *IEEE Trans. on CAD*, 26(11) (2007), pp. 1947–1956.

[13] B. Greskamp and J. Torrellas, "Paceline: Improving Single-Thread Performance in Nanoscale CMPs through Core Overclocking", *Proc. PACT*, 2007, pp. 213–224.

[14] B. Greskamp, L. Wan, W. R. Karpuzcu, J. J. Cook, J. Torrellas, D. Chen and C. Zilles, "BlueShift: Designing Processors for Timing Speculation from the Ground Up", *Proc. HPCA*, 2009, pp. 213–224.

[15] A. B. Kahng, S. Kang, R. Kumar and J. Sartori, "Recovery-driven Design: A Methodology for Power Minimization for Error Tolerant Processor Modules", *Proc. DAC*, 2010, pp. 825–830.

[16] A. B. Kahng, S. Kang, R. Kumar and J. Sartori, "Slack Redistribution for Graceful Degradation Under Voltage Overscaling", *Proc. ASP-DAC*, 2010, pp. 825–831.

[17] S. Kim, I. Kwon, D. Fick, M. Kim, Y.-P. Chen and D. Sylvester, "Razor-Lite: A Side-Channel Error-Detection Register for Timing-Margin Recovery in 45nm SOI CMOS", *Proc. ISSCC*, 2013, pp. 264–265.

[18] V. Subramanian and A. Somani, "Conjoined Pipeline: Enhancing Hardware Reliability and Performance through Organized Pipeline Redundancy", *Proc. PRDC*, 2008, pp. 9–16.

[19] L. Wan and D. Chen, "DynaTune: Circuit-Level Optimization for Timing Speculation Considering Dynamic Path Behavior", *Proc. ICCAD*, 2009, pp. 172–179.

[20] Y.-M. Yang, I. H.-R. Jiang and S.-T. Ho, "PushPull: Short Path Padding for Timing Error Resilience Circuits", *Proc. ISPD*, 2013, pp. 50–57.

[21] N. E. Young, R. E. Tarjan and J. B. Orlin, "Faster Parametric Shortest Path and Minimum Balance Algorithms", *Networks* 21:2 (1991), pp. 205–221.

[22] F. Yuan and Q. Xu, "InTimeFix: A Low-Cost and Scalable Technique for In-Situ Timing Error Masking in Logic Circuits", *Proc. DAC*, 2013, pp. 183:1–183:6.

[23] *Cadence NC-Verilog User's Manual.* http://www.cadence.com/

[24] *Cadence Encounter Digital Implementation System User's Manual.* http://www.cadence.com/

[25] *ILOG CPLEX.* http://www.ilog.com/products/cplex/

[26] *Sun OpenSPARC Project.* http://www.sun.com/processors/opensparc/

[27] *Synopsys Design Compiler User's Manual.* http://www.synopsys.com/

[28] *Synopsys PrimeTime User's Manual.* http://www.synopsys.com/

[29] *Synopsys SiliconSmart User's Manual.* http://www.synopsys.com/

A Hybrid Framework for Application Allocation and Scheduling in Multicore Systems with Energy Harvesting

Yi Xiang and Sudeep Pasricha
Department of Electrical and Computer Engineering,
Colorado State University, Fort Collins, CO, USA
E-mail: {yix, sudeep}@colostate.edu

Abstract - In this paper, we propose a novel hybrid design-time and run-time framework for allocating and scheduling applications in multi-core embedded systems with solar energy harvesting. Due to limited energy availability at run-time, our framework offloads scheduling complexity to design time by creating energy-efficient schedule templates for varying energy budget levels, which are selected at run-time in a manner that is contingent on the available harvested energy and executed with a lightweight slack reclamation scheme that extracts additional energy savings. Our experimental results show that the proposed framework produces energy-efficient and dependency-aware schedules to execute applications under varying and stringent energy constraints, with 23-40% lower miss rates than in prior works on harvesting energy-aware scheduling.

Categories and Subject Descriptors

C.3 [**Computer Systems Organization**]: Special-Purpose and Application-Based Systems -- *Real-time and embedded systems*. B.8.2 [**Performance and Reliability**]: Performance Analysis and Design Aids

Keywords

Mapping and scheduling, energy harvesting, DVFS

1. INTRODUCTION

Recent years have witnessed a significant increase in the use of multi-core processors in low-power embedded devices [1]. With advances in parallel programming and power management techniques, embedded devices with multi-core processors are outperforming single-core platforms in terms of both performance and energy efficiency [2]. But as core counts increase to cope with rising application complexity, techniques for efficient run-time workload distribution and energy management are becoming extremely vital to achieving energy savings in emerging multi-core embedded systems.

Energy autonomous systems are an important class of embedded systems that utilize ambient energy to perform computations without relying on an external power supply or frequent battery charges. As the most widely available energy source, solar energy harvesting has attracted a lot of attention and is rapidly gaining momentum [3][4][5]. Due to the variable nature of solar energy harvesting, deployment of an intelligent run-time energy management strategy is not only beneficial but also essential for meeting system performance and reliability goals. Such a strategy must possess low overhead, so as to not stress the limited available energy budget at run-time. A few prior efforts have explored workload scheduling for embedded systems with energy harvesting, e.g., [6][7][8]. However, all of these efforts are aimed at idealized independent task models, and cannot be easily extended to more complex application sets that possess inter-node data dependencies, such as the workloads represented by direct acyclic graphs (DAGs).

In this paper, we propose a low-overhead hybrid workload management framework (HyWM) to address the problem of allocating and scheduling multiple applications on multicore embedded systems powered by energy harvesting. Compared to related prior work, the novelty and main contributions of our work can be summarized as follows:

—A novel hybrid workload management framework (HyWM) is proposed that integrates a comprehensive design-time analysis methodology with lightweight run-time components for low-overhead energy management;
—A mixed integer linear programming (MILP) optimization formulation is proposed to solve DAG scheduling problems at design time, generating schedule templates composed of optimized execution schedules for various energy budgets;
—A fast run-time scheduling scheme is proposed that selects the best-fit schedule template based on the available energy budget, which is applied with a lightweight slack reclaiming heuristic for additional energy saving by exploiting slack time of tasks finishing before their worst case execution time (WCET).

2. RELATED WORK

Many prior works have focused on the problem of run-time management and scheduling for embedded systems with energy harvesting. Moser et al. [6] proposed the lazy scheduling algorithm (LSA) that executed tasks as late as possible, reducing task deadline miss rates when compared to the classical earliest deadline first (EDF) algorithm. However, LSA does not consider frequency scaling for energy saving and thus is not suitable for emerging power-constrained environments. Liu et al. [7] exploited scaling capability of processors by slowing down execution speed of arriving tasks as evenly as possible, which saves energy because a processor's dynamic power dissipation is generally a convex function of frequency. Xiang et al. [8] proposed a battery-supercapacitor hybrid energy harvester that helps reduce energy supply variability, allowing tasks to execute more uniformly to save energy. *However, none of these prior works take inter-task dependency into consideration.*

Several other efforts have explored mapping and scheduling for task graph based workloads. Luo et al. [9] proposed a hybrid technique to find a static schedule for known periodic task graphs at design time with the flexibility to accommodate aperiodic tasks dynamically at run-time. Sakellariou et al. [10] proposed hybrid heuristics for DAG scheduling on heterogeneous processor platforms. Coskun et al. [11] proposed a hybrid scheduling framework that adjusts task execution schedule dynamically to reduced thermal hotspots and gradients for MPSoCs. *However, all these prior efforts cannot maintain performance when applied to energy harvesting systems that possess a fluctuating energy supply at run-time. Some of these efforts also do not focus on energy as a design constraint.* Our work is the first hybrid framework that targets the problem of energy-aware allocation/scheduling of multiple co-executing task graphs in energy harvesting based multicore platforms.

GLSVLSI'14, May 21–23, 2014, Houston, Texas, USA.
Copyright is held by the owner/author(s). Publication rights licensed to ACM.
ACM 978-1-4503-2816-6/14/05...$15.00.
http://dx.doi.org/10.1145/2591513.2591527

3. PROBLEM FORMULATION

3.1 System Model

This paper focuses on hybrid allocation and scheduling of multiple task-graph applications with real-time deadlines on multi-core embedded systems with solar energy harvesting, as shown in Figure 1. The key components and assumptions of our system model are described in the following sub-sections.

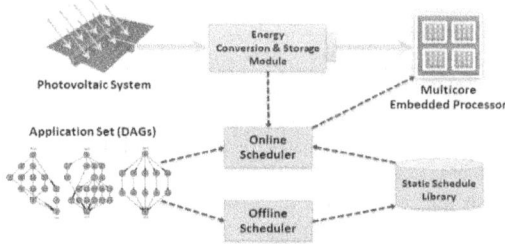

Figure 1. DAG workload based multicore embedded system platform with solar energy harvesting

3.1.1 Energy Harvesting and Energy Storage

A photovoltaic (PV) system is used as the power source for our multicore embedded system, converting ambient solar energy into electric power. Naturally, the amount of harvested power varies over time due to changing environment conditions. To cope with the unstable nature of the solar energy source, an energy conversion and storage module is required to bridge the photovoltaic system with the embedded processor efficiently [21]. We assume that our run-time scheduler can cooperate with this module to inquire about the amount of energy available in storage. We adapt the hybrid battery-supercapacitor energy storage module proposed by Xiang et al. [8] in our work.

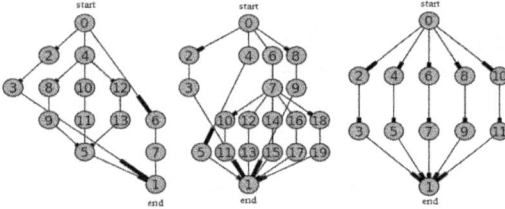

Figure 2. Examples of applications modeled as directed acyclic graphs

3.1.2 Application Workload Model

In this work, we consider multi-core systems hosting multiple recursive real-time applications modeled as periodic task graphs, $\psi: \{G_1, ... , G_{Ng}\}$, such as the examples shown in Figure 2. Each of the N_g applications is represented by a weighted directed acyclic graph (DAG), denoted as $G_i: (t_i, e_i, T_i, D_i)$, $i \in \{1, ..., N_g\}$, which contains a set of task nodes, $t_i: \{\tau_1, ..., \tau_j\}$ with worst-case execution cycles, $WCEC_i$, (number of CPU clock cycles needed to finish a task i in the worst case); and a set of directed edges, $e_i: \{\varepsilon_1, ..., \varepsilon_j\}$, used to represent inter-task dependences with communication (inter-core data transfer) delay from source to destination nodes represented as $COMM_{src,dst}$. A task node can have multiple dependences to/from other nodes, forking/rejoining execution paths in the task graph. We assume that every task graph's execution paths rejoin at its last task node, which accumulate results and conclude execution of the task graph.

Apart from task nodes and edges, every periodic task graph has its unique period, T_i and relative deadline, D_i. At the beginning of each period, a new instance of a task graph will be dispatched to the system for execution. The task graph's relative deadline, D_i, is the time interval between the task graph instance's arrival time and deadline. A task graph instance misses its deadline if it cannot finish executing all task nodes before its deadline. In this work, we assume that D_i equals T_i,

i.e., for a periodic task graph, its instance has to finish execution or be dropped before the arrival of the next instance.

3.1.3 Multicore Platform with DVFS Capability

We consider a homogeneous multi-core embedded processing platform with dynamic voltage and frequency scaling (DVFS) capability at the core level. For inter-core communication, a network-on-chip (NoC) architecture is used with a 2D mesh topology and dimension order packet routing over conflict-free TDMA virtual channels. Each core on the processor has N_l discrete frequency levels: $\varphi: \{L_0, ..., L_{Nl}\}$. Each level is characterized by $L_j: (v_j, p_j, f_j)$, $j \in \{1, ..., N_l\}$, which represents voltage, average power, and frequency, respectively.

Table 1. Processor power and frequency levels [19]

Level	1	2	3	4	5
Power(mW)	80	170	400	900	1600
Frequency(MHz)	150	400	600	800	1000
Energy Efficiency	1.875	2.353	1.5	0.889	0.625

We consider power-frequency levels for each processor core as shown in Table 1. Typically, the dynamic power-frequency function is convex. Thus, a processor running at lower frequency can execute the same number of cycles with lower energy consumption. However, this is not always the case when static power is considered. To find an energy optimal frequency, we represent energy efficiency of a frequency level L_j by $\delta_j =$ cycles executed / energy consumed $= f_j / p_j$. From Table 1 we can conclude that level 2 is the most energy efficient because executing at this level consumes the least energy for a given number of cycles. Besides, we assume idle power of 40mW when no workload is available for execution.

The computation utilization of a periodic task graph (U_{comp}) is defined as the sum of execution times of all its task nodes for the highest processor clock frequency divided by its period:

$$U_{comp\,i} = \frac{\sum_j WCET_{i,j} / f_{max}}{T_i}, i \in \{1, ..., N_g\} \quad (1)$$

Similarly, we define communication utilization of a periodic task graph (U_{comm}) as the sum of the communication times for all of its edges divided by the task graph's period:

$$U_{comm\,i} = \frac{\sum_k COMM_{i,k}}{T_i}, i \in \{1, ..., N_g\} \quad (2)$$

The computation/communication utilization of the entire multi-application workload is simply the accumulation of utilizations for all task graphs, which provides an indication of the overall workload intensity of a given DAG application set.

3.1.4 Run-Time Scheduler

This module is an important component of the system for run-time information gathering and dynamic application execution control. The online scheduler gathers information by monitoring the energy storage medium and the multi-core processor (Figure 1). The gathered information, together with preloaded schedule template library generated by the offline scheduler for the given workload, allows the run-time scheduler to coordinate operation of the multi-core platform at run-time.

3.2 Problem Objective

Our primary objective is to allocate and schedule the execution of a workload composed of multiple application task graphs (DAGs) running in parallel simultaneously at run-time such that total task graph miss rate is minimized. Our workload management framework must react to changing harvested energy dynamics to schedule as many of the task graph instances as possible without overloading the system with complex re-scheduling calculations at run-time.

4. HYBRID SCHEDULING FRAMEWORK

4.1 Motivation and System Overview

The problem of scheduling weighted directed acyclic graphs (DAGs) on a set of homogeneous cores under optimization goals and constraints is known to be NP-complete [12]. This paper addresses the even more difficult problem of scheduling on systems that rely entirely on limited and fluctuating solar energy harvesting. *The limited energy supply prevents the deployment of complex scheduling algorithms at run-time.* Moreover, *execution of applications that will not have enough energy or computation resources to complete due to shortages in harvested solar energy can lead to significant wasted energy with no beneficial outcome.* To address these challenges, we propose a hybrid workload management framework (HyWM) that combines *template-based hybrid scheduling* with a novel *energy budget window-shifting* strategy to decouple run-time application execution from the complexity of DAG scheduling in the presence of fluctuations in energy harvesting.

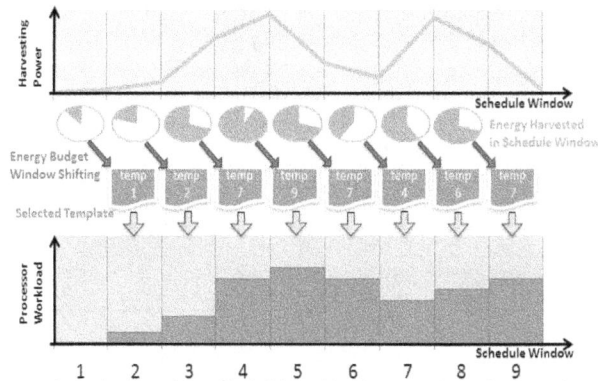

Figure 3. Overview of hybrid workload management framework

An important underlying idea in our framework, as shown in Figure 3, is time-segmentation during run-time workload control that creates an independent stable energy environment for run-time scheduling within each segment. The time of system execution is divided into *schedule windows* with identical length, which is referred to as the *hyper-period* of the DAGs. An energy budget is assigned to a schedule window at its beginning, based on the amount of harvested and unused energy from the previous window. This conservative budget assignment scheme, called *energy budget window shifting*, can delay utilization of harvested energy slightly to ensure that dynamic variations in energy harvesting do not halt executing applications in subsequent windows. The run-time scheduler knows the amount of energy that is available at the beginning of each window, and selects the best-fit schedule template generated at design time based on this known energy budget.

In the rest of this section, we describe our mixed integer linear programing (MILP) formulation for design-time template generation (section 4.2) and the run-time scheduler with a lightweight slack reclamation heuristic (section 4.3).

4.2 MILP for Offline Template Generation

We formulated a mixed integer linear program (MILP) to aid with the generation of optimal task scheduling templates at design time. In this section, we give an overview of our MILP formulation that aims to minimize miss rate for DAG instances in a schedule window under a given energy budget constraint. The constructed formulation is solved multiple times offline with different energy budget constraints to generate a set of schedule templates for the run-time scheduler to select. As our formulation focuses on workload management within an independent schedule window, periodic task graphs in set ψ are unrolled into a set of all task graph instances that arrive within a

schedule window, $\psi^+: \{G_1, \ldots, G_{Ni}\}$. Our target processor is set to have N_c number of cores with N_l discrete frequency levels.

4.2.1 Inputs and Decision Variables

For our MILP formulation, we provide several inputs that represent the energy budget and characteristics of the target workload and platform, as shown in Table 2. The energy budget parameter (*ENGY_BGT*) allows different schedule template outcomes, such that each of them can best match the energy budget available. The $WCET_{j,l}$ and $ENGY_{j,l}$ paramters are calculated based on worst case execution cycles (*WCEC*) of every task node for every frequency level supported by the processor (as per the discussion in section 3.1.3).

Table 2. Inputs for MILP formulation

Inputs	Description
EGY_BGT	energy budget of the schedule template to generate
$ARRIVAL_i$	arrival time of task graph instance i
$DDLINE_i$	deadline of task graph instance i
$WCET_{j,l}$	worst-cast execution time of task node j at frequency level l, $l \neq 0$
$ENGY_{j,l}$	energy consumption of task node j at frequency level l, when $l = 0$, $ENGY_{j,0} = 0$
$COMM_{src,dst}$	communication delay when preceding node src and descendent node dst are allocated to separate cores
$Ni, Nt, Nl, $ and Nc	number of task graph instances, number of task nodes, number of frequency levels, and number of cores

* In our formulation, task nodes can be indexed in two different ways:
(1) Local ID: tuple (i, j) for task node j of task graph i
(2) Global ID: single variable j for task node j in the entire set

For our MILP problem, there are two major requirements for decision variables: firstly, they must form a complete representation of a feasible execution schedule; secondly, they should make it possible to represent all constraints and objective as linear formulations. The decision variables used in our formulation are shown in Table 3. The binary indicators of task graph miss, $miss_i$, are used to construct the major part of the objective function. For $freq_{j,l}$, when $l = 0$, it indicates that the task node j is not scheduled for execution and is thus to be dropped. The two indicators $dec_{j,j'}$ and $bef_{j,j'}$ are used to construct constraints that arrange timing of the task nodes without direct dependencies.

Table 3. Design variables of MILP formulation

Variables	Description
$miss_i$	binary variable to indicate if task graph instance i is missed
$start_{(i,j)}$	Execution start time of task graph i on node j. Note that we also use variable $end_{i,j}$ as the end time of execution. Our schedule does not consider task preemption so that $end_{i,j} = start_{i,j} + WCET_{i,j}$
$freq_{j,l}$	binary variable which indicates if task node j is assigned with frequency level l
$alloc_{j,k}$	binary variable which indicates if task node j is mapped to core k, $k \neq 0$
$dec_{j,j'}$	binary variable which indicates if task nodes j and j' are NOT mapped to the same core (decoupled)
$bef_{j,j'}$	binary variable which indicates if task node j is scheduled before j'

4.2.2 Optimization Objective

In our formulation, the major objective is to minimize the number of misses of task graph instances in a schedule window. Additionally, we include an auxiliary objective: the percentage of energy budget used, so that the MILP optimization also searches for a schedule with the least energy consumption possible. Note that this auxiliary objective does not sacrifice minimization of miss rate for less energy consumption, as the energy minimization term in the objective function always has less impact on the objective function value than any single task graph instance miss. The objective formulation is shown below:

$$\text{Min:} \quad \sum_{i=1}^{Ni} miss_i + \sum_{j=1}^{Nt} \sum_{l=0}^{Nl} (ENGY_{j,l} \times freq_{j,l}) \Big/ EGY\_BGT \quad (3)$$

4.2.3 Constraints

The constraints in our formulation guarantee the satisfaction of the energy budget constraint and correctness of the execution schedule for the target workload and platform. The key constraints are described as follows:

1) Energy constraint for a schedule window: Total energy consumption of all task nodes at their assigned frequency levels should be less or equal to energy budget:

$$\sum_{j=1}^{Nt} \sum_{l=0}^{Nl} (ENGY_{j,l} \times freq_{j,l}) \leq EGY\_BGT \quad (4)$$

2) Timing constraints for task graph scheduling: We formulate multiple constraints, which in combination form a complete timing constraint for all task graph instances and their task nodes, as illustrated in Figure 4.

(2.a) Timing constraints for graph instances: The two constraints below confine start time of the first task node and end time of the last task node to ensure that timing requirements of their task graph instances are satisfied, as illustrated in Figure 4 (a.1, a.2).

$$start_{(i,1)} \geq ARRIVAL_i - M \times miss_i \qquad i \in [1, N_i] \quad (5)$$

$$end_{(i,-1)} = start_{(i,-1)} + \sum_{l=1}^{Nl} (WCET_{(i,-1),l} \times freq_{(i,-1),l}) \quad (6)$$
$$end_{(i,-1)} \leq DDLINE_i + M \times miss_i \qquad i \in [1, N_i]$$

We use a sufficiently large constant, *M*, in the formulation to equivalently represent "if" statements that cancel out constraints when $miss_i = 1$ *(graph instance dropped)*. The constraints can be canceled out when $miss_i = 1$ because large values of *M* ensure that the inequality is satisfied for any variable values in range. In the rest of this paper, we use the same approach for "if" statements. However, for the purpose of intuitive representation, the following sections show "if" statements explicitly.

(2.b) Timing constraints for task nodes with dependencies: The type of constraints shown below model dependencies by forcing destination task nodes to start only after their predecessor nodes have finished. Also it takes communication cost into consideration when two dependent nodes are decoupled (not allocated to the same core), as illustrated in Figure 4 (b.1, b.2):

if $miss_i = 0$: $\qquad\qquad\qquad\qquad\qquad\qquad (7)$
$$end_{(i,src)} + COMM_{src,dst} \times dec_{src,dst} \leq start_{(i,dst)}$$
$$\in [1, N_i], \quad (src, dst) \in edges \ of \ G_i, G_i \in \psi^+$$

(2.c) Timing constraints for task nodes without dependencies: The type of constraints shown below address the fact that task nodes allocated to the same core cannot overlap their execution times, as each core executes only one task at a time without preemption, as shown in Figure 4 (c).

$$dec_{j,j'} \leq 2 - allocs_{j,k} - allocs_{j',k} \quad (8)$$
$$j \in [1, Nt], j' \in [1, Nt], j \neq j', k \in [1, Nc]$$

$$dec_{j,j'} \geq allocs_{j,k} + allocs_{j',k'} - 1 \quad (9)$$
$$j \in [1, Nt], j' \in [1, Nt], j \neq j'$$
$$k \in [0, Nc], k \in [1, Nc], k \neq k'$$

These constraints represent relations between task node allocation variables, $alloc_{i,k}$, and node pair decoupling variables, $dec_{j,j'}$. The constraint in (8) ensures that the pair decoupling variable is equal to 0 when task nodes are on a same core. The constraint in (9) forces the decoupling variable to be 1 when two task nodes are found to be allocated to any two different cores.

With the value of $dec_{j,j'}$ available, the following constraints are used to avoid timing conflicts for every pair of task nodes:

$$bef_{j,j'} + bef_{j',j} - dec_{j,j'} = 1 \quad (10)$$

if $bef_{j,j'} = 1$: $\quad end_j < start_{j'}$ $\qquad (11)$
if $bef_{j',j} = 1$: $\quad end_{j'} < start_j$

$$j \in [1, Nt], j' \in [1, Nt], j \neq j' \ \text{for (10) and (11)}$$

The constraint in (10) implies that the task node *j* should be scheduled either before or after task node *j'* when they are allocated on the same core. Based on the scheduled order of these two tasks, the constraint in (11) ensures that the task node only starts when earlier scheduled task nodes are finished. When two task nodes are decoupled to two different cores, the constraints in (11) cancel out.

3) Constraints for target platform: The type of constraints shown below guarantee that only one frequency level and at most one core are selected for execution of each task node:

$$\sum_{l=0}^{Nl} freq_{j,l} = 1, \qquad j \in [1, N_t] \quad (12)$$
$$\sum_{k=1}^{Nc} alloc_{j,k} \leq 1, \qquad j \in [1, N_t] \quad (13)$$
if $freq_{j,0} = 0$: $\quad \sum_{k=1}^{Nc} alloc_{j,k} = 1, \quad j \in [1, N_t] \quad (14)$

A task is indicated as dropped in the generated schedule when its frequency level is set to 0. The constraint in (14) ensures that all tasks that are not dropped will be allocated to a core; otherwise they may end up being executed on a "ghost core" to escape timing constraints with other tasks.

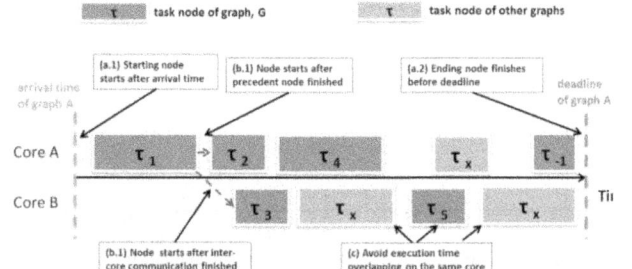

Figure 4. Illustration of timing constraints for periodic task graph set

All of the above constraints are necessary to create a correct, feasible and optimal set of schedule templates. We also establish additional constraints (not shown for brevity) to eliminate obviously sub-optimal solutions and reduce the search space for the MILP solver.

4.3 Online Template and Slack Management

The main goal of our run-time scheduler is to monitor harvested solar energy and select the best-fit template for an upcoming schedule. With schedule templates generated at design time and energy budgets provided at beginning of each schedule window, this is a low-overhead operation, done by selecting the schedule template that finishes the most task graph instances, contingent on the energy budget. Most importantly however, the run-time scheduler must be able to adjust schedule templates as necessary to best cope with system uncertainty at run-time. A typical example of such uncertainty is the actual execution times taken by tasks, which are often shorter than WCET of tasks due to variances in system status and input parameters. [22] In this work, we propose a lightweight run-time slack reclamation heuristic, as shown in Algorithm 1.

Algorithm 1 Run-time slack reclamation

For task τ that finishes at time end'$_\tau$ and has designated finish time end$_\tau$:

1   **if** end'$_\tau$ < end$_\tau$
2   find next task scheduled to execute on the core, τ'
3   **if** task τ' is ready to execute
4   slack_time = start$_{\tau'}$ – end'$_\tau$
5   start$_{\tau'}$ = end'$_\tau$
6   **if** slack_time > WCET$_{\tau', L\tau'}$ – WCET$_{\tau', L\tau'-1}$
7   Lτ' = Lτ' – 1

The heuristic monitors each core separately to find slack

time for additional energy saving. The heuristic is triggered when the actual finish time of a task node is earlier than its schedule finished time based on its WCET. It then finds the next task schedule to execute on the same core and inquires about its precedencies from the run-time scheduler. If the next task is ready to execute, the scheduler will find out if it is possible to execute this task with lower frequency while finishing this task no later than its designated finish time as per the schedule template, reclaiming the slack time for energy savings. Otherwise, this task will execute with its designated frequency immediately, earlier than its designated start time so that it will finish early and pass on the slack time for upcoming tasks.

5. EXPERIMENTAL RESULTS

5.1 Experiment Setup

We developed a simulator in C++ to evaluate our proposed hybrid workload management scheme (HyWM). For offline schedule template generation, we wrote a python script that constructs the data structure of task graphs using the NetworkX package and formulates the MILP problem using a GNU linear programming kit (GLPK) [15]. We chose the Gurobi Optimizer [16] as our MILP solver to generate the optimal schedule templates. We used task graphs for free (TGFF) [18] for pseudo-random task graph generation for most experiments and the distribution of actual execution time of task nodes is obtained from [22]. In addition, we also utilized task graphs of real applications (FFT, Gaussian Elimination, and MPEG) [23]. In the rest of this section, we first analyze characteristics of the generated schedule templates and then study the overall system performance of our proposed hybrid workload management scheme in comparison with prior work.

5.2 Analysis of Generated Schedule Templates

In this set of experiments, we check the quality and optimality of the schedule templates generated using our MILP approach. We randomly generated four periodic task graphs with computation utilization set to 0.8×4 and communication utilization set to 0.15×4, i.e., a total workload utilization of 0.95×4. Based on the periods of the generated task graphs, we set the length of schedule window to be 1 minute, within which 9 task graph instances arrive in the system for execution. We generated 11 schedule templates with energy budgets evenly distributed from 0 to E_{peak}, which is the peak energy budget available from solar energy harvesting (240 Joules).

Table 4. Results of MILP based schedule template generation

Schedule template ID	Energy budget	Objective value	Energy budget usage	Energy usage	Number of misses
0	0J	9.000	NA	0J	9
1	24J	7.788	78.8%	18.9J	7
2	48J	5.838	83.8%	40.2J	5
3	72J	4.867	86.7%	62.4J	4
4	96J	3.882	88.2%	84.7J	3
5	120J	2.891	89.1%	106.9J	2
6	144J	2.743	74.3%	106.9J	2
7	168J	1.940	94.0%	157.9J	1
8	192J	1.823	82.3%	157.9J	1
9	216J	1.739	73.9%	157.9J	1
10	240J	0.957	95.7%	229.6J	0

The results of the schedule template generation for a system with four cores are shown in Table 4. We can observe that schedule template 10, with a peak energy budget can finish all task instances in time, showing the competence of our MILP optimization to deal with stringent timing constraints even for heavy workloads with per-core utilization as high as 0.95. Note also that while 95.7% of E_{peak} is required to finish all instances,

template 3 with energy budget less than $1/3^{rd}$ of E_{peak} managed to successfully schedule more than half of the instances. *Thus our approach can be seen to create superior schedules even under highly constrained energy budget requirements.* The notable schedule performance is a reflection of our MILP optimization approach that finds the optimal schedule by sacrificing more energy-hungry task graph instances, reserving energy for less energy-hungry ones, and scaling down execution frequency whenever possible for optimal energy efficiency, thereby minimizing miss rate of task graphs.

To study the quality of schedule templates from another perspective, we show how our MILP optimization approach selects frequencies for task nodes under different energy budget constraints, as shown in Figure 5. We can observe from the figure that templates with higher energy budgets utilize higher frequency levels more frequently than templates with lower budgets. On the other hand, templates with lower energy budget drop more tasks and slow down execution for better energy efficiency. Note that the 150MHz frequency is never used by any schedule; this is due to the fact that the frequency level of 150MHz has lower efficiency and lower speed than the 400MHz level (see Table 1). Therefore our MILP optimization approach rules out this sub-optimal frequency choice as it is always better to schedule at 400MHz instead.

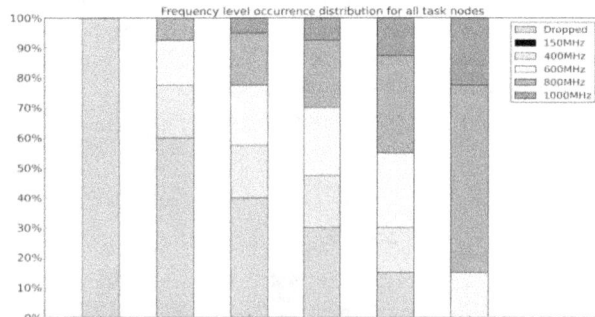

Figure 5. Frequency level occurrence distribution for all task nodes

5.3 Evaluation of System Performance

In this section, we compare the overall system task graph miss rate performance of our hybrid workload management framework (HyWM) against workload management approaches proposed in prior work. Our simulation uses realistic energy harvesting profiles based on historical weather data from Golden, Colorado, USA, provided by the Measurement and Instrumentation Data Center (MIDC) of the National Renewable Energy Laboratory (NREL) [17]. We evaluate the system's performance over a span of 750 minutes, from 6:00 AM to 6:30 PM when solar radiation is available.

To compare our approach with state-of-the-art approaches, we implemented three recent works: 1) UTA [24], which first executes schedulable workload at full speed and then drop tasks when energy is insufficient; 2) SDA [8], which divides system execution time into segments and selects a stable frequency to execute a subset of the workload that can be supported by the assigned energy budget; and 3) LP+SA [20], which finds a feasible but non-optimal schedule using MILP, and uses this schedule as an initial solution to a simulated annealing (SA) based heuristic that finds a near-optimal solution. To compare HyWM with these approaches, we adapt the techniques to our environment and problem formulation. As UTA and SDA are designed for energy-constrained scheduling of independent periodic tasks while our workload consists of multiple task graphs, we enhance these techniques so that our scheduler module analyzes inter-task dependency and provides ready task nodes for the techniques to schedule. In LP+SA, the original approach focuses on task graph scheduling while minimizing

167

energy but without awareness of energy harvesting and not considering task dropping. We enhanced LP+SA by dropping tasks iteratively till the remaining task sets meet the energy budget, and these task sets are then sent as inputs to LP+SA.

The results of our comparison study on random task graphs are shown in Figure 6. The figure shows the total task graph miss rate for three different platform complexities (with 4, 8, and 16 cores). For the platform with 4 cores, it can be observed that UTA has the highest miss rate. This is because UTA executes tasks at full speed and task dependencies in the workload make its slack reclamation techniques practically unusable. The SDA technique generates better results by considering an energy budget for each scheduling window and assigning lower frequencies to avoid violating the budget. However SDA does not consider task dependencies and thus all nodes in the task graph are assigned the same frequencies, resulting in a less efficient schedule. LP+SA outperforms UTA and SDA as it can generate task dependency-aware offline schedules after comprehensive design space exploration unlike in UTA or SDA. However, the superior offline schedules obtained using our MILP formulation in the HyWM framework coupled with its intelligent run-time template selection and slack reclamation techniques allow HyWM to outperform all of these efforts. HyWM reduces absolute miss rate by 9.2% compared to LP+SA, 11.4 % compared to SDA, and 20.2% compared to UTA. In terms of relative performance improvement, HyWM accomplishes an improvement of 23.4%, 27.4%, and 40.1% over LP+SA, SDA, and UTA, respectively.

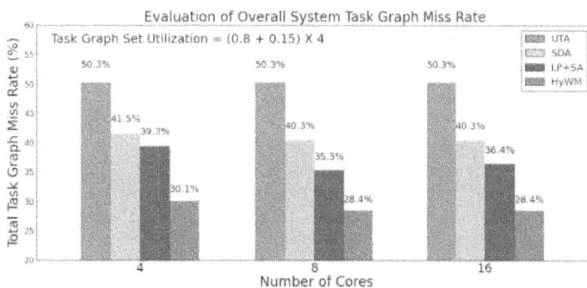

Figure 6. Comparison between proposed HyWM framework and prior work ([8], [20], [24]) in terms of overall system task graph miss rate

Figure 6 also shows the scheduling performance of these frameworks for platforms with a greater number of available cores while keeping the workload and energy budget the same. When the core count doubles from 4 to 8, our *HyWM* framework achieves a lower miss rate compared to other techniques, as it can better distribute workload across more cores, directing these cores to operate at a lower execution frequency and with better energy efficiency. However, the system with 16 cores shows no further improvements because there is no additional parallelism available in our workload to make use of the 16 cores. Note that LP+SA shows a deteriorated result on 16 cores because even though there is no more parallelism to exploit, the search space of its SA heuristic enlarges, leading to slightly worse near-optimal solutions.

We also conducted additional experiments on a real application DAG workload composed of FFT, Gaussian transformation, and MPEG encoder applications running simultaneously. Table 5 shows results for these applications on a 4-core platform configuration. Once again, our proposed HyWM framework can be seen to outperform other frameworks proposed in prior work to generate better quality results.

Table 5. Miss rate on real application DAG set with 4 cores

UTA	SDA	LP+SA	HyWM
52.87%	48.49%	43.02%	35.13%

6. CONCLUSIONS

In this paper, we proposed a novel workload management framework (HyWM) for allocating and scheduling on multi-core embedded systems powered by solar energy harvesting with workload consists of multiple task-graphs that must be executed in parallel in an energy constrained environment. Our experimental results show that the proposed framework produces energy-efficient and dependency-aware schedules to execute task graphs under varying and stringent energy constraints, with 23-40% lower miss rates than the best known recent prior works on energy-harvesting aware scheduling.

REFERENCES

[1] Arm Cortex-A9 Processor, http://www.arm.com/products/processors/cortex-a/cortex-a9.php

[2] "The benefits of multiple CPU cores in mobile devices", http://www.nvidia.com/content/PDF/tegra_white_papers/Benefits-of-Multi-core-CPUs-in-Mobile-Devices_Ver1.2.pdf

[3] C. Li et al., "SolarCore: Solar energy driven multi-core architecture power management", in HPCA 2011, pp. 205-216

[4] X. Lin et al., "Online fault detection and tolerance for photovoltaic energy harvesting systems", in ICCAD 2012, pp. 1-6

[5] Y. Zhang, Y. Ge, and Q. Qiu, "Improving charging efficiency with workload scheduling in energy harvesting embedded systems", in DAC 2013,. article 57

[6] C. Moser, D. Brunelli, L. Thiele, and L. Benini, "Lazy scheduling for energy-harvesting sensor nodes", in DIPES, 2006, pp. 125-134

[7] S. Liu, J. Lu, Q. Wu, and Q. Qiu, "Harvesting-aware power management for real-time systems with renewable energy", IEEE Trans. VLSI Syst., vol. 20, no. 8, pp. 1473-1486, Aug. 2012

[8] Y. Xiang, S. Pasricha, "Harvesting-Aware Energy Management for Multicore Platforms with Hybrid Energy Storage", Proc. GLSVLSI 2013

[9] J. Luo and N.K. Jha, "Power-conscious joint scheduling of periodic task graphs and aperiodic tasks in distributed real-time embedded systems", in ICCAD 2000, pp. 357-364

[10] R. Sakellariou and H. Zhao, "A hybrid heuristic for DAG scheduling on heterogeneous systems", in IPDPS 2004, pp. 111

[11] A.K. Coskun et al., "Temperature-aware MPSoC scheduling for reducing hot spots and gradients", in ASPDAC 2008, pp. 49-54

[12] Y. Kwok and I. Ahmad, "Benchmarking the Task Graph Scheduling Algorithms", in IPPS 1998, pp. 531-537

[13] F. Ongaro, S. Saggini, and P. Mattavelli, "Li-Ion battery-supercapacitor hybrid storage system for a Long Lifetime, Photovoltaic-Based Wireless Sensor Network", IEEE Trans. Power Electron., vol. 27, issue 9, pp. 3944-3952

[14] V. Suhendra, C. Raghavan, and T. Mitra. "Integrated scratchpad memory optimization and task scheduling for MPSoC architectures", in CASES 2006, pp. 401-410

[15] A. Makhorin, "GLPK—GNU Linear Programming Kit," http://www.gnu.org/software/glpk/

[16] Gurobi Optimization. (2009) Gurobi Optimizer Reference Manual, 2nd edn, http://www.gurobi.com/html/doc/refman/

[17] NREL Measurement and Instrumentation Data Center (MIDC), http://www.nrel.gov/midc/

[18] R. P. Dick, D. L. Rhodes, and W. Wolf, "TGFF: task graphs for free", in CODES/CASHE 1998, pp. 97-101

[19] Intel XScale, http://download.intel.com/design/intelxscale/

[20] R. Wtanabe et al., "Task scheduling under performance constraints for reducing the energy consumption of the GALS multi-processor SoC", in DATE 2007

[21] I. Veerachary, T. Senjyu, and K. Uezato, "Maximum power point tracking of coupled inductor interleaved boost converter supplied PV system", IEE Proc. EPA, 2004, vol. 150, no. 1, pp. 71-80

[22] H.F. Sheikh and I. Ahmad, "Dynamic task graph scheduling on multicore processors for performance, energy, and temperature optimization", in IGCC 2013, pp. 1-6

[23] I. Ahmad et al., "CASCH: a tool for computer-aided scheduling," IEEE Concurrency, vol.8, no.4, pp. 21-33, Oct-Dec 2000

[24] J. Lu, Q. Qiu, "Scheduling and mapping of periodic tasks on multi-core embedded systems with energy harvesting," Proc. IGCC, 2011.

Neural Network-Based Accelerators for Transcendental Function Approximation

Schuyler Eldridge*, Florian Raudies†, David Zou*, and Ajay Joshi*

*Department of Electrical and Computer Engineering, Boston University
†Center for Computational Neuroscience and Neural Technology, Boston University
{schuye, fraudies, f2rf2r, joshi}@bu.edu

ABSTRACT

The general-purpose approximate nature of neural network (NN) based accelerators has the potential to sustain the historic energy and performance improvements of computing systems. We propose the use of NN-based accelerators to approximate mathematical functions in the GNU C Library (`glibc`) that commonly occur in application benchmarks. Using our NN-based approach to approximate cos, exp, log, pow, and sin we achieve an average energy-delay product (EDP) that is 68x lower than that of traditional `glibc` execution. In applications, our NN-based approach has an EDP 78% of that of traditional execution at the cost of an average mean squared error (MSE) of 1.56.

Categories and Subject Descriptors

C.1.3 [**Processor Architectures**]: Other Architecture Styles—*adaptable architectures, neural nets*; B.7.1 [**Integrated Circuits**]: Types and Design Styles—*algorithms implemented in hardware*

General Terms

Design, Measurement, Performance

Keywords

Bio-inspired Computing; Neuromorphic Architectures

1. INTRODUCTION

As transistors scale into the nanometer regime, sustaining the scale of energy and performance improvements that were earlier possible with every new technology generation is becoming increasingly difficult [4, 10]. Dennard Scaling-based improvements [8] are approaching their limits and continued improvements are expected to come from "More-than-Moore" architectural improvements [1]. Hence, there is a critical need to develop novel architectures and programming models that can sustain the historic trends of energy and performance improvements in computing systems.

Computational accelerators offer one method of decreasing energy and improving performance. Accelerators can be used alongside traditional processor datapaths to speed up the execution of operations. In such an architecture the processor uses either the traditional datapath or the accelerator during execution. However, most accelerators are special purpose and cannot be leveraged by all applications which limits their use. A truly general-purpose computational accelerator that complements and accelerates the traditional Von Neumann architecture broadly would go a long way towards improving the energy and performance of future computing systems.

One class of accelerators that has the potential to provide general-purpose acceleration are NNs. NNs can be configured to execute a variety of operations to arbitrary accuracy which makes them suitable for general-purpose computation. Unfortunately, the approximate nature of NN-based accelerators limits their potential application. However, the inherent unreliability of current and future nanoscale CMOS devices has prompted researchers to develop a new computational paradigm based on approximate execution of operations. NN-based accelerators, with their approximate nature, can therefore be a good fit for systems based on an approximate computational paradigm.

Bit-level approximation of instructions or functions is an alternative approach to improving performance and reducing energy consumption in current and future CMOS devices. This is particularly appealing when the underlying function can be approximated by simply reducing the number of bits used in the function (e.g., bit truncation of instructions). The large energy requirements of high precision instructions can be significantly reduced if only the necessary precision for an application is used [21]. However, this type of approximation does not reduce the total number of operations that a processor executes. Consequently, large performance benefits and high output accuracies are difficult to achieve.

GPUs and CPUs have dedicated hardware for accelerating certain transcendental functions. However, the large power and data transfer overheads of GPUs make them impractical unless an application has been explicitly written to exploit a SIMD architecture. Additionally, the general-purpose approximate nature of NN-based accelerators has the benefit of allowing one NN-based accelerator to approximate different functions without architectural modifications as would be required of GPUs and CPUs.

In this paper, we present a reconfigurable NN-based accelerator architecture that approximates floating point tran-

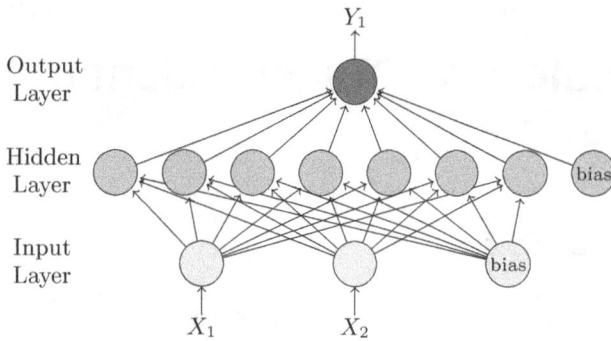

Figure 1: Example two-layer MLP NN.

scendental functions to decrease the EDP of these functions and modern applications. The choice of transcendental functions is driven by two observations. First, floating point instructions show general resilience to approximation [9]. Second, we have found that certain modern recognition, mining, and synthesis (RMS) applications in the PARSEC suite [2] have appreciable numbers of transcendental function calls. Additionally, RMS applications are known to exhibit resilience to approximation [6]. The specific contributions of this paper are as follows:

- We design and implement an accelerator architecture using multilayer perceptron (MLP) NNs in the NCSU FreePDK 45nm predictive technology model [19]. We then compare the execution of transcendental functions using our NN-based accelerator to traditional execution with `glibc`. We compare these implementations using EDP and accuracy as metrics.

- Our proposed accelerator architecture provides close to 2 orders of magnitude improvement in EDP at the cost of an average MSE of 9.04×10^{-3} across five different transcendental functions.

- In addition, we evaluate the EDP benefits and accuracy trade-offs for benchmarks in the PARSEC suite when using our NN-based accelerator to execute transcendental functions.

2. RELATED WORK

The general-purpose approximate nature of NNs has been shown by Cybenko and Hornik [7, 14]. The acceleration of general-purpose applications (e.g. filtering, FFT) by approximating regions of code with MLP networks has been proposed and shown to provide power and performance benefits if the granularity of approximation is sufficiently large and the approximated code is executed frequently [11]. Furthermore, different types of NNs have been used to approximate large regions of code or whole programs in applications [5, 15]. Additional approaches explore alternative benefits that NN-based systems may provide such as fault-tolerance [12, 13, 20].

Our work extends these prior approaches by utilizing NN-based accelerators at the level of library functions as opposed to larger functions or applications. Additionally, our NN-based accelerators are able to run without static/run-time code analysis or application failure.

Table 1: Expected, median, and minimum MSE for 100 2-layer, 7 hidden node, 9 fractional bit MLP NNs trained to execute transcendental functions.

Func.	E[MSE]	M[MSE]	Min[MSE]	Domain
sin	5.3×10^{-4}	4.3×10^{-4}	0.4×10^{-4}	$[0, \frac{\pi}{4}]$
cos	5.6×10^{-4}	4.1×10^{-4}	0.2×10^{-4}	$[0, \frac{\pi}{4}]$
asin	21.7×10^{-4}	18.5×10^{-4}	4.9×10^{-4}	$[-1, 1]$
acos	19.0×10^{-4}	16.5×10^{-4}	5.5×10^{-4}	$[-1, 1]$
exp	6.3×10^{-4}	4.4×10^{-4}	1.0×10^{-4}	$[-\log 2, \log 2]$
log	12.1×10^{-4}	8.4×10^{-4}	0.4×10^{-4}	$[\frac{1}{2}, 1)$

3. NEURAL NETS AS APPROXIMATORS

3.1 Theory

MLP NNs are layered structures that process data in a feedforward manner. The input layer of the NN receives input data, the data is processed by hidden neurons in one or more hidden layers, and the output layer of the NN produces one or more outputs. Figure 1 shows a 2-layer NN[1] with one input layer, one hidden layer, and one output layer. The output, y, of a neuron in the hidden or output layer is determined by an activation function ϕ evaluated using the sum of all N input edges $x_0, x_1, \ldots x_{N-1}$ multiplied by each corresponding edge weight $w_0, w_1, \ldots w_{N-1}$:

$$y = \phi \left(\sum_{k=0}^{N-1} w_k x_k \right) \qquad (1)$$

While the activation function can take many forms, we find that sigmoid hidden units and linear output units are able to accurately approximate the transcendental functions that we analyze:

$$\text{sigmoid:} \qquad \phi = \frac{1}{1 + e^{-2s_1 x}} \qquad (2)$$

$$\text{linear:} \qquad \phi = s_2 x \qquad (3)$$

The steepness parameters that govern the sharpness of the sigmoid, s_1, and the slope of the linear units, s_2, are both set to one. Input neurons are pass-through and do not modify their inputs.

An NN can be trained to approximate a function through error backpropagation that adjusts weights to minimize the output error using a Euclidean distance metric (i.e., gradient descent) [18]. Other algorithms use different distance metrics or approaches to accelerate convergence, i.e., Resilient Backpropagation [17] used by the Fast Artificial Neural Network (FANN) library [16]. The universal approximation ability of NNs can be exploited to enable one NN to approximate different functions. We illustrate this by showing the ability of one NN to approximate several different transcendental functions. We train 100 randomly initialized NNs (1 input neuron, 7 hidden neurons, and 1 output neuron) to separately compute transcendental functions over limited input domains using training and validation datasets. The expected, median, and minimum MSE of the validation datasets are shown in Table 1. The choice of 7 hidden neurons is arbitrary and is only meant to qualitatively validate the ability of NNs to act as generic approximators. Note that the chosen, limited input domains decrease the complexity

---

[1]We use the general convention of counting NN layers as the number of hidden layers plus one for the output layer.

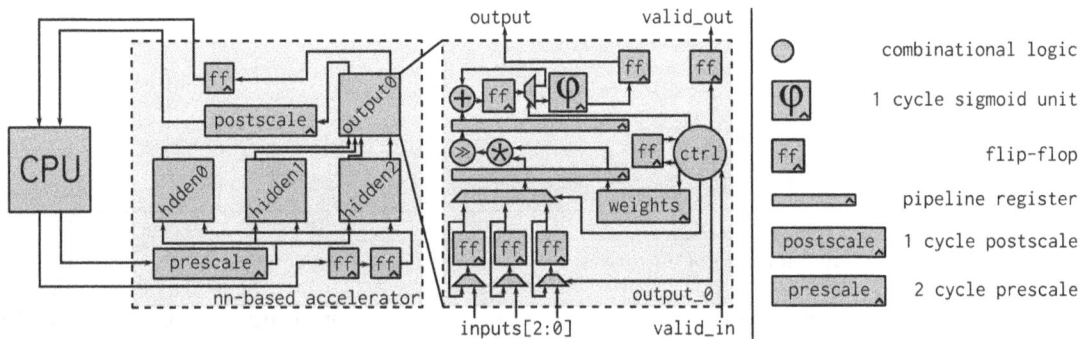

Figure 2: Block diagram of an NN-based accelerator with 3 hidden neurons and 1 output neuron. Input neurons are pass-through and not shown. The internals of an output neuron are shown in the middle and a legend on the right. Each neuron uses a single multiplier, a single accumulator, and a piecewise linear approximation unit. Processing is pipelined within a neuron as well as across layers.

Table 2: Identities from Walther [23] to convert full-domain inputs onto finite domains d for the CORDIC algorithm [7].

Identity		Domain
$\sin(d + \frac{q\pi}{2}) = \begin{cases} \sin(d) & \text{if } q\%4 = 0 \\ \cos(d) & \text{if } q\%4 = 1 \\ -\sin(d) & \text{if } q\%4 = 2 \\ -\cos(d) & \text{if } q\%4 = 3 \end{cases}$		$0 < d < \frac{\pi}{2}$
$\cos(d + \frac{q\pi}{2}) = \begin{cases} \cos(d) & \text{if } q\%4 = 0 \\ -\sin(d) & \text{if } q\%4 = 1 \\ -\cos(d) & \text{if } q\%4 = 2 \\ \sin(d) & \text{if } q\%4 = 3 \end{cases}$		$0 < d < \frac{\pi}{2}$
$\log(d2^q) = \log(d) + q\log(2)$		$\frac{1}{2} \le d < 1$
$\exp(q \lg 2 + d) = 2^q e^d$		$\|d\| < \log 2$

Table 3: Scaling steps using Table 2 identities.

Step	$\sin x, \cos x$	$\exp x$	$\log x$
$f(d, q)$	$x = d + \frac{q\pi}{2}$	$x = d2^q$	$x = q \lg 2 + d$
pre-1	$q = \lfloor \frac{2x}{\pi} \rfloor$	$q = \lfloor \frac{x}{\log 2} + 1 \rfloor$	$q = \lceil \lg x \rceil$
pre-2	$d = x - \frac{q\pi}{2}$	$d = x - q\log 2$	$d = x << q$
NN	$y = \text{NN}(d)$	$d = \text{NN}(d)$	$d = \text{NN}(d)$
post	not needed	$y = d << q$	$y = d + q\log 2$

of the input-output surface that the NNs need approximate. Training an NN to directly approximate one of these functions, e.g., $\sin x$, on an unbounded domain is intractable. So long as the input-output surface of the NN is representative of the whole function, input prescaling and output postscaling methods can be developed that allow an NN, that computes over a limited domain, to effectively compute over the full input domain of the whole function.

For our NN-based approximator, we implement prescaling and postscaling steps using mathematical identities and scalings of the CORDIC algorithm [22, 23] and shown in Tables 2 and 3. For example, say we want to compute $\sin x$ for any x using our NN, but our NN cannot handle unbounded inputs. We train our NN to compute $\sin d$ and $\cos d$ for all d on the limited domain $(0, \frac{\pi}{2})$. Knowing that we can compute $\sin x$ as $\sin(d + \frac{q\pi}{2})$ we find d and q and compute the answer for any x using our limited domain NN.

The two prescaling steps in Table 3 are used to find q and d using computationally easy operations, i.e., multiplication with a constant, addition/subtraction, and bit manipula-

tions. Post scaling operations are necessary for exp and log, but not sin and cos. The pow function cannot be computed using an identity. However, it can be computed as a combination of log and exp as follows:

$$a^b = e^{b \log a} \tag{4}$$

We use these identities and scalings to implement an NN-based accelerator for transcendental functions.

3.2 Implementation

In this section, we describe the architecture of our proposed NN-based accelerator. The architecture for log and exp is shown in Figure 2. The architecture is composed of prescaling and postscaling units, hidden neurons (`hidden0`, `hidden1`, and `hidden2`) and an output neuron (`output0`). The input layer is pass-through and not shown. Processing is pipelined across neurons, i.e., the hidden layer can operate on data while the output layer is operating on the previous data. Additionally, weight–input multiplication and accumulation is processed in a 3-stage, internal neuron pipeline. The accelerator works alongside a CPU and operates as follows.

When the CPU encounters one of the transcendental functions supported by our NN-based accelerator, the input values are passed to the accelerator by means of multiplexed connections. The NN-based accelerator thereby acts as an additional execution unit. We consequently assume this connection is implemented with combinational logic and does add to the latency and energy of the architecture. Data arriving at the NN-based accelerator passes through a 2-cycle prescaling stage (see Table 3) before entering the network along with a data valid flag. Each hidden neuron then operates in parallel on its inputs. A neuron latches input data and begins computation when it sees a data valid signal (`valid_in`). A neuron then multiplies each input by its corresponding weight in a 3-stage pipeline. The input from the bias neuron is implemented as the starting value for the accumulation flip-flop. The accumulated sum is passed through a 1-cycle activation function, ϕ. Each hidden neuron output is then sent to the output unit while a data valid signal (`valid_out`) is asserted. The output unit processes data similarly and returns data to the CPU through a postscaling unit (see Table 3). In the case of sin and cos, postscaling is not necessary and data is returned directly to the CPU. Processing is pipelined across NN layers and within a neuron.

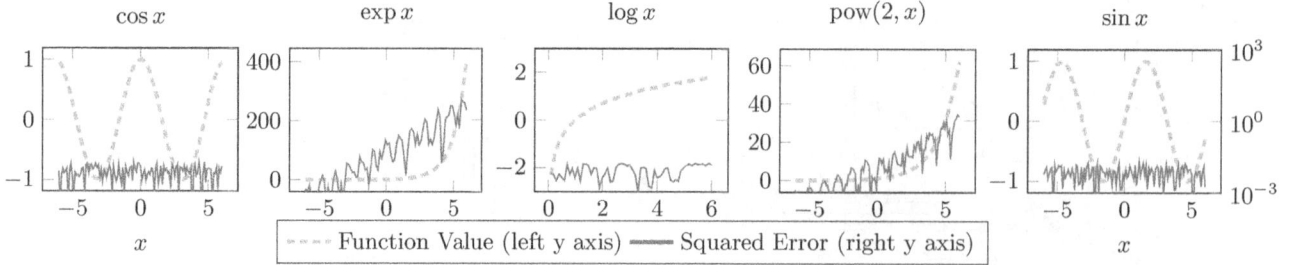

Figure 3: NN-based functions and their errors. Note: Error is plotted on a log scale using the right y axis.

The latency and throughput for a single neuron can be defined as follows, where N is the number inputs to a neuron:

$$\text{latency} = 6 + N - 1 = N + 5$$
$$\text{throughput} = \frac{1}{N + 5} \quad (5)$$

The latency of the entire NN is a function of the number of inputs to the NN (N_i), the number of neurons in the hidden layer (N_h, i.e., the number of inputs to the output neuron), and the latency of the scaling stages (L_s). The throughput is the inverse latency of the longest stage (i.e., either the hidden layer or the output layer). The scaling latency is two for cos and sin and three for log and exp.

$$\text{latency} = L_s + (N_i + 5) + (N_h + 5)$$
$$\text{throughput} = \frac{1}{\max(N_i, N_h) + 5} \quad (6)$$

4. EVALUATION

In this section, we compare accelerator-based execution with traditional execution of transcendental functions using EDP and accuracy metrics. We also explore the impact of NN-based accelerator usage on overall application behavior.

4.1 Accelerator-Based Execution versus Traditional Execution

To compare the accelerator-based execution and the traditional execution of transcendental functions, we use the Verilog hardware description language (HDL) to implement 2-layer NN designs in hardware with 1–15 hidden neurons and 6–10 fractional bits. We select these ranges because we find that NNs with too many hidden neurons are prone to overtraining and NNs with fewer than 6 fractional bits show high error rates. NNs are then synthesized and placed-and-routed (PnR) using a Cadence toolflow that uses the NCSU FreePDK 45nm predictive technology model to generate the final hardware design. All designs are run at their maximal possible frequencies as determined by the Cadence tools. We determine the energy using PnR tools with random data applied to input neurons. We evaluate the accuracy of these configurations by testing 100 trained instances of each NN configuration for each transcendental function. We use the FANN library to implement train and test these NNs in software.

For each transcendental function we select the NN configuration that minimizes the Energy-Delay-Error Product (EDEP) metric, which we define as follows:

$$\text{EDEP} = \text{energy} \times \frac{\text{latency in cycles}}{\text{frequency}} \times \text{MSE} \quad (7)$$

Table 4: NN-based accelerator hardware parameters with minimum EDEP for sin, cos, log, and exp.

NN	Func.	Area (um²)	Freq. (MHz)	Energy (pJ)
h1_b6	cos,sin	1259.50	337.38	8.30
h3_b7	exp,log	3578.50	335.80	24.81

Table 5: MSE and energy consumption of our NN-based implementation of transcendental functions.

Func.	NN	MSE	Energy (pJ)
cos	h1_b6	9.38×10^{-4}	8.30
exp	h3_b7	1.68×10^{-4}	24.81
log	h3_b7	1.45×10^{-4}	24.81
pow	h3_b7	4.32×10^{-2}	101.67
sin	h1_b6	7.37×10^{-4}	8.30

The parameters of the networks with a minimum EDEP for sin, cos, log, and exp are shown in Table 4. We find that sin and cos have minimal EDEP for a network with 1 hidden neuron and 6 fractional bits (abbreviated h1_b6). A network with 3 hidden neurons and 7 fractional bits (h3_b7) has minimal EDEP for log and exp. Using prescaling and postscaling, the outputs and squared error of these networks are shown in Figure 3. Error is plotted on a log scale on the right axis. We additionally show the output and error for pow which is computed using a combination of log and exp. Figure 3 shows that our NN-based accelerator can be used to approximate these five transcendental functions. Additionally, error and output scale together, i.e., a small output has a small error and a large output has a larger error. Table 5 shows the NN configuration, MSE and energy consumed by the NN-based execution of the transcendental functions.

Traditional execution of the transcendental functions involves executing a series of floating point instructions including addition, subtraction, and multiplication. Table 6 shows the average number of instructions that are executed for each transcendental function. We generate this table using the gem5 simulator [3] to trace small programs that repeatedly call transcendental functions with random inputs. We process these traces to pull out only those instructions related to transcendental function calls. Control, integer, and move instructions are aggregated in separate columns. Instructions executed less frequently than floating point subtraction are not shown in the table. Due to random inputs, the average number of instructions per function is not an integer. This is expected because glibc executes different code paths depending on input value.

For a valid EDP comparison of the NN-based execution with traditional glibc execution, we compute the energy per

Table 6: Mean floating point instruction counts (ss denotes single precision and sd denotes double precision) in single precision (e.g., cosf) and double precision (e.g., cos) glibc transcendental functions. Fractional instruction counts occur because glibc takes different code paths based on the random input values used. The estimated energy per function is shown using energy per instruction data from Table 7.

Func.	addsd	addss	mulsd	mulss	subsd	subss	Total Instructions	Energy (pJ)
cos	7.42	0.00	11.64	0.00	8.41	0.00	114.55	966.61
cosf	0.00	3.00	0.00	10.00	0.00	7.03	103.45	365.13
exp	11.00	0.00	14.00	0.00	6.00	0.00	159.97	1158.10
expf	5.00	1.00	5.00	1.00	2.00	1.00	218.00	453.16
log	18.06	0.00	11.79	0.00	5.09	0.00	226.86	994.72
logf	0.00	7.69	0.00	11.38	0.00	3.65	143.09	415.44
pow	32.46	0.00	30.54	0.00	20.54	0.00	337.53	2561.33
powf	0.00	23.32	0.00	35.00	0.00	26.32	354.56	1292.49
sin	8.17	0.00	10.97	0.00	5.99	0.00	109.40	909.30
sinf	0.00	3.00	0.00	8.54	0.00	5.16	96.68	311.42

Table 7: Parameters of traditional glibc implementations of floating point instructions.

Instruction	Area (um^2)	Freq. (MHz)	Energy (pJ)
addss	635.5	388	1.00
addsd	1466.7	388	2.20
mulss	6505.3	283	35.51
mulsd	16226.5	135	80.05

Table 8: EDP of NN-based and traditional glibc execution of transcendental functions.

Func.	EDP-NN	EDP-Single	EDP-Double
cos	3.44×10^{-19}	1.89×10^{-17}	5.54×10^{-17}
exp	1.26×10^{-18}	3.62×10^{-16}	9.26×10^{-17}
log	1.26×10^{-18}	2.97×10^{-17}	1.13×10^{-16}
pow	1.05×10^{-17}	2.29×10^{-16}	4.32×10^{-16}
sin	3.44×10^{-19}	1.51×10^{-17}	4.97×10^{-17}

Table 9: Percentage of total application cycles spent in transcendental functions and the estimated EDP of an NN-based accelerator implementation normalized to traditional, single precision floating point execution. Applications in the lower division have no transcendental functions.

Benchmark	% Total Cycles	Normalized EDP
blackscholes	45.65%	0.5583
bodytrack	2.25%	0.9783
canneal	1.19%	0.9885
swaptions	39.33%	0.6191
dedup	0.00%	1.0000
fluidanimate	0.00%	1.0000
freqmine	0.00%	1.0000
raytrace	0.00%	1.0000
streamcluster	0.00%	1.0000
x264	0.00%	1.0000
vips	0.00%	1.0000

floating point instruction using the same Cadence toolflow. The area, maximum operating frequency, and energy for floating point addition and multiplication is shown in Table 7. Floating point subtraction is taken to be equivalent to floating point addition. Other instructions are not evaluated as we find that floating point addition, multiplication, and subtraction are the most frequently executed instructions (after move instructions) in glibc transcendental functions.

Using the floating point addition, multiplication, and subtraction instruction counts and energy per instruction in Table 7, we calculate the energy per traditional transcendental function. Energy per transcendental function is shown in the last column of Table 6. We then compare the EDP of traditional and NN-based implementations. We did not use EDEP as the comparison metric because the MSE of a glibc implementation is effectively zero. We assume that instructions in transcendental functions can achieve an IPC of one at 2 GHz. The EDP comparison against single and double precision glibc implementations is shown in Table 8. The EDP value for our NN-based execution is, averaging between single and double precision, 68x lower than that of traditional execution. Our NN-based design trades off an average transcendental function MSE of 9.04×10^{-3} for this EDP savings.

4.2 NN-Based Accelerators in Applications

We analyze the EDP versus accuracy trade-offs associated with using our NN-based accelerators in applications. We execute benchmarks in the PARSEC suite using the gem5 simulator and record cycle counts. We then determine the percentage of total cycles that benchmarks spend executing transcendental functions. The EDP savings for each benchmark then follow an Amdahl's law convention—total EDP savings are limited by the number of cycles each benchmark spends executing transcendental functions. Table 9 shows the normalized EDP savings by applying the single precision floating point EDP reductions in Table 8. Results for facesim and ferret are excluded because cycle counts were not able to be obtained using gem5. Some applications do not use transcendental functions. However, NN-based accelerators may be reconfigured to approximate small or large portions of these applications for EDP savings.

We then build a software library that redefines the execution of selected transcendental functions (cos, exp, log, pow, and sin). Our software implementation uses the NN configurations listed in Table 5 for executing each transcendental function. We execute benchmarks in the PARSEC suite and compare their outputs to those of traditional execution of PARSEC benchmarks that rely on traditional glibc. For

Table 10: Application output MSE and percent error using NN-based accelerators.

Benchmark	MSE	E[|%error|]
blackscholes	4.48×10^{-1}	24.6236%
bodytrack	2.07×10^{-1}	29.6321%
canneal	2.89×10^{8}	0.0025%
ferret	1.03×10^{-3}	1.9633%
swaptions	5.59×10^{0}	36.8205%

this analysis, we only execute benchmarks that have transcendental function calls: blackscholes, bodytrack, canneal, ferret, and swaptions. We report the MSE and expected percent absolute error of application outputs in Table 10. The MSE and expected percent absolute error for all benchmarks is in an acceptable range. The output for canneal is a single large value, hence the large MSE, but low percent error.

Overall, NN-based accelerators approximating transcendental functions are able to provide substantial EDP reductions over standard glibc implementations. However, EDP and performance gains (and accuracy trade-offs) are explicitly governed by an Amdahl's law convention—any gains or losses that NN-based accelerators provide are directly proportional to the percentage of time that an application spends using the approximated functions. Benchmarks blackscholes and swaptions spend approximately 40% of their execution time computing floating point transcendental functions and can consequently decrease their EDP substantially. Benchmarks dedup, freqmine, raytrace, streamcluster, and x264 do not use any of the transcendental functions that we approximate. These benchmarks consequently see no EDP improvements or accuracy reductions. Benchmarks bodytrack and canneal make limited use of approximated transcendental functions and see modest EDP gains and small accuracy losses. All applications executed ran to completion without runtime errors.

5. CONCLUSION

NN-based accelerators provide a malleable substrate on which different types of approximate computations can be executed. Our work demonstrates that their inclusion in future architectural designs has the potential to reduce EDP at the cost of application output error. A hardware-level comparison of NN-based and glibc execution of transcendental functions shows that the EDP for NN-based execution is, on average, 68x lower than that of glibc execution. Moreover, the use of an NN-based accelerator to approximate transcendental functions in PARSEC benchmarks uses, averaged across the 5 benchmarks with transcendental functions, 78% of the EDP of a traditional glibc implementation. Output MSE and percent absolute error are, on average, 1.56 and 0.24, excluding canneal. These results indicate that library-level approximation may be a viable direction for leveraging energy reductions while maintaining safe program execution. This work can be furthered by using NN-based accelerators to approximate additional functions in glibc and other libraries.

6. ACKNOWLEDGMENTS

This work was supported by a NASA Office of the Chief Technologist's Space Technology Research Fellowship.

7. REFERENCES

[1] W. Arden, et al. More-than-moore. *International Technology Roadmap for Semiconductors*, 2010.

[2] C. Bienia et al. *Benchmarking modern multiprocessors*. Princeton University, 2011.

[3] N. Binkert, et al. The gem5 simulator. *ACM Comp. Ar.*, 39(2):1–7, 2011.

[4] S. Borkar et al. The future of microprocessors. *Comm. ACM*, 54(5):67–77, 2011.

[5] T. Chen, et al. Benchnn: On the broad potential application scope of hardware neural network accelerators. In *IISWC*, 2012.

[6] V. K. Chippa, et al. Analysis and characterization of inherent application resilience for approximate computing. In *DAC*, 2013.

[7] G. Cybenko. Approximation by superpositions of a sigmoidal function. *Math. Control Signal*, 2(4):303–314, 1989.

[8] R. H. Dennard, et al. Design of ion-implanted mosfet's with very small physical dimensions. *IEEE J. Solid-St. Circ.*, 9(5):256–268, 1974.

[9] H. Duwe. Exploiting application level error resilience via deferred execution. *Master's thesis, University of Illinois at Urbana Champaign*, 2013.

[10] H. Esmaeilzadeh, et al. Dark silicon and the end of multicore scaling. In *ISCA*, 2011.

[11] H. Esmaeilzadeh, et al. Neural acceleration for general-purpose approximate programs. In *MICRO*, 2012.

[12] A. Hashmi, et al. Automatic abstraction and fault tolerance in cortical microachitectures. In *ISCA*, 2011.

[13] A. Hashmi, et al. A case for neuromorphic isas. *ACM SIGPLAN Notices*, pages 145–158, 2011.

[14] K. Hornik. Approximation capabilities of multilayer feedforward networks. *Neural Networks*, 4(2):251–257, 1991.

[15] B. Li, et al. Memristor-based approximated computation. In *ISLPED*, 2013.

[16] S. Nissen. Implementation of a fast artificial neural network library (fann). Technical report, Department of Computer Science University of Copenhagen (DIKU), 2003. http://fann.sf.net.

[17] M. Riedmiller et al. A direct adaptive method for faster backpropagation learning: The rprop algorithm. In *ICNN*, 1993.

[18] D. E. Rumelhart et al. *Parallel distributed processing: explorations in the microstructure of cognition. Volume 1. Foundations*. MIT Press, Cambridge, Ma, 1986.

[19] J. E. Stine, et al. Freepdk: An open-source variation-aware design kit. In *MSE*, 2007.

[20] O. Temam. A defect-tolerant accelerator for emerging high-performance applications. In *ISCA*, 2012.

[21] S. Venkataramani, et al. Quality programmable vector processors for approximate computing. In *MICRO*, 2013.

[22] J. E. Volder. The cordic trigonometric computing technique. *IRE Tran. Comput.*, EC-8(3):330 –334, sept. 1959.

[23] S. Walther. A unified algorithm for elementary functions. *AFIPS*, 1971.

Efficient Parallel Beamforming for 3D Ultrasound Imaging

Pirmin Vogel[1], Andrea Bartolini[1,2], Luca Benini[1,2]

[1]Integrated Systems Laboratory
ETH Zurich, Switzerland
{vogel,bartolini,benini}@iis.ee.ethz.ch

[2]Electrical, Electronic, and Information Engineering
University of Bologna, Italy
{a.bartolini,luca.benini}@unibo.it

ABSTRACT

One of the most demanding tasks in state-of-the-art medical ultrasound systems is the localization of possible scatterers in the body based on received echoes. Digital beamforming involves the summation of all received echoes in each image point according to their time of flight, i.e., their delay. This requires the knowledge of the delays for all combinations of ultrasound transmitters, image points and receivers. Recent three-dimensional (3D) systems comprise thousands of transducer elements and millions of image points. Compared to traditional 2D systems, the total number of delays is several orders of magnitude larger.

In this paper, we present a new beamforming algorithm that exploits the inherent locality in the image formation and efficiently approximates the delays. Compared to latest proposed architectures, this results in 20 percent less arithmetic operations, and a reduction of the input/output (I/O) bandwidth and the total memory size by factors of 30 and 50, respectively.

Categories and Subject Descriptors

F.2.0 [**Analysis of Algorithms and Problem Complexity**]: General; B.2.1 [**Arithmetic and Logic Structures**]: Design Styles—*Parallel*

General Terms

Algorithms, Design, Performance

Keywords

Digital Beamforming; Ultrafast Imaging; 3D Ultrasound

1. INTRODUCTION

Since its first medical applications around 70 years ago, ultrasound imaging has undergone significant development and experienced many innovations and improvements which paved the way for new imaging modalities and applications.

Today, it is one of the main techniques used for medical imaging and offers several advantages compared to conventional X-ray imaging, CT and MRI. These include lower cost, smaller size, real-time applicability, user friendliness, no exposure to ionizing radiation, and compatibility with magnetic materials [8, 13].

During the past decade, 3D ultrasound imaging started to gain popularity. Compared to its 2D counterpart, it allows for the visualization of arbitrary 2D images through the volume [13]. Moreover, it is suggested to reduce the operator dependence in the scanning process, scan times, and costs by dissociating acquisition and reporting. The deskilling could even lead to the adaption of ultrasound imaging as a simple diagnostic tool in doctor's offices and thereby avoiding the need for a referral to the hospital [17]. Providing a repeatable and more accurate way to evaluate anatomic structures, 3D ultrasound allows for accurate volumetric measurements of cysts and tumors [16].

However, these advantages are accompanied by notably increased hardware requirements, especially when opting for real-time imaging. A research system for real-time 3D ultrasound imaging has been presented in [9]. Being designed for research purposes only, the system can be used with transducers having up to 128 elements, uses 80 signal processing units and weights several hundred kilograms. Dealing with recent 2D transducer arrays comprising several thousand transducer elements [18], it is obvious that probably only dedicated hardware architectures can offer the required processing power at reasonable power consumption. In fact, a parallel hardware architecture for low-power 3D ultrasound beamforming has been proposed recently [16].

The contribution of this paper is a new algorithm for 3D beamforming which introduces a novel per *nappe* based image point computation. This leads to a significant reduction of the memory footprint, the I/O bandwidth and the overall number of computations compared to per scanline based approaches. We introduce a novel approximation strategy for the delay computation. With respect to state-of-the-art solutions [16], this allows to reduce the memory footprint and the I/O bandwidth by factors of 50 and 30, respectively. Moreover, as the delay approximation coefficients and the data received by the transducer elements now fit into the local SRAM available in today's field-programmable gate arrays (FPGAs), the use of an external DRAM can be avoided. In addition, our novel architecture reduces the total number of arithmetic operations by roughly 20 percent. Finally, we show that the required computational resources fit into today's high-end FPGAs.

Section 2 gives an introduction to conventional and ultrafast ultrasound imaging. The current state of the art is described in Section 3. In Section 4, we describe the key features and overall architecture of the proposed solution. Section 5 finally gives a comparison of the presented architecture with a recently proposed solution and an FPGA design feasibility study.

2. PRELIMINARIES

The basic principle of medical ultrasound imaging is to excite the target body volume with acoustic, high-frequency pulses and to form an image using the back-reflected echoes. Next, we give a brief introduction to ultrasound imaging.

2.1 Conventional Imaging

Conventional ultrasound systems acquire 2D images sequentially line by line. Per image line, a couple of subsequent transducer elements are used to transmit focused pulses into the tissue. The back-reflected echoes are recorded using all transducer elements, and the corresponding image line is obtained by properly delaying and adding the individual receive signals [5]. This relatively simple step is called receive beamforming. Due to the very limited image acquisition speed, conventional ultrasound imaging is not suitable for real-time 3D imaging [11].

2.2 Ultrafast Imaging

Systems for ultrafast imaging are capable of reconstructing the whole image from a single transmit. For synthetic aperture imaging, an unfocused spherical wave is emitted from a single or a few transducer elements [10, 9], whereas all transducer elements are used to transmit an unfocused plane wave when doing coherent plane-wave compounding [5, 7]. In both cases, the echoes received on all transducer elements need to be digitized and stored. Digital beamforming can then be performed by a parallel computing platform by properly delaying and adding the individual receive signals in each image point. Ultrafast imaging allows for significantly higher frame rates compared to conventional imaging. In fact, [7] suggests that the number of insonifications for coherent plane-wave compounding can be 10 times lower as for conventional imaging while achieving similar image quality. Moreover, ultrafast imaging allows to trade image quality for frame rate. Reaching frame rates of up to a few thousands of Hz, ultrafast imaging paved the way for new ultrasound imaging modalities and led to significant improvements in existing imaging modes such as shear wave elastography and Doppler flow analysis, respectively [5]. However, there are several challenging aspects associated with ultrafast imaging and digital beamforming in particular.

- **Interdependency:** To compute the intensity in one image point, all received signals need to be accessed, and every receive signal contains samples that need to be added to every image point. This aspect makes it difficult to efficiently parallelize digital beamforming.

- **Data Transfer and Storage:** Digital beamforming basically operates on the raw radio-frequency (RF) signals acquired by the transducer elements. In practice, millions of samples need to be transferred to the computing engine for each transmit. To allow for a fast image acquisition and reconstruction, either a large and

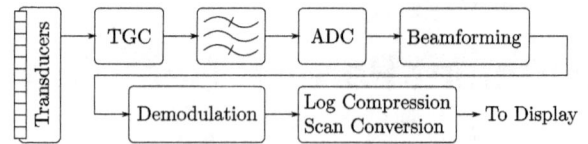

Figure 1: Receive chain for ultrafast imaging.

expensive local memory or an external memory with a huge bandwidth is required.

- **Processing Power:** Recent 3D systems comprise thousands of transducers and millions of image points. Beamforming then means to add thousands of samples to each of the millions of image points and consequently requires the execution of billions to trillions of operations.

In the past, ultrafast imaging had therefore been limited to research and to applications where fast image acquisition is important and real-time operation not required [15]. But due to the emergence of graphics processing units (GPUs) offering sufficient processing power and high-speed interconnects in the past decade, real-time ultrafast imaging has become feasible at least for 2D imaging [8].

2.3 System Overview

A simplified block diagram of an ultrasound receive chain for ultrafast imaging is shown in Fig. 1. After transmitting the pulses, the operating mode of the transducers is switched to receive mode and the back-reflected echoes are recorded. Time gain compensation (TGC) amplifies the received signals as function of time to reduce the dynamic range of the received signals. The signals are then bandpass filtered to avoid aliasing during analog-to-digital conversion (ADC). Now, the signals are ready to be used for digital beamforming. This operation is described in more detail in the next section. Since beamforming acts on the RF signals, its output needs to be demodulated before display. Finally, logarithmic compression reduces the dynamic range of the image and scan conversion is used to generate the final pixel image ready for display.

2.4 Digital Beamforming

The conversion of the received signals from time domain to the spatial image domain is a very demanding task. To localize possible scatterers in the image, all received echoes need to be summed in each image point according to the time of flight. This process is illustrated in Fig. 2. For the sake of simplicity, only a 1D array is shown.

Fig. 2 a) shows the image geometry for a phased array. By applying the same pulse with varying phase to several transducer elements, the ultrasound beam can be steered over the image while always originating from the same location. This is accounted for by the radial scanlines originating from the center transducer element. Phased arrays produce a fan beam and can therefore be used to generate sector images and, e.g., to send the beam between the ribs. Traditional systems process each scanline independently. They do insonification, beamforming and demodulation line by line [15]. Each scanline consists of several image points in which the system can detect scatterers (black dots).

In Fig. 2 b), the insonification is visualized. The figure shows the transmission of a spherical wave from a single

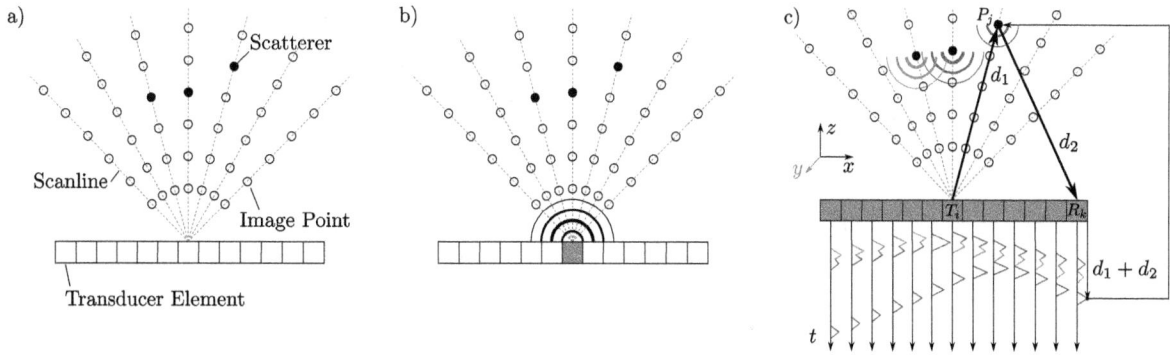

Figure 2: Principle of ultrasound imaging. a) 2D imaging geometry and terms. b) Emission of a spherical wave in the transmit phase. c) The spherical wave is reflected by the scatterers in the body. Depending on the time of flight, the echoes from different scatterers arrive delayed and amplitude scaled at each receiver.

transducer element. After transmission, the wave propagates into the body and as it encounters an interface between materials of different density, part of the wave is reflected back to the transducer array. Each transducer element gets to see a superposition of delayed and amplitude scaled echoes which is recorded as shown in the lower part of the Fig. 2 c). Beamforming means to reconstruct the material interfaces in the image points by computing their contribution to the received echoes. This is done by summing all the echoes in each image point according to their time of flight, i.e., their delay. If for example the contribution of Point P_j to the echo seen by Receiver R_k is to be computed, the Delay d_1 from the Transmitter T_i to P_j and d_2 from P_j to R_k needs to be known. These can be determined to be

$$d_1 = \frac{1}{c}\sqrt{(x_j - x_i)^2 + (y_j - y_i)^2 + (z_j - z_i)^2} \qquad (1)$$

and

$$d_2 = \frac{1}{c}\sqrt{(x_k - x_j)^2 + (y_k - y_j)^2 + z_j^2} \qquad (2)$$

where $c = 1540\,m/s$ is the speed of sound in tissue. Then, the sample recorded by R_k at time instant d_1+d_2 is added to the intensity value in Point P_j. To obtain an intensity map for the whole image, this operation needs to be repeated for all combinations of transmitters, image points and receivers.

3. RELATED WORK

Digital beamforming for ultrafast ultrasound imaging is a very demanding task, especially if it comes to real-time 3D imaging. A research system capable of handling 128 transducer elements is presented in [9]. The system can be used for real-time data acquisition but it does not offer sufficient processing power for real-time 3D image reconstruction, despite its 80 signal processing units. An open ultrasound research platform is presented in [14]. This system is smaller, can handle up to 64 transducer elements at a time, and is able to do real-time image reconstruction. However, it cannot be used for 3D imaging.

The emergence of GPUs offering immense processing power and high-speed interconnects in the past decade paved the way for software implementations of digital beamforming algorithms for 2D ultrafast imaging [8]. In contrast to traditional systems that independently process the individual scanlines [15], these systems split the whole image into many sections according to a 2D grid which are computed in paral-

lel. This allows for the reconstruction of more than 3000 ultrasound images acquired by 32 receive channels per second. With Aixplorer [1], the first software-based ultrasound system for ultrafast imaging has been introduced. In this system, all the processing including beamforming is performed by CPUs and GPUs.

Recent 2D arrays for 3D imaging comprise thousands of transducer elements [18] to compute millions of image points. Compared to 2D imaging, the amount of data to process, the number of delays, and the computational complexity are orders of magnitude higher. Offline computation and storage of all the delays would require a memory with a size of several GBytes and an exorbitant bandwidth for fast processing. Instead, the delays could be computed online. However, this not a trivial task either, mainly due to the square roots in Eq. 1 and 2. There are several approaches to mitigate this problem. For example, [4] suggests to approximate the delay computation using a Taylor series and [12] iteratively approximates the delays on a scanline basis.

Recently, a dedicated hardware architecture for beamforming in low-power, real-time 3D imaging has been proposed [16]. Per second, the Sonic Millip3De reconstructs one volume consisting of 10 million image points out of the signals acquired with a transducer array consisting of 128×96 elements. The delays are approximated on a scanline basis which requires a large external memory with a high bandwidth. As the system processes only a bunch of scanlines and receive signals at a time, the received signals as well as the image data needs to be traversed several times which requires a lot of memory bandwidth. After exciting the target and receiving the back-reflected echoes, the transducer must wait for the beamforming of the current transmit to finish before launching the next transmit. Consequently, the many transmits required to form a single volume are distributed in time which makes the system prone to motion blur.

As opposed to that, the architecture presented in this paper uses a simple but efficient delay approximation scheme and makes use of the inherent locality by computing the image points on a depth basis. The number of approximation constants is orders of magnitude lower which allows to dispense with external DRAM. Furthermore, the total number of arithmetic operations can be reduced by roughly 20 percent, and the required computational resources including the memories containing the data received by the transducer elements fit into today's high-end FPGAs.

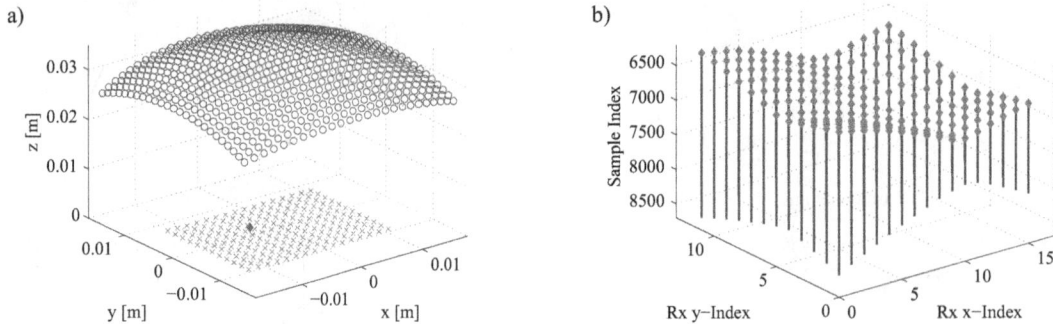

Figure 3: a) Spatial image geometry: transducer elements (red crosses), virtual source (green diamond), image points forming a nappe (blue circles). b) Blanket: first sample of each transducer (red diamonds).

4. EFFICIENT PARALLEL BEAMFORMING

In this section, we present our new beamforming algorithm and the corresponding hardware architecture.

4.1 Inherent Locality in Beamforming

As shown in Fig. 2 c), the echo of a single scatterer arrives slightly delayed at the different transducers, which leads to the arc shape in time domain. Each scatterer in the spatial image domain corresponds to a different arc in time domain. The arcs of scatterers located at similar depth are almost parallel and intersect (red and blue). They form a stripe of varying thickness. The samples required to compute the intensities of the corresponding image points are located nearby in the memories containing the received signals. For scatterers with sufficiently different depths, the arcs do not intersect (green). The corresponding samples are located further away in memory.

The basic principle of our algorithm is to make use of this relationship between depth and time by doing the beamforming on a depth instead of a scanline basis. As can be seen in Fig. 3 a), the image points located at the same distance from the center of the 2D transducer array form a *nappe*. Each of these image points corresponds to a separate surface in time domain. The surfaces of all image points in a nappe form a *blanket* of varying thickness in time domain. Fig. 3 b) shows the blanket for the image points in the nappe of Fig. 3 a). Out of the samples of one blanket, the intensities of all image points in the corresponding nappe can be computed.

Doing the beamforming depth by depth allows to cope with both interdependency and data storage challenges. Only the samples of the blanket contributing to the current nappe need to be kept in the upsampled form in a fast and local but relatively small memory. Once a sample has been loaded to this memory, it is not discarded until all operations involving this sample have been performed. Since the blankets of two subsequent nappes overlap, only a few samples need to be upsampled and loaded to proceed to the next nappe. This is a major improvement over scanline based approaches, which traverse all the receive signals once per scanline.

4.2 Simple Delay Approximation

Computing the intensities of all image points in a nappe in series allows for the use of a very simple delay approximation scheme. We propose to solely use a piece-wise linear

Table 1: System parameters.

Parameter	Value
Transducer elements	128×96
Virtual sources	16
Sub-apertures	12
Image points [M]	10.24
Image points per nappe	2500
Nappes	4096
Samples per receive signal	4096
Sampling rate [MHz]	40
Interpolation factor	4

approximation for the square root function in Eq. 1 and 2. For sufficient accuracy, the function needs to be split into many sections, which requires the use of a large look-up table (LUT) containing the approximation constants for all sections. Since the inputs of the approximation function for all image points in a nappe vary only by small amounts, the approximation can be designed such that the computation of the delays for two sequentially computed image points requires the use of the same or at most of two subsequent sections, and that the approximation section needs to be changed as little as possible for the computation of one nappe. This allows for the use of many small, local LUTs that obtain their content from a shared, global LUT containing the approximation constants for all sections.

4.3 Hardware Architecture

To ease comparison with Sonic Millip3De [16], we use the same system parameters shown in Tab. 1. We use 12-way sub-aperture multiplexing to reduce the number of connections to the transducer array, the number of ADCs, the peak data rate, and the number of parallel processing pipelines. We split the transducer array into 96 rows of 128 elements each. Per transmit, there are only 8 rows active (every 12th). Since 16 virtual sources are used, 192 transmits are used to acquire 1 volume. We consider an ADC sampling rate of 40 MHz and a resolution of 12 bit. For digital beamforming, it has been shown that the sampling rate of the receive signals should be 4 to 10 times the carrier frequency for acceptable performance in terms of random timing errors [19]. To enable the use of typical carrier frequencies up to 15 MHz [16], the signals are upsampled and interpolated to 160 MHz prior to beamforming. To acquire 500 wavelengths, which is the maximum practical travel distance of ultrasound pulses in tissue, about 4000 samples are recorded per transducer element and transmit [6].

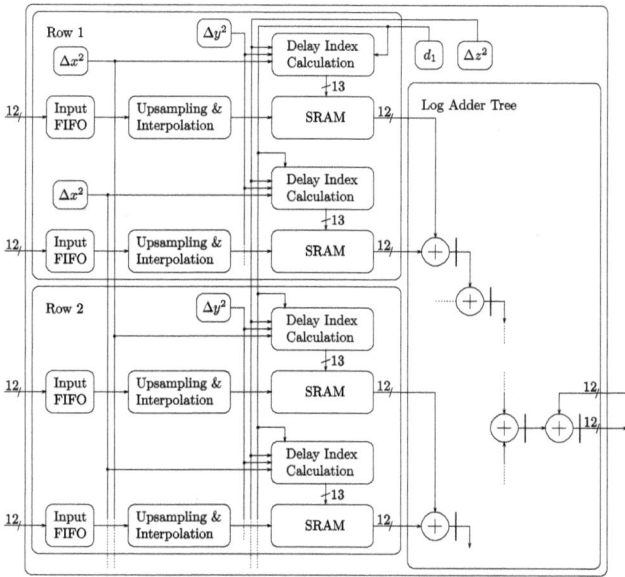

Figure 4: Data path of the hardware architecture.

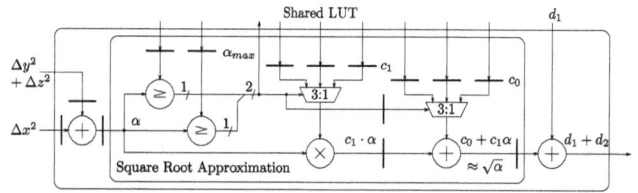

Figure 5: Delay index calculation block architecture.

The data path of the hardware architecture is shown in Fig. 4. There is a separate processing pipeline for each active transducer element including a first in, first out (FIFO) input memory holding up to 4096 samples, a unit for upsampling and interpolation of the received samples, a static random-access memory (SRAM) holding the samples required to compute the image points of the current nappe (≈ 3840 samples per transducer element), and a delay index calculation block to compute the memory address of the samples to add to a particular image point. Per cycle, one sample of each SRAM is read and fed to the logarithmic adder tree to compute the intensity of one image point.

After launching a transmit, the transducers are switched to receive mode and the digitized samples are written to the 1024 FIFOs at the input of the architecture. As soon as the FIFOs are no longer empty, the samples are upsampled, linearly interpolated and transferred to the SRAMs. The beamforming starts by computing d_1 for the first image point in that nappe according to Eq. 1 using the square root approximation unit shown in Fig. 5. The Δx^2, Δy^2 and Δz^2 for both d_1 and d_2 are computed from the x,y, and z coordinates of the virtual sources, image points and transducer elements. The coordinates of the virtual sources and transducer elements are stored as such in memory. For the image points, the coordinates for the first nappe and the increments in x, y and z direction need to be stored. Since these increments are constant for all points on the same radial scanline, the coordinates of the image points in the upper nappes can be iteratively computed. Due to the symmetry in the problem, only one fourth of the coordinates and increments need to be stored.

After having computed Δx^2, Δy^2 and Δz^2 using the coordinates of the virtual source and the image point, the three terms are summed and compared with the section borders of the currently loaded approximation constants. The square root approximation unit can hold the approximation constants of three subsequent sections. Depending on the results of these comparisons, one of the three loaded sets is used. If not the middle one is used, this is signaled to a

shared LUT containing the constants for all approximation sections, which then delivers the proper constants in one of the following cycles. The design of the approximation sections and constants means to find a compromise between approximation error and the number of sections. Confining the maximum approximation error to half a sample led to 64 approximation sections and a maximum delay error of 1 sample in the whole volume. It is sufficient to store three sets of constants locally, since at most two subsequent sections are required for the delay approximation of two subsequent image points. On average, the approximation section needs to be changed less than once every 5 image points. Consequently, if the square root approximation unit signals the request for a new section, the shared LUT needs to deliver the section within 5 cycles. Hence, 1 shared LUT is sufficient to serve 5 square root approximation units. In total, 205 shared LUTs of 288 Bytes each are required.

Once d_1 has been computed, it is fed to all pipelines. At the same time, every pipeline computes d_2 according to Eq. 2. Per cycle, 128 values for Δx^2, 8 values for Δy^2, and 1 value for Δz^2 need to be computed using the coordinates of the current image point and the active transducer elements. These terms are fed to the different pipelines according to the coordinates of the corresponding transducer elements. Each pipeline contains a delay index calculation unit shown in Fig. 5 that combines these terms, approximates d_2 and adds it to d_1 to get the memory address of the sample to select. Next, the proper samples can be read from the SRAMs and fed to the logarithmic adder tree at the output. The intensity of the image point is then accumulated by adding the sum of the selected samples to the corresponding sum obtained from the last transmit. After repeating this procedure for all image points in the current nappe, the SRAMs need to be updated by deleting samples that do not contribute to the next nappe, and by loading new samples from the input FIFOs. On average, only one new sample is read from every input FIFO when advancing to the next nappe. After the last samples have been read from the input FIFOs, the next transmit is launched.

5. RESULTS

In this section, we compare our beamforming architecture with Sonic Millip3De [16]. The required memory sizes are given in Tab. 2. The size of the internal SRAM nearly doubles to due the memories containing the samples of the current blanket. On the other hand, the size of the approximation constants is orders of magnitude lower. The memory footprint of the system is reduced by a factor of 50 which allows to completely dispense with off-chip DRAM. Sonic Millip3De requires 6 DRAM parts connected via 192 links to meet the stringent bandwidth requirements. Together with the 192-bit wide on-chip interconnect, these DRAMs

Table 2: Memory sizes.

Purpose	Value	Millip3De
Input samples	6 MB	6 MB
Blanket samples	5.33 MB	0
Blanket borders	16 KB	0
Coordinates & Increments	14.5 KB	0
Approximation constants	58 KB	1.2 GB
Image points	14.65 MB	14.65 MB
Total	26.07 MB	1.22 GB

Table 3: Arithmetic operations in G (10^9), T (10^{12}).

Function Block	Type	Value	Millip3De
Interpolation	Shift	0.81 G	125.83 G
	Add	3.22 G	503.32 G
Delay index calculation	Comp	4.03 T	10.07 T
	Add	6.35 T	6.04 T
	Mult	2.29 T	0
Logarithmic adder tree	Add	2.01 T	2.01 T
Total		14.68 T	18.75 T

account for half of the system's total power consumption. To reconstruct one volume per second, our architecture requires a total I/O bandwidth of 6.61 GB/s compared to 186.07 GB/s for Sonic Millip3De. This significant reduction has two reasons. First, the received signals are traversed only once. Second, all the constants can be stored on-chip.

In Tab. 3, the number of arithmetic operations per volume are shown. Since our architecture traverses the received signals only once, the number of operations due to upsampling and interpolation are much smaller. However, these numbers are negligible compared to the number of operations required for the delay index calculation and the summation. Compared to Sonic Millip3De, our architecture requires 20 percent less arithmetic operations. However, about 16 percent of all operations are multiplications which is not desirable in a dedicated hardware architecture.

For a fully parallel implementation of the delay index calculation units, 2050 comparators, 3226 adders and 1165 multipliers are needed. The logarithmic adder tree requires additional 1024 adders. Today's high-end FPGAs such as the devices of the Xilinx Virtex UltraScale family offer up to 115.2 Mb of block memory and 2880 digital signal processors (DSPs) [3]. To store the image points, a relatively small, external SRAM such as [2] can be used. The image points are accessed in a circular fashion and per clock cycle, only one value is needed for the processing. Consequently, a single chip suffices to stream the image points in and out. Therefore, our architecture can even be mapped to an FPGA which enables portable 3D ultrasound systems.

6. CONCLUSION

In this paper, we have presented a new beamforming algorithm that exploits the inherent locality in the image formation and efficiently approximates the delays. This is achieved by computing the image points on a per *nappe* base. This approach leads to a reduction of the memory footprint by a factor of 50, an I/O bandwidth that is 30 times lower, and 20 percent less arithmetic operations. The corresponding architecture fits current high-end FPGA's hardware capabilities without the need of an external DRAM.

7. ACKNOWLEDGMENTS

This work was funded by the project UltrasoundToGo, financed with a grant from the Swiss Nano-Tera.ch initiative, and evaluated by the Swiss National Science Foundation.

8. REFERENCES

[1] SuperSonic Aixplorer, http://www.supersonic imagine.com/.

[2] Cypress 144-Mbit QDR II SRAM two-word burst architecture. Datasheet, Nov. 2012.

[3] Xilinx UltraScale architecture and product overview. Product Specification, Dec. 2013.

[4] M. Ali, D. Magee, and D. Udayan. Signal processing overview of ultrasound systems for medical imaging. White Paper, Nov. 2008.

[5] J. Bercoff. Ultrafast ultrasound imaging. In *Ultrasound Imaging - Medical Applications.* InTech, Aug. 2011.

[6] E. Daigle, Ronald. Ultrasound imaging system with pixel oriented processing. U.S. Patent, US 8,287,456 B2, Oct. 2012.

[7] G. Montaldo et al. Coherent plane-wave compounding for very high frame rate ultrasonography and transient elastography. *IEEE Trans. Ultrason., Ferroelectr., Freq. Control,* 56(3):489–506, Mar. 2009.

[8] H. K.-H. So et al. Medical ultrasound imaging: To GPU or not to GPU? *IEEE Micro,* 31(5):54–65, 2011.

[9] J. A. Jensen et al. Ultrasound research scanner for real-time synthetic aperture data acquisition. *IEEE Trans. Ultrason., Ferroelectr., Freq. Control,* 52(5):881–891, May 2005.

[10] J. A. Jensen et al. Synthetic aperture ultrasound imaging. *Ultrasonics,* 44, Suppl.:e5–e15, Dec. 2006.

[11] G. R. Lockwood, J. R. Talman, and S. S. Brunke. Real-time 3-D ultrasound imaging using sparse synthetic aperture beamforming. *IEEE Trans. Ultrason., Ferroelectr., Freq. Control,* 45(4):980–988, July 1998.

[12] D. P. Magee. Iterative time delay values for ultrasound beamforming. U.S. Patent, US 2010/0249594 A1, Sept. 2010.

[13] O. V. Solberg et al. Freehand 3D ultrasound reconstruction algorithms–a review. *Ultrasound in Med. and Biol.,* 33(7):991–1009, July 2007.

[14] P. Tortoli et al. ULA-OP: an advanced open platform for ultrasound research. *IEEE Trans. Ultrason., Ferroelectr., Freq. Control,* 56(10):2207–2216, Oct. 2009.

[15] J. Powers and F. Kremkau. Medical ultrasound systems. *Interface Focus,* May 2011.

[16] R. Sampson, et al. Sonic Millip3De: a massively parallel 3D-stacked accelerator for 3D ultrasound. In *HPCA2013,* pages 318–329, 2013.

[17] R. W. Prager et al. Three-dimensional ultrasound imaging. *Proceedings of the Institution of Mechanical Engineers, Part H: Journal of Engineering in Medicine,* 224(2):193–223, Feb. 2010.

[18] S. Freeman et al. Third generation xMATRIX technology for abdominal and obstetrical imaging. White Paper, Aug. 2012.

[19] B. Steinberg. Digital beamforming in ultrasound. *IEEE Trans. Ultrason., Ferroelectr., Freq. Control,* 39(6):716–721, 1992.

A Task-Oriented Vision System

Yang Xiao, Kevin Irick, Jack Sampson,
Vijaykrishnan Narayanan
Department of Computer Science and Engineering
Pennsylvania State University
{yux106, irick, sampson, vijay}@cse.psu.edu

Chuanjun Zhang
Intel Science and Technology Center for Embedded
Computing
Pittsburg, PA, USA
chuanjun.zhang@intel.com

ABSTRACT

Recently, biologically inspired vision systems have been the focus of intense research effort to emulate the high energy-efficiency, performance and robustness of mammalian vision systems. However, previous vision accelerators have only focused on speeding up computationally intense portions of the system without exploiting effects seen in the human brain that demonstrate the task influence in the vision mechanism. In this paper, we propose a task-oriented two-level vision system which is composed of Saliency and SURF. To the best of our knowledge, our design is the first embedded system that utilizes task influence in the computation of visual attention and recognition. As a result, we show that the new system can achieve at most 12.75% accuracy improvement while saving 25% computation work.

Categories and Subject Descriptors

C.3 [**Computer Systems Organization**]: Special-Purpose and Application-Based Systems – Real-time and embedded system

General Terms

Not available

Keywords

Top-down; Saliency; SURF; Visual Attention; Embedded System

1. INTRODUCTION

Real time object recognition is emerging as a necessary function for mobile low power devices. Wearable glasses [1] with camera can help people who are blind or visually impaired to navigate or experience the environment. A robot can help retail store staff on real-time product location and inventory information. Autonomous cars must detect and recognize objects in real time that are critical for safety driving, e.g. traffic signs, other cars, bicycles, pedestrians that are crossing the street, etc. It is obvious that these applications need to find targeted objects in real time to meet diverse requests of such applications.

Previous neuromorphic vision systems have focused on either the recognition paths [2] or attention paths [3], or required significant hardware resources to attempt to do both in real time. Kestur et al.

GLSVLSI'14, May 21–23, 2014, Houston, Texas, USA.
Copyright © 2014 ACM 978-1-4503-2816-6/14/05...$15.00.
http://dx.doi.org/10.1145/2591513.2591602

[4] used several FPGAs to embody a system that mimics both the attention and recognition paths of mammalian vision, employing the Saliency [5] and HMAX [6] algorithms developed by Itti and Mutch, respectively. In [7], a network-on-chip based parallel processor is demonstrated for vision tasks that require an ARM10 core and eight single-instruction multiple-data (SIMD) clusters to cooperate in order to fulfill the real-time processing requirements of bio-inspired object recognition.

An very important factor in the human vision system, however, is task influence, and it has been paid little attention in previous system designs. Figure 1 illustrates the idea of the experiment conducted by Yarbus [8] to demonstrate the different patterns of eye fixations (attention) changes when human test subjects were asked to perform different tasks in the same scene. Figure 1(a) here is the original picture. When no task is assigned to the test subjects, human visual attentions are randomly located at different places in the scene as Figure 1(b). When tasks are assigned, subject's attention is focused on certain locations of image that are relevant to the given task. For example, when subjects were asked to describe the girl, attention is mainly focused on the girl rather than on the food on the table in the room as depicted in Figure 1(c). In contrast, Figure 1(d) shows the case when the task is to identify the food on the table.

In this paper we propose a visual attention and recognition system which ties the task influence to digital human visual system in a straightforward way. We also show that by integrating the

Figure 1: Different attention location movement based on different task.

knowledge of a given task into our system, it can pay more attention to a specified task than a system that purely depends on the response of low level features of a scene. The rest of the paper is organized as follows: Section 2 provides a fundamental introduction of the vision algorithms and learning algorithm we used. Section 3 describes the complete system architecture in detail. Section 4 shows our experiments and results, and we conclude with Section 5.

2. MODEL OF NEUROMORPHIC VISION

In this section, the attention model, feature extraction model and learning method we used are described in detail.

2.1 TD-Saliency Core

The saliency-based attention model originates from the work of Itti, Koch, and Niebur [5]. The model mimics the early stage visual pathway in a human brain, e.g the LGN, V1 and V2 brain regions. During processing, the low level features of color, intensity, and orientation are gathered together via a bottom-up path to predict the attention location in a scene. Borji, in [9], takes this one step further by integrating the task information into the system. As shown in Figure 2, the system itself contains five steps to reach the final saliency map.

First, the original image is decomposed into three feature channels: intensity, orientation, and color. The intensity channel contains the image's intensity array; the color channel contains *RG* and *YB* arrays; the orientation channel contains four arrays generated via Gabor filtering at degrees of [0°, 45°, 90°, 135°]. Low-pass filtering and subsampling are applied to three channels' arrays for generating intensity, orientation, and color image pyramids (9 scales per pyramid). Second, the surround inhibition is then applied to every pixel of at each scale of the image pyramids to form the feature pyramids. Third, within each feature pyramids each scale is multiplied with its task weight, and then all the scales are summed up, and normalized to create a single feature map. Fourth, feature maps of each channel are then multiplied with their task weights, summed and normalized again to create three individual conspicuity maps. Finally, all the conspicuity maps are biased by the task weights and summed to form the final saliency map.

2.2 SURF Core

SURF, developed by Bay et al [10], is a novel detector and descriptor with scale and rotation robustness. It allows the same objects to be recognized even when observed under significantly different lighting and pose conditions. The algorithm uses the approximated 2nd order Gaussian response via utilizing integral images and Fast Hessian filters for detecting interest points in an image. Here, we decompose the algorithm into two stages with detailed explanation below.

1. Interest Point Detection Stage:

   - First, the integral image of the input image is computed.

   - Second, three octaves, each containing 4 scale responses, are created via Fast Hessian matrix filter with size of {9, 15, 21, 27}, {15, 27, 39, 51} and {27, 51, 75, 99}

   - Third, every pixel of two middle scales in every octave (for example, scale of 15, 21 in {9, 15, 21, 27}), is evaluated with its 3×3×3 surrounding cube for the local maximum.

   - Fourth, the located local maximums are compared with the Hessian threshold, the points with their value above the

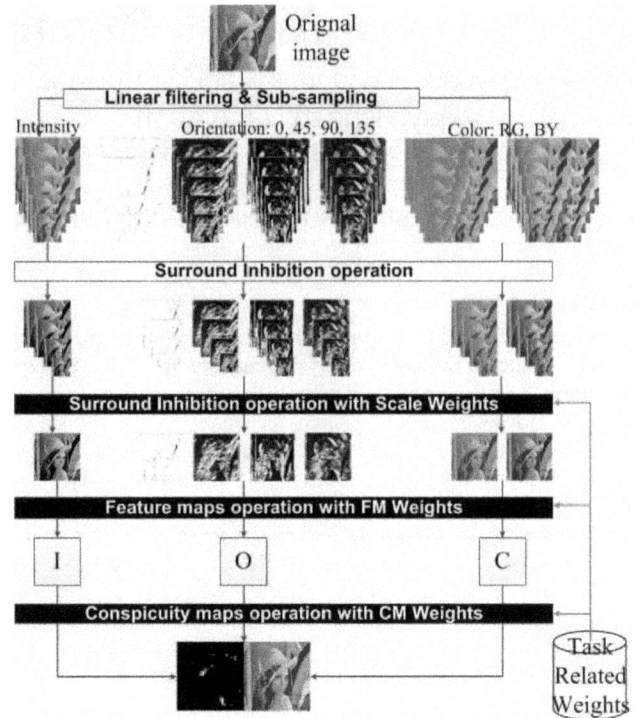

Figure 2: Top down Saliency concept

threshold is consider as interest points (IPs) of input image. At the same time, the scale and image space information will also be stored for processing in next stage.

2. Interest Point Description Stage:

   - First, the dominant orientation of every IP is located by using Haar wavelet filtering.

   - Second, for each IP, descriptor is computed based on IP's dominate orientation via Haar wavelet response. The descriptor can be a 64-value/128-value vector based on whether the extended feature is required. Those descriptors will be sent to classifier/matcher for recognition processing.

2.3 Comprehensive Learning Particle Swarm Optimizer (CLPSO) Algorithm

To realize task-related saliency processing, it is very crucial to find the proper weights associated with a task. As described in Section 2.1, the image pyramids generated in the second stage need to go through three stages of task processing before reaching the final saliency map. Since there are nine scales in the pyramids, 9 weights are used to combine them together into the feature map. For generating the conspicuity map, 7 feature maps (1 in intensity channel, 2 in color channel, and 4 in orientation channel) needs 7 weights. At the final stage, 3 more weights are used to bias the three channels to reach the final top-down saliency map. In total, there are 17 weights used to represent task information. We should note that, in the third and fourth stage, a normalization operation is also applied. The reason for doing this is to promote the response maps that only have sparse strong feature responses while suppressing other maps with large amounts of peak response. It takes three steps to do the normalization: (1) clamp all the values in the map to a range [0, *Max*]; (2) calculate the average value *Avg* of all the local maxima except the ones with Max value; (3) multiply all the value of the map by *(Max - Avg)²*. Since the normalization operation here is not a linear process, a linear regression method is not applicable. More complex search algorithms like particle swarm optimizations, genetic algorithms, and simulated annealing should be used to find a good solution. To train our weights, we use CLPSO algorithm provided in [11] for our task weights searching. The distance between the most salient pixel and task's geometric center is used as a measure of how good our task weights are. Theoretically, this distance can be 0 which means the salient pixel is just at the task center. The parameters used for CLPSO are listed in Table 1.

Table 1: CLPSO parameters used for training

PARAMETER	VALUE
Max generation	30
Population size	100
Dimensions	19
Variable range [min, max]	[0, 6]
Acceleration constants C_1, C_2	1.49445, 1.49445

3. SYSTEM DESIGN OF TDS-SURF

The proposed system is called TDS-SURF which stands for top-down Saliency+SURF. The system overview is provided in Figure 4 and it is composed of (1) a top-down saliency accelerator that identifies the task-related region of interests (ROIs); (2) three SURF accelerators that extract descriptors from the ROIs; and (3) an evaluation module responsible for Euclidean distance computing and task class labeling.

3.1 Architecture of TD-Saliency

As we discuss in Section 2.1 and 2.3, the TD-Saliency module incorporates task object information to compute the attention locations on input image for further detail processing. There are 17 weights to control the low level feature responses for generating the final saliency map which represents visual attention of a corresponding scene. Based on the object's properties, different task objects are represented as different 17×1 weight vectors with elements ranging from 0 to 6 in our TD-Saliency. Two examples with weights ranging from 0 to 6 are shown in the Figure 3. The red dots represent the task weights for

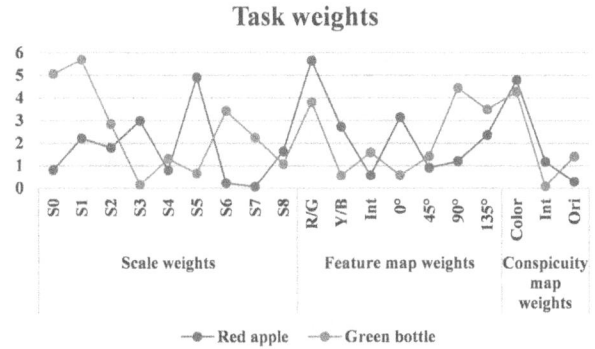

Figure 3: Task weights Example

recognizing a *red apple*, while the green dots represent the weights of finding a *green bottle*. The weights closely representing the target have high weights, like the weight of the R/G channel of feature map for *red apple*, and the weight of the 90° channel at the feature map for *green bottle*.

Inspired by the suppression theory provided by Tsotsos in [12], we performed further analysis of how the suppression affects the task-related attention. We define locating a special object in a sense as a task and we chose 8 different objects for this experiment. 10 images purely containing specified object are used for training and 50+ extra images containing object and distractors for testing. We also gradually suppress the components whose weight value is below a weight threshold pre-set to 1, 2, and 3 respectively. In this experiment, both the specified objects and the computed saliency regions in the test images are annotated by boxes (saliency boxes are placed at the center of saliency regions). We collected two types of information for each class. First, we collect how many saliency boxes overlap with the task boxes for the top three most salient regions. Second, we collect the ratio of the total overlap area of the boxes of the top three saliency ranking to the area of saliency box. The reason for collecting the second type of information is to make sure that the overlapping happens at the main body of the task rather than at the corner. The average result across all the classes is shown in Figure 5. The stacked bar diagram, to the left Y-axis, summarizes the first type information across bottom-up saliency to top-down saliency with different weight thresholds. We can see a significant improvement when we used top-down saliency for our attention computing. However, the benefit from suppressing the

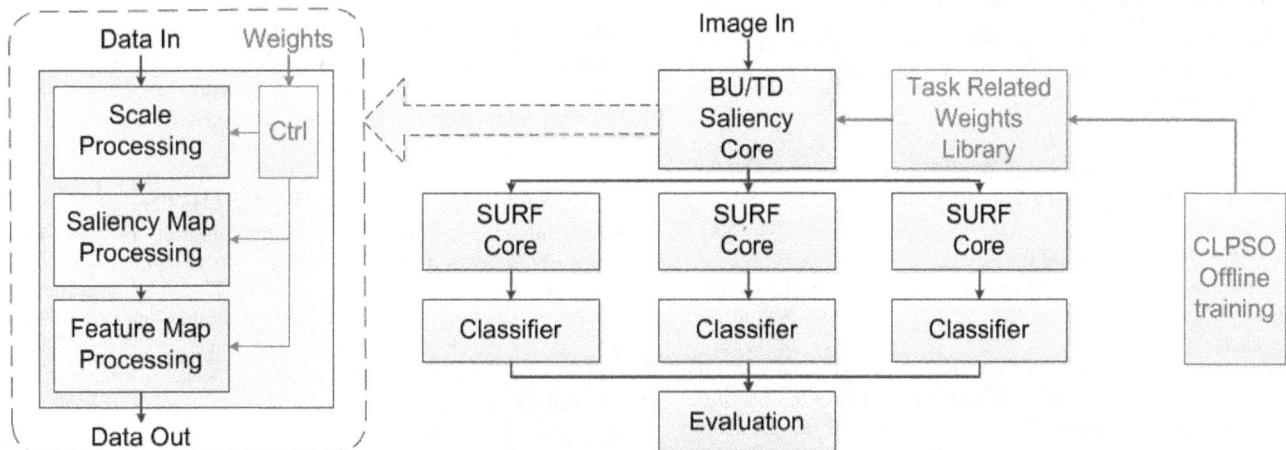

Figure 4: System Overview

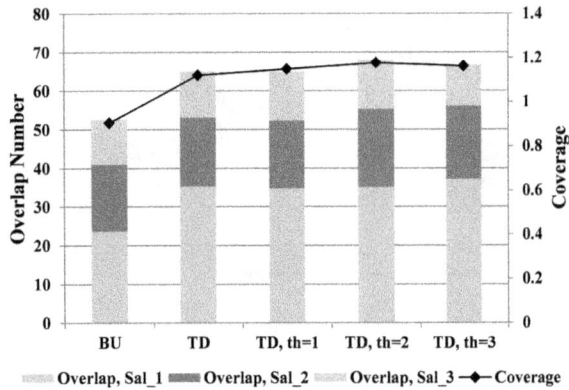

Figure 5: Overlap results between BU-Saliency and TD-Saliency with different weight threshold (1, 2, and 3)

components with higher task threshold doesn't seem significant. The coverage line, to the right Y-axis, shows the second type of information. We can notice that when the weight threshold is set to 3, the overlap number of the 3rd saliency region and total coverage begin to decline. This is because we over-suppress the system too much so that a distractor with one/several same low level feature(s) will be wrongly predicted as task. For example, if we focus too much on the R/G channel to find red apple the system may take a distractor, like a red rectangle box, with the same color feature as our task. Based on these results, we use TD-Saliency without considering task weights suppression.

3.2 Architecture of SURF

The system overview is shown in Figure 6. The upper part stands for the interest point detection stage and it contains the integral image (II) module, Fast Hessian (HS) module, and localization (LOC) module. The interest point description stage is represented in the lower part of the graph, and its components are orientation assign (OA) module and feature extraction (EX) module. The runtime configurations of SURF are listed below:

- Input image size: the accelerator can support different image with size of 128×128, 256×256, 512×512, 640×480, 800×600, and 1024×1024.

- Hessian threshold: a tuning knob that can determine working effort of IP detection. A large threshold will loose the system and reduce the total number of IP found in image; the system will operate in an opposite way with a small threshold.

- Extended-SURF: the accelerator will generate 128-value descriptors when this setting is turned on, and will generate 64-value descriptors otherwise.

In our system, we set SURF as non-extended with the input image size of 256×256. The Hessian threshold is chosen from [0.001, 0.002, 0.003 and 0.004] based on system needs.

3.3 Evaluation Core

The Evaluation core is the last stage of the system, and it contains three brute-force matchers implemented in software. Within each matchers, every given task object is represented as a set of descriptors from its own IPs computed by SURF. The matching begins when the descriptor extraction is done for all the IPs of the incoming ROI. For every IP detected in the ROI, the Euclidean distances are computed with all the IPs of the current-checking

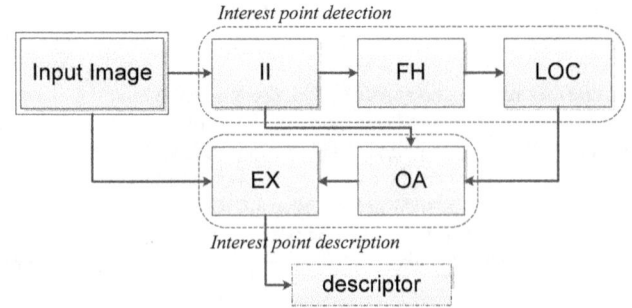

Figure 6: SURF system overview

task object. The task object's IP with the shortest distance is considered as matching point to ROI's IP. After finding matching points for all IPs of the input ROI, sorting is applied to IPs based on the distance to their matching points. The first 50 IPs with the shortest distances are picked and their values are averaged to stand for the closeness between input ROI and the current-checking task. This operation goes through all the task objects in the database, and the ROI will be recognized as the task object whose average distance is shortest. Since we process ROIs of the top three saliency regions from the TD-saliency, the chosen task will be considered as found in scene when any of three matchers has a positive response.

3.4 System Integration

Without reliable pre-processing stages, recognition systems need to go through the whole image exhaustively to find the right feature vector/descriptor. This is not only computationally intensive but also very power hungry. Therefore, as shown in Figure 4, we have a two level system. The first stage is the Saliency core that pre-processes the input image to locate the attention locations. For each attention location a ROI of size 256×256 will be used to extract the information from the original picture. ROIs will be further processed by SURF cores and Evaluation core to decide whether there is a task object in the image and where that object is. The baseline system, BUS-SURF (bottom-up Saliency+SURF), contains 1 BU saliency core and 3 SURF cores and is shown in the Figure 4 with all the black boundary components. The reason to have 3 SURF cores is although the BU-Saliency can't always locate the given object in the most salient region, at most situation it can locate it in the three most salient regions. Passing the ROIs from the three most salient regions can prevent us from missing the task object which is not treated as the first in saliency ranking.

The dedicated components of TDS-SURF are annotated in red in Figure 4. The major differences are: (1) for each special task, the task weights trained by CLPSO can be loaded to the system for saliency computing; (2) The SURF can be configured online with different Hessian thresholds.

4. EXPERIMENT AND RESULTS

The whole system is developed on the Dinigroup DNV6F6-PCIe multi-FPGA platform [13]. It contains six compute FPGAs, and each one is a Xilinx Virtex6 SX475T device operating at 100MHz. The board is mounted on the mother-board via a PCIe x8 link for the host-accelerator communication. The results for TD-Saliency, SURF, and the whole system are evaluated individually in this section.

4.1 TD-Saliency Accelerator

Our saliency accelerator can be configured to bottom-up mode or top-down mode based on the user's need. When the task-oriented property is required for the saliency processing, the red-annotated logic components in Figure 4 will be turned on. The resource utilization of this accelerator on Xilinx 6 SX475T is provided in Table 2:

Table 2: Resource Utilization of TD-Saliency

Slice REGs	Slice LUTs	BRAM36s	DSPs
26%	58%	64%	39%

Figure 8 compares the results of BU and TD saliency. In the pictures, we show three different tasks: red bottle on the top, green round plate in the middle, and green rectangle plate at the bottom. In each task, two pairs of result are displayed. In the top row, Figure 8(a) and 8(c) are the outputs of the original bottom-up saliency method, while Figure 8(b) and 8(d) are the outputs of the top-down saliency. The index within the yellow circle tells the ranking of the saliency regions. With original saliency core, the saliency region located at red bottle has the lowest ranking among the top three regions. When the task information is considered, the top-down system gives a significant improvement: double coverage in Figure 8(b) and 1st saliency ranking at 8(d). The same trend can be also seen in the middle row and bottom row where the task is not considered as a saliency region in bottom-up saliency (Figure 8(e) and Figure 8(k)) while top-down saliency can locate the task at the top saliency ranking (Figure 8(f) and Figure 8(I)).

4.2 SURF Accelerator

The SURF accelerator is developed on Xilinx 6 SX475T with its resource utilization shown in Table 3. We verified implementation of SURF with the model from OpenSURF, and no significant interest point mismatch can be found in our

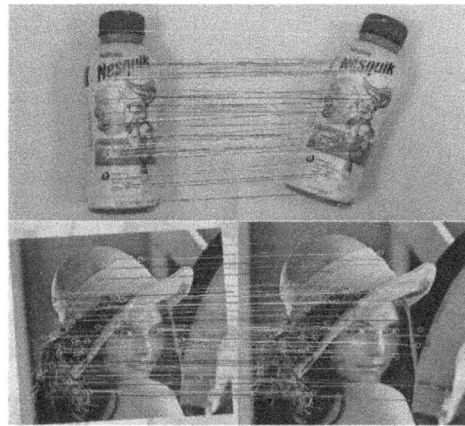

Figure 7: Sample results for SURF IP detection

hardware's result. The Figure 7 shows the two sample tests of our SURF system. In each test, the interest points of one object are marked out by small circles in 2 different images, and the matching pairs are connected by color lines. It can be seen that our system effectively locate interest points of a given object in different poses.

Table 3: Resource Utilization of SURF

Slice REGs	Slice LUTs	BRAM36s	DSPs
20%	59%	78%	62%

4.3 TDS-SURF System

Like we talked before in Section 3.1, TD-Saliency has a high possibility to locate the task at 1st saliency box or 2nd saliency box (Figure 5). Based on this observation, we assign different working effort to three SURF accelerators based on the saliency ranking for their input ROI. Hessian thresholds of SURFs of 1st, 2nd, 3rd ROI are set to {0.0001, 0.0002, and 0.0003} or {0.0002, 0.0003,

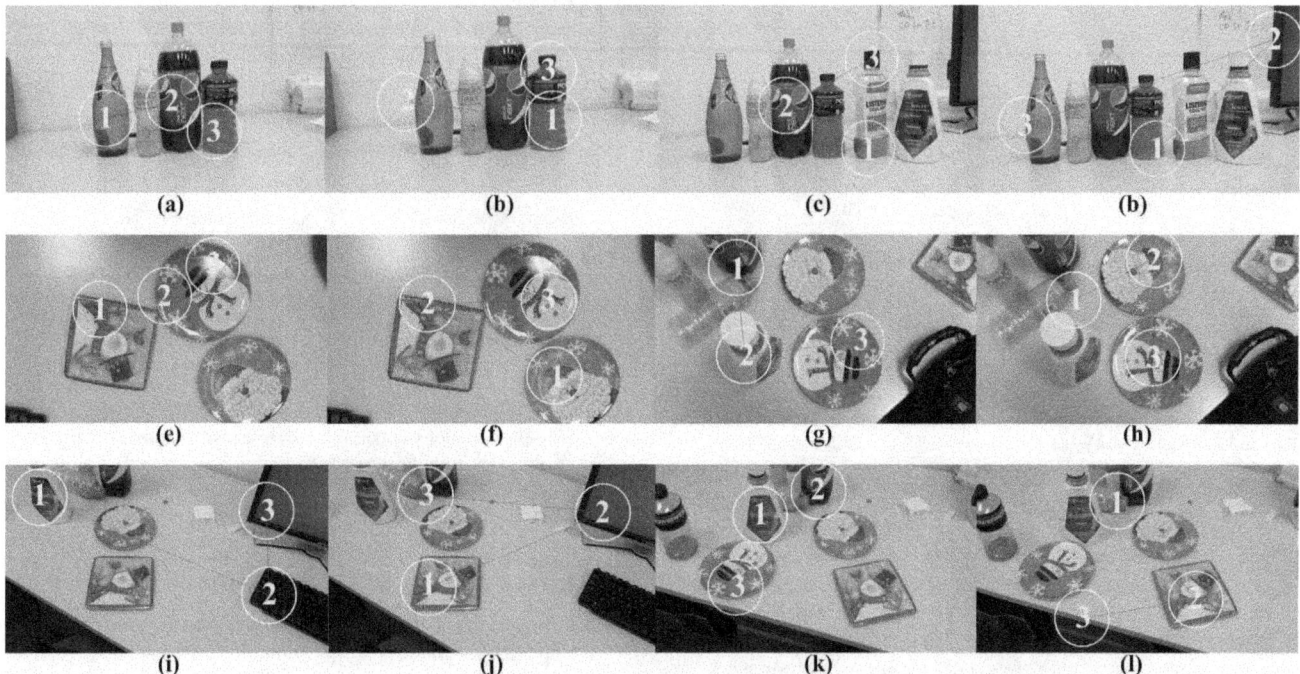

Figure 8: Result comparisons between bottom-up saliency and top-down saliency

task of top row: red bottle; task of middle row: green round plate; task of bottom row: green rectangle plate

and 0.0004}. This is done since the 2nd and 3rd ROIs have low probabilities of locating the task object compared to 1st ROI and as a result we want to spend the less computing effort on them.

We picked six classes of objects listed in Table 4 for the system testing. During training, we loaded the task weights of our task object from the weights library. Then the test images containing both task object and distractor are sent to TDS-SURF for processing. Three ROIs are extracted and sent to the SURF for descriptor generation. The evaluation core collects information that determines whether or not the task object is in the scene. In our experiment, we don't consider the false positive case since we always have the task object in our test images. The average accuracy rate and the average number of computed interest points is shown in Figure 9. Compared to BUS-SURF's 59.39% accuracy rate, the correct task locating rates of the two TDS-SURF's configurations are 64.98% and 66.96%. Furthermore, around 25% computation time is saved when Hessian thresholds of 0.0002, 0.0003, and 0.0004 are used in our SURF implementation. This is due to the fact that 25.7% fewer IPs need to be analyzed in the system.

Table 4: Test Class and Test Number

Class	Test number
Red bottle	54
Red round plate	51
Green round plate	50
Blue round plate	42
Green rectangle plate	55
Yellow bottle	51

Average accuracy rate & total IP computed

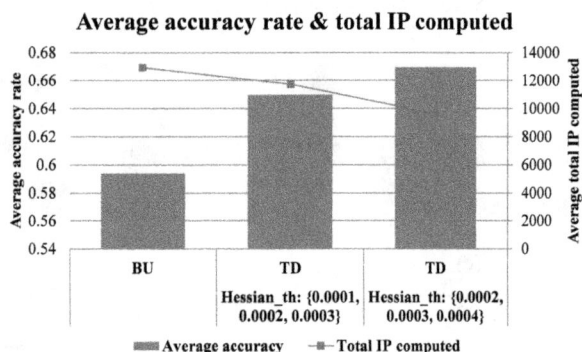

Figure 9: Experiment results between BUS-SURF and TDS-SURF

5. CONCLUSION

As biologically inspired vision systems become increasingly attractive for employing in daily life, there has already been a substantial research effort in developing prototypes mimicking the human visual mechanism. In this paper, we present a two-level hierarchical embedded system that integrates knowledge of a given task into attention/recognition computing. Compared to the baseline vision system, our system can achieve at most 12.75% accuracy improvement with around 25% less computation work.

6. ACKNOWLEDGEMENT

This work was supported in part by US NSF awards 1317560, 1213052, and an award from the Intel Science and Technology Center for Embedded Computing.

The authors also would like to thank Dr. Ahmed Al Maashri for his work on SURF implementation.

7. REFERENCES

[1] http://www.google.com/glass/start/

[2] Maashri, A.A., DeBole, M., Cotter, M., Chandramoorthy, N., Xiao Y., Narayanan, V., and Chakrabarti, C. 2012. Accelerating neuromorphic vision algorithms for recognition. In *Proceeding of Design Automation Conference (DAC)*.

[3] Bae, S., Cho, Y. C. P., Park, S., Irick, K. M., Jin, Y., and Narayanan, V. 2011. An FPGA implementation of Information Theoretic Visual-Saliency System and Its Optimization. In *IEEE International Symposium on Field-Programmable Custom Computing Machines (FCCM)*.

[4] Kestur, S., Park, M. S., Sabarad, J., Dantara, D., Narayanan, V, Chen Y., and Khosla, D. 2012. Emulating Mammalian Vision on Reconfigurable Hardware. In *IEEE International Symposium on Field-Programmable Custom Computing Machines (FCCM)*.

[5] Itti, L., Koch, C., and Niebur, E. 1998. A Model of Saliency-Based Visual Attention for Rapid Scene Analysis. *IEEE Trans on Pattern Analysis and Machine Intelligence*, vol. 20, pp. 1254-1259.

[6] Mutch, J. and Lowe, D. G. 2008. Object Class Recognition and Localization Using Sparse Features with Limited Receptive Fields. *International Journal of Computer Vision (IJCV)*, vol. 80, no. 1.

[7] Kim, K., Lee, S., Kim, J.-Y., Kim, M., and Yoo, H.-J. 2009. A 125 GOPS 583mW Network-on-Chip Based Parallel Processor With Bio-Inspired Visual Attention Engine. In *IEEE Journal of Solid-State Circuits*, vol.44, no.1, pp.136-147.

[8] Yarbus, A. L. 1967. *Eye Movements and Vision*. New York, Plenum Press

[9] Borji, A., Ahmadabadi, M. N., and Araabi, B. N. 2011. Cost-sensitive learning of Top-down Modulation for Attentional Control. *Machine Vision and Applications*, 22(1): 61-76.

[10] Bay, H., Ess, A., Tuytelaars, T., and Gool, L. V. 2008. SURF: Speeded Up Robust Features. *Computer Vision and Image Understanding (CVIU)*, Vol. 110, No. 3, pp. 346-359.

[11] Liang, J. J., Suganthan, P. N., and Baskar, S. 2006. Comprehensive Learning Particle Swarm Optimizer for Global Optimization of Multimodal Functions. *IEEE Transactions on Evolutionary Computation*, vol.10, no.3, pp.281-295.

[12] Tsotsos, J. K. 2011. Chapter 8. In *A Computational Perspective on Visual Attention*. The MIT Press.

[13] Dinigroup DNV6F6-PCIE Documentation. http://www.dinigroup.com/product/data/DNV6F6PCIe/files/DNV6F6PCIe_v14_lo.pdf

A New DRAM Architecture and its Control Method for the System Power Consumption

Yoshiro Riho
Department of Electrical Engineering and
Computer Science, Graduate School of
Engineering, Nagoya University, Nagoya,
464-8603, Japan

Kazuo Nakazato
Department of Electrical Engineering and
Computer Science, Graduate School of
Engineering, Nagoya University, Nagoya,
464-8603, Japan

ABSTRACT

Demands have been placed on dynamic random access memory (DRAM) to not only increase memory capacity and data transfer speed but also to reduce operating and standby currents. When a system uses DRAM, the restricted data retention time necessitates a re-write operation because each bit of the DRAM is stored as an amount of electrical charge in a storage capacitor. Power consumption for the refresh operation increases in proportion to memory capacity. According to a new proposed method the refresh operation frequency and its power consumption reduce to $1/2^N (N = 1, 2, 3, 4)$ when full memory capacity is not required, by effectively extending the refresh operation interval. The proposal includes the conversion from 1 cell/bit to 2^N cells/bit, which reduces the variation of retention times among memory cells. This leads the refresh operation frequency from $1/2^N$ to $1/2^N \times 1/2^N$, while it accompanies the additional charging power for the composed memory cell. A system can select the best way of 1 cell/bit and 2^N cells/bit from the total viewpoint, while all conventional functions and operations in the full array access mode are fully compatible.

Categories and Subject Descriptors

B.3.1 [**Semiconductor memories**]: Dynamic memory (DRAM)

Keywords

self refresh (SELF); composed memory cell; partial access mode 0/1/2 (PAM0/1/2)

1. INTRODUCTION

Dynamic random access memory (DRAM) has been playing the main role of storage in computer systems. The memory capacity of DRAM has been increased to meet system demands due to the miniaturization, which semiconductor process technology has brought. In fact, system demands include not only memory capacity but also data transfer

GLSVLSI'14, May 21–23, 2014, Houston, Texas, USA.
Copyright © 2014 ACM 978-1-4503-2816-6/14/05 ...$15.00.
http://dx.doi.org/10.1145/2591513.2591516.

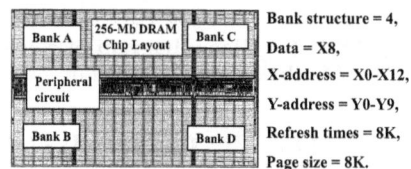

(a) 256-Mb DRAM (CAD data)

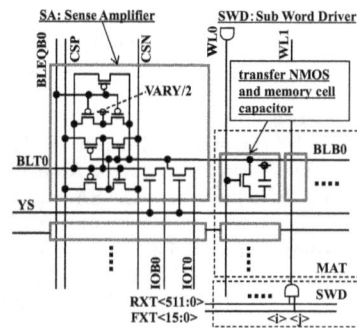

(b) Array Circuit

Figure 1: 256-Mb DRAM: (a) Chip layout, implemented and evaluated, (b) Array circuit.

speed, operation current reduction, and standby current reduction. Since a re-write operation is necessary for DRAM in which all memory cells are constructed by a capacitor, the increase in memory capacity has directly caused two problems: disturbance and power consumption [4-7].

This paper proposes a new method to reduce the re-write operation current when full memory capacity is not required, while maintaining all traditional functions and operations of the full array access mode. The proposed method, called partial access mode (PAM), is based on the extractable memory array structure. The restricted memory array can reduce the re-write power consumption to $1/2^N$. Moreover, the conversion from 1 cell/bit to 2^N cells/bit enables the extension of the refresh operation frequency from 2^N times to $2^N \times 2^N$ times, even though it accompanies 2^N times charging power for the composed memory cell. We prove that PAM, including the conventional low power mode (SELF) can be applied to different kinds of system examples: memory module and wireless system. The minimum power consumption is realized in each system condition through different ways.

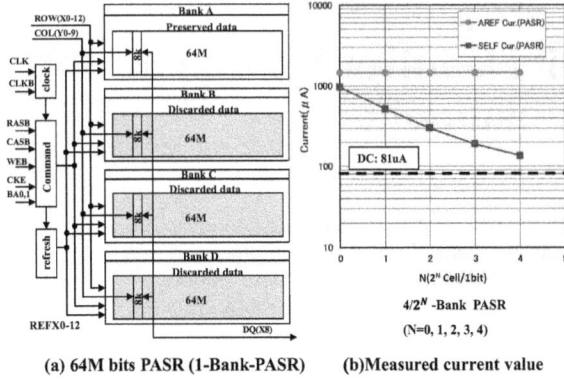

(a) 64M bits PASR (1-Bank-PASR)   **(b)Measured current value**

Figure 2: PASR: (a) Block diagram of conventional 256-Mb DRAM, (b) Measured current.

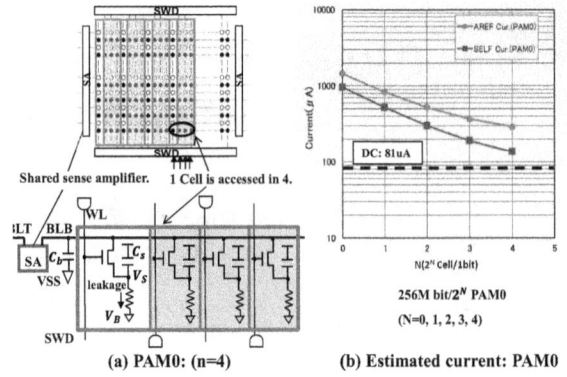

(a) PAM0: (n=4)   **(b) Estimated current: PAM0**

Figure 3: PAM0: (a) Array circuit, (b) Estimated current.

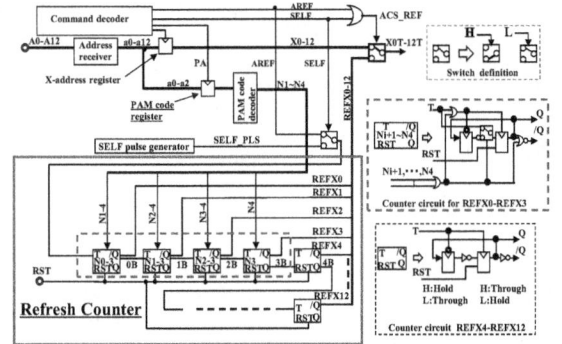

Figure 4: PAM0: Circuit implementation.

2. REFRESH OPERATION AND POWER

2.1 Refresh Operation

DRAM stores a single bit in a memory cell as the amount of electrical charge on a storage capacitor. The leakage current collapses charged data. This means that DRAM needs a rewrite operation before the memory cell loses its storage charge. This re-write operation is called *refresh*. A refresh is performed by the sub-word driver (SWD) and the sense amplifier (SA), shown in Fig. 1(b). An external auto-refresh command (AREF) activates the SA, which amplifies bit lines (BLs). Since refresh is a type of disturbance in a system where normal operation, i.e., read or write, is forbidden, the frequency of the AREF command should be minimized. In the case of 256-Mb DRAM with four banks in Fig. 1(a), the refresh of all memory cells is completed by issuing $2^{13} = 8,192$ AREF commands, called an 8-K AREF operation, which means one AREF operation causes one word line (WL) refresh in 8-K WLs per bank. Each data retention time of a cell is generally expressed by t_{ret}. The minimum retention time of the memory cell, $t_{ret,min}$, during which all memory cells keep their own charges, should be longer than 64 ms, as standardized by the cell refresh time t_{ref}. Thus, the maximum time interval of an AREF command, t_{REF}, is 64 ms/2^{13} = 7.8 μs in an 8-K AREF operation [1].

2.2 Self Refresh Mode

DRAM has the specification of a low power mode (SELF), and does the refresh operation by itself after receiving a SELF command. If it is known in advance that DRAM is not accessible in a certain interval, the system issues the SELF command and DRAM reduces the power consumption by setting t_{REF} to the longest value of pause time ($= t_{ret,min}$), during which the storage charge is not lost. Once the DRAM receives a SELF ENTRY command, it remains in the SELF mode until receiving a SELF EXIT command, and it accepts no commands except SELF EXIT.

2.3 Conventional Method

A system usually demands much greater power reduction than that in the SELF mode. A partial array self refresh (PASR) is added to the DRAM specification. In the case of the 1-bank PASR in Fig. 2(a), the refresh operation is abandoned for three banks in the four banks. Both the memory

capacity and the refresh current decrease by a factor 4 in the SELF mode. The power consumption in Fig. 2(b) is given by the measured standby current of 256-Mb DRAM. The memory capacity in SELF is limited to 256-M/n, where $n = 2^N$ ($N = 0, 1, 2, 3, 4$). The constant power consumption in AREF is estimated from the maximum AREF interval t_{REF}. PASR has no regulation in the normal mode, and experiences the following problems with the system-side viewpoint.

(1) A mismatch exists in the number of banks between the AREF operation in the normal mode and PASR. Fig. 2(a) shows the block diagram for a one-bank PASR. At the first refresh after SELF EXIT, an AREF command is issued to select the WLs of all four banks, although three of those do not keep data. This means that the power consumption is four times larger than needed, since a refresh operation for three banks is not necessary.

(2) The system usually activates the SA for all banks and accesses four pages (8-K $\times$ 4 = 32-K size) of four banks, because the frequency of the disturbance factor, i.e., precharge, should be less. However, the PASR mode cannot preserve all 32-K data in all banks, so four pages must be activated separately with four pre-charge operations before entering the SELF mode to preserve the 32-K accessed data.

2.4 The Proposed Base Circuit

The PASR features of (1) and (2) are caused by the way of preserved data allocation corresponding to the banks. The

Table 1: PAM0/PAM1/PAM2 specification.

A2-A0	Access Array	N	n	Capacity	times	PAM0/PAM1		PAM2	
						$t_{ref0/1}$	$t_{REF0/1}$	t_{ref2}	t_{REF2}
000	All Arrays	0	1	256M	8Kref	64ms	7.8µs	64ms	7.8µs
001	128M(X0=0)	1	2	128M	4Kref	64ms	15.6µs	128ms	31.2µs
010	64M(X0=X1=0)	2	4	64M	2Kref	64ms	31.2µs	256ms	125µs
011	restriction	—	—	—	—	—	—	—	—
100	restriction	—	—	—	—	—	—	—	—
101	32M(X0=X1=X2=0)	3	8	32M	1Kref	64ms	62.4µs	512ms	500µs
110	16M(X0=X1=X2=X3=0)	4	16	16M	512ref	64ms	125µs	1024ms	2000µs
111	restriction	—	—	—	—	—	—	—	—

Table 2: Partial Access Conversion

partial access conversion	partial access re-conversion
Command: partial access conversion(PAC)	Command: partial access re-conversion(PAR)
Example: from N=0 (1 cell/bit) to N=2(4 cells/bit)	Example: from N=2 (4 cells/bit) to N=0 (1 cells/bit)
Operation: $8K/2^N$ times continuous copy	Operation: $8K/2^N$ times continuous refresh

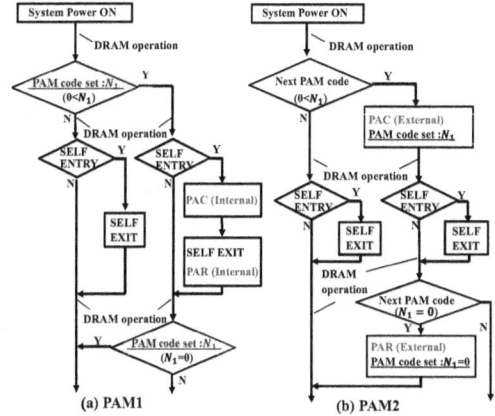

Figure 5: PAM1/2 flows

array circuit structure in Fig. 1(b) has several important features that the refresh operation times increases in proportion to the exponential of X-address number and SA is shared among memory cells in the same array unit. We propose partial access mode 0 (PAM0) which has next features.
(1) The position to control the restricted capacity is higher than that to control SELF Entry or SELF Exit.
(2) X-addresses X0-X3 which decide the memory cell position in the same array unit, allocate the preserved area of total capacity (Fig. 3(a)).

The reception of PAM0 ENTRY/EXIT in normal operation enables (1) and (2), those realize the $n = 2^N$ times t_{REF0} extension and the $1/2^N$ times refresh current reduction (Fig. 3(b)) in the normal, compared to the constant t_{REF} and current of PASR. Moreover, Fig. 3(a) shows the written data on mulch banks can be preserved through SELF mode. The implemented circuit modification is expressed in Fig. 4. A system issues PAM0 ENTRY/EXIT with code A0-A2 in Table 1. Then, the DRAM changes the lowest bit for the refresh operation by N0-N4, the output of the PAM code decoder. This brings t_{REF0} extension and refresh power reduction instead of capacity reduction.

2.5 The Concept for Retention Time

PAM0 gives the selection, whether a DRAM holds a data with $n = 2^N$ cells to extend retention time or not. The added operations to PAM0 ENTRY/EXIT are shown in Table 2 where partial access conversion (PAC) and partial access re-conversion (PAR) are defined as commands of the continuous copy operation and the continuous refresh operation, respectively. The parameter n indicates both the composed cell number and the division number of the memory capacity. The array structure Fig. 1(b), Fig. 3(a) and the right panel of Fig. 9 enable the sharing of a data with 2^N cells due to the shared sense amplifier [2-3].

A PAC command in the normal operation indicates the conversion from 1 cell/bit to 2^N cells/bit. This is simply a copy operation from a memory cell connected with 1 WL to 2^N- 1 memory cells connected with 2^N- 1 WLs in the same mat. Table 2 ans Fig. 3(a) show how this operation is simply achieved by only a delayed WL selection. PAC is completed through 8-$K/2^N$ times copy operations applied to all memory cells in 256-Mb DRAM. In the 2^N cells/bit access mode, 2^N memory cells compensate for each other's storage charge by selecting 2^N WLs at the same time. The PAR in Table 2 indicates re-conversion from 2^Ncells/bit to 1 cell/bit, which is necessary because the stored charge in 1 memory cell is not enough to read for 1 bit. This operation is continuous 8-$K/2^N$ times refresh operations to all memory cells [2-3].

2^N cells/bit access mode enables the extension of the refresh operation interval, t_{REF0}, by dual effects: the retention time extension and the reduction of memory capacity. In the 256-Mb DRAM example, the retention time is 64ms$\times 2^N$ at least and the accessed data capacity is 256-$M/2^N$. However, 2^N cells/bit access mode accompanies the $(2^N - 1) \times 10\%$ charging current increase per SA amplification, which is executed by the refresh operation and X-addressing, IE; AREF command and ACT command.

3. NEW ARCHITECTURE: PAM1/2

3.1 Current component

2^N cells/bit access mode lowers the refresh operation disturbance and refresh power consumption to $1/(2^N \times 2^N)$, when compared to a conventional DRAM. But it needs the SWD to drive 2^N WLs and the SA to charge 2^N cell capacitors for the refresh operation and X-addressing. They are 2^N times larger than before. In case of refresh, the power consumption decreases to $1/2^N \times 1/2^N$ in total, since the extra power for charging is only $(2^N - 1) \times 10\%$, which is a minor portion of the total current. X-addressing accompanies SA activation, too. In this operation, the power consumption is dependent on the frequency of the different X-addressing. In the SELF mode, the power consumption decreases due to the refresh operation interval t_{REF} derived from t_{ret} of the composed memory cell, since no X-addressing is executed.

The quantitative estimated current is derived from the measured refresh operation current (1377 μA) on the condition that t_{REF}=7.8 μs and measured DC current (81 μA),

(a) $I_{ACT}(t_{ACT}, \text{N}) + I_{AREF}(\text{N})$
: 1 cell/bit access mode (PAM0/1)

(b) $I_{ACT}(t_{ACT}, \text{N}) + I_{AREF}(\text{N})$
: 2^N cells/bit access mode (PAM2)

(c) $I_{SELF}(\text{N})$

(d) PAM1/2 comparison

	Normal	SELF
(PAM0)	1 cell/bit	1 cell/bit
PAM1	1 cell/bit	2^N cell/bit
PAM2	2^N cell/bit	2^N cell/bit

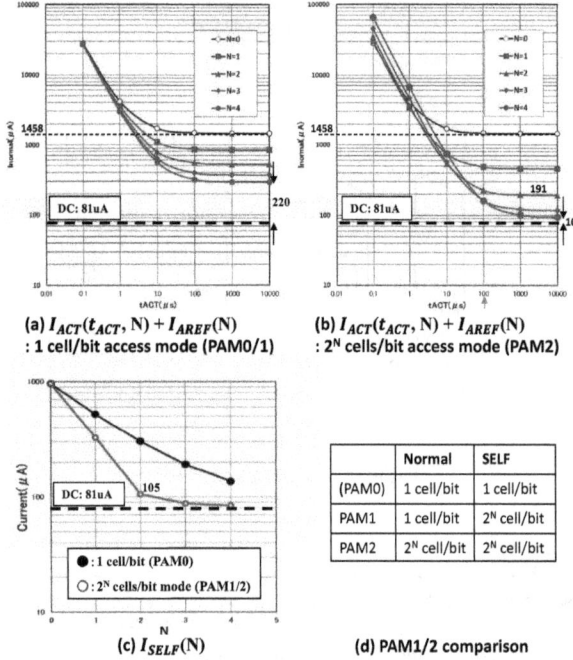

Figure 6: Current estimated result: PAM1/2.

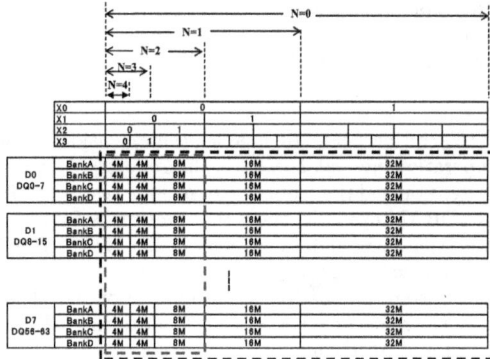

Figure 7: Personal computer: Memory module.

which is the summed value of the transistor OFF current, the operating current for internal voltage generators, and the current for the refresh period oscillators. We obtained the current data from the evaluation of the 256-Mb DRAM in Fig. 1(a). The increasing current per $n = 1$ in a composed memory cell is estimated in (1) and (2) below.

(1) Storage capacitance effect: The storage capacitance C_s is 32 fF from the measured data, and VARY is 1.8 V. The average number of driven capacitors is 8K × 4 banks × 1/2 = 16K. The total current to charge all storage capacitors for $t_{REF} = 7.8$ μs is 32 [fF] × 1.8 [V] × 16K/7.8 [μs] = 121 μA.
(2) Effect of driven WLs: The WL capacitance is 136.5 fF per WL from the design parameters. VPP is 3.6 V and is generated from VDD = 2.5 V at 1/3 efficiency. The number of driven WLs is 16 WLs × 4 banks. The total current for driving all WLs at the same time for $t_{REF} = 7.8$ μs is 136.5 [fF] × 3.6 [V] × 3 × 16 × 4/7.8 [μs] = 12 μA.

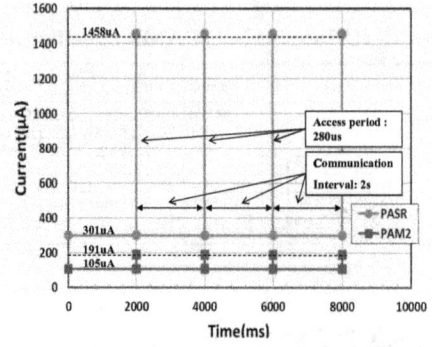

Figure 8: Mobile phone: Current waveform.

(1) and (2) show that the increasing current per $n = 1$ is 133 μA, which is 10% of the full array refresh current (1377μA).

The normal operation current I_{normal} is composed of the X-addressing current, the refresh operation current including the DC current (81μA), and the current for READ or WRITE data transfer. We define their time-averaged values, which depend on the operating frequency, as I_{ACT}, I_{AREF}, and I_{DATA}. Here, we assume that I_{DATA} is constant. I_{normal} in Eq. (1) is the function of composed cell number $n = 2^N$ and X-addressing interval t_{ACT}.

$$I_{normal}(N, t_{ACT}) = I_{ACT}(N, t_{ACT}) + I_{AREF}(N) + I_{DATA}. \quad (1)$$

$I_{ACT}(N, t_{ACT})$ and $I_{AREF}(N)$ are given by next Eqs. (2)(3), where the bank number: $N_{BANK} = 4$ and $t_{REF} = 7.8[\mu s] \times 2^N \times 2^N$.

$$I_{ACT}(N, t_{ACT})[\mu A] = \frac{1244 + 133 \times 2^N}{N_{BANK}} \frac{7.8}{t_{ACT}[\mu s]} \quad (2)$$

$$I_{AREF}(N)[\mu A] = [1244 + 133 \times 2^N]\frac{7.8}{t_{REF}[\mu s]} + 81. \quad (3)$$

Fig. 6(b) shows I_{normal} with the exception of I_{DATA}. I_{ACT} has a strong t_{ACT} dependency that decides the features of I_{normal}, where the minimum t_{ACT} is 100 ns, decided by the minimum X-addressing interval. In the area of $t_{ACT} \geq 100\mu s$, I_{normal} depends on composed cell number $n = 2^N$ of I_{AREF}. A system operation to the DRAMs decides t_{ACT}, which greatly increases I_{normal} above to 100 ns owing to the increasing current factor.

The current of the SELF mode is compared in Fig. 6(c).

$$I_{SELF}(N)[\mu A] = [1244 + 133 \times 2^N]\frac{7.8}{t_{REF}[\mu s]} + 81. \quad (4)$$

$I_{SELF}(N)$ of Eq. (4) is strictly smaller than that of 1 cell/bit access mode by the dual effect $1/2^N \times 1/2^N$.

3.2 New Concepts for PAM0

There should be 2 modes in PAM in the normal operation. The estimated results $t_{ACT} \leq 100$ μs in Fig. 6(b) lead one specification of PAM, PAM1 in Table 1; as shown, the standardized retention time is constant ($t_{ref1} = 64ms$) and the refresh operation interval in normal operation is extended ($t_{REF1} = 2^N \times 7.8\mu s$) by the accessed capacity reduction. This extension brings the current reduction in any case of t_{ACT} in Fig. 6(a). Fig. 5(a) shows the flow of PAM1, in which SELF is formed through internal command, partial access conversion (PAC) and partial access re-conversion

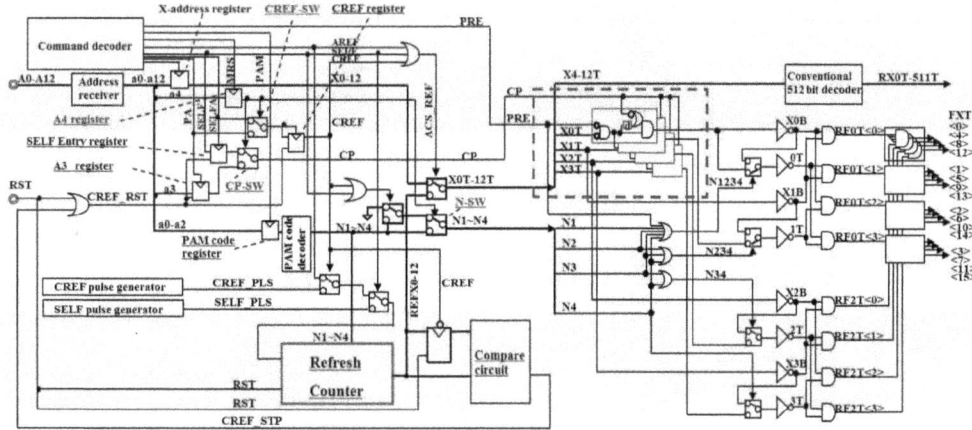

Figure 9: Circuit modification for PAM1/2.

(PAR) in Table 2. The refresh operation interval is extended by the dual effect only in the SELF mode.

By contrast, the area of $t_{ACT} \geq 100 \ \mu s$ in Fig. 6(b) leads the other mode of PAM, PAM2 in Table 1 which is defined in detail here, the standardized retention time is extended ($t_{ref2} = 2^N \times 64ms$) and the refresh operation interval is extended ($t_{REF2} = 2^N \times 2^N \times 7.8\mu s$) by the dual effect of retention time extension and accessed capacity reduction. In Fig. 6(b), the extension of PAM2 brings a significant current reduction in the area of $t_{ACT} \geq 100\mu s$, where I_{normal} is close to DC current. But I_{normal} increases with the N increment in the area of $t_{ACT} \leq 100 \ \mu s$ due to the current increase of SA activation, X-addressing causes. Fig. 5(b) shows the flow of PAM2, in which PAM is formed through external commands, PAC and PAR, which contribute the dual t_{REF} extension for both of the normal and SELF. Data access methods for PAM1 and PAM2 are summarized in Fig. 6(d).

3.3 Example PAM1: Memory Module

In a personal computer system, the demand for the system frequently changes the used memory capacity. It is reasonable to use DRAMs in the PAM1 mode from the viewpoints of both power consumption and system performance. The DRAM is typically used in the set of 8 DRAMs in a module. The memory module of 8 DRAMs has 64 I/O pins, which is the sum of 8 I/O pins in each DRAM. The address pins are shared between the 8 DRAMs. This example is explained in Fig. 7, which is one set of modules from multiple modules. The memory capacity of Fig. 7 is 8 times larger than that of the 1 chip DRAM. If a system uses PAM1 in the form of a module, the memory capacity reduction and current reduction are 8 times that of the 1 DRAM case of Fig. 6(a)(c). The standby current of the memory module can be lowered to just the sum of the DRAM's DC current, if the SELF of PAM1 is used as N $\geq$ 2.

3.4 Example PAM2: Wireless System

Mobile phones are now widely used all over the world. DRAM is the main memory in each phone. This system has a big problem, which is, the system must reduce power consumption for the wireless condition, even though the system must detect all incoming phone calls. This means that the power consumption for detection should be lowered as much as possible. Fig. 8 shows the current waveform of the wireless system. Each mobile phone communicates with a radio station for 280 μs with an interval of 2 s. The communication interval 2 s and the communication time 280 μs are defined by the specification of the wireless system. The mobile phone judges whether a phone call to itself can come in communication time 280 μs.

The small memory capacity is only used to detect an in-coming phone call. It is reasonable to use DRAMs in the PAM2 mode. The current consumption used in PAM2 (N=2) becomes 191 μA and 105 μA, respectively, from Figs. 6(b)(c). The 10 % of 256-Mb memory capacity is large enough to be accessed in the call-waiting state. The t_{REF} of AREF (PAM) at the point of N = 3 is 500μs in Table 1, which is larger than the communication time 280 μs. This means the mobile phone system does not have to issue the AREF command in every communication time of 280 μs.

3.5 Circuit Implementation

In this subsection, we show a few easy modifications enable DRAMs to be selectable for PAM1 and PAM2. In the case of PAM1 external commands, PAC and PAR do not exist. Fig. 5(a) shows the SELF ENTRY includes PAC and SELF EXIT includes PAR. In contrast, external commands PAC after PAM ENTRY and PAR before PAM EXIT execute the operations for the composed memory cell in the case of PAM2, expressed in Fig. 5(b). All that is needed for the mode register set (MRS) concerning PAM1/2 are the selection of SELF ENTRY and external PAC, and the selection of SELF EXIT and external PAR, as shown in Fig. 9 including Refresh Counter of Fig. 4.

In PAM1, A4=L for the MRS. The output signal L of the A4 register selects SELFA through CREF-SW as the flag for a continuous refresh for the composed memory cell, and also selects SELF through CP-SW for a continuous copy. The L of the A4 register sets the configuration for the composed memory cell only in the SELF mode through N-SW.

Fig. 10(a) shows these signal transitions in the case of (N=0 → N=2 → N=0). When the DRAM receives SELF ENTRY, the command decoder generates SELFA, a one-shot pulse, which enables CREF = H and CP = H (set

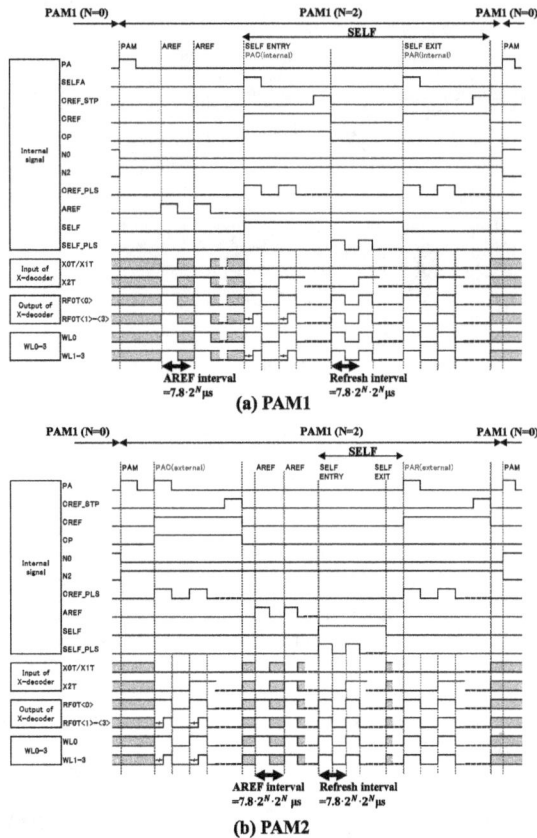

Figure 10: Functional waveform: PAM1/2.

ation. CREF = H selects CREF_PLS as the input signal into the refresh counter, which sends the pulses for continuous copy operation in the 100 ns interval repeatedly until the compare circuit outputs CREF_STP = H, which stops continuous copies at the point of full array copy completion. The reset operation of the PA register changes CREF to L and that of the A3 register changes CP to L. When the DRAM receives the PAR, the circuit operation about CREF is the same. But the A3 register decides CP = L.

4. CONCLUSION

DRAM has been increasing its capacity and X-address numbers with process miniaturization. The current consumption for the refresh operation has been increasing, too. But the frequency and the current for the refresh operation can be decreased efficiently by using the DRAM array circuit structure when its full capacity is not used. PAM brings a new low-power mode to conventional DRAM without die size overhead, although the traditional functions and operations in the case of the full array access mode are fully maintained. The structure of the DRAM array circuit enables the conversion for the 2^N cells/bit memory cell through very simple operations.

The first proposed partial access mode, PAM1, decreases the refresh operation current to $1/2^N$ due to the capacity restriction in the normal mode and to $1/2^N \times 1/2^N$ in the SELF mode. PAM1 needs no current increment per SA activation. The second proposed partial access mode, PAM2, decreases both the refresh currents of the normal and SELF modes to $1/2^N \times 1/2^N$. But, PAM2 needs a 2^N times more current increment per SA activation. Depending on the DRAM usage, a traditional computer system can choose either PAM1/2 effectively owning to the implementation of this new architecture.

5. REFERENCES

[1] N. C. C. Lu and H. H. Chao, "Half-V/SUB DD/ bit-line sensing scheme in CMOS DRAMs," IEEE Journal of Solid-State Circuits, vol.SC-19, No.4, pp.451-454, Aug. 1984.

[2] Y. Riho, K. Nakazato, "A New Extension Method of Retention Time for Memory Cell on Dynamic Random Access Memory," GLSVLSI2013 Conf., May 2013.

[3] Y. Riho, K. Nakazato, "Partial Access Mode: A New Method for Reducing Power Consumption of Dynamic Random Access Memory" IEEE trans. on TVLSI Systems, Published, 2013.

[4] T. Ohsawa, K. Kai, K. Murakami, "Optimizing the DRAM Refresh Count for Merged DRAM/Logic LSIs" ISLPED1998 Conf., 1998.

[5] J. Liu, B. Jaiyen, R. Veras, O. Mutlu, "RAIDR: Retention-Aware Intelligent DRAM Refresh" ISCA2012 Conf., 2012.

[6] R. K. Venkatesan, S. Herr, E. Rotenberg, "Retention-Aware Placement in DRAM (RAPID): Software Methods for Quasi-Non-Volatile DRAM" HPCA2012 Conf., 2012.

[7] J. Liu, B. Jaiyen, R. Veras, O. Mutlu, "An Experimental Study of Data Retention Behavior in Modern DRAM Devices: Implications for Retention Time Profiling Mechanisms" ISCA2013 Conf., 2013.

by SELF) to decide the continuous copy operation. CREF = H selects CREF_PLS as the input signal in the refresh counter, which sends the pulses for the continuous copy operation in 100 ns interval repeatedly until the compare circuit outputs CREF_STP = H, which stops continuous copies at the point of the full array copy completion. The reset operation changes CREF to L and CP to L. In the SELF ENTRY operation, the N0-N4 signal selects not only the lowest bit of the refresh counter among X0T-X4T, but also selects the right panel X-decoder circuit that enables the simultaneous WL selection for $n = 2^N$ cells/bit of the composed memory cell. When the DRAM receives the SELF EXIT, the circuit operation about CREF is the same. But the SELF ENTRY register keeps CP to L by SELF = L.

In PAM2, A4=H for the MRS. The H of the A4 register selects PA through CREF-SW as the flag of the continuous refresh, and selects the A3 register output through CP-SW as the flag of the continuous copy. The H of the A4 register sets the configuration for the composed memory cell in both the normal and the SELF modes through N-SW.

Fig. 10(b) shows these signal transitions in the case of (N=0 → N=2 → N=0). When the DRAM receives the PAC, the command decoder generates PA, a one-shot pulse, which enables receipt of the identification code A3. PA connects to the CREF register, whose output signal CREF = H decides the continuous refresh operation. The A3 register outputs CP = H, which decides the continuous copy oper-

A Memory Mapping Approach based on Network Customization to Design Conflict-Free Parallel Hardware Architectures

Saaed Ur Rehman   Cyrille Chavet   Philippe Coussy

Lab-STICC laboratory / Université de Bretagne Sud
Centre de recherche Christiaan Huygens, 56100 Lorient (France)
{ saeed-ur.rehman@univ-ubs.fr; cyrille.chavet@univ-ubs.fr; philippe.coussy@univ-ubs.fr }

ABSTRACT

Parallel hardware architectures are needed to achieve high throughput systems. Unfortunately, efficient parallel architectures require removing memory access conflicts. This is particularly true when designing turbo-codes, channel interleaver or LDPC (Low Density Parity Check) codes architectures which are one of the most critical parts of parallel decoders. Many solutions are proposed in state of the art to find conflict free memory mapping but they are either limited to a subset of constraints, or result in high architectural cost. These drawbacks come from the interleaving law and the incompatibility between this law and the targeted interconnection network (in coder/encoder architecture). In this paper we propose a conflict free memory mapping approach that is able to generate optimized hardware architectures by limiting these drawbacks. The proposed solution constructs a customized interconnection network by analyzing data access patterns defined in the interleaving law. Our approach is then compared to state of the art methods and its interest is shown through the design of parallel interleavers for HSPA.

Categories and Subject Descriptors

J.6 **Computer-Aided Engineering**: Computer-aided design (CAD); B.7 **Integrated Circuits**: General

Keywords

Parallel architectures, interleavers, memory mapping, FEC.

1. INTRODUCTION

We are living in the era of high data rate wireless applications (smart-phones, net-books, digital television, mobile broadband devices...). The enormous and rapid increase in data traffic strains network capacity and researchers are developing new techniques to deal with this high throughput requirement. As a result, advanced technologies are included in different telecommunication standards such as OFDM, MIMO and advanced error correction techniques to reliably transfer data at high rates on wireless networks. Among these techniques LDPC (Low Density Parity Check) [6][7] and Turbo-codes [8] are able to achieve very low bit error rates for low Signal-to-Noise Ratio (SNR) applications. They are used in various application standards and domains such like [1]-[9] digital video, broadcasting (DVB-S2DVB-T2...), high-speed wired links (10GBASE-T, ADSL...), wireless accesses (WiMAX,Wifi...), telecommunications systems (UMTS, HSPA, LTE...) or magnetic

GLSVLSI'14, May 21–23, 2014, Houston, Texas, USA.
Copyright © 2014 ACM 978-1-4503-2816-6/14/05...$15.00.
http:////dx.doi.org/10.1145/2591513.2591532

storage in hard disk drives. These codes are implemented on architectures composed of two or more processing elements PE (encoders/decoders), one interconnection network composed of steering components (multiplexers, butterflies, barrel shifters...) and memory elements (registers, RAMs...), see Fig. 1 in which 4 PEs are connected to 4 RAMs (i.e. *A,B,C,D*) through a dedicated interconnection network. This network interleaves the data blocks exchanged by the PEs according to a predefined rule named interleaving law or permutation law. To satisfy the aforementioned throughput requirements with an affordable implementation complexity, the iterative nature of these algorithms is a severe constraint. Hence, parallel architectures must be employed to speed up the decoding process. Unfortunately this kind of parallel architectures generates memory access conflicts when the interleaving law requires simultaneous accesses to the same memory block. This problem is called *"collision problem"* [21].

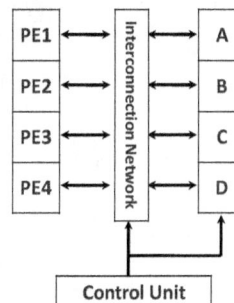

Fig. 1. General architecture of Parallel Decoders

In this paper we propose to introduce a new approach to find conflict free memory mapping based on network customization. This methodology leads to optimized architecture compared to state of the art approaches. The paper is organized as follows: Section II summarizes the different state of the art approaches whereas Section III gives the motivation by explaining memory mapping problem. The proposed approach is presented in Section IV with a pedagogical example. Experiment and results are given in Section V and finally Section VI draws some conclusions.

2. RELATED WORK

In order to overcome collision problem present in parallel architectures, the three kinds of solutions exist:

- Designing architecture and sometimes the interleaving law in order to ensure conflict-free memory accesses. This task is often complex, but more over a designer is rarely free to define his own interleaving law.
- Using fixed architectures, i.e. numbers and architectures of PEs, interconnection network and memory banks are considered as constraints and are not modified. In this case, conflict free memory mapping are obtained through dedicated algorithms, but the resulting architecture cannot be optimized.

• Customizing architectures i.e. numbers and architectures of PEs, interconnection network or memory banks are considered as *soft* constraints and can be modified. These approaches focus on adding buffers in the design to handle conflicts.

The first family of approaches to get rid of collisions consists in designing a dedicated architecture from scratch, or a specific interleaver rule that will natively avoid memory conflict accesses. In [21], the authors propose a deterministic methodology to design collision-free interleavers. In [22] and [23] the authors define collision-free permutations thanks to a combination of a spatial and a temporal permutation. Of course, these solutions are viable if and only if the designer is free to choose the permutation law to be used in the system. As a consequence, the resulting architecture may not be standard compliant.

The second family includes solutions that uses fixed architectures i.e. these approaches use an architecture without making any changes to it (e.g. [10][11][13] or [16]). A solution is proposed in [10] to solve the memory mapping problem under network constraint. Unfortunately, this approach is dedicated to Turbo-codes and is not able to deal with LDPC memory mapping constraints. Simulated annealing approaches like [13] (in place memory mapping) are also able to find a conflict free memory mapping for both Turbo-codes and LDPC. But, in order to apply this algorithm for LDPC, the authors modify memory access schedule by using a Static Single Assignment (SSA) form. Of course, this results in oversized memory architecture to store data. Authors of [16] use a dual-access memory mapping approach in order to map the data in minimum number of memory banks. The approach has been developed using polynomial time algorithm to target both Turbo and LDPC codes. Unfortunately, none of these memory mapping approaches takes into account the interconnection network, its controller or the memory controller. Hence, each processor have to access to each memory bank (to read and/or to write its data). Thus, even if the designer would prefer to use an optimized network (e.g. Butterfly, Barrel-shifter...), the interconnection network must be a full crossbar or a Benes network. In addition, since no dedicated approach has been used, data are randomly stored in memory banks. Parallel interleaver architectures could thus be significantly optimized in terms of interconnection network and network and memory controller costs.

The third family includes [12][14][15] or [19]. These approaches generate conflict-free architectures by adding memory components (buffers) in the interconnection networks and/or memory to manage conflicts. These kinds of approaches increase the cost and/or latency of the system due to presence of complex interconnection network and additional buffer management mechanisms to deal with conflicts. Similarly in [14], multistage interconnection network architectures are presented in order to handle on-chip communications in multiprocessor parallel turbo decoders. They are based on a dedicated network and associated routers. The main feature of these network architectures (Benes or Butterfly based topologies) is their scalability enabling seamless trade-off between hardware complexity and available bandwidth for turbo decoding. However, the proposed approaches still need additional buffering to deal with conflicting memory accesses. In [12] the authors proposed to use additional buffers within the interconnection network in order to store conflicting data during interleaved order access, until the targeted processor can process it. This increases the additional network buffering resources and consequently the time needed to interleave information. This is a suboptimal strategy, in terms of latency and thus throughput which avoids collisions at the expense of area and memory. In [19] the authors present a memory mapping approach to find conflict-free memory mappings for both Turbo-codes and LDPC codes that

generates architectures, with limited network controller cost and that respect a targeted interconnection network defined by the designer. This is possible by adding registers in the memory architecture to deal with conflicting data.

The source of conflicts is the interleaving law, but the final cost of the architecture is also due to the incompatibility between this interleaving law and the targeted interconnection network. Our proposal is to introduce a new approach based on a conflict free memory mapping that could take advantage of adding degree of freedom in the interconnection network in order to optimize the resulting architecture.

3. MOTIVATION

Let us consider a parallel turbo decoder architecture composed of P processing elements $PE=\{PE_1,...PE_p\}$ and P memory banks $B=\{b_1,...b_p\}$ to store $L=\{e_1,...e_L\}$ data elements. In order to balance the number of data among memory banks, each of them has to store $M=L/P$ data.

PE₁	0	1	2	0	6	4
PE₂	3	4	5	8	5	7
PE₃	6	7	8	2	10	1
PE₄	9	10	11	11	3	9
	t_1	t_2	t_3	t_4	t_5	t_6

Time

Fig. 2. Memory access schedule

Fig. 2 models memory accesses schedule as a table for a parallelism $P=4$. Lines represent the set of data used by each processing elements (for example PE_1 accesses data *0, 1, 2, 6* and *4*. Columns represent computation instants needed to process the $L=12$ data, e.g. at time instance t_1 data *0, 3, 6* and *9* will be accessed concurrently by PE_1, PE_2, PE_3 and PE_4 respectively. This example mimics a turbo application where each data is accessed two times e.g. data *0* is accessed, processed and updated 2 times i.e. at times t_1 and t_4. Objective of memory mapping methods is to find a conflict-free memory mapping given memory access schedule (i.e. interleaving law and parallelism) and optionally interconnection network.

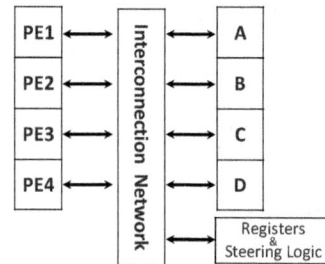

Fig. 3.- Architecture generated by memory relaxation approach

By using a classical memory mapping approaches (e.g. [13]), the resulting architecture (see Fig. 1) will include a memory controller composed of four dedicated control ROMs. Each ROM contains the control bits and address sequences for the memory bank it is associated to (i.e. in this figure the memory banks are labeled by *A, B, C* and *D*) and each command word is randomly stored. Thus, no regularity can be easily extracted from the control words generated by the memory controller, and as a consequence, no optimization can be performed. On the contrary, if such regularity could be extracted, the addressing sequence, and the associated controller could be greatly reduced. Such regularity could be obtained applying the approach described in [19], but the final architecture suffer from additional cost due to new registers inclusion and their dedicated additional steering logic (see Fig. 3). Based on [19] these

194

additional registers are used to store the conflicting data accesses. Therefore, if the targeted interleaving law is strongly incompatible with the targeted interconnection network the additional costs will be high. We will refer this approach as *memory relaxation.*

These added steering logic and registers could be avoided thanks to [13]; however the final architecture is based on Benes network and still require additional buffers between the interconnection network and the memory banks (see Fig. 4). Moreover the total latency of the system is increased since each conflicting data access must travel these buffers before being stored in the memory banks. We will refer this approach as *time relaxation.*

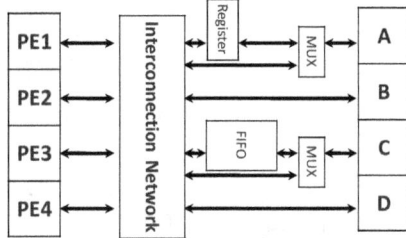

Fig. 4. Architecture generated by time relaxation based approach

As a conclusion, it can be noticed that the targeted interconnection networks has a large impact on the final cost of the architecture, since additionally to parallel interleaving conflicts to be solved, the set of possible permutations offered by the network could strongly restricts architectural design space exploration. Hence, since this interconnection network has a great impact on the final architecture, it seems to be a cause of the problem that is not taken into account in the state of the art approaches. A clever memory mapping approach should also focus on this network in order to adapt the network constraint to the interleaving law as much as possible. We call this *network relaxation.*

4. PROPOSED APPROACH

3.1. Memory Mapping with Network Relaxation

Our proposed approach aims to take advantage of network relaxation principle, see Fig. 5. This figure presents an approach by considering the customization of the interconnection network and reducing the cost of the controller architecture. The mapping relaxation is provided by modifying the original network by adding additional multiplexers/switches to the network. The idea is to keep the advantage of memory mapping approaches like [10] or [13] in terms of architectural cost and latency, while proposing an approach that is able to target any application as [12] or [19]. Starting from the description of an interleaving law (# of data, interleaving law, parallelism) and a targeted interconnection network (*NULL, Barrel-Shifter(BS), Butterfly(BF), Benes(BEN)* or *Cross-Bar(CB)*), the set of input memory mapping constraints is generated and provided to our memory mapping algorithm. Then, the next step consists in applying a memory mapping algorithm under network constraint. In the network library, all classical permutations offered are stored separately for each network. This mapping step aims to fully explore the memory mapping solution space by checking all the networks. If no memory mapping solution exists for this network, then the set of permutations will be extended by addition of a steering component, resulting into customized network architecture with enriched set of permutations (see Fig. 8). At the end the resulting architecture is generated. By applying this process for all available networks in the library, the designer is able to widely explore the design space and to select the best solution.

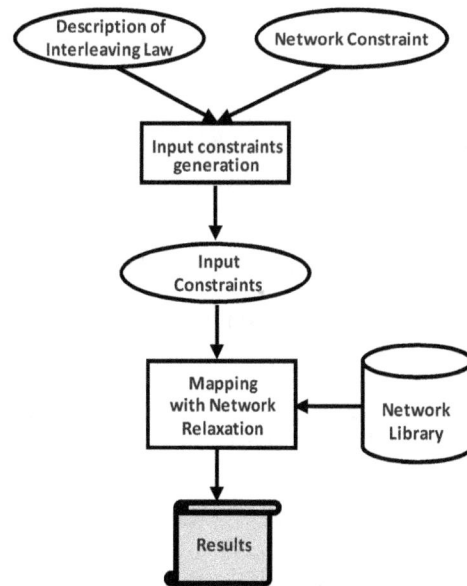

Fig. 5. Proposed Design Flow

The proposed algorithm uses a memory mapping matrix in which each data access is associated to two memory banks (one for the read access to the data and one for the write access of the result, see Fig. 6) as proposed in [19]. In order to guarantee a valid memory mapping, constraints have to be respected for a given parallelism and interleaving law.

Fig. 6. Memory Mapping matrix

Memory constraints:

1- Data processed at the same cycle (i.e. data that are read or written concurrently at time instance) have to be stored in different memory banks.

2- The ith read access to a given data must be performed in the same memory bank that its $(i-1)^{th}$ write access i.e. a data must be read in the same memory location it has been written.

Network objective:

The memory mapping has to respect the set of supported permutations (i.e. this set is initialized with permutations of user-defined network constraint topology).

The proposed memory mapping algorithm (cf. Fig. 7) first selects the most constrained column (i.e. the most constrained read or write access column in a given cycle) in the memory mapping matrix. Then the algorithm generates the subset of valid permutations for this column from the set of supported permutations in the targeted interconnection network. If this subset is not empty (i.e. conflict free memory mapping solution could be obtained for the selected column, with respect to the set of possible permutations) then each possible permutation from this subset is explored one by one, until a final conflict-free memory mapping is generated by our recursive algorithm. If no such valid memory mapping can be found with the targeted network then the set of

```
1. Start ;        // Boolean value initialized with TRUE
2. S_{Perm} ;     // Set of possible permutations in the selected network
3. M_{Map};       // Memory Mapping matrix
4. C_i;           // Selected column i in M_{MAP}
5. LVP_{C_i} ;    // List of valid permutations for column C_i
6. VP_{C_i} ;     // An element of LVP_{C_i}

7. Algorithm Map&NetRelax (S_{Perm}, M_{Map}, Start)
8. C_i = SelectColumn(M_{Map});
9. LVP_{C_i} = SelectValidPerm(S_{Perm}, C_i, M_{Map});
10. If ((LVP_{C_i} is not empty) and not (FullyMapped(M_{MAP}))) Then
11.     Do
12.        VP_{C_i} = Select&RemoveFirstPerm(LVP_{C_i});
13.        MapColumn(C_i, VP_{C_i});
14.        Start = FALSE;
15.        Map&NetRelax (S_{Perm}, M_{Map}, Start);
16.        If ((Start = FALSE) and not (FullyMapped(M_{MAP}))) Then
17.           RemoveMapColumn(C_i, VP_{C_i});
18.        End if;
19.     While ((Start = FALSE) and (LVP_{C_i} is not empty) and
20.        not(FullyMapped(M_{MAP})));
21.     If ((Start = FALSE) and not (FullyMapped(M_{MAP}))) Then
22.        AddNewNetComp(S_{Perm});
23.        EraseMap(M_{Map});
24.        Start = TRUE;
25.        Map&NetRelax (S_{Perm}, M_{Map}, Start);
26.     End if;
27. End if;
```

Fig. 7. Mapping algorithm with network relaxation

possible permutations must be extended by adding a new network component (i.e. multiplexer or switch, see Fig. 8) to the existing network, and the control ROMs that pilot the network is extended. In that case the memory mapping algorithm restarts from the beginning with this new extended set of permutations.

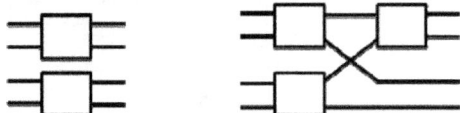

(a)Initial network architecture   (b) Extended network
Fig. 8. Network Customization

The architecture generated with network relaxation is composed of a classical interconnection network (i.e. BS, BF…) along with additional steering component(s) named *customized network*. Then, since the source of the memory conflicts is relaxed, it is possible to find optimized conflict free architecture compared to [12] or [19].

3.2. Pedagogical Example

In order to fully elaborate the proposed approach, the data access pattern example shown in Fig. 2 (and Fig. 6) is considered. Firstly, a Barrel-Shifter *BS* is considered as input network constraint for this example. Hence, the set of permutations offered by a *BS* is selected from the library. The general architecture targeting *BS* is shown in Fig. 9(a). Let suppose that after few iterations of our algorithm, the partial memory mapping described in Fig. 9(b) is achieved. At this step, there is no permutation from *BS* which could results in valid mapping according to the mapping constraints. So an additional steering component (i.e. a switch) is needed with the Barrel-Shifter network and an extended set of permutations is generated. Then, the memory mapping process is restarted with this new set of permutations. This process continues recursively until a valid memory mapping for the all matrix is reached. The resultant conflict free memory mapping and the architecture using network relaxation are shown in Fig. 10.

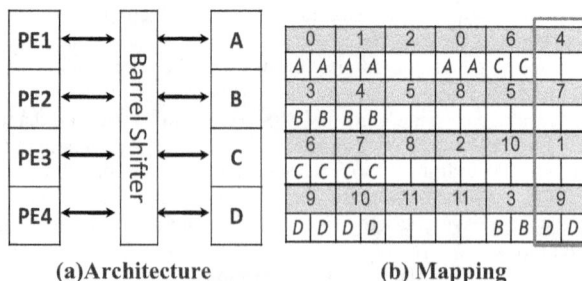

(a)Architecture   (b) Mapping
Fig. 9. Mapping with standard BS

Next, if no network constraint is defined by the designer, the algorithm start from scratch considering no network constraints, i.e. start mapping with NULL network (each PE is directly connected to a single memory bank through a wire).

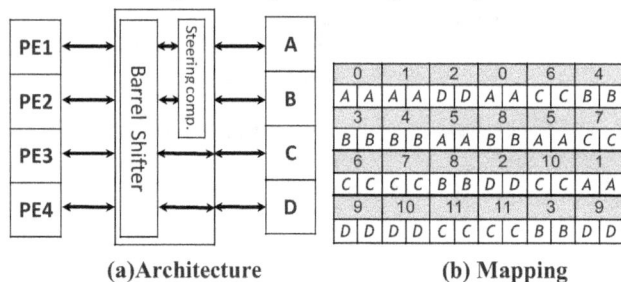

(a)Architecture   (b) Mapping
Fig. 10. Network relaxation with BS

The algorithm will add new steering component to the network when needed, until a valid memory mapping is achieved. As a result a fully customized network is developed. The final mapping for the considered example can be seen in Fig. 11.

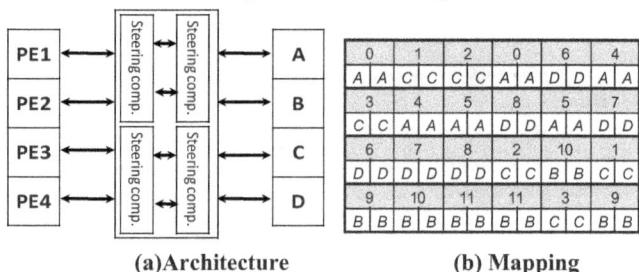

(a)Architecture   (b) Mapping
Fig. 11. Network relaxation without any NW constraints

5. EXPERIMENTS AND RESULTS

This section presents the different experiments we performed and shows the interest of the proposed approach. 90nm technology from STMicroelectronics has been used to calculate area of different components of resultant architecture. The area is given in NAND-gate equivalent to respect non-disclosure agreement. Currently turbo codes are used in different standards. However, interleavers used in these standards are not conflict free for every type of parallelism used in turbo decoding. The proposed approach is able to find conflict free memory mapping for any type of interleaver and for any type of parallelism. However, for experimental purpose, we implemented interleavers used in one of the most widely used standards: HSPA Evolution [1].

Fig. 12 shows comparison of the proposed network relaxation approach with different state of the art approaches. Different HSPA block lengths L with $P=4$ are considered. Fig. 12(a) shows comparison of area in *logarithmical* (base10) scale and Fig. 12(b) shows latency comparison in term of cycles.

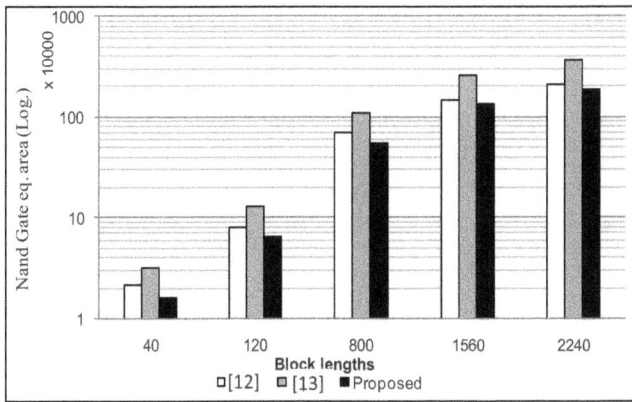

(a) Area comparison

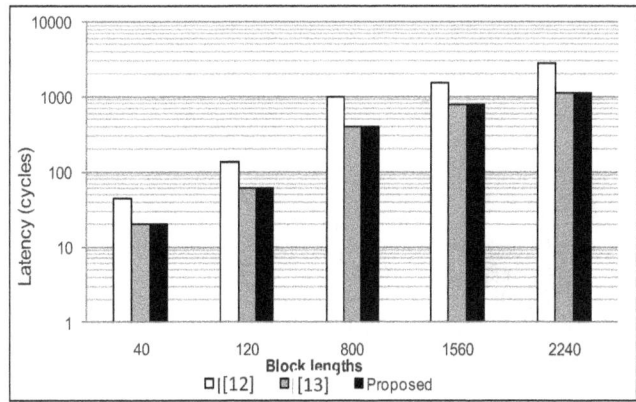

(b) Latency comparison

Fig. 12. Comparison with different approaches

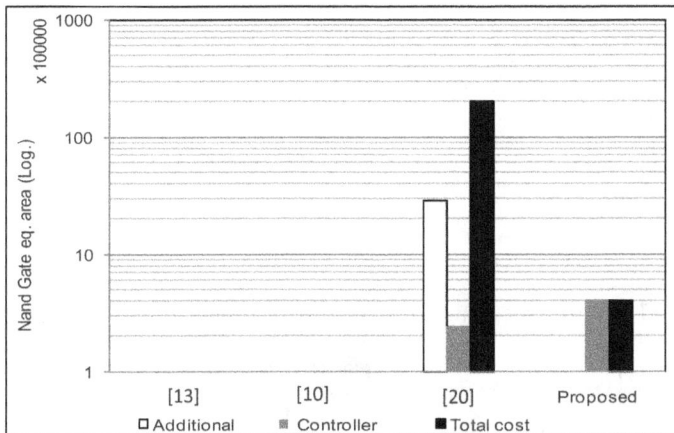

(a) With BS constraint(L=2240,P=4)

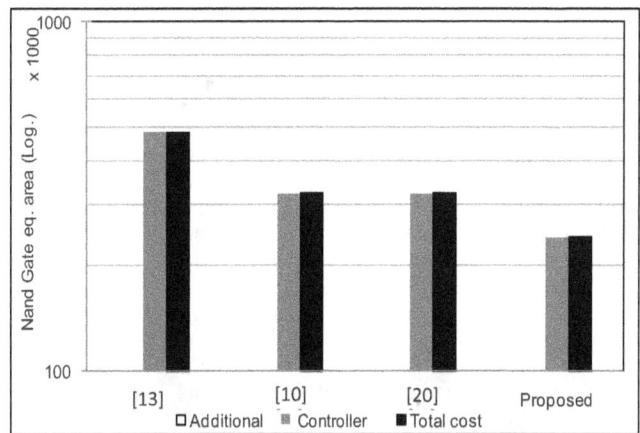

(b) Without any constraint(L=2240,P=4)

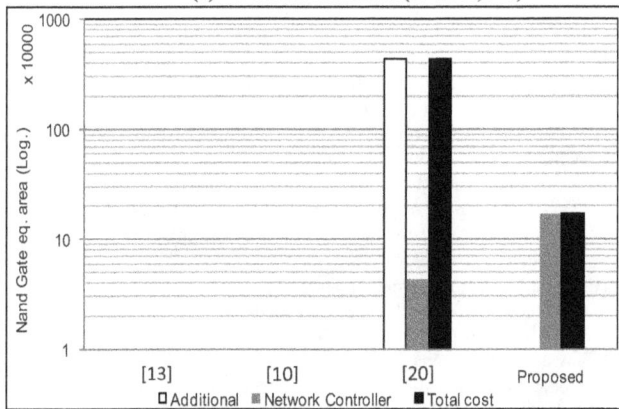

(c) With BS constraint(L=800,P=8)

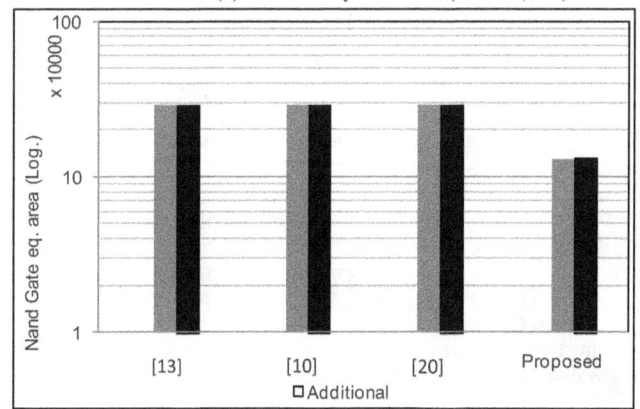

(d) Without any constraint(L=800,P=8)

Fig. 13. Cost comparison HSPA

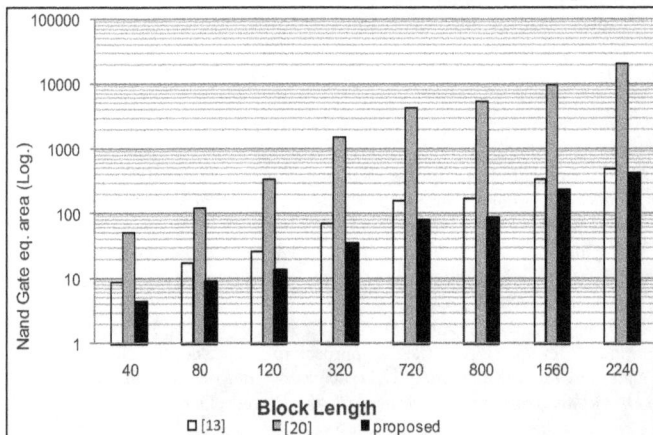

(a) Results *P=4*

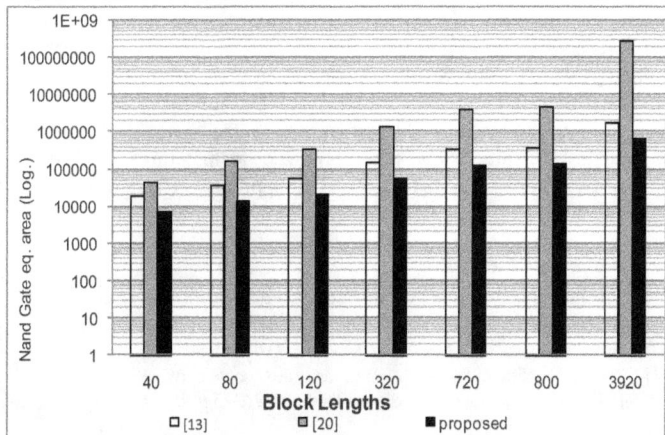

(b) Results *P=8*

Fig. 14. Cost comparison for different block lengths

Our proposed approach has 50% (average) lesser area with equivalent latency as compared to [13] and 18% lesser area with 56% lesser latency as compared to [12]. Therefore, the proposed approach significantly reduces the cost as compared to [13] with the same latency. On the other hand as compared to [12] our proposed approach reaches small reduction in terms of area, but without any additional latency (i.e. our architecture will achieve higher throughput) leading to a better performance/area tradeoff. Moreover, we compared our proposed approach with existing approaches [10], [13] and [19]. These experiments was performed for all block length from HSPA and for parallelism $P=4$ and $P=8$. Since the area for the memory banks is the same for each test case, it is not taken into account in these results. This simplification is fair since from [24] it can be observed that these extrinsic memories represent about 10% of the total area (also 10% of total area for PEs, 1% for the interconnection network and the rest - 79%- for the control unit).

Fig. 13(a) and (c) show typical results obtained in this case for 2240 and 800 data and a unique Barrel Shifter *BS* network constraint. Here, [10] and [12] are not able to find conflict free memory mapping. However, [19] is able to find the solution with the use of additional registers. As shown in this figure our proposed approach can find an optimized solution with an area divided by about 66 as compared to [19] (cf. Fig.13(a)) and by about 20 as compared to [19] for (cf. Fig.13(c)). In Fig. 13(b) and (d), the best results for each approach are presented. In this test case, the interconnection could be different for each, since for example [10] and [13] are not able to find a solution with a Barrel Shifter interconnection network. Then, [13] gives solution only with a fully connected network like Benes and [10] is able to find a solution with a Butterfly *BF* network, for $L=2240$ and $P=4$. Whereas for the second example with $L=800$ and $P=8$ in Fig. 13 (d), the minimum cost is achieved with Benes *BEN* for [10][13] and [19]. Our approach is able to find the conflict free memory mapping for all the considered examples with an area reduction of 34% in average for Fig. 13(b) and 50% in average in Fig. 13(d).

In order to fully explore our approach we have considered different block lengths from *HSPA* with $P=4$ and $P=8$. The results for $P=4$ is shown in Fig. 14(a) and for $P=8$ in Fig. 14(b). Like in the previous experiments, these figures show the best result for each approach. The results clearly show that our proposed network relaxation method always gives lower cost solution as compared to existing approaches. For $P=4$, our solution reduces the total area 21 times in average for all the experiments. Compared to [13] the area is divided by 1.8 in average and compared to [19] the area is divided by 41 in average. For $P=8$, network relaxation reduces the total area 40 times in average for all the experiments. Compared to [13] the area is divided by 2.6 in average and compared to [19] the area is divided by 76 in average.

6. CONCLUSION

In this paper, we proposed a new approach for conflict free memory mapping based on network customization. It systematically allows the generation of a conflict-free memory mapping which also respect targeted network architecture or modify it by adding steering components. Our approach has been compared through industrial test-case with the state of the art approaches. Results show that optimized architectures can be obtained by proposed network relaxation approach with significant area reduction without any loss in terms of throughput.

7. REFERENCES

[1] "Technical Specification Group Radio Access Network; Evolved Universal Terrestrial Radio Access; Multiplexing and Channel Coding (Release 8)", *3GPP Std. TS 36.212*, Dec. 2008.

[2] 3GPP, "Technical specification group radio access network; multiplexing and channel coding (FDD)"*(25.212V5.9.0).June* 2004.

[3] *DVB DocumentA122*. "Frame structure channel coding and modulation for the second generation digital terrestrial television broadcasting system (DVB-T2)," 2008.

[4] *IEEE P802.11n/D5.02, Part 11*. "Wireless LAN Medium Access Control (MAC) and Physical Layer (PHY) specifications: Enhancements for Higher Throughput", July 2008.

[5] *IEEE P802.16e, Part 16*. "Air Interface for Fixed and Mobile Broadband Wireless Access Systems," Amendment 2: Physical and Medium Access Control Layers for Combined Fixed and Mobile Operation in Licensed Bands, and Corrigendum 1, Feb. 2006.

[6] J.C. MacKay David and R.M. Neal, "Near Shannon limit performance of low density parity check codes", *Electronics letters*, July 1996.

[7] I. Gutierrez, A. Mourad, J. Bas, S. Pfletschinger, G. Bacci, A. Bourdoux, H. Gierszal, "DAVINCI Non-Binary LDPC codes: Performance and Complexity Assessment", *proc of Future Network & Mobile Summit, Italy*, June 2010.

[8] C. Berrou, A. Glavieux, and P. Thitimajshima, "Near-Shannon limit error-correcting coding and decoding: Turbo codes", *Proc. IEEE Int. Conf. Commun., vol.2*, 1993.

[9] http://www.ict-davinci-codes.eu/

[10] C. Chavet, P. Coussy, E. Martin and P. Urard, "Static Address Generation Easing: a Design Methodology for Parallel Interleaver Architectures", *proc of the International Conference on Acoustics, Speech, and Signal Processing (ICASSP), pp. 1594-1597*, Dallas, March 2010.

[11] L. Dinoi, S. Benedetto, "Variable-size interleaver design for parallel turbo decoder architecture", *IEEE Trans. Communication,Vol.53, No11*, 2005.

[12] N. When, "SOC-Network for Interleaving in wireless Communications", *MPSOC*, 2004.

[13] A.Tarable, S.Benedetto, and G.Montorsi, "Mapping interleaving laws to parallel turbo and LDPC decoder architectures", *IEEE Trans. Inf. Theory, vol.50, no.9*, Sept. 2004.

[14] O. Muller, A. Baghdadi, M. Jezequel, "ASIP-based multiprocessor SoC design for simple and double binary turbo decoding", *DATE*, 2006.

[15] H. Moussa, A. Baghdadi, M. Jezequel, "Binary de Bruijn on-chip network for a flexible multiprocessor LDPC decoder", *45th DAC Design Automation Conference*, 2008.

[16] A.H. Sani, C. Chavet and P. Coussy, "A First Step Toward On-Chip Memory Mapping for Parallel Turbo and LDPC Decoders: A Polynomial Time Mapping Algorithm", *IEEE Transactions on Signal Processing, vol. 61, issue: 16, p.4127 - 4140*, 2013.

[17] V.E. Benes, "Mathematical Theory of connecting network and telephone trafic", New York, N.Y.: *Academic*, 1965.

[18] A.La Rosa, C.Passerone, F. Gregoretti, L. avagno, "Implementation of a UMTS turbodecoder on dynamically reconfigurable platform", DATE, 2004.

[19] A. Briki, C. Chavet, P. Coussy and E. Martin, "A Design Approach Dedicated to Network-Based and Conflict-Free Parallel Interleavers", In *Proceedings of the 22th ACM Great Lakes Symposium on VLSI (GLSVLSI)*, Salt lake City, USA, may 2012

[20] S Cheng-Chi Wong and Hsie-Chia Chang, "Reconfigurable Turbo Decoder With Parallel Architecture for 3GPP LTE System" *IEEE Trans. Circuits Syst. II, Exp.Briefs, vol. 57, no. 7, pp. 566–570*, Jul. 2010.

[21] A.Giulietti, L.Van Der Perre and M.Strum, "Parallel turbo coding interleavers: avoiding collisions in accesses to storage elements", *Electronics Leters, vol. 38, no. 5, pp.232–234*, Feb. 2002

[22] D. Gnaedig, E. Boutillon, M. Jezequel, V. C. Gaudet, and P. G. Gulak, "On multiple slice turbo codes," in *Proc. 3rd Int. Symp. Turbo Codes, Related Topics, pp. 343–346*, Brest, 2003.

[23] R. Dobkin, M. Peleg, and R. Ginosar, "Parallel VLSI architectures and parallel interleaving design for low-latency MAP turbo decoders", Tech.Rep. CCIT-TR436.

[24] O. Sanchez, S. ur Rehman, A. Sani, C. Jego, C. Chavet, P. Coussy, and M. Jezequel, "A dedicated approach to explore design space for hardware architecture of turbo decoders", *In Proc. of IEEE Workshop on Signal Processing Systems*, Quebec, Oct. 17-19, 2012

New 4T-Based DRAM Cell Designs

Wei Wei
ECE Dept, Northeastern University
Boston, MA 02115, USA
+1-617-373-7780
wei.w@husky.neu.edu

Kazuteru Namba
A.I.S, Chiba University
Chiba, Japan
+81-43-290-3255
namba@ieee.org

Fabrizio Lombardi
ECE Dept, Northeastern University
Boston, MA 02115, USA
+1-617-373-4854
lombardi@ece.neu.edu

ABSTRACT

Dynamic Random Access Memories (DRAM) are widely used in processor design. Different cells have been proposed in the past to overcome concerns associated with low retention time, degradation in performance due to process variations and susceptibility to soft errors. This paper proposes two novel DRAM cells (referred to as 4TI and 4T1D) that utilize the techniques of gated diode and forward body-biasing to overcome the above issues. The designs of these cells are evaluated by HSPICE simulation; different figures of merits (such as Read delay, Write delay, retention time, power dissipation, critical charge and layout area) are assessed and a comparative analysis of the proposed cells with existing cells is pursued. The 4TI cell achieves the best power dissipation, while the 4T1D achieves the best retention time, the highest critical charge and the least average Read delay. An extensive simulation based evaluation of process variations is also presented to confirm that using static and Monte Carlo based analysis, the proposed cells are likely to be less affected by process variations (in threshold voltage and effective channel length) than the other cells found in the technical literature.

Categories and Subject Descriptors

B.7.1 [**Integrated Circuits**]: Types and Design Styles – *Advanced Technologies, Memory Technologies, VLSI (Very Large Scale Integration).*

General Terms

Design

Keywords

Memory Design, HSPICE, Dynamic random-access-memory (DRAM), Process variability

1. INTRODUCTION

Reduced scaling in nanometric technology has the potential to substantially increase the density and performance of digital circuits and systems. While in today's microprocessors, on-chip memory occupies a significant portion of the overall die area; it is extensively used to provide high system performance, while considering low power requirements [1, 2]. Dynamic memories have been extensively used for data storage structures in the processor core due to the transient nature of the data flow. Different designs of a Dynamic Random-Access Memory (DRAM) cell have been proposed; among them, the 3T1D DRAM cell [1] is a promising scheme due to the small area, the non-destructive read process and the good retention time. However, the operation of this cell is heavily influenced by process fluctuations [3-5] and external induced phenomena.

Among these fluctuations, the so-called random dopant fluctuation (RDF) results from a process variation in the implanted impurity concentration and plays a significant role in CMOS performance [6]; the RDF in the channel region may alter the MOSFET properties, especially its threshold voltage [6]. If more advanced process technologies are utilized, the RDF has a stronger effect, because the total number of dopants is small and the addition or deletion of a few impurity atoms can significantly alter the transistor properties [6]. In addition to process fluctuations, DRAMs are also susceptible to so-called soft errors due to externally induced upsets, such as those generated from alpha particles and atmospheric neutrons [7-9]. [10, 11] have shown that neutron induced soft errors dominate over alpha particle upsets in the deep sub-micron range.

A further area of concern in memory design is the increase in leakage current (so contributing to power dissipation) due to short channel effects in which the drain potential lowers the source junction barrier to the minority carriers [12]. Although this phenomenon (referred as to drain induced barrier lowering, or DIBL) has been extensively investigated in the past [13-15], the leakage problem has become a prominent cause of high power consumption for CMOS technology at nano scaled feature sizes. New schemes such as those utilizing the provision of a gated diode in a 3T1D cell [1], have been proposed to mitigate the above problems for designing a reliable, low power and high retention DRAM cell. The addition of transistors also contributes to a better tolerance to a Single-Event Upset (SEU) [16, 17].

The objective of this manuscript is to propose new DRAM cells; in this paper, the 3T DRAM cell is used as core. The techniques of gated diode and forward body-biasing are then applied by utilizing schemes that improve over the circuits of [1] in most figures of merit for performance. The operations of the proposed DRAM cells are analyzed, simulated and compared in detail using HSPICE tool.

2. REVIEW

In this section, the DRAM cells proposed in [1] and relevant techniques are reviewed.

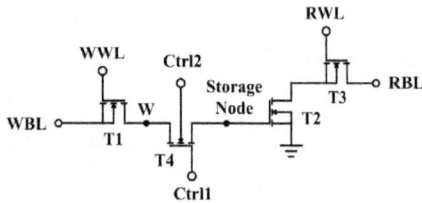

Figure 1. Proposed 4TI DRAM cell circuit

Table 1. Parameters for DRAM Cell HSPICE Simulation

Parameter	Value
Temperature	25 C
MOSFET Feature Size	45 nm
Vdd	1 V
Control	1 V
Ctrl1	1 V
Ctrl2	0.1 V

2.1 3T1D DRAM Cell

Different from a traditional 3T DRAM, the 3T1D DRAM cell [1] requires an additional NMOS transistor, whose source and drain are connected together for "Read". This gated diode configuration acts as a storage device and amplifier for the cell voltage. This raises the voltage at the gated-diode to reduce the read time and achieve a better retention as well as a higher tolerance to process variations than a 3T cell at the same voltage and cell size [3, 18].

2.2 4T DRAM Cell

In addition to the 3T1D cell presented previously, [1] has also presented a 4T DRAM cell; this cell does not suffer from the significant leakage encountered with the 3T1D cell. The gate-diode configuration is replaced with a NMOS pass transistor to decouple the leakage paths in the 3T1D cell. However, this cell requires an extra signal to refresh the stored data. So the NMOS pass transistor avoids the sub-threshold leakage that may also improve the retention time of the DRAM. The 4T DRAM cell [1] is simulated using the parameters of Table 1. For the "Read" 0 operation, the voltage of RBL is discharged to 0 and the voltage of SN is larger than the threshold voltage of transistor T2. The operations of "Write" and "Read" 1 operations are correctly; however, the cell is not fully capable to execute the "Read" operation for a 0 due to the above mentioned problem at the reduced MOSFET feature size.

3. Proposed DRAM Cells

Next two new DRAM designs are proposed in this section.

3.1 4TI DRAM Cell

The first proposed DRAM design is shown in Figure 1 and it is referred to as the 4T Improved DRAM cell (denoted as 4TI). Two control signals (given by Ctrl1 and Ctrl2) are required. Ctrl1 is

used the same as the Control signal for the 4T DRAM cell [1] to refresh the stored data at the storage node. Ctrl2 is connected to the body of the transistor T4 to replace the original proposed connection of RWL proposed in [1]. Therefore, Ctrl2 is equal to RWL but it has a different lower voltage value to improve the "Read" operation. The simulation of Figure 2 shows the correct operation of the proposed 4TI DRAM cell using the parameters in Table 1 and a 45nm MOSFET feature size [22].

From this timing diagram, the first two cycles perform the operations of "Write" and "Read" 0, respectively. During the "Read" operation, although the voltage of RBL is discharged, it is still significantly different from the voltage of the "Read 1" operation. Therefore, this voltage variation can be recognized by the Sense Amplifier to read at the output the stored data. This also shows that the technique of forward-biasing body is effective in improving the "Read" operation. Moreover, the body biasing voltage of transistor T4 in the 4TI DRAM cell has been varied to assess its role on the threshold voltage, as a further parameter for the correct execution of the "Read" operation. Under the parameters of Table 1, the simulation results show that the RBL voltage decreases from 220mV to 0V when the voltage of Ctrl2 increases from 0V to 0.4V. This makes possible a correct "Read" operation using a Sense Amplifier (SA) at the output of the memory. Different circuits can be used to provide the different levels for the above voltage requirements, such as a DC-DC converter [26] and a voltage reference source [27].

3.2 4T1D DRAM Cell

The proposed 4T1D DRAM cell is shown in Figure 3 by incorporating the gated diode technique; in this cell, an additional gated diode is connected to the SN to improve its retention time and speed of operation. The two signals Ctrl1 and Ctrl2 use the same parameters as in Figure 1. Also as for the 4TI cell, the technique of forward-biasing body is still used to improve the "Read" operation. The simulated operation of the proposed 4T1D cell is given in Figure 4. The timing diagrams of the signals are very similar to the ones in Figure 2 confirming the correct operations of "Write" and "Read". The voltage on RBL changes, because the value of Ctrl2 is now given by 0.1V.

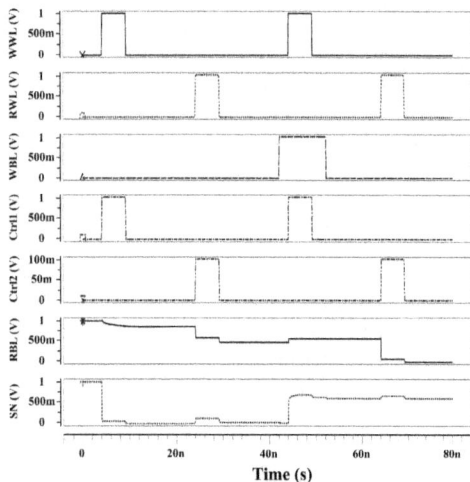

Figure 2. Simulated waveforms of 4TI DRAM cell at 45nm

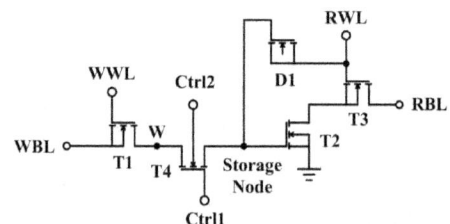

Figure 3. Proposed 4T1D DRAM cell circuit

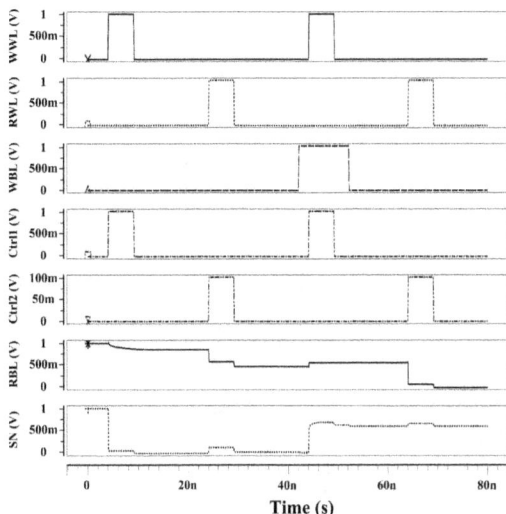

Figure 4. Simulated waveform of 4T1D DRAM cell at

4. Performance Evaluation

The DRAM cells (in Figures 1, 3 and [1]), company with different SRAM cell schemes (6T, 7T [24] and 8T [25]) are simulated to evaluate their performance using different figures of merit.

4.1 Performance

Initially, the delay values for the "Read" and "Write" operations for 0 and 1 are established. Figure 5 and 6 show the average values, company with each delay value for both the "Write" and "Read" 0/1 operations. The newly introduced transistor T4 in a 4T DRAM cell improves the retention time, but it also accounts for a penalty in the write access time [1] compared with the 3T1D cell. Moreover, the utilization of the two control signals used for transistor T4 in the 4TI cell results in an improved average "Read" delay, because the forward-biased body is beneficial to this operation compared to a 3T1D cell. However, due to the small voltage value used for the Ctrl2 signal (i.e. 0.1V), the improvement in the "Read" operation is less than for the 4T cell of [1]. The proposed 4T1D cell has the least average "Read" delay among the four DRAM cells memory types by incorporating both the gated diode and the body biasing voltage of transistor T4. The evaluation of the 6T SRAM is also included. Compared with other DRAM cells, the 6T presents few advantages, but it has few disadvantages such as a larger number of transistors. The other SRAM cells show also better performance than the DRAMs.

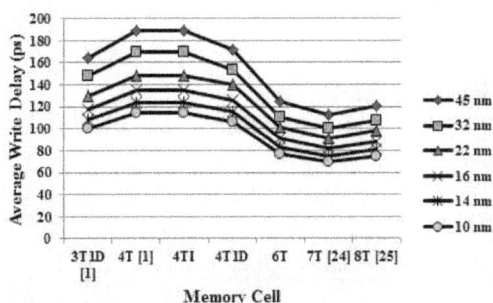

Figure 5. Average write delay vs type of memory cell

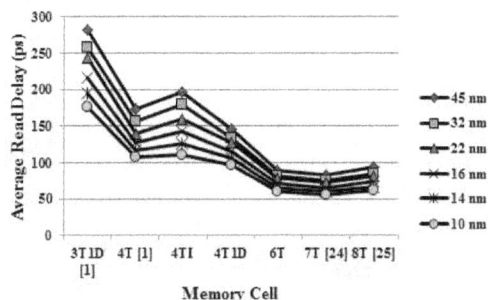

Figure 6. Average read delay vs type of memory cell

4.2 Power Dissipation

Power dissipation is defined for each operational cycle, shown in Figure 7; there is no significant difference among the cells, since they incorporate four devices in their operation. On a marginal basis, the value of the proposed 4TI cell is the best, since it uses two control signals and a low voltage value for one of them, thus reducing the dynamic power consumptions during a "Read". Compared with the other DRAMs, the proposed 4T1D cell has the largest power consumption due to largest number of devices in its design; however, the difference is very marginal. The three SRAM memories incur in larger power dissipation, because of they require a larger number of transistors and suffer from the leakage. Therefore, the proposed DRAM cells have the advantage of low power consumption when compared with the SRAM.

4.3 Retention Time

The retention time is defined as the time such that the minimum voltage Vmin has a value to distinguish the current (high voltage value) "1" state from the (low voltage value) "0" state [19]. The low retention time in a 3T1D cell (Figure 8) is mostly caused by the sub-threshold leakage due to the weak read access transistor [1], leading to most of the charge flowing into the bit lines. The retention time of the proposed 4TI is significantly higher than the 3T1D, because it effectively mitigates the leakage. The proposed 4T1D DRAM cell has the highest value, because the gated diode significantly increases the internal capacitance at the Storage Node. Similar to power dissipation, the reduction in feature size reduces the retention time (due to the decrease of the internal capacitance of the transistors).

4.4 Critical Charge

The evaluation of the charges of the internal nodes of the DRAM cells is also evaluated as a measure of tolerating soft errors. The two nodes (Figures 1 and 3) W and SN represent the critical pair by which the minimum charges (Qw and Qs respectively) are found to flip the stored data. The tolerance to soft errors of the

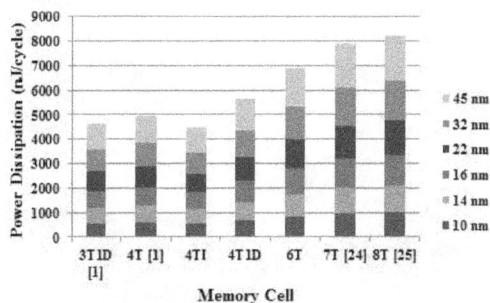

Figure 7. Power dissipation vs type of memory cell

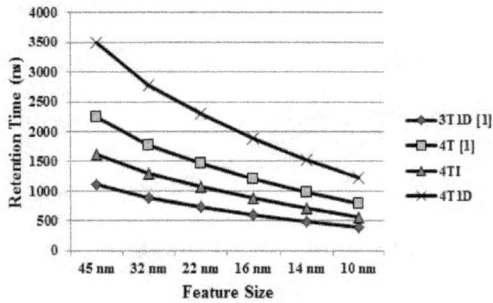

Figure 8. Retention time vs feature size for DRAMs

SRAM cells (6T, 7T and 8T schemes) is better than the DRAMs due to the cross-inverting circuit, so the discussion in this section is only concentrated on the evaluation of the DRAMs.

The results of the charges of the critical pairs are shown in Table 2; the value of Qs is significantly smaller than Qw for the 4T, 4TI, 4T1D DRAM cells, i.e. node W has a better tolerance than the Storage Node (SN) to soft errors. Note that the 3T1D DRAM cell has only the SN node (no node W). As in the 4T cell, the body of transistor T4 is connected to RWL, then the tolerance to soft errors deteriorates compared with the proposed 4TI cell. Finally, the proposed 4T1D cell has the highest charge values for both nodes, because D1 is connected to the SN as gated diode and increases the node capacitance, leading to the improvement of the tolerance to soft errors.

4.5 Area

The layouts of the four DRAM cells have been demonstrated using Cadence Virtuoso [20]. In general, the NMOS transistors are fabricated on a p-type substrate that has a shared body [20], as in the layout of the 3T1D cell. However, due to the utilization of the forward body-biasing technique, the transistor T4 in the 4T cell is fabricated on a separate p-type well, because the body voltage of T4 is changed. Hence, the layout of 4T is split into two parts, the first part is for the NMOS transistor on a separate p-type well defined by the Body Biasing MOS (BBMOS). In the second part, the 4TI has the same layout as the 4T cell, because the difference between them is the biasing voltage variation; so, the layout of the proposed 4T1D DRAM also requires the BBMOS. The comparative results are shown in Figure 9 based the areas of the 3T1D, 4T/4TI and 4T1D cells (given by $1162\lambda^2$, $1304\lambda^2$ and $1531\lambda^2$, respectively) as well as the areas of 3T [21], 6T [21], 7T [24] and 8T [25] cells. Therefore, the SRAMs account for a significant area penalty. The improvements in performance and tolerance to soft errors incur in an area overhead for the DRAMs.

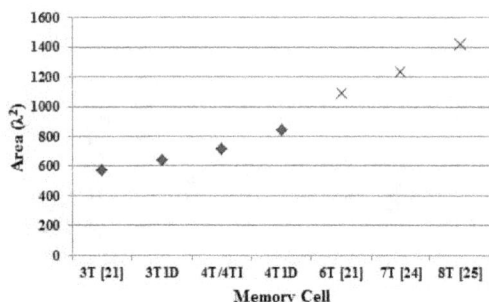

Figure 9. Area vs type of memory cell

Table 2. Charges of DRAM Cell Types

Cell	Node	Charges (aC)					
		45 nm	32 nm	22 nm	16 nm	14 nm	10 nm
3T1D [1]	Qs	19.55	16.33	14.28	7.303	3.867	2.144
4T [1]	Qs	10.71	7.946	6.043	3.091	1.636	0.907
	Qw	106.4	99.21	92.86	47.49	25.14	13.94
4TI	Qs	18.43	15.67	13.42	6.863	3.634	2.015
	Qw	122.6	115.4	110.8	56.67	30.00	16.63
4T1D	Qs	**48.96**	**44.23**	**24.75**	**12.66**	**6.701**	**3.715**
	Qw	**140.3**	**131.9**	**73.80**	**37.74**	**19.98**	**11.08**

5. Process Variability

The process variability of the DRAM cells is evaluated by Monte Carlo simulation at nanoscaled ranges. Table 3 shows the variability (measured by the standard variation in percentage) of V_T and L_{eff} for the technology nodes as reported in [23]. A Gaussian distribution is assumed as characterized by the mean value (μ) and the standard deviation (σ) from that mean. Hence, the $3\sigma/\mu$ ratio will be used to quantify the variability.

5.1 Device Considerations

Simulation is performed to study the influence produced by the variability of each individual transistor/diode on the performance of the whole DRAM cell. Variations of the effective channel length (L_{eff}) and the threshold voltage (V_T) using the data of Table 3 are introduced to determine their effect. The simulation results at 45nm feature size (with the parameters in Table 1) are reported in Table 4 to show the variability caused by each device on the performance of the proposed 4T1D DRAM cell as per different metrics (bold entries in Table 4 show the largest values in percentage of variability, hence the worst cases). The simulation results for the other three DRAM cells are shown in Table 5. For the 4T1D cell, T4 has the most significant impact on the "Write" delay and retention time (followed by T1) while the "Read" delay is mostly influenced by a variation of T3; this is applicable independently of the parameter variation, i.e. both for L_{eff} and V_T. Similar dependencies are exhibited for the 4T and 4TI cells. For the 3T1D, T1 is critical because it has the most significant impact on the "Write" delay and the retention time of 3T1D.

On a comparative basis, the 4T1D cell shows the least impact of process variation at 45nm; V_T (L_{eff}) significantly affects the "Write" operation (retention time). Moreover, the "Read" delay is influenced by both parameter variations and T3/T4 are the most critical transistors for all four memory cells. Hence, T3 for the "Read" operation, T4 for both the "Write" operation and the retention time of the 4T1D, 4T and 4TI cells will be investigated further by reducing the feature size.

5.2 Feature Size

The DRAM cells are simulated to characterize the process

Table 3. Standard deviation for variability (in percentage) of each Technology Node

Parameter	σ (%)		
	45nm	32nm	22nm
L_{eff}	2%	2%	2.5%
V_T	4%	6%	8%

Table 4. Variability (in percentage) of each transistor in 4T1D cell at 45nm

$3\sigma/\mu$ (%)	T1	T2	T3	T4	D1
L_{eff}					
Write Delay	3.135	0.457	0.256	**5.004**	0.119
Read Delay	2.138	4.589	**13.47**	1.515	1.023
Retention Time	17.02	1.539	0.213	**19.82**	8.539
V_T					
Write Delay	1.308	0.180	0.032	**8.244**	0.092
Read Delay	1.302	0.583	**27.92**	7.749	1.628
Retention Time	0.942	0.955	0.220	**3.485**	0.296

variability by reducing the feature size and by concentrating on the most critical transistor variations (as reported previously).

- T4 is varied for both the "Write" delay and the retention time of the 4T1D, 4T and 4TI cells.
- T1 is varied for both the "Write" delay and the retention time of the 3T1D cell.
- T3 is varied for the "Read" delay for all the four memory cells.

The results are presented in Table 6; the $3\sigma/\mu$ ratio increases by decreasing the MOSFET feature size, thus having a more pronounced impact on cell performance. Also, the proposed 4T1D cell shows the least value in variability for the "Write" delay and retention time. This is caused by the utilization of both forward

Table 5. Variability (in percentage) of each transistor in the other three DRAM cells at 45nm

$3\sigma/\mu$ (%)	Parameter	T1	T2	T3	D1(T4)
L_{eff}					
3T1D [1]	Write Delay	**5.347**	0.673	0.241	0.164
	Read Delay	2.597	5.601	**15.38**	1.049
	Retention Time	**26.73**	3.750	2.611	9.603
4T [1]	Write Delay	**3.983**	0.436	0.215	6.218
	Read Delay	2.197	3.651	**20.57**	1.476
	Retention Time	17.59	2.597	1.636	**24.33**
4TI	Write Delay	3.849	0.417	0.179	**5.955**
	Read Delay	1.959	2.473	**16.43**	1.571
	Retention Time	17.30	2.601	1.349	**22.61**
V_T					
3T1D [1]	Write Delay	**9.469**	0.609	0.127	0.289
	Read Delay	2.394	7.592	**29.46**	2.677
	Retention Time	**8.212**	0.783	0.236	1.576
4T [1]	Write Delay	5.871	0.780	0.459	**11.54**
	Read Delay	1.962	3.583	**27.61**	2.769
	Retention Time	3.594	1.796	0.254	**6.377**
4TI	Write Delay	5.774	0.732	0.483	**10.68**
	Read Delay	1.865	2.203	**25.79**	2.873
	Retention Time	3.323	1.664	0.242	**6.028**

Table 6. Variability (in percentage) of four DRAM cells for various MOSFET feature size

$3\sigma/\mu$ (%)	Feature Size	Write Delay	Read Delay	Retention Time
L_{eff}				
4T1D	32nm	**6.943**	**19.82**	**23.03**
	22nm	**13.34**	**46.57**	**29.80**
3T1D [1]	32nm	7.535	22.72	31.27
	22nm	16.59	49.42	38.64
4T [1]	32nm	8.059	29.88	29.77
	22nm	18.76	58.63	36.51
4TI	32nm	7.844	23.97	27.12
	22nm	18.32	51.26	35.16
V_T				
4T1D	32nm	**13.50**	35.74	**5.820**
	22nm	**16.11**	45.50	**9.063**
3T1D [1]	32nm	14.82	36.88	13.92
	22nm	18.92	46.32	17.75
4T [1]	32nm	17.39	35.56	11.34
	22nm	23.83	45.29	15.59
4TI	32nm	16.77	**34.95**	10.89
	22nm	22.61	**44.03**	15.22

body-biasing and the gated diode. The proposed 4TI cell improves over the 4T cell of [1]. As expected, the "Read" operation is substantially affected by the variation of both L_{eff} and V_T while the retention time is more affected by L_{eff}. Additionally, the reduction in feature size increases the variability in all cases. Finally in all cases, the proposed 4T1D DRAM cell shows the least variability to these variations, thus confirming its viability for implementation.

6. Conclusion

This manuscript has proposed two additional cell designs referred to as 4TI and 4T1D. An extensive evaluation has been pursued at nano feature sizes (from 45 to 10 nm) using HSPICE as simulation tool with the relevant PTMs [22]. Table 7 shows the ranking of the proposed two DRAM cells and two cells of [1], i.e.

Table 7. Ranking of DRAM Cells

Metrics		3T1D [1]	4T [1]	4TI	4T1D
Write Delay		1	2	2	3
Read Delay		4	2	3	1
Power Dissipation		2	3	1	4
Retention Time		4	2	3	1
Critical Charge		2	4	3	1
Area		1	2	2	3
Process Variability (L_{eff})	Write Delay	2	4	3	1
	Read Delay	2	4	3	1
	Retention Time	2	4	3	1
Process Variability (V_T)	Write Delay	2	4	3	1
	Read Delay	4	2	1	3
	Retention Time	4	3	2	1

3T1D and 4T. So although the proposed 4T1D DRAM cell requires acceptable penalties in area and power dissipation, it also achieves the best performance for most of the metrics considered inclusive of retention time when compared with the other three cells. The proposed 4TI represents a compromise in design when compared with the cells of [1]; the 4TI cell is ranked in the middle (i.e. 2nd or 3rd) for most metrics, thus avoiding the bottom performance (i.e. the 4th ranking) often encountered for the 4T and 3T1D cells. In conclusion, this paper has demonstrated through an extensive analysis and simulation assessment that the proposed two DRAM cells offer significant improvements for implementation at nanoscaled CMOS.

7. REFERENCES

[1] S. Ganapathy, R. Canal, D. Alexandrescu et al., "A Novel Variation-Tolerant 4T-DRAM Cell with Enhanced Soft-Error Tolerance," *2012 IEEE 30th International Conference on ICCD*, pp. 472-477, 2012.

[2] B. Cheng, S. Roy, and A. Asenov, "CMOS 6-T SRAM cell design subject to 'atomistic' fluctuations," *Solid-State Electronics*, vol. 51, no. 4, pp. 565-571, 2007.

[3] W. K. Luk, J. Cai, R. H. Dennard, et al., "A 3-Transistor DRAM Cell with Gated Diode for Enhanced Speed and Retention Time," *2006 Symposium on VLSI Circuits Digest of Technical Papers*, pp. 184-185, 2006.

[4] E. Amat, C. G. Almudever, N. Aymerich et al., "Variability mitigation mechanisms in scaled 3T1D-DRAM memories to 22nm and beyond," *IEEE Transactions on Device and Materials Reliability (T-DMR)*, issue 99, pp. 1-6, 2012.

[5] X. Liang, R. Canal, G. Y. Wei et al., "Replacing 6T SRAMs with 3T1D DRAMs in the L1 data cache to combat process variability," *IEEE Computer Society on Micro*, vol. 28, issue 1, pp. 60-68, 2008.

[6] A. Asenov, A. Huang, "Random dopant induced threshold voltage lowering and fluctuations in sub-0.1 μm MOSFET's: a 3-d 'atomistic' simulation study," *IEEE Transactions on Electron Devices*, vol. 45, issue 12, pp. 2505-2513, 1998.

[7] J. F. Ziegler, "Terrestrical cosmic rays," IBM Journal of Research and Development, vol. 40, no. 1, 1996.

[8] Y. Tosaka, S. Satoh, K. Suzuki, et al., "Impact of Cosmic Ray Neutron Induced Soft Errors on Advanced Submicron CMOS circuits," *1996 Symposium on VLSI Technology. Digest of Technical Papers*, pp. 148-149, 1996.

[9] L. Borucki, G. Schindlbeck, "Impact of DRAM Process Technology on Neutron-Induced Soft Errors," *2007 IEEE International integrated reliability workshop final report*, pp. 143-146, 2007.

[10] P. Hazucha and C. Svensson, "Impact of CMOS technology scaling on the atmospheric neutron soft error rate," *IEEE Transactions on Nuclear Science*, vol. 47, no. 6, pp. 2586-2594, 2000.

[11] G. Schindlbeck, "Types of soft errors in DRAMs," 8th European Conference on Radiation and Its Effects on Components and Systems (RADECS), pp. PE1-1 – PE1-5, 2005.

[12] W. K. Henson, N. Yang, S. Kubicek et al., "Analysis of leakage currents and impact on off-state power consumption for CMOS technology in the 100-nm regime," *IEEE Transactions on Electron Devices*, vol. 47, no. 7, pp. 1393-1400, 2000.

[13] T. Y. Chan, J. Chen, P. K. Ko, "The impact of gated-induced drain leakage current on MOSFET scaling," *1987 International Electron Device Meeting*, vol. 33, pp. 718-721, 1987.

[14] K. Roy, S. Mukhopadhyay and H. Mahmoodi-Meimand, "Leakage Current Mechanisms and Leakage Reduction Techniques in Deep-Submicrometer CMOS Circuits," *Proceedings of IEEE*, vol. 91, issue 2, pp. 305-327, 2003.

[15] M. Anis and M. H. Aburahma, "Leakage Current Variability in Nanometer Technologies," *Proceedings of Fifth International Workshop on System-on-Chip for Real-Time Applications*, pp. 60-63, 2005.

[16] S. Lin, Y.B. Kim and F. Lombardi, "An 11-Transistors Nanoscale CMOS Memory Cell for Hardening to Soft Errors," *IEEE Transactions on VLSI*, vol. 19, no. 5, pp. 900-904, 2011.

[17] S. Lin. Y.B. Kim and F. Lombardi, "A Novel Design Technique for Soft Error Hardening of Nanoscale CMOS Memory," *Proc. IEEE MWSCAS*, pp. 679-682, Cancun, August 2009.

[18] W. K. Luk, and R. H. Dennard, "Gated diode amplifiers," *IEEE Trans on Circuits and System II: Express Briefs*, pp. 266-270, 2005.

[19] J. C. Koob, S. A. Ung, B. F. Cockburn et al., "Design and Characterization of a Multilevel DRAM," *IEEE Transactions on Very Large Scale Integration (VLSI) System*, vol. 19, no. 9, 2011.

[20] "Cadence Virtuoso," *www.cadence.com*.

[21] J. M. Rabaey, A. Chandrakasan and B. Nikolic, "Digital Integrated Circuits: A Design Perspective (Second Edition)", *Prentice Hall*, pp. 665, ISBN: 0130909963, 2003.

[22] "Predictive Technology Models (PTM)," *http://ptm,asu.edu*.

[23] A. Rubio, J. Figueras, E. I. Vatajelu et al., "Process variability in sub-16nm bulk CMOS technology," *Online. Available: http://hdl.handle.neu/2117/15667*, 2012.

[24] K. Takeda et al., "A Read-Static-Noise-Margin-Free SRAM Cell for Low-Vdd and High-Speed Applications," *IEEE JSSC*, pp. 113-121, 2006.

[25] L. Chang et al., "Stable SRAM Cell Design for the 32nm Node and Beyond," *Symp. VLSI Tech. Dig.*, pp. 292-293, 2005.

[26] V. Kursun et al., "High Input Voltage Step-down DC-DC Converters for Integration in a Low Voltage CMOS Process," *Proceedings of 5th International Symp. On Quality Electronic Design*, pp. 517-521, 2004.

[27] K. S. Park et al., "A Design of Temperature-compensated CMOS Voltage Reference Sources with a Small Temperature Coefficient," *7th International Conference on ASIC*, pp. 711-714, 2007.

MB-FICA: Multi-bit Fault Injection and Coverage Analysis

Chen Jiang, Mojing Liu, Brett H. Meyer
Department of Electrical and Computer Engineering
McGill University
Montréal, QC H3A 0E9 Canada
{chen.jiang2, mojing.liu, brett.meyer}@mcgill.ca

ABSTRACT

Recent studies have shown a dramatic increase in multi-bit upset (MBU) events and related errors as transistors continue to shrink. To assist designers with addressing MBU in microprocessor register files, we have extended an architectural description language, ADL, to simulate and analyze the effect of MBU on the fault coverage of hardware mitigation techniques. Our approach (a) considers the effect of SRAM layout on MBU patterns, (b) considers the data-dependent nature of transient upsets, and (c) runs benchmarks to completion to accurately evaluate coverage. To accelerate fault injection campaigns, we propose a suite of techniques that reduce the execution time of individual trials without compromising accuracy by only simulating mitigation techniques when faults are present and stopping simulation entirely when all errors have been detected or corrected. When evaluating parity, SECDED, and 2-bit 2D ECC, we achieve a mean fault injection performance speedup of $5.1\times$, but up to nearly $60\times$ in one case.

Categories and Subject Descriptors

B.8.1 [**Hardware**]: Performance and Reliability—*Reliability, testing, and fault-tolerance*

General Terms

Algorithms, Design, Measurement, Reliability

Keywords

Single-event multi-bit upset, Transient fault injection

1. INTRODUCTION

As semiconductor manufacturing processes scale to smaller feature sizes, device reliability has become more difficult to achieve: the critical charge Q_{crit}, the minimum charge needed to change the output logic level of a gate, has reduced to the point that phenomena such as neutron or alpha particle strikes regularly result in data corruption [1].

GLSVLSI'14, May 21–23, 2014, Houston, Texas, USA.
Copyright is held by the owner/author(s). Publication rights licensed to ACM.
ACM 978-1-4503-2816-6/14/05 ...$15.00.
http://dx.doi.org/10.1145/2591513.2591538.

In particular, the frequency of multi-bit upsets (MBU), defined as simultaneous errors in more than one bit induced by a single upset event, increases dramatically with transistor scaling [2]. MBU, by definition, are spatially correlated, and therefore layout dependent, as n- and p-well placement can constrain charge collection [3]; furthermore, recent advances suggest that soft-error vulnerability is data-dependent [3]. Such clustered, application- and layout-dependent failures can easily overwhelm traditional error mitigation techniques designed and evaluated under the assumption of independent single-bit flips, with catastrophic consequences for systems operating under a reliability constraint. New strategies are needed for evaluating the effect of MBU on microprocessors and the resulting effectiveness of mitigation technologies intended to improve their robustness.

In this context, we propose MB-FICA (available at `http://bhm.ece.mcgill.ca/~mb-fica`), a novel framework for multi-bit fault injection and coverage analysis. MB-FICA extends ADL [4], an architectural description language, with support for MBU fault injection campaigns to assist designers with early exploration and evaluation of mitigation techniques. MB-FICA injects MBU in microprocessor register files (RF) during benchmark execution, models application- and layout-dependent data corruption, and simulates the corresponding behavior of arbitrary mitigation techniques described in ADL, making it possible to determine pre-RTL MBU coverage. Different studies report different MBU distributions, and the observed fault behaviour depends on the number of bits corrupted by an event; to support coverage estimation under an arbitrary MBU distribution without requiring costly fault injection campaign re-execution, MB-FICA supports fault behavior re-sampling.

Full benchmark MBU analysis is both necessary—we observe that the rate of masking is substantially overestimated when benchmarks are not executed to completion—and computationally expensive: (a) costly sub-campaigns are needed for the different possible MBU that might manifest, and (b) benchmarks may run for millions of cycles after fault injection; our framework therefore implements several techniques for accelerating fault injection campaigns. Our acceleration techniques leverage information about the injected fault (when it is injected, the data-dependent effect of the fault, and when all injected faults have been detected) to dynamically enable and disable fault mitigation technique simulation, and terminate trials as early as possible. Our results show that this improves simulation performance by $5.1\times$ on average across several RF coding techniques (e.g., parity) and a variety of embedded benchmarks.

2. RELATED WORK

AVF analysis [5] is widely used by computer architects for evaluating computer system reliability, and estimates system vulnerability to error by estimating the probability that a fault affecting system state results in an observable system failure. AVF is founded on the principle that each bit is independent; under the threat of MBU however, this is no longer the case [6], and prior work has observed that AVF is inconsistent as well as inaccurate in the context of layout- and data-dependent two- and three-bit faults [3, 7, 8]. Recent work has attempted to apply AVF to MBU, but without addressing the above, fundamental shortcomings [9].

Fault injection is a technique for validating the dependability of a system by introducing faults into the target system and observing the resulting behavior. Touloupis *et al.* [10] used RTL-simulation-based fault injection techniques to study the effect of faults in registers. The required design effort and computational cost of RTL-based fault injection, however, limits its applicability.

Scan-chain-based techniques have been employed to emulate faults [11, 12]. Faults are injected via built-in self-test logic, i.e., boundary and internal scan chains. Scan-chain fault injection has good reachability and observability, as any locations accessible by scan-chains can be corrupted and subsequently monitored. However, this method is only available when a prototype of the system has been implemented.

Hardware fault injection has also been used to test the response of fabricated designs to actual radiation [13]. The primary disadvantage of such an approach is that the device-under-test must be manufactured at great effort and cost.

In this paper, we present MB-FICA, a comprehensive framework that considers data- and SRAM-layout-dependence of MBU, and simulates application-specific fault effects, to estimate the fault coverage of mitigation technologies based on a given arbitrary MBU distribution. Unlike the prior work, MB-FICA targets pre-RTL evaluation by leveraging the flexibility of ADL-based fault injection to enable designers to quickly define and test fault mitigation techniques across a wide variety of benchmarks and port them from architecture to architecture. MBU fault simulation is not new, and has been previously studied in the context of circuits and pipeline registers [14, 10]. These works, however, lack the general applicability of our model to arbitrary failure models (i.e., fault patterns) and mitigation technologies. Futhermore, while fault injection acceleration has been studied in the past [15, 16], these efforts have focused on hardware support for acceleration, such as with GPGPU and compute clusters. Our work is largely orthogonal, as knowledge of the injected faults and their effects are utilized for accelerating each individual trial.

3. MB-FICA

We have developed a coverage rate analysis tool for error mitigation models based on new fault injection extensions to Architecture Description Language (ADL) [4]. MBUs are injected in the register file of the modeled microprocessor; data corruption is based on both data values at the time of injection and SRAM layout. Benchmarks are then simulated to completion to accurately determine whether faults (a) are *masked*, (b) are detected and corrected (*DCE*), (c) are detected but not correctable (*DUE*), or (d) result in silent data corruption (*SDC*).

Currently, our framework focuses on faults and mitigation in the microprocessor register file (RF). The RF is more vulnerable to soft errors than other processor components, due to the fact that it is one of the hottest [17, 18], and soft error rates increase exponentially with temperature [19]. As the RF is typically made from SRAM it is also particularly vulnerable to MBU (as the storage cells are closer together). MB-FICA currently supports 1-3 bit faults in the RF, but may be extended to consider a much more broad set of possible errors and hardware targets.

Exhaustive fault injection is intractable. For instance, there are over 1B possible fault locations in time and space for a 32 word × 32 bit register file and 1M cycle application. Consequently, we sample the space of all possible fault injections and use this sample population and a given target MBU distribution to determine the average coverage rates for each different mitigation technique. Even after sampling, fault injection campaigns remain time consuming. We have therefore developed techniques that accelerate individual trials by (i) disabling error checking within ADL before errors are injected, and (ii) terminating trials once either it is observed that faults do not manifest as register file errors or all errors have been accounted for.

3.1 Architectural Description Language

Architectural Description Language (ADL) [4] defines the behavior of an ISA by describing architecturally-visible hardware (such as the general-purpose and special-purpose registers) and expressing how the operations of each possible instruction interact with that hardware, including exception handling. In our simulations, we utilized a 32-bit implementation of the PowerPC ISA, though our framework is portable to any ISA that can be modeled in ADL.

ADL models register files as an array of variables; architectural register files further define read and write hooks used by instruction definitions to access and modify register state. Consequently, implementing an RF fault mitigation technique is a simple matter of extending the read and write hooks to incorporate the desired functionality, such as checking or setting bits in auxiliary register files that store parity values. The obvious advantage of modifying read and write hooks is portability: once defined, a fault mitigation technique can be moved to any ISA in ADL with little or no modification (except, for instance, when register width differs between ISAs, as this likely influences the implementation of the mitigation technique).

Fault injection in MB-FICA is managed through ADL's interactive command line interface (CLI), and is therefore also portable. Through the CLI, RF values are read and written to simulate single event upsets (SEU); we automate this process with natively supported TCL/Tk scripts.

3.2 Fault Model

The manifestation of MBUs is dependent upon SRAM cell (a) layout and (b) state at the time of the upset [3]. MB-FICA is capable of modeling an arbitrary SRAM cell organization; in this paper, we assume that SRAM uses thin cells and that neighboring bits are mirrored [3]. One bit-cell consists of two cross-coupled inverters statically holding complementary values at circuit nodes Q and QB. The NMOS transistor of the Q node of one bit is in the same p-well as the NMOS transistor of the Q node for a neighbouring bit; this also applies for the QB node. In this case, if a Q node is

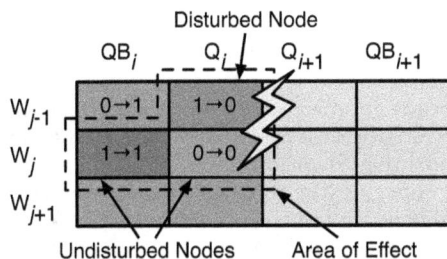

Figure 1: The location and orientation of an upset, and data prior to its occurence, all affect MBU manifestation.

affected by an upset, the Q node of a neighboring bit in the same diffusion, either vertically or horizontally in the array, may also be affected; we assume that the electrical isolation established by the neighboring n-wells means that Q nodes outside of the affected diffusion will not be disturbed [3]. We also assume that node values are driven to 0 (by the parisitic bipolar transistor that briefly shorts the node to the bulk); if a node is already at 0 V, then the node is not disturbed by a fault injection [3]. Consider the example in Figure 1.

Figure 1 illustrates the circuit nodes of three register words W_{j-1} to W_{j+1} and two bit columns i, and $i + 1$. A 3-bit fault is affecting the array, centered at W_j, Q_i (green square, hereafter $Q_{i,j}$); nodes $QB_{i,j}$ (blue square) and $Q_{i,j-1}$ (red square) are additionally affected. Different orientations of the fault pattern would result in different sets of nodes being affected. Despite the fact that three nodes are affected by the given fault pattern (or Area of Effect), due to the location and orientation of the fault and data at the time, only one node is disturbed, resulting in a 1-bit error. In this way, a 3-bit MBU may result in 3-, 2-, 1-, or 0-bit errors.

3.3 Fault Injection and Simulation

We implement fault injection in ADL using a TCL script that accesses the RF using the CLI. We first execute a "golden" (fault-free) run of each benchmark to determine the number of required simulation cycles and to record the final memory state under fault-free operation. We then perform a number of fault injection trials. A single fault is injected in each trial, at a time and location selected randomly by the TCL script. For each fault injection trial, we inject one fault by generating several random variables:

- N: a random instruction count, $N \in n = [1, max]$;
- X: a random general-purpose register (GPR), $X \in x = [0, 31 + v]$;
- Y: a random bit location, $Y \in y = [0, 31 + h]$;
- Q: a random bit, $Q \in q = \{0, 1\}$, determining which complementary node of the circuit is effected; and,
- P: a fault pattern is selected from p, determining the neighboring bits also affected by the fault.

n is determined by a golden run of a given benchmark. The range of x and y are determined by the architecture; h and v are the number of horizontal rows and vertical columns of code bits, respectively. The composition of p varies based on the MBU being injected; in the case of single-bit upsets, there is only one fault pattern affecting a single bit. 2-bit MBU can affect nodes that are horizontal or vertical neighbors. 3-bit MBU take the form of an L (Figure 1), with varieties rotated 90, 180, and 270 degrees.

After a fault is injected the simulation is advanced until the benchmark terminates; approaches in the literature reduce the computational cost of fault simulation by truncating benchmark execution a fixed number of cycles (e.g., 1M) after fault injection [3]. However, prior work has shown that up to 10% of errors do not appear until after one million cycles of execution [20]. Truncated execution is expected to give an optimistic view of fault coverage, converting SDC, DUE, or DCE events into masked errors, since the result of a latent error has yet to be observed.

3.4 Error Mitigation Models

To implement fault mitigation techniques in the general-purpose register file (GPRF), we (a) modified its read and write hooks to perform error detection or correction, and (b) added auxiliary check bit register files (CBRF) to store the required redundant (check) bits. The flexibility of ADL means that any mitigation technique that can be described as a manipulation of register file and check bits can be implemented, and therefore evaluated. We have only implemented (a) parity, (b) SECDED, and (c) 2D ECC; any fault mitigation technique that is invoked when registers are accessed can be modeled. The ADL implementations have been omitted due to space constraints, but are publicly available.

3.4.1 Parity

Parity uses a single bit to encode the bit-wise XOR of a register, and is able to detect an odd number of bit flips. Parity requires the least significant changes to the ADL source: the read hook re-computes the parity bit and compares it with the check bit stored in the CBRF; the write hook computes the parity bit and sets it in the CBRF. When an error is detected, the *DUE* condition is set. If corrupted data makes its way to memory (determined with a memory state comparison against the result of the golden run), *SDC* results. Otherwise, the fault is said to be *masked*.

3.4.2 SECDED

Single-error correct, double-error detect (SECDED) codes can correct 1-bit errors and detect 2-bit errors. As with parity, CBR bits are calculated when a GPR is written and verified when a GPR is read; we utilized the Hsiao parity check matrix [21]. If a one-bit error is detected, it is corrected and the *DCE* condition is set. If a two-bit error is detected, the *DUE* condition is set. As the assumed SRAM layout ensures no more than two bits per word are corrupted, SECDED never encounters an undetectable error (*SDC*).

3.4.3 2D ECC

To improve the efficiency of ECC in the presence of MBU, recent work has utilized two-dimensional interleaved error correcting codes (2D ECC) [22, 23]. 2D ECC makes use of a combination of row and column code bits to more cost- and performance-efficiently detect and correct MBU.

In ADL, 2D ECC requires an additional CBRF for column check bits. As with SECDED, both row and column code bits are updated each time a GPR is written. Likewise, error detection and correction are performed when a GPR is read. Similar to SECDED, 2D ECC never encounters an uncorrectable error (*DUE*) or *SDC*.

3.5 Fault Injection Acceleration

While modifying the GPRF is the best choice for ease of use and reuse, doing so adds considerable overhead, as

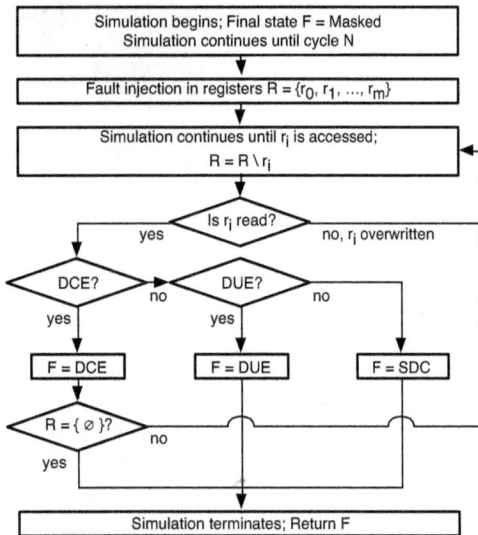

Figure 2: Fault injection is accelerated by simulating mitigation techniques only when faulty data is accessed and terminating simulations once all faulty data has been accessed.

the read (write) hook is executed each time a register is read (written). This is unnecessarily time-consuming: before fault injection and after fault correction, detection, or masking, the simulated error mitigation techniques are not needed. To improve efficiency we propose an acceleration approach which reduces the aggregate execution time of a fault injection campaign without sacrificing coverage analysis accuracy. Our acceleration techniques leverage information about the injected fault (when it is to be injected, the data-dependent effect of the fault) to dynamically enable and disable fault mitigation technique simulation. Mitigation technique simulation is a significant overhead, and only necessary for a small fraction of simulated cycles. We further track if and when corrupted data is detected or corrected; when further simulation will yield no further information about the result of a trial (e.g., it is known it will cause a DUE, and therefore not SDC), trials are terminated early. We conservatively assume that if faulty data not detected or corrected and is subsequently used, the result is SDC.

Figure 2 illustrates the operation of a single trial in a fault injection campaign. Simulation begins with mitigation techniques disabled: there are no faults to detect or correct. Simulation time advances to cycle N and the fault is injected in the set of registers R. If data bits are affected, they are modified using the CLI. As the read hook cannot be called from the CLI, check bits are not updated at this time; instead, the location(s) and effect of the fault are recorded within new ADL registers. If the fault does not corrupt any bits, or if no affected registers are ever read, $F = Masked$ is returned (these cases not shown in Figure 2). Otherwise, simulation advances until an affected register $r_i \in R$ is accessed. For a read access, the read hook first computes check bits based on the original, uncorrupted data. If the fault affects check bits directly, the check bits are corrupted at this point, and the read hook subsequently determines whether the fault can be detected or corrected. This determines the state of the trial F after this access, $F \in \{DCE, DUE, SDC\}$ (the fault has not been masked). If $F = DUE$ or SDC, simulation ter-

minates and F is returned; otherwise, simulation continues until $R = \{\emptyset\}$, at which point F is returned.

Under the accelerated model, fault mitigation code only executes when an affected register is read, and once either (a) all errors have been overwritten or corrected, or (b) another termination condition (DUE or SDC) arises, simulation ends; consequently, trials only run to completion when an injected fault corrupts one or more registers but these registers are never accessed. As our fault injection framework is ISA-independent, this acceleration approach can be easily ported from one architecture to another. Furthermore, the same techniques apply to any fault injection technology that are able to control fault values and monitor registers.

3.6 MBU Distribution Emulation

MB-FICA supports fault campaign *re-sampling* to enable the consideration of arbitrary MBU distributions. A variety of studies in the literature have measured different multi-bit upsets rates under different operating conditions and using different systems implemented in different process technologies [7, 8, 24, 25]. Re-sampling not only addresses the fact that not all n-bit faults result in n-bit errors, ameliorating the need to determine how many 1-, 2-, and 3-bit faults to inject to create a target distribution; it also makes it possible to consider any desired MBU distribution without requiring the costly re-execution of fault injection campaigns.

After each trial finishes, we record both the number of corrupted bits and the corresponding final state F. The final states of each trial, independent of the injected fault (1-, 2-, or 3-bit), are grouped by the fault that manifested (0-, 1-, 2-, or 3-bit). Given a particular manifested MBU distribution and re-sampling size, the final state distribution for each manifested fault cluster (1-, 2-, or 3-bit) is subsequently sampled at the appropriate rate (*e.g.*, 63% 1-bit, 25% 2-bit, and 12% 3-bit [7, 8]) in order to determine the aggregate rate of *masked*, DCE, DUE, and SDC under the target distribution of manifested faults. It should be noted that MBU distributions are determined under different conditions than those present in our experiments, and the effect of this has not been evaluated; estimating and improving the fidelity of re-sampling is the subject of future work.

4. EXPERIMENTS AND RESULTS

We used our framework to conduct fault injection experiments using seven benchmarks for each of Parity, SECDED, and 2D ECC. We use benchmarks from the Mibench benchmark suite [26]: *bitcnts, susan_corner, crc, dijkstra, basicmath, rijndael_decode*, and *qsort*. To manage benchmark execution times, we used small input data sets when available (basicmath, bitcnt, and dijkstra), and further reduced the size of the small input data sets in other cases (susan_corner, crc, rijndaeal_decode, and qsort). We compiled each benchmark with gcc 4.1.2 and optimization -O2.

4.1 Experimental Setup

To demonstrate the use of our framework and the performance of our acceleration techniques, we performed a series of fault injection campaigns. 10K trials were simulated for each of 1-, 2-, and 3-bit fault injections for each benchmark-mitigation combination. The number of corrupted bits (less than or equal to the number of injected faults), final error condition and execution latency of each trial were recorded. The 95% confidence interval around each error condition is

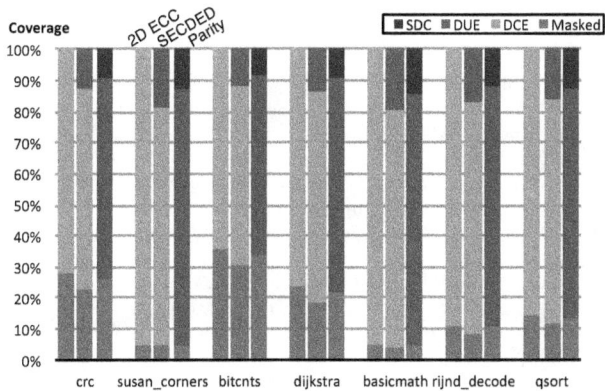

Figure 3: Re-sampled coverage results for 2D ECC, SECDED, and parity for each benchmark.

Table 1: Truncated Fault Injection False Masking Rate (%)

Benchmark	2D ECC	SECDED	Parity
crc	15.05	16.02	17.09
susan_corners	5.41	4.32	5.98
bitcnts	7.09	8.85	9.50
dijkstra	6.18	5.38	7.53
basicmath	4.07	4.62	4.91
rijndael_decode	2.67	1.09	0.97
qsort	1.96	0.77	0.23

less than 0.2% using 10K trials. We then re-sampled the error condition results to emulate a given MBU distribution.

4.2 Coverage Results

We conducted fault injection experiments to estimate the fault coverage of the implemented mitigation techniques, and compare the resulting coverage with those estimated when benchmark execution is truncated. Our fault coverage results, based on an MBU distribution of 63% 1-bit, 25% 2-bit, and 12% 3-bit errors [7, 8], are illustrated in Figure 3. The 95% confidence interval around each fault condition is less than 0.5% using a re-sampled population of 100K.

We first observe that the rate of *masking*, *DCE*, *DUE* and *SDC* vary from benchmark to benchmark, demonstrating the importance of application-specific coverage estimation. For instance, the rate of SDC varies from 8.0% to 14.0% for parity. The rate of error masking also changes significantly, from 4.1% to 35.7%, reflecting the application- and data-dependent nature of fault manifestation.

Truncated trials terminate execution early, before the effect of a latent error is observed, converting SDC, DUE, or DCE events into masked errors. To quantify the fault coverage estimation inaccuracy that results from running truncated trials, we set their maximum execution cycle count to the fault injection time $t + 1M$ cycles and compare the resulting estimated coverage with that derived from our approach. For each benchmark and mitigation combination, Table 1 reports the increase in estimated masking rate when benchmarks are not run to completion.

We observe that when benchmarks are truncated, masking rates are overestimated. The resulting error varies significantly between benchmarks (from 0.23 to 17% for qsort and crc respectively) and within benchmarks (from 7 to 9.5%

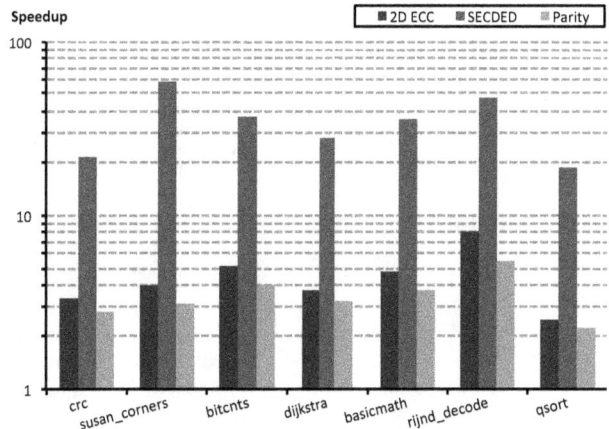

Figure 4: SECDED performance increases dramatically, by 31× on average, due to the complexity of check bit decoding.

for bitcnts). As expected, running trials to completion is the only way to accurately estimate coverage.

4.3 Acceleration Results

Running trials to completion is computationally expensive. We performed analysis to determine the benefit of acceleration compared with a baseline (no acceleration), and two different truncation approaches. The baseline is the time taken to execute a golden run of a benchmark with fault mitigation enabled for the duration.

Figure 4 illustrates the speedup MB-FICA achieves relative to a baseline that executes benchmarks to completion without acceleration. Accelerated fault injection trials execute in 2.5s each, on average, while the baseline requires 30s. Infinite loops resulting from undetected errors are addressed by simulating no more than $max + 1$ cycles where max cycles are executed by a golden run.

We observe in Figure 4 that SECDED performance increases dramatically under acceleration, achieving a 31× speedup on average (harmonic mean), and as much as almost 60× in the case of susan_corners. 2D ECC and parity trials are accelerated to a lesser extent, 4.0× and 3.3× respectively, on average. The difference comes from the complex procedures required to encode (when writing) and decode (when reading) SECDED's check bits.

The high computational cost of SECDED encoding and decoding translates into substantial opportunity for acceleration. During encoding, SECDED computes the value of seven check bits, each requiring 13 XOR operations (91 in total). Parity and 2D ECC require only 31 XOR and 30 XOR operations in total respectively to compute row check bits. Column check bits for 2D ECC can be updated without further XOR operations; if a bit is corrupted, the corresponding column bit changes. While these bitwise operations are relatively inexpensive in hardware, they prove costly in simulation. During decoding, SECDED performs matrix multiplication $((32 \times 7)(7 \times 1))$ to obtain the syndrome vector (32×1) used for fault detection. SECDED decoding represents over 80% of its overhead. In contrast, Parity and 2D ECC still use bitwise operations (32-bit XOR) to check for errors.

Table 2 compares the average execution time of MB-FICA simulating SECDED with that of two different truncation methods. T-1M continually simulates fault mitigation tech-

Table 2: Average Per-Trial Execution Time (s)

Benchmark	MB-FICA	T-1M+Dyn	T-1M
crc	4.620	4.365	47.302
susan_corners	0.425	0.492	8.130
bitcnts	0.261	0.252	6.538
dijkstra	5.506	4.393	71.265
basicmath	1.538	1.493	26.808
rijndael_decode	2.368	2.083	52.027
qsort	2.204	1.999	21.629

niques and terminates simulations 1M cycles after fault injection. T-1M+Dyn, like MB-FICA, dynamically enables and disables mitigation simulation as needed, but does not run trials to completion (resulting in lower accuracy, see Table 1). We observe that MB-FICA achieves 15× speedup on average compared with T-1M. While truncation improves performance modestly, mitigation technique simulation remains a significant source of overhead.

When truncated trials dynamically enable and disable fault mitigation, MB-FICA 9% slower on average. We hypothesize that this slowdown is related to register usage patterns in benchmarks, and that in many cases faults may sit latent in registers for more than 1M cycles. The notable exception is that MB-FICA 16% faster in the case of susan_corners; susan_corners has the fewest trials run to completion, 10% on average, indicating that a large set of registers are frequently used, reducing the likelihood of masking.

5. CONCLUSIONS

We have presented MB-FICA, a new framework for simulating MBUs and evaluating the relationship between application software and faults in microprocessor register files (RF). Our framework models mitigation techniques, and performs SRAM layout- and application-data-dependent MBU fault injection in order to estimate fault coverage; re-sampling makes it possible to model the effects of different MBU distributions without additional simulation costs. Though in this work we present results for parity, SECDED, and 2-bit 2D ECC, our framework, built within the architecture description language ADL, makes it possible to implement arbitrary RF fault mitigation strategies and SRAM layouts.

MB-FICA meets a critical need in early design evaluation by reducing the time required to perform the architectural fault injection experiments needed to achieve high-accuracy coverage estimates. Relative to complete benchmark execution with MB-FICA, truncated benchmark execution introduces varied and at times significant coverage estimation error: from 0.23% in masking rate for qsort, up to 17% CRC. Since executing benchmarks to completion is computationally expensive, MB-FICA accelerates fault injection trials by (a) simulating mitigation techniques only when faulty data is accessed, and (b) terminating simulation after all errors have been accounted for. On average this improves performance by 5.1×, and for complex mitigation models, such as SECDED, results in a speedup of up to 60×.

When (a) above is applied to a typical approach in the literature which truncates benchmark execution rather than run benchmarks to completion, MB-FICA executes 9% slower on average. While MB-FICA may be slower than benchmark truncation techniques, the volatility of coverage estimation suggests the modest performance degradation is a small price to pay for improved accuracy.

6. REFERENCES

[1] R. C. Baumann, "Radiation-induced soft errors in advanced semiconductor technologies," *IEEE Trans. Device Mater. Rel*, vol. 5, no. 3, 2005.

[2] E. Ibe, *et al.*, "Impact of scaling on neutron-induced soft error in SRAMs from a 250 nm to a 22 nm design rule," *IEEE Trans. Electron Devices*, vol. 57, no. 7, 2010.

[3] N. J. George, *et al.*, "Transient fault models and AVF estimation revisited," in *DSN'10*, 2010.

[4] B. Kahne and J. Huang, "Architectural description language," http://opensource.freescale.com/fsl-oss-projects/.

[5] S. Mukherjee, *et al.*, "A systematic methodology to compute the architectural vulnerability factors for a high-performance microprocessor," in *MICRO'03*, 2003.

[6] H. Ando, *et al.*, "Validation of hardware error recovery mechanisms for the SPARC64 V microprocessor," in *DSN'08*, 2008.

[7] N. Mahatme, *et al.*, "Analysis of multiple cell upsets due to neutrons in SRAMs for a deep-n-well process," in *IRPS' 11*, 2011.

[8] G. Georgakos, *et al.*, "Investigation of increased multi-bit failure rate due to neutron induced SEU in advanced embedded SRAMs," in *VLSI'07*, 2007.

[9] M. Maniatakos, M. K. Michael, and Y. Makris, "AVF-driven parity optimization for MBU protection of in-core memory arrays," in *DATE'13*, 2013.

[10] E. Touloupis, *et al.*, "Study of the effects of SEU-induced faults on a pipeline protected microprocessor," *IEEE Trans. Comput*, vol. 56, no. 12, 2007.

[11] P. Folkesson, *et al.*, "A comparison of simulation based and scan chain implemented fault injection," in *ISFTC'98*, 1998, pp. 284–293.

[12] Abbas Mohammadi, *et al.* , "SCFIT: A FPGA-based fault injection technique for SEU fault model," in *DATE'12*, 2012, pp. 586–589.

[13] J. Karlsson, *et al.*, "Application of three physical fault injection techniques to the experimental assessment of the MARS architecture," *DCFTS'98*, vol. 10, 1998.

[14] M. A. Aguirre, *et al.*, "Selective protection analysis using a seu emulator: testing protocol and case study over the leon2 processor," *IEEE Trans. Nucl. Sci.*, vol. 54, no. 4, 2007.

[15] Silvio Misera, *et al.* , "Fault injection techniques and their accelerated simulation in systemc," in *DSD'07*, 2007.

[16] K. Gulati, *et al.*, "Towards acceleration of fault simulation using graphics processing units," in *DAC'08*, 2008.

[17] J. Lee and A. Shrivastava, "Compiler approach for reducing soft errors in register file," *IEEE LCTES*, 2009.

[18] K. Skadron, *et al.*, "Temperature-aware microarchitecture," in *ACM COMP AR*, vol. 31, no. 2, 2003.

[19] P. E. Dodd and L. W. Massengill, "Basic mechanisms and modeling of single-event upset in digital microelectronics," *IEEE Trans. Nucl. Sci.*, vol. 50, no. 3, 2003.

[20] B. H. Meyer, *et al.*, "Rapid, tunable error detection with execution fingerprinting," in *SAE 2013 AeroTech*, 2013.

[21] M.-Y. Hsiao, "A class of optimal minimum odd-weight-column SEC-DED codes," *IBM J RES DEV*, vol. 14, no. 4, 1970.

[22] J. Kim, *et al.*, "Multi-bit error tolerant caches using two-dimensional error coding," in *MICRO'07*, 2007.

[23] K. Mohr, *et al.*, "Delay and area efficient first-level cache soft error detection and correction," in *ICCD'06*, 2007.

[24] J. Autran, *et al.*, "Real-time soft-error testing of 40nm SRAMs," in *IRPS'12*, 2012.

[25] A. Dixit and A. Wood, "The impact of new technology on soft error rates," in *IRPS'11*, 2011.

[26] M. R. Civera, *et al.*, "Mibench: A free, commercially representative embedded benchmark suite," in *WWC-4*, 2001.

On-Line Detection of the Deadlocks Caused by Permanently Faulty Links in Quasi-Delay Insensitive Networks on Chip[*]

Wei Song, Guangda Zhang and Jim Garside
School of Computer Science at the University of Manchester
Manchester M13 9PL United Kingdom
{songw, zhangga, jdg}@cs.man.ac.uk

ABSTRACT

Asynchronous networks on chip (NoCs) are promising candidates for supporting the enormous communication needed by future many-core systems due to their low-energy and high-speed. Similar to synchronous NoCs, asynchronous NoCs are vulnerable to faults but their fault-tolerance is not studied adequately, especially the quasi-delay insensitive (QDI) NoCs. One of the key issues neglected by most designers is that permanent faults in QDI NoCs cause deadlocks, which cripples the traditional fault-tolerant techniques using redundant codes. A novel detection method has been proposed to locate the faulty link in a QDI NoC according to a common pattern shared by all fault-related deadlocks. It is shown that this method introduces low hardware overhead and reports permanently faulty links with a short delay and guaranteed accuracy.

Categories and Subject Descriptors

B.8.1 [**Performance and Reliability**]: Reliability, Testing, and Fault-Tolerance

Keywords

Deadlock, permanent faults, detection, asynchronous, quasi-delay-insensitive, network on chip

1. INTRODUCTION

Current semiconductor technology has enabled tens even hundreds of cores to be integrated on a single chip. The enormous amount of information exchanged on-chip cultivates the demand for energy-efficient, scalable and reliable networks on chip (NoCs). Most existing NoCs are synchronously built. Custom calibration of the global clock tree is usually required in high performance designs [18]. As an alternative, asynchronous NoCs divide a chip into synchronous islands, which enables individual frequency/voltage control and simplifies chip-level timing closure [3]. They also convey data in a speedy and energy-efficient fashion [5].

The increasing size of NoCs brings reliability issues. Compared with designs using earlier technologies, current submicron designs demonstrate reduced yield, worsened process variation, increased rate of faults and shortened device lifetime [4]. Future NoCs are expected to operate reliably in the presence of faults.

Fault-tolerance issues have been extensively studied in synchronous NoCs but rarely in asynchronous NoCs, especially in quasi-delay insensitive (QDI) NoCs [16, 6, 5, 15]. The natural tolerance to delay variations of QDI circuits provides the innate protection from delay-related faults [10]. However, they are extremely vulnerable to permanent faults because these faults break the handshake protocol and cause deadlocks. Unlike synchronous circuits, where redundant coding schemes can be employed to detect permanently faulty links or switches [12, 9, 7], the deadlock in QDI NoCs prohibits the propagation of data and therefore disables any data checks. Although off-line scan techniques can locate permanent faults [17], detecting them on-line remains difficult. Timeout is a common way to detect the existence of deadlocks [8]. However, it is difficult to locate the source of a deadlock because the congestion caused by the deadlock will spread over the whole network, leading to timeout in multiple locations.

This paper tries to resolve this problem by on-line detecting the deadlocks caused by permanently faulty links in QDI NoCs. A common pattern has been found in all deadlocks caused by a single permanent fault. Using this pattern, a simple detection circuit is able to report the exact location of a faulty link in the presence of a deadlock. Utilizing the location, further research can be done to retain the network functionality by isolating the faulty links [21, 7, 8].

[*]This work is supported by grants from the National Natural Science Foundation of China (61272144), the China Scholarship Council, and the Engineering and Physical Sciences Research Council (EP/I038306/1).

GLSVLSI'14, May 21–23, 2014, Houston, TX, USA.
ACM 978-1-4503-2816-6/14/05.
http://dx.doi.org/10.1145/2591513.2591518.

2. RELATED WORK

Fault-tolerance is a well-studied topic in synchronous NoCs. Transient faults can be dynamically detected using redundant coding schemes. If a data packet is found corrupted, it can either be corrected using the redundant code or retransmitted [19]. On the other hand, permanent faults can be checked off-line using self-test mechanisms, such as scan chains [21], or detected on-line by searching persistent errors using certain coding schemes [12, 7]. Although per-

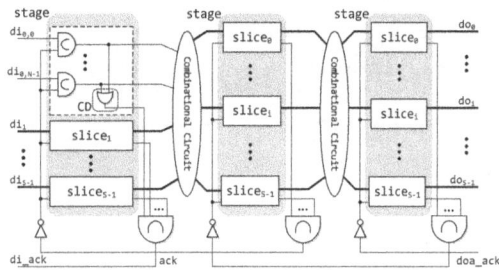

Figure 1: A 4-phase 1-of-N pipeline

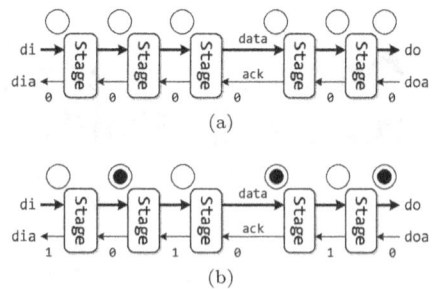

Figure 2: Simplification of an empty (a) / full (b) pipeline

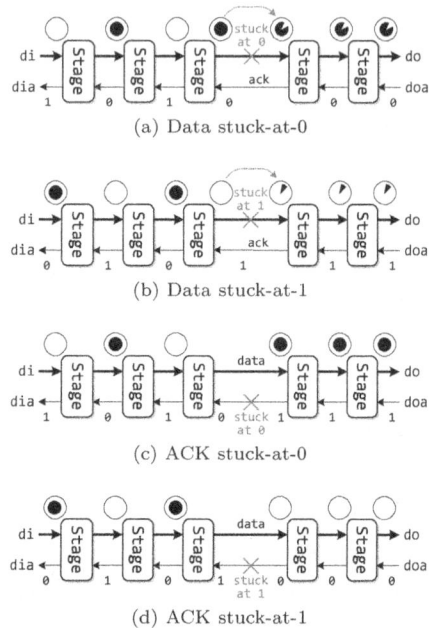

(a) Data stuck-at-0

(b) Data stuck-at-1

(c) ACK stuck-at-0

(d) ACK stuck-at-1

Figure 3: Patterns of deadlocks caused by permanently faulty links

manent faults cannot be recovered, a network may survive with reduced resources. The faulty components can be replaced with spares [12] or isolated using adaptive routing algorithms [21, 7].

Providing fault-tolerance for self-timed NoCs is considered easier compared with QDI NoCs. Since self-timed pipelines have clock-like latch triggers and directly use binary-encoded data, most synchronous techniques can be directly adopted to cope with transient and permanent faults [11, 8].

In QDI NoCs, several unordered redundant coding schemes have proposed to detect and correct transient faults [13, 1, 20]. However, all of them cease to work when the network is deadlocked due to permanent faults. To our best knowledge, there is no code scheme able to detect permanent faults in QDI NoCs. The most effective method existed so far is to detect permanent faults off-line using scan chains [17] while no method has been proposed for on-line detection.

The most related work is the timeout mechanism proposed by Imai and Yoneda [8] in a self-timed NoC using QDI inter-router links. A delay line is used to detect the abnormal data skew among the data wires of the same pipeline stage. However, this method does not work in a pure QDI NoC. Since self-timed pipelines are used inside the router of Imai's NoC and they do not latch incomplete data, the fault-caused partial data (which leads to the large skew) is isolated in the QDI inter-router link. In a pure QDI NoC, this partial data will propagate to all downstream stages as long as they are ready (see Section 3.2). As a result, all the downstream stages are timeout and multiple faults are reported.

3. DEADLOCKS CAUSED BY PERMANENT FAULTS

3.1 Pipeline model

Since most QDI NoCs use 4-phase pipelines [6, 5, 15], this paper is focused on detecting faulty 4-phase pipelines. A 4-phase 1-of-N pipeline is shown in Figure 1. A wide pipeline is usually built from multiple 1-of-N pipelines, shown as slices in Figure 1. Each slice contains several C-elements acting as data latches. A wide OR gate is used to detect the data-completion in each slice. A common ack signal is then generated using a multi-input C-element to synchronize the data transmission of all slices. Although this paper uses 4-phase 1-of-N pipelines, the proposed method is applicable to all M-of-N pipelines.

To provide an easy way for analysing the deadlocks caused by faulty links, Figure 2 simplifies a general 4-phase pipeline into a sequence of places where each place stores a data token or a space (token). In an empty pipeline (Figure 2a), all

stages store space tokens, also denoted by the low ack signals. When a pipeline is full of data (Figure 2b), data tokens are stored alternatively because data must be separated by space in 4-phase pipelines. The pipeline stages with data tokens return positive ack to their predecessors.

3.2 Fault analyses

Most permanent faults on wires can be transformed into stuck-at faults [2]. A stuck-at-0 fault denotes a faulty wire that outputs 0 regardless of its input while a stuck-at-1 fault denotes a faulty wire that always drives its output high. According to the types and the locations of stuck-at faults, Figure 3 depicts all the four possible patterns of deadlocks caused by a single permanent fault:

Data stuck-at-0 (Figure 3a) With a data wire is stuck at 0, the pipeline is blocked when a 1 occurs on that bit. As a result, all downstream stages eventually go into a temporary state storing a partial data and waiting for the missing 1.

Data stuck-at-1 (Figure 3b) If a data wire is stuck at 1, the pipeline is blocked when it should reset to a space. Consequently, downstream stages will gradually enter another temporary state waiting for the withdrawal of the faulty 1.

212

(a) Router structure

(b) Connection between two adjacent routers

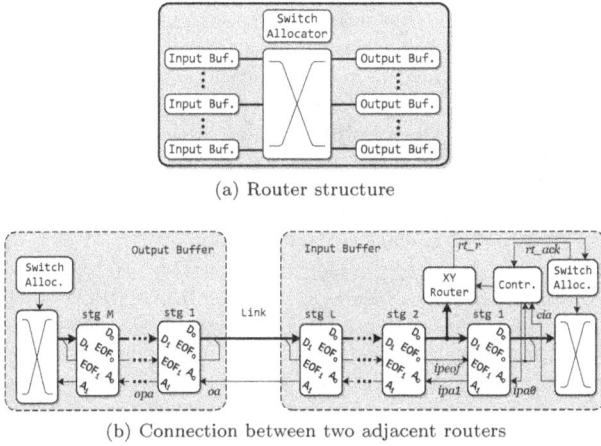

Figure 4: Wormhole router

ACK stuck-at-0 (Figure 3c) Assuming the *ack* is stuck at 0, its receiving stage will not withdraw its data. As a result, soon all downstream stages will return positive *ack* and wait for space tokens.

ACK stuck-at-1 (Figure 3d) Assuming the *ack* is stuck at 1, the receiving stage of the faulty *ack* would fail to store any incoming data. Consequently all downstream stages will be empty and wait for new data.

It can be observed from the four cases of deadlocks that they share a common pattern: the *ack* of all downstream stages have the same value while they are alternatively valued in upstream stages. Detecting such pattern, a 4-phase pipeline can tell when and where there is a deadlock.

4. DEADLOCK DETECTION IN ROUTERS

A QDI NoC can locate a faulty link by searching the common pattern. In this paper, the detection technique is applied to a 5-port router [15] but it can be used in any routers using 4-phase asynchronous pipelines.

4.1 Router structure

As presented in Figure 4a, the router has five bidirectional ports. Every port is 32 bits wide using 4-phase 1-of-4 pipelines. Each buffer contains one to several pipeline stages depending on its configuration. A switch allocator controls the connection between input and output ports through the central crossbar. Packets in this network are divided into flits. Address information is stored in the head flit, which is followed by a sequence of data flits. The packet is terminated by a tail flit which contains a single positive bit on the end-of-frame (EOF) wire.

The structure of, and the connections between, the input and output buffers of adjacent routers is illustrated in Figure 4b. Other relevant information about this router can be found in Song and Edwards [15].

An output buffer contains only a few pipeline stages directly connected to the crossbar. An input buffer comprises several pipeline stages, an XY router and a controller. When a new packet arrives, its head flit is blocked in the second stage (stg 2) awaiting the XY router to produce a request (rt_r) to the switch allocator. After an output buffer is allocated, denoted by a positive rt_ack, the controller enables the pipeline until a tail flit is noticed through the EOF wire.

Working in a QDI fashion, the controller ensures that no data is sent to the crossbar before a path is allocated and the path is not deallocated until the tail flit is safely delivered. For this purpose, the controller controls the enable/reset of the XY router and the ACK $ipa0$ to the first stage (stg 1).

4.2 Deadlock detection

To detect deadlocked faulty links, extra circuits are added as shown in Figure 5a and 5b. An error detector (Figure 5b) is added in each input buffer to detect deadlocks in the connected link. Since the common pattern deduced in Section 3.2 is valid only when the status of the pipeline is stable (deadlocked), a timeout mechanism is utilized to monitor the activities in the input buffer. If the buffer is inactive/paused for a certain timeout period, the detector is assumed safe to sample the ACK values. To achieve this timeout, an external clock (clk) is introduced. The timeout period is controlled by the counter as shown in Figure 5a.

The connection and the internal structure of the error detector are shown in Figure 5b and 5c. It is a sync/async hybrid module where the asynchronous-related signals and circuits are coloured in grey. The three flip-flops ($start$, err_r, and $erpt$) forms a state machine which controls the timeout process. Its state transition graph is revealed in Figure 5e with cross-references in Figure 5c. Several motion detectors (MDs) are used to monitor the activities on certain asynchronous signals. As shown in Figure 5d, if there is any transition on sig when $start$ is high, act is set positive.

Bearing in mind that the input buffer is downstream to the possibly faulty link (Figure 5b), the timeout process can be described as follows:

Idle: After reset, the error detector enters the **Idle** state and all registers are low.

Start: After a timout period (necessary for the reset of MDs), register $start$ is set high (state transits to **Timeout**) to enable all MDs to monitor the activities of $ipa0$ (new data transmission), $ipa1$ (new incoming data) and rt_ack (new path allocation).

Timeout: Monitoring for a whole timeout period, if any MD outputs high (case ①), the input buffer is not deadlocked and the state returns to **Idle**. Otherwise, the buffer may be deadlocked due to a fault if one of the following three cases is true: ② the buffer is transmitting a packet (denoted by the path allocation rt_ack+) and the pipeline stage 1 (downstream to the fault) has equal input/output ACKs ($ipa0 = ipa1$), matching the downstream part of the shared pattern of deadlocks; ③ an ACK stuck-at-1 or a data stuck-at-0 fault may cripple a head flit causing an empty input buffer (unallocated rt_ack- and negative ACKs $ipa1-$, $ipa0-$); ④ an unallocated input buffer (rt_ack- and $ipa0-$) with an arriving tail flit ($ipeof+$) can be caused by a fake tail flit produced by a data stuck-at-1 fault on the EOF wire. In the presence of any of the three cases (②, ③ or ④), err_r is set high (state transits to **Test**) to check the upstream pattern in the adjacent output buffer (Figure 5b). If none of the three cases appears (case ⑤), the input buffer is paused due to congestion and the state returns to **Idle**.

Test: In this state, the error detector waits for the adjacent output buffer (upstream pipeline stages) to verify the upstream part of the deadlock pattern. The C-element in the output buffer (Figure 5b) is enabled (err_r+). It returns a positive err_ack if stg 1 has equal ACKs ($opa = oa$ violates the deadlock pattern). Consequently the state machine

(a) Router structure

(b) Connection between two adjacent routers

(c) Error detector

(d) Motion detector
(MD)

(e) State machine

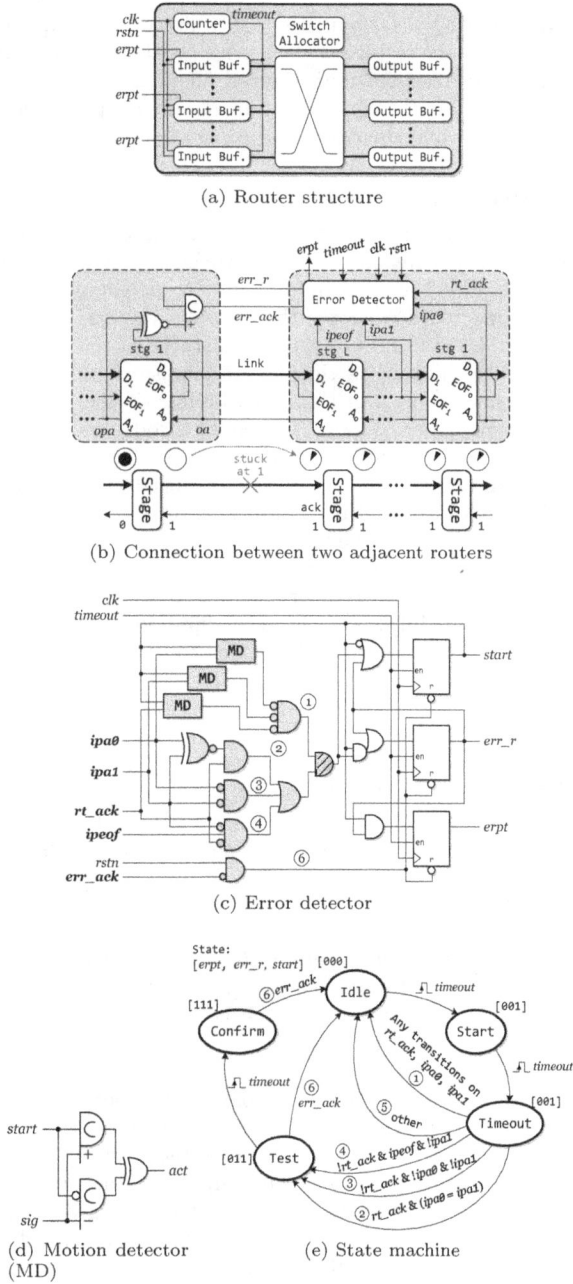

Figure 5: Deadlock detection

is reset through the asynchronous reset shown in the bottom of Figure 5c (case ⑥). If err_ack remains low for a whole timeout period, denoting the deadlock pattern has been stable for a long time, the link is confirmed deadlocked due to a permanent fault. In this case, the error detector reports the deadlock through $erpt+$ (state transits to **Confirm**).

Confirm: The link is confirmed deadlocked. If the fault is intermittent and recovered, err_ack would be positive afterwards, which then resets the state to **Idle** (case ⑥).

4.3 Other technical issues

The mixture of sync/async circuit is one of the difficulties of this design. The sync/async interface in the error detector requires no synchronizer and metastability does not

affect the detection accuracy. The asynchronous MDs and the central AND gate (highlighted with slash lines) in Figure 5c act as a shield to ensure that the values of the three cases (②, ③ and ④) are read only when they are assumed stable as they have been inactive for a whole timeout period. Even under extreme conditions when the input buffer suddenly resumes after congestion and the state mistakenly enters **Test**, the C-element in the upstream output buffer (Figure 5b) will correct the mistake by setting err_ack to high, which then asynchronously resets state machine (the bottom of Figure 5c, case ⑥). Moreover, the error detector ensures its accuracy by reporting a deadlock only when the deadlock pattern has been found and remained stable for a whole timeout period (in state **Test**).

The total latency T_f of reporting a fault from its appearance has two parts:

$$T_f = T_d + T_r \tag{1}$$

where T_d is the time used to form a deadlock and T_r is delay of reporting this deadlock. T_d is out of the control of the deadlock detection. It is short on a busy link but infinite on an idle wire. Nevertheless, no damage is made if no deadlock is formed. The report latency T_r is a more important factor in evaluating the detection speed. The upper and lower bounds of T_r can be described as:

$$2T_t \le T_r \le 4T_t \tag{2}$$

where T_t is the timeout period. The lower bound is achieved when the deadlock is formed just before state transits to **Start** and the upper bound is reached when the deadlock occurs at the beginning of **Start**.

There is no strong constraint on the period of clk (T_c) and $timeout$ (T_t) but several issues should be considered. Obviously reducing T_t decreases the report latency T_r. However, T_t should be larger than T_c and the latency of transmitting one flit through one pipeline stage (usually several nanoseconds, to allow a stable sample from motion detectors). Since clock is used only to drive the state machine, there is no requirement on its frequency, skew or jitter. In fact, users can use any clock sources in the NoC, such as the local clock from the processing element or a slow global clock. Also since every error detector works independently, it can has its own counter to generate a $timeout$ at arbitrary frequencies or share the counter ($timeout$ as well) among arbitrary number of neighbours for area efficiency. For example, Figure 5a shows a way of sharing one counter in one router.

The extra wires added by the deadlock detection (err_r and err_ack) are not protected due to their low activities. Assuming a large T_t, the two wires are triggered every $2T_t$ in the worst case, which is hundreds to thousands times smaller than the toggle rate of data wires. However, a large T_t leads to long T_r. A way to keep a small T_r while reducing the wire activities is to gate the clock and detecting deadlocks only when a permanent fault is indicated by upper layers (receiving an error packet or losing a packet).

Since the deadlock detection does not rely on any coding scheme, it can work together with all unordered redundant codes [13, 1, 20] to provide tolerance to both permanent and transient faults in QDI NoCs. Although the common pattern is deduced from the deadlocked links caused by a single permanent fault, the deadlock detection also detects multiple faults occurring in the same link as this does not alter the ACK pattern. If multiple faults occur on adja-

Table 1: Overhead of deadlock detection

	Original	Detection	%
Area (μm^2)	33,881	34,629	2.2
Throughput (MByte/s/node)	503.2	483.9	-3.8
Latency (ns)	61.5	64.1	4.2

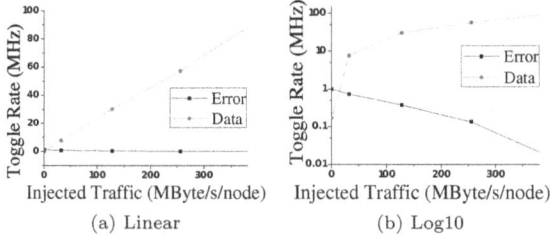

Figure 6: Toggle rates with various traffic loads

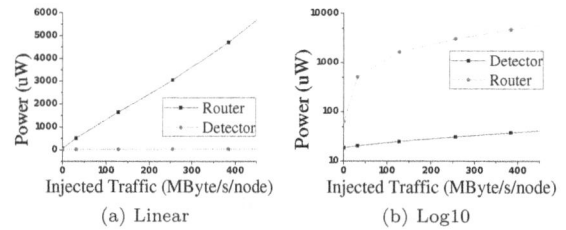

Figure 7: Power with various traffic loads

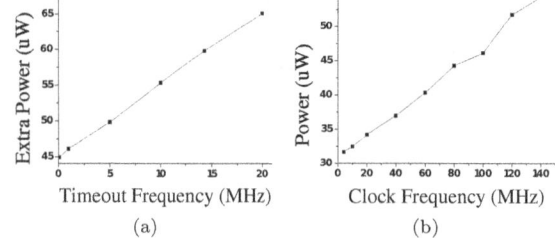

Figure 8: Detection power with various timeout frequencies (a) and clock frequencies (b)

cent pipeline stages, it is possible that only one faulty link is reported as the other one is considered paused by the reported one. In a NoC, this indicates that a permanent fault inside the router (which is adjacent to the inter-router links) may cause a missing fault report. Extending this method to detect faults inside routers is one of the future works.

As mentioned in state **Confirm**, the error detector can also be used to detect the withdrawal of long lasting intermittent faults. When a fault disappears, the resumed link will trigger *err_ack* and reset the state machine, which then withdraws the fault report (*erpt−*).

5. PERFORMANCE ANALYSES

The routers with and without deadlock detection have been implemented using a 130 nm standard cell library and synthesized by the Synopsys Design Compiler. Both routers share the same configuration of five ports, one pipeline stage in output buffers and two in input buffers. The post-synthesis netlist, annotated with gate latency, is simulated in a SystemC/Verilog mixed environment where network interfaces and processor elements are implemented in SystemC.

Table 1 reveals the performance overhead of adding deadlock detection. The extra logic leads to a marginal area increase of 2.2%. Its speed overhead is negligible as well. Collected from 4x4 networks injected with uniform random traffic (using 128-byte fixed-length packets), the saturation throughput per node drops by 3.8% while the average minimum packet transmission latency is prolonged by 4.2%.

The extra wires added by the error detector are unprotected as they are assumed significantly less active than data wires. Using two y-scales (linear and Log10), Figure 6 reveals the average toggle rates of the extra wires (Error) and the data wires (Data) in a NoC injected with various loads. The timeout and clock frequencies are set to 2 MHz and 100 MHz respectively. It is shown that the extra wires have the highest toggle rate of 1 MHz in an idle network and the activity decreases with the increased traffic. The highest rate is exactly half of the timeout frequency because the detector is constantly checking ACK stuck-at-1 deadlocks (case ③ in Section 4.2), which may cause empty input buffers, and this check always turns out negative in $2T_t$. With increased traffic, the state machine in the error detector rarely enters the **Test** state and the toggle rate of the extra wires thus

drops significantly until it is nearly zero in a saturated network. In a network with 26% load (128 MByte/s/node), the toggle rate of the extra wires is only 1.2% of that of data wires. If this rate is still considered high or the rate in idle networks is unacceptable, they can be further reduced by increasing the timeout period T_t.

The power overhead of the deadlock detection is also examined and revealed in Figure 7 using the same configuration of Figure 6. It is shown both the router and deadlock detection circuit consume more energy with increased traffic. The power of the detection logic is 18.6 μW (29.7%) in an idle network while it increases to 43.4 μW (0.7%) in a saturated network, however the rate compared to the total router power deceases from 29.7% to only 0.7%.

It is found that the power overhead of the deadlock detection is linear with the timeout and the clock frequencies. Figure 8a shows the detection power with various timeout frequencies in a saturated network (clock frequency set to 100 MHz) and Figure 8b reveals the increased power with increased clock frequency also in a saturated network (timeout frequency set to 2 MHz). According to the results, as long as the clock has a higher frequency than *timeout*, a slow clock should be used for low power consumption.

To test permanent faults, a fault injector is attached to each link wire in the NoC. It randomly generates a permanent fault (stuck-at-1 or stuck-at-0) according to a preconfigured mean time between failures (MTBF). Note that the error detector is able to detect a fault only when a deadlock is caused, the faults on unused wires are not detectable and the faults on infrequently used wires are slow to detect. However, as long as a fault causes a deadlock, it is found and accurately reported soon after. In the simulation, the location accuracy is 100% and no flawless links have been reported faulty. Setting the MTBF to 5 ms in a saturated network, Figure 9 shows the average report latency, which is the delay between the occurrence of a deadlock and the corresponding report. The average report latency approximately increases proportional to $3T_t$. The latency variation also matches the estimation in Equation 2.

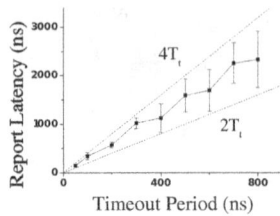

Figure 9: Report latency

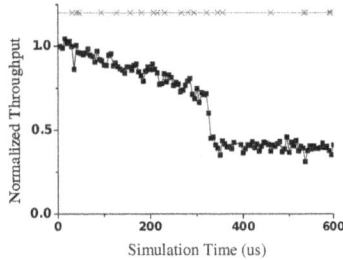

Figure 10: A permanent fault-tolerant SDM NoC

As mentioned in Section 4.2, the error detector is able to withdraw its report when an intermittent fault dissolves. The disappearance of an intermittent fault always triggers the C-element in the output buffer (Figure 5b) when a fault is reported. This consequently activates err_ack which then asynchronously resets the state machine and withdraws the report. In one simulation, the faults are set to fade away in 0.5 ms. The latency of withdrawing the fault report is found around 2.2 ns in our implementation.

To demonstrate the potential uses of the deadlock detection technique, the SystemC model of the spatial division multiplexing (SDM) router of Song and Edwards [15, 14] has been modified to utilize the fault report for isolating permanent faulty links. Since each link between two routers in an SDM NoC is divided into several independent virtual circuits, a link can survive from a permanent fault using remaining virtual circuits. By isolating the faulty virtual circuit and releasing the healthy links blocked by the deadlock, a NoC can retain its function with reduced resources.

In the SystemC model, an individual error detector is added in the input buffer of each virtual circuit. When a deadlock is detected, the deadlocked packet transmitting through the virtual circuit is dropped and the virtual circuit is prohibited from being allocated to other packets. A 4x4 SDM NoC is built with 2 virtual circuits in each link. Setting the MTBF to 2 ms, the runtime throughput is depicted in Figure 10 with the sequence of faults illustrated by crosses in the line above. It is shown that the network has remained functional until 13 faulty virtual circuits. At around 250 μs when both virtual circuits of a link are faulty, the link is broken and around half of the network using this link is paralysed (XY routing is used). As a result, the throughput drops significantly. Adaptive routing can be adopted for further fault-tolerance [21, 7].

6. CONCLUSION

Permanent faults are a significant threat to QDI NoCs as they cause deadlocks. This paper proposed a novel deadlock detection method which reports the accurate location of the permanent faults occurring on inter-router links of a QDI NoC. The detection circuit is light-weighted which introduces low area, speed and energy overhead. As long as a deadlock is caused by a faulty link, the location of the faulty link is reported in a maximum of four timeout periods. Thanks to deduced common deadlock pattern, the faulty location is accurately identified and no flawless link is mistakenly reported. It is shown that an SDM NoC can use this method to survive from multiple permanent faulty virtual circuits.

7. REFERENCES

[1] M. Agyekum and S. Nowick. Error-correcting unordered codes and hardware support for robust asynchronous global communication. *IEEE Trans. CAD*, 31(1):75–88, 2012.

[2] S. A. Al-Arian and D. P. Agrawal. Physical failures and fault models of CMOS circuits. *IEEE Trans. Circuits and Systems*, 34(3):269–279, March 1987.

[3] E. Beigné, F. Clermidy, and *et al*. Dynamic voltage and frequency scaling architecture for units integration within a GALS NoC. In *Proc. of NoCS*, pages 129–138, April 2008.

[4] S. Borkar. Designing reliable systems from unreliable components: the challenges of transistor variability and degradation. *IEEE Micro*, 25(6):10–16, 2005.

[5] F. Clermidy, C. Bernard, and *et al*. A 477mW NoC-based digital baseband for MIMO 4G SDR. In *Proc. of ISSCC*, pages 278–279, 2010.

[6] T. Felicijan and S. B. Furber. An asynchronous on-chip network router with quality-of-service (QoS) support. In *Proc. of SoCC*, pages 274–277, September 2004.

[7] C. Feng, Z. Lu, and *et al*. Addressing transient and permanent faults in NoC with efficient fault-tolerant deflection router. *IEEE Trans. VLSI*, 21(6):1053–1066, 2013.

[8] M. Imai and T. Yoneda. Improving dependability and performance of fully asynchronous on-chip networks. In *Proc. of ASYNC*, pages 65–76, 2011.

[9] A. Kohler, G. Schley, and M. Radetzki. Fault tolerant network on chip switching with graceful performance degradation. *IEEE Trans. CAD*, 29(6):883–896, 2010.

[10] C. LaFrieda and R. Manohar. Fault detection and isolation techniques for quasi delay-insensitive circuits. In *Proc. of International Conference on Dependable Systems and Networks*, pages 41–50, 2004.

[11] T. Lehtonen, P. Liljeberg, and J. Plosila. Online reconfigurable self-timed links for fault tolerant NoC. *VLSI Design*, page 13, 2007.

[12] T. Lehtonen, D. Wolpert, and *et al*. Self-adaptive system for addressing permanent errors in on-chip interconnects. *IEEE Trans. VLSI*, 18(4):527–540, 2010.

[13] J. Pontes, N. Calazans, and P. Vivet. Adding temporal redundancy to delay insensitive codes to mitigate single event effects. In *Proc. of ASYNC*, pages 142–149, 2012.

[14] W. Song and D. Edwards. Asynchronous SDM NoC. http://opencores.org/project,async_sdm_noc,Overview, 2011.

[15] W. Song and D. Edwards. Asynchronous spatial division multiplexing router. *Microprocessors and Microsystems*, 35(2):85–97, 2011.

[16] J. Sparsø and S. B. Furber. *Principles of Asynchronous Circuit Design: a Systems Perspective*. Kluwer Academic Publishers, 2001.

[17] X. T. Tran, Y. Thonnart, and *et al*. Design-for-test approach of an asynchronous network-on-chip architecture and its associated test pattern generation and application. *IET Computers & Digital Techniques*, 3(5):487–500, 2009.

[18] S. R. Vangal, J. Howard, and *et al*. An 80-tile sub-100-W TeraFLOPS processor in 65-nm CMOS. *IEEE Journal of Solid-State Circuits*, 43(1):29–41, January 2008.

[19] Q. Yu and P. Ampadu. Dual-layer adaptive error control for network-on-chip links. *IEEE Trans. VLSI*, 20(7):1304–1317, 2012.

[20] G. Zhang, W. Song, and *et al*. Transient fault tolerant QDI interconnects using redundant check code. In *Proc. of DSD*, pages 3–10, September 2013.

[21] Z. Zhang, A. Greiner, and S. Taktak. A reconfigurable routing algorithm for a fault-tolerant 2D-mesh network-on-chip. In *Proc. of DAC*, pages 441–446, June 2008.

A Novel Parallel Adaptation of an Implicit Path Delay Grading Method

Joseph Lenox
ECE Department
Southern Illinois University–Carbondale
Carbondale, Illinois 62901
lenox@engr.siu.edu

Spyros Tragoudas
ECE Department
Southern Illinois University–Carbondale
Carbondale, Illinois 62901
spyros@engr.siu.edu

ABSTRACT

For large modern circuits, it is desirable to trade hardware cost for time when making path delay fault coverage estimates, especially as a subroutine for ATPG and timing analysis solutions. A parallel adaptation of an established framework for implicit path delay fault grading on with a GPGPU implementation is presented. Experimental evaluation on a NVIDIA Tesla C2075 GPU shows on average 50x speedup against the basic version for the framework on an Intel Xeon E5504 host system. Over a 1200x speedup is observed against a single-threaded, more complex version in the framework which grades more faults.

Keywords

GPGPU;path delay fault grading;fault simulation

Categories and Subject Descriptors

B.8.1 [**Hardware**]: PERFORMANCE AND RELIABILITY—*Reliability, Testing, and Fault-Tolerance*

1. INTRODUCTION

Temporal verification and correctness are simultaneously critical and very challenging problems in deep sub-micron. It is widely accepted that timing analysis or testing for delay defects is very accurate as long as all or a large portion of the sensitized paths–preferably the longest (or so-called *critical*) paths–are sensitized by the targeted sensitization method by the application of a collection of tests (or a test set)[1, 2]. A path delay fault is a physical path in the circuit that has rising or falling logic transitions on its lines when a test pattern t from T is applied to the inputs of C. Different tests may sensitize a path robustly, non-robustly or functionally [3, 4, 5].

The path delay grading problem formulation is essential for simulation-based timing analysis, path delay test pattern generation, and path delay test diagnosis. In grading it is desired to identify, accurately and quickly, the quantity of paths sensitized by a test set. Formally, the input is a set of binary input vectors (or tests) T for a circuit C. The goal with fault grading is to count the number of path delay faults that are detected by the set of tests T. Unfortunately, the number of possible paths in a circuit can be enormous (often larger than 2^{30} for small circuits). Even only considering the longest paths in a circuit can result in too many paths to consider (especially in optimized circuits where the delay on many paths is the same [6]).

For this reason, faults are often graded in an implicit (that is, non-enumerative) manner so that the algorithms are not limited by *a priori* fault lists. This is important because the number of path delay faults in modern designs quickly become too many to enumerate, even when restricting to critical paths (see [4, 7]). The increased complexity of modern designs indicates a need for implicit fault coverage tools that can work with large test sets and large designs.

Two classes of grading methods exist: exact heuristics and approximate heuristics. [8] has shown that problem of obtaining exact coverage is NP-hard. Work in exact heuristics [9, 10, 11] that employ binary decision diagrams (or variants thereof) are memory-intensive on certain designs, while approximate heuristics [12, 13, 8, 14, 2] must pay additional time penalties if more accuracy is required. If it is desired to use these path coverage estimates in a larger algorithm (such as test pattern generation or timing analysis) as a subroutine, such penalties are unacceptable. A speedup for path grading also accelerates algorithms for test pattern generation, timing analysis, and timing verification. The emergence of general-purpose computing on graphics processing units (GPGPU) offers the possibility to trade hardware investment for time. The challenge is that the routines must be distributable.

In this work, we present a novel method to parallelize the fault grading method originally presented in [13], along with a path delay fault grading tool implemented for the NVIDIA CUDA GPGPU architecture. Similar to previous work in fault simulation for GPGPUs, our method simplifies the state-keeping mechanisms and efficiently resolves the serial dependencies inherent in the original work while maintaining the sequence of operations in [13]. It is able to distribute delay fault simulation and grading across the many processors on a GPGPU in a batch-parallel manner. Device memory bandwidth is conserved where possible by treating

GLSVLSI'14, May 21–23, 2014, Houston, Texas, USA.
Copyright 2014 ACM 978-1-4503-2816-6/14/05 ...$15.00.
http://dx.doi.org/10.1145/2591513.2591539.

the GPU device memory as a cache and minimizing the number of transfers and maximizing the size of data transfers.

The work in [13] describes a heuristic to estimate the number of path delay faults present in a circuit under test (CUT) without enumerating the faulty paths. This avoidance is critical because the total path count in a circuit increases quickly with circuit complexity. Their approach simulated each test vector application, serially, to the CUT. The sensitized lines in the CUT from that test vector were then removed from a master list of all lines in the CUT. All paths that went through a line that was removed were counted. Thus, over-counting is not possible (because a path re-encountered for another test vector would not sensitize any remaining lines in the master list). Essentially, when a test vector is applied, path are counted only through lines that were not removed in earlier steps. In [13] these are called new lines. Although the approach avoids double-counting, it is pessimistic. Numerous improvements have been made targeting this basic heuristic, ranging from finding better cutsets for grading over [15] to grading over sub-path segments [16].

This paper shows that the algorithm in [13] cannot be accelerated by parallel architectures unless an additional method is used to cope with determining which lines are new lines for a test $T_i \in T$.

We show improvements to the execution time [13] as an example of a class of algorithms. Importantly, it is fault-implicit and is not limited by *a priori* fault lists. Additionally, targeting full path-delay faults also covers small-delay defects. This work is organized as follows. The proposed method is given in Section 2. Section 3 presents experimental results for our work. Section 4 concludes the paper.

2. PROPOSED PARALLEL APPROACH

Due to space limitations, we outline the approach but implementation details for GPGPU architectures will not be presented. The following presents a logical argument for enabling data parallelism for the fault grading problem.

DEFINITION 1. *A new line L is one that is sensitized by T_i and not by any $\{T_0, \cdots, T_{i-1}\}$.*

[13] maintains a list, G_{new}, of all lines that have not been sensitized up to T_i, and only counts paths that contain at least one line in G_{new}.

LEMMA 1. *Logic simulation of T_i is independent of T_j, $j \neq i$.*

Lemma 1 is straightforward to show, as there is no dependency between the two-pattern test T_i and T_j for logic simulation and determining which paths are sensitized. Thus, T_i and T_j are independent.

LEMMA 2. *A list of possible new lines G_{new} can be described by the pair (L, i), where i is the first test that sensitizes L.*

Lemma 2 can be shown by considering the state of G_{new} at the application of T_i and then T_{i+1}. If T_i sensitizes L and L was present in G_{new}, then L will not be present in G_{new} during the application of T_{i+1}. The difference between $G_{new,i}$ and $G_{new,i+1}$ can be written as (L, i).

LEMMA 3. *The list of (L, i) pairs can be calculated in a parallel fashion.*

1. Simulate circuit, in parallel, for every $T_i \in T$.
2. For every T_i in parallel, mark every line that is sensitized by that T_i.
3. Determine the minimum test $T_i \in T$ for every line L in the circuit using procedure MINT in Fig.2a
4. COUNT paths detected by new lines in T_i. Number of path delay faults is sum of all detected path faults at primary inputs for all T_i.

Figure 1: Outline of the Implicit Parallel Grading Algorithm

Lemma 3 follows from the observation that logic simulation of T_i is independent of T_j. The problem of determining the first test T_i that sensitizes L, given a fixed test order, is equivalent to determining the lowest i of all tests that sensitize L. This operation is a simple reduction for which there exists a parallel method [17].

LEMMA 4. *A complete list of (L, i) pairs, is sufficient to determine whether not a line L sensitized by T_i is a new line.*

Lemma 4 follows from Definitions 1 and Lemma 2. We may simplify and assume that we instead label the L with the minimum T_i that sensitizes it. If L not labeled, then it is implied that L is not in $G_{new,i}$. If Lemma 4 were false, then there would exist a test T_i that, when applied, has some *new line L*. This would require that L be present in $G_{new,i}$, but this would contradict Lemma 2.

THEOREM 1. *Counting the path faults detected by T_{i+1} over T_i may be done independently of T_i.*

The proof of Theorem 1 follows from Lemma 4 and Lemma 1, if L is labeled by the minimum T_i that sensitizes L prior to counting detected path faults.

Our proposed algorithm, given in Fig.1, is built upon Theorem 1 and consists of four phases. First, logic simulation is performed on the circuit netlist for each T_i in parallel. The sensitized paths are determined for every T_i in parallel. Then, each line L in the circuit netlist is labeled by the minimum T_i that sensitizes it. Finally, the labels are used to determine in parallel the coverage of T_{i+1} over T_i for all $T_i \in T$.

The details of Steps 1,2 in Fig.1 follow straightforward data parallelism. In particular, logic simulation uses parallel arguments made in [18, 19, 20, 21]. Sensitization and path counting benefit from implementation details that allow us to perform these tasks compactly on the GPU architecture. Our implementation also exploits model-parallelism.

2.1 Step 3 of the Implicit Parallel Algorithm

This procedure is given in Fig.2a. Procedure MINT, is a reduction for all lines L in Ckt, determining the minimum i for where T_i has sensitized L. As the rule is to only keep the minimum test vector identifier, we are guaranteed to maintain the behaviour of [13]. For a line $l \in Ckt$, we reduce as per Fig.2b across all T_i, and then store it in MERGE[G].

The following illustrates Step 3 on the circuit in Fig.3. This circuit consists of 6 gates labeled $G_1, G_2, G_3, G_4, G_5, G_6$. In our illustration lines correspond to the fan-out stems of the gates.

```
procedure MINT(Ckt, T)
    for all G ∈ Ckt in parallel do
        T_min ← REDUCE(T, min)
        MERGE[G] ← T_min
```

(a) MinT

```
function REDUCE(x, op)
    for d := 0 to log₂n − 1 do
        for k from 0 to n1 step 2d + 1 in parallel
do
```

$$x[k + 2d + 1 - 1] \leftarrow op(x[k + 2d - 1], x[k + 2d + 1 - 1])$$

(b) Reduction [22]

Figure 2: Procedures for Step 3 of Implicit Parallel Algorithm

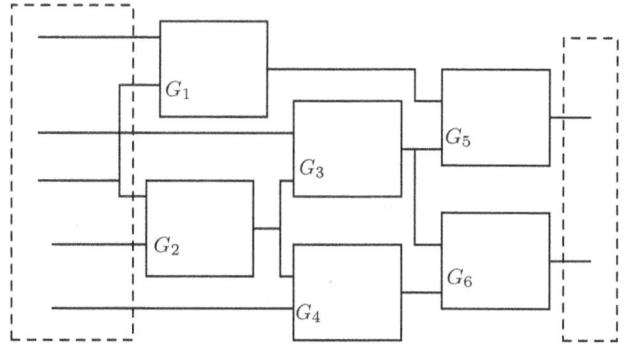

Figure 3: Example Circuit

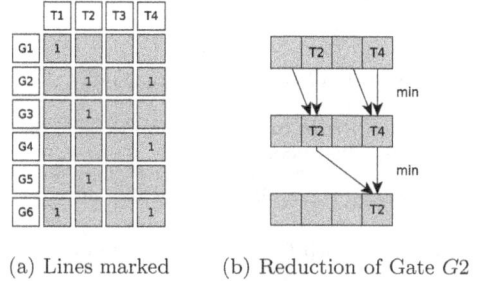

(a) Lines marked   (b) Reduction of Gate $G2$

(c) Results of MinT procedure

Figure 4: MinT Example

We need to determine which test T_i marked a given gate G first. Assume that tests $T_i \in T$ are ordered in a monotonically increasing manner. The algorithm examines all lines (gates) in parallel. For each gate the test are applied in parallel. The following shows the result of MINT on every gate. We consider a test set T consisting of four patterns T_1, T_2, T_3, T_4. Fig.4a lists the tests that mark each line (in our example, gate).

- G_1: Consider the pair T_1, T_2. T_1 marks G_1 and T_2 does not, so $T_{min,G_1} = T_1$. Neither T_3 nor T_4 mark G_1, so they are not considered.

- G_2: The earliest test between T_1, T_2 that marks G_2 is T_2. The earliest test between T_3 and T_4 is T_4. Now consider T_2, T_4. Both mark G, but the test ordering places T_2 before T_4, so $T_{min,G_2} = T_2$. A graphical rendition of this reduction is given in Fig.4b.

- G_3: Consider the pair T_1, T_2. T_2 marks G_3 and T_1 does not, so $T_{min,G_3} = T_2$. Neither T_3 nor T_4 mark G_3, so they are not considered.

- G_4: Consider the pair T_1, T_2. Neither marks G, so we consider T_3 and T_4. T_4 marks G_4 and T_2 does not, so $T_{min,G_4} = T_4$.

- G_5: Consider the pair T_1, T_2. T_2 marks G_5 and T_1 does not, so $T_{min,G_5} = T_2$. Neither T_3 nor T_4 mark G_5, so they are not considered.

- G_6: Consider the pair T_1, T_2. T_1 marks G_6 and T_2 does not, so $T_{min,G_6} = T0_1$. For T_3, T_4, the latter marks G. We now consider T_1 and T_4. T_1 precedes T_4, so $T_{min,G_6} = T_1$.

The final values of the MinT procedure are given in Fig.4c. Note that the evaluation of T_{min} for G_1 is not influenced by the evaluation for any other G, so the steps outlined for each gate may occur in parallel with each other.

2.2 Step 4 of the Implicit Parallel Algorithm

Counting sensitized paths in parallel is a two-phase process, as shown in Fig.5. They are called procedures COUNT and SUM, respectively. COUNT performs a reverse topological traversal over all gates in the circuit netlist. Similar to [13], a path is counted for a test T_i if that test is the first to sensitize at least one line in that path. Because the minimum test that sensitizes each line has already been calculated and stored in Step 3 by MINT, each thread may safely

count sensitized for each test T_i in parallel. The procedure terminates once the primary inputs have been reached for every $T_i \in T$. The procedure COUNT maintains two individual counts, $C_{G,i}$ and $H_{G,i}$. $C_{G,i}$ is the actual paths detected through G by T_i. $H_{G,i}$ is the count of all possible paths detected by T_i through G. The following steps occur for every $G \in Ckt$ and every $T_i \in T$.

1. If G is not sensitized by T_i, then no paths are tested through G and $C_{G,i} = H_{G,i} = 0$.

2. If G is a primary output, $H_{G,i} = 1$

3. Otherwise,

$$C_{G,i} = \sum_{o=1}^{nfo_G} C_{fo,i} \quad (1)$$

$$H_{G,i} = \sum_{o=1}^{nfo_G} H_{fo,i} \quad (2)$$

4. If T_i is the first test to sensitize G (MERGE[G] = T_i), then

$$C_{G,i} = C_{G,i} + H_{G,i} \quad (3)$$

$$H_{G,i} = 0 \quad (4)$$

Require: Gate G is evaluated before its fanin gates.

> **procedure** COUNT(Ckt, l, T)
>> **for all** $G \in Ckt$ **do**
>>> **for all** $T_i \in T$ **in parallel do**
>>>> **if** G is Primary Output **then**
>>>>> $H_{G,i} = 1$
>>>>
>>>> **if** G is sensitized by T_i **then**
>>>>> **if** MERGE$[G] = i$ **then**
>>>>>> **for all** Fanout f_o of G **do**
>>>>>>> $C_{G,i} = C_{G,i} + C_{f_o,i}$
>>>>>>> $C_{G,i} = C_{G,i} + H_{f_o,i}$
>>>>>>
>>>>>> $C_{G,i} = C_{G,i} + H_{G,i}$
>>>>>> $H_{f_o,i} = 0$
>>>>>
>>>>> **else**
>>>>>> **for all** Fanout f_o of G **do**
>>>>>>> $H_{G,i} = H_{G,i} + H_{f_o,i}$
>>>>>>> $C_{G,i} = C_{G,i} + C_{f_o,i}$
>>>>
>>>> **else**   ▷ No Paths through G at T_i
>>>>> $C_{G,i} = 0$
>>>>> $H_{G,i} = 0$

Require: COUNT has evaluated all gates in Ckt.

> **procedure** SUM(Ckt, T)
>> **for all** $G_{PI} \in Ckt$ **in parallel do**
>>> $SUM_G = $ **reduce**(T, sum)
>>>   ▷ Sum intermediate values for all T_i at PIs
>>
>> $N \leftarrow$ **reduce**(SUM_G, sum) ▷ Final add of intermediate values

Figure 5: Path Counting Algorithm COUNT

In the second phase, once all gates in the circuit netlist have been evaluated, the total coverage of $T = \sum C_{G,i}$; (G is a primary input). The parallel reduction procedure SUM then calculates the sum of all detected paths at the primary inputs at each T_i with REDUCE (as a subroutine).

3. EXPERIMENTAL RESULTS

To evaluate the scalability and applicability of the proposed approach, sets of 1024 to 16384 random patterns were processed for the combinatorial cores of the benchmark designs in Table 1 using the a serial CPU implementation and the parallel GPGPU implementation. The list contains the synthesized versions of the largest ITC'99 benchmark circuits (ISCAS'89 BENCH format) [23] and the two largest benchmark netlists in the ISCAS'89 collection. These circuits were chosen for their larger sizes, compared to other available benchmark circuits. a benchmark is the minimum according to our a ASAP placement method; a gate goes into the minimum level that is higher than its fan-ins. In Table 1, the term "Line" refers to the number of internal nodes as reported by our tool; a gate with more than one fan-out is two lines.

The implementation of the serial implicit fault grading algorithm was written for an x86 architecture and uses C++ STL maps to store sensitization information. Both serial and proposed parallel implementations were compiled using GCC 4.6 compiler collection; GPGPU code was compiled with nvcc from the CUDA 5.5 toolkit. "Max Patterns" refers to the maximum number of tests that fit into device memory at once in our experimental setup.

To estimate the size of the active problem set (that is, number of tests simulated in parallel), let Mem refer to the amount of free memory on the GPGPU device (after copying the circuit netlist and test set), and L be the number of lines in the circuit netlist. The number of patterns P that may be simulated in parallel is given by $P = floor(Mem/L)$. The actual numbers used are underestimated, owing to GPU alignment requirements. Exceeding the number of patterns listed results in performance degradation. This is because the test set must be partitioned to fit into device memory and each batch of tests runs in sequence. For each batch, MINT is executed.

Execution times reported are the mean wall clock time, measured as the difference before and after all relevant operations (memory allocation, etc) using the built-in clock_gettime() function. Our GPU platform used for these tests was a Tesla C2075 from NVIDIA. The host machine was a Intel Xeon E5620 2.40GHz workstation with 6GB of DDR3 memory with a 64-bit Debian 7.1.0 GNU/Linux distribution. NVIDIA CUDA 5.5 libraries were used with the official NVIDIA 325.15 Linux x64 driver package for Linux.

3.1 Detailed Analysis on Selected Benchmarks

Table 2 shows the speedup results for our approach for the "0-order" (as termed by [13]) approximation of the circuit. The test coverage reported is for robust sensitization. The test vectors used were subsets of a randomly generated master list: the 2,048-pattern test set includes the 1024-pattern test set. The test set sizes were chosen to be divisible by 32, which is the number of SIMD lanes on each core (in CUDA terms, a *warp*).

The particular circuit topology is more indicative of performance than anything else. The GPU run times remained relatively constant until the amount of available work saturated the available processor cores, and then increased sublinearly. Observe that the average speedup across all of the selected benchmarks was approximately 35x the fault-implicit serial algorithm. The following analyzes the impact of the proposed parallel algorithm on the various benchmarks.

Benchmarks s38417 and s35932 from the ISCAS'89 collection exhibited linear time progression, indicating that the GPU did not have spare processing capacity. While both circuits were similar in size, that s38417 had two-thirds more levels than s35932 meant that there was less model-parallelism to exploit. Our tool performed particularly well with b22_1, which is twice as large and has approximately double the levels of s38417. This difference in size implies that the amount of model-parallelism available in b22 was much lower than s38417. While there is likely lower model-parallelism, b22_1 consists of mostly of gates with small fan-ins, which meant that each gate executed faster. There were many gates in s38417 and s35932 that had large numbers of fanouts, which hurt their performance.

Benchmark b18_C is deep for its size. Our GPU implementation queues up work for as many patterns as possible in each level of the circuit. If the number of gates in a level is low, a low number of patterns would not fully utilize the GPU computational resources. This is why the GPU run times for 1024 and 2048 patterns are nearly identical. At 16384 patterns, there is only an 8x difference in run times over 1024 patterns. Doubling the test set size to 32768 yielded approximately twice the runtime. The 32768 run required 9 "chunks" of tests to execute serially, as the entire working set does not fit into device memory.

Benchmark b19_C, being twice as large as b18_C, performed as expected. The GPU was at nearly full utilization

Table 1: Benchmarks from ITC'99 and ISCAS'89

Benchmark	Line Count	Level Count	Max Patterns	Squareness
b05_C	2245	84	381800	0.0374164811
b15_C	19976	121	42908	0.0060572687
b18_C	250213	236	3425	0.0009431964
b19_C	504948	244	1697	0.0004832181
b22_1_C	47063	120	18212	0.0025497737
s35932	35260	39	24309	0.0011060692
s38417	38261	63	22402	0.0016465853

Table 2: Results for 0-Order Approximation for selected benchmarks (Robust path delay fault Sensitization)

Ckt	Test Count	Coverage	CPU (ms)	GPU (ms)	Speedup
b05_C	1024	446	$1.73*10^2$	$8.00*10^0$	21.63
	2048	514	$3.44*10^2$	$9.00*10^0$	38.22
	16384	585	$2.68*10^3$	$5.10*10^1$	52.49
				Average	37.44
b15_C	1024	2987	$1.66*10^3$	$5.40*10^1$	30.72
	2048	3412	$3.19*10^3$	$6.90*10^1$	46.25
	16384	2987	$1.29*10^4$	$4.48*10^2$	28.77
				Average	35.25
b18_C	1024	17035	$4.12*10^4$	$2.20*10^3$	18.77
	2048	19621	$8.31*10^4$	$2.90*10^3$	28.66
	16384	29635	$6.54*10^5$	$1.65*10^4$	39.68
				Average	29.04
b19_C	1024	33124	$8.91*10^4$	$4.38*10^3$	20.36
	2048	38377	$1.77*10^5$	$8.56*10^3$	20.71
	16384	58994	$9.42*10^5$	$5.80*10^4$	16.25
				Average	19.11
b22_1_C	1024	5231	$6.25*10^3$	$1.23*10^2$	50.78
	2048	6075	$1.22*10^4$	$1.90*10^2$	64.28
	16384	9351	$9.67*10^4$	$1.41*10^3$	68.66
				Average	61.24
s35932	1024	16535	$3.30*10^3$	$1.02*10^3$	3.23
	2048	18253	$6.22*10^3$	$1.04*10^3$	5.99
	16384	16535	$2.50*10^4$	$1.36*10^4$	1.84
				Average	3.69
s38417	1024	11305	$5.20*10^3$	$6.80*10^1$	76.44
	2048	11986	$1.01*10^4$	$1.42*10^2$	71.46
	16384	13395	$7.84*10^4$	$9.29*10^2$	84.38
				Average	75.69
				Total Average	37.35

with the circuit at 1024 tests with a linear progression in time as the test set size was increased.

3.2 Experimental results on an expanded selection of benchmarks

This subsection provides for the following benchmarks from the ISCAS89 and ITC 99 collection: Among those, b10_C and b05_C have fewer than 10,000 lines, b14_1_opt_C, b14_opt_C, b14_1_C, b15_opt_C, b15_1_opt_C, b15_C, b14_C, b21_1_opt_C, b15_1_C, b21_1_C, b20_1_C, b21_opt_C, s35932, s38417, b22_1_opt_C, b20_C, b21_C, b22_opt_C, b22_1_C have fewer than 50,000 lines and b17_opt_C, b17_1_opt_C, b22_C, b17_C, b17_1_C, b18_1_opt_C, b18_opt_C, b18_1_C, b18_C, b19_1_C, b19_C have up to half a million lines.

Fig.6 analyzes the speedup of the parallel 0-order approximation heuristic when 1,024 test patterns are applied. The mean speedup is approximately 49x. Fig.6a shows the speedup of the parallel 0-order approximation heuristic as a function of the circuit size. The dotted line represents the mean speedup across all circuits. It is observed that the speedup tends to be invariant to the circuit size for this test

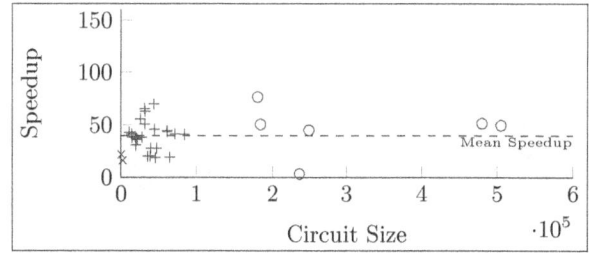

(a) Speedup vs. Circuit Size

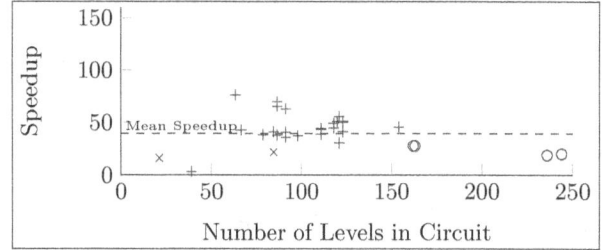

(b) Speedup vs. Circuit Levels

Figure 6: 0-Order Approximation, 1,024 Tests

set. We suspect that for larger circuit we might see less speedup. Fig.6b shows the speedup of the parallel 0-order approximation heuristic as a function of the number of levels in circuit size. A reduction in the speedup is observed for circuits with low or large number of levels.

Fig.7 analyzes the speedup of the parallel 0-order approximation heuristic when 16,384 test patterns are applied.The mean speedup is approximately 56x.Fig.7a shows the speedup of the parallel 0-order approximation heuristic as a function of the circuit size. In general, the speedup tends to decrease as the circuit size increases. Fig.7b shows the speedup of the parallel 0-order approximation heuristic as a function of the number of levels in circuit size,and shows a similar behavior to that in Fig.6b. In particular, a reduction in the speedup is observed for circuits with low or large number of levels. We attempted to identify a circuit parameter for which the speedup tends to be invariant. We consider the ratio "number of levels in the circuit over the circuit size". Fig.7c shows that the speedup tends to be invariant to that quantity.

We have also implemented a parallel version of an enhanced version of the 0-order approximation heuristic of [13] which is more elaborate and grades more faults. It is called the 1-order approximation heuristic. It partitions the circuit into many smaller subcircuits that may share lines. This is favorable to our parallel implementation on GPGPUs.

Fig.8 analyzes the speedup as a function of circuit size of the parallel 1-order approximation heuristic when 1,024 test patterns are applied. The mean speedup is approximately 1,250x. The dotted line represents the mean speedup across all circuits. It is observed that the speedup increases as the circuit size increases but for circuits with more than 500,000 tends to stabilize around 3,500x.

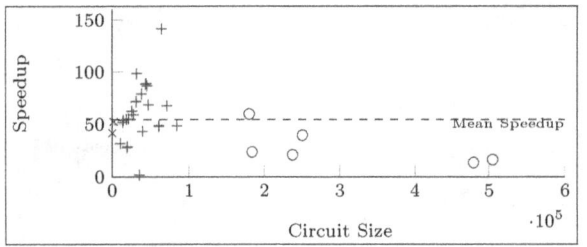

(a) Speedup vs. Circuit Size

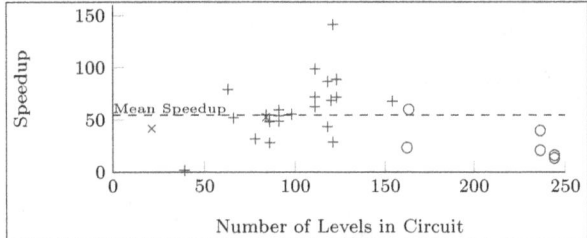

(b) Speedup vs. Circuit Levels

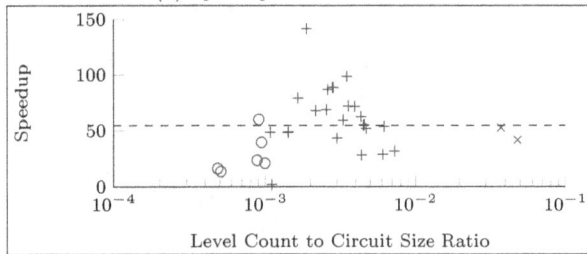

(c) Speedup vs. Circuit Level Count to Circuit Size Ratio

Figure 7: 0-Order Approximation, 16,384 Tests

4. CONCLUSIONS

A methodology to parallelize a wide variety of heuristics for non-enumerative path delay fault grading has been presented. For the most pessimistic heuristic in the framework, a GPGPU-based implementation shows average speedup in the order of 50x. For a less pessimistic in the framework we observe speedups up to 3,500x over a single-threaded serial implementation for the largest benchmarks.

5. REFERENCES

[1] M. Bushnell and V. Agrawal, *Essentials of electronic testing for digital, memory, and mixed-signal VLSI circuits.* Kluwer Academic, 2000.

[2] S. Natarajan, S. Patil, and S. Chakravarty, "Path delay fault simulation on large industrial designs," in *Proceedings of the 24th IEEE VLSI Test Symposium, 2006.*, April-4 May 2006, p. 6.

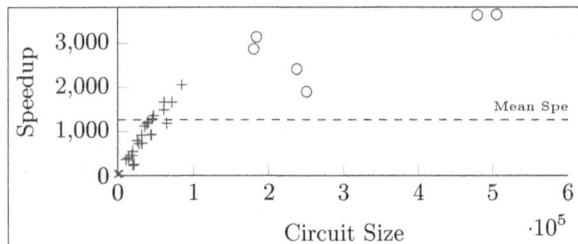

Figure 8: Speedup vs. Circuit Size, 1,024 Tests

[3] A. Majhi and V. Agrawal, "Delay fault models and coverage," in *Proceedings of Eleventh International Conference on VLSI Design*, Jan 1998, pp. 364 –369.

[4] C. J. Lin and S. Reddy, "On delay fault testing in logic circuits," *IEEE Transactions on Computer-Aided Design of Integrated Circuits and Systems*, vol. 6, no. 5, pp. 694 – 703, September 1987.

[5] M. Schulz, F. Fink, and K. Fuchs, "Parallel pattern fault simulation of path delay faults," June 1989, pp. 357 – 363.

[6] T. W. Williams, B. Underwood, and M. R. Mercer, "The interdependence between delay-optimization of synthesized networks and testing," ser. DAC '91. ACM, 1991, pp. 87–92. [Online]. Available: http://doi.acm.org/10.1145/127601.127633

[7] M. Schulz, K. Fuchs, and F. Fink, "Advanced automatic test pattern generation techniques for path delay faults," in *Nineteenth International Symposium on Fault-Tolerant Computing, 1989. FTCS-19. Digest of Papers.*, 1989, pp. 44–51.

[8] D. Kagaris and S. Tragoudas, "On the nonenumerative path delay fault simulation problem," *Computer-Aided Design of Integrated Circuits and Systems, IEEE Transactions on*, vol. 21, no. 9, pp. 1095 – 1101, Sep 2002.

[9] F. Kocan and M. Gunes, "On the zbdd-based nonenumerative path delay fault coverage calculation," *Computer-Aided Design of Integrated Circuits and Systems, IEEE Transactions on*, vol. 24, no. 7, pp. 1137 – 1143, July 2005.

[10] S. Padmanaban, M. Michael, and S. Tragoudas, "Exact path delay grading with fundamental bdd operations," in *Proceedings of International Test Conference, 2001*, 2001, pp. 642 –651.

[11] S. Padmanaban and S. Tragoudas, "An implicit path-delay fault diagnosis methodology," *Computer-Aided Design of Integrated Circuits and Systems, IEEE Transactions on*, vol. 22, no. 10, pp. 1399 – 1408, oct. 2003.

[12] M. Sivaraman and A. Strojwas, "Path delay fault diagnosis and coverage-a metric and an estimation technique," *Computer-Aided Design of Integrated Circuits and Systems, IEEE Transactions on*, vol. 20, no. 3, pp. 440 –457, Mar 2001.

[13] I. Pomeranz and S. Reddy, "An efficient nonenumerative method to estimate the path delay fault coverage in combinational circuits," *IEEE Transactions on Computer-Aided Design of Integrated Circuits and Systems*, vol. 13, no. 2, pp. 240 – 250, Feb 1994.

[14] M. Kumar, S. Tragoudas, S. Chakravarty, and R. Jayabharathi, "Implicit and exact path delay fault grading in sequential circuits," in *Proceedings of Design, Automation and Test in Europe, 2005*, March 2005, pp. 990 – 995 Vol. 2.

[15] D. Kagaris, S. Tragoudas, and D. Karayiannis, "Improved nonenumerative path-delay fault-coverage estimation based on optimal polynomial-time algorithms," *IEEE Transactions on Computer-Aided Design of Integrated Circuits and Systems*, vol. 16, no. 3, pp. 309 –315, Mar 1997.

[16] K. Heragu, V. Agrawal, M. Bushnell, and J. Patel, "Improving a nonenumerative method to estimate path delay fault coverage," *IEEE Transactions on Computer-Aided Design of Integrated Circuits and Systems*, vol. 16, no. 7, pp. 759 –762, Jul 1997.

[17] S. Baxter. (2013) Modern gpu. www. NVIDIA Corporation. [Online]. Available: http://nvlabs.github.io/moderngpu/

[18] M. Li and M. Hsiao, "3-d parallel fault simulation with gpgpu," *Computer-Aided Design of Integrated Circuits and Systems, IEEE Transactions on*, vol. 30, no. 10, pp. 1545 –1555, oct. 2011.

[19] D. Chatterjee, A. DeOrio, and V. Bertacco, "Event-driven gate-level simulation with gp-gpus," in *46th ACM/IEEE Design Automation Conference, 2009. DAC '09*, July 2009, pp. 557 –562.

[20] Y. Zhu, B. Wang, and Y. Deng, "Massively parallel logic simulation with gpus," *ACM Trans. Des. Autom. Electron. Syst.*, vol. 16, no. 3, pp. 29:1–29:20, Jun. 2011. [Online]. Available: http://doi.acm.org/10.1145/1970353.1970362

[21] R. Raghavan, J. Hayes, and W. Martin, "Logic simulation on vector processors," in *IEEE International Conference on Computer-Aided Design, 1988. ICCAD-88.*, Nov 1988, pp. 268 –271.

[22] M. Harris. (2007, April) Parallel prefix sum (scan) with cuda. www. nVidia. [Online]. Available: http://developer.download.nvidia.com/compute/cuda/1_1/Website/projects/scan/doc/scan.pdf

[23] C. Group. Cad group: Itc'99 benchmarks (2nd release). Politecnico di Torino. [Online]. Available: http://www.cad.polito.it/downloads/tools/itc99.html

Simscape Design Flow for Memristor Based Programmable Oscillators

Ebubechukwu Agu[1], Saraju P. Mohanty[2], Elias Kougianos[3], Mahesh Gautam[4]
NanoSystem Design Laboratory (NSDL), University of North Texas, Denton, TX 76203, USA.
eza0001@unt.edu[1], saraju.mohanty@unt.edu[2], eliask@unt.edu[3],
maheshgautam@my.unt.edu[4]

ABSTRACT

In this paper a design optimization flow is proposed for memristor-based oscillators using the Gravitational Search Algorithm. This paper presents for the first time a memristor behavioral model in the Simscape physical modeling language. Using this model, a memristor based Wien oscillator is characterized within the Simscape framework. The oscillation frequency and power consumption of the oscillator for different configurations are explored.

Categories and Subject Descriptors

B.7.1 [**Integrated Circuits**]: Types and Design Styles—VLSI (very large scale integration)

Keywords

Simscape Modeling; Memristor; Programmable Oscillator

1. INTRODUCTION & CONTRIBUTIONS

Simscape is an integral part of the MATLAB framework. It can model multiple-discipline systems including mechanical and electrical. Simulink uses the signal-flow approach which is suitable for high-level system modeling.

A graphical block-based Simulink/Simscape memristor model was presented in [4]. In the current paper a memristor model is presented that is native to Simscape.

As a case study, the design and optimization of a Wien oscillator is presented with the memristor assisted programmability using the proposed Simscape memristor model.

The **novel contributions** of this paper to the state-of-art include the following: (1) The first ever flow for design optimization of memristor-based oscillators. (2) A Gravitational Search Algorithm (GSA) based optimization algorithm for memristor-based Wien oscillators. (3) A programmable oscillator using a memristor is presented. As case study circuit design exploration of the oscillator under five memristor configurations is presented in terms of power consumption and frequency. (4) The first ever Simscape based models for titanium oxide memristors. The Simscape model construction and simulation setup are presented.

GLSVLSI'14, May 21–23, 2014, Houston, Texas, USA.
ACM 978-1-4503-2816-6/14/05.
http://dx.doi.org/10.1145/2591513.2591545.

2. OPTIMIZATION ALGORITHM

The Gravitational Search Algorithm (GSA) is based on the law of gravity and the law of motion of masses [2, 3]. Search agents are characterized as masses, and the interaction between them is governed by Newtonian gravitational force as follows.

$$F = G\frac{M_1 M_2}{R^2}, \qquad (1)$$

where M_1 and M_2 are two masses, G is a constant and R is the Euclidian distance between the masses. The performance of the agents is measured in terms of their masses. All the masses attract each other by force of gravity and objects with heavier mass tend to attract other objects toward them. The heavier mass is considered the optimal solution. With lapse of time, more masses are attracted toward the heaviest mass.

3. SIMSCAPE MEMRISTOR MODEL

The proposed Simscape memristor model is presented in Algorithm 1.

Algorithm 1 Proposed Simscape Memristor Model.

```
1  component memristor<foundation.electrical.branch
2
3    parameters
4        u = { 1e-14,'m^2/s/V' };   % Mobility
5        x0 = { .5,'1' }; % Initial (W/D)
6        d = { 20e-9, 'm' };  % Memristor Width
7        ron = {100,'Ohm'}; % Minimum Resistance
8        roff = {36e3, 'Ohm'}; % Maximum Resistance
9    end
10
11   variables
12       x={.5,'1'};
13       Rmem ={1e3,'Ohm'};
14   end
15
16   function setup
17       x=x0;
18   end
19
20   equations
21     let
22         az = u * ron / d^2;
23     in
24         if(x <= 0 && v <= 0)||(x >= 1 && v >= 0)
25             x.der == 0;
26         else
27             x.der == az * i;
28         end % if
29     end
30     Rmem == ron * x + roff * (1 - x);
31     v == i * Rmem;
32   end % equations
33 end % component
```

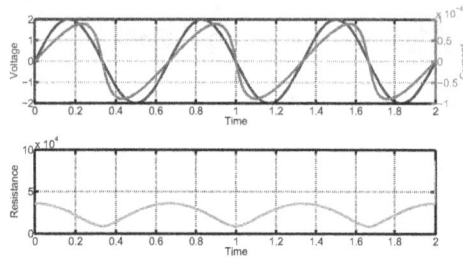

(a) Time-domain simulation result for a 2-V, 1.5 Hz applied sinusoidal voltage.

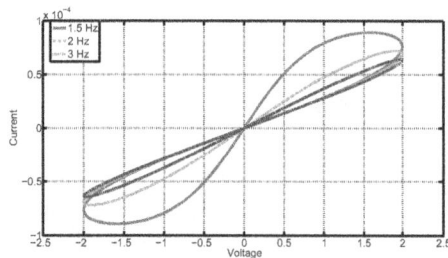

(b) $I - V$ characteristics for various input frequencies.

Figure 1: Simscape memristor simulation.

The memristor model was tested in Simulink/Simscape. The output is shown in Fig. 1. Fig. 1(a) shows the current, voltage, and memristance against time. Fig. 1(b) shows the $I - V$ characteristics of the memristor with three different input frequencies [1].

4. MEMRISTOR-CONTROLLED PROGRAMMABLE OSCILLATOR

A traditional Wien oscillatorcomprises of four resistors and two capacitors. The condition for sustained oscillation is given by:

$$\frac{C_2}{C_1} + \frac{R_1}{R_2} = \frac{R_3}{R_4}. \quad (2)$$

The frequency of oscillation is given by the following:

$$f = \frac{1}{2\pi\sqrt{R_1 R_2 C_1 C_2}}. \quad (3)$$

When the resistors are replaced with memristors, the oscillation frequency can be varied by controlling the memristance according to Eq. (3). Assuming the memristance is not intentionally changed during normal oscillation, the initial condition of memristor determine the frequency of the oscillator. Five different configurations of a memristor integrated Wien oscillator have been studied. In Configuration 1 we replaced R_1 with memristor M_1 whose resistance is labeled as $R_{1,mem}$. In Configuration 2, we replaced R_2 with memristor M_2 whose resistance is labeled as $R_{2,mem}$. In Configuration 3, R_3 and R_4 were replaced with M_3 and M_4, respectively, whose resistance is labeled as $R_{3,mem}$ and $R_{4,mem}$. Similarly in Configuration 4, we replaced R_2 and R_4 with M_2 and M_4 whose resistance is labeled as $R_{2,mem}$ and $R_{4,mem}$ respectively. In Configuration 5 we replaced all resistors with memristors.

Table 1: Oscillating Frequency of Wien oscillators.

Configuration		Frequency		
		Simulated	Calculated	Error %
Traditional		1591.3	1591.54	0.02
Configuration 1	$X_0 = 0$	118.65	118.65	0.01
	$X_0 = 1$	2030.3	2077.3	2.26
Configuration 2	$X_0 = 0$	264.67	265.26	0.22
	$X_0 = 1$	4309	4317.27	0.19
Configuration 3	$X_0 = 0$	1591	1591.54	0.03
	$X_0 = 1$	1591	1591.54	0.03
Configuration 4	$X_0 = 0$	265	265.41	0.15
	$X_0 = 1$	4765.3	4768.44	0.07
Configuration 5	$X_0 = 0$	44	44.23	0.52
	$X_0 = 1$	12388	12791	3.15

Table 2: Optimization Results for Wien Oscillator (Configuration 5).

Metric	Power (W)	Frequency (Hz)
Baseline Design	2.43E-5	88.5
Optimal Design	1.66E-5	57.6
Reduction	32%	35%

Table 1 shows the simulation results obtained from Simscape and calculations obtained using Eq. 3.

5. EXPERIMENTAL RESULTS

The GSA algorithm is applied to the simscape model.

The algorithm took 302 iterations to achieved the optimal power consumption of 16.6 μW. As presented in Table 2, the power consumption is reduced by 32 % at cost of 35 % reduction in frequency.

6. CONCLUSIONS

This paper presented a pure Simscape memristor model for the first time. As a case study, a memristor integrated programmable Wien oscillator is presented. The simulated oscillation frequencies have been verified with the calculated values from mathematical formulas. The paper also presented the power analysis and observations on various configurations of the memristor-based Wien oscillator. Optimization of the memristor-based Wien oscillator circuit using the GSA algorithm is done. The results obtained show that reduction in power consumption can be achieved at the cost of frequency reduction.

7. REFERENCES

[1] Q. Li, H. Xu, H. Liu, and X. Tian. Study of the Noninverting Amplifier Based on Memristor with Linear Dopant Drift. In *Proceedings of the 2nd International Conference on Intelligent System Design and Engineering Application*, pages 1136–1139, 2012.

[2] O. Okobiah, S. Mohanty, and E. Kougianos. Geostatistical-Inspired Fast Layout Optimization of a Nano-CMOS Thermal Sensor. *IET Circuits, Devices Systems*, 7(5):253–262, Sep 2013.

[3] E. Rashedi, H. Nezamabadi-Pour, and S. Saryazdi. GSA: A Gravitational Search Algorithm. *Information Sciences*, 179(13):2232–2248, 2009.

[4] K. Zaplatilek. Memristor modeling in MATLAB® & Simulink®. In *Proceedings of the 5th European conference on European Computing Conference*, pages 62–67, 2011.

Securely Outsourcing Power Grid Simulation on Cloud

Naval Gupte   Jia Wang

Electrical & Computer Engineering Department
Illinois Institute of Technology, Chicago IL 60616, USA
ngupte1@hawk.iit.edu   jwang@ece.iit.edu

ABSTRACT

Power grid (PG) simulation is critical for verification of supply noises in IC design. Computational demands for simulating PG is high. Cloud computing can be leveraged to mitigate these costs. However, simulating on third-party platforms lead to major security concerns. We propose a framework for secure PG simulation on Cloud. Multiple compression strategies are employed to reduce communication overhead. Turnaround time similar to an insecure simulator on Cloud can be achieved, while securing current excitations and output voltage vectors at reasonable costs.

Categories and Subject Descriptors

J.6 [**Computer-Aided Engineering**]: Computer-Aided Design

Keywords

PG simulation, Cloud computing, Security, EDA, SaaS

1. INTRODUCTION

A typical PG is modeled as an RC/RLC circuit with current sources [1,2], and formulated as a system of differential algebraic equations (DAE). With increasing verification complexity, users are forced to spend heavily on computing resources. Cloud computing offers a scalable, customizable and inexpensive computing platform that can be rapidly provisioned and released [3]. Cloud computing for PG simulations raises security concerns, since simulation data typically carry sensitive design information.

We investigate secure outsourcing of system of DAE to a Cloud. Excitations can be transformed, such that all computations are performed on the transformed patterns. Cloud has no access to inputs and outputs of the simulator. This secures the temporal and spatial power consumption profile of the IC. It can be extended to simulate the PG under multiple excitations simultaneously. Our compression algorithms can reduce communication costs by compressing data by 95-99% without affecting the performance. Our approach can be extended to hide the coefficients of equations, thus securing circuit parameters associated with the PG network.

The paper is organized as follows. Problem statement and design goals are introduced in Section 2. Our proposed solution is presented in Section 3. Section 4 depicts our experimental results, followed by our concluding remarks in Section 5.

2. PROBLEM STATEMENT & DESIGN GOALS

2.1. Power Grid Model

The discrete system equation for an RC model with N non-Vdd nodes, using Backward Euler approximation, can be expressed as

$$[\mathbf{G} + \mathbf{C}/h]V_n = I_n + [\mathbf{C}/h]V_{n-1} \qquad (1)$$

where $\mathbf{G}$ is an $N\mathrm{x}N$ conductance matrix, $\mathbf{C}$ is an $N\mathrm{x}N$ diagonal matrix of capacitances, V_n is an $N\mathrm{x}1$ vector of voltage drops and I_n is an $N\mathrm{x}1$ vector of input current excitations at n^{th} instant and h is the time step. Our transformation is also applicable for RLC models of PG, utilizing Trapezoidal Rule for discretization. Direct methods based on LU factorization or Cholesky decomposition for for solving the equations can be prohibitively resource hungry.

GLSVLSI' 14, May 21 – 23 2014, Houston, TX, USA
ACM 978-1-4503-2816-6/14/05.
http://dx.doi.org/10.1145/2591513.2591547

2.2. Cloud-based Simulation

Cloud outsourcing architecture involves two entities, illustrated in Fig. 1, user, and Cloud server (CS). CS refers to an Amazon EC2 instance [4]; a virtual server with predefined configuration.

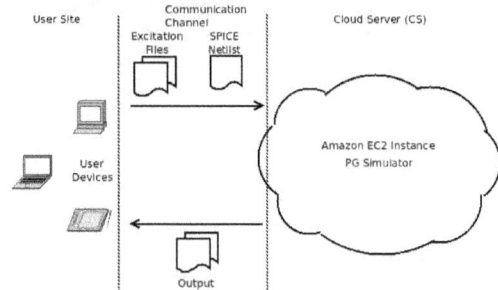

Fig. 1: PG Simulation Outsourcing

User provides input *excitation vectors,* in *excitation files*, at discrete instants to the simulator, running on an EC2 instance. Voltage noises computed by the simulator are written to *output files*. The overall approach can be divided into three phases: current transformation phase, solution phase; and recovery phase.

Our design must ensure that no sensitive data can be derived by the Cloud. Local computations must be substantially lower than solving the DAE and communication and storage costs must be kept minimal. Prior works on scientific Cloud computing do not consider data security [5,6,7]. Secure outsourcing frameworks, proposed in [8,9,10], do not consider costs associated with data encryption. Also, network and storage costs are not considered.

3. PROPOSED SOLUTION

3.1. Current Transformation & Solution Phase

Initial condition vector V_0 and all excitations I_n are embedded in an $N\mathrm{x}k$ matrix $\mathbf{D}_n$, where $k \ll N$, in an arbitrarily selected column, j. These *excitation matrices* are further transformed as

$$\mathbf{D}_0' = \mathbf{V}_0\,\mathbf{P}, \qquad \mathbf{D}_n' = \mathbf{D}_n\,\mathbf{P}, 1 \le n \le L \qquad (2)$$

where $\mathbf{P}$ is an $k\mathrm{x}k$ *transformation matrix*, such that its inverse exist. Matrices in (2) are written to excitation files. $\mathbf{P}$ secures the PG excitations from the Cloud. The simulator returns as outputs solution matrices $\mathbf{V}_n'$, for each time step in the transient simulation

$$[\mathbf{G} + \mathbf{C}/h]\mathbf{V}_n' - [\mathbf{C}/h]\mathbf{V}_{n-1}' = \mathbf{D}_n' \qquad (3)$$

where $\mathbf{V}_n = \mathbf{V}_n'\,\mathbf{P}^{-1}$. The jth column of $\mathbf{V}_n$ is the desired solution vector. The CS has no visibility of the solution vector and hence has no knowledge of the PG outputs.

3.2. Compression Strategies

Each current source can be represented piece-wise as a linear segment. Vectors at which a change in slope or a discontinuity in the inputs is observed are stored in excitation files, as shown in Fig. 2, where the gray columns indicate the vectors written to file. Currents between the two endpoints are computed on-the-fly using the slope-intercept line equation, resulting in an 93-95% reduction in file sizes. Further, excitation matrices are stored in CSC format. Delta compression is employed to store JA and IA. Each value is stored as a delta difference from the previous value, contributing 45-50% reduction in their sizes. AA elements are separated in key-value arrays so that first two bytes of a number form the key and last two bytes are stored in a value array. This avoids storage of redundant key information. A 12-17% reduction is observed in size of AA. An overall reduction of 95-99% is realized.

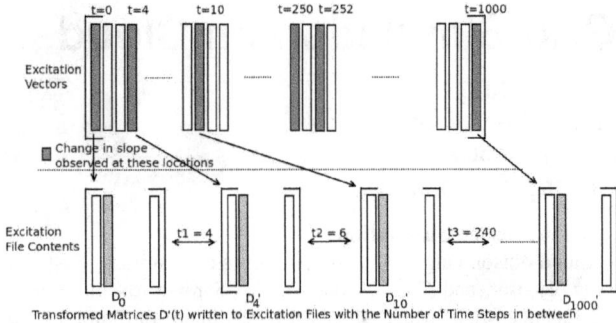

Fig. 2: Compression of Current Vectors as Linear Segments

3.3. Security Concerns And Analysis

Mutual Information is the reduction in uncertainty of $\mathbf{D_n}$ due to knowledge of $\mathbf{D_n}'$ [11,12]. If the distributions are identical, CS cannot derive information about $\mathbf{D_n}$ given $\mathbf{D_n}'$. Elements of $\mathbf{D_n}$ and $\mathbf{P}$ are chosen to be IID with standard Gaussian Distribution (GD). Then, from Central Limit Theorem, $\mathbf{D_n}'$ is also Gaussian [12].

Our transformation is analogous to Blind Source Separation [13]. As concluded in [13,14], Independent Component Analysis results in a good separation only when the signals have non-GD. Since $\mathbf{D_n}$ and $\mathbf{D_n}'$ have GD, they are indistinguishable. Additionally, Dimensionality Reduction-Based Transformation [15] scheme can be used for matrix encoding, expressed as

$$\mathbf{D_n'}_{(N x k)} = \mathbf{D_n}_{(N x d)} \mathbf{P}_{(d x k)}, \ 1 \leq n \leq L \quad (4)$$

where the currents can be embedded into $\mathbf{D_n}$ of dimension Nxd, and then projected to a lower dimension using $\mathbf{P}$ of dimension dxk, such that $k \ll d \ll N$. Security is guaranteed since there can be no invertible linear transformation between Euclidean spaces of different dimensions.

3.4. Securing Coefficients of System Matrix

To secure matrices $\mathbf{G}$ and $\mathbf{C}$, these transforms can be applied

$$\mathbf{G'} = \mathbf{P_1}^{-1}\mathbf{GP_2} \qquad \mathbf{C'} = \mathbf{P_1}^{-1}\mathbf{CP_2}$$
$$\mathbf{D_n'} = \mathbf{P_1}^{-1}\mathbf{D_nP_3} \qquad \mathbf{V_0'} = \mathbf{P_2}^{-1}\mathbf{V_0P_3} \quad (5)$$

$\mathbf{P_1}$ and $\mathbf{P_2}$ are NxN matrices and $\mathbf{P_3}$ is an Nxk matrix similar to the matrix $\mathbf{P}$ presented earlier. Computations can be expressed as

$$[\mathbf{G'} + \mathbf{C'}/h]\mathbf{V_n'} - [\mathbf{C'}/h]\mathbf{V_{n-1}'} = \mathbf{D_n'} \quad (6)$$

where the solution matrix can be derived as

$$\mathbf{V_n} = \mathbf{P_2} \mathbf{V_n'} \mathbf{P_3}^{-1} \quad (7)$$

3.5. Parallel PG Simulation

Each excitation vector can be selected to be a vector from a different current stimulus at the same time step, as depicted in Fig. 3. PG can be simulated under s different stimuli, where $s \leq k$. Vectors corresponding to n=0 in each of the current stimuli can be embedded in the excitation matrix $\mathbf{D_0'}$. Likewise, excitations corresponding to n=500 and n=1000, are embedded, in respective columns, in $\mathbf{D_{500}'}$ and $\mathbf{D_{1000}'}$, respectively.

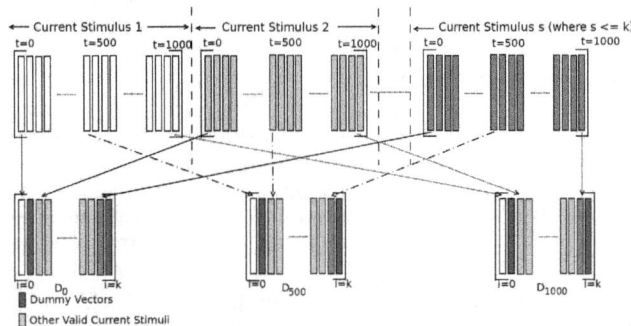

Fig. 3: Embedding for PG Simulation for Multiple Stimuli

3.6. Computational Complexity and Cost

Computational costs can be easily mitigated by simulating the PG under multiple stimuli. Generation of $\mathbf{D_n}$ is straight forward. Multiplication and inversion of $\mathbf{P}$ are simplified by generating it as sparse LU factors, resulting in $O(N^2)$ complexity.

4. EXPERIMENTAL RESULTS

Experiments are based on IBM PG benchmarks, tested on 64-bit EC2 instances with capacity of 13 10.-1.2 GHz 2007 Opteron/Xeon processors, compared to Linux server with 2.67 GHz Intel Xeon X5650. Runtime of insecure simulator is reported in columns 2 and 3. Columns 4 and 5 show runtime of secure simulator for single vector, and communication times in column 6.

Table 1: Simulation and Communication times

IBM PG	Insecure		Secure Simulator (k=10)		
	Server (sec)	EC2 (sec)	Server (sec)	EC2	
				Process (sec)	Comm (min)
ibmpg1t	2.5	1.9	2.6	1.8	1
ibmpg2t	37.6	29.1	38.2	29.3	6
ibmpg3t	89.9	73.1	85.9	72.1	32
ibmpg4t	564.1	387.3	466.3	391.9	14
ibmpg5t	192.2	160.9	171.7	150.7	84
ibmpg6t	281.3	234.4	240.8	219.1	122

5. CONCLUSIONS

Secure framework for PG simulation on the Cloud is proposed. Our transformation is secure and mandates a moderate computation to the user. Our compression allows for efficient management of network and storage overheads. Shielding the coefficient matrices and improvements in turn-around times will be investigated next.

6. ACKNOWLEDGEMENTS

This work was supported in part by the US National Science Foundation (NSF) under grant CNS-1116939.

7. REFERENCES

[1] X. Xiong, J. Wang, "Parallel forward and backward substitution for efficient power grid simulation", *Proc. ICCAD*, 2012, pp.660-663.

[2] J.Yang, Z.Li, Y.Cai, Q.Zhou,"PowerRush:Efficient transient simulation for power grid analysis", *Proc. ICCAD*,2012, pp.653-659.

[3] L. Wang, R. Ranjan, J. Chen, B. Benatallah, *Cloud Computing– Methodology, Systems and Applications*, CRC Press, 2012.

[4] AWS Documentation, https://aws.amazon.com/documentation/

[5] Z. Hill, M. Humphrey, "A quantitative analysis of high performance computing with Amazon's EC2 infrastructure: The death of a local cluster?", in *Proc. Intl. Conf. on Grid Computing*, 2009, pp. 26-33.

[6] A. Iosup, S. Ostermann, M.N. Yigitbasi, R. Prodan, T. Fahringer, D.H.J. Epema, "Performance analysis of cloud computing for many-tasks scientific computing", in *IEEE Trans. on Parallel and Distributed Systes*, Vol. 22(6), 2011, pp. 931-945.

[7] E. Roloff, M. Diener, A. Carissimi, P.O.A. Navaux, "High performance computing in the cloud: deployement, performance and cost efficiency", in *Proc. Intl. Conf. on Cloud Computing Technology and Science (CloudCom)*, 2012, pp. 371-378.

[8] M.J. Atallah, K.N. Pantazopoulos, J.R. Rice, E.H. Spafford, "Secure outsourcing of scientific computations", in *Advances in Computers*, Vol. 54, 2002, pp. 215-272.

[9] M. J. Atallah, K. B. Frikken, "Securely outsourcing linear algebra computations", in *Proc.ACM Symposium on Information, Computer and Communication Security (ASIACCS)*, 2010, pp. 48-59.

[10] C. Wang, K. Ren, J. Wang, Q. Wang, "Outsourcing large-scale systems of linear equations", in *IEEE Trans. on Parallel and Distributed Systems*, Vol. 24(6), 2013, pp. 1172-1181.

[11] C. Cachin, "An information-theoretic model for steganography", in *Information Hiding, Lecture Notes in Computer Science*, Vol. 1525, 1998, pp. 306-318.

[12] T.M. Cover, J.A. Thomas, *Elements of Information Theory*, 2nd ed., Wiley-Interscience, 2006.

[13] A.Hyvarinen, E.Oja,"Independent component analysis: algorithms and applications", *Journal. Of Neural Networks*,Vol.13(4-5), 2000, pp.411-430.

[14] K. Liu, H. Kargupta, J. Ryan, "Random projection-based multiplicative perturbation for privacy-preserving distributed data mining", in *IEEE Trans. on Knowledge and Data Engineering*, Vol. 18(1), 2006, pp. 92-106.

[15] S. R. M. Oliveira, O. R. Zaiane, "A privacy-preserving clustering approach toward secure and effective data analysis for business collaboration", in *Computers & Security*, Vol 26(1), 2007, pp. 81-93.

Layer Assignment of Bus-Oriented Nets in High-Speed PCB Designs

Jin-Tai Yan

Department of Computer Science and Information Engineering

Chung-Hua University

Hsinchu, Taiwan, R. O. C.

ABSTRACT

In this paper, given a set of global routed buses in a high-speed PCB design, based on the concept of a virtual wall between two circuit components and the optimality of interval packing in a left-edge algorithm, the number of the assigned layers can be further minimized and the given bus-oriented nets with crossing constraints can be optimally assigned onto the used layers. As the covering constraint between two bus-oriented nets is released for layer assignment of bus-oriented nets, the number of the assigned layers can be further minimized and all the bus-oriented nets can be assigned onto the used layers by using iterative covering compatibility Compared with Tsai's algorithm[5] and Chin's algorithm[6], the experimental results show that our proposed optimal algorithm reduces 16.2% and 16.2% of the assigned layers and 60.7% and 39.3% of CPU time for six tested examples on the average, respectively.

Categories and Subject Descriptors

B.7.2 [**Integrated Circuits**]: Design Aids – *Placement and routing*

General Terms: Algorithms, Design

Keywords: PCB design, Bus, Layer assignment

1. INTRODUCTION

In general, PCB routing can be divided into net-oriented routing[1] and bus-oriented routing. In net-oriented routing, the nets of two buses may be mixed up and routed in the same layer. Hence, the routing process focuses on the mixing nets of different buses and the other nets of independent buses. In bus-oriented routing, the nets in a single bus are not expected to be mixed up with any foreign net and are routed together. Hence, the routing process only focuses on the nets of any independent bus. Hence, bus-oriented routing is more popular than net-oriented routing in PCB designs.

In layer assignment for bus-oriented escape routing between two circuit components, firstly, Kong et al. [2] proposed an optimal algorithm for bus sequencing. Recently, Yan et al.[3] propose an $O(n^{2.38})$ optimal algorithm in the layer assignment for bus-oriented

GLSVLSI'14, May 21–23, 2014, Houston, Texas, USA.
ACM 978-1-4503-2816-6/14/05.
http://dx.doi.org/10.1145/2591513.2591548

escape routing. Besides that, based on the optimal feature of a left-edge algorithm for interval packing, Yan et al.[4] propose a new $O(n^2)$ optimal algorithm in the layer assignment for bus-oriented escape routing. In layer assignment for bus-oriented area routing in high-speed PCB designs, it is assumed that the nets in a single bus can be represented as an escaped boundary pin. Given a set of unrouted buses, firstly, Tasi et al.[5] introduced the concept of a component connecting point(CCP) between two circuit components to integrate the escaped pins on the two components and the concept of dynamic pin sequence(DSP) to avoid the net crossing in one-layer planar routing. Furthermore, they proposed a global topological routing algorithm for single-layer routing. By using topological routing layer-by-layer, the layer assignment of the given buses can be obtained. However, the proposed approach may not minimize the number of assigned layers for bus-oriented area routing. Besides that, Chin et al.[6] extended the work of Tasi et al.[5] and introduced the concept of transforming chords of a circle to the corresponding circle graph for dynamic pin sequence(DSP). Furthermore, they used Supowit's algorithm[7] to find the maximum number of nets that can be routed on one layer. By using Supowit's algorithm layer-by-layer, the layer assignment of the given buses can be obtained. However, the proposed approach may not minimize the number of assigned layers for bus-oriented area routing.

2. PROBLEM FORMULATION

It is assumed that a pin array is located under any circuit component for IO connections. For bus-oriented escape routing, pins under any circuit component can be grouped into some buses and the pins in a bus must be escaped to the boundary of the circuit component with minimal detours. In a high-speed PCB design, based on the assignment of the escape direction of all the buses, all the buses can be further partitioned and assigned onto different layers. However, the buses on the same layer for bus-oriented escape routing may be really assigned on the same layer because of the global routing result of the buses on the same layer. Hence, it is necessary for bus-oriented area routing to minimize the number of assigned layers and assign all the buses onto the used layers.

Due to the complexity of IO connections among circuit components in a high-speed PCB design, all the buses cannot be assigned onto a single layer at the same time for area routing. It is known that the two buses can be assigned onto the same layer for bus-oriented area routing in high-speed PCB designs if there is no net crossing between two buses on the same layer. If two buses are able to be assigned onto the same layer, the two buses can be defined to be compatible each other. For the layer assignment of the buses in high-speed PCB designs, if any pair of two buses in any assigned layer is compatible each other, the layer assignment can be further defined as a valid layer assignment. It is assumed that the nets in a single bus can be represented as a bus-oriented net between two escaped boundary pins and the global routing result of all the buses can be represented a set of bus-oriented nets for bus-oriented area routing. In a high-speed PCB design, given a set of n bus-oriented nets, $N = \{B_1, B_2,...,B_n\}$, among the boundaries on m circuit components, $C = \{C_1, C_2,...,C_m\}$, and the boundary on the PCB, U, with the consideration of the crossing constraint between two buses, the layer assignment problem for N is to minimize the number of the assigned layers to obtain a valid layer assignment for N and assign all the bus-oriented nets in N onto the used layers.

3. LAYER ASSIGNMENT OF BUS-ORIENTED NETS

In a high-speed PCB design, given a set of bus-oriented nets among the boundaries on some circuit components and the boundary, a proposed algorithm is proposed for the layer assignment of bus-oriented nets and the assignment process is further divided into four sequential phases: *Construction of virtual walls, Transformation from boundary to circle for bus-oriented nets, Optimal layer assignment of bus-oriented nets with covering constraint* and *Iterative covering compatibility for optimal layer assignment* as illustrated in Figure 1. Firstly, it is assumed that the nets in a single bus is represented as a bus-oriented net between two escaped boundary pins and the concept of a component connecting point(CCP) between two circuit components in Tasi's work[5] is modified into the concept of a virtual wall on empty space between two circuit components. Furthermore, the bus-oriented nets on a closed boundary can be transformed into the bus-oriented nets on a circle. Next, the number of the assigned layers can be minimized by using a left-edge algorithm if the covering relation between two bus-oriented nets is set as a constraint for layer assignment of bus-oriented nets. Finally, as the covering constraint between two bus-oriented nets is released for layer assignment of bus-oriented nets, the number of the assigned layers can be further minimized by using iterative covering compatibility.

4. EXPERIMENTAL RESULTS

In the layer assignment of bus-oriented nets in a high-speed PCB design, our proposed optimal algorithm has been implemented by using standard C++ language and run on a Intel Core2 Quad Q9450 2.66GHz machine with 2GB memory. Six tested examples, Board01, Board02, Board03, Board04, Board05 and Board06, are obtained from the used PCB designs. In Table I, "*#Block*" denotes the number of the circuit components "*#Net*" denotes the number of the given bus-oriented nets and "*#Layer*" denotes the number of the assigned layers for the given bus-oriented nets in a tested PCB design. Compared with Tsai's algorithm[5] and Chin's algorithm[6], the experimental results show that our proposed optimal algorithm reduces 16.2% and 16.2% of the assigned layers

and 60.7% and 39.3% of CPU time for six tested examples on the average, respectively.

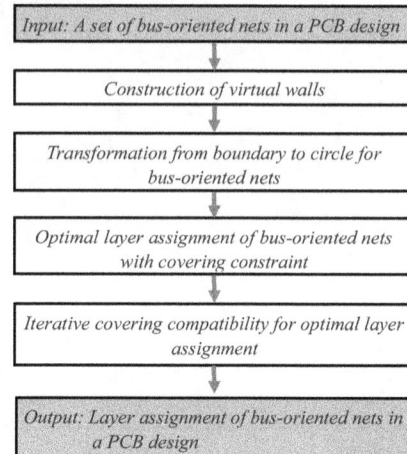

Figure 1 Design flow for layer assignment of bus-oriented nets in a high-speed PCB design

5. CONCLUSIONS

Based on the concept of a virtual wall between two circuit components and the optimality of interval packing in a left-edge algorithm, all the bus-oriented nets can be assigned onto the used layers.

6. REFERENCES

[1] M. M. Ozdal and D. F. Wong, "Simultaneous escape routing and layer assignment for dense PCBs," *IEEE/ACM International Conference on Computer-Aided Design*, pp.822-829, 2004.

[2] H. Kong, T. Yan, D. F. Wong and M. M. Ozdal, "Optimal bus sequencing for escape routing in dense PCBs," *International Conference on Computer-Aided Design*, pp.390-395, 2007.

[3] T. Yan, H. Kong and D. F. Wong, "Optimal layer assignment for escape routing of buses," *International Conference on Computer-Aided Design*, pp.245-248, 2009.

[4] J. T. Yan and Z. W. Chen, "New optimal layer assignment for bus-oriented escape routing" *ACM Great Lakes Symposium on VLSI*, pp.205-210, 2011.

[5] T. Y. Tsai, R. J. Lee, C. Y. Chin, C. Y. Kuan, H. M. Chen and Y. Kajitani, "On routing fixed escaped boundary pins for high-speed boards," *Design Automation & Test in Europe Conference*, pp.461-466, 2011.

[6] C. Y. Chin, C. Y. Kuan, T. Y. Tsai, H. M. Chen and Y. Kajitani, "Escaped boundary pins routing for high-speed boards," *IEEE Transactions on Computer-Aided Design of Integrated Circuits and Systems*, vol.32, no.3, pp. 381-391, 2012.

[7] K. J. Supowit, "Finding a maximum planar subset of a set of nets in a channel," *IEEE Transactions on Computer-Aided Design of Integrated Circuits and Systems*, vol.6, no.1, pp. 93-94, 1987.

TABLE I EXPERIMENTAL RESULTS FOR LAYER ASSIGNMENT OF BUS-ORIENTED NETS

	#Block	#Net	Tasi's Algorithm[5]		Chin's Algorithm[6]		Our Algorithm	
			#Layer	Time(s)	#Layer	Time(s)	#Layer	Time(s)
Board01	6	27	4(100%)	0.06(100%)	4(100%)	0.05(83.3%)	4(100%)	0.03(50.0%)
Board02	10	62	6(100%)	0.14(100%)	6(100%)	0.12(85.7%)	5(83.3%)	0.05(35.7%)
Board03	13	79	7(100%)	0.19(100%)	7(100%)	0.16(84.2%)	6(85.7%)	0.09(47.4%)
Board04	19	92	9(100%)	0.29(100%)	9(100%)	0.23(79.3%)	7(77.8%)	0.13(44.8%)
Board05	21	105	10(100%)	0.41(100%)	10(100%)	0.31(75.6%)	8(80.0%)	0.15(36.6%)
Board06	32	147	12(100%)	0.56(100%)	12(100%)	0.45(80.4%)	10(83.3%)	0.21(37.5%)
Average			8(100%)	0.28(100%)	8(100%)	0.22(78.6%)	6.7(83.8%)	0.11(39.3%)

An Automated Design Approach to Map Applications on CGRAs

Thomas Peyret, Gwenolé Corre, Mathieu Thevenin
CEA, LIST, Electronic Architectures and Sensors Laboratory
F-91191 Gif-sur-Yvette, France
+33 (0)1 69 08 27 85
firstname.lastname@cea.fr

Kevin Martin, Philippe Coussy
Université de Bretagne-Sud, Lab-STICC
Lorient, France
+33 (0)2 97 87 45 65
firstname.lastname@univ-ubs.fr

ABSTRACT

Coarse-Grained Reconfigurable Architectures (CGRAs) are promising high-performance and power-efficient platforms. However, their uses are still limited by the capability of mapping tools. This abstract paper outlines a new automated design flow to map applications on CGRAs. The interest of our method is shown through comparison with state of the art approaches.

Categories and Subject Descriptors

B.5.2 [**Register-Transfer-Level Implementation**]: Design Aids – *Automatic synthesis.*

Keywords

CGRA; Mapping; Scheduling; Binding;

1. INTRODUCTION

For the last two decades, Coarse-Grained Reconfigurable Architectures (CGRAs) have been mainly proposed for accelerating multimedia applications. CGRA are indeed an interesting trade-off between FPGAs and many-core architectures thanks to their power efficiency and programmability [9]. The literature is very rich in CGRAs architectures, which distinguish by different features such as the granularity of the Processing Elements (PE) named *tile*, homogeneity or heterogeneity of PE, type of operators, absence/presence of Register Files (RF) or interconnection network topologies. Figure 1 presents an example of CGRA.

The result of the "compilation" of an application on a CGRA (named *mapping*) is the scheduling and the binding of its operations on operators and registers. This NP-complete process [4] must be automated to allow efficient mapping of complex applications. Several methods have been proposed to tackle this problem. They are split in two categories i.e. (1) approaches that solve scheduling and binding separately with heuristics or meta-heuristics [2, 4, 7] or by combining an heuristic and an exact method [3] and (2) approaches that solve the whole problem entirely with exact method [1] or meta-heuristics [6, 8].

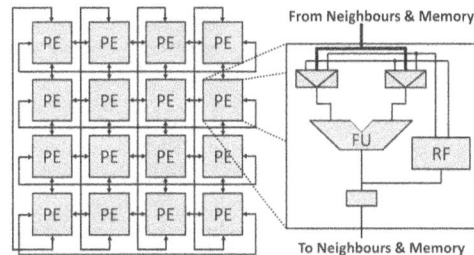

Figure 1 A 4×4 CGRA with 2D mesh torus and RF in each tile

This paper presents a unified approach that maps application on CGRAs. The proposed mapping flow relies on simultaneous scheduling and binding steps respectively based on a heuristic and an exact method followed by a pruning step. The graph of the application is backward traversed and dynamically transformed allowing a better exploration of the design space. This extended abstract paper is organized as follows. Section 2 depicts proposed method. Section 3 presents the experiments and discusses obtained results. Conclusion is given in Section 4.

2. PROPOSED METHOD

Our design flow is presented in Figure 2. Inputs are a C/C++ application code compiled to obtain a formal Control Data Flow Graph (CDFG) and the targeted CGRA's model. Objective of the method is to minimize latency under resource constraint. The proposed mapping approach allows exploring the design space while keeping computation time low.

The key idea is to combine the advantages of exact and heuristic methods while minimizing as much as possible their respective drawbacks. CDFG is mapped by processing each Data Flow Graph (DFG) of basic bloc sequentially. A list-scheduling based algorithm schedules nodes of each DFG. As it is a local greedy method, the binding is made simultaneously to ensure that at least one solution exists, hence avoiding dead-ends, and is realized incrementally by using an exact method derived from Levi's algorithm [5]. However, as exact methods do not scale up [4], a wise pruning step is executed at the end of each scheduling cycle to remove redundant partial mappings and thus keep a reasonable number of solutions during mapping process. Besides, DFGs are dynamically transformed as needed when no mapping (i.e. during scheduling or binding) solution is found. DFGs are also backward traversed to allow for using more different graph transformations.

3. EXPERIMENTS AND RESULTS

The proposed synthesis flow has been fully automated using Java. GCC has been used to generate CDFGs from applications. Five applications from signal processing domain have been used for our experiments: DC filter, Elliptic filter, Moving Exponential

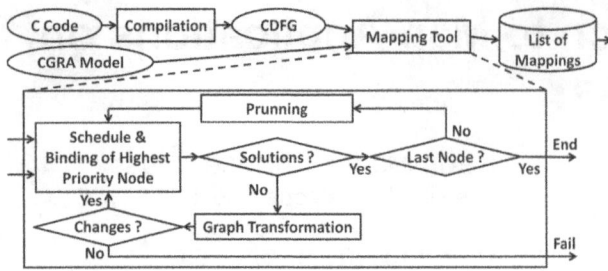

Figure 4 General Flow and Algorithm Core

Average Filter (EMA), Moving Window Deconvolution (MWD) and unsharp mask. To obtain a large spectrum of results, several constraints have been considered: CGRA size, RF size and the number of tiles the final mapping is allowed to use leading to 16 different set of constraints per application and per method.

The proposed approach is compared with two approaches from state of the art. The first, named "Method 1", solves the scheduling and the binding problem separately as the initial step of [4]. It uses a forward list scheduling algorithm and binding is made by using Levi's algorithm. "Method 2" forward traverses the graph, schedules nodes by applying statically graph transformations and tries to find a mapping by using Levi's algorithm as proposed in [3] (that have been shown to provide better results than [8]).

Two metrics were considered: (1) success rate (percentage of time the method finds a solution when at least one of the compared methods succeeds) and (2) percentage of time the method gives the best latency between the compared methods. Figure 3 and Figure 4 give the comparisons between the three methods for the previously defined metrics.

Figure 3 shows that Method 1, which solves scheduling and binding totally separately, leads to the lowest success rate (~56%). Method 2, which transforms the graph *a priori*, provides better results (~67%) but is not as good as the proposed approach (~98%). Figure 4 shows the percentage of time each

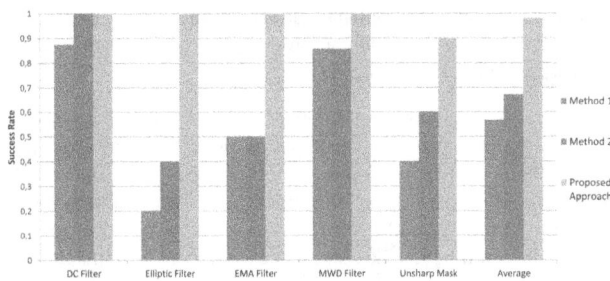

Figure 2 Success Rate

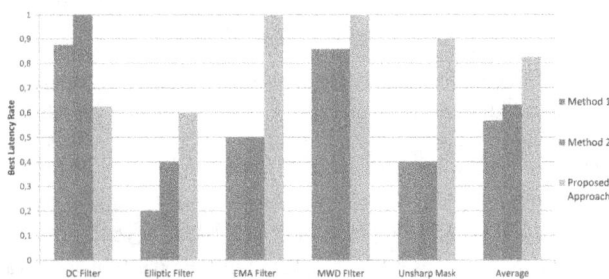

Figure 3 Percentage of a method for obtaining the best latency

method found the best latency and shows that the Proposed Method finds it most of the time (~82%) even if it relies on a heuristic-based scheduling algorithm, while the Methods 1 and 2 find it for respectively 57% and 63% of the benchmark.

4. CONCLUSION

In this paper, a generic method to map applications written in high level language on CGRA architectures has been presented. Experimental results show that this method finds 82% of time the best latency, has the highest success rate and achieves 2.2 times better mappings throughput compared to the other methods and thus achieves a very good exploration of the solution space.

5. REFERENCES

[1] Brenner, J.A., Veen, J.C. van der, Fekete, S.P., Oliveira Filho, J. and Rosenstiel, W. 2006. Optimal Simultaneous Scheduling, Binding and Routing for Processor-like Reconfigurable Architectures. *Field Programmable Logic and Applications, International Conference on* (2006).

[2] Friedman, S., Carroll, A., Van Essen, B., Ebeling, C., Hauck, S. and Ylvisaker, B. 2009. SPR: an architecture-adaptive CGRA mapping tool. *Proceedings of the ACM/SIGDA international symposium on Field programmable gate arrays* (2009), 191–200.

[3] Hamzeh, M., Shrivastava, A. and Vrudhula, S. 2013. REGIMap: register-aware application mapping on coarse-grained reconfigurable architectures (CGRAs). *Design Automation Conference* (2013).

[4] Lee, G., Choi, K. and Dutt, N.D. 2011. Mapping multi-domain applications onto coarse-grained reconfigurable architectures. *Computer-Aided Design of Intergrated Circuits and Systems, IEEE Transactions on*. 30, 5 (2011), 637–650.

[5] Levi, G. 1973. A note on the derivation of maximal common subgraphs of two directed or undirected graphs. *Calcolo*. 9, 4 (Dec. 1973), 341–352.

[6] Mei, B., Vernalde, S., Verkest, D., De Man, H. and Lauwereins, R. 2002. DRESC: A retargetable compiler for coarse-grained reconfigurable architectures. *Field-Programmable Technology, 2002. (FPT). IEEE International Conference on* (2002), 166–173.

[7] Park, H., Fan, K., Mahlke, S.A., Oh, T., Kim, H. and Kim, H.-S. 2008. Edge-centric modulo scheduling for coarse-grained reconfigurable architectures. *Proceedings of the 17th international conference on Parallel architectures and compilation techniques* (2008).

[8] De Sutter, B., Coene, P., Vander Aa, T. and Mei, B. 2008. Placement-and-routing-based register allocation for coarse-grained reconfigurable arrays. *ACM SIGPLAN Notices*. 43, 7 (Jun. 2008), 151.

[9] Taylor, M.B. 2012. Is dark silicon useful?: harnessing the four horsemen of the coming dark silicon apocalypse. *Design Automation Conference* (2012).

He-P2012: Architectural Heterogeneity Exploration on a Scalable Many-Core Platform

Francesco Conti
University of Bologna

Chuck Pilkington
STMicroelectronics

Andrea Marongiu
Univ. of Bologna & ETH Zurich

Luca Benini
Univ. of Bologna & ETH Zurich

ABSTRACT

Architectural heterogeneity is a promising solution to overcome the utilization wall and provide Moore's Law-like performance scaling in future SoCs. However, heterogeneous architectures increase the size and complexity of the design space, and significant enhancements are required to tools and methodologies to explore this design space effectively. In this work, we describe an extension to the STMicroelectronics P2012 platform and simulation flow to support tightly-coupled shared memory HW processing elements (HWPE), we propose a methodology for the semi-automatic instantiation of HWPEs from a C program, and we explore several architectural variants on a set of computer vision benchmarks.

Categories and Subject Descriptors

C.1.3 [**Processor Architectures**]: Other Architecture Styles—*heterogeneous (hybrid) systems*

Keywords

heterogeneous many-core; hardware acceleration; high-level synthesis; HW/SW codesign

1. HARDWARE ARCHITECTURE

We propose here *He-P2012*, an heterogeneous extension to the P2012 platform (see Benini et al.[1]). In He-P2012, the tightly-coupled clusters are augmented with a set of HW accelerators that communicate with PEs via the same shared L1 data memory (a scratchpad) used by the PEs themselves. These tightly-coupled shared memory HW Processing Elements or *HWPEs* [3] address the shortcomings of more traditional copy-based accelerator models, such as the necessity to transfer and maintain coherent multiple copies of data between distinct processor and accelerator memory spaces. In addition, they diminish the semantic gap between executing a task in SW or HW: from a programming perspective, dispatching a HW task on a HW IP is not different from

GLSVLSI'14, May 21–23, 2014, Houston, Texas, USA.
ACM 978-1-4503-2816-6/14/05.
http://dx.doi.org/10.1145/2591513.2591553 .

calling a SW function to perform the same task. The HW IP can be developed directly from the original software function by means of standard methodologies (e.g., HLS tools) with no additional programmer effort, which is connected to a custom wrapper to provide communication with the cluster [2].

2. EXPLORATION FLOW

We automated many of the steps required to create an executable simulation; the user is exclusively responsible for i) writing the application source code, using a programming model such as OpenCL or OpenMP, ii) writing the definition of the HW/SW interface in a custom language, and iii) extracting the functions to be accelerated into separate C files. The tool flow uses this information to automatically generate all of the underlying glue code that is required to execute the application on our heterogeneous platform, using a custom compiler called SIDL.

On the hardware side, the compiler produces scripts to drive the HLS tool (Calypto Catapult) in the synthesis of the HWPEs, and files needed to simulate the hardware models. On the software side, the SIDL compiler generates a C API that can be used by the OpenCL or OpenMP kernels in the simulation.

The output of the tool is a cycle-accurate SystemC model of the HWPEs for the application at hand, plus all the wrappers and other components to bind the HWPEs to the GEPOP platform.

3. RESULTS

For our experiments we considered four applications: *object recognition* (Viola-Jones [6]), *FAST* circular corner detection

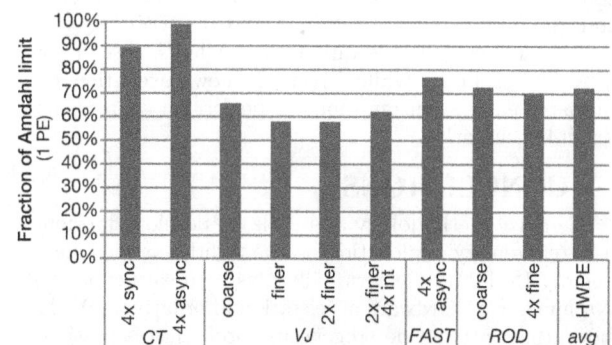

Figure 1: Speedup with 1 PE + HWPEs in % of Amdahl's limit

(a) Execution time

(b) Energy consumption

(c) Performance/Area/Energy

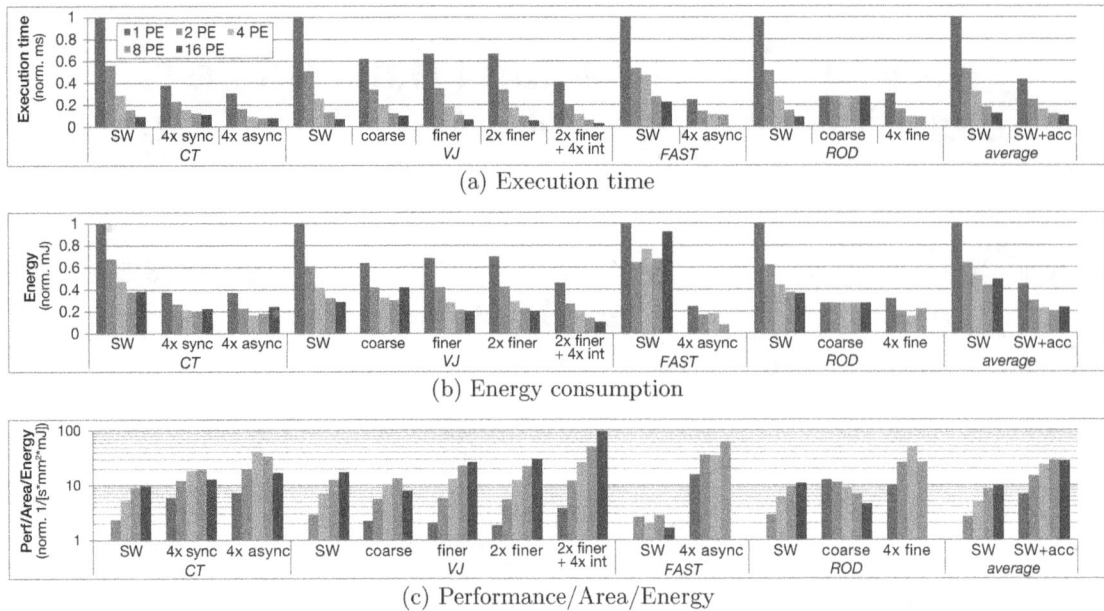

Figure 2: Benchmark results, normalized on SW execution on a single PE. The labels indicate the type and number of the HWPEs used.

[5], *removed object detection* – based on normalized cross-correlation (NCC) [4] – and a parallel version of *color tracking* from the OpenCV library. Object recognition is parallelized with OpenCL, while the other benchmarks use OpenMP.

Color Tracking (**CT**) is composed of three kernels: color scale conversion (*CSC*), color based threshold (*TH*) and moment based center of gravity computation (*MOM*). The most computationally intensive kernel is CSC, which we chose for HW acceleration.

Viola-Jones object recognition (**VJ**) includes two kernels: `cascade` and `int_image`. We accelerated the `cascade` alone at two levels of granularity (*coarse* and *finer* HWPEs), and in one experiment also the `integral_image` (*int*).

FAST circular detection (**FAST**) is composed of two kernels, `detection` and `score`, that were merge in one HWPE.

Removed Object Detection (**ROD**) has one kernel, *NCC*. We accelerated it at two granularities (*coarse* and *fine*). In the *coarse* case, only one PE is used, acting mainly as a controller.

We collect results for three different metrics: execution time, energy, performance/area/energy. We measure execution time as seen by the controlling PEs, and area/energy from the RTL version of the cores and the HWPEs.

Figure 1 shows the speedup in the single-PE case in terms of Amdahl's limit, while Figure 2 shows execution time, estimated energy consumption and performance/area/energy for all benchmarks.

4. CONCLUSIONS

The novel methodology and tools we developed, oriented at heterogeneity exploration on the tightly-coupled shared-memory He-P2012 platform, allow fast and easy exploration of a number of hardware acceleration alternatives. We have shown that with our heterogeneous approach it is possible to obtain a significant advantage with respect to pure software in terms of performance, energy consumption and performance/area/energy.

Our results are promising, as we show an average 4.3x gain in perf/area/energy on the equivalent homogeneous benchmarks, with our HWPEs exploiting on average 71.3% of Amdahl's limit.

5. REFERENCES

[1] L. Benini, E. Flamand, D. Fuin, and D. Melpignano. P2012: Building an ecosystem for a scalable, modular and high-efficiency embedded computing accelerator. *Design, Automation & Test in Europe Conference & Exhibition (DATE), 2012*, pages 983–987, Mar. 2012.

[2] F. Conti, A. Marongiu, and L. Benini. Synthesis-friendly techniques for tightly-coupled integration of hardware accelerators into shared-memory multi-core clusters. In *2013 International Conference on Hardware/Software Codesign and System Synthesis (CODES+ISSS)*, pages 1–10. IEEE, Sept. 2013.

[3] M. Dehyadegari, A. Marongiu, M. R. Kakoee, L. Benini, S. Mohammadi, and N. Yazdani. A tightly-coupled multi-core cluster with shared-memory HW accelerators. *2012 International Conference on Embedded Computer Systems (SAMOS)*, pages 96–103, July 2012.

[4] M. Magno, F. Tombari, D. Brunelli, L. Di Stefano, and L. Benini. Multimodal Abandoned/Removed Object Detection for Low Power Video Surveillance Systems. *2009 Sixth IEEE International Conference on Advanced Video and Signal Based Surveillance*, pages 188–193, Sept. 2009.

[5] E. Rosten and T. Drummond. Fusing points and lines for high performance tracking. *Tenth IEEE International Conference on Computer Vision (ICCV'05) Volume 1*, pages 1508–1515 Vol. 2, 2005.

[6] P. Viola and M. Jones. Rapid object detection using a boosted cascade of simple features. *Computer Vision and Pattern Recognition, 2001. CVPR 2001*, 1:I–511–I–518, 2001.

On Macro-Fault: A New Fault Model, Its Implications On Fault Tolerance And Manufacturing Yield

Tak-Kei Lam
Departmant of Computer
Science and Engineering
The Chinese University of
Hong Kong
Hong Kong
tklam@cse.cuhk.edu.hk

Xing Wei
Departmant of Computer
Science and Engineering
The Chinese University of
Hong Kong
Hong Kong
xwei@cse.cuhk.edu.hk

Wen-Ben Jone
School of Electronic and
Computing Systems
University of Cincinnati
Cincinnati, Ohio
jonewb@ucmail.uc.edu

Yi Diao
Departmant of Computer
Science and Engineering
The Chinese University of
Hong Kong
Hong Kong
ydiao@cse.cuhk.edu.hk

Yu-Liang Wu
Departmant of Computer
Science and Engineering
The Chinese University of
Hong Kong
Hong Kong
ylw@cse.cuhk.edu.hk

ABSTRACT

A macro-fault is defined as a group of signal faults such that the errors induced cannot be observed unless two or more faults (either permanent or temporary) in the group happen simultaneously. Since adding a redundant (alternative) wire for an existing (target) wire can mask some certain faults of these two wires mutually, a macro-fault can be formed by redundant wire addition. The faults that are dominated by or equivalent to the masked faults are also included in the macro-fault. As the feature size of integrated circuit technologies continue to scale down, manufacturing fault-free chips is getting more difficult and fault tolerance techniques will become more critical. In the past, redundancy has been adopted for memory for improving fault tolerance. For critical circuit components, even the costly triple modular redundancy techniques have to be applied. In this work, we study the implications of our new fault model, macro-fault, on the potential impact on fault tolerance and manufacturing yield. Based on the findings, a heuristic approach based on redundant wire addition is designed for improving fault tolerance. The approach can be incorporated with other fault tolerance techniques to form a hierarchical cross-layer fault tolerance scheme.

Categories and Subject Descriptors

B.6 [**LOGIC DESIGN**]: Design Aids; B.6.3 [**Automatic synthesis**]: Optimization

GLSVLSI'14, May 21–23, 2014, Houston, Texas, USA.
ACM 978-1-4503-2816-6/14/05.
http://dx.doi.org/10.1145/2591513.2591556.

Keywords

fault tolerance; redundancy addition; logic synthesis; re-wiring

1. INTRODUCTION

Faults can be made non-destructive by logic masking which can be achieved by redundant wire addition. A logically redundant wire of a circuit is a wire whose existence does not change the correctness of the circuit's function. There are several related works [1] that apply rewiring [2] [3] and other logic restructuring techniques to improve soft error rates. In [4], the authors proposed adding redundant wires selectively to mitigate soft errors. However, the underlying theories of redundancy addition and yield improvement are not much studied in the previous studies. In this paper, we propose a new fault model and a new paradigm for fault tolerance. Redundant wire addition for fault tolerance is analysed by investigating the relationship among fault tolerance, rewiring, and fault dominance.

2. LOGIC REDUNDANCY AND FAULT TOLERANCE

2.1 Macro-Fault

Definition 1. A macro-fault is a set of wire faults such that any single fault in the set, regardless of being soft or permanent, is guaranteed to be masked (untestable). If more than one fault in the set occurs simultaneously, the macro-fault is testable. The size of a macro-fault is the number of faults in the set.

Definition 2. If every pair of faults belonging to two different macro-faults occur simultaneously, and do not produce observable output for any input, these two macro-faults are said to be mutually independent.

LEMMA 2.1. *If there are m independent macro-faults and at most m faults in a circuit, and each of the faults belongs to an independent macro-fault, the faults are unobservable (The circuit behaves as if it is fault-free).*

PROOF. By definition, a single fault of a macro-fault is masked. Since all the faults are contained in a macro-fault, and the macro-faults are independent, no error effects are observable. □

2.2 Constructing Untestable Faults

Suppose faults f_1 and f_2 have sets of test vectors V_{f_1} and V_{f_2} respectively.

LEMMA 2.2. *Suppose a fault f_1 is masked. If the fault f_1 dominates another fault f_2, or if f_1 is equivalent to f_2, it is true that f_2 is also masked.*

PROOF. If f_1 dominates (or is equivalent to) f_2, V_{f_2} must be a subset (same set) of V_{f_1}. When f_1 is masked, there will be no input vector to test it. If f_2 is not masked then it must have some test vectors which should also be able to test f_1, a contradiction. □

In a combinational circuit, the primary inputs and fanout branches are called "checkpoints". According to the Checkpoint Theorem [5], the set of test vectors that detects all single stuck-at faults on all checkpoints of a combinational circuit, also detects all single stuck-at faults in that circuit.

LEMMA 2.3. *All fault dominance paths stop at the checkpoints.*

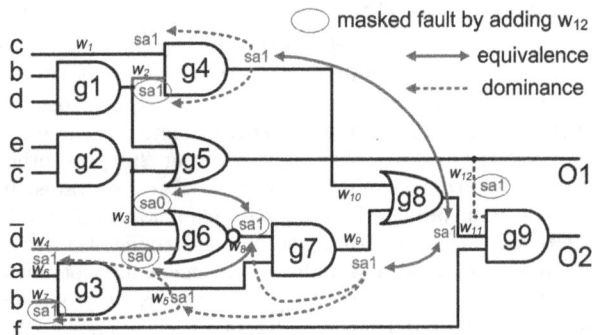

Figure 1: Redundant wire and fault dominance

According to Lemma 2.2, dominating faults should be masked first to achieve higher fault masking rate. Lemma 2.3 suggests we should try to mask faults near POs first. We use Figure 1 to illustrate an example of fault masking by redundant wire addition and dominance relation. Suppose the redundant wire w_{12} does not exist in the beginning. We try to make $sa1(w_{11})$ untestable by rewiring because it is the root of of a fault dominance graph.

2.3 Keeping Untestable Faults

Faults that have previously been made untestable may become testable because of the subsequent redundancy additions. For instance, the fault $sa0(a \rightarrow e)$ in Figure 2 has been untestable in Figure 2a but is no longer untestable in Figure 2b due to the addition of a redundant wire $e \rightarrow a2$. The effect of adding a redundant wire, whether it removes some untestable faults, can be estimated by analysing the logic implication history of the current and all previous wire additions.

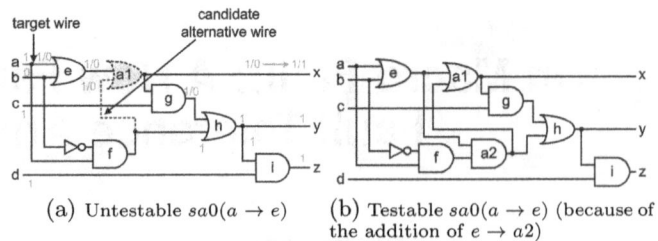

(a) Untestable $sa0(a \rightarrow e)$ (b) Testable $sa0(a \rightarrow e)$ (because of the addition of $e \rightarrow a2$)

Figure 2: Example of rewiring

3. HEURISTIC OPTIMIZATION FLOW

Algorithm 1 is the outline of our greedy incremental optimization flow that aims at increasing the fault masking rate while keeping the cost low.

Algorithm 1: Redundancy addition for improving fault tolerance

input : circuit c
1 **begin**
2    $W = \mathtt{Wires}(c)$;
3   **foreach** *target wire t in W* **do**
4      $AW_t = \mathtt{FindAltWires}(t)$;
5   **foreach** *alternative wire aw_t in AW_t* **do**
6   **if** *aw_t cannot create more or larger macro-faults* **then**
7          $\lfloor$ Skip;
8        $aw_t^* = aw_t$;
9   Break;
10   AddWire (c, aw_t^*);
11 **end**

---

4. CONCLUSION

We have introduced the notion of a new macro-fault model and a heuristic for maximizing the addition of redundant wires. Simulation-based experimental results demonstrate that on average 21.48% of faults can be masked by an addition of 25.16% hardware. How to do a selective and limited redundant addition with a good balance on various objectives, so as to acheive a higher fault tolerance rate would be a non-trivial and worthwhile topic for us to explore next.

5. REFERENCES

[1] S. Krishnaswamy, S. Plaza, I. Markov, and J. Hayes, "Signature-based ser analysis and design of logic circuits," *Computer-Aided Design of Integrated Circuits and Systems, IEEE Transactions on*, vol. 28, pp. 74 –86, jan. 2009.

[2] S. C. Chang and M. Marek-Sadowska, "Perturb and Simplify: Multilevel Boolean Network Optimizer," *IEEE Trans. on Computer-Aided Design of Integrated Circuits and Systems*, vol. 15, pp. 1494–1504, December 1996.

[3] L. Entrena and K.-T. Cheng, "Combinational and sequential logic optimization by redundancy addition and removal," *Computer-Aided Design of Integrated Circuits and Systems, IEEE Transactions on*, vol. 14, pp. 909–916, Jul 1995.

[4] S. Almukhaizim and Y. Makris, "Soft error mitigation through selective addition of functionally redundant wires," *Reliability, IEEE Transactions on*, vol. 57, pp. 23 –31, march 2008.

[5] M. Abramovici, P. Menon, and D. Miller, "Checkpoint faults are not sufficient target faults for test generation," *Computers, IEEE Transactions on*, vol. C-35, pp. 769 –771, aug. 1986.

Transient Analysis of Gate Inside Junctionless Transistor (GI-JLT)

Pankaj Kumar, P. N. Kondekar, Sangeeta Singh
Email:(pankajjha, pnkondekar, sangeeta.singh)@iiitdmj.ac.in

ABSTRACT

In this letter, the transient performance analysis of n-type Gate Inside JunctionLess Transistor (GI-JLT) has been evaluated. 3-D Bohm Quantum Potential (BQP) transport device simulation has been used to evaluate its delay and power dissipation performance. GI-JLT shows better device performance characteristics than GAA-JLT for low power and high frequency applications, because of its larger gate electrostatic control on the device operation.

Keywords

gate-all-around, junctionless transistors, gate-inside.

1. INTRODUCTION

Junctionless field-effect transistors (JL-FET) represent a new class of field effects devices having no abrupt doping junctions. It has been recently revisited by J.-P. Colinge and coworkers [1]. In recent research for area scaling benefits of JLT [2] and gate-all-around (GAA) architecture [3] is reported for fabricating JL devices. To enhance the gate electrostatic control in nano-devices a new kind of structure Gate Inside Junctionless Transistor (GI-JLT) has been proposed. GI-JLT is reported to show better analog and digital performance in comparison with GAA-JLT [4]. In this paper, the transient performance analysis of n-type GI-JLT has been reported.

2. DEVICE STRUCTURE AND SIMULATION

Fig. 1 shows device structure of n-channel GIJLT having the device layer Doping N_d is of uniform profile having the value $3.5 \times 10^{19} cm^{-3}$ and the work-function of gate is $5.1 eV$. Fig. 2 shows the device structure for n-channel GAA-JLT with identical doping profile, and gate workfunction of 4.9 eV. For simulations, TCAD simulator 3-D ATLAS version 2.10.18.R is used.

GLSVLSI'14, May 21–23, 2014, Houston, Texas, USA.
ACM 978-1-4503-2816-6/14/05.
http://cms.acm.org/forms/prform.cfm?confID=020500041C0500040001
&proceedingID=06050009&paperID=0406&sequence=1.

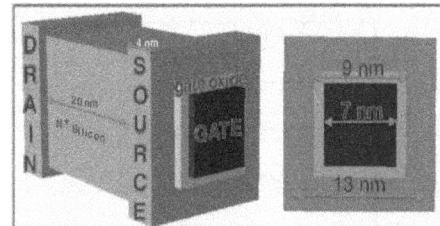

Figure 1: Proposed n-type GI-JLT

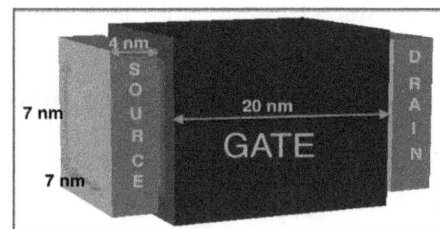

Figure 2: Device structure of n-type GAA-JLT

3. SIMULATION RESULTS AND DISCUSSION

Transient performance parameters of both GI-JLT and GAA-JLT are evaluated and compared in this section. Fig. 3 shows the plot for drain current of n-channel GI-JLT and GAA-JLT as a function of V_{ds}.

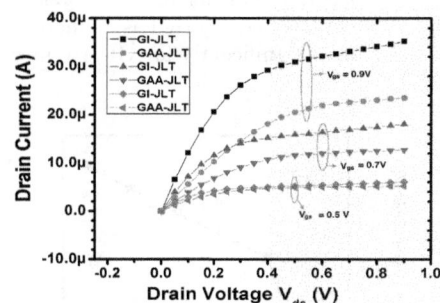

Figure 3: I_d v/s. V_{ds} for n-channel GI-JLT and GAA-JLT.

Fig. 4 shows the plot for C_{gs} and C_{gd} of n-channel GI-JLT and GAA-JLT as a function of V_{gs} for $V_{ds} = 0.9V$. The specific gate capacitance should be as large as possible in order to obtain a very strong electrostatic field-effect modulation for I_d. In JLTs C_{gg} is extracted in similar manner as in the conventional inversion mode device, i.e, oxide capacitance C_{ox} in series with the silicon capacitance (C_{Si}). Hence, minimum gate capacitance $C_{gg,min}$ is defined as

$$C_{gg,min} = \frac{C_{ox} \times C_{Si,min}}{C_{ox} + C_{Si,min}} \qquad (1)$$

where, $C_{Si,min}$ is given by the relation

$$C_{Si,min} = \frac{\epsilon_{Si}}{d_{max}} \qquad (2)$$

where, d_{max} is the maximum depletion region depth.

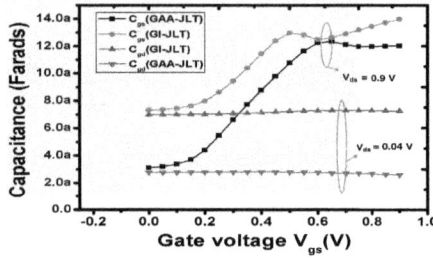

Figure 4: C_{gs} and C_{gd} v/s. V_{gs} for n-channel GI-JLT and GAA-JLT.

Intrinsic gate delay is important as it represents the frequency limit of the transistor operation. In JLTs it is because of its parasitic gate capacitance C_{gg}, it is defined as

$$\tau_{int} = \frac{C_{gg} \times V_{dd}}{I_d} \qquad (3)$$

where, τ_{int} is the intrinsic gate delay. Fig. 5 shows the plot for the intrinsic gate delay as a function of V_{ds} for GI-JLT and GAA-JLT. GI-JLT is showing better intrinsic delay performance for low power applications. Dynamic power dissipation defined as

$$P_{dyn} = C_{gg} \times V_{dd}^2 \times f \qquad (4)$$

where, f is the operating frequency (1 GHz) and P_{dyn} is dynamic power dissipation. It is plotted as a function of V_{ds} in Fig. 6. It is comparable for both at lower V_{ds} values. Power delay product has been plotted as a function of V_{ds} in Fig. 7, that enhances significantly for GI-JLT as compared with GAA-JLT.

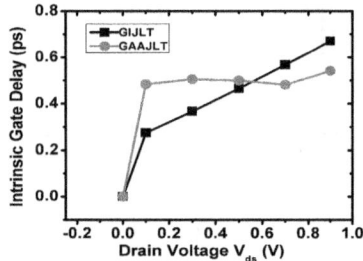

Figure 5: Intrinsic gate delay v/s. V_{ds} for both GI-JLT and GAA-JLT.

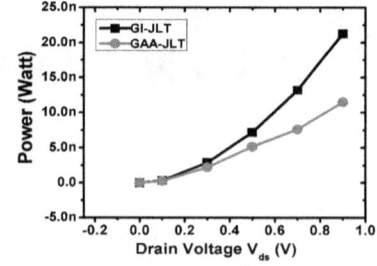

Figure 6: Dynamic power dissipation v/s. V_{ds} for GI-JLT and GAA-JLT

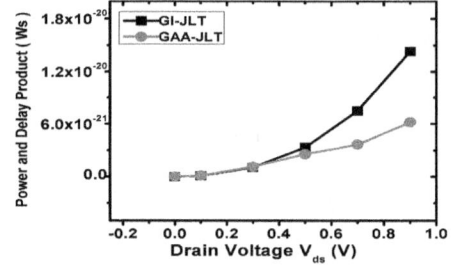

Figure 7: Power delay product v/s. V_{ds} for GI-JLT and GAA-JLT

4. CONCLUSION

In this paper, transient performance analysis of n-type GI-JLT has been reported. GI-JLT exhibits better transient characteristics namely, reduced intrinsic gate delay and dynamic power dissipation for lower V_{ds} values and high frequencies. Hence, power delay product and energy delay product also get enhanced at low power levels. These improvements are because of its larger gate electrostatic control on the device operation. Hence, GI-JLT is the potential candidate for future low power and high frequency applications.

5. REFERENCES

[1] J.-P. Colinge, C.-W. Lee, A. Afzalian, N. D. Akhavan, R. Yan, I. Ferain, P. Razavi, B. O'Neill, A. Blake, M. White et al., "Nanowire transistors without junctions," Nature Nanotechnology, vol. 5, no. 3, pp. 225–229, 2010.

[2] H. M. Fahad, C. E. Smith, J. P. Rojas, and M. M. Hussain, "Silicon nanotube field effect transistor with core–shell gate stacks for enhanced high-performance operation and area scaling benefits," Nano letters, vol. 11, no. 10, pp. 4393–4399, 2011.

[3] B. Sorée, W. Magnus, and G. Pourtois, "Analytical and self-consistent quantum mechanical model for a surrounding gate MOS nanowire operated in JFET mode," Journal of computational electronics, vol. 7, no. 3, pp. 380–383, 2008.

[4] P. Kumar, S. Singh, P. Kondekar, and A. Dixit, "Digital and analog performance of gate inside p-type junctionless transistor (GI-JLT)," in CIMSim2013, 5th International Conference on Computational Intelligence, Modelling and Simulation (CIMSim2013), Seoul, Korea, Sep. 2013.

Built-In Generation of Functional Broadside Tests Considering Primary Input Constraints

Bo Yao*, Irith Pomeranz*, Srikanth Venkataraman[†], and Enamul Amyeen[†]

*ECE Purdue University, [†]Intel Corporation

*{yaob, pomeranz}@purdue.edu, [†]{srikanth.venkataraman, enamul.amyeen}@intel.com

ABSTRACT

This paper describes a method for built-in generation of functional broadside tests for a circuit that is embedded in a larger design, taking functional constraints on its primary input sequences into account. The constraints are captured by functional input sequences of the design. Specifically, the peak switching activity in the circuit under the functional input sequences is used to bound the switching activity during on-chip test generation.

Categories and Subject Descriptors

B.6.2 [**Logic Design**]: Reliability and Testing---Built-in tests; B.7.3 [**Integrated Circuits**]: Reliability and Testing---Built-in tests; B.8.1 [**Performance and Reliability**]: Reliability, Testing and Fault-tolerance.

Keywords

Built-in test generation; functional broadside tests; primary input constraints; transition faults

1. INTRODUCTION

Built-in test generation is cost-effective for delay testing. Using arbitrary states as the scan-in states of the two-pattern tests for delay faults in such techniques introduces non-functional operation conditions during test application. This may lead to higher switching activity (SWA) than normal, and overtesting may occur. To address the issue, the built-in test generation method in [1] generates functional broadside tests [2]. Assuming that the primary inputs (PIs) are unconstrained, a functional broadside test is a broadside test whose scan-in state is a reachable state (a state that the circuit can enter during functional operation). It detects faults under functional operation conditions to eliminate overtesting. In [1], PI sequences are generated on-chip and applied to the circuit starting from a known reachable state. The circuit traverses only reachable states, and functional broadside tests can be obtained from the PI sequences and the corresponding reachable states.

However, a circuit is typically embedded in a larger design that imposes constraints on its PI sequences. Without considering such constraints, certain state-transitions that cannot occur during functional operation may be allowed by the method in [1]. As a result, the SWA during test application may exceed that possible during functional operation, and overtesting may occur. This paper extends the method in [1] to avoid the potential overtesting due to excessive SWA caused by ignoring the PI constraints for a circuit embedded in a larger design. We use functional input sequences of the complete design to capture the PI constraints. The constraints are considered by using the peak SWA that can occur in the

Permission to make digital or hard copies of part or all of this work for personal or classroom use is granted without fee provided that copies are not made or distributed for profit or commercial advantage, and that copies bear this notice and the full citation on the first page. Copyrights for third-party components of this work must be honored. For all other uses, contact the Owner/Author. Copyright is held by the author/owner(s).

GLSVLSI'14, May 21-23, 2014, Houston, Texas, USA.

ACM 978-1-4503-2816-6/14/05.

http://dx.doi.org/10.1145/2591513.2591560

This work was supported in part by SRC Grant No. 2011-TJ-2135.

circuit under these sequences as a bound. The proposed method generates PI sequences under which the circuit only makes state-transitions whose SWAs are no higher than the bound starting from a reachable state. For benchmark circuits, high transition fault coverage can be achieved using simple hardware.

2. BUILT-IN TEST GENERATION WITH UNCONSTRAINED PRIMARY INPUTS

In the method from [1], the circuit is first initialized into a reachable state $s_{initial}$. A PI sequence $P=p(0)p(1)\cdots p(L-1)$ of a fixed length L is generated by a test pattern generator (TPG), where $p(i)$ is the PI vector at clock cycle i, for $0 \leq i < L$. P is applied to the circuit in functional mode and takes it through a state sequence $S=s(0)s(1)\cdots s(L)$, where $s(0)=s_{initial}$ and $s(i)$ is the next-state the circuit enters when its PIs are driven by $p(i-1)$ and its present state is $s(i-1)$, for $0 < i \leq L$. A functional broadside test can be defined by any two consecutive clock cycles from P and S. The test that starts at clock cycle i is denoted by $t(i)=<s(i), p(i), s(i+1), p(i+1)>$ with $s(i+2)$ as its final state. Tests are applied every q clock cycles ($q \geq 2$), and the test responses are compacted by a MISR.

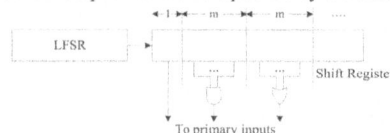

Figure 1. The TPG

Figure 1 shows the TPG in this paper. An LFSR with a fixed number of bits drives a shift register whose states are used as pseudo-random vectors for the PIs of the circuit. The PI sequence is modified by inserting additional logic gates at certain PIs based on a PI cube to avoid repeated synchronization [3]. If a logic gate needs to be inserted at input i, a distinct set of m shift register bits are fed into the m-input gate to bias the probabilities of 0 and 1 on input i. Otherwise, a single shift register bit drives input i. Multiple PI sequences can be applied by using different LFSR seeds.

3. BUILT-IN TEST GENERATION WITH CONSTRAINED PRIMARY INPUTS

Since it is typically not possible to completely represent the PI constraints in closed form and synthesize simple hardware in the TPG to satisfy them [4], we use functional input sequences to capture them. SWA_{func}, the peak SWA that can occur in the circuit under these sequences, is used to bound the SWA of the functional broadside tests generated on-chip so that it will not exceed that possible during functional operation with constrained PIs. Overtesting caused by excessive SWA is therefore alleviated.

For a PI sequence $P=p(0)p(1)...p(L-1)$, we use SWA(i) to denote the SWA in clock cycle i. SWA(i) is defined as the percentage of lines whose values in clock cycle i are different from their values in clock cycle i-1. Let $S=s(0)s(1)...s(L)$ be the state sequence the circuit traverses starting from s(0) under P. It is possible to identify a subsequence $P_{k,w}=p(k)p(k+1)\cdots p(w-1)$ ($0 \leq k < w \leq L$) of P as acceptable if $SWA(i) \leq SWA_{func}$ ($k < i < w$). When $P_{k,w}$ is applied for on-chip test generation, a new LFSR seed should be loaded so that the TPG can generate the subsequence starting from p(k). In addition, the circuit should be initialized into s(k) by scanning in s(k). However, storing the scan-in states requires extra memory.

In this paper, we only use one reachable state $s_{initial}$ to initialize the circuit. We construct PI sequences so that when they are applied to the circuit starting from $s_{initial}$, the SWA in each clock cycle does not exceed SWA_{func}, and the fault coverage is as high as possible. We construct a PI sequence from segments where each segment is obtained through the TPG using a different LFSR seed. We use $P_{multi}=P_{seg}(0)P_{seg}(1)P_{seg}(2)...P_{seg}(N_{seg}-1)$ to denote a multi-segment PI sequence, where $P_{seg}(i)$ is a PI segment ($0 \le i < N_{seg}$), and N_{seg} is the number of segments included in P_{multi}. During the application of P_{multi}, different LFSR seeds are loaded at certain clock cycles to generate the PI segments. The state of the circuit is held when a new LFSR seed is loaded so that the application of the new PI segment can start from the final state of the previous segment. The segments are selected so that during the application of P_{multi}, the SWA in each clock cycle is no higher than SWA_{func}.

A simulation-based procedure selects $P_{seg}(i)$ and constructs P_{multi} as follows. Initially we have $P_{multi}=\emptyset$. A PI sequence P of length L is generated using the TPG based on a random LFSR seed. The procedure applies P to the circuit starting from state s_{start}. If i=0, $s_{start}=s_{initial}$. Otherwise, s_{start} is the final state of $P_{seg}(i-1)$. The procedure examines the SWA in each clock cycle under P until the first violation SWA(j+1)>SWA_{func} is identified at clock cycle j+1. The tests are obtained every two consecutive clock cycles in this paper, so we have $P_{seg}(i)=P_{0,j}$ if j is even, or $P_{seg}(i)=P_{0,j-1}$ if j is odd, so that the final state of $P_{seg}(i)$ is the final state of the last test obtained from $P_{0,j}$. Then the procedure checks whether the tests obtained from $P_{seg}(i)$ detect additional faults. If so, $P_{seg}(i)$ is concatenated to P_{mulit} and the procedure starts selecting $P_{seg}(i+1)$. Otherwise, the current seed fails and a new seed is considered for selecting $P_{seg}(i)$ again. The procedure stops constructing P_{multi} if the last R seeds fail to select $P_{seg}(i)$ for a constant R. To obtain more tests, the procedure attempts to construct multiple multi-segment PI sequences. An attempt fails if $P_{seg}(0)$ cannot be selected. The procedure stops constructing new multi-segment PI sequences if the last Q attempts fail for a constant Q.

4. EXPERIMENTAL RESULTS

The proposed method was implemented and applied to ISCAS89, ITC99 and IWLS2005 benchmark circuits. Fastscan (Mentor Graphics) was used for logic and fault simulation. For area overhead evaluation, the required hardware was synthesized except the MISR and the shift register on the PIs. PIs of an embedded block are typically driven by registers. Such registers can be reused for the shift register. Only benchmark circuits where the area overhead of built-in test generation may be acceptable are considered.

PI constraints are created for a target circuit by connecting it with another circuit such that all of its PIs are driven by the primary outputs (POs) of the driving block. Each benchmark circuit is considered as the driving block if it has no less POs than the PIs of the target circuit. We also consider the case of no PI constraints by using a group of buffers as the driving block. We assume that each benchmark circuit can be initialized into the all-0 state.

To obtain the value of SWA_{func}, the complete two-block design is simulated under 30 functional input sequences of length 30000 generated by the TPG. We use the TPG designed for the driving block as the TPG for the complete design if the target circuit is not driven by "buffers". Otherwise, the TPG for the target circuit is used, and the value of SWA_{func} indicates the peak SWA in the circuit when there are no PI constraints. We use a 32-bit LFSR and m=3 for the shift register configuration. We use R=3 and Q=5 to construct the multi-segment PI sequences. The value of L is selected so that it is suitable for the target circuit.

Figure 2 shows the values of SWA_{func}, given as a percentage of switching lines during a state-transition, and the transition fault coverage achieved on benchmark circuits. For each circuit, we list the case of no PI constraints. We also list the cases where the highest and lowest SWA_{func} occur to show a range of possible results under PI constraints. The lowest fault coverage is always obtained in the case where SWA_{func} is the lowest. It can be observed from Figure 2 that SWA_{func} decreases when PI constraints are considered, compared with the case of no constraints. This demonstrates the influence of PI constraints on the SWA during functional operation. In addition, if SWA_{func} does not decrease much under PI constraints, there is no or a small loss of fault coverage because: (1) Tests whose SWAs are higher than SWA_{func} may not necessarily detect additional faults. The exclusion of such tests does not affect the fault coverage. (2) Multi-segment PI sequences use more LFSR seeds and allow the circuit to traverse longer state sequences to compensate for potential fault coverage loss. Otherwise, a noticeable fault coverage loss may occur since many tests that improve the fault coverage are excluded due to higher SWA.

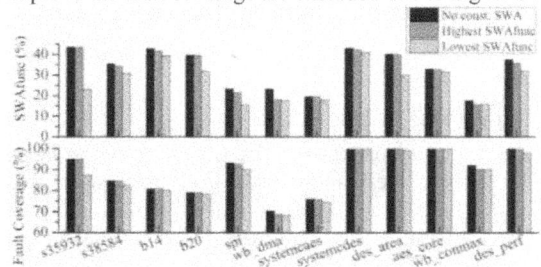

Figure 2. SWA_{func} and transition fault coverage

Figure 3 shows the area overhead, given as a percentage of the required hardware in the circuit. It can be observed that the area overhead is small, especially for larger circuits.

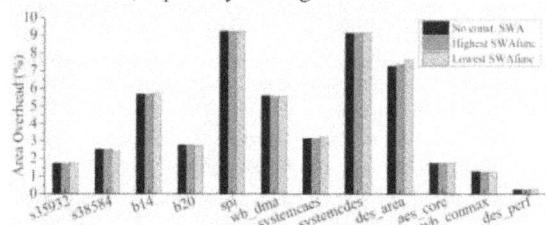

Figure 3. Area overhead

In summary, the proposed method can achieve high transition fault coverage and bounded SWA during test application for the benchmark circuits, using simple hardware.

5. REFERENCES

[1] I. Pomeranz, "Built-In Generation of Functional Broadside Tests Using a Fixed Hardware Structure," IEEE TVLSI Syst., Jan. 2013, pp. 124-132.

[2] I. Pomeranz and S. M. Reddy, "Generation of functional broadside tests for transition faults," IEEE TCAD Integr. Circuits Syst., Oct. 2006, pp. 2207-2218.

[3] I. Pomeranz and S. M. Reddy, "Primary Input Vectors to Avoid in Random Test Sequences for Synchronous Sequential Circuits," IEEE TCAD, Jan. 2008, pp.193-197.

[4] I. Pomeranz, "Generation of Functional Broadside Tests for Logic Blocks with Constrained Primary Input Sequences," IEEE TCAD Integr. Circuits Syst., Mar. 2013, pp. 442-452.

TSV Power Supply Array Electromigration Lifetime Analysis in 3D ICs[*]

Qiaosha Zou, Tao Zhang, Cong Xu, Yuan Xie
Computer Science and Engineering
the Pennsylvania State University
University Park, PA 16802
{qszou, zhangtao, czx102, yuanxie}@cse.psu.edu

ABSTRACT

Electromigration (EM) can cause severe reliability issues in contemporary integrated circuits. For the emerging three-dimensional integrated circuits (3D ICs), the introduction of through-silicon vias (TSVs) as the vertical signal carrier complicates the electromigration analysis. In particular, an accurate EM analysis on TSV arrays that are used in the power supply network is critical since the large current going through those TSVs can accelerate their degradation. In this work, we propose a novel EM analysis framework that focuses on TSV arrays in the power supply network, under the circumstance of uneven current distribution. The impacts of various design factors on the EM lifetime are discussed in detail. Our results reveal that the predicted TSV array lifetime is largely biased without proper current distribution analysis, resulting in an unexpected early failure.

1. INTRODUCTION

Electromigration (EM), which refers to the migration of metal atoms in response to an electric field in a conductor, has been proven to be one of the major factors of interconnect failure [3]. The factors that influence EM lifetime of interconnects have been unveiled in previous studies [1, 5], emphasizing the impact of current density on conductor's EM mean-time-to-failure (MTTF).

In recent years, three-dimensional integrated circuits (3D ICs) have been proposed to overcome the increased interconnect crisis along with technology scaling. In particular, through-silicon-vias (TSVs) have been widely adopted as vertical power and signal carriers. Considering the higher current density requirement on power/ground (P/G) TSVs for the power delivery, it can induce severe EM problems on P/G TSVs [8]. Usually, multiple TSVs are applied for the power delivery due to the limited current delivering capability of a single TSV [10]. Unfortunately, prior studies on EM lifetime modeling and analysis mainly focus on individual TSVs, leaving the EM lifetime analysis on such TSV arrays unexplored. Different from previous work, we model P/G TSV arrays and perform the EM lifetime analysis.

[*]This work is supported in part by NSF 1218867, 1213052, and 1017277 and SRC grants.

GLSVLSI'14, May 21–23, 2014, Houston, Texas, USA.
ACM 978-1-4503-2816-6/14/05.
http://dx.doi.org/10.1145/2591513.2591567.

2. EM LIFETIME CALCULATION

In this section, the 3D power network model is introduced first. Then the framework to calculate the current density and the EM lifetime of TSV arrays is explained. In general, the EM analysis framework contains two stages. The first stage concentrates on the current distribution analysis. The calculated current densities are then used as inputs for the second stage to estimate EM lifetime of the TSV array.

2.1 Power Grid Model

The 3D power network model contains two parts: 2D planar power grids and vertical power connections. We assume two orthogonal metal layers are used for local power or ground rails, which are placed alternately. TSVs connect the global power grid between two adjacent tiers. In the design, only one TSV (*center TSV*) in the array is directly connected to one C4 bump (off-chip P/G pins) while other TSVs (*peripheral TSVs*) are connected to the center TSV with metal wires as proposed by previous study [4].

Because constant unidirectional current stress is applied, the inductance and capacitance are irrelevant to our model, leaving resistance the only parasitic parameter that should be concerned. Due to the resistance network and TSV connections, current is unevenly distributed among TSV arrays. In our framework, the value of voltage drop between two neighboring TSVs is extracted from HSPICE simulation and remains constant during the following EM analysis. TSVs and metal wires are modeled as resistors and the devices powered by the TSV array are abstracted as current sources which are predetermined or extracted from real designs.

2.2 Current Density Calculation

Due to the dependency of TSV's EM lifetime on the current density, the current analysis is performed to generate the current distribution map. In recent studies, in addition to current density, recent studies also reveal other EM driving forces including atomic concentration gradients, thermal gradients, and stress gradients [5]. The detailed EM lifetime calculation considering these factors requires significant computation overhead, which makes it infeasible to model gradual failure in a TSV array. Therefore, in this work, we focus on the impact of current distribution on the EM lifetime, and only use Black's equation [1] to estimate the MTTF.

The current density on TSV is calculated from the voltage difference between two connected nodes. Therefore, the voltage analysis is performed first when the resistance network is known. The voltage analysis contains two steps: 2D power grid voltage analysis and 3D power propagation. We modify the node-based fast algorithm [11] for 2D power grid voltage analysis and voltage propagation method [9] for 3D

TSV voltage analysis. Different from [9], we place the off-chip power supply on the bottom tier and use the distributed TSV array topology to mimic the practical design.

2.3 Array EM Lifetime Calculation

In order to explore the longest possible lifetime, we assume that **a TSV array fails if and only if when the last via in the array is worn out due to EM effect**. We apply the lognormal distribution [3, 2] for the calculation of a single TSV's EM lifetime and combine it with Monte Carlo approximation to generate the EM lifetime distribution of a TSV array.

Since the EM effect is memorizable, the stress time translation is necessary to take the stressed history into account after current redistribution. We leverage the translation rule $\left(\frac{I_{m-1}}{I_m}\right)^2 = \frac{t_m}{t_{m-1}}$ as proposed in previous work [6], where I and t denote the current density and stress time; m represents the timing sequence.

After current densities are generated for the TSV array through the voltage propagation process, one of the possible failure sequences can be determined in the following procedure. First, we select one TSV in each iteration and make it fail with weighted probabilities determined by their current densities in the program. The larger current density one TSV has, the higher probability that it will be selected. The MTTF of the selected TSV is then calculated and the EM failure time is obtained following the lognormal distribution. Then, the stressed time for the remaining TSVs are translated according to the translation rule. The current density calculation process is applied for the rest TSVs to establish the new current density map. The iteration continues until the TSV array fails due to EM degradation. To this end, one sample of array EM lifetime is successfully calculated. Monte Carlo estimation with massive samples is used to generate the MTTF and lifetime distribution for the TSV array.

3. TSV ARRAY EM LIFETIME ANALYSIS

This section shows the TSV array EM lifetime analysis results with various design parameters. For each experiment, we capture massive Monte Carlo samples to calculate the EM MTTF and generate the EM lifetime distribution. A two-tier stacking chip is used as the design target. The TSV diameter is $5\mu m$ and the height is $30\mu m$. The current load of each node in the power grid is assigned assuming an universal activity factor with fixed total current load. Experiment results are normalized to the case with one TSV under the same current load.

3.1 TSV Array EM Lifetime

In this experiment, the target P/G TSV array contains 4×4 TSVs. From the result, we can observe that the TSV array lifetime also follows the lognormal distribution. We also conduct experiments on different TSV counts with the same current load. With more TSVs, the EM lifetime is extended and the distribution variation becomes larger since the number of possible failure sequences is increased, making it harder to predict the exact EM failure time.

When an even current distribution is assumed on the TSV array, the EM lifetime would be overestimated. The results show that for four TSV array configurations (2×2, 3×3, 4×4, and 5×5), the EM MTTF in uneven current distribution is

only 36.79%, 32.02%, 24.38%, and 18.89% of that in even current distribution, respectively. The percentage goes down with larger TSV array because the current distribution is more uneven.

3.2 Other Design Parameters

Filling Materials In this part, we study the impact of TSV filling materials (copper, aluminum, and tungsten [7]) on the EM lifetime. Among these three materials, copper has the smallest resistivity. The result indicates that copper TSV arrays have the longest EM lifetime, whereas aluminum and tungsten TSVs have similar EM behaviors. However, the differences of three EM lifetimes are marginal.

TSV Number and Size Normally, the overall area budget for TSVs is determined at the early design stage. With the fixed area budget, we should make the trade-off between the size and the number of TSVs to achieve the desired EM lifetime. Table 1 shows that as we increase the number of TSVs from 4 to 9, the EM lifetime is improved at first; then, it is shortened if we further increase the number of TSVs to 25.

Table 1: EM MTTF with fixed area budget

TSV count	TSV diameter (μm)	EM MTTF (a. u.)
2×2	10	221.20
3×3	6.67	374.37
4×4	5	219.93
5×5	4	146.52

4. CONCLUSION

Electromigration is an important reliability issue in nanoscale VLSI circuit designs. In this work, we propose an analysis framework for EM lifetime of P/G TSV arrays. The results show that if the current distribution is not evaluated correctly, the estimated EM lifetime is misleading. Sensitivity studies of design parameters are conducted in the paper to show their impacts on EM lifetime. For the future work, we will include the EM influence factors, such as thermal gradients and stress gradients into the EM lifetime analysis.

References

[1] J. Black. Electromigration-A Brief Survey and Some Recent Results. *Electron Devices, IEEE Transactions on*, 16:338–347, 1969.

[2] T. Frank, S. Moreau, C. Chappaz, L. Arnaud, P. Leduc, A. Thuaire, and L. Anghel. Electromigration Behavior of 3D-IC TSV Interconnects. In *ECTC*, 2012.

[3] C. S. Hau-Riege. An Introduction to Cu Electromigration. *Microelectronics Reliability*, 44:195 – 205, 2004.

[4] M. Healy and S. K. Lim. A Novel TSV Topology for Many-Tier 3D Power-Delivery Networks. In *DATE*, 2011.

[5] J. Jing, L. Liang, and G. Meng. Electromigration Simulation for Metal Lines. *Journal of Electronic Packaging*, 132:011002, 2010.

[6] D.-A. Li, Z. Guang, M. Marek-Sadowska, and S. R. Nassif. Multi-via Electromigration Lifetime Model. In *International Conference on Simulation of Semiconductor Processes and Devices*, 2012.

[7] S.-K. Ryu, K.-H. Lu, X. Zhang, J.-H. Im, P. Ho, and R. Huang. Impact of Near-Surface Thermal Stresses on Interfacial Reliability of Through-Silicon Vias for 3-D Interconnects. *Device and Materials Reliability, IEEE Transactions on*, 2011.

[8] K. Tu. Reliability Challenges in 3D IC Packaging Technology. *Microelectronics Reliability*, 51:517–523, 2011.

[9] C. Zhang, V. Pavlidis, and G. De Micheli. Voltage Propagation Method for 3-D Power Grid Analysis. In *DATE*, 2012.

[10] T. Zhang, K. Wang, Y. Feng, X. Song, L. Duan, Y. Xie, X. Cheng, and Y.-L. Lin. A Customized Design of DRAM Controller for On-Chip 3D DRAM Stacking. In *CICC*, 2010.

[11] Y. Zhong and M. Wong. Fast Algorithms for IR Drop Analysis in Large Power Grid. In *ICCAD*, 2005.

A Current-Mode CMOS/Memristor Hybrid Implementation of an Extreme Learning Machine

Cory Merkel
Computer Engineering Dept.
Rochester Institute of Technology
Rochester, NY, USA
cem1103@rit.edu

Dhireesha Kudithipudi
Computer Engineering Dept.
Rochester Institute of Technology
Rochester, NY, USA
dxkeec@rit.edu

ABSTRACT

In this work, we propose a current-mode CMOS/memristor hybrid implementation of an extreme learning machine (ELM) architecture. We present novel circuit designs for linear, sigmoid, and threshold neuronal activation functions, as well as memristor-based bipolar synaptic weighting. In addition, this work proposes a stochastic version of the least-mean-squares (LMS) training algorithm for adapting the weights between the ELM's hidden and output layers. We simulated our top-level ELM architecture using Cadence AMS Designer with 45 nm CMOS models and an empirical piecewise linear memristor model based on experimental data from an HfO_x device. With 10 hidden node neurons, the ELM was able to learn a 2-input XOR function after 150 training epochs.

Categories and Subject Descriptors

B.7.1 [**Hardware**]: Integrated Circuits—*advanced technologies*; C.1.3 [**Computer Systems Organization**]: Processor Architectures—*neural nets*

Keywords

Memristor, extreme learning machine, current-mode

1. INTRODUCTION AND DESIGN

In a conventional feedforward neural network, all of the weights in the network are trained using standard algorithms, such as error backpropagation [8] or one of its variants. These algorithms require computation of error derivatives and are difficult to implement in hardware. ELM networks, introduced by Huang *et al.* [1], circumvent these challenges by fixing the input-to-hidden layer weights and only training those weights connecting the hidden and output layers. In addition, these weights can be adjusted using simple algorithms such as LMS [9, 10]. The CMOS/memristor hybrid design paradigm [3–7] is particularly attractive for ELM implementation because of memristors' small footprint, non-volatility, and ability to store multiple synaptic weight values.

In this work, we have designed current-mode CMOS/memristor neurons and synapses for an ELM. Figure 1 shows the four neu-

GLSVLSI'14, May 21–23, 2014, Houston, Texas, USA.
ACM 978-1-4503-2816-6/14/05.
http://dx.doi.org/10.1145/2591513.2591572.

ron designs. A linear neuron (Figure 1(a)) distributes the ELM's inputs to the hidden layer. Sigmoid neurons (Figures 1(b) and 1(c)) constitute the ELM's hidden and output layers. The sigmoid neuron with no opamp (Figure 1(b)) is used for the hidden layer neurons and the opamp implementation (Figure 1(c)) is used in the output layer. The opamp provides a virtual ground input, which is needed for proper operation of the synapses connecting the hidden and output layer. Finally, a threshold neuron (Figure 1(d)) is used to digitize the output for classification problems. The neurons' transfer functions are shown in Figure 1(e). Here, $s = i_{in}/I_{max}$, and $x = i_{out}/I_{max}$, where $I_{max} = 500$ nA. The a parameter is dependent on the sigmoid neuron's input resistor R_{in} and can be used to adjust the sigmoid's slope. Importantly, the proposed unipolar current mode neurons have a full output swing between 0 and an arbitrary value of I_{max}. Furthermore, the neurons' outputs are easily buffered using current mirrors. Achieving these characteristics (full signal swing and zero-offset buffering) is more challenging in voltage-mode circuits.

The proposed memristive synapse design is shown in Figure 1(f). Two parallel memristors divide the input current, yielding an output of

$$\frac{i_{out}}{I_{max}} = \left(2\frac{G_{m1}}{G_{m1} + G_{m2}} - 1 \right) x_j = w_{ij}x_j, \qquad (1)$$

where G_{m1} and G_{m2} are the memristor conductances, and w_{ij} is the synaptic weight between the jth and i^{th} neurons. As shown in Figure 1(g), the proposed synapse design achieves excellent linearity and bipolar weight values. It also uses fewer devices than voltage-mode bipolar memristor-based synapses. For example, the design proposed by Kim *et al.* [2] requires four memristors and atleast four transistors, if one considers the training circuit.

2. RESULTS AND DISCUSSION

We integrated our circuit-level building blocks into an ELM with 2 inputs, 10 hidden layer neurons, and 1 output. We have used random synaptic weights, implemented with CMOS current mirrors, between the input and hidden layers. The hidden layer neurons are implemented with the no opamp version of the sigmoid neuron, while the output neuron is implemented with the opamp version. Finally, the output is digitized using a threshold neuron. We also designed a novel hardware training algorithm based on LMS:

$$P\left(\frac{|\Delta w_{ij}|}{\alpha} = 1 \right) = \mathcal{B}(1, x_j|x_{iexp} - x_i|) \qquad (2)$$

and

$$\text{sign}(\Delta w_{ij}) = \text{sign}(x_{iexp} - x_i), \qquad (3)$$

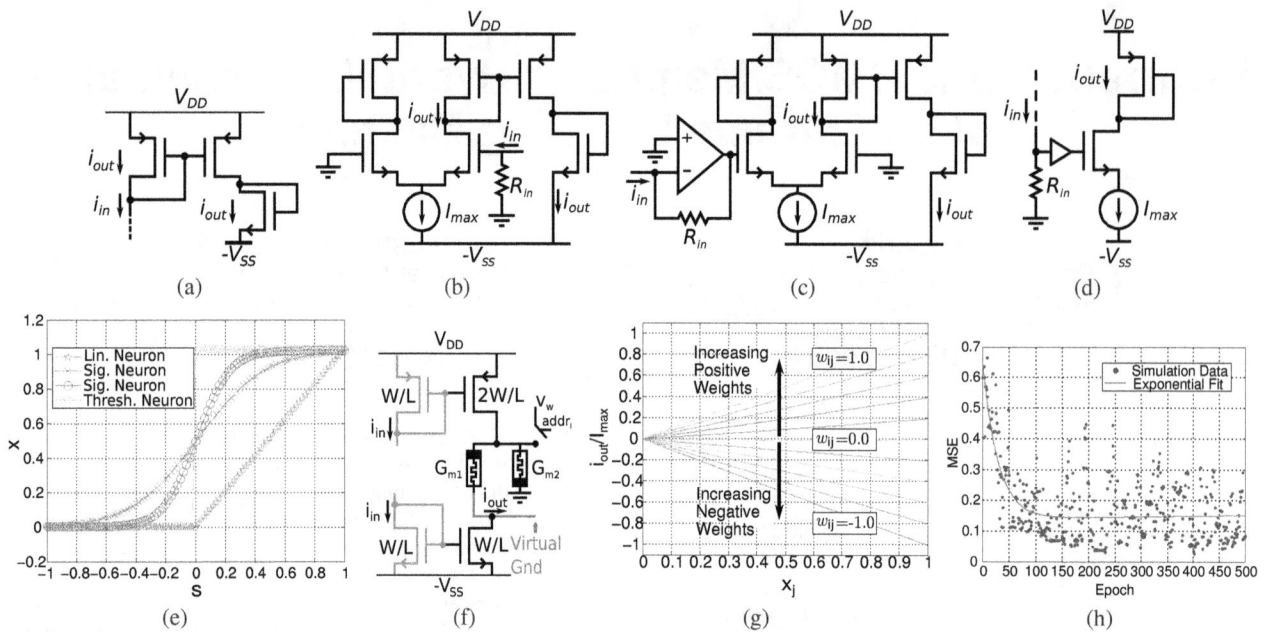

Figure 1: Circuit-level building blocks for a current-mode CMOS/memristor hybrid ELM: Neuron circuits implementing (a) linear, (b)-(c) sigmoid, and (d) threshold activation functions. (e) Neuron transfer characteristics. (f) Bipolar current-mode memristive synapse and (g) transfer characteristics for different weight values. (h) ELM training results for a 2-input XOR gate.

Here, Δw_{ij} is the change in the synaptic weight w_{ij}, P is the probability, α is the learning rate, $\mathcal{B}$ is the binomial distribution, and x_{iexp} is the expected output. This algorithm is much easier to implement in hardware than the original LMS algorithm.

We validated our ELM architecture by training it to perform a 2-input XOR function. This is a standard benchmark for neural networks because of its high non-linearity. The learning curve is shown in Figure 1(h). The y axis shows the mean square error (MSE) between the expected and actual network output, and the x axis is the training epoch. An exponential fit, shown in red, indicates training convergence after approximately 150 epochs. However, due to the stochastic nature of the proposed training algorithm, the MSE oscillates around the exponential fit. This behavior is advantageous as it helps the training algorithm avoid local minima. Note that these oscillations can be reduced by decreasing the learning rate, which can be accomplished by reducing the flux applied to the memristor during training. By the end of the training, the ELM achieves 100% accuracy.

3. CONCLUSIONS AND FUTURE WORK

In this work, we have proposed novel neuron and synapse circuits, as well as a hardware-friendly training approach for a CMOS/memristor ELM architecture. We have shown that the current-mode designs have several advantageous in the design of ELMs due to their easy signal buffering, and simple implementation of constant synaptic weights using current mirrors. The proposed current-mode bipolar synapse design uses less hardware than existing implementations. We have also proposed the first ELM architecture based on the circuit-level designs. The architecture was validated by training the ELM network to perform a 2-input XOR function. Future work will include scaling the proposed designs to address the requirements of more complex applications such as optical character recognition and object classification.

References

[1] G.-b. Huang, Q.-y. Zhu, and C.-k. Siew. Extreme learning machine: a new learning scheme of feedforward neural networks. In *International Joint Conference on Neural Networks*, volume 2, pages 985–990, 2004.

[2] H. Kim, M. P. Sah, C. Yang, T. Roska, and L. O. Chua. Neural synaptic weighting with a pulse-based memristor circuit. *IEEE Transactions on Circuit Theory*, 59(1):148–158, 2012.

[3] D. Kudithipudi, C. Merkel, M. Soltiz, G. S. Rose, and R. Pino. Design of neuromorphic archtectures with memristors. In R. Pino, editor, *Network Science and Cybersecurity*, pages 93–103. Springer, 2014.

[4] D. Kudithipudi and C. E. Merkel. Reconfigurable memristor fabrics for heterogeneous computing. In R. Kozma, R. E. Pino, and G. E. Pazienza, editors, *Advances in Neuromorphic Memristor Science and Applications*, pages 89–105. Springer Netherlands, Dordrecht, 2012.

[5] C. Merkel, D. Kudithipudi, and N. Sereni. Periodic Activation Functions in Memristor-based Analog Neural Networks. In *IJCNN*, number x, 2013.

[6] M. Soltiz, S. Member, D. Kudithipudi, C. Merkel, G. S. Rose, and R. E. Pino. Memristor-based Neural Logic Blocks for Non-linearly Separable Functions. *IEEE Transactions on Computers*, 62(8):1597–1606, 2013.

[7] M. Soltiz, C. Merkel, D. Kudithipudi, and G. S. Rose. RRAM-based adaptive neural logic block for implementing non-linearly separable functions in a single layer. In *IEEE/ACM International Symposium on Nanoscale Architectures*, pages 218–225, 2012.

[8] P. Werbos. *Beyond regression: New tools for prediction and analysis in the behavioral sciences*. Ph.d. dissertation, Harvard University, 1975.

[9] B. Widrow. An adaptive "ADALINE" neuron using chemical "Memistors". Technical report, Stanford University, 1960.

[10] B. Widrow, A. Greenblatt, Y. Kim, and D. Park. The No-Prop algorithm: a new learning algorithm for multilayer neural networks. *Neural Networks*, 37:182–188, Jan. 2013.

Modelling and Mitigation of Time-Zero Variability in sub-16nm FinFET-based STT-MRAM Memories

Matthias Hartmann[*,†], Halil Kukner[*,†], Prashant Agrawal[*,†], Praveen Raghavan[*],
Liesbet Van der Perre[*,†], Wim Dehaene[*,†]
[*] IMEC vzw., Leuven, Belgium, [†] KU Leuven, Leuven, Belgium
Matthias.Hartmann@imec.be

ABSTRACT

Spin-transfer torque magnetic RAM (STT-MRAM) is one of the most promising non-volatile memory technologies and shows potential as an SRAM replacement. However, targeted for advanced CMOS technologies such as the 14nm FinFET node, time-zero variability is a major concern for these memory technologies. In this paper, we investigate the STT-MRAM variability with respect to different technology scenarios. We show the impact of these variations on the bit error rate of the emerging STT-MRAM memories.

1. INTRODUCTION

Multiple emerging, non-volatile memories, such as Spin-transfer torque magnetic RAM (STT-MRAM) [1], have been proposed in the recent past. These memories decrease the leakage power, improve the scaling with technology nodes and increase the area density compared to traditional embedded SRAM memories, which also suffer from increased variability and supply voltage scaling causing severe sensing problems and an increase in read errors. However, STT-MRAM also suffers from process variations.

Process variation has been extensively researched in the past addressing the parameter variations in nanoscale technology nodes [2]. The random process variations for an SRAM memory module have been presented in [3]. In addition, multiple work has been done in the field of STT-MRAM variability. [4] discusses the breakdown behavior of the magnetic tunnel junction and [5] provides a case study for the 32nm CMOS technology node. However, to the best of our knowledge, ours is the first work which focuses on variability issues for embedded NVMs in 14nm FinFET technology and below and discusses multiple technology scaling scenarios.

2. VARIABILITY IN STT-MRAM

The STT-MRAM cell, selected for this work, is a 1T1MTJ memory cell and operates with one FinFET nMOS access transistor. The time-zero variability of this FinFET transistor reflects mainly on its intrinsic V_{th} value. Figure 1

GLSVLSI'14, May 21–23, 2014, Houston, Texas, USA.
ACM 978-1-4503-2816-6/14/05.
http://dx.doi.org/10.1145/2591513.2591573.

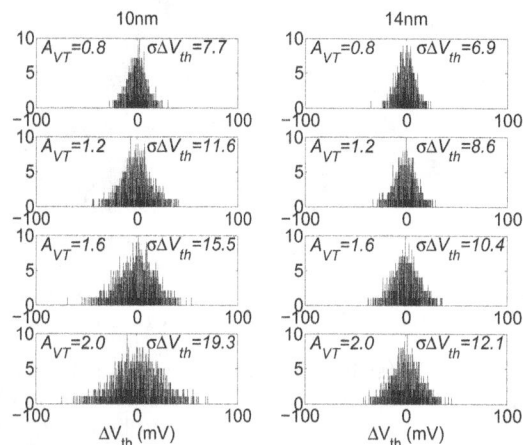

Figure 1: V_{th} spreads for a 10nm and 14nm nMOS FinFET transistor

shows the spread in V_{th} obtained from Monte-Carlo simulations for 1000 nMOS transistors using the transistor model of [6]. For each node, several scaling scenarios are considered. Each scenario is characterized by a scaling parameter A_{VT}. A_{VT} defines the intrinsic process variations for a specific technology process. In general, a higher A_{VT} value implies more random process variations. Moreover, switching from the 14nm technology node to the 10nm technology node also increases the random process variations captured by the σV_{th} of each scenario. A variation in the V_{th} of the access transistor causes a shift in the access time of this transistor leading to insufficient timing margins in the sense amplifier and causing a read error.

In a manner similar to the access transistor, the MTJ is also impacted by process variations. The resulting failure to write to the MTJ and to modify its conductivity leads to an inherent bit error rate (BER) of the memory element. [7] shows the BER for several operating voltages and pulse widths.

3. VARIABILITY MITIGATION

A commonly used method to improve the yield for memory modules is error control coding (ECC). ECC allows the recognition and correction of read/write errors by encoding additional bits with each data word in the memory. These bits introduce redundancy to detect and possibly correct errors. Typically, the overhead of the ECC is largely based on the additional memory cells needed and depends on the error correction/detection strength of the ECC.

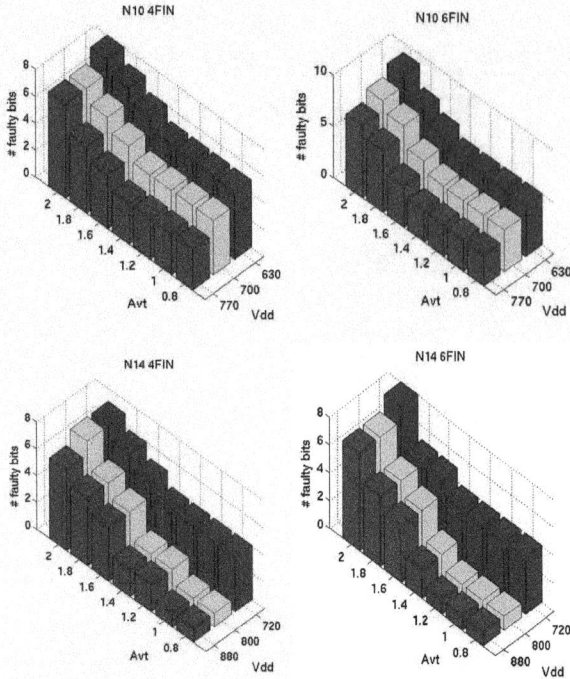

Figure 2: Required ECC bit correction capability for 6σ performance of the STT-MRAM memory module

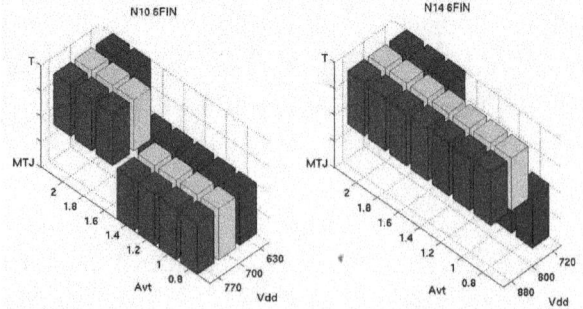

Figure 3: Dominating contributor to the BER of the memory cell in 10nm and 14nm FinFET technology

delay spread of the access transistor. A lower A_{VT} represents a better process, resulting in less random variations in the FinFET transistors.

However, the extent of variance in N_{FB} varies across 14nm ($N14$) and 10nm ($N10$) FinFET technology. $N14$ achieves best case value of $N_{FB} = 1$ whereas it is 3 in case of $N10$. The impact of the number of fins on N_{FB} is similar for both $N14$ and $N10$.

The extent of the impact on variability differs across MTJ and the access transistor, as shown in Figure 3. For both $N14$ and $N10$, we show whether the variability of MTJ or the access transistor T is dominant. In the 10nm technology node, the voltage of the MTJ is significantly reduced due to the lower supply voltage V_{DD} and a higher threshold voltage V_{th} of the access transistor.

6. CONCLUSION

In this paper, we explore the time-zero variability of STT-MRAM and showed multiple scaling scenarios for advanced CMOS technology nodes (10nm and 14nm FinFET technology). We address both the process variations in the access transistor as well as in the MTJ and evaluate the effects of the combined BER in a case study for a 64bit data memory. In addition, we present the trade-off space in terms of supply voltage, technology scaling and required ECC correction capabilities in order to achieve the targeted yield for the memory module.

7. REFERENCES

[1] M. Hosomi et al. A novel nonvolatile memory with spin torque transfer magnetization switching: spin-ram. 2005.

[2] K.J. Kuhn et al. Process technology variation. 2011.

[3] Y. Wang et al. A 4.0-ghz 291-mb voltage-scalable sram design in 32-nm high-k metal-gate cmos with integrated power management. 2009.

[4] Chih-Hsiang Ho et al. A physics-based statistical model for reliability of stt-mram considering oxide variability. 2013.

[5] Y. Emre et al. Enhancing the reliability of stt-ram through circuit and system level techniques. 2012.

[6] P. Schuddinck et al. Standard cell level parasitics assessment in 20nm bpl and 14nm bff. 2012.

[7] Tai Min et al. A study of write margin of spin torque transfer magnetic random access memory technology. 2010.

Besides ECC, resizing of the access transistor is also used to improve the yield of the memory module. In FinFET technologies, the size of the transistor can be configured in discrete steps by increasing or decreasing the number of fins. Typically, larger transistors suffer less from time-zero variability.

Other variability mitigation techniques include (a) configuring the write pulse width to improve the BER of the MTJ, (b) configuring the supply voltage to improve the time-zero variability of the access transistor as well as the write failure rate of the MTJ.

4. EXPERIMENTAL SETUP

For our case study, we selected a typical L1 data memory (L1-D), which implements the baseband processing of recent wireless communication standards. The size of the L1-D is 8Mbit and its interface is 64bit wide. We define a scaling scenario using a 4-tuple $<\lambda,V,A,F>$, where λ represents the technology node (10nm, 14nm); V the supply voltage of the memory module; A the technology scaling based on the parameter A_{VT} and F the number of fins used in the FinFET access transistor. For each of those scenarios, we calculate the following metrics (1) the BER of the access transistor, (2) the BER of the STT-MRAM cell and (3) the required ECC strength.

5. RESULTS

Figure 2 shows the number of faulty bits (N_{FB}) that the ECC for the selected memory module needs to be able to correct in order to achieve 6σ performance. The higher the N_{FB}, the higher will be the requirement on the ECC error correction capabilities for the memory module.

It can be seen that, across all the scaling scenarios, N_{FB} reduces with decreasing A_{vt} and increasing V_{dd}. The increase in V_{dd} will lower the BER of the MTJ and reduce the

A Design Flow for Physical Synthesis of Digital Cells with ASTRAN

Adriel Ziesemer Jr. and Ricardo Reis
Universidade Federal do Rio Grande do Sul
(UFRGS), PGMicro
Av. Bento Gonçalves 9500
Porto Alegre, RS, Brazil
{amziesemerj,reis}@inf.ufrgs.br

Matheus T. Moreira, Michel E. Arendt
and Ney L. V. Calazans
PUCRS, PPGCC
Av. Ipiranga 6681
Porto Alegre, RS, Brazil
{matheus.moreira,ney.calazans}@pucrs.br

ABSTRACT

As the foundries update their advanced processes with new complex design rules and cell libraries grow in size and complexity, the cost of library development become increasingly higher. In this work we present the methodology used in ASTRAN to allow automatic layout generation of cell libraries for technologies down to 45nm from its transistor level netlist description in SPICE format. It supports non-complementary logic cells, allowing generation of any kind of transistor networks, and continuous transistor sizing. We describe our new generation flow which is currently being used to generate a library with more than 500 asynchronous cells in a 65nm process.

Categories and Subject Descriptors

B.7.2 [**INTEGRATED CIRCUITS**]: Design Aids-*Layout*

Keywords

EDA; CAD; cell synthesis; layout generation; standard-cell

1. INTRODUCTION

Cell library-based synthesis flows for ASICs is one of the most used methodologies in both industry and academia for design of VLSI circuits. It is known to be very reliable and predictable since the same cell library can be characterized and used in several different designs. However, the number of cells available in the library can limit the quality of the circuit, specially facing specific problems like: asynchronous circuits design, leakage reduction, SEU, NBTI, etc. Moreover, the layout of these cells is usually designed by hand, which also limits the adoption and development of promising technologies.

Layout Design Automation (LDA) is a challenge since the beginning of the silicon era. In technology nodes below 130nm, the number of new design rules increased considerably due to lithography issues. As a consequence, the com-

GLSVLSI'14, May 21–23, 2014, Houston, Texas, USA.
ACM 978-1-4503-2816-6/14/05.
http://dx.doi.org/10.1145/2591513.2591577.

plexity of layout generation is increasing, which demands new techniques for the generation of dense layouts. Previous works with layout migration [3,9] and cell synthesis [4,5,10] do not support layout generation for newer technology nodes bellow 130nm. Celltk [6] supports 90nm but presents a large area overhead compared to standard-cells. Nangate [2] has a cell synthesis tool capable of producing dense layouts but there is not detailed information regarding their flow.

In this work we present the cell synthesis flow used in AS-TRAN, which is capable of generating dense cell layouts using simultaneous two-dimensional (2-D) layout compaction and support most of the conditional design rules that applies to recent technology nodes. We detail aspects of the layout generation flow, highlighting improvements over our previous work [11].

2. OVERVIEW

ASTRAN [1] is an academic netlist-to-layout synthesis tool. It has a cell library creator module called CELLGEN [10] which is capable of synthesizing cell layouts in technologies down to 65nm (commercial) or 45nm (freePDK45). The tool generates layouts under a linear (1-D) layout style and supports unrestricted circuit structures, continuous transistor sizing, folding, poly and over-the-cell metal 1 routing, as well as rule relaxations for DFM. It is capable of generating dense layouts when compared to high quality standard-cells and improve productivity allowing generation and characterization of around 25 cells per day on average considering a single designer work.

The input of ASTRAN is a transistor level description of a circuit in SPICE format. Each circuit can be synthesized into a standard cell-level layout. The technology rules are set according to the values defined by the foundry. The cell topology (height, routing grid, wells/power rails position and other library specific aspects) are defined according to the target library and can be configured. The layout style used by ASTRAN is detailed in [11]. We managed to make it as flexible as possible in order to be able to generate hard to route cells and produce dense layouts.

3. GENERATION FLOW

The flow employed by ASTRAN is illustrated in Figure 1 and is discussed bellow:

Cell Area Estimation

ASTRAN first estimates the maximum transistor width and the routing resources in order to create a graph that can be

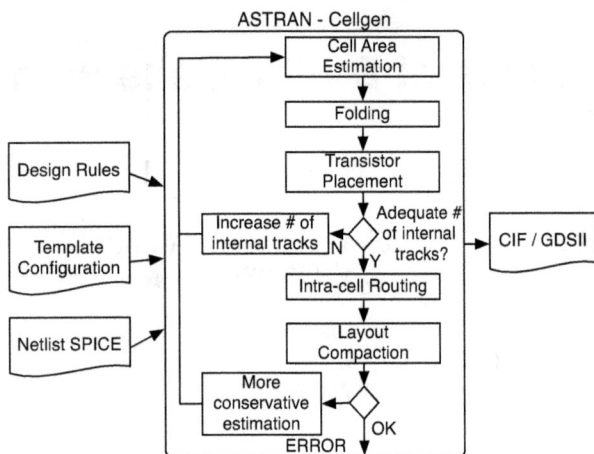

Figure 1: Cell generation flow employed by AS-TRAN

compacted to the layout level afterwards. Because the tool can under or overestimate the number of horizontal tracks that fits in the cell height, we usually start with an optimistic approach (maximizing both the PMOS/NMOS diffusion regions and number of tracks) and then become more conservative (reducing the number of tracks and the size of the PMOS/NMOS regions) if the tool is not able to compact the layout. Such choices are parameterizable for each layout.

Folding

Given the diffusion rows height limits calculated during the previous step, transistors can require to be folded. ASTRAN folds transistors by modifying the cell netlist, creating new transistors in parallel, before the execution of the placement step.

Transistor Placement

The purpose of the transistor placement step in the 1-D layout style is to find out a transistor ordering for the PMOS and NMOS networks that leads to a better design. We use a multidimensional cost function to evaluate the placement quality as described in [11].

Intra-cell Routing

The abstract cell layout representation obtained in the placement step is translated into a routing graph. The graph is generated according to the number and position of the tracks calculated in the cell area estimation step, the placement result and the width of the transistors.

Layout Compaction

Layout compaction is the process of translating the abstract cell representation produced by the previous steps into the cell layout. ASTRAN compacts the layout in 2-D simultaneously using Mixed-Integer Linear Programming (MILP). It was achieved using binary variables to model mutually exclusive constraints.

4. INCREMENTAL GENERATION FLOW

Recently we implemented a new feature that allows ASTRAN to automatically iterate with different parameters in case it fails to complete the cell generation process, as shown in Figure 1. Our incremental generation flow starts with an optimistic approach, attributing the maximal height for the PMOS and NMOS regions of the cell in order to minimize the number of transistor folding. After the placement step is completed, it evaluates the channel density of the current solution and increases the number or internal tracks if it exceeds the capacity of the cell, re-executing the flow from the beginning. At the end, the layout compaction step is called to generate the actual layout of the cell. Models which the MILP solver proves to be infeasible are aborted and re-started using a more conservative approach: reducing the height of the diffusion areas of the cell and the number of horizontal tracks.

5. CONCLUSIONS

This work details optimizations in a previously existing design flow for synthesizing the layout of digital cells. The addition of the incremental generation flow allowed a better automation of the generation process which is currently being used in ASCEnD [7,8] to automate the layout generation of over 500 asynchronous cells with the use of scripts.

6. REFERENCES

[1] Astran - automatic synthesis of transistor networks. https://code.google.com/p/gme-ufrgs/.

[2] Nangate library creator. http://www.nangate.com/.

[3] D.-S. Fu, Y.-Z. Chaung, Y.-H. Lin, and Y.-L. Li. Topology-driven cell layout migration with collinear constraints. In *IEEE ICCD*, pages 439–444, 2009.

[4] M. Guruswamy et al. CELLERITY: A fully automatic layout synthesis system for standard cell libraries. In *ACM DAC*, pages 327–332, Anaheim, California, United States, 1997. New York: ACM.

[5] T. Iizuka. *Optimal Layout Synthesis of Standard Cells in Large Scale Integration*. PhD thesis, Department of Electronic Engineering, Graduate School of Engineering, The University of Tokyo, Tokyo, Japan, 2007.

[6] R. Karmazin, C. Otero, and R. Manohar. celltk: Automated layout for asynchronous circuits with nonstandard cells. In *IEEE ASYNC*, 2013.

[7] M. Moreira, B. Oliveira, J. Pontes, F. Moraes, and N. Calazans. Adapting a c-element design flow for low power. In *Electronics, Circuits and Systems (ICECS), 2011 18th IEEE International Conference on*, pages 45–48, Dec 2011.

[8] M. T. Moreira, B. Oliveira, J. Pontes, and N. Calazans. A 65nm standard cell set and flow dedicated to automated asynchronous circuits design. In *International SoC*, pages 99–103. USA: IEEE, 2011.

[9] H. Said, M. Dessouky, R. El-Adawi, H. Abbas, and H. Shahein. Analog layout retargeting. In H. E. Graeb, editor, *Analog Layout Synthesis*, pages 205–242. Springer US, 2011.

[10] A. Ziesemer, C. Lazzari, and R. Reis. Transistor level automatic layout generator for non-complementary cmos cells. In *VLSI-SoC*, pages 116 –121. IEEE, 2007.

[11] A. Ziesemer, R. Reis, M. T. Moreira, M. E. Arendt, and N. L. V. Calazans. Automatic layout synthesis with astran applied to asynchronous cells. In *LASCAS*, 2014.

A Semi-Formal Approach for Analog Circuits Behavioral Properties Verification

Ons Lahiouel, Henda Aridhi, Mohamed H. Zaki, and Sofiène Tahar
Dept. of Electrical and Computer Engineering, Concordia University, Montréal, Québec, Canada
{lahiouel, h_aridh, mzaki, tahar}@ece.concordia.ca

ABSTRACT

We propose an environment for the verification of analog circuits behavioral properties, where the circuit state space bounds are first computed using qualitative simulation. Then, their specified behavioral properties are verified on these bounds. The effectiveness of the method is illustrated with a tunnel diode oscillator.

Categories and Subject Descriptors

B.7.2 [**Integrated Circuits**]: Design Aids—*Simulation, Verification*

Keywords

Analog Circuits; Global Optimization; Qualitative Simulation; Tunnel Diode Oscillator

1. INTRODUCTION

The analog circuit design process is becoming very complex and therefore new verification approaches are very much needed. Simulation [8] is the most used technique to compute the behavior of a circuit model. Statistical methods like Monte Carlo rely on repeating numerical simulations for a random sampling of parameters. They serve better for fine-tuning parameters and generation of test cases from probability distributions [2]. These two verification methods are not exhaustive and cannot guarantee the coverage of all important corner cases. Formal verification on the other hand ensures exhaustiveness and completeness [10]. For example, in [1, 9] the authors applied formal methods to verify start-up and stability conditions for oscillators. In [4], a formal analysis of SPICE simulation traces was utilized to verify oscillation properties of the Tunnel Diode Oscillator (TDO) with temperature variations. Such contributions are noticeable but they require designer expertise and they poorly scale with the circuit size. Qualitative simulation [7], on the other hand, is a semi formal method for fuzzy dynamical system simulation. It is capable of generating over

GLSVLSI'14, May 21–23, 2014, Houston, TX, USA.
ACM 978-1-4503-2816-6/14/05.
http://dx.doi.org/10.1145/2591513.2591578.

approximated envelopes of system trajectories when its parameters and initial conditions are specified as fuzzy distributions. In this work, we propose a framework for modeling and verifying analog circuits behaviorial properties based on qualitative simulation.

2. PROPOSED METHODOLOGY

An overview of the proposed methodology, implemented in MATLAB [5], is shown in Figure 1. The first block is responsible for generating an augmented differential model for analog circuits described in a SPICE Netlist. To this end, we generate device level models through Modified Nodal Analysis [6]. Then, we augment the obtained differential model with the connection matrix derivatives necessary to compute the circuit behavior for a defined continuous set of conditions. In fact, the elements of this matrix express the sensitivity of the solution. An example of the augmented differential model for the TDO in Figure 2 is shown in Equation (1) (cf. Section 3). The second block computes the state variables bounds of the obtained circuit model for a continuum set of their initial conditions, parameters, inputs or any variable that triggers a specific behavior of the circuit. This block is based on global optimization theory [3] and is inspired from the method for qualitative simulation of fuzzy systems proposed in [7]. The augmented differential model is not solved for every possible situation, but it uses the interior point algorithm to optimize the search for the global extremum. In fact, only the minimum and maximum of each state variable are determined for all specified time points. The result is an over-approximated envelope of all possible model trajectories. Finally, the verification block outputs a pass or fail conclusion when verifying the model properties formulated by the user. The property that can be verified includes model sensitivity, start-up delay, state bounds, or oscillation, as given in Equation (2) (see Section 3).

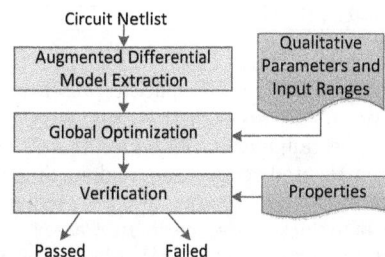

Figure 1: Semi-formal Verification Approach

3. APPLICATION

We consider the TDO shown in Figure 2 and modeled with the augmented differential model given in Equation (1).

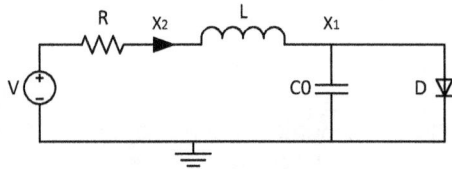

Figure 2: Tunnel Diode Oscillator Schematic

$$\dot{x}_1 = \frac{1}{C0}(-I_d(x_1) + x_2) \qquad (1)$$

$$\dot{x}_2 = \frac{1}{L}(-x_1 - \frac{1}{G}x_2 + V)$$

$$\dot{C} = C \cdot \begin{pmatrix} -\frac{1}{C0}I_d'(x_1) & \frac{1}{C0} \\ -\frac{1}{L} & -\frac{R}{L} \end{pmatrix}$$

where x_1 is the voltage across the capacitor $C0 = 1pF$, x_2 is the current through the inductor $L = 1\mu H$, I_D is the current through the diode and C is a 2×2 connection matrix.

We are interested in the effect of the conductance $G = 1/R$ and the initial conditions $x_0 \in [[0.4; 0.5]V, [0.4; 0.5]mA]$, at a nominal temperature ($T = 200K$), on the TDO oscillation property of x_1 and x_2 in $[0; A_1]$ and $[0; A_2]$, $A_1 = 0.5V$, $A_2 = 1mA$, as given in Equation (2).

$$(|mean(x_{imin}) - \frac{A_i}{2}| \leq \varepsilon_1 \wedge |mean(x_{imax}) - \frac{A_i}{2}| \leq \varepsilon_2) \wedge \quad (2)$$

$$(|std(x_{imin}) - \frac{A_i}{2}| \leq \delta_1 \wedge |std(x_{imax}) - \frac{A_i}{2}| \leq \delta_2), \ i = 1, 2$$

Table 1 reports that the TDO oscillates (Case 1) and locks up (Case 2) and compares our results with the formal method in [4]. In contrast to their method, our approach requires only the differential model and the property expression and covers automatically a complete set of circuit conditions, in reasonable run time and memory usage.

Table 1: TDO Oscillation Property Verification

	Case 1	Case 2
G	$5m\Omega^{-1}$	$4.13m\Omega^{-1}$
Method in [4]	Oscillations	No oscillations
Run time[s]	6505.36	83835.00
Proposed method	Oscillations	No oscillations
Run time[s]	4076.87	3049.95
Mem usage[MB]	0.046	0.050

Figure 3 shows a $2-D$ state space representation of the oscillation Case 1. By construction, any trajectory originating from the rectangular initial region travels necessarily through the represented rectangular region. Since the complete envelope of the TDO trajectories is oscillating, there is no chance of a lock up scenario in Case 1. Although spurious values which cannot be real solutions of the model are included, the generated boxes are kept tight during the whole simulation time. Figure 4 shows a $2-D$ state space representation of the lock up Case 2.

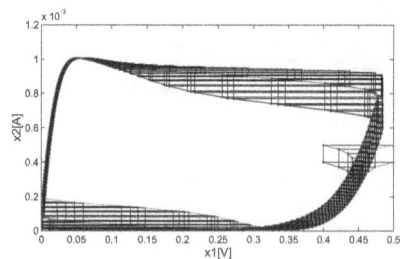

Figure 3: State Space Representation for Case 1

The generated state space regions show that the possible TDO states settle to a fixed region in the state space which eliminates the possibility of a stable oscillation.

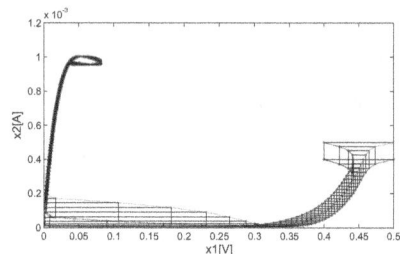

Figure 4: State Space Representation for Case 2

4. CONCLUSIONS

We proposed a verification environment to validate behavioral properties of analog circuits based on qualitative simulation. The main advantage of the method is the good coverage of the state space which is sufficient to verify candidate circuit properties in an acceptable run time. The application on the TDO circuit showed that our method is accurate and appealing in terms of efficiency. Future work include the verification of a larger suit of problematic circuits and automating their properties formulation.

5. REFERENCES

[1] M. Greenstreet and S. Yang. Verifying start-up conditions for a ring oscillator. *ACM Great Lakes Symposium on VLSI*, pages 201–206, 2008.

[2] M. Hazewinkel. *Monte-Carlo method*. Springer, 2001.

[3] R. Horst, P. M. Pardalos, and N. V. Thoai. *Introduction to Global Optimization*. Kluwer Academic Publishers, 2000.

[4] K. Lata and H. Jamadagni. Formal verification of tunnel diode oscillator with temperature variations. In *Asia and South Pacific Design Automation Conference*, pages 217–222, 2010.

[5] MATLAB. Documentation center, December 2013.

[6] F. N. Najm. *Circuit Simulation*. Wiley-IEEE Press, 2010.

[7] M. Nikravesh, L. A. Zadeh, and V. Korotkikh. *Reservoir Characterization and Modeling Series: Studies in Fuzziness and Soft Computing*. Springer Verlag, 2004.

[8] SPICE. User's guide and manuals, December 2013.

[9] C. Yan and M. Greenstreet. Oscillator verification with probability one. In *Formal Methods in Computer-Aided Design*, pages 165–172, 2012.

[10] M. H. Zaki, S. Tahar, and G. Bois. Formal verification of analog and mixed signal designs: A survey. *Microelectronics Journal*, 39(12):1395–1404, 2008.

Reconfigurable STT-NV LUT-based Functional Units to Improve Performance in General-Purpose Processors

Adarsh Reddy Ashammagari[1], Hamid Mahmoodi[2], Tinoosh Mohsenin[3], Houman Homayoun[1]

[1]Dept. of Electrical & Computer Engineering, George Mason University, Fairfax, VA
[2]Dept. of Computer Engineering, San Francisco State University, SF, CA
[3]Computer Science & Electrical Engineering Dept., University of Maryland Baltimore County
E-mail: {aashamma, hhomayou}@gmu.edu, mahmoodi@sfsu.edu, tinoosh@umbc.edu

ABSTRACT

Unavailability of functional units is a major performance bottleneck in general-purpose processors (GPP). In a GPP with limited number of functional units while a functional unit may be heavily utilized at times, creating a performance bottleneck, the other functional units might be under-utilized. We propose a novel idea for adapting functional units in GPP architecture in order to overcome this challenge. For this purpose, a selected set of complex functional units that might be under-utilized such as multiplier and divider, are realized using a programmable look up table-based fabric. This allows for run-time adaptation of functional units to improving performance. The programmable look up tables are realized using magnetic tunnel junction (MTJ) based memories that dissipate near zero leakage and are CMOS compatible. We have applied this idea to a dual issue architecture. The results show that compared to a design with all CMOS functional units a performance improvement of 18%, on average is achieved for standard benchmarks. This comes with 4.1% power increase in integer benchmarks and 2.3% power decrease in floating point benchmarks, compared to a CMOS design.

Categories and Subject Descriptors

C.1.1 [PROCESSOR ARCHITECTURES], Single Data Stream Architectures: Pipeline processors Systems; C.4 [Performance of Systems]

Keywords

STT Technology, Reconfigurable Functional Units, Performance

1 INTRODUCTION

With the current shrinking trend in CMOS technology, larger processing capabilities can be incorporated within the same die footprint. At the same time, the number of functions that are now computationally realizable has also increased in leaps and bounds. Therefore, an efficient allocation of functional resources becomes crucial to the overall performance of any processing unit [3, 4, 5]. Under limited functional resources available to general-purpose processors, major performance bottlenecks arise from functional units unavailability. There are two ways to look into this problem (i) one to increase the number of functional units in a general-purpose processor (ii) transform and adapt the functional units to serve different function needs. The first solution however is not design efficient as will be discussed in Section 2. The next alternative that we have addressed in this paper is adaptability and reconfigurability

GLSVLSI '14, May 21 – 23, 2014, Houston, TX, USA.
Copyright 2014 ACM 978-1-4503-2816-6/14/05...$15.00.
http://dx.doi.org/10.1145/2591513.2591535

between functional units. Incorporating adaptable functional units results in better utilization of hardware, which leads to performance improvement. Reconfiguring a unit to multiple functions requires an on-chip programmable fabric. This reconfiguration is performed on a Spin Transfer Torque Random Access Memory based look-up table (STT-NV-LUT) that is a composed of Magnetic Tunnel Junctions (MTJs). The advantages of using STT-NV technology are its zero standby power and thermally robust behavior. Recently use of MTJs has been explored for realizing low power programmable Look Up Tables (LUT) in processor and Field Programmable Gate Arrays (FPGAs) [12, 14, 16]. MTJs have been mainly used to design low power and thermally robust logics [12, 16]. In latest work MTJs has been used to reduce power and temperature in processor architecture [12, 17]. MTJs therefore have computing ability in addition to non-volatile storage property [12, 14, 17]. MTJ based clocking and logic architecture have already been developed in integration to CMOS [16]. In this paper, we utilize the STT-NV based look up tables [12, 16], to build on-chip adaptable functional units. Such look up tables show very little leakage power. Mapping a function to look up tables generally results in lower performance as compared to the custom implementation using standard cell logic gates; however, the ability to reconfigure the function itself in real time can potentially result in system performance improvement when running applications.

In this paper, we have investigated adaptation and reconfiguration from two perspectives: (i) in a static way (ii) in a dynamic way. In the static way, reconfiguration of all idle units is done at the end of a learning phase in the order of their activities. In this process, only one reconfiguration is performed during program execution time. In the dynamic mechanism, functional units are continuously monitored and the reconfiguration decision is made periodically. All of the functional units are reconfigured back to their original functions in the reset mode, before applying the new reconfiguration.

This is the first research paper that explores the opportunity and benefits of deploying adaptable STT-NV logic in general-purpose processors. While in this research we mainly focus on functional units there are several other processor units that will benefit from a reconfigurable and adaptable design. In general, some of the benefits that stem from adaptable logic are (i) activity migration based on thermal profiling of the processor (ii) failure tolerance by segregating faulty units and performing fine grain reconfiguring over good ones. For example, the integer ALU is one of the hottest spot on the processor. Reconfiguring the int/multiply units and applying activity migration can reduce the temperature significantly. Such run-time reconfiguration would help migrate some of the adder functionalities onto the multiply/divide unit and help reduce the overall temperature of all units. Fine grain reconfiguration possible through MTJ based coupling would enable reconfiguration between an adder/multiplier and help segregate the faulty units by reconfiguring some of the idle good ones while maintaining the chip functionality. The novel contributions of this work are statically and dynamically adaptive reconfiguration algorithms of functional units and exploiting the STT-NV LUT properties to perform the algorithms. The rest of the paper is organized as follows. Section 2 illustrates the functional unit conflict issue. Section 3 presents LUT based reconfiguration circuitry and the circuit performance and overhead metrics. Section 4 presents the proposed adaptive algorithms. Section 5 discusses the results. Finally, section 6 concludes the work.

2 MOTIVATION

Functional unit unavailability (or alternatively functional unit conflict) is one of the major performance bottlenecks in embedded and high performance processors [1, 2]. Functional unit conflicts occur when the processor pipeline has ready instructions, but not available functional units of particular type (multiplier, for instance) to execute. Note that in spite of high functional unit conflicts, it is not design efficient to increase the number of functional units in processor pipeline, as the complexity of additional functional unit will be significant [6, 13, 15]. As studied in several works, increasing the number of functional units not only increases the power consumption of the processor but also significantly affects the complexity of several back-end pipeline stages including instruction queue, write-back buffers, bypass stage, register file design and could severely affect the processor performance, as the number of write-back ports increase significantly [6]. As the number of functional units decides processor issue width, increasing the total number of functional units (which is equivalent to the maximum issue width) from 2 (which is very common in many embedded processors) to 4, increases the critical path delay and the total power of the processor by 15% and 18% accordingly [6]. The major increase is due to the impact on the wakeup and bypass logic of the processor. In addition, several studies indicated that the utilization varies significantly across various functional units [10, 11]. In Figure 1(a) we report the percentage of execution time each of 4 groups of functional units are idle in our studied architecture. While in some architecture some functional units such as multiplier and adder can be shared in our studied architecture we assume that there is no sharing between functional units. As shown, on average integer multiply and divide unit is idle most of the time. Except from apsi which is idle for 96% of the time, for the rest of the benchmarks this unit is idle more than 99% of time. The idleness is lower for floating point add and floating point multiply and divide with average of 95% and 98% respectively. Integer add is the least idle unit; average 66% of program execution time. Such a large idle time in all functional units provide an opportunity for applying reconfiguration when the functional unit is not being used.

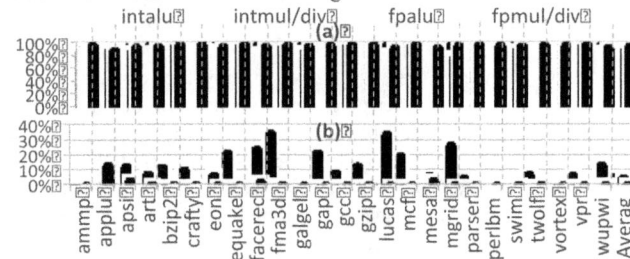

Figure 1. (a) % execution time, for which each group of functional unit is idle (b) % times with functional units conflicts.

Now the question is to which unit the idle unit needs to be reconfigured so that the performance benefit is maximized. To provide more insight in Figure 1(b) we report the percentage of times each group of functional units has been requested but was not available (functional unit conflict) during program execution time.

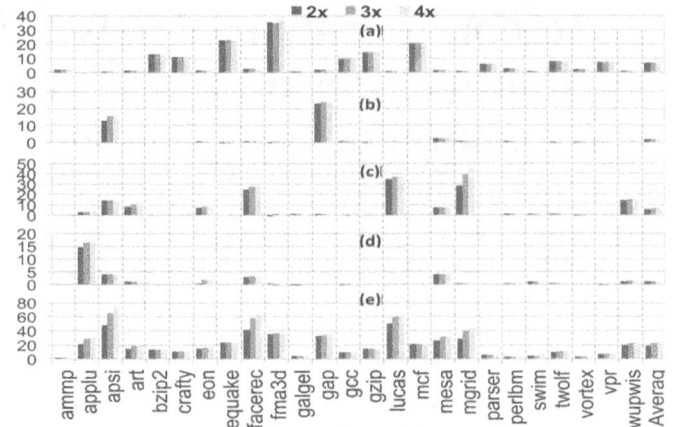

Figure 2. Relative performance improvement when the number of (a) int add (b) int mul/div (c) fp add (d) fp mul/div, and (e) all units increase by 2X, 3X and 4X {vertical bar shows the % of performance improvement}

Across most benchmarks mainly a single unit has a high conflict and therefore is the performance bottleneck. Interestingly, this unit is not the same for all benchmarks; i.e. in different benchmarks different functional unit is the performance bottleneck. While in many benchmarks integer add is the high conflict unit, in many others this is the case for floating point adder; examples are apsi, art, eon, facerec, lucas, mgrid, and wupwis. There are also few benchmarks that integer and floating point multiply and divide are the performance bottleneck units. Examples are applu, apsi and gap. Another interesting observation can be seen by comparing the results in Figure 1(a) and (b). For almost all benchmarks the same unit that is the performance bottleneck is also idle for more than 80% of program execution time. For all of these cases such a large conflict in spite of low utilization indicates that in most occasions functional units are accessed in burst. Therefore there is no single unit that is the performance bottleneck across different benchmarks. Thus finding a performance bottleneck unit to reconfigure the idle unit is a challenging problem and requires adaptive technique as we are presenting later in section 4 of this paper.

2.1 Potential for Improving Performance

In spite of large idle time for the functional units, increasing the number of functional units improve performance significantly. In Figure 2 we report the performance improvement in terms of IPC (average number of instruction committed per processor cycle) as the number of functional units increase to 2X, 3X and 4X times.

Figure 2(a) shows that increasing the number of int add improve performance significantly across many benchmarks. Interestingly, in spite of a very high idle time of integer mul/div, floating point add and floating point multiply and divide, increasing the number of these units, improve performance significantly for many benchmarks, as well. For instance in apsi and gap while int mul/div is idle for more than 96% of the time, doubling the number of this unit increase the performance by 13% and 23% respectively. To better understand this we provide the functional unit conflict results in Figure 1(b). Interestingly in these two benchmark the int mul/div unit is the main source of conflict with 11% and 22%, respectively. In fact in these benchmarks the int mul/divide is requested in burst. While the average idle time is almost 95%, there are some intervals that the unit is being accessed very frequently and therefore additional int mul/divide unit during those intervals could reduce the conflict and potentially improve performance.

Also in Figure 2(e) we report the speed up when increasing the number of all functional units at the same time. Doubling the number of functional units improve performance significantly by as

250

much as 50%. The average speedup is 19%. While there are some benchmarks that tripling and quadrupling the number of functional units improve their performance substantially (applu, art, facerec, lucas, mesa, mgrid), the largest speed up is achieved when doubling the resources. Further gains are seen with increased number of functional unit, but the marginal gains drop off.

3   LUT BASED FUNCTIONAL UNITS

STT-NV technology utilizes Magnetic Tunnel Junctions (MTJ) to realize nonvolatile resistive storage. There have been several attempts to use MTJs for building logic circuits with the hope of exploiting the leakage benefit of MTJs in order to reduce the power [12, 16]. However, due to the significant energy involved in changing the state of an MTJ, circuit styles that rely on changing the state of MTJs in response to input changes do not show any power and performance benefits [16]. An alternative to this approach has been to realize logic in memory by using LUTs that are built based on MTJs [12]. Resistive computation [12] replaces conventional CMOS logic with Magnetic Tunnel Junction (MTJ) based LUTs; it has been proposed for tackling the power wall.

3.1   Estimate of Area, Power, and Performance

To obtain an estimate of area, power, and performance of an LUT based adder as compared to a static CMOS (ASIC) counterpart, we have performed a case study on a 64-bit ripple carry adder and a multiplier implemented in static CMOS, CMOS LUT based, and the STT-NV LUT styles in a 32nm predictive technology node [19]. We used a commercial FPGA tool in order to get a count of LUTs and switch boxes (for routing) needed for each design. For static CMOS design we used design compiler to synthesis functional units (DesignWare) in a commercial 45nm technology and scaled the results to 32nm. Table 1 shows the results of the 64-bit adder and multiplier implemented in both styles. The results indicate that except for the leakage power, the STT-NV design has overhead in other metrics (especially for the adder).

Table 1. Comparison of adder and multiplier results in alternative styles

Metric	Unit	STT-NV LUT style	CMOS LUT style	Static CMOS style
Delay	adder	2.89	3.24	1
	multiplier	2	3.73	1
Active mode power	adder	6.46	6.70	1
	multiplier	0.74	1.26	1
Standby mode (leakage) power	adder	0.17	3.87	1
	multiplier	0.23	1.42	1
Area	adder	3.89	4.61	1
	multiplier	0.90	1.83	1

That means the performance of the reconfigurable adder in STT-NV style will be 2.89X lower than that of the static CMOS adder counterpart. Its standby mode power is 0.17X lower, but its active mode power is 6.46X higher. Due to a larger delay of reconfigurable STT-NV multiplier compared to the baseline CMOS style, the STT-NV multiplier implementation needs to be pipelined two times deeper than the original CMOS based implementation. However this has shown to impact performance minimally [12]. Also in spite of the advantage of a static CMOS based multiplier over the STT-NV based design in terms of delay, it still makes a lot of sense to replace it with the STT-NV design due to significant leakage advantage of the STT-NV design. Due to low utilization and high operating temperature of the multiplier, the standby power becomes the major component of the total power. Also as results in the table 1 suggests, the CMOS LUT based style has no obvious advantage over the static CMOS style. While both STT-NV LUT and CMOS LUT are reconfigurable, STT-NV LUT has advantage over CMOS LUT in

several metrics, noticeably leakage power. The leakage power of a STT-NV style is at least 6X lower than the CMOS LUT counterpart. Based on the results presented in table 1 we select IntALU to be a non-reconfigurable static CMOS as the power and area increase for a reconfigurable IntALU is significant. Other functional units including multiplier and divider (Int and FP) are implemented with STT-NV LUT reconfigurable style where they do not incur area overhead (the area of STT-NV LUT style is even smaller than the CMOS counterpart).

3.2   Estimate of Reconfiguration Overhead

The reconfiguration energy and performance estimation is performed for configuring a 64X64 multiplier unit to a 64-bit adder unit. This represents the worst-case scenario as reconfiguration between any other pair of functional units takes less energy and delay. Reconfiguring a LUT-based multiplier to an adder unit involves programming the LUTs. We have taken the HDL of the multiplier and adder units and synthesized them using a commercial FPGA (with 6 input LUT) synthesis tool in order to get a count of LUTs needed for each design. We have also taken into account the routing overhead including the switch boxes. The multiplier unit can be realized using 437 4-input LUTs and the adder using 65 such LUTs. Hence, we assume reconfiguring the multiplier unit to the adder or vice versa involves writing to at most 65 LUTs. Therefore, the total number of STT-Non-Volatile (STT-NV) bits to be written is 65 * 16 = 1040 bits or roughly 1 Kbits. The write access time to a single bit STT-NV is estimated to be 25ns [9], which are 25 cycles for 1GHz system clock. If LUTS are written in parallel using a 128-bit wide data bus, the reconfiguration is estimated to take about 8 write operations (i.e. 200 cycles). The configuration bits for the LUTs that are different between the adder and multiplier configuration need to be stored in a ROM. A controller will read the configuration bits from ROM and write to the STT-NV LUTs. For the configuration energy estimate, we have ignored the energy of reading the configuration bits from the ROM, since the configuration energy is expected to be dominated by the energy of writing to the STT-NV cells. Using the NVSIM tool, the write energy per bit cell is estimated to be 7.9 pJ [9]. Hence, the total energy estimated for the reconfiguration of LUTs is 1040 * 7.9 pJ = 8.2 nJ. The above estimates are conservative because we assume all the bits of those 65 LUTS need to be re-written; whereas, in reality some of the bits could be same between the two configurations. In addition to programming LUT we also need to program the router and switchboxes. The routing power overhead is not trivial. We used the results of FPGA synthesis to estimate the routing energy as 3.7nJ.

4   ADAPTIVE RECONFIGURATION

In this section we are presenting the algorithms for the functional unit reconfiguration to improve performance. The adaptive algorithm we are proposing is derived from the observation made from Figure 1 where multiply and divide units (both floating point and integer) are idle for a substantial part of program execution time – more than 95% of time for many applications. Note that in spite of such high underutilization we would still need these types of functional units. However due to the infrequency of multiply and divide operations these functional unit are remaining idle for most of program execution time. Since the adder units (float and integer) are active noticeably compared to multiply and divide units, we only make multiply and divide units reconfigurable – therefore only integer and floating point multiply and divide operation can be reconfigured to either int/fp adder or to each other, for instance a multiplier to a divider. Also we have shown in Figure 2 the speedup when increasing the number of int and fp adder and we found a large performance benefit across most benchmarks. Therefore a straightforward reconfiguration mechanism is to reconfigure multiplier and divider at run-time to an adder. Note that as shown in Figure 2 increasing the number of adder beyond a certain limit does not improve performance noticeably for many benchmarks. Therefore, it is not much performance beneficial to reconfigure all idle integer and floating point multiplier and divider to an adder.

Also as seen in Figure 2 there are few benchmarks such as applu, apsi and gap, which benefit significantly from increasing the number of multiply and divide units. Based on all of these observations, in this section we propose several algorithms to capture each benchmark behavior and adapt the number of functional unit required to maximize performance accordingly. We categorize these algorithms into static and dynamic algorithms. The goal of these algorithms is to find the idle functional units and reconfigure them to the active units to improve performance. Note that in all of these algorithms when a unit that has been reconfigured is requested and therefore is not available it needs to be reconfigured back to its original function. We refer to this re-reconfiguration as adjustment process. The adjustment process is asynchronous - For example if a multiplier is reconfigured to an adder and later in the program execution a multiply operation request a multiply unit, then the reconfigured adder need to be adjusted back to a multiplier, immediately.

4.1 Static Adaptive Algorithm

In this algorithm the application is being profiled for an initial phase (learning phase) and based on the profiling information the reconfiguration decision is being made for the rest of program execution. During the learning period active and idle functional units are being identified. At the end of the learning period all idle units are reconfigured to active units in the order of their activity. The reconfiguration pseudo-code is shown in Figure 3.

```
For the first 100M cycles:
-Monitor functional units
-Identify the idle units: idle [1, 2, 3, … i]
   (i is the total number of idle units)
-Identify the active units: active [1,2,3, … j]
   (j is the total number of active units)
-Order active units based on their activity: active_order [i]
At the end of 100M cycles:
Loop: for all idle units (i)
-Reconfigure idle units to active units: idle[i] → active_order [i%j]
```

Figure 3. Static Adaptive Algorithm pseudo code.

Note that the reconfiguration decision is made only once and after an initial learning period (after the first 100M cycles which for many benchmarks is larger than the initialization period). Since only one reconfiguration is allowed at the end of the learning phase, at most one adjustment process is performed during program execution time.

4.2 Dynamic Adaptive Algorithms

We present two dynamic algorithms shown in Figure 4. We refer to these algorithms as balanced idle to active and biased idle to most active algorithms. In both of these reconfiguration algorithms the functional units are monitored periodically and the reconfiguration decision is made every N cycles based on the functional unit activity in the previous N interval (due to space limitation we only report the results for N=100K interval). Then, at the beginning of each 100K interval, all idle functional units are reconfigured to the active ones. Such a periodic monitoring and reconfiguring process is based on the fact that many standard programs execute as a series of nonstationary phases. Each phase is very different from the others, while the program behavior within a phase is homogeneous. The goal of these periodic algorithms is to capture program behavior to find the right number of each type of functional unit for each program phase. In both of these algorithms, in the beginning of

monitoring interval all units are reconfigured back to their original functions (reset process) before applying the new reconfiguration – for example if a multiplier reconfigured to an adder, then in the beginning of every monitoring interval it should be first reset back to a multiplier. Then, the dynamic reconfiguration based on the monitoring information collected in the previous interval is applied.

Balanced idle to active (Dynamic-BIA): In this algorithm all idle functional units are reconfigured to the active units in a balance way. This is shown in Figure 4(a). The order of reconfiguration is based on the activity results presented in Figure 1– first we reconfigure the idle unit to int add, then the remaining idle units are being reconfigured to fp add, fp multiply, int multiply, int divide and fp divide, respectively. This algorithm implementation is simple – we require a single bit for recording the idle functional unit during every monitoring interval. If during the monitoring intervals the functional unit was busy (even for a single cycle) we set the idle bit to busy, otherwise the functional unit is idle.

Biased idle to most active (Dynamic-BMA): In this algorithm (shown in Figure 4(b)) all idle functional units are reconfigured to the most active units in a biased way and based on their activity. From results reported in Figure 1 we observed that the integer adder unit is always the most active unit therefore it make a lot of sense to reconfigure most of idle units to an integer adder.

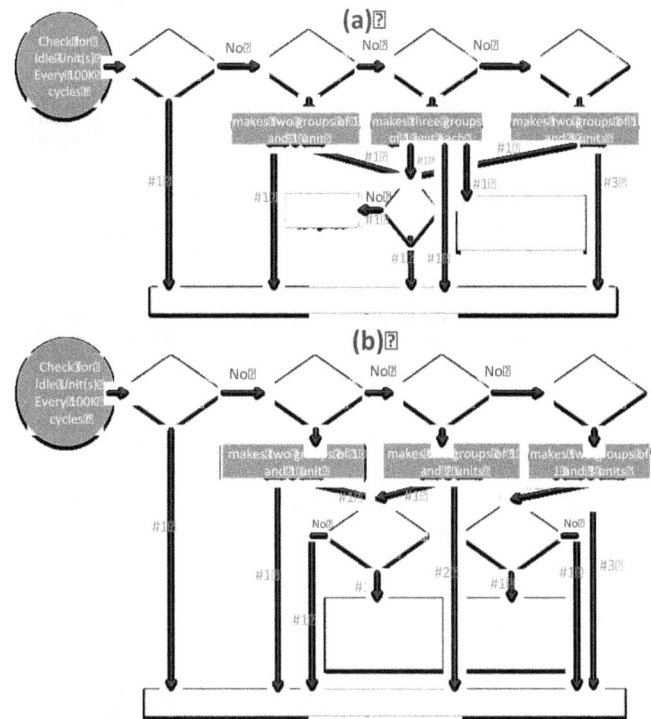

Figure 4. Dynamic Adaptive Algorithms (a) Balanced idle to active, and (b) Biased idle to most active.

For the rest of the units including fp adder, int/fp multiplier and divider the activity is monitored periodically and if they are busy more than 10K cycles in a 100K cycles monitoring interval they are considered as highly active unit. An idle unit will be then reconfigured to the most active unit out of the highly active units. The rest of idle units are reconfigured to int add. This algorithm is more complex than the Balanced algorithm as it requires constant monitoring of functional units activity, finding the highly active units, and selecting the most active among the highly active units.

5 METHODOLOGY AND RESULTS

In this section we present our simulation methodology and the results demonstrating the performance benefit of a reconfigurable STT- logic when deployed in the functional unit of the processor.

Table 2. Baseline Processor Configuration

Number of cores	4	Register file	64 entry
L1 I-cache	8KB, ,4 way, 2 cycles	Memory	50 cycles
L1 D-cache	8KB, 4 way, 2 cycles	Instruction fetch queue	8
L2-cache	256KB, 15 cycles	Load/store queue	16 entry
Pipeline	12 stages	Complex unit	2 INT
Processor speed	1 GHz, 1V	Issue	dual, out-of-order
Fetch, dispatch	2 wide	Arithmetic units	3 integer

As discussed earlier we only replace the integer and floating point multiply and divide CMOS unit with a reconfigurable STT-Logic. The int add and fp add remain unchanged in CMOS technology. Our baseline architecture parameter is shown in Table 2. We model a 4-core chip multiprocessor architecture using gem5 simulator. Each core is a dual issue processor similar in functionality to IBM PowerPC 750 FX architecture. We used SPEC benchmarks suite for evaluation. The benchmarks were simulated for 2 billions instructions after fast forwarding for 2 billions instructions. For the power and delay overhead associated with reconfiguration we used the results reported in sections 3.1 and 3.2.

5.1 Results

In this section we report the performance and power for the five following architecture:

-*Baseline-1X*: All functional units are implemented in CMOS and there is no reconfiguration. We assume that in baseline architecture leakage power is suppressed by power-gating technique reported in [8] with the performance loss below 2%.

-*Baseline-2X*: All functional units are implemented in CMOS and the number of functional units increased by 2X compared to baseline. As discussed in [6] in superscalar processors increasing the number of functional unit impact the processor operating clock frequency. Based on [6] we assume the clock operating frequency in this design is reduced by 15%. Similar to Baseline-1X leakage power in functional unit is being suppressed [8].

Static-Reconfig: Except int add and fp add other functional units are implemented in STT-NV technology and therefore they are reconfigured using static technique.

Dynamic-BIA-Reconfig: Except int add and fp add other functional units are implemented in STT-NV technology and therefore they are reconfigured using dynamic Balanced idle to active technique.

Dynamic-BMA-Reconfig: similar to *Dynamic-BIA-Reconfig* except that the reconfiguration algorithm is dynamic Biased idle to most active technique. In Figure 5 we report the performance improvement of the static and dynamic algorithms normalized to the CMOS baseline architecture with no reconfiguration (Baseline-1X). We also report the performance impact of doubling the number of functional units. Since doubling the number of functional unit increases the issue width [6] and therefore impacts the operating clock frequency, for all cases we report the IPC x Clock-Frequency as a performance metric to account for the frequency impacts. In Baseline-2X design, while 2X number of functional units could potentially provide more opportunity to improve performance, in many benchmarks we observe an overall performance loss. The largest performance loss is in ammp, galgel, perl, and vortex; with more than 10% performance degradation. Interestingly these are the

benchmarks where increasing functional unit does not improve IPC significantly – therefore when taking into account the impact on frequency (15%) we observe a large loss in terms of IPC x Clock-Frequency. On average a Baseline-2X can only improve performance by 2%. However, in a reconfigurable STT-NV design since there is no impact on the clock frequency we can see a noticeable performance improvement across most benchmarks. In STT-NV reconfigurable architecture, for most integer benchmarks including bzip2, crafty, eon, gap, gcc, gzip, mcf, parser, perlbmk, twolf, vortex and vpr the static technique almost match the more complex dynamic techniques. In fact for these benchmarks we observed a lot of underutilization in the functional unit and the fp units are not used for the entire program execution time. Therefore, by simply monitoring during the learning phase we can identify these idle units and reconfigure them to the heavily utilized units like int adder/multiplier and divider. Since these benchmark behavior remain almost the same after the learning phase, the simple static technique can identify the best reconfiguration and apply it for the entire program execution time. Unlike integer benchmark, for floating point benchmark the static technique cannot capture the program behavior in terms of functional unit utilization by simply monitoring the processor during learning phase. This is particularly the case for applu, mesa, mgrid, and wupwise. For these benchmarks the static algorithm during the learning phase cannot capture the performance bottleneck unit(s) (Figure 2(b)). In fact for these benchmarks the behavior of the program changes significantly after the learning phase. Comparing the two dynamic algorithms show interesting results – in many cases the Dynamic-BIA algorithm is able to capture program behavior at run-time and accordingly reconfigure the idle functional unit to the performance bottleneck ones. However there are few cases that this algorithm also cannot find the performance bottleneck units. Examples are applu, apsi and facerec where the dynamic-BIA algorithm attempts to balance the reconfiguration instead of being biased towards the performance bottleneck unit: fp add, fpmul, and fp add, respectively. On the other hand, the dynamic-BMA is biased towards performance bottleneck functional units by constantly monitoring all functional unit activities. In Figure 6 we present the power dissipation breakdown of functional units in Dynamic-BMA-Reconfig and Baseline-1X designs. To have a better understanding of the power dissipation among several benchmarks, we have separated integer benchmarks (top) from floating point benchmarks (bottom). Note that for Baseline-1X CMOS based design we assumed an state-of-the-art power gating technique has been applied to suppress the leakage power by up to 90% in floating points units and up to 45% in integer units. [6]. In both integer and floating point benchmarks, for IntMUL, IntDIV units the leakage power reduces in STT-NV Reconfigurable based design compared to a CMOS based design (results per unit not presented due to space limitation). In integer benchmarks, for IntALU, the leakage power is lower in Dynamic-BMA-Reconfig compared to CMOS Baseline-1X design. Note that in CMOS based design there is small opportunity to suppress leakage using power-gating techniques, as integer unit is busy most of the times. Overall in integer benchmarks the total leakage power of all functional units increase in Dynamic-BMA-Reconfig design compared to CMOS Baseline-1X design. In fp benchmarks the total leakage power of all functional units in Dynamic-BMA-Reconfig design reduces substantially by up to 51% compared to CMOS Baseline-1X design. The dynamic power increases in both integer and floating point benchmarks in reconfigurable design. This is somewhat expected as STT-NV reconfigurable design attempts to put more functional units into work and therefore they have higher dynamic power dissipation compared to a CMOS based design. In integer benchmark Dynamic-

BMA-Reconfig design has on average 61% higher total power dissipation compared to CMOS+PG design. This is mainly due to significant rise in dynamic power and improving in performance for STT-NV designs compared to a CMOS based design. In floating point benchmark, the total power reduces by 22% in STT-NV design compared to CMOS Baseline-1X design. Using McPAT power simulator [7] we estimated the total processor power dissipation to be increased on average by 4.1% in integer benchmarks and to be reduced on average by 2.3% in floating point benchmarks compared to a CMOS based design.

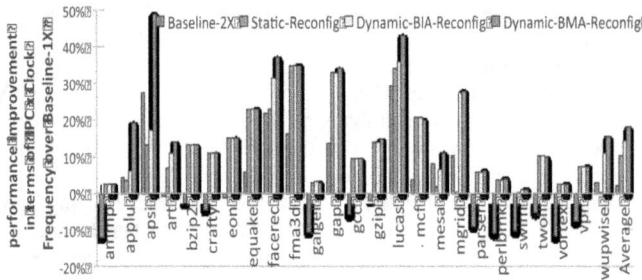

Figure 5. Relative performance improvement of various architecture with and without STT-NV.

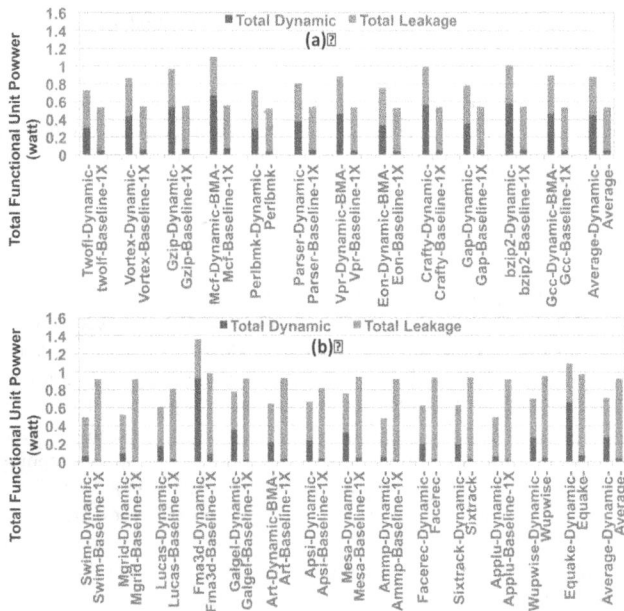

Figure 6. Total power (dynamic and leakage) of functional units for Dynamic-BMA-Reconfig and Baseline-1X in (a) Integer and (b) floating point benchmarks.

6 CONCLUSION

This paper proposes the novel concept of adaptive functional units for improving performance in general-purpose processor. Unavailability of functional units is a main source of performance bottleneck in general-purpose architectures. With functional unit adaptation we overcome this challenge. A selected set of complex functional units that might be under-utilized such as multiplier, divider, etc. are replaced with a programmable STT-NV based look up table fabric. This allows for run-time reconfiguration of such functional units to the functional units that might be creating performance bottleneck, and hence improving performance via functional redundancy and parallel computation. The results show

significant performance improvement across standard benchmark. In addition to performance benefit, the new STT-NV based design and architecture is more power-efficient in floating point benchmarks compared to the a CMOS based design. Our future work will study how STT-NV reconfigurable logic can be deployed in other performance/power/temperature bottlenecks in processor architecture to improve efficiency.

7 REFERENCES

[1] Kejariwal. A., et al., "Comparative Architectural Characterization of SPEC 2000 and 2006 Benchmarks on the Intel Core Processor," SAMOS, 2008.

[2] Folegnani, D., and A. González. "Energy-effective issue logic.". Proceedings. 28th Annual International Symposium on. IEEE, 2001.

[3] A. Kulkarni, H. Homayoun and T. Mohsenin "A Parallel and Reconfigurable Architecture for Efficient OMP Compressive Sensing Reconstruction", The 24'th Annual Great Lakes Symposium on VLSI (GLSVLSI'2014).

[4] Kulkarni and T. Mohsenin "Parallel and Reconfigurable architectures for OMP compressive sensing reconstruction algorithm", In proceedings of The SPIE Sensing Technology and Applications Conference, May 2014.

[5] Adam Page and Tinoosh Mohsenin, "An Efficient & Reconfigurable FPGA and ASIC Implementation of a Spectral Doppler Ultrasound Imaging System", IEEE International Conference on Application-specific Systems, Architectures and Processors (ASAP 24), June 2013.

[6] Palacharla, Subbarao, Norman P. Jouppi, and James E. Smith. Complexity-effective superscalar processors. Vol. 25. No. 2. ACM, 1997.

[7] Sheng Li, et al. "McPAT: An Integrated Power, Area, and Timing Modeling Framework for Multicore and Manycore Architectures", in Micro 2009

[8] Anita Lungu, Pradip Bose, et al, "Dynamic Power Gating with Quality Guarantees" ISLPED, 2009.

[9] X. Dong, et al. "NVSim: A Circuit-Level Performance, Energy, and Area Model for Emerging Nonvolatile Memory." TCAD, 2012.

[10] Homayoun, Houman, and Amirali Baniasadi. "Reducing execution unit leakage power in embedded processors." Embedded Computer Systems: Architectures, Modeling, and Simulation (2006).

[11] Homayoun, Houman, Kin F. Li, and Setareh Rafatirad. "Functional units power gating in SMT processors." Communications, Computers and signal Processing. 2005 IEEE Pacific Rim Conference on. IEEE PACRIM

[12] Guo, X., et al., 2010: Resistive computation: Avoiding the power wall with low-leakage, stt-mram based computing. Power, 371–382.

[13] J. Bisasky, H. Homayoun, F. Yazdani and T. Mohsenin, "A 64-core platform for biomedical signal processing", In proceedings of The International Symposium on Quality Electronic Design (ISQED), 2013.

[14] H. Mahmoodi, S. Lakshmipuram, M. Arora, Y. Asgarieh, H. Homayoun, B. Lin, D. Tullsen, Resistive Computation: A Critique, IEEE Computer Architecture Letter, 2013.

[15] J. Stanislaus and T. Mohsenin, "Low-complexity FPGA implementation of compressive sensing reconstruction," IEEE International Conference on Computing, Networking and Communications, (ICNC'13), January 2013.

[16] F. Ren and D. Markovic. True energy-performance analysis of the mtj-based logic-in-memory architecture (1-bit full adder). Electron Devices, IEEE Transactions on, 57(5):2010.

[17] Adarsh Reddy Ashammagari, Hamid Mahmoodi, Houman Homayoun, Exploiting STT-NV Technology for Reconfigurable, High Performance, Low Power, and Low Temperature Functional Unit Design, DATE 2014.

[18] J. Bisasky, J. Chander, and T. Mohsenin, "A many-core platform implemented for multi-channel seizure detection," In proceedings of The IEEE International Symposium on Circuits and Systems (ISCAS'12), 2012.

[19] Predictive technology models. http://ptm.asu.edu/.

A Generic Implementation of a Quantified Predictor on FPGAs

Gervin Thomas
Technische Universität Berlin
Embedded Systems
Architecture
Berlin, Germany
gervin.thomas@tu-berlin.de

Ahmed Elhossini
Technische Universität Berlin
Embedded Systems
Architecture
Berlin, Germany
ahmed.elhossini@tu-berlin.de

Ben Juurlink
Technische Universität Berlin
Embedded Systems
Architecture
Berlin, Germany
b.juurlink@tu-berlin.de

ABSTRACT

Predictors are used in many fields of computer architectures to enhance performance. With good estimations of future system behavior, policies can be developed to improve system performance or reduce power consumption. These policies become more effective if the predictors are implemented in hardware and can provide quantified forecasts and not only binary ones.

In this paper, we present and evaluate a generic predictor implemented in VHDL running on an FPGA which produces quantified forecasts. Moreover, a complete scalability analysis is presented which shows that our implementation has a maximum device utilization of less than 5%. Furthermore, we analyze the power consumption of the predictor running on an FPGA. Additionally, we show that this implementation can be clocked by over 210 MHz. Finally, we evaluate a power-saving policy based on our hardware predictor. Based on predicted idle periods, this power-saving policy uses power-saving modes and is able to reduce memory power consumption by 14.3%.

Categories and Subject Descriptors

B.0 [**Hardware**]: General

1. INTRODUCTION

Right now, we are living in a time where the complexity of computer systems and embedded systems increase very fast, since more computational components are integrated on smaller and smaller chips. This high complexity allows us to develop embedded systems which have high computational power in small hand-held devices like tablets and smartphones. However, with this high degree of complexity, problems like a high amount of data transfer between components inside these embedded systems or the high power consumption which drains the battery of these portable devices arise. Some of these problems can be reduced or solved with a good estimation of the prospective behavior of such components. This is the point where predictors come into the focus. The well known predictors in the field of computer engineering are usually simple branch predictors which decide if a branch is taken or not. This is a binary decision perfectly suitable for branch predictors. However, if the problem becomes more intricate and a binary decision is not sufficient, more complex predictors are required which can quantify forecasts. These types of predictors allow developing of strategies and policies that can increase system performance or reduce power consumption. For example, in [14] a power-saving policy was presented that reduces the *dynamic random-access memory* (DRAM) power consumption tremendously. The whole power-saving policy is based on a predictor which forecasts the length of the memory idle periods. Using this idle period length, a memory power-saving mode is applied to reduce the memory power consumption and wake up the memory before the next request arrives to avoid wake-up penalties. However, the authors did not present a hardware implementation for this predictor and the power consumption of the predictor itself. In order to fill this gap, we present an implementation of a generic predictor in *very high speed integrated circuit hardware description language* (VHDL). The three main contributions of this paper can be summarized as follows: (1) The *register-transfer level* (RTL) implementation of the generic predictor is introduced in detail. (2) A complete scalability analysis for the RTL implementation of the generic predictor is presented, which includes resource, frequency and power consumption analysis for a *field programmable gate array* (FPGA). (3) We evaluate the hardware predictor by applying the power-saving policy presented in [14]. This shows the efficiency of this policy by predicting the memory idle periods for three different multimedia benchmarks including the power consumption of the predictor itself

This paper is organized as follows: Section 2 presents a brief overview of related work. Afterwards, we present the required background knowledge in Section 3 to understand all following sections. The VHDL implementation of the predictor is described in Section 4 including the whole data path as well as the control unit. Section 5 depicts the complexity, frequency and power consumption analysis as well as the evaluation of the power-saving policy from [14]. Finally, Section 6 summarizes and highlights the contributions of this work.

GLSVLSI'14, May 21–23, 2014, Houston, Texas, USA.
Copyright 2014 ACM 978-1-4503-2816-6/14/05 ...$15.00.
http://dx.doi.org/10.1145/2591513.2591517.

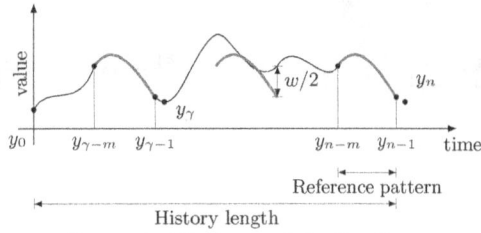
Figure 1: Working of the Predictor

2. RELATED WORK

Predictors are used in many areas of computer architecture. For example in [20] and [13] a predictor was used to reduce average DRAM access latency by forecasting whether an open DRAM row should be closed. Both predictors can therefore only forecast a binary result, whether an action should take place or not. Similarly in [1], a predictor is used to predict DRAM locality to perform page closing decisions.

Another field for predictors is to forecast traffic patterns in networks. In [11] a predictor was used to predict switch-to-switch traffic in a *network on chip* (NoC). A table-driven predictor was presented in [6] to forecast end-to-end traffic. In [4] the authors presented a fuzzy-based predictive traffic model to avoid congestion while maintaining high quality service in *Asynchronous Transfer Mode* (ATM) networks. However, all these mentioned predictors did not present a hardware implementation or any kind of power analysis for their predictors. In [15], a predictor was applied to forecast traffic in NoC, however the authors presented only results based on a software implementation. In [14], the same predictor was used inside a memory controller to snoop memory access. With this data, the predictor forecasts memory idle periods and based on this forecasts a power-saving policy was presented to achieve significant power reductions with only a marginal performance penalty. However, the authors did not present a power analysis for the predictor itself. The authors in [5] presented a fuzzy logic controller running on an FPGA. This controller used a similar technique like [15] and [14] to forecast data points. In [7] the authors presented an implementation of intelligent predictors for solar irradiation running on FPGA. However, both did not provide any analysis on power consumption for their work.

All mentioned predictors were either not able to perform quantified forecasts, the predictor was not implemented in hardware or does not include a complete scalability and power analysis. In contrast, we address all these points in our paper.

3. BACKGROUND

The generic history-based predictor used in this paper was originally proposed in [15], where it was used to forecast traffic pattern for rerouting in networks. In [14] this predictor was used to forecast memory idle periods. Based on this forecast a power-saving strategy was developed to reduce the energy consumption of memory for a *multiprocessor System-on-Chip* (MPSoC). However, the authors did not present a hardware implementation of the predictor. This paper presents a fully synthesizeable VHDL implementation of this predictor. To understand this implementation, the theoretical background of the predictor is introduced in this section.

The general structure of the predictor is depicted in Figure 1. The predictor builds up a history of data points (y_0

to y_{n-1}) before forecasting the next future data point (y_n). Afterwards, the predictor probes the history of data points, considering a current set of reference data points between (y_{n-1}) and (y_{n-m}) and searches for similar patterns in the history. If there is a similar pattern in the past that is very similar to the reference pattern, like the pattern between ($y_{\gamma-m}$) and ($y_{\gamma-1}$), the algorithm weights the next data point (y_γ) depending on the similarity. The matching to past data points is not limited to just one occurring pattern set in the history. Once the predictor has probed the whole history, the next future data point (y_n) is calculated by considering all weighted data points from the history.

The prediction is done in 5 steps. To understand the RTL implementation of the predictor these steps are explained in more detail:

1) Build history: Before the predictor is able to forecast data points, a set of n data points is required (*history length*).

2) Calculate absolute differences: Next, the algorithm considers the latest m data points between (y_{n-1}) and (y_{n-m}) as *reference pattern*. These reference patterns are subtracted iteratively from the history data points.

$$D_i = Y[n-m-i-1, n-2-i] \qquad (1)$$
$$- Y[n-m, n-1] \qquad i \in [0, n-m-1]$$

3) Determine weight/similarity: A parameter *width* (w) is used to identify whether a set of differences fits the reference pattern. A triangular function $\mu(x)$ is applied to all data points to weight all similar ones and set all other which differs by more than $|w/2|$ to zero. To determine the weight for each set of absolute differences, all single weights within this set are multiplied among each other.

$$\beta_i = \prod_{k=0}^{m-1} \mu(d_{i,k}) \qquad (2)$$

4) Weight past data points: In the following, each weight is multiplied with the corresponding data point and summed up. In addition, the sum of all weights is calculated. Both steps are necessary to forecast the next data point and are shown in next step as numerator and denominator.

5) Forecast data point: In the last step N is divided by D and calculates the next future data point.

$$y_n = \frac{N}{D} = \frac{\sum_{\gamma=0}^{n-m-1} \beta_\gamma \cdot y_{n-\gamma-1}}{\sum_{\gamma=0}^{n-m-1} \beta_\gamma} \qquad (3)$$

This operation matches the calculation of the weighted mean.

4. IMPLEMENTATION

To implement the predictor in VHDL, several constraints are made. The introduced algorithm works on rational numbers. However, in [14] the predictor was used on unsigned integer and was, nevertheless, able to predict all necessary values. Moreover, the realization for unsigned integer decreases the complexity, since components like adder and multiplier are easier to build. Hence, the predictor is implemented to work on unsigned integer.

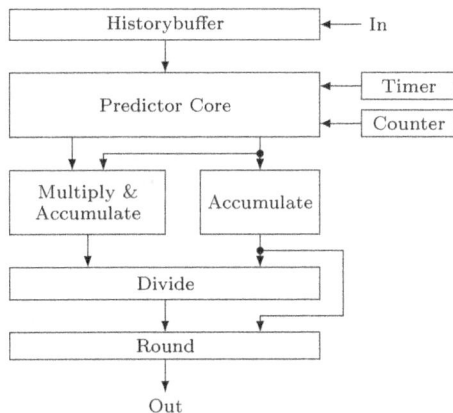

Figure 2: Components in the data path of the predictor

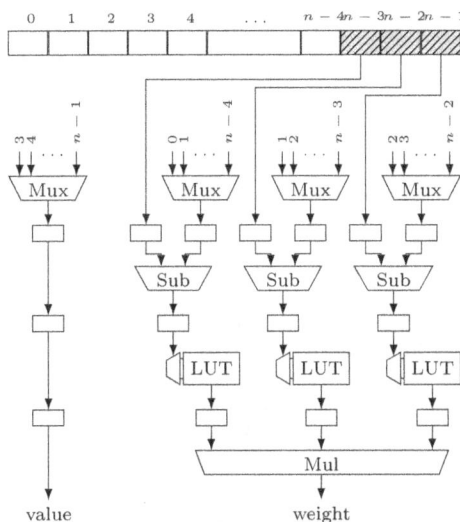

Figure 3: Predictor Core in detail

Figure 2 gives an overview of all components necessary to realize the data path of the predictor. First, a description of all components is provided to realize steps (1) to (5) from Section 3. Afterwards, the control unit is introduced and explained in detail to complete the full predictor unit.

4.1 Data Path

To build up a history as described in Section 3, a generic FIFO buffer is used, where each element is also placed on the output. Step (2), calculate absolute differences, and (3), determine weight/similarity, are both performed in the component *predictor core* which is depicted in Figure 3. The latest entries are the *reference pattern* and are depicted as crosshatched lines. The predictor is generic in terms of the *reference pattern* but set to three in this figure. Each element of the reference pattern is connected to a *subtractor* (sub), respectively. The other input of the subtractors are all possible past data points connected via *multiplexer* (mux) which is controlled by the counter shown in Figure 2. Every clock cycle another set of absolute differences between the reference pattern and the past data points is calculated.

The triangular function from step (3) must be adapted to handle unsigned integers. By extending the Y-range from $[0, 1]$ to $[0, w/2]$ all differences can still be weighted due to their similarity using unsigned integer. The weighting is realized as *lookup table* (LUT). Next, all single weighted

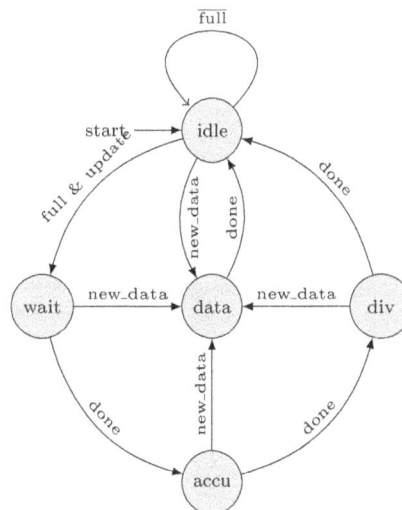

Figure 4: Predictor FSM

values are multiplied among each other to weight the corresponding past data point named as *value*. The design is pipelined to increase clock frequency. As an additional component, a timer is connected to the *predictor core* as depicted in Figure 2. The timer can be used to delay the prediction process by a user defined amount of clock cycles. In [14] this functionality was needed to apply a standard time-out strategy. For step (4), a standard accumulator, taken from [17], is used to sum up all weight and calculate the denominator D. Additionally, a standard multiply and accumulate component was taken from [17] to determine the numerator N by summing up the product of each single weight and the corresponding past data point. Finally for step (5), the devision is realized by using a modified and extended version of the radix-2 divider, presented in [10]. An additional *rounding unit* was implemented which computes, based on the quotient and the remainder, a rounded unsigned integer as result.

4.2 Control Unit

The component depicted in Figure 2 shows the data path of the predictor. A control unit is needed so that all single components work together. The *predictor control unit* is realized as *finite-state machine* (FSM) and is depicted in Figure 4.

The FSM consists of 5 states, namely **idle**, **data**, **wait**, **accu** and **div**. Starting with the state **idle** the FSM is waiting for data input. Independent from the state, every time a new value arrives the FSM changes the state to **data**, add the value to the historybuffer and returns to the **idle** state. As long as the historybuffer is not full and no new data arrived the FSM stays in **idle**. Once the historybuffer is full the FSM changes the state to **wait** to delay the prediction process for a user chosen amount of clock cycles. Following, the FSM goes to state **accu** which triggers the *predictor core* as well as the accumulators. Once the whole history is processed, the FSM changes to state **div** to calculate the final result. After the prediction process has finished, the FSM stays in state **idle** until new data arrives.

5. RESULTS

In this section, first the experimental setup is presented. Afterwards, experiments are shown to analyze the predictors

Table 1: Parameter configuration for the predictor scalability

Parameter	Range
History length (hl)	$10, 20, 30, 40, 50$
Pattern length (pl)	$2, 3, 4, 5$
Width (w)	$2, 4, 6, 8$
Register size (rs)	$4, 5, 6, 7, 8$ bit

Table 2: Usage of slice registers/LUTs to implement the predictor on an Spartan-6 FPGA

	Usage	Spartan-6	Utilization[%]
#LUT	$245 \ldots 1278$	27288	$0.9 \ldots 4.68$
#Register	$186 \ldots 891$	54576	$0.34 \ldots 1.63$

scalability due to the variation of the different predictor parameters. Finally, we apply the generic hardware predictor to analyze the power consumption for the power-saving policy introduced in [14] using real multimedia benchmarks. For more information about the predictor like the accuracy, we refer to [15], since this analysis was already done in detail.

5.1 Experimental Setup

The predictor is implemented as a generic and fully synthesizeable VHDL implementation. As described in Section 3 the predictor has four parameters which have a huge influence on the predictor performance. The parameters are *history length (hl), register size (rs), pattern length (pl)* and *width (w)*. For the rest of this paper, we refer to an instance of the predictor with fixed set of parameters as *predictor configuration*.

To analyze the influence of these four mentioned predictor parameters on the scalability, power consumption and maximum frequency, the design space depicted in Table 1 is used. The predictor is set up with a parameter set, synthesized with the help of the Xilinx ISE Design Suite 14.6 [18] as well as placed and routed. As target device a Spartan-6 FPGA [19] is used. After the place and route, the scalability of the design is analyzed. To determine the maximum frequency, the design is iteratively synthesized using a constraint on the frequency. Section 5.2 presents the results for the device utilization, run time and maximum frequency.

In Section 5.3 the power consumption is analyzed using the lowest frequency (50 MHz) achievable for all configurations within the design space as well as the same 4 bit input sequence to achieve comparable results. The power consumption is determined by simulating each configuration with Mentor Graphics ModelSim 6.6SE [8] and analyzed afterwards using the XPower Analyzer [18].

Finally, in Section 5.4 results are presented by applying the predictor to real multimedia benchmark. In [14] a power-saving policy was presented to reduce memory power consumption for DRAMs applying the same predictor on memory idle cycles. Based on the predicted length of these idle cycles one of two memory power-saving modes is used to reduce power consumption with a negligible performance penalty. However, this work does not consider the power consumption of the predictor itself. The determined data from [14] are taken and validated against the power numbers from a predictor configuration running on an FPGA.

5.2 Device Utilization Analysis

The parameter w has only a minor influence on the predictor complexity and is therefore not shown in any figure. Increasing the width influences the complexity of all following components only marginally. As shown in previous works [14, 15] the parameter w ranges between 4 to 6 in most cases which gives a maximum bit size of 3. We analyze all *predictor configurations* with a *width* of 4.

Figure 5 depicts the device utilization of all analyzed *predictor configurations* by giving the number of used slice reg-

isters and slice LUTs. The x-axis gives the *pattern length* and *register size* (e.g. 2-4 equals a pattern length of 2 and each register in the history buffer has 4 bit). Each stacked bar gives the device utilization by depicting the slice register (R) in the lower and the slice LUTs (L) in the upper part for a certain *history length*.

For a given *pl* and *rs*, the number of used slice registers and slice LUTs grows with the increasing *history length*. This reflects the growing history buffer since a longer *history length* requires more registers inside the history buffer to store the past data values. However, the *predictor core* and the following computational components do not become larger, since the *history length* has no influence on these components.

Also the influence of the *register size* on the history buffer can be seen in Figure 5. A larger *register size* results in an increasing complexity, not only because of the history buffer becoming more complex but because of the *predictor core* and the computational components doing so as well.

The increase of the *pattern length* at fixed size *hl* and *rs* cause also a growing complexity, since the *pl* equals the number of chains (mux, sub, LUT) inside the predictor core as can be seen in Figure 3. However, the bit size of the calculated value *weight* increases and causes an increased complexity of all following components, since more values have to be multiplied . The available and used slice registers/LUTs for the Spartan-6 FPGA are shown in Table 2. As can be seen, most of the FPGA is not used and the device utilization is always below 5%.

The predictor has a certain latency to finish the forecast, which ranges between 28 cc for smaller configurations and 120 cc for the maximum configuration. There are two main contributors to the total latency: (1) The historybuffer, since all elements need to be probed clockwise and therefore the number of clock cycles equals the *hl*. (2) The latency of the divider equals the maximum bit size of both input vectors, which is identical to the output vector of the *Multiply & Accumulate* component. The size of this vector can be estimated by the following formula:

$$\text{div}_{cc} = r + \left\lceil \log_2 \left(\frac{w}{2} \right) \right\rceil \cdot pl + (hl - pl)$$

The total latency for the predictor can be estimated as sum of both main contributors.

We also determined the maximum frequency for each predictor configuration. The frequency ranges between 210 MHz and 85 MHz depending on the configuration's complexity. With growing complexity the maximum frequency drops, since operations performed by the predictor's components increase, too.

5.3 Power Consumption Analysis

To achieve comparable results for the power consumption all predictor configurations run with the same frequency and the same test pattern as described in Section 5.1. Figure 6 depicts the power consumption for different *predictor configurations*. One stacked bar depicts the total power consumption for a certain *history length, pattern length* and *register*

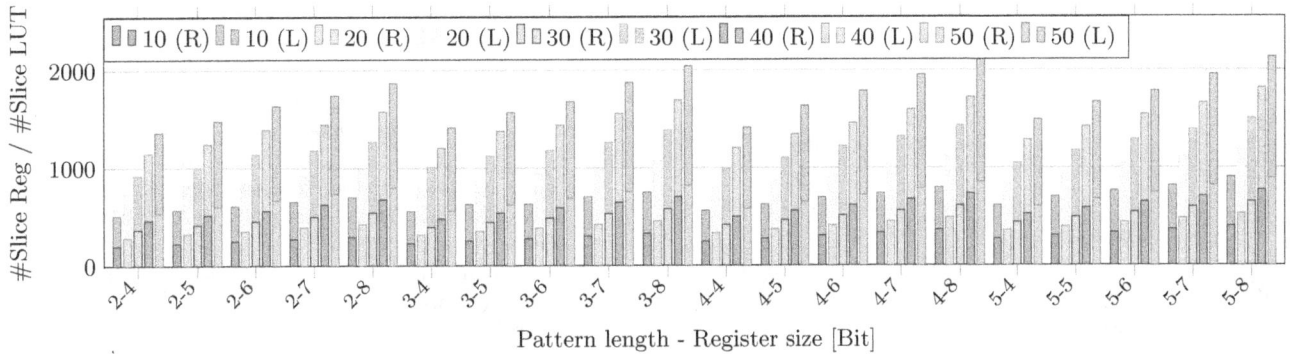

Figure 5: Number of used slice registers and slice LUTs

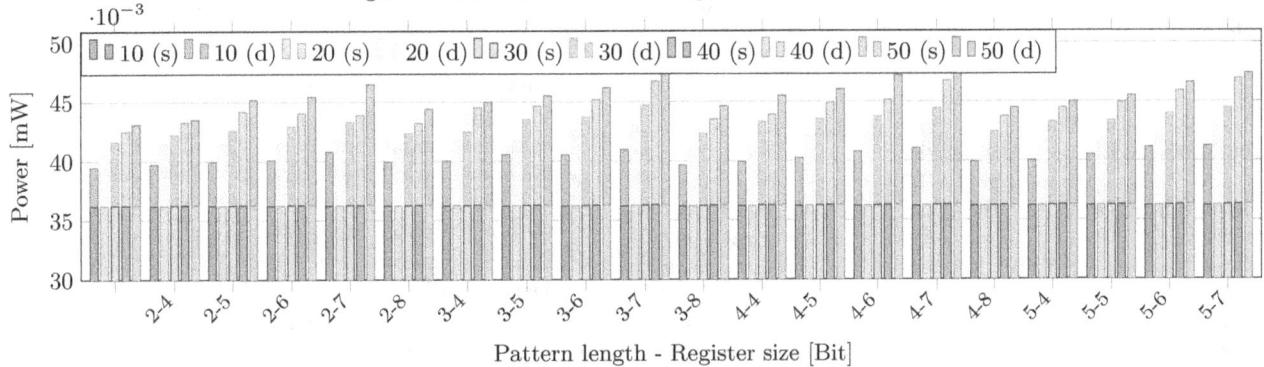

Figure 6: Spartan-6 FPGA Power Consumption

size in Watts. The lower part of each bar gives the static power consumption and the upper half the dynamic one. For better presentation, the y-axis starts at 30 mW. Again, the x-axis shows the *pattern length* and the *register size*.

It can be seen clearly that the static power consumption for each configuration is almost constant. There are some variations for each configuration, however this can not be seen in the figure, since they are in ranges around ±0.1 mW. The reason for almost constant static power is that the predictor is running on an FPGA. Independent from the size of the predictor design, the basic static power consumption for the Spartan-6 FPGA is at 31 mW [16], since the whole FPGA has to be powered. Moreover, our design contributes to the static power only by approximately 6 mW.

The dynamic power consumption is heavily influenced by the *predictor configuration*. The higher the complexity of the design, like longer *history length*, higher *pattern length* or a larger *register size*, the higher the dynamic power consumption.

However, it is important to point again to the high static power consumption compared to our small predictor design as shown in the previous section. Around 85% of total static power consumption is needed to power the whole FPGA and only the remaining 15% is consumed by our design. This power can be decreased tremendously if a smaller or more power efficient FPGA is used. Moreover, also the realization as *application-specific integrated circuit* (ASIC) would decrease the power consumption.

5.4 Memory Idle Prediction

In this section, we evaluate the impact of the predictor forecasting on memory idle periods, based on the approach presented in [14]. The predictor was integrated in the memory controller and used to forecast the length of memory idle periods. Based on this prediction the used memory (Micron DDR3-800 [9]) was set to one of two power-saving modes (power-down or self-refresh). However, selecting the best power-saving mode depends on the length of the idle period, the power-down mode is more gainful for short periods and self-refresh for longer one. Both modes have a wake-up penalty if the memory was not powered up in time before the next request arrives. A power-saving policy was presented that combines the best of both power-saving modes.

To validate this power-saving policy [14], the authors presented results for three multimedia benchmarks (H263 decoder, Ray Tracer and JPEG encoder) running on the CompSOC platform [12] and using [2, 3] to analyze power. The predictor was set up with the following configuration [14]: $hl = 50$, $pl = 2$, $w = 4$ and $rs = 4$ bit. The authors reduced the energy consumption between 68.8% and 79.9% with only a marginal increase in execution time form 0.3% up to 2.2%, but did not consider the power consumption of the predictor itself.

The power saving policy used in CompSOC system [14] required the forecast of the idle time to be delivered after a specific period of time after the last activity of the memory. In order to meet this requirement, the predictor presented in this paper was configured as described earlier, synthesized and implemented to target operation frequency of 180 MHz. A test bench was used to insert the same multimedia benchmarks. To analyze the power consumption the same setup presented in Section 5.1 is used.

Figure 7 depicts the results of the power analysis for the three different multimedia benchmarks. The y-axis gives the power numbers and the x-axis the different benchmarks. The first bar (Base) in each set gives the power consumption of the memory without predictor for the corresponding benchmark and is considered as baseline. The second bar for

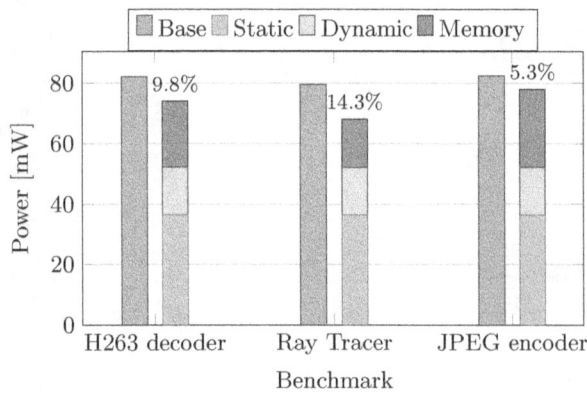

Figure 7: Power consumption analysis for multimedia benchmarks running on the CompSOC platform

each benchmark gives the power consumption of the memory using the power-saving policy from [14] (Memory) as well as the static (Static) and dynamic (Dynamic) power consumption of the predictor itself.

Figure 7 shows that approx. 50% of the total power consumption is caused by the static power of the FPGA. Despite this high static power consumption, the presented power-saving policy [14] still produces beneficial results, since the power consumption of the memory can be reduced by up to 14.3%. However, as already mentioned in previous sections, the whole FPGA has to be powered and therefore 31 mW are needed [16], even if only a small part is used for the design. In our case, this predictor configuration needs less than 5% of the FPGA and consumes only approx. 6 mW. This high basic static power consumption from 31 mW can be reduced by using a more power efficient or smaller FPGA. Moreover, another option to reduce the static power consumption is the realization of predictor as an ASIC which can reduce the power consumption drastically.

6. CONCLUSIONS

In this paper, we have presented a RTL implementation of a generic predictor in VHDL. This predictor is able to produce quantified forecasts and not only binary ones. Furthermore, we have shown how the data path as well as the control unit is implemented. Therefore, we have shown how an algorithm working on real numbers is mapped to hardware working only on unsigned integer numbers. Moreover, we demonstrated that the whole VHDL implementation uses less than 5% resources of an FPGA and still runs with over 210 MHz. We presented power analyses which show the distribution of dynamic and static power when running on an FPGA. Finally, we evaluated a power-saving policy with different multimedia benchmark to reduce the memory power consumption. Using the generic hardware predictor, this power-saving policy reduces the memory power consumption of a DDR3-800 memory by up to 14.3%.

7. REFERENCES

[1] M. Awasthi, D. W. Nellans, R. Balasubramonian, and A. Davis. Prediction Based DRAM Row-Buffer Management in the Many-Core Era. In *20th International Conference on Parallel Architecture and Compilation Techniques (PACT)*, Galveston Island, Texas, October 2011.

[2] K. Chandrasekar, B. Åkesson, and K. Goossens. Improved Power Modeling of DDR SDRAMs. In *14th Euromicro Conference on Digital System Design (DSD)*, 2011.

[3] K. Chandrasekar et al. DRAMPower: Open Source DRAM Power & Energy Estimation Tool. *www.es.ele.tue.nl/drampower*, 2012.

[4] B.-S. Chen, Y.-S. Yang, B.-K. Lee, and T.-H. Lee. Fuzzy Adaptive Predictive Flow Control of ATM Network traffic. *IEEE Transactions on Fuzzy Systems*, 2003.

[5] K. Deliparaschos, F. Nenedakis, and S. Tzafestas. Design and implementation of a fast digital fuzzy logic controller using fpga technology. *Journal of Intelligent and Robotic Systems*, 2006.

[6] Y. Huang, K.-K. Chou, C.-T. King, and S.-Y. Tseng. NTPT: On the End-to-End Traffic Prediction in the On-Chip Networks. In *47th Design Automation Conference (DAC)*, 2010.

[7] A. Mellit, H. Mekki, A. Messai, and S. Kalogirou. Fpga-based implementation of intelligent predictor for global solar irradiation, part i: Theory and simulation. *Expert Systems with Applications*, 2011.

[8] Mentor Graphics. ModelSim, 11 2013.

[9] Micron Technology Inc. *DDR3 SDRAM 1Gb Data Sheet*, 2006.

[10] L. Miller. Division in VHDL, February 2009.

[11] U. Y. Ogras and R. Marculescu. Prediction-based Flow Control for Network-on-Chip Traffic. In *43th Design Automation Conference (DAC)*, New York, NY, USA, 2006. ACM.

[12] B. Åkesson, A. Molnos, A. Hansson, J. Ambrose Angelo, and K. Goossens. Composability and Predictability for Independent Application Development, Verification, and Execution. In *Multiprocessor System-on-Chip — Hardware Design and Tool Integration*, chapter 2. Springer, 2010.

[13] V. Stankovic and N. Milenkovic. DRAM Controller with a Complete Predictor: Preliminary Results. In *7th International Conference on Telecommunications in Modern Satellite, Cable and Broadcasting Services*, volume 2, sept. 2005.

[14] G. Thomas, K. Chandrasekar, B. Akesson, B. Juurlink, and K. Goossens. A Predictor-Based Power-Saving Policy for DRAM Memories. In *15th Euromicro Conference on Digital System Design (DSD)*, 2012.

[15] G. Thomas, B. Juurlink, and D. Tutsch. Traffic Prediction for NoCs using Fuzzy Logic. In *2nd International Workshop on New Frontiers in High-performane and Hardware-aware Computing*, San Antonio, USA, February 2011. KIT Scientific Publishing.

[16] Xilinx. *Xilinx Power Estimator 14.3*, October 2012.

[17] Xilinx. *XST User Guide for Virtex-6, Spartan-6, and 7 Series Devices*, 14.3 edition, October 2012.

[18] Xilinx. ISE Design Suite 14.6, 11 2013.

[19] Xilinx. Spartan-6 FPGA Family, 11 2013.

[20] Y. Xu, A. S. Agarwal, and B. T. Davis. Prediction in Dynamic SDRAM Controller Policies. In *Proc. 9th International Workshop on Embedded Computer Systems: Architectures, Modeling, and Simulation*, 2009.

A Dual-Rail LUT for Reconfigurable Logic using Null Convention Logic

Jing Yu
School of Electrical & Computer Engineering
RMIT University
Melbourne, Australia, 3000
s3336504@student.rmit.edu.au

Paul Beckett
School of Electrical & Computer Engineering
RMIT University
Melbourne, Australia, 3000
pbeckett@rmit.edu.au

ABSTRACT

Both asynchronous and reconfigurable techniques are likely to become increasingly important in the future due to greater device unreliability and variability at nano-scale dimensions. One promising asynchronous technique, Null Convention Logic (NCL) is a symbolically complete quasi-delay insensitive logic system that is inherently self-determined, locally autonomous and self-synchronizing. As current FPGA devices are set up for clocked synchronous logic they are not well suited to reconfigurable asynchronous systems. A reconfigurable block supporting NCL that is intended to form one component of a FPGA organization is proposed and analyzed. Both single-rail and dual-rail LUTs are described. The block design and layout is described and analyzed using an advanced 45nm bulk CMOS fabrication process.

Categories and Subject Descriptors

B.7.1 [**Integrated Circuits**]: Types and Design Styles – *VLSI (very large scale integration)*

Keywords

Null convention logic, reconfigurable, asynchronous logic

1. INTRODUCTION

For many years the semiconductor industry has been able to simply exploit ever smaller transistor sizes to improve computational performance and electrical characteristics [1]. However, this is unlikely to continue as escalating silicon complexity invalidates many of the key design abstractions that have been taken for granted over the last 30 years.

The International Technology Roadmap for Semiconductors (ITRS) [2] identifies a huge list of technical challenges that represent critical "road-blocks" to be solved if the industry is to continue to meet the demands of its customers for cheaper, faster and more capable embedded electronic systems into the future.

Amongst these challenges are the interrelated issues of power

and performance in conventional clocked processor systems. Techniques such as power gating, that switch off unused functionality are becoming common in synchronous designs [3]. However, these various techniques are, at best, ad hoc solutions that impact on performance and can greatly increase hardware and software complexity. It is becoming clear that power consumption can be managed only by careful application of on-chip processing parallelism [4, 5] and by reducing the impact of the global clock.

An obvious solution to the problems of clocked systems is to eliminate the clock i.e., to use an asynchronous approach, even if the removal of the synchronous assumption makes the design process significantly harder. In contrast to a synchronous approach, asynchronous circuits reveal both their timing and data explicitly at their interfaces [6]. Asynchronous signaling (handshaking) tends to be based on a protocol involving requests and acknowledgments that identify the beginning and end of an action to transfer a logic value. Thus, the primary difference between the various asynchronous techniques reduces to variations in the way that the handshaking process is managed.

Null Convention Logic (NCL) [7, 8], is a symbolically complete logic system that implicitly and completely expresses logic processes. It therefore represents a convenient way to describe asynchronous digital logic. In common with other asynchronous styles its advantages include the lack of a global clock, thereby eliminating a major source of power dissipation in synchronous systems.

Asynchronous techniques such as NCL can tolerate wide variability arising from both manufacturing (dopant levels, line roughness, mask alignment errors etc.) and environment (voltage, temperature, etc.). The intrinsically uncorrelated switching noise in asynchronous systems also tends to generate less electromagnetic interference. Finally, because NCL is delay-insensitive and essentially correct-by-construction, it can be more straightforward to achieve a working system using pre-built IP blocks, which can be connected in "plug-and-play" manner, eliminating many of the problems related to synchronous timing closure. While some of these advantages are shared by asynchronous techniques in general, NCL systems can be said to exhibit specific behavior that is self-determined, locally autonomous, self-synchronizing, delay insensitive and inherently fault detecting.

Typical reconfigurable devices, such as FPGAs, tend to be not well suited to asynchronous techniques, due to their fine-grained logic topologies and the need for the place and route tools to identify and maintain tightly constrained delays in both logic and handshake paths. In this paper, we propose and analyze a configurable logic block that is intended to form the basis of a reconfigurable array directly supporting NCL. The block can be configured to represent any of the 27 basic functions that have been defined for 2 to 4 inputs in NCL and has been implemented in an advanced 45nm bulk CMOS process.

The remainder of the paper proceeds as follows. In Section 2, the overall concept of Null Convention Logic is introduced and we identify some of the prior work on reconfigurable NCL logic systems. Section 3 presents the circuit design and layout of our reconfigurable cell and Section 4 illustrates the concept with a simple example of a mapped full adder function. Finally, Section 5 concludes the paper and identifies future work.

2. RECONFIGURABLE NCL

In this section we introduce the overall concept Null Convention Logic and identify existing proposals covering reconfigurable NCL logic systems

2.1 Null Convention Logic

There are two main categories of asynchronous circuit models in common use: bounded-delay and delay-insensitive. The micropipeline technique [9], for example, uses a bounded-delay model, in which it is assumed that delays in both gates and wires are bounded. On the other hand, delay-insensitive circuits such as NCL make no assumptions about the delays in their logic or interconnects beyond a requirement that local wire forks (signals within basic components that fanout to two or more destinations) exhibit equal delays (i.e., are "isochronic"). It is this requirement that is hard to achieve in a FPGA unless the various timing parameters of the interconnection paths are tightly constrained during the place and route stage. This can be extremely difficult to achieve for complex logic functions.

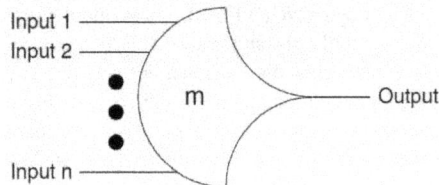

Figure 1. NCL THnm Threshold Gate

Null Convention Logic is a symbolically complete logic system that implicitly and completely expresses logic processes. In this sense, Boolean logic is not complete as it requires the inclusion of an independent time variable (i.e., a clock) that has to be very carefully coordinated with the logic part of the expression to completely and effectively express an operation. NCL adds the control value NULL (i.e., not valid) to the Boolean set to create a symbolically complete and delay insensitive three-value logic system. A gate will only assert its output data when a complete set of (valid) data values is present at its input, thereby enforcing a "completeness of input" criterion. Thus, a key difference between NCL circuits and those of other delay-insensitive methods is that instead of incorporating a single type of state element (i.e., the Muller C-element [10]), all NCL gates exhibit built-in hysteresis or state-holding behavior.

The basic circuit element of NCL is the TH_{mn} threshold gate (Figure 1) [11], where $1 \leq m \leq n$. These gates have n inputs of which at least m must be asserted for the output to respond. The

hysteresis implicit in each gate circuit ensures that the inputs must then all transition back to NULL before the output does the same. Four-input threshold gates with different values of m (i.e., TH_{m4} gates) can generate all functions of four or fewer variables so that complete logic coverage can be established using only 24 basic gate functions.

Table 1 illustrates a subset of NCL gates that illustrate this idea. As can be seen, for a given n, additional terms are added to the function for each increase in m. The *weighting* term, w, $(1 < w \leq m)$ implies that one of the inputs will add two or more "units" to the input. For example, the TH23w2 function describes a 3-input gate with a threshold of 2, where the input A exhibits a "weight" of 2 (equal to the threshold, m, in this case), such that the equivalent Boolean logic function becomes $A + B.C$. NCL gates are considerably more complex than their Boolean counterparts but, at the same time, offer a higher level of functionality to the logic decomposition process. In this context, it can be noted that the final three macro functions listed in Table 1 (making a total of 27 NCL basic gates) could be readily derived from combinations of the remaining 24, but are implemented as standard gates for completeness and to potentially reduce logic complexity.

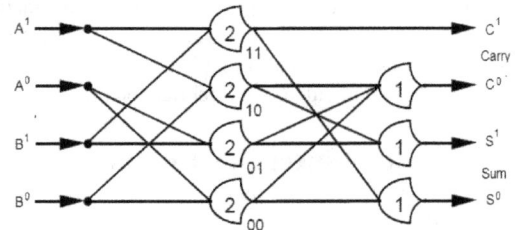

Figure 2. Example NCL Half Adder Circuit

Table 1. Equivalent Boolean Functions of a Partial Subset of 4-Variable NCL Macros

TH_{mn} Gate	Boolean Function	
	Z^1	Z^0
TH12	$A^1 + B^1$	$A^0 B^0$
TH13	$A^1 + B^1 + C^1$	$A^0.B^0.C^0$
TH22	$A^1.B^1$	A^0+B^0
TH23	$A^1.B^1+A^1.C^1+B^1.C^1$	$A^0.B^0+A^0.C^0+B^0.C^0$
TH33	$A^1.B^1.C^1$	$A^0+B^0+C^0$
TH23w2	$A^1+B^1.C^1$	$A^0.B^0+A^0.C^0$
TH33w2	$A^1.B^1+A^1.C^1$	$A^0+B^0.C^0$
TH54w32	$A^1.B^1+A^1.C^1.D^1$	$A^0.+B^0.C^0+B^0.D^0$
TH44w322	$A^0.B^0+A^0.C^0+$ $A^0.D^0+B^0.C^0$	$A^0.B^0+A^0.C^0+$ $A^0.D^0+B^0.C^0$
TH54w322	$A^1.B^1+A^1.C^1+$ $B^1.C^1.D^1$	$A^0.B^0+A^0.C^0+$ $A^0D^0+B^0.C^0$
THxor0	$A^1.B^1+C^1.D^1$	$A^0.C^0+A^0.D^0+$ $B^0C^0+B^0.D^0$
THand0	$A^1.B^1+B^1.C^1+A^1.D^1$	$A^0.B^0+A^0.C^0+B^0.D^0$
TH24comp	$A^1.C^1+B^1.C^1+$ $A^1.D^1+B^1.D^1$	$A^0.B^0+C^0.D^0$

As NCL signals are defined in terms of three values (two data and NULL), multi-bit 'rails' are required to transfer each signal. In this case, we assume that a single NCL signal is transferred on a 2-bit rail, comprising a '0' and a '1' line (e.g., S^1, S^0 and C^1, C^0

of the example in Figure 2). A NULL is defined when the signals are both zero. The remaining possible value (11) is typically reserved for special signaling events such as error conditions. It can be seen from Table 1 that the elements of a 'rail', Z^1 and Z^0, exhibit the same logic forms, albeit with different functions.

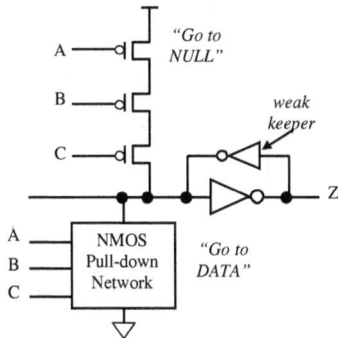

Figure 3. NCL 3-Input Semi-Static Threshold Gate

NCL gates can be implemented in either a fully static or semi-static style. The latter uses a weak feedback inverter to achieve latching behavior (Figure 3) so that only the set (go to DATA) and reset (go to NULL) equations need to be explicitly implemented. Overall, this circuit is slightly faster and requires fewer transistors than its static counterpart. This so-called "weak keeper" maintains static operation by supplying charge lost through leakage at the output node of the array and is typically implemented with transistors that are long (e.g., W:L in excess of 5:1) so that they are easily driven by the pull-up or pull-down circuits.

Numerous example of asynchronous reconfigurable circuits have been developed, based on both bundled data protocols (e.g., STACC [12]), phased logic [13, 14] and NCL [15]. A major problem with bundled data in this context is the need to match the delays in the data and control paths. Systems based on fine-grained look-up tables such as Montage [2] have to synthesize the required state behavior using configured feedback paths and thus rely implicitly on the quality the placement and routing tools to ensure that all delays are matched correctly.

An early reconfigurable NCL system was described in [16] and was based around a 32 transistor LUT that can implement a small range of threshold gates (eight of the possible 27) plus their inverted functions, and with reset and registered outputs. Cell layouts were demonstrated in a 0.5μm 2-layer metal Silicon on Insulator process. The reconfigurable logic element described in [17] uses a Look-up Table organization that is identical to a conventional FPGA in which a tree of pass transistors is used to decode the *minterms* of a particular NCL function that are, in turn, enabled by setting the corresponding configuration register group. The LUT output then drives a single pull down transistor that forms the equivalent to the pull-down network shown in Figure 3. The overall logic block is able to generate the full 27 fundamental NCL gate functions, including resettable and inverting variations.

It can be seen from Figure 3 that the PMOS pull-up circuit ("go to NULL") is the same for all NCL logic functions. Thus, the design problem here reduces to the organization of the reconfigurable NMOS pull down network. In the next section, we describe a simplified single-rail implementation before moving on to the proposed dual-rail solution and a brief look at the LUT configuration system.

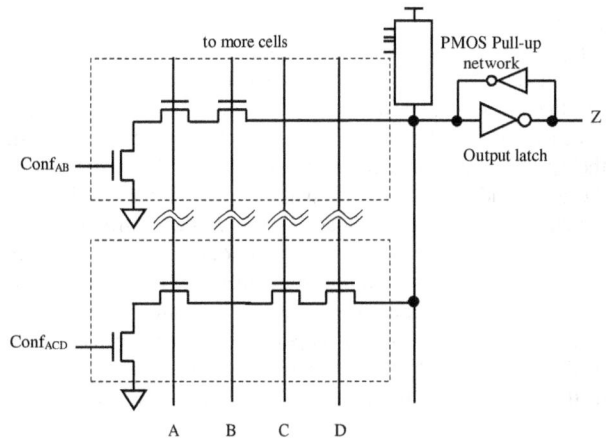

Figure 4. Partial NCL Gate Circuit

3. NCL LUT COMPONENTS

In a similar way to [17], the reconfigurable LUT network proposed here is based on the decomposition of the NCL functions. However, rather than simply decompose the function into its minterms, we start by recognizing that there are only 15 combinations of terms used in the 27 NCL functions defined for four input values of both Z^1 and Z^0 (i.e., A, B, C, D, AB, AC, AD, BC, BD, CD, ABC, ABD, ACD, BCD, ABCD). In this way it is unnecessary to develop the inverse of the input literals ($\overline{A}, \overline{B}$ etc.), the LUT is simplified and decoder tree can be made more regular. Figure 4 illustrates the basic idea. The configuration memory lines (Conf$_{ABCD}$) enable a particular term in the function. For example, the partial circuit of Figure 4 shows the two terms (A.B, A.C.D) that when enabled together form the Z^1 function of the TH54w32 gate in Table 1. As can be seen, the configuration memory simply enables a path to ground for that term in the given function to form: $\overline{A.B + A.C.D}$, which is then inverted by the output latch.

3.1 Single-rail LUT Layout Example

We begin with a simplified example of the single-rail approach to demonstrate the idea. These layouts were performed using the Cadence Virtuoso® design system based on a generic 45nm 6-metal, single-polysilicon bulk CMOS process.

Logic array cells of this type have always tended to exhibit very regular layouts and for that reason were amongst the first structures to be generated algorithmically. However, design for manufacture (DFM) considerations at deep-submicron feature sizes mandate a number of additional layout rules that force even greater regularity. Put simply, even small deviations from regular repetitions of particular features will result in manufacturing difficulties. For example, a "classical" method of creating regular logic array structures (PLAs) of this type is to run (vertical) lines of metal and provide "stubs" of polysilicon where necessary to create a pass-gate. However, this layout technique is not suitable at 45nm and would require additional "dummy" stubs of polysilicon and/or metal 1 (M1) to be inserted to fill the empty space on that layer in order to correct the resulting spatial modulation and to simplify the following oxide growth and planarization stages in manufacture.

As shown in Figure 5, we chose the alternative of creating a complete array of transistors for each term and simply tying the unused devices to V_{DD} (i.e., turning them on permanently). In practice, this is achieved by inserting additional V_{DD} lines between each input line (A..D at the top of Figure 5) and choosing the appropriate connection to the gate stub. This technique has the added advantage that all paths to ground become identical, which makes it easy to adjust the width/length ratio of the LUT transistors to optimize its propagation delay. At the same time, obeying the isochronic timing requirement of NCL is made easier careful control of signal skew (i.e. the variation in propagation delay) between the various outputs. The technique has resulted in signal skews of less than 50pS. Adding configuration registers to the LUT brings its overall size up to approximately 21µm x 28µm ($\cong$590µm^2).

3.2 Dual-rail LUT Layout

The requirements for maintaining isochronic forks in NCL places significant constraints on the place and route process in both FPGA and ASIC environments. One key reason why asynchronous logic has rarely been implemented successfully on standard FPGA parts is the widely variable skew caused by divergent routing paths, and the consequent need to identify and constrain these individual paths. Applying these timing constraints within a conventional FPGA environment represents a significant amount of work and is not always entirely successful [18].

The simplified organization shown in Figure 5 can be extended to handle the full dual-rail signals by including the remaining input signals (A^0..D^0) and connecting these to the corresponding output line (Z^0, in this case). However, it is not necessary for the dual-rail implementation to be constrained to be a simplistic doubling of the single-rail case. Rather, we may take advantage of the extra logic available to extend the functionality of the block. For example, Figure 6 illustrates two important functions required by NCL systems: asynchronous "registers" and completion detection logic (NACK). These form the basis of a hand-shaking mechanism that controls dataflow through the NCL paths.

It can be seen that NCL registers are formed from an array of TH22 gates (eight in this case) where one input is derived from the completion signal from following NCL logic. Implementing these with an array of single-rail reconfigurable gates would result in an extremely inefficient implementation. One option would be to include these specific register structures as part of the LUT cell, to be enabled or disabled as required. We have taken an alternative approach that enhances the connectivity of the LUT structure so that individual terms (A—D) can be combined with the completion detection (NACK) signal to create these register structures within a single LUT. The NACK (*Acknowledge*) signal can be implemented as a 4-of-8 NCL function with inversion. The objective is to detect when all active input rails are carrying data and transmit this completion signal to the previous stage, as shown. Similarly, the asynchronous registers for this stage are controlled by the completion detection signal from a following stage.

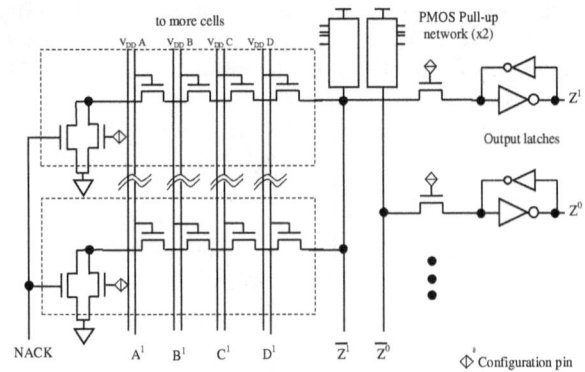

Figure 5.   Simplified LUT Organization

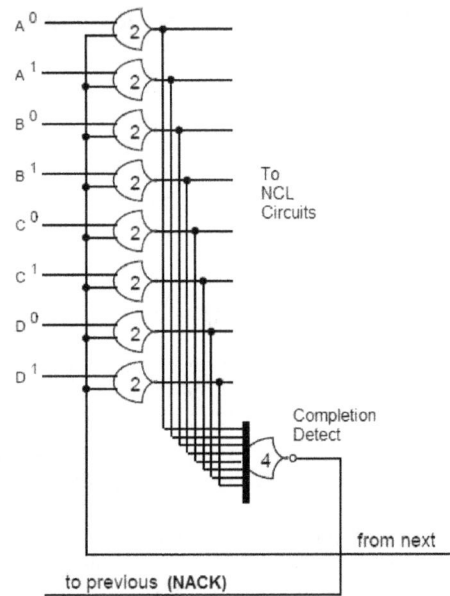

Figure 6.   NCL Register Structure and Completion Detection (NACK)

Figure 7 illustrates a trial layout of the complete LUT using a generic 45nm process. This layout illustrates a number of the key characteristics of the LUT cell including its overall regularity and the fact that the configuration switches occupy more than half the LUT area. It can be seen that the overall dimensions of the block are approximately 28µm x 10.5µm. However, the latches controlling the configuration switches (not shown here) are formed from a dynamic latch array with a second static "shadow" latch to maintain the configuration state. There are about 128 configuration latches controlling this LUT block and their area is about twice that of the LUT block itself, something that is fairly typical of FPGA devices [19]. Taken together, a LUT and its configuration latches are approximately 50% larger in this technology: about 30 x 30µm ($\cong$900µm^2) compared with just less than 600µm^2 in the single rail case.

3.3 Dual-rail LUT Application Example

In this section, we briefly examine a simple example of a one-bit full adder, which has been mapped onto the dual-rail LUT.

$$
\begin{aligned}
D^1 = C_{out}^0 &= A^0B^0 \;+\; A^0C_{in}^0 \;+\; B^0C_{in}^0 \\
D^0 = C_{out}^1 &= A^1B^1 \;+\; A^1C_{in}^1 \;+\; B^1C_{in}^1 \\
S^0 &= A^0D^0 \;+\; B^0D^0 \;+\; C_{in}^0D^0 \;+\; A^0B^0C_{in}^0 \\
S^1 &= A^1D^1 \;+\; B^1D^1 \;+\; C_{in}^1D^1 \;+\; A^1B^1C_{in}^1
\end{aligned}
\tag{1}
$$

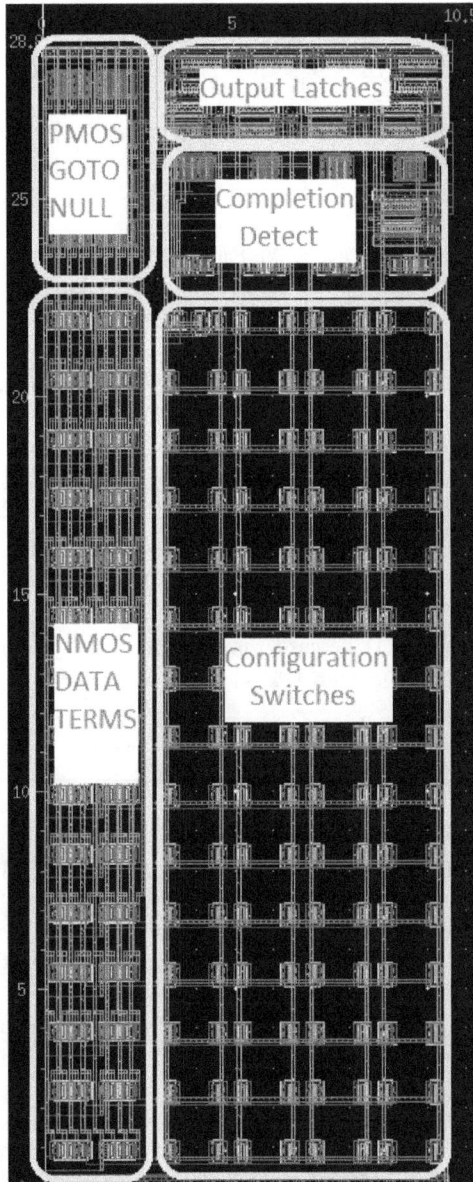

Figure 7. Dual-rail LUT Layout

It can be seen from the logic equations of the full adder outlined in (1) that this particular mapping has optimized the use of the LUT by exploiting an unused input (D) to feed back the carry out terms $\overline{C_{out}^0}$ and $\overline{C_{out}^1}$ to develop the sum terms. The signals therefore pass twice through the LUT to develop the sum terms S^1, S^0. A feature of the dual-rail convention used here is that inverting the logic signal becomes a simple matter of swapping the two lines using external routing switches, such

that $D^1 = C_{out}^0$ and $D^0 = C_{out}^1$. The mapping of the various full adder terms onto the LUT is shown in Figure 8, while Figure 9 shows a partial view of a simulated timing waveform. In this case, the value $ABC_{out}=110$ is applied to the adder so the expected result is S=0, C_{out}=1. In this case, the output signal C_{out}^1 transitions to 1 after about 400pS while C_{out}^0 (not shown) remains at 0. The transition on C_{out}^1 then causes the subsequent transition on S^0 (i.e., Sum = 0), after approximately 430pS. It can also be seen in Figure 9 that the NACK signal becomes active (low) about 350pS after the final sum is valid signaling to the previous stage that this transaction is complete and the input signals can return to NULL.

Over the complete *Null→Data→Null* cycle illustrated in Figure 9, the unloaded cell consumed approximately 10.5µW (with a 1V supply), although its final in-circuit power consumption will obviously increase depending on its post-mapping output load. The average static power for this LUT, based on the 45nm planar CMOS process used for these experiments, was in the region of 900nW.

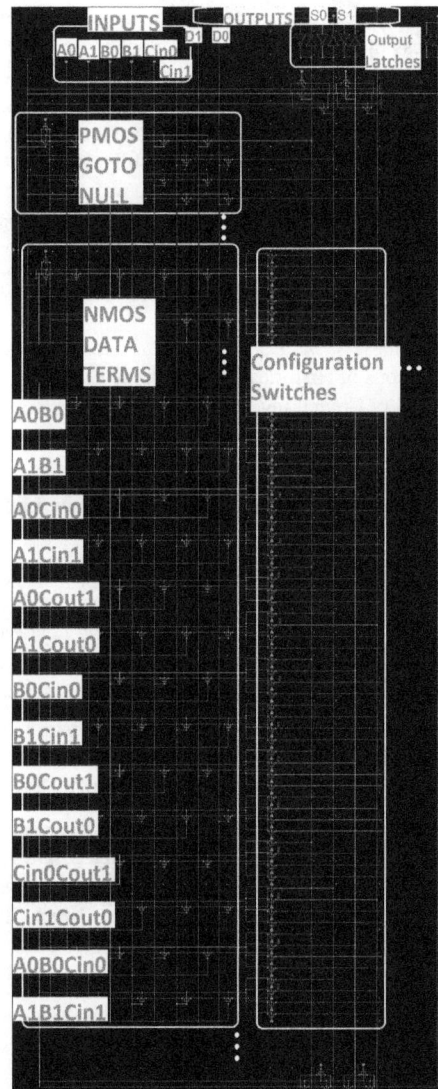

Figure 8. Full Adder Mapped onto Dual-rail LUT

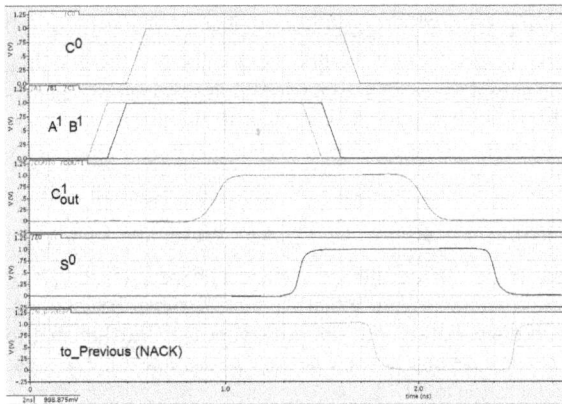

Figure 9.   Dual-rail Full Adder Waveforms

4. CONCLUSIONS

We have presented the design of a reconfigurable block supporting Null Convention Logic that is ultimately intended to form one component of a complete asynchronous FPGA organization. The block has been constructed using a generic 45nm bulk CMOS process that results in a LUT area of around 30μm square and an average propagation delay in the range 400—450pS. While the layout using the 45nm process is very regular, this design style was adopted particularly to ease the transition to our subsequent work which will use a 28 nm fully-depleted thin-body silicon on insulator process. In this case, we expect the overall area of the block to be below 400μm^2 due at least in part to the increased layout densities achievable using SOI technologies.

5. REFERENCES

[1] J. G. Koomey, S. Berard, M. Sanchez, and H. Wong, "Implications of Historical Trends in the Electrical Efficiency of Computing," *IEEE Annals of the History of Computing,* vol. 33, pp. 46-54, 2011.

[2] (2011). *International Technology Roadmap for Semiconductors.* Available: http://www.itrs.net/Links/2011ITRS/Home2011.htm

[3] B. H. Calhoun, F. A. Honore, and A. Chandrakasan, "Design Methodology for Fine-Grained Leakage Control in MTCMOS," in *International Symposium on Low Power Electronics and Design*, Seoul, Korea, ACM Press, 2003, pp. 104-109.

[4] P. Beckett, "Low-Power Spatial Computing using Dynamic Threshold Devices," in *International Symposium on Circuits and Systems, ISCAS'05*, Kobe, Japan, 2005, pp. 2345-2348.

[5] P. Beckett and S. C. Goldstein, "Why Area Might Reduce Power in Nanoscale CMOS," in *International Symposium on Circuits and Systems, ISCAS'05*, Kobe, Japan, 2005, pp. 2329-2332.

[6] A. Davis and S. W. Nowick, "An Introduction to Asynchronous Circuit Design," University of Utah, Salt Lake City, UT, UUCS-97-013, September 19 1997.

[7] K. M. Fant and S. A. Brandt, "Null Convention Logic System," US Patent 5,305,463, 1994.

[8] K. M. Fant and S. A. Brandt, "NULL Convention Logic^{TM}: a complete and consistent logic for asynchronous digital circuit synthesis," in *Proceedings of International Conference on Application Specific Systems, Architectures and Processors, ASAP 96.* , 1996, pp. 261-273.

[9] I. E. Sutherland, "Micropipelines," *Communications of the ACM,* vol. 32, pp. 720-738, 1989.

[10] D. E. Muller, Ed., *Asynchronous logics and application to information processing* (Switching Theory in Space Technology. Stanford, CA: Stanford University Press, 1963, p.^pp. Pages.

[11] G. E. Sobelman and K. M. Fant, "CMOS circuit design of threshold gates with hysteresis," in *IEEE International Symposium on Circuits and Systems (II)*, 1998, pp. 61-65.

[12] R. E. Payne, "Self-Timed FPGA Systems," presented at the 5th International Workshop on Field Programmable Logic and Applications, 1995.

[13] M. Aydin and C. Traver, "Implementation of a Programmable Phased Logic Cell," presented at the 45th Midwest Symposium on Circuits and Systems, Vol. 2, 2002.

[14] C. Traver, R. B. Reese, and M. A. Thornton, "Cell Designs for Self-Timed FPGAs," presented at the 14th Annual IEEE International ASIC/SOC Conference, 2001.

[15] K. Meekins, D. Ferguson, and M. Basta, "Delay Insensitive NCL Reconfigurable Logic," presented at the IEEE Aerospace Conference, Vol. 4, 2002.

[16] D. R. Lamb, "Self-Timed Circuits for Adaptive Processing Systems," presented at the Military and Aerospace Applications of Programmable Devices and Technologies Conference, 1998.

[17] S. C. Smith, "Design of a logic element for implementing an asynchronous FPGA," presented at the Proceedings of the 2007 ACM/SIGDA 15th international symposium on Field programmable gate arrays, Monterey, California, USA, 2007.

[18] M. Rajgara, "Implementation of Null Conventional Logic in COTS FPGA's," Electrical Engineering Masters, Wright State University, 2008.

[19] A. DeHon, "Balancing Interconnect and Computation in a Reconfigurable Computing Array (or, why you don't really want 100% LUT utilization)," in *Proceedings of the International Symposium on Field Programmable Gate Arrays*, 1999, pp. 125-134.

A Complete Electronic Network Interface Architecture for Global Contention-Free Communication over Emerging Optical Networks-on-Chip

Marta Ortín-Obón[§], Luca Ramini[†], Herve Tatenguem Fankem[†], Víctor Viñals[§], Davide Bertozzi[†]

[§] gaz-DIIS-i3A, University of Zaragoza, Spain. {ortin.marta, victor}@unizar.es
[†] ENDIF, University of Ferrara, Italy. {luca.ramini, herve.tatenguemfankem, davide.bertozzi}@unife.it

ABSTRACT

Although many valuable research works have investigated the properties of optical networks-on-chip (ONoCs), the vast majority of them lack an accurate exploration of the network interface architecture (NI) required to support optical communications on the silicon chip. The complexity of this architecture is especially critical for a specific kind of ONoCs: the wavelength-routed ones. From a logical viewpoint, they can be considered as full nonblocking crossbars, thus the control complexity is implemented at the NIs. To our knowledge, this paper proposes the first complete NI architecture for wavelength-routed optical NoCs, by coping with the intricacy of networking issues such as flow control, buffering strategy, deadlock avoidance, serialization, and above all, with their codesign in a complete architecture.

1. INTRODUCTION

The current research frontier for on-chip interconnection networks consists of assessing the feasibility of the optical interconnect technology, by exploiting the recent remarkable advances on silicon photonics [7]. The literature on this topic is becoming quite rich, mainly projecting superior bandwidth, latency and energy with respect to electrical wires beyond a critical length [12]. This benefits are extended to on-chip communication architectures, either as standalone optical networks (ONoCs) [13], or as hybrid interconnect fabrics [4]. Nonetheless, projected quality metrics are overly optimistic for a number of reasons extensively discussed in [1], including optimistic technology assumptions, use of logical topology designs instead of physical ones, and overlooking static power. A big approximation of many projected results is the lack of a complete and accurate network interface architecture for driving on-chip optical communication, which may account for a large fraction of the overall network complexity. This is especially true for a particular category of ONoCs: the Wavelength-Routed ones (WRONoCs). These networks deliver contention-free global connectivity without need for arbitration or packet routing by replicating the amount of wavelengths used, and by associating each wavelength with a different and non-conflicting optical rout-

ing path. Despite their limited scalability, these networks are attractive for specific application domains, where performance predictability and ultra-low latency communications are a must (e.g. data center applications [11]).

WRONoCs can be conceptualized as non-blocking crossbars. Therefore, all the complexity of the control architecture is located at the boundary of the interconnect fabric. To our knowledge, no complete NI architecture has been reported so far in the open literature, with the exception of NIs for space-routed ONoCs. However, these are conceptually simpler due to the intuitive conversion of electrical bit parallelism into optical wavelength parallelism [9]. In contrast, WRONoCs rely on serialization or on a limited bit parallelism, which questions the achievement of performance goals. Even neglecting this difference, the NI design for an optical medium is a non-trivial task due to the interdependent issues that come to the forefront: end-to-end flow control, buffer sizing, clock re-synchronization, and serialization ratio.

This paper takes on the challenge of designing and characterizing the complete NI architecture for emerging WRONoCs, in an attempt to validate whether (and to what extent) the projected benefits of optical NoCs over their electrical counterpart are still preserved with the NI in the picture. The distinctive feature of this work is the completeness of the architecture, including both initiator and target side. Especially, the digital architecture to enable optical NoC operation has been designed out of state-of-the-art basic building blocks (e.g., mesochronous synchronizers and dual-clock FIFOs), thus reflecting realistic quality metrics. The system-level requirements of a target multi-core processor with cache-coherent memory architecture have a large impact on the interface footprint. Finally, for the optical and opto-electronic components, we used a consistent set of static and dynamic power values from the same literature source [2, 1].

Our evaluation methodology consists of 2 steps: first, we synthesize and characterize latency, and power for all of the architecture components on a low power industrial 40 nm technology; second, we set up a complete SystemC-based simulation infrastructure (for both the optical and electronic parts) with RTL-equivalent accuracy, thus enabling to capture fine grained performance effects associated with the microarchitecture.

2. RELATED WORK

Early ONoC evaluation studies rely on coarse, higher-level models and/or unrealistic traffic patterns [19, 23, 10, 18], while more recent ones come up with complete end-to-end evaluations using real application workloads [14] and/or more accurate optical network models [5]. Looking in re-

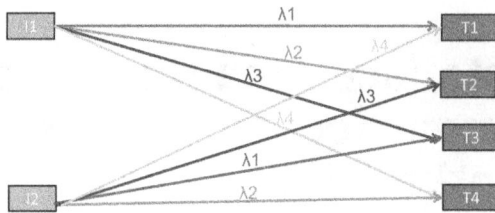

Figure 1: Wavelength-selective routing

trospect, early results have been only partially confirmed, nonetheless showing the potential of ONoCs for on-chip communication.

The refinement of comparative analysis frameworks is far from stabilizing. In fact, other missing aspects are progressively coming to the forefront as the ONoC research concept strives to become an industry-relevant technology. So far, the NI architecture has been overlooked in most evaluation frameworks, or in the best case, only considered in the early stage of design. Some pioneer works account for the NI in their network analysis for wavelength-routed optical networks [17, 1, 3], or space-routed ONoCs [9]. In every case, they suffer from one of the following weaknesses: first, they model NI components only at behavioural level [17], or they target only the more abstract level of formalization of interface specification [3]; second, they consider only the signal driving section of the ONoC, basically up to the (de)serializers. This way, higher-level network architecture design issues such as flow control, synchronization, or buffering architecture are overlooked.

The distinctive features of our approach are: architecture completeness, comparison with electrical interface counterparts, physical synthesis of digital components, RTL-equivalent SystemC modeling for microarchitectural performance characterization, and analysis of the impact of NI quality metrics on global network ones.

3. BACKGROUND ON WRONOCS

Wavelength-routed optical NoCs rely on the principle of wavelength-selective routing. As it is conceptually showed in Figure 1, every initiator can communicate with every target at the same time by using different wavelengths. The topology connectivity pattern is chosen to ensure that wavelengths will never interfere with each other on the network optical paths. This way, all initiators can communicate with the same target by using different wavelengths. WRONoCs support contention-free all-to-all communication with a modulation speed of 10 Gbps/wavelength. Our NI can work with any WRONoC topology. Without lack of generality, we model a wavelength-routed ring inspired by [15] implemented on an optical layer vertically stacked on top of the baseline electronic layer.

4. TARGET ARCHITECTURE

During the design of the NI, we consider a high-impact system requirement: message-dependent deadlock avoidance. Message-dependent deadlock arises from the interactions and dependencies created at network endpoints between different message types (as depicted in Figure 2) [6, 8]. In a complete system, the combination of these effects may lead to cyclic dependencies and block resources at both network endpoints and inside the network indefinitely. When we apply these considerations to WRONoCs, the problem gets simplified by the fact that there is no buffering inside the network, which means messages don't stop along the path, and, therefore, can't get blocked. However, we must break the dependency cycles at the boundaries of the

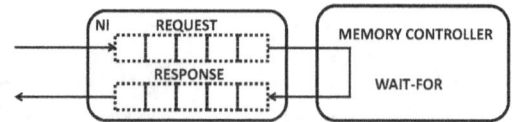

Figure 2: Dependence between a request and reponse at the NI.

NoC by allocating a different buffer for each kind of message in the NI. This has direct implications on the buffering architecture of our target NI (that is, on the number of virtual channels), depending on the communication protocols the WRONoC needs to support.

As a consequence, we make an assumption on a target system architecture. Without lack of generality, we focus on a homogeneous chip multiprocessor with 16 cores, similar to the Tilera architecture [22]. Each core has a private L1 cache and a bank of the shared distributed L2 cache, both connected to a common NI through a crossbar. The system has directory-based coherence managed with a MESI protocol. By analysing the dependency chains of the protocol and deadlock-free buffer sharing opportunities, we came up with a requirement of 3 VCs for deadlock avoidance. Proof is omitted for lack of space.

5. NI ARCHITECTURE

This section presents, to the best of our knowledge, the first complete network interface architecture for wavelength-routed optical networks, as depicted in Figure 3. As a consequence, the objective is not to present the best possible design point, but rather to start considering the basic components, and deriving guidelines about which ones deserve the most intensive optimization effort. Clearly, ONoCs move most of their control logic to the NIs, which should therefore not be oversimplified with abstract models.

To avoid message-dependent deadlock, every NI needs separate buffering resources (virtual channels, VCs) for each one of the three message classes of the MESI protocol. This should be combined with the requirements of wavelength routing: each initiator needs an output for each possible target, and each target needs an input for each possible initiator. As a result, each target comes with 3 FIFOs for each potential initiator. In the transmission side, the same 3 FIFOs are shared for all destinations and flits are sent to different paths afterwards (all the logic components after the 1x15 demultiplexers are replicated for each destination). All the FIFOs at both the transmission and the reception side must be dual-clock FIFOs (DC FIFOs) to move data between the processor frequency domain (we assume 1.2GHz) and the one used inside the NI. As hereafter explained, the latter depends on the bit parallelism. We used the DC FIFO architecture presented in [21].

To size the DC FIFOs, we considered the size of the packets that would use each of the VCs: control packets need 2 flits, while data packets need 21 flits assuming flits are always 32 bits long. The FIFO depth will be assessed in the experimental results. The minimum size for the DC FIFO to achieve perfect throughput is 5 slots [21], so all the VCs in the transmission side have been sized this way. For the reception side, we sized the data VC based on the round-trip latency in order to allow uninterrupted communications, ending up with 15-slot DC FIFOs. However, for the control VCs we decided to keep small 5-slot DC FIFOs because they can already fit two complete packets and we do not expect to send many back-to-back control packets with the target cache-coherence protocol.

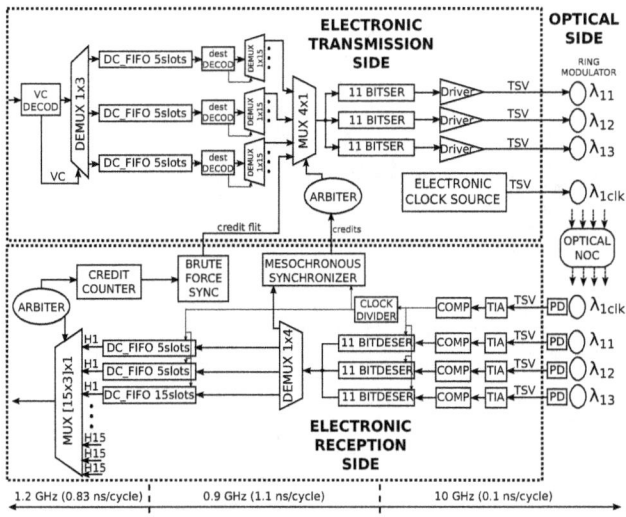

Figure 3: Optical Network Interface Architecture for 3-bit parallelism

After flits are sent to the appropriate path depending on their destination, they must be translated into a 10 GHz bit stream in order to be transmitted through the optical NoC. This serialization process is parallelized to some extent to increase bandwidth and reduce latency. 3-bit parallelism means that 3 serializers of 11 bits each work in parallel to serialize the 32 bits of a flit, resulting on a bandwidth of 30 Gbps. The bit-parallelism determines the frequency inside the optical NI: 1.1 ns (0.1*number of bits) are needed to serialize a flit with 3-bit parallelism, but only 0.8 ns are needed with 4-bit parallelism. In turn, this also impacts the size of the reception DC FIFO based on round-trip latency, which increases from 15 to 17 slots when moving from 3 to 4-bit parallelism.

Another key issue to be considered in NIs is the resynchronization of received optical pulses with the clock signal of the electronic receiver. In this paper we assume source-synchronous communication, which implies that each point-to-point communication requires a strobe signal to be transmitted along with the data on a separate wavelength. With current technology, this seems to be the most realistic solution, even considering the promising research effort that is currently being devoted to transmitting clock signals across an optical medium [16]. The received source-synchronous clock at the reception side of the NI is then used to drive the de-serializers and, after a clock divider, the front-end of the DC FIFOs. We assume that a form of clock gating is implemented, so when no data is transmitted, the optical clock signal is gated.

Another typically overlooked issue is the backpressure mechanism. We opt for credit-based flow control because credit tokens can reuse the existing communication paths. Besides, the low dynamic power of ONoCs can easily tolerate the signalling overhead of this flow control strategy. Credits are generated at the reception side of the NI when a flit leaves the DC FIFO (at the processor frequency) and forwarded to the transmission side so that they can be sent back to the source (at the NI frequency). To synchronize between different frequency domains, we used brute force and mesochronous synchronizers.

6. BASELINE ELECTRONIC NOC

The baseline electronic switch architecture is the consolidated ×pipesLite architecture [20], which represents an

ultra-low complexity design point. Each 32-bit switch includes 3 VCs to avoid message-dependent deadlock, with 5 slots each. It takes one cycle to traverse the switch and one cycle to traverse each link.

When it comes to the network interface, it consists of two parts [14]. The first one is a packetizer, which acts as protocol converter from the IP core to the network. This block is also required for the ONoC, so it is not considered in this comparison framework The second one is the buffering stage. In order to preserve the generality of the design and support cores with different operating frequencies that access an ENoC with fixed common frequency, dual-clock FIFOs have been included at the electronic network interfaces, similar to the ONoC NI design. However, in this case all DC FIFOs have 5 slots at both initiator and target side, because round-trip latency does not require larger buffers for maximum throughput operation.

7. EVALUATION

This section characterises the most important network-quality metrics for the electro-optical NI. Results for an ENoC configured with typical parameters from [20] are also included. This aims to set the bases for a future comprehensive crossbenchmarking study, which is out of the scope of this paper.

7.1 Methodology

To obtain accurate latency results, we implemented detailed RTL models of the optical and electronic network interfaces and NoCs using SystemC. We instantiated a 4x4 2D mesh for the electronic NoC, and a similar system connected by the optical ring. The network-wide focus, well beyond the NI, aims at relating NI quality metrics to network ones. Delay values for the optical ring have been backannotated from physical-layer analysis, and have been differentiated on a per-path basis.

For power modeling, every electronic component has been synthesized, placed and routed using a low power 40 nm industrial technology library. Power metrics have been calculated by backannotating the switching activity of block internal nets, and then importing waveforms in the *Prime-Time* tool. We have applied clock gating to achieve realistic static power values. Energy-per-bit has been computed by assuming 50% switching activity. Table 1 sums up the static power and energy-per-bit for all the electronic and optical devices. For the fast developing optical technology, we consider a coherent set of both conservative and aggressive parameters [2, 1].

7.2 NI Latency Breakdown

Figure 4 presents the latency breakdown for the NI components and the ONoC, obtained from our accurate RTL-equivalent simulations. We clearly see that the latency of the network is negligible, but it requires support from a time consuming NI. Inside the NI, the DC FIFOs are the components with the largest latency.

7.3 Transaction Latency

We simulate the most common traffic patterns generated by a MESI coherence protocol in our RTL models without contention. The increased accuracy of our analysis stems from the fact that our packet injectors and ejectors model actual transactions of the protocol, as well as their interdependencies. Table 2 describes the analysed compound transactions and Figure 5 presents the zero-load latency results. The messages included in these patterns amount to

Table 1: Static Power and Dynamic Energy of Electronic and Optical Devices.

HARDWARE COMPONENTS	3-bit parallelism			4-bit parallelism		
	count per NI	STATIC POWER (mWatts)	DYNAMIC ENERGY (fJ/bit)	count per NI	STATIC POWER (mWatts)	DYNAMIC ENERGY (fJ/bit)
DC_FIFO 5slots (TX)	3	0.12	10.65	3	0.12	12.72
DC_FIFO 5slots (RX)	30	0.12	8.54	30	0.12	10.2
DC_FIFO 15-17 slots	15	0.12	26.50	15	0.12	31.65
DEMUX1x3	1	0.000725	0.92	1	0.000725	0.92
DEMUX1x15	3	0.0021	25.21	3	0.0021	25.21
DEMUX1x4	15	0.00056	6.72	15	0.00056	6.72
MUX4x1 + ARB	15	0.08	0.36	15	0.11	0.49
MUX45x1 + ARB	1	0.9	5.09	1	0.9	5.09
SERIALIZER	45	0.0475	9.41	60	0.0417	2.63
DESERIALIZER	45	0.0289	7.74	60	0.0281	6.12
MESO-SYNCHRONIZER	45	0.041	8.00	45	0.0565	11.1
COUNTER 2bits	45	0.01482	1.014	45	0.01482	1.014
BRUTE FORCE SYNC	15	0.004234	1.4	15	0.00503	1.66
CLOCK DIVIDER	15	0.01172	0.6	15	0.0139	0.714
TSV	120	/	2.50	150	/	2.50
TRANSMITTER aggressive	60	0.025	20	75	0.025	20
TRANSMITTER conservative	60	0.100	50	75	0.100	50
RECEIVER aggressive	60	0.050	10	75	0.050	10
RECEIVER conservative	60	0.150	25	75	0.150	25
THERMAL TUNING/RING 20K	180	0.020	/	225	0.020	/
LASER POWER aggressive	/	0.0421	/	/	0.0525	/
LASER POWER conservative	/	0.308	/	/	0.385	/
E-SWITCH (3VCs)	/	17.9	193	/	17.9	193

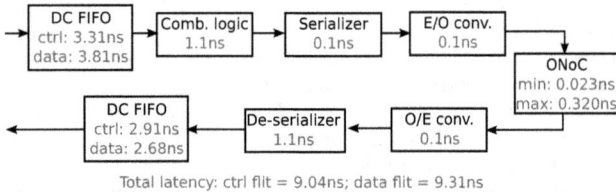

Figure 4: **Latency breakdown of the optical NI with 3-bit parallelism and the optical ring.**

an average 99.9% of the total network traffic, as we observed from full-system simulations of realistic parallel benchmarks from PARSEC and SPLASH2 and multiprogrammed workloads built with SPEC applications (we only exclude communication with the memory controllers). Therefore, they are a very good indicator of the network latency improvements we can expect from the optical network, including its (non-negligible) network interface overhead.

We observe that in all the patterns except the last one, the ONoCs either beat or obtain equal results to the ENoC with all path lenghts. As opposed to the ENoC, most of the latency of the ONoC is spent in the NI, which is needed to support the low latency optical communication. The tendency changes in pattern 5 because the replacement packet is using a VC designed for control to transmit data, and the smaller FIFO cannot store enough flits to support the round-trip latency. However, this messages are only 7.4% of the total network traffic.

7.4 Throughput

We test the behaviour of the electronic and optical networks under contention. To do that, we focus only on requests and data replies. We leave the ACKs out because they are not in the critical path of the communications. We monitor transactions between an L1 and an L2 located in different nodes, and gradually insert congestion by sending requests from the other nodes to the same L2.

Figure 6 presents the results for the ENoC and the 3, 4 and

Table 2: **Messages generated by the coherence protocol.**

id	Event	Sequence of messages
P1a	L1 miss	1. Request from L1 to L2 2. Data reply from L2 to L1 3. ACK from L1 to L2
P1b/c	L1 write miss, 1/2 sharers	1. Request from L1 to L2 2. L2 sends data reply and invalidates 1/2 sharers 3. Sharers sends ACK to L1 req. 4. ACK from L1 to L2
P2a	L1 needs upgrade to write	1. Request from L1 to L2 2. ACK reply from L2 to L1 3. ACK from L1 to L2
P2b/c	L1 needs upgrade to write, 1/2 sharers	1. Request from L1 to L2 2. ACK reply from L2 to L1 and invalidates 1/2 sharers 3. Sharers send ACK to L1 req. 4. ACK from L1 to L2
P3	L1 write miss, another owner	1. Request from L1 to L2 2. L2 forwards request to owner 3. Owner sends data to L1 4. ACK from L1 to L2
P4	L1 read miss, another owner	1. Request from L1 to L2 2. L2 forwards request to owner 3. Owner sends data to L1 and L2 4. ACK from L1 to L2
P5	L1 replacement	1. Writeback from L1 to L2 2. ACK from L2 to L1

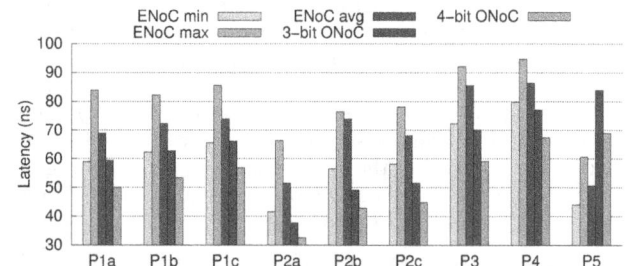

Figure 5: **Latency of the most common communication patterns. For the ENoC, we include minimum, maximum, and average paths.**

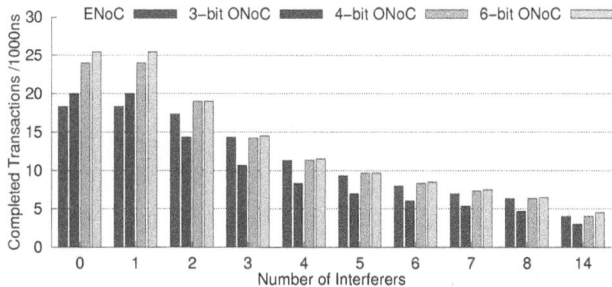

Figure 6: Number of completed transactions per 1K ns between two nodes as the number of interferers increases.

6-bit parallelism ONoCs. Without contention, more transactions get completed in the optical NoC because their latency is lower. As we keep increasing the number of interferers, the throughput for the 3-bit parallelism ONoC drops much faster than for the ENoC. This is because the former can eject a maximum of 30 Gbps, while the latter transmits flits at 38.4 Gbps. For this reason, replies need to wait much longer until they can be transmitted. However, when considering the 4-bit parallelism ONoC, which has a bandwidth of 40 Gbps, we see results comparable and even superior to those of the ENoC. At 6-bit parallelism, the increased bandwidth (60 Gbps) only gives the ONoC a slight advantage, which is not enough to justify the increase in static power (as later documented).

7.5 Buffer Size Exploration

In this section we analyse the effect of modifying the buffering of the optical network interface. We fix the bit parallelism at 3 and explore all the buffer size combinations detailed in table 3. Figure 7 shows how buffer size in the NI affects transaction latency, using the same request-reply pattern as in the previous section.

In case A, the minimum buffering has a very negative impact on performance, because data packets are stalled waiting for credits from the reception side FIFOs, which can only store 2 flits. This effect is slightly mitigated when we increase the buffer size for this VC to 5 slots in case B. Even though the DC FIFOs can achieve perfect throughput, backpressure is still preventing faster communications. We don't see any difference by increasing the size of control VCs in case C because the bottleneck is in the data VC. However, in case D, the reception side has been sized based on the round-trip latency and we achieve the maximum possible throughput. The larger buffers in cases E and F do not show any further improvements because the network is already using up all the bandwidth.

7.6 Power and Energy-per-Bit

Figure 8 depicts the static power and (dynamic) energy-per-bit for the ENoC vs. the 3 and 4-bit parallelism ONoCs. We do not consider ONoCs with less than 3-bit parallelism because the bandwidth of the optical paths would be too low, or ONoCs with more than 4-bit parallelism, because the static power becomes unacceptable (we can see a clear trend in Figure 8). We present a breakdown of the contributions of the NIs (electronic and optical components) and NoCs. The optical NoC is solely composed of laser power, so it has no impact on dynamic energy.

We observe that the electronic switches dominate the static power, accounting for 95.8% of the total. However, this trend is reversed in the ONoC, with a contribution of only

Table 3: Buffer sizes explored for the 3 VCs at each side of the NI. Note that the actual capacity of the DC FIFOs is one flit less than the number of slots.

id	Transmission side	Reception side
A	3, 3, 3	3, 3, 3
B	3, 3, 5	3, 3, 5
C	5, 5, 5	5, 5, 5
D	5, 5, 5	5, 5, 15
E	5, 5, 22	5, 5, 15
F	10, 10, 44	10, 10, 44

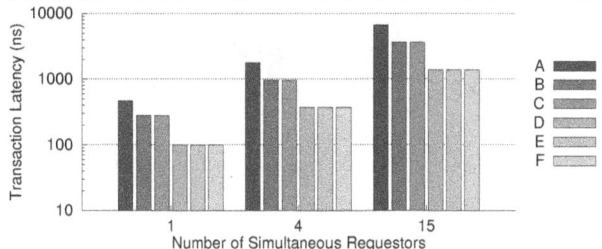

Figure 7: Transaction latency with varying buffer sizes.

10.6% and 11.8% for the aggressive technology with 3 and 4-bit parallelism, respectively. It is worth highlighting that most of the static power of the electronic components in the NI comes from the DC FIFOs. Also, the savings in execution time of the ONoC vs the ENoC may compensate the higher static power and result in overall energy reductions. This is especially true when we consider the power of the system as a whole [14].

For energy-per-bit we included minimum, maximum and average path lengths for the ENoC and specific values for control and data packets for the ONoC (which change due to the different size of the reception DC FIFOs). We clearly see that the ONoC has significantly lower energy-per-bit than the ENoC, which confirms the trend from previous literature. Apart from that, we still see how the main contributor for the ENoC energy is the NoC, while the NI carries all the complexity for the ONoC.

8. CONCLUSIONS

This paper presents an accurate design of NIs for WRONoCs, captures the effect on the most important network-quality metrics, and sets the scene for further comparative ONoC analysis. Regarding latency, the ONoC is always faster than its electronic counterpart even considering the NI, thus preserving the primary goal of a WRONoC. The behaviour under contention depends mainly on the available bandwidth of the interconnect technologies under test. For the WRONoC, such bandwidth can be modulated by tuning the bit parallelism, and adjusting buffer size to flow control requirements for maximum throughput operation. Similar tuning knobs do exist for ENoCs, namely flit width and buffer sizes. Therefore, the ultimate question is whether such tuning knobs are energy efficient in comparative terms, which depends on the sensitivity of system performance to such knobs for the application at hand. This is left for future work.

When we consider power figures, we notice that, while switches are the main contributors in ENoCs, the NI has the largest share in ONoCs. For static power, this contribution is in the same order of magnitude than that from laser sources with conservative optical technology parameters. However, by further improving the optical technology, the role of the NI becomes dominant, thus making it the main target for future optimizations. Finally, the ONoC pre-

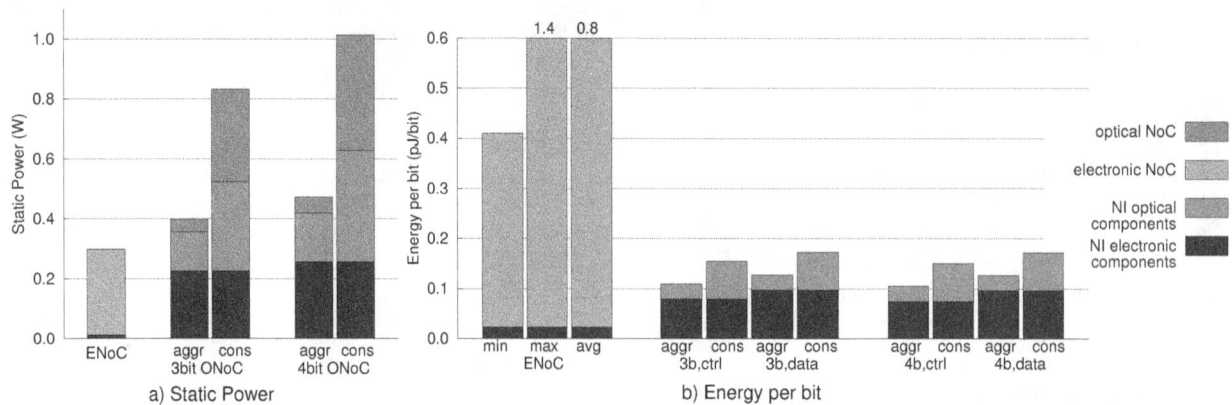

a) Static Power

b) Energy per bit

Figure 8: Static power and Energy-per-Bit of the NIs and the electronic and optical NoCs.

serves its superior dynamic power properties over its ENoC counterpart, even in the presence of its NI.

This paper shows that the NI architecture should not be overlooked for realistic ONoC assessments, and comes up with new insights not provided by earlier photonic network evaluations. The most important one is that NI optimizations perhaps have higher priority over the relentless search for ultra-low-loss optical devices.

9. ACKNOWLEDGMENTS

This work was supported by grants TIN2010-21291-C02-01 (Spanish Government, European ERDF), IT FIRB Photonica (RBFR08LE6V) project, and HiPEAC-3 NoE (European FP7/ICT 217068).

10. REFERENCES

[1] C. Batten, A. Joshi, V. Stojanovic, and K. Asanovic. Designing chip-level nanophotonic interconnection networks. *IEEE Journal on Emerging and Selected Topics in Circuits and Systems*, pages 137–153, 2012.

[2] S. Beamer, C. Sun, Y.-J. Kwon, A. Joshi, C. Batten, V. Stojanovic, and K. Asanovic. Re-architecting DRAM memory systems with monolithically integrated silicon photonics. In *ISCA*, pages 129–140. ACM, 2010.

[3] M. Biere, L. Gheorghe, G. Nicolescu, I. O'Connor, and G. Wainer. Towards the high-level design of optical networks-on-chip. Formalization of opto-electrical interfaces. In *Int.Conf. on Electronics, Circuits and Systems.*, pages 427–430, 2007.

[4] J. Chan, G. Hendry, A. Biberman, and K. Bergman. Architectural design exploration of chip-scale photonic interconnection networks using physical-layer analysis. In *Optical Fiber Communication (OFC)*, pages 1–3, 2010.

[5] J. Chan, G. Hendry, A. Biberman, and K. Bergman. Architectural exploration of chip-scale photonic interconnection network designs using physical-layer analysis. *Journal of Lightwave Technology*, pages 1305–1315, 2010.

[6] W. Dally and B. Towles. *Principles and Practices of Interconnection Networks*. Morgan Kaufmann Publishers Inc., San Francisco, CA, USA, 2003.

[7] C. G. et al. A cmos-compatible silicon photonic platform for high-speed integrated opto-electronics. *Proc. Integrated Photonics: Materials, Devices, and Applications*, 2013.

[8] A. Hansson, K. Goossens, and A. Radulescu. Avoiding message-dependent deadlock in network-based systems on chip. *VLSI Design*, 2007.

[9] G. Hendry, J. Chan, S. Kamil, L. Oliker, J. Shalf, L. Carloni, and K. Bergman. Silicon nanophotonic network-on-chip using TDM arbitration. In *Annual Symp. on High Perf. Interconnects (HOTI)*, pages 88–95, 2010.

[10] A. Joshi, C. Batten, Y.-J. Kwon, S. Beamer, I. Shamim, K. Asanovic, and V. Stojanovic. Silicon-photonic clos

networks for global on-chip communication. In *Int. Symp on Networks-on-Chip*, pages 124–133, 2009.

[11] R. Kapoor, G. Porter, M. Tewari, G. M. Voelker, and A. Vahdat. Chronos: Predictable low latency for data center applications. In *Procs of the ACM Symp. on Cloud Comp.*, pages 9:1–9:14, 2012.

[12] P. Kapur and K. C. Saraswat. Optical interconnects for future high performance integrated circuits. *Physica E: Low-dimensional Systems and Nanostructures*, pages 620 – 627, 2003.

[13] S. Koohi, M. Abdollahi, and S. Hessabi. All-optical wavelength-routed NoC based on a novel hierarchical topology. In *Procs of the Int. Symp. on Networks-on-Chip*, NOCS '11, pages 97–104, 2011.

[14] G. Kurian, C. Sun, C.-H. Chen, J. Miller, J. Michel, L. Wei, D. Antoniadis, L.-S. Peh, L. Kimerling, V. Stojanovic, and A. Agarwal. Cross-layer energy and performance evaluation of a nanophotonic manycore processor system using real application workloads. In *Int. Parallel Distributed Processing Symposium (IPDPS)*, pages 1117–1130, 2012.

[15] S. Le Beux, J. Trajkovic, I. O'Connor, G. Nicolescu, G. Bois, and P. Paulin. Optical ring network-on-chip (ORNoC): Architecture and design methodology. In *Design, Automation Test in Europe Conference Exhibition (DATE)*, pages 1–6, 2011.

[16] J. Leu and V. Stojanovic. Injection-locked clock receiver for monolithic optical link in 45nm soi. In *Solid State Circuits Conference (A-SSCC), 2011 IEEE Asian*, pages 149–152, 2011.

[17] I. e. a. O'Connor. Towards reconfigurable optical networks-on-chip. *RECO SoC*, pages 121–128, 2005.

[18] Y. Pan, J. Kim, and G. Memik. Flexishare: Channel sharing for an energy-efficient nanophotonic crossbar. In *Int. Symp. on High Performance Computer Architecture*, pages 1–12, 2010.

[19] Y. Pan, P. Kumar, J. Kim, G. Memik, Y. Zhang, and A. Choudhary. Firefly: Illuminating future network-on-chip with nanophotonics. In *Procs. of the Int. Symp. on Computer Architecture*, ISCA '09, pages 429–440, 2009.

[20] S. Stergiou, F. Angiolini, S. Carta, L. Raffo, D. Bertozzi, and G. De Micheli. xpipes lite: a synthesis oriented design library for networks on chips. In *Design, Automation and Test in Europe*, pages 1188–1193 Vol. 2, 2005.

[21] A. Strano, D. Ludovici, and D. Bertozzi. A library of dual-clock fifos for cost-effective and flexible mpsoc design. In *Int. Conf. on Embedded Computer Systems (SAMOS)*, pages 20–27, 2010.

[22] TileraCorporation. Tile-Gx8016 specification. http://www.tilera.com/sites/default/files/productbriefs/Tile-Gx-8016-SB011-03.pdf.

[23] D. Vantrease, N. Binkert, R. Schreiber, and M. Lipasti. Light speed arbitration and flow control for nanophotonic interconnects. In *MICRO-42*, pages 304–315, 2009.

A Design Approach to Automatically Generate On-Chip Monitors during High-Level Synthesis of Hardware Accelerator

Mohamed Ben Hammouda
Lab-STICC UMR CNRS 6285
Universite de Bretagne Occidentale
benhammoud@univ-brest.fr

Philippe Coussy
Lab-STICC UMR CNRS 6285
Universite de Bretagne-Sud
philippe.coussy@univ-ubs.fr

Loic lagadec
Lab-STICC UMR CNRS 6285
ENSTA-Bretagne
Loic.lagadec@ensta-bretagne.fr

ABSTRACT

Embedded systems often implement safety critical applications making security a more and more important aspect in their design. Control-Flow Integrity (CFI) attacks are used to modify program behavior and can lead to learn valuable information directly or indirectly by perturbing a system and creating failures. Although CFI attacks are well-known in computer systems, they have been recently shown to be practical and feasible on embedded systems as well. In this context, CFI checks are mainly used to detect unintended software behaviors while very few works address non programmable hardware component monitoring. In this paper, we present a hardware-assisted paradigm to enhance embedded system security by detecting and preventing unintended hardware behavior. We propose a design approach that designs on-chip monitors (OCM) during High-Level Synthesis (HLS) of hardware accelerators (HWacc). Synthesis of OCM is introduced as a set of steps realized concurrently to the HLS flow of HWacc. Automatically generated OCM checks at runtime both the input/output timing behavior and the control flow of the monitored HWacc. Experimental results show the interest of the proposed approach: the error coverage on the control flow ranges from 99.75% to 100% while in average the OCM area overhead is less than 10%, the clock period overhead is at worst less than 5% and impact on the synthesis time is negligible.

Categories and Subject Descriptors

B.5.2 [RTL implementation]: Design Aids, B.5.3 [RTL implementation]: Reliability and Testing
General Terms Algorithms, design, security, performance.
Keywords High-Level Synthesis, Hardware Monitoring, Security.

1. INTRODUCTION

In our today's always more connected world, embedded systems are increasingly used in various domains like transportation, industrial automation, healthcare or telecommunications to execute critical applications and manipulate sensitive data. These systems often involve financial and industrial interests but also human lives which impose strong safety constraints. Hence, a key issue lies in the ability of such systems to respond safely when errors occur at runtime, to prevent further unacceptable behaviors.

Errors can be due to natural causes such as particle hits as well as internal noise (integrity problems) but also due to malicious attacks. Embedded system architectures typically include processor(s), memories, I/O controller(s) to run software

application but also non programmable hardware accelerator(s) to improve energy efficiency and performance. Runtime and control-flow integrity (CFI) attacks constitute one of the most severe threats to software programs. Although CFI attacks are well-known in computer systems, they have been recently shown to be practical and feasible on embedded systems as well [5][6][22]. Such attacks are used to modify application behavior and can lead to learn valuable information directly or indirectly by perturbing a system and creating failures. Several research works on the software components security according to the Control Flow Integrity have been proposed. The most common approach consists in applying signature analysis. Software applications are seen as control flow graph exhibiting the skeleton of the execution flow signatures identify these nodes. Signatures are generated off-line to serve as a comparison basis, and on-line, to be checked against the references. Any deviation from the expected behavior is detected and failure is reported. Analysis approach can be classified into two categories according to how the signature and the comparison references are stored. The Embedded Signature Monitoring (ESM) approaches [1][2] directly include data related to signature (reference plus signature generator) in the main program as parameters (reference) or specific instructions (generator and comparison). The Disjoint Signature Monitoring (DSM) [3][4] stores reference signatures and the skeleton of the application in an external memory. The skeleton of the application drives the timestamp when the signature is generated and compared to the stored reference signature. Signatures generation and comparison are handled by an external hardware component (called monitor or watchdog). Another alternative to perform CFI uses Monitoring System Call Sequence (MSCS) [5][6] technique. MSCS relies on properties and makes sure any faulty behavior violates one or many properties. These properties are extracted through static program analysis that outputs a FSM called Syscall Sequence Recognizer, which enumerates the legal sequences of system calls. In addition, authors of [23] introduce a new approach to allow detecting data errors. They analyze static traces of application execution to generate properties. Those properties are used to detect a divergence in data values which affects the expected program execution.

However, there are classes of attacks that do not target the software, but the hardware component [7] instead. In this paper, we focus on non-destructive invasive attacks which typically consist in tampering with the hardware so as to make it malfunction. Such attacks include RAM overwriting [8] that can be used to force the state of a static RAM point, optically induced faults [9] that cause a target transistor to conduct by illuminating it thereby inducing a transient fault and Clock or power glitch attacks [10] that induce internal system errors by introducing glitches on clock or power supply. A wide range of techniques has been proposed to enhance hardware verification at the low level i.e. Register Transfer Level (RTL). Assertion Based Verification (ABV) [14] has been proposed to allow the designer to capture specification and design intents and can be used to monitor hardware's behavior. Many languages and libraries exist such as Property Specification Language (PSL)[15], SystemVerilog Assertion (SVA)[16] or Open Verification Library (OVL)[17]. Assertions can automatically be converted into hardware monitors by using dedicated synthesis tools like [18][19]. On the other hand, ESL (Electronic System Level) design approaches are gaining momentum and High-Level Synthesis (HLS) is more and more used to design complex hardware accelerators (HWacc)[11]. Unfortunately, few automated design approaches have been proposed to automatically generate, from high-level specification, hardware monitors that verify at runtime the evolution of complex HWaccs. Works from [12] synthesize ANSI-C assertions (assert() functions) into if-then instructions understandable by the Impulse-C compiler. Authors of [13] propose an extension of traditional HLS flow to support generation of ANSI-C assertions as monitors for simulation purpose only. These techniques allow checking at runtime high-level properties via a set of assertions introduced inside the high-level specification of HWaccs. Therefore, they mainly target algorithmic properties and do not allow detecting problems such like infinite loops or errors in branch instructions which are part of CFI.

In this paper, we present a synthesis approach to automatically generate On-Chip Monitors (OCMs) during the HLS of hardware accelerators. Generated OCM allows checking at runtime both I/O timing behavior errors and control flow errors. Control flow error can be errors in branch instruction or non-branch instruction. To this end, important application's information are automatically determined during HLS, from which the monitor's architecture is finally generated. The OCM synthesis is introduced as a set of steps realized concurrently to the HLS flow of HWacc. OCM generation is completely transparent for designer and no modification of the specification used as input of the HLS is required. OCM synthesis flow hence uses information coming from a classical HLS flow to design incrementally the OCM FSM controller that will drive a template-based OCM data-path. It should be noticed that the objective of the OCM we generate is currently to detect errors. Counter reaction i.e. the way how the chip react if an error is detected is out of the scope of this work and is not addressed in this paper. Thus, a flag that can be used by the HWacc to crash or to reset to a safe state for example is raised when an error is detected.

This paper is organized as follows. The proposed approach is introduced and detailed in Section 2. Experimental results are exposed in Section 3. Conclusion is provided in Section 4.

2. PROPOSED APPROACH

2.1 HLS Overview

HLS process consists of several steps [11]: compilation, allocation, scheduling, binding and RTL architecture generation (see left part of Figure 1).

Compilation translates the specification, describing the expected algorithmic behavior of the target application, from a programming language such as C into a formal representation. This formal representation is generally a Control and Data Flow Graph (CDFG). Figure 2.a presents the description of an application to synthesize i.e. the C code of FIR filter algorithm in

our example. This specification is transformed by compilation step into the CDFG as illustrated in Figure 2.b and Figure 2.c. Figure 2.c. presents the Control Flow Graph (CFG) of the application. Figure 2.b depicts the Data Flow Graph (DFG) of the basic block BB3 of the CFG (BB3 includes statements of line 5, instruction to update the value of the induction variable i of loop2 and to check the bound of loop2).

Allocation defines how many instances of each type of resource are required. In our example, two adders (ADD#0 and ADD#1), one multiplier (MUL#1) and one memory bank have been consider as resource constraint.

Scheduling determines the states i.e. control steps (denoted s1, s2...) during which operations start their execution. Once all operations have been scheduled, the timing behavior is classically modeled as a Finite State Machine with Datapath (FSMD) referred as FSMD_s in this paper. FSMD_s handles variables and operations when binding has not yet been done. Each state of FSMD_s is associated to a unique BB and each BB can contain several states (see Figure 2.d). Each FSMD_s state is associated to at least one operation and several operations can be scheduled in the same state. In our example (see Figure 2.d), BB3 is split into four states: s7, s8, s9 and s10.

Binding assigns operations to operators / data to registers and allows resource sharing. Result of binding step can also be modeled as a FSMD wherein variables have been merged and replaced by storing elements (registers, etc.) and operations have been replaced by operators they have been assigned to. In our example (see Figure 2.b), operations + are performed on operator ADD#0 and data C is stored in register REG#4...

Architecture generation includes the data-path generation and the controller synthesis that determines the logic to issue operations based on the control flow (the command words).

2.2 On Chip Monitor Synthesis Flow

Similarly to the HLS flow, the OCMS flow splits into several steps, as illustrated in the right part of Figure 1. First, CDFG Analysis step analyzes the formal representation generated by the compilation step of the HLS flow in order to detect Control Structures (loop and conditional constructs), to extract their parameters and to identify input and output data of the HWacc. Next, FSMD Annotation step analyzes and annotates a copy of the HWacc FSMD_s generated by the scheduling step of the HLS flow. This step identifies all the states (later referred to as notable states) that require particular attention such as fork/join states or states reading input and/or writing output data. This information is used to verify at runtime that I/O timing behavior and jumps between BBs are correct. Afterward, the ID Generation step assigns to each state of the FSMD_s a unique identifier in order to later detect illegal jumps inside BBs. Finally, the OCM Generation step couples the annotated FSMD_s with the results provided by the binding step of the HLS flow to produce the RTL description of the monitor as Finite State Machine (FSM) and Data Path (DP).

2.2.1 CDFG analysis

CDFG analysis is the first step of the OCMS flow. Analysis starts after the CDFG has been generated by the compilation step of the HLS flow. Both input and output data of HWacc and Control Structures (CS) are detected. CS parameters are also identified. Control structures and associated parameters are:

- Loop constructs (for, while, do-while...): initialization, test condition and increment

- Conditional constructs (If-else, switch-case...): operands and test condition

All this information is stored in a dedicated database DB.

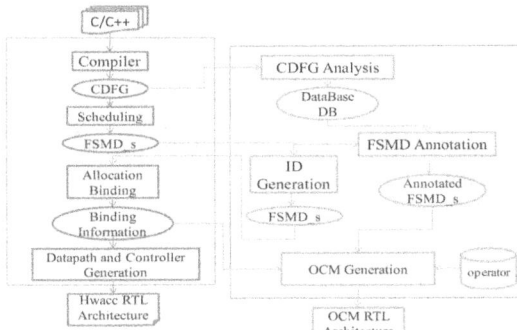

Figure 1: Proposed design flow

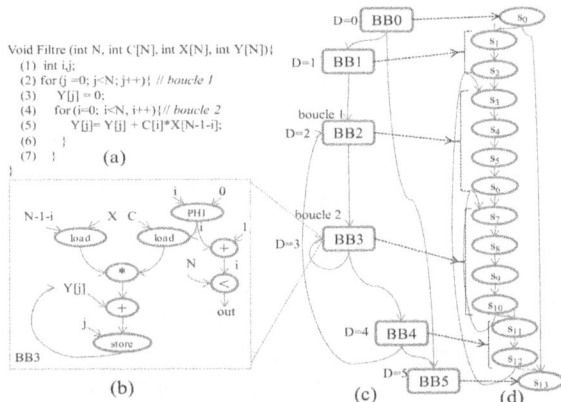

Figure 2: Application and associated CDFG and FSMD_s (a) source code, (b) DFG, (c) CFG, (d) FSMD_s

Loops are detected when identifying back arcs in the CDFG. Thus, the first step in the CDFG analysis is to find back arcs. For this reason the basic blocks BB of the CDFG are numbered by using a Depth-First Search (DFS) algorithm [20]: each BB has a unique DFS-number D (see Figure 2.c). Given that BBs are numbered in preorder, back arcs are identified using the following criterion: for each disjunction BB (a disjunction BB is a BB having more than one outgoing arc), if there is a BB among its immediate successors that has a DFS-number less than or equal to its own DFS-number, then a back arc is detected. Each loop has one entry BB named header and back arcs named latches starting from an inner BB of the loop construct and reaching the header BB. The sink BB of a back arc is referred to as Loop Header (LH) and the source BB of a back arc (i.e. the disjunction BB) is referred to as Loop Latch (LL). The disjunction BB that does not satisfy the previous condition is referred to as Condition Block (CB). Figure 2.c illustrates the CDFG of our FIR filter example. The set of disjunction BB is {BB0, BB3, BB4}. According to the previous criterion, the set of LL is {BB3, BB4}, the set of LH is {BB2, BB3} and the set of CB is {BB0}.

The next step in the CDFG Analysis extracts the parameters of each detected control structure. In detail, loop constructs are classically modeled in the CDFG by three parameters: initialization, test-condition, and increment statements [21]. Test-condition statement is modeled as 3-tuple <f1, f2, CMP> where f1 and f2 are the operands of the comparison operation and CMP is the operation that compares f1 and f2. When detecting a back arc, f1 is identified as the basic induction loop variable and f2 is

identified as the loop bound (that can be constant or variable). Hence, the algorithm searches for the f2 and CMP parameters of the current loop from the last node of LL. Afterwards, the algorithm searches for initialization by looking for the update induction node inside the LH. In fact, the update induction node has two arcs: the first comes from its LL and the other from outside of the loop body which defines the value of initialization parameter. Then, the algorithm extracts the increment information i.e. all the operators OP and the STEP (constant or variable) that are used to compute the next value of the induction variable. In our example, the parameters of the loop2 are "0" for initialization, "N" for f2, "<" for CMP and "+" for increment. Conditional constructs (if-else and switch-case) are simply modeled by a test-condition. Hence, the algorithm searches for the f1, the f2 and CMP for the current conditional construct starting from the last node of the CB. Parameters of each control structure detected during the CDFG analysis step are stored in the database (see Figure 1). Finally, each parameter and each BB is associated to a given control structure through a control identifier Control_ID. This number is later used during FSMD annotation step.

2.2.2 FSMD Annotation

FSMD Annotation starts after the FSMD_s has been generated by the scheduling step of the HLS flow (see Figure 1). This step analyzes the FSMD_s and identifies all notable states that allow tagging initial and final states, recognizing the I/O timing behavior and the timing of the loops increment functions. In addition, some notable states serve as a support for the control flow description. Notable states are:

- The initial and the final state of the FSMD_s in order to synchronize the execution of the OCM with its HWacc to monitor;
- Communication State (ComS): the set of states where an input data is read for the first time per control path and/or where an output data is written;
- Loop Increment Function State (LIFS): the set of states that perform one or more operations of the loop increment function extracted from the database;
- Plus control flow notable states, as itemized below.

The control flow is composed of a set of paths which are interconnected, every of which is started by either a control successor state or a conjunction state and is ended by either a control flow state or a predecessor of conjunction state. Hence, control flow related notable are:

- Control Flow State (CFS): the set of states having more than one going arc;
- Control Successor State (CSS): the set of states whose predecessors are CFS;
- Conjunction States (CjS): the set of states having more than one incoming arc.

Figure 3.b shows the annotated FSMD_s of FIR filter example. The set of ComS is {s1, s4, s6, s7, s10}, the set of CFS is {s0, s10, s12}, the set of CjS is {s3, s7, s13}, the set of CSS is {s1, s3, s7, s11, s13} and the set of LIFS is {s4, s9}.

Each state is associated to a unique basic block (BB) of the CDFG. Thus each Control Flow State of the FSMD_s is associated to a unique BB. Parameters of control structures are identified and extracted from the database thanks to the Control_ID they are associated to. More precisely, each loop has a single entry state named Header State (HS) which is a Control Successor State and a single exit state named Latch State (LS) which is a Control Flow State. Then, the next task of the FSMD

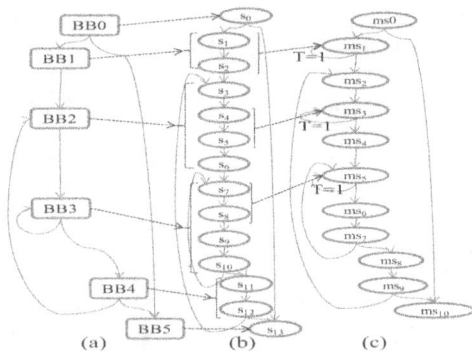

Figure 3: (a) CDFG, (b) Annotated FSMD_s, (c) OCM FSM

annotation step is to identify the HS and the LS of each detected loop in order to check the problem of infinite loops. Thanks to the relation that exists between BB and state, Control Flow State is identified as LS and Control Successor State is identified as HS.

Finally, FSMD annotation detects the LIFS by scanning the set of states that belong to the list of the LS's predecessors and to the list of the HS's successors. In our example presented in Figure 3.b the set of LS is {s10, s12} and the set of HS is {s3, s7}.

2.2.3 ID Generation

Similarly to the FSMD Annotation step, ID Generation step starts after the FSMD_s has been generated by the HLS flow. This step produces for each FSMD_s state of a unique identifier by using the DFS algorithm. Once each state has been processed, the updated FSMD_s is as usual used as input by the allocation and binding step of the HLS flow (see Figure 1). ID is later used during the generation of HWacc architecture by being concatenated to the command word of the HWacc FSM state it is associated to. This ID is used at runtime by the OCM to check that no illegal jump has been done inside a BB (see Basic Block Control Unit BBCU in the next subsection). Inter-BB jumps are checked differently in the Jump Control Unit (JCU) of the OCM as explained later.

Once CDFG analysis, FSMD annotation and ID generation have been carried out, notable states have been detected and control structure parameters have been extracted and stored in the database. Hence, all the information needed to generate an On-Chip Monitor able to check the I/O timing behavior and the control flow of HWacc have been collected.

2.2.4 OCM Generation

OCM generation is the last step of the OCMS flow. It generates the RTL specification of the OCM. OCM architecture includes a Data Path DP and a FSM controller. The approach we propose to generate an OCM FSM is as follow: HWacc FSMD_s generated by the HLS flow is traversed to construct OCM FSM and each time a new notable state of the FSMD_s is visited, a new state is created in the OCM FSM. This new state is associated to the proper monitoring operations to be performed when entering this state as illustrated by Figure 3.c. Hence, if the visited FSMD_s state is:

- a Communication State then the corresponding monitoring operation checks that the related load signal(s) of the HWacc register(s) containing I/O data is correctly driven;
- a Loop Increment Function State, then the monitoring operation applies the increment function to the loop's induction variable;

- a Latch State, then associated monitoring operations compare, using a CMP operator, the stored loop's induction variable with the loop bound f2;
- a predecessor of Header State i.e. PHS, then the associated monitoring operation sets the loop's induction variable to its initial value;
- a Control Flow State, then associated monitoring operations compare the operands of the condition transitions (f1 and f2) by using a CMP operator;
- a Control Successor State, then the associated monitoring operation verifies the result of the comparison realized in the associated Control Flow State or Latch State with the STATUS provided by the HWacc, disables the check operations of Basic Block Control Unit (BBCU) and upload the ID Control Successor State inside the BBCU;
- a Conjunction State, then the associated monitoring operation disables the check operations of BBCU and upload the ID Conjunction State inside the BBCU;

Monitoring operations are executed only when entering a new OCM FSM state. Instead, when staying in the same state, nothing (i.e. NOP operation) happens. Every OCM FSM state owns a counter value T representing the number of merged states from HWacc. This counter decreases when staying in the same state until it reaches zero, then a transition to the next state is activated.

Figure 3.c illustrates the results of OCM FSM when OCM generation is applied to the FSMD_s of Figure 3.b. For example, states s1 and s2 have been merged to create OCM FSM state MS1 with a loopback (T=1). MS1 has also been tagged as Predecessor Header State because the successor of s2 is a Header State.

The OCM FSM inputs are the STATUS signals coming out from the HWacc and a comparison result provided by OCM DP.
OCM DP consists of four modules. The Delay Control Unit (DCU) is used to count NOP operations the current OCM FSM state has to execute thanks to the current value of T. This module ensures that a proper delay is introduced during run-time, to keep the HWacc and OCM synchronized. The I/O Control Unit (IOCU) checks that LOAD signals associated to I/O registers are performed in time in HWacc. The Basic Block Control Unit (BBCU) verifies that there has been no illegal jump inside the current Basic Block. To do this, for all HWacc FSM states (except Control Successor States (CSS) and Conjunction States (CjS)), it compares the identifier of the state ID extracted from the COMMD signal with the one of the previous state or with the ID coming from the OCM FSM uploaded by the CjS or CSS. If the difference between these two identifiers is not one, the BBCU recognizes an illegal jump inside a Basic Block.

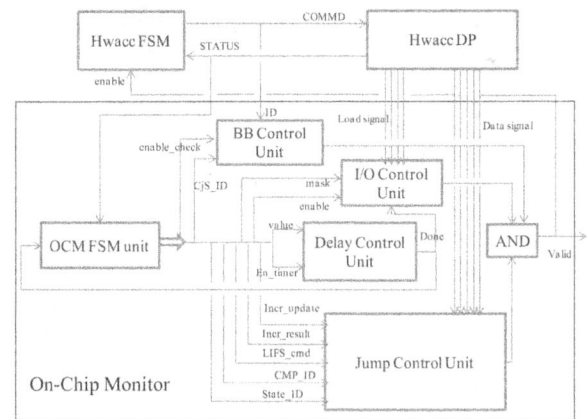

Figure 4: OCM Architecture

276

Application	C code lines	Loop constr.	Cond. Constr.	#I/O
FIR	17	2	0	4
FIR_unroll_4	23	2	0	4
FIR_unroll_8	27	2	0	4
DCT-2D	56	4	2	3
DCT_unroll_4	65	4	2	3
DCT_unroll_8	76	4	2	3
MatMult	20	3	0	6
MatMult_unroll_4	32	3	0	6
MatMult_unroll_8	37	3	0	6
SAD	22	1	1	3
SAD_unroll_4	43	1	4	3
SAD_unroll_8	71	1	8	3
FFT	55	5	1	2
FFT_unroll_4	82	5	1	2
FFT_unroll_8	115	5	1	2
Conv	22	6	0	6
Conv_unroll_4	55	6	0	6
Conv_unroll_8	73	6	0	6
Sobel	82	4	11	4
Sobel_unroll_4	284	4	44	4
Sobel_unroll_8	522	4	88	4
Blowfish	201	11	1	7
AES	213	19	2	5
ADPCM	1097	23	50	5

Table 1: Applications Characteristics

Basic Block	State	Notable State
7	25	12
7	32	15
7	40	19
13	31	19
13	43	21
13	51	21
12	43	23
12	46	26
12	54	30
5	23	12
5	25	10
6	33	12
15	52	31
16	66	39
16	82	47
21	70	41
22	78	48
22	104	62
28	127	45
66	223	108
117	390	191
76	179	66
13	159	76
124	871	358

Table 2: CDFG and architecture characteristics

HWACC without OCM (ms)	HWACC with OCM (ms)	%Time Overhead
1521	1544	1,51%
1488	1507	1,28%
1429	1457	1,96%
1354	1379	1,85%
1588	1611	1,45%
1570	1597	1,72%
1567	1584	1,08%
1604	1631	1,68%
1633	1657	1,47%
1728	1747	1,10%
1453	1476	1,58%
1564	1592	1,79%
1472	1493	1,43%
1483	1510	1,82%
1821	1852	1,70%
1561	1582	1,35%
1764	1793	1,64%
2269	2321	2,29%
1578	1604	1,65%
2345	2396	2,17%
3821	3974	4,00%
7997	8048	0,64%
120411	120623	0,18%
104541	104684	0,14%

Table 3: Synthesis time

Application	SEU	MBU2	MBU3	MBU5	MBU10	MBU20
FIR	3,07E-04	5,38E-04	7,68E-04	1,15E-03	1,77E-03	2,17E-03
DCT-2D	1,62E-04	3,12E-04	4,43E-04	6,68E-04	1,06E-03	1,49E-03
MatMul	7,27E-05	1,36E-04	1,95E-04	2,95E-04	4,61E-04	6,24E-04
SAD	7,74E-04	1,25E-03	1,60E-03	2,02E-03	2,38E-03	2,48E-03
FFT	4,53E-05	8,68E-05	1,21E-04	1,85E-04	3,05E-04	4,42E-04
Conv	8,45E-05	1,04E-04	1,24E-04	1,58E-04	2,28E-04	3,13E-04
Sobel	6,25E-05	6,41E-05	6,72E-05	7,34E-05	8,06E-05	9,33E-05
Blowfish	2,22E-06	3,33E-06	4,44E-06	7,78E-06	1,26E-05	2,17E-05
AES	3,58E-07	3,58E-07	3,58E-07	3,58E-07	6,23E-07	1,16E-06
ADPCM	2,29E-07	2,29E-07	2,29E-07	2,29E-07	4,91E-07	8,72E-07

Table 4: Error Detection mismatch

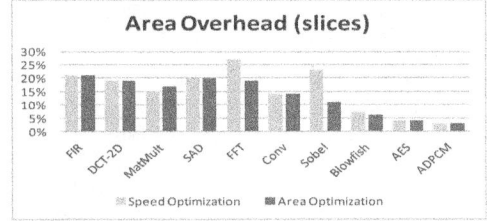

Figure 5: Slice overhead without loop unrolling

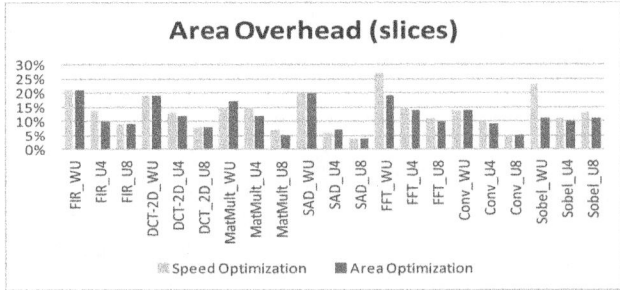

Figure 6: Slice overhead with partial loop unrolling

The Jump Control Unit (JCU) checks the induction variable and the exit condition of loops and checks conditional construct parameters. OCM DP inputs are the control signals COMMD coming from the HWacc FSM and the primary inputs of OCM i.e. Data signals (f1 signals, f2 signals and STEP signal) and Load signals coming from the HWacc. OCM DP output (i.e. signal Valid) can beconnected to the enable signal (which authorizes the state transition) of the HWacc FSM to stop it when an invalid condition is encountered (Valid ='0'), see Figure 4.

3. EXPERIMENTAL RESULTS

In this section, we present the error coverage, as well as the hardware (area) overhead incurred by the proposed on chip monitor. We implemented in java and EMF (Eclipse Modeling Framework) the HLS flow and the on-chip monitor synthesis flow presented in this paper. The HLS compilation step uses GCC 4.7.2 to generate the CDFG. For the purpose of our experiments, we chose ten applications out of well-known DSP applications, HLS benchmarks and encryption standards: Finite Impulse Response filter (FIR), Discrete Cosine Transform (DCT-2D), Matrix Multiplication (MatMult), Sum of Absolute Difference (SAD) of the MPEG-2 application, Fast Fourier Transform (FFT), Convolution Product (Conv), Sobel filter (Sobel), Encryption Standards (Blowfish and AES) and Adaptive Differential Pulse Code Modulation Application (ADPCM). All the applications have been kept parameterized i.e. sizes of the structured data (array, etc.) are variable.

In order to design HWacc using HLS, one functional unit has first been allocated for each type of operation type i.e. addition,

subtraction, etc. The functional unit each executes in one clock cycle apart from multipliers that take two clock cycles. All the RTL architectures generated by the proposed flow have been synthesized using 64-bit ISE 14.5 suite from Xilinx, with a Virtex 5, Device XC5VLX110T (Package FF1136) as target.

3.1 Coverage Analysis

We considered a fault model that includes control flow errors of following types: Register State (SR), state identifier (ID), STATUS signals, command words (COMMD) alteration. Two types of alterations have been considered: single and combined. Single refers to potentially multiple alterations, but on a single element (e.g. on SR but with no impact on the other three types). Combined refers to alteration crossing over several types at the same time. For combined alterations, the only undetected cases are either alteration of commands in non-notable states or a combination of ID and SR alterations which mask each other. However, alteration of commands in non-notable states is out of the scope of this paper as we focus on control flow and I/O behavior. These errors can be detected through data based assertions (e.g. PSL assertions like in [12] or [18]). Combined ID and SR alterations are handled by our approach. As states within SR are one-hot encoded, odd numbers of bit flips in SR lead to illegal states that are immediately detected. Instead, the worst case is when the altered state appears as legal. As an example, after 2 bit flips, one to reset the current bit, and another one to set a new bit high. This occurs with a probability of $2*(n-1)/n^2$, n being the number of states. More generally the asymptote is $1/n^{\log(bitflip)}$. Besides, to get a silent error, the ID must match this new state, so its binary encoding should be altered accordingly. Then the higher number of alterations over ID, the higher chance to hide the faulty behavior. To evaluate the error detection capability of the OCM, we led simulations on the worst case (2 bit flips). Then, faults injection sequences - single (SEU), or multiple (MBUx; x={2,3,5,10,20}) bits upset - have been performed on the ID and commands encoding word. Table 4 summarizes these results. The error detection capability of the OCM slowly decreases with the higher number of alterations over ID to lead to a minimum error detection capability of 99.75%. This conforms to theoretical expectations. For single alterations, if the modified value comes to be locally inconsistent, our solution immediately detects the alteration. On the contrary, be the faulty value correct within its type, the inconsistency is globally detected based on the unaltered three types. As an example, even if an alteration over SR unlikely produces a valid state, detection happens due to a mismatch with the current ID. The theoretical detection rate is 100%, what is confirmed by our measurements.

3.2 Hardware Overhead Analysis

Two optimization options have been considered for logic synthesis: area and speed. All the experimental results were obtained on a laptop with Intel® Core™ i3-2330M Processor (4 GB RAM, 2.20 GHz).

Table 1 gives an overview of the application complexity in terms of number of C code lines, loop constructs, conditional constructs and I/O parameters. Benchmarks range from simple (1 loop, 1 if-else and 3 I/O) to more complex (23 loops, 50 if-else and 5 I/O) applications. Table 2 presents CDFG, FSMD_s and annotated FSMD_s characteristics in terms of number of basic blocks, states and notable states. Table 3 summarizes the synthesis times running HLS alone and HLS with OCMS flow in order to generate the OCM architecture. As stated, the overhead ranging from 0.13% to 4.06% is negligible and decreases when the applications' complexity increases.

Figure 5 presents the area overhead in slices when OCM is added to the HWacc. Results are given for the two optimization options of logic synthesis. For speed optimization, the overhead can go up to 27% while for area optimization the overhead is up to 20%. Peak overheads are obtained when considering OCM DPs that implement complex loop increment functions – that must be computed twice to detect single error over *STATUS* despite their area is important - like multiplications (e.g. the FFT). The second characteristic that impacts the overhead is the application's complexity. HWaccs that implement low complexity applications, with only one functional unit for each type of operation, exhibit high overhead. On the contrary, the OCM overhead is less than 4% for applications of higher complexity like AES, ADPCM and blowfish. Figure 6 demonstrates the same effect when loops are partially unrolled to make HWacc more parallel, more powerful and thus more realistic. For that purpose, loops of FIR, DCT-2D, SAD, MatMult, Conv, Sobel and FFT have been unrolled by a factor of 4 and 8. Partial unrolling brings potential parallelism. Our scheduler is aware of this and allocates as many functional units as required to fully exploit this parallelism This allowed reducing the area overhead down to 13% (speed opt.) and 11% (area opt.) on average for these applications.

Our experimental results demonstrate that our approach leads to a small average overhead in terms of slices, with no significant impact over clock frequency, 0.12% on overage. Moreover, the two optimization options are compatible with our OCMS flow hence enabling designers to keep their optimization objectives unchanged.

4. CONCLUSION

In this paper, we proposed an automated methodology that generates On-Chip Monitors (OCM) during High-Level Synthesis (HLS) of hardware accelerators. The generated OCM checks at runtime both I/O timing behavior errors and control flow errors in order to enhance embedded system security. The OCM architecture is composed of control part (FSM) and a Data-Path (DP). The OCM FSM skeleton is an optimized copy of the HWacc FSM. Our experimental results show that the error coverage on the control flow ranges from 99.75% to 100% while in average the OCM area overhead is less than 10% and decreases

when the application gains in complexity. In addition, the average OCM clock overhead is 0.12% and thus negligible. Finally, our approach has no impact on synthesis time of HLS flow. Our approach thus offers a transparent path to runtime monitoring since the process is fully automated and over cost is negligible.

REFERENCES

[1] R. Vemu; J.A. Abraham; "CEDA: Control-Flow Error Detection Using Assertions," *Computers,IEEE Transactions on* , vol.60, no.9, pp.1233,1245, Sept. 2011

[2] N. Oh; P.P. Shirvani; E.J McCluskey; "Control-flow checking by software signatures," Reliability, *IEEE Transactions on* , *vol.51, no.1, pp.111,122, Mar 2002*

[3] A. Benso; S. Di Carlo; G. Di Natale; P. Prinetto; "A watchdog processor to detect data and control flow errors," *On-Line Testing Symposium, 2003.9th IEEE* , *vol., no., pp.144,148, 7-9 July 2003*

[4] T. Michel; R. Leveugle; G. Saucier; "A new approach to control flow checking without program modification," Fault-Tolerant Computing, 1991. FTCS-21. Digest of Papers., *Twenty-First International Symposium* , *vol., no., pp.334,341, 25-27 June 1991*

[5] D. Arora; S. Ravi; A. Raghunathan; N.K. Jha;"Secure embedded processing through hardware-assisted run-time monitoring," *DATE, 2005. Proceedings* , *vol., no., pp.178,183 Vol. 1, 7-11 March 2005*

[6] M. Rahmatian; H. Kooti; I.G. Harris; E. Bozorgzadeh; "Hardware-Assisted Detection of Malicious Software in Embedded Systems," *IEEE, Embedded System Lettre, vol.4, no., pp.94,97, Dec. 2012*

[7] Sylvain G., Renaud P. , "SoCs security: a war against side-channels ", *Annales Des Télécommunications Juillet/Aout 2004, Volume 59, Issue 7-8, pp 998-1009*

[8] M. Nueve, E. Peeters, D. Samyde, and J.J. Quisquater; "Memories: *a Survey of their Secure Uses in Smart Cards"; Proc. of IEEE SISW 2003, October 2003. Washington DC, USA.*

[9] S.P. Skorobogatov and R.J. Anderson; "Optical Fault Induction Attacks". *Proc. of CHES'02, 2002.*

[10] O. Käommerling and M. Kuhn;"Design Principles for Tamper-Resistant Smartcard Processors". *Proc. of the Usenix Workshop on Smartcard Technology (Smartcard'99), pages 9{20, May 1999.*

[11] P. Coussy and A. Takach, Special Issue on High-Level Synthesis, *IEEE DTC . IEEE Computer Society*, 2009, vol. 25

[12] J. Curreri; G. Stitt; A.D George, "High-level synthesis techniques for in-circuit assertion-based verification," *in Proceedings of the 17th Reconfigurable Architectures Workshops,* April 2010, pp. 1-8

[13] A. Ribon; B. Le Gal; C. Jego; D. Dallet; , "Assertion support in high-level synthesis design flow," *in Proc. Specification and Design Languages,* Sept. 2011, pp. 1-8.

[14] T. Yunfeng, "An introduction to assertion-based verification," *IEEE 8th International Conference on ASIC, 2009,* pp. 1318-1323

[15] Accellera, "Property Specification Language Reference Manual, version 1.1," , 2004

[16] Accellera, "SystemVerilog 3.la language reference manuall," 2001

[17] Accellera, "Open Verification Library, Reference Manual," 2009

[18] D. Borrione, K. Morin-Allory, Y. Oddos, "Property-Based Dynamic Verification and Test", in "Design Technology For Heterogeneous Embedded Systems", Springer 2012

[19] M. Boule; Z. Zilic, "Efficient Automata-Based Assertion-Checker Synthesis of PSL Properties," *IEEE International High-Level Design Validation and Test Workshop,* Nov. 2006, pp. 69-76

[20] H. Paul, "Nesting of Reducible and Irreducible Loops," *ACM Transaction on PLS,* vol. 19, 1997, pp. 557-567

[21] P. Coussy, A. Morawiec, "High-Level Synthesis: From Algorithm to Digital Circuit," Springer, 2008

[22] L. Davi , R. Dmitrienko , M. Egele, T.Fischer, T.Holz, R.Hund, S.Nurnberge, A.Sadeghi "MoCFl: A framework to mitigate control-flow attacks on smartphones", In Proc of the NDSS Sym, 2012.

[23] K.Pattabiraman, G.P.Sagesse, Z.Kalbarczyk, R.Iyer; "Dynamic Derivation of application-Specific Error Detectors and their Implementation", Proceedings EDCC, 2006, p97-108

Thermal-aware Phase-based Tuning of Embedded Systems

Tosiron Adegbija and Ann Gordon-Ross*

Department of Electrical and Computer Engineering, University of Florida, Gainesville, FL 32611, USA

tosironkbd@ufl.edu & ann@ece.ufl.edu

*Also affiliated with the NSF Center for High-Performance Reconfigurable Computing (CHREC) at UF

ABSTRACT

Due to embedded systems' stringent design constraints, much prior work focused on optimizing energy consumption and/or performance. However, since embedded systems have fewer cooling options, rising temperature, and thus temperature optimization, is an emergent concern. We present thermal-aware phase-based tuning—TaPT—that determines Pareto optimal configurations for fine-grained execution time, energy, and temperature tradeoffs. Results show that TaPT reduces execution time, energy, and temperature by as much as 5%, 30%, and 25%, respectively, while adhering to designer-specified design constraints.

Categories and Subject Descriptors

B.3.2 [**Hardware**]: Memory Structures: Design Styles – *cache memories*.

Keywords

Dynamic thermal management, phase-based tuning, thermal-aware tuning, energy savings, configurable caches, dynamic optimization.

1. INTRODUCTION AND MOTIVATION

Embedded systems have been the focus of much optimization research due to these systems' pervasiveness and intrinsic design constraints. Since most embedded systems are battery operated, reducing energy consumption without significantly degrading system performance is a key design optimization. However, temperature is also a growing issue in embedded systems optimization research since most embedded systems have fewer cooling options as compared to general purpose computers due to area/size, cost, and energy constraints. Most embedded systems only dissipate heat by passive convection, thus necessitating efficient thermal management methodologies.

Increased chip temperature in an embedded system can result in increased cooling costs, reduced mean time to failure (MTTF), reduced reliability, etc. Increased temperature can also lead to thermal emergencies, which can result in an exponential increase in leakage power and compounding temperature increases (i.e., thermal runaway), leading to permanent chip damage. To address these issues, several dynamic thermal management (DTM) techniques have been proposed for managing chip temperature, most of which leverage clock gating [5], dynamic voltage scaling (DVS), dynamic

GLSVLSI'14, May 21–23, 2014, Houston, Texas, USA.
Copyright 2014 ACM 978-1-4503-2816-6/14/05 ...$15.00.
http://dx.doi.org/10.1145/2591513.2591586

frequency scaling (DFS), dynamic voltage and frequency scaling (DVFS) [19], and task migration [11].

DTM techniques have been successful in reducing chip temperature, however, some DTM techniques consider temperature in isolation [16], which may adversely affect other design objectives, such as execution time and/or energy consumption. Furthermore, the applications' execution characteristics (e.g., cache misses, instructions per cycle (IPC), branch mispredictions, etc.) can affect the temperature [21], and even though some DTM techniques consider inter-application characteristic variations [12], these techniques do not consider intra-application characteristic variations, which can significantly limit optimization potential [7].

To increase optimization potential using fine-grained system tuning (i.e., specialization) to varying application characteristics without incurring significant tuning overhead in terms of energy, area, and/or performance, previous work has proposed phase-based tuning [6]. A phase is a length of execution where an application's characteristics remain relatively stable, and therefore the best system configuration, or specific parameter values (e.g., cache size, associativity, line size, clock frequency, etc.), that adhere to the design constraints also remain relatively stable. Phase-based tuning requires configurable hardware with tunable parameters where the parameter's values can be specified/changed during runtime. Phase-based tuning also requires a mechanism to evaluate the application's characteristics to determine the best system configuration for each phase of execution to best satisfy design objectives (e.g., minimize energy, execution time, etc.) and design constraints (e.g., temperature thresholds). Previous work showed that phase-based tuning significantly reduced energy consumption in embedded systems [6]. For example, Gordon-Ross et al. [8] showed that phase-based cache tuning saved as much as 62% of the memory access energy. However, little work studied the combination of phase based-tuning and DTM.

Since prior work showed that phase-based cache tuning significantly impacts energy consumption and execution time, and DTM techniques can significantly impact temperature, energy consumption, and execution time, we combine phase-based cache tuning and DFS for fine-grained and efficient temperature, energy, and execution time optimization. However, since optimizing one design objective may adversely impact the other design objectives, combining these techniques presents a multi-objective optimization problem. The solution to a multi-objective optimization problem is the Pareto optimal configuration set, which enables designers to choose the system configuration that best meets the design constraints.

We present thermal-aware phase-based tuning (TaPT), which dynamically determines the Pareto optimal system configurations trading off execution time, energy, and temperature design objectives. TaPT is based on the strength Pareto evolutionary algorithm II (SPEA2) [23], which is a well-known and effective evolutionary algorithm for solving multi-objective optimization problems. We modify SPEA2 to implement phase-based tuning and consider designer-selected priority settings. These priority settings allow designers to prioritize a design objective, thus trading off/degrading non-prioritized design objectives to increase the prioritized design objective based on design constraints. TaPT's runtime automation aids designers in adhering to design constraints with no design time effort. TaPT leverages previously proposed/existing configurable hardware, thus minimizing the additional hardware overhead with respect to these prior techniques. Experimental results show that compared to using the same system configuration throughout an application's execution, TaPT reduces execution time, energy consumption, and temperature by as much as 5%, 30%, and 25%, while adhering to designer-specified design constraints.

2. BACKGROUND AND RELATED WORK

Since much previous work focuses on phase-based tuning [1][6][8] and DTM [5][11][19] separately, and to the best of our knowledge, our work is the first to combine phase-based tuning and DTM, we present related work and background in these two areas. We also present background and key concepts for SPEA2, which serves as the basis for TaPT.

2.1 Phase-based Tuning and DTM

To facilitate phase-based tuning, hardware- or software-based phase classification partitions an application's execution into intervals, measured by the number of instructions executed. Intervals showing similar characteristics can be clustered into phases. Balasubramonian et al. [3] used cache miss rates, cycles per instruction (CPI), and branch frequency characteristics to detect changes in application characteristics for cache tuning, and found that these characteristics were effective for phase classification. Since we utilize cache tuning in this work, for brevity, we limit our review to phase-based cache tuning.

Phase-based tuning can leverage any configurable cache architecture (e.g., [7]) and tuning method to search the configuration design space, which consists of all the different system configurations/combinations of tunable parameter values. Zhang et al. [22] proposed a low energy and area overhead configurable cache architecture that provided runtime-configurable total cache size, associativity, and line size using a small, hardware-settable bit-width configuration register. Motorola's M*CORE processor [14] provided per-way configuration using way management, which allowed ways to be shut down or designated as instruction only, data only, or unified.

A major challenge of phase-based tuning is tuning the configurable hardware to the best configuration for each phase without incurring significant tuning overhead. Gordon-Ross et al. [6] presented cache design space exploration heuristics that when used for phased-based tuning, realized as much as 39% energy savings on average as compared to non-phase-based tuning (i.e., using a single configuration for the entire application). Hajimir et al. [10] presented a dynamic programming-based algorithm to find the best cache configuration for each phase. However, these methods only focused on energy savings and did not consider thermal issues.

To reduce chip temperature dissipation, several DTM techniques have been proposed. Brooks et al. [5] investigated clock gating, which turns off the clock signals during thermal emergencies. Heo et al. [11] proposed task migration, which migrated tasks from a hot core to a cooler core to avoid a thermal emergency. However, these works did not explicitly consider the tradeoffs between energy, temperature, and execution time, thus increasing the possibility of significantly degrading one design objective while optimizing other

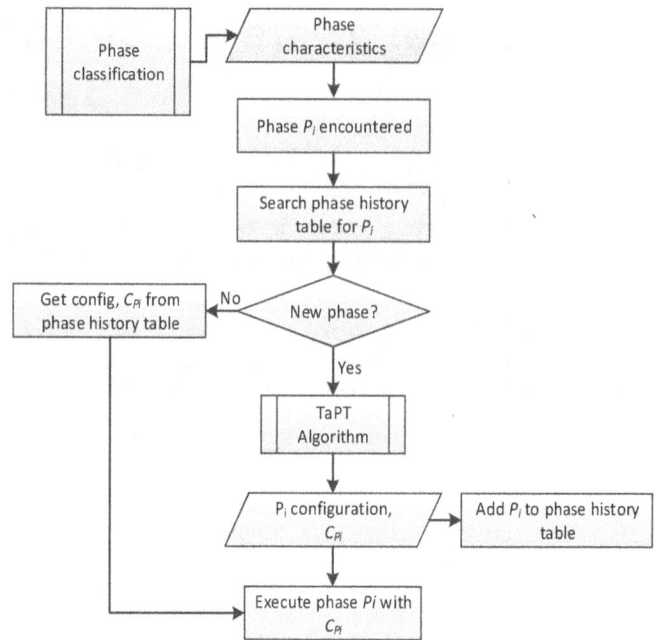

Figure 1. TaPT overview

design objectives. Furthermore, these methods were not phase-based and did not consider intra-application variations.

Our work differs from previous works by combining phase-based cache tuning and DFS to achieve Pareto optimal configurations that trade off execution time, energy, and temperature, thus achieving fine-grained multi-objective optimization.

2.2 SPEA2 Algorithm

Evolutionary algorithms leverage biological evolutionary concepts, such as population, reproduction, mutation, selection, etc., for efficiently determining Pareto optimal solutions to multi-objective optimization problems. The solution space consists of all of the possible solutions to the optimization problem, the population is a subset of the solution space, and the population's solutions are referred to as individuals. A solution's fitness dictates the solution's quality and represents how well the solution adheres to design constraints. Evolution iterates over successive generations of populations, where each evolution considers the population's individuals' finesses and replaces the least fit individuals with new solutions from the solution space, and interjects random solution mutations to create the successive generation.

Prior work shows that SPEA2 outperforms most other evolutionary algorithms for solving multi-objective optimization problems [23]. SPEA2 uses *elitism*, which maintains an external set of non-dominated solutions, called an *archive*. A solution is non-dominated (or Pareto optimal) if none of the design objectives can be improved without degrading another design objective. For example, given two configurations C_x and C_y, C_x dominates C_y (written as $C_x \succ C_y$) if and only if:

$$\forall i \in \{1, 2, ..., k\} : f_i(C_x) \geq f_i(C_y) \quad \exists j \in \{1, 2, ..., k\} : f_j(C_x) > f_j(C_y) \quad (1)$$

where k is the number of objectives and f_k represents the design objectives' objective functions, and $f_k(C_x)$ characterizes how well C_x achieves the design objectives.

For brevity, we present an overview of SPEA2, and refer the reader to [23] for additional details. SPEA2 takes the solution space as input and outputs the Pareto optimal solution set. SPEA2 generates

Input: n, s, A_{size}, G, Q
Output: Pi's best configuration

```
0       t ← 0
1       for i ← 1 to s do
2           C_i ← rand() / s + 1
3       end
4       population is {C_1, C_2, ..., C_s}
5       for j ← 1 to n do
6           D_j ← d(P_i, P_j)
7       end
8       A_msp ← archive(P_j) | D = min(D_j)
9       if n == 0 && t == 0 then
10          archive ← Ø
11      else if k > 0 && t == 0 then
12          archive ← A_msp
13      end
14      else
15          archive ← archive(t-1)
16      end
17      U ← population + archive
18      for (C_i ∈ U) do
19          fit(C_i) ← calculateFitness(C_i)
20      end
21      archive ← getNonDominated(U)
22      size(archive) ← A_size
23      if t == (G – 1) then
24          bestConfiguration(P_i) ← min(f(Q))
25          exit
```

an initial population and creates an empty archive and populates the first generation's archive with the population's non-dominated individuals. For subsequent generations, SPEA2 calculates the population's and archive's individuals' finesses, and populates the next generation's archive with the population's and archive's non-dominated individuals. When the maximum number of generations has been reached and/or number of solutions that satisfy the design objectives have been determined, the current archive contains the Pareto optimal set.

3. THERMAL-AWARE PHASE-BASED TUNING (TAPT)

TaPT leverages several fundamental assumptions based on mechanisms that have been widely studied and implemented in embedded systems [15][22]. Since our work is independent from the specific phase classification technique leveraged and prior work presents many phase classification techniques, we assume phase classification has already been performed and the applications' phases and the phases' instruction and data cache miss rates and IPC characteristics are input into phase-based tuning. We also assume that DFS is enabled, and the system has a temperature sensor, a hardware tuner [7] to orchestrate phase classification and implement TaPT, and a hardware-tunable cache with tunable size, associativity, and line size. In this section, we present an overview of TaPT and details of the TaPT algorithm.

3.1 Overview of TaPT

Figure 1 depicts an overview of TaPT. TaPT takes as input the classified phases' characteristics, which are output from phase classification. To minimize tuning overhead, a phase history table stores information about previously executed phases and the phases' best system configurations. When a phase P_i is executed, if P_i is in the phase history table, P_i has been previously executed (i.e., P_i is a not new phase) and the stored best system configuration C_{Pi} is used to execute P_i. If P_i is not in the phase history table (i.e., P_i is a new phase), TaPT determines P_i's best system configuration C_{Pi}, P_i is executed with C_{Pi} and C_{Pi} is stored in the phase history table for subsequent executions of P_i.

3.2 The TaPT Algorithm

TaPT contains three designer-specified priority settings, X, N, and T, which prioritize execution time, energy, or temperature minimization, respectively. These priority settings enable TaPT to efficiently determine the best system configuration C_{Pi} for a phase P_i while adhering to designer-specified constraints. The priority settings trade off the non-prioritized design objectives in favor of the prioritized design objective. For example, X trades off increased execution time and increased temperature for minimized energy. If the designer does not specify a priority, the priority setting defaults to S, which prioritizes energy delay product (EDP) minimization to account for both energy consumption and execution time while also reducing temperature and/or preventing a significant temperature increase. TaPT also allows the designer to associate a peak temperature threshold with each priority setting, such that TaPT determines Pareto optimal configurations that do not exceed the temperature threshold.

To ensure equal probability of selection for all configurations when generating the population, TaPT uses random uniform distribution, and on system startup, the initial archive is an empty set since there are no previously executed phases. TaPT generates P_i's archive from P_i's population's and archive's non-dominated configurations (Equation (1)) using the configurations' fitness and stores P_i's final archive in the phase history table. A configuration C_i's fitness is the sum of C_i's dominators' strengths, and a configuration's C_i's strength $S(C_i)$ is the number of configurations dominated by that configuration such that:

$$S(C_i) = |\{C_j \mid C_j \in P \cup A \,\forall\, C_i \succ C_j\}| \qquad (2)$$

where P and A are P_i's population and archive, respectively. C_i's fitness $R(C_i)$ is:

$$R(C_i) = \sum S(C_j) \,\forall\, C_j \in P \cup A, C_j \succ C_i \qquad (3)$$

where $R(C_i) = 0$ indicates that Ci is non-dominated.

To implement phase-based tuning, TaPT calculates the phase distances [1] between the currently executing phase P_i and all of the previously executed phases P_{i-1}, P_{i-1}, ..., P_{i-n}. The phase distance is the difference between two phases' characteristics, which the authors in [1] calculated using the normalized difference between the two phases' cache miss rates. However, since TaPT tunes multiple hardware parameters (instruction and data cache configurations and clock frequency), TaPT calculates the phase distance using the Euclidean distance between the instruction cache miss rate (iMR), data cache miss rate (dMR), and the instructions per cycle (IPC). The phase distance D between two phases P_i and P_j is:

$$D = \sqrt{(iMR_{Pi} - iMR_{Pj})^2 + (dMR_{Pi} - dMR_{Pj})^2 + (IPC_{Pi} - IPC_{Pj})^2} \qquad (4)$$

TaPT uses the most similar phase's archive as the currently executing phase's initial archive, where the most similar phase has the minimum D from P_i. Since phases with stable characteristics require similar configurations, using the most similar phase's archive as P_i's initial archive starts the TaPT algorithm with solutions that are presumably closer to P_i's Pareto optimal solutions, as compared to an archive from the randomly-generated initial population.

Algorithm 1 depicts the TaPT algorithm, which executes for each new phase P_i. The algorithm takes as input the number of previously executed phases n and a designer-specified population size s, archive size A_{size}, number of generations G, and priority setting Q. The algorithm outputs P_i's best system configuration. The product of s and G defines the maximum number of configurations explored/executed during tuning, which limits the tuning overhead, and A_{size} specifies the size of the archive and ensures that only the most fit configurations (Equations (2) and (3)) are stored in the archive. Given the nature of evolutionary algorithms, the archive does not necessarily contain the actual Pareto optimal solutions. In general, larger s and G values determine solutions that are closer to the Pareto optimal solutions, but also increase tuning overhead. Alternatively, smaller s and G values reduce tuning overhead, but may also determine configurations that are farther from the Pareto optimal solutions. We extensively evaluated different values of s, G, and A_{size} and observed that s and G values that explored 4% of the design space and $A_{size} = 5$ yielded an efficient balance between determining Pareto optimal solutions and reduced tuning overhead.

First, TaPT generates an initial population from the configuration space and calculates the phase distance D between the currently executing phase and all of the previously executed phases (lines 1 – 7). Next, TaPT initializes P_i's archive to P_i's most similar phase's archive (i.e., the phase with the minimum distance D from P_i) (lines 8 and 16). At system startup ($n = 0$), there are no previously executed phases ($D =$ null), and the archive is initialized to an empty set (lines 9 – 10). For each generation, TaPT uses the previous generation's Pareto optimal set as the current generation's initial archive (line 15). TaPT calculates each population's and archive's configuration's fitness using Equations (2) and (3), and updates the current generation's archive with the non-dominated configurations (lines 17 – 21). TaPT maintains P_i's archive's size at A_{size} by

discarding the least fit configurations or adding the most fit configurations from the population (line 22).

On the final generation, TaPT selects the *best configuration* from the archive that optimizes the specified priority setting (line 24). Finally, TaPT stores C_{Pi} in the phase history table (Figure 1) for P_i's subsequent executions.

3.3 Computational Complexity and Hardware Overhead

TaPT calculates $S(C_i)$ and $R(C_i)$ with worst-case time complexity $O(m^2)$, where m is the sum of the population and archive sizes, and calculates D with worst-case time complexity $O(n)$, where n is the number of previously executed phases. Thus, since these calculations dominate TaPT, TaPT results in minimal computation overhead. Furthermore, since TaPT utilizes previously proposed and implemented hardware, such as a DFS mechanism, phase history table, and configurable caches, TaPT imposes no additional hardware overhead as compared to prior work.

4. EXPERIMENTAL RESULTS

4.1 Experimental Setup

We evaluated TaPT's execution time, energy, EDP, and temperature savings by comparing a system that switches to the best configuration, as determined by TaPT, for each phase to a base system with a fixed system configuration. The base system had 32 Kbyte, 4-way private level one (L1) instruction and data caches with 64 byte line sizes, and a processor clock frequency of 2 GHz . This configuration is similar to current embedded systems (e.g., Motorola RAZR XT890 [15]), and thus serves as a good base comparison to a commercial off-the-shelf (COTS) system.

We modeled an embedded processor architecture, similar to the ARM Cortex A9 [2], consisting of a 4-width out-of-order issue processor with 8 pipeline stages and 45 nm technology. Our experiments represent state-of-the-art embedded systems, and our results and analyses extend to future and/or more complex systems (e.g., n-core processors, heterogeneous systems, etc.) because TaPT is independent of these system characteristics. The processor's

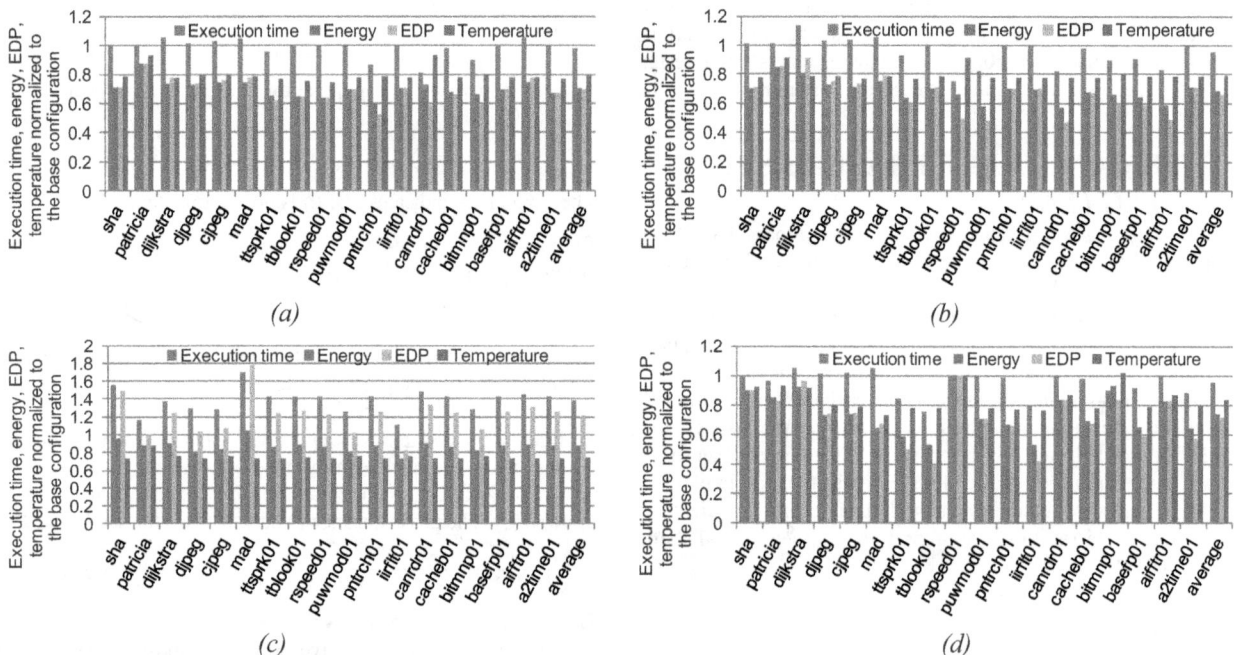

(a)

(b)

(c)

(d)

Figure 2. Execution time, energy, EDP, and temperature normalized to the base configuration for priority settings (a) S, (b) N, (c) T, and (d) X.

configurable L1 instruction and data cache sizes ranged from 8 to 32 Kbyte, line sizes ranged from 16 to 64 byte, and associativities ranged from 1- to 4-way, all in power-of-two increments. The processor offered seven clock frequencies ranging from 800 MHz to 2 GHz in 200 MHz increments. Given these parameter values, the design space contains 1,701 configurations.

We modeled the processor using GEM5 [4] and generated cache miss rates and core statistics, which we used to calculate the execution time. We also used these statistics to calculate the system's total energy consumption and EDP with McPAT [13]. We used Hotspot 5.0 [20] as the thermal modeling tool to measure the temperature using a floorplan and silicon chip area similar to the ARM Cortex A9 processor. We ran thermal simulations and sampled the application's power consumption at 10 ms intervals, similar to modern operating systems (e.g., Linux) [18]. Previous work [18] showed that this fine-grained sampling accurately depicted the application's temperature characteristics during execution. To simulate an embedded system without cooling mechanisms, such as an heat sink and/or spreader, we set the convection resistance to 4K/W and the heat sink and spreader thickness to 1 mm and 0.1 mm, respectively, which are considered negligible in Hotspot.

To model a variety of real-world embedded system applications, we used eighteen benchmarks: twelve EEMBC [17] Automotive benchmarks (the full suite could not be evaluated due to compilation errors) and six MiBench [9] benchmarks selected to represent different application domains. The benchmarks were specific compute kernels performing specific tasks in different application domains, such as networking, image processing, security, etc.

We implemented TaPT using Perl scripts to drive simulations and executed each phase once to completion. To implement phase classification, we ran execution trace simulations on each benchmark using GEM5 to generate cache miss rates and IPC statistics, and grouped intervals with similar characteristics as phases using variable-length intervals [7], which previous work found to be effective for phase classification. Since the benchmarks were specific compute kernels, our experiments revealed that the benchmarks exhibited relatively stable characteristics throughout execution. Without loss of generality, this characteristic stability enabled us to consider each kernel/benchmark as a different phase of execution.

To determine appropriate values for s, G, and A_{size}, we ran extensive experiments with different values and observed that $s = 20$, $G = 3$, and $A_{size} = 5$ achieved a good balance between Pareto optimal solutions and tuning overhead. These values explored only 4% of the design space, while larger values increased tuning overhead without significantly improving the Pareto optimal solutions and smaller values reduced tuning overhead, but achieved sub-Pareto-optimal solutions. s and G are system dependent and can be scaled appropriately for different design spaces.

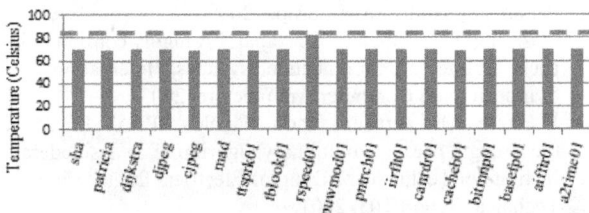

Figure 3. Peak temperatures with respect to a temperature threshold of 82°C (broken horizontal line).

To explore several diverse design objectives, we modeled all of TaPT's priority settings using these values of s, G, and A_{size}. To evaluate the impact of designer-specified temperature thresholds lower than the base configuration's average peak temperature of 89°C (determined by simulation), we evaluated empirically-determined high and low temperature thresholds set at 82°C and 65°C, based on the range of temperatures observed during simulation. The high 82°C threshold illustrates a system where the primary concern is for the temperature to be maintained below 82°C to prevent overheating damage, while the low 65°C threshold represents a strict temperature-constrained system to illustrate how maintaining a low temperature impacts the other objective functions.

4.2 Results

Figure 2 depicts the execution time, energy, EDP and temperature of the best configurations as determined by TaPT normalized to the base system configuration for a single execution of each benchmark/phase for each priority setting. Figure 2 (a) depicts a zero-designer-effort system, with a default priority setting S (EDP prioritization) and no temperature threshold. The results show average EDP, energy, execution time, and temperature reductions of 31%, 30%, 2%, and 21%, respectively, with maximum reductions of 48%, 35%, 19%, and 5%, respectively. For some phases, prioritizing EDP minimization only slightly reduced the temperature. For example, candr01's EDP, energy, and execution time reduced by 40%, 27%, and 18%, respectively, while reducing the temperature by only 8%. However, other phases suffered increased execution time, up to 6%, to prioritize EDP minimization, but gained significant reductions in energy and temperature. For example, mad's EDP, energy, and temperature reduced by 23%, 26%, and 21%, respectively, while increasing the execution time by 4%. In general, priority setting S minimizes EDP, and reduces the energy consumption and temperature for all phases, with only minor increases in execution time for some phases.

Figure 2 (b) shows that priority setting N (energy prioritization) and a temperature threshold of 82°C resulted in average execution time, energy, EDP, and temperature reductions of 4%, 31%, 34%, and 20%, respectively. Figure 3 illustrates the impact of a high temperature threshold, and depicts the phases' peak temperatures with respect to the threshold temperature 82°C. For all of the phases, the temperature never exceeded 82°C, because rather than minimizing temperature, TaPT maintained the temperature at or below 82°C, which allowed for further execution time, energy, and EDP reduction since the temperature threshold was relatively high.

Figure 2 (c) depicts a much lower temperature threshold set at 65°C and priority setting T (temperature prioritization). On average over all of the phases, the energy and temperature decreased by 13% and 25%, respectively. However, the execution time and EDP significantly increased by 39% and 22%, respectively. TaPT maintained a peak temperature for all the phases within 65°C to 68°C, however, to maintain this low peak temperature, TaPT traded off execution time and energy consumption. Increasing the temperature threshold to 70°C (results not shown for brevity) decreased the energy, EDP, and temperature by 27%, 26%, and 21%, respectively, while the execution time only increased by 2%. These results show TaPT's ability to trade off objective functions in order to adhere to design constraints. The results also show the extent to which some objective functions may be adversely affected in a multi-objective optimization problem where one of the objective functions is significantly constrained.

Figure 2 (d) shows that using priority setting X (execution time prioritization) with no temperature threshold decreased execution time, energy, EDP, and temperature by 5%, 26%, 29%, and 16%, respectively. For example, TaPT significantly decreased *tblook*'s execution time, energy, EDP, and temperature by 24%, 47%, 60%, and 22%, respectively. However, for some phases there was no execution time decrease, such as *mad*, which increased by 5% while the energy, EDP, and temperature decreased by 36%, 32%, and 27%, respectively. Even though TaPT achieved significant execution time improvement for some phases, the base configuration performed well in terms of execution time for most phases. Thus, for those phases, TaPT determined configurations that did not significantly increase the execution time, while also reducing the energy and temperature. Therefore, even though TaPT emphasized execution time minimization in this experiment, since the base configuration was a high performing configuration on average, the relatively low execution time reduction was expected. In general, TaPT successfully achieved significant savings in terms of execution time, energy, and temperature while adhering to specified design constraints.

4.3 TaPT Exploration Time

We evaluated TaPT's exploration time by comparing how much time TaPT required to determine a phase's best configuration with how much time was required to determine the phase's best configuration using an exhaustive search of the design space. On average over all the phases, TaPT reduced the exploration time from 142 seconds to 6 seconds, with the longest and shortest exploration reductions being from 321 seconds to 13 seconds and from 25 seconds to 1 second, respectively. Thus, on average, TaPT reduced the exploration time by 96%, translating to a 25 times speedup in exploration time.

5. CONCLUSIONS

In this paper, we presented thermal-aware phase-based tuning, TaPT, which combines phase-based cache tuning and dynamic frequency scaling (DFS) to determine Pareto optimal configurations for different application phases of execution. We show TaPT's effectiveness in determining Pareto optimal configurations that significantly reduce execution time, energy, energy delay product (EDP), and temperature, with minimal computational complexity, while adhering to specified design constraints. Future work includes incorporating runtime phase classification into TaPT to provide optimization for systems where the executing applications are not known and/or classified a priori. Additionally, we plan to verify TaPT's scalability to more complex systems with much larger design spaces (e.g., heterogeneous multi-/many core systems).

6. ACKNOWLEDGMENTS

This work was supported by the National Science Foundation (CNS-0953447). Any opinions, findings, and conclusions or recommendations expressed in this material are those of the authors and do not necessarily reflect the views of the National Science Foundation.

7. REFERENCES

[1] T. Adegbija, A. Gordon-Ross, and A. Munir, "Dynamic Phase-based Tuning for Embedded Systems Using Phase Distance Mapping," International Conference on Computer Design, 2012.

[2] ARM, http://www.arm.com/products/processors/cortex-a/cortex-a9.php.

[3] R. Balasubramonian, D. Albonesi, A. Byoktosunoglu, and S. Dwarkada, "Memory hierarchy reconfiguration for energy and performance in general-purpose architectures," International Symposium on Microarchitecture, 2000.

[4] N. Binkert, et al, "The gem5 simulator," Computer Architecture News, May 2011.

[5] D. Brooks and M. Martonosi, "Dynamic thermal management for high performance microprocessors," International Symposium on High-Performance Computer Architecture, 2001.

[6] A. Gordon-Ross, J. Lau, and B. Calder, "Phase-based cache reconfiguration for a highly-configurable two-level cache hierarchy," ACM Great Lakes Symposium on VLSI, 2008

[7] A. Gordon-Ross and F. Vahid, "A self-tuning configurable cache," IEEE Design Automation Conference, 2003.

[8] A. Gordon-Ross, F. Vahid, and N. Dutt, "Fast configurable-cache tuning with a unified second level cache," International Symposium on Low Power Electronics and Design, 2005.

[9] M. R. Guthausch et al., "Mibench: a free, commercially representative embedded benchmark suite," IEEE Workshop on Workload Characterization, 2001.

[10] H. Hajimir and P. Mishra, "Intra-task dynamic cache reconfiguration," International Conference on VLSI Design, 2012.

[11] S. Heo, K. Barr, and K. Asanovic, "Reducing power density through activity migration," International Symposium on Low Power Electronics and Design, 2003.

[12] R. Jayaseelan and T. Mitra, "Temperature aware task sequencing and voltage scaling," International Conference on Computer-Aided Design, 2008.

[13] S. Li, et al, "McPAT: an integrated power, area, and timing modeling framework for multicore and manycore architectures," International Symposium on Microarchitecture, 2009.

[14] A. Malik, W. Moyer, and D. Cermak, "A low power unified cache architecture providing power and performance flexibility," International Symposium on Low Power Electronics and Design, 2000.

[15] Motorola RAZR i XT890 - http://www.gsmarena.com/motorola_razr_i_xt890-4998.php.

[16] M. Pedram and S. Narian, "Thermal modeling, analysis, and management in VLSI circuits: principles and methods," Special Issue on Thermal Analysis of ULSI, Vol. 94, No. 8, pp. 1487-1501, 2006.

[17] J. Poovey, M. Levy, and S. Gal-On, "A benchmark characterization of the EEMBC benchmark suite," International Symposium on Microarchitecture, 2009.

[18] S. Sharifi, A. Coskun, and T. Rosing, "Hybrid dynamic energy and thermal management in heterogeneous embedded multiprocessor SoCs," Asia and South Pacific Design Automation Conference, 2010.

[19] K Skadron, "Hybrid architectural dynamic thermal management," Design Automation and Test in Europe, 2004.

[20] K. Skadron, et al., "Temperature-aware microarchitecture: modeling and implementation," Transactions on Architecture and Code Optimization, March 2004.

[21] I. Yeo and E. Kim, "Temperature-aware scheduler based on thermal behavior grouping in multicore systems," Design Automation and Test in Europe, 2009.

[22] C. Zhang, F. Vahid, and W. Najjar, "A highly configurable cache architecture for embedded systems," International Symposium on Computer Architecture, 2003.

[23] E. Zitzler, M. Laumanns, and L. Thiele, "SPEA2: Improving the strength pareto evolutionary algorithm," Swiss Federal Institute of Technology, Dept. of Electrical Engineering, Technical Report 103, 2001.

EDA for Extreme Scale Systems: Design Abstractions, Metrics, and Benchmarks

Alex K. Jones
University of Pittsburgh
1140 Benedum Hall
Pittsburgh, PA
akjones@pitt.edu

ABSTRACT

The context for EDA research is rapidly changing thanks to enhanced and novel switching devices, manufacturing technologies, new application targets, and the increasing software development effort required for new ICs. These trends continue to expand the gap between the capabilities of systems and what can be utilized by designers. To address these problems requires a collaborative effort with industry researchers, academics, and funding agencies working together in close partnership. This talk describes recommendations from the recent CCC workshop series on EDA in the Extreme Scale era for improving the collaboration between IC designers and EDA. There remains a continued importance of effective design abstractions that facilitate research on EDA advances that can be effectively translated to actual design flows for relevant technologies. Further, these abstractions must be accompanied by (i) effective design metrics, especially for new technologies where optimization objectives may not be obvious, and (ii) appropriate benchmarks, especially for more established technologies where alternative optimization techniques must be carefully compared. Focus on these research directions for EDA will have direct impact to reduce the existing capabilities gap between tools and designers.

Categories and Subject Descriptors

B.m [**Hardware**]: Miscellaneous—*Design management*

Keywords

Design Automation; Tools; Designers; Community-wide Collaborative Efforts; Extreme Scale Design; Hybrid Design; Emerging Technologies

GLSVLSI'14, May 21–23, 2014, Houston, Texas, USA.
ACM 978-1-4503-2816-6/14/05.
http://dx.doi.org/10.1145/2591513.2597170.

BIOGRAPHY

Alex K. Jones received the BS degree in 1998 in physics from the College of William and Mary in Williamsburg, Virginia, and the MS and PhD degrees in 2000 and 2002, respectively, in electrical and computer engineering at Northwestern University. He is currently the director of computer engineering and an associate professor of electrical and computer engineering and computer science at the University of Pittsburgh, Pennsylvania. He is a Walter P. Murphy Fellow of Northwestern University. He is a senior member of the IEEE and ACM. Dr. Jones' research interests include compilation techniques for configurable systems and architectures, behavioral and low-power synthesis, parallel architectures and networks, RFID and wireless sensor networks, sustainable computing, and embedded computing for medical instruments. He is the author of more than 100 publications in these areas.

Dr. Jones is also an active leader in the community. Dr. Jones has been leading an effort in visioning for the electronic design automation community funded by the Computing Community Consortium (CCC). Dr. Jones is also actively involved in efforts to improve the scientific method for experiments in computers science and engineering. He has recently been funded by the US National Science Foundation to develop OCCAM (www.occamportal.org) to develop methods reproducible research and a centralized hub for computer architecture simulators, emulators, benchmarks and experiments. His activities are funded by the NSF, DARPA, CCC, ACM/SIGDA, and industry. Dr. Jones' contributions have received several awards including a most influential paper of the first 20 years of the FCCM Conference, the ACM/SIGDA Distinguished Service Award, Best Paper Award of the 2013 GLSVLSI Symposium, , the University of Pittsburgh Innovator Award, and the Dominion VITA award.

ACKNOWLEDGMENTS

The material for this talk was developed in part from the CCC and ACM/SIGDA sponsored visioning effort on *Extreme Scale Design Automation* [2].

The workshop co-organizers:

R. Iris Bahar: Brown University, **Srinivas Katkoori**: University of South Florida, **Patrick H. Madden**: SUNY Binghamton, **Diana Marculescu**: Carnegie Mellon University, and **Igor L. Markov**: University of Michigan contributed significantly to the consolidation of this material and preparation of this talk. In particular, Patrick Madden and Igor Markov provided particularly valuable material and insights based on their considerable work in the area of designing contests and developing appropriate benchmarking in EDA [1].

References

[1] S. Adya, M. Yildiz, I. Markov, P. Villarrubia, P. Parakh, and P. Madden. Benchmarking for large-scale placement and beyond. *Computer-Aided Design of Integrated Circuits and Systems, IEEE Transactions on*, 23(4):472–487, April 2004.

[2] A. K. Jones, R. I. Bahar, S. Katkoori, P. Madden, D. Marculescu, and I. Markov. Extreme Scale Design Automation: A CCC Visioning Effort. http://www.cra.org/ccc/visioning/visioning-activities/esda.

Hardware Trojan Attacks in FPGA Devices: Threat Analysis and Effective Countermeasures

Sanchita Mal-Sarkar
Cleveland State University
Department of CIS
Cleveland, Ohio, 44115
s.malsarkar@csuohio.edu

Aswin Krishna, Anandaroop Ghosh and
Swarup Bhunia
Case Western Reserve University
Dept. of EECS, Cleveland, Ohio, 44106
{ark70, axg468, skb21}@case.edu

ABSTRACT

Reconfigurable hardware including Field programmable gate arrays (FPGAs) are being used in a wide range of embedded applications including signal processing, multimedia, and security. FPGA device production is often outsourced to off-shore facilities for economic reasons. This opens up the opportunities for insertion of malicious design alterations in the foundry, referred to as hardware Trojan attacks, to cause logical and physical malfunction. The vulnerability of these devices to hardware attacks raises security concerns regarding hardware and design assurance. In this paper, we analyze hardware Trojan attacks in FPGA considering diverse activation and payload characteristics and derive a taxonomy of Trojan attacks in FPGA. To our knowledge, this is the first effort to analyze Trojan threats in FPGA hardware. Next, we propose a novel redundancy-based protection approach based on Trojan tolerance that modifies the application mapping process to provide high-level of protection against Trojans of varying forms and sizes. We show that the proposed approach incurs significantly higher security at lower overhead than conventional fault-tolerance schemes by exploiting the nature of Trojans and reconfiguration of FPGA resources.

Categories and Subject Descriptors

K.6.5 [**Security and Protection**]: Authentication

General Terms

Design, Security

Keywords

Hardware security, FPGA, Trojan, Trust

1. INTRODUCTION

Reconfigurable hardware platforms are integrated circuits (ICs), consisting of an array of logic blocks and distributed interconnect structure, which can be programmed and, in

GLSVLSI'14, May 21–23, 2014, Houston, Texas, USA.
Copyright 2014 ACM 978-1-4503-2816-6/14/05 ...$15.00.
http://dx.doi.org/10.1145/2591513.2591561.

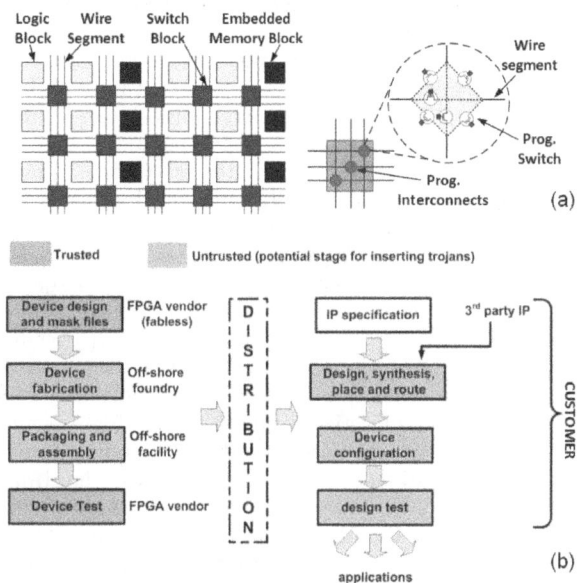

Figure 1: (a) Conventional island-style FPGA architecture with programmable interconnects; (b) FPGA design flow from device design to deployment showing potential stages for malicious alterations.

many cases, re-programmed to implement logic functions. FPGAs dominate the space of reconfigurable hardware. They are increasingly used in diverse embedded applications for improving performance and/or energy efficiency compared to software-based execution. Additionally, designs implemented on FPGAs do not suffer from the increasing non-recurring engineering (NRE) costs of ASIC production. Figure 1(a) shows a high-level block diagram of an FPGA and illustrates the structure of a programmable interconnect. They are typically designed as an interleaved array of configurable logic blocks and programmable interconnects.

The growing use of FPGAs in diverse and critical applications has urged designers to think about security. In this context, security refers to protecting the intellectual property (IP) of the design mapped to a FPGA device from being stolen. However, little attention has been directed towards security and assurance of the FPGA device itself. Malicious alteration to the device is possible at several stages of design/fabrication flow of FPGA as shown in Fig. 1(b). Security in every stage of the design flow is of growing importance. After all, the security of a design mapped to FPGA is only as good as the security of the system itself.

FPGA system protection has been investigated earlier in different contexts [1, 3, 2, 4]. In [2], the authors describe the various logical and electrical attacks possible to cause malfunction and physical destruction of a FPGA device caused by creating internal conflicts in the device by inserting malicious code in the configuration files. Earlier works also present attack models such as replay attacks, cloning, power analysis attacks, invasive and semi-invasive attacks, and radiation attacks as related to the security of FPGA design [3]. None of these existing works, however, discusses hardware attacks in the foundry to cause malfunction and leak IP.

Malicious modifications of ICs, referred to as Hardware Trojans, have emerged as a major security threat due widespread outsourcing of IC manufacturing to untrusted foundries [7, 8, 9, 10, 11]. An adversary can potentially tamper with a design in these fabrication facilities by inserting malicious circuitry, intended to cause malfunction or leak secret information from inside a chip during field operation. Conventional post-manufacturing testing often fail to detect hardware Trojans due to their stealthy nature, complex structure, and inordinately large number of possible instances [10]. The condition of Trojan activation is referred as the triggering condition and the node(s) affected by a Trojan is referred to as its payload. Fig. 2(a) illustrates the general scenario of a Trojan attack in a design. Fig. 2(b) shows example of a combinational Trojan, which activates on simultaneous occurrence of a set of node conditions and a sequential Trojan, which activates on a sequence of rare events.

The issue of foundry trust related to the fabrication of FPGAs has been discussed in [1]. It argues that hardware attacks on FPGA devices in the foundry to tamper with the functionality of the final design are slim due to: (1) the foundry does not know about the design being implemented; (2) exhaustive testing of the bitstream security features to ensure that any attacks on them are detected during testing; and (3) possible destructive testing of a large number of chips to identify any extraneous logic.

In this paper, we present comprehensive analysis of hardware Trojan attacks in FPGA devices and propose effective protection approaches. To our knowledge, this is the first effort to analyze Trojan attacks in FPGA hardware and develop countermeasures against them. We show that even with the above-mentioned security features to ensure the integrity of FPGA devices, a variety of attacks are possible in the foundry. Firstly, we show that not all attacks have to depend on the final design and it is possible to insert malicious logic which are "independent" of the design and can also be used to leak the intellectual property implemented in the device. Moreover, an attacker in the foundry can distribute Trojans dependent on the internal logic values all over the chip. Secondly, even though bitstream security functions can be fully tested to ensure that no attacks are made on the FPGA's security, an attack can be made to steal a key and not cause malfunction. Thus, thoroughly testing the security functions may not help in protecting the IP from being copied by an attacker. Finally, even though number of FPGAs can be exhaustively (possibly through destructive process) tested after production, a Trojan may exist in only a subset of chips which may not be fully tested. In particular, the paper makes the following major contributions:

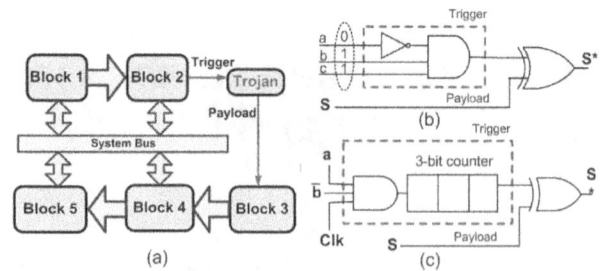

Figure 2: (a) General model of a hardware Trojan realized through malicious design modification; example of (b) combinational, (c) sequential Trojan.

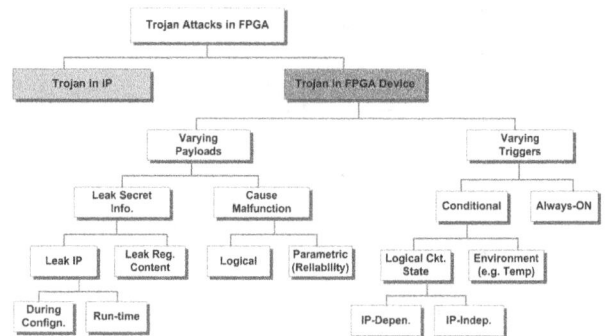

Figure 3: Taxonomy of hardware Trojan attacks in FPGA devices.

- It identifies the vulnerabilities; analyzes the spectrum of Trojan attacks on FPGA hardware; and provides Trojan models along with examples. It presents a taxonomy of Trojan attacks in FPGA which categorizes possible Trojan attacks in FPGA into different classes based on activation and payload characteristics.

- It presents a novel low-overhead redundancy based Trojan tolerance scheme for effective protection against diverse Trojan attacks in FPGA. It takes inspiration from existing run-time fault tolerance approaches [12, 13]. However, compared to these approaches (in particular, Triple Modular Redundancy or TMR), the proposed scheme has the following distinctions: (1) it leverages on dynamic reconfiguration capability of FPGA to minimize the overhead; and (2) it uses a novel variant-based redundancy scheme to maximize protection against Trojan attacks. The later enables detection of similar Trojan instances in multiple regular structures (e.g. CLBs or clusters).

2. HARDWARE TROJANS IN FPGA

Reconfigurable hardware consists of a regular array of programmable cells and other modules (e.g. decryptor, clock manager, DSP cores, block RAMs) connected through a distributed programmable interconnect structure. Since most of the chip is occupied by the regular structure of logic blocks and interconnect, it is relatively easy (compared to ASICs) for an attacker to reverse engineer the device and identify the components. For example, a DSP core or clock manager can be easily identified from the layout of the FPGA and can be potential target for Trojan attacks.

We have developed a taxonomy of FPGA-specific hardware Trojans that alter the programmed state of its logic, memory, interconnect and I/O blocks. We classify the FPGA hardware Trojans into two main categories as shown in Fig. 3, according to their activation and payload characteristics. Activation characteristics refer to the triggers or conditions that make a Trojan active while payload characteristics refer to the signal(s) that the Trojans affect. While it may be possible to classify FPGA Trojans based on other characteristics such as size, distribution, we believe that the proposed classification comprehensively covers FPGA Trojans and is adequate to evaluate the capabilities and limitations of detection methods.

2.1 Activation Characteristics

Based on the activation characteristics, Trojans can fall into two subcategories marked as *condition-based* and *always-on* in Fig. 3. Always-on Trojans are always active while condition-based FPGA Trojans wait until a particular condition is met before causing malfunction or leaking information. At this level, Trojans can be further classified as *logic-based* and *sensor-based* (e.g. temperature, delay). At the lowest level, logic-based FPGA Trojans can be further divided into *IP dependent* and *IP independent* categories as explained next.

IP-dependent Trojans: IP dependent Trojans represent ones whose trigger signals depend on the design implemented in the device. As shown in Fig. 4, an adversary can insert malicious circuit which monitors the logic values of several nodes such as configuration cells in the logic modules and interconnect structures, outputs of logic modules, look-up table (LUT) values. When triggered, such a Trojan can cause malfunction in many different ways, e.g. by altering the values stored in LUTs or configuration cells to cause incorrect routing between logic blocks or writing wrong values into block-RAMs (BRAM). These Trojans are highly likely to evade conventional FPGA testing, which cannot sensitize all possible trigger conditions of a Trojan.

Since the IP to be mapped is not available to the foundry during device fabrication, an attacker who plans to insert design-dependent hardware Trojans must do so without assuming any characteristic of the IP. Even though the probability of such a Trojan becoming active is very low, an attacker may distribute many such Trojans over the entire chip to increase chances of causing malfunction. A possible goal for the attacker in this case can be giving competitive edge to one FPGA vendor by creating bad reputation to another. Given the countless designs that can be mapped and the growing field of applications of FPGAs, IP dependent Trojans can be a practical threat that should be considered for hardware assurance.

IP-independent Trojans: An intelligent attacker can also insert Trojans whose activation conditions do not depend on the final design. Such Trojans can be inserted to alter the functionality of critical modules of the device. For example, Xilinx Spartan-3, Virtex-II, Virtex-II Pro FPGAs contain a separate module for clock management known as digital clock manager (DCM) as shown in Fig. 5. It contains a frequency synthesizer for producing a multiple or division of the input clock. The amount of phase shifting required and the amount of clock division or multiplication required

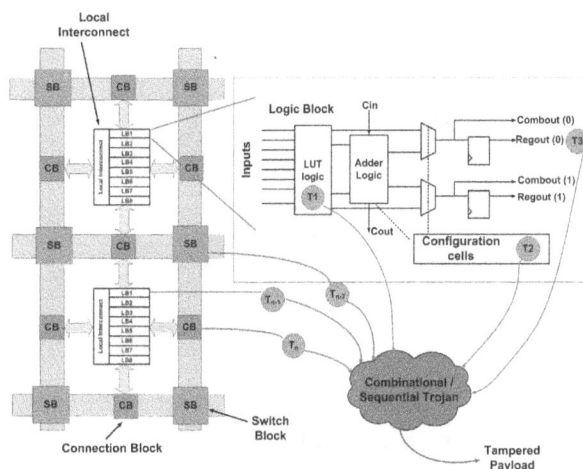

Figure 4: Simplified architecture of an FPGA showing the trigger points that a Trojan may use.

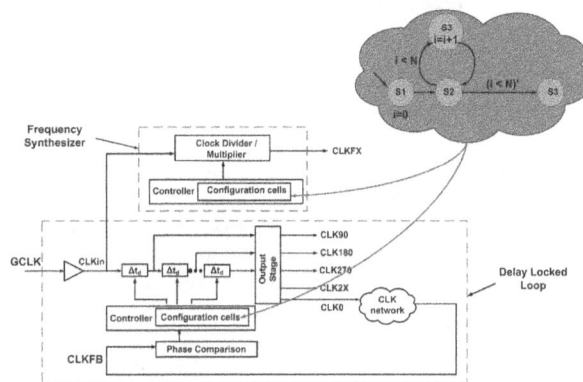

Figure 5: Schematic of digital clock manager (DCM) which can be affected by Trojan attack.

are stored in SRAM cells in the DCM. A possible Trojan design could be a counter that counts the clock edges to a specific number and then modifies the values of the SRAM cells to increase clock rate. A faster clock can cause delay failure in a sequential circuit. For a N-bit counter, since the final output occurs once in every 2^N clock cycles, even a reasonably large counter could evade conventional logic test methods.

2.2 Payload Characteristics

Hardware Trojans can also be classified into two categories based on their intended behavior.

Trojans for malfunction: Trojans in this class can be further classified into two subcategories based on whether they cause *logical* malfunction or *physical* malfunction. Trojans presented in the previous sections cause logical malfunction by modifying the values in the LUTs, causing undesired routing between two logic modules, etc. Fig. 6 shows additional examples of payloads affected by Trojans. Trojans intended to cause physical damage can create electrical conflicts at the I/O ports or at the programmable interconnects. Consider a typical programmable I/O block in FPGA. When a I/O port is configured to be an input by a design, the configuration cells in the I/O block should disable the output

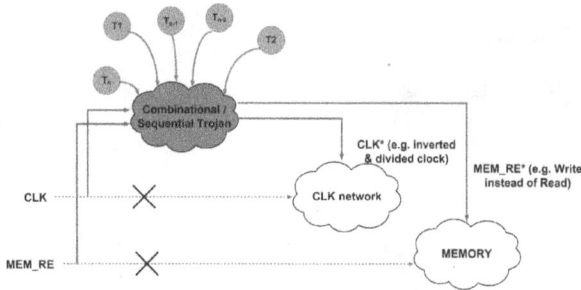

Figure 6: Diagram showing examples of payloads that can be altered by Trojans.

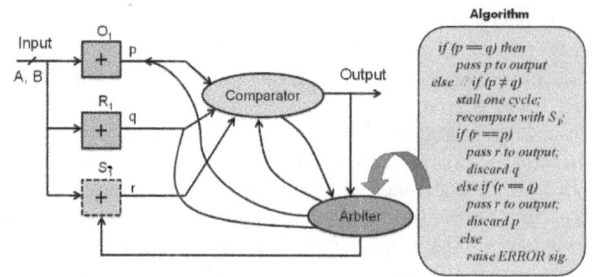

Figure 8: Proposed Trojan-tolerant application mapping scheme using redundant computing blocks and the output routing algorithm in arbiter.

block to prevent internal conflicts. A counter-based Trojan can be inserted in the foundry which detects the state of the I/O port (i.e. I or O) and begins counting. When the counter counts to the final value, the Trojan may enable the output logic when the port is configured as an input. This would cause a high short-circuit current to flow between the FPGA and the external device, thus damaging the system.

IP-leak Trojans: Since IP designs involve a high development cost and contain sensitive information, security of IP is of critical importance against theft and reverse engineering. Many high-end FPGAs such as Xilinx's Virtex5 and Altera's StratixIII offer bitstream encryption to prevent unauthorized cloning of the bitstream. Fig. 7 shows the security features in a generic FPGA device which contains the programmable logic array (bottom right in the figure), configuration logic which controls the programming of the SRAM cells in the logic array, interconnect network and additional modules in the device [6, 5]. The device also contains a decryptor module for decrypting the bitstream using a key stored in a non-volatile memory. Security measures in the device (1) prevents the key from being read and sent to a port by clearing the configuration data and keys when an attempt is made, (2) prevents readback of the configuration data, and (3) restricts decryptor access after configuration [1]. However, all these measures only prevent malicious code in an IP from accessing the key or configuration data.

Hardware Trojans can leak an IP in two ways by leaking either (1) the decryption key, or (2) the design itself. An attacker in the foundry can insert extraneous circuit as shown in the Fig. 7 to tap the wires connecting the non-volatile memory and decryptor module. Even if the decryptor module is implemented in the logic array by using a decryptor bitstream as mentioned in [5], such an instantiated module must have access to the non-volatile key for decryption.

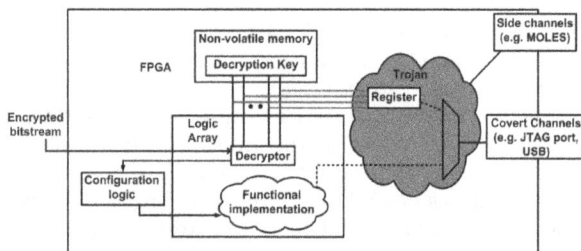

Figure 7: FPGA device with security features for bitstream decryption.

A copy of the key can be stored in the Trojan which may then leak it through side-channels or covert-channels. For example, the MOLES Trojan presented in [9] uses a spread-spectrum technique to leak the key in the power traces over several clock cycles. Alternatively, a Trojan may also mux the JTAG port, USB port, or any ports to leak the key through I/O channels when they are not being used.

3. HARDWARE TROJAN TOLERANCE

In this section we introduce a novel protection approach against Trojan attacks in FPGA devices through tolerance of Trojan effects during operation. It works by either containing the Trojan effect or bypassing the effect of Trojan using spare units. We propose a hybrid scheme of hardware Trojan tolerance that combines an efficient redundancy based mapping approach with dynamic reconfiguration.

3.1 Adapted TMR (ATMR)

TMR is a well-known fault mitigation technique that masks circuit faults by using redundant hardware [12, 13]. A TMR circuit has three redundant copies of the original circuit and a majority voter. A single fault in one of the redundant hardware modules will not produce an error at the output as the majority voter selects the result from the two working modules. Use of TMR has been explored earlier in FPGA in the context of tolerating run-time failures e.g. soft error. However, it typically comes at the cost of about three times the size and power of the original circuit.

We note that appropriate adaptations in TMR for Trojan tolerance can make significant improvement on redundant hardware usage and power consumption by employing two modules at a time, instead of three. The outputs of the modules are compared using a comparator circuit. The third module is used on demand when the comparator circuit detects a mismatch in outputs. With the help of an arbiter, the comparator determines which module is in error; discards it; and then creates correct output using the third one. It, however, requires to halt the circuit for few cycles (typically 1-2) in order to transfer control to the arbiter on a mismatch and to include the third spare component in computing.

Fig. 8 shows three adders (O_1, R_1, and S_1) that are mapped to the Trojan infected region of an FPGA and their corresponding outputs (p, q, and r). The comparator will compare the outputs (p, q) of the first two adders (O_1, R_1). The third adder (S_1) will not be used unless there is a mismatch between the two outputs p and q. In case of a mismatch,

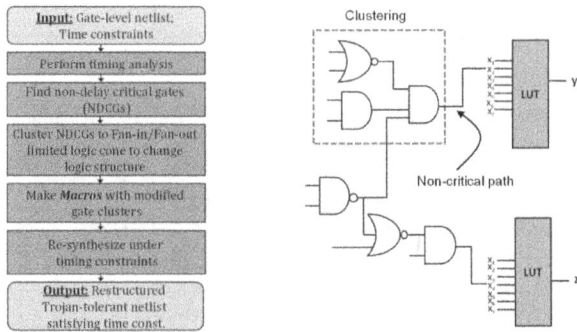

Figure 9: Flowchart showing a variant generation approach from a gate-level design and an example.

the comparator with the help of the arbiter continues comparing the output r with the outputs (p, q) until it finds a match and it determines which adder is in error. Then the comparator outputs the correct result and prevents the propagation of erroneous data. Note that although the third replica is required to determine which one is in error, only two are enough to flag that one of them is infected with a Trojan, prevent the propagation of the Trojan's payload in the system and/or stop leakage of potentially sensitive data. Therefore the scheme we have proposed, even without the third replica, will be of particular interest to many mission-critical applications.

3.2 Improving Protection through Variants

The Trojan tolerance scheme proposed in Section 3.1 cannot protect against simultaneous activation of identical Trojan instances in O_i and R_i. An adversary can incorporate the same Trojans in two or more clusters or CLBs in an FPGA, so that both O_i and R_i can be similarly affected. For example, this can happen if O_i and R_i are identically mapped in two different clusters, both of which has a combinational Trojan triggered by specific combination of LUT content. In such a scenario, two Trojans in O_i and R_i would trigger at the same cycle with identical malicious effect and the proposed tolerance approach would fail to detect it. To address this scenario, we enhance the proposed scheme by implementing *variants* of a module e.g. the adders for O_i and R_i to ensure that O_i and R_i functionally compute the same result, but the adders are implemented in a structurally different manner. It is highly unlikely that both adders (O_i and R_i) will simultaneously trigger the same Trojan because different implementations involve different logic blocks, storage elements, logic structures, and memory locations. Thus we can assume that both O_i and R_i cannot simultaneously trigger the same Trojan.

A judicious design of structural variants can tolerate simultaneous activation of Trojans in both original and replica modules. The variants need to differ in both LUT and interconnect structures while maintaining the functional behavior and parametric specifications (e.g. critical path delay). Fig. 9 shows the flow chart and an example for implementing the variants. It starts with finding non-delay critical gates (NDCGs) and regrouping them into clusters. The clusters are derived using a hypergraph partitioning approach with specific fan-in/fan-out limits. It ensures that the content/type/number of the LUTs, and interconnections

among them are changed while critical path delay remains unchanged. Next, we convert the regrouped LUTs as "hard macros" (to avoid re-optimization during synthesis). The last step is to re-synthesize the circuit including the macros with the original time constraints. Hence, even when both replicas are infected with a Trojan, the Trojan is very unlikely to be simultaneously activated during operation in both original and replica modules. Hence, the proposed scheme can overcome the limitation of TMR since it can protect against multiple Trojan effects in functional units.

3.3 Trojan Tolerance in the controller/arbiter

If the arbiter or the comparator is compromised i.e. has Trojans, we can: (a) use majority voting also for comparator and arbiter, or (b) exhaustively test the them to validate their trustworthiness. The first approach can improve the integrity of the system but hardware overhead can be considerable. The second one, however, can be more attractive to designers since the small comparator and arbiter circuits are amenable for exhaustive testing at modest test cost.

4. SIMULATION RESULTS

In this section we present case studies with a commercial FPGA device (Altera Cyclone IV GX) and a large benchmark design (32-bit pipelined DLX processor) to analyze the effectiveness of the proposed Trojan tolerance approach. The processor pipeline is broken into five stages (Fetch, Decode, Execute, Memory Access, and WriteBack). We applied both TMR and ATMR to the combinational logic for each sequential boundary to mitigate the effect of hardware Trojans in them. First, we present the mapping results for the processor execution unit followed by results for the entire processor. Area, delay and power overhead for the proposed scheme are compared with those for conventional TMR.

Figure 10 show the variation in area requirement, power consumption and delay of the mapped ALU in original mapping scheme (using area constraint) and variant mapping scheme (using delay constraint). Table 1 compares the overhead, in terms of power, resources, and performance of TMR and our hybrid tolerance scheme (ATMR). It illustrates that ATMR requires 1.5X less power than TMR to achieve the same level of security while maintaining equivalent resource and performance requirements as in TMR. This result is expected given that ATMR, unlike TMR, uses the third spare resources/replicas only when Trojans are activated and a mismatch occurs in the outputs of the initial two replicas. Similar performance (delay) of TMR and ATMR indicates that ATMR does not require additional processing cycle.

Table 2 presents the overhead of TMR and ATMR when a judicious design of structural variants is introduced in FPGAs. As shown in Table 2, ATMR with variants requires 1.5X less power than TMR with variants with similar performance and resource usage. Moreover, ATMR with variants provides higher level of security since it can protect against simultaneous activation of identical Trojan instances in two or more clusters or CLBs. The improvement in power consumption in ATMR is due to the use of the third spare resources/replicas only in case of Trojan activation.

5. CONCLUSION

We have presented possible malicious changes i.e. hardware Trojan attacks in FPGA that can be inserted during

291

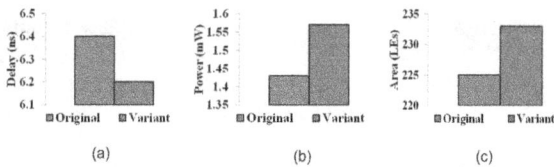

Figure 10: Single ALU (a) delay (b) power and (c) area results in conventional and the proposed variant-based mapping scheme.

Table 1: Comparison of design overhead between TMR and ATMR

	TMR	ATMR	Times Impr.
Power	4.70 mW	3.15 mW	1.5X
Resource	850 LEs	856 LEs	1X
Performance	6.7 ns	6.7 ns	1X

*LEs = Logic Elements in FPGA

Table 2: Comparison of overhead between TMR and ATMR with variants

	TMR with Variants	ATMR with Variants	Times Impr.
Power	4.95 mW	3.26 mW	1.5X
Resource	860 LEs	872 LEs	1X
Performance	6.4 ns	6.4 ns	1X

device production. As FPGAs are being increasingly used in wide array of applications including many defense and other security-critical applications, vulnerability of FPGA devices against hardware Trojan attacks pose a major security threat. We have presented a taxonomy of hardware Trojan attacks in FPGAs, including models and specific examples of Trojans that cause logical malfunctions and/or physical damage. We have also shown the possibility of Trojan attacks targeting information leakage from inside an FPGA during operation. Next, we have proposed a novel Trojan tolerant application mapping scheme that can effectively protect against Trojan attacks of varying sizes and functionalities. We compared our scheme with the conventional redundancy-based error tolerance approach. The proposed Trojan tolerance scheme incurs significantly less power overhead, while providing higher level of security. It is easily scalable to larger designs. Future work will include efficient detection of hardware Trojans in FPGA and developing a metric for estimating FPGA trust.

6. ACKNOWLEDGMENTS

This work is funded in part by National Science Foundation (NSF) Grant #1245756 and #1054744. The authors acknowledge valuable suggestions by Dr. Seetharam Narasimhan.

7. REFERENCES

[1] S. Trimberger, "Trusted design in FPGAs," *Design Automation Conference*, 2007.

[2] I. Hadzic, S. Udani, and J. Smith, "FPGA viruses," *International Workshop on Field Programmable Logic and Applications*, 1999.

[3] S. Drimer, "Volatile FPGA design security: a survey," Cambridge University, 2008.

[4] T. Huffmire, "Handbook of FPGA design security," *Design Automation Conference*, 2007.

[5] S. Trimberger, "Method and apparatus for protecting proprietary decryption keys for programmable logic devices," US Patent 6654889, 2003.

[6] Aletar: Military Anti-Tampering Solutions Using Programmable Logic. [Online]. Available: http://www.altera.com/literature/cp/CP-01007.pdf.

[7] D. Du, S. Narasimhan, R. S. Chakraborty, and S. Bhunia, "Self-referencing: a scalable side-channel approach for hardware Trojan detection,", *Workshop on Cryptographic Hardware and Embedded Systems*, 2010.

[8] R. S. Chakraborty, S. Narasimhan, and S. Bhunia, "Hardware Trojan: Treats and Emerging Solutions," *International High Level Design Validation and Test Workshop*, pp. 166-171, 2009.

[9] L. Lin, W. Burleson, and C. Paar, "MOLES: malicious off-chip leakage enabled by side-channels," *International Conference on Computer-Aided Design*, 2009.

[10] R.S. Chakraborty, F. Wolff, S. Paul, C. Papachristou, and S. Bhunia, "MERO: A Statistical Approach for Hardware Trojan Detection," *Workshop on Cryptographic Hardware and Embedded Systems*, 2009.

[11] F. Wolff, C. Papachristou, S. Bhunia, and R.S. Chakraborty, "Towards Trojan-Free Trusted ICs: Problem Analysis and Detection Scheme," *Design Automation and Test in Europe*, 2008.

[12] H. Kubatova and P. Kubalik, "Fault-Tolerant and Fail-Safe Design Based on Reconfiguration," *Design and Test Technology for Dependable Systems-on-Chip*, pp. 175-194, 2011.

[13] N. Gaitanis, "The Design of Totally Self-Checking TMR Fault-Tolerant Systems," *IEEE Transaction on Computers*, vol. 37, no. 11, 1988.

Forward-scaling, Serially Equivalent Parallelism for FPGA Placement

Christian Fobel
cfobel@uoguelph.ca
School of Computer Science
University of Guelph
Guelph, Ontario, Canada

Gary Grewal
gwg@uoguelph.ca
School of Computer Science
University of Guelph
Guelph, Ontario, Canada

Deborah Stacey
dastacey@uoguelph.ca
School of Computer Science
University of Guelph
Guelph, Ontario, Canada

ABSTRACT

Placement run-times continue to dominate the FPGA design flow. Previous attempts at parallel placement methods either only scale to a few threads or result in a significant loss in solution quality as thread-count is increased. We propose a novel method for generating large amounts of parallel work for placement, which scales with the size of the target architecture. Our experimental results show that we nearly reach the limit of the number of possible parallel swaps, while improving critical-path-delay 4.7% compared to VPR. While our proposed implementation currently utilizes a single thread, we still achieve speedups of 13.3x over VPR.

Categories and Subject Descriptors

J.6 [**Computer-Aided Engineering**]: Computer-aided design (CAD); D.1.3 [**Programming Techniques**]: Concurrent Programming—*Parallel programming*

General Terms

Algorithms; Design; Performance

1. INTRODUCTION

In *Field-Programmable Gate Array (FPGA)* design, *"placement"* is an NP-complete problem[5], which assigns each block in a netlist to a position on the target architecture, while minimizing one or more objective costs. Heuristic and analytic[7] methods have been developed to provide approximate solutions. However, with the size of target architectures growing exponentially, placement can already take hours or even days to perform for large designs. Thus, it is essential to develop parallel methods for placement that will scale along with the growth of FPGA architectures.

Despite recent work developing parallel techniques, placement times continue to dominate the runtime of the FPGA CAD flow. Several attempts have been made to improve the performance of simulated annealing for placement, which is the most common heuristic applied to placement, but with

limited success. In the best cases, the performance improvements either do not scale to more than a few cores[2], or the quality of solution degrades as the parallelism increases, where eventually synchronization overhead limits the available speedup[6]. The production trends from leading hardware vendors, such as Intel and NVIDIA, continue to push an ever-increasing number of cores. To write efficient code for these new architectures, it is crucial to generate as much parallelism as possible, and to have the amount of parallel work *grow with the problem size* to take advantage of as many of the available parallel resources as possible. In fact, Intel specifically encourages developers to generate as many opportunities for parallelism as possible, going well beyond the number of cores in present-day CPUs, to allow programs to seamlessly "forward-scale"[1] to future architectures. Scaling parallel work for placement along with the size of the architecture requires a different approach to parallelism, compared to the traditional, thread-parallel programming models found in the literature[2, 6]. As such, **the amount of potential parallelism that existing methods make available plateaus at a level that does not scale with the size of the FPGA**. For example, in [2, 6], the amount of parallel work is directly correlated to the number of threads, with either performance gains or quality diminishing as thread-count is increased, preventing these approaches from scaling forward.

In contrast, in this paper, we propose a novel method of generating a large amount of parallelism for performing FPGA placement, where the amount of parallel work directly scales with the size of the target architecture. Our approach is based on generating very large sets of *non-overlapping* swaps that may be evaluated, and conditionally applied, in parallel. Using these large sets of swaps, we propose an algorithm inspired by the annealer in VPR[3] to perform FPGA placement. In this paper, we focus on our method of generating opportunities for parallelism that scale with the size of the FPGA. While our experimental results (discussed in Section 4) are from a serial implementation of our proposed algorithm, our approach is designed using structured parallel programming patterns, which may be mapped naturally to both multi-core and many-core architectures *(i.e., NVIDIA CUDA, Intel MIC)* using mature parallel frameworks, such as Cilk Plus, Threading Building Blocks, and NVIDIA CUDA[4]. Furthermore, our proposed method is designed such that parallel implementations may be easily implemented ensuring serial-equivalency, regardless of the number of computing cores, similar to the method proposed by Altera[2].

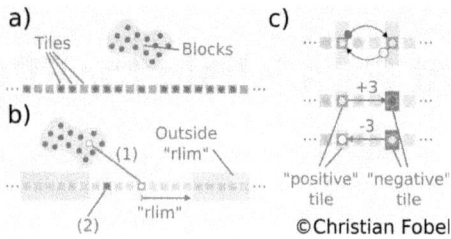

Figure 1: A swap as performed by VPR's annealer.

The remainder of this paper is laid out as follows. Section 2 describes our method for generating large sets of non-overlapping swaps, while Section 3 discusses how we apply these swaps in our *move-pair* annealer. In Section 4 we present our experimental results and in Section 5 we conclude our discussion and present future work.

2. PARALLEL MOVE-PAIRS

In this section we describe our method for generating parallelism in the context of FPGA placement, where the amount of parallel work scales *directly* with the *size of the target architecture*. In discussing our approach, we define the grid of the target architecture as a set of what we call *"tiles"*, where each *tile* represents a potential location on the FPGA where a block from the netlist can be placed. Furthermore, we assume that we are targeting an *island-style* FPGA[3].

Let us consider a hypothetical placement architecture that consists of a series of tiles, which could be a part of a row on an FPGA. Figure 1a, illustrates the layout of our hypothetical architecture. We will describe our approach, first in terms of this one-dimensional grid, after which we will extend the core concepts to the bounded two-dimensional architecture used in our algorithm described in Section 3.2.

As depicted in Figure 1b, the VPR annealer starts by *(1)* randomly selecting a block from the netlist and retrieving the index of the tile that the block is currently occupying. At this point, *(2)* a second tile is randomly selected within a bounded region[1] surrounding the first tile. The contents of the two tiles are then swapped, and the difference in cost caused by the swap is calculated. The difference in cost is assessed using acceptance criteria described in Section 3.1. If the swap is deemed to be rejected, the content of each tile involved in the swap is returned to its original position.

We have developed a novel method to quickly generate many *(i.e., hundreds to thousands of)* pairs of tiles, where each pair may be considered for swapping contents, similar to a swap operation in VPR, but where the definition of our swaps guarantee that each block belongs to *at most* one pair. This ensures that multiple swaps may be applied from the set concurrently without the risk of a *hard-conflict*[6]. A hard-conflict occurs when a block is involved in more than one concurrent move, resulting in an inconsistent placement. In addition to *hard-conflicts*, *soft-conflicts* may arise when applying concurrent moves to blocks which are connected to the same net[6]. However, as shown in our results in Section 4, we find, as in [6], these soft-conflicts have little

to no appreciable impact on solution quality. In fact, our experiments show a marked improvement in critical-path-delay compared to VPR's annealer.

Since each swap may be viewed as the result of moving two blocks with equal, *but opposite*, displacements, we redefine each swap as a *"move-pair"*, which consists of two ordered *tile indexes* and a *displacement-magnitude*. In Fig. 1c, we illustrate the swap from Fig. 1b, as a move-pair with a displacement-magnitude of 3. Within a *move-pair*, we call the tile corresponding to the lowest tile index the *"positive"*-tile, and the tile corresponding to the highest tile index the *"negative"*-tile. Note that the *positive-tile* is assigned a *positive* displacement while the *negative-tile* is assigned a *negative* displacement. The index of the *negative-tile* can be reached by *adding* the displacement-magnitude to the index of the *positive-tile*.

By mapping move-pairs with the same displacement-magnitude to consecutive tiles in the grid in a specific pattern, we can create non-overlapping pairs of tiles, completely avoiding hard-conflicts. For example, let us consider a move-pair with a *displacement-magnitude* of 2, as shown in Fig. 2a, between tiles with indexes `i` and `i+2`. As shown in Fig. 2b, a second move-pair can be defined using the tile with index `i+1` as the positive-tile. Note that the second move-pair shares the same displacement-magnitude used for the first move-pair. As shown in Fig. 2c, the next tile in the grid, with index `i+3`, already belongs to a move-pair. Note that assigning a second move-pair to tile `i + 3` would result in a hard-conflict. In general, we skip tiles that already belong to a move-pair and seek the next available tile to create a new move-pair with the same displacement-magnitude, as shown in Fig. 2d. This process can be repeated to create a series of move-pairs which are grouped in contiguous sets where the tiles in the first half of each set have a positive displacement *(i.e., +d)*, and the tiles in the second half of the set have an equal displacement, but in the opposite direction *(i.e., −d)*. As shown in Fig. 2f-g, the displacements of contiguous tiles follow a cycle, where the period is twice the displacement length. We refer to each period of alternating displacements *(half positive, then half negative)* as a *"displacement-pattern"*. These *displacement-patterns* have a length of twice the corresponding displacement-magnitude *(i.e., 2d)*. The patterns continue in a repeated sequence to fill the placement grid. Fig. 2g illustrates how this concept can be extended to any selected displacement-magnitude. In Section 2.1, we discuss displacement-patterns in more detail, including how to handle sections of a displacement-pattern that result in a move with a target that is out of bounds, i.e., beyond the edge of the FPGA.

2.1 Series of displacement-patterns

In the previous section, we introduced the concept of a *displacement-pattern*, which consists of a set of displacements, with the first half in the positive direction and the second half in the negative direction. While the displacement-patterns in Fig. 2 are relative to an *unbounded* grid, Fig. 3 illustrates a scenario where a series of displacement-patterns with the same magnitude are applied to the tiles in a *bounded* one-dimensional placement grid, which could be a row of a FPGA. Note that the series of displacement-patterns begins in Fig. 3a at the tile index 0 in the grid. However, we may apply a *shift* to the series, such that the first *complete* displacement-pattern starts at the position corresponding to

---

[1]VPR defines a parameter called 'rlim', which acts as limiting radius on the displacement applied to the contents of a tile.

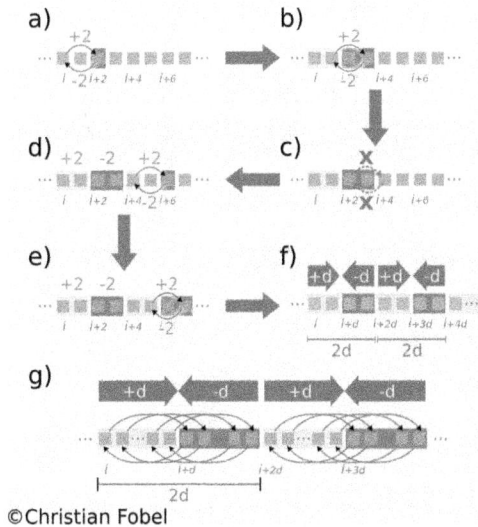

©Christian Fobel

Figure 2: Move-pairs generated by applying a repeated *displacement-pattern* along a one-dimensional grid

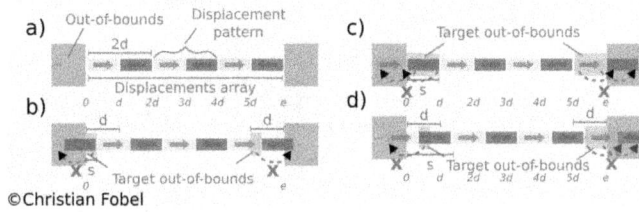

©Christian Fobel

Figure 3: Any tile assigned a move with a target that is outside the placement grid has its displacement set to zero.

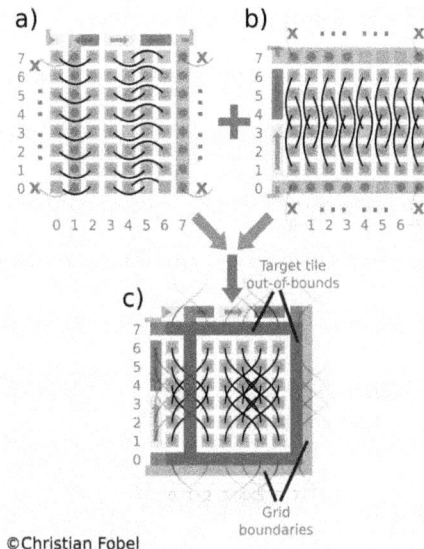

©Christian Fobel

Figure 4: Two-dimensional displacement vectors, created by combining two orthogonal one-dimensional displacement components.

the specified *shift* value, as shown in Fig. 3b-Fig. 3d. The pattern produced by increasing the shift repeats at every multiple of $2d$. Therefore, each effective shift value, which we denote as s, falls within a range such that $0 \leq s < 2d$. Notice that in some cases, a section of one or more displacement-patterns that overlap with either the upper- or lower-boundary of the placement grid cause some moves to target positions that are outside the grid boundaries. The largest number of moves that can be out-of-bounds at each edge of the grid is equal to d. To ensure moves remain within the FPGA, d is set to zero for each tile originally assigned a target that is out-of-bounds. This includes any *negative-tile* with an index less than d, or any *positive-tile* with an index that is within d positions (*i.e., half the period of the displacement-pattern*) from the end of the grid. Note that the same rules apply when the extent, *i.e.,* e, is not a multiple of $2d$. In general, any tile assigned a move with a target tile index, i, where $i < 0$ or $i \geq e$ has its displacement set to zero.

2.2 Extending to two-dimensions

The examples considered so far only target a *one-dimensional* placement grid, whereas a placement grid is typically *two-dimensional*. However, the concepts described can easily be extended to support two *(or more)* dimensions. As shown in Fig. 4, we can generate a *series of displacement-patterns* along *each dimension* of the grid, creating an *array* of displacements, defining the displacement to be applied to each tile. Note that every curved line within the grid represents a *move-pair*, that is, a pair of tiles and the magnitude of the displacement that must be applied to the tiles to exchange contents between them. We call this array of tile-displacements the *"displacement-array"* for each dimension. Each *displacement-array* defines the displacement to be applied to each tile position along the corresponding dimension. In the case of two-dimensions, this results in each tile being assigned two *orthogonal* displacement components, which we call d_x and d_y, that combine to form a two-dimensional *displacement-vector*, which we denote as d_T. We denote the extent of each row as e_x and the extent of each column as e_y.

For example, consider the tile at grid row 6 and column 0, shown in Fig. 4c. According to the orthogonal displacement-patterns, this tile is assigned displacements $d_x = +2$ (*see Fig. 4a*) and $d_y = -3$ (*see Fig. 4b*). However, if we consider the tile at row 1 and column 7, the lateral displacement assigned in Fig. 4a would result in a target that is outside of the FPGA (i.e., $x_i > e_x - 1$). Similarly, the tile at row 0 and column 2 has a vertical displacement of $d_y = -3$ assigned, as shown in Fig. 4b, that would result in a target position outside the FPGA (i.e., $y_i < 0$).

To deal with tile displacements resulting in target positions that are out of bounds, we assign no displacement at all to any tile with a displacement that targets either a row or column that is out-of-bounds. The resulting tile displacements from applying this method are depicted in Fig. 4c. Notice that two rows and two columns of tiles are assigned *no displacement at all* (i.e., $d_T = (0,0)$), since the corresponding tiles would be moved out-of-bounds in at least one dimension based on the original displacements.

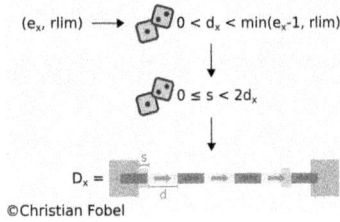

©Christian Fobel

Figure 5: Generate displacements-array for x-dimension

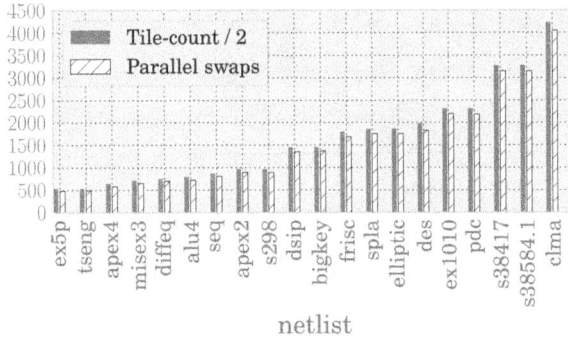

netlist

Figure 6: Architecture tile-count and the median number of parallel swaps available.

2.3 Generating sets of move-pairs

As shown in the previous section, a two-dimensional displacement can be generated for a tile by combining two completely independent, orthogonal displacement components. Moreover, provided with a displacement-magnitude, we can create consecutive, non-overlapping move-pairs to cover an entire row or column of an FPGA. Figure 5 illustrates how to generate a displacements-array for the x dimension, given the current annealing radius-limit parameter (i.e., $rlim$) and the extent of the x-dimension of the FPGA architecture, e_x. First, a displacement-magnitude, d_x is randomly selected, bounded by both e_x and $rlim$. Based on the selected value of d_x, a shift value, s, is randomly chosen, bounded by the period of the corresponding displacement-pattern, $2d_x$. Using the randomly selected d_x and s values, we can construct the displacement-array for the x-dimension, as described in Section 2, which we denote as D_x. The same procedure is applied to the y-dimension to generate D_y. Each tile, t_i at position (x_i, y_i) on the FPGA is then assigned the displacement (d_{xi}, d_{yi}), where $d_{xi} = D_x[x_i]$ and $d_{yi} = D_y[y_i]$.

Using this approach, we generated sets of non-overlapping swaps for each of the 20 MCNC netlists, while running our move-pair annealer (which we discuss in Section 3.2). For each netlist, Fig. 6 shows the median number of swaps generated through each D_x/D_y definition, i.e., the median number of swaps available for concurrent evaluation during each iteration of our move-pair displacements annealer. As shown in the figure, the number of swaps available for parallel evaluation scales directly along with the half the number of tiles in the target FPGA architecture. Since each swap involves two tiles, this shows that we are very close to exposing the maximum amount of parallel swaps during each iteration.

3. PARALLEL ANNEALER

3.1 VPR annealer

Using our method, described in the previous section, for generating large sets of non-overlapping move-pairs, we propose a parallel variant of simulated annealing based on the annealer from VPR. Program 1 describes the annealing process implemented in VPR.

Program 1 VPR anneal pseudo-code.

```
1   moves_per_temperature = inner_num * (netlist.block_count ^ 1.333)
2
3   # Perform one round of 'moves_per_temperature' moves, and record
4   # change in cost due to each move.
5   delta_costs = random_swaps(netlist.block_count)
6
7   starting_temperature = 20 * stddev(delta_costs)
8
9   # Initialize annealing schedule:
10  #  - Set starting temperature.
11  #  - Initially, allow moves to cross the entire grid area.
12  schedule.temperature = starting_temperature
13  schedule.rlim = max(architecture.dims)
14
15  while schedule.temperature > 0.005 * mean(net_costs):
16      accepted_swaps = 0
17
18      for i in 0 to moves_per_temperature:
19          source_block = select_random_block(netlist.blocks)
20          # Look up the tile where the randomly-selected source
21          # block is currently located.
22          source_tile = get_tile_position(source_block)
23          # Randomly select a target tile position within the
24          # current radius-limit (i.e., 'rlim').
25          target_tile = select_random_tile(source_tile,
26                                            schedule.rlim)
27
28          delta_cost = swap_tile_contents(source_tile,
29                                           target_tile)
30
31          accept = assess_swap(delta_cost, schedule.temperature)
32          if not accept:
33              undo_most_recent_swap()
34          else:
35              accepted_swaps += 1
36
37      # Update temperature and radius-limit based on acceptance
38      # rate of most-recent round of swaps.
39      schedule.update(accepted_swaps / moves_per_temperature)
```

Lines 1-13 initialize the state of the annealer based on the *netlist* and on the `inner_num` parameter, which scales how many moves are applied at each temperature state. We refer to the code from Lines 18-35 as the *"inner-loop"*. The *inner-loop* evaluates the calculated number of random swaps at the current temperature state. The tiles involved in each swap are randomly selected, by first randomly selecting a block *(Line 19)* and then selecting a a random target tile *(Lines 25-26)* within a radius-limit displacement from the current position of the selected block. Any swap resulting in a cost improvement is accepted *(Line 31)*, while non-improving blocks are conditionally accepted based on the current temperature and a stochastic variable [3]. The anneal continues by updating the current temperature and radius-limit parameters after every *outer-loop* iteration, before stopping once the temperature is very low compared to the average cost of a net.

3.2 Move-pair annealer

Our annealer is based on the VPR[3] annealer described in Program 1. The key difference in our annealer is the implementation of the *inner-loop* section, which corresponds to Lines 18-35 in Program 1. Instead of evaluating many *serialized* swaps during each *inner-loop* iteration, we operate on a large set of *non-overlapping* move-pairs (*i.e., swaps*) which may be evaluated and applied concurrently, since all instructions in the inner-loop of our implementation map to structured parallel patterns, including *map, pack, prefix sum, gather, and vector arithmetic operations*[4]. By using such patterns for all operations in the inner-loop, we ensure the serial run-time complexity of Lines 5-28 is $O(N)$, where N is the number of tiles in the target architecture, while providing opportunities for parallelism using a wide variety of parallel platforms that support such standardized parallel patterns and constructs.

Program 2 Move-pair anneal inner-loop pseudo-code.

```
1   total_accepted_swaps = 0
2   evaluated_swaps = 0
3
4   while evaluated_swaps < moves_per_temperature:
5       # Compute a displacement for each tile in the grid.
6       # Note that a tile may have a displacement of zero.
7       tile_displacements = get_random_displacements(schedule.rlim)
8
9       # Since each tile assigned a positive displacement _must_
10      # have a corresponding tile with a negative displacement,
11      # the number of positive displacements is equal to the
12      # number of move-pairs (i.e., swaps) being evaluated.
13      evaluated_swaps += count_positive(tile_displacements)
14
15      # Compute difference in cost for each tile based on moving
16      # the tile's contents by the corresponding computed
17      # displacement.
18      tile_delta_costs = evaluate_displacements(tile_displacements)
19
20      # Sum the cost changes for each pair of tiles belonging to
21      # the same move-pair.
22      swap_delta_costs = combine_move_pair_deltas(tile_delta_costs)
23      move_pair_accept_mask = assess_swaps(swap_delta_costs,
24                                           schedule.temperature)
25
26      accepted_swaps, affected_nets = apply_swaps(swap_accept_mask)
27      update_net_costs(affected_nets)
28      total_accepted_swaps += accepted_swaps
29
30  # Update temperature and radius-limit based on acceptance
31  # rate of most-recent round of swaps.
32  schedule.update(accepted_swaps / evaluated_swaps)
```

Program 2 lists the pseudo-code for the *inner-loop* of our proposed annealer. Line 7 computes a displacement to apply to each tile according to the process described in Section 2.3. Line 18 computes the change in cost due to applying the displacements from Line 7 to the contents of the corresponding tiles. Where Line 18 computes the changes in cost relative to each tile, Line 22 combines the cost changes from tiles belonging to the same move-pair to obtain a change in cost based on the associated swap being applied. On Lines 23-24, each swap is assessed based on the corresponding difference in cost to determine if the swap should be applied or not (*i.e., if the tile contents should be exchanged*). The assessments from Lines 23-24 result in a binary mask, where each position in the mask corresponds to an evaluated swap (*i.e., move-pair*) and a value of one in a position indicates that the related swap should be applied. The move-pairs that are marked in the acceptance mask are applied on Line 26 while recording the number of swaps applied and the indexes of any nets that were affected by any of the swaps applied. The costs of the affected nets are recomputed on Line 27. Since the number of non-overlapping move-pairs

is not likely to be equal to the moves-per-temperature parameter, Lines 5-28 are repeated until the desired number of evaluated moves is reached.

4. EXPERIMENTS

To evaluate the efficacy of our proposed *move-pair annealer*, we conducted several sets of experiments. First, we ran VPR using the bounding-box cost function with `inner_num=1` and `inner_num=10`, across the set of 20 MCNC[8] benchmark netlists, ranging from 1135 blocks to 8445 blocks. For each netlist, we ran ten trials, each with a different seed for the random-number generator. Next, we ran ten trials using our *move-pair annealer* for each netlist in the same set of benchmarks, with `inner_num=1`. Note that we ran all experiments using a single thread on an Intel Core i7-3517U processor running 32-bit Ubuntu 12.04.3. All code was compiled using Intel's `icc` compiler, version `13.1.3 20130607` with the `-fast` flag.

4.1 Post-routing critical-path-delay

After performing placement under each of the configurations described above, we routed each placement using VPR's router. Since the minimum routable channel-width varies between placements, to compare the routed results between the various annealer configurations, for each netlist, we selected the maximum channel-width required to route any of the placements produced by any of the annealer configurations. We then routed all placements for each netlist using the corresponding largest minimum channel-width to provide the same conditions for routing all placements of the respective netlist.

The resulting routed critical-path-delays for VPR and our proposed move-pair annealer are listed in Table 1, where μ_{cpd} represents the mean critical-path-delay (in nanoseconds) for each placer configuration across 10 trials for each netlist. The last two columns in Table 1 show the percentage difference in the resulting critical-path-delay from VPR versus our move-pair annealer, denoted as Δ_{cpd}. Note that a negative value in a Δ_{cpd} column indicates that the move-pair annealer improved upon the critical-path-delay from VPR running the corresponding `inner_num` configuration. Bold values in a Δ_{cpd} column denote cases where, based on the results of a Wilcoxon sign-ranked test, the distribution of critical-path-delay values produced by our move-pair annealer is deemed to not be the same as the distribution produced by the corresponding VPR `inner_num` configuration, with an α-value of 0.05. From the table, we can see that in the case of VPR with `inner_num=1`, our move-pair improves the critical-path-delay compared to VPR with statistical significance for 15 out of 20 netlists, with an overall improvement of 11.5% in critical-path-delay. Furthermore, in the case of VPR with `inner_num=10`, the behaviour of the move-pair annealer is deemed to statistically differ from that of VPR in 11 of 20 cases, resulting in an overall improvement in critical-path-delay of 4.2%. These results clearly show that our move-pair annealer is able to effectively explore the placement solution space, despite the soft-conflicts introduced by evaluating swaps in concurrent sets and any bias introduced by the regularity of the applied displacement-patterns.

Table 1: Mean placement run-times and routed critical-path-delays for VPR with inner_num=1, inner_num=10 vs. our move-pair annealer.

Netlist	VPR i=1 μ_{cpd} (ns)	VPR i=1 μ_{tp} (s)	VPR i=10 μ_{cpd} (ns)	VPR i=10 μ_{tp} (s)	Move-pair μ_{cpd} (ns)	Move-pair μ_{tp} (s)	% versus VPR i=1 Δ_{cpd}	% versus VPR i=10 Δ_{cpd}
ex5p	115.6	0.9	117.5	9.3	101.6	0.9	**-12.1**	**-13.5**
tseng	80.5	1.0	74.8	9.5	81.8	1.2	1.6	**9.3**
apex4	130.6	1.1	120.1	11.0	103.6	1.0	**-20.7**	**-13.7**
misex3	111.1	1.2	105.3	12.5	94.6	1.1	**-14.9**	**-10.2**
alu4	115.3	1.3	114.9	13.3	102.2	1.3	**-11.3**	**-11.0**
diffeq	106.8	1.5	93.2	15.1	99.7	1.5	**-6.6**	7.0
dsip	81.2	1.4	91.0	13.5	76.6	2.1	**-5.6**	**-15.9**
seq	123.4	1.8	119.9	18.0	102.0	1.6	**-17.3**	**-14.9**
apex2	127.0	2.0	125.8	19.9	107.2	1.6	**-15.6**	**-14.8**
s298	232.3	1.6	196.5	16.0	214.0	1.6	**-7.9**	8.9
des	130.1	1.7	127.2	17.3	130.3	2.3	0.2	2.4
bigkey	97.0	1.8	92.8	18.5	79.9	2.3	**-17.6**	**-13.8**
frisc	241.8	5.2	185.1	51.7	202.3	3.9	**-16.3**	9.3
spla	210.3	5.4	182.5	53.3	176.8	3.7	**-15.9**	**-3.2**
elliptic	242.3	5.2	199.4	51.9	232.4	4.4	**-4.1**	16.6
ex1010	219.0	7.4	211.0	74.2	191.2	4.7	**-12.7**	**-9.4**
pdc	256.4	7.3	218.7	73.1	213.7	4.9	**-16.7**	**-2.3**
s38417	195.6	12.7	171.9	126.4	164.2	8.0	**-16.0**	**-4.5**
s38584.1	127.6	12.6	121.6	125.3	113.3	8.9	**-11.2**	**-6.8**
clma	261.6	17.6	246.5	175.9	237.4	11.4	**-9.2**	**-3.7**
Mean	-	-	-	-	-	-	**-11.5**	**-4.2**
Sum	3.2e3	90.8	2.9e3	905.5	2.8e3	68.3	-	-

4.2 Run-time

Columns two, four and six in Table 1 show the mean placement run-times in seconds, denoted as μ_{tp} using VPR with inner_num=10, VPR with inner_num=1, and our *move-pair annealer* (with inner_num=1), respectively, across the ten trials for each of the 20 MCNC netlists. By observing the summed total run-time for each placer configuration in the last row, we can see that the move-pair annealer is faster than VPR with inner_num set to either 1 or 10. Though not shown in the table due to space restrictions, compared to VPR running with inner_num=1 and inner_num=10, our move-pair annealer achieves an overall speedup of 1.3× and 13.3×, respectively.

As shown in the previous section, the critical-path-delay values reached using our move-pair annealer rival VPR running with inner_num=10. This means that our annealer is able to produce comparable critical-path-delay results using approximately 10x *fewer* swaps overall. This dramatic reduction in total swaps evaluated results in a significant reduction in run-time for our move-pair annealer compared to VPR run with inner_num=10, resulting in the observed 13.3× speedup.

Again, we would like to emphasize that although the work in our move-pair annealer is organized using structured parallel pattern operations that lend themselves to high levels of parallelism, the speedups discussed in this paper are a result from running our algorithm using a single threaded implementation only. While further work is required to characterize which aspects of our annealer lead to improved critical-path-delay overall, we conjecture that the observed performance improvements are due to improved data-locality introduced by using structured parallel patterns, even when running with a single thread.

5. CONCLUSIONS AND FUTURE WORK

In this paper, we proposed a novel method for generating parallel work in the context of placement, which we have demonstrated scales with the size of the target FPGA architecture. Furthermore, we have developed a simulated annealing variant, which we call *move-pair annealer*, that eval-

uates and applies the generated sets of swaps using structured parallel programming patterns. Although the implementation described in this paper only utilizes a single thread, by using structured parallel patterns which can be implemented using various parallel frameworks (e.g., Cilk Plus, CUDA, etc.), there is a straight-forward path to implement our annealer on many different parallel platforms, including multi-core CPUs and many-core architectures, such as GPUs or Intel MIC. We are currently working to develop a Cilk Plus implementation of our move-pair annealer, targeting multi-core processors as well as a GPU implementation using NVIDIA CUDA. Since both of these parallel frameworks provide support for the structured parallel patterns used in our implementation, we expect to significantly reduce run-times while maintaining *serial equivalency*, ensuring that, unlike other parallel placement approaches[2, 6], our annealer will improve run-times without sacrificing quality. In fact, as our results show, our annealer is capable of out-performing VPR in terms of critical-path-delay, even when evaluating as little as one-tenth of the swaps overall.

6. REFERENCES

[1] A. Ghuloum, T. Smith, G. Wu, X. Zhou, J. Fang, P. Guo, B. So, M. Rajagopalan, Y. Chen, and B. Chen. Future-proof data parallel algorithms and software on intel multi-core architecture. *Intel Technology Journal*, 11(4), 2007.

[2] A. Ludwin, V. Betz, and K. Padalia. High-quality, deterministic parallel placement for FPGAs on commodity hardware. In *Proceedings of the 16th international ACM/SIGDA symposium on Field programmable gate arrays*, pages 14–23, Monterey, California, USA, 2008. ACM.

[3] J. Luu, I. Kuon, P. Jamieson, T. Campbell, A. Ye, W. M. Fang, and J. Rose. VPR 5.0: FPGA cad and architecture exploration tools with single-driver routing, heterogeneity and process scaling. In *Proceeding of the ACM/SIGDA international symposium on Field programmable gate arrays*, pages 133–142, Monterey, California, USA, 2009. ACM.

[4] M. McCool, J. Reinders, and A. Robison. *Structured Parallel Programming: Patterns for Efficient Computation*. Access Online via Elsevier, 2012.

[5] K. Shahookar and P. Mazumder. VLSI cell placement techniques. *ACM Comput. Surv.*, 23(2):143–220, 1991.

[6] C. C. Wang and G. G. F. Lemieux. Scalable and deterministic timing-driven parallel placement for FPGAs. In *Proceedings of the 19th ACM/SIGDA international symposium on Field programmable gate arrays*, FPGA '11, pages 153–162, New York, NY, USA, 2011. ACM. ACM ID: 1950445.

[7] M. Xu, G. Gréwal, and S. Areibi. Starplace: A new analytic method for FPGA placement. *Integration, the VLSI Journal*, 44(3):192–204, 2011.

[8] S. Yang. *Logic synthesis and optimization benchmarks user guide: version 3.0.* Citeseer, 1991.

A Parallel and Reconfigurable Architecture for Efficient OMP Compressive Sensing Reconstruction

Amey Kulkarni
Department of Computer
Science & Electrical
Engineering
University of Maryland,
Baltimore County
Baltimore,USA
ameyk1@umbc.edu

Houman Homayoun
Department of Electrical &
Computer Engineering
George Mason University
Fairfax,USA
hhomayou@gmu.edu

Tinoosh Mohsenin
Department of Computer
Science & Electrical
Engineering
University of Maryland,
Baltimore County
Baltimore,USA
tinoosh@umbc.edu

ABSTRACT

Compressive Sensing (CS) is a novel scheme, in which a signal that is sparse in a known transform domain can be reconstructed using fewer samples. However, the signal reconstruction techniques are computationally intensive and power consuming, which make them impractical for embedded applications. This work presents a parallel and reconfigurable architecture for Orthogonal Matching Pursuit (OMP) algorithm, one of the most popular CS reconstruction algorithms. In this paper, we are proposing the first reconfigurable OMP CS reconstruction architecture which can take different image sizes with sparsity up to 32. The aim is to minimize the hardware complexity, area and power consumption, and improve the reconstruction latency while meeting the reconstruction accuracy. First, the accuracy of reconstructed images is analyzed for different sparsity values and fixed point word length reduction. Next, efficient parallelization techniques are applied to reconstruct signals with variant signal lengths of N. The OMP algorithm is mainly divided into three kernels, where each kernel is parallelized to reduce execution time, and efficient reuse of the matrix operators allows us to reduce area. The proposed architecture can reconstruct images of different sizes and measurements and is implemented on a Xilinx Virtex 7 FPGA. The results indicate that, for a 128×128 image reconstruction, the proposed reconfigurable architecture is $2.67 \times$ to $1.8 \times$ faster than the previous non-reconfigurable work which is less complex and uses much smaller sparsity.

Categories and Subject Descriptors

B.2 [**ARITHMETIC AND LOGIC STRUCTURES**]: Design StylesParallel,Pipeline; B.2.4 [**High-Speed Arithmetic**]: Algorithms

GLSVLSI'14, May 21–23, 2014, Houston, Texas, USA.
Copyright 2014 ACM 978-1-4503-2816-6/14/05 ...$15.00.
http://dx.doi.org/10.1145/2591513.2591598 .

Keywords

OMP;Compressive Sensing; FPGA; High Performance and Reconfigurable Architecture

1. INTRODUCTION

In recent years, Compressive Sensing (CS) has emerged as a novel technique which enables reconstruction of sparse signals sampled at sub-Nyquist rates. Reducing the number of measurements can reduce the time and cost of signal acquisition. CS reduces the amount of data collected during signal acquisition thereby, eliminating redundancy. Reducing the number of measurements can significantly reduce the communication power (e.g. space applications, wearable biomedical devices), scanning time (e.g. MRI) and cost of signal acquisition.

CS is used for radar imaging applications due to its fast and efficient signal processing ability. Radar Signal Processing encompasses a wide range of applications in processing techniques, sensing objectives, propagation media etc. Recently, it is mainly being used in military and civilian applications. The signal in these applications needs to be of high resolution. Therefore, it requires wider bandwidth and hence necessitates large amount of data for transmission, reception and processing. Similarly, applications such as Inverse Synthetic Aperture Radar (ISAR) imaging used for maritime targets, and through-the-wall Radar (TWR) imaging used to get vision into obscured areas. Therefore, both the systems need to reconstruct the signal in real-time to be effective.

On the other hand, in Medical Resonance Imaging (MRI), CS reconstructs the image from sparse measurements and reduces scan time, which is proportional to the number of samples acquired. Long term functional MRI requires continuous high speed imaging. The continuous acquisition of images results in high volume of data. Therefore, instead of considering the whole image, most of the devices allow pre-determined rectangular region of interest (ROI) to be sampled. In medical imaging, ROI is the area of an image which is very important for diagnosis. The ROI is variable and is based on the stage of disease. For example, Benign lesion has less ROI as compared to malignant lesion. Hence, the size of image to be sampled and reconstructed is dependent on ROI. Therefore, CS reconstruction is in intense need of reconfigurable architectures.

Though CS has several advantages, reconstruction of CS is very complex and computationally intensive. Recently, there have been several reconstruction algorithms proposed which show trade-off between complexity and accuracy. Two such algorithms are ℓ_1–minimization and Orthogonal Matching Pursuit (OMP) [11]. ℓ_1–minimization algorithm is better in terms of accuracy, but its implementation is very complex and time-consuming. OMP is a greedy algorithm of less complexity that finds closely correlated values in each iteration. The complexity of the design increases with data length and sparsity number. OMP contains iterative interdependent modules which repeat iteratively up to sparsity count makes parallel implementation of the algorithm challenging. OMP has matrix multiplication, sort and inversion, which are known to be operator consuming operations. Therefore, the signals with large matrix lengths will require more resources and hence larger chip area. This motivates us to consider a semi-parallel architecture wherein operators are reused, thereby reducing chip area.

To address these challenges, this paper present a low complexity, parallel and reconfigurable architecture to accept variable matrix image lengths and measurements as input. In the OMP algorithm, at each iteration, matrix sizes vary. Therefore, the main challenging blocks in making the architecture reconfigurable are dot product calculations and least square block. Since the iteration count is dependent on sparsity, it is fixed to 32 based on our prior experiments and analysis.

The structure of this paper is as follows: in Section 2, paper overviews trends and related work. Section 3, goes over the OMP algorithm. Section 4 proposes the architecture for reconfigurable and parallel OMP reconstruction algorithm. Finally, in Section 5 paper discusses the FPGA implementation results and analysis.

2. BACKGROUND

The basic theory behind compressive sensing lies in solving Equation 1. Let ϕ be the measurement matrix of dimension $M \times N$, where M is the number of measurements to be taken and N is the length of the signal and x be a m-sparse signal of length N. Multiplying these two vectors yields y of length M, which contains the measurements obtained by the projection of ϕ onto x.

$$y = \phi x \qquad (1)$$

Orthogonal Matching Pursuit (OMP) is a greedy algorithm, which performs the signal recovery from random measurements [20]. For the first few years, research on the CS OMP reconstruction algorithm was focused on reducing latency of operations. The focus has shifted over the past few year to reducing energy consumption as CS is implemented for wireless and battery operated devices [9], [10]. Most of the OMP designs are implemented on FPGA [12] [17], [18],[5], [1], some implement the designs on ASIC [12] [17], [21], [9] and others implement the architecture on ASIP [6]. Similarly, most of the papers compare their results with previous architectures and show improvements in terms of speed (latency of operations) [18]. Some prior work also shows the improvement in speed on software [1]. To the best of our knowledge, this is the first implementation which targets reconfigurability for OMP algorithm.

The first basic implementation of OMP is presented [17], which shows interdependence between modules. It implements OMP with sparsity up to $m = 5$ and input vector of 128 size on FPGA. OMP with QR decomposition is proposed in [18], to speed up the algorithm. The paper implements the design on CMOS 65nm and FPGA and is 2.4 times faster than [17]. Black et.al. [5] segregates OMP algorithm in three kernels and each kernel is parallelized to reduce latency of operations. The paper compares the speedup with a software implementation, and performs 38 times faster. L.Bai et.al. [1] propose the design and implementation of OMP and AMP algorithms on FPGA and compare hardware with software implementations. In contrast to other VLSI implementations, this implementation can deal with less sparse signals, which enables fast image reconstruction. The architecture works at 100MHz with a reconstruction time of 0.63 msec.

Tsai et.al. [21] present a versatile signal reconstruction platform. It is implemented in three different blocks. Pseudo Random Number Generator generates random numbers on the fly to reduce memory complexity. Matrix factorization engine contains Cholesky based linear solver and the multi-processing core performs the other operations. The design is implemented in TSMC 40nm CMOS process and runs at 250 MHz.

The trend to reduce latency of operations and energy consumption begins with [9]. This work proposes OMP with Matrix Inversion Bypass to reduce computational complexity. The paper targets battery or renewable energy powered cyber-physical systems. It compares with OMP Batch algorithm, which is less complex and performs the operation in one iteration. The paper implements Moore-Penrose pseudo inverse referred to as the updated pseudo inverse solution, that utilizes the matrix $G - 1$ available from the previous operation to obtain current matrix $G - 1$. Specifically, this method calculates $G-1$ using the Schur-Banachiewicz block wise inversion (due to low complexity) . In other words, the computation of $G - 1$ for current inversion can be bypassed. As $G-1$ is only needed in the $(k-1)^{th}$ iteration, it can be computed in parallel with the computation of X to improve the speed of signal reconstruction. The design is implemented on 65nm CMOS process with the clock frequency of 500MHz.

Soft thresholding OMP technique to reduce the energy for reconstruction of the signal is implemented in [10]. This paper targets CS to exploit renewable energy sources in autonomous and distributed wireless sensor networks. The threshold of employing the efficient reconstruction is made dynamically adjustable according to the performance requirements and energy levels. The paper takes motivation from the fact that last iteration usually recovers less significant elements of the signal. Hardware is implemented on 65nm CMOS process with clock frequency of 500MHz. It achieves significant reduction in computational complexity in particular when sparsity of signal is high because the low complexity procedure recovers more elements in such signals. The implementation of ST-OMP takes 0.16 msec to recover a signal and consumes 0.0205 mJ energy.

OMP algorithm with a sub-V_t Application Specific Instruction set Processor (ASIP) for exploiting specific operations of CS is implemented in [6]. The paper mainly targets battery operated devices i.e., sensing environment systems and wireless body sensor networks (WBSNs), where portable and autonomous devices are expected to operate for an ex-

Algorithm 1 OMP Reconstruction Algorithm

1: Initialize $R_0 = y$, $\phi_0 = \emptyset$, $\Lambda_0 = \emptyset$, $\Phi_0 = \emptyset$ and $t = 0$
2: Find Index $\lambda_t = max_{j=1...n}$ subject to $| < \phi_j R_{t-1} > |$
3: Update $\Lambda_t = \Lambda_{t-1} \bigcup \lambda_t$
4: Update $\Phi_t = [\Phi_{t-1} \ \phi_{\Lambda_t}]$
5: Solve the Least Squares Problem
$x_t = \min_x \| y - \Phi_y \ x \|^2$
6: Calculate new approximation: $\alpha_t = \Phi_t \ x_t$
7: Calculate new residual: $R_t = y - \alpha_t$
8: Increment t, and repeat from step 2 if t<k
After all the iterations, we can find correct sparse signals.

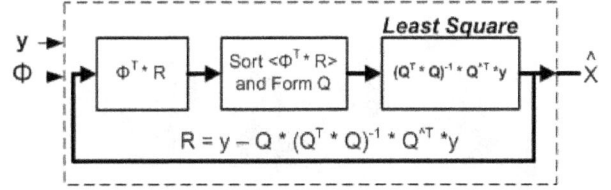

Figure 1: Basic Block Diagram for OMP Reconstruction Algorithm

tended period of time with limited energy resources. Hence, an ultra low power (ULP) CS implementation is crucial for these energy limited autonomous systems. The processor has sleep mode which allows external clock gating of the entire core. The processor has sub-V_t latch-based memories. The paper shows power and performance trade-off. The simulation result shows that CS processor operates at 0.37 V for required clock frequency of 100KHz with total power 288nW and critical path of 5.2 nsec.

3. ALGORITHM

OMP takes two inputs: the measured signal (y) and the measurement matrix (ϕ). At each iteration (t), column of ϕ is chosen which is most strongly correlated with y. Least square algorithm is used to obtain a new signal estimate. In the next step, the amount of contribution that column y provides is subtracted to obtain a residue which is used for the next iteration. Finally, after k iterations, correct set of columns are determined [20] [11].

The variables used in the algorithm are defined below:

- N$\times$ N = Images Size (e.g $128 \times 128...768 \times 768$)

- M = Measurements (e.g 42...252)

- k = Sparsity (e.g 32)

- R = Residual Matrix ($size : M \times 1$)

- ϕ = Measurement Matrix ($size : M \times N$)

- λ = Maximum Index after Dot Product

- t = No. of iterations (k)

4. PROPOSED WORK

Based on the algorithm description, OMP is partitioned into three main kernels: *dot product, sort and least square* (which involves *matrix inversion*). These blocks are shown in Fig. 1. As shown in the figure, these three kernels are interdependent, therefore OMP cannot be fully parallellized. This paper implements a semi-parallel architecture for each of the kernels to fit different data sizes of reconstruction.

4.1 Sparsity Analysis

Computational / hardware complexity is a major factor in parallel implementation of the design on FPGA for different sizes of a matrix. From Fig. 1,it is observed that Least Square is the most complex kernel of the three. In OMP algorithm, each column is repeated k (Sparsity) times. Therefore, $\phi^T \times \phi$ increments in each iteration till $k \times k$. Therefore,

Table 1: PSNR and Sparsity Analysis numbers for variety of Image Sizes with OMP Reconstruction Algorithm

Image Sizes	Sparsity k	PSNR (dB)
256×256	8	27.22
256×256	**32**	**34.70**
256×256	48	34.89
384×384	8	21.24
384×384	**32**	**22.88**
384×384	48	22.91
512×512	8	21.19
512×512	**32**	**25.65**
512×512	48	25.71
768×768	**32**	**22.55**
768×768	90	22.95

complexity of Least Square algorithm is dependent on the size of sparsity. Hence, the primary focus is to reduce the hardware complexity by setting the sparsity to a constant value. This reduces the size of the matrix during inversion.

In this paper, the sparsity of the matrix is set based on experimenting on the different sizes of images while observing satisfactory range of PSNR. The random measurement matrix (One of the input to the OMP) changes each time while running the experiment and hence the result may vary from 0.09% to 0.158%. Therefore, average Peak Signal-to-Noise Ratio (PSNR) is calculated by repeating the experiment 100 times. Setting sparsity size to 32 helps to reduce operations of the complex Least Square algorithm. Table 1 shows different sizes of images (N × N) with different sparsity and their PSNR results. It clearly indicates that variation in image sizes for a constant sparsity has minimal effect on PSNR. However, from a hardware stand point, it is advantageous since it reduces memory transfers, area and speed.

4.2 Fixed Point Optimization

Floating point arithmetic is complex and requires more area. At the same time, OMP algorithm requires huge number of multiplications and additions. Hence floating point operations increase hardware complexity. This motivates the selection of fixed point arithmetic. As shown in fig. 3, fixed point arithmetic increases the hardware complexity when accuracy reaches threshold. In this paper, we experimented output accuracy and hardware complexity with different binary points. The quality of reconstructed image is mainly dependent on accuracy of the fixed point output. Hence, binary points are chosen close to their corresponding floating point numbers (100 % accuracy) at the output. Ac-

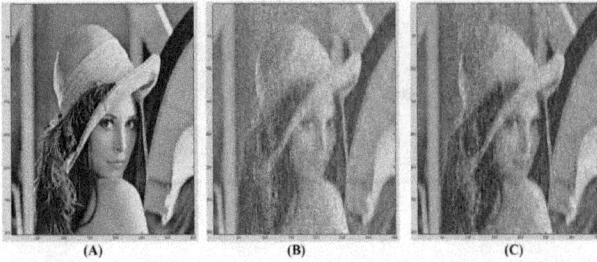

Figure 2: (A) 256 ×256 Original Image, (B) and (C) reconstructed images with sparsity values of 8 and 32.

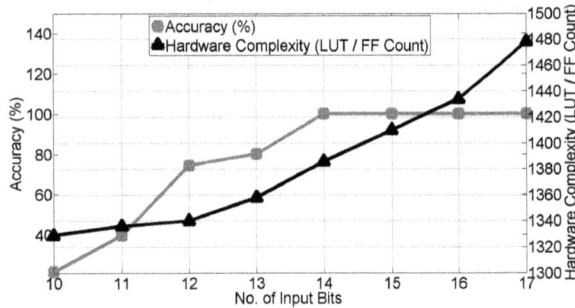

Figure 3: Hardware complexity (LUT/FF count in *Virtex-7* FPGA) and accuracy (fixed point vs floating point) of OMP CS Reconstruction algorithm when the number of input bits increases Accuracy with 0.0005 margin of error

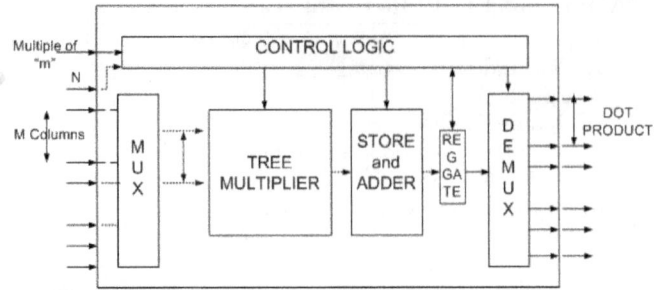

Figure 4: High level block diagram of Reconfigurable Dot Product

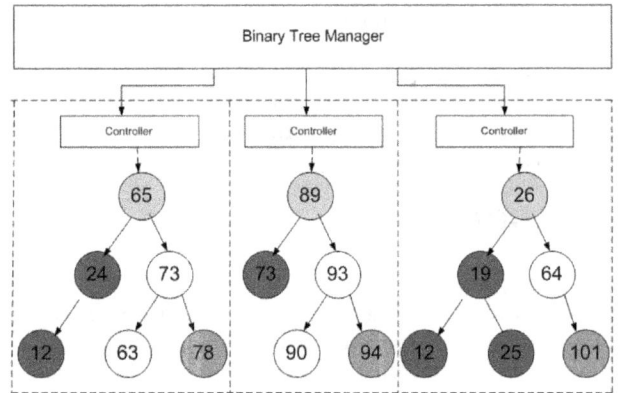

Figure 5: Example of Parallel Implementation of Binary Tree

curacy of the output is verified at each hardware step along the data path post truncation/saturation. Similarly, by incrementing bits at the input, the data path word width is changed. This affects area of an architecture and the amount of switching activity on wires and logic gates, consequently affecting the power dissipation.

4.3 Reconfigurable DOT Product

At each iteration, OMP computes dot product of ϕ^T, which is a N × M matrix, with a residual matrix R, which is a M×1 vector. This has a computational complexity of O(MN). Tree multiplier is implemented to leverage the parallel and pipeline architecture (Figure 4). It is implemented for each 42×1 size array. For our implementation measurements are 30% of image sizes.

Tree multiplier requires N multipliers and $N - 1$ adders where, N is the number of columns. Thus total number of operations come to be $2N - 1$. As discussed earlier, this architecture considers N columns, which are multiple of 42. Therefore, at every cycle dot product of 42×1 and 1×42 is available. For the image size of 128×128, column size of ϕ^T is 42. Therefore, the dot product of 128×42 and 42×1 is computed in 128 clock cycles.

4.4 Sort Algorithm

The operation of the second kernel is to locate the maximum of $|<\phi R>|$ (N×1 vector). This has a computational complexity of O(N). Sort algorithm is implemented by using

a binary tree structure [15]. $N/2^S$ trees are implemented, where S is variable and dependent on size of an image. Concurrent sorting is applied to $N/2^S$ to efficiently use parallelism as shown in Fig. 5. In this architecture, since the algorithm needs only the highest number, we could reduce the memory usage as compared to [15], by pruning the left sub-tree. Each concurrent binary tree gives highest number, thereby generating $N/2^S$ highest numbers which are fed to another binary tree. Reconfigurability is achieved by changing the number of trees in parallel, dependent on the size of an image. Since the architecture is two staged, for every two cycles, a maximum of 128 elements is obtained.

4.5 Least Square Method

This is the most important kernel of the algorithm. As mentioned, $(\phi^T \phi)^{-1}$ has the highest hardware implementation complexity. At each iteration t, ϕ has t columns of size M. Hence, the new matrix, ϕ, is of size t×M. Computing $(\phi^T \phi)$ gives a t×t resulting matrix. Least square $(x=(\phi^T \phi)^{-1} \phi^T y)$ has three sub-blocks. Matrix transpose is achieved by calling matrix index in transpose order, which reduces the hardware complexity and utilizes minimal resources. Matrix multiplication is based on tree architecture mentioned previously in section 4.3. Whereas, matrix inversion is obtained by LU decomposition leveraging the symmetric matrix. As shown in Fig. 6, blocked algorithm for LU decomposition is used for efficient parallel implemen-

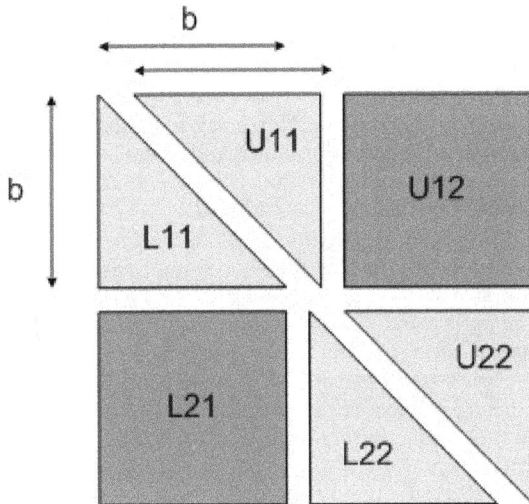

Figure 6: Blocked LU Algorithm for Parallel Implementation of Matrix Inversion

Table 2: *Virtex-7* post layout implementation results of DOT product for different image sizes

$< \phi R >$	Parallel Implementation		Serial Implementation	
	Time (ns)	Dynamic Power(W)	Time (ns)	Dynamic Power(W)
42×128	3.67	0.032	0.76	0.012
84×256	7.34	0.032	1.52	0.012
168×512	14.72	0.034	3.04	0.013

tation [14]. Finally, the resources are reused to reduce the area of the architecture.

5. IMPLEMENTATION RESULTS

The proposed reconfigurable architecture is implemented on a *Xilinx XC7VX485T Virtex-7* FPGA, which uses the sparsity of $k = 32$ for different size of images.

Parallel dot product implementation, gives one results each cycle. Therefore, after n cycles, the dot product for the whole image will be obtained, where n is the row size of an image. Table 2, shows the implementation results for serial and parallel architecture for different sizes of matrix.

As discussed in section 4.4, sort algorithm is implemented in parallel. Each binary tree sorts 32 elements. Therefore, for 128 × 1 array , the architecture has four concurrent binary trees in first stage. Second stage has a simple comparator tree to segregate the last four elements from each binary sub-tree.

For the sparsity of $k = 32$ (i.e 32 iterations), OMP takes 6208 cycles to reconstruct each column of image and hence $8.97\mu S$ for a 128 × 128 image, 9.32 μS for a 256 × 256 image and 10.12 μS for a 512 × 512 image size. The 256 × 256 reconstructed image has the PSNR of 35 dB , and 512 × 512 image achieves the PSNR of 26 dB in both fixedpoint hardware and floating point software. Post place and route timing results show that the proposed architecture is 62.62 %

Table 3: *Virtex-7* post layout implementation results of Sort algorithm for different image sizes

$\lambda_{j=1...n}$	Parallel Implementation		Serial Implementation	
	Time (ns)	Dynamic Power(W)	Time (ns)	Dynamic Power(W)
128	3.85	0.041	9.47	0.010
256	8.7	0.083	19.25	0.010
512	10.48	0.16	23.1	0.010

(2.67 ×) faster than the previous implementation [17], which takes 24 μS to reconstruct a 128 × 128 image, whereas 43.93 % (1.8 ×) faster as compared to [5]. Both previos work use a fixed image with much smaller sparsity (i.e. k=5).

6. CONCLUSION

The paper presents the first reconfigurable architecture for the OMP compressive sensing reconstruction algorithm. The hardware can take different image sizes with sparsity up to 32. The accuracy of reconstructed image is analyzed for different sparsity values and fixedpoint wordlength reduction. The results indicate that OMP peforms well with fixing the sparsity to be 32 for different image sizes of 128×128 to 768× 768. This reduces the hardware complexity in terms of the number of iterations as well as matrix inversion size. Datapath wordlength is optimized such that the hardware has minimum area with a highly accuracy reconstructed image. Different parallelization techniques are used for implementing the main three kernels of OMP algorithm which are dot product, sort and matrix inversion. The reconfigurable architecture is implemented on a Xilinx Virtex 7 FPGA. The results indicate that, for a 128×128 image reconstruction, the proposed architecture is 2.67× to 1.8× faster than the previous non-reconfigurable works which use much smaller sparsity.

7. REFERENCES

[1] L. Bai, P. Maechler, M. Muehlberghuber, and H. Kaeslin. High-speed compressed sensing reconstruction on fpga using omp and amp. In *Electronics, Circuits and Systems (ICECS), 2012 19th IEEE International Conference on*, pages 53–56, 2012.

[2] A. BanaiyanMofrad, H. Homayoun, and N. Dutt. Fft-cache: A flexible fault-tolerant cache architecture for ultra low voltage operation. In *Compilers, Architectures and Synthesis for Embedded Systems (CASES), 2011 Proceedings of the 14th International Conference on*, pages 95–104, Oct 2011.

[3] J. Bisasky, D. Chandler, and T. Mohsenin. A many-core platform implemented for multi-channel seizure detection. In *Circuits and Systems (ISCAS), 2012 IEEE International Symposium on*, pages 564–567, May 2012.

[4] J. Bisasky, H. Homayoun, F. Yazdani, and T. Mohsenin. A 64-core platform for biomedical signal processing. In *Quality Electronic Design (ISQED), 2013 14th International Symposium on*, pages 368–372, March 2013.

[5] P. Blache, H. Rabah, and A. Amira. High level prototyping and fpga implementation of the

orthogonal matching pursuit algorithm. In *Information Science, Signal Processing and their Applications (ISSPA), 2012 11th International Conference on*, pages 1336–1340, 2012.

[6] J. Constantin, A. Dogan, O. Andersson, P. Meinerzhagen, J. Rodrigues, D. Atienza, and A. Burg. Tamarisc-cs: An ultra-low-power application-specific processor for compressed sensing. In *VLSI and System-on-Chip (VLSI-SoC), 2012 IEEE/IFIP 20th International Conference on*, pages 159–164, 2012.

[7] H. Homayoun, V. Kontorinis, A. Shayan, T.-W. Lin, and D. Tullsen. Dynamically heterogeneous cores through 3d resource pooling. In *High Performance Computer Architecture (HPCA), 2012 IEEE 18th International Symposium on*, pages 1–12, Feb 2012.

[8] H. Homayoun, S. Pasricha, M. Makhzan, and A. Veidenbaum. Improving performance and reducing energy-delay with adaptive resource resizing for out-of-order embedded processors. *SIGPLAN Not.*, 43(7):71–78, June 2008.

[9] G. Huang and L. Wang. High-speed signal reconstruction with orthogonal matching pursuit via matrix inversion bypass. In *Signal Processing Systems (SiPS), 2012 IEEE Workshop on*, pages 191–196, 2012.

[10] G. Huang and L. Wang. Soft-thresholding orthogonal matching pursuit for efficient signal reconstruction. In *Acoustics, Speech and Signal Processing (ICASSP), 2013 IEEE International Conference on*, pages 2543–2547, 2013.

[11] A. Korde, D. Bradley, and T. Mohsenin. Detection performance of radar compressive sensing in noisy environments. *International SPIE Conference on Defense, Security, and Sensing*, May 2013.

[12] A. Kulkarni and T. Mohsenin. Parallel heterogeneous architectures for efficient omp compressive sensing reconstruction. *International SPIE Conference on Defense, Security, and Sensing*, May 2014.

[13] A. Kulkarni, J. Stanislaus, and T. Mohsenin. High performance architectures for omp compressive sensing reconstruction algorithm. *39th Annual GOMACTech Conference*, April 2014.

[14] M. Kumar Jaiswal and N. Chandrachoodan. Fpga-based high-performance and scalable block lu decomposition architecture. *Computers, IEEE Transactions on*, 61(1):60–72, 2012.

[15] D. Mihhailov, V. Sklyarov, I. Skliarova, and A. Sudnitson. Parallel fpga-based implementation of recursive sorting algorithms. In *Reconfigurable Computing and FPGAs (ReConFig), 2010 International Conference on*, pages 121–126, 2010.

[16] A. Sasan, H. Homayoun, A. Eltawil, and F. Kurdahi. Inquisitive defect cache: A means of combating manufacturing induced process variation. *Very Large Scale Integration (VLSI) Systems, IEEE Transactions on*, 19(9):1597–1609, Sept 2011.

[17] A. Septimus and R. Steinberg. Compressive sampling hardware reconstruction. In *Circuits and Systems (ISCAS), Proceedings of 2010 IEEE International Symposium on*, pages 3316–3319, 2010.

[18] J. Stanislaus and T. Mohsenin. High performance compressive sensing reconstruction hardware with qrd process. In *Circuits and Systems (ISCAS), 2012 IEEE International Symposium on*, pages 29–32, 2012.

[19] J. Stanislaus and T. Mohsenin. Low-complexity fpga implementation of compressive sensing reconstruction. In *Computing, Networking and Communications (ICNC), 2013 International Conference on*, pages 671–675, Jan 2013.

[20] J. Tropp and A. Gilbert. Signal recovery from random measurements via orthogonal matching pursuit. *Information Theory, IEEE Transactions on*, 53(12):4655–4666, 2007.

[21] Y.-M. Tsai, T.-J. Yang, and L.-G. Chen. A 401gflops/w 16-cores signal reconstruction platform with a 4g entries/s matrix generation engine for compressed sensing and sparse representation. In *VLSI Circuits (VLSIC), 2013 Symposium on*, pages C256–C257, 2013.

Generation of Reduced Analog Circuit Models using Transient Simulation Traces

Paul Winkler[1,2], Henda Aridhi[1], Mohamed H. Zaki[1], and Sofiène Tahar[1]

[1] Dept. of Electrical and Computer Engineering, Concordia University, Montréal, Québec, Canada
[2] Dept. of Electrical Engineering and Information Technology, University of Applied Sciences, Leipzig, Germany
{pwinker, h_aridh, mzaki, tahar}@ece.concordia.ca

ABSTRACT

The generation of fast models for device level circuit descriptions is a very active area of research. Model order reduction is an attractive technique for dynamical models size reduction. In this paper, we propose an approach based on clustering, curve-fitting, linearization and Krylov space projection to build reduced models for nonlinear analog circuits. We demonstrate our model order reduction method for three nonlinear circuits: a voltage controlled oscillator, an operational amplifier and a digital frequency divider. Our experimental results show that the reduced models lead to an improvement in simulation speed while guaranteeing the representation of the behavior of the original circuit design.

Categories and Subject Descriptors

B.7.2 [**Integrated Circuits**]: Design Aids—*Simulation*

Keywords

Analog Circuits; Curve-Fitting; Model Order Reduction; Krylov Space

1. INTRODUCTION

Device level simulation is a main step to validate electronic circuits before their fabrication. This step became very computationally expensive because of the large size and nonlinearity of their models. Therefore, researchers are looking for methods to build faster circuit models which preserve the same device level accuracy. Such models are needed to fasten simulation and enhance verification methodologies. Model abstraction, simplification and linearization are methods to deal with the complexity of large dynamical models. However, for the case of analog circuits they can lead to inaccurate models which do not preserve their characteristic nonlinear behaviour. Model Order Reduction (MOR) [1] is an attractive technique which consists in transforming a mathematical circuit model into a macromodel using a well defined algorithm. The resulting reduced model simulates

in much smaller time than the full order model while reproducing the same behaviour. The most promising MOR algorithms for the reduction of analog circuits are the Trajectory Piece-Wise Linear MOR method (TPWL) [13], the General-Purpose Nonlinear MOR using Piecewise-Polynomial Representations [7] and the MOR method for nonlinear circuits based on state space clustering [2]. These methods employ Taylor expansions representations and Krylov space projection to reduce dynamical circuit model in the form of Ordinary Differential Equations (ODEs).

Curve-fitting is a very powerful method used in different scientific areas to construct models from a series of data points [12]. It is a very effective approach especially for partially known models. This is the case of analog circuit models generated through Modified Nodal Analysis (MNA), when their semiconductor devices I-V characteristics are not completely specified or are missing some parameters [6].

In this paper, we propose an automated approach to build reduced models for nonlinear analog circuits, based on curve-fitting, clustering, linearization and MOR via Krylov space projection. Parametric nonlinear models are built via MNA and are curve-fitted using SPICE circuit simulation traces to obtain accurate nonlinear dynamical models. Then, linearization and state space reduction via Krylov space projection are applied at different state space clusters to obtain circuit reduced models.

In what follows, the related work is briefly reviewed in Section 2. Then, Section 3 details our method to generate circuit reduced models using their netlist and simulation traces. After that, our experimental results are shown in Section 4 for three nonlinear circuits: a voltage controlled oscillator, an operational amplifier and a frequency divider. Finally, our conclusions and future work are presented in Section 5.

2. RELATED WORK

In the last two decades many researchers realized the possibilities offered by MOR and tried to improve and apply these methods. There have been different successful methods to approximate transfer functions of linear circuits like the Singular Value Decomposition (SVD) and the Krylov Space projection methods [1]. However, for the case of nonlinear circuits, MOR methods are still in development phase. The Proper Orthogonal Decomposition (POD) that is the adaptation of the SVD method for nonlinear models is being used to reduce Partial Differential models successfully [1]. For the case of weakly nonlinear circuits, a MOR based on approximating nonlinear terms with quadratic Taylor approximations and Krylov space projections is proposed in [4]. Also, the TPWL MOR, based on linear Taylor approximations, was applied to nonlinear transmission lines, amplifier chains and Micro-machined devices [13]. The general purpose MOR method, based on piecewise polynomial representations [7], and the MOR method, based on state space clustering [2], improve the TPWL by addressing the problem of input dependency. Recently, three different MOR methods called ManiMOR, QLMOR and NTIM were proposed to derive reduced models for circuits and biology models [8]. Their accuracy is enhanced by using nonlinear manifolds projection, canonical representation and Volterra analysis. However, the resulting reduced models are intended for a specific type of analysis: DC, AC responses and timing/phase responses.

Curve-fitting is an inverse-problem where the objective is to determine parameters of a candidate model given a desired system response. For analog circuits, curve-fitting was used to determine a power MOSFET model parameters using experimental results [3]. Also, a piecewise curve-fitting modelling technique was proposed to determine accurate low order impedance transfer functions for capacitors and inductors from experimental data [11]. Recently, a method for parametric fault detection based on polynomial curve-fitting was applied to the case of a biquad filter [10]. However, none of these approaches can be used to curve-fit a large size analog circuit model.

In this paper, we are rather interested in determining dynamical model parameters for large analog circuits using a nonlinear curve-fitting constrained to a minimum mean squared error and reducing these models using a projection type MOR approach.

3. MOR METHODOLOGY

The proposed methodology for the generation of reduced models of large analog circuits using their transient simulation traces and their netlist is depicted in Figure 1. We apply first MNA to elaborate a mathematical model for the given circuit netlist, after replacing each active device with an equivalent circuit. The I-V-characteristic parameters of each equivalent circuit are unknown which leads to a parametric nonlinear differential model describing the circuit dynamics. Then, we use curve-fitting to extract the missing parameters from the circuit simulation traces performed in SPICE. The obtained circuit model is validated through simulation and comparison with the original simulation traces. In parallel, we perform clustering of the simulation traces in order to select linearization points which will be used for a piecewise linear description of the nonlinear differential model obtained via curve-fitting. After that, we compute a Krylov space projection matrix using the Arnoldi algorithm and reduce the local linearized models via projection, as described in [2]. Finally, the obtained reduced model is validated against the original nonlinear model within a testbench. We simulate the reduced model for different inputs and conditions and check its accuracy, input sensitivity and speedup.

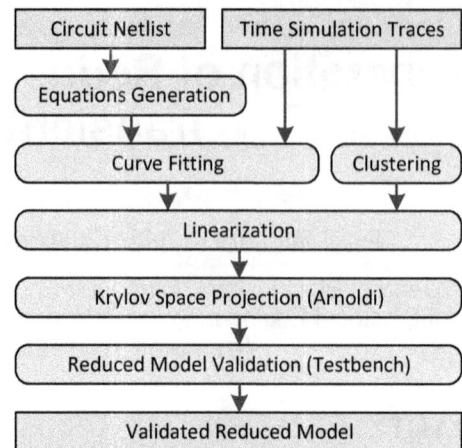

Figure 1: Model Order Reduction Methodology

3.1 Equations Generation

In order to perform an accurate curve-fitting, the generation of a good function guess is essential. In fact, the function guess must be capable of reproducing the main transient characteristics of the active devices. Semiconductor devices can include hundreds of parameters. In our approach, these elements are modeled using basic transient equivalent circuits consisting mainly of Voltage Controlled Current Sources (VCCS) and possibly some constant parasitic capacitances and resistances. The VCCS models are piecewise defined functions with linear and quadratic terms for MOSFETs and exponential terms for diodes and BJTs. The parameters of these models have to be determined using curve-fitting. The replacement of the active elements leads to a circuit consisting only of the following two-port elements: capacitances, resistances, inductances, independent voltage and current sources and VCCS. The input voltages and currents as well as the passive elements models are extracted from the netlist. Having a two port elements equivalent circuit, we extract the differential model using the MNA formulation.

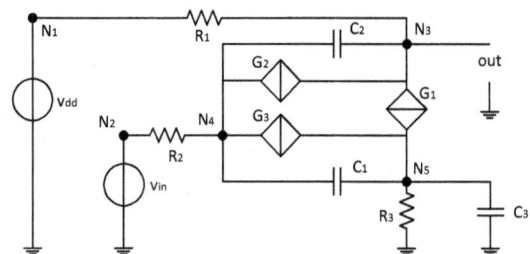

Figure 2: One-BJT Amplifier Circuit with VCCS

We demonstrate the equation generation step on a single BJT amplifier circuit, shown in Figure 2. The BJT element was replaced by its transient equivalent circuit and the MNA formulations leads to the set of matrices, shown in Equation (1).

$$
\begin{aligned}
C &= A_C \cdot C_0 \cdot A_C^T \\
G &= A_R \cdot R^{-1} \cdot A_R^T
\end{aligned}
\qquad (1)
$$

$$R = \begin{bmatrix} R_1 & 0 & 0 \\ 0 & R_2 & 0 \\ 0 & 0 & R_3 \end{bmatrix} \quad C_0 = \begin{bmatrix} C_1 & 0 & 0 \\ 0 & C_2 & 0 \\ 0 & 0 & C_3 \end{bmatrix} \quad I = \begin{bmatrix} G_1 \\ G_2 \\ G_3 \end{bmatrix} \quad V = \begin{bmatrix} v_{dd} \\ v_{in} \end{bmatrix}$$

$$A_R = \begin{bmatrix} 1 & 0 & 0 \\ 0 & 1 & 0 \\ -1 & 0 & 0 \\ 0 & -1 & 0 \\ 0 & 0 & 1 \end{bmatrix} \quad A_C = \begin{bmatrix} 0 & 0 & 0 \\ 0 & 0 & 0 \\ 0 & -1 & 0 \\ 1 & 1 & 0 \\ -1 & 0 & 1 \end{bmatrix} \quad A_I = \begin{bmatrix} 0 & 0 & 0 \\ 0 & 0 & 0 \\ 1 & -1 & 0 \\ 0 & 1 & 1 \\ -1 & 0 & -1 \end{bmatrix}$$

- The resistance, capacitance and inductance matrices R, C, L are ordered diagonal matrices.
- Dependent and independent current and voltage sources are merged to the row vectors I and V, respectively.
- The incidence matrices for all elements A_R, A_L, A_C, A_I and A_V are built based on their nodes information.

The matrices C and G are reduced to C_{cut} and G_{cut} by removing the lines related to the supply and input voltages, which are not considered as state variables. Then, the differential model is formed as given in Equation (2).

$$\dot{e} = C_{cut}^{-1} \cdot \left(-G_{cut} \cdot \begin{bmatrix} V \\ e \end{bmatrix} - A_I \cdot I(e, c) \right) \quad (2)$$

where $e = [v_{N_1}, v_{N_2}, v_{N_3}]^T$ is the state variables vector and $I(e, c)$ are the parametric VCCS models which depend on the state variables and the undefined parameters c. The matrix C_{cut} has to be nonsingular to generate an ODE system and avoid a DAE system, which is not always solvable. For this purpose, very small parasitic elements can be considered, as C_3 in Figure 2. If the circuit contains inductances, their currents have to be added as state variables to Equation (2), which leads to one system of Equation (3).

$$\begin{aligned} \dot{e} &= C_{cut}^{-1} \cdot \left(-G_{cut} \cdot \begin{bmatrix} V \\ e \end{bmatrix} - A_I \cdot I(e, c) - A_L \cdot i_L \right) \\ \dot{i_L} &= L^{-1} \cdot A_L^T \cdot \begin{bmatrix} V \\ e \end{bmatrix} \end{aligned} \quad (3)$$

The general form of the differential model is given in Equation (4).

$$\dot{x} = f(x, c, u(t)) \quad (4)$$

3.2 Curve-Fitting

The curve-fitting step is performed as detailed in Figure 3. It requires the circuit transient simulation traces (state variables snapshots) and a function guess f which is the incomplete circuit model given in Equation (4). After that, we approximate the state variables derivatives by finite differences approximation $\dot{x} \approx (\frac{\Delta x}{\Delta t})_s$ for different time samples s. The approximated state variables time derivatives provides a set of valuations of the function guess f. Then, the best-fit model parameters c_{opt} are determined automatically using the Levenberg-Marquardt curve-fitting method [12]. It is also called the least-squares curve-fitting algorithm since it determine local best-fit parameters which minimize the least-square residual between the function guess values and the approximated time derivative, as shown in Equation (5).

$$c_{opt} = \min_c \| f(x_s, c, u_s) - (\frac{\Delta x}{\Delta t})_s \|_2 \quad (5)$$

The accuracy of the curve-fitting algorithm depends on the function guess choice, the approximated state variables time derivatives and the initial parameters guess c_{init}. Because of that, we solve numerically the differential model in Equation (4) with the obtained best-fit parameters and compare

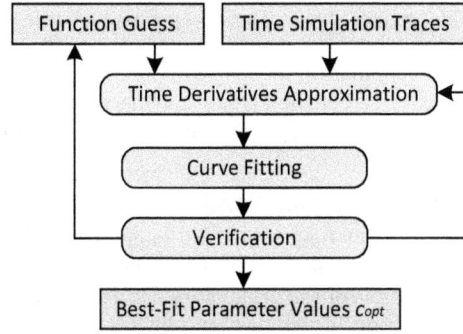

Figure 3: Curve-Fitting Model Parameters

the result with the time simulation traces. If the model is accurate, we proceed to the model reduction step. Otherwise, we add more training points x_s which leads to the maximum error values, during the verification step. At the end, if the previous test did not improve the accuracy of the models, we change the initial function guess. In fact, the use of a proper function guess is necessary for a successful curve-fitting of the nonlinear behavior of analog circuits. For that reason, we use device models similar to the SPICE model but with a smaller set of parameters. Using only polynomial function guess, as the Vandermodes interpolation method [9], we do not get best fit-parameter set which can reproduce the large signal transient behaviour of the circuit devices. The reason is that some device I-V characteristics have piecewise exponential functions with different parameters and coefficients. Piecewise local interpolation also fails to approximate the states behavior as it leads to a linear dependent system of equations which does not have a unique solution. Using the described curve-fitting approach, we determine the complete differential model given in Equation (6).

$$\dot{x} = f(x, u(t)) \quad (6)$$

3.3 Linearization and Krylov Space Transformation

We select k linearization points via Kmeans clustering of the simulation traces [12] and linearize the differential model in Equation (6), as detailed in [2, 13]. This leads to k local linear models as given in Equation (7).

$$\dot{x} = f(x_l, u_l) + J_{x_l} \cdot (x - x_l) + J_{u_l} \cdot (u - u_l) \quad (7)$$

where the Jacobian $J_{x_l} = \frac{\partial f}{\partial x}(x_l)$ and $J_{u_l} = \frac{\partial f}{\partial u}(u_l)$ are computed numerically for each cluster (x_l, u_l), using the Romberg extrapolation [5]. The piecewise weighted sum of the previous few local models is a good approximate of the differential model in $\mathbb{R}^n$. This intermediate model is reduced via Krylov space projection to get a smaller size differential model in $\mathbb{R}^m$, $m < n$, as given in Equation (8). A local $n \times m$ orthogonal projection matrix, which is necessary to do such a transformation, is computed using the Arnoldi algorithm [14]. Then, the main singular vectors of these local matrices form the unified projection matrix U. The reduced differential model is given in Equation (8).

$$\dot{z} = R_l + A_l \cdot (z - z_l) + B_l \cdot (u - u_l) \quad (8)$$

where $R_l = U^T \cdot f(x_l, u_l)$, $A_l = U^T \cdot J_{x_l} \cdot U$, $B_l = U^T \cdot J_{u_l}$ and $\vec{z}$ is the reduced state space vector that can be projected back to the original state space to approximate the original full order state variable x using the relation $\hat{x} = U \cdot z$. During the numerical simulation of Equation (8), the closest cluster $z_l = U^T \cdot x_l$ to the current state z is determined and the local model around it is evaluated in order to determine the next state.

3.4 Reduced Model Validation

The reduced model must fit some requirements to be usable in practice. Its simulation time must be smaller than the simulation time of the original model. It has also to preserve the input-output behavior and be accurate for a range of input signals. We use a testbench environment to automatically check the generated reduced models and compare them to the original model simulations. For our applications, we measure the closeness of the reduced simulation output vector $\hat{x}_o(t)$ and the original simulation output vector $x_o(t)$ with Equation (9).

$$error = \frac{\sum_{i=1}^{nt} ||x_o(i) - \hat{x}_o(i)||}{\sum_{i=1}^{k} ||x_o(i)||} \quad (9)$$

where nt is the number of time sample points. If different sample times are used for x_o and $\hat{x}_o$, we interpolate $\hat{x}_o$ at the time i using the closest trajectory points. The simulation speedup can be affected by the numerical integration method. Therefore, we use the same backward differentiation algorithm for both the reduced and the original model version in MATLAB [12]. Note that we cannot force the solver to use the same internal steps as it affects the solution accuracy. Also, the determination of the closest linearization point, which is done at every time step, can be time consuming if the current state is compared to a large number k of linearization points. Even though, we do not have the original SPICE circuit models coded in the MATLAB environment, we still can illustrate the speedup of the simulations of our generated reduced models using models expressed in the original state space using SPICE-like equivalent models for active devices.

4. APPLICATIONS

In this section, we apply the current method to a two-stage operational amplifier, a $90 - nm$ $CMOS$ voltage controlled oscillator (VCO), and a frequency divider. We show that the simulations of the generated reduced models are faster than that of the original models, while the error due to the reduction, evaluated using Equation (9), is minimal. Equation (10), illustrates a two parameters VCCS equivalent model for an $NMOS$ transistor used during the equation generation step, for all applications. The set of parameters $c_{1,2}$ is determined during the curve-fitting step and x and y are the gate to source and the drain to source transistor terminals voltages which values are extracted from the simulation traces.

$$I_{FET} = \begin{cases} 0 & if \quad x < c_1 \\ c_2 \cdot 0.5 \cdot (x - c_1) & if \quad y > x - c_1 > 0 \\ c_2 \cdot y \cdot (x - c_1 - \frac{y}{2}) & if \quad y < x - c_1 \end{cases} \quad (10)$$

For each of the following applications, a table shows the mathematical model size of the original state space (Equation (2)) and the reduced state space (Equation (8)).

4.1 Two Stage Operational Amplifier

Operational Amplifiers (OA) are extensively used in analog circuits applications such as communications and signal conversion. We use the two stage OA, in Figure 4, as an application to prove the effectiveness of the proposed reduction method. Its bias current is provided by a constant current source built by an $NMOS$ transistor and a resistance. The open loop gain of this OA is of the order of $6.6 \cdot 10^5$ at $1 MHz$ operating frequency.

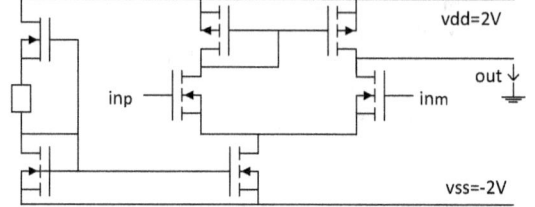

Figure 4: Two Stage Operational Amplifier Circuit

The number of best-fit parameters determined, during the curve-fitting step, is eight, as there are four different types of transistors in this circuit. The curve-fitted model have been validated against the original SPICE simulation traces. Table 1, gives the size of the original and reduced OA mathematical models. The reduced models 1 and 2 in rows 4 and 5 refer to the open loop OA and feedback loop OA configurations, respectively. The open loop OA configuration consists in grounding the negative input and connecting a sinusoidal input source to its positive input. The feedback loop OA configuration consists in connecting a resistance between the output node and the negative input which leads to a limited gain non-inverting OA.

Table 1: Original and Reduced OA Sizes

Original	C_{cut}^{-1}	G_{cut}	$[V; e]$	A_I	$I(e)$
	30×30	30×34	34×1	30×7	7×1
Reduced	R_l	A_l	z	B_l	u
1	27×1	27×27	27×1	27×4	4×1
2	25×1	25×25	25×1	25×4	4×1

The reduction of the feedback loop OA model needed 30 linearization points. However, we used 79 points for an accurate reduction of the open loop OA which can be explained by its very high gain and its strongly nonlinear behavior. This results in a much smaller speedup of the open loop OA as shown in row 2 of Table 2. Table 2, provides also in row 3 and 4 the results for the feedback loop reduced OA models simulations. In this configuration the reduced OA model is accurate and much faster that the OA original model.

Table 2: OA Simulation Results for $(in_p - in_m) = A \cdot \sin(2\pi \cdot f \cdot t)$

A[V]	f[MHz]	Run Time[s]		Speedup	Error [10^{-2}]
		Original	Reduced		
18μ	1	10.93	2.90	3.70	0.02
$45m$	1	142.20	4.13	34.43	0.07
$45m$	0.5	66.51	3.07	21.66	0.01

Figure 5 shows that the reduced and the curve-fitted OA models are accurate compared to the SPICE model.

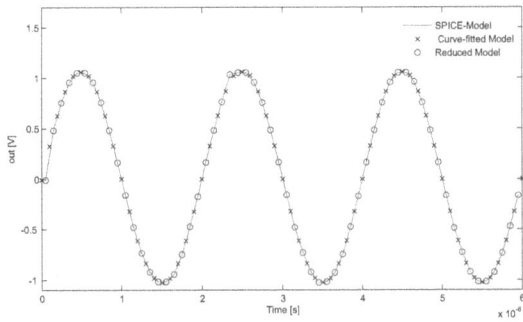

Figure 5: Operational Amplifier Output Signal

4.2 Voltage Controlled Oscillator

The Voltage Controlled Oscillator (VCO) is an ubiquitous circuit used for applications requiring an adaptive clock frequency, such as PLL. It generates a square output voltage with a frequency controlled by its input voltage. We applied our approach to the VCO given in Figure 6. It is implemented as a ring oscillator (central inverters chain $PMOS$ and $NMOS$ transistors) and a large current mirror (upper $PMOS$ and lower $NMOS$ transistors), which limits the current mirrored in each of the ring oscillator inverters. The curve-fitting of the VCO model requires 4 parameters

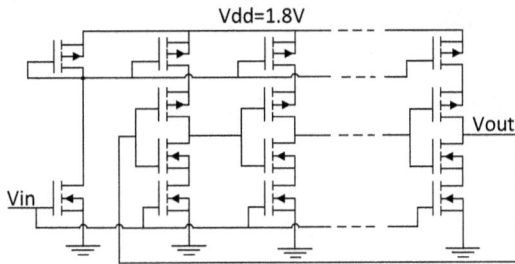

Figure 6: Voltage Controlled oscillator Circuit

for each of the equal size and same type transistors, leading to 16 parameters in total. The size of the original and reduced VCO models are given in Table 3. Table 4 reports the

Table 3: Original and Reduced VCO Sizes

Original	C_{cut}^{-1}	G_{cut}	$[V;e]$	A_I	$I(e)$
	48×48	48×50	50×1	48×62	62×1
Reduced	R_l	A_l	z	B_l	u
	33×1	33×33	33×1	33×2	2×1

different simulations results of the generated reduced VCO model. The reduced VCO model runs 5 times faster than the original VCO model for a reduction of the state variable size from 48 to 33. Reducing further the VCO leads to higher speedup values but requires also an adjusting of the set of linearization points. In all experiments, the accuracy of the reduced VCO model is good compared to the VCO original model. The last row of Table 4 shows also that the reduced VCO model is able to increase its output signal frequency after a step increase in its input frequency. This feature has been enabled because of the input dependent terms, in Equation (8), which makes the reduced models sensitive to small input variations. Figure 7 illustrates the output volt-

Table 4: VCO Simulation Results

Input	Run Time$[s]$		Speedup	Error
$Vin[V]$	Original	Reduced		$[10^{-2}]$
1.2	21.75	2.70	5.85	0.45
1.3	21.49	6.73	3.15	0.28
$step(0.9, 1.1)$	21.72	5.38	4.03	0.23

ages behavior of the reduced VCO model, the curve-fitted model and the SPICE model. It shows that the three models are oscillating at the same frequency for the specified input voltage. The slight deviation from the SPICE simulation traces is mainly due to the accuracy of the curve-fitting step which uses different active device models than that of SPICE.

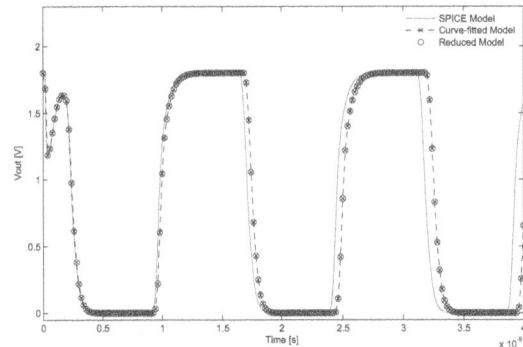

Figure 7: VCO Output Signal

4.3 Frequency Divider

We consider a Frequency Divider (FD) which is a highly nonlinear circuit commonly used for both analog and digital applications. It inputs a signal of a frequency f_{in} and outputs a signal of frequency f_{out}, where $f_{out} = \frac{f_{in}}{n}$ and n is an integer. A typical FD operating frequency ranges from $100MHz$ to $5GHz$. We applied our methodology to reduce

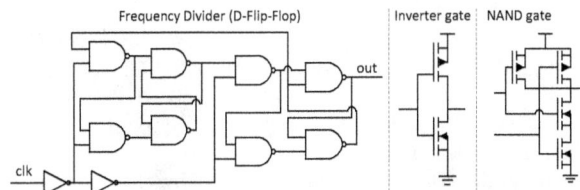

Figure 8: Frequency Divider Circuit

the FD implemented using one D-Flip-Flop (eight NAND gates and two inverters), as detailed in Figure 8. This FD is sensitive to the high flank of the input clock signal and output a rectangle signal whose frequency is half of the input clock frequency. The size of the original and reduced FD models are given in Table 5.

Table 5: Original and Reduced FD Sizes

Original	C_{cut}^{-1}	G_{cut}	$[V;e]$	A_I	$I(e)$
	53×53	53×55	55×1	53×36	36×1
Reduced	R_l	A_l	z	B_l	u
	48×1	48×48	48×1	28×2	2×1

Table 6 summarizes the different simulations performed with the generated reduced FD models for a set of clock frequencies ranging from $0.5GHz$ to $2GHz$. The FD reduced model runs three times faster than the FD original model for a reduction of the state variable size from 53 to 48. The simulation speedup can be increased to higher values by reducing further the state space size and using a sufficient number of linearization points to reproduce the FD behavior at the clock rising and falling edges. Figure 9 shows a snapshot

Table 6: FD Simulation Results

| Frequency | Run Time[s] | | Speedup | Error |
[GHz]	Original	Reduced		[10^{-2}]
2.0	46.80	14.56	3.21	0.18
1.0	43.26	15.08	2.87	0.73
0.5	24.52	7.49	2.90	0.06

of FD simulation results reported in row 3 of Table 6. The input clock has a frequency of $2GHz$ and the FD model output has a frequency of $1GHz$. The reduced FD model is as sensitive to the clock edge as the curve-fitted and SPICE models and its output signal accurately reproduces the main frequency component of the SPICE simulation traces.

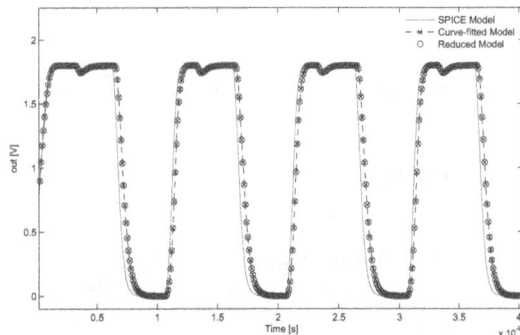

Figure 9: Frequency Divider Output Signal

5. CONCLUSION

In this paper, we proposed an approach to extract reduced analog circuit models using their SPICE simulation traces. The main challenges of the method are the creation of simplified circuit models via a curve-fitting procedure and their reduction using a Krylov space projection method. Guess functions required by the Levenberg-Marquardt curve-fitting algorithm were obtained with the help of MNA and the use of parametric equivalent models for the active devices. The accuracy of the curve-fitted models was measured by comparing them with the original simulation traces. For that reason, these models are intended to be used for the same input and environment conditions as during the initial SPICE simulation. Otherwise, accuracy issues might raise. The curve-fitted differential models of the circuit are linearized at different points of the state space and are reduced locally via Krylov space projections. The application of the method on three different circuits showed that our reduced models are accurate compared to the simulation traces and are faster than their original models. However, to improve the presented method, curve-fitting could be applied in a hierarchical way after subdividing the original circuit model into sub-circuits with a limited number of active

devices. This will reduce the MOR effort and make the method scalable to much larger and complex circuit models. Also, limiting the number of linearization points in each integration time step and using computationally inexpensive weight-functions, which can smooth the model between local regions, can lead to better accuracy and speedup. Finally, to fully automate our methodology, an algorithm has to be implemented for the prediction of the total required linearization points as well as the size of the reduced model based on the information within the simulation traces and the number of nonlinear devices in the circuit netlist.

6. REFERENCES

[1] A. C. Antoulas. *Approximation of Large Scale Dynamical Systems.* Society for Industrial and Applied Mathematic, 2005.

[2] H. Aridhi, M. H. Zaki, and S. Tahar. Towards Improving Simulation of Analog Circuits Using Model Order Reduction. *IEEE/ACM Design Automation and Test in Europe,* pages 1337–1342, 2012.

[3] I. B. Aris, L. N. Hulley, N. B. Mariun, and R. K. Z. Sahbudin. Using Curve-Fitting Optimisation Technique to Estimate Power MOSFET Model Parameters for PECT II System. *IEEE International Conference on Semiconductor Electronics,* pages 157–161, 1998.

[4] Y. Chen. Model Order Reduction for Nonlinear Systems. M.s. thesis, Massachusetts Institute for Technology, United States, 1999.

[5] J. D'Errico. Adaptive Robust Numerical Differentiation. Technical report, MATLAB Central, 2013.

[6] C. Desoer and E. Kuh. *Basic Circuit Theory.* McGraw-Hill Education, 2009.

[7] N. Dongi and J. Roychowdhury. General-Purpose Nonlinear Model-Order Reduction Using Piecewise-Polynomial Representations. *IEEE Transactions on Computer Aided Design of Integrated Circuits and Systems,* 27(2):649 – 654, 2008.

[8] C. Gu. *Model Order Reduction of Nonlinear Dynamical Systems.* PhD thesis, EECS Department, University of California, Berkeley, United States, 2012.

[9] D. W. Harder. Numerical Analysis, 5.1 Vandermonde. Technical report, University of Waterloo, 2013.

[10] A. Kumar and A. P. Singh. Neural Network based Fault Diagnosis in Analog Electronic Circuit using Polynomial Curve Fitting. *International Journal of Computer Applications,* 61(16):28–34, 2013.

[11] C. C. Kuo, M. Y. Kuo, and M. S. Kuo. Modeling of Capacitors and Nonlinear Inductors using Piecewise Curve Fitting Technique. In *IEEE Computers in Power Electronics,* pages 133–138, 1994.

[12] MATLAB. Documentation Center, December 2013.

[13] M. Rewienski and J. White. A Trajectory Piecewise-Linear Approach to Model Order Reduction and Fast Simulation of Nonlinear Circuits and Micromachined Devices. *IEEE Transactions on Computer-Aided Design of Integrated Circuits and Systems,* 22(2):155–170, 2003.

[14] W. Schilders, H. V. D. Horst, and J. Rommes. *Model Order Reduction: Theory, Research Aspects and Applications.* Springer, 2008.

A Novel Mixed-Signal Self-Calibration Technique for Baseband Filters in Systems-on-Chip Mobile Transceivers

Yongsuk Choi and Yong-Bin Kim [*]
Northeastern University
360 Huntington Ave.
Boston, United States

ABSTRACT

This paper presents a novel digitally-assisted automatic frequency tuning technique, and the self calibration technique is verified for a 130nm CMOS 4-th order biquad baseband low-pass filter case with 20MHz cut-off frequency, which satisfies the typical LTE receiver specifications. The proposed tuning method includes hardware reduction methods, coherent sampling, and magnitude calculator using 'alpha max plus beta min' algorithm for significant chip area reduction with negligible accuracy degradation. The cut-off frequency turns out to be tunable in the range of 16.2MHz to 24.4MHz, and the tuning error is less than 0.4% over the whole frequency tuning range. The estimated area consumption is $0.027mm^2$ with 80% device density, and power dissipation is 0.16mW at 128MHz clock speed with a 1.2V supply voltage.

Categories and Subject Descriptors

B.7.1 [**Integrated Circuits**]: Types and Design Styles—*Algorithms implemented in hardware, VLSI*; B.7.3 [**Integrated Circuits**]: Reliability and Testing—*Built-in tests*; B.8 [**Performance and Reliability**]: General

Keywords

Analog/mixed-signal Testing; Built-in Calibration (BIC); Digitally Assisted Calibration; Off-line Testing Technique

1. INTRODUCTION

Taking advantage of continuous advances in the integrated CMOS technology, systems-on-chip (SoC) designs that include analog mixed-signal (AMS) circuits are widely used.

[*]The authors are with the Department of Electrical and Computer Engineering, Northeastern University, Massachusetts, USA (e-mail: ychoi@ece.neu.edu; ybk@ece.neu.edu).

At the same time, their applications in communications, signal processing, and embedded systems are also increasing. As higher specifications are required for analog circuits due to new applications, the performance of the circuits has kept improving. Nevertheless, the analog circuits still suffer from process variations, and performance-tuning is required after fabrication to increase yield and to maintain the high performance. Therefore, testing the integrated circuits is becoming increasingly complicated and costly [1].

Conventionally, one of the low-cost testing solutions is automated test equipment (ATE) and device interface boards (DIBs). The most common way is to use an AMS ATE tester with an analog DIB [17]. However, the tester needs to have much better performance than the circuits under test (CUTs) in terms of accuracy, speed and noise. In addition, DIBs should be designed carefully, considering the CUT. Therefore, it is a challenging and time consuming work. As another possible solution, digitally-assisted calibration of analog integrated circuits is gaining popularity. The on-chip built-in calibration (BIC) turns out to be an effective solution to reduce test time and cost, to improve test accuracy, and to eliminate the necessity of the external test equipment. Existing digitally-assisted analog circuit calibration and recovery mechanisms include gain and linearity tuning of low-noise amplifies [11], second-order nonlinearity and mismatch correction for mixers [5] as well as linearity enhancements for baseband filters [14].

However, the analog BIC techniques used to be challenging because data converters (ADCs) and digital signal processing (DSP) resources such as fast Fourier transform (FFT) engines are required for accurate analysis in frequency domain and tuning of analog circuits. This makes the BIC approach unrealistic due to power and silicon area overhead. In SoC designs, these blocks are embedded in a single chip. In the example of the 4G LTE standard transceivers, which adopts an orthogonal frequency-division multiple access (OFDMA) scheme, a 2048-points FFT is used in 20MHz channel bandwidth [16]. Also, a 12-bit ADC with 65-MSPS sampling speed can be used. It also includes RF front-end blocks such as LNAs, mixers and analog filters with digital resources for the built-in calibration such as FFT engines and ADCs. In [10, 6], calibration methods have been proposed, which incorporate existing ADC and DSP resources to directly quantize the output signals of the analog circuits for computation of the FFT and automatic tuning with DAC. These methods provide not only a solution to minimize hardware complexity and silicon area but also to maintain analog circuit performance by off-line tuning mechanisms. In this paper, a performance tuning algorithm with minimally embedded hardwares is focused.

In the LTE transceiver, the analog baseband channel filter is responsible for adjacent channel selectivity, anti-aliasing and dynamic range maximization [12]. A channel filter with low input-referred noise (IRN) and high linearity is important for the performance of the whole RF front-end. In terms of the channel selectivity, adjusting the cut-off frequency is essential. A robust, accurate, reliable and low-cost automatic tuning technique for fine tuning of the analog baseband filter's cut-off frequency is proposed. This paper includes the control circuit design of the tuning algorithm and the calculation block circuit implementation for the magnitudes of FFT engine's complex number outputs.

2. PROPOSED FREQUENCY TUNING TECHNIQUE FOR CONTINUOUS-TIME FILTERS

2.1 Principle of Proposed Algorithm

In general, the cut-off frequency in a low-pass filter is defined as a boundary between a passband and a stopband. In the filter response, it is the frequency at which the output power has dropped to half of the nominal passband value. This occurs when the output voltage level dropps by

$$1/\sqrt{2} \quad \text{or} \quad 20\log(\frac{1}{\sqrt{2}}) \cong \text{-3dB} \qquad (1)$$

from the passband value. Therefore, if the power level or the voltage level of the filter output in the passband and the desired cut-off frequency can be compared, it is possible to tune the cut-off frequency of the low-pass filter.

To precisely measure and compare the peak voltage amplitude of the filter output at specific frequencies, the analysis region has to be converted from time domain to frequency domain. Although there are several methods to measure the peak voltage amplitude [9, 7], they are limited by signal harmonics and ripples, which leads to less accuracy when measuring the voltage amplitude in the transient domain because of noise and interference signals. Therefore, the desired signal should be separated from them in order to extract accurate information.

Transformation is used to convert a time domain function to a frequency domain function and vice versa. The most common time-to-frequency transformation for this purpose is the Fourier transformation. Since analyzing sinusoidal functions is easier than analyzing general-shaped functions, this method is very useful and widely used. Theoretically, the Fourier transformation is used to convert a signal of any shape into a sum of infinite number of sinusoidal waves. However, implementation and size of the Fast Fourier Transformation (FFT) engine is related to its resolution and the number of high-order harmonics of interest. Our research group developed a sampling technique to reduce the required size of the FFT for spectrum analysis with negligible accuracy degradation, which is introduced [8]. The reduced size of FFT engine is used in this work. The size of FFT in current transceivers is generally 512 to 2048 points in different channel bandwidth [16], but a 64 points FFT is selected in this research using the coherent sampling technique.

Frequency spectrum analysis can be realized by utilizing the existing resources on a transceiver chip, such as the ADC

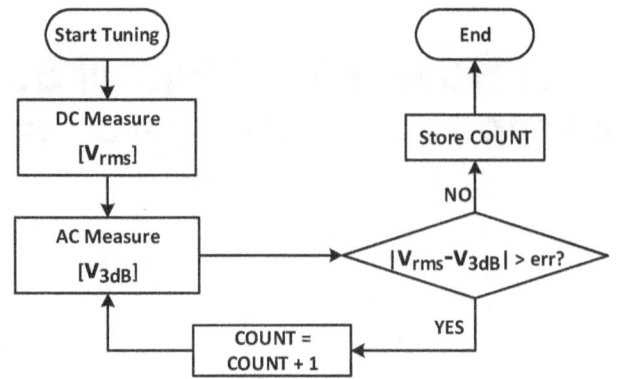

Figure 1: Conceptual flowchart of cut-off frequency tuning

and FFT engine for quantization of the filter output signal and frequency analysis. It is possible to adjust the cut-off frequency of the filter by analyzing and comparing the frequency domain information.

The conceptual flow chart of cut-off frequency tuning is shown in Figure 1, and the detailed algorithm will be discussed in the next Section.

2.2 Tuning Algorithm

A block diagram of the proposed frequency tuning algorithm is shown in Figure 2, which includes external equipment such as the clock generator and the sinusoidal signal generator. The AC source is a sine wave signal generator as an input signal to the low-pass filter. It generates the desired frequency to be tuned, cut-off frequency of the filter, and a low frequency sine wave signal which has negligible power loss from the DC power level. The low frequency sine wave signal is used as a DC measurement input source because the actual DC voltage is for a circuit biasing (not for an input testing tone).

Once the tuning mode is turned on, the DC measurement mode is turned on to start measurement of the filter output at the passband. The filter input node is disconnected from the previous stage, and connected to the tuning blocks.

In addition, two different clock frequencies are needed for each of the DC and AC measurement mode. The clock period used in the DC measurement mode is chosen as an integer multiple to simplify the clock divider circuit. Therefore, the clock signal is passed to the clock divider which provides a divide-by-8 signal from the input reference clock. It is used as a clock signal for the ADC and digital blocks through the multiplexer.

The digitized output of the ADC is passed to the input nodes of the FFT block to analyze the filter output in the frequency domain. Since the FFT outputs are complex numbers, consisting of real and imaginary values, the magnitudes of the complex numbers have to be calculated to compare their voltage levels at certain discrete frequencies (called as FFT bins). The calculated DC value is stored in the register and compared continuoulsy with the results from the AC measurement mode after the AC measurement mode is turned on.

In the AC measurement mode, the array switch controls a capacitor array of the low-pass filter circuit and changes the capacitor value that affects the cut-off frequency of the

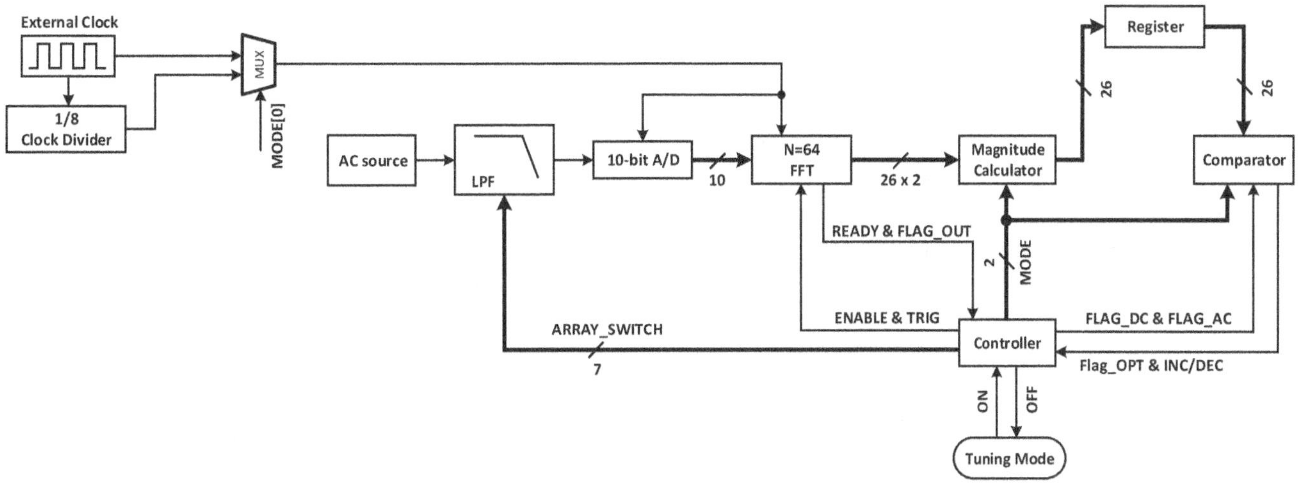

Figure 2: Block diagram of the proposed cut-off frequency tuning algorithm (bold lines - buses with multiple bits)

filter. In the next step, the magnitude in the AC measurement mode is calculated again in the same way, and those two values are compared at the comparator block. The output signals of the comparator block indicate that the AC value is smaller or larger than the RMS of DC value. If the comparator result converges within a specified range, it sends a signal to the controller. Then the controller informs that the filter is optimized and the tuning flow will stop. Otherwise, if all the capacitor array combinations cannot meet the accuracy requirement, the least difference value is stored in the register and it will be adopted at the end of the tuning mode.

3. HARDWARE REDUCTION TECHNIQUE

Additional technical challenges as well as significant increase in cost are incurred when estimating the voltage amplitude at radio frequencies. However, cost effective and computationally inexpensive techniques are used based on mathematical analysis, proper frequency selection, and formulation of appropriate algorithms. Two efficient methods, coherent sampling and 'alpha max plus beta min' algorithm, are addressed in this section.

3.1 Coherent Sampling of FFT

Coherent sampling is a useful and efficient technique to evaluate the spectral performance of analog/mixed signal circuits [2, 3] because it increases the FFT accuracy and eliminates the need for a window function if certain conditions are met. Coherent sampling of a single tone assures that its power in the spectrum is contained in exactly one frequency bin. The condition for coherent sampling is given as

$$\frac{f_{1^{st}\text{bin}}}{f_{sample}} = \frac{N_{cycle}}{\text{NFFT}} \quad (2)$$

where $f_{1^{st}\text{bin}}$ is the fundamental frequency bin after the DC value, f_{sample} is the sampling frequency, N_{cycle} is the integer number of cycles of the signal to be sampled, and NFFT is the length of the FFT engine.

To ensure coherent sampling, one should first determine the number (usually a prime number) of integer cycles (N_{cycle})

that fits into the predefined sampling window, and use it to approximate the input frequency to the near optimal frequency that exactly matches with one of the discrete frequency bins in the spectrum for the given FFT length [4]. Under the condition in equation (2), there will not be any leakage because the coherent sampling guarantees an exact integer number of input signal cycles.

In the proposed algorithm, 64 is used as the NFFT and one cycle is taken for the sampling window. The sampling frequency (f_{sample}) is different in the DC and AC measurements. For the DC measurement mode, 125KHz is taken as the first bin ($f_{1^{st}\text{bin}}$), resulting in the $f_{sample} = 16$MHz. In the AC measurement mode, the 10-th frequency bin is selected such that the $f_{sample} = 128$MHz with $f_{1^{st}\text{bin}} = 2$MHz can be used.

3.2 Implementation of Magnitude Calculator

The key elements of the proposed tuning algorithm shown in Figure 2 are the magnitude calculator and digital calibration control. In the tuning block, the FFT engine produces a complex output, $Z(Re, Im)$ consisting of real and imaginary parts represented by Re and Im, respectively. The mathematical way of calculating the magnitude of a complex number requires an adder, a multiplier, and a square root operation as defined by

$$Magnitude\{Z\} = \sqrt{Re^2 + Im^2}. \quad (3)$$

The real and the imaginary parts themselves at the output of the FFT engine are less meaningful as the power level of the spectral components are calculated based on the equation (2). In order to determine the power level of the spectral components, it is required to calculate the magnitude of the each spectral component. To achieve the desired measurement accuracy, the numbers are usually represented in fixed-point or in floating-point notation which poses a significant area and power overhead for on-chip estimation of the magnitudes. Therefore, the traditional way to extract the power spectrum from the FFT output is to transfer the numbers generated at the FFT output to the off-chip resources such as PC and to exploit mathematical tools to calculate the power spectrum. However these approaches are very in-

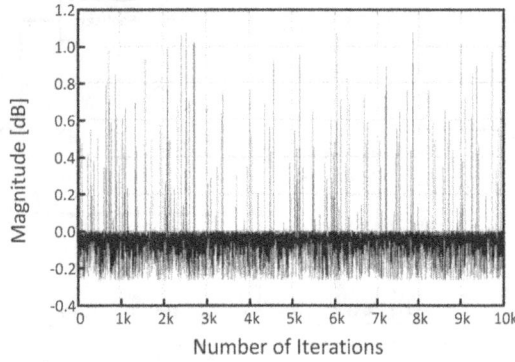

Figure 3: Error in the approximated magnitude

efficient and put limits on on-chip built-in-calibration (BIC) and built-in-test (BIT) approaches where it is critical to obtain an estimation of the spectral characteristics for dynamic tuning of the circuit under test (CUT).

An alternative way to determine the magnitude of a complex number based on the 'alpha max plus beta min' algorithm is adopted and is defined in [13]:

$$Magnitude\{Z\} \cong \alpha \cdot max(|Re|, |Im|) + \beta \cdot min(|Re|, |Im|), \quad (4)$$

where $max(|Re|, |Im|)$ and $min(|Re|, |Im|)$ represent the maximum and the minimum absolute values of the real and imaginary parts, respectively. The approach represented by equation (4) is a linear approximation of the magnitude of a complex number. The above approximation is simple and can be efficiently implemented for on-chip estimation of the magnitude.

In terms of implementation, the absolute values (| |) are easily calculated by just dropping sign bits or bit conversion. Both the $max(|Re|, |Im|)$ and $min(|Re|, |Im|)$ calculations can be done with one comparison. However, the two coefficients, α and β are introduced in the approximation. They can be determined depending on the desired accuracy, and other performance parameters such as area, power and the available computational resources. From MATLAB simulation results, the coefficients are determined to achieve good accuracy in this research. In the simulation, the α and β are randomly generated from a Gaussian distribution with different mean and standard deviation, and the error introduced by the approximation is estimated. The error introduced by the equation (4) is around 1dB, which is shown in Figure 3 with 10K samples superimposed on the actual magnitude with $\alpha = 1$ and $\beta = 1/4$. The coefficient values help to reduce the count of the fixed point-point multiplication, allowing the binary calculation (divide by 2^2) to be simply and efficiently implemented by a bit-shift operation.

4. SIMULATION RESULTS

The proposed tuning algorithm have been simulated with a reference filter. A reference fourth-order Bessel baseband filter satisfying typical LTE receiver specifications has been designed as a cascade of two single-branch cells. The filter with 20MHz corner frequency is displayed in Figure 4. A 130nm standard CMOS technology was used to design with a supply voltage of 1.2 V. All the transistors are designed with $0.5\mu m$ (non-minimum) channel length to reduce output impedance effects. The first stage is composed of PMOS

transistors and the second stage is designed with NMOS transistors. Equation (5) is in terms of the transconductance, where the output conductance of transistors are not ignored:

$$\begin{cases} \omega_0 = 2 \cdot \pi \cdot f_0 = \dfrac{g_m}{\sqrt{C_1 \cdot C_2}} \\ Q = \sqrt{\dfrac{C_2}{C_1}} \\ |K| = 1 \end{cases} \quad (5)$$

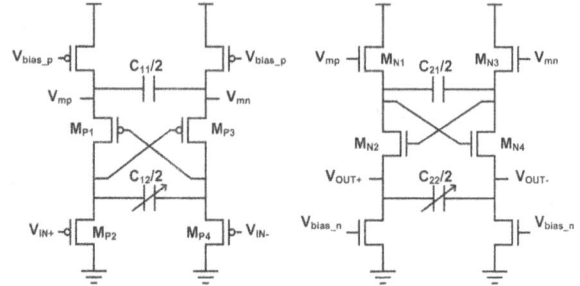

Figure 4: Fourth-order filter schematic

All filter parameters are listed in Table 1. The parameters for the first cell are for the biquad cell on left side in Figure 4, and the bottom half of the table presents the biquad cell design with NMOS transistors (on the right side in Figure 4). The simulation results are summarized in Table 2 for the filter performance parameters such as loop stability, noise and linearity.

4.1 Capacitor Array Design

The cut-off frequency of the filter is tuned by changing the capacitors C_{12} and C_{22} in Figure 4. The fixed capacitor corresponds to 20MHz bandwidth of the filter. To achieve 50% of tuning range, from 15MHz to 25MHz, a 7-bit capacitor array was designed, which is visualized in Figure 5. The capacitance is increased and hence the filter bandwidth is reduced from equation (5) by switching the binary-weighted unit capacitors (C_ks). C_1 is the minimum unit capacitor with 80 fF and the other capacitance are set as $C_k = 2^k \cdot C_1$.

In principle, all of the capacitors in the filter could be implemented with four parallel capacitor matrices. However, this would lead to a large chip area. Therefore, the design

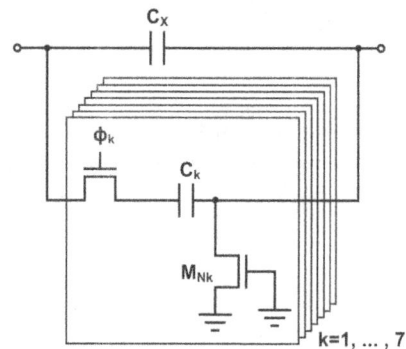

Figure 5: Implementation of a 7-bit binary-weighted capacitor array

Table 1: Biquad filter parameters

		g_m [mA/V]	g_{mb} [mA/V]	$C_{n1}/2$	$C_{n2}/2$	Q	f_0
1st cell	M_{P1}, M_{P3}	2.0	0.35	5.5 pF	19.2 pF	0.54	19.5 MHz
	M_{P2}, M_{P4}	2.0	0.27				
2nd cell	M_{N1}, M_{N3}	2.0	0.26	6.1 pF	11.2 pF	0.74	24.2 MHz
	M_{N2}, M_{N4}	2.0	0.33				

Table 2: Summary of the filter parameter

Technology	CMOS 130 nm
Power supply	1.2 V
Current consumption	0.427 mA
Power consumption	0.513 mW
DC gain	-5.8 dB
f_{-3dB}	19.6 MHz
f_{-3dB} tuning range	16.2 - 24.4 MHz
Input Referred Noise	11.86 nV/$\sqrt{Hz}$
in-band IIP3 (f_1, f_2 = 10, 11 MHz)	23 dBm
1dB compression point	4.46 dBm

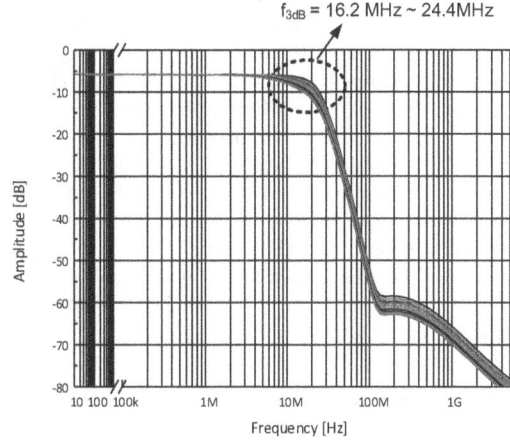

Figure 6: Magnitude responses of the filter for different capacitor array settings

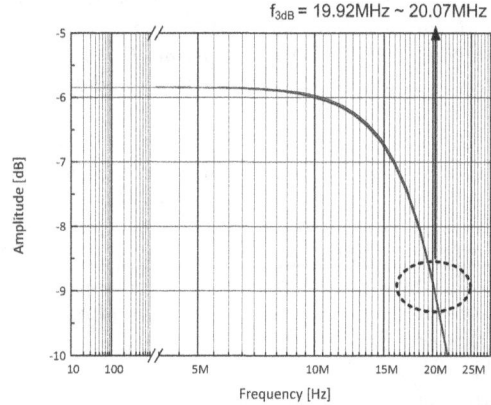

Figure 7: Simulation results of magnitude responses after tuning

was finalized to minimize the number of capacitors and the area by merging the separate capacitor arrays. In the final design, the frequency response is tuned with 7-bit binary-weighted switched-capacitor matrices and the default value is C_X in parallel with C_7 (C_k=0 for k=1 to 6). During the phase ϕ_k, the capacitor C_k is connected to the fixed capacitor C_X in parallel. On the other hand, in the phase $\overline{\phi_k}$, the C_k is disconnected from the C_X and the transistor M_{Nk} is used to avoid charge accumulation [15]. The implementation of the small unit capacitors demanded careful layout design in order to minimize the parasitic capacitance.

4.2 Simulation Results for the Closed-Loop Tuning Algorithm

The simulated AC frequency responses with different capacitor array settings are shown in Figure 6. The initial cut-off frequency of the filter is set in a range of 16.2MHz to 24.4MHz. The simulation results of the magnitude responses after the automatic tuning is shown in Figure 7. The cut-off frequency of the low-pass filter is tuned between 19.92MHz to 20.07MHz.

This corresponds to 0.4% tuning error with 50μs of typical tuning time at 16MHz of reference clock speed for DC measurement mode and 128MHz for AC measurement mode, respectively. All digital blocks are implemented in verilog-HDL and synthesized to the gate level netlist using 130nm standard CMOS technology PDK. The generated gate level netlist was ported to the place and route tool to complete the physical layout of the digital blocks and to evaluate the overall area and power requirements. The layout of these blocks are displayed in Figure 8. The estimated area consumption is 0.027mm^2 with 80% device density, and power dissipation for the 128MHz clock speed (with 1.2V supply voltage) is 0.16mW.

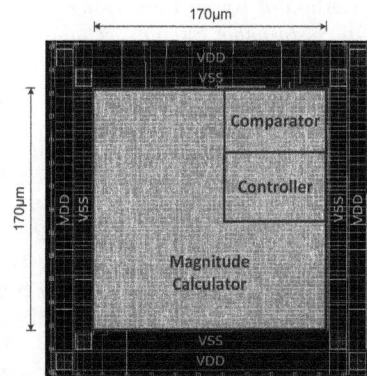

Figure 8: Layout of tuning blocks

5. CONCLUSIONS

A digitally assisted on-chip built-in self-calibration algorithm for cut-off frequency tuning of baseband filters was proposed. This method uses the relationship between the power values at the DC and at cut-off frequency. It has an advantage of using the existing DSP engines to achieve hardware complexity minimization and the high tuning accuracy. To verify the tuning algorithm, a 4-th order source-follower based biquad filter was used as a reference baseband low-pass filter. The analog continuous filter with 20MHz cut-off frequency for a standard LTE analog front-end application has been designed using 130nm standard CMOS technology at 1.2V supply voltage. Its 3dB frequency tuning range is from 16.2MHz to 24.4MHz. The frequency of the filter was changed with a 7-bit binary weighted capacitor array.

A digital controller and tuning blocks were synthesized and implemented. The estimated area is 0.027 mm^2 with 80% placement density, and the estimated total power consumption with a 128MHz clock speed is 0.16mW. The simulation results show that the errors of the automatic frequency tuning algorithm are within 0.4%.

6. REFERENCES

[1] *International Technology Roadmap for Semiconductors*, 2012. [Online]. Available: http://public.itrs.net/.

[2] *IEEE Standard for Digitizing Waveform Recorders.* IEEE Standard 1057−2007, Apr. 2008.

[3] *IEEE Standard for Terminology and Test Methods for Analog to Digital Converters.* IEEE Standard 1241−2010, Jan. 2011.

[4] J. J. Blair. Selecting Test Frequencies for Sinewave Tests of ADCs. In *Instrumentation and Measurement Technology Conference, 2002. IMTC/2002. Proceedings of the 19th IEEE*, volume 1, pages 189–193 vol.1, 2002.

[5] C.-H. Chang and M. Onabajo. IIP3 Enhancement of Subthreshold Active Mixers. *Circuits and Systems II: Express Briefs, IEEE Transactions on*, 60(11):731–735, 2013.

[6] H.-M. Chang, M.-S. Lin, and K.-T. Cheng. Digitally-Assisted Analog/RF Testing for Mixed-Signal SoCs. In *Asian Test Symposium, 2008. ATS '08. 17th*, pages 43–48, 2008.

[7] S. Change, X. Yan, Q. Zhang, H. Liu, H. Zhao, and L. Li. A Method of Rapid Detection of the Grid Voltage. In *Sustainable Energy Technologies (ICSET), 2012 IEEE Third International Conference on*, pages 426–431, 2012.

[8] H. Chauhan, Y. Choi, M. Onabajo, I.-S. Jung, and Y.-B. Kim. Accurate and efficient on-chip spectral analysis for built-in testing and calibration approaches. *Very Large Scale Integration (VLSI) Systems, IEEE Transactions on*, 22(3):497–506, March 2014.

[9] H.-Y. Chu, H.-L. Jou, and C.-L. Huang. Transient Response of a Peak Voltage Detector for Sinusoidal Signals. *Industrial Electronics, IEEE Transactions on*, 39(1):74–79, 1992.

[10] D. Han, B.-S. Kim, and A. Chatterjee. DSP-Driven Self-Tuning of RF Circuits for Process-Induced Performance Variability. *Very Large Scale Integration (VLSI) Systems, IEEE Transactions on*, 18(2):305–314, 2010.

[11] C. hsiang Chang and M. Onabajo. Linearization of subthreshold low-noise amplifiers. In *Circuits and Systems (ISCAS), 2013 IEEE International Symposium on*, pages 377–380, 2013.

[12] D. Kaczman, M. Shah, M. Alam, M. Rachedine, D. Cashen, L. Han, and A. Raghavan. A Single-Chip 10-Band WCDMA/HSDPA 4-Band GSM/EDGE SAW-less CMOS Receiver With DigRF 3G Interface and + 90 dBm IIP2. *Solid-State Circuits, IEEE Journal of*, 44(3):718–739, 2009.

[13] R. G. Lyons. *Understanding Digital Signal Processing.* 3rd Edition: Prentice Hall, 2010.

[14] M. Mobarak, M. Onabajo, J. Silva-Martinez, and E. Sanchez-Sinencio. Attenuation-Predistortion Linearization of CMOS OTAs With Digital Correction of Process Variations in OTA-C Filter Applications. *Solid-State Circuits, IEEE Journal of*, 45(2):351–367, 2010.

[15] J. Ryynaı̀Lnen, M. Hotti, V. Saari, J. Jussila, A. Malinen, L. Sumanen, T. Tikka, and K. Halonen. WCDMA Multicarrier Receiver for Base-Station Applications. In *Solid-State Circuits Conference, 2005. ESSCIRC 2005. Proceedings of the 31st European*, pages 515–518, 2005.

[16] M. Suarez and O. Zlydareva. LTE transceiver performance analysis in Uplink under various environmental conditions. In *Ultra Modern Telecommunications and Control Systems and Workshops (ICUMT), 2012 4th International Congress on*, pages 84–88, 2012.

[17] H. Xing, H. Jiang, D. Chen, and R. Geiger. High-resolution adc linearity testing using a fully digital-compatible bist strategy. *Instrumentation and Measurement, IEEE Transactions on*, 58(8):2697–2705, Aug 2009.

A Qualitative Simulation Approach for Verifying PLL Locking Property

Ibtissem Seghaier, Henda Aridhi, Mohamed H. Zaki, and Sofiène Tahar
Dept. of Electrical and Computer Engineering, Concordia University, Montréal, Québec, Canada
{seghaier, h_aridh, mzaki, tahar}@ece.concordia.ca

ABSTRACT

Simulation cannot give a full coverage of Phase Locked Loop (PLL) behavior in presence of process variation, jitter and varying initial conditions. Qualitative Simulation is an attracting method that computes behavior envelopes for dynamical systems over continuous ranges of their parameters. Therefore, this method can be employed to verify PLLs locking property given a model that encompasses their imperfections. Extended System of Recurrence Equations (ESREs) offer a unified modeling language to model analog and digital PLLs components. In this paper, an ESRE model is created for both PLLs and their imperfections. Then, a modified qualitative simulation algorithm is used to guarantee that the PLL locking time is sound for every possible initial condition and parameter value. We used our approach to analyze a Charge Pump-PLL for a $0.18\mu m$ fabrication process and in the presence of jitter and initial conditions uncertainties. The obtained results show an improvement of simulation coverage by computing the minimum locking time and predicting a non locking case that statistical simulation technique fails to detect.

Categories and Subject Descriptors

B.7.2 [**Integrated Circuits**]: Design Aids—*Verification, Simulation*

Keywords

PLL; ESRE; Qualitative Simulation

1. INTRODUCTION

The verification of Analog and Mixed Signal (AMS) designs is challenging and time-consuming because of their infinite state space, the fundamental differences of their digital and analog components operating modes, and their sensitivity to initial conditions uncertainties, process variation, device jitter and noise [5]. Phase Locked Loops (PLLs) are one of the basic and widely used AMS circuits in modern electronic systems. They are used as modulators and demodulators in wireless systems, frequency synthesizer in communication systems, and clock-acquisition in high-speed links. Several research activities have been done to model PLLs at high abstraction levels [3, 7, 13] in order to identify their functional errors at early design stages. These abstracted models offer a good accuracy and can serve as a reference to check the behavior of the device level PLL implementation. The required time for PLLs to lock is a key property in their verification. Typically, numerical simulation techniques are conducted to check the PLL locking for a finite number of initial conditions and parameters values. However, simulation cannot guarantee that there are no other possible initial conditions and parameters values that can derive the PLL into unlocking. In order to overcome this verification coverage shortcoming, the circuit should be verified for entire intervals of possible initial conditions and parameter values. Qualitative Simulation is a method for the simulation of continuous dynamical systems whose parameters and/or initial conditions are modeled by fuzzy distributions [10]. Interestingly, this method provides a phase space representation of dynamical model sensitivity to parameters which can be used to verify PLL locking property.

In this paper, a new modeling and verification methodology for PLL designs is proposed. The PLL design is described in terms of Extended System of Recurrence Equations (ESREs) (to be mathematically defined later). These equations offer a unified language to describe both analog and digital blocks of PLLs as functions of the preceding state variables terms. Moreover, Extended SREs offer a means of modeling more abstracted designs which significantly speed up the verification execution time. Our ESRE PLL models include the effect of accumulating and synchronous jitter as well as process variation. The Qualitative Simulation algorithm proposed in [10] has been reformulated for the case of discrete models expressed using ESREs to enable the verification of PLL locking behavior over entire ranges of initial conditions and parameter values. To illustrate the use of our methodology, we study the lock time property of a third order dual path charge pump PLL. The obtained results show that we can predict unlocking corner cases which cannot be determined via nominal parameters simulation nor statistical simulation.

The rest of the paper is organized as follows: related work is discussed in Section 2. Then, Section 3 provides an overview of the proposed methodology. After that, we report experimental results for the analysis of the lock time

GLSVLSI'14, May 21–23, 2014, Houston, TX, USA.
Copyright 2014 ACM 978-1-4503-2816-6/14/05$15.00.
http://dx.doi.org/10.1145/2591513.2591593.

of a third order dual path charge pump PLL in Section 4. Finally, the concluding Section 5 summarizes the contributions of this paper and provides future work.

2. RELATED WORK

Simulation based techniques provide an insight of the circuit behavior only for particular values of parameters and initial conditions. Therefore, they suffer from uncertainty about verification coverage. Indeed, running multiple simulations cannot guarantee the absence of corner cases where the subject property is not satisfied [4]. To improve the coverage of analog circuits state space, the authors in [12] proposed an algorithm that guides the input stimuli but falls short to address the effect of Process Variation (PV). In [9], the PLL is modeled using Stochastic Differential Equations (SDE). Then, it is verified using a statistical runtime verification approach that combines Monte Carlo/Bootstrap techniques with hypothesis testing. The accuracy of the verification technique is directly related to the confidence level which depends on the number of simulation runs [9]. In addition, this technique introduces randomness in the simulation but fails to cover all possible design behaviors.

The use of formal methods is another paradigm that has been adopted by many researchers [15]. For instance, an equivalence checking formal technique has been used in [11] where the authors verify the equivalence of a Verilog AMS PLL behavioral model against its Spectre netlist electrical implementation for a limited set of input conditions and without imperfections. In [14], the authors proposed a method for reachability analysis of AMS designs, such as sigma delta converters, using Taylor approximations and interval arithmetic. However, this method suffers from dependency and wrapping effect problems. In [3], a reachability analysis technique has been proposed to verify the locking of a PLL circuit (which we intend to also verify in this paper) under parameters and initial condition variations. Taylor approximation was used to model the PLL design and a method called continuization was proposed to over-approximate the reachable state based on a geometrical representation namely polyhedra in the multidimensional space. This technique has the following shortcomings: first, it does not consider jitter which is the major concern in the locking of PLLs [2]. Second, their proposed model and algorithm are not scalable to handle other PLL designs.

3. PROPOSED METHODOLOGY

An overview of our proposed methodology for modeling and verifying PLL designs is depicted in Figure 1. This methodology can be split into two main phases: a modeling phase that results in an ESRE model including process variation and two different jitter models and a Qualitative Simulation based verification which assess the effect of PLLs imperfections on its locking time. We have implemented this methodology using the numerical computation environment MATLAB.

3.1 Modeling Phase

PLL designs contain both analog and digital modules that are interconnected and interrelated. Hence, it is not appropriate to model these modules separately. Therefore, we have to describe the continuous (analog) signal and the discrete (digital) signal using the same language in order to

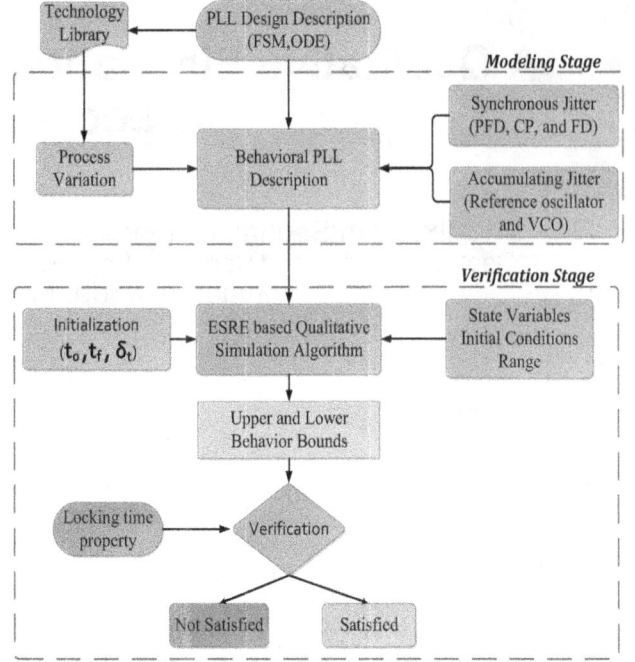

Figure 1: PLL Modeling and Verification Methodology

exhibit the interrelationships between the two. The behavior of analog circuits can be mathematically modeled by Ordinary Differential Equations (ODEs). Since a close-form solution for these ODEs is not always obtained, a numerical approximation is needed. Using System of Recurrence Equations (SREs) [1], it will be possible to handle continuous behaviors like that of currents and voltages in discrete time intervals which can be done for a non-trivial class of analog circuits. An SRE is a set of relations between consecutive elements of a sequence. It is mathematically defined as a system consisting of a set of equations of the form:

$$x_i(n_t) = f_i(x_j(n_t - \delta)), \forall n_t \in \mathbb{Z} \qquad (1)$$

where $x_i(n_t) \in \mathbb{R}$ is a state variable with $i, j \in 1, .., k$ and $n_t \in \mathbb{Z}$, and $\delta \in \mathbb{N}$ represents the delay. On the other hand, digital designs are described using various frameworks such as Finite State Machines and Petri nets. To alleviate the modeling gap between the digital and analog models, we use the notion of Extended SRE (ESRE) for interleaving the two [1]. ESREs offer a means of modeling more abstracted PLL designs which will significantly speed up the verification execution time. In [1], the authors define the notion of ESREs: *"Generalized If-formula is a class of expressions that extend SREs to describe digital systems"*. Mathematically, it is defined as follows: let $\mathbb{K}$ be a numerical domain ($\mathbb{B}, \mathbb{N}, \mathbb{Z}, \mathbb{Q}$ or $\mathbb{R}$), a *generalized If-formula* is one of the followings:

- A variable $x_i(n)$ or a constant $C \in \mathbb{K}$.
- Any arithmetic operation $\Diamond \in (+, -, \times, \div)$ between variables $x_i(n) \in \mathbb{K}$.
- A logical formula: any expression constructed using a set of variables $x_i(n) \in \mathbb{B}$ and logical operators : not, or, and, nand, nor, etc.
- A comparison formula: any expression constructed using a set of $x_i(n) \in K$ and comparison operators $\alpha \in (<, =, >, <>)$.

- An expression $If(x, y, z)$, where x is a logical formula or a comparison formula and y, z are any generalized If-formula. Here, $If(x, y, z) : \mathbb{B} \times \mathbb{K} \times \mathbb{K} \to \mathbb{K}$ satisfies the axioms:

$$If(True, x, y) = x$$
$$If(False, x, y) = y$$

To accommodate the imprecise nature of PLL designs, design imperfections will be taken into account and will be considered as an integral part of the design modeling method. As a next step, we append to the generated PLL ESRE model two imperfections effect. The process variation due to $0.18\mu m$ process [8] and the jitter (a.k.a phase noise). Depending on the fabrication technology and the circuit configuration, we include process variation in some or all circuit components. We assume that the parameter values adhere to a Gaussian distribution with mean equal to their nominal values and a standard error σ equal to the deviation percentage extracted from the technology library.

As characterized by Kundert in [6], there are two types of jitter that impact the locking property of PLLs: synchronous jitter exhibited by driven blocks such as the Phase Frequency Detector (PFD), Charge Pump (CP) and Frequency Divider (FD), and accumulating jitter exhibited by autonomous blocks such as the Voltage Controlled Oscillator (VCO) and the reference oscillator (Ref). As a next step, we include the synchronous jitter as a phase modulation. The accumulating jitter is modeled as frequency modulation since in its presence the frequency of a signal fluctuates randomly [6].

3.2 Verification Phase

The behavior of a PLL design cannot be precisely defined in many cases due to inherent initial conditions uncertainty. For that reason, complete ranges of the PLL initial conditions are considered, as done in [3]. They are generated as ranges of values that follow uniform probability distribution as done in [3]. Also, the simulation parameters such as the step-size δ_t, the initial simulation time t_o, and the simulation end time t_f are specified.

Thereafter, the proposed ESRE based Qualtitative Simulation algorithm is used to generate a lower and an upper bounds for the transient behavior of each of the ESRE PLL

Algorithm 1 ESRE based Qualitative Simulation

Require: $ESRE(X)$, $ESRE_{property}$, $T = [t_1, t_2, ..., t_N]$, IC

1: **for** $n_t \leftarrow t_2$ to t_N **do**
2:    **for** $n_{t^*} \leftarrow t_1$ to n_t **do**
3:       $X_{min}(n_t) \leftarrow +\infty$
4:       $X_{max}(n_t) \leftarrow -\infty$
5:       $\Delta t \leftarrow n_{t^*} - n_{t^*-1}$
6:       $X_{min}(n_t) \leftarrow \min(X(n_{t^*})) \ |X(n_{t^*}) = f(X(n_{t^*} - \Delta t)) \wedge If(LB_{IC} < IC < UB_{IC}, true, false)$
7:       $X_{max}(n_t) \leftarrow \max(X(n_{t^*})) \ |X(n_{t^*}) = f(X(n_{t^*} - \Delta t)) \wedge If(LB_{IC} < IC < UB_{IC}, true, false)$
8:    **end for**
9:    $B_L(n_t) \leftarrow X_{min}(n_t)$
10:   $B_U(n_t) \leftarrow X_{max}(n_t)$
11: **end for**
12: $Evaluate \leftarrow If(ESRE_{property}, true, false)$

---

model state variables (see Figure 1). These envelopes over-approximate the behavior of the PLL design without using any geometrical representation, as in [3]. The behavior of the circuit is tracked over a range of conditions in one execution. In this paper, we extend the Qualtitative Simulation algorithm proposed in [10] to support the verification of PLL designs described with ESREs (see Algorithm 1). Algorithm 1 requires: an ESREs model of the circuit with imperfections denoted by $ESRE(X)$, the desired property to be verified $ESRE_{property}$, which is the locking property for PLL (for example: the required number of cycle for the PLL to lock), the sampling time vector T of size N, and the initial conditions IC, which are m number of intervals for the state variable vector X of size m. The algorithm uses a global optimization technique to compute the minimum X_{min} (line 6) and maximum X_{max} values (line 7) of the state variable X such that they are a solution of the ESRE model for the initial conditions ranges. For each time instant n_t, the computation of X_{max} and X_{min} is done by evaluating all solutions starting from the first sampling instant (see lines 2-8 in Algorithm 1). To do so, the time step Δt is not equidistant; it is adaptatively refined in order to ensure accuracy while optimizing computations. Thereafter, the algorithm affects the obtained values of X_{min} and X_{max} to the lower bound B_L (line 9) and the upper bound B_U (line 10), respectively. Therefore, the behavior of the PLL design is bounded between the B_U and the B_L for each state variable. These envelopes are used in an offline based verification of the locking property $ESRE_{property}$ (line 12). The B_U and the B_L are involved to verify if the PLL locking property is satisfied or not, as depicted in Figure 1.

4. CHARGE PUMP PLL

In this section, we apply the proposed methodology on the dual path third order Charge Pump PLL depicted in Figure 2 [3]. It is comprised of five blocks: a reference signal oscillator, a phase frequency detector, charge pumps, a low pass filter, and a voltage controlled oscillator. By placing a frequency divider in the feedback path, the PLL can be used as a frequency synthesizer that multiplies the low frequency of the reference oscillator to generate a higher output frequency signal. Locking is a key property for all PLL based frequency synthesizers. This property is defined as the synchronization of the VCO frequency f_{VCO} being equal to N_D times the input reference frequency f_{ref}.

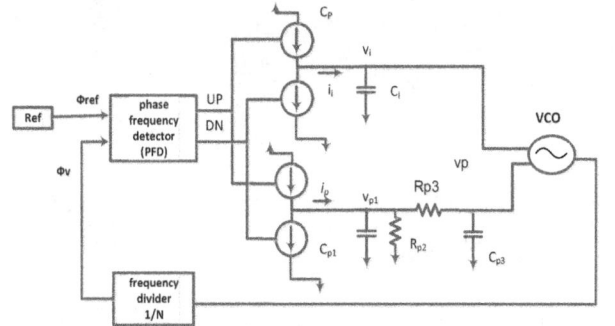

Figure 2: CP-PLL Based Frequency Synthesizer [3]

4.1 Behavioral Model

The CP-PLL based frequency synthesizer schematic, shown in Figure 2, has two different models:

1. Continuous Time Dynamic Model which is a set of first order ODEs (Equation (2)) that describes the behavior of the analog components namely, the Ref, the CPs, the LPF, the VCO, and the FD.

$$\dot{x} = Ax + Bu + c \tag{2}$$

where $x = [v_i\ v_{p1}\ v_p\ \phi_v\ \phi_{ref}]^T$ denotes the continuous state vector and u is the input vector $u = [i_i\ i_p]^T$

$$\mathbf{A} = \begin{bmatrix} 0 & 0 & 0 & 0 & 0 \\ 0 & -\frac{1}{C_{p1}}(\frac{1}{R_{p2}}+\frac{1}{R_{p3}}) & \frac{1}{C_{p1}R_{p3}} & 0 & 0 \\ 0 & \frac{1}{C_{p3}R_{p3}} & -\frac{1}{C_{p3}R_{p3}} & 0 & 0 \\ \frac{Ki}{N_D} & 0 & \frac{Kp}{N_D} & 0 & 0 \\ 0 & 0 & 0 & 0 & 0 \end{bmatrix}$$

$$B = \begin{bmatrix} \frac{1}{C_i} & 0 \\ 0 & \frac{1}{C_{p1}} \\ 0 & 0 \\ 0 & 0 \\ 0 & 0 \end{bmatrix} \qquad C = \begin{bmatrix} 0 \\ 0 \\ 0 \\ \frac{2\pi}{N_D}f_0 \\ 2\pi f_{ref} \end{bmatrix}$$

We keep the same notations in Figure 2 for the circuit variables (voltage and current nodes) and components (capacitor and resistors). The VCO frequency f_{VCO} can be determined as follows:

$$f_{VCO} = \frac{1}{2\pi}(K_i v_i + K_p v_p) + f_0 \tag{3}$$

where f_0 stands for the offset frequency and K_i and K_p represent the VCO gain.

2. Discrete Event Dynamic Model which characterizes the digital component PFD behavior. Its operation is described by the four states Finite State Machine (FSM) shown in Figure 3. After comparing the VCO phase (ϕ_{VCO}) with the phase of the reference oscillator (ϕ_{ref}), two state sequences are possible:

- *Both_off* $\rightarrow$ *Up_active* $\rightarrow$ *Both_on* $\rightarrow$ *Both_off*: if the reference oscillator leads the feedback signal ($\phi_{ref} = 2\pi$ is reached first), then the CP injects a current to charge the LPF capacitor, which increases the VCO control voltage.

- *Both_off* $\rightarrow$ *Dw_active* $\rightarrow$ *Both_on* $\rightarrow$ *Both_off*: if the reference oscillator lags the feedback signal ($\phi_v = 2\pi$ is reached first), then the CP injects a current to discharge the LPF capacitor, which decreases the VCO control voltage.

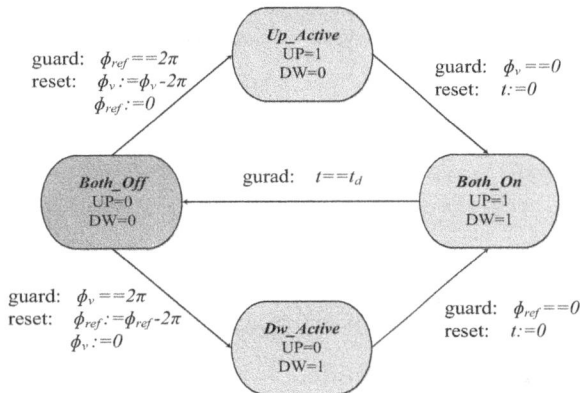

Figure 3: PFD Dynamic Model [3]

As illustrated in Figure 3, the phase values are reset to $(\phi - 2\pi)$ after the leading signal, whose phase reaches 2π first, is identified. Therefore, the same transition condition can be used for the next cycle. At the zero crossing of the lagging signal, the FSM passes to the state *Both_On*. After a time delay t_d, which represents the time required to switch off the charge pumps, the FSM enters the *Both_Off* state. The input vector u changes according to the PFD FSM states, as follows:

$$u = \begin{cases} \begin{bmatrix} 0 & 0 \end{bmatrix}^T & \text{if Both\_Off} \\ \begin{bmatrix} I_i^{DW} & I_p^{DW} \end{bmatrix}^T & \text{if Dw\_active} \\ \begin{bmatrix} I_i^{UP} & I_p^{UP} \end{bmatrix}^T & \text{if Up\_active} \\ \begin{bmatrix} I_i^{UP}+I_i^{DW} & I_p^{UP}+I_p^{DW} \end{bmatrix}^T & \text{if Both\_On} \end{cases}$$

with $I_i^{DW} = -I_i^{UP}$ and $I_p^{DW} = -I_p^{UP}$

Extended System of Recurrence Equations Model
The analog behavior of the PLL (described by the linear continuous dynamic model) and the digital behavior of the PFD (described as FSM) are transformed into ESREs using the approach defined in Section 3.1, as follows :

$$\begin{aligned} v_i(n+1) =\ & if((Both\_On \vee Both\_Off), \\ & v_i(n) + f_1(n,0), if(Up\_active, v_i(n) \\ & + f_1(n, I_i^{UP}), v_i(n) + f_1(n, I_i^{DW}))) \end{aligned}$$

$$\begin{aligned} v_{p1}(n+1) =\ & if((Both\_On \vee Both\_Off), \\ & v_{p1}(n) - f_2(n,0), if(Up\_active, v_{p1}(n) \\ & - f_2(n, I_p^{UP}), v_{p1}(n) - f_2(n, I_p^{DW}(n)))) \end{aligned}$$

$$v_p(n+1) = if(true, v_p(n) + f_3(n), 0)$$

$$\phi_v(n+1) = if(true, \phi_v(n) + f_4(n), 0)$$

$$\phi_{ref}(n+1) = if(true, \phi_{ref}(n) + f_5(n), 0)$$

where
$$f_1(n,I) = \frac{1}{C_i}I\delta_n \tag{4}$$

$$f_2(n,I) = \frac{1}{C_{p1}}[(\frac{1}{R_{p2}}+\frac{1}{R_{p3}})v_{p1}(n) - \frac{1}{R_{p3}}v_p(n) - I]\delta_n \tag{5}$$

$$f_3(n) = [\frac{1}{C_{p3}R_{p3}}(v_{p1}(n)-v_p(n))]\delta_n \tag{6}$$

$$f_4(n) = [\frac{Ki}{N_D}v_i(n) + \frac{Kp}{N_D}v_p(n) + \frac{2\pi}{N_D}f_0]\delta_n \tag{7}$$

$$f_5(n) = 2\pi f_{ref}\delta_n \tag{8}$$

4.2 Verification of the Locking Property

In this Section, the verification of the locking property of the PLL is discussed in detail. If the phase difference between the reference signal and the feedback one is within the tolerated bound $[-0.2°, 0.2°]$, then the PLL is "locked", otherwise the PLL is "not locked". The PLL locking property in ESRE form is given in Equation (9).

$$If(|\phi_v(n) - \phi_{ref}(n)| < 0.2°, PLL\ locked, PLL\ not\ locked) \tag{9}$$

Figures 4 and 5 depict the analysis of the locking property of the CP-PLL without imperfections for the design parameters listed in Table 1. We notice that the VCO frequency stabilizes to 27 *MHz* after about 756 *cycles* which correspond also to a zero phase difference between the reference signal and the feedback signal. However, such analysis can only be performed for one possible initial conditions vector which is in this case $x = [0.35\ 0.01\ -0.01\ -0.3\ 0]$. We now verify the locking property of the PLL using our ESRE based Qualitative Simulation algorithm. The verification is performed for a range of the voltage nodes initial conditions ($v_i(0) \in [0.34, 0.36]$ and $v_p(0), v_{p1}(0) \in [-0.01, 0.01]$), and the feedback phase ϕ_v. The initial reference phase $\phi_{ref}(0)$ is fixed to zero.

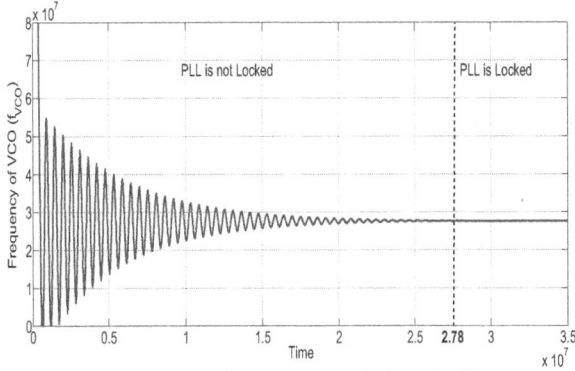

Figure 4: Frequency of the VCO

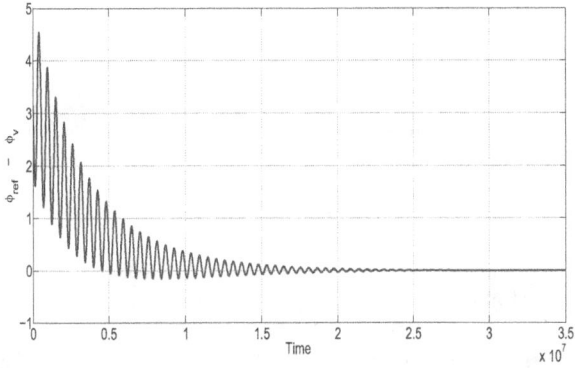

Figure 5: Phase Difference Between the Reference and Feedback Signals

Figure 6 shows the upper and the lower bounds of the VCO phase state variable. We remark that the phase is always between 0 and 2π because the reference and feedback phase are reset to $\phi = \phi - 2\pi$. Thus, the same phase crossing can be used in the next cycle. One of the advantages of our methodology is verifying the PLL locking property based only on the phase difference ($\phi_{ref} - \phi_v$) state variable. In other words, if the upper and the lower bounds of the phase difference are in the tolerated region $[-0.2\,^\circ, 0.2\,^\circ]$, then we claim that the PLL is locked. A comparison of the required number of cycles ($t_{cycle} = \frac{1}{f_{ref}}$) for the PLL locking between our Qualitative Simulation (QS) methodology (ESRE-QS) and the Monte Carlo (MC) simulation technique (MC-S) is depicted in Table 2. The simulation was carried out first in the ideal case (row 1), then with process variation (PV) in the VCO (row 2), the CP (row 3), and the LPF (row 4), finally with synchronous jitter (row 5), and accumulating jitter (row 6). Our methodology analyzes the locking property for an entire initial conditions range of the normalized phase ϕ_v. On the other hand, the Monte Carlo technique analyzes the locking property for only one possible initial condition value in each trial. Therefore, MC simulations are performed for 10 times and the maximum

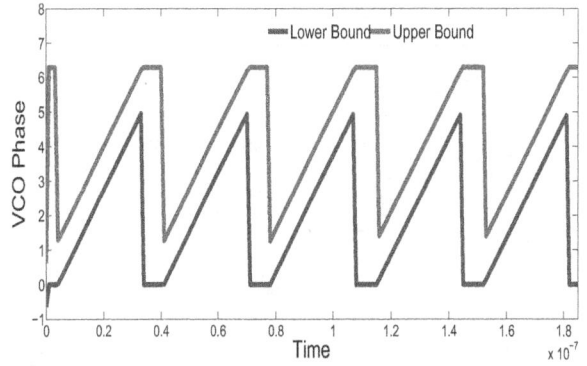

Figure 6: Bounds of the VCO Phase State variable

number of cycles found is compared with our results. In other words, the reported number of cycles for MC technique are performed by randomly choosing the initial value of $\phi_v^i \in 0.1 \times [i, i-1]$, $i = 1, 2, .., 5$.

From Table 2, it can be noticed that our Qualitative Simulation approach provides a greater number of required locking cycles compared to the MC technique. Unless an infinite number of simulations is conducted, the MC simulation technique cannot provide the maximum clock cycles required for the PLL to be locked in an initial condition interval. We also see that the number of lock cycles increases with the initial phase difference ($\phi_{ref}(0) - \phi_v(0)$).

Table 1: Parameters for the CP-PLL Model [3]

Name	Value	Unit
f_{ref}	27	KHz
f_0	26.93	MHz
N_D	1000	–
K_i	200	MHz/V
K_P	25	MHz/V
I_i	[9.9, 10.1]	μA
I_p	[495, 505]	μA
C_i	25	pF
C_{p1}	6.3	pF
C_{p3}	2	pF
R_{p2}	50	KΩ
R_{p3}	8	KΩ
t_d	50	ps

Moreover, we remark that the jitter performance, and more specifically the synchronous jitter in the VCO and the reference oscillator (row 6), are of great concern in PLL locking. For these imperfections, the PLL fails to lock as represented by the "dashed entry" in Table 2. More importantly, when considering phase modulation jitter and for $\phi_v \in [-0.5, -0.4]$, our Qualitative Simulation technique finds values of ϕ_v where the PLL fails to lock, while the MC technique was not able to detect this violation (shaded region).

5. CONCLUSIONS

In this paper, a new methodology to verify the locking property in PLL designs based on Qualitative Simulation technique is proposed. The PLL design is modeled using Extended System of Recurrence Equation in the presence of accumulating jitter, synchronous jitter, and process variation. Thereafter, the verification algorithm based on Qualitative Simulation is conducted to analyze the behavior of

Table 2: Required Cycles for PLL Locking

$\phi_v \in -0.1\times$	[5,4]		[4,3]		[3,2]		[2,1]		[1,0]	
Experiment	ESRE-QS	MC-S	ESRE-QS	MC-S	ESRE-QS	MC-S	ESRE-QS	MC-S	ESRE-QS	MC-S
No imperfections	1454	883	1389	832	1313	709	1247	676	1169	628
PV in VCO	1827	1228	1763	1117	1718	1001	1652	972	1574	946
PV in CP	1576	1066	1514	913	1479	894	1406	837	1367	779
PV in LPF	1681	1157	1629	1007	1580	994	1516	956	1489	913
Synch. jitter only	–	1763	2513	1546	2337	1481	2284	1405	2162	1379
Accum. jitter only	–	–	–	–	–	–	–	–	–	–

the PLL ESRE model over a range of initial conditions. The algorithm computes the envelopes that enclose all possible behaviors of the PLL state variables. This methodology has been gainfully employed on a third order Charge Pump PLL verification. The required locking cycles of the PLL design were computed over a range of parameters due to $0.18\mu m$ technology process, and a range of initial conditions of node voltages and feedback phase. Our methodology proved a better coverage compared to simulation methods. Indeed, a locking failure case was found using our approach that was not predicted by 10 Monte Carlo simulations of randomly chosen initial values of the normalized feedback phase $\phi_v \in [-0.5, -0.4]$.

As future work, we are planning to improve the imperfections models by deriving them directly from device level simulations and integrating them in the ESREs behavioral model. Moreover, we are working on the application of the proposed method to larger and more complex AMS designs and the verification of their functional properties. By doing so, we will be able to measure and assess the limitation of the proposed methodology.

6. REFERENCES

[1] G. Al-Sammane, M. H. Zaki, and S. Tahar. A symbolic methodology for the verification of analog and mixed signal designs. In *IEEE Proceedings of the Conference on Design, Automation and Test in Europe*, pages 249–254, 2007.

[2] A. Aloisio, R. Giordano, and V. Izzo. Phase noise issues with FPGA-embedded DLLs and PLLs in HEP applications. *IEEE Transactions on Nuclear Science*, 58(4):1664–1671, 2011.

[3] M. Althoff, A. Rajhans, B. H. Krogh, S. Yaldiz, X. Li, and L. Pileggi. Formal verification of phase-locked loops using reachability analysis and continuization. *Communications of the ACM*, 56(10):97–104, 2013.

[4] R. Alur. Formal verification of hybrid systems. In *IEEE Proceedings of the International Conference on Embedded Software*, pages 273–278, 2011.

[5] M. Fulde. *Variation aware analog and mixed-signal circuit design in emerging multi-gate CMOS technologies*, volume 28 of *Springer Series in Advanced Microelectronics*. 2010.

[6] K. Kundert. Predicting the phase noise and jitter of pll-based frequency synthesizers. *Available from: www.designers-guide.com*, 2003.

[7] W. Li and J. Meiners. Introduction to phase-locked loop system modeling. *Analog Applications Journal, Texas Instruments Incorporated*, 2:5–10, 2000.

[8] R. Narayanan, B. Akbarpour, M. H. Zaki, S. Tahar, and L. C. Paulson. Formal verification of analog circuits in the presence of noise and process variation. In *Proceedings of Design, Automation and Test in Europe*, pages 1309–1312, 2010.

[9] R. Narayanan, I. Seghaier, M. H. Zaki, and S. Tahar. Statistical run-time verification of analog circuits in presence of noise and process variation. *IEEE Transactions on Very Large Scale Integration Systems*, 21(10):1811–1822, 2013.

[10] M. Nikravesh, L. A. Zadeh, and V. Korotkikh. Fuzzy partial differential equations and relational equations. *Reservoir Characterization and Modeling Series: Studies in Fuzziness and Soft Computing*, 142, 2004.

[11] A. Singh and P. Li. On behavioral model equivalence checking for large analog/mixed signal systems. In *IEEE Proceedings of the International Conference on Computer-Aided Design*, pages 55–61, 2010.

[12] S. Steinhorst and L. Hedrich. Improving verification coverage of analog circuit blocks by state space-guided transient simulation. In *IEEE Proceedings of International Symposium on Circuits and Systems*, pages 1811–1822, 2010.

[13] Z. Wang. Runtime verification of analog and mixed signal designs. Master's thesis, Concordia University, 2009.

[14] M. H. Zaki, G. Al-Sammane, S. Tahar, and G. Bois. Combining symbolic simulation and interval arithmetic for the verification of ams designs. In *IEEE Proceedings of International Conference on Formal Methods in Computer Aided Design*, pages 207–215, 2007.

[15] M. H. Zaki, S. Tahar, and G. Bois. Formal verification of analog and mixed signal designs: A survey. *Microelectronics Journal*, 39(12):1395–1404, 2008.

Optimal Power Switch Design Methodology for Ultra Dynamic Voltage Scaling with a Limited Number of Power Rails

Yanzhi Wang, Xue Lin, and Massoud Pedram
University of Southern California
Los Angeles, CA 90089 USA
{yanzhiwa, xuelin, pedram}@usc.edu

ABSTRACT

Many burst-mode applications require high performance for brief time periods between extended sections of low performance operation. Digital circuits supporting such burst-mode applications should work in both the near-threshold regime and the super-threshold regime for brief time periods. This work proposes the structure support of fine-grained ultra dynamic voltage scaling (UDVS) from the traditional strong-inversion region to the near-threshold region, with limitations on the number of power rails. The number, type, and size of the power switches are jointly optimized to minimize the overall energy consumption of the UDVS circuit block, meanwhile satisfying the target delay or frequency requirement at each DVS level. The proposed optimization framework properly accounts for the dynamic energy consumption as well as the leakage energy consumption through all the power switches during both the operation time and stand-by time of the circuit block. Experimental results on 22nm Predictive Technology Model demonstrate the effectiveness of the proposed optimization framework.

Categories and Subject Descriptors

B.8.2 [**Performance and Reliability**]: Performance Analysis and Design Aids

Keywords

Ultra dynamic voltage scaling (UDVS); power switch; near-threshold

1. INTRODUCTION

Aggressive voltage scaling from the traditional super-threshold region to the near/sub-threshold region has been shown to be very effective in reducing power consumption in digital circuits [1][2][3]. It is especially beneficial for applications such as wireless sensor processing and RFID tags where performance is not the primary concern. The operating frequency of near/sub-threshold logic is much lower than that of regular strong-inversion circuits ($V_{DD} > V_{th}$) due to small transistor current, which consists mostly of leakage current. Authors of [4][5] derived analytical expressions of the optimal V_{DD} to minimize energy, i.e., the minimum energy point or MEP, and showed that the MEP for CMOS circuits typically occurs in the near-threshold region.

Many burst-mode applications require high performance for brief time periods between extended sections of low performance operation [6]. Digital circuits supporting such burst-mode applications should work in both the near-threshold region and super-threshold region (for brief time periods.) Therefore, traditional dynamic voltage scaling (DVS) method should be extended to include near-threshold operation, but the overhead of providing the necessary voltages can be large. Adjustable DC-DC converters tend to have limited efficiency over broad output voltage ranges, and they take hundreds of micro-seconds to switch between different V_{DD} supply levels especially in the near-threshold regime [6]. An alternative implementation approach called local voltage dithering (LVD) uses header power switches to connect circuit blocks to one of the several power supply rails, thereby allowing for faster switching [7][8]. The LVD approach supports application of fine-grained ultra DVS (UDVS) down to the near-threshold regime and to smaller internal circuit blocks. As the required operating frequency changes, each circuit block spends a different fraction of its operating time at different voltage levels. However, the area overhead of LVD can be significant when the number of required virtual-V_{DD} levels becomes relatively large, since a separate power rail is required for each virtual-V_{DD} level.

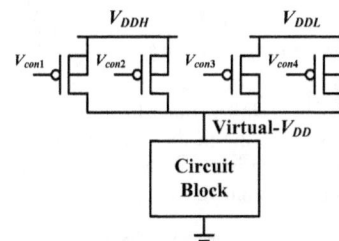

Figure 1. Architecture of fine-grained UDVS to generate six different virtual-V_{DD} levels using two supply power rails.

In this paper, we propose an implementation structure for UDVS with a limited number of power rails. The proposed structure is a generalization of the LVD structure and induces less area overhead than the LVD structure when the number of required virtual-V_{DD} levels is large. We use parallel, independently controllable power switches with different widths connecting between each V_{DD} supply rail and the circuit block. During circuit operation, we turn on a subset of the parallel-connected power switches and turn off the rest to vary the effective size dynamically, in order to generate an appropriate operating voltage level for the circuit block. The circuit block is therefore not constrained by the available voltage rails. Figure 1 illustrates an example of the proposed structure, which provides up to six different virtual-V_{DD} levels for the circuit block from two V_{DD} supply rails if the power switches are properly sized.

The introduction of a power switch device between V_{DD} and the circuit block creates an IR drop across the header, thereby resulting in a reduced virtual-V_{DD} value. Power switch sizing is critical to maintain low power consumption and expected performance. An undersized power switch results in large performance degradation, whereas an oversized power switch results in increased leakage and increased area overhead. Power switch sizing methodologies have been examined in depth to support techniques such as multi-threshold CMOS (MTCMOS), which uses high-V_{th} power switches to reduce leakage [10][11][12]. In this work, we propose an optimization framework of the UDVS implementation structure. We jointly optimize the supply voltage V_{DD} levels as well as the number, type (PMOS or NMOS), and size of the power switches. We minimize the overall energy consumption of the UDVS circuit block satisfying the target delay or frequency requirement at each DVS level. We take into account the additional constraints on the number of V_{DD} power rails and the total area overhead. The proposed optimization framework also properly accounts for the dynamic energy consumption as well as the leakage energy consumption through all the power switches during both the operation time and stand-by time of the circuit block. Experimental results on HSpice simulation of 22nm Predictive Technology Model (PTM) [14] show that the proposed optimization framework achieves up to 19% reduction in energy consumption or 74% reduction in area overhead compared with the baseline method.

The rest of this paper is organized as follows. Section 2 presents the transistor and circuit models operating in the sub/near-threshold regime. In Section 3, we propose the structure support for UDVS over a wide supply voltage range. Section 4 discusses the design considerations and optimization variables. Section 5 provides the optimization framework and algorithm. Experimental results and conclusion are presented in Section 6 and Section 7, respectively.

2. NEAR-THRESHOLD COMPUTING

2.1 Transistor Modeling

First, we use NMOS transistors as an example. We know that the MOSFETs satisfy the α-power law model in the traditional super-threshold regime [15]. On the other hand, the drain current I_{ds} of NMOS transistors operating in the subthreshold or near-threshold regime obeys an exponential dependency on the gate drive voltage V_{gs} and drain-to-source voltage V_{ds}, given by:

$$I_{ds} = \mu C_{ox} \frac{W}{L} (m-1) v_T^2 \cdot e^{\frac{V_{gs}+\lambda V_{ds}-V_{th}}{m \cdot v_T}} \left(1 - e^{\frac{-V_{ds}}{v_T}}\right), \quad (1)$$

where μ is the mobility, C_{ox} is the oxide capacitance, m is the subthreshold slope factor, λ is the DIBL coefficient, and v_T is the thermal voltage $\frac{kT}{q}$. Given a specific technology node (e.g., the 22 nm PTM), we can rewrite Eqn. (1) as follows:

$$I_{ds} = I_0 W \cdot e^{\frac{V_{gs}+\lambda V_{ds}-V_{th}}{m \cdot v_T}} \left(1 - e^{\frac{-V_{ds}}{v_T}}\right), \quad (2)$$

where I_0 is a technology-dependent parameter.

2.2 Circuit Modeling

In the circuit level, let $P_{CB,dyn}(V)$ and $P_{CB,sta}(V)$ denote the average dynamic (switching) power consumption and static (leakage) power consumption of the circuit block in the UDVS structure, respectively, when the virtual-V_{DD} value is V. Let $P_{CB}(V)$ denote the average power consumption of the circuit block during operation time, and we have

$P_{CB}(V) = P_{CB,dyn}(V) + P_{CB,sta}(V)$. Similarly, we define the average current values $I_{CB,dyn}(V)$, $I_{CB,sta}(V)$, and $I_{CB}(V)$. Furthermore, let $T_{CB}(V)$ denote the worst-case delay, i.e., the clock period, of the circuit block when virtual-V_{DD} value is V. We characterize from ISCAS benchmarks and typical circuits and derive the corresponding functions. Figure 2 shows the measured and fitted dynamic and leakage power v.s. virtual-V_{DD} of a typical circuit using 22nm PTM. Figure 2 also shows measured and fitted delay v.s. virtual-V_{DD} of that circuit.

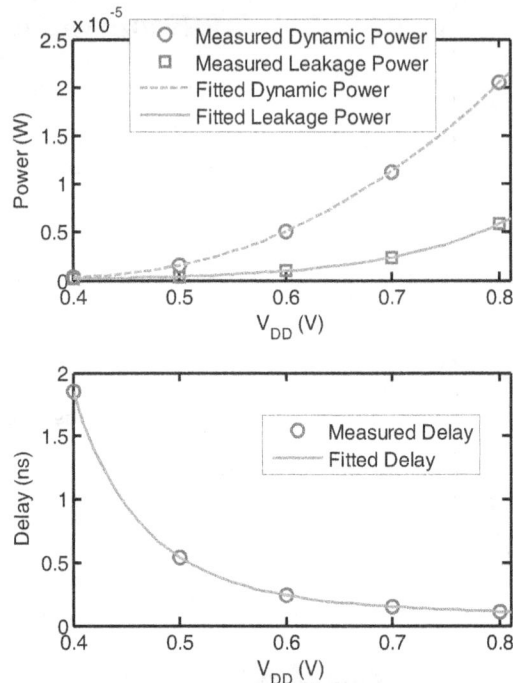

Figure 2. Characterization results of the circuit block in the UDVS structure.

3. STRUCTURE SUPPORT FOR FINE-GRAINED ULTRA DYNAMIC VOLTAGE SCALINGS

In this section, we propose the structure support for fine-grained UDVS over a wide voltage range from the traditional super-threshold regime down to the near-threshold regime. The proposed structure support induces less area overhead especially when the number of required virtual-V_{DD} levels is relatively large. Please note that the determination procedure of the number of required virtual-V_{DD} levels is out of the scope of this paper. Figure 1 shows an example with two V_{DD} power rails and four PMOS switches with different width values. We number the four PMOS switches as shown in Figure 1. We can generate three different virtual-V_{DD} levels for the circuit block using the 1st and 2nd PMOS switches and the higher supply voltage rail V_{DDH} by turning on the 1st switch only, turning on the 2nd switch only, and turning on both switches, respectively. When both power switches are activated, the effective width is the sum of the width values of the two power switches. Similar observation also applies for the 3rd and 4th switches. Therefore, we can generate six potentially different virtual-V_{DD} levels, denoted by V_1 through V_6 in the descending order, for the circuit block using this example structure. The three higher virtual-V_{DD} levels, i.e., V_1, V_2, and V_3, are generated by the first two switches and V_{DDH}, whereas the rest are generated by the last two switches and V_{DDL}. Proper sizing of the header switches is critical in order to generate the appropriate virtual-V_{DD} levels for the circuit block to satisfy the target delay requirement at each DVS level.

Consider the 3rd and 4th PMOS switches that are connected to the lower supply voltage rail (V_{DDL}). The body of these PMOS switches is tied to the virtual-V_{DD} to avoid forward body bias, which results in a significant increase in the leakage current through these switches when the 1st and/or the 2nd switches are activated [7]. The gate drive signals of the 3rd and 4th PMOS switches are either connected to the ground when they are activated or to V_{DDH} if they are inactivated. These signals cannot be connected to V_{DDL} to be inactivated. This is because it will result in high ON-current flowing from the virtual-V_{DD} to V_{DDL} when the 1st and/or the 2nd switches are activated (it is highly likely that the virtual-V_{DD} level is higher than V_{DDL} in this case.)

4. DESIGN CONSIDERATIONS AND OPTIMIZATION VARIABLES

In this section, we provide the design considerations and optimization variables for UDVS in the following four aspects: the number, type, and size of the header power switches, as well as the V_{DD} levels.

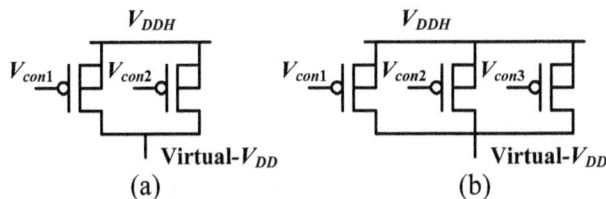

Figure 3. (a) Two parallel power switches and (b) three parallel power switches to achieve three different virtual-V_{DD} levels.

Number of Header Power Switches: Consider only the header switches connecting to V_{DDH} as an example. Suppose that we are required to generate three different virtual-V_{DD} levels, i.e., V_1^{req}, V_2^{req}, and V_3^{req}, using these switches and the V_{DDH} power rail in order to satisfy the corresponding frequency requirement at each DVS level. Then we may use either two parallel switches (as shown in Figure 3 (a)) or three parallel switches (as shown in Figure 3 (b)) to achieve this goal. When three parallel switches are utilized, we can achieve **exactly** the three required virtual-V_{DD} levels by proper sizing of the parallel switches (even when leakage is considered.) On the other hand, when only two parallel switches are utilized, we can reduce the area overhead but may not generate exactly the three required virtual-V_{DD} levels. In this case, one or two virtual-V_{DD} levels generated by this structure may be inevitably higher than the required values in order to satisfy the three requirements simultaneously, which induces higher power/energy consumption. Utilization of two parallel switches will have another effect of reducing the leakage power consumption. In general, the former effect outweighs the latter effect, and therefore application of only two parallel switches will increase the overall power/energy consumption. Similar observation also applies to the header switches connected to V_{DDL}. Hence, the number of header power switches is an important design variable to achieve a desirable tradeoff between lower power/energy consumption and less area overhead.

Type of Header Power Switches: Consider the four power switches in Figure 1. We may replace some PMOS switches by NMOS switches and reduce area overhead while maintaining the same performance and power consumption, as illustrated in [7].

The 1st and 2nd PMOS switches cannot be replaced by NMOS ones. This is because an NMOS switch with a much larger size is required due to the relatively minor difference (less than the threshold voltage $V_{th,n}$) between V_{DDH} and the required virtual-V_{DD} level when the 1st and/or the 2nd power switch are activated. On the other hand, the 3rd and 4th PMOS switches, which are connected to V_{DDL}, may be potentially replaced by NMOS power switches as shown in Figure 4. In general, an NMOS switch induces less area overhead and is more desirable than its PMOS counterpart when

$$V_{DDH} - \text{Virtual\_}V_{DD} - V_{th,n} > V_{DDL} - 0 - |V_{th,p}| \qquad (3)$$

where $V_{DDH} - \text{Virtual\_}V_{DD}$ is the V_{gs} value when the NMOS switch is turned on, whereas $V_{DDL} - 0$ is the $|V_{gs}|$ value when the PMOS switch is turned on. Please note that Eqn. (3) is an approximate criterion since some secondary effects, such as the effect of body biasing or DIBL (drain-induced barrier lowering), are not accounted for. Moreover, utilizing NMOS switches will have another benefit of reducing the leakage power consumption mainly due to the reverse body biasing at any operation mode. Detailed discussions are omitted in this paper due to space limitation.

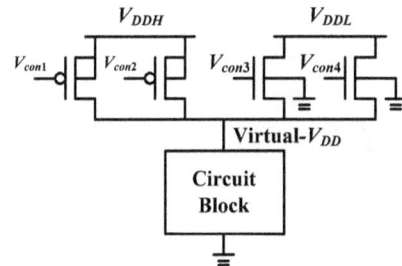

Figure 4. UDVS structure support with NMOS power switches.

Sizing of Header Power Switches: Appropriate sizing of the header power switches is crucial to maintain low power consumption and expected performance. Generally speaking, an undersized power switch results in large performance degradation, whereas an oversized power switch results in increased leakage and increased area overhead. We need to perform joint sizing optimization of all the power switches in the proposed structure of UDVS, since the sizes of those power switches affect the virtual-V_{DD} values in an interleaved manner. Let us consider the structure for UDVS in Figure 1 or Figure 4 again. Then we have the following two cases:

Case I: In this case the 1st and/or 2nd switches are active and V_1, V_2, or V_3 are generated as the virtual-V_{DD} value. Increasing the size of the 1st or the 2nd power switch will result in an increase in the virtual-V_{DD} level, whereas increasing the size of the 3rd or the 4th switch will result in a decrease. This is because current flows from V_{DDH} through virtual-V_{DD} to V_{DDL} in this case (virtual-V_{DD} is higher than V_{DDL}.)

Case II: In this case the 3rd and/or 4th switches are active and V_4, V_5, or V_6 are generated as the virtual-V_{DD} value. Increasing the size of any power switch will result in an increase in the virtual-V_{DD} level. This is because virtual-V_{DD} is lower than both V_{DDH} and V_{DDL} in this case.

Because we need to satisfy the corresponding required virtual-V_{DD} value at each DVS level, we should perform elaborate optimization on the sizes of power switches.

Supply Voltage Levels in the Power Rails: The supply voltage levels in the power rails, i.e., V_{DDH} and V_{DDL} in Figure 1 or Figure 4, need to be jointly optimized with the power switches to achieve the globally optimal UDVS structure. A higher V_{DDH} or V_{DDL} value will reduce the required total width of power switches but incur higher power consumption, whereas a lower V_{DDH} or V_{DDL} value will have the opposite effect.

5. OPTIMIZATION FRAMEWORK

In this section, we propose the optimization framework of UDVS. We jointly optimize the supply voltage V_{DD} levels as well as the number, type (PMOS or NMOS), and size of the header power switches. We minimize the overall energy consumption of the UDVS circuit block, subject to the constraints on the number of supply power rails and the total area overhead. We account for both the dynamic energy consumption and leakage energy consumption through all the power switches during both the operation time and stand-by time of the circuit block. We formally describe the design optimization problem for UDVS as follows:

Given: M supply power rails (we use $M = 2$ in the experiments); N different required virtual-V_{DD} values, i.e., $V_1^{req}, V_2^{req}, \dots V_N^{req}$, which correspond to the N different required frequency/latency values at different DVS levels (we use $N = 6$ in the experiments)[1]; the circuit block characteristics obtained from our characterization procedure.

Find: Number (K), type (PMOS or NMOS), and width (W_1, $W_2, \dots W_K$) of all power switches, as well as the voltage supply levels V_{DDH} and V_{DDL}.

Objective Functions: We define two objective functions for minimization as follows. Let $V_1, V_2, \dots V_N$ denote the **actually generated** virtual-V_{DD} levels using the UDVS structure. Let $P_{DVS}(V_i)$ denote the (average) power consumption of the whole UDVS structure (including PMOS headers) during operation time when the generated virtual-V_{DD} level is V_i, and let $T_{DVS}(V_i)$ denote the corresponding latency value (clock period.) We know that $P_{DVS}(V_i) \cdot T_{DVS}(V_i)$ is the energy consumption of the UDVS structure in one clock cycle, which has accounted for the conduction loss in PMOS headers. Then the first objective function, named the *weighted energy consumption*, is given as follows:

$$\sum_{i=1}^{N} \alpha_i \cdot P_{DVS}(V_i) \cdot T_{DVS}(V_i) + \alpha_0 \cdot P_{DVS,sta} \quad (4)$$

where α_i $(1 \leq i \leq N)$ are the number of clock cycles when the circuit block operates at the ith DVS level; α_0 is the idle time of the circuit block; $P_{DVS,sta}$ is the leakage power consumption value of the UDVS structure.

For the second objective function, we know that the energy consumption per clock cycle of the circuit block (the power switches are not considered here) is given by $P_{CB}(V_i^{req}) \cdot T_{CB}(V_i^{req})$, when the supply voltage is V_i^{req}. Then the second objective function for minimization, named the *maximum energy overhead*, is given as follows:

$$\max_i \frac{P_{DVS}(V_i) \cdot T_{DVS}(V_i)}{P_{CB}(V_i^{req}) \cdot T_{CB}(V_i^{req})} \quad (5)$$

Subject to:

(i) *Virtual-V_{DD} constraints:* $V_i \geq V_i^{req}$ for $1 \leq i \leq N$.

(ii) *Area overhead constraint:* $\sum_{i=1}^{K} W_i \leq W_{max}$, where W_{max} is the maximum total width of the power switches.

Consider a UDVS structure with K_1 power switches connected to V_{DDH} and K_2 power switches connected to V_{DDL}, satisfying $K_1 + K_2 = K$ and $K \leq N$. We name (K_1, K_2) a *configuration* of the N-level UDVS structure. For example, the UDVS structure with six required virtual-V_{DD} levels has four configurations $(2, 2)$, $(2, 3)$, $(3, 2)$, and $(3, 3)$, if we generate the same number of virtual-V_{DD} levels from V_{DDH} and V_{DDL}.

The proposed joint optimization algorithm consists of an outer loop and a kernel algorithm. The outer loop finds the best-suited configuration of UDVS structure as well as values of V_{DDH} and V_{DDL}. The kernel algorithm finds the optimal type and size of each power switch. The general procedure of the proposed joint optimization algorithm is shown in Algorithm 1.

Algorithm 1: Brief procedure of the joint optimization algorithm.

For each configuration of the UDVS structure:

> **Perform** ternary search to find the optimal V_{DDH} and V_{DDL}:
>
> > *The kernel algorithm:*
> >
> > Step I: Generate initial sizing of all power switches.
> >
> > Step II: Generate feasible sizing of all power switches.
> >
> > Step III: Determine the types of power switches
> >
> > Step IV: Refine the sizing of all power switches

Find the optimal configuration and values of V_{DDH} and V_{DDL}, such that the objective function is minimized and constraints are satisfied.

The proposed kernel algorithm consists of four steps as shown in Algorithm 1. Without losing generality, we describe these four steps using configuration $(3, 2)$ of the 6-level UDVS structure as an example. In this example, the 1st, 2nd, and 3rd power switches are connected to V_{DDH}, whereas the 4th and 5th power switches are connected to V_{DDL}. Similar optimization steps can also be applied to the other configurations.

Step I (Generating the initial sizing of all power switches): In the first step, we generate the initial sizing of all power switches only considering the ON-currents of the power switches that are turned on, while neglecting the leakage currents of the other power switches. We continue with the above-mentioned example.

Let $I_{PMOS}(V_s, V_d, V_g, V_b)$ denote the source-to-drain current of a unit-size PMOS switch with voltage levels at source, drain, gate, and body given by V_s, V_d, V_g, and V_b, respectively. Then for the three switches connected to V_{DDH} $(1 \leq i \leq 3)$, we generate an initial sizing as follows:

$$W_i = \frac{I_{CB}(V_i^{req})}{I_{PMOS}(V_{DDH}, V_i^{req}, 0, V_{DDH})} \quad (6)$$

In this way, we have $V_i = V_i^{req}$ for $1 \leq i \leq 3$ because the current flowing through the ith PMOS switch matches the current flowing through the circuit block (leakage currents through other PMOS switches are ignored here.) On the other hand, the initial sizing of

---

[1] Please note that the focus of this work is to reduce the energy and area overhead in implementing the UDVS requirements. In the proposed framework, M and N can be general values. Necessities of multiple power rails and virtual-V_{DD} values as well as the derivation procedure of the optimal M and N values are out of the scope of this paper.

the two switches connected to V_{DDL} is more involved because the initial sizing should satisfy the following three constraints simultaneously:

$$W_4 + W_5 \geq \frac{I_{CB}(V_4^{req})}{I_{PMOS}(V_{DDL}, V_4^{req}, 0, V_4^{req})} \qquad (7)$$

$$W_4 \geq \frac{I_{CB}(V_5^{req})}{I_{PMOS}(V_{DDL}, V_5^{req}, 0, V_5^{req})} \qquad (8)$$

$$W_5 \geq \frac{I_{CB}(V_6^{req})}{I_{PMOS}(V_{DDL}, V_6^{req}, 0, V_6^{req})} \qquad (9)$$

If (8) and (9) are the dominant constraints, we can set (8) and (9) to be equalities and W_4 and W_5 achieve the minimal possible value in this case. However, if (7) is the dominant constraint, we need to find the optimal W_4 and W_5 values such that the objective function (4) or (5) is minimized and constraints (7) – (9) are satisfied. Details are omitted due to space limitation.

Step II (Generating a feasible sizing of all power switches): In this step, we generate a feasible sizing of all power switches in the sense that the virtual-V_{DD} constraints, i.e., $V_i \geq V_i^{req}$ for $1 \leq i \leq N$, are satisfied simultaneously. We consider both the ON-currents of the turned on switches and the leakage currents of the other power switches in this step. We continue with the above-mentioned example.

This step is based on the following observation from Section 4: Increasing the width of the 1st, 2nd, or 3rd switch can only increase the V_i values for $1 \leq i \leq 6$, whereas increasing the width of the 4th or 5th switch will increase V_4, V_5, and V_6 but decrease V_1, V_2, and V_3. Hence when we check the virtual-V_{DD} constraints taking into account the leakage currents, only the constraints on V_1, V_2, and V_3 may be violated. After we identify the virtual-V_{DD} constraints that are violated, we increase the corresponding width of switches until there is no violation. Detailed procedure is omitted due to space limitation. The proposed procedure guarantees to find a feasible sizing of all power switches with no violation on virtual-V_{DD} constraints. This is because increasing the width of the 1st, 2nd, or 3rd power switch will only increase the V_i values.

Step III (Determining the type of each power switch): In this step, we determine the type (NMOS or PMOS) of each power switch. Originally we set each power switch as PMOS switch. We continue with the above-mentioned example. We know from Section 4 that the 1st, 2nd, and 3rd power switch, which are connected to V_{DDH}, can only be implemented using PMOS switch. On the other hand, the 4th and 5th power switch can be potentially replaced by NMOS switch. For the 4th or 5th power switch, if we find out that NMOS power switch can achieve the same current driving capability with less width value, we conclude that NMOS is more suitable. We replace the original PMOS power switch by the NMOS one.

Step IV (Refining the sizing results of all power switches): Please note that we have the opportunity of refining, i.e., reducing, the sizing results of all power switches due to two reasons: (i) Some V_i values (such as the V_4, V_5, and V_6 values in the above-mentioned example) are higher than those calculated in Step I due to the effect of leakage; (ii) Potential width increase of some power switches in Step II will further increase those V_i values. If no violation of virtual-V_{DD} constraint will be resulted in, refining/reducing the width of a power switch will have two

benefits: (i) reducing the ON-current and hence the power/energy consumption and (ii) reducing the leakage power consumption. In this step, we find and exploit the opportunity in reducing the sizing results of power switches derived from the previous steps. The detailed procedure is shown in Algorithm 2.

Algorithm 2: Refining the sizing results of power switches.
Do the following procedure:
Identify the set of power switches where reducing width by $\Delta\%$ (a small amount) will not cause violation of virtual-V_{DD} constraint.
Identify the power switch from the set where reducing width will result in the minimal objective function value.
Reduce the width of the identified power switch by $\Delta\%$.
Until the sizing results cannot be further reduced, i.e., any futher size reduction will cause violation in virtual-V_{DD} constraint.

6. EXPERIMENTAL RESULTS

We test the proposed optimization framework of UDVS on the 22nm PTM [14]. We consider two supply power rails V_{DDH} and V_{DDL}, and six required virtual-V_{DD} values, i.e., $V_1^{req} = 0.85$ V, $V_2^{req} = 0.8$ V, $V_3^{req} = 0.7$ V, $V_4^{req} = 0.6$ V, $V_5^{req} = 0.5$ V, $V_6^{req} = 0.4$ V. Our proposed optimization framework finds the number, type and width of power switches as well as the values of V_{DDH} and V_{DDL} for the UDVS structure. The baseline UDVS structure also generates the same six required virtual-V_{DD} values from two supply power rails V_{DDH} and V_{DDL}. In the baseline structure, the configuration is fixed at $(3, 3)$, PMOS switches are used, and the values of V_{DDH} and V_{DDL} are fixed. We generate feasible sizes of power switches in baseline UDVS structure using the kernel algorithm up to Step II.

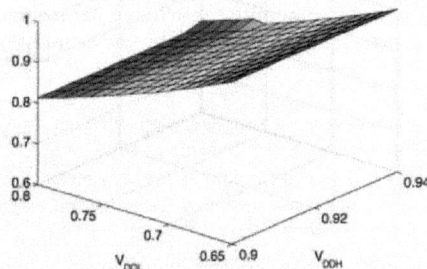

Figure 5. The ratio of "maximum energy overhead" of the proposed UDVS structure to that of the baseline structure under the same area overhead constraint.

We compare the baseline UDVS structure with different pairs of (V_{DDH}, V_{DDL}) values with the proposed UDVS structure. We plots the ratio of the maximum energy overhead of the proposed UDVS structure to that of the baseline UDVS structure under the same area overhead in Figure 5. The proposed optimization framework can reduce the maximum energy overhead by up to 19% (occurs when $V_{DDH} = 0.9$ V and $V_{DDL} = 0.8$ V) compared to the baseline.

Figure 6 plots the ratio of area overhead of the proposed UDVS structure to that of the baseline UDVS structure, when they have the same maximum energy overhead. As can been seen in Figure 6, the proposed optimization framework reduces the area overhead of UDVS structure by up to 74% (occurs when $V_{DDH} = 0.9$ V and $V_{DDL} = 0.8$ V.) Figure 7 plots the ratio of the area overhead of the proposed UDVS structure to that of the baseline

UDVS structure, when they have the same weighted energy consumption. In this case, the proposed optimization framework reduces the area overhead of UDVS structure by up to 70%.

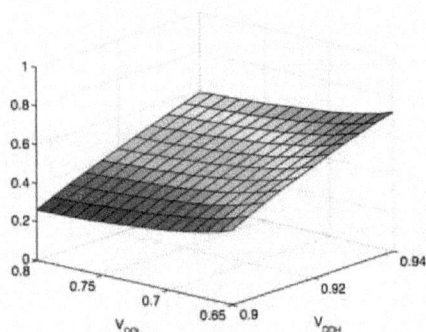

Figure 6. The ratio of area overhead of the proposed UDVS structure to that of the baseline structure under the same constraint of "maximum energy overhead".

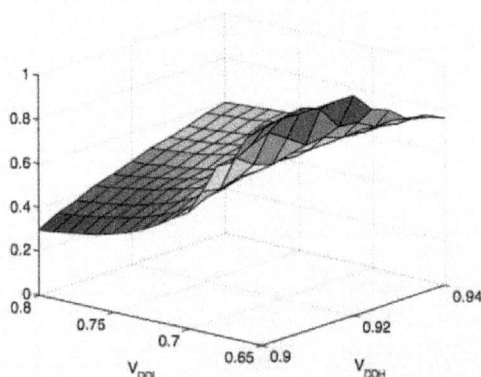

Figure 7. The ratio of the area overhead of the proposed UDVS structure to that of the baseline structure under the same constraint of "weighted energy consumption".

7. CONCLUSION

In this paper, we propose a structure support of fine-grained ultra dynamic voltage scaling (UDVS) with a limited number of power rails. The proposed structure support induces less area overhead than the reference methods especially when the number of supply voltage rails is relatively large. Moreover, we provide an optimization framework to jointly optimize supply voltage levels as well as the number, type (PMOS or NMOS), and size of the power switches. We minimize the overall energy consumption of the UDVS circuit block satisfying the target delay or frequency requirement at each DVS level. We take into account the additional constraints on the number of supply power rails and the total area overhead. The proposed optimization framework also properly accounts for the dynamic energy consumption as well as the leakage energy consumption through all the power switches during both the operation time and stand-by time of the circuit block.

8. ACKNOWLEDGMENTS

This research is sponsored in part by grants from the PERFECT program of the Defense Advanced Research Projects Agency and the Software and Hardware Foundations of the National Science Foundation.

9. REFERENCES

[1] R. Dreslinksi, M. Wiekowski, D. Blaauw, D. Sylvester, and T. Mudge, "Near-threshold computing: reclaiming Moore's law through energy efficient integrated circuits," *Proc. of IEEE*, Feb. 2010.

[2] D. Markovic, C. Wang, L. Alarcon, T. Liu, and J. Rabaey, "Ultralow-power design in near-threshold region," *Proc. of IEEE*, Feb. 2010.

[3] X. Lin, Y. Wang, and M. Pedram, "Joint sizing and adaptive independent gate control for FinFET circuits operating in multiple voltage regimes using the logical effort method," *ICCAD*, Nov. 2013.

[4] B. Zhai, D. Blaauw, D. Sylvester, and K. Flautner, "The limit of dynamic voltage scaling and insomniac dynamic voltage scaling," *IEEE Trans. on VLSI*, vol. 13, no. 11, pp. 1239 – 1252, Nov. 2005.

[5] B. H. Calhoun, A. Wang, and A. Chandrakasan, "Modeling and sizing for minimum energy operation in subthreshold circuits," *IEEE J. Solid-State Circuits*, vol. 40, no. 9, pp. 1178 – 1786, Sept. 2005.

[6] B. H. Calhoun, A. Wang, N. Verma, and A. Chandrakasan, "Sub-threshold design: the challenges of minimizing circuit energy," *Proc. of International Symposium on Low Power Electronic Design*, 2006.

[7] K. Craig, Y. Shakhsheer, and B. H. Calhoun, "Optimal power switch design for dynamic voltage scaling from high performance to subthreshold operation," *Proc. of International Symposium on Low Power Electronic Design* (ISLPED), 2012.

[8] K. Craig, Y. Shakhsheer, S. Khanna, S. Arrabi, J. Lach, B. H. Calhoun, and S. Kosonocky, "A programmable resistive power grid for post-fabrication flexibility and energy tradeoffs," *Proc. of International Symposium on Low Power Electronic Design* (ISLPED), 2012.

[9] Y. Shakhsheer, S. Khanna, K. Craig, S. Arrabi, J. Lach, and B. H. Calhoun, "A 90nm data flow processor demonstrating fine grained DVS for energy efficient operation from 0.25V to 1.2V," *CICC*, 2011.

[10] E. Pakbaznia and M. Pedram, "Coarse-grain MTCMOS sleep transistor sizing using delay budgeting," *Proc. of Design, Automation, and Test in Europe* (DATE), 2008.

[11] M. Seok, S. Hanson, D. Sylvester, and D. Blaauw, "Analysis and optimization of sleep modes in subthreshold circuit design," *Proc. of Design Automation Conference* (DAC), 2007.

[12] K. Shi and D. Howard, "Challenges in sleep transistor design and implementation in low-power designs," *DAC*, 2006.

[13] D. M. Harris, B. Keller, J. Karl, and S. Keller, "A transregional model for near-threshold circuits with application to minimum-energy operation," in *International Conference on Microelectronics*, 2010.

[14] W. Zhao and Y. Cao, "New generation of Predictive Technology Model for sub-45nm early design exploration," *IEEE Transactions on Electronic Devices*, vol. 53, no. 11, pp. 2816 – 2823, Nov. 2006.

[15] T. Sakurai and R. Newton, "Alpha-power law MOSFET model and its applications to CMOS inverter delay and other formulas," *IEEE J. Solid-State Circuits*, vol. 25, no. 2, pp. 584 – 594, April 1990.

Level Shifter Planning for Timing Constrained Multi-Voltage SoC Floorplanning

Zhufei Chu, Yinshui Xia, and Lunyao Wang
School of Information Science & Engineering
Ningbo University, Ningbo, Zhejiang, P.R. China
chuzhufei@mail.nbu.edu.cn, {xiayinshui, wanglunyao}@nbu.edu.cn

ABSTRACT

To implement multi-voltage technique in SoC designs, level shifters (LSs) are essential modules which translate signals among different voltage domains. However, inserting LSs requires non-negligible area and timing overhead. In this paper, we study LS planning (LSP) method for timing constrained multi-voltage SoC floorplanning problem. The design flow consists of two phases. In phase I, to reserve the desired white space for the placement of LSs, the netlist is modified by assigning *virtual LSs* in the nets. In phase II, the main floorplanning loop is implemented. Different from previous works which do voltage assignment without physical information feedback, we build an inner loop between voltage assignment and LS placement under the constraints of both timing and physical layout. Experimental results on Gigascale Systems Research Center (GSRC) benchmark suites indicate the proposed approach can improve power saving by 15% with 4% area increase.

Categories and Subject Descriptors

B.7.2 [**Integrated Circuits**]: Design Aids—*Layout*

Keywords

multi-voltage; floorplanning; level shifter; SoC

1. INTRODUCTION

Multi-voltage technique is an increasingly attractive design option to balance the requirements of performance and power of system-on-a-chip (SoC). The technique assigns high voltage to critical modules while low voltage to non-critical modules, so that the power can be saved without performance degradation [2]. To ensure the right functionality, level shifters (LSs) should be inserted when low voltage modules driving high voltage modules. Since the LSs have area and timing overhead, an effective LS planning (LSP) algorithm is desirable to optimize power consumption under both the timing and physical constraints.

GLSVLSI'14, May 21–23, 2014, Houston, TX, USA.
Copyright 2014 ACM 978-1-4503-2816-6/14/05 ...$15.00.
http://dx.doi.org/10.1145/2591513.2591587.

There are several challenges in LSP. First of all, as the required number of LSs can only be determined after the voltage assignment stage, the final LSs requirement is unknown in advance. Hence, to allocate "just enough" white space resource is a tough task. Moreover, the placement of LSs has a significant impact on timing. If the LSs are placed at improper locations, the timing closure may hard to satisfy or power optimization quality is degraded.

Considerable literature works address the multi-voltage driven SoC design problem at floorplanning stage [7, 8] or post-floorplanning stage [5]. But few of them actually consider the LS placement, which makes the generated results may limit the potential applications. Yu et al. [11] first considers the LS placement problem during floorplanning. For each candidate solution, the voltage assignment and level shifter placement are carried out. They restrict the LSs must be placed in the white space which inherent generated by the floorplan. Hence, it may cause extra wirelength and timing overhead if there are no proper spaces for budget. Zhang et al. [12] proposed an LS floorplanning algorithm for a given multi-voltage design. Based on sequence pair representation, the LSs are greedily pre-placed in the white space. Then, a floorplanning algorithm is used to re-optimize the locations of LSs. Lin et al. [6] proposed two ways, named LS channel and LS island, to allocate regions for LSs during floorplanning and then a two-stage approach is adopted to place LSs. However, both [6] and [12] place LSs under the assumption that the operation voltage of each module is determined and the LS impact on timing is not considered. In contrast, Lee et al. [3] proposed a three-stage algorithm to handle the voltage assignment problem under timing constraints. They first do voltage assignment in netlist level by dynamic programming heuristic. Then the netlist is updated by inserting LSs in the required nets. At last, a power-network-resource (PNR) aware floorplanning algorithm is applied to place the modules and LSs in the netlist. The main drawback is the voltage assignment is done without the feedback of physical information, which may prevent better solutions.

In this paper, we propose a design flow for timing constrained multi-voltage SoC design. Our method consider voltage assignment, LSP and voltage island generation simultaneously under both timing and physical constraints during floorplanning. Since the LSs should be placed in the white space of the floorplan, apart from the inherent white space generated by the floorplanner, we propose a heuristic method to assign virtual LSs in the netlist to reserve the required white space. To satisfy both timing and physical constraints, the voltage assignment and LS placement

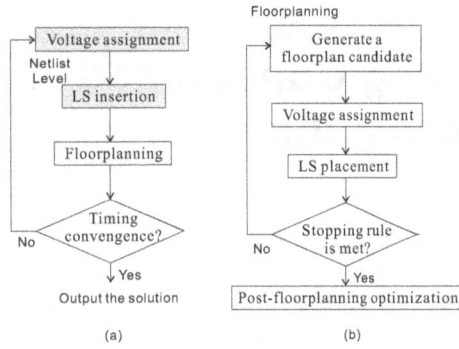

Figure 1: Design flows proposed by other works. (a) [3]. (b) [11].

are operated iteratively until no constraint violations exist, which is different from previous works that do voltage assignment without the feedback of LS's physical information.

2. PROBLEM FORMULATION

We are given a set of n hard modules $m_1, m_2, \cdots, m_n$ with areas. Each module m_i has k_i voltage supply choices, under which the module's delay varies. The power-delay tradeoff is represented by the discrete delay-power (DP) curve, $\{(d_i^1, p_i^1), \cdots, (d_i^{k_i}, p_i^{k_i})\}$, where each pair (d_i^j, p_i^j) denotes the delay and power values of module m_i operating at voltage VDD^j, $1 \leq j \leq k_i$. Modules are connected by the nets. A set of multi-pin nets is decomposed into a set of source-sink two-pin nets. Generally, the netlist can be formulated as a directed acyclic graph (DAG) $G = (V, E)$ with vertexes set V to represent modules and edges set E to denote nets. For multi-voltage designs, apart from modules from the netlist, LSs are essential modules at floorplanning stage. Hence, the DAG $G = (V, E)$ can be extended to $G' = (V', E')$ such that $V' = \{V_m, V_l\}$ contains both modules set V_m from netlist and LSs set V_l. The nets set E' are updated by the original nets and the LSs nets.

Let t_a^i denotes the arrival time of each vertex in V' while t_r^i denotes the required arrival time, the static timing constraints of the netlist is $t_a^i \leq t_r^i$ for each vertex. The calculation of t_a^i can be finished by topological sorting algorithm when $t_a^i = 0$ for all primary inputs (PIs). By setting the required arrival time of primary outputs (POs) to T_{cycle}, the t_r^i can be also determined by reverse topological sorting algorithm. To formulate the interconnect delay, the wire-delay scaling method is used. Assume that the Manhattan distance of modules m_i and m_j is $dist_{ij}$, then the wire delay d_{ij} is calculated as follows.

$$d_{ij} = \delta \times dist_{ij} \qquad (1)$$

where δ is a constant to scale wirelength to delay [3, 7].

Definition 1. (**The Multi-voltage Floorplanning Problem**): Given the DAG G, DP curves, the timing constraints T_{cycle}, and scaling constant δ, the problem is to assign each module with a supply voltage and coordinates so that no two modules are overlapped and power consumption, PNR are optimized with the timing, fixed-outline constraints are satisfied.

Moreover, at the floorplanning stage, the LS must be inserted to accomplish multi-voltage design after voltage assignment step. Hence, we define the LSP problem as follows.

Definition 2. (**The LSP Problem**): For each floorplan candidate, the supply voltage and coordinates of each module are determined, the problem is to place the required number of LSs within the remaining white space so that no two LSs are overlapped and the static timing constraints are satisfied.

Definition 3. (**Feasible Region, FR**): The FR for an LS is defined as the maximum region where the LS may be placed such that by inserting the LS into any candidate location in that region, the delay constraint can be satisfied.

3. MOTIVATIONS

The design flows proposed by [3] and [11] are shown in Figs. 1 (a) and 1 (b), respectively. Lee et al. [3] did voltage assignment and LS insertion in netlist level. The operation voltage of each module and required LSs were determined before floorplanning. If the timing constraints unable be satisfied, the voltage must be reassigned to reserve more timing slack. Moreover, the floorplanning also need be re-operated. Therefore, the design convergence speed severely determined by the number of iterations.

In contrast, Yu et al. [11] did voltage assignemt and LS placement during floorplaning. Given a floorplan candidate, the positions and connections of modules were fixed. Then, the voltages were assigned under the timing constraints. Next, for LS placement, [11] tried to assign as many level-shifters as possible. In other words, the timing may not converge after floorplanning. Therefore, an additional post-floorplanning optimization step was required to further handle LS placement issue.

In our work, we investigate physical constraints of LS that account for design convergence and power consumption. We first develop probabilistic based virtual LS insertion method to reserve the required place for LSs. Then, taking advantages of enough white space, the voltage assignment and LS placement are operated iteratively to make both timing and physical constraints satisfied.

4. ALGORITHM

Fig. 2 shows our design flow for solving the multi-voltage floorplanning problem. The flow consists of two phases: netlist modification and floorplanning. For Phase I, we present a probabilistic based method to insert the virtual LSs into the selected nets to maintain the required white space for subsequent LSP. In Phase II, we perform floorplanning on all modules including the original circuit modules and the additional virtual LSs.

For each floorplan candidate, we first assign supply voltages for all the original circuit modules. Because the LS's locations still unknown, this voltage assignment is somehow a rough estimation. Then, based on the voltage information, the LSs are placed. Taking advantages of the white space inherent existed in the packing and occupied by our virtual LSs and the feature of the FR, we first figure out the possible insertion sites for LS budget, and then the LSs are efficiently placed. Next, we check if the timing converges. If not, the placement information of LSs is fed back to voltage assignment step to make voltages reassigned to reserve

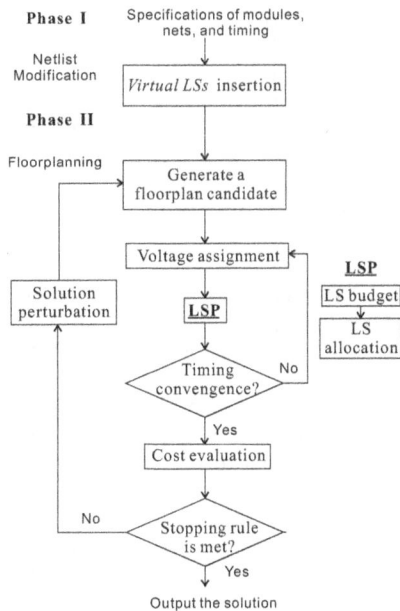

Figure 2: The proposed design flow for the multi-voltage floorplanning problem.

more timing slack. After LSP, the candidate is evaluated by a weighted cost function which considers power, wirelength, and power network resource simultaneously. The algorithm is terminated and output the solution when the stopping rule is met.

4.1 Virtual LSs Insertion

Newly inserted LSs must be given valid locations in the remaining white space. In previous work [11], authors use the space inherent existing in the design as the possible location resources. However, due to insufficiency white space resource, there exists amounts of LSs be placed out of the FR, which makes the algorithm hard to converge and a post-optimization method is required to fix the violations. For the better allocation of the remaining white space, the technique we propose intends to maintain the white space throughout the layout by pre-processing.

Definition 4. (**Virtual LS**): We define the virtual LS as the module which is inserted into the nets without changing the netlist, but accounts for their impact on area and timing.

Now, the problem is how to determine the nets that proper for virtual LS insertion. At first, we review the LS insertion cases. The LS is necessary only when a low-Vdd node drives a high-Vdd node and unnecessary for other cases such as high-to-low, high-to-high, and low-to-low. Therefore, an effective method is required to detect the low-to-high driving nets.

Based on topological estimation without considering the false path and the interconnect delay, we can evaluate the circuit by static timing analysis (STA). The module is referred to (non-)critical module if it is on the (non-)critical path after STA. Since the physical information is not known at the netlist level, we can not accurate determine which net is the low-to-high driving net. However, we can alternatively detect it by probabilistic analysis.

For critical modules, based on the rule of multi-voltage technique, the supply voltage of those modules are likely to be set high. If we use $P(i = s|s \in (low, high))$ to indicate the probability of module i working in voltage state s, then

$$\forall j \in critical, P(j = low) = 0, P(j = high) = 1; \quad (2)$$

For non-critical modules, the one which has larger timing slack has relatively large probability to be set low. Based on this assumption, we randomly assign the voltage state by computing the probability mass function $pmf(x)$, which is

$$pmf(x) = 1 - exp(-x) = 1 - exp[-\frac{sck_i - sck_{min}}{\alpha \times sck_{avg}}] \quad (3)$$

where sck_i is the timing slack of module i and sck_{min}, sck_{avg} are the minimum and average timing slack of all modules, respectively; α is user defined parameter that determines the total number of virtual LSs. By generating a random floating point number $rand()$ between 0 and 1, the voltage state of module i is set to be low if $rand() \leq pmf(x)$. Otherwise, the voltage state of module i is set to be high. Finally, according to above probabilistic voltage assignment, the virtual LSs are inserted for all low-to-high driving nets and the netlist are updated.

4.2 Voltage Assignment

In Phase II, the main floorplanning loop is implemented. For each floorplan candidate, we first assign voltages for each module under the timing constraint. In this stage, the positions of modules and interconnect are determined. Hence, different from probabilistic voltage assignment described in Section 4.1, we can perform voltage assignment in a more accurate way.

With the feedback of physical information of LSs, we use an iterative method to solve voltage assignment shown in Fig. 2. Initially, we obtain the voltage assignment result without considering LS's physical location impact. The ILP (integer linear programming) formulation proposed in [4] is used to obtain such voltage assignment. Then, after LSP (detailed in next subsection), if the LSs can not be successfully placed within the FR, the voltages should be reassigned to reserve more timing slack. The iterations will be terminated until the timing converges.

4.3 Level Shifter Planning (LSP)

In this section, we describe the LSP algorithm in detail. Firstly, the possible insertion sites for LS budget are figured out. Next, we place the LSs within their FRs to meet the delay constraints.

4.3.1 White Space Detection

Recall that the white space in each floorplan candidate can come from two sources: the place occupied by virtual LSs and the white space generated by packing. Hence, the first task is white space detection. As shown in Fig. 3, this can be done by drawing non-uniform grids on the floorplan and making the grid cells covered by modules. The grid cells that remain unmarked are detected as white space [9]. Next, the white space are partitioned into LS sites where LS can be placed.

The introduction of virtual LSs can significantly increase the number of possible LS sites. Firstly, one virtual LS may result in far more than one LS site. As shown in Fig. 3 (a), only one virtual LS is placed between two modules, the

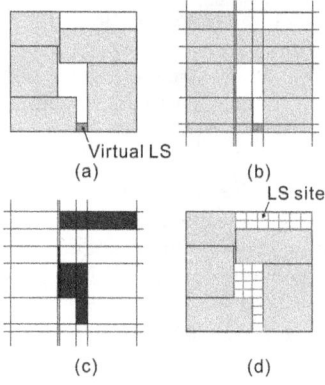

Figure 3: Deadspace detection. (a) initial floorplan. (b) drawing non-uniform grid lines. (c) white space detected. (d) possible LS sites.

number of LS sites resulted by virtual LS shown in Fig. 3 (d) is more than one. This is because the virtual LS can also account for the white space along the boundaries of the two modules. Secondly, the shape of the white space generated by packing may small than the LS size. In such case, the LS can not be placed for non-overlapping violation. But it is not an issue for the virtual LS method since it has the same size as the placed LS.

4.3.2 Detailed LSP

Definition 5. (**Wire Slack**): After voltage assignment, the arrival time, required arrival time, and slack of each module are determined. For $e(u,v) \in E$, the wire slack of e is defined as

$$WR_{slack}(e(u,v)) = tr_v - d_{uv} - ta_u \qquad (4)$$

LEMMA 1. *For $e(u,v) \in E$, suppose that it needs an LS insertion and $\Delta = WR_{slack}(e) - d_{LS}$.*

1. *If $\Delta < 0$, there is no FR for e.*

2. *If $\Delta = 0$, the FR is the white space surrounded by the net bounding box of (u,v).*

3. *If $\Delta > 0$, the FR is the white space surrounded by the region which consists of net bounding box of (u,v) and an additional $\frac{\Delta}{2\delta}$ offset from the four edges of the net bounding box, where δ is the same as that in (1).*

PROOF. When $\Delta < 0$, then $tr_v < ta_u + d_{uv} + d_{LS} = ta_v$, which means the arrival time is later than the required arrival time of module v. Hence, the timing is violated and no FR exists. When $\Delta = 0$, it means the timing is satisfied. According to (1), the Manhattan distance between modules is scaled to evaluate the wire delay. Therefore, if the LSs are located within the net bounding box, the timing is satisfied. Otherwise, the timing may be violated for the extra wire delay. When $\Delta > 0$, apart from the LS's delay, it permits Δ wire delay for LS's connection, which transformed to $\frac{\Delta}{\delta}$ wirelength. Since the connection detours, there are $\frac{\Delta}{2\delta}$ offsets from the edges of net bounding box, as shown in Fig. 4. $\square$

From Lemma 1, we know the Δ must not less than 0 if we should insert an LS into the net. Furthermore, the larger Δ

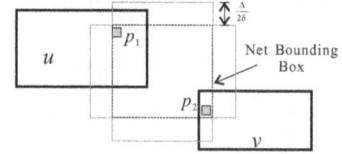

Figure 4: Example of FR.

leads to larger FR. Hence, the LSP has higher probability to satisfy the timing. Before detailed LSP, the Δ value of all nets, which need an LS insertion, should be checked and the FRs are recorded.

Next, we formulate our LSP problem under the timing constraints. Given an LS set V_l in the netlist and a collection of LS sites set Ψ, we need to find a mapping from vertices (LSs) to the LS sites

$$p : V_l \to \Psi \qquad (5)$$

such that

$$\forall i, j \in V_l : (i \neq j) \Rightarrow (p(i) \neq p(j)) \qquad (6)$$

$$\forall j \in V_l : p(i) \in FR(i) \qquad (7)$$

where $FR(i)$ is the feasible region of LS i. Equation (6) indicates that each LS in V_l must be mapped to one-and-only-one LS site while each LS site should be occupied by at most one LS. Under the timing constraint, we aim at finding a solution such that all LSs in the netlist can be mapped within their FRs ((7)).

We solve LSP by an ILP formulation. By introducing a binary variable p_i^j to denote whether a LS l_i is assigned to a LS site s_j, the determination of the locations of LSs can be defined as follows:

$$\sum_{i=1}^{|V_l|} p_i^j \leq 1, j \in [1, |\Psi|] \qquad (8)$$

$$\sum_{j=1}^{|\Psi|} p_i^j = 1, i \in [1, |V_l|] \qquad (9)$$

Equation (8) indicates each LS site can be occupied by at most one LS, while (9) denotes each LS must be assigned to one LS site. Besides, to make the LSs be assigned within its FR, we must set the binary variable of every LS out of its FR to FALSE.

$$p_i^j = 0, \forall j \notin FR(i), i \in [1, |V_l|] \qquad (10)$$

The timing constraint can be satisfied if all the LSs are assigned within its FR. However, if the placed LS site is out of the net bounding box, it may cause extra wirelength. Regarding this issue, the objective function can be

$$MIN : \sum_{i=1}^{|V_l|} \sum_{j=1}^{|\Psi|} p_i^j \times ct_i^j \qquad (11)$$

where ct_i^j is the cost when LS i placed at LS site j. If the LS is placed within the net bounding box, it equals 0; otherwise, it equals a big constant value.

Table 1: Comparison Between Our Method and Previous Work [11]

Circuit	#VLS	#Sites	Power		PNR		#LS		WS (%)		CPU time	
			[11]	Ours	[11]	Ours	[11]	Ours	[11]	Ours	[11]	Ours
n10	3	157	189142	178626	1007	981	9	5	9.44	6.02	2.85s	0.46s
n30	19	290	146483	140610	1436	1257	25	19	11.32	10.38	30.90s	73.26s
n50	29	234	135316	136080	1460	1457	114	30	16.66	10.56	102.93s	467.22s
n100	71	250	123526	107156	1354	1418	153	78	26.71	12.86	605.55s	1316.71s
n200	71	171	130050	103334	1763	1618	203	134	29.66	12.25	28min	616min
n300	40	273	234389	148133	1997	1954	337	128	37.74	13.57	35min	77min
AVG.	–	–	1.00	0.85	1.00	0.96	1.00	0.47	1.00	0.50	1.00	9.64

Table 2: Comparison Between Our Method and No Virtual LS Method

Circuit	No virtual LS						Our method					
	#Sites	Power	PNR	#LS	WS(%)	CPU time	#Sites	Power	PNR	#LS	WS(%)	CPU time
n100	75	110368	1494	75	9.24	991.47s	250	107156	1418	78	12.86	1316.71s
n200	88	144005	1665	87	11.16	419min	171	103334	1618	134	12.25	616min
n300	125	163926	2100	125	9.69	66min	273	148133	1954	128	13.57	77min
AVG.	1.00	1.00	1.00	1.00	1.00	1.00	2.40	0.86	0.95	1.18	1.28	1.42

4.3.3 LS Physical Information Feedback

Based on above formulations, if the ILP solver returns a feasible solution, then we can conclude that the LSP is successful implemented under timing constraint. Otherwise, there must be some LSs not legally mapped to LS sites, such as insufficient LS sites in FR. In that case, we feed back the current physical information of LS to voltage assignment step to reserve more wire slack, hence larger FR.

LEMMA 2. *Given T_{cycle}, the wire slacks of partial edges $e \in E$ will be increased if the voltage level of one module has changed from low to high.*

PROOF. For $e(u, v) \in E$, referring (4), the wire slack of e is $tr_v - d_{uv} - ta_u$. Given T_{cycle}, the tr_v is invariant. Since the interconnect length of (u, v) remains, the d_{uv} still unchanged. If the voltage level of module u has changed from low to high, from DP curves definition, the delay is reduced. Hence, the ta_u decreases and $WR_{slack}(e(u, v))$ is increased. For other edges $e' \in E$, $e' \neq e$, the wire slacks may also improved for the reduction of the arrival time and the increased required arrival time, which can be verified by STA. Therefore, the wire slacks of partial edges $e \in E$ will be increased. □

Definition 6. (**Effective number of LS sites**): Note that one LS site may be shared by several different FRs simultaneously. Assume that one LS site s_j is within θ different FRs, we define the effective number of s_j in one FR as $eff(s_j) = 1/\theta$. Then, the effective number of each FR is the sum of the effective number of all LS sites.

$$eff(FR(i)) = \sum_{j, s_j \in FR(i)} eff(s_j) \quad (12)$$

Therefore, we can use following equation to denote the feasibility that the LSs can be successfully placed.

$$f(i) = \frac{eff(FR(i))}{|\Psi|} \quad (13)$$

To summary, once the ILP solver returns an infeasible solution, we first calculate $eff(FR(i))$ and sort them in an ascending order. The one which has the minimum value is chosen for proceeding. By changing the voltage level of the corresponding module, more wire slacks can be reserved.

Hence, the probability to obtain a feasible solution becomes large.

4.4 Floorplanning Implementation Details

In this paper, we adopt DeFer [10] as our floorplanner to validate our LSP problem. The slicing tree is used for floorplan representation. To perturb the floorplan solution, the sub-tree is swapped or mirrored from top-down. The stopping rule is met when all the sub-tree is traversed. For more details, please refer to [10] due to the limitation of space.

After voltage assignment and LSP, the floorplan candidate is evaluated by the weighted cost function.

$$cost = P + \beta \times W + \gamma \times \Phi \quad (14)$$

where P is the total power consumption, W is the total wirelength, and Φ is the power network routing resource, which is estimated by the sum of half-perimeters of the bounding boxes of the modules working at the same voltage levels. The parameters β and γ are the weights which are set at the beginning of the algorithm by random walks to make the three terms similar in weighting.

5. EXPERIMENTAL RESULTS

In this section, experimental results of the proposed approach are presented. The algorithm is implemented in C under Linux operating system with 3.40 GHz CPU and 4 GB RAM. The benchmark suites and DP curves information are obtained from the authors of [7]. The Gurobi Optimizer [1] is employed as our ILP solver.

The approach is firstly compared to the latest previous work [11] which also tried to solve timing constrained multi-voltage SoC floorplanning and LSP problem. The comparison results are shown in Table 1, where "#VLS" and "#Sites" stand for the number of virtual LS in the netlist and the resulted LS sites in the floorplan, respectively; "Power" is the total power consumption; "PNR" lists the power network routing resource; "#LS" represents the required number of LS; "WS" and "CPU time" are the white space and runtime, respectively. Our method improves power saving by 15%. For larger circuits such as n100, n200, and n300, the power improvement is significant. The main reason is that the virtual LSs are distributed in the floorplan adequately

Table 3: Comparison of Power & Area by Different α Settings

Circuit	No virtual LS			$\alpha = 0.5$			$\alpha = 1.0$ (Our method)			$\alpha = 2.0$		
	Power	Area	#VLS	Power	Area	#VLS	Power	Area	#VLS	Power	Area	#VLS
n100	110368	196080	0	106126	211519	81	107156	206514	71	105200	207390	42
n200	144005	195300	0	104562	202930	110	103334	201122	71	134197	199252	48
n300	163926	299646	0	158480	328792	60	148333	312465	40	159047	310969	34
AVG.	1.00	1.00	–	0.88	1.08	–	0.86	1.04	–	0.95	1.04	–

to reserve possible LS sites for LSP. Therefore, the required number of LSs may be placed within its FR and more modules be assigned lower voltage under the timing constraints. In contrast, without enough LS sites, some modules in [11] must work at a higher voltage to satisfy timing constraints. For other parameters, our method generates 4% less PNR and 50% less white space. In terms CPU time, note that we adopt ILP method for voltage assignment, the method in [11] is almost 10X faster than us. The CPU time may be improved if the voltage assignment is operated by other techniques, such as the promising network flow based method in [7].

To validate the effective of virtual LS, the comparison between our method and no virtual LS method, which does not insert virtual LS in Phase I, is carried out. The results on large circuits are shown in Table 2. Without virtual LS to reserve white space, the resulted number of LS sites dramatically reduced compared to our method. Influenced by this, our method improves the power saving by 14% and PNR by 5%, with a 18% increase of required LS number. In terms of white space and CPU time, since our method should handle more modules (including virtual LSs), the white space and CPU time is increased by 28% and 42%, respectively. For small circuits which need fewer LSs, our method has no advantages on power saving. This is because the inherent white space generated by packing can provide enough space for LSs placement. In contrast, after adding virtual LSs by our method, the floorplan area becomes larger and longer CPU time is consumed.

At last, we report the comparison by different α value in (3). The α value can control the total number of the virtual LS in the netlist. Generally, a lower α leads to more virtual LS. The results are shown in Table 3. As the number of virtual LS increase, the area of the resulted floorplan increases by 4%–8%. However, the power is not liner improved. Although more virtual LS may reserve more LS sites, the wirelength is also increased since the area of the floorplan becomes larger. Referring (1), the wire delay is thus increased. Therefore, under the given T_{cycle}, the power saving may not be so much.

The floorplan results of circuit n50 and n200 are shown in Fig. 5, in which the modules working in high voltage are painted red, the low voltage are painted light-blue, and the LSs are painted yellow.

6. CONCLUSIONS

In this paper, the timing constrained multi-voltage SoC floorplanning problem is studied. The proposed design flow considers voltage assignment, LSP, and voltage island generation simultaneously during floorplanning. To reserve enough white space for LS placement, the virtual LSs are inserted into the netlist based on probabilistic method. During floorplanning, the voltage are assigned with the feedback of physical locations of LS. Experimental results on GSRC benck-

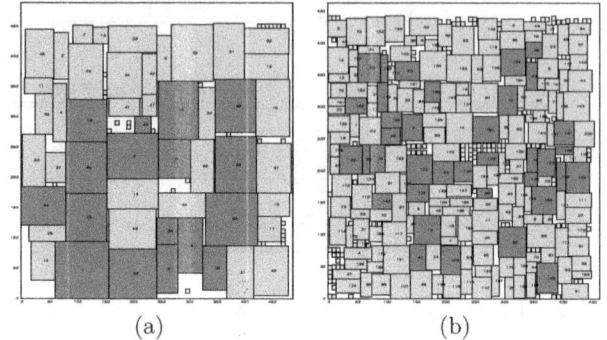

Figure 5: The floorplan results. (a) n50. (b) n200.

mark suites indicate we achieves lower power cost by considering the placement of LS.

7. ACKNOWLEDGEMENTS

This work is supported by the NSFC under Grant Nos. 61131001, 61228105, SRFDP under Grant No. 20113305110001, the ODGR of Ningbo University under Grant No. PY20110001.

8. REFERENCES

[1] Gurobi optimizer. http://www.gurobi.com.
[2] D. E. Lackey, P. S. Zuchowski, T. R. Bednar, D. W. Stout, S. W. Gould, and J. M. Cohn. Managing power and performance for system-on-chip designs using voltage islands. In *Proc. IEEE/ACM ICCAD'02*, pages 195–202, 2002.
[3] W.-P. Lee, H.-Y. Liu, and Y.-W. Chang. Voltage island aware floorplanning for power and timing optimization. In *Proc. IEEE/ACM ICCAD'06*, pages 389 –394, nov. 2006.
[4] W.-P. Lee, H.-Y. Liu, and Y.-W. Chang. An ILP algorithm for post-floorplanning voltage-island generation considering power-network planning. In *Proc. IEEE/ACM ICCAD'07*, pages 650 –655, nov. 2007.
[5] M. K. Y. Leung, E. K. I. Chio, and E. F. Y. Young. Postplacement voltage island generation. *ACM Trans. Des. Autom. Electron. Syst.*, 17(1):4:1–4:15, Jan. 2012.
[6] J.-M. Lin, W.-Y. Cheng, C.-L. Lee, and R. C. Hsu. Voltage island-driven floorplanning considering level shifter placement. In *Proc. IEEE ASP-DAC'12*, pages 443–448. 2012.
[7] Q. Ma, Z. Qian, E. Young, and H. Zhou. MSV-driven floorplanning. *IEEE Trans. Comput. Aided Des. Integr. Circuits Syst*, 30(8):1152 –1162, aug. 2011.
[8] Q. Ma and E. Young. Multivoltage floorplan design. *IEEE Trans. Comput. Aided Des. Integr. Circuits Syst*, 29(4):607 –617, april 2010.
[9] E. Wong and S. K. Lim. Whitespace redistribution for thermal via insertion in 3D stacked ICs. In *Proc. IEEE ICCD'07*, pages 267–272. IEEE, 2007.
[10] J. Yan and C. Chu. Defer: Deferred decision making enabled fixed-outline floorplanning algorithm. *IEEE Trans. Comput. Aided Des. Integr. Circuits Syst*, 29(3):367 –381, march 2010.
[11] B. Yu, S. Dong, S. Goto, and S. Chen. Voltage-island driven floorplanning considering level-shifter positions. In *Proc. ACM GLSVLSI'09*, pages 51–56. ACM, 2009.
[12] X. Zhang, Z. Lin, S. Chen, and T. Yoshimura. An effecient level-shifter floorplanning method for multi-voltage design. In *Proc. IEEE ASICON'11*, pages 421–424. IEEE, 2011.

Exploiting Heterogeneity in MPSoCs to Prevent Potential Trojan Propagation across Malicious IPs

Chen Liu and Chengmo Yang
Dept. of Electrical and Computer Engineering, University of Delaware
Newark, DE, United States
{liuchen, chengmo}@udel.edu

ABSTRACT

Multiprocessor System-on-Chip (MPSoC) platforms face some of the most demanding security concerns, as they process, store, and communicate sensitive information using third-party intellectual property (3PIP) cores. The trend of outsourcing design and fabrication strongly questions the assumption of 3PIP components being trustworthy. While existing research focuses on addressing hardware trojans in individual IPs, this paper improves MPSoC security from another perspective. Specifically, our goal is to prevent trojans in malicious IPs from triggering each other and leading to severe system-wide degradation in security and reliability. We propose to impose trojan isolation constraints during static task scheduling, ensuring that all legal communications on the target MPSoC are between IPs of different types. This in turn enables the runtime system to monitor and detect undesired communication paths, if any. We furthermore pose the security-constrained MPSoC task scheduling as a multi-dimensional optimization problem, and solve it through Integer Linear Programming (ILP), thus minimizing the associated performance, power, and hardware overhead. The results show that trojan isolation can be achieved within one extra vendor and nearly no performance overhead.

1. INTRODUCTION

Advances in VLSI have accelerated the integration of processing, storage, and communication capabilities onto a single chip. Multiprocessor System-on-Chip (MPSoC) architectures have become a routine way of building embedded systems such as smart phones, network routers, storage & web servers, and gaming systems. Through integrating third-party intellectual property (3PIP) cores and outsourcing fabrication and testing steps, MPSoC designers can quickly respond to the increasing demands in functionality, power consumption and programmability without sacrificing design productivity. Unfortunately, using 3PIP cores and outsourcing design steps also make MPSoC platforms vulnerable to malicious modifications (also known as *Hardware Trojan Horses*), leading to severe security concerns.

Hardware trojans in 3PIPs may cause system failures at some critical points during application execution or could create backdoors to leak confidential information back to the attacker. Existing research shows that trojans, from the perspective of their activation method, can be classified into three categories: *always-on*, *externally triggered*, and *internally triggered* [1]. In an MPSoC, not only may each individual 3PIP core have these three types of trojans, but also the interactions between cores should be taken into consideration. A trojan, once activated, can send messages to trigger those hibernating trojans in other cores. We name this triggering method as "**trojan propagation**".

Trojan propagation can lead to crucial security and reliability issues, as it introduces correlation between unexpected events. MPSoC architectures usually exploit hardware redundancy to improve reliability, such as duplicating a program on two cores [2], or providing spare cores in case of failures [3]. Yet the effectiveness of these techniques hinges on an underlying assumption of failures being random and the probability of correlated failures being extremely low. Unfortunately, this assumption no longer holds when considering trojan propagation. IP cores with the same type of trojans may fail at the same time, thus causing two cores to produce the same wrong results or resulting in no healthy spare core left in the system.

Trojan propagation could be prevented if an already activated trojan is isolated from those hibernating trojans. Typically different vendors do not share back-doors or trigger patterns in common since to do so, a rogue element has to expose itself to the other rogue elements. This implies that trojan propagation could be prevented if every single core on an MPSoC is from a distinct vendor. Unfortunately, as MPSoCs may have tens or even hundreds of cores, it is infeasible to find so many IP vendors. In light of this observation, we propose a collaborative strategy that embeds certain property within the target MPSoC at design-time, and checks such property at runtime to detect inter-vendor communications and isolate trojans, if any. The proposed technique exploits the flexibility that MPSoC designers usually have in choosing cores and vendors based on the task graph information of their applications. In a nutshell, the technical contribution of this paper consists of the following three aspects:

- At the MPSoC design stage, security constraints are embedded into the task scheduling process. Tasks of the target application are bound to cores and vendors in a way that all necessary communications are between cores from different vendors.
- The underlying communication framework is extended to enable the runtime system to easily monitor the types of source and destination cores of every communication. Undesired intra-vendor communications, if any, will be detected, thus preventing triggers from being sent to their destinations.
- The security-constrained task scheduling is posed as a multi-dimensional optimization problem and solved through Integer Linear Programming (ILP), thus enabling trojan isolation to be achieved within minimum overhead in schedule length, energy consumption, vendor and hardware cost.

2. TECHNICAL BACKGROUND

To reduce costs and meet the tight time-to-market deadlines, companies such as *Apple Inc.* purchase IP cores from third parties, integrate these cores, generate the layout, and send it to foundries for fabrication. This globalized design trend makes MPSoCs prone to insider attacks. A rogue insider in the foundry may make subtle mask changes, or alter chemical compositions to accelerate failures in critical circuitry [4]. A rogue insider in a third-party design house may insert malicious logic in an IP [4, 5, 6] to modify functionality, deny service, or create a backdoor to leak confidential information.

From the perspective of their activation method, hardware trojans can be classified into three categories: *always-on*, *externally triggered* and *internally triggered* [1]. Always-on trojans are always active. In order to avoid being detected during testing, an always-on Trojan needs to be inserted in rarely accessed places and its footprint needs to be kept small, which in turn limits its functionality [1]. In comparison, externally triggered trojans are to be activated by the trojan implanter. This implies that a trojan needs to have access to the I/O in order to receive activation messages from the implanter [7]. Finally, internally triggered trojans are to be activated by internal triggers, such as on-chip sensors, a segment of cheat codes or ticking timebomb [5], when they reach certain conditions. Same as always-on trojans, the triggering conditions should be relatively hard to reach so as to prevent these trojans from being detected during testing.

A wealth of trojan detection techniques target malicious modifications during fabrication. Through performing functional testing or side-channel analysis, manufactured chips are measured and compared against the expected values. Hardware trojans are identified by detecting their impact on power [8, 9, 10], delay [11], and a combination of them [12, 13]. Yet side channel analysis is usually limited by the measurement capabilities of the analog probes. For trojans of small size, the subtle differences in power and delay can be masked by process variations and measurement errors, which can be as high as 5% [14]. In [14], several techniques combining algebraic, numerical, and statistical methods with power and delay measurements have been proposed to detect hardware trojans in the presence of process variations.

Detecting hardware trojans in 3PIPs is even more challenging, since there is no golden (trojan-free) model for the designer to refer to. In [15], a trojan detection and prevention scheme is proposed for homogeneous systems. Each program is partitioned into segments and redundantly executed on three or more cores, aiming at limiting the data access capability of each core. In [5], a register transfer level technique is proposed to monitor inter-component communications to detect malicious behavior. This work is extended in [16] to prevent trojans from being triggered through obfuscating and scrambling the inputs to infected hardware units. As these techniques require detailed RTL information, their application to third-party IP cores is limited. Another related work [17] requires the check of a 3PIP against pre-defined agreements on security-related properties provided by the vendor. Yet developing security-related properties for a 3PIP is still in its infancy. Further, there may still be opportunities for the rogue designer to deliver malicious 3PIP cores that honor these security properties.

3. TECHNICAL MOTIVATION

The growing complexity of MPSoCs, along with the fact that hardware trojans are purposefully inserted by an attacker in hard-to-detect sites in the design, makes it almost infeasible to fully test or analyze the system to guarantee trustworthiness (i.e., 100% trojan freeness) of 3PIPs. More crucially, as most MPSoC platforms employ a centralized bus or on-chip network that physically connects cores to each other, it is possible that undesired communication paths may be formed between malicious 3PIPs, leading to potential trojan propagation that the designer is not aware of. Trojan propagation is a serious security issue, as it not only makes triggering conditions easier to meet but also may lead to multiple trojans being activated at the same time, as discussed below:

For externally triggered trojans, their activation requires receiving messages through the I/O. In most MPSoCs, only a limited number

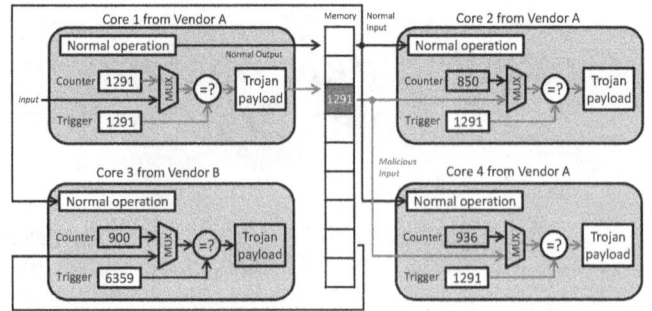

Figure 1: An example of a trojan propagation. $Core1$ maliciously writes the trigger value to a memory location that is accessed by $Core2$ and $Core4$, triggering trojans in them. $Core3$ does not access this location since it is produced by a different vendor.

of cores are directly connected to I/O devices. However, with trojan propagation, the triggering message can be sent from one core to another. The trojan therefore can be triggered as long as it can receive activation messages from a core that has access to the I/O.

For internally triggered trojans, they will be activated when the temperature sensor or time bomb counter reaches a specific value or when a certain code is being processed. A concrete example is shown in Figure 1, wherein $Core1$, $Core2$, and $Core4$ share the same trigger value. During normal execution these cores will receive different inputs and will have different temperature and power values (also influenced by process variation) that diversity their triggering conditions. However, with trojan propagation, if any core (e.g., $Core1$ in Figure 1) reaches the triggering condition, it can send messages to other cores through secretly writing in a memory location (shown in red). As a result, all trojans of the same type became active within a short while.

To prevent trojan propagation, one solution that may seem feasible is to check the content of every single inter-core communication message to ensure its cleanness. However, this approach is impractical since the associated transmission delay and energy consumption can be prohibitive. Also it may not be able to detect the triggers that are camouflaged as normal messages. Another possibility is to exploit *vendor diversity*. Usually different vendors do not share a backdoor or a trigger pattern in common. This is shown in Figure 1, wherein the triggering condition of $Core3$ is different from the other three cores. Given this fact, trojan propagation could be prevented if the designer ensures that no cores on an MPSoC are from the same vendor, Unfortunately, for MPSoCs with tens or even hundreds of cores, this approach is infeasible.

To prevent trojan propagation while minimizing the request for extra vendors, we propose a collaborative strategy. Given the fact that only 3PIPs from the same vendor may share common triggers, we consider communication paths between cores from different vendors as *trustable*, and the paths between cores from the same vendor as *untrustable*. At the design stage, the proposed technique schedules tasks of the target application in a way that all necessary inter-core communications are mapped to trustable paths on the target MPSoC. Then, at runtime if any communication occurs on those untrustable paths, it must be malicious and hence a security flag will be raised. In this way, even if a core (e.g., $Core1$ in Figure 1) silently produces unexpected data at runtime, such data are only accessible to cores from different vendors (e.g., $Core3$ in Figure 1) which will not use them for trojan triggering.

4. SECURITY-CONSTRAINED SCHEDULING

This section describes the static scheduling part of the proposed collaborative hardware trojan isolation technique, which is to be adopted at the MPSoC design stage. In our threat model, the attacker is a rogue insider in the 3PIP house who may insert malicious logic in the 3PIP cores. The defender is a designer who has the information of task graph and the flexibility of binding tasks to cores, choosing cores from different vendors, and developing glue logic for security enhancement.

To protect an MPSoC against system-wide trojan propagation, the propose technique isolates trojans through exploiting *vendor diversity*. Companies such as Microchip Technology, Altera, Sony and Ingenic provide cores sharing the same instruction set (i.e., MIPS). These diverse cores can be integrated on the target MPSoC to meet the requirement of diverse vendors. However, an increased level of diversity elevates the design cost. To enable the designer to consider security along with the traditional scheduling metrics, we formulate the security-constrained task scheduling problem through integer linear programming (ILP).

4.1 Scheduling Problem Formulation

Task scheduling is a critical step in MPSoC design [18]. Given the task graph of an application, the designers bind tasks to cores and coordinate the communications between cores. This step determines the performance and power consumption characteristics of an application, as well as the types and number of the 3PIP cores needed in the MPSoC. Compared to homogeneous MPSoCs, heterogenous MPSoCs furthermore offer the flexibility of using the most suitable core for each task to improve overall performance or energy efficiency [19].

The scheduling problem can be formalized as the association of a start time and the assignment of a core with each task of the application. The target platform is modeled as an MPSoC with m cores $Core_i$ ($1 \leq i \leq m$), and each core may be produced by one of the p available vendors $Vendor_k$ ($1 \leq k \leq p$). The parallel application can be represented as a weighted *directed acyclic graph* (DAG) $G = (V, E)$. The graph has n vertices. Each vertex $Task_i \in V$ represents a task, with a weight $exeT_i$ ($1 \leq i \leq n$) denoting its execution time. Each edge $Dep_{i,j} \in E_c$ represents a communication from $Task_i$ to $Task_j$, with a weight $comT_{i,j}$ ($1 \leq i,j \leq n$) denoting the inter-core communication overhead.

To model binding relations, a set of variables $T2C_{i,j}$, $C2V_{j,k}$, and $T2V_{i,k}$ are used:
- $T2C_{i,j} = 1$ if $Task_i$ is bound to $Core_j$ and 0 otherwise.
- $C2V_{j,k} = 1$ if $Core_j$ is from $Vendor_k$ and 0 otherwise.
- $T2V_{i,k} = 1$ if $Task_i$ is bound to $Vendor_k$ and 0 otherwise.

Clearly, every task is bound to a single core, and every core is bound to a single vendor. Analogously, each task should be bound to the vendor of the core it is scheduled on. These properties can be modeled using the following three ILP constraints:
- $\forall Task_i$:

$$\sum_{j=1}^{m} T2C_{i,j} = 1 \tag{1}$$

- $\forall Core_j$:

$$\sum_{k=1}^{p} C2V_{j,k} = 1 \tag{2}$$

- $\forall Task_i$ and $\forall Vendor_k$:

$$T2V_{i,k} = \sum_{j=1}^{m} T2C_{i,j} * C2V_{j,k} \tag{3}$$

Equation (3) ensures that $T2V_{i,k}$ is 1 if and only if $Task_i$ is scheduled on $Core_j$ and $Core_j$ is from $Vendor_k$.

In addition to task binding properties, it is necessary to ensure that tasks scheduled on the same core should not overlap in their execution time. To model this constraint, we introduce another set of variables:
- $Order_{i,j} = 1$ if $Task_i$ and $Task_j$ are scheduled on the same core AND $Task_i$ is before $Task_j$, and 0 otherwise.

Using these variables, the non-overlapping property is to be modeled through the following three constraints: First, a child task cannot be put before any of its parent tasks:
- $\forall Dep_{i,j}$:

$$Order_{j,i} = 0 \tag{4}$$

Second, the order relation is transitive such that if, on a single core, $Task_i$ is before $Task_k$ and $Task_k$ is before $Task_j$, then $Task_i$ must be before $Task_j$.
- $\forall Task_i, Task_j, Task_k$ that $i \neq j \neq k$:

$$Order_{i,j} \geq Order_{i,k} * Order_{k,j} \tag{5}$$

Third, the order relation between two tasks is mutually exclusive:
- $\forall Task_i, Task_j$ that $i \neq j$:

$$Order_{i,j} + Order_{j,i} = \sum_{k=1}^{m} T2C_{i,k} * T2C_{j,k} \tag{6}$$

If $Task_i$ and $Task_j$ are scheduled on the same core, the right hand side of Equation (6) will be 1 and hence exactly one of $Order_{i,j}$ and $Order_{j,i}$ is 1. Otherwise if they are on different cores, both $Order_{i,j}$ and $Order_{j,i}$ are 0.

Once the order relationship between tasks is defined, the start and finish time of each task can be constrained. For $Task_j$, its start time ST_j is constrained by the finish time of all its predecessors and the ready time of all the incoming data. Here, the communication overhead $comT_{i,j}$ is imposed only when $Task_j$ and its predecessor $Task_i$ are scheduled on different cores, that is, $Order_{i,j} = 0$. FT_i denotes the finish time of $Task_i$.
- $\forall Dep_{i,j}$:

$$ST_j \geq FT_i + comT_{i,j} * (1 - Order_{i,j}) \tag{7}$$

Moreover, $Task_j$ cannot start if any $Task_i$ that is scheduled before it on the same core (therefore $Order_{i,j} = 1$) have not finished execution:
- $\forall Task_i, Task_j$ that $i \neq j$:

$$ST_j \geq FT_i * Order_{i,j} \tag{8}$$

Finally, the finish time of a task is the sum of its start time and its execution time. Yet the heterogeneity in cores affects task execution time. Here we adopt a matrix representation, wherein $exeT_{i,k}$ denotes the execution time of $Task_i$ on a core from $Vendor_k$. If $Task_i$ cannot be executed by cores from $Vendor_k$, the execution time of $Task_i$ on $Vendor_k$ will be set to an extremely large value, enabling the scheduler to automatically avoid such binding during task assignment. Using this matrix representation of task execution time, the finish time of $Task_i$ is given by the following equation:
- $\forall Task_i$:

$$FT_i = ST_i + \sum_{k=1}^{p} exeT_{i,k} * T2V_{i,k}; \tag{9}$$

Since $T2V_{i,k} = 1$ only for a single vendor, one and only one value of $exeT_{i,k}$ will be added to ST_i, thus effectively modeling core heterogeneity and its impact to task execution time and finish time.

4.2 Security-Constrained Task Scheduling

The isolation of potential hardware trojans requires the exclusion of all communications between cores from the same vendor. Extra security-driven constraints need to be added to the heterogeneous MPSoC scheduling problem, which can be achieved at **two different granularities**. At the finest granularity, trojan isolation can be added to each communication path. In other words, all the communications are forced to be between 3PIP cores produced by different vendors, thus providing strongest protection against trojan propagation between malicious 3PIPs:

- $\forall\, Dep_{i,j}$ and $\forall\, Vendor_k$:

$$T2V_{i,k} + T2V_{j,k} \leq 1 \qquad (10)$$

Equation (10) constrains that for any pair of dependent tasks i and j, $T2V_{i,k}$ and $T2V_{j,k}$ can never be 1 at the same time. In other words, the constraint prohibits dependent tasks from being scheduled on cores from the same vendor and hence on the same core. Therefore, $comT_{i,j}$ is always imposed in Equation (7), which in turn may increase the schedule length. Also, the energy consumption becomes higher, not only because of the increased amount of inter-core communication, but also because cores need to be active for longer time due to the increased schedule length. What is more, because dependent tasks need to be bound to different vendors, the minimum number of vendors needed in the target MPSoC platform may increase. Specifically, the lowest vendor count is constrained by the the minimum number of colors needed to color the task graph of the application[1]. As long as there is dependency (i.e., edges) in the task graph, more than one vendor is required.

Given the elevated performance, energy, and vendor overhead imposed by the fine-grain trojan isolation, we also exploit the alternative of satisfying trojan isolation constraint at a coarser granularity, allowing dependent tasks to be scheduled on the same core to reduce such overhead. This can be achieved by allowing both $T2V_{i,k}$ and $T2V_{j,k}$ to be 1 if $Order_{i,j}$ is 1 (implying that $Task_i$ and $Task_j$ are on the same core):

- $\forall\, Dep_{i,j}$ and $\forall\, Vendor_k$:

$$T2V_{i,k} + T2V_{j,k} \leq 1 + Order_{i,j} \qquad (11)$$

Compared to Equation (10), Equation (11) also ensures that all inter-core communications are between different vendors, but does not force every communication to be inter-core. The relaxed constraint in turn provides more flexibility in scheduling, which could be exploited to reduce communication overhead and energy consumption, and to improve performance and the flexibility in coloring the task graph.

4.3 Multi-Dimensional Optimization Process

Up until now we have presented the ILP constraints for formulating heterogenous MPSoC scheduling and the proposed trojan isolation constraint. An ILP solver can then solve this multi-dimensional optimization problem by optimizing the schedule based on the following three objective functions:

The performance of the schedule is defined as the overall schedule length, which is computed as the finish time of the last finished task among all the tasks.

$$\textbf{Goal1: } minimize \max_{1 \leq i \leq n} FT_i$$

The number of vendors is crucial to the design cost of the target MPSoC. For a given schedule, the vendor count can be computed by summing up the maximum value of $C2V_{j,k}$:

$$\textbf{Goal2: } minimize \sum_{k=1}^{p} \max_{1 \leq j \leq m} C2V_{j,k}$$

If $Vendor_k$ is not used, then $C2V_{j,k}$ should be 0 for all cores. In contrast, if $Vendor_k$ is used, then there should be at least one $C2V_{j,k}$ equals to 1. Therefore, by summing up the maximum value of $C2V_{j,k}$ across all vendors, the total number of vendors used in a schedule can be obtained.

The energy consumed in executing an application is composed of three parts: the energy in executing all the tasks, the standby energy

---

[1]Graph coloring [20] is the problem of finding the minimum number of colors that ensure adjacent vertices in a graph do not share the same color.

---

when a core is idle, and the energy in sending/receiving all communication data.

$$\textbf{Goal3: } minimize \sum_{i=1}^{m}(T_i^{busy} * P_i^{busy} + T_i^{idle} * P_i^{idle}) + E_{comm}$$

Here, T_i^{busy} and P_i^{busy} respectively denote the length of time that $Core_i$ is busy and its power consumption during that time, while T_i^{idle} and P_i^{idle} denote the corresponding values when $Core_i$ is idle. The first two product terms give the energy consumed when $Core_i$ is busy and idle, respectively. E_{comm} represents the energy consumed by all the inter-core communications. It can be computed by summing up the communication energy between all pairs of dependent tasks $Task_i$ and $Task_j$ if and only if $Order_{i,j}$ is 0.

The proposed ILP model provides designers with flexibility to adjust the priorities of the various objective functions. In our study, the schedule length is considered as the most important optimization goal since increasing it will also increase energy consumption. The vendor count is the second important goal since increasing it will sizably elevate the design and hardware cost. The energy consumption is ranked third. These three goals can be optimized one by one in a 3-step optimization process. First, the ILP solver minimizes the schedule length given the maximum number of cores that the target MPSoC can hold and an upper-bound of vendor count. This value is set to the theoretical upper-bound, which is the minimum number of colors required for coloring the task graph, as mentioned in Section 4.2. Subsequently, the ILP solver minimizes the vendor count within a fixed core count and the schedule length obtained at the first step. Here it is possible to allow a degradation of the scheduled length at an amount specified by the designer (e.g., 5%). Finally, the ILP solver minimizes the energy consumption while leaving the schedule length and vendor count intact.

5. COMMUNICATION MONITORING

The security-constrained task scheduling performed at MPSoC design stage guarantees that all the expected inter-core communications are between 3PIPs from different vendors. This effectively simplifies the runtime communication monitoring process. There is no need to check the content of every message to distinguish legal and illegal communications. Instead, only the producer and consumer 3PIPs need to be monitored to ensure that they are not from the same vendor. This can be easily accomplished through a lightweight extension to the underlying communication framework, within only negligible hardware overhead. In the following parts of this section, we outline possible extensions to two commonly adopted communication approaches, namely, *shared memory* and *message passing*.

5.1 Shared memory based MPSoC

A communication in shared memory MPSoC is performed through two operations: a write to a memory location followed by a read from another core. To detect undesired communications, each data block is extended to include an *owner* field of $\lceil \log_2 m \rceil$ bits (for an MPSoC with m cores). This field uniquely specifies the owner of each data block. It is to be updated by the memory controller whenever a 3PIP writes the data block, and to be checked whenever a 3PIP tries to read the data block. The memory controller checks the data producer against the 3PIP requesting the data, and raises a flag if their core IDs differ but their core types are identical.

For some MPSoCs, each 3PIP core has its local cache, and these caches can communicate through a coherence protocol [21] without writing/reading data objects to/from memory. To record data producer information, not only the memory but also the local cache should include *owner* fields for each cache line. While these fields are still updated upon write accesses, they only need to be checked upon read misses, as reads hitting in the local cache are not involved in inter-core communication. A detailed example is shown in Fig-

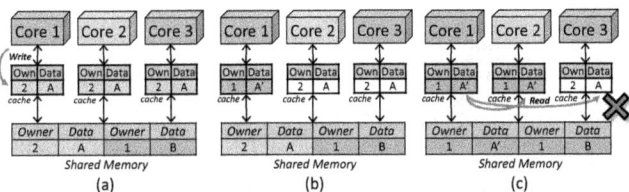

Figure 2: Monitoring inter-core communication through the owner fields. In (a), $Core1$ tries to update data A. In (b), the owner field of A is updated, while the old copies in $Core2$ and $Core3$ are invalidated. In (c), Read from $Core3$ to A is blocked since it is from the same vendor as $Core1$.

ure 2, assuming the use of a write-back cache and a standard write-invalidate MSI coherence protocol [21].

- The owner field is updated upon $Core1$ issuing a write request to location A, as shown in Figure 2(a). After this write, the data field and the owner field in the local cache of $Core1$ are updated, as shown in Figure 2(b). The old copies of A in $Core2$ and $Core3$ are invalidated, thus preventing incorrect data sharing.

- The owner field is checked upon $Core2$ and $Core3$ issuing read requests to location A, as shown in Fig. 2(b). The read issued by $Core2$ is granted since it is from a different vendor. Yet the read issued by $Core3$ will be denied since $Core3$ is from the same vendor as $Core1$, the owner of A. A security flag will be raised to report this illegal read request.

5.2 Message passing based MPSoC

In this scheme, messages can be passed through either an on-chip network or a centralized bus structure. In both cases, extra logic can be attached to the routers or the bus controller to act as a "firewall".

The communication pattern can be either point-to-point or broadcasting. For a point-to-point communication, both the sender and the receiver are explicit. By checking the source and the destination 3PIPs of each message, an illegal communication can be easily detected and the unexpected, malicious messages can be intercepted. In comparison, for a broadcasting communication, only the sender is explicit. It is impossible to differentiate legal and illegal messages since they all share the same broadcasting channel. However, the router or the bus controller can still block, given the message sender, all the receiver cores that are from the same vendor as the sender. This way, the runtime system is still able to prevent a hibernating trojan from being triggered.

6. EXPERIMENTAL RESULTS

6.1 Methodology

To show the impact of the security constraints, we compare **three** schedules. The first is a baseline schedule for heterogeneous MP-SoCs without any security consideration, while the second and the third schedules have the trojan isolation constraint satisfied at fine and coarse granularities, respectively. The corresponding ILP constraints and optimization functions are generated according to the equations shown in Sections 4. These ILP problems are solved using LINGO [22].

The propsed technique is effective for MPSoCs with a wide range of core counts. In our experiments, it is assumed that the underlying MPSoC platform can hold up to 8 cores. Our study indicates that this value is sufficient for confining the complexity of ILP within a reasonable range, while at the same time allowing the three schemes to generate distinguishable results.

To model a diverse set of cores, we utilize the data of a set of real-world processors, including AMD ElanSC520, IBM PowerPC 405GP and NEC VR5432. These values are obtained from the E3S

Table 1: Schedule lengths of the three schemes

	Not-secured	Fine-grained		Coarse-grained	
	length	length	ratio	length	ratio
Auto-indust	22695	22727	1.01	22695	1
Consumer	14530	32580	2.24	14530	1
Networking	5136	5168	1.01	5136	1
Office	12620	14525	1.15	12620	1
Telecom	4288	4429	1.03	4288	1
Random1	32695	34878	1.07	32696	1
Random2	33712	39826	1.18	33712	1
Random3	44684	54447	1.22	44684	1
Random4	27863	34306	1.23	28174	1.01
Random5	34816	39798	1.14	34816	1
Average			1.23		1.00

benchmark suite [23], which includes not only task graphs of real-world applications, such as *auto-indust, consumer, networking, office-automation,* and *telecom,* but also the performance and power information of each task on these given processors. Such information allows us to model and study the variations in task execution time and energy consumption when generating the three different schedules. Furthermore, as the task graphs in the E3S benchmarks are relatively simple, we additionally use 5 random parallel task graphs to evaluate the proposed scheduling scheme. These task graphs, generated using TGFF [24], are more complex and diverse than those E3S benchmarks. Values of task execution time, communication latency, and energy consumption are also randomly generated.

6.2 Results

Our first set of experiment compares the optimal schedule lengths of the not-secured and the two secured schedules. The energy consumption is not constrained and the upper bound of vendor count is set to three in these studies. Our studies show that three vendors are sufficient for representing the diversity of heterogeneous MPSoCs and satisfying trojan isolation constraints.

Table 1 lists the lengths of the three schedules obtained for the E3S benchmarks (first 5 rows) and the random task graphs (next 5 rows). For the two security schedules, their schedule length ratio over the baseline is also provided. It can be clearly seen that the fine-grained security scheme, as it requires the separation of all dependent tasks to different types of cores, has the longest schedule length for all the benchmarks (1% – 124% longer than the baseline). In comparison, the schedule lengths of the coarse-grained scheme are almost the same as the baseline. This confirms that the coarse-grained scheme effectively exploits the flexibility of core to vendor mapping during the scheduling process, thus eliminating intra-vendor communications and fulfilling security constraints without sacrificing performance.

As a crucial factor that impacts both the design cost and the hardware cost, vendor count should be controlled within a reasonable range. Using the optimal schedule length in Table 1 as a constraint, the number of vendors required for the three schedules is minimized and reported in Table 2. As can be seen, without sacrificing the schedule length, all the benchmarks can be scheduled within three vendors. As expected, on average the two security-driven schemes need more vendors than the baseline, non-security scheme. Yet when the trojan isolation constraint is fulfilled at the coarse granularity, fewer vendors are needed. Compared to the baseline, the coarse-grained scheme needs no extra vendor for 8 out of the 10 benchmarks, and only one extra vendor for the other two benchmarks. We believe that this small cost for extra vendors is acceptable for building a trustworthy MPSoC, especially when it is used in critical infrastructure.

Using the optimal schedule length and minimum vendor count as constraints, the last step in the optimization process is to minimize the total energy consumption, a factor crucial to most embedded systems. The obtained values are also shown in Table 2, computed using

Table 2: Vendor count and energy consumption

	Vendor count			Energy Consumption		
	No	Fine	Coarse	Not-secured	Fine-grained	Coarse-grained
				total = busy + idle + comm	total = busy + idle + comm	total = busy + idle + comm
Auto-indust	2	2	2	1 = 0.789 + 0.210 + 0.001	1.002 = 0.790 + 0.211 + 0.001	1 = 0.789 + 0.210 + 0.001
Consumer	1	2	1	1 = 0.703 + 0.297 + 0	1.678 = 0.659 + 0.164 + 0.855	1 = 0.703 + 0.297 + 0
Networking	2	2	2	1 = 0.866 + 0.125 + 0.009	1.439 = 1.210 + 0.191 + 0.047	1 = 0.866 + 0.125 + 0.009
Office	2	3	2	1 = 0.877 + 0.123 + 0.000	0.909 = 0.726 + 0.183 + 0.000	1 = 0.877 + 0.123 + 0.000
Telecom	1	3	2	1 = 0.820 + 0.179 + 0.001	1.559 = 1.229 + 0.317 + 0.013	1.214 = 0.994 + 0.218 + 0.002
Random1	3	3	3	1 = 0.757 + 0.222 + 0.021	1.106 = 0.790 + 0.239 + 0.077	1.021 = 0.749 + 0.239 + 0.033
Random2	3	3	3	1 = 0.693 + 0.257 + 0.050	1.200 = 0.812 + 0.303 + 0.085	1.048 = 0.747 + 0.250 + 0.051
Random3	2	3	2	1 = 0.755 + 0.221 + 0.024	1.235 = 0.843 + 0.297 + 0.095	1.080 = 0.806 + 0.249 + 0.025
Random4	1	3	2	1 = 0.686 + 0.304 + 0.010	0.886 = 0.519 + 0.292 + 0.075	0.816 = 0.633 + 0.172 + 0.011
Random5	3	3	3	1 = 0.660 + 0.296 + 0.044	1.092 = 0.662 + 0.348 + 0.082	1.045 = 0.711 + 0.290 + 0.044
Average	2	2.7	2.2	1 = 0.761 + 0.223 + 0.016	1.210 = 0.823 + 0.254 + 0.133	1.022 = 0.787 + 0.218 + 0.017

the formulas listed in Section 4.3. The busy and idle energy is respectively proportional to the busy and idle time of each core, while the communication energy is proportional to the number of inter-core communications. These values are normalized to the total energy consumption of the baseline scheme. It can be seen that for each scheme, the total energy is the sum of core busy energy, idle energy, and communication energy.

For almost all the benchmarks and almost all the individual energy types, it can be seen that the not-secured scheme consumes the lowest amount while the fine-grained scheme consumes the highest amount. This is due to the fact that the fine-grained scheme separates all the dependent tasks to different cores, forcing every pair of dependent tasks to consume communication energy. Meanwhile, the separation of dependent tasks also forces cores to wait longer for incoming data, thus making the idle time and idle energy larger. In some cases, if the fine-grained scheme utilizes more vendors than the baseline scheme, it is possible that a relatively slower core may be very power-efficient and hence offers energy reduction. The examples are benchmarks *Consumer*, *Office* and *Random4* in Table 2, for which the fine-grain scheme consumes less amount of core busy energy than the baseline. This in turn results in less amount of total energy for *Office* and *Random4* achieved by the fine-grain scheme. Yet for *Consumer*, the fine-grained scheme consumes significantly high communication energy, resulting in a higher total energy than the baseline.

Overall, the three sets of results confirm that the proposed security-driven task scheduling schemes effectively eliminate undesired communication paths and hence prevent potential trojan propagation across malicious 3PIPs within reasonable overhead in performance, power, and design cost.

7. CONCLUSIONS

We have presented a task scheduling based approach that a designer can take to protect MPSoCs against potential collusion between malicious 3PIPs. Security constraints have been proposed, ensuring that all valid communications are between 3PIPs from different vendors. This security-constrained task scheduling problem has been modeled and solved through integer linear programming. Hardware support for detecting undesired communication paths has also been discussed for various communication protocols. The experimental results show that using the proposed ILP model, the security constraint can be fulfilled with one extra vendor and nearly no performance and energy overhead. We believe that this extra cost is acceptable for building a trustworthy MPSoC, especially when it is used in critical infrastructure.

8. REFERENCES

[1] X. Wang, M. Tehranipoor, and J. Plusquellic, "Detecting malicious inclusions in secure hardware: Challenges and Solutions," in *1st Intl. Symp. Hardware-Oriented Security and Trust (HOST)*, pp. 15–19, Jun. 2008.

[2] C. Yang and A. Orailoglu, "A light-weight cache-based fault detection and checkpointing scheme for MPSoCs enabling relaxed execution synchronization," in *Intl. Conf. Compilers, Archit. & Synthesis for Embedded Syst. (CASES)*, pp. 11–20, Oct. 2008.

[3] S. Shamshiri, P. Lisherness, S. Pan, and K. Cheng, "A Cost Analysis Framework for Multi-core Systems with Spares," in *Intl. Test Conf. (ITC)*, pp. 1–8, Oct. 2008.

[4] S. Bhunia, M. Abramovici, D. Agarwal, P. Bradley, M. S. Hsiao, J. Plusquellic, and M. Tehranipoor, "Protection against Hardware Trojan Attacks: Towards a Comprehensive Solution," *IEEE Des. & Test.*, vol. 30, pp. 6–17, Mar. 2013.

[5] A. Waksman and S. Sethumadhavan, "Tamper Evident Microprocessors," in *31st Intl. Symp. Security & Privacy (SP)*, pp. 173–188, May 2010.

[6] C. Sturton, M. Hicks, D. Wagner, and S. T. King, "Defeating UCI: Building Stealthy and Malicious Hardware," in *32st Intl. Symp. Security & Privacy (SP)*, pp. 64–77, May 2011.

[7] M. Tehranipoor and F. Koushanfar, "A Survey of Hardware Trojan Taxonomy and Detection," *IEEE Des. & Test. Comput.*, vol. 27, no. 1, pp. 10–25, 2010.

[8] M. Banga and M. S. Hsiao, "A Novel Sustained Vector Technique for the Detection of Hardware Trojans," in *22nd Intl. Conf. VLSI Design*, pp. 327–332, Jan. 2009.

[9] Y. L. Gwon, H. T. Kung, and D. Vlah, "DISTROY: Detecting Integrated Circuit Trojans with Compressive Measurements," in *20th USENIX Workshop on Hot Topics in Security (HotSec)*, pp. 47–50, 2011.

[10] D. Agrawal, S. Baktir, D. Karakoyunlu, P. Rohatgi, and B. Sunar, "Trojan Detection using IC Fingerprinting," in *29th Intl. Symp. Security & Privacy (SP)*, pp. 296–310, May 2008.

[11] Y. Jin and Y. Makris, "Hardware Trojan detection using path delay fingerprint," in *1st Intl. Workshop Hardware-Oriented Security and Trust (HOST)*, pp. 51–57, Jun. 2008.

[12] S. Narasimhan, D. Du, R. S. Chakraborty, S. Paul, F. Wolff, C. Papachristou, K. Roy, and S. Bhunia, "Multiple-parameter side-channel analysis: A non-invasive hardware Trojan detection approach," in *3rd Intl. Symp. Hardware-Oriented Security and Trust (HOST)*, pp. 13–18, Jun. 2010.

[13] F. Koushanfar and A. Mirhoseini, "A Unified Framework for Multimodal Submodular Integrated Circuits Trojan Detection," *IEEE Trans. Information Forensics and Security*, vol. 6, pp. 162–174, Mar. 2011.

[14] M. Potkonjak, A. Nahapetian, M. Nelson, and T. Massey, "Hardware Trojan horse detection using gate-level characterization," in *46th Design Autom. Conf. (DAC)*, pp. 688–693, Jul. 2009.

[15] M. Beaumont, B. Hopkins, and T. Newby, "SAFER PATH: Security architecture using fragmented execution and replication for protection against trojaned hardware," in *Design Autom. & Test in Europe (DATE)*, pp. 1000–1005, Mar. 2012.

[16] A. Waksman and S. Sethumadhavan, "Silencing Hardware Backdoors," in *32nd Intl. Symp. Security & Privacy (SP)*, pp. 49–63, May 2011.

[17] E. Love, Y. Jin, and Y. Makris, "Proof-Carrying Hardware Intellectual Property: A Pathway to Trusted Module Acquisition," *IEEE Trans. Information Forensics and Security*, vol. 7, pp. 25–40, Feb. 2012.

[18] C. Yang and A. Orailoglu, "Predictable execution adaptivity through embedding dynamic reconfigurability into static MPSoC schedules," in *5th Intl. Conf. HW/SW Codesign & Syst. Synthesis (CODES-ISSS)*, pp. 15–20, 2007.

[19] A. Schranzhofer, J. J. Chen, and L. Thiele, "Dynamic Power-Aware Mapping of Applications onto Heterogeneous MPSoC Platforms," *IEEE Trans. Industrial Informatics*, vol. 6, pp. 692–707, Aug. 2010.

[20] D. Brelaz, "New methods to color the vertices of a graph," *Comm. of the ACM*, vol. 22, pp. 251–256, Apr. 1979.

[21] D. E. Culler, J. P. Singh, and A. Gupta, *Parallel Computer Architecture: A Hardware/Software Approach*. Morgan Kaufmann, 1999.

[22] "Lindo software, lingo," http://www.lindo.com.

[23] R. P. Dick, "Embedded System Synthesis Benchmarks Suite," ziyang.eecs.umich.edu/~dickrp/e3s.

[24] R. P. Dick, D. L. Rhodes, and W. Wolf, "TGFF: Task graphs for free," in *Workshop on Hardware/Software Codesign*, pp. 97–101, Mar. 1998.

Optically Reconfigurable Gate Array with an Angle-Multiplexed Holographic Memory

Retsu Moriwaki[1], Hikaru Maekawa[2], Akifumi Ogiwara[2], and Minoru Watanabe[1]
(1) Electrical and Electronic Engineering, Shizuoka University
(1) 3-5-1 Johoku, Hamamatsu, Shizuoka 432-8561, Japan
(2) Kobe City College of Technology
Email: tmwatan@ipc.shizuoka.ac.jp

ABSTRACT

Optically reconfigurable gate arrays (ORGAs) have been developed to achieve a high-performance FPGA with numerous configuration contexts. In the architecture, an optical memory technology or a holographic memory technology has been introduced so that the architecture can have numerous configuration contexts and high-speed reconfiguration capability. Results show that the architecture can achieve a large virtual gate count that is much larger than those of currently available VLSIs. To date, ORGAs with a spatially multiplex holographic memory have been reported. However, the spatially multiplexed holographic memory can only have a small number of configuration contexts, which are limited to about 256 configuration contexts. To implement more than a million configuration contexts, an angle-multiplex holographic memory must be used. However, no ORGA with an angle multiplex holographic memory that can sufficiently exploit the huge storage capacity of a holographic memory has ever been reported. Therefore, this paper presents a proposal of a novel ORGA with an angle-multiplexed holographic memory. The architecture can open the possibility of providing a million configuration contexts for a multi-context FPGA.

Categories and Subject Descriptors

B.7 [**Hardware**]: INTEGRATED CIRCUITS

General Terms

Design, Experimentation, Reliability.

Keywords

Field programmable gate arrays, Holographic memory, Optically reconfigurable gate arrays

1. INTRODUCTION

Recently, studies of accelerating a software operation on a personal computer using a field programmable gate array (FPGA) have progressed [1]–[4]. Reportedly, various hardware implementations

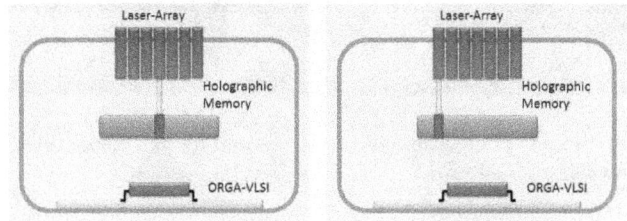

Figure 1: Cross-section view of an ORGA architecture with a spatially multiplexed holographic memory.

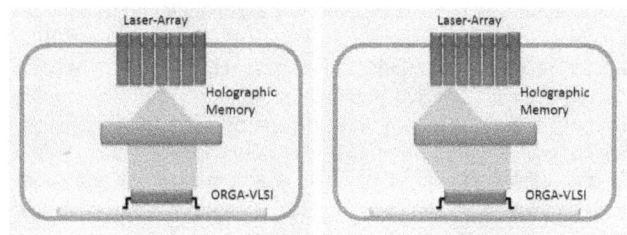

Figure 2: Cross-section view of an ORGA architecture with an angle-multiplexed holographic memory.

are useful. Their operations are superior to the corresponding software operations even on a latest personal computer with a latest processor. Therefore, FPGA is extremely useful as an accelerator of software operations.

However, such acceleration applications are always limited to some dedicated software algorithms expecting a parallel operation. To accelerate a general-purpose operation on a processor, a quick change of such hardware operations is frequently necessary. However, current FPGA reconfiguration times are longer than 100 ms [5][6]. Reconfiguration overhead caused by a function change between dedicated operations can increase the total operation time. Such overhead cannot be neglected.

Therefore, to date, optically reconfigurable gate arrays (ORGAs) have been developed to achieve a high-performance FPGA with numerous configuration contexts [7]–[10]. In the architecture, an optical memory technology or a holographic memory technology has been introduced so that the architecture can have numerous configuration contexts and a high-speed reconfiguration capability. As a result, the architecture can achieve a large virtual gate count that is much larger than those of currently available VLSIs and FPGAs. In addition, the reconfiguration time of ORGA is less than 10 ns. Therefore, the quick function change of dedicated hardware on a programmable gate array is possible. Such high speed re-

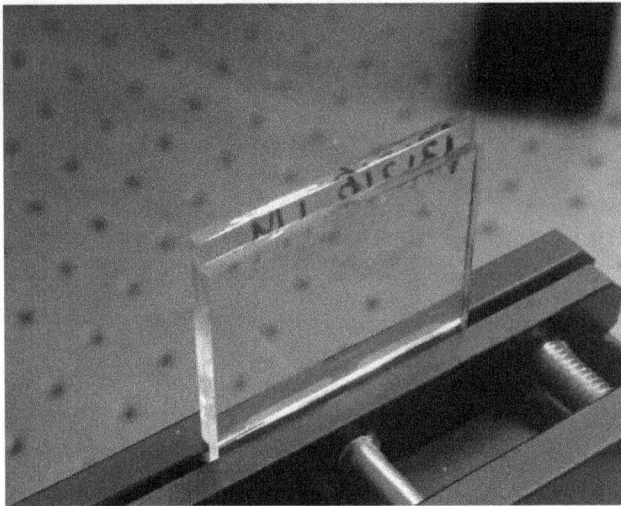

Figure 3: Photograph of an angle-multiplexed holographic memory

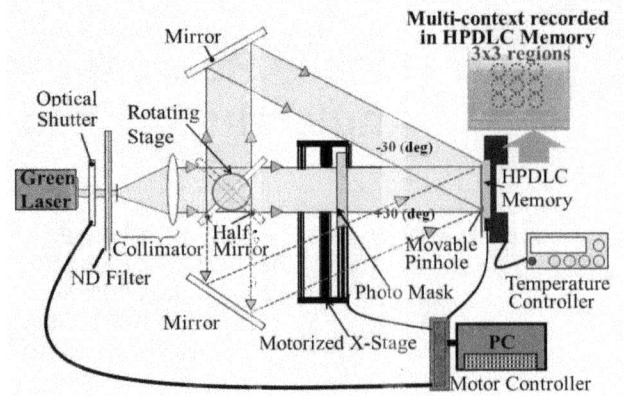

Figure 4: Recording system for an angle-multiplexed holographic memory.

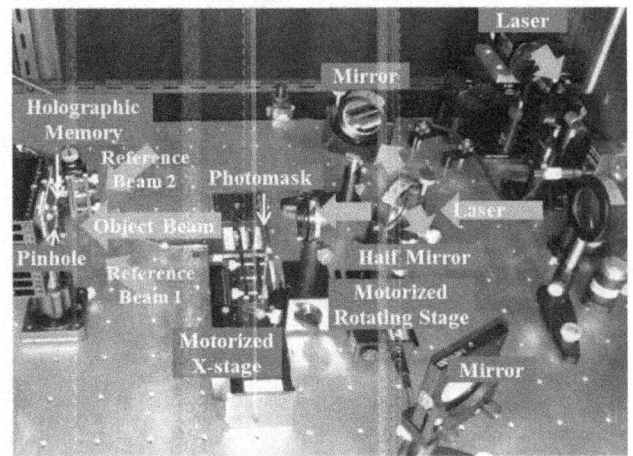

Figure 5: Photograph of the recording system.

configuration enables that the acceleration targets can be extended from limited algorithms to non-limited general-purpose algorithms or general-purpose operations of processors.

To date, ORGAs have been developed based on a spatially multiplexed holographic memory. However, spatially multiplexed holographic memory can only have a few configuration contexts. It is limited to about 256 configuration contexts. In the ORGA with the spatially multiplexed holographic memory, each holographic memory region includes one configuration context. It is not allowed to be overlapped on any other holographic memory region as presented in Fig. 1. The number of storable configuration contexts is always limited. Therefore, the capability of ORGAs with a spatially multiplexed holographic memory is not high.

To implement over a million configuration contexts to achieve a tera-gate count VLSI, an angle-multiplex holographic memory must be used as presented in Fig. 2. In this case, each holographic memory region can overlap the other holographic memory region and can store one or more configuration contexts. As a result, an ORGA can have over a million configuration contexts. The necessary conditions are only one: it needs a thick holographic memory material instead of the thin holographic material of a spatially multiplexed holographic memory. A thick holographic memory, for example, a cube of 1 cm × 1 cm × 1 cm can be fabricated easily.

However, no ORGA with an angle-multiplex holographic memory that can sufficiently exploit the huge storage capacity of a holographic memory has ever been reported. Therefore, this paper presents a proposal of a novel ORGA with an angle-multiplexed holographic memory. The architecture can open possibilities of providing a million configuration contexts for a multi-context FPGA.

2. ANGLE-MULTIPLEXED HOLOGRAPHIC MEMORY

2.1 Material

Here, we use a polymer-dispersed liquid crystal holographic memory including the prepolymer composed of dipentaerythritol hydroxyl penta-acrylate (Wako Pure Chemical Inds. Ltd.) with liquid crystal materials. The mixture ratio of the prepolymer was 60 wt%. A liquid crystal material (DIC RDP98487) was added to the previously described prepolymer mixture at 40 wt % in the frac-

tion of all ingredients. N-phenylglycine and xanthene dye (dibromofluorescein) were introduced, respectively, as a co-initiator and a photo-initiator. Then, the mixture of the liquid crystal material and prepolymers was injected and poured into the 10 μm air gap separating two glass plates. The glass plate cell was fabricated by two glass plates with dimensions of 25 mm × 20 mm × 1 mm. The photograph is depicted in Fig. 3.

2.2 Recording system

Figure 4 shows an optical recording system set up to record an angle-multiplexed holographic memory. The photograph is portrayed in Fig. 5. The light source is a green laser (Nd:YVO4) of 150 mW with 532 nm wavelength. The laser source for photopolymerization was collimated and linearly polarized perpendicularly to the grating vector. The laser light was divided into two parallel beams: a reference beam and an object beam. The object beam is incident to a metal photomask including configuration context information of a logical circuit. The reference beam is incident on the holographic memory by switching the slanted angles at ±30° to implement the angle-multiplexed recording of multi-context for an optically reconfigurable gate array. The temperature condition in the device fabrication was adjusted to 25°C using the temperature controller with a Peltier element. The photomask pattern designed to record the information of the configuration context was

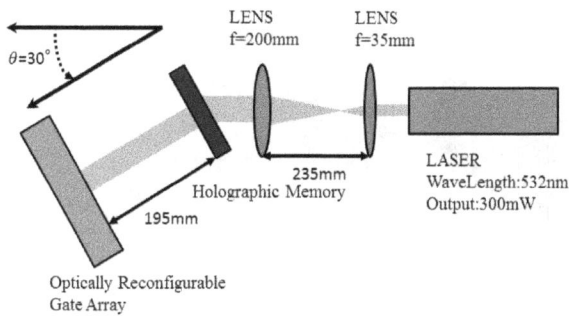

Figure 6: Block diagram of the reconfiguration system in which a light source was placed at +30°. The configuration is executed with a +30° incident angle for a holographic memory.

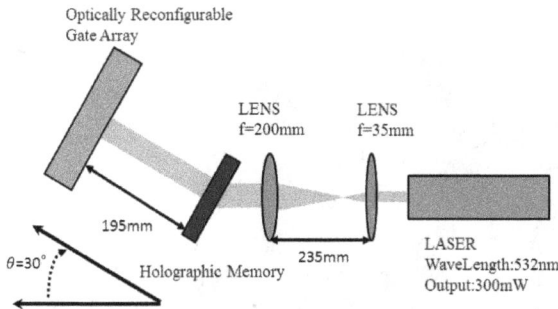

Figure 7: Block diagram of reconfiguration system in which a light source was placed at -30°. Configuration is executed with a -30° incident angle for a holographic memory.

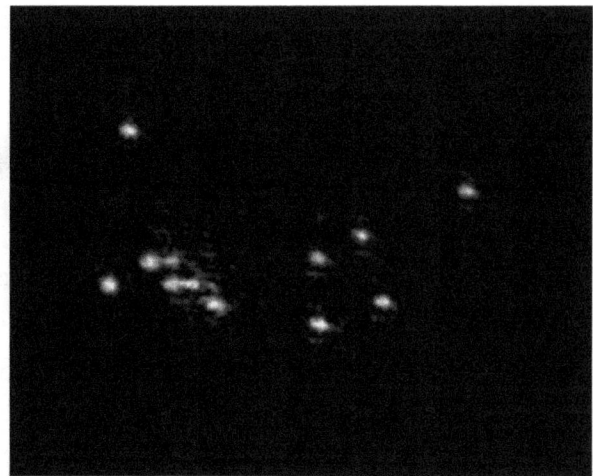

Figure 10: CCD-captured configuration context pattern of a two-input AND circuit in the case in which the laser beam is incident to region 1 on a holographic memory at +30°.

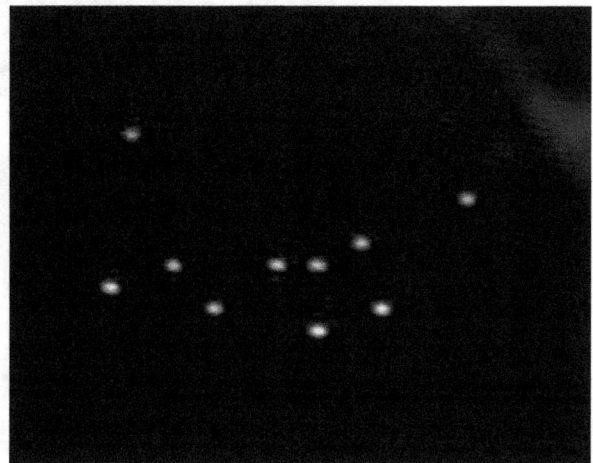

Figure 11: CCD-captured configuration context pattern of a two-input NOR circuit in the case in which the laser beam is incident to region 1 on a holographic memory at -30°.

used in the laser path as an object beam at the location of 200 mm in front of the liquid crystal composite sample. The configuration context for a logical circuit was defined by the number and location of transparent circles to lead the laser beams to the photodiode array in the VLSI chip.

As shown in the photograph in Fig. 4, the multi-context information is written to the isolated regions at the photo area of 25×20 mm^2 in the angle-multiplexed holographic memory. The angle-multiplexing recording of multi-context is described as follows. After the position of movable pinhole for the laser exposure is fixed at the specific region on the liquid crystal composites by driving the X–Y stage, the configuration context in the photomask is selected by shifting the photo area using the motorized X-stage. Then, the laser light is illuminated for 2 min by opening of an optical shutter. After the first exposure of laser interference at a slanted angle of 30°, the second exposure is implemented in the same photo area at the symmetric angle of -30° by controlling the location of half mirror using the motorized rotating stage. The formation of the holographic memory by angle-multiplexing recording of a multi-context is fabricated by repeating the previously described process successively.

3. RECONFIGURATION SYSTEM

The constructed optical system is presented in Figs. 6 and 7. In addition, these photographs are shown in Figs. 8 and 9. A laser of the same wavelength as that of the recording system, 532 nm, was used. The ORGA reconfiguration system was constructed simply using a laser, an angle-multiplexed holographic memory, and an ORGA-VLSI including a fine-grained programmable gate array. The laser beam was collimated and was then incident to an angle-multiplexed holographic memory, as depicted in Fig. 3. The ORGA-VLSI was placed 195 mm distant from the angle-multiplexed holographic memory. The ORGA-VLSI was fabricated using a 0.35 μm three-metal 4.9×4.9 mm^2 CMOS process chip. In this fabrication, the distance between photodiodes was designed as 90 μm. Each of the 340 photodiodes is 25.5×25.5 μm^2 to ease the optical alignment. The configuration context size is 20×17 bits. The gate array's gate count is 68. Results of preliminary experiments confirmed that the ORGA-VLSI itself can be reconfigured in nanoseconds.

4. EXPERIMENTAL RESULTS

The angle-multiplexed holographic memory shown in Fig. 3 recorded 18 configuration contexts. The holographic memory has nine holographic memory regions. Each holographic memory region includes two configuration contexts that are read out by a

Figure 8: Photograph of an experimental system in which a light source was placed at +30°. The configuration is executed with a +30° incident angle for a holographic memory.

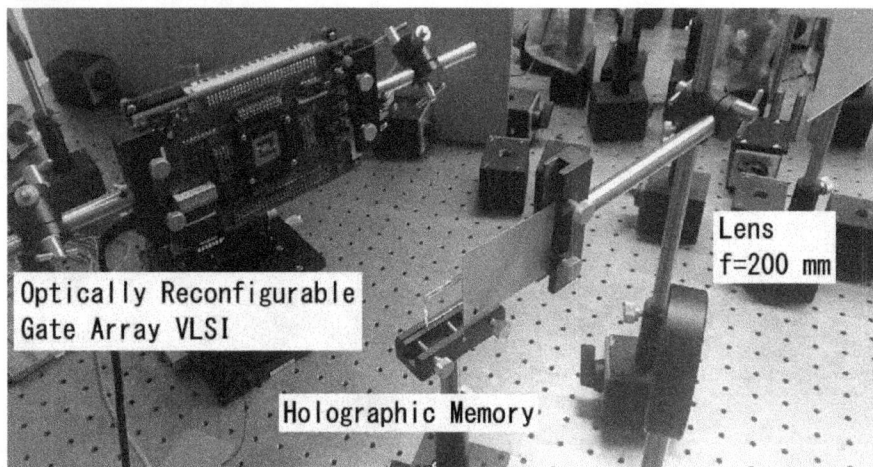

Figure 9: Photograph of the experimental system in which a light source was placed at -30°. The configuration is executed with a -30° incident angle for a holographic memory.

$\pm 30°$ reference laser beam. To confirm the angle-multiplexed holographic memory reading operation, we used a configuration system with two lasers, which make $\pm 30°$ reference laser beams as shown in Figs. 6, 8, 7, and 9. Here, among the 18 configuration contexts, reconfiguration experiments were done for only 4 configuration contexts. The CCD captured configuration context patterns which were generated from the angle-multiplexed holographic memory are shown in Figs. 10, 11, 12, and 13. The configuration contexts shown in Figs. 10 and 12 were generated by laser beams that are incident to region 1 and region 2 on a holographic memory at -30°. The configuration contexts shown in Figs. 11 and 13 were generated by laser beams that are incident to region 1 and region 2 on a holographic memory at +30°. All CCD captured configuration context patterns were clear. All configuration contexts can be programmed onto an ORGA-VLSI correctly. The programmable gate array on the ORGA-VLSI could work correctly.

5. CONCLUSION

Optically reconfigurable gate arrays (ORGAs) have been developed to achieve a high-performance FPGA with numerous configuration contexts. In the architecture, an optical memory technology or a holographic memory has been introduced so that the architec-

ture can have numerous configuration contexts and a high-speed reconfiguration capability. To date, ORGAs with a spatially multiplex holographic memory have been reported. However, the spatially multiplexed holographic memory required large space inside an ORGA. Therefore, this paper has presented a proposal of a novel ORGA with an angle-multiplexed holographic memory. In this experiment, we demonstrated 18 configuration contexts on an angle-multiplexed holographic memory. Therefore, although the number of configuration contexts is not sufficient currently, numerous configurations will be realized in the future. The architecture opens the possibility of providing a million configuration contexts for a future multi-context FPGA that can achieve an over-1-tera-gate count programmable gate array.

Acknowledgment

The VLSI chip in this study was fabricated in the chip fabrication program of VLSI Design and Education Center (VDEC), the University of Tokyo in collaboration with Rohm Co. Ltd. and Toppan Printing Co. Ltd.

344

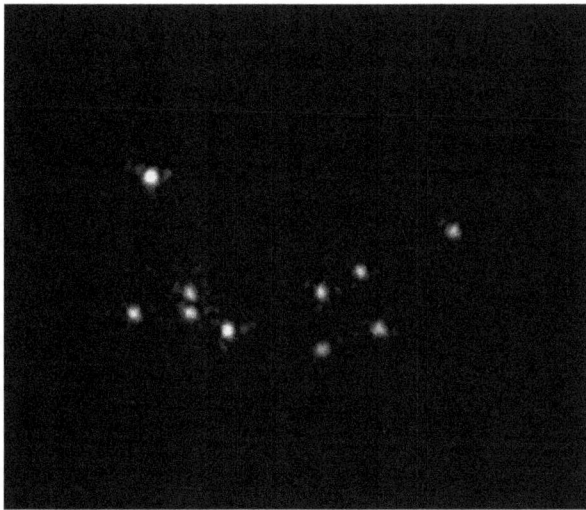

Figure 12: CCD captured configuration context pattern of a two-input AND circuit in the case in which the laser beam is incident to region 2 on a holographic memory at +30°.

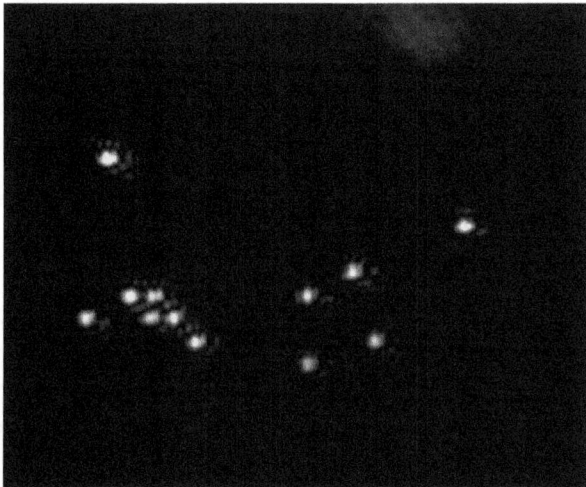

Figure 13: CCD captured configuration context pattern of a two-input OR circuit in the case in which the laser beam is incident to region 2 on a holographic memory at -30°.

6. REFERENCES

[1] N, Dave, K. Fleming, K. Myron, M. Pellauer, M. Vijayaraghavan, "Hardware Acceleration of Matrix Multiplication on a Xilinx FPGA," IEEE/ACM International Conference on Formal Methods and Models for Codesign, pp. 97-100, 2007.

[2] T. Drahonovsky, M. Rozkovec, O. Novak, "Relocation of reconfigurable modules on Xilinx FPGA," IEEE 16th International Symposium on Design and Diagnostics of Electronic Circuits & Systems, pp. 175-180, 2013.

[3] I. Yasri, N. H. Hamid, N. B. Z. Ali, "VLSI based edge detection hardware accelerator for real time video segmentation system," International Conference on Intelligent and Advanced Systems, Vol. 2, pp. 719-724, 2012.

[4] X. Jiang, X. Liu, L. Xu, P. Zhang, N. Sun, "A Reconfigurable Accelerator for Smith-Waterman Algorithm," IEEE Transactions on Circuits and Systems II: Express Briefs, Vol. 54, Issue 12, pp. 1077-1081, 2007.

[5] A. Jara-Berrocal, A. Gordon-Ross, "Runtime Temporal Partitioning Assembly to Reduce FPGA Reconfiguration Time," International Conference on Reconfigurable Computing and FPGAs, pp. 374-379, 2009.

[6] B. Schulz, C. Paiz, J. Hagemeyer, S. Mathapati, M. Porrmann, J. Bocker, "Run-time reconfiguration of FPGA-based drive controllers," European Conference on Power Electronics and Applications, pp. 1-10, 2007.

[7] S. Kubota, M. Watanabe, "A four-context programmable optically reconfigurable gate array with a reflective silver-halide holographic memory," IEEE Photonics Journal, Vol. 3, No. 4, pp. 665-675, 2011.

[8] M. Nakajima, M. Watanabe, "Fast optical reconfiguration of a nine-context DORGA using a speed adjustment control," ACM Transaction on Reconfigurable Technology and Systems, Vol. 4, Issue 2, 2011.

[9] D. Seto, M. Nakajima, M. Watanabe, "Dynamic optically reconfigurable gate array very large-scale integration with partial reconfiguration capability," Applied Optics, Vol. 49, Iss. 36, pp. 6986-6994, 2010.

[10] H. Morita, M. Watanabe, "Microelectromechanical Configuration of an Optically Reconfigurable Gate Array," IEEE Journal of Quantum Electronics, Vol. 46, Issue 9, pp. 1288-1294, 2010.

Variability-Aware Design of Double Gate FinFET-based Current Mirrors

Dhruva Ghai[1], Saraju P. Mohanty[2], Garima Thakral[3], Oghenekarho Okobiah[4]
Dept. of Electronics and Communication Engineering, Oriental University, Indore, India.[1]
Dept. of Computer Science and Engineering, University of North Texas, Denton, USA.[2,4]
Department of Computer Science, Oriental University, Indore, India.[3]
dhruvaghai@orientaluniversity.in[1], saraju.mohanty@unt.edu[2],
garimathakral@oriental.ac.in[3], oo0032@unt.edu[4]

ABSTRACT

With the technology trend moving towards smaller geometries and improved circuit performances, multigate transistors are expected to replace the traditional bulk devices. The double-gate FinFET lends itself to a rich design space using various configurations of the two gates. Accurate current mirroring is a critical analog design requirement in many applications. Current mirror is an essential component in analog design for biasing and constant current generation. This paper presents the exploration of different configurations of a double gate fully depleted SOI based FinFETs for efficient design of current mirror designs. In particular, comparison among the important Figures-of-Merit (FoMs) current mirror designs including mismatch, variability, output resistance (r_0), compliance voltage (V_{CV}) is presented for: (1) shorted-gate (SG), (2) independent-gate (IG), and (3) low-power (LP) configurations. Based on the results obtained, guidelines are presented for the designer for current mirror design using FinFET.

Keywords

Analog design; current mirrors; FinFET; mismatch; independent-gate

1. INTRODUCTION

The current mirrors are essential building blocks in analog integrated circuits which affect the qualitative performance of the system. The current mirrors are used as active loads as they offer high impedance. They are also used as biasing structures as they provide better tolerance to the variations in power supply and temperature [2]. An ideal current mirror, which may not be practically realized, has the following:

- Infinite output resistance ($r_0 = \infty$).
- Provide the same current regardless of voltage across it, in other words, there are no compliance range requirements ($V_{CV} = 0$).
- No sensitivity to real-world effects like mismatch (mismatch = 0) and process variations.

The major drawbacks of conventional bulk CMOS current mirrors in analog design tend to be the following: mismatch, output resistance degradation and compliance voltage increase, which is due to aggressive technology scaling. One of the candidates to replace planar bulk CMOS technology is the double gate FinFET (DG-FinFET) technology [3, 4]. FinFETs are particularly appealing because they allow suppression of short channel effects (SCE), high transconductance and optimal subthreshold voltage. In DG-FinFETs, there is reduced mismatch from random dopant fluctuations due to undoped or lightly doped body and reduced carrier mobility degradation. DG-FinFETs also provide design flexibility at circuit level with two gates as the threshold voltage can be adjusted using bias applied on the back-gate [22]. This feature offers the following advantages: versatile functionality from the same set of devices, and reduction of layout area and a higher speed/lower power consumption over equivalent conventional circuits [12]. The current mirror circuit is implemented using the FinFET technology to explore these advantages.

The following modes of DG-FinFET configurations are considered for circuit design: (1) the shorted-gate (SG) mode with transistor gates tied together, (2) the low-power (LP) mode where the back-gate is tied to a reverse-bias voltage to reduce leakage power, and (3) the independent gate (IG) mode where independent signals are used to drive the two device gates [3, 4]. In the current paper we consider these configurations for current mirror designs to study their impact on current mirror design. The objective is the comparative analysis of the various DG-FinFET configurations and trends of the FoMs of the current mirrors to evaluate the advantages of FinFETs on analog designs.

The remainder of this paper is organized as follows: Section 2 summarizes the contributions of this paper. Section 3 presents the related research. A discussion of the FinFET models and FinFET configuration-based current mirrors is presented in Section 4. Section 5 presents discussions on variability and mismatch for the various DG-FinFET configuration-based current mirrors. A performance analysis for FoMs under consideration is presented in Section 6. Section 7 discusses the design guidelines for FinFET based current mirrors. This is followed by conclusions and directions for future research in Section 8.

2. CONTRIBUTIONS OF THIS PAPER

The *novel contributions* of this paper include the following:

1. A comparative study is presented among the SG, IG and LP configurations of the double gate FinFET device for current mirror design. A 32nm n-type FinFET current mirror has been used for this comparison.

2. Study of mismatch, variability, output resistance (r_0), compliance voltage (V_{CV}) is presented for SG, IG and LP mode double gate FinFET current mirrors.

3. A novel algorithm is presented for measuring mismatch in the configurations of double gate FinFET current mirrors using Design of Experiments (DOE) and polynomial modeling. Mismatch models are developed for each configuration.

4. A novel algorithm is presented for measuring variability in the various double gate FinFET configuration-based current mirrors. The coefficient of variation (c_v) is presented for each configuration.

5. Guidelines are formed for current mirror design using double gate FinFET current mirrors.

3. RELATED PRIOR RESEARCH

The feasibility of FinFET based digital and analog circuits has been well established in [11, 17, 4, 3, 7]. In [6], a back-gate voltage tuning based statistical optimization is performed in a FinFET-based SRAM array. In analog design, the exploration has also been done at the device level [16, 15]. The impact of fin width on FinFET characteristics is analyzed in [13]. The analog performance of Double Gate, Tri-Gate FinFET and single-gate (SG) SOI MOSFETs are compared in [20]. The performances of FinFET are studied for analog/RF circuits in [21, 8, 18]. The various configurations of the FinFET device for analog applications are presented in [12, 9]. However, the main focus is on forward bias configurations and not reverse bias configurations, which are becoming increasingly popular for digital applications and are covered in the current paper.

The research presented in this paper is the advancement of research in [5], in which a comparison of the SG, IG and LP FinFET modes is presented for analog design using FoMs like open circuit gain, transition frequency, and variability. The current paper deals with current mirror design focusing more on the relevant FoMs like compliance voltage and output resistance. Apart from variability, current mismatch is measured which is crucial for current mirror design.

4. DOUBLE GATE FINFET-BASED CURRENT MIRRORS

Current mirrors work on the principle that if the gate-source potentials of two identical FinFET devices are equal, the channel current is equal. For a good current source, the devices must operate in the saturation region. In case of the reference transistor (REF) of the mirror, the drain current $I_D = I_{REF}$. Reference current I_{REF} is a known current (I_{REF}=35μA), provided by the current source ensuring that it is constant and independent of voltage supply variations [2]. Using $V_{DG-REF} = 0$ for transistor REF, I_{REF} sets the value of V_{GS-REF}. The circuit in figure 1 forces the same V_{GS-REF} to apply to the output transistor OUT. If OUT is also biased with V_{DG-OUT}=0 and provided REF transistors and OUT have good matching, we have $I_{OUT} = I_{REF}$, i.e. the output current is same as the reference current when V_{DG-OUT}=0 for the output transistor, given both transistors are matched.

Fig. 1 shows shorted-gate (SG), independent-gate (IG), and Low-Power (LP) n-type FinFET current mirrors, where V_{gf} denotes the voltage applied at the front gate, and V_{gb} denotes the voltage applied at the back gate. In the SG mode, the front and back gates are tied together, while in the independent-gate (IG) mode, the top part of the gate is etched out giving rise to two independent gates and the back-gate voltage (V_{gb}) is set to 0 V [15]. The low-power (LP)-mode applies a reverse-bias voltage of -0.2V to the back-gate.

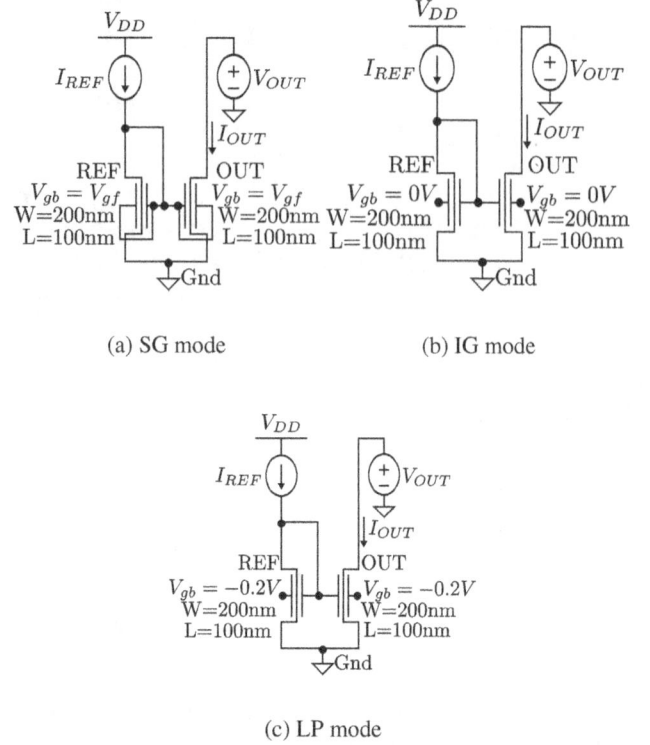

(a) SG mode   (b) IG mode

(c) LP mode

Figure 1: Circuit diagram and simulation setup for (a) SG mode, (b) IG mode and (c) LP mode DG-FinFET based current mirrors.

We use an equivalent sub-circuit model for a FinFET device instead of TCAD simulators as the existing compact models are accurate and simple to use [1]. The FinFET is inherently an SOI transistor as the bottom of a FinFET structure sits on top of a layer of SiO$_2$. The SOI thickness (T_{si}) is very thin in a typical FinFET process making the silicon body fully depleted. The fully depleted SOI model of BSIM (BSIM FD SOI) is used as the model basis for each sub-transistor. Two fully depleted SOI devices have been used as the front and back transistors, respectively. To make this sub-circuit compatible with standard circuit simulators (SPICE), BSIM SOI has been used as the model for each device. The current conduction controlled by the front and back gate in a FinFET [22] is captured by using two single-gate transistors. Each sub-transistor has its own definitions of gate voltage (V_g), threshold voltage (V_{Th}), and gate-oxide thickness (T_{ox}). The key parameter values for the FinFET models at 32nm node are shown in Table 1. The body thickness (T_{Si}) of a single fin is equal to the silicon channel thickness.

Table 1: 32nm n-type FinFET Device Nominal Values.

Parameter	Value
Oxide Thickness T_{ox}(nm)	1.4 nm
Threshold voltage V_{Thn}	0.28 V
Channel doping $N_{ch}(cm^{-3})$	2×10^{16}
Fin-Height H_{fin}(nm)	50 nm
Body Thickness T_{Si}(nm)	8.6 nm

5. VARIABILITY ANALYSIS OF FINFET CURRENT MIRRORS

This section presents the mismatch and process variation study for the various configuration-based current mirrors.

5.1 Mismatch

We use a Design of Experiments (DOE)-based setup to understand the effect of mismatch on the FinFET-configuration current mirrors. A detailed discussion of DOE assisted method for process variation analysis is presented in [19]. A $\pm30\%$ gate oxide thickness mismatch between the REF transistor (nominal value: $T_{ox-REF} = 1.4$ nm) and OUT (nominal value: $T_{ox-OUT} = 1.4$ nm) devices of the current mirror has been considered, with $T_{ox-REF_L} = 1$nm and $T_{ox-OUT_L} = 1$ nm as the low values, and $T_{ox-REF_H} = 1.8$ nm and $T_{ox-OUT_H} = 1.8$ nm as the high values. A 3 level-2 factors leads to $3^2=9$ states in the design matrix (shown in Table 2). Algorithm 1 shows the detailed steps. The proposed algorithm affords designers an efficient process to understand the effects device and process parameters mismatch on device performance.

Algorithm 1 Mismatch in FinFET configuration current mirrors

1: **Objective:** Mismatch in SG, IG and LP configuration-based FinFET current mirrors.
2: **Input Factors:** T_{ox-REF}, T_{ox-OUT}.
3: **Output Responses:** Transfer ratio$=\frac{I_{OUT}}{I_{REF}}$, mismatch$=\frac{I_{OUT}-I_{REF}}{I_{REF}} \times 100\%$.
4: Setup experiment using 3 level-2 factors ($3^2=9$ states).
5: **for** each FinFET configuration **do**
6:     **for** each 1:9 state of experiment **do**
7:         Run simulation.
8:         Record $\frac{I_{OUT}}{I_{REF}}$, mismatch.
9:     **end for**
10: **end for**
11: Form regression-based mismatch models.

The mismatch is calculated as $\frac{I_{OUT}-I_{REF}}{I_{REF}} \times 100\%$. Table 2 presents the current transfer ratio$=\frac{I_{OUT}}{I_{REF}}$ and mismatch values for each of the configurations. Nominally, the point where $V_{OUT}= V_{DS-REF} = V_{GS-REF}$ is where the transfer ratio $\frac{I_{OUT}}{I_{REF}}=1$, leading to a mismatch of 0%. We have not taken into consideration the mismatch between front (T_{oxf}) and back (T_{oxb}) gate oxide thicknesses within each device in this study and assume they are identical ($T_{oxf}= T_{oxb}= T_{ox}$) as the theme of this section is to study inter-device mismatch, and not intra-device mismatch.

To understand the behavior of configurations, we present the threshold voltage as a function of the back-gate voltage (V_{gb}) [10]:

$$\frac{\partial V_{Thn}}{\partial V_{gb}} = -\frac{\epsilon_{si} \times T_{ox}}{\epsilon_{si} \times T_{ox} + \epsilon_{ox} \times T_{si}}, \quad (1)$$

where $\frac{\partial V_{Thn}}{\partial V_{gb}}$ is called the back-gate effect. The negative sign in equation 1 implies that the direction of the threshold voltage change is opposite to that of the back-gate change. So, a negative back gate bias results in a threshold voltage shift towards a positive direction. We can also see that the back-gate effect becomes dominant as the gate oxide thickness increases. If the oxide thickness is reduced, the front surface potential is more dominantly controlled by the front gate than the back gate, and the back-gate effect becomes weaker. We can see from Table 2, that the mismatch is lowest when the oxide thicknesses are low, and the back-gate effect is minimized. Also, LP mode has highest mismatch, followed by IG

Algorithm 2 Process variation in FinFET configuration current mirrors.

1: **Objective:** Coefficient of variation (c_v) in SG, IG and LP configuration-based FinFET current mirrors.
2: **Input Factors:** $\mathcal{N}(\mu_{T_{ox-REF}}, \sigma_{T_{ox-REF}})$, $\mathcal{N}(\mu_{T_{ox-OUT}}, \sigma_{T_{ox-OUT}})$.
3: **Output Responses:** $\mathcal{N}(\mu_{\frac{I_{OUT}}{I_{REF}}}, \sigma_{\frac{I_{OUT}}{I_{REF}}})$.
4: Setup Monte-Carlo experiment.
5: **for** each FinFET configuration **do**
6:     **for** each 1:1000 Monte-Carlo run **do**
7:         Run simulation.
8:         Record $\frac{I_{OUT}}{I_{REF}}$.
9:     **end for**
10: **end for**
11: Report $\mu_{\frac{I_{OUT}}{I_{REF}}}, \sigma_{\frac{I_{OUT}}{I_{REF}}}$ and $c_{v \frac{I_{OUT}}{I_{REF}}}$

---

and SG mode, where the back-gate effect is not present. Also, in the case of SG mode, the gate work function and the bias applied are the same for both gates. However, in the IG and LP modes, the gate work function is different for the 2 gates, giving rise to a flat-band voltage difference (ΔV_{fb}) [10]. This leads to the prediction that LP mode will suffer the highest mismatch followed by IG and SG mode.

Using the data in Table 2, we develop mismatch models for each configuration. Fig. 2(a), 2(b) and 2(c) show the surface fit for the data points in SG, IG and LP mode, respectively. Polynomials of the order 2 are developed for each configuration of the form: Mismatch (in %) $= p_{00} + p_{10} \times T_{ox-REF} + p_{01} \times T_{ox-OUT} + p_{20} \times T_{ox-REF}^2 + p_{11} \times T_{ox-REF} \times T_{ox-OUT} + p_{02} \times T_{ox-OUT}^2$. The mismatch models are accurate with low values of RMSE ≈ 0.0614 and $R^2 \approx 0.999$. The coefficient matrices for each DG-FinFET configurations are presented in the following equations:

$$p_{ij}(Mismatch_{SG}) = \begin{bmatrix} 0.01144 & -4.173 & -1.787 \\ 3.256 & -0.1163 & 0 \\ 1.488 & 0 & 0 \end{bmatrix} \quad (2)$$

$$p_{ij}(Mismatch_{IG}) = \begin{bmatrix} 0.011 & -5.328 & -1.203 \\ 4.385 & 0.004158 & 0 \\ 0.988 & 0 & 0 \end{bmatrix} \quad (3)$$

$$p_{ij}(Mismatch_{LP}) = \begin{bmatrix} 0.005834 & -11.4 & -0.7874 \\ 9.573 & 0.128 & 0 \\ 0.5752 & 0 & 0 \end{bmatrix} \quad (4)$$

5.2 Process Variation

For process variation, we consider T_{ox-REF} and T_{ox-OUT} variations having a Gaussian (normal) distribution with mean (μ) values as specified in Table 1 and standard deviation (σ) as 10% of the mean. 1000 Monte Carlo simulations are performed. Algorithm 2 shows the steps.

Fig. 3(a), 3(b), 3(c) show the probability distribution function (PDFs) with Gaussian fit of the transfer ratio ($\frac{I_{OUT}}{I_{REF}}$) for SG, IG and LP modes, respectively. Table 3 shows the mean (μ), standard deviation (σ) and the coefficient of variation ($c_v = \frac{\sigma}{\mu} \times 100\%$) values for the configurations. We use the c_v value to compare the variability of the configurations as it shows the extent of variability in relation to mean of the population. Overall, it is observed that the LP mode shows the highest variability, followed by the IG mode and the SG mode. This trend is due to discrepancy of the work function between the two gates in the IG and LP modes of

Table 2: T_{ox} Mismatch effect on FinFET Configuration-based Current Mirrors

REF	OUT	$\frac{I_{OUT}}{I_{REF}}$(SG)	Mismatch(SG)	$\frac{I_{OUT}}{I_{REF}}$(IG)	Mismatch(IG)	$\frac{I_{OUT}}{I_{REF}}$(LP)	Mismatch(LP)
T_{ox-R_L}	T_{ox-OUT_L}	1.00555	+0.555%	1.00845	+0.845%	1.0208	+2.080%
T_{ox-REF}	T_{ox-OUT_L}	1.02402	+2.402%	1.04573	+4.573%	1.12182	+12.182%
T_{ox-REF_H}	T_{ox-OUT_L}	1.08352	+8.352%	1.10897	+10.897%	1.23643	+23.643%
T_{ox-REF_L}	T_{ox-OUT}	0.982087	-1.791%	0.962083	-3.792%	0.89517	-10.483%
T_{ox-REF}	T_{ox-OUT}	1	0%	1	0%	1	0%
T_{ox-REF_H}	T_{ox-OUT}	1.05793	+5.793%	1.06459	+6.459%	1.12034	+12.034%
T_{ox-REF_L}	T_{ox-OUT_H}	0.911764	-8.824%	0.88536	-11.464%	0.75459	-24.541%
T_{ox-REF}	T_{ox-OUT_H}	0.928658	-7.134%	0.922524	-7.748%	0.857361	-14.264%
T_{ox-REF_H}	T_{ox-OUT_H}	0.983526	-1.647%	0.986101	-1.390%	0.977039	-2.296%

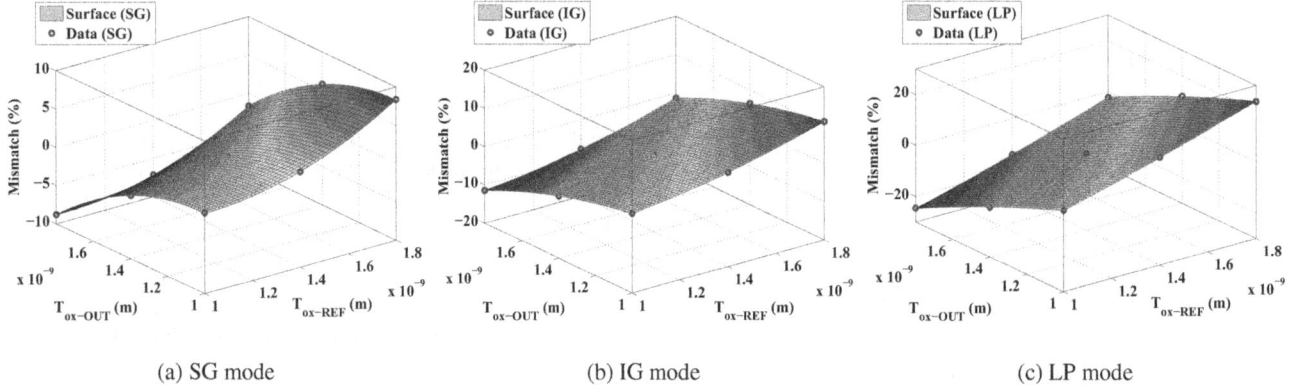

(a) SG mode   (b) IG mode   (c) LP mode

Figure 2: Mismatch models for (a) SG mode, (b) IG mode and (c) LP mode FinFET current mirrors.

DG-FinFET, as discussed in Section 5.1. This difference in work function leads to a difference in the threshold voltage as [10]:

$$\Delta V_{Thn} = \frac{\epsilon_{si} \times T_{ox}}{\epsilon_{si} \times T_{ox} + \epsilon_{ox} \times T_{si}} \times \Delta V_{fb}. \qquad (5)$$

According to Eqn. 5, the impact of the work function difference on the threshold voltage gets weaker as the gate oxide thickness reduces.

Table 3: Process variation statistical data for DG-FinFET current mirrors.

Mode	μ	σ	c_v(in %)
SG	1	0.0252	2.52
IG	1	0.0309	3.09
LP	1	0.0637	6.37

6. PERFORMANCE ANALYSIS OF DG-FINFET BASED CURRENT MIRRORS

This section discusses the FoMs such as output resistance (r_0) and compliance voltage (V_{CV}). The simulation setup used is the same as shown in Fig. 1, where V_{OUT} is varied from 0 to V_{DD} (1V), and I_{OUT} is recorded.

6.1 Output resistance (r_0)

r_0 is measured by taking the reciprocal of the output current's derivative from I_{OUT}-V_{OUT} curves. Using the well known long-channel relationship: $r_0 \propto \frac{1}{I_{OUT}}$[2] (also used for understanding short channel behavior), we can understand the trend observed. As the best drive strength is offered by SG-mode [3], I_{OUT} increases at a faster rate with increasing V_{OUT}, we obtain the lowest r_0 for this configuration, followed by the IG and LP modes, where I_{OUT} reduces [3] compared to SG mode. Figure 4 shows the trend, and Table 4 shows the values of r_0 recorded at a biasing point of $V_{OUT} = 0.4$ V. As r_0 dominates the open circuit gain: $(g_m \times r_0) \propto \frac{1}{\sqrt{I_{OUT}}}$ [12], we can infer that the open circuit gain also follows the same trend as r_0 for the configuration-based current mirrors.

Table 4: r_0 for FinFET configuration-based current mirrors.

Configuration	r_0
SG mode	20.43 kΩ
IG mode	24.58 kΩ
LP mode	26.33 kΩ

6.2 Compliance Voltage (V_{CV})

The output compliance range for a current mirror is the range of output voltages where the current mirror behaves like a current

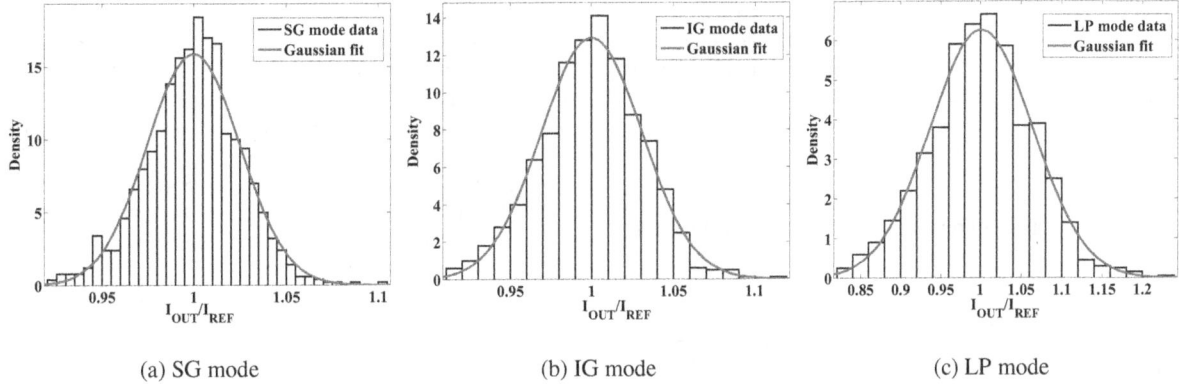

(a) SG mode   (b) IG mode   (c) LP mode

Figure 3: Distribution Functions for $\frac{I_{OUT}}{I_{REF}}$ for (a) SG mode, (b) IG mode and (c) LP mode FinFET current mirrors.

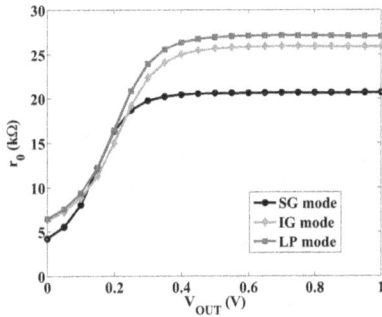

Figure 4: r_0 for FinFET configuration-based current mirrors.

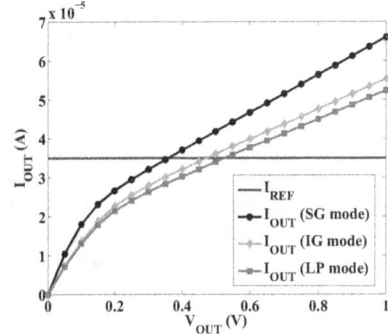

Figure 5: V_{CV} for FinFET configuration-based current mirrors

source and not an open or a resistor. To keep the output transistor in saturation, $V_{DG-OUT} = 0$ V. Hence, the lowest output voltage that results in correct mirror behavior, the compliance voltage, is $V_{OUT} = V_{CV} = V_{GS-OUT} = V_{DS-OUT}$ for the output transistor at the output current level with $V_{DG-OUT} = 0$ V. A lower value of V_{CV} is recommended as it leads to a higher compliance range. Figure 5 shows the intersection points where $I_{OUT} = I_{REF}$, and V_{CV} is recorded at these points. Table 5 shows the exact values. We can observe that SG mode offers the best (lowest) compliance voltage followed by IG and LP modes.

Table 5: V_{CV} for FinFET configurations based-current mirrors.

Configuration	V_{CV}
SG mode	0.359
IG mode	0.473
LP mode	0.528

This observation can be explained as follows: In FinFET, the effect of back-gate biasing is that the threshold voltage (V_{Thnf}) of the front-gate increases as the reverse-biasing (V_{gb}) of the back-gate increases [6]. The front-gate threshold voltage (V_{Thnf}) for the IG and LP mode is related to the back-gate voltage (V_{gb}) as [14]:

$$V_{Thnf(IG,LP)} = V_{Thn} - m \times V_{gb}, \qquad (6)$$

where m is the gate-to-gate coupling factor given by:

$$m = \frac{3 \times T_{oxf}}{3 \times T_{oxb} + T_{si}}, \qquad (7)$$

where T_{oxf} and T_{oxb} are front and back gate oxide thicknesses, respectively. The threshold voltage of IG, LP modes is related to the SG mode configuration as:

$$V_{Thnf(IG,LP)} = (1 + m) \times V_{Thnf(SG)}. \qquad (8)$$

It is evident that SG mode has the lowest V_{Thnf}, resulting in the lowest V_{CV} as it turns on faster than the IG and the LP mode and offers the largest compliance range. As the LP mode has the highest reverse bias (V_{gb}=-0.2V), it is the slowest giving rise to the largest V_{CV}, hence offering smallest compliance range.

7. CURRENT MIRROR DESIGN GUIDELINES USING DG FINFET

This section presents the guidelines for current mirror design using DG-FinFET configurations. The experimental results obtained in section 5.1 and Section 6 are used in the realization of the guidelines. Table 6 shows the design trade-offs between the three DG-FinFET configurations under consideration. There is a trade-off between the output resistance and the compliance voltage for current mirrors. The LP mode current mirror offers high gain (high

r_0) making it suitable for application in a common source amplifier. However, it has high variability and high V_{CV}. The SG mode current mirror offers low gain (r_0) making it suitable for use in a common drain amplifier for a voltage buffer. SG mode current mirror also offers the lowest variability and V_{CV}. The IG mode offers a compromise between the LP and SG mode with medium variability, r_0 and V_{CV}.

Table 6: Guidelines for current mirror design using FinFET configurations.

Variability	r_0	V_{CV}	Configuration
High	High	High	LP
Medium	Medium	Medium	IG
Low	Low	Low	SG

8. CONCLUSIONS

In this paper, we have studied current mirrors based on 3 configurations of the double gate FinFET device for analog circuit design. 2 novel algorithms are presented for measuring mismatch (using DOE and polynomial modeling) and variability in the double gate FinFET current mirrors. The future work will involve exploring advanced current mirror architectures such as cascode current mirror, regulated drain current mirror, supply independent biasing circuits using the various configurations studied in this paper. Mixed mode current mirrors may be proposed where certain devices are operated in the LP mode for high output resistance, and other devices in the SG mode for lower mismatch and higher compliance range.

9. REFERENCES

[1] Predictive Technology Model. http://ptm.asu.edu.

[2] R. J. Baker. *CMOS Circuit Design, Layout, and Simulation.* Wiley-IEEE Press, 2010.

[3] S. Chaudhuri and N. K. Jha. 3D vs. 2D analysis of FinFET logic gates under process variations. In *Proceedings of the 29th International Conference on Computer Design*, pages 435–436, 2011.

[4] S. Chaudhuri, P. Mishra, and N. K. Jha. Accurate Leakage Estimation for FinFET Standard Cells Using the Response Surface Methodology. In *Proceedings of the 25th International Conference on VLSI Design*, pages 238–244, 2012.

[5] D. Ghai and S. P. Mohanty and G. Thakral. Comparative Analysis of Double Gate FinFET Configurations for Analog Circuit Design. In *Proceedings of the 56th IEEE International Midwest Symposium on Circuits & Systems (MWSCAS)*, pages 809–812, 2013.

[6] B. Ebrahimi, M. Rostami, A. Afzali-Kusha, and M. Pedram. Statistical Design Optimization of FinFET SRAM Using Back-Gate Voltage. *IEEE Transactions on VLSI Systems*, 19(10):1911–1916, 2011.

[7] M. Fulde. *Variation Aware Analog and Mixed-Signal Circuit Design in Emerging Multi-Gate CMOS Technologies.* Springer, 2009.

[8] M. Fulde, J. P. Engelstädter, G. Knoblinger, and D. Schmitt-Landsiedel. Analog Circuits using FinFETs: Benefits in Speed-Accuracy-Power Trade-Off and Simulation of Parasitic Effects. *Advances in Radio Science*, 5:285–290, 2007.

[9] H. F. A. Hamed, S. Kaya, and J. A. Starzyk. Use of nano-scale double-gate MOSFETs in low-power tunable current mode analog circuits. *Analog Integrated Circuits and Signal Processing*, 54(3):211–217, 2008.

[10] J. W. Han, C. J. Kim, and Y. K. Choi. Universal potential model in tied and separated double-gate MOSFETs with consideration of symmetric and asymmetric structure. *IEEE Transactions on Electron Devices*, 55(6):1472–1479, 2008.

[11] R. V. Joshi, K. Kim, and R. Kanj. FinFET SRAM Design. In *Proceedings of the 23rd International Conference on VLSI Design*, pages 440–445, 2010.

[12] S. Kaya, H. F. A. Hamed, and J. A. Starzyk. Low-power tunable analog circuit blocks based on nanoscale double-gate MOSFETs. *IEEE Transactions on Circuits and Systems II: Express Briefs*, 54(7):571–575, 2007.

[13] V. Kilchytska, N. Collaert, R. Rooyackers, D. Lederer, J. P. Raskin, and D. Flandre. Perspective of FinFETs for analog applications. In *Proceedings of the 34th European Solid-State Device Research conference*, pages 65–68, 2004.

[14] K. Kim and J. G. Fossum. Double-gate CMOS: Symmetrical-versus asymmetrical-gate devices. *IEEE Transactions on Electron Devices*, 48(2):294–299, 2001.

[15] A. Kranti and G. Armstrong. Design and optimization of FinFETs for ultra-low-voltage analog applications. *IEEE Transactions on Electron Devices*, 54(12):3308–3316, 2007.

[16] A. Kranti and G. Armstrong. Source/Drain extension region engineering in FinFETs for low-voltage analog applications. *IEEE Electron Device Letters*, 28(2):139–141, 2007.

[17] Z. Liu, S. A. Tawfik, and V. Kursun. Statistical Data Stability and Leakage Evaluation of FinFET SRAM Cells with Dynamic Threshold Voltage Tuning under Process Parameter Fluctuations. In *Proceedings of the 9th International Symposium on Quality of Electronic Design*, pages 305–310, 2008.

[18] A. Marshall, M. Kulkarni, M., Campise, R. Cleavelin, C. Duvvury, H. Gossner, M. Gostkowski, G. Knoblinger, C. Pacha, C. Russ, et al. Finfet current mirror design and evaluation. In *Proceedings of the 2005 IEEE Dallas/CAS Workshop on Architecture, Circuits and Implementtation of SOCs*, pages 187–190, 2005.

[19] S. P. Mohanty and E. Kougianos. Incorporating Manufacturing Process Variation Awareness in Fast Design Optimization of Nanoscale CMOS VCOs. *IEEE Transactions on Semiconductor Manufacturing*, 27(1):22–31, Feb 2014.

[20] J. P. Raskin, T. M. Chung, V. Kilchytska, D. Lederer, and D. Flandre. Analog/RF performance of multiple gate SOI devices: wideband simulations and characterization. *IEEE Transactions on Electron Devices*, 53(5):1088–1095, 2006.

[21] V. Subramanian, B. Parvais, J. Borremans, A. Mercha, D. Linten, P. Wambacq, J. Loo, M. Dehan, C. Gustin, N. Collaert, et al. Planar Bulk MOSFETs Versus FinFETs: An Analog/RF Perspective. *IEEE Transactions on Electron Devices*, 53(12):3071–3079, 2006.

[22] B. Swahn and S. Hassoun. Gate sizing: finFETs vs 32nm bulk MOSFETs. In *Proceedings of the 43rd annual Design Automation Conference*, pages 528–531, 2006.

A Comparison of FinFET based FPGA LUT Designs

Monther Abusultan   Sunil P Khatri

ECE Department, Texas A&M University, College Station, TX 77843.

ABSTRACT

The FinFET device has gained much traction in recent VLSI designs. In the FinFET device, the conduction channel is vertical, unlike a traditional bulk MOSFET, in which the conduction channel is planar. This yields several benefits, and as a consequence, it is expected that most VLSI designs will utilize FinFETs from the 20nm node and beyond. Despite the fact that several research papers have reported FinFET based circuit and layout realizations for popular circuit blocks, there has been no reported work on the use of FinFETs for Field Programmable Gate Array (FPGA) designs. The key circuit in the FPGA that enables programmability is the n-input Look-up Table (LUT). An n-input LUT can implement any logic function of up to n inputs. In this paper, we present an evaluation of several FPGA LUT designs. We compare these designs from a performance (delay, power, energy) as well as an area perspective. Comparisons are conducted with respect to a bulk based LUT as well. Our results demonstrate that all the FinFET based LUTs exhibit better delays and energy than the bulk based LUT. Based on our comparisons, we have two winning candidate LUTs, one for high performance designs ($3\times$ faster than a bulk based LUT) and another for low energy, area constrained designs (83% energy and 58% area compared to a bulk based LUT).

Categories and Subject Descriptors: B.7.1 [Types and Design Styles]: VLSI (very large scale integration)

Keywords: FPGA LUT Design and Layout; FinFET based LUT; High Performance FPGA; Low Power FPGA

1. INTRODUCTION

In recent times, a new type of transistor, called the FinFET [1, 2], has been developed and has gained significant attention in the literature and in industrial practice. The FinFET (also called the Tri-Gate transistor by Intel), essentially stands the transistor on its edge, making the resulting structure appear like a fin protruding from the IC surface. Conduction in a FinFET is along the fin, rather than along the surface of the IC (in case of a traditional bulk MOSFET). Figure 1 illustrates a bulk MOSFET (left), along with a FinFET (right). The gate of the FinFET then essentially wraps around the fin, covering it on three sides (hence the monicker "Tri-Gate"). Because the gate essentially wraps around the fin, the FinFET achieves significantly lower leakage currents for a constant speed than a bulk MOSFET with the same effective dimensions. This has the desirable effect of thereby reducing both dynamic and leakage power and alleviating thermal issues which are significant in today's designs. In general, many of the problems associated with bulk MOSFETs (which originate from the short channel effects in bulk processing [3, 4]) are significantly alleviated with the FinFET. An additional benefit is that transistors can be packed more densely, since the device width of the FinFET is substantially equal to twice the height of the fin (which can be narrow). The regular arrangement of the fins also eases lithography problems that plague bulk CMOS designs. Electrically, FinFETs are more tolerant to threshold voltage variations as well. A key restriction in FinFET based design is that gate width can be incremented in quanta of fins, and hence continuous gate sizing is not easily possible. The effect of continuous gate sizing can be approximated by increasing the channel length of specific FinFETs, however.

For radiation heavy operating environments (military or space applications, for example), FinFETs demonstrate improved performance as well. This is mainly because the volume of the fin is significantly lower than the volume of the bulk node in bulk MOSFETs. The improved radiation tolerance of FinFETs occurs for the same reason that Silicon-on-Insulator (SOI) MOSFETs exhibit better radiation tolerance than bulk MOSFETs.

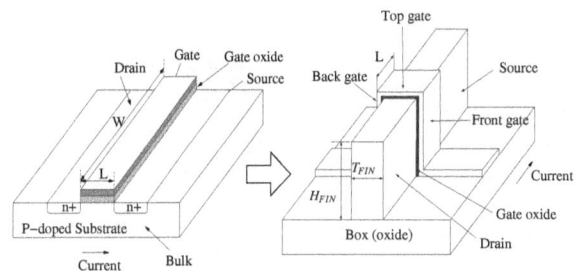

Figure 1: Bulk NMOS versus FinFET

Field Programmable Gate Arrays (FPGAs) [5, 6] are a popular platform to implement digital circuits. Their popularity has been growing recently, due to the fact that the non-recurring engineering (NRE) cost of implementing a design with FPGAs is low. Also, for the same reasons, FPGAs tend to have rapid turn-around-times (TATs) as well. In contrast, an ASIC or custom IC implementation of the same design requires a larger engineering effort for the design, verification, layout, testing and qualification of the resulting IC. Also, since the cost of fabrication of an IC has been increasing significantly over the last few technology generations [7], ASIC or custom IC designs have become less popular, except for very high volume parts. The fact that FPGAs have become faster and more dense over the years further fuels their popularity.

The core circuit in an FPGA is called a Lookup Table (LUT). A n-input LUT can realize any logic function f of up to n inputs, by using a recursive Shannon expansion based realization of the function f, and by storing the resulting minterm values in SRAM cells. In practice, recent FPGAs choose LUTs with n between 4 and 6. Since the LUT is the key circuit in the FPGA, an efficient design of the LUT is a key design requirement. Efficiency is measured in terms of area, delay, and power consumption.

This paper is the first (to the best of the authors' knowledge) to study the design of the FPGA LUT using FinFETs. The focus is on super-threshold operation of the FPGA LUT, and several candidate LUT topologies are studied. We compare five candidate FinFET based LUT designs, and compare their delay, power and layout area. A comparison with a bulk based LUT is also conducted.

The key contributions of our paper are listed below:

- This paper is the first to systematically evaluate several LUT designs for use in a FinFET technology.

- We present layout configurations for the five candidate LUTs, and show that for FinFET based design, simple circuit level simulations are not sufficient to compare designs, since the relatively strict FinFET layout rules have a significant bearing on the LUT parasitics and area, and hence its design characteristics.

- We compare our 5 FinFET based LUT configurations with a bulk based LUT in terms of delay, power and layout area of these LUTs.

- Our results demonstrate that *all* the FinFET based LUTs exhibit better delays and energy utilization than the bulk LUT. One of our FinFET based LUTs (LUT-P) is significantly faster than all other designs ($3\times$ faster than the bulk based LUT) with a penalty of higher energy utilization and circuit area compared to the other FinFET based LUTs. Compared to the bulk based LUT, LUT-P has slightly lower energy, and about 65% of the area utilization. Hence LUT-P is the LUT of choice for high performance applications. LUT-S (about 83% of the energy of the bulk based LUT) has the best energy utilization with low circuit area (about 58% of the bulk based LUT) making it the LUT of choice for energy/area critical applications.

The remainder of this paper is organized as follows. Section 2 discusses some previous work in the area of FinFET based design. Section 3 describes our candidate LUT designs, while Section 4 reports the results of experiments we performed to compare the candidate designs. Conclusions are drawn in Section 5.

2. PREVIOUS WORK

An excellent reference on FinFETs (and multi-gate MOSFETs in general) can be found in [1]. This book discusses FinFETs from several angles – the physics, compact modeling aspects, radiation effects and circuit design issues as well. An additional reference article on FinFETs is [2], which provides an overview of FinFET devices, the challenges associated with them, the FinFET process flow, and future prospects. A discussion of circuit design with FinFETs is also presented in these works. The authors of [8] discuss a lookup table-based FinFET compact modeling approach. Their idea is implemented in a circuit simulator. Although the title discusses the lookup table based compact modeling framework, it has no connection with the LUTs in FPGA design.

There has been a rich body of work in the area of SRAM cell design using FinFETs. In [9], IG FinFET based memory cells were discussed, and compared in terms of speed, area, dynamic power, leakage power, read stability, and tolerance to process variations. The authors of [10] compare IG and tri-gate (TG) FinFET based SRAM designs. Two IG-FinFET 6T SRAM cells described. Results show reduced leakage compared to a TG-FinFET SRAM cell. The SRAM design of [11] evaluated the trade-off between supply voltage, fin height and threshold voltage for a 65nm FinFET SRAM. The approach of [12] used the back gate to minimize power, and presented a 8T SRAM cell with better static noise margin (SNM). The effect of transistor stacking along with IG operation of FinFETs was studied in [13]. The authors demonstrate a sleep transistor based source biasing technique to control leakage in IG FinFET based SRAMs.

In addition, there have been several papers dealing with logic cell design in FinFET based technologies. In [14], layout results for several FinFET based cell libraries were discussed. The authors of [15] show that the width quantization property of FinFETs has a large

impact on the device leakage under VT variations. They offer a new model which can predict leakage more accurately than simple-minded Monte-Carlo, and this was validated on a dynamic logic circuit. Another paper which presents high speed domino logic circuits using FinFETs is [16]. In this paper, IG-FinFET based keepers are used to improve noise immunity. The threshold voltage of the keeper is modified to reduce contention, but not hamper noise immunity. Speed and power are shown to be improved by about 50%. The authors in [17], proposed a technique for low power dynamic domino circuits using IG FinFETs. By clocking the back gate of the FinFET, they are able to modulate the threshold voltage to improve speed. Several other papers present FinFET based design of logic and latch or flip-flop cells [18, 19, 20]. However, none of the papers discusses the design of an FPGA LUT.

The only work in the literature which discusses the FinFET based FPGAs is [21]. In this thesis, however, the focus is on process voltage variation experiments, single event upset (SEU) experiments, and sub-threshold leakage experiments. The authors do not focus on the FinFET based LUT design at all, and do not present a comparative study of alternate LUTs, or a discussion about the power, delay or layout area of these LUTs unlike this paper.

3. APPROACH

In this section, we first describe the TG FinFET device, followed by a brief discussion of the design of an FPGA LUT. Next, we discuss the layout design rules we used, followed by a description of the 5 candidate FinFET based LUTs and the (reference) bulk based LUT.

The basic structure of a TG FinFET is illustrated in Figure 1 (right). The FinFET consists of a fin of width T_{FIN}, and three gates as shown. The three gates are electrically "tied" in the TG FinFET. The tied gate wraps around the fin, and it's W is twice the height of the fin plus the fin width T_{FIN}. In other words, $W = 2 \cdot H_{FIN} + T_{FIN}$. The L dimension of the TG FinFET is illustrated in Figure 1 (right) as well.

3.1 FPGA LUT Design

The design of a conventional 3-input FPGA LUT is shown in Figure 2. The LUT consists of three stages of NMOS passgates, one for each input of the FPGA. For any one of the eight values of the inputs {a, b, c}, exactly one path from a single SRAM cell to the output is enabled, and all 7 other paths have at least one NMOS passgate that is turned off. Let's assume that this value of {a, b, c} is called v. In that case, the corresponding SRAM cell Sv contains the value of the output function of the LUT, evaluated at v. In this way, the LUT of Figure 2 can implement any of the 2^{2^3} logic functions of 3 variables. The same argument holds for a LUT which has n inputs, allowing it to implement any one of 2^{2^n} logic functions. When used in the context of our LUT, a single fin of the TG FinFET is used for each passgate of the LUT.

In a circuit sense, it would seem intuitively beneficial to implement complementary passgates in the LUT design instead of NMOS passgates. However, as was shown in [22] the NMOS passgate based LUT is superior to the complementary passgate based design, for several reasons. First, the area of NMOS passgate based design is smaller on account of fewer devices. Also, the area of a complementary passgate design tends to increase since the well spacing rules have to be adhered to. Finally, even though the complementary passgates have a smaller on-resistance, the increased capacitance on the internal nodes of the LUT actually results in a slower LUT. As a consequence, all the LUT designs we explore are based on NMOS passgates. The use of an NMOS passgate, however, results in a voltage drop at the output (by V_T), since NMOS passgates drop V_T when passing a VDD value. A full rail voltage swing at the output is ensured by using a lowered switch-point inverter at the output node

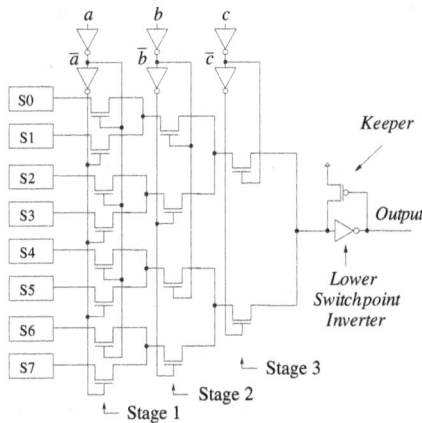

Figure 2: Basic 3-Input LUT Structure

of the LUT, along with a PMOS keeper device, shown in Figure 2. The low switch-point inverter and the PMOS keeper were sized to achieve lower power consumption while maintaining substantially equal rise and fall times. Despite this additional buffering delay, the NMOS based LUT structure is still faster than the complementary LUT design.

Parameter Description	Symbol	Dimension (nm)	Reference
Gate Length	L	21	[23]
Fin Thickness	TFIN	12	[23]
Fin Height	HFIN	26	[23]
Fin Pitch	FP	42	[23]
M1 Pitch	M1P	48	[24]
M1 Width	M1W	24	[24]
Contact Size	C	47	[24]
Contact Pitch	CP	50	[24]
Contact Hole Size	CH	18	[25]
Uncontacted Poly Pitch	PP	34	[24]
Metal Contact-Fin Spacing	CFS	24	[25]
Metal Contact-Gate Spacing	CGS	24	[25]
Gate Edge-Fin Edge Spacing	FGES	12	[25]
Metal Hole-Metal Hole Spacing	CHS	12	[25]
Metal Contact-Fin Spacing at Gate	CFS2	24	[25]

Table 1: Design Rules Used for FinFET Layouts

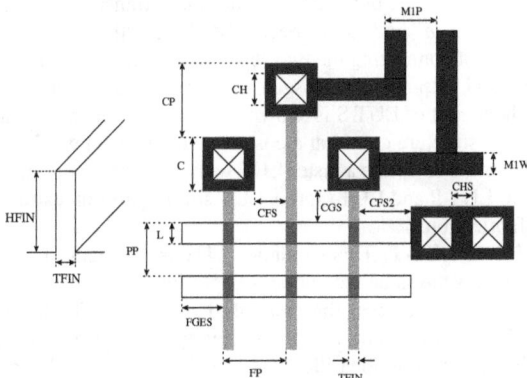

Figure 3: Design Rules Used for FinFET Layouts

3.2 FinFET-based Design Rules

In this section, we discuss the layout design rules we followed. Figure 3 illustrates the design rules we used, with the parameter description and its dimensions listed in Table 1, along with the reference which yielded the data for each design rule. Most of these rules were obtained from ITRS 2012 specifications [24]. Some of the rules were obtained from [23] for a 16nm FinFET process. For a few design rules, the data is obtained through discussions with a senior design engineer at a leading microprocessor company [25].

These design rules were also used to determine RC parasitics for the simulation of each of the LUT structures presented in this pa-

per. The HSPICE [26] simulator supports a MOSFET model level 72 (BSIM-CMG), using a set of parameters to define the geometries of the FinFET based structure simulated. The main parameters used were PDEO, PSEO, ADEO, ASEO, NRS and NRD. PDEO (PSEO) defines the perimeter of the drain (source) to substrate overlap region through oxide, while ADEO (ASEO) defines the drain (source) to substrate overlap area through oxide. NRD (NRS) defines the number of drain (source) diffusion squares, which is used to model the fin resistance. The BSIM-CMG model was used in SOI mode for all the FinFET based simulations conducted in this paper.

3.3 Candidate TG FinFET-based LUT Designs and Layouts

In this paper, we present our comparisons using a 4-input LUT. We have 5 candidate TG FinFET based LUTs in all, and one bulk based (reference) LUT. In this section, we present the circuit level designs and the layout of the 5 candidate LUTs. The candidate LUTs are named alphabetically – LUT-P, LUT-Q, LUT-R, LUT-S and LUT-T.

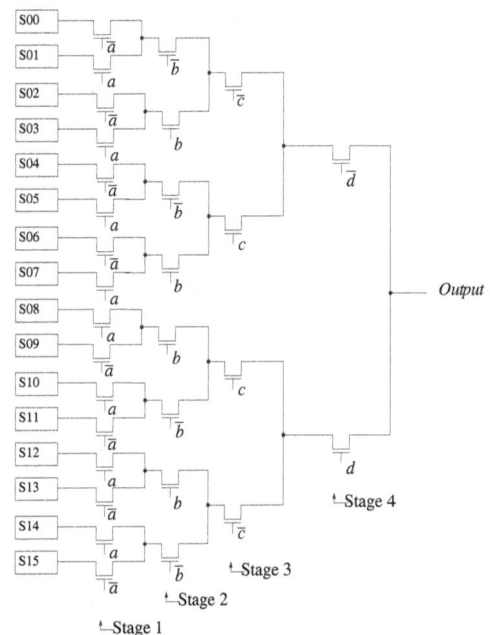

Figure 4: Candidate LUT-P circuit diagram

Candidate LUT-P: The circuit structure of this LUT is shown in Figure 4, and is the traditional design for a 4-input LUT. The layout of the passgate portion of LUT-P is shown in Figure 5. In each successive stage of passgates, the number of transistors is reduced by a factor of 2, and hence paths from any given SRAM cell to the output actually share passgates and wires. For example, each passgate at the last stage (at the output side), will be shared by half of the paths from the SRAM inputs to the output, as shown in Figure 4.

The layout for this candidate LUT accomplishes some area reduction by reordering the inputs from the SRAM cells. The output node of LUT-P is at the bottom of Figure 5. We organize the layout of LUT-P in a triangular manner, so that another LUT might use that space if it were flipped along the x-axis. Despite the fact that this structure utilizes the least number of transistors, it has a relatively large area, which is due to the existence of the metal contacts being required on the internal nodes. In addition, the (horizontal) gate signals need to form transistors over selected (vertical) fins, and need a thick oxide layer over other fins in order not to form transistors over these fins. For example, the gate for signal "a" forms transistors with every alternate fin. This would require an additional mask for a (horizontal) gate signal not to form a transistor over a (vertical) fin, by

355

depositing an additional amount of field oxide (which increases the cost of device fabrication). The advantage of LUT-P is the minimal capacitance at the output, making it a faster LUT candidate.

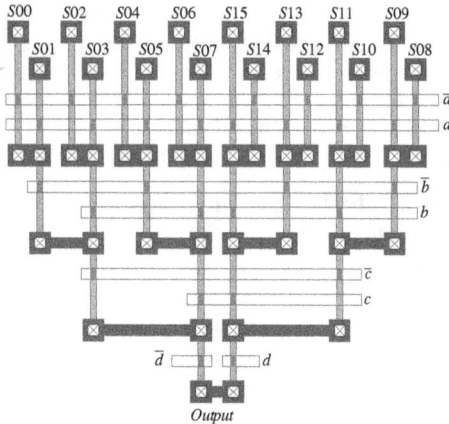

Figure 5: Candidate LUT-P passgates layout sketch

Candidate LUT-Q: The circuit for this candidate is shown in Figure 6, while the layout of the passgate portion of LUT-Q is illustrated in Figure 7. The output node for LUT-Q is at the bottom of Figure 7. In this LUT structure, each SRAM input has its own separate path to the output. This path is not shared with the paths of other SRAM inputs, unlike LUT-P. Although this design results in the use of more transistors (asymptotically, LUT-Q needs n times more transistors than LUT-P), it does not require internal nodes in the LUT to be connected using metal contacts. This results in a significant reduction in area over the LUT-P structure. The main disadvantage for this structure is the extra capacitance at the output of the passgate structure, which results in a slower operation (but with a slightly lower energy consumption) due to the extra charging/discharging needed. This structure also requires an extra mask during fabrication, since the (horizontal) gates in the LUT-Q need to selectively form transistors over specific (vertical) fins in the layout.

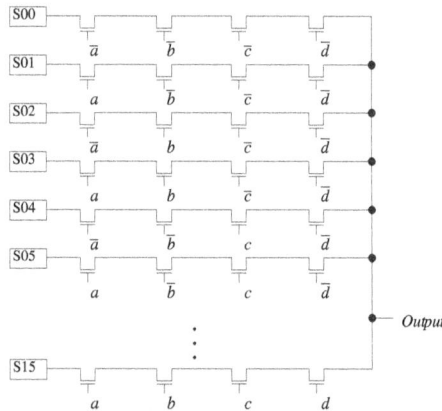

Figure 6: Candidate circuit diagram for LUT-Q, LUT-R

Candidate LUT-R: The circuit for candidate LUT-R is illustrated in Figure 6, while the layout of its passgates is shown in Figure 9. The layout structure of this candidate LUT is a modification on the layout of LUT-Q. The key goal of LUT-R is to eliminate the need for the additional mask layer (which is required by LUT-P and LUT-Q) for a (horizontal) gate signal not to form a transistor over a (vertical) fin, by depositing an additional amount of field oxide. It turns out that by changing the arrangement of the input signals of the LUT (as shown in the layout of Figure 9), we can accomplish this goal. This candidate LUT structure uses slightly higher area (about 2% more than LUT-Q). However, it requires one less mask, reducing

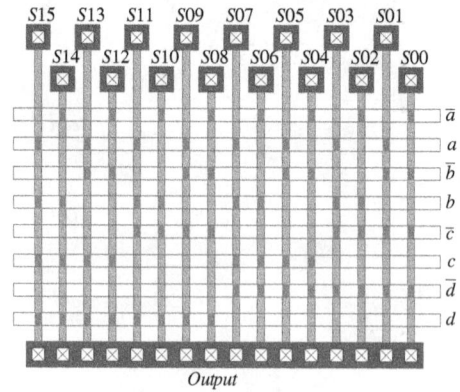

Figure 7: Candidate LUT-Q passgates layout sketch

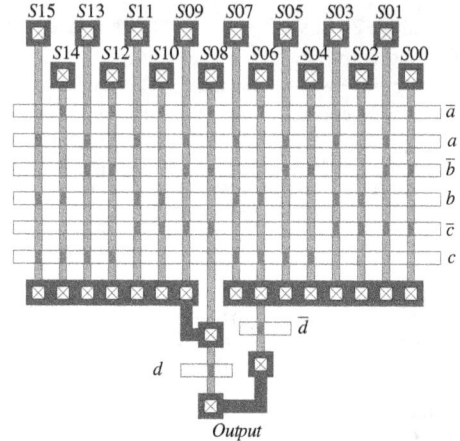

Figure 8: Candidate LUT-S passgates layout sketch

fabrication cost. The output terminal of LUT-R is at the top of the layout shown in Figure 9.

Candidate LUT-S: Candidate LUT-S is a variant of LUT-Q. As mentioned earlier, one of the disadvantages of LUT-Q is the large output capacitance compared to LUT-P. In order to reduce the capacitance at the output, LUT-S modifies the last stage of LUT-Q design. The fourth (last) stage in LUT-S has one pair of transistors driven by the input signal "$\bar{d}$" and "d" respectively. The fourth stage in LUT-S does the job of connecting the two separate parts in the third stage to form the final output of the passgates. This reduces capacitive parasitics. The layout of LUT-S is shown in Figure 8. This modification on the LUT structure comes at a cost of increased area which has to be paid in order to obtain a faster LUT with lower energy utilization. Similar to LUT-P and LUT-Q, this LUT still requires an extra mask during fabrication.

Candidate LUT-T: This candidate LUT is a variant of LUT-R. LUT-T applies the same technique (of splitting the last stage so that it only uses two devices) that was used in LUT-S. The layout of this LUT structure is not shown for brevity, but it can be realized by applying the same idea illustrated in Figure 8, to the layout of Figure 9. To obtain LUT-T, we split the output terminal of Figure 9 into two halves, and connect each half to a passgate that is connected to "$\bar{d}$" and "d" respectively. The row of devices connected to "$\bar{d}$" and "d" in Figure 9 is eliminated in LUT-T. Similar to LUT-R, this LUT structure does not require an extra mask during fabrication.

Reference bulk-based LUT: For our experiments, we also realize a reference bulk-based LUT. This LUT is based on the circuit shown in Figure 4. The layout of this LUT also has a substantially triangular nature, and is omitted for brevity.

4. EXPERIMENTS

In this section, we present a comparison of the delay, area, power and energy of the 5 candidate LUTs, along with a traditional bulk

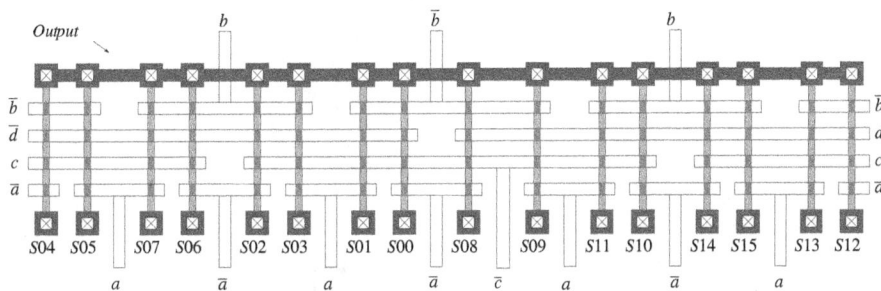

Figure 9: Candidate LUT-R passgates layout sketch

based LUT. All simulations were performed using HSPICE [26]. We implemented our candidate designs using the 16 nm PTM [27] high performance TG FinFET model card for the FinFET based LUTs, and the 16 nm PTM high performance bulk model card for the traditional bulk based LUT. The full supply voltage used in our experiments was 0.7 V.

The configuration inputs of all LUTs were driven by minimum size inverters for all the designs, to model the output drive of the SRAM cells. The inputs of the LUTs were driven by means of optimally sized inverter chains, to drive the (different) input capacitance of each stage of every LUT.

4.1 Sizing of the Output Buffer

As mentioned earlier, a low switch-point inverter and a long channel PMOS keeper device are required at the output of each of the LUTs described in this paper (as shown in Figure 2). The low switch-point inverter and the PMOS keeper allow us to obtain a full rail output signal with approximately equal rise and fall times. The inverter and the keeper were sized based on the characteristics of the output of the last stage of the NMOS passgates.

The input of the inverter is the signal from the output of the last stage of NMOS passgates of the LUT. This signal has a slower risetime and a degraded voltage when driven high. Taking this into consideration, the inverter is designed with a lower switching voltage. This is obtained by using a stronger NMOS transistor than its PMOS counterpart. Based on HSPICE simulation sweeps, we determined the proper sizing of the first inverter. We noted that after a certain point, an increase in the size of the NMOS device only resulted in a small improvement in the falltime at the output of the inverter, due to the increase in the diffusion capacitance of the output node. In this paper, for the bulk based LUT, the sizes used for low switch-point inverter are Ln = 16 nm, Lp = 32 nm, Wn = 128 nm and Wp = 32 nm. For the FinFET based LUTs, the inverter had a length of 34 nm for both of the NMOS and PMOS devices with 1 fin each.

The optimal length of the channel of the keeper was also determined based on HSPICE simulation sweeps. For the bulk based LUT, a keeper with length 2× and a 2× width was used, while a keeper of length 21× and 1 fin was used for the FinFET based LUTs. The need for an extra long channel keeper in the FinFET based LUT was due to the increase in the drive strength of the FinFET transistor compared to the bulk (planar) transistor.

4.2 Operating Frequency

Some of the candidate LUTs can be faster than others. Hence, if a fixed operating frequency is used, the faster LUTs will finish their computation earlier than the slower LUTs, causing the faster LUTs to spend more time waiting for the next clock edge to switch, and hence consume more static energy. Hence, instead of using a fixed clock frequency, we select the clock frequency for each LUT such that 5 LUTs can switch in one clock period. This makes the energy metric fair across all LUTs. Hence, the operating frequency of each LUT is calculated using the equation $Freq = 5 * max(Tplh, Tphl)$. In this case, in our simulations, all the candidate LUTs spend time in

the static operation region equivalent to a logic depth of 4 (since a time equal to one logic depth will be spent in the dynamic operation).

4.3 Simulation Results for Candidate LUTs

For all 5 TG FinFET based LUT configurations as well as the bulk based LUT, we measured the risetime (Tr), falltime (Tf), propagation delay (Tplh and Tphl), power, energy and total layout area (including the area of the low switch-point inverter and keeper at the output of the LUT). Note that all of the delay parameters were extracted at the final output of the LUT (i.e. the output of the low switch-point inverter). All the different input switching scenarios were considered in our simulations, but we only report the results from the input vector that had the highest total energy consumption.

Table 2 summarizes the results of our experiments. This table presents the risetime Tr (Column 2), the falltime Tf (Column 3), propagation delay Tplh (Column 4), propagation delay Tphl (Column 5), dynamic power (Column 6), dynamic energy (Column 7), static power (Column 8), static energy (Column 9), total power (Column 10), total energy (Column 11) and total layout area (Column 12) for each candidate LUT structure, reported at full supply voltage (0.7 V). The results of the bulk based LUT are reported as absolute values, while the results for the FinFET based LUT candidates are reported as a ratio of the value to the corresponding value for the bulk based LUT.

From Table 2, we note that all the FinFET based LUTs are faster than the bulk based LUT in terms of rising and falling delays (LUT-P, LUT-S and LUT-T are about 4× faster while LUT-Q and LUT-R are about 3× faster than the bulk based LUT). The propagation delay of LUT-P is at least 3× faster than the bulk based LUT. LUT-S and LUT-T are more than 2× faster while LUT-Q and LUT-R are about 37% faster than the bulk based LUT. LUT-P has significantly lower propagation delay due to the fact that the capacitive load at the output of LUT-P is lowest, resulting in faster switching. The dynamic energy of LUT-S and LUT-T is the lowest (∼14% lower than the bulk based LUT) while the dynamic energy of LUT-Q and LUT-R are slightly lower than the bulk based LUT by ∼2%. In general, the dynamic energy of the FinFET based LUTs is lower than that of the bulk based LUT, except for LUT-P, which is slightly higher than the bulk based LUT. As for the static energy, LUT-P has the least leakage current, with almost half of the leakage of the bulk based LUT. LUT-S and LUT-T have 62% of the leakage of the bulk based LUT, while LUT-Q and LUT-R have slightly less leakage than the bulk based LUT (8% lower). LUT-Q, LUT-R, LUT-S and LUT-T have a higher leakage than LUT-P (due to the additional active devices they need). Looking at the total energy, we clearly see that both LUT-S and LUT-T use 17% lower energy than the bulk based LUT. The other FinFET based LUTs are still better than the bulk based LUT, but not as energy efficient as LUT-S and LUT-T. The results yield two key conclusions. For a high performance FPGA, the LUT of choice would be LUT-P, with slightly higher energy than the other candidate FinFET based LUTs (yet, comparable energy with respect to the bulk based LUT), but at the same time, LUT-P provides considerably faster operation (∼3× faster than the bulk based LUT and more than 1.2-2× faster than the other FinFET based

357

Configuration	Tr (ps)	Tf (ps)	Tplh (ps)	Tphl (ps)	Dyn Pwr (uW)	Dyn Energy (aJ)	Static Pwr (uW)	Static Energy (aJ)	Total Pwr (uW)	Total Energy (aJ)	Total Area (nm^2)
Bulk	191.03	215.27	279.54	134.43	4.89	3372.90	0.72	500.59	2.79	3873.50	1113828
P	0.14×	0.23×	0.21×	0.32×	4.74×	1.06×	2.87×	0.55×	4.79×	0.99×	0.65×
Q	0.19×	0.34×	0.36×	0.73×	2.58×	0.98×	2.48×	0.92×	2.60×	0.97×	0.49×
R	0.19×	0.34×	0.36×	0.73×	2.58×	0.98×	2.48×	0.92×	2.60×	0.97×	0.62×
S	0.15×	0.26×	0.24×	0.46×	3.24×	0.86×	2.94×	0.62×	3.48×	0.83×	0.58×
T	0.15×	0.26×	0.24×	0.46×	3.24×	0.86×	2.94×	0.62×	3.48×	0.83×	0.60×

Table 2: Delay, Power, Energy and Area of the Candidate FinFET based LUT structures and the Bulk Based LUT

LUTs). For an energy optimized FPGA, the LUT of choice would be either LUT-S or LUT-T (with a 17% lower energy, and ~54% lower delay than the bulk based LUT).

Next, we will integrate the area trade-off in our analysis in order to find the optimal LUT of choice. The area of each of the candidate LUTs is estimated based on the layouts shown earlier. The estimation of the area also accounted for the area of the low switch-point inverter and the long channel keeper at the output of the LUT. The area was computed as the area of their enclosing rectangle for each of the FinFET based LUTs. For the bulk based LUT, the area was computed as half of the area of the enclosing rectangle (due to the substantially triangular footprint of the bulk based LUT). Table 2 shows the area of all the candidate LUTs (Column 12) as a ratio of the area of the bulk based LUT (which is listed as an absolute value). All the FinFET based LUTs use a much smaller area than the bulk based LUT. LUT-Q has the smallest area footprint (about 49% of the bulk based LUT) followed by LUT-S (about 58% of the bulk based LUT). LUT-P has the largest area among the FinFET based LUTs (due to the internal metal contacts). However, LUT-P is still smaller than the bulk based LUT by 35%.

The delay, energy and area results suggest that the optimal LUT of choice depends on the target application. For a high performance application LUT-P is the best choice. For a lower energy and area application, LUT-S is the optimal choice, since it has a lower area than LUT-T, with the same energy.

5. CONCLUSIONS

In this paper, we present 5 candidate designs (and their associated layouts) for a TG FinFET based FPGA LUT implemented in a 16nm technology. We compare these designs with a bulk based FPGA LUT as well. Our metrics for comparison are the delay, energy and layout area of each design. HSPICE simulations are performed to measure the delay and energy. Our results indicate that all the FinFET based LUTs exhibit better delays (Tr, Tf, Tplh and Tphl) than the bulk LUT, and show that the best candidate LUT structure varies depending on the application. For a high performance application with less emphasis on energy, LUT-P is the best choice with 3× faster operation than a bulk based LUT and 1% lower energy. On the other hand, LUT-S has the lowest energy utilization across all the candidate LUTs (17% lower than the bulk based LUT) as well as small area (about 58% of the area of the bulk based LUT). Hence LUT-S is a desirable choice for low power and area constrained targeted applications.

6. REFERENCES

[1] J.-P. Colinge, *FinFETs and Other Multi-Gate Transistors*. Springer Publishing Company, Incorporated, 2007.

[2] T.-J. King, "FinFETs for Nanoscale CMOS Digital Integrated Circuits," in *Proceedings of the 2005 IEEE/ACM International conference on Computer-aided design*, ICCAD '05, 2005.

[3] T.-J. King, "FinFETs for nanoscale CMOS digital integrated circuits," *Computer-Aided Design, 2005. ICCAD-2005. IEEE/ACM International Conference on*, pp. 207–210, 2005.

[4] M. Turi, J. Delgado-Frias, and N. Jha, "Low-Power FinFET design schemes for NOR address decoders," *VLSI Design Automation and Test (VLSI-DAT), 2010 International Symposium on*, pp. 74–77, 2010.

[5] S. Trimberger, ed., *Field-Programmable Gate Array Technology*. Netherlands: Kluwer Academic Publishers Group, 1994. ISBN: 9780792394198 (0792394194).

[6] S. D. Brown, R. J. Francis, J. Rose, and Z. G. Vranesic, *Field-programmable gate arrays*. Norwell, MA, USA: Kluwer Academic Publishers, 1992.

[7] A. Sangiovanni-Vincentelli, "The tides of EDA." Keynote Talk, Design Automation Conference, June 2003.

[8] R. Thakker, C. Sathe, M. Baghini, and M. Patil, "A Table-Based Approach to Study the Impact of Process Variations on FinFET Circuit Performance," *Computer-Aided Design of Integrated Circuits and Systems, IEEE Transactions on*, vol. 29, no. 4, 2010.

[9] S. A. Tawfik and V. Kursun, "Robust FinFET Memory Circuits with P-Type Data Access Transistors for Higher Integration Density and Reduced Leakage Power," *J. Low Power Electronics*, vol. 5, no. 4, 2009.

[10] S. Tawfik, Z. Liu, and V. Kursun, "Independent-Gate and Tied-Gate FinFET SRAM Circuits: Design Guidelines for Reduced Area and Enhanced Stability," in *Internatonal Conference on Microelectronics (ICM)*, 2007.

[11] H. Ananthan, A. Bansal, and K. Roy, "FinFET SRAM - Device and Circuit Design Considerations," in *Proceedings of 5th International Symposium on Quality Electronic Design*, 2004.

[12] Y. B. Kim, Y.-B. Kim, and F. Lombardi, "Low Power 8T SRAM Using 32nm Independent Gate FinFET Technology," in *SoCC*, 2008.

[13] T. Cakici, K. Kim, and K. Roy, "FinFET Based SRAM Design for Low Standby Power Applications," in *8th International Symposium on Quality Electronic Design (ISQED)*, 2007.

[14] M. Alioto, "Comparative Evaluation of Layout Density in 3T, 4T, and MT FinFET Standard Cells," *IEEE Transactions on Very Large Scale Integration (VLSI) Systems*, vol. 19, no. 5, 2011.

[15] J. Gu, J. Keane, S. Sapatnekar, and C. Kim, "Width Quantization Aware FinFET Circuit Design," in *Custom Integrated Circuits Conference (IEEE CICC)*, 2006.

[16] S. Tawfik and V. Kursun, "High Speed FinFET Domino Logic Circuits with Independent Gate-Biased Double-Gate Keepers Providing Dynamically Adjusted Immunity to Noise," in *Internatonal Conference on Microelectronics (ICM)*, 2007.

[17] Y. B. Kim, Y.-B. Kim, and F. Lombardi, "A technique for low power dynamic circuit design in 32nm double-gate FinFET technology," *Circuits and Systems, 2008. MWSCAS 2008. 51st Midwest Symposium on*, pp. 779–782, 2008.

[18] C.-H. Pao, M.-L. Fan, M.-F. Tsai, V.-N. Chen, V.-H. Hu, P. Su, and C.-T. Chuang, "A Comprehensive Comparative Analysis of FinFET and Trigate Device, SRAM and Logic Circuits," in *2012 IEEE Asia Pacific Conference on Circuits and Systems (APCCAS)*, 2012.

[19] A. N. Bhoj and N. K. Jha, "Design of Ultra-low-leakage Logic Gates and Flip-Flops in High-performance FinFET Technology," in *IEEE ISQED*, 2011.

[20] K. Roy, H. Mahmoodi, S. Mukhopadhyay, H. Ananthan, A. Bansal, and T. Cakici, "Double-Gate SOI Devices for Low-Power and High-Performance Applications," in *IEEE/ACM International Conference on Computer-Aided Design (ICCAD)*, 2005.

[21] M. U. Mushtaq and Y. Xie, "Reliability and Power Analysis of FinFET-Based FPGAs," Master's thesis, Pennsylvania State University, 2008.

[22] P. Chow, S. O. Seo, J. Rose, K. Chung, G. Paez-Monzon, and I. Rahardja, "The design of a SRAM-based field-programmable gate array-Part II: Circuit design and layout," *IEEE Trans. on Very Large Scale Integration (VLSI) Systems*, pp. 321–330, Sept. 1999.

[23] S. Sinha, G. Yeric, V. Chandra, B. Cline, and Y. Cao, "Exploring Sub-20nm FinFET Design with Predictive Technology Models," in *49th ACM/EDAC/IEEE, Design Automation Conference (DAC)*, 2012.

[24] "ITRS website." http://www.itrs.net/.

[25] Private communication, senior microprocessor design engineer.

[26] I. Meta-Software, "HSPICE user's manual," Campbell, CA.

[27] "PTM website." http://www.ptm.asu.edu/.

Author Index